To Chris and Melissa

"In its evocative power, its understated skill, the vividness of its description, its noncosmopolitan setting and its orientation toward the next-to-immediate past, *During the Reign of the Queen of Persia* takes its place among several other recent works that are also concerned with the female matrix: Anne Tyler's *Dinner at the Homesick Restaurant*, Marilynne Robinson's *Housekeeping*, Alice Munro's *Lives of Girls and Women*, and, in a Southern variant, Helen Henslee's *Pretty Redwing*. This is excellent company, and *During the Reign of the Queen of Persia* is an important debut by a fine new writer."

Margaret Atwood
The New York Times Book Review

"An original portrait of a modern rural matriarchy . . . Chase's . . . dialogue sparkles and her characters live. A highly recommended first novel."

Los Angeles Herald Examiner

"Remarkable . . . one must emphasize the writing itself—not everyone can write this kind of prose. It is made of rhythms, images and metaphors that involve both sense and spirit and allow the reader, through the narrator, to experience a tone of the keenest excitement and awe . . . this saga by Joan Chase . . . is informed by her elegant, formal language . . . the book is broader than the battle of the sexes or even the world of women."

Chicago Tribune Book World

During the Reign of the Queen of Persia

JOAN CHASE

BALLANTINE BOOKS • NEW YORK

Library of Congress Catalog Card Number: 82-48680

ISBN 0-345-31525-1

This edition published by arrangement with Harper & Row, Publishers, Inc.

Manufactured in the United States of America

First Ballantine Books Edition: June 1984

I want to express my thanks to the Yaddo Corporation and the Ragdale Foundation for the time they gave me, and to the Vermont Council on the Arts and the Illinois Arts Council for project grants. To Hayden Carruth and Ted Solotaroff—inexpressible gratitude.

PART ONE

Celia

In northern Ohio there is a county of some hundred thousand arable acres which breaks with the lake region flatland and begins to roll and climb, and to change into rural settings: roadside clusters of houses, small settlements that repose on the edge of nowhere, single lane bridges, backwater country stores with a single rusting gas pump, barns advertising Mail Pouch in frayed and faded postings. These traces of human habitation recede, balanced by the luxuriant curving hills, cliffs like lounging flanks, water shoots that rapidly lose themselves in gladed ravines. Fields of wheat or oats surrounded by dark trees seem to unreel as part of a native flair. Occasionally, gloomy forgotten farmsteads loom. There are a few proud spreads, fastidiously tended enclaves of the Amish and the Mennonites.

Deep into the country originates the hump of railroad lines circling the market town that is the county seat; a small denominational college distinguishes it as the center of culture as well. The downtown square is a brisk trading area, its broad avenue resolving into a central square which, framed by three-story buildings, seems as though it is entirely walled. Within the sandstone blocks, stripped off the hillsides and mined from mountains to the south, glistens still the jewel dust of crushed quartz. All the streets are brick-paved. A dark earthen red, they bear the imprint of their manufacture—Metropolitan, Canton, 1905 Cleveland Block, Egyptian, Sciotoville.

On Saturdays in the 1950s, there was a policeman to direct traffic; the sidewalks were crowded with country people, lopsided buckboards vied with flying Oldsmobiles for the right-of-way, the clip-clop of horses sounding on the brick, drawing the wagons and the black-canopied buggies of the plain people, whose faces reflected the timeless, ordered certainty of their innocence. Stone-hewn, stone-blind Samsons of bulging strength ornamented the county courthouse, adding to the general impression of stability and sanctioned self-interest. When we lived there, on the farm which was right on the edge of the city limits, we thought it the very center of the world, and the green and golden land and wooded hollows which began two blocks over from the railroad loop and then rolled off to obscurity formed a natural barrier to the rest of existence, which we dismissed as the outer darkness.

Our Uncle Dan had his butcher shop on that town

square. It was on the backside, beside the newsstand, beyond which the city buses loaded. When we went inside after the picture show or from shopping at Fitchberg's Dry Goods, we'd finger pennies out of the cup he kept on the shelf and have a round pop of colored gum from the machine while we waited for Aunt Libby to drive from our farm to pick us up. If Uncle Dan was busy with a customer he wouldn't say a word to us, wouldn't seem even to recognize us, going on with his practical and patient advice to any of his familiar clientele; he knew them all— their eating habits, the states of their gallbladders, pocket-books and marriages.

There were the four of us then, two his own daughters, two his nieces, all of us born within two years of each other. Uncle Dan treated the four of us the very same and sometimes we thought we were the same—same blood, same rights of inheritance. Some part of each year, mostly summers, all four of us lived with Uncle Dan, or rather with Gram, for he lived with her too. Gram was the queen bee—that was what Uncle Dan called her. That, or the Queen of Persia, the Empress herself. Or just Queenie for short. Our pony was Queenie too. Uncle Dan said they had a lot in common, and although he didn't say exactly what, we knew Queenie was nearly impossible to catch, had thrown every one of us, racing for the barn. We knew she had what was called a high head.

At last, after Uncle Dan had satisfied Mrs. Wheeler or Mrs. Smucker and they had left the shop, he would look over the rim of the porcelain display case and say, "And now what can I do for you busybodies today?" His hat was perched at a jaunty slant over his lacquered, vein-domed head. "Today's specials: pickled pigs' feet and blood pudding."

"We have to wait," Jenny would say, sounding like her mother, Aunt Libby, ignoring her father except for the fractures of light in her black and almond-slanted eyes.

"Can we see the meat?" we'd ask.

"Vultures," he'd say, and then go before us into the back room and open the heavy door to the walk-in cooler. From that small room issued the cold and bloody reek of a consuming rawness. We'd breathe one enormous breath, perhaps our last, and step inside to confront the stiff, hanging carcasses. The air congealed, prickly cold on our bare summer arms. Under our sandals the floor was scummy from the tatters of fat and bristles of hair rolled in the sawdust. We'd shiver going out, and look sideways at Uncle Dan. He would latch the door, standing before us, shorter even than we were, yet fearless—in his blood-smeared apron and his sailor hat, dressed for anything.

During the war Uncle Dan had been a Marine. Although he'd lived on a ship, he had never left the port of San Francisco. He sent for his wife and two small children across all that distance from Ohio, causing them to sit on suitcases in the aisles of packed train cars and Aunt Libby to have adventures—too many, she said, her smooth face registering the folly of camp following. Once she'd had to assist at the birth of a baby during one of the endless waits at some nameless siding, so no one was able to decide which state the baby had been born in. They had pictures from that time, of themselves swimming in the Pacific in brilliant winter sunlight, Uncle Dan in his sailor hat, Aunt Libby, dark-tanned, her fine hair windblown, sweet-smiling in a one-piece swimming suit. When they were free to return to Ohio, Uncle Dan joined his father at the store, just until he'd got his feet on the ground, his same reason for moving his family into the big house with Gram and the various members of the family who regularly came and went. But both places yielded their convenience and they stayed on—Uncle Dan counting the years, planning that one day he would take another job, would move, that his life would begin.

Uncle Dan would talk to us about this sometimes while he was feeding his lustrous Irish setter, which lived a high-strung life of his own tied to the doghouse at the edge of the lawn. Uncle Dan always said it was a mystery to him how a man with a redheaded daughter could end up with a red-haired nervous wreck of a dog. He fed "the beast" when he got home at night, serving him a broth-warmed mash in a tin pan, assuring us as he mixed and brewed that the dog ate better than the rest of us, though at first sniff he'd turned up his nose, and Uncle Dan had confessed that it was probably not exactly what the dog had had in mind. He spoke as though he knew his dog inside and out. But gradually the setter would eat faster, going into the pan with increasingly desperate gulps. When he'd finished, Uncle Dan let him free for a time, his long red streamered plumes racing over the shine of evening grass in spumes of flight, circling, leaping. Until with murmured affection and resignation, Uncle Dan secured him again with the links of steel chain that seemed strong enough to hold a gorilla.

But when Uncle Dan talked to us about his job, his life, as though he too were secured with a chain, which, though invisible, bound as securely, we never worried: he was forever joking, complaining—"thrashing at the bit," he called it. Nevertheless, when he was at home we would hear him whistling up from the cellar, where he worked on his projects, and over the years he turned out an assortment of goods, one enthusiasm finding its way into another—cowhide wallets succeeded by chair caning, hand-crafted furniture, poured candles, eventually oil painting. And he knew the meat-cutting business through and through. We could see that in the patient way he could slice off chops or hook up a side of beef—as though it were all as natural and disheartening as his brown hairs sliding off on the comb.

We went into the alley behind the market to wait for Aunt Libby to come for us and we felt these lonesome things about Uncle Dan. Finally the car would come easing through the shaft, taking up nearly the entire path against the garbage cans, Aunt Libby with one bare arm resting on the open window, already, even in early summer, darkly tanned, her other arm back over the seat. Only a slight drift of a smile would acknowledge us waiting there. With the motor left running she'd seem just to pause, idly, her glance fixed off to where the sunlight chinked through at odd intervals between the brick buildings. We might scatter for a moment then, to get candy at the newsstand or look at the magazines. And Uncle Dan might slip out for a quick second to lean on the car door with his arms folded, flirting with her every chance he got. His nudges for her attention seemed to distract her only fractionally from the dark and dappled path of the alley. Then abruptly she would decide she had had enough, it was time to leave, and she would blow the horn with a sharp fret of irritation, the way Gram always did, and we'd dive out of the newsstand and jump in the car just as she started to move off. Behind us Uncle Dan would vanish as we turned into the square and then onto Main Street, one of the two parallel roads going north, the ruddy road underneath us seeming to spread out before us like a royal carpet; one which was rolled up as quickly from behind, so that we were the only ones who knew about it—another secret part of our knowing that where we were going no others could follow.

All the car windows were down, the sweetness of mowed grass and flowering lawn beds blowing through while we were in the town, and then richer meadow clovers and the cool wooded hummocks scented with needles and vine, an interval of two miles or so that separated us from the business district of the town, a distance never calculated exactly, because it wasn't a matter of space or time but one of difference. A lane of white oaks bordered our lawn. Those oaks, perhaps fifteen of them, standing out against the open fields as far as we could see on either side, fixed for us the entrance to our farm, and even after there was a gas station built on the north corner and a restaurant beyond the hedge, those trees still loomed like a massive gate.

When almost into the house, Aunt Libby would often stop short and look at us, baffled and almost accusing. "Damn it, girls. Do you know? I was right there and forgot entirely about supper. And I suppose we do have to eat"—spoken as though it mystified her, this matter of appetite. "Well, Dan will just have to bring something home with him."

Gram, it seemed to us, watched out for Uncle Dan more than Aunt Libby did. She made us pipe down when he was home, spoke up for the privileges of a man after a day's work. We watched her sideways, suspecting her motives, her sincerity. What did she know? There were times when Uncle Dan was the only male in a household of ten or more. It was Gram's house, had been so even when Grandad was alive, for she had bought it with her own money, as we had often enough heard her say. And any of her five children was welcome to move in with her at any time, displacing one another, squeezing in as best they could, using any of the three floors and the fourteen rooms. At different times one or the other or all of her five daughters might choose to come back home: some had married and came with children, some had had husbands but lost them; Aunt Elinor married late. So, often it was one or another assortment of us females living there, and Uncle Dan when he came home from the market.

His arrival was around six-thirty in the evening. Those years two of us, Uncle Dan's nieces, daughters of Gram's dead daughter, Grace, ate an early dinner with Gram, who would be already bathed and dressed to go off for her evening's entertainment: bingo parties, horse racing, roulette at a private club—anything exciting. She cooked us a dinner before she left, something that she didn't have to think about, something she had fixed for sixty years or more. She only did it, she said, for our mother who had died, for she herself was plain fed up with cooking. She told us that nearly every day. Fed up with cooking, with work—had worked for sixty years, cooking for more damn unappreciative men, thrashers, hired hands, in addition to squalling brats, starting from age eleven, when she had been sent across two miles of meadow to help a neighbor woman with her nine children. So now she just put food out on the table: fried-down salt pork, chops or ground meat, boiled potatoes and cabbage. She ate scarcely any of it herself, preferring to have a slab of her Dutch bakery bread, dipped into coffee blanched pale with cream. She didn't care if we wanted what she'd fixed or even if we ate it; it was just put on the table at five o'clock.

Uncle Dan's two daughters, Celia and Jenny, waited for him to come home and when they were all at the table they made a romantic picture of a family, the three of them around the big farm kitchen table with a surviving male figure. We weren't supposed to interrupt them since it was Uncle Dan who put meat on the table, their table, and Gram thought he deserved that much real family life. We liked to sit there in the dark stairwell while they ate, our own mouths dark, running as if with a juice, as we watched them cut into the thick soft sirloin and lift pieces of it on the red-handled forks. Uncle Dan brought home the best cuts and gave himself up to a wholehearted appreciation of his appetite, belching out loud whenever he felt like it, talking with his mouth full, stabbing his fork across the table for extras. After they were finished we went in to help our cousins clear the table and we would pop yellow scraps of fat into our mouths, spitting it out only if it had gone cold and lardy.

During the evening Uncle Dan sat in his recliner and made his remarks over the paper—he was famous for that. Often it seemed to us that we talked or perhaps lived to inspire his comments—repetitive yet always new, his tone conveying a total although good-natured abdication, a comical weariness.

Aunt Libby would ask what they might have for supper the next evening. Feeding other people was for Aunt Libby a constant preoccupation, though, like Gram, she had little interest in food for herself. Uncle Dan would consider aloud the little difference the menu would make, since one thing burned or neglected tasted pretty nearly as bad as another.

"I've had my disappointments," he would say with a pointed melancholy, so that we would all know he was thinking again of Hedy Lamarr and her falsies. And the house brimful of females—he had really hoped for sons when Celia and then Jenny were born. And Aunt Libby did have a boy later, and another, but they were stillborn and after that she couldn't have another child, something Uncle Dan never mentioned. Every evening he entertained us, making it like a party, because later he would go out to the kitchen and make popcorn and serve Cokes to all of us, or some special concoction he was promoting at the market— for a while we had homemade root beer made from a syrup and a seltzer bottle. Then he would go off to bed, hours before the rest of us, since he had to leave at six in the morning to open up the store.

But sometimes he would bring out his trombone, the one thing left from his year at the local college, when he'd played in a jazz combo. He would get Celia to play the piano and they would try for a while to bring their two instruments and interpretations into harmony, finally breaking down into solos, each one playing for the other. Uncle Dan listened to Celia attentively, helped her with the dotted notes and syncopation. "You should have kept up your lessons," he lamented, and played for her what he still recalled of "Lady Be Good." While they worked over the music he had that same intense absorption he had when he played his Peggy Lee records. He said she was the very best. "You've got it in you to be good," we'd hear him say to Celia when they'd finished and she'd folded down the cover on the piano and spread out her polished nails to admire against the dark mahogany. She'd smile and lithely dip her head, pleased and flattered. And then she would go to her room to be alone. Uncle Dan would finish the session by himself with one of Peggy Lee's records. He would listen with his trombone laid over his knees, transfixed, his thoughts far away from us.

One early spring evening when Celia was fourteen and the rest of us girls thirteen or nearly so, Uncle Dan came home, carrying the sack of groceries Aunt Libby had ordered over the phone, and saw a troop of boys sprawled around on the porch or hanging from the railings and balustrades. He stopped and asked them if there was some problem, had their mothers forgotten something at the market. They slunk off sideways and kicked the porch steps. But when Celia walked through the front door they came alive and in a fevered sprint backed away, running and hollering, to the far road, their speeding eyes in retreat still fastened on Celia, who smiled vaguely with a certain regal privilege. For a moment Uncle Dan's face was strange to us, unshielded by his bright mocking ironies. Then he recovered. Knew what was what. He appraised her long bare legs, asked it she had taken to going about half naked because of internal or external heat. She huffed, "Oh, Daddy! Don't be so old-fashioned," her face golden-lighted in the sun's reflection off her apricot hair, and she went inside tossing that mane, her legs slightly rigid at the knee, like a leggy colt. Uncle Dan flicked his gray, dust-colored eyes over the rest of us, who were dark-haired, with sallow complexions, or altogether too high-colored; he

13

smiled outright, also an expression rare for him, and he seemed newly primed for the changed direction life was taking.

And after that we knew too that there was something different in Celia. It wasn't just that she was older. It was a confidence that came upon her, suddenly and entirely, so that it didn't matter that summer after summer her hair had swung out with more sun-riffled gleam or that her body had swelled here and tightened there into a figure that was at the same time voluptuous and lissome. Effortlessly she appealed to boys, boys who ever after seemed to wander our place with the innocent milling confusion of lambs for the slaughter. That was what Aunt Libby called them, gazing out. "Those poor souls. They don't know what's hit them." She shook her head and sometimes found fault with Celia as if she were too provocative. "Just look at that butt": she'd frown out toward where Celia was talking fifty miles an hour to some boy, leaning on a car window, her body swiveling, her hair swooping in dips, her smiles tossed like fanciful flowers. We couldn't tell for certain whether Aunt Libby was angry or proud.

Celia's change separated her from the rest of us. She seemed indifferent, didn't need us anymore. We fell back, a little in awe. Where she was bold we were unsure, wondering what Aunt Libby would say. Anxiously we tried for Celia's attention, wanted fiercely to be included. But it was no use, that desire; we could not reach her, or be content without her. So we watched her life ravenously while waiting for her to make some slip.

But increasingly from afar, as though we were only strangers from the town. Outsiders. Even a horseback ride with Celia, something we'd done all our lives together, would take an unexpected turn, would become an excuse for an entirely different purpose—a forbidden rendezvous. We would find ourselves following Celia down an unknown back street of the town, where the factory people lived—where we remembered our family had once lived. Then, swarming from out of nowhere, came the dark-eyed foreign boys, drawn by the hooves clipping the brick and by some invisible vibration Celia set up in which the air quivered as if with a snare, or bridle bells. Ambling over to us from their slumped grimy houses, the boys would slouch against a post or picket in lazy wonder, lifting their gaze to Celia like an offering. Only the uneasy shifting of her horse, its prance, suggested any nerve or breaking through of impulse. We, her followers, subjects, were openly disheartened, far from home, uneasy about disobeying Uncle Dan, who had warned us to visit the blacksmith before we rode on pavement, to stick to known territory. It seemed Celia had forgotten Uncle Dan for good, had left everyone behind.

Still the day came when we had to face him. A customer at the market mentioned she'd seen his girls riding on South Belmont Street. He eyed us, angry and cold. Celia searched her nails for imperfections in the polish, then excused herself and left the table. Going under the door lintel, she appeared to be framed in the varnished oak. But the rest of us were still his little girls, the three of us stricken and despairing that all his goodness to us, the freedom we had, had been treated as nothing. After that we tried to avoid Celia—who didn't care and always did exactly as she wished, all her energy and her allegiance straining away toward a destiny we did not share or even understand. It was as though she trained obsessively for an event, a challenge we had heard of only distantly without comprehending any of our own desire. But when we dreamed, it was as though we too, like her, had been transformed.

Everything was changed. At the swimming pool Celia no longer entered the water unless she was thrown in by some boisterous youths, and then she let them, as eagerly, assist her in getting out, their hands now lingering and gentle on her. We peered out onto the front porch, the pack of boys more distant, even as we desired them more. It was seeing the way they waited, with a patient wistfulness for any attention Celia might chance to offer, boys who before had not wanted anything from a girl, that defeated us finally: Celia, in impartial imperious command, standing among them, her hands fixed like delicate fan clasps upon her jutting hips, her mouth small and yet full and piquant, like two sections of an orange. It seemed then that we were the intruders on our front porch, that everything belonged to Celia. We went into town, leaving her the porch while we sneaked into the swimming pool at night, or waited at the "Y" for the arrival of a few boys so that then we could walk the two miles home with our girl friends shadowed by the boys, who circled round us, calling out of the dark, fresh whoops coming nearer then moving further into the dark. Sometimes when we got home we'd stand behind the parlor drapes, up against the climbing roses of the wallpaper, and peek out onto the porch to watch Celia. Then we didn't laugh even to ourselves and there would be the run of saliva inside us, as though we were watching her eating steak.

*   *   *

Around us and behind us, Aunt Libby and Uncle Dan lived their married lives. There in Gram's big old house it seemed they had no relationship between themselves that wasn't ours as well, no function beyond their making up part of the life of the house. Uncle Dan usually came home from the market for lunch, still in his apron and hat, Aunt Libby parading around half dressed or not dressed at all, calling up through the attic stairwell—calling us girls to get up.

It was summertime and we girls talked most of every night (except Celia, who had begun to sleep alone in the room by the back stairs which had been Grandad's before he died), and it would be very late, nearly dawn, when we fell asleep. Then we slept on and on, through the mornings into the noon hours, while the increasing heat stifled us into a further resistance to waking. Off and on Aunt Libby would rouse herself to call us. Then she would sleep again too. We felt Aunt Libby could have slept forever. And perhaps Uncle Dan suspected as much, because usually he came home with something from the store for lunch. Aunt Libby would call out sharply that this time she meant business. We were already talking even as we lay waking, the two iron-frame double beds arranged side by side in the attic room, and then we would go down and Aunt Libby would be dressing herself as though her body belonged to all of us.

Aunt Libby left the bathroom door open; she talked to us while we sat on the tub or stood in the doorway; sometimes we would see a Kotex dangling between her legs. We felt sickened by the sight of it. Then she stood and arranged a fresh pad to ride amidst her prickly black hairs, between her olive stretch-marked cheeks. She dropped her used pads in the trash unwrapped; she said being female was a dirty business, no use trying to hide it. She pouted disdainfully, none of it her fault. Uncle Dan said that somehow none of this fit his particular notion of a child of nature; but he was never really offended, it seemed, although his own personal habits were discreet and modest. Perhaps to a butcher—stuffing entrails, grinding meat—such things were common enough.

But while she dressed, Aunt Libby reminded us of some swarthy half-wild gypsy woman, her face, partly obscured by her morning tumble of hair, conveying a mysterious charm as she stood by the closet door with her bra dangling from her hand, her smooth olive skin glowing around the pointed wrinkled berries of her nipples. Standing half in and half out of the closet, with no trace of self-consciousness, she appeared almost to reflect the flickering shadows of woods, while from the edge of a clearing all of us watched. Uncle Dan breezed in and out, whistling and razzing, and then he went down to the kitchen to make the meat sandwiches, talking to Gram, that old farm woman who hadn't been up that long herself but was already tapping her foot, impatient for the passing of time until she could bathe herself and put on her silken-jersey dress and go to the matinee at the Coronet or off to the races in Franksville.

Infrequent and bitter, Aunt Libby's and Uncle Dan's fights astonished us. A stifled row, overheard from the kitchen, a door slamming into its frame—then Aunt Libby shouting "goddamn" and "shit" and "turd," and Uncle Dan thundering down the stairs and out the side door, spitting gravel back at us as he disappeared up the drive in his delivery truck. Soon Aunt Libby would come down and tear into the sack he'd left on the counter and slam down the meat and pickles, the soft white bread. Gram, if she was there, her bottom lip out a mile, would take up for Uncle Dan, as if she knew all about it. We always heard her say that he was all right for a man, the best of the lot, and that Libby was too much of a damn fool to know when she was well off. Aunt Libby ignored her. Beneath the smoothness of her skin, more often sallow than golden, an undercurrent of turbulence ran now and it lit her eyes with a passion she seldom allowed to show, with a delight in the battle which had just belonged to her.

Their making up was in secret too, perhaps accomplished over the phone when Aunt Libby called the store to order the steak; usually by the time Uncle Dan drove in at evening it was as if nothing had happened. But sometimes we would hear Aunt Libby talking to her sisters while they canned peaches or boiled jam, or just drank coffee; saying that it was Dan's fault she had become so droopy-chested, a consequence of his ardent making up. It pleasured her, though, to be so desirable, fully mature and tempting, with even her brown eyes gold-shot at times like the ripe skins of the pears simmering, spiced dark with cinnamon and cloves.

There was one memorable fight; it lasted two days. Uncle Dan came home with groceries and a flowered lounge for the yard or porch and Aunt Libby hit the roof the second she saw him unloading it, yelling from the window, "We can't afford that kind of thing. You have no business. What would we do anyway with a piece like that?" Going on to tell Uncle Dan that he was forever needing some new trinket for amusement. When would he ever grow up? And when had he ever had a spare minute to lay in the sun?

"In California," he said, as he worked to adjust the mattress, "they're set up for this kind of thing. They don't mind a little fun. A fellow works all his life. What's the harm?" His face looked as though it had rained all his summers, his eyes gray from clouds that had passed over his heart.

Aunt Libby's voice spurted anger and something of alarm too. "You! You have a sudden uncontrollable notion to lay in the sun. What are you, a beach boy? Use a blanket. A towel, for God's sake. I don't live at home with my mother, scrimping and saving, to look out the window and see you snoozing on a bed of roses—orange roses at that. That thing reminds me of an orgy, just looking at it."

"That thing reminds me of everything I'll never have," Uncle Dan said.

"Then why didn't you stay the hell in California? You liked it so well."

Uncle Dan was silent, looking up at her from the yard at the bottom of the porch.

"Then don't complain. A bargain's a bargain." Aunt Libby went back inside, letting the door slam hard, as hard as her set face.

But Uncle Dan did keep it; it rested on the lawn through sun and storm until the cushions erupted soggy cotton swabs that we kids threw at each other. We used it in various ways until the frame finally cracked clear through and it wouldn't stay upright. Then we dragged it over into the high weeds by the doghouse and no one ever mentioned it again.

Just once we saw Uncle Dan make use of it: the first

Wednesday afternoon after he had bought it, the afternoon when all the stores in Sherwood regularly closed. He came home from the market, changed into a black knitted bathing suit which was a little tight, the front buckle digging into his stomach. It was the one he'd had in California. He wore a pair of dark glasses we didn't know he had and he took out a bottle of baby oil, pink with iodine, and a towel. He set the chaise precisely near the shadow of one of the spruce trees, which were taller than the house, right at the edge of the pool of darkness it made on the grass at noontime, and he turned on his portable radio, opened a beer and lay down. We wandered over near him and sat in a semicircle on the grass to watch him take his sunbath. He took a long drink from the bottle. His eyes were obscured behind the smoked glass. Perhaps they were closed. After a while, when he didn't move again or talk to us, we asked right out was he really going to tie one on. He raised up his glasses and peered at the four of us and his eyes were nearly lidless slits of slivered light. "Now that's some kind of talk. Whatever gave you that idea?" Then, his voice weary: "No, don't tell me." And we didn't want to say any more of the things Aunt Libby had muttered while she was crying and shoving the carpet sweeper over the floor. The air was stifling under the trees, drenched with resin and sap, Uncle Dan glistening with oils and sweat; for a moment we too seemed rooted together, captured in the presence of the dense trees, while beyond the swags of branch the blackbirds skimmed the field. Soon afterward he picked up all the things he'd carried out and went back inside the dark house. We sat on, transfixed before the flowered canvas mattress, until the advancing shadows covered us. Uncle Dan didn't come back to his lounge, although he left it sitting there, in plain sight, a reminder of California, of another life.

An accomplished seamstress, Aunt Libby spent much of her time in a little upstairs room, the room so littered with snips of thread, pins, scraps, it seemed she sat in an intricate nest of her own design. There was a green couch, old and sagging, a chintz-covered chair and the sewing machine console, a good one, modern and dependable. A silent, diffident, ill-at-ease woman outside the family group, with us she was absolutely herself, hardly capable of restraint. We girls flopped all over the furniture or the floor while Aunt Libby, a brace of pins in her teeth, embroidered her tales of disillusionment as with tiny needle tacks she tied off her threads. She whacked away at her own remnants of romanticism as if she could still be caught off guard and swallowed whole.

We might have passed Rosalie Morgan on the street that morning. Now she told us that Rosalie was "getting it." For shame, Rosalie Morgan. There was a thrill in it, no mistaking Aunt Libby's tone; but the peril of it was absolutely certain and without remedy. There rose in us a longing commensurate with our deprivation and fear. We blamed Aunt Libby. Wise and embittered herself, she would deny us even our early innocence so that, just as she intended, we would never learn for ourselves the full fascination and implication of her knowledge.

We accused her. "How do you know a thing about it? You don't even know Rosalie Morgan."

"I can smell it," she said. "Besides, I've known her mother since before you were born. Just take a good look at her eyes." Rosalie had larkspur eyes sunk in the bluish-brown circlets of their own thrown shadow. Those were the shadows of despair, Aunt Libby said. "For where can it lead, girls? Either Sammy will waltz off with the next one he spies, free and clear, or he'll hang around until he ends up having to marry her. And which is worse, I ask you?" She'd seen more than enough of that particular misery—wedlock forced on a resentful man who would never let you forget it.

There was never any hiding from Aunt Libby, sniffing and patrolling, everything figured out. Other people talked, around her, of weather or shopping. Aunt Libby half listened, preoccupied with her own divinations and prophecies. There was no arguing with her. So we didn't try—better silence and subterfuge. Someday we would escape. In the meantime we would lie low, guarding secrets and longings even from ourselves or we would have nothing left when she was done with us.

"You girls make me sick. Mooning around here. Swallowing all that crap." The machine whirred under her touch with the murmurous precision of a loom.

We reminded her of Aunt Rachel, who had remarried the summer before. That was love and she was blissful on account of it. Aunt Libby had to admit that. Right then, without her makeup, her mouth pinched, yellow-skinned, sepia-splotched, her tucked chin reminding us of Gram's fallen face, she was ugly to us—a woman spurned and rejected. Poisoned, she would poison us. She raised her eyebrows; we could see the stubble stumps, unplucked, in the glare from the window. "I s'pose," she snorted, two words, her tone bleak as ditch water in November. And we knew there was something more to it, more than we would ever know or want to, Aunt Rachel self-deceived, no happier than the whole love-lost world.

"There's one true love in the world, someone for everyone." We declared things like that. Then we would stand on our heads on the back of the sofa cushions, feeling the blood rush, our bare feet slapping the wall, so we didn't have to look at Aunt Libby's face, though still we could hear her derision in the mechanical and unerring drive of the needle down a seam.

"Don't think I don't know the charms of young men," Aunt Libby said, and we knew she did; beautiful again, a trace of blood spurting from her cold heart, illuminating the texture of her skin, warming yellow to gold. And her eyes softening like a melting amber. They hardened again. We trembled to hear her. In Aunt Libby there was none of Gram's flip "You may as well fall for rich as poor." For Aunt Libby it was a matter of outrage and contest.

She spoke to us incessantly of love. Endless betrayal, maidens forsaken, drowned or turned slut, or engulfed by madness. Most chilling were the innocent babes—stabbed with scissors and stuffed into garbage cans, aborted with knitting needles. In all this, love was a blind for something else. For sex. Sex was trouble and when a girl was in trouble, sex was the trouble.

Nor would Aunt Libby allow us the miscalculation that marriage put an end to trouble. Men were only after what they could get. When they got it they didn't want it anymore. Or wanted what someone else had. The same as the cars they bought and used. It was their nature. Some got nasty about it. That she attributed mostly to liquor—which men turned to out of self-pity and petty vengeance.

These matters were serious enough so that once the lid

was off she began to reveal family secrets. Long silences would punctuate her stories or comments, but we didn't harry her with questions, reminding her we were there, making her self-conscious. We waited. And finally she would continue, plainly needing to. "Dad would come in at night. When he was drunk. Fit to be tied. Get me and Rachel out of bed and beat us. For nothing."

She would begin another seam, her concentration flowing between her thoughts and the work. "He liked doing it, somehow. Like it worked through him and made him feel powerful. So then he would take on Momma afterwards."

Didn't she save you, we thought, Gram fierce as anything; we'd heard of her, straggle-haired and screeching, heading with the lye toward Grandad at the table, her daughters struggling with her for the can, rusted and half eaten through.

"He'd lock Momma out. And she'd stand beyond the door and pound and scream. After she got her money she dared him to try it again. 'Lay a hand on them kids.' But he was too smart for that. Or maybe it had all just been too much for him before. Seven of us. No money." Under the steady run of the sewing machine and her remembering, Aunt Libby seemed to open as though she were scratching old wounds. "Selma, my cousin. She told me once: her mother hid out in the barn when Uncle Del came home late from drinking. Only this time he caught her and took hold of her and forced her hand against the lantern globe until the flesh just melted. I remember seeing the mark of it when I was little." The mark of a man. Our own flesh burned.

"There's been more than one woman, I can tell you,

25

has come to feel so degraded and hopeless she can't go on. Your father," she would begin, looking at the two of us who were her dead sister's daughters, then biting her lip. "Well. She always went back." She didn't want to say more.

"Weren't you ever in love?" we asked her.

"More than once." She smiled downward at her own admission. "Or thought I was. Those Italian boys from the old neighborhood on North Street—beautiful dark boys." She wouldn't say more about that. We imagined for her a love that had killed love. We pitied her.

"Love," she spit out. "Sex is what it was and is and will be." The way she said "sex," we knew it was something wonderfully powerful, rising with a naturalness like the deep cold suck of water at the barnyard spring on a hot day. Love, on the other hand, she told us, was something you had to learn. "Love takes time. You learn it over a long time of being with a good man." It sounded like hard work and cold potatoes.

"Marry a man who loves you more than you love him"—that summed it up. And we thought of Uncle Dan down at the market, coming out of the food locker with a slab of meat over his shoulder, his eyes fathomless, glimmering under the bare bulb, inside him a heart raw with love for Aunt Libby.

"Don't let it fool you—sweet looks and sweet talk." What were we to do, desiring desire more and more as she paraded it before us in all its allurements; even her warnings were tempting. Sometimes now, by chance, we would see, in the appraisal of a male, a vision of ourselves changing, illuminated. Playing at the brook we saw a condom, flushed down the house sewage system, floating in the slime. Sex was going on all around us, in spite of danger and disruption; in spite of love.

Aunt Libby would push harder at the machine, driving it faster and faster as if she were getting someplace; we could see sparks spray off the wheel. "Oh my God, look what I've done now," the possibilities for disaster at her fingertips—perhaps a sleeve secured to a neckline, a collar binding a trouser leg. "See what I get for not paying attention," she said meaningfully, resigning herself to the punishment of painstaking backwork. Everything she made had to be just so, otherwise she would worry it endlessly, never forgive herself. Such was the discipline required to master the upheavals of passion, constantly lurking.

As we grew older, Celia was more and more absent from our sessions with Aunt Libby. All the time, though, we were thinking of Celia and Aunt Libby was too, for it was all coming due—Celia was now attracting college men who had cars and money they had earned themselves, pumping gas or cutting hay. They took her away from the farm, the town—dancing at a lake near Cleveland, out to restaurants where there was a wine list. Celia was forbidden to touch a single drop of the stuff and furthermore to ride in a car with anyone who did. "Two dead last night over in Mullerstown. Girl fifteen. Boy seventeen. And the other will wish she'd died, five hundred pieces of glass in her face." Aunt Libby looked over at Celia as though she had counted every sliver herself, but Celia didn't seem to care much, while she ironed each tuck down the front of a blouse, evidencing the perfectionism of her mother. Her face was still so clear and abstracted it could have been made of glass. Aunt Libby increasingly made mistakes in her sewing, threw four yards of misstitched dimity into the trash, then cried. She lost the thread of her hemstitch, the thread of her conversation. Agitated and distracted, she left the iron turned on for days at a time.

"I should have locked that one in a convent," she would say. This from a woman who thought the Catholic Church primarily responsible for the suppression of women, the promulgation of all claptrap. "Ever since she was little it was always the men. Climbing on their laps, teasing their whiskers. It's a family disease, I guess." But one she would cure if it killed her.

Yet there was something else in Celia, which wasn't pure obstinacy or boldness, something Aunt Libby couldn't touch because it was natural to Celia, coming as it did from her father. That was a kindheartedness, an absence of self-regard if any creature aroused her pity. A stray cat, a toddling baby—these had her attention while the rest of us failed. She would turn down dates to baby-sit for a relative's young children and once she sat all night with an injured dog from the highway, until even Gram relented and let her bring its basket out of the cellar. When it recovered, that dog took the place of the red setter that had once lived at the back of the yard; though the dog was a mangy mongrel now dragging a leg, Celia devotedly fed and groomed it, whispered into its ear, making the rest of us seethe with jealousy so that we ignored the dog completely. It wasn't that she disliked the rest of us, or the girls at school; it was more an absentness, an inability to focus her attention. As if we didn't need her.

At school this vagueness caused the teachers to give her nearly failing grades. It shamed Celia that they called her frivolous, using her red hair against her. Miss Warren,

who had once taught Aunt Libby too, kept Celia after
school day after day—she would teach her to name the
oceans and the continents. Celia gave it up and let them
think what they would. "By God, honey, don't let it go,"
Uncle Dan would plead if he came in while she was idling
away at the piano, working out by ear and feel some
melody line with rhythmic variations, useless though it
was to urge on her an ambition she couldn't feel. Perhaps
in another time she would have gone off to nurse the
wounded on the fields of battle, founded an orphanage.
Now she comforted those she saw in need. Those she
could help. And they approached her almost reverently, as
if simply to be in her presence were a healing thing; and
she made it so, boys so uncomplicated, their needs so
apparent and her hand so easily gentling. For a while she
responded to them all with the same exquisite sensitivity,
no favorites, although that changed when she was sixteen
and started going out with Corley, pouring her whole self
out, or so Aunt Libby feared.

Though Celia stayed alone in her room, we were no less
conscious of her, heard her phonograph playing, the strident riffs of Stan Kenton's saxophones and horns reaching
us. We imagined Celia in there upon her bed while around
her and within her everything was in motion, mounting,
going toward the time of fulfillment. She had only to make
herself ready. It was as though she were primed by that
music and by the surrounding aromatic dark-needled trees
with their depths and peaks, and then the fields and woods
that slid off to become transparent at the horizon, all
making for the unfolding and accomplishment of what was
growing unwaveringly within her and would have her yet.
Aunt Libby stitched away on tulle gowns draped with net

and flounces, finely bordered with sequins, each whirl arranged to dramatize the gown's colors of limed yellow or pale melon—all of it to enhance the evanescent dangerous glory of her first daughter. Her lips pursed under her squinted eyes, intent on the meticulous needlework, and with each yank of the thread she pulled from herself knowledge of the most intimate kind.

"Don't give it away," she told us. Did she want us to be misers? She might never have heard of love, sacrifice. We said nothing, afraid to hear. But bound to stay. Aunt Libby never spoke of sin, as though she knew nothing of that and didn't need to. She warned of impulse and consequence. Flattery and humiliation. "You'll learn fast enough; once he's gotten what he wants you're finished. He'll be gone. Or worse, you'll have him for good, and something else you didn't plan on and can't get rid of."

We were fourteen and then fifteen, sixteen. Aunt Libby was still sewing and instructing us, her younger daughter, Jenny, her two nieces, Anne and Katie, the daughters of her dead sister, Grace, while Celia stayed shut away in her room, carving and buffing her nails, rearranging her snapshots to frame the mercury-splotched looking glass, laying out on the tatted runner covering the bureau the different lucky charms, menus and dance favors. As though from a faraway tower, we heard June Christie singing "Something Cool."

"Don't be a man's plaything. Make him pay a good price—that way he'll value you more." Did Celia hear?

But if you love each other? We dared only think it, but she answered as though she'd heard. "Love"—two pins held in her lips while we listened to a trombone slide in the pause—"love is what they say. What they mean is an entirely separate thing.'' She smiled, the pins like bared fangs, like Gram when she talked about money. Her money. Then Aunt Libby's smile failed, went slipping away as if she had unpredictably lost the grip on her own bitterness.

We asked about Uncle Dan. ''You love him.'' We made it sound like an accusation.

''Shit,'' she yelped, the machine jamming. ''Look at this!'' She despaired over the pucker in the blue silk and for a time she strained over the mass of thread caught in the feed plate, digging with a darning needle. When it was dislodged, she went on sewing for a while, then said, ''Loving isn't anything easy.''

It was beginning to storm; the oak trees up by the road tossed to silver foam, fell back green again. There had been a lover once. An Italian boy with ardent glowing eyes. We imagined him for ourselves. The purple clouds were plowing in on the wind from the darker distance, weaving into garlands that hung over us like terraces as though we dwelt in Babylon. All at once, moving as one spirit, we did what we had not done for years: we dropped our clothes on the floor, on the stairs, as we ran down, and then on the porch, so that we were fully naked by the time we leapt onto the grass. The rain chilled, stung against our skin, turned to hail. Then Celia came out too, with us again after long years, flying over the grass, prancing, flowing with rain, her golden-red hair streaked dark with rain, streaming out. She was like a separate force quickening us, urging us further by her possibilities. Over the grass we ran and slid until it churned, spattered and oozed with mud; we painted ourselves, each other, immersed in the driveway ditch of foaming brown for a rinsing, before we took the mud slide again. We formed a whip, flung ourselves over the grass. Until Celia stopped and looked up the drive, sideways, hiding herself. A car passed on the highway, silent and distant as though driven by a phantom. Celia stood covered with her crossed arms and like that, suddenly, we all ran onto the porch and grabbed for towels or rags from the shelf, shivering gooseflesh like a disease.

Celia had him in the parlor. We stayed in the living room across the hall and were quiet, listening for any sounds they might make. We never heard any talking. This night Aunt Libby and Uncle Dan had gone out and Corley had come later, so we were the only ones who saw him go into the parlor with Celia and close the door.

The hall light was out. Across the darkness we could see the slight border of light under the double panel doors and between them where they pulled together. There was no hurry. We waited.

Going out of the room, Celia left the door open so we could see Corley waiting there while she was in the kitchen. She didn't even glance at us. Corley was her new boyfriend and already she was different with him. The other boys didn't come to the house now and she saw him every night Aunt Libby would allow it. Celia arguing nonstop all afternoon, then over supper. Corley wore his wavy hair in a slick ducktail, which he was constantly combing; we watched the muscles in his arms quivering even from that little bit of movement. When he smiled, his full lips barely lifted and there was no change in the expression of his thick-lidded eyes. Aunt Libby said he was lazy as the day is long, you could tell that by looking at him, and he wouldn't ever get out of bed once he'd got Celia into one.

She said he dripped sex. To us that seemed to go along with his wet-looking hair.

Still we thought he was cute and Celia was lucky. He grinned now, combing his hair. "How you all doing?" His family had come up from Kentucky and he still talked that way, with a voice mushy and thick like his lips.

"Fine." We shrugged.

"Here's some money," he said. "You want to get some ice cream?" He must have thought we were still kids. There was a Dairy Delight now on the far lot beside the gas station; Gram spoke of her fields and meadows as lots now.

Sure, we said, knowing he wanted to get rid of us, knowing too what we'd do when we got back. We took our time walking there because there were a lot of cars driving in and out of the parking lot on a Saturday night and we knew some of the guys. Walking back, we felt the connection with the rest of the world sever as we left the high lamps and passed beyond the cedar hedge onto the dark gravel, the house shadowy too now, with only one small glow of light in the front hall.

We needed no words. We moved to the grass to quiet our walking. Through the gap in the honeysuckle we sneaked and climbed over the railing and stood to one side of the window, where we could see at an angle past the half-drawn drapes. At first we could scarcely make them out where they were on the floor, bound in one shape. We licked our ice cream and carefully, silently dissolved the cones, tasting nothing as it melted away down inside us. Tasting instead Corley's mouth on ours, its burning wild lathering sweetness. In the shaft of light we saw them pressed together, rolling in each other's arms, Celia's flowery skirt pulled up around her thighs. His hand moving there. Then she pushed him away, very tenderly, went to sit back on the couch while Corley turned his back and combed his hair. He turned and started toward her, tucking his shirt in. We stared at the unsearchable smile that lifted from Celia's face like a veil and revealed another self, as she began to unbutton her blouse, undressing herself until she sat there in the half-dark, bare to the waist, bare to the moon which had come up over the trees behind us. She drew Corley to her, his face after he'd turned around never losing its calm, kissed him forever, it seemed, as long as she wanted to. Then she guided his mouth to press into first one and then the other cone-crested breast, her own face lake-calm under the moon. Then she dressed again. Our hearts plunged and thudded. At that moment we were freed from Aunt Libby. We didn't care what it was called or the price to be paid; someday we would have it.

Terrible battles began between Aunt Libby and Celia. Breaking out anywhere—in the kitchen, the hall—night or day, their screaming and slamming rocked the entire house, made Uncle Dan say he had a headache all the time just waiting for them to get started. Something had alerted Aunt Libby; she wouldn't leave the house at night in case Corley came over, and she made Celia leave the parlor doors ajar. They fussed over how wide a crack it should be, the dimensions of privacy. When Aunt Libby sniffed that she didn't hear much talking going on, Celia snapped back that they couldn't talk when they were under surveillance like prisoners by an old busybody. Old! Aunt Libby's eyes sealed, impenetrable.

Celia came into the living room one night, leaving

Corley behind in the parlor. "Mom, we're driving to Abnerville." Corley's married sister lived there.

Aunt Libby wanted to say no, never. We watched her struggle. She fastened her attention on Celia's legs, long and tanned below her white shorts. "You're not going like that," she said, her voice, once found, taking the bull by the horns.

"Mother." Celia ground her teeth. The clock ticked as firmly as Aunt Libby's mind was made up. Celia went upstairs and put on a skirt. Then they fought over the time she was to be home. "Eleven," Aunt Libby insisted. "Twelve," Celia said, and banged out the door.

"Goddamn little rip," Aunt Libby said to us.

At eleven-thirty Aunt Libby was drinking hot milk in the kitchen. She kept her eyes on the table. Now and then we looked up at the clock, high over the painted wainscoting; never washed, its face was fuzzy with soot and grease. It was past midnight when the lights at last came down the drive. They lighted up the orchard as the car made the wide circle and left again. Celia came in. Aunt Libby looked pasty sick. Celia glanced at her and said, "What's the matter with you, old sourpuss?" but smiling. Her face was pale and tired, her mouth blurred at the edges from all the kisses we imagined there.

Aunt Libby got up, deliberately, and went over and slapped Celia's face. "Bitch," she hissed at her, and slapped her again, harder. "Tramp."

The slaps rushed the blood to Celia's face. It fell as fast, leaving her gray as ash dust save for her smeared orange mouth, tangled hair. "I could have, you know," she screamed, crying at the same time. "I wanted to, but I

35

didn't. Now I wish I had. I will for that," and she ran up the stairs.

Aunt Libby was after her, her aqua cotton dress pulling up and showing her brown thighs which slapped together as she went, her face horrible in dismay, in fear of the worst, of what she'd done herself. "Well, I'll kill you first myself, if it comes to that." We could hear her, although what she said came in a low guttural moaning from the hall. "Throw yourself away, will you! Open this door, I tell you. Open it!"

We were left in the kitchen with the black sea of night awash at the screens. Fireflies like flying phosphorescent fishes sailed through the orchard. Apples fell to their ruin. We could smell them softening in their own brine.

Later Celia and Aunt Libby made up. Uncle Dan had roused himself and declared through his door, "I don't ask for a whole hell of a lot around here," and Aunt Libby quit screaming and pounding and Celia opened her door and they went in together. Once again, it was over. They seemed to us like lovers who quarrel for the sake of reconciliation.

We sat on in the kitchen until another car came creeping down the drive. We listened for the slight scratching sound of Gram coming up on the granite stoop, her step silent on the carpet, slow and halting.

"There was a fight," we told her, wanting to say more.

She snorted once, didn't ask a thing. "I'm tired. You kids turn out them lights." She'd seen a million fights.

"Did you win?" We always asked her that, although from her evasive answers there was no real telling; sly and secretive, apt to lie, we thought, to protect her little bit of magic. "Maybe," she said. "Well, I'm going up to roost.

Night now.'' She hung her light woolen coat in the closet and treaded her way up the long curved stair toward the darkness of her room; with everybody home, we felt the fields and sky fold inward to wrap up the house for bed. Gram had survived more battles than we had dreamed of, a regular old war-horse, Uncle Dan called her. Gluey-eyed, longing for sleep, we followed her.

After Corley there was Mike. Then Bud, Roger, Hal—strange boys whose last names we never knew, only the names of the towns they came from: Oakfield, Madison, Peru. Later, for a long time, there was Jimmy, for such a long time we thought Celia would marry him—forsaking all others, finally letting Aunt Libby settle down. Aunt Libby had started to have stomach trouble; she burped so regularly that she didn't try to hide it or excuse herself, allowing the burning gas to erupt from her, the signal of her own wretchedness. She dosed herself with chalky liquids and chewed on saltines. She was already thin as a girl and grew thinner. When we went places out of town, people thought she was our older sister. But they saw her high-heeled, made up, brown eyes aglow. They didn't know the source of that fire; didn't watch her trembling over the kitchen sink, her body heaving dry and empty.

It was as though that first open battle with Celia had broken some reserve and refinement in Aunt Libby; we never knew after that when another fight would rage. The waiting for them and preparing for them preoccupied Aunt Libby, further sapping her strength. She left off talking to the rest of us about love and sex. She stopped fighting with Uncle Dan and he seemed to spend the late hours of every night getting in and out of bed by himself, trying to get things to quiet down so he could sleep a little before he had to open up the store in the morning. Out many nights ourselves by then, although never as regularly or extravagantly entertained as Celia, we were content to go around in groups and to get home on time.

Ordinarily we came home about the time Aunt Libby got out of bed to wait up for Celia and sometimes to fight. Our hearts would draw into silence until some exhausted tension or battered anxiety would give way and there would be peace again—Celia and Aunt Libby talking far into the night, an intimacy feeding off secrets and mysteries. To the rest of us Aunt Libby vowed she would protect her daughter. Die trying. We went our own ways—denied now her confidences and cautions. It was the fiery and reckless Celia whom she braced for, boasting of it too. Had any other daughter in the whole world ever been such a handful, so wondrously alluring? We went riding with Aunt Rachel and when we cantered the horses along the north pasture, sometimes caught by dark and the rising moon, still letting them have their heads as we raced toward the shed we used as a barn, calling back and forth through the urgent dusk, our blood would sing, unvoiced: "Oh, Johnny is my darling, my darling, a Union volunteer" —just then we felt we had everything that Celia had, through her.

Still we hated Celia, hated what she was doing to her mother. Once when Aunt Libby knocked the skillet to the floor and then drove off in the car, screaming and sobbing— drove the way Grandad used to career past when he'd been drinking what Gram called firewater—we thought she would kill herself. We envisioned her lurching over hill and dale until she sailed off the cliff of the ravine.

Frightened, divided in loyalty, we fumed at Celia through the door of the bathroom where she'd shut herself. Told her she was cruel and selfish, was killing her mother. When she came out, pale and cold-eyed, she continued to prepare for the forbidden dance, refused to answer.

"You spoil her," we accused Aunt Libby. "If we ever so much as thought . . ." But we couldn't get Aunt Libby to pay attention to us, other than a vague distracted smile of gratefulness for our goodness, for sparing her.

She lived through her wild ride, lived to call and calmly tell us she was with Aunt Rachel, who now lived in a small house on the edge of the farm with her son Rossie and her new husband, Tom Buck. Had we found anything to eat? It was Uncle Dan's late night at the store, something he now had to do to compete with the supermarkets in outlying shopping centers.

When we were home nights with Uncle Dan, it was like old times. He popped corn by the bowlful, brought home chips and cheese spread, fixed icy Cokes and made his remarks, generally reflecting on the level of confusion around the place, which made him feel that at last, years after the war, his ship had left the port of San Francisco. He'd bought a television set just as soon as the price came down, just like a kid, Aunt Libby said, and we watched together in the dark living room with Uncle Dan serving us, doing his best to entertain us. Aunt Libby, passing by, would pause a moment in the doorway, half amused in spite of herself, and would then go on shaking her head as Uncle Dan called after her, "Honey, all of us can't continually ponder the darker side." When she didn't answer he would shrug and be thoughtful for a while—until *Broadway*

Open House came on and he could watch Dagmar, whose tits he said always put things in perspective.

About eleven o'clock, Uncle Dan would carry the bowls and glasses to the kitchen and go up to bed and we would feel a little lonely, although not ready to leave ourselves, Gram and Celia yet to come home, perhaps the real drama of the evening still to happen. Our entertainment with Uncle Dan was the beginning of the night and as he was on his way up to bed, Aunt Libby was on her way down from reading in bed—passing like ships in the night, Uncle Dan called it. There in the downstairs hall Aunt Libby would position herself with her needlework and then later, when Celia would be parked out in the drive, staying in the car with whoever her current boyfriend was, she would begin to flip the porch light switch every five minutes, until Celia would fling herself in for a moment, demanding more time, pleading for it, then disappear again, finally to be forced in by the light signaling in warning across the dark like a lighthouse probe. Aunt Libby figured that Celia wasn't going to get too carried away in her own driveway with her mother announcing her presence. Sometime in there Gram would come home. Uncle Dan always said what a pi̱ it was that an old woman like that had to work the night shift. When he couldn't sleep because of all the commotion, the comings and goings, he would appear on the stairs, decently wrapped in his bathrobe, and announce to one and all that there was more going on in his house after dark than in a whorehouse.

One night we overheard him talking to Aunt Libby, serious for once. "Let her be. Let her live her own life. You had your chance."

"Yes, and see where it got me."

We couldn't hear what he said next, but we knew his mild and quizzical expression.

"Oh, shut up, Dan," she said. "You know very well what I mean. It's just that I think Celia has a real good chance. Better than most."

"You've got two daughters," he reminded her.

"Jenny's like me. She can compromise if she has to. She's got good sense. Celia's different. It's the waste I object to. Pure waste. If I can just get her married to a good man. Before it's too late."

"Wouldn't hurt her to lose a little blood first. I've heard of worse things."

"Dan Snyder, are you crazy?"

"Probably am. Always was, about you."

We heard the familiar capitulation in her tone, a warming current touching her place of love. "Well, I always knew I got better than I deserve. I'm not easy."

Later we heard Uncle Dan whistling his way down the stairs to the cellar, where he was learning to draw. Following an open workbook, using an arc and a ruler, he was trying a vase of flowers. In the dimness beyond the aimed desk lamp, he told us, there were sometimes rats that scurried past, though there was no longer food stored there. Uncle Dan said he didn't mind sharing, made him feel he was suffering for art, and anyway they were a lot less troublesome than a pack of overheated females. All the same, we thought he might amount to something, mastering sepals and petals with mechanical precision in a dungeon.

When Celia was a senior in high school she met Phillip. He was going to study law when he was through at the college, and already he had more money to spend than anybody we knew, including Gram, and he took Celia to dinners in Mencina and Cleveland, for Swedish smorgasbord at country inns. During the summer he drove up the fifty miles from his hometown. Increasingly he spent time talking to Aunt Libby and after a while he was even stopping off at the store to pick up things she needed. Theirs were serious talks, Aunt Libby confiding her concerns about Celia, her high-strung nature, her willfulness, her sympathetic heart. It was as though Celia were a bred filly that Aunt Libby was handing over to an experienced trainer; Phillip had gained her confidence. There were fewer fights. He brought Celia home on time, soothing them both, the go-between.

Phillip would say, "We'll be a little late tonight; the dance is in Oakland," and Aunt Libby would nod, agreeable and relaxed, her legs hooked up over the side of the armchair, showing most of her thighs, the way she sat when she felt peaceful. Her stomach settled more easily now and her face had regained that glow, hint of gilt, suggesting the edges of pages in an old cherished romance.

"Is she smoking?" Aunt Libby would ask.

Phillip had the smoking in hand, allowed her only four an evening. Celia's best interests were his.

He was undeniably handsome, and his whole bearing expressed his instinct for command. Well-clothed and organized, he didn't interest us the way Corley had, or the other boys. Already he seemed as settled in as Uncle Dan. Uncle Dan said he certainly had the gift of gab; he said it as if it were nothing he had ever wanted for himself. But for Aunt Libby Phillip was a godsend, someone who understood Celia, and although there was plenty in him smoldering just beneath the surface, he was content to wait. She liked that in a man—self-control.

Phillip had his eye on the future and on his path for getting there in law, real estate, politics. Aunt Libby's gaze inched over him. She squinted, as though she were measuring him against a pattern she had in mind. She accepted his prospects as good ones; hazy about the particulars of that future he anticipated, she put her stock in her judgment of the man. It was as though that future time need not concern her, after she had turned Celia over to him.

Those two would talk comfortably and confidentially while waiting for Celia to appear. She was always late. Then at last she would be coming down the stairs, calling ahead with her rattling excitement so we'd be expecting her, straining toward her.

She stood in the doorway, dressed in a gathered print skirt, newly made, the colors clear as fresh-cut flowers, her white blouse starched, open at the throat.

"I guess you just had to iron it a second time," Aunt Libby said. "And no stockings." We all looked with her at Celia's fine-boned ankle, circled by a mesh chain dangling a tiny locket heart. As yet no man's, she was ours, our achievement, our possibility. This wealth was ours— the hundred acres of woodland and field, Gram's fortune, Celia's bewitching charm. Her hand drooped against her skirt. Phillip reached for it. We could have stabbed him. But she went with him out the side door onto the solid cut-granite stoop and down the four steps. The car started up and left. We heard the leaves fanning against the screens. And smelled Celia's perfume lingering on the air, as though all of nature were excited too.

"That man is a blessing," Aunt Libby said.

"Too bad you can't have him for yourself," Uncle Dan answered, dead level, carrying a tray of Cokes into the room. "What our Libby needs is a honey-tongued talking mule." He winked at us.

"Oh, hush," she said, but he couldn't make her mad. She said, "If that's what I need, then I've already got it." And she went on peaceful, gazing into the evening light which filtered across the gray ferns of the wallpaper, bending them up and down.

"I'm just so thankful she didn't marry Corley," Aunt Libby said one afternoon while she did some hand stitching on a bridesmaid dress she had designed in pale rose silk, with insets of lace taken from an old gown of Gram's. "I wouldn't doubt he's partly Italian. Dark like that." Now that Celia was preparing for her wedding, Aunt Libby was regaining some of her old style, thinking out loud to us, her fingers advancing over the fine silk, the rose ruffled against the ivory lace.

"He loved her a lot," we said, recalling his masking indolence, the half-glutted lion roaming behind the grass-cover of his lashes.

"I never doubted that. And I thought I'd never stop her. Doubling all the time with that Ruthie Thompson and Rossie and heaven knows what they were up to. That winter her nerves were terrible; she was thinner and wilder every day. I just don't know."

We knew——for once, more than Aunt Libby maybe—— what Rossie and Ruthie were up to. Ruthie told us that once when she was sitting on his lap he said for her to look down and she'd about died laughing after she got over the shock of it; because he'd opened up his pants and it was standing up beside her elbow, fresh as a daisy. We were so embarrassed for Rossie, our cousin, we could hardly think about it, but Ruthie got a kick out of it—always jolly and easygoing. About sixteen, she dropped out of high school, pregnant. "Right on schedule," Aunt Libby said.

"There's nothing to be done about it," Aunt Libby said now. She meant us, our family. Being female. She referred to it as if it was both a miracle and a calamity, that vein of fertility, that mother lode of passion buried within us, for joy and ruin. "None of us can no more than look at a man and we're having his baby. Look at Florence"— Aunt Libby's cousin, who still took in ironing to help support over a dozen children. And there was Gram with her soiled and faded apron and her exhausted face, marked like an old barn siding that had withstood blasts and abuse of all kinds, beyond any expression other than resignation and self-regard.

"It will be my release, the day I hand her over to Phillip," Aunt Libby said, molding a rose out of scrap velvet, to set in the bodice on a green-piped stem. We remembered Corley, his lips hot as a brand on Celia.

Then Uncle Dan came home right in the middle of a Friday afternoon. We knew something had to be wrong. He called out once, "Libby," crossed the dining room and went up the stairs to their room.

Before she followed him, Aunt Libby glanced out at the meadow dripping in the rain, beyond the thin aisle of lawn that every year Uncle Dan was making narrower, mowing less, leaving Gram's peony bushes as the border. It was as though it fortified her, that swell of meadow; already she looked resigned to the worst, something she'd half ex-

pected all along. Often she'd warned us that moments of
happiness hang like pearls on the finest silken thread,
certain to be snapped, the pearls scattered away. Up the
stairs she went, from the back, in her shorts, looking like a
girl, her face, reflecting darkly in the hall mirror, capable
of any age.

And we were waiting, afraid; it might have been a long
time, the pale rain rills sliding hypnotically over the glass.
Then we heard water running above us, Aunt Libby in the
bathroom splashing and blowing, and then she came down.

"Oh, God." She sobbed away, hugging her tumultuous
stomach. "How will I ever tell her? And I trusted him.
Fool." Our wise conspiratorial Libby thrown. Still we
were giddy with excitement, deliciously free to mourn
openly with her over her wounded pride and bitter
disillusionment, although we didn't know exactly what the
trouble was. Which caused Uncle Dan to examine us for
an instant as he strode over to the high shelf where the
unused milk crocks were lined up and brought down the
whiskey bottle hidden there, and drank off in front of Aunt
Libby one gulp which went on so long and seemed so
agreeable to him that right then we understood something
of her vigilance, knew we'd be just like her. His eyes
darkened, then, taking on that same bordering indigo of
the crocks, subject to his grim drinking mood. He drank
again. Then capped the bottle. "I'm going now, Libby,"
he said, and so we imagined his departure for war, before
they knew he would be in California for the duration.

Gradually, Aunt Libby calmed. Told us what a woman
from Millersburg, Phillip's aunt by marriage, had come to
town to tell Uncle Dan that afternoon. She could not stand
across the counter and ask for a pound of hamburger and

not tell Uncle Dan that Phillip Masterson was the uncontested father-to-be of Louanne Price's child, which was no longer anybody's little secret. At one time Phillip had gone steady with Louanne. But this pregnancy had happened recently, since his engagement to Celia. Everybody was counting. Aunt Libby said that Uncle Dan was so fired up she didn't know what he might do, and we all remembered Grandad's rabbit gun still leaning against the back of the pantry closet.

Gram came in from the matinee while we sat at the kitchen table. We could smell the rusty screening at the windows and the stale stained cloth as she pulled her apron off the hook. She reached into the potato bin and started a curl of peeling toward the drain.

"Well," she said as she plopped the first one in a pan of cold water and began a second. " I already heard. Reckon scandal borrows wings."

In the presence of her mother Aunt Libby was nearly herself again, restored to the stability of hard knocks and no nonsense. "I guess we've been fooled."

"Some fool easier than others. But sooner's better than later, I'd say. Don't ask me why she's in such an all-fired hurry to get hitched anyways. Lasts too long as it is." Gram turned the fire sky-high under the pork chops and they began to smoke and scorch right off. She couldn't wait to get them on the table. Under the potatoes she raised a great flame, setting the pan on the burner with a bang as though she still cooked on an iron stove. "Have fun while you're young, I say—not much you can do when you're old and ugly."

"You're beautiful to us," Aunt Libby said, and indeed the afternoon sun turned Gram's coiled iron-gray curls to a crinkly crimson when she stood just so in the light. But only an instant; she was in a great hurry, dropping plates on the table, dealing tableware like cards.

"You're not going out tonight—not tonight?"

"Am too."

"But, Momma. Celia's going to take it hard."

"Phooey. She's well rid of him. Ain't nothing I can do anyways. Maybe she'd like to come along with me," she added, offering a real prize, her own one reliable pleasure.

"The roads are terrible. Twenty's closed on account of water."

"Don't matter to me. It's clear to the west. I'll take number thirty. I've gone through worse, I suspect, and the horse was scared too." Gram was proud of what she'd survived; once she'd turned eighty she boasted of her age, couldn't tack on another year soon enough. She poured water on the chops to stop the burning and clamped on a lid, opened green beans she'd canned the last year she had a garden—they had to boil fifteen minutes and she'd wait for that. She'd known more than one family that had died, every last one, from a taste of spoiled green beans. Everything was now frying and boiling at top speed. Sow-bellied, spike-legged, there was still something about her tough management of the supper that stirred like an exuberant passion that had not been so much used up as outlived.

We tried to eat what she'd cooked, working down small bits of the hard dry pork with lots of milk. Gram ignored the meat and ate through a plate of green beans with vinegar ladled on it and then cut herself two slabs of the white Dutch loaf. Its powdery dusting of flour sprinkled the table and her front; she cut it, cradling it in her arms, sawing the iron butcher knife back and forth across the front of her sunken breasts, squeezing the bread against herself. "I swear, Momma. Someday . . ." Aunt Libby flinched and held her own two breasts in her hands. But Gram paid no attention, knew what she was doing. She saw us watching her and, for once, in a shy flash of generosity, offered each of us a thin slice. "Don't pester me for more, though, or the next time you'll get nothing." The country butter had little specks of white whey. The bread was so soft we hardly had to chew it. Maybe it was because Gram had lived so long and had so much trouble that she subsisted almost entirely on these soft white loaves. As she mouthed the bread her mouth gleamed with the fat of cows—content as a ruminant herself, forgetful. But then she startled: the pale watery veiling of sunlight over the orchard struck the hammered brass planter hanging between the two windows. That reminded her. Time to be gone. She gathered the plates in one sweeping motion while we were still chewing, rested them on the hump of her stomach and pushed what remained into a slop pail, as if she still had chickens and hogs to feed. "Now I done enough. You gals, wash them dishes. Boil that cloth. It stinks like shit." She winked her childlike pleasure in her little joke, which had made Aunt Libby frown. She added then, "In my next house I'm going to have one of them dishwashers."

Then a car came down the drive and Celia got out. We heard her ring of good cheer as she called goodbye. Since her future was settled with Phillip she had become friendlier with other girls; they weren't so afraid of her now. She was even more outgoing around the house. But when Celia came into the room she knew by looking at her mother that something had gone wrong with her life. We didn't know until then that Celia was like the rest of us, always waiting for something terrible to happen.

"Goddamn it, Libby," Gram said, "tell her"—nearly mad with impatience, Celia her favorite out of all her grandchildren. She moved toward Celia with her neck extended, taut as a goose's and using every bit of her waggle of extra chin. "You ain't going to fall to pieces because of a man's fool doings." And she told Celia, just that way, telling her what was wrong, and at the same time telling her how she was to take it. "Ain't a man born yet that's interested in more than a couple of inches of a gal anyway. So now you know it too," she ended up, red as the fires she cooked over, as if to cauterize the whole house with the rage and passion that still persisted in her.

Gram laid her old work-worn hand on Celia's arm. "You go on and cry. Cry your eyes out and then get over it!" Before she left she took four nickels from her pocketbook and put them on the sink, as though we were still little kids.

Celia sat and lit a cigarette, the first time she'd smoked in front of her mother since she had learned to do it from Corley. Although she didn't cry, her face was mottled with the sudden splotch and bruise of high feeling which redheads show. Aunt Libby whispered to the rest of us, talking of Celia's nerves so that we almost felt we could see them tracing her fragile skin, the way veins are visible on the surface of leaves held against the light. The way Aunt Libby talked, we expected Celia to blow up, smoking and sizzling, her nerves shorting out.

"I can't imagine what Dan's doing," Aunt Libby fretted. The wet orchard grass and briers gleamed like washed planking, while above, the branches held green sails to the wind. Aunt Rachel had fancied that once and we didn't forget, never let ourselves forget any of it; we knew we'd have to live our whole lives off what they'd said and done around us.

"Look," Aunt Libby said. At the edge of the field two does stood. Their ears flicked. None of us moved. Gram banged out the side door.

"Momma." Aunt Libby pointed toward the vanishing tails. "You scared them."

"Ain't nothing. Come for apples. You could see them on any morning, if you'd get out of bed before noon. Makes them sick, though. Tipsy. But they always come back for more. Like some fool man." She choked a declarative roar from the car. She felt relieved, released, we could tell—getting away from us.

Aunt Libby turned back to Celia, who smoked her cigarette with a fervent concentration. "Try to get it out, dear," she told Celia. "Cry." Then Aunt Libby released a long rumble of her own discomfort.

"Mother." Celia spoke for the first time, her nerves threatening.

"I can't help it. I should eat something."

"Then do." Celia got up and went toward the stairs. "And see if you can find Daddy, before he does something stupid."

But we just sat on at the table. For hours. Aunt Libby drank milk, which we warmed for her. "I don't know how much she can stand," she said.

There were things we could tell, wanted to tell. We closed our mouths and watched Aunt Libby clutching her stomach, which we imagined tight and cramping like her desiccated mouth. We could tell about Celia, but we had promised. With Aunt Libby we stared toward the highway, expecting Uncle Dan.

"It's just like him to disappear like this and worry me to death. Up to God-only-knows-what." She told us that Uncle Dan always had had a fresh streak in him: the night she met him he'd told her she would end up married to him. "Keep on hoping," she'd said. A little dandy, not a hair taller than she was, clowning for attention all the time. A party drinker too. But of course he'd given that up for her; one way and another he'd had his way, wormed himself into her affections. "Well, I'll walk on over to Rachel's." She put on her sweater. We stared after her as she went, slender with the last light absorbing her into its quiet grasp, walking through the orchard where the deer had stood.

Aunt Libby hadn't been gone long when what Uncle Dan called the nightly excitement began. First we thought we heard Celia talking on the upstairs phone. So when we heard the car on the gravel, we ran to the parlor window in time to see her opening the door and slipping in as the car barely paused to scoop her up and continued the circle of the drive, speeding toward the highway. We could tell from Phillip's face that he'd heard what had happened. They didn't greet or even look at each other. In the silence they left behind, we felt the trees and early stars and land pitch together. Only the brick house stood firm against it, stretching away up over us, cold and empty as though it had felt each desertion, slow death and failure that had occurred and, like someone with a stern character, had been made stronger yet numb from having suffered them. "Celia's gone," we imagined Gram saying, "and she ain't never coming back." Seeing Phillip made us feel for the first time that something had really changed, feel it more than Uncle Dan's coming home in the middle of the afternoon. Like selfish and evil stepsisters, spurned and embittered, we wanted Phillip for ourselves, lusted after his newly blemished self. Now we could tell Aunt Libby—about Corley, Jimmy, the others too whom Celia still met, sneaking and lying herself, while pretending to be so blameless and true. And now broken-hearted. False herself, she played men for fools. While we, constantly nagged by an old biddy, protected ourselves for nothing, against nothing. Although it was early, we locked all the doors that were never locked and went up to our attic room.

But there was someone else on the drive. This time it was Jimmy, lurching toward the house on foot, muttering, "I'll kill him. Fucking son-of-a-bitch. Kill him." The lights from the dairy across the road glinted on the rifle he was carrying, the bottle he drank from. "Celia," he yelled. Then, "Celia," wavering to aim the gun toward the house as if he didn't know whom or what he was going to shoot. We didn't call down. He stumbled around and we could hear him crying and muttering her name and then we heard him farther away again, his voice trailing back to us from the lane leading toward the woods. Sometime later we woke up. Because we heard someone with a key scratching on the side door, trying to unlock it. Uncle Dan was talking then in the front hall. In the dark we edged, half sliding down the banister so the stairs wouldn't creak, to the landing on the second floor. Down below, through the railing, we saw Uncle Dan's bald spot under the globe and his elbows stabbing out as he made a strange girl comfortable, helping her remove her sweater, fixing a cushion for her back. Sure as anything, we knew it was Louanne

Price. On her face were the inescapable purple shadows of despair and poor judgment. We couldn't see her stomach.

"Want a Coke or something while we wait?" Uncle Dan asked.

She closed her eyes. "No, thank you."

They seemed to know already that Celia had gone out with Phillip.

"Don't mind if I do," he said, and went into the kitchen. Below us Louanne's face rested so deeply she looked like a child in a dreamless sleep. When Uncle Dan returned she didn't open her eyes and he sat at the other end of the sofa, drinking calmly, his mouth holding the warming liquid; he could have been almost contented. Once he looked up toward where we were in the dark. Then at Louanne. "It won't be long, I guess," he assured her.

The leaves outside the landing window began to rustle without a perceptible rise in the wind, without force, just marking the later hour, the shifting balance, cooler air coming in. Everything seemed more peaceful as we waited.

We heard another car on the drive. We didn't move to look—leaving everything to Celia, the way we always had. She came in with Phillip, holding his hand; solemn and spent-looking, they seemed about to announce some momentous decision to their grave and startled audience. Until Celia saw Louanne. Then she stepped away from Phillip, while Louanne rubbed her eyes with her fists like a newly awakened child. Uncle Dan watched everything, a curious onlooker, relatively unconnected with a complicated affair. Phillip looked as before, stern and hopeless. He left abruptly, telling Celia that he would call her tomorrow, saying something about not being railroaded.

Louanne began to shed the tears of a child. And soft-hearted Celia, devoted to dogs and small children, all needful things, a nurse in wartime, a camp follower for ravaged men, took Louanne in her arms and told her everything would be all right. "He still cares for you. He told me so tonight," she murmured in ballad-like cadence. Celia's clear voice rose out of the column of her throat in unfaltering renunciation of whatever was trivial and low. Only her skin, blanched white as a substratum of exposed bone, showed the strain of her feelings.

"But he seems to hate me," Louanne got out. "He was so angry when I told. I just had to tell somebody, you know. I was so afraid that he might try to kill me, like that girl in the movies. And he says he won't ever marry me."

"Of course he will." Celia stroked her hair. "He has to." She had learned some things from Aunt Libby. She was still comforting Louanne when Aunt Libby came in. With one glance she knew everything—"it" written all over Louanne, while we were thinking that if that was how "it" made you look, then who would ever want it. Uncle Dan gazed straight up at us then and said, "You might as well get in on the act." So we went down. Jimmy had wandered back into the yard and we could hear him muttering and cursing. Uncle Dan said some people had the damnedest notions of being useful; then he said he might as well take Louanne on home, and when they left, Celia gave her a final hug and promised to call her the next day. Louanne was slumped into a tiny little nobody of shame and grief, a lesson to all. We could sense Aunt Libby thinking that, after she'd shut the door behind them. But Celia said nothing and went straight upstairs; from her room we soon heard the wail of a saxophone.

Aunt Rachel came in then and we went with them to Aunt Libby's bedroom, where the two sisters flopped on the bed to talk. Aunt Rachel lay across the bed that had been hers for so long before she had married Tom Buck and moved to the other side of the farm. Now Aunt Libby was saying that Dan had been right after all. Celia would have to live her own life. Sometimes it took a real shock to make you see things.

And Aunt Rachel said, "There isn't any shock greater than a baby coming."

"Celia still sees the other guys," we broke in, at last saying it out loud, telling on her. "Not only Phillip! Corley, Jimmy and Roger." Aunt Libby gave us a scorching look.

"And I'd like to know why she wouldn't," Aunt Rachel said. "A young girl like that tying herself down. That's the silliest thing I ever heard of." Aunt Rachel had been married herself for a short miserable spell at eighteen. That was when she'd had Rossie. She asked then "You ever noticed how that water stain on the ceiling looks like a big tit?" Changing the subject, something droll like that popping out of her like a surprise butter rum drop. She reached over and tickled Aunt Libby under the arms. "Smile, you old sourpuss."

"You're as bad as Dan," Aunt Libby said, twisting around, and then she did laugh. "Only one thing on your mind."

"Lucky you," Aunt Rachel said, and gave her the sideways slanted look from her tilted green eyes which made us think of jade pagodas and gold-threaded cloth.

"I'll have to put that bottle away where he can't find it." Aunt Libby didn't seem worried now but only resigned.

"Maybe I worry so much about her because she was sick for so long and I got into the habit." Long ago Celia had had asthma and had nearly died more than once.

"It's that new baby I'm worrying about," Aunt Rachel said. Uncle Dan agreed with her as he came into the room that was full of females.

"You look awfully pleased with yourself," Aunt Libby said while he stood in the doorway, her arms propping up her head while she eyed him from the bed. But it was as though through her elongated, half-closed almond eyes she was openly envying him something he had that she didn't, only usually she didn't think about it. Then she got up and started to take off her clothes. Aunt Rachel said, "Well, excuse me!" Anyway, she ought to be going on home and Uncle Dan said he didn't know why—certainly Libby didn't mind who stayed. He said that he for one was glad he didn't have to leave the house for a strip show and Aunt Libby said she hadn't ever asked anybody to watch. Which made Uncle Dan call back from the hall that he was hardly able to take his eyes off her for even a second. And we saw a little private smile float in her eyes before she slipped her gown over her head.

Aunt Rachel walked off alone into the darkness toward home. She refused any company, saying that nobody was ever going to catch her on her own land. She would probably run just for fun, the way she let her horse stretch out over the fields night and day. There was always that something in Aunt Rachel that we felt drove and bedeviled her. We let her go. Aunt Libby was saying to Uncle Dan when we passed their room, "Sometimes I want him horsewhipped and then I feel there probably wasn't a thing he could do about it. Poor fool."

Phillip didn't marry Louanne. Nothing could make him do it. Celia gave him back his ring and wouldn't see him or talk on the phone, and one day when he stepped out in front of her downtown, she let him have it right there. He got a flash flood of her temper—the temper, Uncle Dan said, that was not so much the fault of red hair as of all the extra attention that went with it. Anyway, her tirade shocked Phillip and soon after that he left the college and then the state. He kept staunchly to his word and never married Louanne, though he never failed to send her money for the baby, no matter where he was, Alaska or Europe. Gram said right there was the sum difference between a father and a mother.

"The son-of-a-bitch," Uncle Dan always called him after that, with something like admiration along with just plain amazement in his voice. Phillip wrote Celia once but she tore up the letter without looking at it and we never heard directly from him again. She said she didn't think she'd ever really known him, could scarcely remember what he'd looked like.

From the first Celia considered herself kind of a god-mother to Louanne's baby. Aunt Libby taught her to knit, skillfully managing the gauge, and Celia knitted a pair of booties and then other garments in delicate pastels, attempting more complicated patterns as she got better.

Once in a while she still shut herself into her room with the mournful jazz she'd loved, but more often she sat with the rest of us, her fingers flying faster and faster with the needles and her tongue loosened, trying to catch up on everything she had missed, as if she'd come out of a daze or dementia. Even stories we told her of times she'd been with us fascinated her, because she didn't clearly remember.

She questioned Gram too, patient with Gram's rambling and disjointed tales, got excited over old recipes, and watched Gram cook as though she might imitate the same rapid-fire style. She even got Gram to talk a little about the time when Aunt Grace lay dying.

Aunt Libby still fretted over Celia, a set habit, focusing now on her health, for rather quickly the bloom of Celia's face and figure was gone. She looked wilted by her misfortune. Aunt Libby hid her cigarettes but Celia accepted the intrusion as love-inspired, and just bought some more. Celia had developed a persistent allergy to pollens and grasses and her blue eyes seemed to have lost a portion of sight, were streaked with irritated vessels that accentuated the paleness of her skin, the prominence of her thin nose. It didn't help her sneezing that she smoked so continually. Aunt Libby coaxed her to eat.

Jimmy began to come around the house again. To us Celia was almost like another aunt, her life settling into a foreseeable pattern; she could have been the one having a baby with the father thousands of miles away. She seemed to allow Jimmy to take her out because he wanted to so much, doing it for him rather than for herself.

Sometimes Celia would go out gambling with Gram in the evenings. Then, one day, Gram said, "I'm thinking of taking me a little trip before I die," which was partly a taunt to Aunt Libby, who never wanted to think it was possible for Gram to die, who said Gram would outlast the whole bunch of us. Gram took Celia along to Hawaii. They brought home a coconut and snapshots of the two of them wearing leis around their necks, with the other people on the tour, older men in flowered shirts and their wives, who watched the hula girls with careful smiles on their faces. Celia's smile was much the same.

Jimmy, pitifully missing her, not eating, almost as distraught as when she had been engaged to Phillip, took leave from his job and flew out to Los Angeles to meet her. And when they came back they were engaged. Kindhearted Celia, no longer beautiful, devoted to needy creatures, blew her nose continually; all the flowering tropical plants had been wretched for her condition. Again she suffered asthmatic attacks. Jimmy displayed the patience and devotion of a saint, qualities she said she expected would make for a fine father. Celia's obsession with motherhood, which she got from Louanne's pregnancy, remained her lone passion and she had questioned Gram almost nonstop about the rearing of children. Gram was reluctant and gruff, because she was done with that business, thought children pretty much raised themselves if you had plenty of them. Good riddance—one compensation for being old and ugly.

Afterwards Gram referred to the trip as Celia's wedding present. Uncle Dan said it was just like her to think up a wedding gift that left out the husband entirely, but then again he couldn't think of a more appropriate introduction to the family. Jimmy was just grateful that Celia at last was his. He must have noticed, as we did, that she was not the same girl he had first loved; we talked of her bygone beauty and charm in legendary terms, as if it might have been something we made up. Their wedding was quiet, in front of the fireplace, beside the dried-up coconut, and right away they left for Beaumont, Texas, where Jimmy had been transferred by his company.

After they drove away we went up to Celia's room and

lay on the bed, still in our good clothes. The call or the mourning doves across the fields went back and forth; we wondered whether we were the only ones to hear it. Jenny got up and turned on Celia's phonograph. She dropped the needle and then all we heard was Dave Brubeck.

PART TWO

Grandad

*F*or as long as we could remember we had been to-gether in the house which established the center of the known world. When we were younger we woke in the mornings while it was still dark. Grandad would be clump-ing out of his back room and down the hall to the bathroom, phantom-like in his long underwear. He wore it because he was a farmer, which was why he got up before first light to do the chores. In the two iron beds in the attic room there were the four of us—Celia and Jenny, who were sisters, Anne and Katie, sisters too, like our mothers, who were sisters. Sometimes we watched each other, knew differences. But most of the time it was as though the four of us were one and we lived in days that gathered into one stream of time, undifferentiated and communal.

Beyond the window glass the spruce trees were black and the sky ran silver around their silhouettes. The day smelled like clear water coming in through the open window which our mothers said must be raised at night for health and inspiration. Our mothers believed in nature, its curative and restorative power, trusted its beneficent guardianship. We were given fresh-squeezed juice with breakfast, two vegetables with every dinner, and were put to bed early. Other than that, we were left alone. They spoke among themselves in whispers, they who had their own mysteries, concerns; they left us to the tutelage of the wild and natural world. The doors of the house were always open to the drive, which turned at the lilac and rose hedges, and led to the barn at the head of the ravine and woods, the barn there like an outpost, mysterious and alluring.

One thing was forbidden. Any fighting among ourselves was punished consistently and severely—no listening to "She did this," or that. We were to protect each other, they seemed to say, for who else would? So we bit and scratched each other at night in bed under the covers, hiding the marks from our mothers.

When we heard Grandad again, the stairs creaking, we slipped out of bed, snatching our jeans and cotton shirts off the floor, nothing more to dressing than that. We were mixed up as sisters, Jenny and Katie with dark skin and eyes and Anne and Celia redheads; but we were alike in other ways, tall for our ages with long legs and large hands, like our Grandad. Passing along through the second-floor hall we saw bad-tempered Rossie asleep in his bed. If we woke him, later in the day one or all of us would pay for it. We tiptoed by; Rossie's head was a silky brown fluff on the pillow, snuggled like a little creature out of the woods. Katie thumbed her nose. Anne grabbed her as though she'd made a noise.

Next to Rossie was Aunt Rachel's door, closed; all the doors would be closed until late morning if no one disturbed the sleepers: Aunt Libby, Celia and Jenny's mother, asleep in another room, soon to be alone because Uncle Dan would leave for the store. Gram in her room, alone, because she and Grandad had two separate rooms at opposite ends of the hall. And then Aunt Grace, Anne and Katie's mother, alone too because her husband, Neil, was at their home in Illinois. She had come back to the farm for some reason we didn't know. All the sleeping around us: we were aware of the peacefulness like a transforming mist, the waiting house rapt.

Down the drive we hurried after Grandad, still fastening our pants, pulling on a sweater. We could see him in his black barn boots taking great strides, which Katie mocked. When we moved alongside him he didn't say anything and we didn't either. Grandad did not talk to girls or women. Unless he was fighting with Gram—then he yelled. That was one of the reasons we weren't allowed to fight. "We've seen too much of that," our mothers said.

Grandad picked up his hickory stick from the lean-to shed and opened the wide-boarded gate, letting it swing for us to come through, showing us that he knew we were there. We fastened it with the tied sock. He was watching for that. Once we'd forgotten and the pigs got loose; for a long time after, Grandad wouldn't let us near the barn. "Damned little hellions," he'd snarl at us. Now we went

67

behind him into the pasture although we couldn't keep up and he never waited. We heard his voice calling out, "Sucky, sucky," suppliant on the morning's silence, seeming to originate from the wooded hollow; but already the waiting cows heard him and were coming toward us out of the faint dawn light, answering back to Grandad's call, coming like his love-tamed creatures out of the mist. Other times we were afraid of the cows and ran from them, climbed high up into trees, shivering at their wild rolling eyes, but with Grandad we stayed close, letting them come all around us, and then we turned with him and started up the incline of pasture, going back to the barn that was still dark, with the lighter sky banking it.

"Ho now," Grandad would say every little bit, talking easy so as not to disturb them. His breath lifted into the air with the cows' steamy breath, with ours, veils drawing from the earth, its sleeping solitude removed. "Blow away the morning dew," we could remember Aunt Elinor singing.

"Sweet Sal, Daisy, Belle, Matty," they were Grandad's gals; we could hear it as he urged them along, although they were going forward, as anxious as he. Golden brown or spotted black and white, they all looked pretty much alike to us. Gradually, as it lightened up, he said more to them and it was peculiar at first, always hard for us to know he was the same man who was otherwise so silent— sitting in his window corner up at the big house, listening to the radio and playing endless rounds of solitaire.

"Git on over there," he snarled to the heifers in the barnyard, who hadn't learned yet; sometimes he'd strike them across their foolish gentle-looking faces and they'd leap up and scatter out of his way. "Now you just stand still here," he'd murmur to the cow he was fixing to milk, and he'd draw up the old backless chair to sit on and settle the pail into the straw. "You always got to fight me," he'd say, and soothe the beast with his huge knowing hands before drawing downward for the milk to come. "Now, now . . . you want old Jake to help ya, don't ya? Ya little cross-eyed daughter of a whore," his hands and voice stroking. Then we would hear the milk spraying, making the zinc pail sound. By then it was almost bright day outside the windows. Where the glass was broken we could see clearly through the broken webs and feel the cool fresh morning. Around us we could hear the exultation of waking creatures, so distant from the house full of sleeping women. "Stingy dried-down bitch," Grandad cooed. When the calico cat slinked past he squirted milk right into her expectant mouth.

Now Grandad was really talking. He had forgotten we were there. He talked to himself. Up at the house our mothers laughed about it, not for him to hear. To us it came natural enough from him, seemed another of the low brute voices, more felt or sensed than heard—the animals nudging their boxes, chewing, mouthing the grain Grandad handed around. "Yepee," he said. "Snavely won't git this one here. Not for free. He'll have to pay the piper, all righty. Ninety myself, oughta bring at least double that, maybe he'll take to your looks, though—string-bean yeller gal." He'd slap the cow on her flank for emphasis and she glanced around as if she was ready to skedaddle. But Grandad was already her familiar and she only hitched her feet around on the straw and flicked her tail. Grandad was bigger than the cows, it seemed, bigger than all the other men we saw who came around the farm, except maybe Tom Buck, who'd played tackle in college. It was a bigness of bone, as though he were solid calcium with only skin stretched over him. Sitting on the manger ledge across from him, we half listened. "Now, Miss Betsy, I'm going to braid up this here nothing of a tail with a silky piece of ribbon and put ye on the block. I reckon the day will come when you'll wish yourself back with ol' Jake." More than the milking business, Grandad was in speculation: buying and selling cattle for profit, wheeling and dealing. We'd seen him at an auction, taller, darker than anyone else, gypsy dark and silent, a man to be reckoned with. Until he got to drinking. Then, Gram told us, he'd lock in on some notion and outbid for pure stubbornness, more than once ending up in terrible fights. Or coming home with the most dearly bought, driest cow in the county.

After a while of watching the milk foam to the top of the pails, Katie would lean over to Anne, pointing to the soft pink teat with Grandad's hand on it, and say, "Someday somebody's going to do that to you." Anne was eleven, developing breasts already and ashamed of it, hiding when she dressed, so that Aunt Rachel would tease, "What do you think you've got there that we haven't seen a million· of?" Anne with her red hair and most of the time her face red, because she was what Gram called a wild hyena, forever excited, talking all the time, flashing with anger. Or ashamed. Katie said those things to rile her—she knew that, we knew that. Sometimes two of us or three would watch each other, watching the differences, feeling the differences working. We could watch Anne burning. She was big like Grandad, big-boned, way bigger than she should have been at eight, nine and ten. Katie was younger and quiet but in a sly way was mean sometimes, like Grandad too in her way, bad on purpose like an outlaw, and would sometimes say anything, do anything, pull her pants down for anybody to see—she had done that once for the colored boys who lived over the hill. No one had moved or laughed, them or us, all of us shocked. She drank out of the creek where the sewage drained. Once, on a dare, she took a barn spike and whacked Jenny with it, the wound requiring five stitches. Gram said it was Anne and Katie's father, Neil, who made them act so wild.

Now Anne was steaming, holding back but poised, so that we thought one more thing and she would leap on her sister and strangle her to death. It was like watching Gram and Grandad get ready to fight.

But the moment passed without death. Anne flew up the ladder to the loft, running from her hate and shame, and we followed. From the distant rafters we heard the soft call of the doves. We forgot what had happened, running over the upper floor, making the cows edgy so that Grandad snarled out, poking with his pitchfork on the ceiling boards, "You goddamn kids. I'll hide ye," which made us go faster away from him. Into the hay. With all our scraping and scrambling we set the rafter birds into flight, wraithlike through the half dark with their sad and dreamy cries, the darkness glowing like a picture of night with the light starred through a million chinks. We lay on the hay, resting, suspended. We strained toward that deep night as if we might lift into unfathomable reaches of delight. "Hi," we heard Grandad down below, "hold up there sweet little bitch-gal," calming the beasts. Katie said, "Grandad loves Daisy," and giggled so that we all started to laugh.

We went up farther into the barn, to the top level, where the little slatted windows blazed in a luminous stillness.

71

The sun was full up. We began flinging ourselves off into the darkness below the loft; faster and farther, spinning in the dust clouds we raised out of the hay, and then Anne began to bounce off the bales onto the second level and then to the wagon and the floor. We all did it. We would never fall. "Watch out," we cried, and left the world behind.

It was the city dummies who came to visit us sometimes who made mistakes. They'd try to outshow us, just because they were boys; we who lived there, who belonged there, knew where all the posts stood, the holes, and could have jumped out the windows into the valley of Lost Creek, far below, and never been hurt. Once a distant cousin came and Rossie sneered right off that he wouldn't be able to make the leaps, even to the first level. We all showed our style, calling out how easy it was. But the cousin was more daring than we expected and he followed everything we did. Finally he swung himself on the grappling fork rope, higher than any of us, then let go. At the second-story beam he grazed against the side of the stacked bales, lost his balance and fell all the way, lying still and white with a thread of scarlet seeping from his mouth.

"He's died," Katie said, as if we were just waiting for somebody to be dead.

For a while after that we were forbidden to play there, but the cousin recovered and as Gram said, "All's well that ends well. Damn fool younguns." Soon they forgot us again, forgot to notice where we played or what we did, as long as we were together. We went back to the haymow and learned to ride the grappling fork better than anybody.

We kept our deck of cards hidden on the rafter ledge, which we could reach only when the barn was full of hay, as sometimes it was for years, because Grandad was regularly selling off his stock and then changing his mind and starting over. Gram said she didn't care what he did as long as he left her out of it. Katie started to talk a little dirty; she said there were poo-poos on the floor. And with that we were climbing up to the level where we stashed the cards, reaching up quickly into the dark rafters where the rats clawed their swift way. The limp sour deck of cards was Grandad's and they smelled the way he did, as did the corner of the living room where he sat to play solitaire and nod off to sleep, spitting from time to time into a Maxwell House coffee tin. It was rusty and stank, Gram said, made her living room a filthy pisspot. Once when they fought over the can, Gram picked it up and headed out to the kitchen. She said she was not having it anymore; she said it was enough to put up with him. Grandad just kept sitting in the green plush chair, chewing. Then he aimed, spat directly where the can should have been. We heard the splat of it when it hit the wall and watched it dribble down onto the carpet.

Aunt Grace was crying while she scrubbed at the carpet, but she didn't make any noise; you could hear just the rag moving. Gram was still standing in the back doorway, screaming down the drive toward the barn, where Grandad had vanished as if swallowed up, his fist still raised after he'd snarled "Jezebel!" back at her. "Horse-piss, shit-face," Gram repeated until finally she choked into silence and hurled the tin can after him onto the dirt.

Our mothers wouldn't allow us to talk like Gram though they did themselves when they were mad enough. When we were alone we did it for fun. It made us feel bold and powerful. In the same way we played strip poker; it was just something that came over us, the wanting to play, the knowing we were going to, only putting it off for a little, so we could feel the excitement working in us. We were breathing hard, trembling even, when Katie threw the crumpled deck among us. Jenny might say, "Maybe we shouldn't." But there was no stopping us.

Katie started to deal the hands. Because the cards had been through so much already, it took a long time. "You're slower'n shit," Anne barked, tough as nails, grabbing the cards. Taking over. Whenever we acted movie scenes she had to be the cowgirl or the streetwalker or she wouldn't play. Now she pretended she knew how to play poker, but she didn't. None of us did. We just made up rules as we went along, proprietary and quarrelsome about them. We called the game five-card draw and used kernels of corn for chips, only we didn't know what to do about them. None of that mattered, because all we wanted to do was undress in front of each other. First our barrettes and shirts went into the center, except Anne's, for she was winning every hand. Then Celia called "Double or nothing" and Anne lost, which meant we could get dressed again, while she had to get naked in front of us.

The smartness ran out of her face. She looked at us. Nobody could help her. We didn't move even for our shirts, while the slants of light glinted off the silver hair clasps.

Anne stood up. "I know what you're thinking, about me." Even though Celia was the oldest, Anne was more developed than the rest of us, who had hardly started. When she went into the bathroom she shut the door, would have locked it if she could. Rolfe Barker, a boy from down the highway, had taken her into a back room once and put his hands on her; had made her bleed. It was wildness in her that had made her sneak off with him into that far back room. Then he'd forced her. We were thinking of that now and the rats, swollen big as cats, that swam in the grain bins, maybe blood trickling in their fur, human blood, like on the posters tacked up at the fairgrounds.

"Fraidy cat," Katie whispered. She snickered.

The blood made a splash over Anne's face then and she leaned over to unfasten her sandals, when Katie, with that ornery streak aroused, scrawny as broom straw, snatched the cards out of the center, crying, "Fifty-two pickup." They went sailing and spinning into the air, setting the birds in their restless circles overhead while the cards settled somewhere in the dark; last of all the six of spades fluttered back into the midst of us as though it bore a significant numerology. But we were having to tear Anne off Katie, who was on her back with her arms and legs flailing, blurred so that it seemed she'd grown extras, Anne holding her down with one arm and socking into her stomach. "You spoiled it," she was yelling. Anne never knew what she wanted. Katie was moaning, "Doesn't hurt, can't hurt, won't hurt." We yanked Anne's hair.

"Caught ya," Rossie said, and we nearly fell off the edge of the high platform, because we hadn't put our shirts on yet and his face was grinning up over the shelf—he was getting his eyeful. "I'll tell if you don't," his eyes were saying, coaxing us to do more; Rossie, even bigger than Anne and after us for peep shows all the time. "I'll tell," he said, knowing our fighting was forbidden. We laughed right out, the fight between Anne and Katie stopped for that time at least, although we knew it could start up again quicker than fire. We knew he'd never tell. Ha! He'd be the lucky one if *we* didn't. And right then he started to roll a cigarette as he leaned up against the bales, every little while spitting off into the hay, clear spit, white like sea foam. But if Grandad caught him smoking in the barn we knew it would be something awful; something like the time we'd heard of when he'd rammed Uncle Gabe up into the radiator and banged his head time and again against it while Aunt Elinor clawed at his back and some of the others ran to the neighbors for help. We didn't dare tell. When Rossie struck up the match the smoke was spiraling on the air. It smelled strong, streaming blue toward the high slatted window. He sat and stretched out his legs and then folded one over the other; he looked like a man himself, already taller than his mother, Aunt Rachel, and solidly built. It was scary to smell smoke in the barn. And we were afraid to tell.

"Grandad'll tan you," Katie said.

Rossie narrowed his eyes. "Fuck you." That was the most powerful thing a man could say. When Rossie said it, it was like something he'd stabbed right into the center of us. In the quiet now, listening for him, we could hear Grandad discussing matters with his cows.

"I'm telling," that renegade Katie said, the impudent gleam in her eyes that made "tattletale" no abuse at all once she got going, that made no amount of punishment too much. Katie was the youngest of us all and we were supposed to watch out for her, take care of her. But we couldn't do any more with her than we could with the weather or time.

Rossie sat and began to pull on each of his fingers so they made a popping noise. He smoked and spit. Then we heard Grandad's talking coming nearer, toward the ladder, and Rossie looked as if he was going to swallow the cigarette and we left him, went flying down the levels and across the scarred planking and leaped out over the two-foot-high doorsill, transformed by the freshness, the immaculateness, whirled into the forgetfulness of each new moment.

We went around the side of the barn. Inside, Grandad was telling himself, "By spring it'll fetch a dollar." Trying his best to outsmart the world, Gram said. She usually added that he'd never been smart enough nor had the foresight to bring in anything before it rained. Still Grandad had bought a pair of glasses at the five-and-dime store and there were evenings when he mumbled to himself over the farm journals, making notes with the stub of a pencil. Gram said it was typical of a man that now he was on easy street, where she'd put him, he figured to improve himself.

Behind the barn was Grandad's personal graveyard, boneyard really. Whatever he slaughtered or when one of the animals just fell dead, like Sally did when she got the blind staggers, still in the traces, Grandad would haul the part that was left to the back and leave it, and soon enough the buzzards and weather took care of it.

"The smell is terrible," his daughters said. "It's disgraceful." Their faces showed it, screwed up against him.

Grandad didn't answer them. Sometimes he'd sprinkle white lime over the ground and the decaying flesh. The smell was a little like what came from the eggs Rossie took out of the nests of the broody hens and smashed up against the side of the barn, so he could show us the little chicks inside and the blood they fed on. When Grandad found out, that was the only time we saw him smash anybody; he just raised his hand and Rossie went flying up against the side of the barn and then lay there.

As we walked, the calcium dust blew up white onto our feet. The bones crunched and splintered and teeth rolled loose on the ground. We could have been walking in the valley of Gehenna. Rossie had disappeared. Then Katie jumped out; she came from behind one of the spindly locust trees that grew there in a single clump. "The Philistines are coming," she yelled, jabbing a jawbone within inches of us, spiking around with a sawed-off horn.

"I'm Delilah," Celia said, and went over to couch herself where the cornfield began. The rest of us sprang at each other with spears of bone. Teeth toppled from jaws as we kicked them. Celia fanned herself with a fern frond. Anne ran into the middle. She'd taken leaves and sticks and stuck them into her wild red hair. Content for once not to squabble with Celia over who would be the great beauty, she was a mighty Samson. She'd tied her tee-shirt around her chest, uncovering one shoulder. Twirling a cow tail, she snapped it on the air. "I have slain the lion with my bare hands," she cried. "My strength is in my hair, lips that have never touched wine." Sometimes we played to the end of the story, with Samson's terrible blinding and God's revenge. But this time, when we were jabbing around, Katie rushed right into Anne on purpose and rammed her leg, which brought a quick spurt of blood. "Her tittie's showing," Katie smirked, and we looked at the unsightly lump of white flesh plopped out over the tied shirt.

"That hurt," Anne screamed, tears in her eyes, and she kicked Katie so that she fell backwards and then she shoved her down, smearing Katie's black hair into the dust. Katie kicked and flailed like an overturned bug. Anne was crying and gasping and Katie was screaming. We yanked at Anne but she was strong and kept on pounding. Then Rossie was there; he'd probably been spying the whole time. He whacked Anne's breath out of her with one powerful sock so that she fell on the ground, not moving except to double up her knees, gagging out of her mouth. Then Rossie kicked her chest, his brown boots falling like smashing rocks. "Filthy slut. Whore," he said, looking down on her.

He went away. Anne cried for a long time, the tears rilling through the pale dust film on her face, which was ordinarily so pink and warm-looking. We helped her up. Straightened out her hair, unfastening twigs which broke off some of the ends.

"I'll tell what he did," Jenny said, and she would; at times she was like a mother, protecting us when no one else would.

When Anne could speak she sobbed out, "He kicked me, kicked and kicked. I'll die. I couldn't breathe. I wanted you to help but I couldn't breathe." Sorrow for her swept over us.

"Come on, we'll wash your face," Jenny said. We trudged through the bones, down the grassy hill beside the barn and then into the barnyard where the water ran. It was from a wellspring which came through an iron pipe under the barn and ran continually into a black and rusted caldron. We splashed our faces where the animals put their tender spongy faces and sucked. Like them we laid our lips across the surface of the water. When we had enough we took turns standing in the pot and soaked our jeans through, getting all of ourselves clean and cold. We waded barefoot, sloshing in manure up to our ankles, then washed again. The swamp of manure was warm and sucked around us as if in some way it could hold us safe in that time and place.

Under the corncrib a batch of kittens drank from their mother. When we tried to reach them the mother scratched out at us. The kittens were newborn, with tiny squinched-up eyes. "We'll be back later," we told them. "We'll have to hide you." Gram didn't like so many cats hanging around; sometimes there were as many as thirty on the back porch. They were diseased, she told us. Distemper. When she couldn't stand it anymore she had Grandad put all he could fit into a gunnysack and take them to the pond. "We'll save you," we promised, going out of the entrance shed into the bright morning. Over the tin barn roof the sun gleamed so that, wet and shivering from the cold water, we were irridescent too.

"I'm starved," Anne said. We remembered—the house, mothers; up the gravel, our shoes in our hands, we raced over long morning shadows, after Anne, the biggest and fastest with the toughest feet, the most delirious, the wild hyena. She bragged all the time that she could whip any boy with one hand, sometimes doing it. She would shake out her storm of red hair, boast that she hadn't combed it in a week, in a year, would never comb it, climbed all the way to the rafters to jump. Jenny tried to calm her down, warning in black-eyed seriousness, "Sometimes things happen. Be more careful."

Before we got into the house there was the smell of coffee coming onto the porch. Grandad's straw-and-manure-crusted boots were set beside the fir-board cupboards and the shelves that overflowed with so much junk nobody could find anything. So we knew that he'd come up for his coffee and that this morning there wouldn't be a fight. It was a kind of signal that he hadn't worn the boots inside, soiling the rugs. "You got up," we cried to our mothers, Libby and Grace, who were at the table. "You got up early," we raved, finding their unexpected appearance something marvelous. They were in their bright-colored robes, drinking the lovely strong coffee, their eyes dark and shiny just out of sleep. The printed oilcloth was in the sun, the myriad surface cracks interfacing.

"High time," Gram said from the pantry, where she was peeling apples. "And you younguns ramming already. Dripping on my floor."

"Gram's baking pies," we sang as we raced up the stairs to change, with still a full day ahead, a day holding everything we could ever want. Behind us she hollered, "Goddamn it, stop that running. You, Anne." Because whenever there was noise and commotion she blamed Anne, knew without looking, she said, that Anne was in the thick of it.

"Up with the birds," Aunt Grace said to Anne when we came back. They all thought Anne was the first to wake, woke the rest of us. "It's no wonder your hair stands on end," she said, and tried to smooth it with her long-boned and frail-looking hand, graceful motion like strumming a harp. Still she was smiling along with us, as if it were of no importance, this untidiness and flightiness of her first child, not when we were all together. So they laughed at our long feet, careless spelling, dancing fits, saw us as natural wonders.

"What have you been up to?" Aunt Libby asked, halfheartedly, as if she knew we wouldn't tell.

" Just playing," we said.

"Rossie kicked Anne," Jenny said. "He kicked her over and over. Hard. For nothing." We felt the prickling of fear, revenge. The two sisters exchanged a frown. "It's not right," Aunt Grace said, "beating on girls." We were safe. We all began to accuse him.

"More'n likely she deserved it," Gram said from the pantry, as if she'd like to kick something needing it.

"She couldn't breathe," Jenny insisted. Anne sat quietly knotting her shirt over and over.

"Quit your wrangling," Gram said. "Ain't nobody hurt. Now where in hell's that Rachel. It's time she's up . . . we've got to be going."

"You get her," Aunt Grace told Anne. "You tell her what he did."

Then Anne was racing up the back stairs. We could hear her crashing, like the wild Injun Gram said she was. "Why don't she learn?" Gram asked nobody, said it like all the things she said, as though responding to a steady inner annoyance like heartburn.

It was quiet upstairs; already Aunt Rachel had lured Anne into her bed. We'd all been sent there by Gram with that same mission: Rachel was always having to be dragged out of bed in the mornings. She'd be late—for work, for church, for life. But Aunt Rachel with her siren charms adroitly seduced the one that had been sent to rouse her. And always we succumbed. In her bed it was soft and warm and she put her arms around us and snuggled up. Enclosed in her den of curves and billows, we were tempted to melt into sleep, to be absorbed into her dreams. But we were embarrassed too, too close, and we squiggled and tossed about. Then she would tickle us on the feet or under the arms, her hand moving lightly while the rest of her lay still, pretending sleep, her rosy cheek into the sheet with her dark hair in unrestrained spirals about her heart-shaped face. As we started to giggle and lurch about the bed she would begin to croon some childish song in her liquid and throaty alto. "Cat's in the cream jar, what'll I do?" tickling us out of the covers and onto the floor. It was hopeless. Anne would never get it told about Rossie; Aunt Rachel didn't want to hear it because she didn't know any more than anyone else what to do about her son.

She came into the kitchen through the back-stairway door. Anne behind her, bounding down the stairs. "Can't that youngun walk?" Gram muttered. She was scooping lard from the five-gallon pail by the stove, taking it in her hands. Aunt Grace said to Anne as she came, "Come over here and sit. I want you to calm down."

"I am calm, Mother," Anne said. We all laughed in her face. Then she sat down. On her red face was the hard crystal glitter we'd seen when she was pounding Katie.

"Anne hit me," Katie said then, trying for trouble in her own sly way. But this morning nobody listened to her. We were making toast, piece after piece, while Gram was whirling her way through four pies at once, asking Celia to light the oven, to hand her the plates. Gram liked Celia best, maybe because she was quieter than the rest of us, and didn't mind doing errands—Gram always had one of us getting her glasses from the bureau or walking for the mail, one thing or another fifty times a day.

"We oughta leave soon," Gram said to Aunt Rachel.

Aunt Rachel smiled lazily over her coffee cup, legs crossed. She lit up a cigarette, the only one of the five sisters who smoked. "And what's the point of being early and sitting around in Cleveland all day? Doctors are never on time. It's much nicer here." She had drawn around her the raspberry silken robe and we could see the creamy fullness of her bosom, bare where it strained at the fabric. All of Aunt Rachel was swelling, white and soft. "Anyway, the trip's not long when I'm driving."

"I ain't going if we're flying," Gram said.

"Of course you're going." Aunt Rachel looked around at us. "You'd go with me, wouldn't you, girls?"

We'd go with her. Anywhere. Every Sunday it was Aunt Rachel who took us to Sunday school while the others slept. With her we were always late, eating toast in the car and helping her to zip her dress while she was driving, and laughing at the fun of it, of being nearly too late to bother going, the car rattling over the brick street, down Belden and Highland, over the iron bridge at Keeler. We'd see the speedometer go over eighty more than once on every trip. When she'd parked, the doors sprang open and we spilled onto the sidewalk, chattering and laughing at her because now she put her nose high into the air and walked stuck-up, whispering to us to be quiet and act right, because Mrs. Peabody had nominated her as president of the Ladies' Aid. "You don't want them to think I'm not fit,' she said. The very idea was absurd. She belonged only to us and she could never be a lady. And neither would we. We spread our legs to wrap around the chair legs.

"I need to stop downtown first," Gram said.

"I never heard of such a thing. Can't it wait?"

"No. It can't."

"Well, I'd like to know why not," Aunt Rachel said, more seriously.

"I've got business." Business. The three women at once looked concerned.

Aunt Libby sniffed. "It's that Hank Browning. You're selling him that field."

"I am." Gram looked stubborn enough to hang herself.

"Does Dad know?" Aunt Grace asked.

"I told him. Likely he's heard one way or another by now. He don't use it anyhow. Not for anything that counts. Piddling."

"He won't like it," Aunt Grace said.

Gram stuck her neck out toward the other room, where Grandad slept in his chair, and she spoke as if to him, for him. "I'd like to know what he can do about it. It's mine. The whole place is. He can count himself lucky if I don't sell it all. One day I will too." She marched across the kitchen with the rolling pin and splashed flour on the sideboard, her stuck-out lip giving her face the spouting look of a teakettle.

Aunt Grace went over close beside her and stood with her head pressed against the cupboards, but Gram elbowed her aside, moving the rolling pin sideways, then back and forth.

"Mama," she said. "You don't need the money. Not now. And Dad is looking after the place. It's important to him."

We could hear Gram, though her voice was now low, without anger or blame, just resignation. "And who do you think's going to pay your bills, Grace? Not likely that husband of yours. Someone's got to think of that."

"Shut up, Momma," Aunt Rachel snapped. "Just shut up."

"That's not your only reason," Aunt Grace said to

Gram. Tears were spilling down her face while her fingers automatically crimped the edges of the crust Gram had cut to fit the bottom of the pie tin. There was flour on both of them.

"No, it ain't. Maybe I've got about a million. And you've dug yourself into the same hole, Grady." Gram had used the name the little girls had called Aunt Grace when she was the oldest girl at home, the one taking care of them while Gram had been boiling herself into old age over a washtub and the canning baths. Just then it seemed that Gram and Aunt Grace might still be the ones taking care of all of us, seeing to the wash and meals a long time ago.

"Sometime in there I quit," Aunt Grace said. "Just lost my fight, I guess." She was looking down but not noticing what she was doing, for she was going over and over the same edge and Gram saw that and for the first time put her hand out and touched Aunt Grace. They smiled at each other. Then Aunt Grace threw back her head and her arms started flying out and she finished up another crust nearly as fast as Gram could do it. Aunt Rachel and Aunt Libby stared in pure amazement, which made Aunt Grace and Gram shrug and eyebrow each other. The respect between them was evident then, because each knew the other could be depended on, had been depended on in fact, to work from dawn until dark without a rest and without making a big to-do about it, all the while listening out for the kids and having supper on the table for a man when he came home. Gram said to Aunt Grace, smiling openly, "Them two was raised with silver spoons. What do they know?"

She whipped through the pies and put them into the oven and hung up her apron. She looked at Aunt Grace and decided to finish saying what she had on the tip of her tongue. "I seen more damned men than you would believe, drinking themselves crazy, killing each other over nothing. And their women dying with babies or something else unnecessary. But you can't tell them. I'm through trying. You can't tell a young gal nothing, nor an older one neither. Not anything she don't want to hear." First they had been talking about Grandad but now Gram was trying to talk about something more, though Aunt Grace wasn't listening and instead put her finger to her lips and frowned in toward the room where we could hear Grandad snoring. "Don't do anything to get him mad, Momma," she said.

Gram sighed as if she'd worn out suddenly. Then she was rushed again. "I need to leave early, I'm telling you. Either that or I won't go." She flared up at Aunt Grace. "And when I need your advice, young lady, I'll ask for it."

"Is May coming?" Aunt Grace asked, and went to sit down. Her eyes were sunken in, looked darker than we'd ever seen them.

"She's not sure yet that she can get away."

"She shouldn't," Aunt Grace said. "It's too much. I've got the rest of you with me. There's always somebody who doesn't show up and then May has to do either the cleaning or the laundry." Aunt May was the oldest sister. Her husband had died just after he quit his regular job to build and operate the hotel business, which now Aunt May was dependent on, the twenty rooms more than she could manage. It told on her, the muscles in her face and body often twitching, her slenderness already gaunt.

We sat and watched the horses in the orchard. Before the apples dropped, Grandad let his workhorses graze among the trees and they, in sublime goodwill, glided in and out of sight. Gram came down from dressing and put her apple and cherry pies on the sill to cool. Then she went to sit in the car. Every few minutes she would lean on the horn and yell for the others to come, getting the names all confused, the living and the dead.

Right before they were ready, Aunt Rachel still in her slip, the phone rang. It was Uncle Dan, asking to speak to Aunt Grace. We heard her saying, "I know you do. There isn't anything else to say. I guess we'll know this evening." When she hung up the phone she stared out the window of the dining room. We were watching from the stairs. Then Gram snapped her out of her thoughts by drumming on the horn.

Aunt Rachel had been staring at Aunt Grace and the horn made her furious. She raised the window as if she would tear it from the sash and screamed out, "Momma, for God's sake." Tears were suddenly running down her face. She bent over and wiped her eyes with one finger, using the hem of her slip.

Then Aunt Grace was saying goodbye to Anne and Katie. "You two be good now and no fighting. Aunt May will call later." To Anne: "Try to stop hopping up and down, and comb your hair, dear. Maybe you could read for a while. And be good to your sister. Remember, she's the youngest." Aunt Grace wore a dark blue linen dress with embroidered white silk birds flying up at the throat. Smiling tremulously, she opened the back door to the car and slid in. Aunt Rachel drove. The car started up the drive, all the sisters turning to wave their hands out the back. Gram bolt upright beside Aunt Rachel, face forward, her summer-white pocketbook upright on her lap. We ran behind the car, up the drive as fast as we could go, barefoot, running through the dust and cinders thrown up by the speeding car. The horses in the orchard began to trot toward the highway too.

"Where are they going?" Katie asked, her face tear-streaked.

"Don't be dumb," Anne said. We all knew that Aunt Grace was going to Cleveland. She'd been there before, when she had her operation. We didn't want to talk about it. We lay on the grass under the oak trees which were in a line at the edge of the highway. The grass was pale and feathery. Cars passed on the road, the ground vibrating, and it felt as though we were still connected with the car that had left us behind.

We hung around the house. Aunt May called to see how we were doing and said she'd be over later with some ice cream. She said Valerie was under the weather. Valerie was her daughter, another cousin, a little older than we were.

"Is she sick?" We wondered if Valerie had locked herself in the bathroom again.

"No, it's just her time of the month. Is Dad there?"

We'd forgotten Grandad. We wanted to go with him to the mill. He would leave us. "We have to go," we told Aunt May, and grabbed our shoes. In the hall we nearly collided with Grandad, who was padding in his stocking feet, his long underwear showing like a shirt under suspenders. He wore it all summer long.

"Quit your rammin'." He went into the kitchen and carried a few things to the table and sat down. We stopped, uneasy about being alone with him in the house. His lunch was cold cereal with half the sugar bowl emptied on top of it. "If you're going to do it why don't you stab yourself. It's quicker," Gram would snarl at him.

"Where's Rossie?" we asked. Grandad didn't answer, the question gone as though it had fallen down a well. He finished his cornflakes, then filled the bowl with Ritz crackers and dumped his coffee over them. They bloated and dissolved. Gram said he'd been feeding pigs so long he ate like one; sometimes he cooked a rank mash for them on a hot plate in the cellar.

Since no one was there to care, we made ourselves sugar sandwiches on white bread and went onto the back porch to eat. Grandad went to the sink and began to splash and snort, washing up. Gram would have had a hissy, him spitting there, using her sink for his slops the minute her back was turned. Other times she swore at him for not washing all over except a few times a year, when he changed his underwear. She made a great fuss over the event—once she held his long johns suspended from a stick to burn in the trash can. After Grandad washed, we heard him shuffle toward the living room and later he snored. Peaceable, we waited on the porch in the dappling noontime. In the Mason jars stacked up dusty and fly-specked on the side shelves, in the broken-webbed snow-shoes hung there, the heap of rusty hinged traps waiting this long time to be oiled and set to catch something in the night, was the visible imprint of the past we were rooted in.

The way Gram told it was that all she had ever had in life was kids and work and useless men and what she wanted, and had earned besides, was to be left alone. Part of that was nobody accusing her or expecting anything

90

from her. She took care of herself, did her own personal laundry, cleaned her room, cooked her own supper, and what's more, did the breakfast dishes for the whole family. Plenty. Beyond that she felt put upon, although she continually nagged her daughters and grandchildren to see to one chore or another, as if she couldn't rest easy, didn't really believe anyone else would take responsibility. At eleven she had been sent out to work on a nearby farm, to take on many of the household duties of a mother of nine children who was dying of tuberculosis. That was the end of her childhood. "My ma hated it," she told us, "but they was feeding me instead of me taking from the family. All the same my ma hated it."

We were about eleven ourselves when we first paid attention, playing all day, quarreling over our share of the supper dishes. The stories she told seemed made up to impress us, to wheedle sympathy and make us feel guilty. But we knew for certain how she'd felt about one thing, staying with a dying woman, because Aunt Grace was already sick.

Gram had been Lil Bradley then, and the two miles she walked or rode, clutching the mane of an unsaddled horse, was usually covered in the dark—going before sunrise, returning after nightfall. As soon as she got there she took up the baby, shook down the ashes in the cook stove and, the baby on her hip, prepared breakfast for the family—this only the beginning of a day that wouldn't end until the dark miles home.

In later years Gram liked to be driven the thirty miles south to Marland, where she was raised, and she would point out the fields she'd crossed then and we would wonder how she'd ever been a thin wiry girl in a cotton wash dress. She would point proudly to the house where she was born, by now refurbished with a grandness she had never known. Though her father had built it, he had been unable to give it the touches—small-paned windows, shutters and lattice detailing—which made it, when we saw it, so substantial and original-looking. Gram was possessive about it, even then, as though in some way it still belonged to her and affirmed what she had become. She would smile out of her late-model Pontiac, nod and point. Even if the present owners were in evidence, she would stare just as greedily, bold by right, so that Aunt Libby would have to get out of the car and explain our interest. Or rather hers and Gram's, because we kids were only thinking of the ice cream Gram would buy us at the dairy. We had already seen her old house a hundred times. It was not until we were much older that we wished we'd paid attention, although Gram was always more interested in how people had improved things than in what the house had been like before—rather like appreciating her connection with a friend who had risen in the world. We had to dig her past out of ourselves as much as out of her.

For the most part, Lil had grown up without her father. The 1890s were a time of speculation and fortune hunting and her father was one of the many men who couldn't stay home. Lil's uncle, her mother's brother, had gone to California in the years of building the cross-country railroads and the family heard all sorts of reports about his associations with the wealthy and famous. They didn't believe most of what they heard, but Lil's father developed a frantic anxiety that he might miss the boat—remain at home in poverty and wistfulness.

Time and time again he went out to the oilfields of the

West. Back home, out of money and chagrined, he stayed and worked the land awhile, until it seized him, the urge to try again, and then he would be gone. They might not hear from him for a year or longer. At first a little money would come for Lil's mother and her six children. Then nothing, until he was back with them once more. Until the time he was gone for so long they thought he might be dead and later heard word he was. He had been killed sinking a dry hole in east Texas.

Then Lil's mother became ill and it wasn't long before she was dead too, another victim of tuberculosis. Lil gave up working for the neighbor and went to stay with her older sister, Hat, who lived in town. It was the first Lil had lived anyplace but on an isolated farm and it was a lot more lively than any life she'd known before, different young men seeing her home from church or visiting her in the evening. It was then that the piano arrived, first evidence that her rich uncle might not be entirely a family myth. Ordered from New York, the piano was a gift for their mother. But, too late for her, it was brought down from Cleveland on a wagon bed by Hat's husband and put into her parlor, up against the plank walls, with a rag rug under the stool. Lil took in washing and ironing and with the little extra money she kept, above room and board, paid a woman to start her on the piano.

Then Hat's husband lost an arm in a farm accident and Lil was forced to take another job, to contribute what she could to Hat. By now seventeen, Lil went to live away from home again, six miles out of the town, where she cooked in a farm kitchen, peeling a peck of potatoes before noon, and boiling tubs of salt pork and greens, finally to bed down in a blanketed-off section of a barn loft, where she froze in winter and melted in summer. Once more she was excluded from the little bit of town social life, but she was too exhausted to care, certainly too tired to walk the six miles, and there was no one to take her.

Unless she favored Jacob Krauss. She didn't think much of it at first, his still wanting to see her in the evenings, now riding out from the town, but she figured if it was worth it for him to travel that distance to sit and watch the fire, there wasn't any harm in it. He never did have much talk in him, even as a young man. He was out of the plain people, maybe shunned for something, folks suspected, though no one ever knew his past for sure. But Lil was seventeen and the mystery of Jacob's past was part of what intrigued her—she liked the different way he dressed, in shirts of home-dyed indigo and suspenders, and she liked his quaint old-fashioned manners, so at odds with his rough hard look. Tall and lean, he had straight dark hair falling to frame both sides of his face, and the little habit he had of tossing his hair back showed the strong bones clearly and his slanted, long-lashed eyes; and she began to want him in the way you want something you think will occupy you until Doomsday. The wanting felt like enough. There was no mother to warn her, and the other girls she knew were thrilled with Jacob too and envied her, though there was not a father or mother who would have sanctioned his attentions to their daughter. Lil did not desire the children that would come in a marriage; already she knew their demands well enough. But neither did she fancy the endless monotony of cooking for twenty farmhands every day while guarding herself against the teasing, fresh-mouthed married ones who, sensing her loneliness, determined to break her off and make use of her. Better that she should have her own man and the life he would bring her.

She did not deny it—Jacob drew her. He would sit with no words for her before the wood stove, watching her continually with his dark, dark eyes, and she began to feel his hunger, so that often she would get up to put more wood in the stove or busy herself at the sink, just to avoid his eyes and hide her trembling. Every night his eyes were watching, wanting her and letting her see it in him; but he wouldn't touch her, not so much as to let a hand graze hers, though when she would pass close beside him she would hear his breathing, harsh and quick. It nearly drove her wild and her mind came to dwell on him nearly every second. Sometimes, when she lifted up the handle of the stove to stir the wood, the glutted, ashy coals crumbled at the slight touch and something inside her seemed to fragment in the same way.

Lil would plot to forget him. During the day, going about her work, she would plan how she would be gone in the evening when he came. But she never was, and again she'd open the door to him, to his silent and steady need. It got so peculiar between them that neither of them said a word to the other through whole evenings. Lil would back against the wall when he entered and feel the exact dimensions of his body, the insistent presence of his nature. He would pass close to her, nearly touching her, his eyes locking on her, where they would stay fastened through whole evenings. Eons. She forgot time.

It took Hebbard Watson coming to court to change things, or else, Lil thought, they might have jumped together off a cliff to end it, both of them stubborn beyond belief. But Hebbard tied his horse by the gate a time or two, and although Jacob didn't even come to the door, his feelings were plain enough on his face as he stood outside and glared as if he wanted to strangle the horse. Then he tore away in the direction of town without a further glance, though Lil was certain he'd known she watched from behind the parlor curtain. After a third evening of that, Lil was in the kitchen in the morning, peeling through a pail of early yellow apples, thinking about Jacob and his silent withholding, when she heard a commotion on the road. She went to the door and then out in the yard, wearing her flowered apron, her braids frayed with curl. Coming along was a wagon team of six horses driven by Jacob, who was so intent on managing things he didn't even glance up to see her, though they both knew she was there, the same as when they sat beside each other at the fire. The piano from her sister's house was strapped onto the wagon bed, swaddled with quilting and roped down to keep it steady. She watched it pass, slow and resounding, the wagon out of sight but the raised dust keeping its memory a little longer, almost like a song resonating, and Lil knew they would be married. It was the only semblance of a proposal that passed between them.

Married, they moved into rooms up over a store on the town's one street and in the secret dark Jacob touched her and moved himself in her, and though she got accustomed to it, a part of her was more aggravated by his touch than satisfied, and then it came to seem more invasion than touch, his need something he took care of, quick and by dark, by daylight no trace left, as though it had never happened between them. Lil felt resentment rising in her; his tacit denial shamed her, convinced her that he felt he stole something from her, was taking without asking. Every night, nearly, he turned to her and held her against him while, rapid and brutish, he moved in her. She began to be sick to her stomach nearly all day long. Afraid that it was a baby coming, dreading it, she lay under his heaviness, which blocked out any trace of light, and thought: Soon I'll be dead.

Then Jacob became more active in his cattle business. He left her alone, stayed away for days at a time, and Lil began going out to the church for prayer services or hymn sings, a little society one way to distract her mind from continual hating and grieving. Jacob didn't like going to church. He'd left his own religion but some of the teaching stayed with him, that fancy music mixed with religion was an abomination. Though he didn't try to stop her, a few times she'd seen him standing outside the church window staring in. Sometimes she was harmonizing with the schoolteacher and she felt it served Jacob right to see her with another man, for she had come to hate him for his neglect.

One night Lil watched him standing outside the church window for a long time. She trembled, knowing something was changing. When she got to their rooms, she felt certain of it, smelled the strong drink in the air though he stayed hidden and didn't answer when she called, "Jacob." She built up the fire because of her shivering, though that wouldn't touch the part that came from fear. She felt him watching her again. Waiting. Wanting her and still hiding it like a thief. She would give him something to want, and she began to remove her clothes, with the fire hot and dancing over the walls, shattering the shadowy places. Lil excited, knowing she was beautiful and that he had never seen her and that it would be a power over him and would

97

cause something between them to change. The thought of it made her fumble over the layered items of winter clothing and her nipples stood erect, chafed by the fabric. It came into her mind that she would take his head in her two hands and place it against her breasts, each one in turn, press his mouth to suck on her, his tongue to lick her nipples. Wanting that all through her, she turned, fully naked, toward the doorway, where she heard his step.

By firelight all his need was finally visible in his face, what she'd longed to see. But there was such anger in it too that she tried to cover herself. When she saw the kindling hatchet raised in his hand, she thought that would be the end of it and part of her was glad, fire staining the blade red before blood. She couldn't get her breath even to scream. He brought the hatchet down then, on the piano, and twice more he struck, to leave it then, anchored in the wood, the piano vibrating as though it shrieked out and held to its voice long afterwards, as though it were her voice. Still she seemed to hear it, after he'd gripped her to bring her hard against him and then carried her to the bed. She couldn't take breath but repeated wordlessly: why didn't you, why didn't you?

The piano quieted and while Jacob strained into her, Lil's breath regained its regular and solitary pattern and, quieted, she heard in the distance the repeated howling of a dog left out in the cold. She began to count the times it sounded while Jacob finished and rolled off her. Then she went on counting. Sometime in the night she was sick, threw up everything she had eaten, and let herself think about the baby that was growing in her. Then she went on counting. It was a fearful and lonesome thing but finally she went to sleep and it was possible to imagine how its small eager mouth would fasten on her and pull at her breast. She never told Jacob a baby was coming. She let him see it for himself as if it had nothing to do with him.

Lil and Jacob went on living and sleeping together for more than twenty years and they never spoke of these things between them. For Lil there were the children they had, seven finally, although the two boys died in infancy, and they meant more to her than she had expected, kept her too busy for worry and lamenting. Looking around, who had it any better? It was the lot of women. Who among them wasn't stuck with something she couldn't abide? She, for one, determined to forget it. Sometimes she knew it hurt her children, to see her with bruises or a swollen face, or to find something in the house smashed while there was never any money to give them even the little they needed for school. But she wouldn't ever give Jacob the satisfaction of showing that she cared, that he could hurt her.

She left him only once. The children were young and he had started drinking hard and coming home staggering and falling dead asleep. This night, though, she had awakened in the night and found him gone from their bed and she'd followed him to the end of the hall where the little girls slept, hardly knowing where he was or what he was doing. Something in that scared her and she left the house as soon as she got him asleep in their bed again, and went to stay with her sister. But she couldn't stay on there indefinitely, crowding in with the four children she had then, and when word reached her that Jacob had stopped drinking, she went back to him. He was soon drinking again but he didn't wander through the house at night; in fact, he often stayed away at night, drunk, or on business. It was a relief to Lil, although the money, always short, became even more scarce. But Lil kept a large garden to feed them and she took in washing along with the Italian women in the neighborhood. Most of those women had it worse than she did.

It satisfied Lil to do so well without Jacob and for him to see it plain when he came home. Their girls were nicer than there was reason to hope for. They helped her, were bright in school, and all of them were good-looking. And they were with her, set against Jacob, ashamed of his ways and determined to better themselves. The more crude and brutal he became, the more they locked against him. None of his abuse could touch them. Spitting in the wind. About the sum total of all his whammings—save a moment's hullabaloo. She would show him. There was always the hope, too, that like her own father, he might one day go away and never return.

Of her children, Grace helped Lil the most and seemed to feel the closest to her, always hanging around and taking an extra chore. She would say to Lil, her black eyes concerned, appealing, "When I grow up I'll buy you the prettiest dress in the world and we'll wear hats and go to tea."

"Phooey," was all Lil would reply, impatient with romantic nonsense. Better put your money in the bank or buy a spread of land. You'll be needing it. As for putting Lil in a silk dress, you may as well dress up a sow and put it in the parlor: she hated the way she'd come to look so soon, all stomach and a wrinkled face.

Mostly she tried to ignore her appearance, the way she ignored whatever she couldn't mend. If Jacob would finally come home and then, for spite, spill the evening's milk over the floor, or do some other fool trick, Lil would scream at him until she choked, while beside her on the floor, cleaning up, Grace would cry, making something hurt worse inside Lil so that she'd snarl for her to get away. The child's sympathy weakened her, another female groveling at the foot of a man. The very effort of cleaning up, though, was relieving in its own way, and Lil let her flare-ups with Jacob slide out of her mind, and planned for the children. She kept them in school, sewed their clothes, raised chickens out back for the egg money that would give Eleanor (as she spelled her name then) music lessons. It was indulgent and the others resented the favoring, but Lil figured Eleanor to be the most promising, the one who might eventually get away altogether. The piano could still be played; a draped shawl concealed the disfigurement. For Lil it was a reminder that changes can come in the twinkling of an eye.

And her life did change just about that fast and that miraculously. When Lil was our Gram, this was the one story she relished telling, the one she treasured. There she was, as she saw it, living her whole life up to her elbows in a copper washtub, her face hag-lined from steam and exposure, as though it bore the punishment directly for what it had brought her, when her entire prospect changed and she, like the Goose Girl, was acknowledged as the true princess.

"It begun at the reunion," Gram started the story. "Naturally the old chap"—she meant Grandad, this tale making her more tolerant than usual—"wasn't nowheres about, off helling. But I had my children with me, even May from over yonder where she'd gone to live with her husband. And they was all looking right, clean, with here and there a touch of fashion to show they were somebody. We went over in the wagon and it was the nicest sort of a day. The girls felt it too, and when we stopped to rest on the way, Grace and Eleanor picked bunches of daisies and lace out of the fields so that when we pulled into my aunt's yard, we were singing, all of us wearing flowers, including the horse.

"I was having my first day off in a while, though I was busy enough chasing after Libby and Rachel. Of course I did my share, helping the women with the dinner too. Along in the late afternoon, when all the food was a shambles and we was sitting on the grass resting, some of the younguns asleep and nearly all of the men, who hadn't done a thing all day but stuff themselves, we heard one of them new motorcars on the road, chugging along. And then it pulled up our road and stopped in front. We was too startled to even tidy our hair, just staring. Out of this car steps a fine-dressed man, wearing a tailored suit with starched cuffs and collar, purely white. It didn't take but a second for Aunt Molly to know it was her brother Burl come back from California, New York City, the world. She was on him quick as a wink, hugging and crying over him, saying, 'Now ain't he the limit,' over and over. She took him around to visit with all of us and he made a great fuss over Hat and me especially because of our mother, who was his favorite sister. My girls was always a credit to me, pretty and sweet-natured, none of them a bit lazy. He seemed to notice they was a cut over the others and everyone knew I'd never had it easy with Jacob. I thanked him for the piano and pointed out Eleanor, who could play it—she was always the prettiest thing too, with that bright hair, like my ma's. And Grace had that dimple in her chin and was so devoted to the others; I could see how taken Uncle Burl was with watching her and Libby playing, daisies still wound through their hair. He give every one of them kids a silver dollar, and they come up to show me, big-eyed. A little shamefaced too, so I figured they'd been telling him how we lived on North Street with the Italians. But I spoke right out to them, same as always: 'You just be proud you have such a fine uncle and don't ever let being poor shame you, unless you never tried not to be.'

"Uncle Burl ate some of the dinner that was left and then looked at his gold watch and said he had to leave. Before that, he went with Molly on a tour through the house, and after coming out he stared at it awhile, the house he'd been born in, hunkering down under two maples with sunset bringing out the windows' gleam more than Aunt Molly could, and she was famous for the way she kept that house. He made all of us a sort of bow, formal and dignified. Kissed his sister. I was standing off to one side of the car, holding Rachel, who was asleep on my shoulder, and he come over to look me directly in the eye. 'I'm taking care of you, Lil,' he says. His exact words. And by the dead serious way he said it, I knew it was so. I thought to myself: I'm going to be all right. I am. And maybe I'm even going to be rich. One day. It was coming to me from a man and it was going to save me from one, just like the world was paying me a debt. Inside I felt so free, thinking: How do you like that, old mister? I wanted to see his face when he got the news.''

But when she did see Jacob he seemed more pathetic than dangerous and she didn't have the energy to tell him what was what. Not just then. Until he made her furious enough to pitch him out; then she told him that she didn't have to answer to him no more, that he could leave and never come back, far as she cared. He went off for a while but was home before long, dragging his tail, no place to go, and it didn't seem worth it to rile him again. And when he came to her unsteady and flushed, impatient and harsh with her, the way he always was when he was wanting that one thing, she took a backward glance at pride and ultimatums and shut her mouth. If it hadn't killed her by then, likely it wouldn't. And she didn't figure getting maimed or having the children hurt on account of him. Not when life was finally starting to happen to her. With one of the early checks from Uncle Burl she had bought a brand-new nightdress. She lay in the dark wearing it, and Jacob never saw it or felt the difference in the material, and Lil cried some of the tears she'd stored up —the last time she would cry over that. After Jacob dropped off to sleep she removed the gown and put on the old one. It could wait until she slept alone. After that, his wanting her seemed as perverse as tales she'd heard of men desiring the dead. She felt that hard.

Once Uncle Burl was dead the money came in fast. It took the old Nick out of Jacob quicker than Lil's patience was being used up, and he began to let her alone. By the time she bought the farm and they moved into the big brick house, he went off to the back bedroom meek as a lamb and never bothered her again. Not in that way, though he was resentful to the end of his days and stood up against her for meanness and spite. Lil would ignore him and fight him by turns. Feel sorry for him. More than anything she seemed to feel he was a nuisance, getting in her way, trying to get attention like one of the kids. Partly, though, it made her feel stronger to have Jacob around.

There he was, living proof of where she had been. "I felt like I'd been let out of a prison."

Eventually Gram owned, beside the farm, three houses in town, four places of business and later another couple of farms to the south, bought for speculation in gas and oil. Sundays she would drive to see the tenants there to talk about the crops and the nearby wells that were coming through. While she talked we stared away at the tiered steel rigs poking up out of the rolling pastureland, steeple-like spires that could have been proclaiming a new religion, higher than the corn and wheat. And more productive too, Gram said, when afterwards we'd drive around to see if more land was for sale. She vowed it was peculiar—her father spent his life in the West, searching for oil, when all along it was right out back under the corn crib. Now wasn't that just like a man? Like life.

We were still waiting for Grandad to go to the mill. It seemed he would never wake up. We walked down to the barn so he couldn't run out on us. From where the house sat, the land sloped at a gradual downward tilt and didn't become really level again until the far creek bottom. The barn was built into a mound of earth, with a stone foundation and then boards dried to tinder, topped off by a cupola. It belonged to Grandad and Grandad to it; it seemed in the same opposition he was to the encampment of fun-loving females who had seized the manor house and held it by superior numbers and adaptability. Just going down there made us feel adventurous. Made us feel divided. We sat on the barnyard railing and dared each other to touch the single-strand electric fence Grandad had newly installed to keep the horses in the orchard. An old hired hand had coaxed Katie to grab hold of it. He'd pointed out the birds sitting there, not feeling a thing. The trick was to put your whole hand around it and take hold. He did it, standing regularly, with a grin. So Katie did the same, clasped the wire and held on. As the current went through her, she stood as if she'd been planted in the ground. The man thought it was funny, Katie standing like that. We laughed too.

Grandad didn't call to us, just suddenly appeared, got into the cab of the ramshackle truck and started it up. We scrambled over the side rails while he was cursing to himself, bitter, unlike his casual bovine profanity at milking time. "You'll goddamn buck me, will you?" as he overshifted the gears. He had put on a striped shirt and a dark broadcloth coat that had once belonged to a suit. In the rearview mirror, we saw his eyes beneath the brim of his tweed schoolboy's cap. Abruptly we knew he was a man, braced in the iron strength of his willfulness.

At first we lay among the hunks of dung-soiled straw. We rolled into the boards when the truck lurched forward, clutching each other. Then we looked and the house was out of sight; with it receded our mothers' warning: "Don't stand up, it isn't safe. The way he drives." We did, as soon as the house wasn't watching us anymore. Grandad never told on us. We felt he didn't notice. The wind was in our hair and through the crazed glass of the window we could watch Grandad, who seemed to control the vehicle as though it were some fiercely independent creature that battled with him. His head jolted violently as we bucked over the bricks of the road until we reached the smoother blacktop. Between the floorboards we could see the road's black streaming under us; surrounded by the dung-crusted slats of the truck bed, we identified with the innumerable pigs and cattle, rams too, that had ridden in it to their final destination. The oaks that lined Summer Street dropped their branches low so that sometimes we could catch them, stinging and staining our hands with the blood of leaf veins. After we reached the back dirt roads again, we lay down to give ourselves up to the dust and thudding stones, daydreaming into the forever fleeing land.

At the mill, Grandad stomped up the ramp in his knee-length boots, a burlap sack of wheat loaded high on his squared shoulder like a young ram tied up for slaughter. We went behind him, more slowly, hesitant to enter the large frame building, dark beyond the entrance ramp, bare-looking without shutters or trim. Inside, the air glowed in a white powdery radiance that reflected off every surface. Down below, the miller stood, a ghostly figure, overseeing the grinding of the stones. We could feel their heave and shudder, on and on.

Grandad greeted the men standing in the yard and those inside with a nod of his head as he dropped the sack to the floor and kicked it right as though it had become the fit object of his contempt. Grandad had a reputation in the county for being still, even in his seventies, a strong man; and the farm was beautiful and they admired his family. We'd heard them, some of these same men, at threshing time when they ate their noontime dinner at our kitchen table, which had been opened up and boarded to sit twenty or more hired hands, Gram herself cooking, without a word to anyone, and us girls waiting on them. "Save that redheaded gal for me, Samuel," one would say with a wink. "I'll take me a black-eyed Susan anytime," another joked; but with one eye out for Grandad, for the talk was serious and respectful when he was there with the women around. Now, with his cap on, tall and lean, and his expression proud and distant, he made us all uneasy, wondering what might be in him, what he might do.

He stomped out for another sack. The men eyed us. "There's shorly a fire," one said because of Celia's and Anne's hair, and they all gave a spurt of something like laughter, though it mixed with another thing we couldn't name. But Grandad was coming back in, nodding and grinning at us, and it was as if we'd been set loose about the place. We watched the sacks of wheat or other grain descend on the conveyor and disappear below. On another belt the sacked flour ascended. Grandad handed each of us a penny for the gum machine, feeling good now, forgiving us abruptly and with as little reason as he'd had for conceiving his grudge. Or maybe his anger had never really had anything to do with us. When he went over to stand with the men, they offered him a bottle to drink from. After that we saw him drinking from it again and again.

An Amish boy stood off to one side with his father. The man's face was frizzled with an untended beard, but it seemed that underneath, his bare face would have had an innocence identical to the boy's. The boy was trying to conceal it, but we could tell he was watching us, wishing he could be with us. We felt exhilarated ourselves, with ourselves, in our blue jeans, tee-shirts, with the shiny thick hair of our family. Whenever we caught his eyes we'd smile, coaxing him.

Then his father went off a moment and Celia walked over. "Want some gum?" she asked, and held out her piece, which she had saved. The boy got red against his blue home-dyed shirt and stared blankly into the floor.

"Well, I don't want it," Celia said, and looking up at the father, who came then, she threw back her head with its lush fall of red-gold hair. He flushed too, looked as unsettled as the boy, his eyes blinking rapidly. Celia kept standing there, the gum offered, and they both stood, father and son, heads hanging before the round satiny piece of blue enamel. The wide brims of their hats cast a dark ellipse of shadow to hide their eyes. We pulled at Celia finally, to make her come away with us. "He's not allowed to have it," we whispered, reminding her, embarrassed over the fuss. The round of gum seemed unnatural, a wicked worldly thing resting on her delicate hand, and we saw—was it the first time?—that her nails were polished scarlet, long and crescent-shaped.

"All right," Celia said at last. "But I'll leave it here, in case you change your mind," and she placed it on the oak railing where, grained with sifted flour as though bleached for effect, the wood gleamed so the gum seemed precious. In our relief, released from the stricken pair, we chased after Celia, pushing and running, and raced out onto the ramp, oblivious of Homer Snavely, who was coming up with a load of grain, until we were right on top of him and he was already fighting for his balance, then he gave up half jumping and let himself roll off the ramp onto the ground. We went rolling and skidding after him. We saw his set of teeth pop out of his mouth and sail away.

Grandad was standing at the top of the ramp. We could see him from where we lay in the dust. He didn't say a word. We could scarcely breathe in the quiet that Grandad held in deliberate tension. Right then he could have come

at us with a horsewhip and we would only have waited. He
leaned over the railing and spouted a brilliant stream of
amber into the dust near us, raised a flask and drank, then
turned his head back toward the men, who must have
waited too, knowing about him what everybody knew, and
said sometimes even for us to hear: that he was as mean as
a man could be who hadn't yet been brought in for actual
murder, though men might have died because of things
he'd done. We could hear then the loud, relieving guffaws
at whatever he said to the men above the tireless scraping
of the stones. With his stick he reached down to help
Homer Snavely pull himself to standing. There on the
ground were the false teeth, grinning with embarrassment,
it seemed. Grandad speared them on his stick and went
swaggering inside, diving left and right to balance them
there. "Lookie what I catched," he said. The men were
stomping with the fun of it.

But we were uneasy still and slunk around the yard,
feeling that something had really just begun more than
finished with Grandad, who stood apart from the rest, and
superior, until he started to drink whiskey with them, and
then something stirred in him that still set him apart but
was what excited them. Homer Snavely disappeared inside.
"I wonder you didn't swaller them," somebody cackled.

Beyond the fence the Amish boy and his father were
loading their buggy with tied-up sacks, neither of them
looking away from their concentration on positioning the
load, as if they wore blinders, like the standing, well-
groomed horse. Everything about them was intentionally
dark, even the buggy's curtains, except the blue shirts—
quite like the fierce blue of the boy's blue eyes when he
tilted back his hat and looked at Celia once, before he

pulled up beside his father and took the reins. The heavy-spoked wheels creaked through the dust and the tussocks of grass bent and sprang back. In a while we heard the clip of the horse's hooves, after they had disappeared and gone over the dirt to the paved road on the rise that led to Orsonville Flats.

"His hat was funny," Katie said, and we giggled. Celia said, "I thought his eyes were fine." And then she went inside and we got the same idea and ran after her, but taking care this time, going in at the side door. Even before we looked at the railing, we knew the gum would be gone, because we saw first, from the landing, the expression on Celia's face, her calm acknowledgment. That was the first time we saw it in her, that sureness. "Celia's sweet on a plain one," we teased, trying to bring her back to us, make her blush and deny it.

"And I'll have anyone I want," she said.

We squatted in the yard and chewed on oat grass, the way we saw the men do, chewed and spit, long-legged, bony, the daughters of our family, like Grandad, waiting for him. He came then with two sacks of grain mash loaded on his shoulders. One of the laughing men leaned out the doorway, swaggering, and called after him in a slurred voice, "My woman goes to the bank, she just better keep on a-going, she knows what's good for her." Then he ducked inside. Grandad didn't pause even, but we could see he was furious—so quickly, as though he had been astonished to have the men, loud and drunk, laugh together like that. His face was dark but he went on throwing the sacks into the back and then headed for the cab, leaving us again, and we had to spring onto the slats and scramble in, even as the engine sputtered and the truck began to lurch across the uneven dirt. His face was visible in the rearview mirror. Though the crazed glass faded him, we could see the muscle beside his mouth twitch and pop. We recalled how Gram said he'd sold his soul to perdition. And this day she had sold land.

And from the way he drove we were certain he had been taken by a power, going like something suddenly pushed over a dam, carried by a force beyond himself and mere machinery. The truck swayed and bumped. We tumbled about and stared at the road flying beneath us, sickened almost, and on into the gray opening the road made through the corn and scattered grasses and flowers that disguised the steep pitch of the roadside ditch.

We were looking back toward the retreating and lost distance when the truck settled down to a more even ride. So it was all the more startling when the truck suddenly swerved. We half tipped over and then we heard the horse, its squeals like our own screams. Beside us then, nearly under us, the Amish buggy was fighting to stay upright on the road. The horse, blinded to the sides, threw back its head, trampled into the roadside weeds, stumbled and lunged for balance, the man now pulling on the reins, heaving backwards, trying to steady and slow him. We watched then as we moved away, the horse losing its battle, overwhelmed by the earth giving way, so that he went sliding into the ditch and fell sideways, the entire buggy tipping over. Scenes we'd watched in the movies at the dime theater came to us as we gazed back, watching the two figures in black moving around the downed buggy. We couldn't tell what had happened to the horse. We could see his legs, though, thrashing as if he still intended to travel. We never heard a single word or oath from the man or boy, even as we'd passed and they were struggling with the horse, trying to avoid Grandad's truck, the unprovoked assault. Their faces weren't anything other than intent.

After they had disappeared we clung to the rails, not looking even at each other. We felt the rude shifting of the boards beneath us and sometimes our bodies hit against the slats.

It was only when we reached the final turn into the drive at home that we stood up. Again the truck picked up sudden speed. We were flung against the cab. There was a streak of fresh blood on Celia's cheek. Now Grandad was making a final lurching run toward the barn, and we spurted past the haven of home we now yearned for, followed down the drive, past the house, by the three grown women, mothers and aunts, who came first onto the porch and then on the lawn, furiously following behind us to the barn, where the truck slammed to a stop like the sudden cessation of a scream. But it was we who screamed then, crying while scrambling again over the rails. We sobbed, disconsolate, shamed before the women who reached us at last and held us in their arms, crooning. Grandad was gone somewhere into the depths of the barn, or into the woods, or off into the arms of faithless women. We'd heard Gram's disdain.

"Even today," Aunt Libby said. And then we remembered this was the day they had taken Aunt Grace to the Cleveland Clinic.

"Where's Mother?" Katie asked.

Before anyone could answer, Gram came straggling along, her gray tangle of curls damp on her hot face and the low sun shadowing through her loose hair, wrinkling her face absolutely. Breathing painfully, she stood before the empty cab. The door dragged off its hinge, desolate. She jerked her head toward the dark barn, shook her fist and yelled, "And that's only the first part, mister." From the near pasture a cow began to low, the sun setting down the wood's line. "Well, he'll not neglect them. That I know," she said, all her resignation at what she considered his myriad other neglects in her tone.

"Where's Mother?" Katie repeated, singsong, until someone would pay attention. Aunt Rachel was staring toward the darkening barn. Then she put her arm around Katie's shoulder. "She's stopped off at Aunt May's and we came on to fix supper. She'll be here soon."

Anne called down from the tiptop of the sour cherry tree. In the evening light with the sun striking there, her hair was brighter than the cherries; with the leaves twined and shadowed about her face it seemed the spirit of the tree had materialized out of the gold-spun air. The tree was swaying from Anne's being so near the top.

"Goddamn it. Git down from there," Gram yelled, the way she always yelled at Anne. "You'll tumble. Then we'll see who's the smarty pants." She was so angry it was like a curse. Anne swung down. We could see her white arms winding against the black form of the tree.

Gram started up the drive. She called back to us while we still gazed at the barn: "Don't look up a dead horse's behind," and went marching on. She had her good dress on under her apron.

"Hey, old woman," Aunt Rachel called in her loving mocking way. "Where's the fire? She's just too fast for us," she reminded us, her pride strong.

"You younguns dawdle all you like." Gram marched on. "I got things to do."

"You're not going to go!" Aunt Libby snapped in disbelief. Her eyes flashed at Aunt Rachel, who shrugged.

"I am. It's an early party and I'll be back before she will. I know what you're thinking, but I can't help it. I've got to go." She stopped by the house yard, catching her breath, eyeing her daughters straight on.

We followed up the back steps onto the porch and then into the house. Already it was dark in there, and muffled too, as if nobody was saying what they were thinking. Almost out of a dream we heard Grandad's call: "Sucky, sucky." He was going to milk.

"Work me clear to death," Gram said, her recent fury at him dissolved, absorbed into the usual unremitting discontent. "There's two gallon already standing," she muttered. Now that Grandad was old and good for nothing, as Gram told him and us, his cows gave up their milk so lavishly that Gram, curdling with resentment but country bred, still skimmed the blooms of yellowed cream from the sideboard crocks and churned butter by the back door in the late mornings; the rhythm of the paddle hitting the wooden bottom seemed to calm her for a time. When the butter came she felt it and washed it, slapping it into a crockery bowl, washed the churn and banged the whole assembly into the corner. All her hours at home were restless ones, tasks to rush through. Others would have done them for her, but too slowly to suit her, the family a relentless nuisance to be coped with, so that time would roll by and take her away.

Aunt Libby asked, "Why does Dad have to be like this? Of all times."

"I quit asking that long before. There's never any right time for it, I reckon. It's drink every time, one way or another. Should've pitched him out."

"Don't any of you kids tell Dan what happened," Aunt Libby told us. "He'd want to kill him." Uncle Dan had all the equipment for killing in the way of tools, but we couldn't imagine his doing it.

But Gram said, "Since I ain't done it already, there's none that's likely to." She said it in braggadocio, exactly the way she described Grandad as the handsomest man in Marland County when she married him. Now she maintained he couldn't be beat for his meanness either, or herself for long-suffering. "He'll sleep it off. Then maybe won't even recollect. Wisht I could sleep that good."

Aunt Rachel was on the phone, calling all over for Rossie. Nobody had seen him. She said she couldn't eat and went off to find him.

Anne and Katie ate with Gram. She put a big plate of food in the oven for Grandad. She had made fried cabbage with cream and dumped on pepper to suit her—her own tastes the ones that mattered. Katie wouldn't eat it. Anne moved hers around with her fork. Gram merely raised up her chin and ate as fast as she'd cooked, smacking her lips. *Eat it or starve*, her manner said. *That's all there'll be*. She carried her dish to the sink, swallowing off the remainder of her coffee as she went, and hung up her apron. "In my next house I'll have electric," she said, as if that would make all the difference.

Aunt Libby went toward her. "We need you," she said.

"You! Shut up! I told you I need to go." The webbing of veins on her cheeks popped red. "Probably I'll beat her home anyways." Before she left the room she told Aunt

Libby, "They count on me," meaning the women she went out with at night.

"So do we," Aunt Libby said, but Gram had already turned away.

"You feel lucky?" we asked her when she was waiting by the front door, holding her lightweight coat, her neck craned up the drive, her pocketbook at the ready in her lap like a shotgun. She didn't answer, her thoughts withdrawn, owing us nothing. Sometimes she seemed as unapproachable as Grandad.

He came in the kitchen with the milk pails clattering. "You gals show him his supper," Gram said over her shoulder as she saw a car turn into the drive.

Aunt Libby went into the kitchen with us. She whispered, "Now forget it. There's to be no trouble tonight." Grandad was straining milk through the cheesecloth he kept washed and drying over the cleaned pails. Some bits of straw and a dead fly came out in the mesh. He poured himself a glass of the milk warm from the cows. The back counter was lined with crocks of milk and there was more overfilling the refrigerator. "Confounded lazy women," he muttered. "Too busy putting on paint and powder."

"There's your supper," we said.

"Where's she at?" He was still looking at the milk. Behind his spectacles, when he glanced at us, we saw his eyes. They were the brown eyes of his children, except Aunt Rachel, and they were the eyes of a real person.

We couldn't answer. Gram was just out. She always went out. Aunt Libby answered, though. "She stayed over with May. She'll be home later." Then we knew he had meant Aunt Grace. Where was she, his daughter? We'd never known before that he noticed her, or any of us, just

117

as we'd hardly noticed him, unless he was nearly killing someone or something, as he had that day.

The supper Gram had fixed he ate with the same hungry indifference with which he ate what he fixed for himself in the morning. There was one of Gram's pies for dessert. They were her crowning achievement, the pastry tender with dissolving layers, the filling both tart and sweet. Grandad plopped his piece into his bowl of coffee and spooned it up as though it were his usual Ritz crackers.

Nearly in darkness, we played croquet beside the spruce trees. Uncle Dan came out and sat on the back steps. The hollow sound the balls made knocking together or against the mallets was lonely, and with Uncle Dan just sitting there, not wisecracking for once how darkness improved our game, we lost interest ourselves and quarreled over whether the balls were in or out of the wickets. Grandad had gone, the kitchen light snapped off. He would sit up against the radio with the cards laid out and fall asleep. We started hide-and-seek. But we stayed in the yard this evening.

Aunt Rachel came home with Rossie. She marched him straight past us into the house. She said he had to practice his piano lesson. Right then. Before he could eat. We saw the light go on in the parlor. Their shadows streaked the driveway and Rossie's yelps and whines reached our hiding places. We quit the game and went onto the front porch to watch him get it.

"Thick-headed dunderhead." Aunt Rachel sat on the bench beside him. She held the wooden ruler, tapped out the time. And when he blundered, she rapped him, tweaked his ear. Rossie scowled into the book. His fingers were dirty and stubby against the white keys. The ruler cracked against his knuckles. "Two-four": Aunt Rachel beat the accent on her palm. She hit him again because he looked out the window. We moved further into the shadow.

Rossie shrieked and rubbed his hand. "What'd you do that for? I did it right." He was sobbing a little. We giggled. Aunt Rachel only pursued the measured beat, arching her eyebrows toward the score.

We made faces into the window and Rossie caught us once, almost as if he'd felt them land on him. He stuck out his tongue. We did it back. Aunt Rachel hit him again. "Play," she commanded. Rossie took a last glance at us and then sat up straight, collecting himself, and began "Stepping Stones." We'd all learned it.

"There now," Aunt Rachel said when she was finished with him for the night. "That wasn't so bad. Before long you'll be another José Iturbi." She brushed his fine hair out of his face, while her tilted mocking eyes lingered on him lovingly, as if she doubted herself that he'd ever amount to anything. As he left the room, Rossie shook his fist, and then he went to the kitchen for supper.

We were all waiting in the night, not thinking for what. Then a car was once again steering the turn off the highway, its lights spiraling the dark, washing over the trees. Aunt Grace was coming home. Aunt Rachel and Aunt Libby came out under the carport. We all called out together, against the silence, against the dread we felt. Aunt Rachel opened the car door and helped Aunt Grace, holding her arm and supporting her, as if she had become very ill since going away to Cleveland. We stood back a little, watching. All their faces, lit by the parlor light, seemed briefly to glow. Aunt Grace hugged us as together we went crowding into the narrow hallway. "Sh," we said. "Grandad."

But right away we heard another car on the drive, the formal lumbering swing and crawl of the sedan bringing Gram home. The hall was ghostly, lit by the replica of a lighthouse in pink-veiled marble which cast a steady beam onto the marble rocks sculpted at its base. Rossie had appeared from somewhere, and Grandad rose from his sleep, adjusting his spectacles as he came. He looked solemn and uneasy with all the family around him, and rubbed his gnarled hands together in mute supplication, as though he were sorry—for sleeping, for everything. Aunt Grace went over to him and put her arms around him. "Somebody will have to call Neil," she said. "And Elinor."

On the stone steps we heard the little scratching sounds of Gram's feet and then the opening of the screen. She stood before us, her pocketbook dragging from bone handles, her woolen coat sagging with her shoulders. In one hand she held a silver-painted candy dish which was mounted on a pedestal base.

Grandad lifted one hand toward her without any particular directive force but in appeal to her—as if in losing land he felt a part of himself was going too. Gram took offense, said, "Leave me alone, old man." Then her face softened as if she remembered why we were all waiting for her. "Phooey anyways. You'll scarcely notice any of it's gone. I can't see why all the fuss over a little scrap of meadow."

Then Anne shrieked out, "Oh, I hate it, I hate it," clutching her stomach, and we thought she meant selling the land or something else that was terrible which we didn't know yet. But then we saw a mouse dive down into the dark space under the sliding parlor doors.

"For crying out loud," Aunt Rachel said, laughing a

little. We all did, relieved by Anne's well-known terror, its insignificance. "That child has the Saint Vitus' dance."

But Gram wasn't paying attention. She had her hand on Anne's arm, gentle this once. "There, there," she crooned. "There's worse than that to cry over, girl." Her hand continued to stroke Anne while everyone hushed and looked with her at Aunt Grace.

"Well, you're back," Gram said.

Aunt Grace nodded. "Yes. It's all done. I called up there from May's. The tests were ready. Not good, I'm afraid." It seemed that her hair, so black that in sunlight it shimmered blue, was folded in two glistening wings that held her face, protecting her slender throat. We saw how her chest heaved so that the embroidered birds in flight over the bodice of her dress seemed to vibrate, although underneath was the unyielding rubber cup she wore to simulate the live flesh which had been cut away in an operation three years earlier. We wondered how she could still look so alive with all that gone.

But Aunt Grace wasn't looking afraid or sorry now. She looked steadily more amused, with some mock horror showing too as she reached for the silver-painted candy dish. "I do believe. Momma, that this is very nearly the worst thing you have ever won. I guess if we have to keep it we'll think of it as a kind of trophy won in the wars and handed down to us for what we have to go through." In the light which trailed over the sculpted marble rocks, Aunt Grace's oval fingernails shone transparent, and the half-moons at their base seemed mystical and unearthly. Beyond that bit of light our eyes dilated to form one dark place. Gram kept stroking Anne's arm. The tears running from her eyes immediately filled the crevices of her ancient face the way rain first puddles clay seams.

PART THREE

Grace
and
Neil

*O*ur mothers and aunts were all proficient swimmers, although neither Gram nor Grandad had set foot in open water, if they could help it, since they were children. It was not a skill common to country people. Aunt May had been taught by a college student who boarded with the family one summer and she taught Aunt Elinor, who passed it on to Aunt Grace, who worked with the two younger girls. Even as grown women, they liked to go to a lake or swimming hole, just to be doing together what they had always enjoyed so much. Usually they didn't want men around, just each other. Perhaps it was that exclusiveness that had prompted Neil to follow them once when they'd gone to the pond at Taylor's farm. This was a remote place and as usual they took off their clothes and swam naked. Although we were told, over the years, only the bare bones of the story, we made up the details and fleshed it out. We seemed to imagine even the thoughts of these women. And we could see them, young, well-formed, water-licked and dazzling.

Aunt May and Aunt Elinor, the two competitors, would have challenged each other to repeated speed trials, while Aunt Grace taught Aunt Libby and Aunt Rachel dives off the limestone boulder which marked the deep end. They would all look at each other openly and appreciatively, strong in their shared beauty.

All the more reason for the shame and fury they felt when they left the pond to dress and found their clothes missing. Right away they knew that it was Neil who had spied on them. While they became hungry and chilled, waiting for the cover of evening, they plotted their revenge. As it approached dark they opened the car, hoping to find a blanket or at least a few oily rags, and found on the floor their carefully concealed clothing.

After that they had to laugh. But their plans were made. They took the back farm road and parked by the barn. Then all together, stifling their laughter, they sneaked up to where Neil's car was parked on the drive, released the handbrake, took it out of gear and pushed and steered it downhill to the barn, where they felt it was safe to start the engine. Both cars proceeded to the next county. By a creek where fishermen left their cars, they hid Neil's, after letting the air out of the tires. Back at the house, they teased and joked with Neil, who was surprised at their good humor.

The next morning he discovered his car was missing. They couldn't imagine why he was accusing them. Neil became furious. Aunt Grace wouldn't let him get her alone. When the sheriff brought the car back, his two suitcases were already set on the porch and he left without a goodbye. The women—what did they care? They had each other.

Aunt Grace had met Neil for the first time at the town lake. She had driven her mother's brand-new white Chrysler convertible on that July day during the Depression when most people in their county considered themselves lucky to have a plow horse. Neil couldn't take his eyes off her, slender, with very dark eyes and hair, and when she went home that day he was sitting up front alongside her and before long he was driving them everywhere.

Neil liked Aunt Grace. He liked the car. He visited the farm and before long he asked to live there. He paid for his board and room; Gram liked putting the empty attic rooms to good use although she didn't care much for Neil from the beginning. She sometimes laughed at him, along with her daughters, but mostly his jokes seemed silly and her girls daft, for Aunt Grace wasn't the only one who encouraged his fooling. All of them, along with their dates, seemed to end up at the house and in the evenings the kitchen was noisy with the cooking and fixing, the card games and the constant horsing around. Aunt Grace's lovely face, nearly always sad-looking when not lit up by her white teeth and sparkling eyes, astonished her mother, who even as she saw the evidence of love became increasingly short-tempered with the cause of it. She said Neil was just hanging around their place for what he could get, that all he was wanting was a good time.

"Well, I hope so!" Aunt Elinor had said. She didn't think any of them should be in a hurry to get married. She was an aspiring actress then and one of the liveliest of the crowd when she was home from New York for a visit. More seriously, she would remind Gram that Neil was in college and that he had been made captain of the baseball team and didn't that show a pretty responsible nature under all the kidding around. Aunt Elinor admired Aunt Grace and thought it appropriate that her beauty and intelligence would have attracted a man who balanced her serious side, someone who could make her laugh. Aunt Elinor was further impressed that Neil was the son of a country doctor and she thought the chances of his eventually making a successful career as a writer were good—heaven knows he had a flair for the dramatic, the gift of gab and a lot of charisma.

"Speak English," Gram told her.

"Well, I'll never marry him anyway," Aunt Grace had said. She had plans for herself, thought someday she would get a master's degree in zoology and maybe teach at a college.

And for three years she held firm, while Neil continued to hang around, sometimes in school, sometimes not, pursuing her in an offhanded way, so that no one could really be certain he wanted to marry her. Off and on he rented one or the other of the attic rooms, whichever was available, and then he might follow Aunt Grace around the place for quite a while, dallying with her, weaving garlands of daisies to hang about her until, sitting in the high meadow grass, she was nearly buried, her chin aglow with pollen. Under the apple trees she took down her hair and he lay with his head in her lap, a buckwheat stalk tickling her throat as he chewed on it and said things that made her push at him and laugh out loud. He followed her into the henhouse when she gathered the eggs, and pretended to block the door, grinning and holding on to her when she tried to leave. Then for a time he might seem indifferent; they would quarrel and he would move into town, and Aunt Grace would not speak of him. They would all feel his absence through her and be relieved when one day he would be there again.

Neil took great liberties to make Aunt Grace laugh. Once when he was renting a room still, although he and Aunt Grace were on the outs, she entertained another young man in the parlor. Neil stopped in the doorway, holding his shoes in his hand, and yawning and stretching, he said, "I'm going on up. Grace. Don't be too long." She was so embarrassed she could have killed him; but she could laugh at it too, her reputation not quite so sacred a thing now that she had a college education and her mother had come into money. It was all new to her, the large house, new clothes and new opportunities. Neil's background as the son of a doctor impressed Aunt Grace also and although he often drank too much at the parties they went to, there seemed little connection between his revelry and her father's drunken isolation. Aunt Grace and her sisters now felt increasingly pity and tolerance as both their father and the past he represented became more distant, less binding.

Sometimes Neil went too far and Aunt Grace would send him away—for good, she said. He would comfort himself any way he wanted, making a scandal of himself in the ingrown town, exaggerating and glorifying his whoring and dissipation to everyone, until there didn't seem that a word of it could be true. Anyway, Aunt Grace and her sisters would be delighted to have him around again and Neil would say he felt like he'd come back home. He always seemed brand-new; though he was never remorseful, he still could convince them that he was just sowing his wild oats and would soon grow up.

Then both Aunt Libby and Aunt Rachel, seven and nine years younger than Aunt Grace, almost her own children from her years of caring for them, were married and pregnant. Neil ruined his knee stealing home; the team star abruptly became a has-been. Aunt Grace, holding on to her teaching job by the skin of her teeth, decided life was passing her by and married him. They ran away in secret because the school board immediately fired any female who was married and gave the job to a man with a family, and they kept their secret for eight more months until school was out, living on Aunt Grace's money while Neil finished college.

When he did, they announced their marriage. Gram was furious and declared she would never contribute to that marriage. She had made no secret of her disapproval, hadn't really imagined that Grace would marry that kind of man—which partly explained why she'd let him hang around the farm in the first place. The further reason was that she didn't pay a whole lot of attention to any of her children after they were grown. But now she couldn't stop talking about how Grace would rue the day! Neil was a trifler, with women and affection, a drinker, and further-more greedy. When this last was repeated to Neil, it made him howl. "Those pitiful pissant dollars. The woman has deluded herself." But soon after their marriage, Aunt Grace and Neil were living back at the farm with Gram and the others; Neil could not find a job and Aunt Grace had compromised hers. Neil and his mother-in-law were locked in open hostility, with Aunt Grace in the middle.

It was hell for everyone: Gram and Grandad still warring, the constant sniping between Gram and Neil, his partying in the kitchen nearly every night and then drunken episodes in which he attacked Aunt Grace. It was a relief to everyone when at last Neil landed a job as a book salesman. They moved away to Chicago and Aunt Grace got substitute teaching work with the expectation that the following year she would have a full-time position, which would allow Neil to quit his sales job and devote himself to his writing.

But before long Aunt Grace was pregnant and unable to work at all, she was so sick. When her time was near she went back to the farm so she could deliver her baby where she was truly happy, in the room where Gram slept, with its open view of fields and woods, above the fireplace mantel the picture of the Indian brave. They called Neil in plenty of time to be there. Two years later, when Katie was born, Aunt Grace's labor was faster and they couldn't contact him in time. Over the phone when finally they reached him and told him he was the father of a second healthy child, another girl, Neil retorted: "How come you bothered to call?" By now Aunt Grace was living back at the farm, on and off, for reasons other than delivering babies, sometimes for as long as a year. There was plenty to do with family always about, Aunt Rachel already divorced and home with Rossie, Aunt Libby and Dan occupying the attic. Aunt Grace couldn't make up her mind. She'd come home furious and depressed, would talk about a divorce, and then would as abruptly go off to join

Neil wherever his job had placed him, and they would begin again. Then something would happen between them and Aunt Grace would show up at the farm. Gram would just say, "Well, it's you back, I see," and take her and her girls in, same as the rest. For all Gram complained about the commotion, it seemed that it was less bother to her than the alternatives of sending money or feeling guilty, as long as she had the room. Besides, she'd told her so.

We would hear the women talk as they went about their work at the farm, as they sat for hours over coffee at the kitchen table. We heard all sorts of things. Once Aunt Libby said that Neil would do anything when he got drunk, that he had stumbled into many beds where he didn't belong and in some he had stayed until morning. She snapped her eyebrows up and down, whispered. We would hear Aunt Rachel's name. Hear that Aunt Grace had left Neil again and again, that it had become a little tiresome—same old thing. Sometimes, though, Neil was a hero in the stories—he'd saved Gram and Aunt Grace from being poisoned by leaking gas and he had saved a little girl from drowning, jumping into the river current in his Sunday best. Once he had fooled Gram into changing her bet to another horse while he stayed with the winner. To us it was all romantic and fun to think about, seemed scarcely to concern us, like fairy tales or cautionary fables that are not to be taken literally or to heart.

But now the Hudson is in the drive and we know that the Neil who is real to us is back. This time he has come because Aunt Grace called him after she came back from the Cleveland Clinic. A buzzard had flapped over the house at dawn with three redwing blackbirds diving and pecking at it, and Gram said that meant the coming of trouble and confusion. Though Gram still hates Neil, she doesn't let his coming bother her. She just goes right on plowing through whatever she has to do, the few chores that occupy her, her struggle with time and the rest of us, until she can get away. We want to be like Gram, who says whenever anyone crosses her, "I know better," her lower lip stuck out a mile. When we are grown up and have been through everything, we'll be like that. We'll order kittens drowned by the bagful. Then at night we'll dress in our silken best, pile on jewels and whiz off to parties, bring home prizes for the family. We'll bet on horses.

We all see the car. Celia says, "He's here. Neil's come." We stop and stare like the mouth-breathers Neil says we are—idiots bound for the cannery, the sweatshop, goods headed downriver. "Well, we're going in": Jenny speaks then like her mother, the expert fatalist. She and Celia go away toward the house.

The Hudson, slouched under its metal visor, the sun shifting over it, gives the impression of a wild beast in repose, the light skimming a fierce though disguised wakefulness. We hear a voice calling us; it is our mother, Grace, calling and calling. Do we only imagine she wants to come out with us and run away? We feel separate from all of them, and we will have to go in alone, stupid and tardy, exposed, the family watching. "Well, if it's not Mutt and Jeff," Neil will say, because one of us is taller and the other shorter. Other times he calls us the two sad sisters, two sad sacks, two milkmaids, two of everything, as if we are just the same, would fetch the same price. The others laugh when he says these things, but they will put their arms around us and whisper for us not to mind, to smile even, although that won't fool Neil. We know that—we know him. Better than anybody.

When we go in, Neil is sitting at the table with his drink before him. No one else is drinking, none of the women. They fear it and keep their distance. They feel that they have the same weakness the men have and must guard themselves from becoming sots. None of the women has a taste for it either. Sometimes Neil coaxes Aunt Grace to loosen up and have some fun; so she drinks and gets glittery and laughs a lot. Later she sometimes gets sick.

Neil notices us the moment we step inside but he doesn't show it to any of the others, goes on teasing Aunt Rachel about her new boyfriend, Tom Buck. Neil knows him from college, when they were on athletic teams together. Also at one time Tom Buck had wanted to marry Aunt Grace. We don't understand exactly what Neil is saying now but we know it has to do with the private, disturbing and exciting things between a man and a woman. That shows, as does the whiskey, he's drunk.

"You know you need it. If you don't I do," he's saying to Aunt Rachel, whose white skin is aglow; the color seems to float on her in blooms like water flowers. Then she isn't laughing anymore, while he raises his glass and drinks a sip with that intimate knowledge of her plain and bold on his face while he stares at her. For all to see. Aunt Grace has her back to him as she works at the sink.

He looks at us now. Before he does we know it is time, feel the connection. "Well, my own two daughters. Come give your old pappy a kiss." He wants us, asking us from deep inside. We feel it. We resist. He tightens his mouth, shrugs, shrinks backward, angry. There is a place hurt in him now. It's like when he sings, "Frankie and Johnny were lovers and oh how that couple could love." He drinks and makes us more ashamed with his high laugh. "I see nothing's changed here. Turning out like the rest of the bunch." When Gram comes into the room he nods toward her: "Here's to the Queen of Hearts," but she's already left without a glance, before he can raise his glass to his lips.

"You know you love all of us." We hear Aunt Elinor, who has also been called home to be with her sister. But still we are eroded by our shame, by the wearing force of our separateness and our attachment to him. In the pantry we stop a moment beside Aunt Grace, watching the arc formed as her long slender arms and hands move quickly and capably. She is too busy to notice us and we are in the way. Supper will be late because he is here and everyone, fascinated, can't break away and says helplessly the things they know he's wanting them to say—their eyes darting and ardent, playful, safe as long as they are together.

Or until something happens to upset them. Neil leans back in his chair and holds his cigarette like a prop in front of his face as he says to his wife, "It's a good thing that the girls' school starts next month. Any longer and I might end up so lonely I'd have to get a girl friend."

Aunt Grace takes a deep breath and says, "I thought I would stay on at the farm for a while, Neil. I have to keep going back and forth to the clinic and the girls might as well begin school here." We are all very still, but by the looks on their faces and the sound of their voices we know that it is best for them to say this to each other in front of everyone.

Neil starts to say that he guesses there aren't any other doctors in the world, then mutters, "Never mind."

Aunt Grace says, "We'll see."

"Yeah," Neil says. "I don't know what more it takes, Grace. A house. A raise." He is weary.

The women get up and find things to do. Aunt Rachel makes coffee and it smells wonderful. We even hear the bell strike from the town clock—the wind amplifies it, or the silence. Uncle Dan rattles into the drive in the delivery truck and we kids run out to greet him. It's like a reprieve, for now Neil will talk to him and be the way we've seen him sometimes, on the street, serious with an acquaintance, or at a table in a room by himself where he fills page after page with his words.

When Neil is on the farm the days begin with a grand breakfast. He says that being here puts him in mind of the summers of his boyhood, though he doesn't know why exactly, since that was a working farm, where his relatives were, not some kind of refuge for misfits or playland for the idle rich. As though it's a holiday, just because he is here to enjoy it, we all eat late, take several fried eggs from the oval ironstone platter, have extra bacon and Aunt Grace's homemade bread toasted, with jam she has boiled from fresh fruit; all except Grandad, who has had his boxed cereal hours before and is already asleep in his chair in the corner of the living room, up against the console radio. It is nearly lunchtime when Aunt Grace goes to the sink to empty the coffee grounds and says, "You go on now," to Neil. "We can't get a thing done with you around." When he rolls up his daredevil eyes at her, she adds, "Certainly nothing useful," letting her hand for a second fondle and caress the back of his neck where his blond hair curls over the pitted scars of acne. Soon afterwards. Neil lifts his straw hat off the rack and says, "I know when I'm not wanted," and strolls out the door, calling back over his shoulder to us, "See you gals in back of the barn." He gives Aunt Grace a saucy look when she says, "Now, Neil. Nothing mean."

"When have I ever?" he asks her in a bold and mocking pretense of disbelief. Already we are thrilling with excitement, fascinated by the blue again burning in his eyes. There is no stopping us either. But Aunt Grace is by now distracted, sorting through laundry on the floor, laundry for ten people that must be bleached and blued, starched, washed and dried, sprinkled and ironed; she scarcely notices when we leave, singing under her breath, quite content. She seems well, like her old self again.

Linked in the force of our expectancy, we go to the back of the barn and sit there to wait for Neil where the cedar log is so dried and whitened with lime and calcium dust it appears to have drifted over the surging sea to rest finally on this desolate shore. Soon we are sweating under the full impact of the sun; the few locust trees scatter a skimpy shade into the quivering heat. Neil takes so long to come to us that we forget almost why we have waited here. But we wait on because he told us to, and then Celia cries out because a hickory burr has struck her head and we glance up just in time to catch Neil's head drawing back out of the eaves window of the hayloft.

"We see you. We see you." We are shrill in relief.

Neil sticks his head out again. From upside down under the brimmed hat, his face appears cloven at the chin, in shadow under the shiny petal yellow of the bleached straw and the surrounding fall of yellow hair. "If you're ready for the spelling bee,'' he says, talking down the hay sprig dangling from his mouth, ''get yourselves lined up.''

We arrange ourselves into formation after finding for Neil the stout stick that he always holds. It is an old-fashioned school, like the one he went to as a boy when, he has told us, the teacher was as mean as Silas Marner, as severe as God and as relentless as the devil. Neil commands his class with the absolute authority of his own justice. During the session we will call him Master Higgenbottom. He knows the name will make us laugh, but only for an instant. Uncannily, his abrupt transformation into the dreaded master completes for us the entire setting of his boyhood—the raised platform where the teacher's desk presides, the central wood stove which must be fed continually although everyone is always either cold or sweltering, and the actual whip, long, of a narrow braided leather, which is hung up in plain sight. He has told us how fortunate we are that he as master does not insist on the complete historical accuracy of employing the strap; although he looks quite capable of resorting to it, should it become necessary. We tremble, waiting in line.

We have entered the school. It is a hundred years ago and we are trapped there, by fate, by our own intention. Before us stands the demoniac Master Higgenbottom; we even conjure for him a tailored rusty black waistcoat. There is now no humor in his name, none in his always unsettling yet once familiar eyes, which now stare from the distance of an incomprehensible lost world. We stagger, almost faint in the glare of high noon. Again, we have not recognized him until it is too late.

''And now, my dears,'' he says, and addresses us especially, his two daughters. ''I have appraised the fact, made known to me through the word of several of your more infatuated and silly admirers, who shall remain nameless, that you, although the erratic disarray of your clothing, your disheveled appearance in general, would deny it''—and here he takes the tip of his stick to flick the dragging hems of our cotton dresses—''that you,'' he repeats, and curls up his top lip, ''have recently entertained aspirations that would forever sever you from the taint of this miserable pig wallow and thrust you into a broader, and presumably receptive, world.''

None of us responds, in part because we have to struggle with the words he uses. He has heard that we have been listening to the country radio broadcasts, coming out of West Virginia, that we have in turn sung in harmony like those pairs of sisters we have listened to, that we have talked of singing on the radio and being famous. Good singers like good actors, he has always told us, are a dime a dozen. If only he had a nickel for every mother's son who wanted to be a star. It seems entirely shameful and ludicrous to us now, this ambition which is against all that Neil has taught us, about vanity and self-denial, humility, against all that he truly admires and has wanted us to be. We have been seduced, spoiled for him. We deserve punishment. We cannot meet his eyes.

''Therefore,'' the master continues, ''duty impels me to uncover this betrayal or else to discover if there is a single shred of evidence that such clandestine hope should reside in the breasts of common farm girls, should be given an iota of encouragement.

''Sing,'' he commands us.

Our mouths hang open, like mouth-breathers', but we have no power to move them. There is a prolonged silence.

"I thought as much," he says finally, himself for an instant, laughing at us. Then he slaps the stick against his open hand, causing it to resound smartly. The master again, he speaks: "I won't flog you this time. But should such vain conceit appear in the future, it would be clearly incumbent upon me to expunge this detestable and affected foolishness which would persuade you from your plain and rightful course. Unless, of course, you should ever wish to perform."

We are humiliated. He has shown again that we are his stupid, flighty, undisciplined daughters, certain to end our days in the laundry or as bar wenches. He has told us so.

"Attention," he begins. We straighten ourselves involuntarily, caught in the flow of his power.

"Was." He gives the first word to Jenny.

"W-a-s," she responds. Nobody smirks although she is by far the most able student among us—only ten months younger than Celia, she seems the older of the two, perhaps because Celia was so sick as a baby. We all know Neil asks Jenny the easiest words, always does, because he admires her sensible ways. She is safe in her role as the prize student, the role he gives her.

To Celia: "Give." Again, what we expect, a simple word which, although she is always pressed to her limits at school, struggling mightily just to pass the grades, he knows she will spell easily.

But for his daughters, the next pause is extended into an unreeling suspense. It could be anything. "Shame": he delivers the word, and we are flooded with the joy of being able to spell it out. After this the game moves easily, and with a skill we seldom manage, we spell all the words he gives us, even multisyllabic ones. Increasingly our voices reflect our assurance and confidence; our disregard of what, underneath, we know is only a temporary respite.

"Symbol," he calls to Celia.

"S-i-m-b-J-e," she tries.

"Come forward." It is very hot in the locust clump, which holds heat and casts a shallow pool of shadow into its own roots with the sun high overhead. Above Celia's pink trembling mouth we see the dewy salt. Master Higgenbottom renders her the punishment—one blow with the stick across her bare calves. Celia's tongue licks over her lips but she does not cry out. The actual blow does not hurt very much; he strikes his own hand harder.

We begin our plunge into the final predictable though unavoidable moments of the session; for in surefire and rapid order we miss each of our next words and suffer the noisy blows. Once. Then again. As we become more flustered we miss even the simple words. And with our mute failure to even attempt "conscience" and "uranium," as though we had been commanded to sing, we have received the ten strikes which end the game. The last are the hardest and we at last break down. He regards us with contempt. "You wanted to play. Nobody forced you. And now you blubber and bawl. Can't take it, can you?" He hurls the stick against the barn siding, turns his back and walks away. He kicks through the bone piles as though he is thrashing willful stupidity.

We four climb up into the haymow, up to the rafter window. We vow we will never forgive him. We swear to avenge ourselves, even if we have to pay with our lives. We tell each other how he'd feel if we died. Dry-eyed, exhausted at last, we lie in the sun-shot darkness of the barn, and the soft cries of the doves seem to be the sound of Neil's grief when he knows that he has lost us, when he views us, innocent girls, cold and still in death.

We are released then, forget again, and begin to descend the levels of the barn, down through the shafts of sunlight, and then we run off down the pasture lane into the woods, walking by the stony shallow stream until it is deeper and runs clean. We slide into the water; our dresses fill and float about us as though we have been altered into water lilies. After our dip, cool, absolved, we lie upon the bank, brushed dry by the coarse grasses, which hold a mosaic of daisies and Queen Anne's lace.

When we hear the rock chuck into the water beside us, we sit up. We don't see anything but we know he is here. Feel him. Somewhere, hiding. When the next throw comes, we are ready and pop up our heads to see a streak of bright blue among the trees, a blue bluer than the sky painted behind the trees, his shirt, and we are up, shrieking, "We see you, we see you," leaping away over the brook with our wet clinging dresses slapping against our legs, going on into the denser woods, where immediately the silence takes hold. We feel lost, stop, strain into the winding tangles of brush and vine. Has he been there? Then from nearly on top of us, from behind, comes a menacing growl. We wheel round. There it is, the leaping blue, and we race after his retreating form. And then he trips or falls somehow and we are upon him. We jump on top of him, seizing a wonderful victory. We have hold of his yellow hair. We tickle under his arms and pinch the loose skin by his belt. He puts his arms around us and rolls over the ground, going downhill toward the creek, and laughs so that we can feel his body shaking, with his hard legs wrapped around us. "Did my little girlies get mad at their daddy?'' he whispers. "Did the little girlies think they would never love him again?" Sky and trees dissolve behind his enclosing shoulders.

At the bottom of the hill we lie, surrounded and quiet. We can smell his tobacco and the wild parsley and clear water. We are at peace, enthralled. Sometime in there he becomes restless and leaves. When we realize he has gone we search and call into the solemnity of the woods. Then we forget again, dreaming.

The sound of the trampling feet rouses us, provokes in us the fear which flickers always just beyond the edge of our senses and which, triggered, drives us crazy. We see them as horned, creatures with foaming mouths breaking through the branches. We dash in circles, scream, laugh and push into each other until we are able to pull ourselves up into an oak tree, to safety, twisting ourselves right out from between the teeth of the beasts that mill about on the ground near the base of the tree right beneath us. But then, laboring painfully, spent, they simply stand there, calming. Grandad would be furious if he knew someone had run his cows. All the same, we want to see them scared and running again, want them to pay. We wonder when we will ever get away—as if, shipwrecked, we're stranded in a swaying oak tree island.

Then Neil is coming down the path swinging his stick, whistling as though he has just happened along. We know better. He walks right into the midst of the cows, pushing at them, poking. With a start they amble on down the curving path along the streambed. Neil is singing about Frankie and Johnny. "Frankie drew back her kimono," he sings. His voice inclines toward us, mellow and insinuating. A certain inflection tells us he knows we are there, although he doesn't look up. It's in the way he lingers over "kimono." Then he says, "Reckon you gals are safe now. Now that I'm here. Whatever do you suspicion commenced them critters to skedaddle like that?" He's mocking Gram now, the way he does sometimes, so we'll join him in laughing at her, even though it makes us feel disloyal, bewildered. Also he wants us to know exactly what he's been doing. Although he'll say we're lying if we tell. We don't know what to think of him, but it doesn't matter and we sail out of the tree and seem nearly to waft to earth. Then with him we follow the path winding along the stream, skipping rocks, jumping the wider banks, naming aloud the meadow flowers for him, to show we remember what he has taught us. And we sing through to the end the long droning ballads of forsaken love, to which he learned all the words when he was a boy. In the shallows where the stream is divided by a sandbar, we take hands and for a while make a bridge the width of the stream, Neil in the middle. It all affects us, the deep of the woods and the songs, as though we are legendary maidens drowned in the deep salt sea.

It is only when we are going up the wooden back stairs onto the porch and then into the house that we know we have been gone longer than long. We smell onions frying. Aunt Grace is preoccupied, moving over the length of the two joined kitchen rooms, for the stove is in the larger room with the table, and the sink and refrigerator are in the smaller pantry room, the countertops here and there. Everybody is at the table. Waiting. When Neil comes in and sits down, still wearing the straw hat, it's as though they relax and tense simultaneously, preparing for him. When he passes Aunt Grace, going for a drink, he slides an ice cube down her dress front and she yelps and squirms around to dislodge it, then leaves the room to remove it. We all laugh like crazy.

Rossie calls from the yard for the four of us to come out. "Hey, I got a new shiner. I want to show you." He sounds friendly and we let him talk us in closer to him, the way we draw Queenie toward us with grain when we want to ride her. He wants us to admire the new marble he has won in a game. We don't understand his moods.

"Honest," he says. He stands across from us, holding out his hand. We stand like draft horses, shifting nervously, unwinking, even afraid of a shadow. Then he empties the whole sack of marbles and we are caught. They roll and spin, are beautiful, some clear as jewels, and in others shattered crystals resemble sugar or milky spills. We are impressed that he has so many, and the shiner is mammoth. He impresses us further by giving each of us one—he lets us pick. We love him again and want to take care of him, this neglected and fatherless boy.

He wants to show us a new trick. He lies on the grass and raises his knees. His plan is for us to balance on the bottoms of his feet, full length, while he gives us rides up and down, back and forth. He wants Jenny to go first because she is his favorite because she is sensible. We all take turns then and we like doing it a lot so that when he offers one of us an honest-to-God flip we all want one. Celia goes first—she asks him to be careful and gives him her hands. The next thing we know, she is off on the ground some distance away, as if she has flown there. Now she is still.

"You killed her," we say, and go to her. She opens her

eyes when we lean over her. "What happened?" Her voice is hollow-sounding. We think she is pretending, trying to get attention. "What do you mean, what happened? You were doing the trick." We want to hit her.

Her face is very white and she doesn't answer. "Don't be dumb," we tell her, and lie down beside her on the grass, watching the first coming of evening, lavender among the dark branches. Rossie has gone away and we wonder about him, how he can be this way and the other way we know him too, the way he is sometimes in bed at night with one of us. Those nights, it seems to us in our attic beds as though we are together and forgotten in an isolated tower. The cars out on the highway that sometimes splash the walls with their lights proceed like our thoughts, solitary and dreamlike, at a great distance. Sometimes there is a mashed and wrecked car brought into the garage down the highway, late at night, and if we wake up we get out of bed to watch the crane drop the car, watch the spinning red light. In the morning we will go across to see the car; sometimes there is blood on the seat or mixed in with the windshield glass. After the night is quiet, we feel lonely and shivery, and if Rossie is there he gets into one of the beds and waits until only one of us is awake beside him. We are so far away from the rest of the world, up in the branches of the trees, it is as if the curving stairway is a fragile mooring line on the end of which we bob and drift. Soft and warm and secret, we touch each other and in that way we are able to fall asleep. In the mornings afterwards we fight. We are ashamed because of what we can mean to each other. We want everyone to believe that we despise Rossie, that he despises us. Everybody is fooled. Except Neil maybe. He knows about boys; his lip curls up at the very mention. He says he wishes Rossie were his own boy—for about five minutes.

Now we get up and walk toward the house and Celia stumbles a little and wants to know what happened. We ignore her, looking at the lights which appear in various rooms of the house, lights that have been left on, for days maybe, a negligence that drives Gram wild with the waste and her bills. As we go in we still hear everybody laughing. We have forgotten for a moment that Neil is here.

"I don't know how Grace does it," Aunt Elinor says. "Do you know that when I'm by myself in the city I don't even boil water." That seems natural enough to us, her New York affairs far removed from the minor concerns of food and drink. We are sitting on the dining room floor, beginning to play gin rummy, but we watch Aunt Grace move back and forth and we listen to their talk.

Neil begins, says, "That never was a favorite of mine anyway," meaning Elinor's boiled water.

Aunt Libby says, "You know, it's the truth—what Momma says: If I used a barrel of butter and cream in everything I make, you'd rave over my cooking too. But I think Grace is the best cook." She says this with the impartiality of someone definitely not in the running.

"Well, I never will understand what all the fuss is about anyway," Aunt Rachel says. "Seems to me anybody that can read can cook."

"Hear, hear," Neil says. This is it, what he's wanted. "That explains it, Ellie. You can't read. And all this time you've hidden it. By golly, I wish one of you barmaids"—he turns away from the table so he can see us watching and listening to him—"would take off a little time and teach your auntie to read. She'd probably be a good study.

147

Although, considering your spelling, I don't know. Maybe none of you can read." He gets the disgusted look that we see sometimes when he says privately to us, "I don't know how I ever got tied up with such a bunch of stupes." Still they all are laughing; it comes out of their love for each other and the keenness of its trance. Aunt Elinor laughs too, expansively and musically, the way she does everything.

Neil stops lifting his eyebrows at us and looks at her, directing the attention of all of us. "It's for certain no one ever said you couldn't *talk*. No siree! Nobody ever said that."

"Now, Neil," Aunt Grace says. "Ellie doesn't talk any more than the rest of us."

"Uh?" He plays dumb. "I declare. That's not exactly what you told me in bed last night." Aunt Grace stops moving at the sink, and we can see the stain of red rise under her dark skin. Her expression darkens too as her eyes seem to sink further back into the hollows around them. Without answering, she goes on with the knife, quick, with Gram's inbred speed, slivering celery on the diagonal, quartering green peppers and tomatoes.

But Aunt Elinor is still genial and Neil looks toward us again, and winks; he knows we are going right along with him, knows what we think. Although we give no sign.

"Now let's get on back to this cooking thing. I'd like to get a few things straight, for once get you girls to admit what you really think. Instead of always this boring wishy-washy sweetness and light. You must have an opinion, May." Neil says.

Neil has told us that Aunt May is the only one of the sisters besides Aunt Grace who showed promise—that she wasn't just an Ohio peasant putting on the dog. Now she gives a gurgle of self-effacing denial of her worth; but we think immediately that her food tastes the best, perhaps because her table is covered with a stiff ironed linen cloth and is set with polished silver and her rose-patterned china is complete with separate vegetable dishes, so spinach or broccoli floats in its own delectable butter sauce. She says only, "I guess we're all good cooks. Must get it from Momma."

"Well, if your preference is for pepper and dough," Neil says. He lets out a prolonged breath, which glides into a whistled rendition of "There's a long, long trail a-winding." It's one of the songs he's taught us, a song from the days when he used to sleep on bare ground under the stars on the lonesome prairie, when he was a vaquero, and learned to distinguish crow bait from bred stock. Sometimes on summer nights he lies beside us on the cooled grass and traces out the constellations, teaching us to find Cassiopeia and Pegasus, telling us of the endless reaches of light that separate us from the stars. We never know when the thing he tells us is true or made up. Now he stops his song for a second and says in rhythm, "Yes. Uh, uh! Guess you get your beauty from your Momma too." Then he goes on whistling until he adds, "From the knees up."

With the cessation of the melody, the silence of the room is such that we can hear the oil scatter in the skillet. Their legs are one of the things we aren't supposed to mention, like their ages. Secrets. Once we found letters to Aunt Rachel which a boyfriend had sent in 1935. She was seventeen then; we figured back and forth, came up with her age, accused her of it. "Sh," she had said, her eyes with their peregrine tilt, conspiratorial. And immediately we forgot because she wanted us to and because we thought of all of them as beyond ordinary time or distance—like movie stars.

"If only I had me a piano": Neil baits them some more. That's the way he describes the dense, heavy, although curved ankles that support their bodies. Again they are laughing, Aunt Elinor the most adventurous, risking the most, because of all the five sisters, she is the one who is somewhat plumpish, although solid-fleshed—a feature, Neil tells us secretly, which would have won her a sure reputation as a lady wrestler. This seems to us particularly funny though our snickers feel nasty, provoking an image of Aunt Elinor, squat and muscular, pinning her opponent. We must hide these jokes from her. Like the others. Aunt Libby Neil privately calls Penelope because he says he doesn't know anyone else who takes so long to get things done, says he figures she'll be there when the last die is cast. Gram is Hecuba—that's when he says he is feeling kindly toward her.

But this summer evening Gram has already flown away to pleasure herself and Grandad is down in the barn milking and Neil lets the feeling in the kitchen become peaceful; for a while he talks seriously to Aunt Elinor about the advertising world. Aunt Grace works hard over a complicated recipe for egg foo yong and we can see her enjoyment in displaying her competence. Neil says she is going through a lot of fuss for an omelet, though he looks proud too, and Aunt Elinor says it is highly regarded at the best restaurants in Chinatown, and Aunt Rachel says she'd stake money on it that we are the only people in Sherwood eating it this night. Which makes Neil say that he's glad to be in such select company. He walks to pour another drink and when he passes Aunt Grace he suddenly gooses her, which makes her startle and glare at him. But he only laughs more determinedly and she puts on a smile for us to see, even while he says to everybody that sometimes he has to go out of his way to liven up old Grace or else she would shrivel into the awfulest old prude. Aunt Grace says, without paying much attention, that she guesses that would be a fate worse than death.

We eat our dinner in stages while Aunt Grace stands at the stove and adjusts the heat under the oil, calculating exactly this final stage in the preparation of the exotic vegetable patties; she seems very pleased to be serving us, and her sisters are raving over this delicacy. When Grandad comes in with the milk, he refuses to try any, and then won't even sit at the table to eat what Gram has left for him from her meal but stands at the sink in the pantry. Aunt Grace doesn't fuss at him but pours coffee into the ironstone mug he prefers, takes it to him, and helps him scald the milk pails. He says then, padding toward the living room in his socks and grinning sheepishly, "Guess you can't teach an old dog new tricks," and she smiles as if she agrees. Still he has learned at last to leave his barn boots on the porch, except for a few times when he goes ahead and stomps his path over the carpet to his corner chair, leaving the scattered chaff and smudges of barnyard waste—which Neil says is done to show that Grandad still has something running in him that makes him feel like a man.

Neil and Grandad like each other well enough, at least we think so, because sometimes they get drunk together on the hard cider Grandad hides in the barn. Uncle Dan has joined them on occasion, but he gets so sick and desperate he prays to die, and since it is as much guilt as octane that gets him, that and Aunt Libby's disapproval, he figures to let the stuff alone and save it for the big boys. But Neil says he can't let old Jake catch all the hell there is around there, and he joins Grandad more than seldom, and then the two of them come up along the drive in the late dark, bellowing Neil's western songs, their arms draped around each other, reeling and hugging. Complaining about the women. "Acting," Aunt Grace says. "Just sheer play-acting," and she fastens the locks on the doors, the only times they are all secured, and turns out all the lights so the house is dark, and then she goes to bed while they pound and sing and get mad. Once Neil had sneaked up onto the porch roof and was climbing in Gram's open window, when she, thinking someone had at last come for her pocketbook, which she kept under the mattress, threw the bedside clock at him. The clock smashed to bits and startled Neil so that he pitched backwards and was saved from sliding off the roof only by the venetian blind cords, which he had grabbed until he caught his balance. Everyone agreed that it was a wonder he hadn't broken his neck. Which, he agreed, was no doubt the case, but it had been outrage alone that had saved him—when he realized that he wasn't taking the old witch along with him. He said that if Gram had risked throwing her pocketbook at him she would have finished him for good, loaded as it must be with gold bullion, considering how closely she guarded it. "Missed your chance," he reminded her from time to time, raising his brows and narrowing his eyes simultaneously.

After we have all eaten the egg foo yong, the special hot

and sour sauce, Aunt Grace is still going between the stove and the sink, stacking the dishes, wiping counters, while Neil is hand-wrestling with the rest of us, using his left arm and letting two of us at a time try to force his lean, hard-muscled arm to the tabletop. He says that none of us knows what hard work is: how many hours of a summer's day have we spent on a haywagon? He challenges Aunt May, who at least, he allows, has put out many a load of washing; after he has played around with her a few minutes he pins her arm abruptly, as though it's no more than a stick. Around her thin wrist is a crimson chafe mark and we see a slight skim of tears fill her eyes. Aunt Grace has put her own plate on the table, getting ready to eat, and says to Neil, "You ought to be ashamed," while he sweeps back his arms to shake hands with himself over his head, declaring his mock victory, and sends her plate and the egg foo yong spinning and crashing to the floor.

Aunt Grace hops up as if she's done it herself; while the rest of us stare, she kneels on the floor beside her ruined dinner, her hair hanging over her face. And then she just collapses into a heap amidst the mess and starts to heave in an odd tearless retching despair. We are still stricken. It's as though she cannot breathe and we cannot move to save her. Aunt May says, "My God in the mountain," as she hurries over to Aunt Grace, lifts her up to sit on the floor, straightens and smooths her hair, murmurs, "You must be so tired. Slaving all afternoon for us while we just sit here enjoying ourselves." By this time all the sisters have come to life and are busy, sweeping the food together and drawing water into the scrub pail. They pull Aunt Grace up and over to the table. Aunt Elinor holds her hand. But Aunt Grace draws away and lays her head down on her

153

folded arms, breaking into sobs again. When everything is cleared away they start the kettle for tea water. Aunt May says she will fix Aunt Grace a regular omelet since the other mixture is all gone, and she starts to beat the eggs. Aunt Grace says that she is too upset to eat, but she lets them bring her a cloth to cool her face and gradually she becomes calm and nibbles on some toast Aunt Libby brings her.

"Oh, I don't know what's the matter with me," Aunt Grace says, a tentative smile oddly combining with her swollen red eyes. The dimple in her chin is like a tiny keyhole. "I don't know. It seemed so sad, the mess and everything. The waste. And after it was all so nice." She looks at Neil for the first time. He hasn't moved or spoken.

His mouth is tight and his eyes are myopic, slitted, as though constricted into a single-minded comprehension. Then he speaks: "I wish to God you could just once get through a simple accident without turning into a martyr." He is furious with her. She lays her head on the table again and we watch her shoulders shake. There is nothing we can ever do to help her. Aunt May strokes her hair and nobody is looking at Neil.

"For God's sake, Grace," he says, "get hold of yourself. If you keep this up, one of the girls here is going to have to offer up a fur coat or something." He rears back his head and drinks, looking down the pitch of his mobile thin nose, and it seems he is inwardly imitating a mirthless laughter for us to see. He glances around, ashamed of nothing, while each of us feels mortified, stripped naked before him and each other.

"Momma gave me that coat because she's giving you

the down payment on your house," Aunt Rachel says to Aunt Grace. "How greedy can you get!"

"I don't care about the coat," Aunt Grace says, while her face is still covered by her disordered hair. "It's not that."

"If it isn't, you sure as hell ought to start getting your stories straight, sister. Makes me look like some kind of liar. Or jackass." Neil says that as quiet as truth.

The rivalry among us is contagious, in our blood, perhaps, as Neil says. Now he sits back to watch. The women forget all about the dishes.

Aunt Grace shakes back her hair and her eyes flash so that we feel the heat, though she speaks to Aunt Rachel. "Don't think I don't know what you're up to. The whole town knows. A married man! But when has that ever stopped you? Hot little dancing girl." Aunt Grace hates Aunt Rachel suddenly, and her voice is clogged and nasal. "Same old thing all over again. Well, you won't have to worry about me much longer. I'm sick, I tell you. Sick." Her sobbing sounds like someone throwing up.

Aunt Rachel hangs her head as though she deserves this abuse. We think of her hasty marriage. Rossie and her divorce. Ever so long ago. We do not understand. Now she teaches ballroom dancing at a local studio. What shame twists her hands in her lap?

This time Aunt Libby flies in to protect Aunt Rachel. "I won't hear it, goddamn it, I won't. You don't like the way things are, well, I won't listen to your bellyaching. You turned Tom Buck down flat after you'd strung him along. Turns out you're not so proud." She looks at Neil—when roused, his rank match in scorn. "Neither of them's worth shit, far as I can see."

Neil tips his hat to her, making a tsk-tsk sound, then slides the brim lower to enhance the wicked pleasure of getting just what he wants. He often wears a hat, playacting with it, sometimes one of Gram's with a stiff netted veil, or a visor which makes him resemble the croupier at a gaming table. He can play all the parts. Aunt Grace gets up from the table and goes to stand at the back door, looking into the dark. In the quiet we hear the crickets.

"Don't be so hard," Aunt May says. "Grace doesn't really mean that. She's tired and under a strain."

"We know that," Aunt Elinor says. "All the same, it's resentment and envy. Self-pity. You have such great blessings, Grace," and she smiles at us, thinking to make everybody grateful with a reminder.

Aunt Grace speaks then with her back turned, wistful and repentant. Sorrowful. "It's not Tom. Or you, Rachel. Nothing you've done, or even money. It's kind of a feeling of being left out and alone and sometimes it seems as if Momma's turned against me. Half the time I'm living back here, doing most of the work. I don't blame you girls; it's always been that way. As if, if I didn't work I couldn't stay. And now I wonder if I'll ever have a chance to live in that house now that we've got it, or enjoy any of the other things I've wanted." With her half smile and her arms raised with empty hands, she turns to look at her sisters, shrugs and says, "I'm awfully nervous."

Then even Aunt Libby stays quiet, though she had seemed about to interrupt when the subject of housework came up, a quarrel between her and Aunt Grace we had often heard. Neil tells us privately, from the days when he had been a time and motion analyst for a large manufacturing company, that Aunt Libby performs motions below a level yet to be measurable, sophisticated calibration notwithstanding. Aunt Grace has finished speaking and returns to the table, staring at her folded arms, so thin that the knobs of her elbows seem almost to pierce the skin; her true-black hair, skin shadowed darker by her lowered head, the taut stretched eyelids, give her the stolid look of a half-breed, as if she is in fact only partly related to the rest of them. "I'm sorry, Rachel," she says. "I didn't mean it."

"By God, sister," Neil says. "You ought to be able to do better than that. I thought that at least I'd picked the one of you that might not be altogether a sniveling momma's baby."

"You bastard." Aunt Rachel speaks for herself now. "Let her alone and shut up." She continues to glare at Neil, a look set enough to last forever, which becomes clear to him and he does not take her dare but snorts, slaps his knee and changes his mood like a wizard. "Hot dog!" he says, and goes on doing the talking then, fast and not waiting for any responses, as though he's on the stage or spinning yarns by a campfire. He says he doesn't think there is anything in the world half so invigorating, or grotesque for that matter, as the female of the species in her native habitat. He is surely glad his little daughters can be there to observe and learn, though neither of them has a snowball's chance in hell; already the air they breathe is treacherous, contaminated with greed, self-pity and the stench of a petty vanity. Puts him in mind of a mule skinner he'd known when he was out in the West, that fellow himself part weasel and part snake. "Once a dude come up to him and asked him for the meanest, sorriest nag on the string. 'You cain't have her right now,' he said.

'She's a-washin' the dishes.' " To Neil we are all horses, skittish, apt to catch our death in a draft.

Neil goes on recounting his adventures in the West, how as a cowboy he learned early that if there was anything more disappointing than humankind it was *Equus caballus*—that on a Saturday night the stench of horseflesh was pretty much just exchanged for another, only this time you had to pay. The sisters ignore him, bustle about, circling around each other in weaving patterns, almost a formal dance figure, their loose dresses and hair like streamers as they pile the dishes and wipe the table and counters. They make Aunt Grace sit still; they say again they have been horribly thoughtless, allowing her to carry the whole burden. Aunt Rachel refills Aunt Grace's teacup, one of the fine rose china cups from the dining room buffet and Aunt Grace lays her hand, bony, with thick-corded veins, on Aunt Rachel's rounded plump one. They sit that way, the trouble between them settled.

Beyond the screen, across the drive, is the rustling orchard, the trees there bent close, entwined in the heavy scent and fester of ripening apples and furrowed earth where the horses tramp. Neil has stopped paying attention. Then he looks at Aunt Grace and takes one of the curls that hang by her throat and cones it over his finger, where it makes a netted veiling. With that touch she trembles and returns his look, her eyes sad. His are humorous, gentle even, as he asks her has she taken to dosing herself with belladonna—her pupils dilated like that. And that word and some love showing in his eyes affects her. Her face loses its despairing drained look and she smiles back a little, saying that there is poison enough as it is in the air we breathe. Then she sends us away, only now really aware that we have been there and seen and heard them—out into the yard, where, she says, in the fresh evening air we will be happy and can wish on stars. Although we are running down the porch steps, released, we can still hear Neil's voice: "God forbid they should ever have to face things just the way they are." Then his embittered laugh. " 'What is truth?' " he asks. "You see, Ellie, you aren't the only one who reads the Bible." After that their voices fall low, soft and intimate, and only sometimes does something of their laughter reach us, penetrating the obliviousness which we find in the fantastic dark.

We hear something move in the weeds at the back of the yard. At first we are scared but when we edge closer we see that it is Rossie leading Queenie. He hardly ever rides her, is considered too heavy, but still he is bossy because she came as a gift from his father. Queenie is the only material evidence we have of that man's existence, other than Rossie, although Gram remembers him and has told us that his friends called him "Dopey." Sometimes we are afraid Rossie will hurt Queenie and we try to protect her, and tell on him. But this night we are too amazed and excited that he would have her here with him in the dark.

"We want a turn," we yelp when we see the two of them clearly.

"Shut up," he says. "Who's there?"

"Us."

"Okay. Today I showed you a trick. Now I'm going to do one. Like they do in the rodeo. And you can watch. Go turn on the light." Celia says she doesn't remember a trick, but the rest of us remember how she flew across the yard.

After that we make a little audience for him between the cornfield and the lawn, where he mounts Queenie. He carries a willow switch. Usually it is the most we can do to get her to move at all, either that or she runs away with us to the barn.

The porch light comes over the lawn and seems like a spotlight for a stage. Rossie draws Queenie up tight on the reins. Then he kicks her and lashes her with the switch. She is so startled she bucks, going straight up, so that Rossie nearly slides off. Even in the faint light we can see his face and something in us cringes. We know that look which comes over his face when things don't go his way, comes on him when he sits on our stomachs and pounds our chests. He slams Queenie again. And, as if recognizing fully her situation, she explodes into motion in the direction of the barn. Rossie is so tall his feet would touch the ground if he didn't hold them up. The empty stirrups slap. The saddle creaks and shifts. We have never seen Queenie go so fast. She races as if Rossie has become too much for her, the way he is too much for his mother and for us.

Then Rossie begins to lift himself to his knees and then, nearing the clothesline post, he is standing in the saddle. Bravo! For an instant. For then he has vanished in the dark as though taken by the hand of God, while Queenie disappears at the corner of the drive. From the orchard comes the pounding of the workhorses as they run beside her, nickering softly.

We stand over Rossie. Beside him on the ground an end of the clothesline still dances. We are scared and sorry we have laughed.

"Leave me alone," he sputters, struggling to sit, brushing tears away with the back of his hand. He lies down again.

"He's dead," Katie says, and we laugh again.

Rossie sits up. "Shut up, dummies." He coughs and it sounds feeble. We laugh some more, skipping back so he can't hit us. When he lurches to his feet we run toward the house. "Mad dog. Mad dog." We can't wait to tell about Rossie's fall. We know that Neil will be secretly glad.

But we don't tell. They are playing a game and have forgotten us. We wonder what Neil knows about Aunt Grace. He seems the same. Now everything has been cleared away from the dinner and all the women sit with Neil at the wide boarded table playing hearts. Grandad is asleep and Uncle Dan is late at the store. Neil tricks the women again and again while they are distracted by the joking and fooling, thankful the trouble is over. Neil takes all the hearts and the queen of spades. They lose, take bunches of hearts, over and over, and act as though they love it. Love him. Don't care. "You girls sure don't take after your mother," he tells them, because Gram gets furious and won't play whenever she loses and she cheats to win at solitaire. Neil remarks that in a curious way he almost misses her. "At least when the old woman's around you know somebody's at home."

We leave them. Upstairs Aunt Rachel's door is open and her porcelain lamps, a shepherd and shepherdess, are illuminated, their innocent faces smiling sweetly under fluted ivory shades. Arranged before the mirror on the dressing table are her creams and perfumes, her gilt dresser set and hairpins. For years we have invaded her room, spilled her powders and worn her pumps and finery up and down the house and drive. She has complained, mildly, in her indulgent way, but we have ignored her and do as we please, use up her favorite cologne. Now Neil is here and has taken control; he says somebody has to protect Aunt Rachel. He has said that we may not even enter her room, that if we do, his two daughters at least, over whom he presumes he still has some authority, will wish for Gehenna as consolation from his wrath. He says that if he were in charge around there, things would be a lot different.

We stand in the doorway, inch nearer. Celia and Jenny try lipsticks. Then Celia smooths her hair with the tortoise-shell comb. Downstairs they are still absorbed. We hear Neil "smoking out the queen." Aunt Elinor is careless and shows her hand. Neil says she should use her mammoth frontispiece for something useful. "Look! Of course I look," we hear him. They laugh and tell him he is impossible. "You women bring out the worst in me," he admits.

Hearing them far away and entertained, we move in closer to the lighted mirrored table. What right does he have to be here? To tell us what to do? We do what we want. They are playing their game and we begin to fix our hair and polish our nails. Celia puts one of Aunt Rachel's records on the Victrola and one by one we dance.

Aunt Rachel's hand mirror falls. Shatters. Then Neil is upon us. He has sprung from the kitchen in one leap, it seems, as though he'd been half waiting. His face is terrible. "You won't rest, will you? Not until you get what you want." He is hardly able to form words but he only dares touch his daughters. We are yanked and dragged through the hall and pushed into a dark room. From a great distance Aunt Grace calls, "Neil."

They don't come. He slams the bedroom door and

shoves us onto the bed. We hear his breath and then the sound his belt makes sliding out of the notches. We are afraid of his belt, plastic with ridges which leave stripes. We wait for its sound on the air. But there is nothing. Just the sound of his breathing and after a while it's quieter and he sits down on the side of the bed, which makes the mattress slant toward him, and he is near us in the dark, quiet now, so that except for the pitch of the bed we would think we had been left alone. It's that way such a long time that we are almost not afraid. Finally he gets up and goes to the door, stands there a moment, his hand on the doorknob. Then he speaks, wearily and without anger: "You know your mother is dying." Light falls on the bed and we see that we are lying on Gram's appliquéd quilt. Then it is dark again as he shuts the door and we begin to sob and sob, sorrow all through us as though it is the only real feeling in the whole house and now we have to accept our share.

When much later we leave the room, Celia and Jenny are waiting at the top of the back stairwell. They go down with us. We have all been crying. We crawl down the tunnel of the stairs and sit on the rubber treads. We can tell that everyone is mad again at Neil, that they are making him pay this time. When he says things, no one laughs or answers. We imagine their faces, hard, eyes downcast. Neil's voice is pitched up higher than usual, as if the strain has affected even him.

They don't respond to the change in Neil but somehow he knows we are there and he begins speaking to us where we are beyond the door in the dark. He tells an old story about his life in the West, the freight cars he hopped to get there. How hungry he was. How lonesome. He describes the flowing prairie and the rising moon, the incomparable sky. Then he asks us can we hear the shy tittymouse. Already we are smirking when he says that; we don't believe any such thing exists in all the world, except in his head. Then he calls out, "Annie. Katie. Stop your sulking and get out here." The women come immediately to the door, surprised, and draw us all out. We are blinded by the light and stagger into the room, like redeemed outcasts. While we drink lemonade we ignore Neil, and the women make a great fuss over us, showing how much they love us, how apart Neil is.

Neil says that if we keep frowning like that we will be wrinkled up by the time we're twenty and won't ever get husbands, that around here we have to be careful or our mouths will be like prunes, that for his money, resentment nursed and cultivated is the fount of all disease, particularly degenerative disease. And perhaps if there were less of that in certain quarters, certain people wouldn't be sick all the time. He comes then to sit on the floor at our feet.

"Help your poor old balding father," he says, and our hands begin their task almost automatically, massaging his head up near the forehead where the fair wavy hair has begun to thin and recede. Soon our palms are slick and rank with the oils from his head and we can smell its sourness as though it is a horse's lather. He tells us that we will become famous in this way, that since the world began man has labored, experimenting endlessly, to restore hair, that we two are engaged in that great family project, magic. Maybe, he says, we have found the answer. This encourages us, so we work all the harder. Strong fingers, he goes on, will pay off at the piano—and elsewhere. His eyes nearly close beneath our stretching, kneading touch and we watch the pulse throb in his veins under the taut skin, which is strawberry pink under the darker spots of freckling. The women go into the other room but we are not afraid now. Neil rests so quietly under our hands that we think he has gone to sleep. We will go on endlessly. He will never release us.

But he is not asleep and begins to tell us another story. He wishes we had known his Aunt Sarah "on the distaff side." She'd been as hardy and capable a woman as could be imagined. Word had it that she'd just stop by the furrow long enough to drop her babies, fourteen of them in all, and then would go on at the plow. When her youngest boy fell out of the barn loft and bit off the end of his tongue, she took it, warm and slippery as it was, and with her needle and thread stitched it back on—while the initial shock still rendered it somewhat numb. Anyway, that boy had lived to tell the tale. This had happened twenty-five miles from any doctor and in the time before women had capitulated to the notion that the chief advantages of civilization were to dress well and have the leisure to be sick.

He asks us to turn off the light. Moonlight, falling in silent silver between the tangled trees in the orchard, fingers across the drive. The silhouetted, discernible forms of the trees suggest personality: Neil always said they reminded him of the family—some a little apart, on the fringes, a few little tots here and there, the gnarled old crone in the center, and then the five sisters, close together, their slender branches intertwined, thrashing in any wind at all, making much ado about nothing. The sawn-off waterlogged stumps he compared to the few men who ever dared to approach. We think now that Neil is not one of the trees at all, but he is like a bold colorful blue jay, sailing and bluffing.

"Oh, the poor sad waifs," he croons under his breath, telling us the ways of the wicked world. "You two better stick with me. You'll find there isn't much more around here to be counted on, unless you want a lot of singing and dancing. With me you know exactly what you're getting."

He is quiet, drinking. "Anyway," he adds, "what other choice do you have really? And I doubt things will ever get as bad for you as they did for your poor old pappy when he ran away from home in nineteen hundred and twenty-five. I don't imagine you girls will want to try that."

We have tried. More than once. Years ago, after he whipped us, we vowed to run far away, to break his heart in pieces. We took out a suitcase and folded up a few socks and some underwear, which seemed as lost in the large case as we would be in the world. Neil walked us to the door. "Long as you're set on going," he said, and frowned. At the end he seemed sad. "I surely hate to see you go. But if you're determined." He shrugged his shoulders and his eyebrows too, which were a frizzled blond. Often we'd heard him lament that he couldn't have them transplanted to the top of his head. He gave each of us a nickel, to make our start in the world, he said. We refused the money, still haughty, making him suffer. Then we were out in the world, in the abrupt dark. The door closed. With the closing of that door it seemed we had gone a million miles. We began to fling ourselves against the door, pounded and cried. But he had locked it and gone away. Frenzied, we beat on, nothing else to do, and then magically he appeared before us, outlined against the warm and lighted room. "Now haven't I seen you before somewhere?" he said.

"Yes, yes," we cried, struggling to speak. "We're Anne and Katie. Your daughters." Saying that made us sob out loud.

"Why, can it be?" He warmed slowly. Looked more and more glad. He embraced us finally, recognized us as truly his two beloved, long-lost daughters. We could feel our fear dissolve in the safety and relief of home, of Neil's love expressed at last, almost as though we had indeed made some long and perilous journey alone.

In the dark now we sit and remember those times, feel his love. Laugh with him about his tricks, the things he's done. From the other room we hear the murmur of the sisters talking, calm and peaceable. "Thick as thieves, aren't they?" Neil says. "Guess I'll have to see about that. Make some impression," and he gets up and slicks back his longish yellow hair. He pinches our legs, says he hopes we don't ever run to fat. "Glad I raised you girls to be tough," he says. "Considering the way things have turned out, I don't think there's a better thing I could have done for you." He sounds proud of us and as if he's never really felt anything else.

PART FOUR

Aunt Elinor

*G*ram sent us with Tom Buck to wait for Aunt Elinor's
train. It was cold in the station and we could see our breath
flaring toward the vaulted ceiling, which had been painted
a heavenly blue with golden rims, like a sun always sinking just out of sight. Tom Buck was going to marry Aunt
Rachel. But she was not the first of the Krauss girls he had
loved. Years before, he had been in love with Aunt Grace
and had tried to marry her, long ago when she had been in
college, before she met Neil. It seemed that the death of
that old love was merged with Aunt Grace's death and
burdened him still as he shuffled over to the wooden
benches, which were sectioned into seats like desks in an

old-fashioned schoolhouse. He slumped, his head in his hands.

He said the train from New York had been delayed because of the night's storm. We said nothing, but knew it would never come. Aunt Elinor had forsaken us; inside us was the thought: if only she had come in time. The train station was stark in snowlight and as immense as a waystation to heaven, under that distant blue dome where we imagined the spirit of the recently departed hovered. And perhaps might be called back. "Come back," we yearned. Tom Buck had to wipe his eyes, as he had all morning.

"I have to go to the bathroom," Katie said. We went with her for something to do. The ceramic tiles were tiny fitted hexagons of black and white, covering the walls and floor in grimy precision. All the stalls had metal lockboxes requiring a dime. Jenny went to ask Tom Buck for the money, but Katie wriggled herself under the door. Anne tried to pull her back, then went after her, only she was heavier and got stuck halfway and Katie was kicking her shoulder. When Jenny came with the dime, they couldn't get the door open, with Anne wedged under it, Katie still shoving her with her feet, just to be mean. But when finally Anne was able to get up she rushed to the sink, raving, "I'm filthy. It's terrible. I touched it. I'll die." She didn't mention Katie at all, scrubbing frantically at her face and hands in the rusty rivulet that was all the faucet would produce. And that was cold. Katie was afraid to come out. We were hating her, as we always did when she turned mean. But Anne was struggling to control herself, scrubbing and scrubbing her hands under the cold water, not even saying shit and damn, the way she wanted to. We could tell that from her face on fire. "Redheads have no secrets," Aunt Rachel said.

We just walked out and left Katie there, went back to Tom Buck. We were glad Aunt Rachel was going to have a husband again and we tried to make him feel included, though Uncle Dan said it was more than he'd been able to feel in thirteen years. Under the circular dome the air took up our voices and expanded them so that they hummed in reverberating lonesomeness. We called out to each other. When Katie came back she stayed away from us, watching Anne as if she couldn't believe Anne wouldn't fight.

Then the floor began to vibrate and then to quake. It was a wonderful sensation; in full power the train materialized, its wheels screeching, blowing steam. We followed Tom Buck to the gate, came face to face with the appalling force of the engine, which was stopped but seemed to pant and gather for another rush forward. Then with more resignation than we had ever felt before, we knew the train from New York wouldn't change anything. They had taken Aunt Grace out of the room before we were awake and it didn't matter if Aunt Elinor had been there or not.

That summer, a year and a half before, when Aunt Grace had gone to the Cleveland Clinic and they had told her what she said she must know, the unvarnished truth, Aunt Elinor had come home from New York with her new religion—almost as if she had been handed it straight from God for this occasion. The doctors could do nothing, they were the first to admit it, and told Aunt Grace that she could live only a few months, that her cancer had spread beyond their ability to treat it. But Aunt Elinor was ready for them, the nay-sayers. She had come armed with Truth against Evil, with Spirit against Matter.

"We must never again believe the physicians. Do they have the power of life and death? Do they note the sparrow's fall?" Christian Science was a science of health, it was the power of God revealed and demonstrated. It would help all of us, as it had helped her; and it was going to cure Aunt Grace completely. Aunt Elinor was absolutely convinced of it. Besides, under the circumstances, "Grace, my dear," Aunt Elinor asked, "what have you possibly got to lose?"

During that summer Aunt Grace sat with her sister in the kitchen until nearly noon every day. No longer did they sleep late; there was work to be done. The Bible and the new book, *Science and Health with Key to the Scriptures*, lay open before them, spiked with the markers that underlined the lesson for the week. Usually we were included too and the day began with reading the lesson designated in the *Christian Science Quarterly*. These lessons had titles such as "Love," "Spirit," "Matter," "Reality." Serious words to meditate on, words that impressed us with their power and ours, if we could only figure them out, feel them profoundly. We took turns with the women, reading from the Bible, selections carefully chosen to extend our thinking, often passages beginning in the middle of sentences; it seemed that each word was significant in itself, so much so that Aunt Elinor perceived meaning upon meaning. But when she read the corresponding portion of *Science and Health*, revelation seized her almost continually, so that she became breathless to declare the surpassing wonder of it—drawing us by the forcefulness of her belief. All of it related to Aunt Grace's healing, to our lives there on the farm at this time, with this mission.

Together we would conquer. Sometimes she would stop suddenly, as if in listening to herself she had become amazed. She'd throw up her hands and laugh out loud.

"Oh, God, I don't know. But isn't it the most thrilling thing you've ever imagined, this tremendous power right here . . . ours." Then we would feel it in the same way, through her, as though a prophet had come among us. She studied tirelessly, into the night, made long, long calls to New York to learn from special teachers and practitioners. The faster she could learn, the better. She was in great haste for Aunt Grace's sake.

Aunt Elinor's own healing was a triumphant testimony to the power of Truth. "You ask Momma," she said to Aunt Grace. "Momma, you saw the X-rays. Momma?"

Gram was washing the breakfast dishes, which, she announced regularly, was her contribution to the housework and should be considered enough, after all the years she'd put in, slaving for kids and a good-for-nothing man. Now she didn't look up from where she was working to answer Aunt Elinor.

"Well. They were clear. All the heart damage? It's gone. Completely." Aunt Elinor spoke for Gram to hear too, firmly, trying to be patient with her mother's peculiar and exasperating reticence.

Gram spoke then over the pot she was scrubbing, her face nearly in the water. "I don't know nothing about them pictures. Can't see a thing in them that makes sense."

Aunt Elinor turned away from Gram and spoke entirely to us. "They were clear. Dr. Alexander said there was no evidence of any damage at all now, and that's only two years after he said I would always have to live as a semi-invalid. He was as amazed as I was." We too felt a part of her victory, her voice like a bellows, full, strong and tireless, her vision burning her eyes to topaz. "And I know that I am well; that is what matters." Her platinum-blond hair, thick-curled in waves, spread above her as though it were a canopy over the temple of the indwelling spirit. We could feel that spirit of hers, a firm foundation for those who were called to believe. We strained to: she was calling us to another, greater victory.

Including us all, still, she drew us into a new, exalted realm of being. It felt as though our entire former lives had prepared us for this. After a while, even Aunt Grace did not question anything during these sessions; her face rapt, she listened, absorbing the power and mystery, the wonder of faith pouring from Aunt Elinor, as over the wooden table bars of sunlight would move, clearing away the dark places until the surface gleamed whole.

Steadily Aunt Grace, her wonder at herself increasing, began to absorb the new metaphysic, to love it, apart from any benefit to herself—for its own sake. She had always been what she called sensible, down-to-earth (although if that was so, why had she married Neil? Aunt Libby asked). But now we glimpsed her bent in study over the books, repeating verses from memory, talking with Aunt Elinor far into the night. Aunt Elinor extended her vacation. The two of them plunged, with what we imagined was a zeal akin to the apostle Paul's, into the work of conversion. All that summer it seemed hardly to rain, only at night, a little for the earth; the leaves glittered with clean clear light as though the world were hung with mirror fragments—such, Aunt Elinor taught us, was the nature of reality, everything reflecting God.

We went to church with her and Aunt Grace, and sometimes Aunt Rachel and Aunt Libby. Gram wouldn't go. "I always been Methodist," she said, although as far as we could tell she wasn't anything, didn't go to church, did as she pleased.

Unexpectedly, Anne was fervently attentive, more so than the rest of us. It was not just that Aunt Grace was her mother. It was, as Anne said, that she felt something herself, which must have been spiritual power coming from God, and although she could not really describe it to us, it was something like when she jumped all the way from the top of the haymow and knew she couldn't miss, could fly, in fact, there being only the tiniest barrier, like a veil of illusion, to prevent her. We found her greatly changed. Subdued and yet, underneath, on fire. We had not felt that. Reading from the Bible, her voice trembled as she uttered the words about the singing of the morning star—as though something within her sang too. The aunts began to regard her with a new seriousness; we heard them say, "She's a deep one. You never know." Aunt Elinor presented Anne with her own set of books and took her to the regular Wednesday-evening testimonials at the church.

Gram wanted no part in it; she left the room if Aunt Elinor started to "preach." "A lot of folks are going to get hurt around here." But we didn't pay much attention to an old woman who grumped over the dishpan and arranged to flee away nearly every afternoon and evening of her life. What did she have to do with us?

Aunt Elinor smiled at Gram's grumbling and said she already had a lot of Science in her, the way worry never got to her. She said the rest of us had some catching up to do. Gram snorted at that, her color-bled eyes cloudy so that she nearly looked blind. Science or whatever you called it, she didn't care; there was a lot in life you just had to swallow, like it or not.

That whole summer we were absorbed by Aunt Elinor, as if her thought made up our world as God's made up hers. When we weren't studying with her, we went on long nature walks, as she called them, or rode the horses into the far woods beyond where we'd ever gone before. She wore satin dressing gowns to the breakfast table and sat for hours drinking cup after cup of coffee, an addiction she had begun to feel guilty about; some mornings she drank plain boiled water. All of us wore something that had been hers at one time—jewelry, gabardine coat dresses, slips, expensive things she had saved and brought home in a special suitcase for us to share. Wearing her things made us feel a part of her glamorous life away from us.

Soon after she would come home on a visit, her sisters disappeared with her into her old bedroom and would begin to bargain over the "spoils." Late into the night we would hear them, arguing sometimes, or there were exclamations of delight and hysterical laughter over the fittings, Aunt Libby rueful that the dresses that fit Aunt Elinor's buxom form so perfectly hung on her like sacks, made her look like a flapper. They all had to agree on what was fair. This year Aunt Grace got the prize, a rectangular silver watch with turquoise inlay, which she took for Anne. They had let her have first pick of everything. All these items were lovely, real gifts, generously given. The sisters praised Aunt Elinor to the skies. Then after that there was further excitement over a display of Aunt Elinor's inarguably superior wardrobe, up to the moment, which they knew would belong to them in due time, certainly soon enough for the glacial progression of fashion to Sherwood.

Every few days Aunt Elinor would talk long-distance to New York. She tried to wait until Gram had left, because Gram couldn't stop interrupting her, reminding her every minute or two that the call was long-distance. And those calls often stretched beyond half an hour. "Dammit," Gram would flare up, "you've talked long enough."

Aunt Elinor would put her hand over the mouthpiece. "Mother, I'm paying for it."

"I don't care. Nobody needs to talk that long."

The calls to the Christian Science doctors, who were called practitioners, were necessarily lengthy, the need for an exacting spiritual examination no less acute than for a medical doctor's to determine the nature of an illness. In this case the treatment was mental—the eradication of error from thought. Then there were many calls about business too, which now Aunt Elinor had to handle from afar.

"Hello, Louie," she would trill into the phone. We could hear her all over the house, but we were drawn in closer to her, would end up right at her feet, lying on the carpet, so we could listen only to her, feel included in the whole of her enchanted life. Her laugh would come often, a musical leisured interruption of serious discussion. She would smile at us and roll up her eyes, joshing the man on the other end of the line, sweet-talking him but enjoying it too. We figured he was in love with her. Everyone was. Men were always calling or coming to visit, knocking themselves out, Uncle Dan said, to become one of her enthusiasms. Now, he added, they were really out in the cold, having to compete with God.

Listening to Aunt Elinor's outbursts of hilarity and the firm commands she gave, we were thoroughly confused and simultaneously enthralled. Finally she might say, "Shoot it," or "Kill it," meaning this or that ad, as she would explain later. "Finish that Motorola commercial by tomorrow. Or else!" With more throaty peals of feeling, she would hang up the phone and turn to all of us, released at last to confide the exact details. She would deliver a full account of "the ad game" in New York, her part in it; all this, like her fashions, light-years from our ordinary preoccupations and understanding, was, through her presence, made accessible—the far border of our lives.

She would end our conversations on a sober note, though. "Girls"—and that included her sisters too—"God never fails. When I think of the years on my feet! Well, you have no idea." She searched our eyes, trying with every fiber of her being to reach us, holding within that passionate stare the meaning and hope that words alone would never convey. The graciousness of Divine Love was evident in the quality of her attention.

Aunt Elinor had an increased authority within the family. She valued her own counsel more highly too, prayer purifying her motives, each thought clarified by the perspective of eternity. The discontent of her sisters was no longer beyond repair; she became impatient with their endless grievances. Whereas before she had insisted they were fools to put up with this or that man's foolish behavior, now she suggested they should count their blessings, rejoice and be grateful to have husbands to work for them, so they didn't have to go out and be shopgirls or typists, or have to sit all day in a casting agency. As she had, for years. Although she had heard herself on the radio, she was still nothing but a failed singer, a second-rate actress. But the really important thing she said was, once dissatisfaction had been replaced by gratitude and gladness, the very evils her sisters had denied would disappear, transcended and defeated by Goodness, which always prevailed, like light over darkness. "Doesn't God want you to be happy?" She asked us that quite sincerely. It seemed blasphemy to disagree.

She reckoned her own increasing success as evidence. In precise detail she told us all the stages of her own career, the developments which had resulted in her present position as creative director with a large advertising agency. She had taken risks, bought stock in various products at just the right times and their values had zoomed with the economy. "Without Science I could not do this, girls. But Science teaches us to hold to the Truth—not for personal gain but for Its own sake. If want and deprivation are your expectations, want and deprivation you will have." She faced us with these terrible choices, the power over our own lives.

Her force in speaking was such that by emphasis she seemed to capitalize the recurring important words; we could sense them in her pauses, her emphatic diction, and knew these words in themselves conveyed power from God. In her presence they seemed emblazoned in our minds. After a time of listening as she went on with exact and stirring recitations of radical conversions, horrible illness and wondrous healings, all punctuated with her full thrilling laugh and presided over by her aura of luxurious well-being, we sank off our chairs onto the green carpet, which was sun-splashed as if licked by warm and gentle waves of salt water—the medium of creation itself.

But certain though Aunt Elinor was in her faith, never doubting Aunt Grace's healing, she seemed to appreciate

Aunt Grace's more cautious attitude, her desire to follow the procedures which the doctors recommended to prolong her life as well as to keep up her spirits. *Let them do what they can,* Aunt Elinor's calm bearing seemed to say. So all that summer while Aunt Grace was taught by Aunt Elinor, she continued to go to Cleveland for radium and other treatments, which deepened her voice and sprouted black hair on her chin and upper lip—yet we all knew that the important work of healing was to be accomplished at home, all of us working for this and praying. The treatments made Aunt Grace weak and sick so that she was unable to eat and her hair fell out in handfuls. Finally they were discontinued. The doctors dismissed her. Now she was entirely in the hands of Aunt Elinor and God.

We would often see Aunt Grace walking the back farm road, deeply concentrated. Once when we were coming home from the dairy with ice cream, we saw her from the highway against the backlight of the sky, there by the barn hill, for the farm track was slightly higher than we were, and to us it seemed her figure was silhouetted, a shadow, indeed the visible incarnation of a present spiritual being. The newly cut grass was redolent of its raked crop and in the golden and purpling passage of evening light over it we perceived again the incorporeal origins of creation. Aunt Grace seemed to move across the edge of that vast stage as though she were already far beyond us on a quest which had already removed her from us as effectively as death. We watched as if from the other side of a chasm, ice cream dripping down our arms.

Aunt Elinor, spiritualized, had time for everything, an unflagging energy which surpassed the physical. "Let's take a ride, girls," she would propose on any afternoon, unmindful of the weather or any demands on her as spiritual guide and New York business executive. And we would be off, two riding double on the bigger horse, one on the pony, Queenie, one on a borrowed horse, and Aunt Elinor astride the high-spirited mount she had leased for herself. Often we went so far, with her in the lead, or in such humid and miserable weather, that all of us were aching and weary, desperate to complain aloud—had God's world, and Aunt Elinor's, permitted any such dissatisfactions. Sometimes Uncle Dan said, "I don't think she notices the difference." He meant the difference between good and bad, hot and cold; and he spent many of his evenings alone in his attic sitting room, where he said it was peaceful to be miserable, pure and simple. But we extended ourselves to be with Aunt Elinor and to live up to her expectations. Enthralled, we wanted that summer never to end.

Once when we were out on a very long excursion, Anne's thirst grew beyond her endurance. She mentioned it uneasily to Aunt Elinor. Aunt Elinor was immediately solicitous, recognized it as a natural thing, not in the category of menstrual cramps and head colds, which had to be vigorously denied. Thirst might even be interpreted as reflecting the spirit's craving for living water. Aunt Elinor was so accessible right then that we all seized the chance to lament our discomforts—guilty that we had ever thought her unsympathetic, that we had misunderstood her. She turned into the first farm road we came to, slid from her horse's back and strode to the back door, where she greeted the bewildered housewife with queenly courtesy, requesting cold water and a resting spot on the grass.

"What a perfectly marvelous place you have here," she

rejoiced with the woman. "You must never tire of the enjoyment." It was obvious from her presence that Aunt Elinor never tired of anything.

"Is a nice place." The woman spoke finally, out of her shy rolling smiles, in rather halting English, patting her disordered hair.

"Why, my dear, you must be Mrs. Chaccio." Aunt Elinor beamed at the embarrassed woman. "Gino's mother. And Angelica's. I taught them in school, you know, years ago, before I went to New York. Of course, you have so many children." Aunt Elinor hesitated as though Mrs. Chaccio had forgotten about them herself. "And what are they doing now?"

Mrs. Chaccio shrugged, her English or some other inhibition not allowing her to tell it. "The farm. Kids." She motioned vaguely.

"Why, yes, of course. This wonderful place. And aren't you fortunate to have them with you. Such a grand family."

"Yes. Big." Mrs. Chaccio grinned broadly at what could not be denied. "Eighteen live. Two gone." Aunt Elinor looked sympathetic for the missing two, yet her expression suggested that there was much to be grateful for in the eighteen who had survived. "They must be a great help to you." She encouraged Mrs. Chaccio as she encouraged everyone. And Mrs. Chaccio opened the screen door and stood aside for us to enter. We hung back from the darkness inside, but Aunt Elinor marched forward, up the broken steps, wiping her feet on the porch boards before she went in. We could hear her silent urging: Never turn down Experience—the stuff of life. We dragged behind her. A chicken stood in the middle of the table; Mrs. Chaccio scooped it aside and spoke to one of the dark-eyed children peeping in at the door. She spoke rapid Italian to the child, who came and took the docile chicken in its arms and carried it out. Aunt Elinor simply beamed then, as if this fluency in Italian were some special gift.

"*Buon giorno*," she said happily, for she had studied Italian when her ambition had been to sing with the Metropolitan Opera. Her word of greeting made Mrs. Chaccio giggle and nod.

Beyond restraint, Aunt Elinor admired the large room, the wall of cupboards, the view of the woods and creek. She proclaimed the joy of family life, including each of us in her enthusiasm. Meanwhile we shrank inward. It seemed we were under the influence of a strange and unholy power in that place, which even Aunt Elinor could not combat. We were fixated by the stare of the unchildish baby Jesus from a calendar, Him crucified and bleeding in another picture. Was this Divine Love? Still Aunt Elinor urged us, nodding significantly, as if she understood but would reassure us that, though distorted and grotesque, the images were evidence of man's eternal striving toward the Infinite. She glowed, smart in the tailored riding habit she wore in Central Park. Mrs. Chaccio began to roll and slice the dough which had been drying on floured cloths. She blew a feather off the table.

"Oh, girls, look." Aunt Elinor tried to rouse us to another wonder—we were always behind her. "Noodles." We gathered with her to watch and give tribute.

"Pasta," Mrs. Chaccio corrected. Her bulk jiggled with the flash of her knife. She sliced with a machine's precision.

"Oh, of course. Did you ever!" Aunt Elinor said meaningfully, meaning for us to note the merits of skill and self-reliance, of service to others. We watched the mound pile high. Then Mrs. Chaccio spread the yellow ribbons of dough over the tabletop and Aunt Elinor asked how long they might last. Mrs. Chaccio said she thought about a meal. Again we had the sense that Aunt Elinor was asking questions and pointing out things primarily to teach us—that Mrs. Chaccio was unwittingly a subject.

Then, with "Come and see us," and exclamations of how delightful it had been, Aunt Elinor decided to leave and swept us out to the lawn and onto our horses and we, glad enough to escape, left at a fast clip, waving grandly behind to the woman and the now seven or eight children and grown girls who came out and waved back. The chickens in the yard scattered and one of the dogs followed us down the road, barking and growling.

Katie, on Queenie, fell behind and we drew up to wait for her. When we were all circled around Aunt Elinor, she gave us the clear, deliberate look we knew. It told us that she intended to be very serious, that although she could carry any role and enjoy any situation, there were always the lessons underneath to be learned, ramifications to seemingly simple occurrences. We took a deep breath because we wanted only to get away from there.

"Do you girls realize that that woman is not much older than I am?" We certainly couldn't believe it. "And she is nearly dead from fatigue. From childbearing. Eighteen, twenty—what does it matter? It's ridiculous! But no one will ever lift a finger to help her, not while she is carrying out the dictates of the Roman Pope. Many Catholics are fine people, don't misunderstand me. But misguided. And her husband? What does he care, worked to death himself, the church always after something. That woman, my dears, is a slave. This may be the twentieth century, but she is in bondage. To her husband, the church, her children. Never forget her.''

We knew we never would. Always and forever we would remember Mrs. Chaccio, old before she had been ripe, with dozens of children, heaps of noodles, chickens underfoot, and on her neck the heavy feet of her husband and the Pope. Neither would we forget what we had seen when we looked back at the barking dogs. Several of the older girls were running in the yard, prancing like high-strung horses, while Mrs. Chaccio laughed and thumbed her nose. We blushed to ourselves, glad that Aunt Elinor was far ahead and wouldn't have to know.

At dinner Aunt Elinor recreated the afternoon, complete with noodles. Gram muttered, ''Humph.'' She'd made as many for threshers. Her noodles, it was clear, were quite different from Mrs. Chaccio's, prepared in freedom and far from Rome. They were the pinnacle of Gram's surviving skill at homemaking. We had only to imagine them, served in fatty streams of milk gravy along with chicken, double fried in the country way, to beg her to make some. Which ordinarily she refused ever to do again—''I'm done with that.'' But now we knew she'd have some noodles drying by midmorning someday soon, the report of Mrs. Chaccio's skill activating an old pride. And we'd swallow our fears, follow after her to see her snatch the hen she wanted and wring its neck with one formidable twist, the life of the tough old bird no concern of hers.

Grandad didn't look up from eating. He and Uncle Dan were very little in our lives that summer, both doing what Uncle Dan called ''laying low.'' Now that we were too busy to play in the barn, with Aunt Elinor filling every hour, Grandad was left to himself. We had nearly forgotten he was there. Perhaps he was often gone, to town or to auctions. What we had noticed, but only to recall later, was that he had to stop to get his breath when he came up the seven steps to the porch, and that sometimes his face bruised purple at something Gram said, though with a glance at Aunt Grace, he'd usually turn on his heel and go away, his anger unspoken. But this night he was there at the table, silent, although he knew the Chaccio family well enough, the men helping him at haying time or with the threshing.

Toward the end of the meal Aunt Elinor excused herself for a moment and came back to the table with a small foil-wrapped packet of cheese. She opened it and the pie-shaped wedge exposed then was uneven and spongy on the surface, riddled with a greenish-blue substance.

"That's the mold," she explained. "But it's perfectly harmless." We were aghast. She smeared some on a cracker, found it edible, in fact delicious. She nibbled appreciatively, wiping her fine thin-curve of mouth daintily, eating as she always did, in the refined way we thought they must eat in New York City, which just then seemed a million miles away.

The summer before, Aunt Elinor had come home with other alluring specialties, yogurt and wheat germ. For a week or two we had traded in our sugar sandwiches for what she assured us were the far superior benefits of raw green peppers and sunflower seeds. Until Rossie got an upset stomach and Gram declared in no uncertain terms that Aunt Elinor could just pack up and leave for New York if things there suited her so much better. We were allowed to go back to our old ways of eating and while the rest of us ate Gram's white-flour biscuits and mashed potatoes, Aunt Elinor ate what she called chef's salad and cottage cheese. Even now that she had come to see that spiritual nourishment was the true bread, she continued to eat her health foods, as if she now preferred them. We wondered if she was afraid to be so alone. It never seemed so.

"You're missing out on so much," she said to everyone at the table, spreading the cheese. She said it was just silly, the family aversion to cheese, just some old-fashioned nonsense, though Uncle Dan suggested she should allow the custom to persist, since as far as he could see it was the only thing Grandad and Gram had in common and they'd passed it on to their children, like a family trait. Though Aunt Elinor laughed at that, she continued to eat the blue cheese for us to see, in order that we might take heart, become braver, dare to begin anew.

"Eleanor." We could tell from the edge Gram put on pronouncing the name that for her it was still spelled the way Gram named her, before she went to the state of New York and had her name officially spelled E-l-i-n-o-r, and her middle name of Myrtle dropped entirely. "If you have to eat shit, do it out of my sight."

Aunt Elinor, her neck arched, poised high, looked at Gram, her mother. We could see by the swell of her bosom how it had shocked her. But she said then, matter-of-fact, "Mother, I don't think it's all that serious a thing," and she went back to her cheese, flourishing her hands with their jeweled rings and sprinkling of freckles.

Gram continued to dip her white bread into her coffee, making sucking noises. Louder than usual, it seemed. Uncle Dan took his plate to the sink and went to his attic room; he went in a hurry. Aunt Elinor was the only one who ever got the best of Gram like that, forcing her to hold her tongue, just as, when Aunt Elinor was a girl, she alone of the five children was selected to exchange the dollar's worth of egg money for a weekly piano lesson, and was then further excused from evening dishes so she could practice. We often heard of this privilege when our mothers were impressing us with the good fortune that was ours, students at the piano from the age of six, in contrast with their musical deprivation. We could almost imagine the two dark-haired and thin older girls, May and Grace, in the rented bungalow on North Street, down with the Italians, scraping and stacking dishes by kerosene light, while in the background Elinor tripped light-fingered over the keys and spread through the house her resonant contralto.

But Gram could get back, anytime she wanted to. She made more than her usual guzzling over her coffee when Aunt Elinor was around and spoke exactly as we figured her people had spoken on the old farm. It was as if she were reminding her daughter: an apple never rolls far from the tree.

Grandad hadn't said one word. But when he'd finished eating he stood up abruptly, his dish in one hand. With the other he reached to pick up Aunt Elinor's cheese, dropped it on the floor, and then mashed it with a hard wiping motion of his heel and tracked it across the linoleum to the sink and out the door toward the barn.

Aunt Elinor had tears standing in her amber-brown eyes. Gram recovered her voice and went to the door, screaming out after the vanished figure, "Goddamned bastard. Swine." She came back in with the scrub pail and told her daughters to shut up. There were four of them standing at the table, Libby, Elinor, Grace and Rachel, all of them furious, railing that it was no fit place to have their children, never had been, that he had ruined their whole lives.

"Then why don't you get the hell out?" their mother said as she slowly let herself down onto her bony knees beside the pail. "You know he can't abide cheese. Never could." Her arm, burdened with its slack quiver of hanging skin, moved the rag in what was still a strong motion, as though habit went beyond the endurance of flesh itself.

"We must forgive," Aunt Elinor said. "None of us is perfect." She wiped her tears then and smiled. We kept absolutely silent so they wouldn't ask us to take sides or send us out, for what we knew about the family was disclosed to us by our being there to see it happen. We had to remain as inarticulate as the mantling walls, silent and watchful—outside the action. The five sisters had guarded their secrets from us, as though we were strangers, as if their loyalty was only to each other and their mother; if further divided, it would dissolve.

Aunt Elinor revived and brought out a fresh package of cheese. She began to spread it on crackers, lining them up before her. "God is our father and our mother," she said then. We heard Gram moving the rag in widening circles over the floor. Aunt Elinor offered us a cracker. Gram went out on the porch. The door slammed behind her. We heard the water slap against the packed dirt by the steps. With the tips of our tongues we tasted the blue cheese. Salt. Gram clanged the pail onto the shelf. Aunt Elinor beamed encouragement.

Gram marched through the door and across the room without looking at us. Ready to go out, she had scrubbed the floor in her good dress. While she washed her hands,

Aunt Rachel went over and brushed off the hemline. "Honestly, Momma. We could have done it."

"I figured you was too busy improving yourselves," she said, and left the room.

Aunt Grace had the cheese in her mouth. She sat there, full-mouthed, as if she couldn't bring herself to move it either way. But then she ran to the sink and spit it out. Aunt Elinor looked patient, as one who had seen a wider world, one she constantly made visible to the rest of us—accepting the fact that a wider world might mean a weaker place in the old one. She left the table to go to Aunt Grace, who still bent over the sink. We waited. Later we would toss our crackers into the trash. Choosing between Aunt Elinor and Gram seemed to us as profound as a choice between good and evil, only we didn't know which was which.

How completely they forgot us. Gram left in her car and Aunt Elinor put her arm around Aunt Grace and led her out. "Who is My mother? our Lord asked. Whoever would follow after Me must forsake all that he has." They were gone into the next room. Already Aunt Elinor had said that we might leave off the Aunt in addressing her: simply call her Elinor. She would consider it no disrespect, for it was our spiritual bonds that mattered, not our human. Yet we never did more than try to say it once or twice, "Elinor." We didn't want to say the bare name, to break the connection. It seemed we might be asked to give up everything.

Aunt Rachel and Aunt Libby still sat at the table, Aunt Rachel eating more of the cheese. She had tried it before, rather liked it. Aunt Libby was looking disgusted, but not about the cheese—she didn't even pretend to taste any. "It would be wonderful if you could believe it. But I just can't understand how a person can turn their back on all the terrible things that happen and say they aren't real. Most of what happens in this world isn't real, then. I will not look at somebody who I can see is sick and say they're well. It's nothing but a damned lie." She gathered up all the crackers and took them to the trash, as though she would thereby strip the world of humbug.

"It appeals to me a little," Aunt Rachel said. "You have to look deeper than that, Libby. It's like that old thing about the chicken or the egg." Her gaze was fixed with Oriental inscrutability upon the elusive figures shadows painted over the orchard grass.

"God," Aunt Libby said. "You ever start in on that"— she motioned with her raised fist toward the front room, from where we could hear Aunt Elinor's strong voice— "I'll leave town, I swear it. Hardly any family left, it seems to me. Most of the time I feel like I'm not even here—as if she sees through us, as though we're all disembodied spirits floating around." There were tears standing in her eyes. A breeze came in at the window, stirring the cloth on the table. When Aunt Elinor was home there were special touches like tablecloths and napkins, what Gram called "airs."

"It's for Grace," Aunt Rachel said, and put her hand on Libby's arm. "Let's just try. See what happens and maybe there will be a miracle and she'll get well."

As if brought down by the Truth, Aunt Libby said nothing to that. They looked at us. "I think we should forget ourselves and have one mind among us." Aunt Rachel addressed us and Aunt Libby. Although two years younger, Aunt Rachel seemed now the older, wiser one.

"After all, I don't see that things turn out so well for most people. Live and die for nothing." We felt at one in a yearning to believe, to transcend the material and false, to perceive the reality of Spirit. Just then over the stove, the opaline salt and pepper shakers, their tin lids marred and bent, appeared to be invested momentarily with an underlying quality, a luminous spirit, as the flood of sun went down.

In the fall, Aunt Grace heard of new treatment centers that might offer some slight hope. She seemed stronger after the summer of religious enlightenment, had more energy, and she accepted Gram's determination that she should try any and every thing. Aunt Elinor concurred. It was a last effort. She would travel with Aunt Grace whenever she could; we watched her usher Aunt Grace, who looked thin and stylish wearing the new fur coat Gram had bought her, into the interior of the prop plane. Aunt Elinor's shoulders squared over her sturdy frame. The size which most of the family carried in a gangling bony height was in Aunt Elinor condensed into a powerful firm fleshiness. She had become more quiet and concentrated in her spiritual quest with the passing months. Always now in speaking to us of Aunt Grace she assumed an intense, solemn tone. But there was a hint of withdrawal too, as if our concern, though loving, contained a fearfulness and worldliness which might be traitorous to the requirements of absolute faith. It could even jeopardize the cure. We felt her drawing away from us, but in the interests of our common struggle we tried to be brave, swallowed our hurt.

It was during that winter that Grandad died. No one expected him to die; Aunt Elinor hadn't even known he needed help or she would certainly have tried to give it. He had heart failure in the downstairs bathroom, a tiny little room made from a back hall, with a curtain in front of a toilet and sink. He had been home alone and when Rossie found him he'd been dead for hours. It was terrible for Rossie. We were all comforting him, trying to help him overcome the shock, the embarrassment of crying so hard. We were waiting for the police to come to help.

Gram exploded: "God almighty. Them cows'll be dead or worse," and she flew straight to the barn as if there she expected to meet a real disaster. But there weren't any cows; Grandad had sold off the last of them. Why had he done that? Perhaps he got sick of spilling perfectly good milk down the drain or feeding it to hogs. "Maybe he knew something was coming." Gram said that. We looked at her, surprised, as if for the first time we realized she might know things about him, more than she'd let on.

After Grandad was gone we didn't notice much that was different. We had to buy milk. There were fewer fights, but that had been true since Aunt Grace got sick. Uncle Dan sat down in the living room more often in the evenings and eventually the furniture in the attic sitting room was distributed around the house. Sometimes we'd wake up around dawn and think we heard Grandad going off to milk. But we didn't get up, so we must have known it was some other sound we heard. Or was some memory the house kept. And there were times when the wild doves seemed to moan "Sucky, sucky," as though Grandad were tramping through the hollow, gathering his cows.

Another summer came and Aunt Grace still lived. She was very thin, with some form of bandage under her dress at the throat. And she carried her left arm in a muslin sling. Her eyes, dark and prominent, were too much for us—she had seen what had burned its own image into her gaze. The first and the last. We held her in great awe. And it was as though her presence and our devotion to her had united us at last in a perfect oneness, we four girls thinking, feeling and moving in a dimension that felt like the exact representation of a greater mind. We had bad dreams, cried out at night. But during the day we guarded every thought about her.

If we met Aunt Grace as she went about the farm on her long solitary walks, we—still dancing and running, coming out of the flowing, dazzling pleasures of the brook, the embrace of vines and roots, the sting of grasses—would fall into silence. Then talk awhile, but carefully, self-consciously, answering her few questions, her smiles with our smiles. At the edge of our awareness we glimpsed the white wrapping at her throat, breathed carefully so we wouldn't smell the abscess underneath. There in the dust-silted track by the barn, ankle-deep, we buried our bare toes, sprayed geyser figures into the air to fall away. While we talked with her, it seemed that our hearts burned within us, as if we were with someone who had come to love the world, inexpressibly yet without entitlement. We made some excuse and ran away. Left her alone to concentrate her entire being toward making manifest the sufficient love of God.

Every morning and afternoon Aunt May left her hotel and came to the house to change Aunt Grace's bandages and help her bathe. Only Aunt May could do this for her; Aunt Grace could not bear for anyone else to see her—not just for the shame of it, but for inflicting the horror of it.

We knew Aunt May had been chosen for this. Perhaps because she was the oldest of the five sisters and part mother to the rest, but there was her nature itself, tender and selfless, revealed in the tone of her voice, the tone the others used in speaking to her.

They were so concerned for her when she came down to the living room after tending Aunt Grace. They would coax her to sit a few minutes. At first there would be silence, all of us thinking of Aunt Grace, in bed for the night, although her light would burn long after everyone else had gone to sleep. Once, Aunt Libby told us, when she was preparing for bed, coming out of the bathroom, she glanced through the crack in the door where Aunt Grace was reading in bed.

"You still awake?" Aunt Libby had asked.

Aunt Grace had stared out with such a look, Aunt Libby told us she felt it penetrate her heart. And Aunt Grace had said, "If you only knew the wonder of it, you wouldn't waste a single instant." While Aunt Grace was with us, when we spoke of her and repeated those things she said to us, it was with the sense that we had had the exquisite visitation of a saint.

Aunt May showed all the strains of her life, a widow at forty, mother to a fatherless daughter, nurse to her favorite, mortally ill sister. We honored her for her place in our lives then, her acts of devotion. But while she sat on the recliner, trying to relax, her legs would spring up and away like parts wound too tightly and she would have to startle up and walk the cramps out of her legs, rubbing her hands through her black hair and along the sides of her neck. Aunt Libby badgered her to get away for a rest.

"How could I?" Aunt May asked, casting her eyes

toward the ceiling. Aunt Grace was now occupying the room directly over the living room, the room where some of us had been born, with its view of the west and the outlying woods beyond the meadows; over the fireplace mantel was the framed picture of the Indian brave. Poised on his horse at the edge of a cliff, the Indian gazed into an endless distance of land and sky, but he seemed equal to that immensity, his back straight and resolute, his attitude dignified.

Toward the end of the summer the sisters decided that we all needed a break from the tension and planned a picnic at the lake. Gram wouldn't come. She was going to the races. Besides, she didn't like the bother of eating outside. It was a special treat for the rest of us, however, something like the Fourth of July, and we stayed around the kitchen to help with the deviled eggs and baked beans, to pack the hamper and wash out the thermos. We felt as if after a long illness or imprisonment we were reentering the world.

At the lake, though, it was crowded and noisy. The county orphanage was having an outing and some of the kids, who seemed backward or maybe even retarded, came over to stare at us, which made Aunt Libby look her most mournful and whisper things like: "Have you ever seen anything more pathetic? Always makes one count one's blessings." One of the kids was sick on the ground near the covered tables and it smelled so bad we had to take our blanket over to the grass. Then Aunt May drove up, alone, because her daughter didn't feel well, had her period, which made Aunt Libby whisper again, this time that she'd never thought of it as either an illness or a holy ritual. The orphans stared at us a lot and some tried to talk to Aunt Libby, who smiled although she couldn't understand a word, and finally Aunt Elinor, home for a weekend, went to the park office and suggested that the orphan children be taken away where they wouldn't disturb people while they were eating. The leaders gathered them together then, but sullenly, and we all felt guilty of a fastidious contempt, devoid of compassion, as though our long vigil, our trial, had as effectively estranged us from the rest of the world as an imprisonment.

"It's spoiled," Aunt Libby said when we were left to ourselves. Aunt May went in the water, where she swam, again and again, the rounds of the buoy ropes. No matter what we did, we couldn't get the feeling right. We sat and thought about Aunt Grace alone in the house, Gram off to the races. Would Aunt Grace think we had deserted her? Did she need us as much as we needed her? After listening to us complain about the reek of vomit and watching us mope around on our patch of blanket. Uncle Dan said, "I can only stand just so much of a good time," and he got up and began to pack things for the trip home.

On the way back, we listened to Aunt Libby speculating to Aunt Rachel that perhaps Valerie, Aunt May's daughter, was jealous of Aunt Grace, getting all her mother's attention and concern. Did Valerie want her to die? It didn't fit, for weren't we all turning everything upside down to save Aunt Grace from death? Aunt Elinor taught us that God is Life. And everyone wanted God—wanted Life. In that way the things Aunt Elinor told us made sense, convincing us with indisputable logic. In such harmonious circularity we were as one; we felt it as always, undaunted by the failure of the outing, when we turned down the gravel drive, passing under the hanging oaks, entering into our own kingdom.

"And tonight?" Aunt Libby asked one evening when Aunt May came down from Aunt Grace. Sometimes now she had to come three and four times a day to change the dressings on Aunt Grace's neck. We would never dare to ask about that lingering abscess. To do so would be as shocking as if we threatened God with a rival power. And no one would ever explain it, thinking, if they thought of it at all, that we were wholly of them, knew what they knew, would fear what they feared, believe or not, by happenstance and accretion, as they did themselves.

"About the same," Aunt May answered.

The silence deadened the air so the ticking of the clock seemed to flow into our emotions and become their exact representation.

"They're going to have to do something about the pain." Aunt Libby said that with the cross and exasperated look she wore when referring to all misery; its meaning in the scheme of things would never be sanctioned by her.

"Elinor has hired a nurse," Aunt May said.

A nurse? It was impossible. Medicine. We thought this must be the end. Did Aunt Grace know?

Aunt May explained: "She's a Scientist, but trained in certain procedures. For cases like this. She'll come with Elinor next week. I don't think you should tell Grace yet. I don't know how she'll take it."

"At least this will mean some rest for you," was all Aunt Libby said, totally disillusioned with living and dying.

"Libby: if it would do any good, I'd crawl on my hands and knees to China," Aunt May said.

Aunt Elinor came to bring the Christian Science nurse.

She made the trip without her suitcase of extra finery, came only with her brave and magnanimous soul; we could see it glowing still, translucent in her gaze. We could scarcely take our eyes off hers. The tiny nurse was a shadowy, inconsequential figure, lost beside Aunt Elinor. Maybe Aunt Grace would hardly notice her.

Aunt Grace slept now on a hospital bed which had been moved into her room and positioned by the west window. Sometimes she sat in the corner armchair, but she seldom left the room, took only a few short walks, leaning on someone's arm. This night the door stood open, but more often it was closed and sometimes we would hear through it her muffled thrashings and moaning. We would stand in the hall, unable to leave. Until Aunt Libby or Aunt Rachel, sometimes even Gram, would come and stand at the crack of the door and say to us, "It's all right. I'm here." Usually in their hands was a piece of the quilt they were making, a way to pass the time and occupy their thoughts. It pleased Aunt Grace to see the pattern emerge and the piece grow larger and when she was well enough she would hem a square herself, each square setting into the point of an emerging star. Gram had begun the quilt years before, then never had the time, or later the patience, to finish it. It was the old pattern "Broken Star," worked in strips of unbleached muslin, the stars of various shades of green, surrounded by a calico border. They had Aunt Grace make the mistake on her first piece, a traditional play for good luck. It was, by Calvinist logic, presumptuous that anything human should strive for perfection—Aunt Grace said that maybe they should try to make a Mary Baker Eddy quilt, one that would be as nearly perfect as possible.

Each morning we were taken in for our separate visits. Aunt Grace would make us feel at ease, her pain less in those hours, or her strength to bear it more certain. She would encourage us to tell her whatever we were doing, and tell us that she thought she was feeling a little better, would soon be up and around. We could not meet her eyes; but she looked away too, out the window as if she might absorb further the health and harmony of the land. Hopes like that she would share with us occasionally. Once she said, "I have come to know that living and dying are a single event when considered by the mind of God." For days we would mention one revelation or another—comforted that Aunt Grace had been privileged to receive, through her suffering, a saintlike character.

· But that night when Aunt Elinor entered the room with the little nurse, out of Aunt Grace's deep eyes, hollowed by an anguish from hell, came such a look that Aunt Libby said it suggested to her the gaze of the prophetess Anne, who had waited in the temple for years and years, not allowing herself to die, not until she saw the Promise of Israel. "So it's come to this," Aunt Grace said, in her voice made husky from the drugs, horror in it. She was not fooled. She knew what it meant.

"Darling," Aunt Elinor cried, and rushed over to seize her sister with an intensity that made us withdraw.

There now began a strange and bitter contest between the two sisters: Aunt Grace seemed to scent betrayal, Aunt Elinor insisted that the time for victory was at hand. The nurse was merely a convenience, a symbol of resolve, if anything. Not failure. But for us, the nurse, gliding about on her soft white shoes, had become the spirit of the house. While we had been diverted, breaking all lesser attachments, the house had been harboring a separate and competing force.

Gram was on Aunt Grace's side. We heard her say to Aunt Libby, "All's she wants is to go in peace. And quickly. It's over a year. Why in God's name won't Ellie leave her be? I can hardly stand it." She didn't even look sorry, just angry, and we hardened ourselves against her.

"What other hope is there, Momma?" Aunt Libby asked.

Gram said, "Sometimes there ain't no hope."

At these outbreaks our alarm held us shuddering and we deafened ourselves. There was no less feeling in Gram's voice, yet all her words seemed severe, harsh. Although she sometimes went out in the evenings, it was just her habit, more restlessness than pleasure, and there was no talk of winning or losing. Still Aunt Libby disapproved, thought she should stay at home.

"I'd like to know what anyone else could do—with her around." Gram would jerk her head toward Aunt Elinor's insistent voice, winding its way down the stairwell.

But Aunt Grace was a captive. No one would interfere with Aunt Elinor really, for she was all we had. Sometimes we'd hear Aunt Grace, defiant and belligerent: "God. Tell me why I have to endure this. And you. You are tormenting me. For your own willfulness. Oh, I can use a knife by myself. How can you ask me to live like this, cut up and stinking?" She would burst into anguished weeping. She no longer tried to hide her pain. We felt she punished us. We could hear her shrieking and storming and we became afraid to visit her in her room, for she would stare at us fiercely, refusing to talk, so that it seemed she wished us ill and would gladly have bargained all our lives to save her own. And hearing her at night, we could not sleep, would take our pillows and blankets and lie in the hallway across from her door, praying for it to end. It seemed that we had lost our lives already.

Through the open door, we saw Aunt Elinor stroking Aunt Grace's arm while murmuring her litany of assurance. Once Aunt Grace sat up and with more strength and fury than we could conceive of, shook off that soothing touch, screamed, "Goddamn you. How can I ever get you to leave me alone? Just let me die. I'm begging you." Then she turned toward the window, that was black against the wall of night. We were astounded.

Aunt Elinor came in and out of the kitchen, running errands in the nurse's stead. They were always trying to get Aunt Grace to eat something. And always Aunt Elinor was struggling against evil, affirming the power of God to save, even while Aunt Grace gnashed her teeth, spit out her food, locked the door against her, and stopped her ears against that voice which, even as Aunt Elinor became outwardly more silent, we seemed to hear more pervasively—the voice of God, as if it had absorbed Aunt Elinor's being.

At the table, in her brief moments with us, Aunt Elinor would sit heavily, she who before had carried herself in almost strenuous erectness. Aunt Libby asked her once what we were all thinking: "How long?"

Aunt Elinor stood and regained almost the bearing we remembered. She paused in the doorway of the kitchen, beyond her the dark hall which, like a path stumbled upon in a wilderness, must be taken, in spite of its uncertainty. No longer did she waste strength to pet us or cheer us on. "Love does not fail." So she said, and in her strong-boned square face, lifted at the chin, we could see the lengths to which love would go.

Then one night Gram came home early. We met her in the hall. Although it was still summer, she wore already her lightweight wool coat. Under the dim bowl of the hanging globe, her slack flesh draped, flaccid, covering a body which could no longer feel the heat. Still there was a moisture, like grease, on her forehead. From that room upstairs we could hear the two sisters. Elinor and Grace. The one spoke seldom and then irritably, waspish, against the other's continual low-voiced intensity. When the door opened we heard Aunt Grace growl, "And Christ I hope you never come back."

When Aunt Elinor came wearily around the curve of the stairway and saw her mother standing below she stopped. In her hands was a basin of unwound and heaped gauze, stained dark. It seemed we could smell it, so we tried not even to breathe. The freckles splotched upon Aunt Elinor's pale face seemed to form into patterns like the outlines of land masses floating upon a map of waters.

Gram started up toward her, such vehemence in her raised fist it reminded us of the time when Grandad was alive. Aunt Elinor was nearly to the bottom of the stairs then and Gram did not strike her but whacked the basin out of her hands. It flew and the contents spread, dark and vile, on Gram's precious carpet. "You'll burn for this," Gram gasped, sobbing. "Pride. Meddling."

Aunt Elinor went past her and knelt on the floor, gathering the wads of dressing back into the bowl. As her hands moved we saw the scarlet lacquer on her nails was jagged and unkempt. Below us her shoulders heaved and shook, as she continued to reach for each piece. She was alone.

We were afraid: of Gram, who stood over her, still panting, but more of Aunt Elinor, who could endure the hatred and misunderstanding of the whole world.

Aunt Grace came down the stairs. She leaned on the banister and her features, illuminated by the globe light, seemed unmarked by suffering. She was like a young girl, slender, her black hair, which had stopped falling out now that the radium treatments were ended, curling again in masses around her throat, hiding the bandage. The dimple set in the center of her chin winked over the deep point of darkness. To Aunt Elinor she said simply, "Come." Her eyes appeared to shine as with tears, but without sorrow or bitterness. There was plain joy in Aunt Elinor's face as she went up to Aunt Grace and encircled her with one arm and helped her back toward her room. From the back, beside Aunt Elinor's sturdiness, we could see how wasted Aunt Grace had become—now both of them held upright, supported by the ballast of indomitable character. Anne said, "Mother," but neither answered.

Gram stood, horribly aged within the folds of her skin and under the layer of her coat. The time she'd survived was like doom upon her head. She jerked up her head as if ready to denounce, then with a sigh lowered herself to finish gathering up the tangle of dressings. There was a brown stain on her hands when she'd finished. She scrubbed at the mess a minute with a clean piece. "What's the use? What happens happens," she said. She looked at our feet, then up at our faces, one by one. "Well, don't just stand there like a bunch of ninnies. Help me." So then we knew we were chained to Gram, having nothing more in us than what she was and hoped for. She had claimed us. We brought her fresh water, emptied the slops, got on our knees beside her and worked until the rags were rinsed clean. When it was finished we followed her into the living room, where she struck the gas jet of the converted fireplace, and lifting her dress and the coat, which she still wore, she stood almost into the asbestos grate of the running flame. "Feels good," she said, and gave her only smile, not to us, but to her own momentary contentment.

After that, a watchful peacefulness settled on the house. Aunt Grace appeared to have more strength, came to the table for dinner sometimes, although her digestion was delicate and even the smell of fried food revolted her, so that we did not have food like Gram's but instead something prepared by Aunt Rachel under Aunt Elinor's supervision—perhaps a clear broth, a green salad. Aunt Grace would just pick. Gram offered her bread and cream but she refused it. None of us could enjoy those elegant simple dishes, the bare skeletons of meals. Not with Aunt Grace wasting beside us.

Uncle Dan, though subdued, could still make us laugh when he wanted. Since we had started going to the Christian Science Church he had some new customers coming to his store to buy meat. He was glad for that, his business steadily falling off because of supermarket competition. But, he said, conversation with the faithful could be awfully risky—a fellow had to watch himself, couldn't hardly say anything right any which way. "Especially that Mrs. Beall from over on the Franksville Road. I say, 'Nice day, isn't it, Mrs. Beall?' She gives me a look. 'All God's days are perfect, Mr. Snyder,' daring me to take issue. But if I try to head her off and say, 'This rain is a blessing,' she says, 'God answers our every need, Mr. Snyder.' " Aunt

Elinor laughed too and agreed that some people were bores on any subject. The woman meant well, no doubt, but being new to Science, she was perhaps overzealous. And for that time, with Aunt Grace a little better, nobody was inclined to quibble. "I'll say black's white," Gram said, "if it'll do any good."

Still there remained beside our posture of confidence phantoms of dread like the hangover of a bad dream or the premonition of a bad day. The house seemed alive with the conflict; we could hear the walls settling and the floor-boards creaking beneath the carpet as we walked. Aunt Rachel packed up Rossie's clothes and he went to stay with his other grandmother, who lived in some other town—bad dreams were keeping him awake for hours every night.

Then Neil came to the farm. When he first went into her room and saw Aunt Grace sitting in the armchair by the window, the white embroidered birds on her dress blazing silver, the dress loose on her form, he went to her, fell on his knees beside her, put his head into her lap and cried. Sobbed out loud. We weren't there to see, but we heard Aunt Libby telling Gram. We couldn't imagine his emotion and it seemed almost unbecoming, as if a perfect stranger were trying to imitate real grief. And we were afraid, as if his coming would make everything worse.

"It's late in the day for tears," Gram said.

Aunt Rachel answered, "Seventy times seven." Since we were all studying the Bible, living and breathing Scripture, we knew that that meant the length and breadth of forgiveness.

Gram flared that she didn't need to hear it. "I'm sick and tired of sermons. When I was a girl I memorized practically the entire Gospel. Christian Scientists don't have a monopoly on the Bible, no matter how high and mighty they think they are. From what I've heard, she wasn't no saint neither, Leader or not. There are some who say she wasn't no better than a heathen herself, married more than once. Vain.''

"Well, Momma," Aunt Rachel said, after a few moments of quiet, plainly offended but not running scared, "I guess we have a lot in common, then." Because Aunt Rachel was soon to marry Tom Buck, who was waiting for his divorce, and he would be her second husband; and vanity—these women knew about that, laughed about it, but couldn't hide it.

Then she told Gram, "I think I feel sorriest for him," meaning Neil. Was that because he loved Aunt Grace the most and had sobbed in her arms? Was that because she had loved him but didn't anymore? We didn't know. Neither did Gram, because her face wasn't even angry but was overcome by a vacant astonishment. Maybe he was the black sheep returned to the flock, the one who required a radical forgiveness.

The day before Neil was going back to his office, Aunt Grace thought she was strong enough to walk a little with us. We had found a special place by the old orchard, up from the duck pond, and we wanted her to see it. They walked very slowly down the drive, Aunt Grace leaning against Neil. Because of Aunt Grace, we didn't go into the ravine but crossed through the meadow, where Grandad's haywagon still sagged, one wheel missing. Neil was very tender toward Aunt Grace, toward us too, a way he'd never been before; we'd heard Gram say that maybe some of the smartness had been knocked out of him. We felt included, as though we shared in the change in him, shared a lover's attentions. Observing him, slim and blond, his blue eyes, which could be so wild, now sobered, we felt in him the miracle we expected, the resurrection of forgotten love.

"See this. And this," we called to them. Nothing mattered now except ourselves, running among the flowers and grass, crossing shale ledges, beneath us the dark ravine with its flickers of leafy light, these ways we'd gone countless times and could always go when we wanted to, the paths gouged through our own flesh. Neil and Aunt Grace wound steadily up the gentle incline, leaned together. We came close and seemed to ourselves to impart, like watchful spirits, strength and reassurance.

So at last when they were lying together in the reedy windbent grasses, thin under the oaks, Aunt Grace rested her head on Neil's shoulder. The oak leaves rippled and the grass too in the touch of breeze that blew continually over this high place above the cooler ravine, its weather entirely its own. We wanted to lie around them, to be done with everything.

But then Anne said, "No, let's go down." We went after her, into the ravine where the vines hung from the tops of trees, and we caught them and swung out over the brook, working up the nerve to let go and sail to the other side. We moved rocks and built a dam to pool the water, planned how deep it would be and how secretive.

Katie stopped then and said, "I'm going back."

"You can't," Anne yelled at her. "You haven't finished your part. We aren't through."

"You aren't the boss. Bossy, bossy. I hate you anyway.

210

You aren't my mother," and Katie went scrambling up the hill.

Anne jumped off the vine she was straddling and lunged forward to leap on Katie, dragging her to the ground. We could hear the sound of Anne's slaps, over and over. "What I say, what I say," she was growling as we worked to haul her off. She lost her balance then on the hillside, and toppled over. Katie lay on the dirt and leaves, crumpled up and playing dead. When Anne stood up she looked like Gram, her face set like a blank painted totem. There was a trickle of blood from her lip.

We'd forgotten Anne was like that. Forgotten we were all like that. Changing and horrible. We could have torn out our eyes. And Katie: she had gone out into the yard and told Rossie and his friends that Anne had her period, that she had become a woman. We'd stood with them below the window, laughing and calling up dirty stuff at Anne, shaming her for what she couldn't help. Later we were ashamed. Aunt Grace had heard Anne pounding Katie that time after she'd caught her. "I'll kill her." Anne was fierce. "Someday I will, too." Aunt Grace had stopped her with a word. But that time she didn't punish her for fighting. Instead she took Anne into her room. Through the closed door we could hear Anne sobbing while Aunt Grace talked in a low careful tone. Later Aunt Grace came out, and before the door closed again we saw Anne lying on the bed with a pillow over her head. "It's a pity she's so young," Aunt Grace said to Aunt Libby; though what we saw in her eyes made us think that something extraordinary had happened to all of us. As now, following Anne and Katie up the hill again, we were feeling uneasy, even about the love that was in us, because of the hate.

Down below us, in the ravine, the quick light flamed, while steadily we rose into the bright noon, onto the plain of flowery grass. Aunt Grace and Neil lay as before, their eyes closed, the oak tree behind them as straight as a marker. If we didn't wake them, they might sleep and never wake. We needed them to get up. We braided a chain of chicory flowers and when Aunt Grace opened her eyes, hearing us, we wound it around her neck and hair and Neil sat up and cupped a blade of grass in his palm and blew over it like a whistle. Going back, we danced around them, trying cartwheels. But Aunt Grace could no longer walk, she was so exhausted, and Neil had to carry her the rest of the way and up to her room. The burden of her life settled over us again, its weight keeping everything in place. We stayed in the kitchen with Gram and Aunt Rachel.

"Maybe she would have been better off to have stayed with him this year," Aunt Rachel mused. "Since they did get the house."

"And maybe you won't have the sense you was born with if you live to be a hundred." Gram sounded angry although she was crying.

Neil left to go back to his job in Illinois. Aunt Elinor was leaving the next day for New York. She had a visitor from the old days when she had tried to be an actress. Pearl, her friend, had made it, Aunt Elinor told us, unlike herself who had grown weary of show business and had instead gone into the world of everyday business. Pearl went into the parlor to sing while Aunt Elinor played the piano. All the doors were left open so Aunt Grace could hear, because her walk in the woods with Neil had seemed to use up what extra strength she had gained and now she left her room only to be helped to the bathroom. Still she looked very peaceful and content listening from her bed, dressed in a powdery blue gown which Neil had bought her.

We stayed in the living room while Pearl sang in the parlor. We wanted to laugh. She had a powerful soprano which must have broken glass more than once, something we'd heard Uncle Dan say about Aunt Elinor, and we were watching the branches of the living room chandelier. Aunt Elinor was very upright and serious over the keys, frowning into the score in her nearsighted way, but when Katie slid out of the recliner in a fit of suppressed giggling, Aunt Elinor gave her an unerring frown without missing a note. We got control of ourselves by ignoring each other and looking out the window, so that the music became part of the sun-warmed landscape which undulated with those same rhythms and passions we had seen move over Pearl's white breast as it lay exposed above her rather low-cut dress. After several classical numbers, long after our impulse to clown had been subdued, then obliterated, Pearl said to Aunt Elinor, who had led us in prolonged applause, "Do sing something for us yourself."

"Oh, I couldn't," Aunt Elinor said, blushing and even lowering the lid over the keys. "It's been years."

"It hasn't," we begged her, only then realizing that the summer had passed without her playing and singing for us. It seemed that if only she would, all that was wrong would vanish. "You always sing," we said, risking her disapproval for putting an adult on the spot, and were supported by Pearl, who said, "I remember when your auntie was on the radio—that Ipana smile."

"This is silly," Aunt Elinor said then, and raised the piano lid. "I'd better play for myself, though. That way I can fake it better." That made her sound like a real musician. When she began to sing, her face became so soft and lovely with the emotions of the songs it was easy to believe what Aunt Libby had told us, that she had had more suitors in her day than most women dreamed of.

Nothing was between us and her singing, our hearts as full as hers, lapped by the same waters. She sang all our favorites: "In the Gloaming," "Annie Laurie," "The Shores of Minnetonka," "Who Is Sylvia?" "Deep River." When she stopped we heard the far fragmentary clapping of Aunt Grace's hands. Aunt Elinor sent one of us to see if she had a request. We all went.

" 'Oh, What a Beautiful City!' " we called down the stairs to her, then we went back into Aunt Grace's room and sprawled over Gram's old bed, where the nurse slept at night. Aunt Grace was over by the window in the metal hospital bed. We could hear Aunt Elinor's every word— Pearl said that our auntie was famed for her perfect diction.

"Three gates to the North, and three in the South,
There's three in the East, and three in the West—
There's twelve gates to the city, O Lord."

From the high windows, looking out to the west, we could see shafts of sunlight dropping in golden bars against the deep blue of the sky, with the forest line glowing too. But when we turned to show this to Aunt Grace, she had fallen asleep. We tiptoed away. Aunt Elinor looked perfectly happy when we told her how deeply Aunt Grace slept. But we must not fall asleep, she reminded us. We were watchers in the garden. "Pray without ceasing. No one knows the hour." We promised her that we would. We wanted to. But we knew that it was partly a lie, that we were as flawed as any of the disciples.

We did the best we could. Aunt Grace went into a period of terrible unrelieved pain. When morphine allowed her some rest, though mostly she refused the drug, it seemed only to make her feel the next seizure more intensely. During the days we were in school, and some nights, Uncle Dan took us over to his mother's house to sleep. But we resisted; we thought we should be there with Aunt Grace. We had promised. Though we could no longer pray, we could watch. We hunched against her cries, but we were there to listen.

The little gray-haired nurse was indispensable now and capable in her ministrations, both physical and spiritual. We saw her hardly at all, mostly bringing trays back and forth to the kitchen, but her calm face affirmed that something was being done, whatever possible, and she would answer Aunt Libby, the only one who dared to ask each time, "How is it?" Aunt Libby's eyes showing a bitter grudging resignation to a superior power. "I think she's coming closer," the nurse answered, her smile kindly and spiritual; though she was not secretive, we felt excluded.

"Closer to what?" Gram would say, spit threading her lips together as if she hadn't been able to swallow in a long time. "I should have strangled her with my own hands," she cried out once, one of her outbursts which came seemingly from nowhere and left her momentarily crushed. Aunt Libby just pressed her hand until Gram pulled away and went to the sink to wash the few dishes. In that time, she seldom left the house, but we couldn't tell from her face what she expected. Uncle Dan said he thought Aunt Grace should be taken to the hospital. Surely they could do something for her—he was a butcher, but so kind-hearted that he had to hire a man to do the actual killing; and it took only one solid blow to fell a steer. He spent most of his time up in the old attic sitting room because, Aunt Libby told us, "He can't take it." Gram said it was too late to send Aunt Grace away. "We've had screaming over babies being born, screaming over pretty nearly everything that could pain a human. Now this." She raised up her fist as if with it she only wished she might bring the whole structure down around us.

Aunt Grace couldn't eat. Nothing appealed to her, and she wouldn't try, not even for Aunt May, who came to the house every minute she could spare. At last, when Aunt May succeeded in feeding a few bites to her, a vile black substance rose out of her, and after that no one coaxed her to eat.

Then one day, mercifully, Aunt Libby said, the pain subsided. Then it stopped entirely. There was no explanation for it. We accepted anything. It was a kind of miracle to Aunt Libby, though not the one we'd wanted, and she was grateful for it. Much of her day was spent with Aunt Grace and she worked steadily, hemming and piecing the quilt. Often they were silent, together and at peace, absorbing the tranquillity that came out of the fields and woods which stretched to the far border of Gram's land. The leaves had already fallen from the trees but winter had held off, and each day the land warmed, the fields the color of sand. Aunt Libby told us she considered those days a privilege—however dearly bought. Never before had she felt so tangibly the actual presence of love in the world, not even when her children were born. And she said it was something you could feel only once in lifetime, because afterwards something in you had been burned away.

Gram told us we should be getting ready to say goodbye. Goodbye? We stared at her, uncomprehendingly. To speak of leaving seemed a treachery, a mockery of all that we had been through together. We thought of what Aunt Elinor had taught us, that both living and dying are a dream. We were bewildered but we would not say goodbye, not for any of them.

Thanksgiving passed, unremarked, except that it was Anne's birthday and Gram remembered that no one had been able to eat that year either. Then one day as Aunt Libby sat with her, Aunt Grace turned her head from the window and said, "Get Neil."

Aunt Libby let her head fall forward, not hiding the tears which spilled fast, wetting the quilt. Aunt Grace reached so slowly, Aunt Libby told us later, and her fingers moved in Aunt Libby's hair. "Elinor too?" Aunt Libby asked when she could.

Aunt Grace nodded, her eyes closed. She sank into a sleep that had the finality of surrender.

The calls were made. "And for God's sake hurry," Aunt Libby said. Aunt Elinor had declared, "Tell her to hold on. I'm coming." But nobody told her, because Aunt Grace was in a coma now and when she did open her eyes she was unable to speak, didn't seem even to hear. Only her eyes, stained black from morphine, seemed alive.

She's still watching, we told each other. And so were we. Then she sank away from us again.

After dark we were led to her room by the women. Was this the time to say goodbye? "She's accepted it," Aunt Libby said. We filed up through the house in the dim light cast from the low-watt bulbs Gram kept in the converted gas wall fixtures. It seemed that we went by candlelight, our unequal heights throwing jagged shadows against the flowing walls. Gram sat by Aunt Grace's bed on a straight chair, but she did not raise her head when we entered. At the doorway began abruptly the sweetish, thick, terrible odor of the abscess, which mingled with that of the sulfur candle Gram had lit to purify the air. For months we had known that smell; to smell it was part of our watching. Under the hung picture of the Indian brave, the fireplace glowed with burning coals. We had never seen it used before, but Aunt Grace had requested a fire and they had moved her bed away from the cold dark windows so that when she opened her eyes she could watch the flames. She had mentioned Neil, just his name—and Aunt Libby reminded everyone how Neil had loved a fire.

When we went in, Aunt Grace seemed to be fully awake. Her lips before, when she had been well, had been bright red, thin and curving. Now they were stained black too and so crusted and shapeless it seemed a hole of nothingness opened there. And her eyes, which had always been brown, were now outraged and empty; they held only the smallest flicker of life, perhaps firelight, perhaps the evidence of salvation.

We wept as though we were doing as Gram said—saying goodbye. But we didn't say anything, just stood shaking, without sound, while Aunt Grace in her slurred and distorted voice, her tongue lacerated, tried to ask us about school, our friends, to show her interest. She could scarcely get the words formed and it was as if already we called to each other from separate worlds. Finally Gram raised her head and with one curt nod dismissed us. We leaned down to Aunt Grace, each in turn, and kissed her cheek, our tears sliding off onto her face. She wiped her finger across then; put her finger to her mouth. She seemed to smile and murmured, "Salt." From the hall we looked back once, but blinded from crying, could not see more than the firelight dashing on the walls. Then we went downstairs together.

We hadn't heard him arrive, but when we came down, Neil was at the kitchen table drinking whiskey. He stared at the table, ignoring even his two daughters, though he had just driven in from Illinois. We stopped crying, shrank from him. We felt that he loathed us as if we had conspired to hold his wife captive and tortured her for amusement. There was an enormous mood in the room, weighing of regret and denial, guilt and anger. Anne and Katie sat at one side of the long table, away from Neil.

Uncle Dan came into the kitchen, walked over to Neil and put his hand on his shoulder. "Come on. I'll take you up." His eyes were their same mild gray again; he'd cried himself out, according to Aunt Libby. But we felt this moment shocked Neil as it did us. Not because his wife was dying but because nothing had been asked from him. He stood and called his daughters. Their heads stayed on the table. Neil shrugged and followed after Uncle Dan.

We waited awhile, but Anne and Katie didn't move. We slipped away and followed up to Aunt Grace's room, where it was quiet, nearly dark, Neil just a shadow by the window, his arms folded, his back to Aunt Grace, who must have been sleeping. Anne and Katie were gone when we got back to the kitchen. Snow blew in the draft of the half-open door. The trail of their steps led us across the porch and down the stairs. We found them crouched on the floor of Neil's car. There was a sound, like singing or wind. Our teeth were chattering.

"She made me." Katie was crying again. Anne said nothing, just got out and stood there. Their eyes looked as if they had tried to die.

"Are you girls crazy?" Aunt Libby came out on the porch. "No coats! No boots!" We went to her and she took us on past Aunt Grace's room to the attic.

Sometime after we had fallen asleep, we heard a loud angry brawling and we thought maybe Grandad had come back and was fighting with Gram. The house was open to all the spirits; gravestones were shifting. From the distance we heard Aunt Grace moaning and crying. Anne slammed a pillow over her head.

We woke again. Heard a swelling sound that was like the murmuring of a great throng. Perhaps we were all going away. Pulled without will or intention, we went from our beds down the attic stairwell and stood at the doorway to Aunt Grace's room, on the edge of the dark. Particles of snow stung on the glass. Neil sat with his head in his hands. A few coals glowed. Anne wasn't with us. Gram said, "Leave her be."

Aunt Grace woke and said, "Hello, Dad," in her recognizable voice.

Aunt Rachel whispered to Gram, squeezing her hand:

"You see, she's passing over." From tears, Aunt Rachel's face shone as though it were a shell clarified in the sea.

Then Aunt Grace looked at her sisters, her mother, husband. Then at us in the doorway. And we knew that at last she was saying goodbye. "Don't be afraid," she whispered, slowly, slowly. "It's like going into another room." There was a strangling catch in her breath and a gurgling noise. Everybody was standing. The snow on the wind made the night seem even deeper. The wind funneling in the chimney fused with our spirits and demanded that we release her. Within ourselves we cried, "We can't hold on." There was a sudden draft as if we had let her go. Gram sat down and put her head on Aunt Grace's bed, pressing up against her leg, one hand folding and refolding the hemline of the woolen blanket. All around the house the wind was moving, swirling and piling the snow.

Led by Aunt Libby again, we went up the stairs to the wide attic landing. Up above, the high window gleamed and sparkled with frost in the dimness. Then we turned and went further up into the last blackness of the unheated attic and the night took hold. We nestled against Anne's body, warm in her sleeping. It seemed that she might never have to know.

The instant Anne sat up in bed we were awake. Katie's eyes watched over the rim of the covers. Beyond the window frost was the concrete-gray light and snow accumulating. Rills flipped on the screens, curving over the sills. We saw Anne's arms, long and white, then her legs, as she sat on the edge of the bed. Katie's eyes closed. Opened again. There wasn't a sign of anything, but Anne ran from us. We heard her bare feet slap on the stairs, and going after her, we saw her standing alone in the doorway of the room where Aunt Grace had been for so long. Anne's braced legs were paler than the faded cotton gown which, outgrown and ragged, made her neglect and outrage palpable. Her hoarse convulsive breaths seemed to injure her. The bed was empty, stripped to the mattress, the blinds lifted and the windows too, so that the fresh light snow was powdered over the dark floor. Even the fireplace had been swept clean.

"You didn't call me. You left me." Anne was screaming at us.

Neil came up the stairs. He lifted his arms toward Anne, but she whirled and hunched her shoulders as if he would hit her and scuttled down the wall. "I'll never. Never. Not for you. Not for her." Anne still screamed. Neil shrugged and went away.

Anne slammed herself into the back room where Grandad had slept on a mattress so ancient it was stuffed with straw. Katie tried the door. It came open and out banged a shoe.

"Don't take it out on me," Katie yelled. "You were the baby that stayed in bed."

We knew the second time the door opened and we saw Anne that we'd better get help. We ran, calling the women. Gram was the first one to reach the stairs and when we caught up, Anne was lying on the floor face down, in her clenched fist a wad of Katie's hair, her fist pounding and pounding on the floor. Katie's neck was flaming where Anne's hands had strangled and at first she couldn't get a breath. She didn't cry. On Anne's shoulder was a welt from the crack Gram had given her with the spatula she still had in her hand. Gram was panting from the tussle and Anne was sobbing and sobbing, banging her fist on the floor.

Katie was just rubbing her neck, her face blank-looking, as though she couldn't figure anything out and had quit trying. "She tried to kill me," she said.

"Now, now," Aunt May said. "We're all broken-hearted." She put her arms around Anne as tenderly as though she were holding pieces of her shoulders together. Anne grew quieter and Aunt Libby pulled back a length of her wet hair and uncovered her red face. "Old sorrel's tail," she said, and switched Anne in the face, which got a little smile. She led Anne off to the bathroom to wash and we overheard Anne say that she would try to be better, to be good, and when she came back her expression proclaimed that the effort would change her drastically. Katie continued to look addlepated, slack-jawed, as if it had all become too much for her. Gram said it wasn't the first fight she'd ended.

The women led us down the back stairway to the kitchen, to the breakfast that was arranged and waiting on the table. We felt formal and shy with each other, arriving in the high-ceilinged room, the pure illuminating snowlight blazing off the walls. Beyond the drive the black-barked apple trees pointed every last twig, it seemed, toward heaven, and its immensity was what was left at the end. Gram lifted a teakettle from the stove to pour boiling water into the coffeepot. She shook the iron burners around—slam, bang. She looked over at Anne and Katie. Her daughter, their mother, was dead. "Eat quick now. You're going to get Elinor." Her voice was hard. We thought that must have been what Aunt Elinor meant about God not telling the difference between living and dying, the way Gram mixed up loving and getting mad.

"You tell Tom he'll be needing them chains," Gram said to Aunt Rachel, who answered that she figured Tom Buck could think that much for himself, which made Gram make a further clatter over the burners as if she were putting down an insurrection.

It took two hours to get through the snow, the forty miles to the station, but the leisurely pace and the uneven rumbling beneath us, together with the air, that was steadily colder and clearer as the snow decreased, then stopped, took us back to another time, one we'd seen in old photographs, the aunts as girls, snuggled to their chins in furs, drawn by horse and sleigh along the drive. We traveled along, swaying and gliding over the snow, wrapped in blankets, letting motion and desire carry us forward into one timeless union.

The first passengers leaving the train from New York seemed to be appearing out of the clouds from heaven, the way the steam billowed. We hurried forward, one last time to enter the fold where we might meet the living and the dead. We saw Aunt Elinor. From the top of the iron steps she regarded us with her eager and yet composed expression. Her eyes touched ours. Then she looked at Tom Buck for the answer to her question, even as her smile for the rest of us came to her lips. We all watched her, as if with her we would at last know.

"Yes." He nodded. "She went in the night, near dawn."

Aunt Elinor accepted it and bowed her head. Then she said each of our names in turn: Anne, Katie, Celia and Jenny, and took our hands in hers and slipped a ring on each of us. They were bits of turquoise on adjustable silver bands. We could see how much she loved us. It was in her face as she gathered us into her arms, welcomed us into the enclosure of the full-flowing black coat with its downy cuffs and collar of ermine. She offered her strength to us, longing to lift us from grief into Life eternal. We could no longer follow her there. We didn't know about divine love, knew only an insufficient human love. But we let her comfort us, her throaty and musical voice, her russet eyes warm in the burrow of her furry coat, starlets of snow blown in her hair.

PART FIVE

Gram

In Tom Buck's Chrysler, going home from the train station, Aunt Elinor and Katie sat in front, holding hands. Turning to take the rest of us in too, Aunt Elinor said, "I made reservations as soon as Libby called me. With the storm, I was lucky to get here. Still it's a long trip at best." There were limitations, even for her.

Tom Buck's silence could have meant he was disappointed too. Or that he was utterly weary. Leaning forward with our chins on the front seat, near to Aunt Elinor, we could see his galoshes flopping open at his ankles. Behind us, the iced back windows enclosed us in a dim sanctuary. The run of chains over the snow seemed all that held us fast to earth.

"If only I'd known sooner. I prayed for her to hold on. To wait." Aunt Elinor would have stopped Aunt Grace from going, she seemed to be saying, her eyes fixed to outdistance the progression of the car. At the edge of the road we saw the snow-filled fields, then the dark solemn woods.

"She gave up," Aunt Elinor said. "Libby told me she had accepted it that morning." We looked down. "We must never give power to evil. It must always be denied." Although she turned toward us, we would not meet her gaze. We were all guilty.

Tom Buck didn't say a word but we felt him wanting to, something stirring inside him. He shifted his body and gripped the wheel so tight his knuckles bulged under his gloves.

Aunt Elinor sighed, then gave us her good warm smile, indicating what we had left between us and the full extent of our darkness. We had wanted to believe. Might still. Perhaps, miraculously, the empty bed in the upstairs room would float out of memory.

"I've never seen the snow so fine," she said. "Remember He said that it was good." Again all things were made new—the long sweeping vista of snow pools iced over and glittering before the motionless woods, the veil of illusion drawn away. We stared and stared, maybe to become snowblind.

"Was she calm at the last?" Aunt Elinor asked Tom Buck. No one wanted to say Aunt Grace's name. Neither would we mention the way she had suffered, although we sensed the memory licking behind the ways we avoided remembering. We had never talked openly of Aunt Grace's pain. We had never been told exactly the name of her disease, as if identifying it would give it a further advantage. So the secret name would bring further evil out of our own knowledge.

At last Tom Buck spoke. "Goddamn, goddamn. I don't know how or why to go on living after any of it." We remembered Aunt Libby saying that his mother had been buried alive in a nursing home. Aunt Elinor reached over to touch his arm, then her own head fell forward. Suddenly we were all crying.

Aunt Elinor blew her nose on a handkerchief of embroidered chambray. "This is the true demonstration. When all is dark. Didn't even the disciples despair? And then there was Easter!" For a time we rode on in silence, pulled both ways. The chains beat around us like nails.

"You couldn't have done anything, Elinor," Tom Buck said. "She wasn't going to get well and she went on too long as it was. I'm goddamn glad it's over, I tell you, and I don't care a whole hell of a lot about anything else."

On Tom Buck's cheek we could see the intricate purple webbing that underran his ruddy color, stark evidence of what everyone said was an incipient weakness for drink which might get worse. Sometimes Gram vowed she would cut Aunt Rachel out of her will for marrying him, for being such a damn fool as to think she could change any man. Hadn't she learned the first time? That marriage had been over in a moment, but all the same Aunt Rachel had nearly lost her mind afterwards. Now this wedding was planned. Watching Aunt Elinor, her eyes staring open to the farthest sky, we knew she was praying for Tom Buck. Pray for us, Aunt Elinor, we yearned. Tom Buck slumped behind the wheel. And we remembered the plain metal bed, the stained mattress, a few snow feathers wafting across.

The house had become surrounded again by unbroken snow and seemed mysterious and melancholy. Right then the granite sills at the window, the solid walls of maroon brick and the towering spruce at the back gave it the appearance of an ancient asylum, as if once committed we wouldn't get out.

"There's relief in it. Christ, there's relief." Tom Buck stopped the car behind Gram's and glared at the house. Tears were flowing down his face, but he didn't brush them away. The remaining sisters were coming out then to greet Aunt Elinor, who left the car with her black ermine-ruffed coat sweeping behind her, walking as though she bore a crown. Into each other's arms they merged, and went toward the house, leaving us with Tom Buck. After a while he got out and we followed him to the kitchen, where Gram was standing at the iron sink. Neil was there too, at the long table with a drink before him.

"Jesus God," Tom Buck said. "Let me fix one of them goddamned things, will you?" He was trying to smile and went over to shake Neil's hand and gave him a clap on the shoulder. The two men looked alike in some ways, with their red faces and their blue eyes blurred with veins. But Neil, still lean, was almost emaciated, while Tom Buck was fat in the middle. Their difference we felt in other ways too, Tom Buck saying whatever came to mind, whether anyone listened or not; but Neil spoke deliberately—a man who meant to be heard.

Gram didn't look up when Tom Buck opened the refrigerator to take out the ice tray, but she said, "There ain't enough for that."

"Hell, Grammy. I don't care. I'll go to the store and get some more for you. Christ, I could take it straight from a nipple if it comes to that." He drank what he poured in one big gulp and then looked ashamed and touched Gram on the arm. "Sorry," he said. Then: "I'll get you some ice, Lil. In a little bit." He poured more of the whiskey and sat down on the step stool, that kept him a little to one side of the table Neil occupied. Both men were smoking; the air held it low because the kitchen was steamy from cooking and the storm windows sealed us in, the smoke blending with the milk smell of the room, that room soured every inch by milk slopped and strained, churned and set by, year after year, maybe seventy of them passed altogether. We sat down on the floor, the four of us, our backs against the radiator, quiet and dulled, hardly there.

"God almighty, Neil, how in hell can you stand it?" Tom Buck was looking out the window when he asked that. Maybe he didn't want to hear really, and Neil didn't answer. "I'll say again, there's relief in it." His eyes slashed around the room but there was nothing he could do, and he clasped his hands as if he might say a prayer, then bent them backwards to crack the knuckles. "There are some around here, given their head, would force the hand of God Himself."

Gram went on moving her rag over the surface of the same dish. Her eyes were red too, the bruised red of sumac cones. Still she hadn't lost sight of us. "You gals fetch me some of them apples from the cellar." The cellar was damp and smelled of dirt and the rotten, punk apples, many of them needing to be pared away to the small good centers left. Gram took the warped pan of them without a word. She sat down away from the table, drawing a

233

chair over by the window. Again we huddled against the radiator.

Neil cleared his throat. He spoke as though for the first time in days. "How's business?"

"Busy. Goddamn, it's busy. Can't keep help. Train a mechanic and he's opening his own shop before you know it." Neil nodded as if he were paying attention, but we felt Tom Buck was just talking away as usual. He owned the Ford dealership in town.

Neil stood up and poured himself another drink from the bottle on the counter. He dropped an ice cube down Katie's neck, which made her yelp and wiggle around; so he knew we were there too. Gram went on moving her knife, without looking up. Neil winked at us, but we looked down: we sensed that Gram and he were just circling around, using us until they got good and ready to fight.

"We're going now." The sisters came into the kitchen. Aunt Rachel stood behind Tom Buck and pressed his head against her so that her throat showed over the collar of her dress, pearly white against his dark hair. She whispered in his ear.

"Jesus," he whispered back. "Don't leave me here for long." She pressed her finger over his lips.

"Can we come?" we asked. We didn't know where they were going, but we felt afraid of the house without them.

"Not this time," Aunt Elinor said. Kind as always, her face bore evidence of some personal obligation she was feeling. "But tonight, when you see her, she'll look lovely. You'll know then how happy she is."

"Shut up," Gram said. Her crinkled old face looked as distorted as the heap of peelings mounding around the pan.

"Momma." Aunt May, the oldest, spoke firmly. "Nobody wants to do this. It simply has to be done and in the best spirit possible. We can do it best. We're going down to the funeral home," she explained to us, and we felt how brave they were, how much love they had.

"I hope when my time comes they'll throw me in a pit," Tom Buck said. "This business makes it just about impossible to die.

"Scientists do cremate ordinarily," Aunt Elinor said, "but in this case . . ."

Gram had refused to pay for that kind of burial. She had said she wasn't going to get mixed up in any heathen ways when not a bit of it meant anything anyhow. "She'll lay up there aside of me, where she belongs," Gram said then. Grandad was already there, on top of the hill at the cemetery, and Gram had bought plots for herself and her five children. "I don't know what the rest of us are supposed to do," Uncle Dan had said. "Just wander, I guess. Outside paradise."

"There's more where that come from," Gram had told him. But Uncle Dan said he wasn't going in the back row and the way he said it, we could tell none of it did matter to him.

As they went out the door, the sisters were crying. Aunt Elinor carried the alligator cosmetic case with the jars of rouges, oils and perfumes which clients in the advertising world had given her. "If Dan calls, tell him we're coming," Aunt Libby said. He had been gone all day, making arrangements.

With their leaving we felt the house more, its great weight on us, heaviness not so much of brick or atmospheric pressure as of experience. We leaned in close to

235

protect Anne and Katie, whose faces were so white and remote, it seemed they felt an incomprehensible freedom.

Gram finished peeling the apples in silence. Her daughters had wanted her to rest, but she had gone on with what she was doing.

"Jesus, Neil. What're you going to do now?" Tom Buck didn't look at him, but got up to pour again from the bottle and then returned to the stool, his elbows propped up on his knees.

"The same," Neil said, pouring whiskey.

"Not around here, you ain't," Gram answered. We'd been waiting for it to happen—all that unresolved bitterness in the angle of her face. We had felt it when her four daughters had left, the persistent past, heavy and actual.

Neil took his careful walk for more ice, going past Gram so quietly he might have walked on tiptoe. Then he sat down again at the table and leaned back against the wall, watching her through eyes narrowed to spell danger. "You never could keep your trap shut, could you?" We felt him taunting her, trying to make her wild, showing in that way that he thought he had the advantage. "Don't worry, though; I'll be gone soon," he said.

"Yeah. I bet you will."

"Now that must mean something. You got something on your mind, Lil?" Neil tilted his chair, forcing her hand, enjoying it too.

"You're a widower now. It's done and finished. So you can pack your bags and git."

"Meaning?"

"Meaning I don't reckon you've got a cent to pay on them bills."

"I might have known." Neil's hand was shaking when

he put his glass down. Then he wagged his head back and forth, with his head lowered and his mouth tight. "Well, maybe"—and he looked up at her, disgust showing in his face openly—"maybe you can return that fur coat. Seems to me it's still nearly brand-new—since she had to be about half dead before you were good for it or any of the other promises."

"That ain't none of your business."

"No, it probably isn't." Neil stood up then and started toward the door as if he were going to leave; he looked suddenly ill.

But Gram had begun. "I told her what she'd get if she married you. Nothing. That's what. Now just go on. Git. Maybe we can have some peace and quiet around here. And decency," she added in a lower, different voice.

Neil turned toward her, stopped in his tracks, and his face was blood red again. "Decency. I declare. Decency. You know, Lil, you rather disappoint me. Just about the time I think you're going to take action, really give it to me, maybe just outright hand me an accounting, you back off and begin to preach. I suppose you have some idea about that. Decency." He sat at the table again.

"Let's go down to the Elks, Neil," Tom Buck said. Gram stood up and looked at Neil, fit to kill. A chalky-white froth was oozing from her mouth, the way it does out of an abused and lathered-up horse.

"When they took her breast, you was told: leave her be. But you wouldn't. Couldn't restrain your manhood, rooting in her—killing her is what it amounts to. Pregnant. She lost it but you killed her, same as if you'd taken a gun."

Neil came out of his chair. Fast. Gram braced herself,

but stood her ground. He pounded on the table once with his fist and the sound was emphatic and alarming. "You don't know what the hell you're talking about." His face was white.

"For Christsake." Tom Buck stood up, wobbled and sat down.

In the quietness, Gram stood facing Neil directly, holding the pan of peelings, the rotten and wasted parts against her stomach, the paring knife in her hand. "They ought to have cut something off of you," she said.

"Maybe you'd like to try your hand at it, Lil." Neil was walking toward Gram. Deliberately. "Come on, let's see what the old war-horse is really made of. Actually you might be doing both of us a service," and this time he laughed, as if he truly meant it, that it was funny to think she could do something he wanted done.

"Christ in heaven." Tom Buck's drink spilled into the lap his legs made perched on the step stool. He gave out a little yelp. "Cold," he explained when we looked up. Then he stared down, wondering at the stain as it spread over his pants. He brushed at it helplessly, shrugged. "Looks like I peed my pants," he said, as if he might have done such a thing to get attention.

We threw ourselves down and laughed our heads off. Raged with laughing, rolling and gasping. It seemed wonderful that he was going to be in the family. When he walked away, he stumbled over a chair and we laughed all the harder.

"Another goddamned drunk," Neil said, and we thought it was funny to hear him sounding like Tom Buck. "Lil, you seem to draw them like flies." Tom Buck was splashing his face at the sink and Neil said seriously, "A legend

that might interest you women—the Amazons. They removed the left breast of their warriors and then they hung
the quiver of arrows there. Now that was a sign of something out of the ordinary. What you might call resolve.
Courage. Seems none of us has what it takes." He followed Tom Buck out of the room. They were talking a
little. Then we heard Neil mounting the stairs, going up
toward the empty room, where the snow blew in the lace
curtains and embellished the netting.

When they had gone and we were left with Gram, she
said, "Anne, quit your howling," though we were all
laughing and fooling around. Anne was quiet then, as
though she'd been slapped. Gram didn't notice, went on
making her pie crusts, not measuring anything, going fast
with a kind of flair, as though all the movements and
ingredients came to her out of a dance she had in her head.
"So that's what he wants," she said out loud, and then
went on to form the dough into generous circles.

Later the sisters came home. Saddened and spent-looking,
they went off to rest. When it was dark, we all left
together for the funeral home.

"She looks so beautiful," Aunt Rachel said. "I'm grateful for that. You did it perfectly," and she buried her face
for a moment into Aunt Elinor's collar. Aunt Libby drove
with her usual inner absorption, like a chauffeur. Gram
didn't say a word.

Aunt Elinor turned back to us. "Now when you go in, I
want you to remember: Life never was or will be in the
body. The body is the outworn shell left when the Soul
flies away. Kind of like moving out of an old house into a
new one."

Aunt Libby almost interrupted her, thinking and saying her own thoughts. "When I see her now. So peaceful and at rest. It's hard to believe how she suffered. Just yesterday. What was it for, I ask you?"

"Maybe it was for us," Aunt Elinor said. "So that we could be brought to know God." Then we thought that maybe it was: Aunt Grace a living sacrifice made perfect and acceptable to God, chosen to bear all for us, who were lost in sin.

But when we walked into the large old mansion that had been converted into the funeral home, we paused in the vestibule; there was in that enveloping silence the profound presence of something more final even than the things Aunt Elinor had told us, in the knowledge of which we felt at last the exceeding wonder of living. We were drawn both ways. Beyond the bank of cut flowers which Gram had wanted, in spite of Aunt Elinor's beliefs, we felt the fascination of it, this dread combining with an exquisite excitement. The women took us in to where the body was.

Since the night before, there had been a transformation; the figure lying there, serene, redeemed, was severed radically from the woman whom we remembered in the darkness. Now those pain-blasted eyes were forever closed and her mouth was a fixed crimson curl, untouchable. They had dressed her in a gown that was ineffably blue. With all pain and desire wiped away, she was now more lovely to us than we could remember, and totally unfamiliar. Anne and Katie were crying.

"Oh, my babies," Aunt Elinor said, and hugged them with tears moistening her smile, the joy she felt at the spirit's release blending with her own human insufficiency, as she called her grief. We stood by Gram. Aunt Rachel said that it was getting too morbid for her. After a while she went for Anne's and Katie's coats and drove them home.

Gram seemed not to notice anything, just nodded whenever anyone came up to offer condolences. Sitting on the straight chair with the hooped baskets of flowers near her, she was strangely like a girl, her feet barely touching the floor, her gaze innocent, without the accretion of her usual expression of impatience.

Aunt Minny came. Huge, almost six feet tall. Gram called her a holy roller. Sometimes Gram warned Aunt Elinor that she could get to be as ridiculous, might even begin to throw fits. We were always hoping Aunt Minny would throw one when we were with her, but she didn't, although Gram said it couldn't be so very much different from the way she generally acted. Right away Aunt Minny leaned down to kiss the face, eagerly, fervently. We imagined her touch—lips unwarmed despite thousands of such encounters.

"She's washing her feet in Jordan tonight. Amen and praise the Lord." Aunt Minny seized Aunt Elinor and, sisters in the faith, they stood together. "Praise Jesus," Aunt Minny exulted, witnessing boldly in the enemy's stronghold.

"Steal away," she crooned, and went over to Gram, pulled her out of her chair to hug her entirely, Aunt Minny enormous all over, so that Gram hung limp against her like a doll. "Lil, the Lord's watching after you for certain. These angels he has provided for your comfort and blessing." That was us somehow. We shrank back, afraid of her touch, but when she'd reached us and had clasped us to her bosom, it was warm and billowy. "Do you recollect the night He washed our sins away?"

Gram looked startled. Then she blurted out what she'd been thinking: "Ain't no sense to it. Leaving me here. An ugly old woman." She turned her back and walked away, then appeared in her coat, her pocketbook dragging. "You come on," she snapped at the rest of us. We took one final look, going toward the door, at the stranger bedded in satin. In her waxed paleness we already imagined her as Snow White, asleep under the dome of eternity, though beyond any charm we knew of.

When we got home, Gram moved straight to the fire-place and struck the gas, yanking up her dress and stand-ing with her legs close up to the spiraling run of blue-gold flame, her expression urgent to feel the heat. She stood on one end of the Persian rug and her feet pointed in the direction of the pattern; she had told us once that the rug was woven so that the design directed the Moslem's prayers to the east. She'd placed her rug that way too. It was one of the only disinterested facts she had ever told us, pure information unrelated to her life or ours, and it amazed us. Just then, her face calm and absorbed by the fire, she could have been facing Mecca, although not kneeling. Anne and Katie sat with Aunt Rachel on the couch. They had stopped crying and even smiled when we came in.

"Momma," Aunt Elinor teased, watching Gram toast herself. "One of these days you're going to set yourself on fire."

"Well, then, lady, you better pray for me." So prayer was on her mind. She looked at Anne and Katie and said, "I wisht it was different." And we thought maybe she was wishing that she was.

When we went to bed we felt the immense absence. Katie woke up screaming, "Don't make me. Don't make me go." Aunt Rachel came up and said hush, rocking her in her arms. She left the hall light on. We were next to Anne while she was crying—we were all more to each other now. And more separate too, for Anne and Katie didn't have a mother anymore. The light in the hall enhanced the height of the stairwell. The four of us got into one bed, and in that closeness, pushed against each other, we forgot about the aloneness of sleeping the unbroken night of eternity.

Sitting at the kitchen table the next morning, we heard Neil run down the stairs, the back uncarpeted ones, and slam out the side door. No goodbye, just his ancient car coughing and lurching out the drive. The sisters shrugged at each other and frowned when Gram gave them a withered I-told-you-so smirk. "Guess he's had his wagon fixed. Knows what's what."

"Now, Momma."

"Don't now Momma me. He's been begging for it."

"I don't think Grace did it for the reasons you think at all," Aunt May said. "She just wanted the girls to have something from her. For when they're older. You know how she hated it, not seeing them grow up."

"All the same, she's left him without his house. Not that anything much that went in it was ever his to begin with. I give it to her. Now he'll have to mend his ways, scramble some. I didn't know she had it in her."

They had found Aunt Grace's will in her Bible, along with instructions for her funeral service, texts she wanted read, everything written out clearly in her schoolteacher's

hand. It hadn't been witnessed by anyone, a simple statement of final wishes bearing an unmistakable intention.
Aunt Grace had amazed everyone by requesting that the
house Gram had helped her buy, the house she had never
lived in, be sold and the proceeds held in trust for her two
girls. We didn't know when they had shown the will to
Neil. They had held it back as long as they could. Now
that he knew, no one was relieved, except maybe Gram a
little.

"But where will they live?" Aunt Rachel asked, and we
all looked at Gram, except Anne and Katie, who looked at
the floor. Gram got up and went to work at the sink. We
were quiet. There was nothing anyone could do, no power
left. With the vanishing of Aunt Grace, something that had
bound us together and had given us strength beyond the
ordinary had vanished too. Now we were simply going on,
with what we'd ended up with, which was not enough but
would have to do.

It was the day of the funeral, the third day. Aunt Elinor
continued to teach. "Your heavenly Father-Mother God
will supply all your needs." She was watching still. We
hid our faithlessness to protect her, as though it would
seem to be her failure too. But when we took our places
beside her in the anteroom by the chapel, set aside for the
family, we doubted our own doubts. We wanted to believe
again. She knew something wonderful. Was wonderful.
The solemn and benevolent Mr. Besaw, director of the
funeral home, would come in, leaping for joy, bearing
witness to the resurrection. It seemed possible, and the
psalms and hymns we had learned by heart during that
long time of devotion seemed now to be our own poems.

Through the brief service we were waiting. Then Mr.

Besaw did come in. We were expecting him. He whispered something to Aunt Elinor and she shook her head after glancing at Gram's lowered head. Leaning forward, we watched him enter the room by the altar, and then he lowered the cover to the coffin, clamping the white satin rim so that the braid of brass made a continuous loop. In that moment there was absolute silence. We looked into his face. Before its clean-shaven acceptance our spirits fell. The glass amethyst lily aglow over his head on a curved leaded stem seemed more intense with life than we would ever be.

We stood for the final hymn:

> Abide with me!
> Fast falls the eventide;
> The darkness deepens:
> Lord, with me abide!

None of us sang, our sorrow accomplished. We heard the footsteps of the men who carried the coffin and the closing of car doors. We went outside with the others, blinking our eyes as if we'd walked into first light. Without a comprehensible past or imaginable expectations, we had entered into another lifetime. We held hands. A family friend drove us home. Rossie came too. It had been so long since he had lived with us that we felt shy; as if we hardly knew him.

After a while cars began to arrive, coming from the cemetery, where they had not wanted us to go. We could not conceive of that place. The women immediately became busy, laying out the food neighbors and friends had brought, finding the good set of dishes in the buffet, everybody acting as if they belonged and knew what to do.

Uncle Dan poured drinks for the men. They stood in the kitchen. "Right in the way," Aunt Libby muttered to us. They drank, their eyes downcast as though they might be doing something even they disapproved of. Perhaps it was that connivance that also lent them a kind of conviviality, although there was none of the usual joshing between the swift-moving women, intent on their preparations, and the drinking men.

Neil came in. Had he been at the funeral? We couldn't remember. We felt afraid of him. There was a hot glitter about him that made him look mean. We thought he might do anything.

But nothing in particular happened. He poured whiskey, his usual pale drink, and took his place at the back of the kitchen table, against the wall, keeping a distance around himself. The men shifted, found excuses to disperse. For the rest of the time, while people were eating, Neil sat there in the black-painted Windsor chair, staring at the glass he slid over the table or moved up and down to his mouth. Most of the time he smoked, quick jabs toward his face. He spoke once to a man he'd known in college.

It was dark and the people were leaving. We saw it was still snowing when the cars turned on their lights and drove away. Neil sat on at the table, his head now resting on his arms. Through the long double room, into the dining room, we could see the baskets of flowers the women had brought from the grave. Aunt Elinor said it would have been a waste to leave them in the cold and she could arrange them to look like regular bouquets. We didn't go near them.

Anne tried on Aunt Elinor's black coat with the ermine collar and cuffs. The collar was slightly raised so that it surrounded her face. She paraded into the kitchen, where the aunts took one look at her and broke into tears. How it suits her, they said, and told her how glamorous she would be, grown up. "Like your mother," Aunt May said. "Only the coloring's different."

"And that mop!" Aunt Rachel said. Anne's hair was dark red and uncut, hanging far down her back. "Something's going to have to be done about that." Aunt Rachel moved her fingers to snip like a scissors.

But Anne, giddy because they found her beautiful, said, "I'll never cut it. I'll let it grow and grow, until somebody will have to walk behind me to carry it. And you can leave me your coat when you die," she said to Aunt Elinor. Whereupon everything was completely quiet, until Aunt Libby opened the door to set out the garbage and a sweep of air danced the snow in at the door so that it seemed we might be snowbound for days.

Then Neil lifted up his head and looked around at all of us. Only Gram was missing. "I guess I know when I'm licked. Though if you don't believe I've tried, then, God knows, you never will. Hell, I never could make enough money to impress any of you and I couldn't keep my wife at home—even to die. Wasn't any competition for you at all." He stood up then and went to the window, his back turned to us, and continued. "Then she took away the one thing I did think was mine. Ours. The house. And probably she thought to give my children away with it. There never was any way to make you or her think I was man enough to handle you or what belonged to you." He turned and nodded his head toward Anne but spoke to the

247

women. "And now this fool girl thinks she's a princess. Expects God knows what. Nothing else anyone will ever try to do for her will ever mean anything, never be enough. She'll always be dreaming about this place and this time, looking backward. Could be all of us should have gone on and died right along with Grace. Might be none of us will ever be quite alive again." We had never heard Neil speak like that, long and serious, not hiding his meaning. We sat as though forbidden to move, while Neil took up the whiskey bottle and, walking over to the sink, stood and poured all of it down the drain. We heard it gurgle going down. He set the empty bottle down with a shrug, then smiled, half amused, and said mostly to himself, "Too bad reform's not that easy," his eyes on the bottle.

Gram came in the doorway, her fists raised, yelling first at us: "You kids go on." But she couldn't stop herself, never could. "Don't you talk sorry, you bastard. Not around here. It don't matter what them doctors say they know. I know. I seen you. Heard." Gram's face was purple. But she was raging into a void, like when Grandad used to walk out on her, because Neil had exited, holding his hands in mockery around his ears, saying to the rest of us, "Here's to female solidarity. May it last forever." When Gram had wound down, she allowed Aunt Elinor to lead her to a chair. We were all quiet, but we scarcely heard Neil's car going through the snow. So many times he had left, furious and outcast, then was back again: a pattern that reminded us of Aunt Grace, as though it was something they had forged together.

He didn't come back that night, and the next morning on his bed, still made up, was a heap of clothing and other things—Aunt Grace's belongings: the fur coat, the silver-linked belt made by Indians in Arizona, her wedding band and a watch, the music box that played "In Springtime." Aunt Libby lifted the lid and it ground feebly, statically, dragging. Inside the box was the confetti-like litter of a sheet of paper torn up. Aunt Libby knew what it was right off. "Makes you want to kill him," she said. "Always the last word."

"Not this time," Gram said, and left for town. She called in the loan she had made to Grace and Neil for the down payment on their house. That house was far off in Illinois—to us it seemed as insubstantial as the torn-up sheet of paper.

"I wonder if we'll ever see him again," Aunt Rachel said when Gram got home.

"We better," Gram said. "There's a thing or two here that belongs to him." She looked at Anne and Katie. "I already had too many kids," she said, then smiled thinly, almost an apology.

"Of course he'll come back," Aunt Elinor reassured us. And then she said, "You know he's no worse than the rest of us. We shut our eyes and tell ourselves we're wonderful. That we're better than everybody else, different. When we've had endless fighting and envy and fear. When some plain honest forgiveness would be truly wonderful." Although her colors—eyes, hair and complexion—were no more vivid than in all her earlier passions, her words were new, fruits of the Spirit, and they unnerved Aunt Libby so that for some reason she threatened Aunt Rachel: "If you ever start in on that religion, I'll move to California and never see you again. A person might as well have died." It was possible; already Aunt May, having lost husband, father and sister within two years, had begun to study

Science with Aunt Elinor. They stayed off together, apart from the rest of us, to read and talk late into the night. Aunt Libby feared that she'd end up with only Gram left.

Later that morning, Gram divided up Aunt Grace's possessions—she said it was her right, not Neil's, since she had paid for most of them. And where was he? Typical! Aunt Elinor whispered to Anne and Katie that she'd see they got something from their mother.

The snow had stopped falling and the day was clearing. The apple trees were rimed in white. The sisters had followed Gram into the parlor and the door was shut. Left alone, we lay on the rugs amidst the gardens of paradise. In front of the window in the dining room were the flowers, gleaming against the light—rigid and priggish in their hothouse satisfaction. We got up and went in where they were. We could smell death, its victory and boast. Scarcely meaning to, but doing it, Katie knocked against one basket and it tipped over, reclining as stiffly as it had stood. We reached in and pulled out a long-stemmed carnation. Anne stuck it into her hair and it suddenly had an urgent beauty, translucent against her red hair. We took all the arrangements apart then. Over Katie's head we draped a circlet of white chrysanthemums and wound a ribbon sash around her waist. When we were all decorated, we filled vases with bunches of flowers and placed them around the rooms, on sills and tables where the snowlight glazed them. Some we put into water glasses. The house looked beautiful again. Anne took one piece of ribbon and tied it like a beauty queen's banner while we sang, "A pretty girl is like a melody."

We didn't see Gram come in. She slapped Anne's hot, still-laughing face, then she clawed the bow from her chest. She slapped out at a vase of flowers and the water sprang up and stained the wallpaper dark. Anne stood with her head bent.

"Can't you never do right?" Gram asked her. Then to Aunt Elinor, who had come in with her sisters, she said, "It's your doings. Them girls don't a bit know how to act anymore." But when she passed her on the way to the stairs, her mood suddenly shifted and she said, "You done the best you could, I reckon," the closest she ever came to admitting that, and went away.

We heard her bath running. A half hour later she came back dressed and powdered, two dots of rouge plopped on her face. Her daughters looked up, amazed to the end at her ways. But Gram said, nice as could be, "All's any of us can do is keep going, though there ain't no sense to it. I'm going to the picture show." She searched her purse and came up with nickels for ice cream—in the dead of winter. She touched Anne's hair, leaving. "You go on outside and play. Try to forget. You'll feel better."

The minute we were out the door, Anne was running, the snow spraying up around her, hightailing it toward the ravine. We followed, at first a little reluctant, wondering how we would ever find the way home. Anne went straight to the big tree which stood at the entrance to the deeper woods. The sun had come out and the light in the silence struck like cymbals as it appeared and disappeared among clouds. The vine ropes that hung down from the nearby trees were more noticeable than ever, more enticing with no leaves hiding them, and we ran and caught them, taking long swings to land in the soft snow. We romped and screeched and got so heated we unbuttoned our coats.

Anne was staring at the big oak. Then she took off her

coat and looped and tied one of the vines around her waist. She began to climb up the steps Rossie had nailed to reach the first branch. We thought she would jump from there but instead she went higher, her feet sliding and scrambling, clinging with her body to the rough snow-layered branches.

"Are you crazy?" we called up to her. "You come down. We'll tell."

"Shut up," Anne snarled down at us. Her teeth were scoured white against her kinky red hair.

"You might fall."

"Never do."

We didn't say anything more but watched Anne going higher than we went even in summer, showers of snow falling down on us. Her feet slipped but then got their grip and pushed higher.

At last she stopped. She grinned at us. "Katie be quiet. I have the rope. I'm coming down now. Bombs away!" She had the scared happy look she had when she took the jumps off the haymow. She pushed off then, swinging far out from the tree, her lurch sending down an enormous fall of snow. Out of that silent storm we heard the crack when the vine snapped, and then Anne's plunging scream, which was cut off as if it too struck the ground. After that it was still again and the snow stopped falling.

Gram said it was the snow that saved Anne, that she might otherwise have ended up dead or wishing she was. She came back to consciousness the next morning and recognized Neil right away. He had come over from Illinois, where they'd finally located him the night before. Everybody had been afraid, the way he'd carried on, mourning at last, almost crazed with grief and begging forgiveness. Pale and tremulous, he didn't seem like the same man.

We went to visit Anne in the hospital. They had cut off her hair and a tiny part of her head was shaved because of the stitches. Her exposed neck seemed too long, livid and dotted as with a rash. We couldn't say anything, for they had warned us and made us promise we wouldn't make fun of her.

Gram pronounced the haircut overdue and quite all right with her. She smoothed the bangs. "It looks real neat. Modern too."

Anne lay glaring toward the window. We talked of other things as best we could. She had lost the ring Aunt Elinor had given her—Gram said that was typical, that Anne never could keep hold of anything. Anne said one thing about her hair, determined and final: "I don't care."

Aunt Rachel wondered if anyone had thought to save some of the hair so Anne could make a hairpiece for when she was older. But Gram said it wouldn't do any good anyway, since her hair was getting darker every year and it wouldn't ever match up. We thought there was something different about Anne altogether, something that would never match up. It had to do with the way she didn't talk or laugh, and nothing Katie did could make her hit her. Neil didn't seem like himself either, bringing Anne a glass of water and adjusting the shade so the light wouldn't glare in her eyes. Even with the view covered up, she kept staring that way. As soon as Anne was well enough, Neil said, he would be taking his girls home to Illinois. Until then he and Katie were staying at a nearby motel.

Neil offered to drive them out to the farm before they left, but Anne said she was still having headaches and wanted to get the trip over with. We went to the hospital the night before they were leaving, to say goodbye. Gram was going over to Kingfield to play bingo, so she was in a rush and we couldn't stay long. Everybody kissed the girls and told them it would soon be summer and they would be back before they knew it. After the women left, we stayed behind a minute. We leaned over to kiss Anne. The smell of the hospital was between us. We looked outside to see the woods, but it was dark and we saw only ourselves and lights in the glass. The hospital bed made everything confused.

It seemed Anne would never speak to us again. "We hate to see you go," we wanted to tell her. "We won't ever forget." But we couldn't, not with her face terrible like that and her arm tied up in a sling. We heard a horn blowing over and over from outside. Knew it was Gram, so anxious to leave that she forgot all about the people in the hospital who were sick. Then it seemed almost that Anne would smile. We said, "Goodbye; see you next summer," and hurried out the door.

Partway down the hall, we heard Anne call out, "I can still climb the farthest of anybody."

"I'd already had too damn many brats," Gram would continue to say, right to our faces, a little wicked pleasure on hers from making the remark. She had let Neil take Anne and Katie away and that seemed cruel. But she reversed herself about the loan on the house. Just said Neil could have it for the girls—after all, she wasn't the meanest person in the world. Reminded of Grace's will, she said, "She didn't know what she was doing. They have to live somewheres."

Gram kept us off guard. We were afraid of her truths and then their reversal. One day she might deny that there was any earthly or heavenly rhyme or reason to anything. The next day she might announce, "I'm going down to see the old nigger."

"She's no better than a witch," Aunt Grace had said once.

"I s'pose since you went to college you know everything," Gram had said. She'd had her fortune told, her palm read, from time to time the tarot. It was a comfort and she wasn't going to stop it. Not for a bunch of uppity know-it-alls. Gram sometimes seemed like the child of her daughters, the bad and willful one they couldn't do a thing with but loved the best because of her charm and daring.

When she went off to see the nigger woman, we sneaked away from the house over the back hill and waited in the lower field for Gram to come in her car. The disrespectful name was a part of the mystery we came to sense in those visits to Della's mother—Della the woman who cleaned for Gram—was part of the great distance we traveled to get there and enter the unpainted shack which stood on stilts on the far border of our land. Gram said she didn't take what the old woman told her as gospel, no more than she took anything. But fortunetelling fascinated her and relieved her some. After Aunt Grace died she recalled that the woman had warned her of heavy sorrowful times to come—had seen a woman, still young, with a dimple on her chin. That had to be Grace. Gram knew it right then, had cried even. We had seen her, coming out wiping her eyes.

Della's mother was so ancient-looking she might have been mother to the whole world, the burden of it wearing down her pigment to a milky-tea color and blinding her eyes. She was nearly bald except for random cotton bolls that sprouted. Her empty cheeks sucked themselves and we wondered if her clouded eyes even saw the light. We could stay with her only a moment. Just for a glimpse. It was too powerful a place to be; the fogging sweet-smelling smoke from the wood stove, ablaze even in summer, filled the cabin and presences beckoned through that haze, disturbing and suggestive, while the old woman, a worn quilt on her knees, sat expectantly.

We waited outside on the sagging porch for Gram to have her reading. Bending around a lopsided icebox which held a nest of kittens, we took peeps at Della's dark lanky boys, who hoed in the garden. They glanced at us shyly too; they knew who we were but we never spoke. The big boy, Jefferson, brought each of us a carrot, which was about an inch long and more golden than orange. We nodded thanks and chewed at it, though a bit of dirt still clung in the root hairs. The boys showed us a human grave where a trampled picket fence about a foot and a half high marked it out of the field and a picked flower waved in a jar.

But Gram knew why she was there and stayed a good while. When she came out she was wiping her eyes, though she only answered, "Never mind," when we asked her what was the matter. She called back to Della, "I'll have them drapes setting on the porch." And Della put her hand up to shade her eyes and called to Gram, "You come on back anytime, Lil"; so there had been an exchange. Just then it seemed that Gram was closer to Della than she would ever be to us. We remembered the wood smoke's lavender haze figured on summer heat while we still flicked flecks of carrot and dirt with our tongues. Afterwards we would wonder if Della's mother had known all that was coming. And had Gram known too when she would eye us and say significantly although enigmatically, "Times change," a calculation in her tone that frightened us.

It was summer and Anne and Katie were back on the farm, so we were all together the night the barn burned. Waking by chance, or intuition, Uncle Dan looked out the window and saw it. Perhaps the flare seemed like dawn. The fire trucks came along soon and the racket had all of us awake, throwing on clothes and running down the drive. Gram was dressed completely, even to her stockings and garters, and carrying her pocketbook. We stood off on the weeds beside the orchard trees and watched the fire engine come speeding along the back way, the clinging men serious and intent, acting as if they didn't know us. Everybody had to tell Rossie ten times to keep out of the way.

An immense heat blasted from the barn so that we could feel it hot against our own bodies. Gram said, "I mind the day this barn was raised. There was a big party." The firemen were hooking up the pumper and dragging hoses. Uncle Dan said they didn't build things that well anymore. Gram agreed, said maybe they didn't need to because progress meant that something a whole lot better would be coming along the next day.

"Did you come to the barn party, Gram?" we asked. We had lost some interest in the barn, for although it was getting hotter and brighter, it seemed it might just go on that way like an eternal flame and never be consumed.

Gram said she had been a nobody then. Nobody to invite. Not then. But she'd remembered the place, the oaks along the front like a high fence.

We looked with her up at the barn. It was heating so fast the sound was like a wild storm. After playing some water onto the siding, which hissed and remained unaffected, the firemen turned and directed all the water onto the nearby orchard trees; the sweet and sour cherry trees, side by side, were flaming. The curled singed leaves decorated them like candles set in the darkness. Another truck came in from Bluerock, and it attempted to go around back, where the locust clump was already smoldering, but it was too hot to pass on the track and they gave it up because it was only scrub growth. They played all their water on the orchard side. Everybody was just waiting for the barn to finish itself off—no houses were threatened, the night was windless and clear, the smoke lifting into the sky over the barn while across the pasture over the old duck pond the moon, calm and indifferent, floated in a few cloud wreaths.

It became quieter and Gram said, "Lightnin's done it, I reckon." It had stormed earlier that evening.

"Or a tramp," Aunt Libby said. "Smoking." She shivered and drew her robe close. The night reminded us of other nights, things that had happened to us.

Gram insisted, "Lightnin' "; her lower lip protruded. "I always told the old man to replace them rods after he'd fixed the roof. But of course he knew better. Well, now he sees." She looked satisfied to be right another time, rubbing in another victory.

At that the whole front side of the barn gave way and the iron wheel that was propped against it, off a carriage, rolled along in a despairing and graceful descent and dropped into the fire, followed by another length of siding. It was proceeding rapidly now, the flames high and outlined in blue.

After the collapse of the final two sides there was a lull while the visible internal structure of the barn, posts and beams, timbered rafters, the metal roof, stood complete, revealing once more, at the end, the original plan.

"I wouldn't have believed anything could happen so fast," Aunt Rachel said.

"And there's all that stuff piled in there. That telescope Grace had for a while. The furniture from North Street, the sleigh." One of the cherry trees, engulfed by flame, was hacked down and dragged in closer to the barn. Then from the lower level a sudden great explosion whooshed upward.

"By Christ," Uncle Dan said. "No wonder they never found that still. Jake must have buried it. Always knew that was powerful stuff."

Aunt May came then, flying over the silt ruts in her roadster. She leapt from the car, fast, because she was thin, all nerve and fiber. "I could see the blaze from in town. Oh, Momma, I'm as sorry as I can be. That beautiful barn." She hugged Gram, who stood it a second, then reared back.

"Ain't no use to cry over spilt milk. It wasn't no good to us anyways. Not anymore."

"Well, Elinor was going to keep a horse again," Aunt May said. "And one for the girls."

"A lot of housing for two critters." Gram seemed to be feeling more and more lighthearted. "Day's commencing," she said, and we looked with her to where the moon had been, the sky now the same silver but without the moon. "You gals," she said, "Lila, Cynthia, Maude, Grace." She called through the family names, the living and the dead. Confused, she gave a little moan of sorrow or impatience and went on, "Goddamn it. You kids." She butted her head at us. "You'uns get on up to bed."

"Aw, Gram." We all said it, knowing she wouldn't really insist, that she was just spent and angry before all that had happened.

The firemen held their hoses and yawned, smoking or squirting little jets of tobacco juice sideways out of their mouths toward the fire, ready to give up and go home. And as though with a similar resignation, the barn gave up and collapsed into itself, one section following upon the next, all of it tumbling into the stone foundation, the sills and lower scaffolding folding into and absorbed within the billowing blooms of fire. In the sudden quiet, something rustled beside us in the dark. We turned a flashlight that way, then screamed and jumped around. It was a rat, grown huge, but dazed and injured; it tottered in a circle while we carried on.

Before the men could even move, Gram snatched the stout stick Rossie held and gave the rat one lick across its head. It staggered around and bled and then fell dead. The firemen, across the silt drive, stared at Gram. So did we, mouths slack before the soot-marked old woman with her white leather pocketbook dangling from her arm, on the ground the dead rat.

"Gawd a'mighty," an old guy muttered. And spit. "Guess we may as well be going on." The men began pulling in the hoses. The smoke was still hanging over the empty place where the barn had been and the roof glowed red. As never before from that place, we could see the faraway lights of the next town across the valley.

"Guess I fixed him," Gram said, looking at the rat. She wanted to be sure we appreciated her.

Rossie took it up on the end of a stick and after trying to scare us with it, so that it kept getting bloodier, he scraped and mauled it until he got it over to the edge of the fire pit and flipped it in. The men were finished and most of them went away, leaving one old man on guard over the remaining smoke and ashes and glowing timbers.

We heard the sparrows and blackbirds beginning to chirp for the new day out in the dark orchard. "Well, I guess that's about it," Aunt Rachel said. Then she got annoyed with Rossie, who was still trying to touch us with the stick. "You big baby. You're too old for that," she said, threatening to whack him with the stick if he didn't settle down. We felt like little kids again, with Rossie there deviling us and catching it from his mother.

We walked along the drive backwards with our eyes on the horizon where the barn had been. One of us tripped and shoved the others. "Watch where you're going, girls," Aunt Rachel said, as if she doubted we ever would. Then she turned to look at Rossie, who was walking ahead of us thumping on the ground with the big stick, reminding us of Grandad going through the hollow. "Tom can't do a thing with him either," she said to Aunt Libby. "Guess he's not a miracle worker. Maybe the best thing for Rossie would be to stay on here and learn to farm, like his granddaddy before him."

Uncle Dan was listening and said, "You better hope to God he finds his way out." Then he added, "We had us some swell times, though." In his voice was the sound of endings, his life something that had happened a long time ago.

From behind us we felt and then heard the thud of hooves striking the ground. We knew her as we turned, recognizing the high wavering squeal. Queenie, thinner and more ornery-looking than ever, but still the same huffy little sprawl-legged pony. We'd been too busy for whole summers to think of her. We all stood and watched her emerge out of the damp of morning. She stopped to watch back, in front of the trees, stiffening with her familiar exasperating caution, calculating our distance, our intentions, ready to vamoose. Her disheveled coarse mane was coiled tight with burrs and debris, her body shaggy and mud-caked. Phantom-like, with mist tatters curling at her ankles, she called out to us again. Years of knowing her, sensing that the slightest movement forward would send her scampering, kept us perfectly still, not even daring to reach out a hand, some distance short of the fence—just sweet-talking her a little, telling her how we'd missed her since we had grown up, that we had dreamed of her.

Queenie snorted, shifting her weight a step nearer, and we could see the loose skin shiver under her neck. Her head was butted down and the thick gray in her forelock and mixing in with the brown fur of her haunches gave her the painted look of an Indian pony.

"You old bag of bones," Aunt Rachel said. "You'd like some sugar, wouldn't you, baby? One of you girls get an apple and see if we can get her."

We brought one from the orchard, tramping the mist-beaded, scorched grass. We held it out, calling in low murmurs, suffering her ways, coaxing. And she moved a yard or two closer, her head snaking just over the ground, stretching toward the apple, toward us—which made us jerk backwards, although she was some distance away.

"For crying out loud," Aunt Rachel said, and tossed the apple to land and roll near her. Queenie judged her chances, rushed forward, snatched it and carried it off, backing away. Then she wheeled and vanished toward the ravine, an old acquaintance, never friend, three-quarters wild and looking, for all the world, Aunt Rachel said, like roast piggy on the hoof, that apple wedged in her lifted jaw.

"Varmint," Gram humphed. We were amazed that she had stopped there with us. "Oughta be sold for glue."

"You never would!" Aunt Rachel said. We vowed to ourselves. No. Never. Before that we would turn fugitive, run into the farthest woods with Queenie and disappear forever.

"I might," Gram said, just being stubborn. "It ain't horses I'm thinking of anyways." She bared her own small yellowed teeth in a mirthless smile, then walked on.

"Just look at that old woman," Aunt Rachel said, trying to get her attention again. "Just like her to be out all hours, gallivanting." We all laughed because Gram was that way, flamboyantly, joylessly unpredictable. Gram marched on. Rossie and Uncle Dan crossed into the yard and disappeared toward the house.

Gram stopped to rest at the top of the drive. We came around her, and Aunt May, who had been driving her car slowly behind us as though we were in a procession, honked and went around to go on home. In the first sight of the house it could have been on fire too, the sunlight striking fireballs at the windows.

"You've got insurance, haven't you, Momma?"

"Course I have it. That and a lot more." She seemed revived then and went on toward the house, moving faster.

"I hope that doesn't mean you're going to be pulling

back all the rugs at this hour, digging things out," Aunt Rachel said.

Gram stopped and faced her. "That ain't none of your affair, young miss."

Uncle Dan called out from the porch, where he stood watching us come up, his face amazed and admiring too. "Glad you women made it back. I don't know whether to think you're a band of witches or ladies of the night." He held open the door and we passed through.

After the barn burned, Gram didn't plant the vegetable garden at the back of the yard and over the next three years she sold off the land where the orchard had been and then she never had apples for pie—that was her excuse anyway. When we complained about the noise and lights from the restaurant built on the other side of the hedge, she snapped out that it was a lot more company than a field of daisies with never a smile in them. All she really wanted, it seemed, was to go out with her friends. Della came to clean every Friday, but still Gram felt the house was getting away from her, the ledge on the back porch stuffed to the ceiling and all the closets bulging. The house had become too much, she said, was too large for only five people. Her daughters were more settled in their own lives now, Aunt Rachel married to Tom Buck, Aunt May a Christian Scientist and married to one now besides, and Aunt Elinor was so successful in business she could hardly get away from New York—after she had her teeth straightened, Gram took one look at her and told her that she had now completed the job, had managed to become a perfect stranger. Still members of the family came often to visit so that sometimes Aunt Libby and Uncle Dan felt robbed of their privacy, interrupted in their family life, not that they would ever have refused anyone who wanted to come.

Every summer Anne and Katie came for a long visit. Gram saw to that. When they would arrive without a dime in their pockets and scarcely a change of clothes, Gram would grumble, "I hate to give him the satisfaction," then would take them downtown and buy what they needed. Nice things, but no more than was essential, suspecting Neil was amused because she had to do it. "I can't let them go 'round like that. He's never thought of anybody but hisself," she said, not minding that he would have said the same of her.

"It won't be that much longer," we heard her say one day when we were helping out by cleaning the living room before we went off to the pool. Celia would be meeting Phillip there, for that was the time when they were engaged to be married, and they were together nearly all the time.

"They're growing up," Aunt Libby said. "Never thought I'd see it happen, or live through it."

"Can't be too soon for me. Gals in the house—I've had my fill. Can't count the years, the numbers. Bleeding and reeking. This place reeks!" From the other room we imagined her eyes gleaming, having said just what she wanted, scaring us to death. "I'm leaving," she said then.

"For heaven sakes, Momma," Aunt Libby said. "Five nights straight."

"Can't help it. I am. But I don't mean that."

"Then what do you mean?"

"I mean I got me a buyer."

We rushed toward the kitchen, as if we could do something. We listened for what she would say next, that old woman holding all the cards, but when we walked in she was just sitting in her chair over by the window. She looked right at us with an expression that closed off any discussion. "I'm tired," she said.

But actually Gram had what she called a new lease on life. She crawled along the borders of the carpeting and rugs, lifting out cash, certificates and deeds. She hired Della for extra days and worked beside her. When we laughed at her getup, bandanna and work shirt and overalls, she just raised her straggly gray-shot eyebrows, an old woman who slept with her pocketbook under the mattress, who, when she was traveling in the West and there was an earthquake, woke up and thought for certain the tumbling about of things was a man going after her purse. She never doubted what she was about, what she was worth and why she'd been able to hold on to it. We were as separated from her as always, living on there, awaiting her decisions, with everything that happened heightened with the poignancy and solemnity of an old tale.

Gram was as close-mouthed about her negotiations on the sale of the farm as she was about the financial details of her gambling—playing ten bingo cards at a time, she won at least once every evening, and that was all she reported to us. If anyone called her to account, costs versus winnings, she was immediately defensive, her stringy neck flushed, the cords throbbing. "Leave me be. Ain't none of it's your business." That was that. Once Gram flared up, she went on until her opposition had been inflamed to a raging equal to her own and the air was blue. But whereas Gram's abuse swelled to support her willfulness, a ready and useful weapon, such displays frightened the rest of us, made us fearful of a likeness to her which shamed us. So Gram always had the last word; no one was up to her.

"I've found me my house," she'd announced a few weeks later. She had Aunt Libby drive us by on a Sunday afternoon. It was a brick ranch house in a new development on the old Masters place. Set on about an acre of lawn with a few wire-steadied saplings arranged around it, it had a large bay window on the front, though all the other windows were high tiny rectangles, suggesting a fetish for privacy since no neighbors were near. The kitchen was tiny too. Uncle Dan said it would feed three people who had already eaten—which, Gram retorted, was more than she intended anyway. But there were two full-sized garages, altogether a space nearly as large as the rest of the house, the curtained windows making them appear like extra rooms from the outside. And Gram was proud of the powder room by the front door and the large basement where company could sleep and Uncle Dan could work on his projects.

It was right after Aunt Elinor called, excited about a client she had obtained for her agency, that Gram said, "The Jew will be here next week." That was the first we'd heard of him. The house was prepared and Gram took the long soak that readied her for her affairs. In the hall we met her, a towel flapping in front, steam rolling out of the bathroom around her, making it seem she was a genie released from a bottle. These baths could never erase completely a pervasive smell that emanated from her, a sourness of teeth and age, of heart. We watched her dress. She lay on the bed to corset herself, then disappeared an instant under the dark green dress with its marble print.

She put on her cameo, rhinestones and pearls. Without a mirror she rouged herself, powdered her still-damp cheeks and brushed at her hair, which was as set in its way as a wig. As the rest of her. Then she smiled vaguely toward us as she put on her glasses, read our expressions and said, "Now wipe off them sourpusses. Ain't a funeral. Besides. I want him to notice how pretty my gals is." So gleeful she was. She might as easily have sold us.

Then the Jew was coming down the drive in a long black car. Quietly it came, as purring and sleek as Mr. Weiner, who stepped from it smiling, paunchy and balding, as we had expected, smoking a cigar. Gram licked her lips. He held out his hand to greet her, but she, the old farm woman, didn't even notice and wiped and twisted hers against her dress, as if she wore an apron.

"You have a beautiful place here, Mrs. Krauss," he said. "Lovely."

Mr. Weiner walked the lawn with Gram. He admired her flowers, perennials planted long before, and then he stood awhile under the rose arbor, looking down toward the unraveling tapestry of undulating hills and cloud shadows staining some fields dark, turrets of far barns, encircling woodland. He took her arm. He might have grasped a railing, her stance was so graceless and unyielding. But he seemed not to notice, courtly, enjoying everything. At the house he remarked on details we had thought only we appreciated or had ever noticed, the prisms, the granite aprons, the solid oak-paneled doors, the planked flooring. He named what we loved so that we trailed after him to hear, bitterness edged aside for now.

"Your girls love this house, Mrs. Krauss," he said as if

in praise of us too. Then he added, "They're beautiful. I lost my own at about this age."

"It's easy for them—sing and dance all day." Gram took no notice of Mr. Weiner's misfortune, assimilating only what concerned her.

Mr. Weiner sat in the living room and looked out the window to the meadow which had once been Grandad's cornfield. He sighed. It emerged from deep inside him and made us feel sorry for him. Already Gram was opening the deed to her land. She began to talk business: the location of the farm relative to the growth spurt the town was making, the time she would need to complete the move. All for a moment wavered, at pause and balance; then Mr. Weiner put on his glasses and picked up the deed. The meadow flowers, in bright yellows, pinks, shades of lavender and ivory, levitated over the grass.

After he had gone, Aunt Libby wondered aloud if he had big-city connections. Maybe he was in the Mafia.

"Botheration," Gram snorted, "he ain't Eye-talian. He's a Jew."

"I know that. But there's something fishy."

"There ain't. No more than him pulling some of his Jew tricks. Trying to." Later we heard her humming "When the Roll Is Called Up Yonder," her first song in years.

"You seemed to like him well enough," Aunt Libby teased Gram. "Walking on his arm. He is kind of nice, though. A gentleman. Liked the girls."

And we liked him. Better and better. Sometimes when he came he brought us things from New York—boxes of special candy, a nicely framed photograph of the house. And even after the shopping center was under construction and we were almost ready to move away, we still heard from him. He invited us to come and visit his home, which, though not as lovely as ours, he said, was on Long Island Sound, and he had a yacht we could sail on. But there was a distance between us that was more than miles now. Without our house and land we had been diminished, stripped of pride and reputation. Once we left the farm we knew we would never see him again.

The last time he came was when the papers were signed. Gram lifted aside the lace cloth on the dining room table and Mr. Weiner handed her a magazine to protect the finish. Her fingers were stiff and there was a discernible tremor over the close work of signing her name on the several documents. When she had finished, the room became quiet, as though even the impassive furniture held its breath, disavowed the transfer.

Gram had her own personal copy of the blueprints for the commercial development of the land, the proposed positions of the IGA, Woolworth's, the bowling alley. "This here's going to be Krauss Drive," she said, proud-sounding, glad to at last have something more enduring than flesh and blood to share her name. Her unblinking eyes, varnished by her glasses, weren't seeing anything but the future, which was taking off like the printed road before her.

"If only I had the money," Aunt Rachel said, after the limousine had taken Mr. Weiner away. It went without sound or disturbance, like a figment, as if in the preceding transaction our land had evaporated and become mere value. Gram snorted to hear Aunt Rachel. Castles in the air—the notion that any of them would ever have money. "If wishes were horses, beggars would ride."

Gram thought of Aunt Elinor. "You call her, Libby.

Right now. About that set of furniture she wants. And while you're at it, you can tell her she's not the only one that can turn a dime.'' She turned to Aunt Rachel, who had said she would have wanted the place and would have bought it and wouldn't ever have sold it. "If you had the money! Pooh. You'd do the same as me. What did we ever have around here but dying and fighting? Work and craziness?'' Off she went to ready herself for the evening, calling back to the rest of us that we were nothing but a pack of dreamy fools. "Wish I could see that old man's face. Reckon we'd see who's the horse dealer now.''

When she came down she went to the kitchen, put on her apron, took the skillet from the oven and turned the gas flame sky high under it. Started for the refrigerator. Then she stopped and looked at us watching her, willowy dips of sunlight fluttering over the table. Maybe we depressed her then, because she hung up her apron and turned off the fire. "I'm going over yonder,'' she said, and soon we heard her car start up to take her the half block to the restaurant on the other side of the hedge. Aunt Libby called Uncle Dan at the market and told him to bring home something to eat. She didn't care what. She laughed, listening to him. He was probably lamenting once again, how cruel a fate that in a household of women he had to plan the meals and do the shopping too. Sometimes he'd ask her if she wanted him to eat for her as well.

We were talking about the shopping center, how funny it was going to look to see a big old brick house poking up in the middle like a sore thumb. Aunt Libby was off the phone by then and she looked peculiar and said she didn't think that was the plan. She figured they were going to knock it down.

After that we sat quietly, imagining the walls around us buckling, the plaster crumbling, all of us diving out the doors and windows to get away. We could see Gram's Pontiac steering for her turn. She drove with the authority of her right to drive on the future Krauss Drive. She parked and drew herself slowly out of the car. At the edge of the parking lot, facing the house, she leaned forward and with two fingers grasping the end of her nose, blew it and expertly flicked the residue into the weeds of the ditch. Then with her pocketbook shelved on her mound of stomach, bespeaking the female condition of multiple childbearing, her pace toward the restaurant for her evening meal unhurried, her expression mild and vaguely pleasant, she proceeded with the assurance of someone who had earned everything she had gotten.

A few months after the final payments were arranged, Celia and Jimmy were married and moved away to Texas. Gram had bought her new house and everything was in an uproar with the tremendous job of moving out of the big house. It was early summer and Anne and Katie were back and they were helping too. We knew it was the last summer we would be together. Celia wrote from Texas that the whole world seemed brown. Then later that she was expecting a baby. If it was a girl she was going to name her Jennifer after her sister. Gram said she had never liked the name, that she thought of it as a mule's name. She looked cross about the whole business. And Aunt Libby got the stomachache.

We didn't know what to think. As we went through the house, packing up, emptying boxes or drawers, we felt as though Celia should still be with us and it would surprise us to go in her room and find the phonograph all dust-coated. And the phone would ring for her sometimes—a guy who hadn't heard that she had gotten married. We didn't know what to do with all the things she'd left behind, so we threw most of them out. She wrote that she was sick all day long and the heat was unbearable. If she had a boy she would name him Kevin. That was a name we'd never heard of.

Gram was impatient with the smallest details of the move, referred to it as "the whole pile of junk," and vowed that she was glad the barn had burned down so she didn't have anything else to worry about. She commanded a truck to be driven up alongside the house and had Aunt Libby and Uncle Dan pitch the entire contents of the attic out the window. At the beginning they dallied over some of the ribbon-tied love letters, some from Neil to Aunt Grace, others that Uncle Dan had written from California; they were amazed at this evidence of their youth. Meanwhile, Gram was tossing away anything that came to hand. She asked if anyone wanted the framed magazine print of the Indian brave which had always hung over the fireplace in her bedroom—she'd looked at it long enough, both of them seeing too much of what she wanted to forget. She paused a second and threw him out the window. The grubby muslin sampler Anne had struggled over went after it. When they couldn't find anyone to take the walnut Queen Anne chairs from the dining room, Uncle Dan hauled them away and set them upright at the dump, to one side, where he said it looked as queer as if a bunch of ghosts were having a banquet.

All that Gram said she cared about saving were her Persian rugs. They were now worth a lot more than what she'd paid for them. Besides, she thought they were bright and colorful, comfortable to stand on.

"Although somewhat lumpy," Uncle Dan reminded her. Because she kept her important papers under them. He said he imagined that without her rugs she might never find anything, might crawl for hours or have to resort to a file cabinet. Gram said she viewed each rug as though it were the layout of the entire farm; she knew that she kept her will under the center, where the barn had been, the birth records where Grandad had experimented with soybeans in the south meadow—that way she could go straight to anything she wanted.

Celia wrote from Texas: "Save me Aunt Elinor's saddle blanket and the marble lighthouse lamp. The coconut from the downstairs hearth." Had anyone found the Sunday school Bible they gave her in the fourth grade? But it was too late; everything had been sorted out and carried away.

On the Sunday they called from the hospital, Uncle Dan was down at the church, singing in the choir, the only one of us who went regularly. Gram watched her services on television, told anyone who questioned her to shut up, that she'd gone to church longer than the rest of us had lived and now she figured God wouldn't begrudge her some comfort and ease. We heard the evangelist fervently exhorting, "Heal! Heal!" when Aunt Libby went to the phone.

Celia would make it. The doctor told her that the first thing, so she wouldn't get hysterical. He asked if Celia had shown signs of serious depression before. Was there a history of that sort of thing in the family? Her husband was far too upset to give them the information they needed, and besides, it seemed that he didn't know that much

274

about her past, about the family. Aunt Libby asked if she should come right down to be with her. No, but Celia wanted to come home. Would she be able to get help there, in such a small town? "We can take her up to Cleveland," Aunt Libby said. We'd gone to Cleveland for help before. Celia would have to remain under a doctor's care for some time—the next time she might succeed. They hadn't been able to save the baby. Aunt Libby asked how Celia had gotten the pills. She'd been saving them up, a few at a time, for quite a while.

That night Uncle Dan shut himself in the parlor and played the trombone sonata he had practiced on and off over the years since his one year at the college. Usually he told us that each time he played he got worse, instead of better, which he thought about summed up life anyway. . But this night he went in without a word. We heard him struggling away. After a while of listening to him, Aunt Libby said she couldn't stand that noise another minute. It was just like crying. "He's such a big baby, you know." She frowned at us, tears clustered thick in her lashes, and she went in with him and closed the doors.

The
Best Modern Fiction
from
BALLANTINE

AMERICAN SOCIAL LEGISLATION

AMERICAN SOCIAL LEGISLATION

HARPER & BROTHERS

HARPER'S SOCIAL SCIENCE SERIES

Under the Editorship of

F. STUART CHAPIN

AMERICAN SOCIAL LEGISLATION

 HARPER & BROTHERS

JOHN D. HOGAN

Associate Professor of Economics, Bates College

AND

FRANCIS A. J. IANNI

Assistant Professor of Anthropology and Sociology, Russell Sage College

PUBLISHERS · New York _____

Library of Congress catalog card number: 56–8845

58674

To Beatrice and Marguerite

contents

Preface

PART V: SOCIAL ASSISTANCE AND SOCIAL INSURANCE

PART VI: ANALYSIS OF AMERICAN SOCIAL LEGISLATION

tables

The authors wish to make certain representations about the work which follows. In the first place, this is a book *about* social legislation in the United States and the forces which have given it its present structure rather than a compendium of laws. Hence, the first part is given over to an analysis of the social system, social thought and social movements, and the legislative process. Second, in recognition of the importance of "employeeism" in American culture, a substantial portion of the book is concerned with the problems which issue from an expansion of employee status. Such topics as income security, social insurance and assistance, and labor law are discussed in relationship to the dependency that has been produced by employeeism. Third, the area of family legislation is dealt with in functional terms, with discussion centering on role changes, need satisfaction, and goal fulfillment. Finally, the book is meant to fill a void in text material which has existed for teachers of social legislation throughout the postwar period.

It is hoped that the book will prove useful in courses that vary in terms of purpose and content. The pattern of development in each substantive area of legislation has sought to provide flexibility. In courses where a survey of social legislation is combined with outside readings, the more technical chapters such as 7, 8, 15, and 16 might be omitted. The three parts which develop family legislation, labor legislation, and social security legislation are each flexible and the omission of chapters will not disturb the continuity of the book.

The authors have collaborated closely in writing this volume. They shared responsibility for the course in social legislation at Russell Sage College. A division of labor was made, however, to draw on each author's specialization. Thus, Mr. Hogan prepared chapters 3, 4, 5, 9, 10, 11, 12, 13, 14, 15, and 18. Mr. Ianni prepared chapters 6, 7, 8, 16, 19, and 20. The remaining chapters were prepared jointly by the authors.

Many colleagues and friends assisted the authors in preparing this

volume. It could not otherwise have been completed. Lewis A. Froman, President of Russell Sage College, was continuously helpful and inspired the authors to prepare the text in the first place. Margaret R. Meyer, Librarian at Russell Sage College; Marion Kenyon, of the Legislative Reference Section, New York State Library; and E. L. Breuer, Law Librarian, New York State Library, all graciously helped the authors. Suggestions for improving the manuscript were given by many persons who, of course, share no responsibility for the final result. Harry J. Carman, Dean Emeritus of Columbia College, read the Introduction and Social Thought and Social Movements chapters and Chapter 9 on the American Labor Movement. James R. Flynn, Professor of Domestic Relations Law, Albany Law School of Union University; the Honorable Marcus L. Filley, Judge of Children's Court, Rensselaer County; Jessie Bernard, Professor of Sociology, The Pennsylvania State University; and Marvin Sussman, Associate Professor of Sociology, Western Reserve University, read the entire manuscript. Robert J. Myers, Chief Actuary, Social Security Administration, and Eveline M. Burns, Professor of Economics, Columbia University, were especially helpful in reading the social insurance chapters. Jesse V. Burkhead, Professor of Economics, Syracuse University, read the chapter on income security. Finally, Mrs. Mary Becraft and Mrs. Dorothy Powers merit special acknowledgment for their work in preparing the manuscript.

J.D.H.
F.A.I.

April, 1956

PART I

INTRODUCTION

PART I

INTRODUCTION

chapter 1

Social Legislation

Every industrialized society has witnessed the changing of social relationships. In some instances this has been an orderly procedure, and in other instances violent. Western nations in particular have been the scene of changing relationships during the last century because the pace of industrialization has become more rapid and the agricultural basis of society has been superseded. The dynamic character of social life is lucidly illustrated in the efforts of legislators to adapt statutes to changing social values. At times the role of legislation has been to lead the community, i.e., to compel large segments of the population to readjust their social relationships. More often, however, its role has been to recognize formally that values have changed for the largest or most vocal segments of the population.

Industrialization has been the prime mover of this process, as we would expect. Value systems fashioned by an agricultural or semi-industrial society are not well fitted to the problems of advanced industrialization. Values of an agricultural society focus on rigidity and individualism, and a striking feature of societies preoccupied with agriculture is a passive disposition toward nature and man. Industrialization, however, pays little heed to rigidity in social values. Among western nations its pace has been very rapid and its essence has been the absence of sentiment in its impact upon social institutions. The family, church, government, and educational system have been required to adjust rapidly to the new industrialized basis of society; but the resources of these institutions which would facilitate rapid adjustment have been inadequate.

Ogburn termed the maladjustment of separate parts within a culture the cultural lag.[1] Serious social problems have arisen because of

---

[1] William F. Ogburn, *Social Change*, New York, The Viking Press, 1922, Part IV.

the tendency of social institutions to lag behind industrial technique. Some institutions should, ideally, resolve the consequences of such maladjustments to the "general advantage." Accordingly, behavior consistent with the new industrial technique but in conflict with the ability of social institutions to adjust should be checked or regulated. The other possibility is to carry out social engineering activities which attempt to bolster the resources of social institutions so that they may be able more readily to adjust.

A careful study reveals that over the largest part of modern history operations to correct for cultural lag have been the prerogative of a minority seeking to preserve its interests in the face of social change. Thus the nobility surrendered its role of prescribing social relationships reluctantly to the bourgeoisie, and the bourgeoisie more recently, but as reluctantly, gave way to the industrial laboring classes. In the past, restrictions on the proportion of society formally engaged in the legislative process have been the major avenue by which the merchant and industrial classes maintained their function of prescribing for social change. Regulation of order has been far more popular than social engineering until very recently.

Complicated and bitter struggles have accompanied the movement from negative (protective) legislation to positive (welfare) legislation. The early part of this book will deal with the forces which brought about the movement for welfare legislation.

Definitions and Content

A definition of social legislation in general terms will add definiteness to the development of our study. Social legislation embraces action by government authority to eliminate elements of the social-economic system which are "objectionable" and provide elements for which the system does not make provision. The medium on which social legislation exerts its force is social relationships. Are all deliberate changes in relationships, then, to be discussed within this book? The answer is that we shall exclude many changes.

The household as it operates through our basic institution, the family, will be the focus of our concern. Our study of social legislation will concentrate on relationships to which household members are a party. We shall begin with domestic relations within the household. A major group of subsequent chapters will deal with income security for the household. Discussion of the relationships between the household and government authority will be limited in general to those

situations wherein the status of family members or their income security is affected. A whole series of relationships will not fall within our area of concern in spite of the connection which they may have for household well-being. The household's buyer relationship to business units, its property-holder relationship to political units, its learner relationship to educational units, and its worshiper relationship to religious units will not concern us. The exclusion of these important relationships is a matter of convenience: it enables our limited subjects to be pursued more thoroughly.

An understanding of social legislation as it *currently* affects relationships is our objective. We might begin studying our first area of social legislation right off; but numerous questions would soon arise concerning background and social processes and we would be very uncomfortable before we were far along. It seems advisable to treat the processes of social change and the peculiarities of American social history as thoroughly as we can prior to entering on the substantive material of social legislation. We may, then, avoid the situation into which a legal student got himself when he undertook to master the statutes on the books of Vermont. A kindly judge pointed out that the legislature might in time repeal everything the young man knew.

Social Legislation and the Social Sciences

It is appropriate to raise this question: With which academic discipline are we dealing? Relationships and institutions have been mentioned, and we might, therefore, conclude that we are dealing with sociology. Legislative processes are at the base of our inquiry, however, and they fall outside of sociology by any traditional reckoning. A part of our discussion will have to do with social values and their effect upon legislation, another with the effect of ideas on social legislation. These are, respectively, the proper provinces of philosophy and intellectual history. Moreover, study of the American cultural pattern draws extensively on the findings of cultural anthropology. We have asserted from the beginning that we shall be preoccupied with the problem of income security for members of the household, which falls within the subject matter of economics.

Clearly we shall often cross subject-matter lines while evaluating social legislation and searching out the forces which motivate social change. Actually, the boundaries of the social sciences have been ill defined for a long time. Large universities have founded social science research centers and institutes of human relations in order better to

study social problems. The public hearing, an important development in the American legislative system, illustrates this disappearance of exclusive boundaries among the social sciences. Experts called upon for testimony in connection with the Social Security Act of 1935, for example, revealed a wide diversity of backgrounds. Traditional boundaries among the social sciences persist only in academic institutions; and the existence of interdisciplinary institutes and subjects (human relations, social psychology, economic history, etc.) suggests that the need for crossing subject-matter lines has been met while separate departmental organization has been maintained.

The social sciences are distinguished by their attention to interaction between the individual and his culture, organic and superorganic. Thus, intensive study has been given to the interaction of the technical order and the social order, the kinship structure and the social structure, and the individual with each of these. In the final analysis, the objective of all the social sciences is to determine what makes people behave the way they do.

Although the human organism is customarily thought of as the "property" of the biologist, each social science is ultimately concerned with the individual organism and its capabilities. Anthropology and psychology are surely as much biosocial sciences as social sciences. In order better to understand the capabilities of the human organism, we shall devote the remainder of this chapter to a description of its nature.

The Human Fabric

Man is the most recent of all creatures to arrive on earth. Fish have been on earth perhaps one hundred times as long as man, reptiles eighty times as long, and the horse twenty times as long. Evidence exists for the presence of Hominidae, the family which man shares with prehuman fossils, in the Pliocene period—more than 1,000,000 years ago. During the Pleistocene, perhaps 500,000 to 1,000,000 years ago, the presence of man has been established from skeletal and cultural materials. Man has not always been the efficient, upright specimen that we know him today, of course, and the modern species of man, Homo sapiens, probably emerged about 50,000 years ago. While the evidence is questionable concerning time relationships, it seems probable that the generalized physical characteristics of modern man are 500,000 years removed from such human fossils as Pithecanthropus erectus and Sinanthropus pekinensis, early men who very probably had the capacity for speech and fashioned crude hand tools.

The feature which is most striking about man is his general physical inferiority to nearly all other animals. Neither a rapid runner nor protected by such devices as a shell or fur, he is peculiarly vulnerable to a wide range of hazards. Basic physical inadequacies of this kind are compensated for by man's brain, which is a far more complex reasoning instrument than the brains of any other animals, and his speech apparatus. The complexity of human material and social inventions depends in a fundamental way on these differentiations from other animals. Man's triumph over physical vulnerability, prolonged infancy, and numerous other inadequacies derives from his ability to reason and communicate, thus enabling him to pass on the fruits of his ingenuity to succeeding generations.

Man's behavior must be learned to an astonishing degree. Unlike the lower animals his behavior is guided by only rudimentary instincts. Furthermore, learning must await physiological readiness and is, hence, a very slow process. Nearly one-third of man's life span is taken up in the process of physiological maturation and the learning which must await its various stages, a period during which he is more or less dependent on other humans. Man is a "social animal" owing in some measure to this prolonged period of dependency on others, a period during which he develops behavior patterns which become habitual with him.

Some insight into man's functioning can be gained if we consider him a bundle of capabilities and energy. Some of these resources must be expended in maintenance of the body mechanism and its "running cost." Physical growth causes an additional drain on energy and capabilities. Even though man is a relatively inefficient mechanical phenomenon and wastes resources, there will be a surplus over physical needs. In a later section we shall devote attention to the dissipation of this surplus. Suffice to say that the surplus can be used in both physical and social pursuits.

Man has a resource-using schedule, then, but we might understand him better if we were to know how he operates in terms of his energy pattern. What guides his actions? We can view man in general as attempting at all times to maintain a balance between the demands made upon him and the resources, physical and social, which are at his command. We can break the demands upon human resources down into specific types. Stimuli which stir the organism to action are called motives by psychologists and three varieties are commonly recognized: drives, appetites, and socially acquired goals. *Drives* are

associated with physiological needs and are expressed as hunger, thirst, fatigue, temperature control, etc. Expenditure of resources by the organism on maintenance and running cost relates closely to drives. Appetites, in contrast to drives, are disassociated from physiological needs in the sense that their satisfaction is not an essential condition of bodily health. The following variations are distinguished: sexual, color, taste, and tone. The vast majority of human motives are socially conditioned. More than any other factor the belief system of the group determines our motives and, hence, our action. Leighton recognizes the following systems of belief:

1. Concepts of right and wrong
2. Concepts of religion and the supernatural
3. Ideas about government, law, and politics
4. Ideas about work and working conditions
5. Family beliefs
6. Ideas about how society is organized
7. Ideas about death, its place in the scheme of things
8. Ideas about health and disease, their causes and cures
9. Ideas about the causes of conflict
10. Ideas about the purpose in the universe and what it is [2]

If we would understand the behavior of modern man, the beliefs of his society must receive our sustained attention. Chapter 2 will deal with social values and describe human action in relationship to values.

The human organism, we have seen, is a very recent addition to the animal world, inferior to other animals in nearly all aspects except in the possession of capacity for speech and a highly complex brain. On the basis of his ability to speak and reason, man has built a highly complex culture. Furthermore, most of man's conduct is regulated by the culture which he builds, and any accounting for his approach to problem solving must take into consideration the beliefs peculiar to his society. His ability to reason and ascertain causal relationships probably led him to develop institutions for the control of force. It is to this development in the history of social legislation that we now proceed.

THE HUMAN FABRIC AND SOCIAL LEGISLATION

Man has established beyond question his domination over all other forms of life in spite of the fact that he was the most recent creature

[2] Alexander H. Leighton, *The Governing of Men*, Princeton, Princeton University Press, 1945, passim.

to arrive on earth. It was stated above that his brain, which is a superior reasoning instrument, and his ability to communicate accumulated knowledge to his offspring are at the base of his success. Man was very slow to utilize his distinguishing characteristics, however. In just what measure he was tardy in utilizing his extraordinary abilities can be shown by an analogy. Let us represent the total period of man's life on earth by a cross-country trip from San Francisco to New York— 1,000,000 years of his existence on earth being equivalent to the 3000-mile-long distance. Departing from San Francisco on the eastward trip, we must reach Oklahoma City before we reach Pithecanthropus erectus and Harrisburg, Pennsylvania, before we approach the beginnings of Homo sapiens. The beginnings of the Neolithic period, during which man learned to domesticate animals and carry on agriculture, brings us to a point already within sight of New York. We must enter New York City to find the beginnings of the Holocene, during which man began his political life; mere city blocks then separate us from the historical period—4000 years ago. In the space of time bearing the ratio of a few city blocks to 3000 miles, man has formulated all that we recognize as modern life—writing, agriculture, the state, and construction of buildings.

Political life constitutes our major interest and, while the evidence is speculative in large part, we can suggest some of the probable factors that motivated man to form political institutions. We recognize political life where provision is made for the legitimate use of force on members of the group. The niggardliness of nature, which prevented a comfortable margin of subsistence, is probably associated with the origin of political life, that is, the state. Hazards associated wth control of subsistence factors probably required that individual wishes be repressed in favor of group welfare where conflicts between the two arose. Group action provides a more efficient method of gaining control over subsistence. Political life may have had its origin in the necessity for coercing clansmen to the end of gaining control over subsistence.

The expanding base of social intercourse from the kinship area to the territorial area is also a probable determinant of political functions. This point of view is developed by Durkheim.[3] Primitive societies are characterized by a homogeneous population and division of labor largely on the basis of age and sex. Under such circumstances group

[3] Emile Durkheim, The Division of Labor in Society. New York, The Macmillan Company, 1933, passim.

opinion, custom, and tradition are sufficient means of guaranteeing group welfare from individual nonconformity. Control thus operates through *collective* moral and legal responsibility; it is based on "mechanical solidarity." Societies characterized by a heterogeneous population, well-developed division of labor, and multigroup loyalties require positive controls in order to guarantee the society against the individual. This type of control is based on "organic solidarity." It is implied that the state has its origin in the necessity for regulating conflicts of interest which result from the presence of diverse groups in society.

Leadership is the office through which the function of coercion is exercised in most societies. We shall understand the multiplicity of factors which give rise to the control of coercion if we discuss leadership briefly. Study of primitive societies reveals that the assumption and exercise of leadership is frequently based on nonrational factors. In times of crisis, for example, the abnormal personality is as apt to find followers as the wise or strong personality. Epileptics, for example, have often found favor because of the supernatural explanations which followers attached to seizures. Functional differentiations among group members influence the exercise of leadership and a strong political leader may wield his power at the sufferance of religious (nonpolitical) leaders whose fundamental roles in the group assure them followers. It should not be assumed, either, that physical strength and prowess are universally characteristic of leaders in primitive society. Generosity, mildness, and ability to reconcile disputes have been the traits sought in their chiefs by the Zuñi, Pawnee, and Winnebago Indians. Ranking of members by status is characteristic of all societies, and it is common for the leadership function to redound only to individuals of restricted status.

In modern society an intricate complex of institutions controls the coercive function of the state. It is suggested that activities of the political unit became more numerous as social intercourse expanded from the kinship area to territorial areas. From the relatively simple function of marshaling clansmen in the common task of assuring control over elements of subsistence, the political unit has come to regulate such varied institutions as the family and the educational system. Part of the explanation for this expansion in authority is related to the increasing specialization of individual roles which broke down the essentially egalitarian nature of primitive hunting bands and promoted diversity in their systems of belief.

It should not be concluded on the basis of this speculative account that man's development of the political institutions took place as a logical series of advances toward greater group security. Government often was ad hoc, responding only to crises, and seldom permanent. It expanded without plan and bears little evidence of deliberate innovation. The attempt has often been made to show how the modern state developed in a series of discrete steps from the primitive hunting band. There has not resulted any pattern of political development which fits all societies.

The Basis of Social Action

Our social system is characterized by countless interactions among individuals, and it appears as though the totality of social action which takes place is the sum of individual interactions. The summing of one-to-one interactions, however, fails to take note of a compounding effect which occurs in social action and which allows us to think of individual actors as "free agents" only in the narrowest sense. There is, in fact, a dimension to individual interactions which is not apparent from an observation of the actors. This additional dimension consists in the belief system of the group, the social norms.

A diagram will enable us to understand better this additional dimension of social action. The accompanying diagram (Figure 1) shows a sphere which is intersected by two planes, giving us a pair of "great circles." Let the shaded plane represent the interactions among individuals who compose an in-group, a family perhaps or an intimate office group. The fact that the interactions of the individuals take place within the same plane signifies a communality of motives and goals. Each event expressed through the interaction among the individuals within the group, however, has another dimension, represented in our diagram by the unshaded plane. This is to say that the total sphere represents a macrocosm of which the shaded plane is a microcosm, the microcosm always existing in relationship to the larger whole. Each interaction of the group members is oriented in the closest sense to a plane of the macrocosm, such as the unshaded plane in our diagram, and takes cognizance of the macrocosmic dimension in selecting means for satisfying needs.

An illustration will help to clarify the point. Assume that the shaded plane represents a family with two minor children. The parents decide that the children should become economic partners in the household in order to relieve financial pressure on the family. Arrangements are

made for the children to stop formal schooling and begin working. The plane of the macrocosm relevant to this decision, however, brings the action to a halt through laws regulating school attendance and child labor and, perhaps, social ridicule from neighbors. The macrocosm is, thus, a party to all social action.

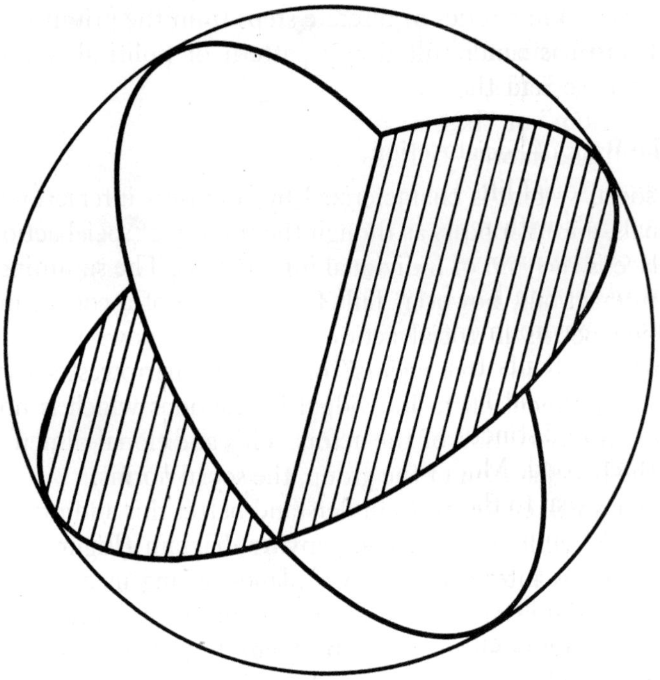

Fig. 1. The Social Microcosm and Macrocosm.

Now our case was unrealistic in that the parents failed to assess properly their orientation to the macrocosm. In the vast majority of instances where economic need was great, the decision to make economic partners of the children would have anticipated the standards and regulations of the macrocosm and the decision, qua decision, probably would not have been made.

It is necessary that we understand the influence of the culture (macrocosm) on decisions that are apparently unilateral. The macrocosm does not, however, have an existence, goals, motives, and equipment of its own. While it gives a dimension to individual decisions beyond the plane of the individual's own group, it reflects group goals and beliefs. Changes in the beliefs of the group thus alter the culture (macrocosm) to which the individual's actions are oriented.

Determinants of systems of belief are seen to be very important from the above illustration. It is not necessary for us to pursue the determinations of systems of belief further at this point because Chapter 2 deals largely with the subject.

Perfectibility of Social Life

Our discussion has carried us through the capabilities of human fabric and the demands of social life. Free play of his imagination will sooner or later lead the reader to speculate about the possibilities of an "equilibrium" or "best relationship" between the social framework and the human fabric. We shall discuss briefly the question of perfectibility in social life, trying to determine wherein it lies.

Experiments with republican systems of government have been undertaken on the premise that the possibilities in the human organism are great. Rousseau had little doubt that man could not be corrupted in a natural environment; his wickedness derived from the unnatural or artificial elements to which he was forced to respond. Republican government does, at least, assume an awareness on the part of the individual of the distinction between the social good and the individual or provincial good. Modern western society does not make it obvious that man is equal to the task of making such a distinction consistently. Conflict and competition seem to characterize modern social life, and this observation is supported by the study of communication media, which report conflict far more often than coöperation. Police annals are not much more encouraging about the possibilities of human coöperation.

Beneath the obviousness of competition, however, basic coöperation of some order enables complex industrial society to function. Our money and credit system would collapse if we did not coöperate in the use of installment credit and checking accounts at least 95 percent of the time. The modern metropolis does not possess the necessary resources to compel obedience to traffic laws or respect for property; a fundamental willingness of most individuals to coöperate enables the city always to underman its police force, as it must. Mutual assistance, moreover, typifies the in-group far more adequately than does competition.

It is of little importance to our present discussion that coöperation may be a learned response to social approval within our society. That man would be brutish and without compassion in the absence of culture is a proposition of only academic interest at this point. Our *modus operandi* is modern western society, wherein culture is compelling and

shapes propensity to coöperate. In fact coöperation and competition are always at work in our society, a comfortable balance of coöperation being maintained a large part of the time. Coöperation consists simply in eliciting general favorable response to the goals and beliefs of the group. The process through which this general response operates will be dealt with in Chapter 2.

One issue remains to be covered. We should inquire into the extremes of coöperation and competition. Obviously, we should avoid extremes of competition in the interest of self-preservation. The notion of perfectibility, however, carries a strong implication that coöperation can know no excess. The argument depends on whether or not desire for recognition is a basic need which must be met. Failure to meet such a basic need is generally thought to account for the economic and social failure of communistic experiments such as Brook Farm and New Harmony.

Equilibrium in social life probably is described adequately in these terms: maximum exercise of human talents and creativeness consistent with maximum conditions of physical and mental health. Guides to the achievement of such an equilibrium condition must be held for another section.

Social Legislation: Concluding Remarks

This is a text designed to describe and analyze the social legislation which has been enacted in American society. Our primary concern will be with social relationships and their alteration by legislation intended to eliminate elements considered "objectionable" and substitute elements considered "desirable" in the social-economic system of the nation. In this analysis we shall concentrate attention on the relationships into which an individual enters as a member of the basic social unit, the family. Our somewhat restricted areas of concern will force us to neglect some of the important relationships which are a part of daily life, but will enable us to deal more thoroughly with relationships of greater importance.

Our plan is to develop the relationship between man, the biosocial animal who has so recently entered into political life, and the institutions of society which direct and order his behavior. We shall be most interested in the basic associations of family, economy, and state and how they have molded human behavior.

To appraise properly man's relationships to the social order we need understand some of his biosocial features. A creature lacking in any

great number of instinctive patterns to guide his behavior, man's dependence on life in an enduring group has been a basic factor in determining state policy. Dependent and helpless in a prolonged infancy, man is forced to remain with the group which satisfies the imperious tissue needs he himself is helpless to serve. But his dependency also provides an opportunity to spend a large portion of his life in social interaction with others. Language, learning, society, and culture have all resulted from this dependency.

Life in groups has additional effects upon behavior. Group activity requires rules of order to ensure the maximum utilization of group effort, and so some system of regulating behavior is born. From this crude beginning develops the normative order of customary rules and eventually the state and law. Conformity to these rules becomes a condition of group membership, and so the authority of the law comes to have meaning for the individual. Lacking efficiency in operation at first, rules eventually become deliberate attempts to order social relations and produce social legislation.

SELECTED REFERENCES

Durkheim, Emile, *The Division of Labor in Society*, New York, The Macmillan Company, 1933.

Homans, George C., *The Human Group*, New York, Harcourt, Brace and Company, 1950.

La Barre, Weston, *The Human Animal*, Chicago, University of Chicago Press, 1954.

Leighton, Alexander H., *The Governing of Men*, Princeton, Princeton University Press, 1945.

chapter 2

Social Values and Social Legislation

We have seen from the previous chapter that man is a highly adapt-able being, favored over all other animals by his well-developed cortex and motivated to act largely by the system of belief to which his cul-ture favorably disposes him. Thus his behavior is largely the result of learning. It is, of course, highly fortuitous that man is not confined by instincts and drives, for, being free of them, he can determine his rela-tive preference among the objects accessible to him. This chapter will explore in some detail the objects he has been led to choose at various times and under various conditions. We shall see that value selection is basic to social legislation, since social legislation presumes certain values to be so essential that the community is prepared to punish failure to conform with them.

Social Values

We shall begin our discussion of social values by suggesting that the reader ask himself: "Of all the objects that man has sought, which should I require present-day society to observe?" A list of some length will be possible. Our exercise in omnipotence has another operation, however. The reader should now decide what form of coercion he is prepared to enlist in enforcing conformity with each of the objects in his list. Should the exercise be completed, the result will be the read-er's preference among the objects he would require, the degree of coercion to enforce conformity being the key to his preferences.

Now it would be extraordinary if any two readers were consistent in the objects which they would require us to observe; and still more extraordinary would be a correlation among the punishments each reader would mete out for failure to conform with the objects of his choice. Some readers would require that we observe the practices of

Biblical fundamentalism, others that we tax ourselves to the end of developing a store of atomic weapons. We can be sure, however, that broad areas of agreement would be found among readers concerning the objects to which the community should require conformity.

A similar polling of a total community, say a city of 100,000 residents, would reveal broad areas of nearly unanimous agreement both as regards objects and "punishment" for nonconformity. We can presume this result because of our knowledge about (1) socialization of the individual and (2) the tendency for the community to disapprove extreme variations in values. Reference has already been made to the fact that man's domination over all other forms of life depends on his ability to communicate the heritage of his ancestors to his offspring. The process through which this occurs is socialization, and one major function of the family, play group, school, and other associations is to prepare the individual to enter society with the least resistance to its demands. If the socialization process were perfectly carried out, the social values as they find expression in the folkways and mores would become personal values for the individual. Society has a stake, then, in molding each individual to the "modal personality" type. As a matter of experience, however, the socialization process is not executed to perfection; every personality deviates from the modal type. In the final analysis social change depends on this failure plus the other elements of personality which permit nonconformity—constitutional factors, environmental factors, and role experiences.

Personality governs the quantum of values and objects to which the individual is favorably or unfavorably disposed and his responses to stimuli. Because individual behavior is conditioned by socialization, there results a high correlation between individual and social behavior. Sapir explains social values in the following passage:

If our attention is focused on the actual, theoretically measurable behavior of a given individual at a given time and place, we call it "individual behavior," no matter what the physiological or psychological nature of that behavior may be. If, on the other hand, we prefer to eliminate certain aspects of such individual behavior from our consideration to hold on only to those respects in which it corresponds to certain norms of conduct which have been developed by human beings in association with one another and which tend to perpetuate themselves by tradition, we speak of "social behavior." In other words, social behavior is merely the sum or, better, arrangement of such aspects of individual behavior as are referred to

culture patterns that have their proper context . . . in historical sequences that are imputed to actual behavior by a principle of selection.[1]

Individual behavior differs from social behavior chiefly in terms of the valued judgments involved. Objects selected by society for conformity constitute the determinants of social behavior.

Conformity to objects which define social behavior depends upon formal or informal sanctions against failure to conform. Few of the objects which our society believes important have escaped codification into law at some level of government. On the other hand, the numerous objects of lesser and often partisan importance are controlled informally by groups that are sometimes difficult to define. For example, deference to females by males is a value which an undefinable group enforces through ridicule and the scornful glance. Between rules of behavior enforceable by the state and rules of courtesy enforced by threat of ridicule from vaguely located group interests lie the vast number of objects to which we conform as a matter of social course. Extreme deviations from the values actively upheld by social entities prepared to disapprove nonconformity are rare so long as the consequences of nonconformity are sufficiently unpleasant to the individual that he is motivated to conform. When society fails by default to reprove nonconformity to a value, even by a scornful glance, the skids are set beneath the value in question. Now, circumstances quite unrelated to the social worthiness of objects operate to permit nonconformity with them.

The advances of technology, urbanization, specialization, and secularization bring about the passive acceptance of nonconformity. In general, forces which are disintegrating in their effect, which operate to lessen the frequency of interaction of individuals known to each other, have this effect. Values highly revered in small-town life—active civic participation, family solidarity, and neighborly assistance—have fallen prey to the anonymity of the great metropolis. These same values are preserved by active disapproval of nonconformity in the small village.

It is not implied that we began with a stock of values relevant to small-village society and proceeded merely to whittle away at them as forces of disintegration had their way. Nonconformity with objects to which the society expects conformity implies the existence of alterna-

---

[1] Edward Sapir, "The Unconscious Patterning of Behavior in Society," Margaret Mead and Nicholas Calas (eds.), *Primitive Heritage*, New York, Random House, 1953, p. 78.

tive objects for the nonconformist. The personality is dynamic, as we have observed, and it responds to new experiences, particularly stress situations, by resistance to the disapproval which socialization has taught will accompany nonconformity with given social values. New possibilities for approval also lead the personality to pressure for conformity with "old" objects.

Interrelationships between culture and personality constitute a new subject of social science inquiry, and the role of such factors as heredity, socialization, experiences, and cultural change in changing personality is largely unknown. For our purposes, however, it is sufficient to recognize that socialization seldom, if ever, produces the truly modal personality, and this fact permits values to change. Ramifications of the questions raised in this section will be dealt with in the remaining sections of this chapter: first, the determination of values, then their changing nature, and finally reasoning from general to particular and guides to values.

Value Determination

Our task in this section is to discuss some of the factors which enter into the determination of values at a given time and place. We would anticipate that crises and the religious and economic inclinations of the community would enter into decisions about social values. In the case of other factors some reminders may be necessary. These less obvious dimensions of value determination will be revealed as we generalize about the value patterns in the several hundred societies of which we have knowledge.

All societies require conformity to designated objects by members. Objects selected by societies differ greatly, however, and our attention is drawn to the bases for differentiation. Certainly these differentiations can be distinguished: the number of objects to which conformity is required, emphasis on means or ends, relative preferences among objects, the type of personality which the objects chosen for conformity tend to perpetuate, and the major preoccupation of those members of society whose objects are served by conformity with social values. We shall examine each of these bases for differentiation in turn.

DIFFERENCES IN THE NUMBER OF OBJECTS

We should expect that social values would be related to needs of the individual in social life. The number of such needs that one might

cite is a matter of taste. W. I. Thomas [2] suggested four and Combs forty.[3] Malinowski has drawn up simple lists of basic needs and derived needs for which provision is made in all societies. First, the basic needs and then the cultural responses:

Basic Needs	Cultural Responses
1. Metabolism (nutritive)	1. Commissariat
2. Reproduction	2. Kinship
3. Bodily comforts	3. Shelter
4. Safety	4. Protection
5. Movement	5. Activities
6. Growth	6. Training
7. Health	7. Hygiene [4]

We need only point out the objects to which conformity would be required in terms of a few of the needs mentioned; objects related to other needs will be self-explanatory. In the case of the basic need for metabolism, the objects to which conformity may be required are that payment must be rendered to a hired worker for work performed, malnutrition should be eliminated in a land of agricultural surpluses, and industries producing food for public consumption must maintain standards of cleanliness. The need for safety gives rise to the following values: individuals possessing instruments which can harm others (e.g., pistols or automobiles) should be regulated in the use of them, employees have a right to protection from dangerous machinery, and an individual is liable for injuries to another person caused by negligence of the former.

Malinowski derives four "imperatives" from the basic physical needs of man for which society must make provision. Values are thus related to these four imperatives:

1. The cultural apparatus of implements and consumers' goods must be produced, used, maintained, and replaced by new production (Economics).
2. Human behavior, as regards its technical, customary, legal, or moral prescription must be codified, regulated in action and sanction (Social Control).
3. The human material by which every institution is maintained must be

[2] W. I. Thomas, The Unadjusted Girl, Boston, Little, Brown and Company, 1923.
[3] Arthur W. Combs, "A Method of Analysis for the Thematic Apperception Test and Autobiology," Journal of Clinical Psychology, April 1946, pp. 164–174.
[4] Bronislaw Malinowski, A Scientific Theory of Culture and Other Essays, Chapel Hill. University of North Carolina Press, 1944, p. 91.

renewed, formed, drilled, and provided with full knowledge of tribal tradition (Education).

4. Authority within each institution must be defined, equipped with powers, and endowed with means of forceful execution of its orders (Political Organization).[5]

Technological state of the arts will be referred to time and again as a factor which gives rise to social change and value reorientation. This is not evidence for the Marxian belief that the mode of production dominates all other determinants of values. Entirely different determinants have given rise to values as complex as those which surround capitalistic production in Western European civilization. Among the Australian aborigines the complexity of objects associated with kinship reckoning to which conformity is required is almost beyond belief. Kinship is related to functions performed by clansmen, not blood relationship, among the Todas. The unindustrialized rural Chinese almost certainly are required to observe more objects than the industrialized urban American. We should not, then, assume that the number of objects correlates with the state of technology or any other index of social advancement. The Australian aborigines, in spite of their elaborate system for reckoning kinship, were admitted to the "human species" only recently by common consent of anthropologists.

The number of objects requiring conformity probably bears a closer relationship to forces which have a centripetal effect on the society, which destroy the unity of agreement concerning objects. Forces having this character operate to obstruct the efficiency of socialization and eventually produce subcultures with objects of their own.

RELATIVE PREFERENCES AMONG OBJECTS

No two societies would agree on a hierarchy of objects or with methods for obtaining conformity with each object. Matters which would be punished as serious felonies in American courts are dealt with by ridicule among the Eskimo. The practice of witchcraft often brings the death penalty among primitives, while in American society the plaintiff in a witchcraft case would stand a good chance of being hustled off to a psychiatric examination. It has been found that primitives often manifest concern for individual values rather than social values; that is to say, torts, or purely private offenses, are recognized instead of crime (social offenses).[6] No single object, even preservation

---

[5] Ibid., p. 125.

[6] Robert H. Lowie, Social Organization, Rinehart and Company, 1949, pp. 160–161.

of the group, is valued highly by all societies. The relative dignity of the individual, the state of scientific technique, the complexity of government, and other factors influence relative preferences among objects. Imperatives described above by Malinowski require the society to make provision for their satisfaction, as mentioned; but the forms in which they can be satisfied constitute a basis for value differentiation. No unanimity of feeling exists as to the "proper" or "normal" method of satisfying these imperatives. The objects to which any society may require conformity in connection with the imperatives will thus differ. Acquisitiveness has a high value in western European culture, but virtually none in the Zuñi culture. Individual property rights are fortified against government encroachment by a voluminous heritage of legal lore in western society, but a Tongan chief may, as Lowie observes, "seize whatever takes his fancy." [7] Furthermore, reciprocal gift giving is a common object to which conformity is required in primitive societies—an object of incidental importance in western society. Responses to the imperative requiring that capital and consumers' goods must be produced and maintained are varied and they become more complex when acquisitiveness gains high approval as a social value. Social control likewise gives rise to quite different objects, as shown by the Eskimos' disregard for rigid legal codes and permanent political officials and the American preoccupation with legalism and political selections. Education can pass on the skills requisite for spearing salmon or for atomic investigation, and each skill is valued equally highly in terms of approval given for accomplishment in different societies. Institutional provision for political authority may be *ad hoc* or surrounded by legal prescriptions.

DIFFERENCE OF EMPHASIS BETWEEN MEANS AND ENDS

Modern western democracies regard ends as subordinate to means as a general condition. This is not the case among all peoples. A minority of societies require trial by one's peers as a prerequisite to punishment for social offenses. The quest for subsistence control is not often of such preëminent importance to primitives (or modern peoples) that they are prepared to surrender other ends, say leisure, in order to institute efficient means of farming, hunting, or marketing. Efficiency is a fetish in the United States; but it appears to be arbitrary to a society where keeping with prescribed methods for gaining

[7] *Ibid.*, p. 154.

a mate, reckoning kinship, or appeasing the gods are objects valued highly.

The Types of Personality Which the Chosen Objects Tend to Perpetuate

Values persist in a society in the measure to which socialization of offspring succeeds. The Zuñi value coöperation and eschew conflict; offspring are, therefore, prepared to enter Zuñi culture with the least possible resistance to its values, and mildness and coöperation are taught the young Zuñi child. The Arapesh "overindulge" their children to the same end. Not far distant from the Zuñi and the Arapesh, urban Americans are taught that competition is the natural order of things; that life exists in a resisting medium wherein it is shameful not to succeed beyond the achievements of one's neighbors. Europeans of the early middle ages valued asceticism highly and sought to prepare youth who would willingly be self-depriving and long-suffering.

In the characteristics of modal personality is reflected the collective social judgment that group life can sustain itself only through dedicated observance of specific objects. Needs must be met only in the approved pattern of relationships and means must be consistent with established practices. Candor leads us to investigate the interests which are served by a process dedicated to preserving the values inherited from the past, and thus blocking social change.

Interests Served by Conformity with Selected Objects

It is not intended that the reader should see a conspiracy in the attempt of social members to prescribe and perpetuate a given value system. History abounds with examples of well-intentioned interest groups making pleas for the retention of old, tried principles. Before Adam Smith gave us the "invisible hand," a long line of thinkers from Epictetus to Thomas Bemis and Martin Luther counseled obedience to the established organs of authority and cheerful acceptance of whatever lot fell to man. Nearly all groups have sought to eliminate extreme deviates from established group objectives; and it is not obvious that selfish interests are always at work in each case. The point here is that organized "self-seeking" is not a sufficient answer to the resistance encountered by the social deviate. Thomas Burke saw in the failure of the eighteenth-century French Revolution a vindication of the "non-interference with events" thesis. The idealized objects liberté, égalité, fraternité had not been achieved after a decade of bloodshed, and ob-

jectionable remnants of the "old regime" persisted in the Napoleonic era. A complex phenomenon occupies our attention when we try to account for partisan influences on social values. A later section will center upon this problem (see "The Fallacy of Composition," pp. 26–28).

Value determination produces patterns of objects which serve essentially similar needs in all societies. The selection of objects is not an exercise in origination and reëvaluation for each generation, but a somewhat passive acquiescence with the heritage of values which are passed on to each group member through socialization. In the failure of socialization to stamp the individual with an immutable conformity with the sum total of social values lies the basis for social change. The degree of change has been held to correspond to the intensity of centrifugal (integrating) as compared with centripetal (disintegrating) forces. Urban industrial life is centripetal, agricultural life centrifugal. Roles of group members are more homogeneous and outside stimuli less frequent and intensive in agricultural life; the failure of socialization is thus less likely to result in social change in such a social environment. Other differentiations apply to primitive societies and change results from essentially the same forces: outside stimuli and inadequate socialization. Perhaps sometime in the past the "first" social values were determined in the absence of outside stimuli and in spite of simple, almost immutable socialization. But the matter is one of speculation, and for all of human history that we can review with confidence values have been dynamic.

The Changing Character of Values

Values change and nonconformity which was punishable yesterday may pass unnoticed today. The nature of our discussion centers attention on legislative activities as they operate to change values (or reflect the reality that values have changed). We should be more comfortable in our discussion of legislative activity if we could identify the process by which values change, if we could isolate the "first cause" so to speak. Inadequate socialization and individual perceptions which were suggested above lack the precision which we should like. There is the danger that we shall oversimplify the process—and we may be forced to do so through lack of knowledge about the "inner process" of social change.

Major changes which have influenced western European civilization have been typified by a slow but very definite break away from established value patterns. Brinton notes that humanism, protestantism,

and rationalism have combined to pave the way for the modern doctrine of progress—the ethos of our culture.[8] Each of these historical changes describes a liberation: humanism from preoccupation with saving our souls, protestantism from preoccupation with one exclusive church and ministry as the avenue to salvation, and rationalism from restraints on human reason as the key to explanations of the operation of the physical universe.

We seem to be on firm ground when we assert that ideas and systems of belief determine human action, not to the exclusion of other factors such as heredity and role experiences, but above their influence. Of far greater consequence for action than other factors are the beliefs which direct efforts and give them a sense of rightness. Leighton confidently asserts that human groups cannot effectively carry out acts for which they do not have a system of belief.[9] Lewin establishes our basic postulate in the following statement: "Since action is ruled by perception, a change in conduct presupposes that new facts and values are perceived." [10] Let us agree that it is systems of belief with which we must deal if we are to explain changes in action. Moreover, changes in action of such a numerical preponderance that the majority of a group is affected will, for us, constitute evidence that changes in values have occurred.

Still to be dealt with is the mechanism by which the "numerical preponderance" is motivated to change its values. Identification with "great men"—the decision makers—by the rank and file of the group offers one explanation. In this approach the changes in value orientation, including changes in the method of gaining conformity, occur in the individual fields of a few and are transmitted to the many. Only the changes in value orientation of the few, the decision makers, must be accounted for. Crises, for example, which endanger the welfare of the group are accompanied by the emergence of strong personalities who point out solutions; response of the threatened population is in the nature of identification with the leaders, and the values of the leaders become the values of the populace at large.

Facts and reasoned thinking have been offered as explanations for social change. This approach draws heavily on the ability of human beings to act logically, to reason cause and effect deliberately. Thus, when it appears to the "majority" that given objects no longer are

[8] Crane Brinton, *Ideas and Men*, New York, Prentice-Hall, 1950, pp. 365–366.
[9] Alexander H. Leighton, *Governing of Men*, Princeton, Princeton University Press, 1945, p. 292.
[10] Kurt Lewin, *Resolving Social Conflicts*, New York, Harper & Brothers, 1948, p. 63.

worth maintaining, they are rejected, and new objects sought. Some historians have found that almost no crises are too great a test for mass perception of the "facts" in the situation. Logical behavior is thought by social psychologists to give way under stress to emotional behavior. Leighton, again, states that belief systems under stress become more emotional and less rational.[11] All determinism, economic, environmental, or other, is confronted with the objection that behavior logically oriented to given (economic) ends fails to appreciate the irrational causative elements in human behavior.

Another method of accounting for social change must be dealt with. It explains changes as owing to an accidental combination of factors. There is no defense against such an explanation; but it is highly suspect on the grounds that it is offered in lieu of explanations less defensible, less defensible in the sense that acceptance rests on worthiness of a theoretical structure rather than its avoidance.

Where it shall be necessary for us to account for changing systems of values, we shall utilize the first approach. All legislated changes in values within republican systems of government involve these two features: majority *ex ante* changes in values and *ex post* reëducation (persuasion) of the minority which has not changed its value orientation.

Changes in the objects to which society requires us to conform permit analysis in many dimensions. In this book we shall be concerned with changing relationships, particularly from the standpoint of income security in recognition of the fact that the vast majority of individuals are economically dependent on others who provide them income-yielding activity. Changing economic relationships constitute simply a point of special emphasis. Other dimensions with which we shall deal are the consequences of changing relationships to physical and mental health, the effect of changing roles on the efficiency with which we respond to the cultural imperatives listed by Malinowski, and the changing *Zeitgeist* which reorientation of values produces. Chapter 4 discusses the American culture pattern and will deal at length with each of these dimensions.

The Fallacy of Composition

We have discussed the determination of values, noting the process through which the community (those who participate in political decision making) requires conformity of all members to certain objects.

11 Leighton, *op. cit.*, p. 299.

Except in the limiting cases of (1) complete unanimity of community judgment wherein all adult members agree on objects, and (2) complete disregard for community involvement in decision making, as in a dictatorship, values cannot properly be said to exist uniformly for the whole group. This fact would not require emphasis but for the frequency with which legislative action is explained as being in the "public interest" or the "general welfare."

Degrees of welfare are to be recognized, and some legislation fulfills the brief held for it—that enforcement of conformity with designated objects is in the public or general interest. Protection of the individual's person and property fulfills this condition. We can agree on this because surrender by the nonconformist of his freedom to prey on individual person and property is of little moment as compared with the security his sacrifice affords the community. This example approaches limiting case (1) above.

Objects which do not closely bear upon preservation of the species create complex problems when an attempt is made to relate them with the general interest. Are zoning laws which restrict the forms of residential and commercial construction in the general interest? Are laws which permit employers to sue labor unions for triple damages, when secondary boycotts reduce business earnings, in the general interests? The simplicity of the case wherein we limit attacks upon the individual's person and property contrasts sharply with required construction standards and labor-union responsibility from the standpoint of their being community objects to the advantage of each and all individuals.

The phrase "fallacy of composition" has been used to describe the sophistry which one indulges when he attributes goal fulfillment or need satisfaction to an aggregate of individuals. For a wide selection of social values the differentiation between partisan objects and social objects is significant. The importance of this assertion is amplified when "failure" of the socialization process and the existence of sub- or part-cultures are related to value determination, as was done previously. When recognition is taken of the near impossibility of objects being in the "general interest," apparent solidarity of purpose masks inevitable compromises in legislation. The group possesses uniform agreement neither in terms of the objects legislation selects nor the type of coercion to be employed in obtaining conformity.

In Chapter 1 it was noted that the movement in recent years from negative (restrictive) legislation to positive (welfare) legislation occa-

sioned bitter conflicts. In large measure these conflicts arose over interpretations of the general-welfare concept. Attitudes of retrenchment with reference to welfare legislation are illustrated by the following quotation from William G. Sumner:

The amateur social doctors are like the amateur physicians—they always begin with the question of remedies, and they go at this without any diagnosis or any knowledge of the anatomy or physiology of society. They never have any doubt of the efficacy of their remedies. They never take account of any ulterior effects which may be apprehended from the remedy itself. It generally troubles them not a whit that their remedy implies a complete reconstruction of society, or even a reconstitution of human nature. Against all such social quackery the obvious injunction to the quacks is, to mind their own business.[12]

Values in Relationship to Manifest and Latent Functions

The process of legislation which we have presented thus far implies that objects, once decided upon, become determinants of action. No allowance has been made for the possibility that the consequences of legislation may be different from the consequences envisaged by the legislators. The facts are obvious: legislation is enacted to require recognition of labor unions, but an unanticipated effect occurs which is unrelated to the original intent of the legislation. The worker slows his working pace in response to the assumption that he has found a champion, or the union proceeds to restrict entry of workers into its ranks, reducing employment. Explanations of the phenomenon are not simple.

Legislators cannot, of course, anticipate all of the consequences of their actions. The unwillingness of the minority to conform with the objects laid down by majority legislative action may produce unanticipated results. Inability of legislators to assess the ramifications of their work sets limits to the extent of correlation between intended results and actual results. Subsequent chapters will deal with the legislative process in political terms. One major political problem is the methods of ascertaining ex ante the consequences of legislation.

Merton has distinguished between the manifest or intended consequences of action and the latent or unintended results.[13] Merton further classifies the latent results of legislation in terms of their func-

12 William G. Sumner, What Social Classes Owe to Each Other, 1920, New York, Harper & Brothers, p. 38.
13 Robert K. Merton, Social Theory and Social Structure, Glencoe, Ill., The Free Press, 1949, p. 61.

tion and dysfunctional contributions to the social structure. He sees these latent functions as being either functional to a given system, dysfunctional to the system, or irrelevant, that is, neither functional nor dysfunctional. By adopting the elements of this analytic tool we avail ourselves of the possibility of extending our view of the consequences of legislation spatially in society. We may, for example, examine the effect of diverse marriage and divorce laws on family behavior, of child labor laws on education. A further advantage is to protract our view in time.

Illustrations of manifest and latent differentiations abound in American welfare legislation. "Social engineering" is a new field, still in its infancy, and this alone would result in latent functions. The Social Security Act of 1935 was passed for the avowed purpose of relieving some of the major hazards to subsistence security. This, then, was the manifest function of the act. Latent functions which have been cited by its critics are that it brought about a reduction in individual incentives, it promoted individual irresponsibility, it promoted habits of dependency upon the state in violation of American tradition, it brought us a step closer to socialism, it advanced secularization, it increased the United States Treasury's control over the monetary system, and it promoted the unity of business and other groups to the detriment of future welfare legislation.

We shall have to be watchful as we discuss social legislation, as the preceding discussion implies. Latent functions of legislation frequently counter the manifest functions almost entirely.

Guideposts to Legislation

There is a tone of "highhandedness" in group action which requires general conformity to objects that are usually less than "general" objects. A necessary precaution in the legislative process would seem to be the establishment of criteria for guidance. Tests for the purpose of determining the adequacy of existing objects and the merits of proposed objects would be wholly preferable to leaving changes in value systems to indeterminate factors. We have discussed determination of values above, and it was pointed out that criteria are used to select objects; but the facility with which the criteria have been articulated leaves ample room for improvement. Criteria can certainly be extended in range and made more explicit.

Professor Leys' analysis of guides for policy decisions is an excellent

approach to our problem.[14] Ethical systems are seen in terms of the "deliberative questions" which they raise rather than in terms of the answers they provide. We shall review briefly most of the ethical systems with which Professor Leys deals.

UTILITARIAN CALCULATION

Jeremy Bentham founded a system of ethics which holds that social decisions should rest on a comparison of "pleasures" and "pains." The maximization of net pleasure is the objective of decision making. Professor Leys describes the questions to which the utilitarian would require answers in making his decisions: "What are the probable consequences of various proposals?" "Which policy will result in the greatest possible happiness of the greatest number?" "What is the factual evidence for assertions about benefits and disadvantages?" [15] The distinctive emphasis of utilitarian ethics is on ends.

CASUISTRY

"Casuistry," says Professor Leys, "is the art of applying authoritative rules and precedents to present cases." [16] The emphasis in this approach to decision making is on legalism and the heritage of values. It raises the questions: "What are the authoritative rules and precedents?" "What authoritative opinions are relevant?" "Which citations are lacking in authority?" [17]

MORAL IDEALISM

Professor Leys associates raising of the following questions with Plato and Kant: "Can you define what you approve?" "Can you bring various approved practices under a general rule?" "What would you approve in an ideal community?" "Can you reconcile conflicting principles?" [18] In essence this approach requires that values be differentiable in terms of higher and lower values; it demands consistency of general principles.

PSYCHOLOGICAL ETHICS

Hobbes and Butler constructed a system of ethics which stresses the capabilities of the organism. The questions to which it gives rise

[14] Wayne A. R. Leys, *Ethics for Policy Decisions*, New York, Prentice-Hall, 1952.
[15] *Ibid.*, p. 189.
[16] *Ibid.*, p. 33.
[17] *Ibid.*, p. 189.
[18] *Ibid.*, p. 190.

are: "What is the nature of human nature?" "What controlling motives have been overlooked in your deliberations?" "Are the motives which are being considered influenced or influenceable by cool reflection?" [19] It is implied in this series of questions that the disposition of man to act is based on nonrational elements; that man does the things he does because of how he feels rather than because of what he knows.

HISTORICAL LOGIC OF HEGEL

Hegel emphasizes the "laws of history" in his approach to social decisions, and the questions to which his system of ethics gives rise are described by Professor Leys as follows: "What are the main historical trends of institutions?" "How are our partisan causes related to this larger picture?" "To what can we all be loyal?" "What synthesis has overcome the opposition of thesis and antithesis?" [20]

HISTORICAL LOGIC OF MARX

Marx built an ethical system on Hegel's historical logic; but the questions to which the Marxian system requires answers are different from those cited by Professor Leys in connection with Hegel: "What are the fundamental changes in the mode of economic production?" "What economic classes are created by these changes?" "How are all the issues related to the class conflict?" "What action in the immediate situation will hasten the final showdown in the class war . . .?" [21]

DEWEY'S INSTRUMENTALISM

The American, John Dewey, made a heroic effort to relate historical logic to the operations of institutions. Professor Leys describes the questions to which the Dewey system requires answers: "What is the problematic situation that gave rise to deliberation?" "What will satisfactorily terminate deliberation, that is, relieve the conflicts and tensions of the situation?" "Does the proposed solution anticipate consequences in the larger environment as well as in the immediate situation?" [22]

SEMANTIC ANALYSIS

Semantic analysis has pointed out this important factor about words: they have emotion-bearing capabilities as well as fact-bearing

[19] *Ibid.*, p. 190.
[20] *Ibid.*, p. 191.
[21] *Ibid.*, pp. 190–191.
[22] *Ibid.*, p. 191.

capabilities. Professor Leys describes the questions to which semantic analysis gives rise: "Is your knowledge of fact confused by emotional language?" "Does the language that you use pre-judge the issues?" "In choosing your course of action, do you select words (as part of your action) to which other people will respond rationally?" "Are you expecting words to do things that words cannot do?" [23]

We shall have frequent recourse to Professor Leys' approach to decision making—the raising of deliberative questions in terms of an ethical system. It will be apparent from this brief review that welfare legislation has defended itself on utilitarian grounds, the greatest good for the greatest number. Until recently less emphasis has been placed on Hegelian historical logic and Platonic-Kantian moral idealism. We should accept these observations only as a statement of tendency and not in an exclusive sense.

Social Legislation and Social Values: Concluding Remarks

Little of man's activity is completely arbitrary. His activity is functional, with some end or goal in mind. This chapter has attempted to demonstrate how man chooses among the multiplicity of objects presented by his environment, and how valuation of these objects shapes the character of social legislation.

Man as a solitary animal would, in all probability, choose those objects which best satisfied his immediate needs, but group life has taught him that there is a hierarchy among these objects and that some objects have a higher priority than his immediate needs. The process by which man is transformed from a self-satisfying to a socially concerned animal is socialization. In his contacts with other group members, particularly in the intimacy of the family, he acquires a preference for objects "valued" by his society and comes to eschew those objects condemned. Socialization is never complete, owing to individual differences and discontinuities in individual exposure to culture, and the value system of a society can change to include new objects and to discard those which have become dysfunctional, but some values obtain such a sanctified status that they are considered indispensable and form a hard core of "ultimate" values for the society. These ultimate ends serve as the basis for judging the relative merits of newer, less traditional ends introduced by social change.

Social legislation has an intimate and functional relationship with the system of social values. As a deliberate attempt to produce change

[23] *Ibid.*, p. 191.

in the social system, it requires some definitive set of standards in choosing the ends toward which it directs its activity. The value system, and the "ultimate" values in particular, provide such a standard. There is seldom complete consensus among the various interest groups in a society as to what values serve best to orient legislation. Thus conflicts may arise between social elements seeking more restrictive legislation as a means of promoting individual sufficency and those that would legislate for the "general welfare" of society. Some criteria of guidance for the measurement of the relative merit of these various proposals are needed beyond the interpretation of values by special-interest groups. Ethical systems which select objects for the community's guidance have seldom received the attention they deserve.

SELECTED REFERENCES

Brinton, Crane, *Ideas and Men*, New York, Prentice-Hall, 1950.

Lewin, Kurt, *Resolving Social Conflicts*, New York, Harper & Brothers, 1948.

Leys, Wayne A. R., *Ethics for Policy Decisions*, New York, Prentice-Hall, 1952.

Lowie, Robert H., *Social Organization*, New York, Rinehart and Company, 1949.

Malinowski, Bronislaw, *A Scientific Theory of Culture and Other Essays*, Chapel Hill, University of North Carolina Press, 1944.

in the social system. It requires some definitive set of standards in choosing the ends toward which it directs its activity. The value system, and the "ultimate" values in particular, provide such a standard. There is seldom complete consensus among the various interest groups in a society as to what values serve best to orient legislation. Thus conflicts may arise between social elements seeking more restrictive legislation in the interests of promoting individual autonomy and those that would legislate for the "general welfare" of society. Some criteria of guidance for the measurement of the relative merit of these various proposals are needed beyond the interpretation of values by special interest groups. Ethical systems which select objects for the community's guidance have seldom received the attention they deserve.

SELECTED REFERENCES

Bruton, Crane, Ideas and Men, New York, Prentice-Hall, 1950.

Lewin, Kurt, Resolving Social Conflicts, New York, Harper & Brothers, 1948.

Lepawsky, Albert, ... New York, Prentice-Hall.

Lewis, ... Social ..., New York, Alfred Knopf and Company, 1949.

Malinowski, Bronislaw, A Scientific Theory of Culture and Other Essays, Chapel Hill, University of North Carolina Press, 1944.

PART II

SOCIAL THOUGHT AND SOCIAL MOVEMENTS

The Development of Social Thought

This chapter will carry us farther toward an understanding of social change. In the preceding chapter it was pointed out that objects of interest to the community change through time, owing, in the first instance, to the unique experiences of individuals and the failure of the socialization of the new generation to be perfectly effective. Other influences, such as changes in the economic order of life and the occurrence of catastrophes, promote change on the basis of these primary factors.

Of major importance in social change are the suggestions that inform change and determine its direction, suggestions concerning the goals to be implemented in departing from the previous structure of action. These suggestions have often been provided by one or a few individuals, and are referred to as social thought when they concern social relationships. The striking feature of social thought is its individual character, and the greatest social ideas, as Whitehead notes, "start as speculative suggestions in the minds of a small, gifted group." [1] Perhaps the number of persons in any age who are able to break away from the relative security of conforming behavior and set down their thoughts to influence others is necessarily small.

The stimuli that have caused individuals to make new departures in social thinking have been diverse. In the case of Plato and Aristotle the appearance of their social thought may lie in the fact that Athens was located on much-used trade routes with a consequent quickening of city life. The volatile social thought of Karl Marx owes its origin in part to the sensitivity of Marx to certain features of the social order which meted a great deal of suffering out to him. St. Augustine's social

[1] Alfred North Whitehead, *Adventures of Ideas*, New York, The Macmillan Company, 1933, p. 17.

thought illustrates logical deductions from a faith. William Ellery Channing and Ralph Waldo Emerson sought to redirect social thought in consideration of the changing order of life brought by industrialization. Variations of these illustrations will become apparent as the major figures in social thought are discussed.

The publication of heterodox views on social questions has nearly always been a challenge to the existing social structure, and only rarely have the new views been accepted and implemented immediately. More often, contributions to social thought appear to be inconsequential. But, in time of need—following a crisis—the previously ignored suggestions may be seized upon and implemented with a burst of reforming energy. Dissatisfied social groups are likely to concern themselves with heterodox social views, with the intention of pressing them into service when the opportunity arises. Opposed to such groups are the defenders of the *status quo* and those who are indifferent to social issues; the opponents are thus nearly always more effective than the proponents of social change. Certain themes of social thought have shown a cumulative growth through the centuries in spite of opposition. In this connection we should mention the preference for persuasion over force, the desirability of a broad base of decision making, and the expanding idea of human rights. The social conscience to which these ideas appeal seems to include a majority of interest groups.

Social thought includes so many themes that a simple classification of them is difficult to frame. However, most social writing has been concerned with one of the following matters: (1) pointing out new social interests which should be served, (2) defining anew what is social truth and social virtue, and (3) explaining social catastrophes.

Folkthought

We will begin our discussion of social thought with folkthought, the unsystematic lore about tested practices which primitive peoples invoke. Primitive peoples, to a greater extent than people in modern societies, are concerned with results because, as Sumner observed, "the first task of life is to live. Men begin with acts, not thoughts." [2] The limits of tolerance, one might say, are drawn very close for primitive peoples because inefficiency might threaten life itself. Among the alternative actions which might insure effective regulation of such matters as food supply, marriage, protection of the person, etc., those

[2] William Graham Sumner, *Folkways*, Boston, Ginn and Company, 1907, 1930, p. 2.

are apt to be chosen which prove most effective with the least disutility. In time a body of thought arises to inform future generations of the wisdom gained in past experiences and to justify procedures that the group associates with its preservation.

The form of folkthought may vary from simple proverbs to elaborate ceremonial invocations. Not only the form but also the substantive content of folkthought may vary even among groups situated geographically near to each other and, presumably, faced with the same problems. The Zuñi, Hopi, and Navaho have opposing ideas about death and competition although they live in similar environments.

Folkthought is unsystematic and its major shortcomings consist in the arbitrary assignment of cause and effect and its origins, which are often aleatory. Man's development of social thought beyond this stage depended in some measure upon his attention to these inadequacies. The accomplishments of folkthought are not to be dismissed, however, because, as Bogardus observes, folkthought produced "fundamental social concepts such as kinship, authority, dependence, and tribal loyalty." [3]

Hebraic Social Thought

About twelve centuries before the birth of Christ, there arose in Egypt a system of thought centering about the theme of social justice. An inspired development which went far beyond the tribal folkthought of the Israelites, it has survived to mitigate the harshness of life in western civilization. Important in its own right, the social thought of the Hebrews becomes crucial when it is properly viewed with Graeco-Roman thought as an abutment upon which rests the Christian church. Charles F. Kent has referred to the Hebrews as the "leading social teacher of the human race." [4] Stirred by the centuries-old problem of surviving the harsh dictates of nature's niggardliness and the cruelty of conquerors, a succession of great Hebrew prophets challenged the rectitude of a social system that permitted so much suffering. Whitehead describes these prophets as "one of the few groups of men who decisively altered history in an intimate sense." [5] They proclaimed the sovereignty of Yahweh over all men and clothed

---

[3] Emory S. Bogardus, The Development of Social Thought, New York, Longmans, Green and Company, 1948, p. 26.

[4] Charles Foster Kent, The Social Teachings of the Prophets and Jesus, New York, Charles Scribners Sons, 1917, p. 4.

[5] Whitehead, op. cit., pp. 62–63.

him with a responsive concern for the social conditions of the Hebrews under Egyptian tyranny. The prophets condemned unequal
distribution of wealth, deceit, and lack of compassion for human suffering. To all forms of selfish privilege the prophets held up the threat
of Yahweh's wrath. In place of avarice and self-seeking, Hebrew social
thought put justice and love, with the attendant obligations which
justice and love implied.

Slavery was accepted in the Old Testament—and it would remain
for the Greeks to discover freedom as an intellectual ideal, an ideal
that required more than 2,000 years for its realization. Furthermore,
the prominent place given to personal relationships and individual
ethics in Hebrew thought resulted in the virtual absence of a true
social philosophy. The contribution of the Hebrews is the "heart"
of modern social thought, a legacy of the awakening urged by the
prophets.

Graeco-Roman Social Thought

The six centuries that preceded, and the four centuries that followed, the birth of Christ saw the flowering of Greek and Roman culture, and then their synthesis. The social problems of this period
produced responses that profoundly influenced the social basis of
modern thought. An explosion of genius in the fourth century before
Christ saw the Greeks throw off the restraints of hand-me-down codes
and shibboleths, and turn instead to a complete trust in human reason. The guides to social action that the Greeks prepared were beyond
human realization, perhaps because the Greeks, particularly Plato and
Aristotle, realized the many threats to the survival of the Athenian
democracy and constructed an ideal deliverance from them. The deliverance would rely heavily on the freedom of human intelligence
and the willingness of persons to restrain emotional dispositions. Few
would deny that the theoretical constructs of Plato and Aristotle addressed complete answers to the problem of human emotions, even
though the implementation of their ideal patterns would violate the
sanctity with which western civilization has clothed individual choice.

Humanism and respect for reason had received attention from the
Greek literati and occasional leaders prior to the fifth-century enlightenment. Aeschylus had lamented that brotherhood and harmony
could not come into fruition for the human race. Euripides anticipated
the feminist movement and also spoke in favor of the poor and the
feeble. Solon, in the office of dictator, took state action to mitigate

the harshness of the laws. But the generation of Pericles (469–431 B.C.) saw Athenian democracy perfected, and when it deteriorated, the tyranny with which it was displaced stimulated the profound reflections of Plato and Aristotle.

It is important to understand the nature of the tyranny from which Plato and Aristotle recoiled. The many city-states were, in the beginning, monarchies and notable chiefly for their separateness from each other. Within the city-states crises—usually in the form of severe food shortages—drove the populace to seek relief through a change of government. Thus, the monarchies were succeeded by oligarchies and military dictatorships, a few eventually becoming democracies. Among those few that became democracies. Athens is singularly noteworthy for the excellent achievements of her citizens in many fields of endeavor. Our concern is with the excellent thought produced by the Athenans in connection with social relationships.

Early in the seventh century B.C. a harsh code of laws had been developed by Draco which materially strengthened the power of the state. The code was a necessary supplement to the customary law, since the latter had proved powerless in dealing with feuds and tribal murder. In the following generation a reaction against the harsh principles of the code brought Solon into power. He broke the power of the nobility by reforming certain features of the slave code, limiting land ownership, and extending citizenship to artisans. The fifth century B.C. was a century of struggle against Persia, and the successful conclusion of the war by Athens brought with it the brief "golden age" of Pericles. The aristocracy broken, the commercial and industrial classes came into power and pressed for democratic reforms. But this era also marked the beginning of fratricidal war between Athens and Sparta. This turn of events upset the moody Plato, who withdrew from Athenian affairs and set about the formulation of principles that would guide the ideal state, the Republic, with human relationships based on human reason. The fundamental principle was that, knowing what is virtuous, a wise man could only act virtuously. The idea had been Socrates,' and for his pains in rousing the Athenians against ignorance he became the victim of a judicial murder. Plato made the disjointed arguments of Socrates into a system. Citizens do depend on each other for mutually supporting conduct, he reasoned, and citizens will behave to the social advantage when they have been instructed to recognize the social good. But the capacity to know and understand is not general, as Plato inferred from his deteriorating Athens. Hence,

the ideal Republic must ascertain the qualifications of those who would make decisions, and educate those who do not participate in the making of decisions nonetheless to obey them for the good of the state.[6] The Republic is an ideal recipe for the state—unrealizable, but useful in the sense that earthly states (mere shadows of the ideal Republic) may be compared with it.

In addition to the *Republic*, Plato made contributions to social thought in other dialogues. The *Phaedo* contains sentiments that are less authoritarian than those in the *Republic*. Plato observes that a general harmony of inharmonious parts cannot exist; that "a harmony does not lead the parts or elements which make up the harmony, but follows them." [7] The concept of the *general* welfare being dependent upon mutually coöperative *specific* welfares is implied in this statement. Plato developed the idea of the human soul and reasoned that human souls were equivalent. He was a slaveowner; but it is difficult to read the *Phaedo* and others of his dialogues without gaining the impression that slavery and the compulsory subordination of individual wills to the state will are logical inconsistencies. Whitehead sums his impression of Plato's essence in these words:

> The creation of the world—said Plato—is the victory of persuasion over force. The worth of men consists in their liability to persuasion. They can persuade and be persuaded by the disclosure of alternatives, the better and the worse. Civilization is the maintenance of social order, by its own inherent persuasiveness as embodying the nobler alternative. The recourse to force, however unavoidable, is a disclosure of the failure of civilization . . .[8]

Whitehead's analysis shows Plato approaching the idea of freedom as an ideal in a hesitant way. Slavery was a functional requisite of the Athenian society and Plato was himself a slaveowner; but the ideal which he derived went beyond these familiarities and endured until a later period when men would be more willing to square ideals and actualities with each other.

---

[6] Plato's ideal state is authoritarian, with the emphasis upon each participant knowing his proper station. At the small, decision-making top are the philosopher-kings, especially selected for their tasks and provided with sufficient income and power so that they have no unsatisfied passions. Free from fear, avarice, and all base passions, they can then only serve the public good. Plato sought through just laws and education to remove all causes of disharmony among men. Neither wealth nor power could be too sparse or become too great; land and even wives and children were held as wards of the state at the ruling-class level.

[7] Plato, *Republic*, The Harvard Classics, New York, P. F. Collier's Sons, 1909, Vol. II, p. 86.

[8] Whitehead, *op. cit.*, p. 105.

Plato's student, Aristotle, also concerned himself with the social good, starting with the actual and the concrete and proceeding in the manner of the inductivist. That is to say, he began with live problems rather than with abstract generalizations. Man, he observed, was necessarily a social animal because his needs were so vast and his means of satisfying them so inadequate. Aristotle appeared able to accept the authoritarianism of his teacher's *Republic*, but he rejected communism in property and wives. Moreover, Aristotle's *Politics* lacks the exclusiveness of the *Republic*, he being willing, for example, to accept any of three forms of government as good under appropriate conditions.

Aristotle was not a system builder but an "anatomist" who skipped around among various topics in political and moral philosophy, giving of his comments. His major theme is the golden mean, the concept of avoiding both excess and insufficiency. Gross inequities in wealth, power, fear, honor, respect for the law, etc., would, he thought, bring decay and revolution. Aristotle would, therefore, give a very large role to the middle class in state affairs. In their hands change would be gradual and the state would be secure. No organizational form for the state could be proof against individual passion and chicane; but a virtuous middle class, wherein the extremes of poverty, fear, etc., were absent, might make any political form effective.

The social thought of Plato and Aristotle dealt primarily with the definition of the elements of social organization that would best accommodate man. Their judgments share many common elements and are in each case based on a view of the nature of human nature. Plato was explicit about human nature; men might look alike, but they conceal three creatures: a many-headed monster with both tame and wild heads (desires and passions), a lion (the spirited quality which will fight for food, country, and an ideal), and a human being (the rational element). The task of life, according to Plato, was the elevation of the rational man. This view is shared by Aristotle. Happiness depends upon understanding, and the implication is that the many, the aggregate population, cannot understand. Their task, once their intellectual measure has been taken by the state, is to assume their place, whatever it be in the social system.

Many profound thinkers have probed the meaning of Hebraic and Hellenic thought for western civilization. The two strains entered Europe via the Roman conquerors and Christianity. Their fusion into

Christianity is yet to be discussed; but certain contrasts and meanings might well be pointed out at this point.

Wrongdoing was viewed by the Hebrews as an insult to Yahweh, hence was horrible and nonerasable; the Greeks viewed wrongdoing with permissiveness and tolerance. The Hebrews began with God, the Greeks with man. Matthew Arnold analyzes the contrasts in these words: "The uppermost idea with Hellenism is to see things as they really are; the uppermost idea with Hebraism is conduct and obedience. The Greek quarrel with the body and its desires is that they hinder right thinking; the Hebrew quarrel with them is that they hinder right acting." [9] Another viewpoint stresses the extremely high regard with which the Greeks held man. "What is man that thou art mindful of him? The Greeks gave proud answers to this question. . . . From the beginning they said in effect that man is the proper study of mankind, if not the measure of all things. Man was the main actor in Homer; the heroes were dearer to him than the gods. Man was the subject of the incomparable sculpture of the Greeks. . . . For all their living ideals they looked to great men, who spoke for themselves rather than as privy councillors of deity." [10] In the survey of social thought that follows, it will be seen that a view of man approximating the Hebraic appears to have dominated western social thought for nearly twelve centuries after the birth of Christ; but the development of western thought since the Renaissance has been along Hellenic themes.

The route by which Hebraic and Hellenic thought entered the culture of Europe was Rome. Rome, the sole survivor of three centuries of international wars, constructed a vehicle of authority which provided for the transmission of selected and modified Greek thought to the future. Greek thought influenced a wider audience after the Roman conquest and its concepts became more legalistic. The Christianization of Rome in the fourth century admitted the influence of Hebraism with the Greek, both of which were by this time fused in Christian thought.

The Roman contribution in law is often cited as its greatest contribution to western civilization; but the social thought of such men as Cicero, Marcus Aurelius, and Epictetus should not be obscured by this fact. Cicero discoursed on human nature and the fundamental sameness of men, concluding that they were led by common urgings

---

[9] Matthew Arnold, *Culture and Anarchy*, New York, The Macmillan Company, 1896, pp. 111–112.

[10] Herbert J. Muller, *The Uses of the Past*, New York, Oxford University Press, 1952, p. 137.

and would respond to humane treatment. In the spirit of Plato's *Republic*, Cicero sought to discover those principles of conduct which would make Rome the ideal state. His principles deal largely with that technique of administering justice which would inspire continuous loyalty. It was the Stoics, chiefly Marcus Aurelius and Epictetus, who enriched Roman social thought with their ethical system which stressed human similarities. Brinton credits the Stoics with the foundation of natural law, natural law defined as "not what is, but what ought to be" for all peoples.[11] Stoicism had its origin with the Greek philosopher Zeno, but its real value was achieved after the Roman conquest.

Wrongdoing was clearly a failure of reason in the view of the Roman Stoics, and they always referred to reason as "the ruling faculty." Stoics assumed that the most coveted possession was a virtuous soul— "Have I done something for the general interest? Well then I have had my reward"[12]—and their distinguishing idea is personal resignation to whatever life should mete out to the individual. Thus, Marcus Aurelius says: "If gods care not for me and my children, there is a reason for it."[13] Vengeance was excluded from the stoicism of Epictetus and Aurelius; Epictetus illustrates the principle as follows: " 'My brother ought not to have treated me thus.' True: but *he* must see to that. However he may treat me, I must deal rightly with him. This is what lies with me, what none can hinder."[14]

In brief, the Stoics supposed evil to be within man, and the ideal was to conquer the evil, live virtuously the part that is given to one, and know that one is then living as best he can—reward enough. Marcus Aurelius Antoninus as emperor practiced his philosophy, approaching the ideal of compassion in the Christian sense. No libertarianism emerged from Roman Stoicism; however, harsh judgment of the Roman military dictatorship is somewhat moderated by the maturation of Zeno's ideas among the Romans.

Christian Social Thought

Adolf von Harnack describes Christianity as the "fruit of Hebrew prophecy, growing in the soil of Greek philosophy, cultivated by Ro-

---

[11] Crane Brinton, *Ideas and Men*, New York, Prentice-Hall, 1950, p. 133.

[12] Marcus Aurelius Antoninus, *The Meditations of Marcus Aurelius*, The Harvard Classics, New York, P. F. Collier's Sons, 1909, Vol. II, p. 290.

[13] *Ibid.*, p. 251.

[14] "The Golden Sayings of Epictetus," from abstract of Arrian's *Discourses and Encheiridion*, The Harvard Classics, New York, P. F. Collier's Sons, 1909, Vol. II, p. 153.

man administrative genius." [15] Atkins notes that Christianity began with three great inheritances: a hope (expectation of the Messiah as promised by the prophets), a song (the Hebraic psalms sounding the heights and depths of the ways of God), and its law (ethics of the Old Testament).[16] The synthesis of the Greek philosophy and Hebraic testament in Christianity is accepted by all modern scholars. One has not dealt at all with the essence of Christianity, however, merely by searching out its origins. The persuasiveness of its major theme and the authoritativeness of its ethical constructs have extended its influence many times beyond the influence of those themes and constructs which it borrowed. It is hardly an exaggeration to say that the primary agency in humanizing western social thought has been Christianity. Whitehead sees the appeal of Christianity in the simple affective symbols of its story: ". . . there can be no doubt as to what elements in the record have evoked a response from all that is best in human nature. The mother, the child, and the bare manger: the lowly man, homeless and self-forgetful, with his message of peace, love, and sympathy: the suffering, the agony, the tender words as life ebbed, the final despair: and the whole with the authority of supreme victory." [17]

The teachings of Jesus were as simple as the symbols of the Christian story: love of one's neighbor and one's enemies; compassion for the poor, the meek, and the humble; and the life of service. If the themes are simple, they have also proved unattainable—perhaps progressively so—and the impossible height of Christianity's ideals has constituted a gadfly to those peoples who have come under its influence, ever holding up critically the distance that needs be traveled to the ideal society. One should expect that the social implications of Christianity would be immense, but the gospel of love scarcely fired multitudes of people to assume lives of charity and self-sacrifice in its early history. And the survival of Jesus' teachings as reported in the Gospels of Matthew, Mark, Luke, and John seems to have depended upon some stalwart practitioners, among them Saul of Tarsus.

Saul was a Neoplatonist and through his efforts Christianity entered the Roman empire with added Hellenism, mysticism, and authoritativeness. The product was harsh and inconsiderate of the problems with which this world saddled the average man, probably because Saul

---

[15] Adolf von Harnack, *Die Mission und Ausbreitung des Christentums in den ersten drei Jahrhunderten*, Leipzig, J. C. Hinricks, 1902, p. 12.

[16] Gains Glenn Atkins, *Making of the Christian Mind*, New York, Richard R. Smith, 1931, p. 1.

[17] Whitehead, *op. cit.*, p. 214.

thought the apocalyptic end of the earthly kingdom was near at hand. His contribution was to give the teachings of Jesus unity, appeal, and authority. He probably did no greater service to the Christian religion than to add to it the promise of posthumous salvation which he inferred from the Gospels. Through his efforts the Christian movement was kept alive while it achieved an organization based on the model of civil government in the Roman empire. The organization was achieved at the hands of the Christian Fathers, whose first important success came in 325 with the recognition of the Bishop of Rome as chief spokesman for Christianity. Under the guidance of the sympathetic Constantine a creed was formulated that all Christians could profess in common. During the next century, although the destruction of the Roman empire was complete, the Christian religion gained increased significance as agencies of secular authority disappeared.

Medieval Social Thought

On the ruins of Rome, plundered by the northern barbarians, a new culture arose. Throughout the eight centuries during which this culture matured, the single principle of continuing authority was Christianity as it had developed at Rome. Social thought was largely influenced by one man—Augustine. No period in history shows the dominance of a single man's thought in the way that the medieval period was dominated by the thought of St. Augustine. The deductions of Augustine, Bishop of Hippo, gave final, authoritative cast to the work of the Church fathers.

Augustine's *Church History, Confessions, City of God,* and other works set forth the formula for salvation, a concern which loomed preëminently in the minds of medieval men. The pagans at Rome had sought to explain the destruction of Rome in 410 by the fact that their placations of the gods had been forbidden. Augustine came to the defense of the Christian faith with his masterful differentiation between the city of men and the city of God.

An understanding of the consuming importance with which the salvation of the soul was viewed by the medieval Church, following Augustine, accounts for the unwillingness of the Church to meliorate the pain and suffering of this world; by comparison with deserving the eternal kingdom, reducing earthly suffering was an insignificant operation.

Men were by nature wicked, according to Augustine; they had been cursed with original sin from the start. Furthermore, they could be

delivered from this curse only through the grace of God. The medieval Christian set himself to the task of beseeching God's pardon for sinfulness. Sin stood between man and salvation and sin was a matter of personal responsibility, no excuses accepted. The pitfalls of the environment were part of the accepted vale of tears and were to be avoided. To assist him, the medieval Christian was provided with priests and sacraments, both exclusive with the Roman Church. The latitude permitted men in the exercise of creative thought was slight for the obvious reason that it was unnecessary, the primary values of life having already been authoritatively determined. A serious change in this official viewpoint did not take place until the thirteenth century, when Thomas Aquinas defended the thesis that God intended the world to be a livable place, and implied the use of human reason to fulfill man's mission on earth.

It would be erroneous to view society during the Middle Ages as though the individual were wholly a pawn in the quest for personal salvation. The security which a well-stratified society under a "revealed" charter affords must be appreciated. Brinton summarizes a defense of medieval society: "In ideal the Middle Ages provided for men on earth a well-organized and orderly life: the Church took care of men's souls, the feudal nobility preserved civil order, the peasants and craftsmen worked unenviously at useful tasks; a beautifully ordered nexus of rights and duties bound each man to each, from swineherd to emperor and pope; each man knew his place, was secure in his place, happy in it." [18] Brinton goes on to observe that "there were gangster wars among the feudal barons, corruption, laziness, worldiness, and worse among the clergy, poverty among the great masses, endemic disease, frequent famine, outbursts of class warfare—in short, and at best, the customary misbehavior and unhappiness one finds in the human race, perhaps in some ways rather worse than usual." [19] If this system of social relations placed people in a structure which provided stability, a high price was paid for the stability thus gained. The price consisted of the creative energy that was not employed and the cures, beneficent social practices, and goods which went undiscovered. One should not hold up to medieval society the ideal of egalitarianism; but the stability and moderation which are associated with the existence of an articulate middle class in nineteenth-century Europe were sorely lacking in medieval society. The status of knight was

[18] Brinton, *Op. cit.*, p. 201.
[19] *Ibid.*, p. 201.

ideally open to all males on the basis of ability, though it was the rare peasant's son who made his way to knighthood—a consummation virtually assured the male progeny of nobility. Certain rights were guaranteed the peasant—against arbitrary treatment by his lord and against forfeiture of his land—but it is important that the basis for these rights was traditional and had no substance in humane consideration of the peasant as a person. The ideal life in medieval society was permitted two forms—the warrior knight or the cloistered monk. Typically, the fundamental Christian doctrine of love was ignored in pursuit of the forms which, through the agency of the Church, would assure salvation. Randall, describing the plight of the peasant, observes: ". . . the knight and the Crusader took his place in the Christian tradition beside the monk and saint. He was the goal of the upper, landholding class. If we turn to the peasant and his aspirations, the darkest side of the Middle Ages is revealed. For him, strictly speaking, there could be no ideal; Christian resignation was his lot, and human contempt." [20] While the medieval Church urged care of the poor and the destitute, the objective was the well-being of the benefactor's soul, not the relief of human misery per se. James Westfall Thompson analyzes the role of the Church in social service:

The charity of the Church was not wholly disinterested. One may readily admit its large activities in poor relief, the social service afforded by its hospitals and orphanages. But its own practices of economic exploitation often induced the poverty which it was called upon to relieve, and it is questionable whether in proportion to its enormous resources the Church actually contributed as much as lay society to poor relief. The social dimension of chivalry in which the knight was bound to service of the weak and defenceless was accomplished by the Church in part to protect its own property and peasants, who were being destroyed in the fratricidal wars of otherwise unoccupied barons.[21]

It can be concluded that the vast power of the medieval Church might have been used to moderate the misery of life for the mass of people, but was not. The blame rests on the assumptions of the Christian faith as fashioned by Augustine. But two monks, Saints Francis and Dominic, denounced the preocupation of the Church with its economic fortunes and turned their attention to the poverty-stricken. The

[20] John Herman Randall, Jr., The Making of the Modern Mind, Boston, Houghton Mifflin Company, 1926, p. 88.
[21] James Westfall Thompson, An Economic and Social History of the Middle Ages, New York, Century Company, 1928, p. 684.

lives and teachings of the Begging and Teaching Friars were devoted
to the idea of humanity to man for its own sake. Thompson maintains
that St. Francis and the movement he inspired saved the Church from
extinction through corruption.[22] In spite of the Franciscans, the human spirit found few ministers to aid its earthly misfortunes, since
they were not eternal misfortunes, and the medieval *Zeitgeist* must be
indicted for its cruel omissions. To the apologist's insistence that the
"times" were cruel, Muller remarks: "It remains cruelty, however; if
'the times' make men what they are, they are also made by men; and
in any event these were religious times when Christianity was at the
peak of its power. They force the question of the quality of medieval
religion." [23]

The social and economic policies of feudalism gave way before the
quickening of trade and commerce which characterized the twelfth
and thirteenth centuries. A social system based on town life brought
a new set of interests which opposed the papal bureaucracy. A world
view which stressed the worth-whileness of life on earth arose in defense of commercialism. In its broad sweep from the twelfth century
to the sixteenth, this movement is called humanism.

Humanism

Virtually the whole of modern social thought can be referred to as
humanistic, signifying the acceptance of man in terms of his possibilities rather than of his wickedness. On the assumption that man's
possibilities were very great, movements developed which sought to
enlarge the area of his choices and cushion somewhat the hazards of
this world. Abelard began this reëxamination of basic assumptions
when he called attention to the numerous contradictions within the
medieval Church. Some of those who heard him returned to the
Greek literati for their answers to the goals of life. Out of the activities of many Abelards and those who responded to them, there developed a "Renaissance" of Greek thought and a serious questioning of
the old social order. The groups to whose interests government had
been most sympathetic were replaced by new groups, first the mer-
chants and later the industrialists and financiers. The working out of
this succession of the bourgeoisie to power left the masses of people
dependent on new masters; and the new masters possessed neither the

[22] *Ibid.*, p. 694.
[23] Muller, *op. cit.*, p. 259.

tradition of chivalry nor the *noblesse oblige* which had existed under the suzerainty of Mother Church.

The new commercial and industrial order developed its own thought about social relationship. New concepts of God and the state and the relationship of each to men arose. The dominant theme of social thought was individualism—a reaction from ecclesiastical socialism and a direct product of the Renaissance. In its wake fell monarchies, landed aristocracies, and ecclesiastical privilege. The specific encroachments of this powerful awakening cannot be reviewed here; but the several new beliefs about social relationships which fulfilled individualism can be recalled briefly. One note of caution is to be observed: it should not be thought that those who were immediately inspired by the Renaissance and Reformation arrived at our modern concepts of man's importance. Such libertarian notions as self-government and the social-welfare state are three centuries ahead of our present discussion. Into the eighteenth century common men obeyed absolutely a monarch whose power was absolute. However, the steps toward the modern conception of human "just deserts," though hesitant, were positive.

The Protestant Reformation gave rise to a positive doctrine which neatly fitted the interests of the new commercial and industrial age— Calvinism. So much of this doctrine as dignified work and busyness, and held sloth and disorganized activity the worst of sins, gave a bend to social thought and thinking which survives to this day in countries that came under the Puritan influence. The results were profound. Those countries which lived under Puritanism gained a head start in moneymaking and the elaboration of a political and social creed that would support this master goal. The Reformation thus both fed on and reinforced concepts of individualism.

The humanists had prepared a path which the two generations that included Huss and Wycliffe broadened. The Reformation was in the direct line of this tradition, as has been observed. A whole line of political thinkers, moreover, drew on the same source of sustenance, but with a more secular interest. Nicolo Machiavelli dramatically broke from the unquestioning acceptance of divine causation and described in *The Prince* how harshly human nature actually operated as he observed it. The same work is a guidebook to monarchs on the methods whereby underlings may be manipulated. In various works he anticipated the authoritarian and the paternalistic states of the modern era. The social thought of Thomas Hobbes is similar to that of Machia-

velli, though a century later. He described a most uninspiring view of human nature, being no more sanguine about human compassion than Machiavelli. He assumed human motives to be dominated by desire for gain, safety, and reputation. In his essay on the state of human nature, Hobbes insists that "during the time men live without a common power to keep them all in awe, they are in that condition called war, and such a war as is every man against every man." [24] Men naturally inveigh against each other, and their conduct is punctuated by "force and fraud" except as they are cowed by a superior force. It remained, in Hobbes' view, only for men to endow an absolute authority with power over all. Absolute authority also received approval from John Locke, who so profoundly influenced the American Constitution of 1787, but with many reservations. The protection of property —foremost among the interests of the state—might require absolute authority; but only as freely determined by free men. Once the authority had been determined, however, the duty of absolute obedience remained, at least until the authority should transgress the limits of right conduct in office. The duty of authority was to protect the basic rights of man—life, liberty, and property. Both Hobbes and Locke had suggested a type of social compact between authority and the governed. But in the hands of Rousseau this contract became founded on an amended view of basic rights, the "life, liberty, and property" becoming "life, liberty, and the pursuit of happiness." Simply on the fact of his humanity man had these rights. The social contract came about between an authority bound to observe these basic rights and the governed through the governed voluntarily surrendering personal liberty in favor of liberty to obey the duly constituted authority. Rousseau adds a factor lacking in the social thought of Machiavelli, Hobbes, and Locke—an optimistic view of human nature. If man were corrupt, it could not be owing to his nature, but rather to the unnatural condition of his environment. Rousseau struck at many social evils, most important of all slavery.

The generation which followed Rousseau was stirred by the compulsory degradation of men into slavery, and the British government abolished the slave trade in 1808 and 1833. In the nineteenth century this great step which had found its first inspiration in Plato would be accomplished by all major nations. It would be erroneous to assert that the writings of sensitive men produced this result without assist-

---

[24] Thomas S. Hobbes, "Of Man, Being the First Part of Leviathan," The Harvard Classics, New York, P. F. Collier's Sons, 1909, Vol. 34, p. 404.

ance. Steam power and democracy played the major roles; but democracy was itself a formulation of sensitive souls. Whitehead gives the movement of democracy in the nineteenth century the credit for facing the question of slavery "explicitly and with thoroughness"; but it is to the Methodists led by John Wesley that the "supreme achievement" owes its power. The Methodists, says Whitehead, "made the conception of the brotherhood of man and the importance of men, a vivid reality. They had produced the final effective force which thereafter would make slavery impossible." [25] In their ministry among the common men the Methodists effectuated an idea 2,000 years old.[26]

It is highly fortuitous that the humanitarian doctrines of democracy, Quakerism and Methodism, successfully produced the British decrees of 1808 and 1833. Opposed to its outlook were arrayed a host of social theorists who drew their philosophical underpinnings from the eighteenth-century Enlightenment. Throughout the nineteenth century they promulgated doctrines inimical to social ministry and humanitarian relief of human misery. In common with humanitarianism they share a belief in the natural goodness of man, man liberated not from social misery but rather from interference of the state and from the meddling of social reformers. In this tradition were Adam Smith, Thomas Malthus, David Ricardo, John Stuart Mill, and Charles Darwin. They differed from the humanitarian theorists in terms of the avenues through which progress would be assured.

Adam Smith, the first of these tough-minded rationalists, sought to ride two horses simultaneously—one of compassion and the other of individual aloofness from social misery. He thought that men, under the minimum of government restraints, could produce the best social good through individual action. He defended selfish, personal quest because the individual self-seeker was "led by an invisible hand to promote an end [the social good] which was no part of his intention." [27] No believer in subsidization of separate classes and always fearful of antisocial control, public or private, Smith assumed that enlightened self-interest would produce a larger net progress for mankind than restrained self-interest. The state could not interfere to relieve social misery else the beneficial results of self-seeking be upset. On the heels

[25] Whitehead, op. cit., p. 28.

[26] The formulation of a modern movement to secure the abolition of slavery probably belongs to John Woolman, an American Quaker, who viewed it as an anti-Christian practice (1793).

[27] Adam Smith, The Wealth of Nations, The Harvard Classics, New York, P. F. Collier's Sons, 1909, Vol. 10, pp. 351–352.

of Adam Smith, Thomas R. Malthus wrote his famous *Essay on Population*, the effect of which was to remove any lingering doubts about the efficacy of the individualistic order. In brief, Malthus argued that human fecundity always would outstrip the food supply, for the simple reason that the former increased according to geometric progression, and the latter according to arithmetical progression, and a geometrical progression will always outstrip an arithmetical progression. Thus, any social doctoring to meliorate suffering would be self-defeating, since it would increase population growth, pressure on the food supply, and thus eventual starvation. It remained only for Charles Darwin to publish in 1859 his meticulous findings about evolution of species. His followers then inferred that through the extermination of the unfit the progress of the human species was assured. Spencer offered the solace that "nature is a little cruel that it may be very kind." [28] In part this harsh doctrine was worked out through application to larger units such as nations and races, though the results were scarcely more considerate of the human rights offered by Rousseau. It seems a tribute to the compassion in men's souls that they were stirred to hold the humanitarian fort against the new scripture of natural law. With Jeremy Bentham, John Stuart Mill, and August Comte, the humanitarian case received considerable support, and the movement would gain a militant ideal with the socialists.

Jeremy Bentham and John Stuart Mill might be discussed at length in another kind of survey of social thought. But it is enough to observe here that they championed an organization of English working men called the Chartists, Bentham arguing that human affairs should be guided through government to the ideal of "the greatest good for the greatest number" and Mill questioning whether it were not social laws, rather than natural (unchangeable) laws, that stood behind human misery. Auguste Comte drew up a hierarchy of the sciences, putting at its apex a new "science of society" called sociology. The goal of the sciences was nothing less than the reconstruction of society. Commenting on the role of Bentham and Comte in social thought, Whitehead asserts: "Most of what has been practically effective in morals, in religion, or in political theory, from their day to this derived strength from one or the other of these men." [29]

At the beginning of this chapter it was stated that the quickening of pace in human affairs might result in social ideas that departed sub-

---

[28] Herbert Spencer, *Social Statics*, New York, D. Appleton Century, 1896, p. 149.
[29] Whitehead, *op. cit.*, p. 46.

stantially from previous expositions. The nineteenth century was such a period. Exercising harsh justice according to the formulas of beneficence prepared by Adam Smith, Thomas R. Malthus, Charles Darwin, and others, the factory system swallowed up the meager control which men had over their affairs, deprived them of their craftsmanship, and bade their forbearance in the face of periodic economic crises. No social vestige of pastoral life was so sacred that it escaped sacrifice to the new industrial age. In men of Alexander Hamilton's stature it produced advocacy of child labor.

The bitterness of the new industrial order produced inflammatory doctrines in some sensitive souls. Karl Marx was one of these. From the social theory of Smith, Ricardo, and Mill, the philosophy of process fashioned by Hegel, and the indictments of exploitation of Sismondi and Rodbertus, Marx gave to the world a bitter *Weltanschauung*. He advocated revolution to rid the world of capitalism. All evils, Marx observed, were related to the class struggle which was the activating element in human history. The new capitalistic order was torn with internal inconsistencies, hence it would fail; but in its death throes it would inflict ever greater miseries on the wage slaves, dominion over which it would not surrender. The proletariat, therefore, should seize the reins of power and strive for the egalitarian society promised in the final stage of socialism, communism. Possibly the two most influential men of the nineteenth century were Darwin and Marx, and the movements to which they gave rise (social Darwinism and socialism) are the obvious antitheses of the twentieth century. Marxism rejected the individualism drawn from the Renaissance and Reformation, which would liberate one's talents to the end of winning the competitive race, and in its place put an "upside down" medieval society—service to the central principle of authority, but with the "have-nots" at the helm. The debate still rages as to whether the present-day advocates of Marxism in the Soviet Union and Chinese People's Republic truly draw their spirit from his doctrine. The debate concerns such questions as, Was it really Marx's wish that, since the existing social system corrupted men, it should be stamped out in blood? Did he intend that the hard-core cadre should dedicate itself to oversee the achievement of communism under tyranny? The answers, if negative, are of only academic interest, for the governments of the Soviet Union and the Chinese People's Republic have removed the sanctity of the individual and his choices which required twenty-five centuries for their establishment. The doctrines of Lenin, Trotsky,

and Stalin properly belong not within the present discussion of humanitarianism, but with modern authoritarianism.

The mid-nineteenth century saw the idea of man's worth established and his natural rights accepted. The logical next step was the extension of the decision-making process to include the mass of citizens. In Britain this quest occupied the whole nineteenth century, but was complete (except for the granting of the franchise to women) by 1884. Other European states sought the same democratic processes more hesitantly. But it was in the United States that the movement for effecting government by the whole of the citizenry called forth the most colorful advocates. The sponsorship of the humanitarian and democratic ideals passed into American hands for nearly a century, beginning about 1850. It was based upon European thought and, of course, was paralleled by less forceful movements in Europe. We shall trace the several major phases of American social thought, considering the European counterpart only in terms of the reversion to authoritarianism in Italy, Germany, and Russia.

It is common to separate the development of American thought into twenty or more discrete phases, beginning with the colonial era. We cannot afford the luxury even of an adequate sampling of the rich literature in this survey. Our analysis, therefore, will be restricted to the great contributions since Jefferson which, in the opinion of the authors, have carried the European heritage of the social conscience closer to maturity. Specifically, our concerns will be the place of the common man and his social and economic roles, the supplementation of "natural order" to arrive at a higher "moral order," the alleviation of social misery through state action, and the American compromise with extremes of European socialism and authoritarianism.

American Social Thought

Many factors combined to give a new, extra-European cast to American social thought. The tradition of dissent and venturesomeness, the continent waiting to be exploited, the opportunities for the persevering worker, and the behavior patterns that grew out of the frontier—all gave an enthusiasm to American individualism that was unmatched in Europe. Furthermore, when the need for reform became widely recognized, the reforming energy of American social leaders displayed a vigor hardly approached in Europe.

We shall begin with Thomas Jefferson because he was the first to break from the economic and social doctrines of Europe which based

their appeal on the fact that they were consistent with natural laws. It is important, also, that the fundamental beliefs which he entertained about the rights of man are the beliefs which have endured and guided social thought in America. The Piedmont-bred Jefferson chose the natural rights of man as posed by Rousseau rather than the statement of Locke, and his choice has endured in the Declaration of Independence. A quarter century later, when Jefferson was elected President, he stood at loggerheads with snobbery, special privilege, concentrated economic and political power, and limitations on popular decision making. Professor Parrington paints this picture of Jefferson:

Back of the figure of Jefferson with his aristocratic head set on a plebeian frame, was the philosophy of a new age and a new people—an age and a people not yet come to the consistency of maturity, but feeling a way through experience to solid achievement. Far more completely than any other American of his generation he embodied the idealisms of the great revolution—its faith in human nature, its economic individualism, its conviction that here in America through the instruments of political democracy, the lot of the common men should somehow be made better.[30]

Jefferson's "common man" was a yeoman farmer, and a search of his writings will scarcely reveal a love for humanity irrespective of some qualifications—a conviction which will be encountered later. He thought, rather, that in comparison with artificial aristocracies (based on wealth and birth rather than on talent and virtue) and monarchy, popular decisions would better check the powers of greed and avarice. A letter written by Jefferson in January 1787 contains one of his numerous statements on the subject: "I am persuaded myself that the good sense of the people will always be found to be the best army. They may be led astray for a moment, but will soon correct themselves. The people are the only censors of their governors. . . ."[31] With the lines of communication between legislators and citizens free, Jefferson expected extraordinary results from popular government. Apparently he did not foresee the domination of political life by the townsmen, and he judged the possibilities of democracy only as the agrarian citizenry should predominate. But the full force of "French ideas" entered America through Jefferson (and Thomas Paine) and informed subsequent generations of the right of all men

[30] Vernon Louis Parrington, *Main Currents of American Thought*, New York, Harcourt, Brace and Company, 1930, Vol. I, p. 343.

[31] Philip S. Fower (ed.), *Basic Writing of Thomas Jefferson* (letter to Colonel Edward Carrington, January 16, 1787), New York, John Wiley & Sons, 1944, p. 550.

to the "pursuit of happiness." It is Parrington, again, who pays Jefferson the highest respect, observing: "To all who profess faith in the Democratic ideal Jefferson is a perennial inspiration. A free soul, he loved freedom enough to deny it none; an idealist, he believed that the welfare of the whole, and not the prosperity of any group, is the single end of government. He was our first great leader to erect a political philosophy native to the economics and experience of America, as he was the first to break consciously with the past." [32]

Two generations after Jefferson's inauguration, his social viewpoint was expressed by Abraham Lincoln under conditions which Jefferson had not anticipated. The industrial basis of future American society was already clear and the "townsman" was the typical citizen. Lincoln accepted the realities of moneymaking as the source of American strength, but believed sufficiently in the French ideas underlying the Declaration of Independence to place them ahead of laissez-faire considerations. In a famous speech opposing the Dred Scott decision he observed, concerning the authors of the Declaration of Independence:

They meant to set up a standard maxim for free society, which should be familiar to all and revered by all. The assertion that "all men are created equal" was of no practical use in effecting our separation from Great Britain; and it was placed in the Declaration, not for that, but for future use. Its authors meant it to be—as, thank God, it is now proving itself—a stumbling block to those who in after times might seek to turn a free people back into the hateful paths of despotism. They knew the proneness of prosperity to breed tyrants, and they meant when such should reappear in this fair land and commence their vocation, they should find at least one hard nut to crack.[33]

A conservative lawyer who believed in the property rights of masters to their slaves, Lincoln also reaffirmed, in his first inaugural address, Jefferson's belief in the right of the people to overthrow the government by revolution. When the moral urgency of the slave issue became too great, and the union was imperiled, he seized the power necessary to achieve the course of action that was consistent with Jeffersonian tradition. Lincoln's speech at Gettysburg, familiar enough to the reader, is a classic of American democratic thought and Jeffersonian idealism.

[32] Parrington, *op. cit.*, Vol. I, p. 355.
[33] Abraham Lincoln, "Speech at Springfield, Ill." June 26, 1857, *The Collected Works of Abraham Lincoln*, Vol. II, Roy P. Basler (ed.), New Brunswick, N.J., Rutgers Univ. Press, pp. 327–328.

EARLY NINETEENTH-CENTURY CRITICISM

The first half of the nineteenth century saw the appearance in America of the belief that all men's entitlements to consideration were a function of their humanness, and that men were not naturally wicked, but perfectible. William Ellery Channing, Ralph Waldo Emerson, and Walt Whitman represented this view. Each of them stood opposed to servitude, broadly defined, and each helped make American slavery untenable.

William Ellery Channing founded Unitarianism and interpreted the views of the French *philosophes* in the American nineteenth-century setting. He broke away from the Calvinistic view of man's natural wickedness and taught the French view that human nature was perfectible, perfectible because it was divine. The new religion was bound to concern its practitioners with social evils. Emerson, Theodore Parker, and others were moved by its belief in human goodness. Parrington notes that the master passions of Channing's life ultimately reduced to two: "respect for human nature, and reverence for human liberty—passions which were inseparable in all his thinking." [34]

In 1840 Channing delivered a series of lectures under the title "On the Elevation of the Laboring Classes." He gave to an association of apprentice workmen his counsel concerning how they might achieve their real worth:

Leave men to the free use of their powers and some will accumulate more than their neighbors. But to be prosperous is not to be superior, and should form no barrier between men. Wealth ought not to secure to the prosperous the slightest consideration. The only distinctions that should be recognized are those of the soul, of strong principle, of incorruptible integrity, of usefulness, of cultured intellect, of fidelity in seeking for truth. A man in proportion as he has these claims should be welcomed and honored everywhere. [35]

Insistent that men have equal access to the perfectibility which alone deserved honor, impatient with artificial distinctions, Channing carried the French view of man far beyond the Puritan view and profoundly influenced all of New England at a time when his influence was crucial. He had willing and able cohorts, and Emerson was the giant among them.

Emerson assumed the complete sufficiency of the individual and

[34] Parrington, *op. cit.*, Vol. I, p. 333.
[35] William Ellery Channing, "On the Elevation of the Laboring Classes," The Harvard Classics, New York, P. F. Collier's Sons, 1909, Vol. 28, p. 356.

called attention to the lowly, the near, and the common. Parrington asserts, "For a generation he was the conscience of America, a pricker of inflated balloons, a gauger of the national brag and cant and humbug. With keen insight he put his finger on the mean and selfish and the great and generous." [36] The mean and selfish were due, in Emerson's view, not to any failings of men, but to failings of social institutions which encouraged men to behave in a manner injurious to their fellow men. He set the example for social criticism, and in a famous address to the Phi Beta Kappa Society in 1837 he clarified the principle which obligated the scholar to criticize and decry: "The world is nothing, the man is all; in yourself is the law of all nature . . . in yourself slumbers the whole of reason; it is for you to know all, it is for you to dare all." [37] Emerson disparaged alike the social insensitivity of the Whig and the demagoguery of the Democrat as he judged each during his lifetime. Self-government was his ideal political system, and in the "Essay on Politics" he proclaims: "It [self-government] promises a recognition of higher rights than those of personal freedom or the security of property. A man has a right to be employed, to be trusted, to be loved, to be revered." [38] Nearly one hundred years passed before serious attempts were made to put this amended statement of natural rights into law.

Those thousands of persons who heard Emerson from the lyceum platform very likely failed to grasp the transcendental character of his social thought. The lessons which it implied were clear and incisive, however, and disturbed the complacency of the rising middle class. Many men of letters followed in his tradition, but we shall deal only with Walt Whitman.

Walt Whitman was more emotional and less erudite than Emerson; but he almost certainly dealt with the themes of humanitarianism in a more basic way. He penetrated the very marrow of the nation. Whitman arrived matter-of-factly at a concept of love for common men, the disinherited. He left the carnage of the Civil War with his love for men *en masse* vindicated, and secure in his belief that a redeemer of the unfulfilled American promise had arrived in Abraham Lincoln. The spirit which he tried to extend is illustrated best by the preface to his work, *Leaves of Grass:*

[36] Parrington, *op. cit.*, Vol. II, p. 391.
[37] Ralph Waldo Emerson, "The American Scholar," The Harvard Classics, New York, P. F. Collier's Sons, 1909, Vol. V, p. 23.
[38] Ralph Waldo Emerson, "Essay on Politics," The Harvard Classics, New York, P. F. Collier's Sons, 1909, Vol. V, p. 260.

. . . the genius of the United States is not best or most in its executives or legislatures, nor in its ambassadors or colleges or churches or parlors, nor even in its newspapers or inventors . . . but always most in the common people. Their manners speech dress friendship—the freshness and candor of their physiognomy—the picturesque looseness of their carriage . . . their deathless attachment to freedom—their aversion to anything indecorous or soft or mean—the practical acknowledgment of the citizens of one state by the citizens of all other states—the fierceness of their roused resentment—their curiosity and welcome of novelty—their self-esteem and wonderful sympathy—their susceptibility to a slight—the air they have of persons who never knew how it felt to stand in the presence of superiors— the fluency of their speech—their delight in music, the sure symptom of manly tenderness and native elegance of soul . . . their good temper and open handedness—the terrible significance of their elections—the President taking off his hat to them, not they to him—these too are unrhymed in poetry.[39]

The preoccupation of the gilded age with securing the interests of wealth provoked Whitman's denunciation. In laissez-faire capitalism as the generation following the Civil War knew it, he saw only the reversal of those ideals for which Jefferson and Emerson had spoken.

We have passed over figures whose penetrating criticisms had enduring importance in American social thought, a necessary omission in providing this overview. Josiah Royce, Theodore Parker, Wendell Phillips, Herman Melville, and others supported and extended the belief that extraordinary possibilities inhered in common men, given a social milieu that would promote their influence. Excellent anthologies of the middle period in American literature have been prepared for the student who wishes to enjoy a complete analysis.

The post-Civil War period in America witnessed the triumph of Whigism and the convenient laying to rest of the social criticism of the ante-bellum period. The northern industrialists accepted the defeat of the southern agrarian interests as a signal that industrialization should be the first concern of American social institutions. The value system of agrarian life should make way for progress. William Graham Sumner and Herbert Spencer were the theorists for the new age, and a whole generation stood firm in the conviction that social classes owed naught to each other, and that sentiment must be banished from social affairs to provide for the working of natural laws. But this last surge of effort in behalf of a system of values already a

[39] Walt Whitman, "Preface to the Leaves of Grass" (1855), The Harvard Classics, New York, P. F. Collier's Sons, 1909, Vol. 39, p. 410.

century in the wane hardly survived the nineteenth century. Lester Ward in sociology, Thorstein Veblen in economics, and Oliver Wendell Holmes, Jr., and Roscoe Pound in law set themselves in opposition to this harsh disposal of mutual social obligations.

Lester Ward selected a position diametrically opposed to Herbert Spencer. In contrast to Spencer's "evolutionary process," automatic, undisturbed dispenser of progress, Ward offered "social telesis" providing for progress through the purposeful guidance of social change. Ward based his theory of social engineering on a systematic account of the bases of human action, its sets and meliorates, which he believed should be sluiced into the channel of social welfare. There was no reason to believe that this harmonizing of conflicting interests would proceed automatically from the "natural order."

Ward's life work constituted a stern, though fairly stated, indictment of the ruthlessness which characterized the last quarter of the nineteenth century. His creative approach marks him off from those who were mere critics. Henry Steele Commager links Ward with twentieth-century social planning: "He was the prophet of the New Freedom and the New Deal, of all those movements looking to the reconstruction of society and economy through government intervention which is the most striking development in the political history of the last half-century in America." [40]

On a foundation to which the humanists had raised the first stone, and Lester Ward one of the final ones, economics, history, and political science prepared a new social science, teleological, humanitarian, pragmatic, unencumbered by mechanistic formulations of natural law. The principals in this approach were Thorstein Veblen and John R. Commons, Frederick Jackson Turner, Vernon Louis Parrington and Charles Beard, Oliver Wendell Holmes, Roscoe Pound, Woodrow Wilson, and Franklin Delano Roosevelt.

Economic thinking until the close of the nineteenth century had nursed a system of principles which were sacrosanct because of their harmony with "nature." People, according to the prevailing view, made responses in terms of a pleasure-pain calculus to immutable economic laws. Economics was unwilling to believe that the new industrial order of society might invalidate the principles laid down by Smith and Ricardo a century before. Antagonistic toward government intervention, unyielding in their attachment to economic laws, econo-

[40] Henry Steele Commager, *The American Mind*, New Haven, Yale University Press, 1950, pp. 215–216.

mists were the Swiss guards of the pre-progressive industrial order. Private property for private purposes never had more self-righteous champions.

In the closing years of the nineteenth century, the state of economic theory came under the criticism of Veblen and Commons. For support they could look to the heretical charter of the newly formed American Economic Association. It held that "the doctrine of laissez faire is unsafe in politics and unsound in morals; and that it suggests an inadequate explanation of the relations between the state and its citizens." [41] Furthermore, the economists went on to reject the "final statements" which had guided the economists of the past generation.[42]

Veblen turned his immaculately phrased contempt on the complacency of the late nineteenth century. The "pecuniary man," whose grasping crassness made regulation by government a farce, "conspicuous leisure" and "conspicuous consumption," "machine process thinking," and the whole maze of purely monetary standards received his scorn. In the *Theory of the Leisure Class* and the *Theory of Business Enterprise* he made obvious the fact that the economic system and its parts might well get out of "natural harmony"; well-being in the former did not even assure sufficient-being in the latter. Production for profit, the sole incentive for undertaking production under pure competition, particularly received his condemnation. It seemed to Veblen more natural that production should be for need than for profit, and he held that a corps of "technics" (technicians) could, if freed from the profit motive, better provide for the nation's economic needs. Commager pays tribute to this observation:

It [technician-directed production] was adopted . . . by the United States Government during the second World War with spectacular success. If engineers were not put in control of the nation's economy during this crisis, they were at least given a free hand; if profits were not eliminated— far from it—they were not permitted to dictate production. Yet the most illuminating aspect of this capitulation to the exigencies of war was not the spectacular success with which the technicians organized the economic resources of the nation for victory but the decisiveness with which the experiment was abandoned and its lessons repudiated once victory had been achieved.[43]

John R. Commons represents the spirit of inquiry which the eman-

[41] *Report of the Organization of the American Economic Association* (1886), Anniversary Meeting Publications, American Economic Association, 1911.
[42] *Ibid.*, p. 2.
[43] Commager, *op. cit.*, p. 242.

cipated economics fostered. Economic and moral ethics were not separate in Commons' view and he gave the industrial practices of his generation a searching examination. As a member of the Industrial Commission of Wisconsin he investigated and reported on conditions of work, race relations, housing, banking, etc., areas of social affairs with which economists would not have deigned to concern themselves in the nineteenth century. Commons found a role to play in the New Freedom of Woodrow Wilson, and his venerable, learned "muckraking" was a necessary preparation for the Mitchells, Douglases, Arnolds, Tugwells and Clarks who followed him in the same kind of economic thinking.

While sociology found its Ward and economics its Veblen and Commons, no deliverance such as these stalwarts rendered to their social sciences appeared for history. The dismal prophecies of the Adamses—Henry's awesome physical force and Brooks' awesome military force—failed to survive the nineteenth century; but not because some academic leader put the task of history right. Rather, the complex vagaries of history seen in its mounting accumulation of data caused the search for laws and single answers to be abandoned in favor of the narrative account. The objective was to determine, according to the German techniques, what had happened. The work of Beard, Turner, and Parrington, however, gave history new perspective. All three tended toward an impersonal history of forces and trends rather than the history of colorful heroes and drama.

Turner dealt with American character in terms of the forces which had produced its peculiar dimensions. From the frontier experience, from "an abundance of natural resources open to a fit people," something wholly unique to America had been achieved in the way of national character. American character had thus become emancipated from its European roots, and America was, therefore, neither to be swept up in historical currents nor to be given a stage in the world pattern. Recent scholarship on the role of the frontier in American history does nothing to invalidate the central point of Turner's work. If the American character was, as he said, a wholly unique product, then the "natural laws" developed in European conditions could not hold.

Parrington was a historical genius, a student of the vast literature of America in its broadest sense, including all forms of literary endeavor. The complete literary record was his field, and he was as much at home with Thorstein Veblen as with Harriet Beecher Stowe. His sen-

sitive social conscience produced a masterpiece of American history in *Main Currents in American Thought*, which was a contribution to philosophy, history, economics, and politics alike. Commager calls the study "a monument to all that had been pledged and sacrificed that America might continue to mean liberty and democracy; it was a magnificent tract calling upon Americans to be true to their past and worthy of their destiny." [44]

The most omniscient of all American historians, at home in several fields, was Charles A. Beard. He gave history and his fellow citizens a jolt when he published the *Economic Interpretation of the Constitution* (1931). The twentieth century having made abundantly clear the role to be played in political and economic institutions by property and wealth, Beard sought to show that the role played by these same forces probably had not changed a great deal during our history. Parrington makes these observations about Beard's work:

The earlier group of liberals were ill-equipped to wage successful war against plutocracy. Immersed in the traditional equalitarian philosophy; they underestimated the strength of the enemies of democracy. They did not realize what legions of Swiss Guards property can summon to its defense. They were still romantic idealists tilting at windmills, and it was to bring them to a sobering reality that the *Economic Interpretation of the Constitution* was written. If property is the master force in every society one cannot understand American institutional development until he has come to understand the part that property played in shaping the fundamental law. [45]

Social legislation was affected in two ways by Beard's work: first, the venerable past, always called upon to thwart this or that new social departure, became less venerable, and in fact fully as mischievous as the present; second, the whole materially oriented American culture experienced a feeling of guilt over the disclosure that men had been Whigs while preparing the nation's most sacred document.

It was in the field of law that the breakaway from the old postulates proved most consequential, because its effect on political science was direct. No appreciation of the dramatic importance that attached to the "new jurisprudence" can be enjoyed unless one appreciates also the extraordinary respect with which Americans have always held "the law." Only in the United States did a court possess a veto over resolutions duly legislated by the people's own representatives. It was of

[44] *Ibid.*, p. 303.
[45] Parrington, *op. cit.*, Vol. III, p. 409.

staggering importance that the "rules" whereby the stamp of legal approval might be obtained should themselves undergo change. In fact, law was the last social science to abandon "natural," mechanistic formulae to decide worthiness and justice.

The legal propositions which filtered into American law were English, of course, and even after the revolution English precedents were used to determine justice in American courts. The English legal background is of utmost importance, therefore, to an understanding of that body of propositions from which American law broke away in the first quarter of the present century, forming what has been called the sociology of jurisprudence.

Anglo-American law was by 1787 a doctrine of double-distilled strictness. In the first instance this was owing to the essentially Germanic character of the English common law; it was owing also to the Puritan influence in America. The sovereignty of the common law in America issued from the apostle-like following by American jurists of the major British architects of the harsher common law, Sir Edward Coke and Sir William Blackstone. Not until the turn of the nineteenth century did their influence in America wane, their works being the first requirements of the law schools. When the general approach of the common law is understood, many of the impediments to social welfare legislation and humanitarian state practice also are clarified.

In legal philosophy the eternal, universal ideals of justice are known as natural law; in the Anglo-American tradition, the common law was thought to be the embodiment of these ideals. The United States, moreover, developed in the first sixty years of its history the belief that the Constitution of 1787 contained the essence of natural law, complete and immutable. Our legal tradition preserved such a rigidity well into the present century. Roscoe Pound, who did as much as anyone to change the common law tradition, says with reference to it:

It is concerned not with social righteousness but with individual rights. It tries questions of the highest social importance as mere private controversies between John Doe and Richard Doe. Its respect for the individual makes procedure, civil and criminal, ultra-contentious and preserves in the modern world the archaic theory of litigation as a fair fight, according to the canons of the manly art, with a court to see fair play and prevent interference. Moreover it is so zealous to secure fair play to the individual that often it secures very little fair play to the public.[46]

[46] Roscoe Pound, *The Spirit of the Common Law*, Francistown, N.H., Marshall Jones Company, 1921, p. 13.

In other works Professor Pound points out that common law is not *made* but is *found*. The judge is not a lawgiver but rather ideally a practiced minister of revealed jural truths, the common law. Not a jurist, he is a guardian. From the principle that the essence of justice lies within the common law there is derived the judgment that legislation is unnecessary, superfluous. The heyday of this judgment embraced the last third of the nineteenth century. Professor Pound describes this stage of our legal history as ". . . the professional feeling that there ought to be little or no legislation on legal subjects, the attitude of resentment toward legislation on the part of the bench and bar that has led so often to the failure of legislative attempts to simplify procedure, and has made so much of the labor of social workers nugatory after they have put it upon our statute books." [47]

The spadework which brought a reversal of this legal tradition is associated with the work of Oliver Wendell Holmes, Jr., Louis Brandeis, and Benjamin Cardozo; but the reworking of the common law into a climate that would admit to legal relevance the gradually maturing American social conscience was in large part due to Professor Pound's efforts. Professor Pound called his philosophy "sociological jurisprudence," whereby he intended the adjustment of law to people and their living conditions rather than vice versa.

A bitter struggle between the executive and judicial branches of our government prefaced the assumption of sociological jurisprudence as a guide. But this triumph had to be enjoyed in the memory of a half-century of obstruction of social legislation by the judiciary. Professor Laski's indictment cannot be thought too harsh under the circumstances:

To protect the property of the few against the will of the people has remained the function of the lawyer in most American courts and, above all, on the Supreme Court of the United States. . . . That function has been to arrest the pace of dynamism inherent in American society. It is not merely that it has arrested obvious techniques like the income tax or the abolition of child labor. . . . The courts have been hostile to trade unionism almost throughout its history. They have used the idea of liberty of contract to strike down measure after measure which a legislative assembly believed, after careful consideration of the evidence, to be necessary to the social welfare. . . . Their hostility to the development of an effective administrative law has been nothing so much as a method by which they

[47] *Ibid.*, p. 45.

could strike into impotence the first efforts to develop in the great society of the United States the obvious implications of the positivist state.[48]

With the reinforcements provided by the new sociology, the new economics, the new history, and the acceptance by law of its social responsibilities, the way was open for a development of the American political system that would leaven the harshness produced by unrestrained laissez-faire capitalism. The actuating force would be the Presidency, an office without strict legal limits to its activities, and a succession of strong Presidents carried out the appointed task. Theodore Roosevelt, Woodrow Wilson, and Franklin Delano Roosevelt are of such great importance in the completion of that task that the central contributions of each must be reviewed briefly here.

THEODORE ROOSEVELT, WOODROW WILSON, AND FRANKLIN DELANO ROOSEVELT

With the departure of history, sociology, economics, and law in America from the autonomous connection each had assumed with natural law and preëstablished harmony, the way was cleared for public policy to redefine social relationships. The essential concepts of man's obligation to man had been formulated and the fact of a new (industrial) order of life was widely recognized. It remained only for reforming energy to be directed against existing social evils through effective leadership. This necessary ingredient was provided by a series of strong Presidents, each of whom broadened the activities of his predecessor. Theodore Roosevelt, then Woodrow Wilson, and finally Franklin Delano Roosevelt developed the instrument of government to social needs.

Theodore Roosevelt was the first President to dramatize effectively the need for government assistance to the downtrodden, the human refuse of the new industrial order. The psychological effect of a President—particularly one of aristocratic family background—championing progressivism was of profound importance. Progressivism gained respectability thereby. In a 1910 speech at Ossawattamie, Kansas, Roosevelt declared it essential that "property shall be the servant and not the master," and he thought that the Constitution of 1787 might very well prove too rigid for the needs of twentieth-century industrial life and require changes. It would require extension of governmental authority to accomplish legislation commensurate with the needs of the

[48] Harold J. Laski, *The American Democracy*, New York, The Viking Press, 1948, pp. 30–31.

time. Labor conditions brought about by the arrival of the giant corporation as an employer especially required intervention by government on the side of labor, Roosevelt reasoned, and in his annual messages to the Congress he repeatedly asked for workmen's compensation legislation.

Woodrow Wilson brought to the Presidency a great erudition and a sensitive social conscience for the problems with which industrial life overwhelmed the workingman. His analysis of the basic social problem was succinct:

> Yesterday, and ever since history began, men were related to one another as individuals. To be sure there were the family, the Church and the State, institutions which associated men in certain wide circles of relationship. But in the ordinary concerns of life, in the ordinary work, in the daily round, men dealt freely and directly with one another. Today, the everyday relationships of men are largely with great impersonal concerns, with organizations, not with other individual men.[49]

At the base of twentieth-century social problems was a changing structure of social relationships which saw a masterful organization of business enterprise, and no similar organization of workingmen. The evil, Wilson thought, was in the system and he said: "We are all caught in a great economic system that is heartless." [50] So great were the abuses which the social order visited on the lower classes that Wilson believed the situation fraught with danger. Change must be introduced through legislative machinery or it will come violently. His warnings were not lost on the generation to which he spoke:

> Don't you know that some man with eloquent tongue, without conscience, who did not care for the nation, could put this whole country into a flame? Don't you know that this whole country from one end to the other believes that something is wrong? What an opportunity it would be for some man without conscience to spring up and say: "This is the way. Follow me!"—and lead in paths to destruction.[51]

That kind of leadership which would make revolution unnecessary Wilson provided. When the severe crises of 1929–1939 came, the precedent of his New Freedom instructed a generation to apply legislative measures again to adapt the social-economic system to new needs.

[49] Woodrow Wilson, *The New Freedom*, New York, Doubleday, Page and Company, 1913, pp. 6–7.
[50] *Ibid.*, p. 18.
[51] *Ibid.*, pp. 28–29.

Franklin Delano Roosevelt succeeded to the Presidency at a time when the social-economic machinery had halted at dead center. The New Deal which he promised was named after the earlier Roosevelt's Square Deal and Wilson's New Freedom. The assumptions upon which he proceeded had the closest connection with those of Theodore Roosevelt and Woodrow Wilson—relief from the miseries surrounding the country required government action; the system was wrong; and the focus of legislative activity should be the workingman. Franklin Roosevelt's first inaugural address made the dimensions of the problem clear:

Values have shrunk to fantastic levels; taxes have risen; our ability to pay has fallen; government of all kinds is faced by serious curtailment of income; the means of exchange are frozen in the currents of trade; the withered leaves of industrial enterprise lie on every side; farmers find no market for their produce; the savings of many years in thousands of families are gone . . . a host of unemployed citizens face the grim problem of existence, and an equally great number toil with little return. Only a foolish optimist would deny the dark realities of the moment. . . . These dark days will be worth all they cost us if they teach us that our true destiny is not to be ministered unto, but to minister to ourselves and to our fellowmen.[52]

The broad program of social legislation to which the New Deal gave rise reconstructed the relationships between family and state, employer and employee, employer and government, and employee and government which had endured since the formation of the Constitution. A generous view was taken of the impact which legislation might have in changing formerly rigid structures, and the nature of the crisis permitted great changes in short periods of time, changes which might otherwise have been a half-century in their accomplishment. In subsequent chapters the specific social legislation to which the New Deal gave rise will be analyzed with the many amendments which have been introduced since 1933. Certainly no aspect of present-day social legislation can be discussed without observing its relevance to the New Deal program.

Social Thought and Social Legislation: Concluding Remarks

We have surveyed the major contributions to social thought from the Hebrew prophets to modern statements by national political lead-

[52] Wilfred Funk (ed.), *Public Papers and Addresses of Franklin Delano Roosevelt*, New York, Random House, Vol. II, 1938, p. 11.

ers. The themes which predominate are clear: persuasion over force, expanding ideas of human rights, acceptance of man's perfectibility, conservation of human resources, and respect for human personality. Thus armed with ideas about human associative living, we are equipped to analyze social problems with a social conscience that is mature. The contributions to social thought upon which our current perspective rests can be summarized briefly: union of Hebraic concepts of social justice with Hellenistic concepts of man's significance under Christianity, humanist emphasis upon the Greek concept of man, the social gospel of Methodism, the natural-rights philosophers, and the keenly sensitive American critics of social life. These movements have brought us to our present outlook. And the accomplishment is more striking in view of developments in some European countries which twisted the European heritage to a justification of tyranny. Italy, Germany, and Russia alike sought to reverse a thousand years of social thought that had come to accept respect for the human personality as the highest object of statecraft. In each of the departures mentioned the state took on goals of its own and bent human personality to its ends. The American contribution is laudatory, then, for its preservation of the social conscience which the last millennium had so painfully sought. That the Declaration of Human Rights adopted unanimously by the United Nations should state the supremacy of human beings above systems testifies to the role played by the world democracies in preserving such elusive concepts.

SELECTED REFERENCES

Bogardus, Emory S., The Development of Social Thought, New York, Longmans, Green and Company, 1948.

Brinton, Crane, Ideas and Men, New York, Prentice-Hall, 1950.

Muller, Herbert J., The Uses of the Past, New York, Oxford University Press, 1952.

Parrington, Vernon Louis, Main Currents in American Thought, New York, Harcourt, Brace and Company, 1927–1930, 3 vols.

Randall, John Herman, The Making of the Modern Mind, Boston, Houghton Mifflin Company, 1926.

Whitehead, Alfred North, Adventures of Ideas, New York, The Macmillan Company, 1933.

The American Culture Pattern
and Social Legislation

This chapter has been prepared in order that the reader will understand how the peculiarities of American culture influence the course of social legislation. Social thought, after all, represents merely the formally expressed sensitivities of individuals in the culture, and characteristically they leave the remainder of the community far behind when they depart from traditional ideas of social relationships. The response of the community to heterodox social thinking, even during crises, rests largely upon the ethos of American culture. We shall first try to describe what the American character is, then analyze the problems to which American culture gives rise, and finally suggest how American social legislation is influenced by these unique factors.

American Character

A major enterprise in cultural anthropology and social psychology over the past two decades has been the analysis of those distinctive dispositions and tendencies which make a given people different from all other peoples. Ruth Benedict, Margaret Mead, Geoffrey Gorer, and others have employed observation, projective tests, and scaling techniques in their studies. Other social scientists have contributed to an understanding of American character through historical search, literary criticism, and observation. Ralph Barton Perry, Denis Brogan, and Henry Steele Commager have made important contributions in this connection. The results of all these endeavors have provided a continuum of traits and tendencies that can be called American character.

Conceding the vastness of the American nation and the quilt of

traits, customs, and sectional peculiarities of which it is composed, can such a concept as American character possibly be useful? Is the result not almost certain to be nebulous and impalpable? It appears, on the contrary, that the concept is congruous and even striking in some respects. There can be no doubt of its usefulness if American character can be described in terms that embrace all Americans. Gunnar Myrdal deals with the apparent heterogeneity of American culture, observing: "The intensities and proportions in which . . . conflicting valuations are present vary considerably from one American to another, and within the same individual, from one situation to another. The cultural unity of the nation consists, however, in the fact that most Americans have most valuations in common though they are arranged differently in the sphere of valuations of different individuals and groups and bear different intensity coefficients." [1] It is American cultural unity which we wish to understand in this chapter.

American character is not a static unity, but a steadily changing one. Many of its aspects have been modified as the agricultural base of the social order has passed to an industrial one, and as crises, chiefly the two world wars and the Great Depression, have tested previous orders in the social structure. Henry Steele Commager begins his study of *The American Mind* with a description of the nineteenth-century American and closes it with a description of the twentieth-century American; the contrasts are illuminating. The earlier American at the conclusion of the nineteenth century was undoubting, supremely confident that the American experiment had been a success. European social misfortunes had been forever banished by the inevitable American progress. He was, Commager notes, "sure that fortitude, together with industry, shrewdness and a little luck, was bound to be rewarded in the end. He preached the gospel of hard work and regarded shiftlessness as a vice more pernicious than immorality. He liked solid evidence of wealth, but distrusted ostentation. . . . He was accustomed to prosperity. . . . Whatever promised to increase wealth was automatically regarded as good. . . ." [2] One sees in this view a dead serious concern with workaday life, as though for the first time common men saw the possibility of gaining control over their economic and social fates, and drank thirstily of the opportunities. The nineteenth-century

[1] Gunnar Myrdal, *An American Dilemma*, New York, Harper & Brothers, 1944, p. xlviii.

[2] Henry Steele Commager, *The American Mind*, New Haven, Yale University Press, 1950, pp. 6–7.

American had little if any impatience with individuals more affluent or highly placed than himself. Such prizes as he lacked would surely be his one day. His egalitarianism was of the mind, not of worldly goods and statuses. Manners, gentility, and snobbishness were lacking at all levels of American society. This American of the last century flouted rules and authority and delighted in cutting pretenders down to size, attitudes which survive in the present day. Individualism was his most obvious characteristic.

It was generally thought by the nineteenth-century American that man was perfectible, that extraordinary possibilities existed in otherwise ordinary people. His heroes were rural and his villains were city-bred or city-tainted. The farm was the sentimental home of America and the values which America professed were those which had been associated with the farm: industry, obedience, cheerful acceptance of one's share, generosity, temperance, the Ten Commandments, and the golden rule. To be a better self and to make one's way fairly were the basic postulates of home education on the farm.

Agricultural social standards passed away in the twentieth century before the urbanizing, mechanizing, dependency-producing industrial era. The security of the farm home and its egalitarian influence were lost and the new era concluded that the old values had been naïve and sentimental anyway. New behaviors surrounded the dynamo, the symbol of the age, which had replaced the Virgin, the old symbol. In the new order of life, petty distinctions and social stratifications gained emphasis in spite of the American tradition.

Two world wars and the Great Depression caused the twentieth-century American to hesitate over the belief in automatic progress. Previously neglectful of his past because he had been so sure his future would be unrelated to it, the new American sought to sanctify and enshrine it. A Whiggish approach to social and economic problems became a necessity in many walks of life, and "individual" points of view on social questions became unpopular. Following both world wars, intolerance became an official point of view, and natural rights seemed to be inviolate only in the absence of crises. Cynicism about American greatness became a popular point of view for the first time in the second quarter of the twentieth century. The relaxation of political and social conduct during the 1920's reflects this general attitude, and many sensitive young people departed for Europe in search of genial permissiveness of heterodoxy no longer to be found at home. The low-water mark of agrarian values was reached at this time.

The observations of foreign social scientists concerning the twentieth-century American character are important to an understanding of its dimensions. Traditionally, they have prepared the most lucid descriptions of American life and character. In general, they have tended to approve American buoyancy and the optimistic approach of Americans to their future. They have nearly always attached significance to child-rearing patterns and the values which Americans associate with the mother. American fear of centralized authority has been baffling to most foreign observers, as has been the national concern with masculinity and masculine virtues. Disapproval has been shown for the sordid picture of American machine politics, the superficial state of American knowledge, and the national inclination to disobedience.

Denis Brogan and Geoffrey Gorer have dwelt on the role of the American mother as socializer of the young and as the national reformer. Brogan notes that in this century the turn of events was away from the essentially male task of settling the frontier, and "American women began to clean up America, to make it less dirty, less sinful, less a boarding house for bachelors and more a home." [3] The brothel and the saloon were the menaces which the American women met successfully, if temporarily. Gorer entitles an important chapter of his work on The American People "Mother Land" and says: "America in its benevolent, high, idealistic aspects is envisaged [by Americans] as feminine; it is masculine only in its grasping and demanding aspects." [4] The consequences for social legislation in this situation where the values that support such legislation are thought of as "feminine" by a culture earnestly protective of its maleness can be imagined. Gorer comments on this fact in connection with the New Deal program of the 1930's: "A great deal of the animus felt and expressed by businessmen and their spokesmen against the New Deal was due to the fact that its social legislation was felt to be introducing into the domain of masculine privilege, the meddling of female morality." [5] Few kinds of chiding in American middle-class male life are resented so strongly as those which suggest effeminacy, and to ward off suspicion concerning his maleness a little boy will go without galoshes in the winter slush and his father will refuse to carry an umbrella. When

[3] Denis W. Brogan, The American Character, New York, Alfred A. Knopf, 1944, p. 48.

[4] Geoffrey Gorer, The American People, New York, W. W. Norton and Company, 1948, p. 53.

[5] Ibid., p. 60.

opponents of the welfare state desire to create resistance to its extension, they warn people about being "kept," which no self-respecting man could permit. Any form of "overprotection" in American life will be thought of as a condescension to feminine values. There can be no doubt that social legislation has been made more difficult to obtain by these aspects of American character.

Concerning the American doctrine of progress—the idea that diligent pursuit of life's aims within the American tradition will inevitably bring progress—many foreign observers have raised questions. Harold Laski discusses the place of this view in American life, noting: "No concept has played a larger part in the shaping of the American faith than the conviction that there is a constant, upward progress. This led to an experimental temper, which did not believe that there were obstacles in any realm capable of hindering permanently the forward movement of mankind, or, at any rate, of American mankind." [6] Brogan also comments on this belief, himself believing that it follows from a simple observation of American experience: "American tradition is tied to the idea of progress. It has grown during the centuries in which the novel and revolutionary idea took possession of man's mind in the West, and all American experience has seemed to confirm the view that the world is advancing towards something better, to a fuller, richer life for more people, more of the time." [7] The essential elements of the American dedication to progress as the destiny of the nation have been observed by many other foreigners. For our purposes the effect of this idea of progress upon social legislation is the major factor. Two views are possible: the inevitability of progress might be assumed a sufficient condition for human life and social legislation deemed unnecessary; or the obligation of the state to make the "inevitability" of progress a fact might lead to the enactment of necessary social legislation. It seems that the American view has tended toward the latter interpretation; that progress is not a gift bestowed on the nation, but must be won and maintained. Ralph Barton Perry's interpretation of this situation is interesting: "They [Americans] do not regard unhappiness as the necessary lot of man, to be accepted as a fatality and sublimated in tragic nobility. Even sin is regarded as curable, if not by divine grace, then by psychoanalysis." [8]

[6] Harold J. Laski, *The American Democracy*, New York, The Viking Press, 1948, p. 259.

[7] Brogan, *op. cit.*, p. 65.

[8] Ralph Barton Perry, *Characteristically American*, New York, Alfred A. Knopf, 1949, p. 12.

American character manifests itself in the twentieth century as a formal intonement of nineteenth-century values, but an actual accommodation to industrial life. The major themes which endure from an earlier age of individualism stress protection of male virtues, accept progress as the natural way of things, and fear the extension of government authority. Two wars and a severe depression have modified the character type produced by the frontier, and Americans have sought to ensure that the future will indeed bring progress by extending government authority. Nonetheless, the post-World War II period has witnessed a retrenchment of the nation against further extension of the welfare state, a subject which will be discussed more fully at a later point.

The American Culture Pattern

Having dealt with the personal common denominator of American culture, the character it produces, we shall now discuss the less personal cultural determinants of American behavior. Such differences in behavior as would result from class, ethnic, sectional, and other differences must be overlooked in order to gain a general sense of the institutional constructs that cause Americans as a whole to do the things they do. To this end we will consider in turn agrarian behavior standards, fears of centralized authority, fluidity of class boundaries, the Puritan ethic, pragmatism, family-structure changes, and the communications system.

AGRARIAN BEHAVIOR STANDARDS

American individualism, which booster organizations never tire of proclaiming, is not simply a figment of commercial imagination. An era merely two generations past knew the savor of individualism well and guarded it jealously. Direction of individual effort was personal, insofar as family needs allowed, and the free surrender of one's will to this or that standard of conduct was deliberate. The results both social and personal were laudable in terms of the stability attained; chicane and treachery were less in evidence, certainly more frowned upon, than at present. Artificial behaviors and synthetic tastes and wants had not been prepared through the instruments of mass communication, and the most descriptive word for this society was "natural." Even the threats which called for one's attention were natural, i.e., related to the forces of nature, and against these forces no protection (as

through government) was asked for or given. The personal and social good were thought of as one, and the line between right and wrong practice was clear and devoid of syllogisms. Sharing of political, religious, economic, and other functions was the rule, and the norms of conduct received unanimous acceptance. The obligations of obedience which the individual owed to his fellow men were equally clear to him and to them.

Within the present century, however, the individualistic structure described above has been greatly modified. In the wake of two world wars and the severe depression of 1929–1939 the vast majority of Americans have agreed to modify individualism in favor of government-provided security. Relationships among individuals take place over a shorter time in present urban society than when the family farm was passed on from generation to generation. The result has been that social norms lack the unanimous acceptance that previously existed, and the tolerable deviations have become more numerous and more extensive. Right and wrong practice shade into each other. Moreover, threats to the individual are thought "unmanageable" and are associated with urban life and the dependency it produces. The personal and social good are less readily seen in their common character, and the obligations which one recognizes toward his fellow men tend to be specific and contractual. Under these conditions of the industrial order, one who seriously abides by the tenets of conduct appropriate to an agrarian age will be scorned for his naïveté, for not "knowing the score."

In this discussion contrasts between the agrarian and industrial conditions of life and their regulation have been deliberately emphasized. The objective has been to make the fact of changing conditions clear in a brief statement. One should not despair that stability of social life has been upset permanently, or at all. The agrarian order has become an industrial order with attendant changes in the norms of behavior. But people change also and will adjust their behavior in time to the new conditions of life. During the transition period an unusual amount of stress will be borne by American social institutions, perhaps the family most of all, and such maladjustments as occur will concern us from the standpoint of government assistance. The section on family legislation (Chapters 6–8) will deal extensively with the implications of the new industrial order for the marital and parent-child relationships.

Eighteenth-century Americans debated briefly over their major political antagonisms—republicanism and monarchy—before deciding to restrain both under a government on the British model. It was an easy decision; Daniel Shays' rebellion removed whatever lingering doubts had existed concerning the vulnerability of property to the mob. The Declaration of Independence had, furthermore, set forth in detail the tyranny of King George III. Of the many legislators who helped select the middle course, most were trained in the law and had a healthy respect for the type of mechanical justice provided in the English common law. We have discussed the growth of sociological jurisprudence as a reaction against the harshness of the common law; but it will be useful to observe here that the common law could so highly regard its mission to protect property that a law prohibiting the payment of workers with "scrip" orders usable only in company stores was held unconstitutional as an infringement on "natural inherent rights and an insulting attempt to put the laborer under a legislative tutelage." [9]

In part this fear of government authority has constituted a misreading of European experience, leading to the conclusion that government per se is evil. But the natural tendency of Americans to view government with suspicion has frequently been exploited by interests which feared the consequences of government efforts to reorder social relationships. Thus, operations of government, from the Public Health Service to the Tennessee Valley Authority, have seldom been evaluated in terms of their contributions, but rather in terms of their dangerous implications as departures from the "American way." The American fear of government has been fed by the fact that the German, Italian, and Russian peoples have been victimized by governments that placed the welfare of the state above that of its citizens. Public administration as an applied social science has nothing less than a herculean task to perform in removing the distrust of government and politics in the nation.

The consequences of the traditional American view of government have nearly always, in combination with other factors, determined that social legislation would come too little and too late. In the period since the conclusion of World War II, the recognition has been general that some variation of national planning would be required to assure the stable social relationships of full employment. Effective use

[9] Commager, op. cit., p. 372.

of national planning, on a scale which would, however, promise beneficial results, would entail an increase in central government authority and thus leave us to bear the consequences of unplanned use of our economic resources. Problems which might be solved at the source are allowed to mature, with resulting social welfare expenses to all government units. Furthermore, the maldistribution of natural resources among the several regions of the United States, the effects of which might be atoned for by the central government, are allowed to persist, and educational opportunities, for example, are unequal among the states.

FLUIDITY OF CLASS BOUNDARIES

It would be difficult to overemphasize the importance to Americans, in the century following Andrew Jackson, of the belief in unlimited mobility upward through the society. Men ignored social problems which they assumed would be merely temporary obstacles in their trip to higher status and would not bother them for any appreciable period of their lives. The simple will to prosper unlocked doors to increasing responsibility and privilege through the first quarter of the present century, and American parents hoped above all else that their children would improve on the social standing which they received by birth. All classes of society except the highest, which based its status claims on the period of time the family had been "upper class," could be entered by the accumulation of wealth. Given sufficient wealth, no other major obstacle (except time) stood in the way of increasing one's family social status.

Numerous influences brought about a reassessment of this American dream. The intense competition among business units, the growth of the giant corporation as an employer, and the decline in availability of cheap farm land all played a part. As agriculture lost its position as the chief source of American national income and industrialization of the nation accelerated its pace, occupations became specialized. The consequent dilution of craftsmanship among skilled laborers is a well-known result; but managerial occupations became specialized also, and a middle class of industrial functionaries came into being. Initially the expansion of industry was so rapid and the need for executive personnel so great that men of positive personality and perseverance were upgraded from skilled labor and minor functionary positions into the managerial ranks. The skills necessary to successful executiveship multiplied, however, and the rendering of men's lives more early useful to

TABLE 1. Level of Schooling Completed by
Major Occupation Group and Income, 1949 [a]

Subject	Completed less than 5 years of Elementary School Percent of Total	Completed 8 Years or More of Elementary School Percent of Total	Completed 4 Years or More of High School Percent of Total	Completed 4 Years or More of College Percent of Total
MAJOR OCCUPATION GROUP				
Total employed	8.9	74.4	37.0	8.0
Professional, technical, and kindred	0.9	95.3	86.8	51.7
Farmers, farm managers	18.2	57.0	16.1	1.5
Managers, officials and proprietors except farm	4.3	85.7	53.0	11.4
Clerical and kindred	1.5	93.1	65.2	6.7
Sales workers	2.9	88.7	54.4	8.2
Craftsmen, foremen, kindred	6.2	76.4	28.6	1.8
Operatives, kindred	10.1	67.7	19.9	0.8
Private household	20.5	48.1	12.3	0.9
Service, except private household	10.5	68.6	24.0	1.5
Farm labor, unpaid, family	18.1	56.6	16.1	0.8
Farm labor, except unpaid foremen	31.8	41.0	10.3	0.8
Laborers, except farm and mine	22.9	49.5	11.9	0.7
Occupation not reported	10.1	62.8	29.0	5.9
INCOME IN 1949				
Male	11.9	68.6	31.5	7.1
Less than $500	28.1	46.1	15.0	3.1
$500 to $1,999	19.4	55.8	18.6	3.5
$2000 to $2999	9.2	71.9	28.0	3.7
$3000 to $3999	4.8	82.2	39.2	6.0
$4000 to $4999	3.2	87.1	48.4	11.0
$5000 to $6999	2.5	89.9	58.5	19.9
$7000 and over	2.3	91.8	69.5	33.8
Not reported	10.0	48.2	24.5	6.4
Female	9.8	72.4	35.1	5.0
None	10.4	72.1	32.4	3.4
$1 to $499	14.9	64.5	27.6	3.9
$500 to $1999	8.8	74.1	34.2	4.5
$2000 to $2999	3.1	88.7	57.8	10.5
$3000 to $3999	2.2	92.7	69.8	22.3
$4000 and over	2.6	91.4	70.9	28.1
Not reported	11.2	52.0	25.5	3.9

[a] Based on 3-1/3 percent sample.

Source: U.S. Bureau of the Census, U.S. Census of Population, 1950, Vol. IV, Special Reports, Part 5, Chapter B, "Education," 5B-14, Table C.

industry prompted formalization of training. To the requisites of talent, energy, and vision was soon added the possession of college graduation for aspirant managers.

The realities of the American social-economic system gave the specialization of training for executive employment significance in connection with traditional American vertical mobility upward. A requisite of mobility had been constructed which could be provided only at extensive cost. Low-income-family youngsters in the American school system showed a far higher attrition than their more fortunate companions. Tutors and special assistance for youngsters from higher-income families further discriminated in their favor. Few families could bear the burden of supporting a youngster through four years of college or, in some instances, even permit the loss of his income contribution to the family. Improving upon the father's occupational status, and thus his class status to a large degree, became progressively less likely for the aspiring youngster from low-income background. For the few who might accept the challenge, however, college graduation promised upward movement in the social class system. Table 1 (p. 81) shows that both income level and occupation (and hence, social class to a large extent) are a function of formal schooling, particularly college.

Data which would permit confident conclusions concerning the equality of opportunity in the United States are wanting. Study of father-and-son occupations in San Jose, California, in 1930 when its growth was already vigorous yielded these results: of adult sons from families wherein the father's occupation was unskilled, 41.7 percent of the sons followed unskilled occupations, 16.5 percent became semiskilled workers, 13.7 percent became clerical employees, 10.3 percent became proprietors, and 4.1 percent achieved professional occupations.[10] Study of urban occupational mobility on a national scale in 1948 yielded the conclusion that two-thirds of white American males have sons whose occupational status is either the same as or no better than their own.[11] These data suggest that vertical occupational mobility is severely limited for youngsters of disadvantageous economic circumstances.

Social mobility in nineteenth-century America frequently turned on

[10] Percy E. Davidson and H. Dewey Anderson, *Occupational Mobility in an American Community*, Stanford University, Stanford University Press, 1937, p. 20.

[11] Kingsley Davis et al., *Modern American Society*, Rinehart and Company, 1949, p. 201.

an individual's ability to accumulate savings and enter business or farming as a small proprietor. In the twentieth century the scale of enterprise became larger and the competition of established organizations acute. Many occupations and lines of business adopted restrictive practices against new entrants which increased the advantage of incumbents over those willing to assume the risks of beginning a business. Special legislation in behalf of certain economic groups, farmers, for example, fortified their position against the competition of newcomers.

The disappearance of immigration as an important source of population increase had implications for the occupational mobility of "native sons": formerly, newly arrived immigrants had assumed unskilled employment which permitted native-born persons and established immigrants holding unskilled jobs to "climb on their backs" and improve their occupational and class positions. Restrictive practices against immigration inaugurated during the 1920's put an end to such techniques of improving occupational status.

One sees the results of college training for occupational specialization and the increased scale of enterprise in the American cultural scene. For the first time in our history we have a large class who expect to be employees throughout their lifetime. Their ability to rise in the social system depends to a large extent upon achievement of a college diploma. Such opportunities have increased with the provision of funds for scholarships by some states, the adult education movement, veteran training programs, and state universities. However, the surrender of income which might be gained through employment is difficult and often impossible for the personal of low-income family background to accept. The advantage which the possession of a bachelor's degree provides, furthermore, threatens to become diluted as the annual number of recipients attains the magnitude of several hundred thousand. Already college graduation is tending to permit the graduate simply a higher type of employee status. The realities of lifelong employee status have caused many traditional attitudes to be cast aside, and employees come to attach more and more significance to income security, protection of seniority, fringe benefits, and union security.

Social legislation has been affected by the decline in upward vertical mobility between class ranks and has in turn provided effects of its own. As mentioned above, workmen facing the prospect of lifelong employee status have demanded legislation from the political unit to

provide them personal income security and security for their labor unions. These objects, once attained, tend to reduce mobility further, with even horizontal mobility among jobs being reduced for fear of loss of seniority rights, pension benefits, and other rewards of enduring employment with a given employer.

THE PURITAN ETHIC

Unappreciated until recently, the close relationship between Puritanism and American culture has been interpreted by legal scholars, historical scholars, and anthropologists, to cite but a portion of the interest centered on the connection. Max Weber had made the relationship between Puritanism and capitalism clear in his classic work, *The Protestant Ethic and the Spirit of Capitalism*, an English translation of which became available in 1930. The most illuminating study of Puritanism and American culture, however, has been written by Professor Ralph Barton Perry—*Puritanism and Democracy*. Some of his observations will help us better to understand American culture and social legislation.

Some effects of Puritanism worked counter to the movement of democracy and humanitarianism in the United States. By maintaining the belief in man's inherent wickedness, Puritanism obstructed humanitarianism. It prolonged authoritarianism, Perry notes, through its rigorism and legalism, "its insistence on duty rather than on desire and love of good." [12] The idea of election into heaven and the sovereignty of the deity "accustomed a Puritan community to privilege, and hardened the hearts of the elite to the plight of the unfortunate." [13] Some of the resistance to social services extended by government authority probably can be traced to survivals of Puritanism in our culture.

The effect of Puritanism on American culture was not wholly obstructive, however, as Professor Perry demonstrates by comparing the many common values which democracy and Puritanism shared. Both shared respect for the dignity of man—their units of responsibility in society being the unit man with a free will; both contained a body of higher truths stated plainly; and both approved the doctrine of laissez faire in which men sought personal gain and at the same time enjoyed

[12] Ralph Barton Perry, *Puritanism and Democracy*, New York, The Vanguard Press, 1944, p. 190.
[13] *Ibid.*, p. 191.

the comforting assurance that they were best serving the will of God and the good of mankind at large.[14] Other elements were similarly comparable about the two movements, as the following quotation suggests:

. . . there was the same sense of destiny felt by a group set apart to realize the moral purpose of the world; and in both cults that sense of destiny was nostalgic—the homing instinct of exiles from Paradise. In both cults man had fallen from grace: in the one case through abuses of institutional authority [democracy]; in the other, through pride and temptations of the flesh. In both cults that condition of man in which the circle is completed, and life ends as it began, was a condition of freedom: in the one case the spontaneous exercise of reason and conscience [democracy]; in the other, the fearless confidence of creatures in the Author of their being. In both cults man was originally endowed with the faculties requisite for his salvation, and by which he might be trusted to govern himself: he sprang into full realization at the dawn of his being, and required no slow and tortuous process of development. If in this doctrine there was a magnificent disregard of historical fact, both cults were guilty: and both were justified in the same manner and degree as having been blinded by a passion for perfection.[15]

In the American consideration of workaday life, the more obvious vestiges of Puritanism are to be observed. There has been a traditional approval of busyness and dutiful work, and traditional condemnation of sloth and work performed without sufficient gravity. A certain incomprehensibility has always surrounded the idea of enjoyable work, work performed in a spirit of gaiety, and the practitioner thereof has been regarded with suspicion. On the assumption that work should be unpleasant and undertaken as a kind of penance, American society took slowly to the idea of fringe benefits, shortening the working day and raising of wages. That injustice was wrought on the individual by tedious employment for long hours at low pay was resisted by those whose system of values contained the central theses of Puritanism. The respectability attached to moneymaking, the eager pursuit of which has always been associated with the middle class in America, has made it difficult for the American social conscience to make an indictment of the business community until its abuses were flagrant or until its miscalculations forced the issue. Traditionally, American business has assumed a moral rectitude which approaches sanctifica-

[14] *Ibid.*, passim, pp. 191–193.
[15] *Ibid.*, pp. 196–197.

tion; and the culture has accepted commercial and industrial definitions of American values almost from the first.

No institution in America was so thoroughly influenced by Puritanism as was American law. Some consideration was given to the common law and its Puritan background in Chapter 3; we shall inquire further into the effect of Puritan individualism on law at this point. Professor Pound's study of the common law properly places Puritanism in the framework of American legal thinking. Puritanism, he notes, "has given us that conception of abstract liberty of contract which has been the bane of all social legislation" and, of its major concepts, "few doctrines have been more irritating than those of assumption of risk and contributory negligence, as applied to injuries of employees." [16] Professor Pound illustrates his point with the following example: ". . . a workman, engaged constantly upon a machine, so that he becomes a part of it and to operate mechanically himself, omits a precaution and is injured. The common law says to him, 'You are a free man, you have a mind and are capable of using it; you chose freely to do a dangerous thing and were injured; you must abide the consequences.' " [17] When one considers the fact that jurisprudence considered legislation unnecessary, because the eternal principles of justice already had been decided, the block which Puritanism laid in the path of social legislation can better be appreciated. As our notions of rights deriving from one's humanness matured, the common law in America constituted a "cultural lag" which has not been entirely spent at the present time. Discussion of social legislation in later chapters, particularly in connection with the shifting of responsibility from the individual to other agencies, will reveal that certain Puritan viewpoints are very much alive in present-day American culture.

PRAGMATISM

Offsetting elements of the American culture pattern which, as with aversion to overprotection, fear of centralized authority, and the Puritan ethic, obstruct social legislation is an American homespun philosophy called pragmatism. The creature of William James and John Dewey, pragmatism is intricate and impalpable in its extensions and overtones, but can be stated simply in its essence. The center of the

[16] Roscoe Pound, The Spirit of the Common Law, Francistown, N.H., Marshall Jones Company, 1921, pp. 44, 47.
[17] Ibid., p. 48.

universe, its disturber and rectifier, is man. In exercising his role he is guided not by universal laws, but by what "works," i.e., is effective, in producing what we desire collectively. William James seems to ask: "Are not men first and foremost the material with which we deal? In the event of their complete extermination, could there possibly be any meaningfulness to the cosmos?"

There is in pragmatism a statement of assumptions and consequences which neatly fits the era of the liberated common man and encourages social engineering. This applied role of pragmatism matured in the hands of John Dewey, who provided whatever it was lacking in the way of workaday practicality. Pragmatism was a democratic philosophy from the beginning, but John Dewey pressed it into social service. Commager sums up the contribution of John Dewey in these terms: "More fully than any other philosopher of modern times, Dewey put philosophy to the service of society. More, he formed a whole network of alliances—with science, with politics, with education, with aesthetics, all directed toward advancing the happiness of mankind." [18] Philosophy, which from the time of the Greeks had been primarily concerned with consoling individuals in their determination to act rightly, extended its orbit to the society. The change in philosophy's scope was merely one novelty introduced by pragmatism; the other consisted in the fact that no system or rigid frame of reference was to guide the extended philosophical concern.

Criticism has been directed at pragmatism to the present day for its disregard of "truth" in the sense of derived values; it seemed that success, satisfactory results, were the ultimate values and no controls on their direction were in evidence. George Santayana described the fallacy in pragmatism as he saw it: ". . . James would have us bet on immortality, or bet on our power to succeed, because if we win the wager we can live to congratulate ourselves on our true instinct, while we lose nothing if we have made a mistake. . . ." [19] It was the uncertainty of success which Santayana criticized. Since he was an "outsider," detached from the American assumption that progress was inevitable, Santayana would necessarily criticize such illusory hopes. However, the experimental, pragmatic attitude of mind has encouraged American venturesomeness and growth. In the case of social legislation, pragmatism was a supporting factor in American culture.

[18] Commager, op. cit., p. 99.
[19] George Santayana, Character and Opinion in the United States, New York, W. W. Norton and Company, 1940, p. 86.

Family Structure Dynamics

Our discussion thus far suggests that the family would be adversely affected by industrialization and the decline of agrarian values. While the functions which have been historically associated with the family have been modified, the family remains one of the most important sentimental referents of the American culture. Perhaps the libertine character of socialization in America and the maternal coddling of youth create an enduring sentiment that is recalled with nostalgia in the tension of urban industrial life. Whatever the cause, it persists in the face of forces which, in the manner of a centrifuge, have torn at its traditional functions. In 1931, John Dollard published his study of the American family, in which the central thesis was the shift from a family based on function to a family based on companionship; and he has not been alone in that observation.[20]

Functions attributed to the family in its historical role have included procreation, economic production, health preservation, religious instruction, education (socialization) of members, protection, status conferment, and affection. In present-day American culture all of these functions have been modified. The nature of these modifications will be discussed at length in Chapter 6; at this point we might simply note some of the factors which have brought about the changes. Industrialization of the nation has been the most important factor and it has issued in most of the centrifugal forces affecting the modern family. In the first place, industrialization made the clan-type rural family obsolete. Reverent deference to nature's imponderable operations no longer could be tolerated, and preservation of timeworn formulas of craftsmanship and human relationships was useless because they failed to fit the demands of industry. Age and control by the aged lost their places as the premium set on youth and vigor rose. Of all the effects industrialization produced, urbanization was by far the most consequential for the family. The family homestead and the institutions surrounding it decayed gradually (although the stem family, in which one child would stay with the farm to preserve the family tradition and enterprise, was a significant adaptation) as young people left the farm to make their (individual) mark in the world of industry

[20] John C. Dollard, *Changing Functions of the American Family*, Chicago, University of Chicago Press, 1931; see also
Ernest W. Burgess and Harvey J. Locke, *The Family*, New York, American Book Company, 1945, and
Ruth S. Cavan, *The American Family*, New York, Thomas Y. Crowell Company, 1953.

and commerce. This tendency gained acceptance very rapidly. David Hatch's study of Hilltown makes the rapidity of family reorientation strikingly clear; for example, Hilltown (a New England farming community) in 1900 contained twenty families whose sons might have carried on the family farm or business; but only five did so, and out of fifty houses identified with particular families in 1900, only three were occupied by members of the same families in 1948.[21] Furthermore, over the decade 1940–1950, while the number of government workers increased 55 percent, and private wage and salary workers 32 percent, unpaid family workers *decreased* by 23 percent.[22] With the decline of the farm homestead, the value system which it had fostered declined also. Competitive striving for the individual recognition which urban society granted replaced coöperative striving in the family enterprise. One generation was born and sternly socialized under the watchful eyes of the rural community; the next was born and permissively socialized in the anonymity of the urban community. The character results could not possibly have been expected to be similar. Among the values which the newer generation would esteem were material success at any cost, independent making of one's way, manipulation of peers and superiors, and judgments in dollar terms. The aged, who had loomed so importantly in the rural community, became a burden in the urban community. Furthermore, each generation had learned the obligations of responsibility for aged family members by observing the practice as worked out between the two preceding generations. No such example guided the dispositions of urban youth, and their reluctance to (and inability to) perpetuate the tradition of family responsibility for its aged created the need for legislation to affect that kind of care. Marriage in the urban environment, which often precluded intimate knowledge of one's mate and his family background, became more risky, and the resources available to newly married couples in the rural community (the "family" pastor and doctor, solicitous relatives, etc.) were largely lacking.

To this gloomy picture should be added some observations that deserve approval. The essential function of the family, by which it is distinguished from all other institutions—procreation within a socially approved relationship—continues for reasons that will be analyzed in

[21] David L. Hatch, unpublished thesis, "Changes in the Structure and Function of a Rural New England Community since 1900" (1948), discussed in George C. Homans, *The Human Group*, New York, Harcourt, Brace and Company, 1950, p. 353.
[22] U.S. Bureau of the Census, *U.S. Census of Population, 1950*, Vol. II, *Characteristics of Population*, Part I, 1953, p. 61.

tracing the natural history of the family. Furthermore, the personality fulfillment of each member has become more probable because the roles which one may perform have multiplied and become more varied. Women especially have profited from the urbanization of life in that roles alternative and complimentary to childbearing and housekeeping have been made available. Because the urban mother marries younger and has fewer children, she can return to employment or other pursuits, thus enabling the family to enjoy a higher material level of life. Cultural acceptance of the women employed in industry and commerce, as well as the invention of household labor-saving devices from automatic washing and drying machines to frozen ("just brown and serve") foods, have brought about this change. The effect on the family larder is suggested by the fact that, in 1949, 20.1 percent of American *families* had incomes over $5000, but only 3.1 percent of unrelated individuals had incomes over $5000.[23] Nearly two families out of five, during 1950, had more than one wage earner.[24] How remarkable is this participation of women in the labor force can be seen from Table 2 below.

TABLE 2. Participation in the Labor Force by Sex, 1900–1970.

Sex	1970	1960 [a]	1950	1940	1920	1900
Both sexes	57.4	56.9	56.8	54.1	55.8	55.0
Males, 14 years and over	79.7	81.1	82.4	80.9	83.4	85.9
Females, 14 years and over	36.2	33.8	31.9	27.4	24.1	20.4

a Estimates for future years are based on projection of the labor force for 1920 and an average of the years 1947-1951, assuming the continuation of past trends and the maintenance of the high-level employment characteristic of the post-World War II period. Data for years prior to 1940 are based on "gainful workers," for years since 1940 on "total labor force."

Sources: Conference Board, *Economic Almanac for 1953–54*, New York, Thomas Y. Crowell Company, 1953, p. 428; and U. S. Bureau of the Census, *Statistical Abstract of the United States, 1954*, p. 00.

It should be further observed that whereas in 1890 4 percent of married women were employed, in 1950 this figure was 25 percent.[25] A complete consideration of the social implications of women, particularly mothers, increasing their participation in the labor force will be delayed until our discussion of family legislation. Essentially this in-

23 *Ibid.*, Table 57.
24 *Ibid.*
25 U. S. Bureau of the Census, *Current Population Reports*, Series P–50, No. 39, May 28, 1952, p. 11.

volves a balancing of the diffusion which occurs in family roles with the desirability of increasing the family's income security.

Modification of the family's traditional functions in the struggle which it has waged with other media for the loyal attention of its members raises several serious questions. One danger is that those media which appear to have won this struggle (movie houses, teen-age peer groups, adult social and business associations, etc.) have motives far less worthy, and cultural merchandise far more shabby, than the family has historically provided. The human fabric is not likely to prove more serviceable to the culture if it trades integrity for popularity, character for sex appeal, long-run security for short-run romantic thrill, and high standards of performance for manipulative skill. These and other bargains struck by modern youth (although youth are not alone in their susceptibility to the centrifugal forces operating on the family) are the wages of a quickening of pace in life ushered in with the commercial and industrial transition of the twentieth century.

COMMUNITY TRENDS

The discussion thus far has alluded to urbanization as a product of twentieth-century industrialization, and an outstanding characteristic of American culture. Table 3 traces the growth of urban areas from 1800 to 1950. The United States was not a predominantly urban nation until the census of 1920; however, in every decade since 1790, with the exception of 1810–1820, the rate of growth of urban population has exceeded that of the rural population. Whereas approximately one person out of every twenty lived in an urban area (population exceeding 2500) in 1790, the relationship had become three persons out of every five in 1950.

TABLE 3.   Urban-Rural Population in the United States, 1800–1950.
Percent of Population

Year	Urban [a]	Rural
1950	59.0	41.0
1940	56.5	43.5
1930	56.2	43.8
1920	51.2	48.8
1900	45.7	54.3
1800	6.1	93.9

[a] Bureau of the Census "old" definition of urban population used throughout, inhabitants of incorporated areas having a population of 2500 or more.

Source: U. S. Bureau of the Census, *United States Census of Population: 1950,* Vol. II, *Characteristics of the Population,* Part I, 1953.

Not only has the proportion of urban population increased, but the proportion in large cities has also increased. This is shown in Table 4. In spite of the movement of people away from central city areas into suburbs, the population of the larger urban centers has shown a tendency to increase.

TABLE 4.   United States Urban Population by Size of Population Area, 1900 and 1950 [a]

Population Area	1950	1930	1900
2,500 or more	49.0	56.2	39.7
1,000,000 or more	11.5	12.3	8.5
500,000 to 1,000,000	6.1	4.7	2.2
250,000 to 500,000	5.5	6.5	3.8
100,000 to 250,000	6.4	6.1	4.3
50,000 to 100,000	6.0	5.3	3.6
25,000 to 50,000	6.3	5.2	3.7
10,000 to 25,000	8.3	7.4	5.7
5,000 to 10,000	5.2	4.8	4.2
2,500 to 5,000	3.7	3.8	3.8

a Bureau of the Census "old" definition of urban population used throughout, inhabitants of incorporated areas with a population of 2500 or more.

Source: U. S. Bureau of the Census, United States Population: 1950, Vol. II, Characteristics of the Population, Part I, 1953.

For many reasons urbanization has created social problems of great importance. In the first place, inhabitants of urban areas are almost completely dependent for their basic needs; the loss of employment, in the absence of social legislation to meet this contingency, threatens life itself. Depressions of the magnitude demonstrated during the decade of the 1930's find subsistence farmers in a less drastic plight than previously high-income people in cities without a source of income. Other problems derive from the proximity of large numbers of people to one another, which leaves the urban area vulnerable to communicable disease, fire, failure of utilities, etc. But, the most significant indictment of urban—particularly metropolitan—areas is what they do to the people of whom they are composed. All kinds of crime, particularly those against the person, increase in direct ratio with the size of the city, rape being an exception in that it has a lower incidence in areas with a population from 10,000 to 50,000 than in areas with a population under 10,000; but for cities with a population above 50,000 the incidence increases rapidly.[26] Considering the growth pattern shown in Table 4, these data are of critical significance. In spite of superior

26 Federal Bureau of Investigation, Uniform Crime Reports, Washington, Government Printing Office, 1949, Vol. 19, p. 78.

medical facilities, the death rate is higher in urban areas, particularly for underprivileged groups, than for nonurban areas. In spite of its varied facilities to accommodate the atypical personality, the incidence of personality disorganization is greater in urban areas than in nonurban areas, although it is not clear whether this is the result of the disorganizing influences of urban life or simply better diagnosis. It must be observed, however, that those circumstances of life which figure heavily in the etiology of personality disorganization are typical of urban, particularly metropolitan, life. Isolation of the self within a metropolis of teeming millions is one of the vagaries of urban culture.

Urban areas have been the shame of the American political system and challenge the art of public administration to make their governments operate at a reasonable cost. Considering the fact that urban governments do not have military items in their budget, their expenses for comparable items (social welfare, education, highways, etc.) have increased since 1940 at a rate exceeding that of the federal government. Viewed simply from the standpoint of geography, the crazy-quilt pattern of urban development suggests an absence of planning. Congestion alone has made the automobile unusable in the largest cities of the United States for driving to one's place of employment, a peculiar circumstance when one considers that the higher incomes enjoyed by inhabitants of large cities would enable them to own an automobile. City planning in geographic terms represents one of the most serious instances of cultural lag in our culture.

Considering now the American class system, it should be noted that inducement for the individual to strive for vertical movement into a higher class is especially strong. Opportunities to "gain points" that would facilitate entrance into the next higher-class level are greatest in urban areas, and those individuals attracted to the urban environment tend to be "mobile." A recent study of urban communities by Hallenbeck makes this observation:

Urbanism brings to a focus such tendencies as rampant individualism, and the concept and feeling of community emerge with difficulty from the conflict of private interests, which are prevalent in the urban culture, because cities harbor the unrestrained egotistic qualities which the culture encourages. But this is not inherent in individualism; rather is it the case that an urbanized society provides the environment which is conducive to the development of any qualities to which an individual is disposed.[27]

[27] Wilbur C. Hallenbeck, *American Urban Communities*, New York, Harper & Brothers, 1951, p. 338.

It may be that rampant individualism is not inherent in the urban community; but the type of personality which emerges from urban upbringing almost certainly will reflect its dominant values. Such selective factors as income, ethnic background, and race foster groupings in urban areas which are mutually exclusive. One product of these groupings is inbreeding of viewpoints, which sometimes obstruct the achievement of unanimous response to some question of truly community interest; political machines and bosses are one result of this stratification, since they are able to organize a majority vote for matters of common interest. More will be said in this connection when the legislative process is discussed in the next chapter.

In the post-World War II period there has arisen a new kind of urban community in which class level and value reinforcement are highly structured; one writer has referred to it as the "mass-produced suburbs." [28] Fringing the nation's larger cities, these housing developments constitute communities of common values, common income, and common strivings—all with the bias of the American middle class. Commuting of fathers to places of employment not infrequently consumes three hours of the day, and children may not have awakened when he leaves in the morning and may go to bed before he gets home at night, leaving only week ends in which to cultivate a father-child relationship. Often these suburban communities lack local government of any kind, as in the case of Levittown, Long Island, which has a population of 70,000, and must attach themselves to established jurisdictions. Offsetting these undesirable features are such factors as the very low crime rate in such areas, and the fact that they were purposely planned for families. They are, furthermore, new and lack such symptoms of economic deprivation as slums, run-down neighborhoods, and high unemployment. Whether or not suburban communities constitute a solution to those problems which we have discussed in connection with urban life depends, as stated before, upon a balancing of the greater income security afforded by metropolitan employment with the consequences of living so far from the father's place of employment, loneliness of the mother, splitting of citizenship interests, and other similar disadvantages.

In conclusion, it should be recalled that the outstanding characteristic of the city, insofar as social legislation is concerned, consists in the dependency it produces. At the personal level the urbanite has

[28] Harry Henderson, "The Mass-Produced Suburbs," *Harper's Magazine*, November, 1953, pp. 25–32.

more freedom and the agencies to satisfy his desires are manifold; however, the urban culture fosters a dilemma. The values which urban industrial society has outmoded survive nonetheless and are pressed before the community by the church, school system, and editorial press. A frustrating situation arises, therefore, when the urbanite attempts to abide by the coöperative values held up by these agencies and at the same time meet the harsh realities of occupational life, which call for intense individual striving.

COMMUNICATIONS SYSTEM

Under this heading will be discussed the multiplicity of means whereby an individual learns (1) what his culture expects of him, and (2) what the responses of his associates to these cultural expectations are. The family, press, government, school, among other agencies, have a hand in this process. No society, of course, is without apparatus to facilitate the process of disposing the new generation favorably toward cultural values, nor are the responses of group members to these values ignored by the new generation. But in the American culture there has arisen a mass concept of this apparatus which has largely replaced the personal concept of a generation ago. Mass-communications media have produced this phenomenon, and the change is not without consequence for American culture.

Let us observe first how the essentials of American character "get into" the child, and how he comes in time to get his "cues" about the culture from impersonal, unidentifiable agencies. The preschool child already has some grasp of the values by which his parents make judgments. Certain of his behaviors gain approval and others do not. Being "all boy" for daddy and "nice" for mommy, not being too easily discouraged with difficult new learning situations presented by parents and originating frequently for the peer group, all will assure parental approval. The reverse of these may result in less than the normal amount of love being manifested by parents. One can say with some certainty that the child, particularly of middle-class parents, arrives at school with the rudiments of predominating cultural values already instilled. School constitutes a learning situation embracing considerably more than the acquisition of information skills. At school the ranking process begins and the child learns his "place" in relationship to the efforts and results produced by his peers. Millard comments as follows on the role of the school system in making cultural values accessible to the child:

In spite of some variation in what they demand of the child in his personal-social behavior, certain patterns seem to be characteristic of conventional schools. Although deplored by certain modern educators, "perfect" attendance is still rewarded. Promptness in school is cherished as is respect toward teachers and authority. Children must say "Excuse me," when they pass in front of an adult, although little is said when the response is lacking in respect to other children. . . . The conventional school has also developed other patterns. Children from "across the tracks" do not surprise anyone when they seem to be guilty of petty stealing, and the child from a "broken home" may be expected to exhibit innumerable kinds of emotional instability.[29]

In his adolescent years the child will begin to appreciate the bombardment of stereotypes directed at him by moving pictures, the broadcasting and television companies, and the press. The personal agency, which had in the home and school allowed him a basis upon which to evaluate the symbols offered by authorities, is lacking, and a situation which David Riesman calls "other-direction" is set up.[30] In this manner the manipulators of public consent press upon their publics the objects which will serve their interests. Happy people are associated in the weekly magazines with this or that brand of electrical appliance, tobacco, or apparel. News articles bear mastheads which upon examination prove wholly erroneous as descriptions of their content. Authoritative pronouncements about "national feeling" on this or that question issue from the pleasant-voiced commentator over radio and television. The results, considering the occupational strata which are most likely to possess the instruments to participate in these media and the time to use them, can be very important: a resistance to change and a complacency in the face of social need may prove to be the wages of this new mass response, and heterodox opinions may become more scarce than ever before. The sheer impersonality and inability to identify sources makes this danger real, and the symbols presented by the mass media in a synthetic situation tend to enjoy the same credibility as those directly perceived by one's own sense apparatus in a nonsynthetic (real life) situation. Thus, the radio commentator's report that the labor leader "was sullen and contemptuous when he called the strike" tends to be accepted by the listeners as though they actually had witnessed the situation and observed the labor lead-

[29] Cecil V. Millard, *Child Growth and Development in the Elementary School Years*, Boston, D. C. Heath and Company, 1951, p. 222.
[30] David Riesman, *The Lonely Crowd*, New Haven, Yale University Press, 1950, p. 34.

er's attitudes. The importance of the influence enjoyed by mass media turns to a large extent on the attitudes of those who control the mass media. We shall deal with this matter below. Reusch and Bateson describe the individual's plight in the face of these developments:

A social event may be characterized by mass communication—e.g., through the media of radio, television, movies, and the press. When exposed to such mass communications, an individual is likely to feel on the one hand, that he is a participant in a larger superpersonal system, and on the other hand, that he is unable to delineate the system. This contradiction is brought about by the fact that in mass communications the originators and recipients of messages are so numerous that they usually remain anonymous. Therefore, under such conditions, the individual is not able to observe the effect of his own messages upon others, nor can he communicate his personal reactions to a message originating from committees, organizations, or institutions. Cause and effect become delayed in time and removed in space; if correction finally occurs, it often is no longer appropriate.[31]

The individual meditative response of the nineteenth-century citizen has been influenced profoundly by the development of mass communications. A more effective instrument to standardize opinion and perpetuate traditional values antithetical to social legislation would be difficult to imagine. Never before in any society has it been possible to "tune in" 48,000,000 households to the same methodically prepared symbols for the purpose of influencing responses and dispositions. Television has both multiplied the symbols and increased the intensity of their appeal.

Accepting the role of mass media as important agencies in the structuring of opinion in American culture, one becomes concerned over the biases which such media represent. In general these are the biases of the middle class, and the American press has historically shared the Whiggish attitudes toward social questions that one associates with business enterprise in general. In fact, the press is more susceptible to the viewpoints of organizations upon which it depends (advertising accounts) than other kinds of business simply because the dependency is so complete. It has been estimated that in 1952 more than four out of five newspapers in the nation opposed the Democratic party, a party which in recent years has been associated with social change in the culture. Even after making allowances for courageous

[31] Jurgen Reusch and Gregory Bateson, Communication—The Social Matrix of Psychiatry, New York, W. W. Norton and Company, 1951, p. 16.

individualism among the press, the viewpoints which reach the individual through his newspaper will more likely than not underplay the need for social legislation. The tendency for several media of communication to be held by a single corporation increases the importance of this tendency, as when the local newspaper, radio station, and television station are owned by a common corporation. On balance, it would seem that mass communications tend to stereotype values and promote resistance to social legislation.

SUPERANNUATION

Several times in this chapter reference has been made to the role of the aged in industrial society and the failure of the new society to support old values, which included care of the aged by the family. So important are the problems created by this change of attitude and other changes in the culture that superannuation calls for discussion at this point. One aspect of the problem derives from the statistical fact that the number of persons aged 65 and over has increased four-fold from 1900 to 1950.

The increase in the number of aged is attributable to advances in public health and medicine which enabled a larger proportion of the population to survive the germ-type killers during their lifetime. In the future, control of nongerm-caused diseases—the so-called degenerative diseases—such as heart disease and cancer may result in additional growth of the aged population in the United States. These facts would not startle us if cultural changes had not taken place during the last quarter-century that created a problem out of a situation in which we might all rejoice—the increase of human life expectation. Our economy has expanded its productivity sufficiently that a larger number of individuals who do not participate in production can be cared for and still permit rising living standards. But in spite of the growth in percentage terms of persons over 65, the American economy is not called upon at the present time to care for a larger percentage of nonproductive inhabitants than formerly. The accompanying table shows the population at dependent ages per hundred persons of productive ages 20–64 from 1850 to the present, and for the future.

Since 1850 the proportion of inhabitants at dependent ages has decreased steadily except for the decade 1940–1950, in which an unusually high birth rate produced a slight increase. On the assumption of the prevailing trend in the birth rate, future years will produce small decreases in these percentages. If the characteristic 2–3 percent

annual increase in American productivity continues, the greater number of persons aged 65 and over will not increase the burden represented by their support.

TABLE 5.   Population at Dependent Ages per 100 Persons of Productive Ages 20–64.

Year	Under 20	65 and Over	Total at Dependent Ages
1850	113	6	119
1900	87	8	95
1910	79	8	87
1920	75	9	84
1930	70	10	80
1940	58	12	70
1950a	59	14	74
1960	58	16	74
1970	53	18	71
1975	53	19	72

a Data for 1950 from U. S. Bureau of the Census *Preliminary Reports, Series PC-7*, No. 1; data for subsequent years from *Forecasts of the Population of the United States, 1945–75*. The forecast assumed high fertility, low mortality, and no immigration. No adjustment for the 1940–1950 increased birth rate has been made for the 1960, 1970, and 1975 forecasts.

Source: Joseph L. McConnell, Janet M. Hooks, *et al.*, "The Changing Family and Its Dependents," *American Income and Its Use*, New York, Harper & Brothers, 1954, p. 286.

The cultural factors, to which reference was made above, are of greater importance in producing the problem of superannuation than are the vital statistics. The age group 35–45 comes more and more to represent the upper limits at which industry wishes to take on new employees, both production and managerial employees. When the number of younger persons available for employment increases, as it is expected to in the period 1960–1970 owing to the higher birth rate of the 1940's, the problem becomes more acute. After we have discussed income security in a later chapter and particularly the cost of retirement annuities (e.g., a $75 monthly annuity for each of two people aged 65 costs about $25,000), the problem will be seen in its full scope. To the threat of economic insecurity must be added the disengagement of age and its status from the central focus of American culture. In an industrial order enthusiastic in its approval of youth and vigorous competition, the aged may well feel that they have been relegated to a subculture that is merely tolerated rather than highly esteemed. It is a rare advertisement which does not utilize happy, youthful persons to get its message across, and most of the products offered by advertisers to enhance the self are aimed at younger people. This tendency to deal out the aged makes the prospect of old age

upsetting to those who, at age fifty, for example, see the writing on the wall.

Aging persons are confronted with problems of income security and status which have become jeopardized by the industrial order. As they become more numerous and their voting power increases (by 1980 one voter in every five will be over 65 years of age), aging people may be expected to use political power more effectively in their own behalf. Additional support for extension of legislation in behalf of the aged may come from those upon whom the aged otherwise would be dependent. It seems assured that the amount and scope of social legislation addressed to the problem of the aged will increase.

The American Culture Pattern and Social Legislation:
Concluding Remarks

This chapter has purposed to relate the essential features of the American culture pattern and the American basic character to social legislation. The American character, expressing as it does a jealous regard for traditionally masculine virtues of individualism and a confidence in future progress, basically opposes the extension of social legislation. The trends in American culture during the twentieth century, however, have wrought a reappraisal of the merits in this basic character. Of primary importance have been American involvement in two world wars and the depression decade of the 1930's. If the traditional American fear of centralization and the Puritan ethic promote a hesitancy on the part of Americans to deal with their social problems through extending the operations of government, then they are offset by the traditional American pragmatism and the reactions in social thought to the crises of this century. By mid-century, in any case, the debate about extending the agency of government centered not on whether such action should be undertaken, but rather on the scope and mode of government participation. In other words, the question had become one of administrative alternatives and the sufficiency of the aid provided.

Other dimensions of American culture might have been substituted for some of those discussed in the preceding chapter. The secular character of our culture, the structure of income distribution, and the stability of personality might have been given the attention which their importance in our culture deserves. For the most part the elements which have been neglected in this chapter will be discussed in subse-

quent chapters, some of which (income distribution, for example) have been accorded an exclusive chapter.

SELECTED REFERENCES

Brogan, Denis W., *The American Character*, New York, Alfred A. Knopf, 1944.

Commager, Henry Steele, *The American Mind*, New Haven, Yale University Press, 1950.

Davis, Kingsley, et al., *Modern American Society*, New York, Rinehart and Company, 1949.

Gorer, Geoffrey, *The American People*, New York, W. W. Norton and Company, 1948.

Homans, George C., *The Human Group*, New York, Harcourt, Brace and Company, 1950.

Laski, Harold J., *The American Democracy*, New York, The Viking Press, 1948.

Perry, Ralph Barton, *Characteristically American*, New York, Alfred A. Knopf, 1949.

Perry, Ralph Barton, *Puritanism and Democracy*, New York, The Vanguard Press, 1944.

Riesman, David, *The Lonely Crowd*, New Haven, Yale University Press, 1950.

American Culture Pattern and Social Legislation   101

quent chapters, some of which discuss income distribution, for example, have been accorded intensive study.

Cochran, Thomas C., *The American Business System* . . . 1900–1955, 1957.

Commager, Henry Steele, *The American Mind*, New Haven: Yale University Press, 1950.

Davis, Kingsley, *Human Society*, New York: . . . , Blakiston and Company, 1949.

Handlin, Oscar . . . and Company, New York: W. W. Norton and Company, 1915.

Homans, George . . . *The Human Group*, New York: Harcourt, Brace, and Company, 1934.

Laski, Harold J., *The American Democracy*, New York: The Viking Press, . . .

chapter **5**

The Political Process and Social Legislation

The objective of this chapter is to examine the nature and functioning of those institutions whereby the state determines which among various objects will be given the force of law. Some objects will, through the legislative process, take on the authority of the state to compel obedience to them; other objects will be discarded because they are not considered of such consequence that conformity should be legally compulsive. The behaviors which influence this selection process are very complex and their nature and operation challenge the efforts of all social scientists. From the vast literature concerning political behavior we shall deal with the constitutional background of the American state and, in a general way, with the behaviors that determine the character of social legislation.

The Functions of the State

The state is distinguished from other associations, as we have learned in preceding chapters, by the fact that it is vested with the ultimate power to use force. As we would expect, the form which this function assumes varies from culture to culture, and the variations concern how, over whom, and to what extent the threat of force shall be used. The organizational machinery and the behaviors which concern themselves with these questions can be referred to as political institutions; they become more complex as society becomes more complex. As with all social institutions, there is an ideal and an operative dimension to the political process. Because the power to compel behavior is so important, the ideal, formal structure of political institutions yields to a great deal of opportunism and adaptation, causing

the operative dimension to be of greater significance than in the case of other institutions.

At times the state has operated as an omnipotent colossus with objects of its own and with little heed to the group over which it exercises power. In contrast, the state has at other times been almost completely subordinate to the group over whom it exercises power. In the modern world, every form of state has been known; but among those states which draw their heritage from western Europe, the predominating characteristic has been the encumberment of state power with extensive safeguards.

Any classification of state forms is vulnerable to criticism; but to distinguish modern states from each other we can use the classification of paternalistic-protective and individualistic-protective. This classification distinguishes among states on the basis of their major assumptions concerning individual action. In the case of the paternalistic state, there is a distrust of the consequences of individual, laissez-faire behavior and the state seeks to control the results of social intercourse by exercising regimen over individuals and groups. In the manorial system of the Middle Ages, for example, the avoidance of starvation and military annihilation demanded preoccupation by the state with the effectiveness of community action. Thus, conduct which did not contribute to subsistence and protection was proscribed. Survival took precedence over individual liberty of action, and the community accepted serfdom and military bondage. This paternalistic form of state has typified "underdeveloped" (economically) cultures and mature, "overdeveloped" (economically) cultures. Each has sought relief from the consequences of underproduction or overproduction through state intervention in individual affairs.

The second classification of state, the individualistic form, is insistent in its protection of the individual from state interference. Guidance, not regimen, is its major function. Individual freedom of action is regarded highly, and it is assumed that the most efficient harnessing of human and natural resources will result from unrestrained "private" action. A development of the period since the thirteenth century, this form of state is comparatively new in man's political history. This individualistic form of state is typical of young, dynamic societies which are confident in the power of individuals over future consequences. Nations which have in their early stages enjoyed the kind of permissiveness which this concept of the state affords have brought the highest standards of living to their citizens. The United States, particularly,

owes the rapid development of its resources in part to the stubborn defense of individual enterprise made by past generations. In the twentieth century, however, the high social costs of the individualistic state have caused its worthiness to be challenged, and the state form in all industrial nations has become, in some degree, paternalistic.

The extension of the paternalistic state form has come about for several reasons. First, we are unwilling to tolerate the capricious and arbitrary consequences of uncoördinated individual action; depressions, for example, seem to bear a relationship to individual freedom. Second, we can no longer tolerate the extremes of inequality which are bred by the individualistic state because the ideas surrounding living standards provide for an ever-increasing margin beyond the necessary subsistence minimum. Third, changes in our cultural outlook upon security have occurred. As pointed out in the preceding chapter, the family no longer is thought of as caretaker for the aged, this function having been shifted to government. Finally, the balance of political power has shifted in favor of those elements of the society, notably organized labor and agriculture, which would benefit from state welfare action in their behalf. In a sense our whole discussion beyond this point rests on these observations since social legislation presupposes a balance of political power in favor of the paternalistic state.

Let us look at the American state in connection with the above discussion. The American state—referring to the association which exercises the legal right of compulsion over the area included in the United States—is unique in many respects. In the first place, the American "experiment" (a mere six generations old) was a deliberate innovation born out of revolution. It lacked the kind of evolution which in Europe saw gradual attrition of the power in the hands of the hereditary nobility. The purpose of those who promoted the new government was to limit both democracy and central authority. If any single event can be cited as the precipitating factor that brought about the constitution of 1787, it was Daniel Shays' attack on the Springfield arsenal in 1786. This attack on property represented, in the eyes of the "fathers," an example of the dangers inherent in too much personal liberty. Central authority was equally suspect for the obvious reason that a war had only recently been fought against King George III, and the "fathers" earnestly sought to ensure that future generations never would be oppressed by another "tyrant," foreign or domestic. Furthermore, the states were not united and they feared the consequences of an efficient central authority, particularly regular tax

collections, regulation of money, and control over property. It required more than a century for sentiment in favor of the paternalistic state to become effective in the United States, and this occurred only after social crises had made the need for change painfully obvious. Because American resources were so bountiful, farmland particularly, changes in the assumptions of the individualistic state were delayed in comparison with the experience of European nations. As various phases of American social legislation are discussed, this delay will be recognized.

Political Procedure

Decision making in the new national government, as the fathers of the Constitution saw it, was to be a coöperative affair. The representatives of the people (in general, property owners) would arrive at conclusions to guide policy matters through more or less public debate. Majority decisions in most cases would decide controversies and the majority stand would represent the wiser stand—owing solely to the predominance of numbers on the assumption that the representatives were identical in ability, integrity, etc.—and the minority was expected to accept the majority position. There is in this procedure an implicit assumption that unanimous judgments would result if time permitted extensive debate and deliberation; but time does not permit, and the majority's position is taken to guide policy in the belief that the minority would have come around to the majority position anyway.[1] By way of restriction the fathers determined that no creed or doctrine should ever bind the people's representatives, and the Constitution specifically forbade state intercourse with a religious sect.

To frustrate the influence of a particular sectional interest for any extended period of time, the fathers gave different terms of office to senators and representatives. The passage of legislation on the basis of majority sentiment was made unusually difficult by separation of government powers and a system of checks and balances, a matter which we shall investigate in detail later. It seems clear that the Constitutional Convention was anxious to frame the governmental apparatus with a view to hindering the passage of legislation based on simple majority sentiment, and, by making legislation difficult, the delegates sought to provide for the slow perfecting of a new order in statecraft based on eternal *legal* principles. Their handiwork, at any

[1] For a discussion of this point, see Ralph Barton Perry, *Characteristically American,* New York, Alfred A. Knopf, 1949, p. 128.

rate, afforded sufficient leeway both for the absolutely necessary legislation to be passed and for the lessons of political experience to be adapted within the political apparatus when that seemed desirable.

Our discussion thus far may have suggested that the political machinery of a modern state functions merely to accomplish deliberate changes in social relationships in response to more or less well-defined social needs. This view is not realistic, as the casual visitor to the national or a state legislature will soon see. The people's representatives are not to be seen at all times earnestly deliberating over proposed solutions to pressing social problems. At times such deliberations actually take place, but the legislatures exist primarily to "get government business done," and only a small part of this business is related to the larger social problems of American society. Of the 10,000 proposals which an average American Congress considers in its two-year lifetime, not more than 1000 find their way to the statute books, and a very large proportion of these deal with the establishment of committees, the approval of appropriations, the correcting of war records, and the relief of citizens engaged in suits against the government. If the reader has uncertainties about the "routine" in Congress, a hurried leafing through the *Congressional Record* will establish the fact that dramatic debates on social issues are far from an everyday occurrence.

The political machinery becomes truly deliberative, however, when something approaching a national consensus on matters such as national health insurance, amendment of basic labor legislation, or a national divorce law becomes clear, or if the President initiates the proposal for social legislation. In these cases the audience is nationwide and interests keen. Distribution of power [2] between states and nation, and among interest groups, lies in the balance of Congressional action, and the determination of a "general" or "public" interest sets the political machinery in motion.

As the above discussion implies, the formal political framework is only part of the picture in our political experience, and adaptations constructed to facilitate "getting political business done" have proved far more important in explaining the response of social legislation to social need. It is to a discussion of the *formal* and *operative* framework that we now turn.

[2] Harold D. Lasswell notes that the "power" for which groups compete consists of three things: safety, deference, and goods. *Politics, Who Gets What, When, and How,* New York, Whittlesey House, 1936, p. 1.

The National Political Framework

The setting within which American political institutions operate is defined formally by the Constitution of 1787. A model of brevity, it has served as a sort of flexible perimeter of state authority. Because the fathers started from scratch in *writing* a constitution, they drew up guidelines with a view to permitting such adaptations as the lessons of practical experience would suggest. The rigidities in the Constitution of 1787, fortunately, concern its spirit rather than its letter. Furthermore, Alexander Hamilton and other strong personalities labored to assert the power of the national government over the states, justifying their efforts by the "implied powers" of the Constitution: the people of the United States having set up the Constitution as a sovereign power, the means requisite to effecting that sovereign power were "implied" and "resulted" from the action of the people. This view was made a part of the Constitution in 1819, when its essentials were upheld by the Supreme Court in the case of McCulloch v. Maryland.[3] By 1800, as a matter of fact, the "liberal" view of national government power was established, a result which the fathers probably had not intended. Some students see the greatness of the American Constitution as resting primarily on its ability to grow with the needs of American society.

Such modifications of the original Constitution as have been described above have altered the formal setting of American government. This is recognized in the "broadly defined" concept of the Constitution—the body of rules that bear upon political practice. The elements which make up this larger concept are stated in the following list:

1. The written constitution, including formal amendments.
2. Important enduring statutes that organize and regulate major branches and departments of the government.
3. Court decisions interpreting and applying the written constitution and basic statutes.
4. Less important, but worthy of mention—the opinions of public attorneys and the rules of major departments insofar as they deal with important matters.
5. The customs and practices that determine the form and operation of government.[4]

The first four elements listed above are parts of the law, while the

[3] *McCulloch v. Maryland*, Wheaton (U.S.) 316 (1819).
[4] William Anderson and Edward W. Weidner, *American Government*, New York, Henry Holt and Company, 1953, p. 101.

fifth is nonlegal. Examples of each category will help clarify the conditions which give rise to expanded bases for government. In the first case, it is noteworthy that even before the Constitution of 1787 was ratified by the required nine states, amendments had been provided for. As a condition of their acceptance the states demanded the first ten amendments, which have since been known as the Bill of Rights. The protection of the rights guaranteed in the Bill of Rights has been a matter of the greatest importance in American government. Other important amendments include the Thirteenth, Fourteenth, and Fifteenth, which respectively prohibit slavery, deprivation of life, liberty, and property without due process of law, and abridgement of suffrage on account of race, color, or previous condition of servitude; the Sixteenth, which permits a federal income tax; the Seventeenth, providing for popular election of senators; and the Nineteenth, which prohibits denial of suffrage on account of sex. The second element is illustrated by the Judiciary Act of 1789, which set up a system of federal courts, and the laws which in the same year created the departments of Foreign Affairs, War, Treasury, and Justice. In the case of court decisions, the *Marbury v. Madison* decision rendered by John Marshall in 1803 is of great importance, for it established the practice of judicial review by the Supreme Court.[5] The decision in the *McCulloch v. Maryland* case, mentioned previously as asserting the supremacy of the national government and recognizing "implied" powers in the Constitution, has frequently been cited as the most important decision ever rendered by the Supreme Court. Other decisions of lower courts, such as the *Santa Clara County v. Southern Pacific R.R.*, have had the effect of giving Constitutional protection to circumstances never intended in the Constitution or its amendments, in this case construing the corporation as a person under the Fourteenth Amendment. The fourth element, opinions of public attorneys and rules of major departments, is illustrated in the former case by the statement of the Attorney General, Caleb Cushing, in 1855 that "no head of a department can lawfully perform an official act against the will of the President, and that will is by the Constitution to govern the performance of all such acts." Opinions of the Department of Justice concerning violation of antitrust legislation, and opinions of the Secretary of the Treasury concerning liability under the tax laws, illustrate the latter. Customs, which complete the elements of the broader Consti-

[5] *Marbury v. Madison*, Cranch 137 (1803).

tution concept, are very numerous. Nomination of candidates by political parties, pledging of Presidential electors to a particular party, and Senatorial courtesy are illustrations.

A changing character is given to political procedure by the factors discussed above. In general, such changes have concerned the extension of the franchise, criteria of constitutionality employed by the Supreme Court, and the extension of functions within the executive branch. Because they have performed so well, these adaptations have enabled the Constitution to grow with social needs. The formal specifications of the Constitution of 1787 are still the basis of American government and they have been adapted rather than altered for the most part.

THE CONSTITUTION OF 1787

The discussion thus far has taken note of the rigidities in the Constitution, and the fact that these rigidities have hindered the accomplishment of social legislation. While in the light of modern industrial conditions this would appear to be the case, in 1787 the Constitution was far more appreciative of democracy than the basic law of any other state. Its basic inspiration had been drawn from English liberalism, and the American Constitution inherited the hard-won accomplishments of the British Parliament. As the oldest written constitution in the world, the American Constitution is living testimony to the fundamental wisdom of the fathers.

Amendment of the national Constitution is an important feature of that document and is specified in Article V. Only one restriction is placed on the process; it requires that "no State, without its Consent, shall be deprived of its equal Suffrage in the Senate." Presumably, then, the entire document might be altered if the legal procedure were followed. Proposed amendments may arise in two ways: by vote of two-thirds of both Houses of Congress, or by a national constitutional convention called by Congress on application of two-thirds of the state legislatures. Ratification of the proposed amendments is likewise possible in two ways: by legislatures in three-fourths of the states, or by conventions called in three-fourths for that purpose. Actually, of the twenty-two amendments to the Constitution, only one has been proposed by Congress and then submitted to state conventions for ratification. All of the others have been proposed by the Congress and then ratified by the requisite state legislatures.

Long periods have intervened between amendments to the Constitution: 1804 to 1865 and 1933 to 1951. The explanation would seem to lie not in the cumbersomeness of the amending procedure, necessarily, but rather in the fact that the Supreme Court has continually reinterpreted the Constitution, which, with other elements in the broader conception of the Constitution, has enabled the document to meet national needs without recourse to the amending process. Only twenty-seven amendments have been proposed and submitted for ratification. But the inability to add the child-labor amendment, which was proposed in 1924 and is still unratified, to the Constitution is an indication of how the Constitution can lag behind the national social conscience.

A FEDERAL GOVERNMENT

It was assumed by the fathers that the states would carry the major burden of legislation, the national government confining its operations to matters of national and international concern. In brief, almost terse, language, the Constitution defined national and state jurisdictions. To the national government was given the control of military affairs, foreign relations, the national currency, interstate and foreign commerce, the adjudication of cases where state courts would be inadequate, and regulation of patents, copyrights, bankruptcy, and naturalization. In the Tenth Amendment the state powers are described: "The powers not delegated to the United States by the Constitution, nor prohibited by it to the States, are reserved to the States respectively, or to the people." Additional groups of powers are exercised concurrently; they include police power, taxing power, and power to adjudicate. Specific prohibitions are made to the states and the national government in the constitution.[6]

While the thirteen states which had entered into the compact remained primarily agricultural in their interests, the scant powers permitted the national government seldom jeopardized social stability. In the War of 1812, however, the refusal of some states to allow their militia to leave the state caused difficulty. As the nation expanded and regional inequalities became pronounced, the national powers permit-

---

[6] Article I, Section 10, and Article IV, Sections 1 and 2, prohibit the states from trespassing on national powers, impairing contracts, and abridging privileges of citizens from the several states. Articles of amendment I through IX, the Bill of Rights, list the prohibitions of the national government.

ted by the Constitution became progressively inadequate and social legislation at the national level would have been impossible without the construction of the "broader concept" of the Constitution.

SEPARATION OF POWERS

In addition to weighting the United States Government strongly in favor of the states, the fathers also endeavored to separate the branches of the national government and define their functions in such a way as to provide a system of checks and balances. Three coequal branches of the national government were created: the legislative, executive, and judicial. In defining powers of the three branches, the fathers switched their logical powers around so as to make each branch incomplete in carrying on its activities; thus, the President as head of the executive branch may propose legislation, conduct foreign relations, and command the armed forces; but the action of the Congress exercising the legislative power is necessary to give effect to any of these actions. The President shares appointive power with the Congress, and impeachment functions are legislative. The role of the Supreme Court exercising the judicial function was vague until 1803. After that date it maintained the right to decide whether national and state laws were consistent with the Constitution and to disallow them if they were not. It was possible, then, for Congress to pass a law, the President to veto it, and the Congress to override the veto with a two-thirds' vote of both houses. Or the Congress could pass a law, the President sign it (or fail to veto it in the required ten days), and the Supreme Court (upon receiving a case involving the law) could disallow the law for being unconstitutional. This extraordinary power of the judiciary has at times been employed in such a way as to make social legislation impossible, although this has not been the case since 1937. The use to which the power has been put in specific instances will be discussed in later sections.

The formal structure of American government favored the legislative branch, which was to determine policy (factions canceling each other out). It was the duty of the President to administer policies of the Congress. He could, of course, initiate the proposals, which became policy through legislative procedure, and veto the policy if he saw fit. In practice the President has most frequently initiated legislation, and only infrequently have Presidential vetoes been overridden. Moreover, the President through the bureaucracy has become a *de*

facto policy maker in many respects without Congressional check, save for Congressional action in setting up the bureaus. Against the Supreme Court individual Presidents have been less successful in making functional inroads, though many commissions under the President have quasi-judicial functions. The long tenure of the venerable men of the bench scarcely ever allows a President to appoint members whose opinions are suitable to his program, and in recent years attempts by the President to counteract opposing views from the Supreme Court by reorganization have failed before the legislature and the public. But the Supreme Court has showed a tendency to keep pace with the social views suggested by the election returns and has not often obstructed the other two branches in giving the will of the voters the force of law.

Much of the growth in Presidential power emanates from the fact that the President is a truly national representative, "all-interested," where the Congress is a body of separate interests. The fathers had supposed (failing to anticipate the two-party system) that the President would be chosen by the House of Representatives and would owe his election to the legislative branch. Since the Presidency has emerged as an independent institution, the power of the executive branch has gone far beyond the original expectations. Given supporting social thought, the President has been able to make much of his office in time of war and social crisis. If the Constitution favored the legislature, it did not restrict the executive branch but merely left its dimensions vague.

THE ELECTORATE

Government by the people's representatives such as the fathers sought to inaugurate rests in a basic sense upon the ability and willingness of the electorate to participate. Concerning the qualifications of the electorate, the fathers left determination to the states with only the restriction that the requirements for participation in national elections be the same as for electing the more populous house in the state legislature. Property qualifications for participation in elections were in force in many states until the mid-nineteenth century; the removal of racial restrictions was brought about by law only after a civil war; and women were enfranchised only in 1920. In spite of formal legal statements, restrictions on suffrage because of race are notorious in some states.

Willingness to participate is another matter. Legal restrictions on persons willing and able to vote account for but a small percentage of the nonparticipation in American national elections. Civic indifference seems to be the major explanation. The fathers expected the vote to be eagerly prized, and self-disenfranchisement is simply another—though negative—example of a political institution supplementing the formal order.

SUMMARY

The formal apparatus which the fathers designed to govern thirteen small agrarian states must be viewed as an unprecedented success in man's political life. It is to be judged by its performance in comparison with the basic law of other states rather than by its failure to foresee the problems that complex industrial society would create. On this kind of comparison the American Constitution has permitted the management of human and natural resources in such a way as to afford the highest standard of living in the world. Rigidities in the Constitution, such as the inability to alter the representation of a state in the Senate without its consent, and the brief terms of office for representatives, are important. That the attitude of reverence with which Americans have regarded their Constitution has handicapped efforts of the national government to deal with social problems can be readily admitted. But such handicaps are scarcely worse than the obstructions affected by supplemental political apparatus, including customs, political parties, and pressure groups which deliberately frustrate social legislation. Following a brief analysis of the political framework general to the states, we will discuss these supplemental factors.

The State Political Framework

It is appropriate to accord the national political framework the most importance in a discussion of political institutions. The supremacy of the national Constitution has been long established. Furthermore, social legislation has become a national matter except for family legislation, and the probable future course of social legislation will be toward exclusive national determination, the states administering programs. But important vestiges of social legislation remain with the states—family legislation, education, labor in intrastate commerce, etc. —and their political institutions deserve brief consideration. Simply on the basis of governmental jurisdictions, the preponderance of units is not national, as the following table discloses:

Table 6. Units of Government, 1951.[a]

Units	Number
Nation	1
States	48
Counties	3,049
Municipalities	16,677
Townships	17,338
School districts	70,452
Other special	11,900
Total	119,465

[a] U. S. Bureau of the Census, *Governments in the United States in 1951*, State and Local Government Special Studies No. 29, 1952.

STATE CONSTITUTIONS

The fathers favored the states over the national government and left the largest number of functions possible with them, except for the minimum uniformities necessary to interstate commerce, which were delegated to the national government. All of the original states have, or have had, constitutions which antedate the national constitution. Following the Declaration of Independence in 1776, Massachusetts and New Hampshire led a movement to reformulate their constitutions under new provisions. The essence of the new provisions consisted in the election of delegates for the purpose of formulating a new constitution and the submission of the new constitution to the voters for approval. The Massachusetts and New Hampshire constitutions later became the models for the other states and, as new states were added to the original thirteen, they also copied the dominant form of basic law. Generalizations about state constitutions are possible, therefore, because the major provisions are so similar.

All state constitutions embody the separation-of-powers principle, and contain statements of basic individual rights which the states shall not abridge. As in the national Constitution, the central (state) power is viewed with suspicion and generous powers are given the legislative branch; but the executive branch has gained power steadily. Even at the present time, however, the governor is in most cases more dependent on the legislature than the President is on the Congress. The senate in most states retains a veto over appointments proposed by the governor; but the control which the national legislature holds over the executive, in that appropriations bills must be accepted or rejected as a whole, is uncommon at the state level—provision being

made in thirty-nine states for the veto of separate items by the governor. Furthermore, the governor may call the legislature into special session, which has become common in recent years (only six states hold annual sessions of the legislature). But these offsets to legislative domination are more than balanced by other factors which limit executive power. The tenure of the executive is only two years in about half the states, and this brief term represents an improvement over the previously common one-year term. More recently the four-year term has been instituted, and a majority of the states provide for such a tenure at the present time. A more severe limitation on the executive power is its dispersion. The governor is not the "executive power" but the "supreme executive power" in most state constitutions, sharing his power with six other elective officials in the substantial majority of states and many more in those states which provide for the popular election of boards and commissions. The executive power is thus diffused to the disadvantage of the governor. When it is also appreciated that the direct primary method of selecting candidates further restricts the governor's choice of personnel in the executive branch, the obstacles to the governor's being a true executive *in fact* become obvious.

State constitutions have been particularly criticized in connection with the procedures stipulated for amendment. In many instances the original handiwork of the framers produced constitutions so ill suited to the complexities of modern state government that amendments became crucial. But the constitution of Tennessee, for example, has never been amended because the procedure for so doing is too complicated. In contrast, the constitution of California has been amended 352 times. Amendments to state constitutions are sufficiently difficult to process that delay may permit abuses and difficulties that derive from the constitution as it exists.

The amendment procedure specified in most constitutions (thirty-six) was for a constitutional convention to draw up proposals, but every state except New Hampshire permitted other means of amendment. Proposals by the legislature are far more important as sources of amendment, but the required vote in favor of proposed amendment seldom is a simple majority, two-thirds or three-fifths often being required. In general, the time required to secure an amendment to the state constitution is far less under the legislative proposal system. One authority estimates the normal amount of time required for changing the constitution by the convention method as more than five years from the proposal for a constitutional convention to the counting of

a popular ballot on the proposed changes by an official group such as
a canvassing board.[7] Even allowing for the provision in some constitutions that proposals for amendment by legislatures be passed by extraordinary majorities in two successive legislatures, the time required
to complete the amendment process will be less if this method is used.
A third method of proposing amendments has been developed, largely
since 1900, and is in use in fourteen states. This provides for proposals
to be introduced by popular petition and it is called the popular initiative method. A relatively small percentage of the voters (8 to 15
percent) may circumvent the legislature entirely in putting proposed
amendments before the people. A majority of voters voting in the
election may, through this procedure, accomplish constitutional reform.

The large number of amendments common to state constitutions
should not be taken to suggest that rigidity is unimportant in state
constitutions. Because the more recent constitutions have been extremely detailed—including provisions better left to legislation—reforms have often been prevented or delayed. A former Oregon state
senator criticizes the states in this connection:

A person unfamiliar with state constitutions would not believe what he
was reading if he had thrust upon him the basic charters which govern
many of the forty-eight states.

The constitution of Oregon restricts the location of all new state institutions such as colleges and mental hospitals to just one out of the state's
thirty-six counties, irrespective of other factors. The constitution of Tennessee makes ineligible for public office any individual who denies "a system
of rewards and punishments." West Virginia's constitution bars officials
of railroads from serving in the legislature. The constitution of Texas forces
the state to maintain five times as many courts and judges as serve the
infinitely larger population of the United Kingdom. California's constitution goes into endless detail regarding such trivialities as the duration of
wrestling matches and the breeding of mollusks and crustaceans.

A matter locked in a state constitution is beyond the touch of the Governor or legislature. Only a referendum vote among a majority of a state's
citizens can set it aside. This involves a minimum of two years' time, frequently more. Emergencies rarely allow such a leisurely pace, which is why
the federal government must step into the breach.[8]

We shall see in the following section that the more odious opera-

---

[7] Anderson and Weidner, op. cit., p. 123.
[8] Richard L. Neuberger, "The Decay of State Governments," Harper's Magazine,
October, 1953, pp. 38–39.

tive political institutions are associated with the states. This is not unrelated to the shortcomings frequently found in the state constitutions. Short tenures, divided executive authority, salary rigidities for legislators, and other antiquated features cause the formal machinery to be circumvented in order to get government business done.

The Operative Political Process

Only rarely do systematic portrayals of formal social apparatus explain actual social behavior. The organizational plan of a corporation scarcely reveals the behavior within the organization, nor does the process chart, with its carefully defined "lines of authority," reveal the operations of national, state, or local government. In the case of political units the stakes of officeholding are so high—power, wealth, prestige—that the nonformal or operative institutions are of enormous importance. The manner whereby officeholders are nominated and elected, and the manner whereby they determine who gets "what, when, and how," are matters which in modern political life cannot be explained by looking into the written national and state constitutions. Because the associations and institutions which effectuate the political process are so important, we will discuss them in the remainder of this chapter.

FEDERALISM AND SEPARATION OF POWERS

These two matters, which assumed great importance in the Constitution of 1787, have been modified in actual practice, as the preceding section suggested. The states, to which the fathers gave the broadest political powers, have seen their preëminence disappear as the nation's problems have grown, chiefly as a result of industrialism and internationalism. From the early nineteenth century on, this tendency was clearly in evidence. Lacking express authority to regulate conditions of employment, railroad rates, agricultural surpluses, etc., the national government passed necessary legislation and defended it as an exercise of the power to provide for the general welfare. This provision is mentioned in the Constitution in two places: in the Preamble as a condition for framing the document, and in Article I, Section 8, as an object to be served by the taxing power of the Congress. The Supreme Court has generally sustained national legislation outside of the delegated powers in accordance with the general-welfare clauses. The most noteworthy penetration of state powers by the national government took place after the onset of the Great Depression. When the inade-

quacy of state resources to cope with such a crisis as a national depression was made obvious, the practice of "matching grants" was expanded; the state could receive moneys from the national treasury if certain standards were met and if the state matched the national sum with a like sum. Various state programs, including highways, health and welfare, housing, and agriculture, are now dependent upon variations of this technique. More subtle has been the effect upon state powers caused by national preëmption of revenue sources. In every major form of taxation except the retail sales tax, the national government presently competes with the states. Simply for lack of necessary revenue the states have been unable to use their full reserved powers. The results are clear—the states have surrendered authority to the national government in many areas, including social legislation, as we shall see in succeeding chapters.

The powers of the President and his office have expanded far beyond the powers that the fathers anticipated. National and international crises have created the need for focused authority, and the Congress has seen fit to delegate its authority generously to the executive branch, retaining something more than nominal power over appointments. The magnitude of its generosity is seen in the several hundred bureaus which have mushroomed at the national level, sixty-five of which report directly to the President. There is little question that the growth of the executive power attained its present proportions because of experiences associated with the Great Depression and the Second World War. In creating the need for *expertise* in government affairs, these crises caused the multiplication of regulatory and fact-finding agencies. So concentrated were such agencies in the executive office that the legislative branch was distinctly handicapped in coping with Presidential proposals of legislation. Proposals buttressed by elaborate statistical documentation were far more formidable than proposals which, in the absence of such documentation, might be taken for unsupported opinion. During the decade of the forties the Congress provided for similar research assistance in its own behalf, the Legislative Reorganization Act of 1946 specifically meeting the need. The result has been wholly favorable in that the prevalence of informed opinion in the executive and the legislative branches has raised the level of information upon which proposals are considered. How this aids legislators in responding to pressure groups will be explained later.

In his office the President now has agencies whose functions bear

upon the great economic and social problems of the nation. The Bureau of the Budget, the National Security Resources Planning Board, and the Council of Economic Advisors are examples of such agencies. Comparable agencies are maintained by the Congress, but the initiative rests with the Presidential agencies, the Congress frequently making defensive use of its agencies. Of enormous importance in accounting for Presidential power is the availability to the President of mass media through which he can seek support for his policies from a nation-wide audience "face to face." The effectiveness of the mass media, particularly television, in gaining support for the President's program has been increased by the role which they play in election campaigns. Frequent televiewing of the President appears to have made him more a national symbol than ever. The advantage which he gains in comparison with the locally representative Congress is considerable. As national head of his political party the President gains additional influence.

POLITICAL PARTIES

The operation of the American political process without political parties would be impossible as presently constituted. No mention of such organizations is made in the Constitution of 1787, however, and the idea of a mere two-party system is only vaguely described in historical documents of the constitutional period. The danger of factions was dealt with, the most famous discussion being in the *Federalist*, Number 10, by James Madison; while warning against the dangers of factions, he concluded that diversity of interests in the nation would prohibit any single one from attaining a majority power. There is no suggestion that the factions might deliberately be organized to the end of attaining a majority power. With the very first administration, however, party lines crystallized on such issues as states' rights, democracy, and Hamiltonianism.

Defining the political party as an organization of individuals having essentially similar views about government would simplify our discussion, but would poorly describe the organization of the two major American parties. The Republican and Democratic parties cut across economic, class, racial, and sectional lines. No brief definition, then, can account for all of the diversities reflected in their programs and membership. Some characteristics of the major parties should be understood, however. First, truly national political organizations come into being only once in four years, at the time of Presidential elec-

tions. Second, the two major political parties are primarily state and local organizations, the locus of power being at the state level. Third, issues which separate the major parties are rarely fundamental, but are rather concerned with administrative alternatives. Fourth, the relationships between political parties and pressure groups are often competitive rather than complimentary. We shall not elaborate on these statements separately at this point, but will deal with them as the functions of parties are discussed.

If defining the political party in America is difficult, such is not the case with its functions. The political party atones for the shortsightedness of the fathers by selecting candidates and mobilizing voting majorities for elections (particularly Presidential elections), operating the government, dichotomizing issues, furnishing an organization responsible to the general will, and acting as a line of communication between citizens and their state. Schattschneider comments on the "natural mistake" of the fathers as follows:

> They made the very natural mistake of underestimating the difficulties arising from the numbers, preoccupation, immobility, and indifference of the people. Everyone took it for granted that the people would assume responsibility for the expression of their own will as a matter of course without so much as dreaming of the intervention of syndicates of self-appointed managers and manipulators who for reasons of their own might organize the electorate and channel the expression of the popular will.[9]

Mobilizing a majority of the electorate has become increasingly dependent on political parties as the number of divisive issues has multiplied. This was a natural consequence of industrialization and its problems. It is the function of the political party to devise a program to the fulfillment of which candidates for political office pledge their energies. Of necessity the program will be a compromise of many points of view because it must appeal to a majority. Each party quilts a program which seldom is strongly partisan on any controversial issue, and contains some objectives that will appeal to each major interest group. Consistency and rational design matter little in this procedure; increased government spending and promises to reduce taxes, higher prices for the farmer and lower ones for the consumer, protection and discipline of labor unions, all are to be found in the program to which the party commits those who run for office under its banner. Since the party is most vital at the local level, however, the greatest service

[9] E. E. Schattschneider, *Party Government*, New York, Farrar and Rinehart, 1942, p. 14.

is rendered by those who at that level "talk up" the party's candidates and program, promise favors in return for votes, and even transport voters to the polls on election day and return them dry and appreciative to their homes. It is inconceivable that the election of candidates to office could be carried on in modern American society without the services performed by the political party. The fortunate circumstance of having two major parties which between them poll 99 percent of the total votes cast (the difference in votes cast for either party rarely amounting to 10 percent and most often less than 3 percent) will be discussed later.

The successful party in an election assumes vast power in the organization and operation of government. The separation-of-powers principle in the national and state governments would, if not controlled, create a divergence of interests among the three branches such that unanimity would be difficult to accomplish. It is necessary for either the executive or legislative branch, in getting its proposals for legislation enacted into law, to convince the other branch of the proposals' merits. Otherwise, obstruction by the President through the veto or by the Congress through various tactics of obfuscation would prevent legislation. Because the political party gives a common hue to the executive and part of each House in Congress, the separation of powers does not so often prevent the enactment of legislation. The actual working groups in the legislature, the committees, are strongly influenced by the political party. Committee chairmanship and membership depend upon which party successfully elects a majority of its candidates to each House. When the importance of committees in the legislative process is discussed in a later section, the considerable role played by political parties will be better understood. Selection of appointive officials in the government is also influenced by political parties, particularly at the state and local levels. The merit system has reduced this influence, but the ability to appoint loyal party workers to government positions is important enough to spur local and state organizations in their quest of political victory at the polls.

Issues which the individual representative might be called upon to decide in enacting laws could be counted in the thousands if the points of view of every interested group were to be submitted to him for judgment. The political party organization sifts the views pressed for enactment and simplifies them into proposals endorsed by the party. Of course, the individual representative may ignore the party proposal and a majority of party proposals seem to be ignored at the

national level. The Congressman does not owe his election to the national party organization; except in closely contested states little financial aid is made available. But the tradition of the party, its past victories and heroes, are important factors in gaining loyalty to party policies. In most matters of national concern the Democratic and Republican parties tend to agree in principle—social security, foreign policy, and agricultural price supports are examples—which makes the legislative pitfalls for proposals less hazardous for such legislation. Debate in these cases concerns administrative alternatives. The party function enables local partisan views to be fused into one or two viewpoints in national government. Furthermore, the views of state party leaders concerning the public's opinion, when transmitted to the national level, are an invaluable aid in determining a party stand on issues. If the state leaders' assessments of sectional opinion are accurate, the party is enabled to encourage the passage of legislation agreeable to national opinion and thus retain power in the national government. Essentially the same relationships exist between cities and counties and the states.

Party responsibility for government activities is a much debated issue among political scientists. The government of Great Britain is the best example of party responsibility, the party in power operating the government. Party responsibility is not wholly absent from the American political scene. It is virtually impossible for a party to reelect its candidates if they have held power at the time a severe depression has set in. A party friendly to labor will have to bear the responsibility for a rash of strikes if they upset the economy and are widely publicized. The inability of the national political parties in the United States to maintain and enforce "party discipline" makes party responsibility somewhat ineffective. It is not without importance nonetheless.

Pressure Groups

Society is best understood in terms of the group orientations of people. Membership in some groups, the family or the neighborhood or the office force, is almost inescapable since it follows from the necessary fulfillment of basic needs. Other group memberships are voluntarily sought: the business association, church, labor union, and political party are examples. Every group is an association of persons who share common activity and are bound together by sentiment (the

affective dimension of their association).[10] It follows that groups have political potential; that is, since they share activity and sentiment in common to some degree, then they must share goals also in some degree. For a group to become political it merely has to articulate its goals and seek their recognition through a political unit. In pressing its case for favor from the political unit, a group becomes a political pressure group. Its goal is to gain security and deference. The labor union thus seeks many kinds of security for its members—against arbitrary dismissal from employment, against loss of income, against regressive taxation, etc.—and deference from "out-groups" such as employers and nonunion employees.

Groups vary significantly in their ability to make political pressure effective. The pressure of the Saturday Garden Club on City Hall to "do something" about the Japanese beetles cannot begin to compare with the pressure of the American Farm Bureau Federation and the National Association of Manufacturers on national and state legislatures to restrict the activities of labor organizations. The political pressures of some groups, such as the National Association of Manufacturers and the American Medical Association, are continuous, professional lobbyists being retained to maintain political pressure on governmental organs in behalf of the goals sought by these two groups. The ability to pressure legislators, educate the public by manipulating symbols, and otherwise affect legislation and political activity is maldistributed to the advantage of national groups favored by money, leadership skill, and other important factors. A bias in legislative activity weighted against the average citizen and his interests is thus formed by pressure groups. As Professor Key has observed:

> Pressure groups in considerable measure advocate action or inaction in conflict with the general welfare. They speak, on the whole, for people who are more aggressive, more privileged, and better off than the average of the citizenry. They eternally seek further advantage and more often than not get it. Their behavior is seldom colored by any genuine concern for the common welfare, though they often claim to carry the burden of the public good.[11]

Pressure groups in the United States fall into five classifications: business, labor, agriculture, the professions, and veterans. Among these

[10] George C. Homans, *The Human Group*, New York, Harcourt, Brace and Company, 1950, pp. 33–40.
[11] V. O. Key, Jr., *Politics, Parties and Pressure Groups*, New York, Thomas Y. Crowell Company, 3rd Edition, 1953, p. 173.

five classifications, only labor groups bring pressure for social legislation. This is not to say that business, professional, and agricultural groups are all opposed to social legislation; but the opposition is consistent among national organizations which represent these groups in national politics.

Business groups in American society have historically enjoyed great prestige, and their aggregate financial power has never had a serious equal. As a group organized for political pressure, business must deal with several kinds of heterogeneity. In no sense could it be maintained that all business enterprises, corporated and unincorporated, have identical interests. Export and import business, agricultural and nonagricultural business, railroad transportation and air or bus transportation business, and "small" and "large" business are examples of business groups with conflicting interests. A sufficient number of interests are held in common by business groups to enable them to influence legislation through national and state spokesmen. Two thousand associations of businessmen active on a national or interstate basis were listed by the United States Department of Commerce in 1949, and this figure does not include groups which characteristically ally themselves with business groups. Two powerful organizations [12] bring pressure for favorable treatment in the national government, the Chamber of Commerce of the United States and the National Association of Manufacturers. The Chamber is a federation of 3000 state and local chambers and allied groups which carries on public-information activities and attempts to influence legislators in connection with those issues on which businessmen have a common view. It is active at every level of government and uniformly hostile to social legislation. The National Association of Manufacturers is an organization of about 17,000 members with considerably more unanimity of purpose than the Chamber. It is controlled by a small proportion of the total membership, less than 1 percent of its members holding more than two-thirds of its directorships in the period 1933–1946.[13] Since the NAM enjoys more unanimity of purpose than the Chamber, its pronouncements tend to be more vehement and its activities more narrowly focused. Since 1932 it has been an unfaltering foe of social legislation in general and labor legislation in particular. Other associations effectively bring pressure in behalf of partisan inter-

[12] Jay Judkins, *National Associations of the United States*, Washington, Government Printing Office, 1949.

[13] A. S. Cleveland, "NAM: Spokesman for Industry," *Harvard Business Review*, May, 1948, pp. 353–371.

ests on which business as a whole would be divided. The National Retail Drygoods Association, the American Petroleum Institute, and the American Bankers Association are examples of such organizations. With a few exceptions these more partisan organizations oppose social legislation.

Labor has been represented in national politics by the two major federations, the American Federation of Labor and the Congress of Industrial Organizations (recently merged), and by independent organizations such as the Railway Brotherhoods. The combined membership of the AF of L and CIO is about 14,000,000 and of the independent unions about 2,000,000. About 25 percent of all persons in the labor force are members of labor unions, and perhaps half of the persons in the labor force are not "organizable" for one reason or another. The effective proportion of organizable labor actually organized, therefore, is closer to 50 percent. The major federations are active in politics at both the state and national levels, their primary functions being public relations. In addition, the national or international unions which make up the federations are active in behalf of their own special problems at the state and national levels.

Vigorous use of pressure techniques to influence legislation has been employed by labor only since the early 1930's. Prior to this time the prevailing labor philosophy had been laissez faire, an insistence that labor be left free of government control in order to use economic weapons such as the strike against employers. The resort to legislation to redress grievances followed the onset of the Great Depression and was intensified by the formation of the CIO in 1936. As late as 1930 the annual convention of the AF of L voted down a proposal to endorse unemployment insurance. Both the CIO and the AF of L intensified their use of political pressure tactics in the 1940's, the CIO forming a Political Action Committee in 1943 to replace its defunct Labor's Nonpartisan League, and the AF of L forming Labor's League for Political Education in 1947. These political arms of the AF of L and CIO have enjoyed moderate success at the national level in electing "friends of labor" and preventing the election of its foes. At the present time labor groups exert their pressures in favor of social legislation and, other than certain nonpartisan groups such as the League of Women Voters, which favor social legislation on the basis of conviction, and government agencies, are virtually alone in exerting such pressures.

Agricultural groups constitute the oldest political pressure system

in the United States. Their activities have been at least partly defensive, seeking to maintain agricultural well-being against the encroachment of new groups, particularly labor. Declining farm population, increased mechanization, parity ratios, and commercialization have beset agriculture in the United States with problems which required the intrusion of the national government with protective legislation. To gain such legislation the farm groups have formed organizations since the mid-nineteenth century. Following the Civil War, the distress of falling farm prices brought about the Granger movement and Farmers' Alliance, and at the turn of the century the Farmers' Union was formed. After the First World War the American Farm Bureau Federation came into existence; it is presently the most powerful spokesman for national agricultural interests. To its credit is the organization in the Senate of members who have become known as the "farm bloc." The Grange and the Farmers' Union are important representatives of sectional interests, the former being strong in the east central states and the latter in the Great Plains. In national politics the American Farm Bureau Federation brings pressure for agriculture as a whole, although it reflects the interests of the Midwestern states where its strength is greatest. The Federation seldom supports social legislation, and Professor Key describes the general tenor of its policies outside of agriculture as follows:

On issues outside the agricultural sphere, the Federation often takes a stand parallel to that of the principal business groups. On labor questions the Federation tends to throw its weight with business, and some state federations have spearheaded movements for legislation to restrict organized labor. Along with business, the Federation, in 1949, opposed taxation of that portion of corporate income distributed as dividends. In general, the Federation probably reflects with fair accuracy the conservatism of its members on matters of general economic policy, although at times Farm Bureau leaders come perilously close to letting their organization become the tool of business interests without much regard to the concern of farmers in the issues at stake.[14]

Among professions, the medical and bar associations have been most active as political pressure groups. Formed initially to ensure the maintenance of standards, these associations have in recent years carried on extensive political activities beyond the safeguarding of standards. At the state level, associations of physicians and lawyers are highly influential, one reason being that standards and related matters

[14] Key, op. cit., pp. 42–43.

are determined at that level. Both the American Bar Association and the American Medical Association, however, exert pressure to influence legislation at the national level. Of the two groups the AMA is more effective in matters relating to its central interest because of the large proportion of the nation's physicians included in its membership, nearly two-thirds, and their loyalty to the Association's views. In contrast, the American Bar Association probably includes less than one-fifth of the nation's lawyers. Both organizations are weighted against social legislation and the American Medical Association's views on national health insurance approach the phobic stage. Lawyers are the most numerous group in both state and national legislatures, and it is fortunate that their convictions are not determinate upon the stand against social legislation traditional with the American Bar Association. It would appear that both organizations tend to be ruled by physicians and lawyers whose practices are sufficiently well established to allow them time for association activities. This results in policy making being carried on by older men of considerable wealth and, very likely, of more conservative judgment than the general membership.

Veterans' associations carry on political pressure activities on a wide front. The primary concern of the American Legion and the secondary associations—the American Veterans of World War II, the Veterans of Foreign Wars, and the American Veterans Committee—is, of course, to secure benefits for members. Pensions, preferences in public housing and civil service examinations, and free medical facilities are among their goals. Outside of these matters, however, the American Legion in particular has displayed little support for, and occasional active hostility to, social legislation. Thus, the Legion joined forces with the American Medical Association in opposition to compulsory health insurance and has at times made common cause with the National Association of Manufacturers in opposition to labor legislation. With perhaps 3,000,000 members drawn together by powerful bonds of sentiment, such opposition attains importance.

A system of pressures that is often not clearly understood is formed by agencies of the national and state governments which already are engaged in the administration of social legislation. The Federal Security Agency (now the Department of Health, Education, and Welfare) for many years exerted pressures in support of social insurance and welfare legislation. Certain bureaus within the Departments of Labor and Agriculture have performed similar functions. The advan-

tages which governmental agencies have are considerable; research carried on more or less continuously provides a source of information about social needs that looms impressively when presented to Congressional-hearing committees. Only rarely are such pressures exerted against social legislation, unless proposals for reorganization threaten to divert energies away from what are considered primary needs.

Other pressure groups should be included in a survey of the political process because of their influence on certain kinds of social legislation. The traditional policy of the Catholic Church in matters of divorce, birth control, sterilization, and child labor makes it a powerful force at the state level. Women's associations are very numerous and form pressure groups of considerable influence. The National Federation of Business and Professional Women's Clubs, the League of Women Voters, the American Association of University Women, and the Women's Trade Union League are examples. Associations of racial and ethnic groups are also active in exerting political pressures, usually in defense of their interests rather than to gain any special consideration from legislation.

Pressure groups active in national and state politics are of the utmost importance in determining the existence and form of social legislation. Because the most powerful and influential pressure groups are in general opposition to social legislation, they add their weight to such other opposing factors as the American cultural bias against government welfare programs, the common law background, Puritanism, and the separation of powers. Labor associations, certain government agencies, and other associations which exert pressures sporadically constitute the major pressures on legislation from outside the legislature. Business groups constitute the greatest pressure against social legislation, as a recent report indicates: "Organized business has always gained the most from lobbying because it has had the best organization, the most money, and the readiest access to publicity. It has had, in addition, the great advantage of seeking generally to prevent rather than encourage action by broadly based popular government. Given the strategic bottlenecks of our legislative procedure, it is far easier to obstruct than to create." [15]

The enactment of social legislation does not depend on so simple a calculus as implied in a comparison of pressures. A simple adding up of strength opposed or in support of social legislation does not explain

[15] House of Representatives, Report No. 3138, Eighty-first Congress, 2nd Session, p. 63.

the considerable legislation that has been enacted in this field. The explanation seems to lie in the legislative process itself, particularly in the kinds of influence to which legislators respond. The executive branch is not unimportant in this process, but the determination of *legislative* action is our primary concern.

The Legislative Process

More clearly than in any other dimension of the political process the distinction between the formal and operative is illustrated in the national legislative process. The fathers, failing to foresee the role which would be played by political parties, provided that "each House may determine the rules of its proceedings" and, consequently, left the legislative process to be determined by experience. An incredibly complex process has evolved, and we can only hope to deal with its fundamentals.

We will begin with the individual legislator and the factors which lead him to propose legislation to his colleagues and to support or obstruct their proposals. Senators and representatives are, first of all, *local* representatives. Each senator represents a constituency which varies from about 90,000 in the case of Nevada to over 7,500,000 million in the case of New York. Representatives have constituencies of about 370,000 on the average, except for the few states which have one representative regardless of population. This local character of legislators is important in that it diverts their attentions from national matters to local matters. Legislation for the "general welfare" is, thus, likely to reflect local biases and interests rather than truly national needs. Much depends on the influences to which the legislator responds. If he would be long a legislator, he cannot ignore local sentiment, although numerous devices which we shall discuss later permit him to "dodge" local sentiment on some questions. The influences to which a legislator responds have been variously described; it is common to include constituency, pressure groups, party, personal conviction, tradition, and the mass media among the major influences.

It is his constituency which primarily influences the legislator's decisions in legislation. If not actually pressured by local groups which have powerful voting strength, he will actively solicit their approval by supporting their interests. Pressure groups beyond the area of their constituency cannot be ignored by representatives, although pressure groups seem always to overestimate the amount of support they can extend or withhold from an uncoöperative legislator at election time.

If the vote-controlling power of a pressure group is real, then the legislator will more likely take the initiative in satisfying its reasonable requests, other things being equal. Some pressure groups are of genuine service to the legislator—preparing data and "model" bills for his use which may fill a gap in his own resources. The introduction of research-staff aid for legislators at both national and state levels, however, has made this service less necessary. When the legislator wishes to avoid submitting to local or national pressure groups, there are various techniques available to him. Ernest S. Griffith has described some of them:

> Against the political power of groups as against the merits of their viewpoints, Congress has employed chiefly the weapons of publicity for group activities and obscurity as regards its own decisions. For the most part, lobbies and lobbyists must register. Such registration includes disclosure of amount and nature of expenditure, source of funds, membership, names and salaries of representatives. On its own part, Congress seeks, if possible, to avoid having to make final decisions on legislation insistently and militantly supported by pressure groups. . . . Devices are numerous. Delays in one House or the other; emasculating amendments; advance assurance of a veto by the President; refusal of the House Rules Committee to grant facilities for floor consideration; substitution of another method of voting for roll call; elimination of objectionable provisions by the conference committee. . . .[16]

If the legislators cannot, for some reason, square the proposals of pressure groups with their concept of the "public interest" or "general welfare," they can prevent the proposals from becoming law. In deciding to avail themselves of these techniques, of course, a minority of legislators can likewise prevent legislation for social needs, their concepts of the general welfare causing them to oppose social legislation. The party line on legislation is an influence to which legislators respond. But the importance of this influence as against local and national pressures and other influences is far from staggering. Within the Congress a core of legislators is always to be found which rarely opposes the party view, but it is only when chairmen of powerful committees are part of this core that party discipline becomes decisive. On nearly every kind of legislative proposal, party solidarity is the exception rather than the rule. Personal convictions of legislators are far more important in determining legislation than is ordinarily recog-

[16] Ernest S. Griffith, The American System of Government, New York, Frederick A. Praeger, 1954, pp. 60–61.

nized. Given the extensive research services available to the legislator and his ability to comprehend the significance of research findings (and it is generally agreed that the average legislator both at the state and national levels is far more capable than the average constituent who elects him), a powerful offset to narrow, partisan causes emerges. Another aid to the legislator is the strength of his party at the national level. In general, the effectiveness of organized pressure groups correlates inversely with the strength of the national parties. The culture of the locality from which he is elected molds the legislator's views and influences his stand on certain issues. Legislators from some constituencies in the South and the Midwest are thus unfavorably disposed toward legislation which favors labor unions, and Midwestern legislators are also disposed to value individualism highly even at the expense of social needs which to others would seem desperate. Finally, there should be mentioned the mass media, particularly the press, which play a role in the legislator's decisions. Probably the columnists of outstanding reputation, such as Arthur Krock, Walter Lippmann, and Marquis Childs, are of more importance than their editors in influencing legislative views. Powerful syndicates of newspapers and other media are not without their influence on local opinion, however, and by withholding or slanting information about a legislator's activities they may do him harm. It would appear, however, that this kind of influence is minor in determining the output of legislation.

We understand, then, the kinds of influences which play a part in the legislator's making up his mind. It does not follow, however, that his mere judgment concerning the desirable course of action to serve the general welfare will prove effective in determining the character of legislation. A bill meeting his views may never reach the Congress for decision or may be offered in a form which provides only token relief for social needs. Whether or not these factors occur depends largely on the work of Congressional committees, particularly standing committees, of which the Senate has fifteen and the House nineteen. At the state level the number of committees averages twice the number at the national level for each house. Membership on legislative committees is only partly a matter of personal choice, the determining factors being party membership and action of the party caucus. The dominant party in each House determines the membership of committees, allowing itself a safe majority, and appoints the chairmen on the basis of seniority. Certain committees, notably the House Rules Committee, wield enormous influence in determining legislation.

Members of the Rules Committee are from "safe" districts and thus less liable to censure at the polls for their actions. The Rules Committee determines when a proposal will be debated, the amount of time allowed for debate, whether or not amendments may be offered from the House floor, and may make the granting of a "rule" dependent upon the inclusion of qualifying phraseology or amendments by the sponsoring committee. A majority petition of the whole House will force a reluctant Rules Committee to grant a "rule," but this action is very rarely undertaken. Important bills reported out by committees usually go directly to the Rules Committee; others go on a complicated system of calendars from which bills are considered according to rules of procedure governing each calendar. In former years the Speaker of the House used the Rules Committee, of which he was a member, in defiance of even the majority view of the House. Without his control at the present time, the Rules Committee still wields great power. Other standing committees have a large part to play in determining the character of legislation. Upon being introduced, a bill is referred to a standing committee by an officer known as the Parliamentarian under the guidance of the presiding officer. A margin of discretion exists with the presiding officer, and it is of importance whether the bill is referred to a committee hostile to the measure in question or to a more favorably disposed committee. On vote of a majority of the House in question, a reference may be changed, but this rarely occurs. After consideration by the standing committee, including public hearings at the discretion of the committee, the bill may be either withheld or "reported out." Bills often die on the calendar to which they are assigned for want of being called up for floor consideration before the end of the legislative session. If this occurs, the bills so stranded must begin all over again at the proposal stage. It will be apparent that committees determine the nature of legislation in an important way. Their actions, if opposed to social needs, can offset the good intentions of individual legislators. Furthermore, committee sessions may be secret, in which case public censure of committeemen at the polls is difficult, and it is the committees of the legislatures which are the primary targets of pressure groups.

The Electorate

The considerable abuse which is continually heaped upon the political process by those who, understandably, decry "machine politics," "pressure politics," and "legislative chicanery" seldom has any definite target. Who, if anyone, must bear the blame if the task of politics

becomes defiled? In a political system which rests on popular sovereignty, the answer is clear. The electorate, the group which, able to be sovereign, exercises its sovereignty without effect, or not at all, is responsible. No more striking illustration of a development beyond the wildest dreams of the fathers could be cited than "citizen passivity" or "self-disenfranchisement" on a mass scale.

The Political Machine

In the recent past the political machine turned this condition to its own advantage. In return for social services and tampering with the intricacies of governmental red tape, including the administration of justice, large groups of voters, particularly immigrants making their way in a hostile environment, have willingly voted for "the machine." Denis Brogan's description of American machine politics is hardly flattering, and suggests the major indictment of the machine: it gains the fruits of political victory without its activities being passed on by the electorate at the polls.

. . . the machines controlling the voters of some of the largest (and many of the smaller) cities of the United States were and largely are an independent force with which the party leadership must deal, must bargain, and it is seldom that the state and national matters that matter to the party, matter much to the rulers of the machines. The machines could neither be ignored nor controlled. They could not be ignored, for they controlled great blocks of voters and voters massed in strategically important places and they could not be controlled, for although every machine professed allegiance to one or the other of the national parties, they never sacrificed, for a moment, the interests of the local organization even to the gravest necessities of the state or national parties.[17]

The same author also pinpoints the factor which alone can deprive the political machine of its awesome strength: "Only when the electors begin to think that giving a vote is not a trifling favor do machines decline." [18]

In his address to the New York Constitutional Convention of 1915, Elihu Root referred to the Platt machine as the "invisible government," and the term has since been applied to those forces in government which circumvent the responsible channels of communication. In brief, it is not that political machines are unresponsive to the public will—they must be in order to continue in power—but rather that their operations short-circuit that deliberative process

---

[17] Denis W. Brogan, *Politics in America*, New York, Harper & Brothers, 1954, p. 80.
[18] *Ibid.*, p. 138.

whereby majority resolutions decide the basis and character of governmental action and, in its place, decide on the basis of expediency. There is no assurance under machine rule that social needs will be met by legislation adequate to their relief, nor that legislative concern with a given social need will be continuous. The same expediency which gives rise to social legislation may also cause its decline, political conditions demanding.

THE BASIC PROBLEM

Political machine power can be seen to rest on well-organized blocks of voters which, though small in number, are strategically located. In some cases this power is the product of gerrymandering (the deliberate drawing of electoral district boundaries to concentrate voting power), but more often it is the result of indifference on the part of the unorganized voters. The extent of this indifference, though large, cannot be measured with accuracy. But for Presidential elections, in which the extent of participation by the eligible voters is highest, participation has varied from less than 50 percent in 1920 and 1924 to more than 60 per cent in 1940. Munro analyzes the 1920 performance as follows:

. . . the census of 1920 showed approximately fifty million Americans of voting age. Of this total, only about twenty-six million voters actually went to the polls in the presidential election of the same year. The successful candidate for the presidency was said to have "swept the country," yet he received the votes of only thirty per cent of the people who were legally qualified to exercise the suffrage. Fifteen per cent of the total population gave the "consent of the governed" for all the rest.[19]

For other than Presidential elections this showing would have been unusually good, for the average participation declines as one goes from the national to state and local elections. It is proper to view the American political system as resting in the hands of the citizens. There is no political condition beyond their influence, including the scrapping of the Constitution or the restriction of government spending to the achievement of social and economic security. But this influence has effect only if citizens avail themselves of the means through which it is exercised. Those factors which determine whether or not citizens will be politically active are not well established. Perhaps 3 to 4 percent of the membership in the two major parties might be described

[19] William B. Munro, *The Invisible Government*, New York, The Macmillan Company, 1928, p. 10.

as continuously active politically; this group forms a quasi-professional core, a majority of whose members hold some form of political office while doing "organization" work. Many motives in addition to a desire for responsible government account for the sustained activity of this group, and persons carrying on political activity outside the major parties constitute an equally large group and are probably more concerned with making government responsible (to their views) than the party professional staff. Political activity in the simple sense of casting a ballot is better understood than professional activity, and conclusions of importance have been produced by political scientists and other social scientists.

The factors which differentiate the participation of eligible voters are the common factors which differentiate the activities of large groups in any other area of mass social activity. Professor Key has summarized the major factors as follows:

> Perhaps the most significant differentials in voting participation are those associated with economic status, educational level, and occupation. The body of participating electors consists disproportionately of persons in the upper half of the economic spectrum, of persons who have completed high school, and of persons in the so-called higher occupations. Contrariwise, the poor, those of little education, the unskilled and manual worker participate in elections in lesser degree.[20]

It should also be noted that participation is much higher for members of the Republican party than for the Democratic party. Studies of American and European society have revealed data which yield conclusions similar to those cited by Key. A summary of these conclusions shows that:

1. A group will have a higher rate of voting if its interests are more strongly affected by government policies.
2. A group will have a higher rate of voting if it has more access to information about the relevance of government policies to its interests.
3. A group will have a higher rate of voting if it is exposed to social pressures demanding voting.
4. A group will have a higher rate of voting if the pressures to vote are not directed in different political directions so as to create conflict over which way to vote.[21]

[20] Key, op. cit., p. 573.
[21] Seymour M. Lipset, Paul F. Lazarsfeld, Allen H. Barton, and Juan Linz, "The Psychology of Voting: An Analysis of Political Behavior," Handbook of Social Psychology (Gardner Lindzey, ed.), Cambridge, Addison Wesley Publishing Company, Vol. II, 1954, p. 1128.

An analysis of voting participation reveals the differentiations shown in Table 7.

TABLE 7.   Factors Influencing Participation and Non-Participation in Elections.

High Level of Participation	Low Level of Participation
High income	Low income
High education	Low education
Occupational groups:	Occupational groups:
Businessmen	Unskilled
White collar	Servants
Government employees	Service workers
Commercial crop farmers	Peasant subsistence farmers
Miners	
Jews	Catholics
Protestants	
Whites	Negroes
Men	Women
Middle-aged (35–55)	Young people (under 35)
Older people (over 55)	
Old residents	Newcomers to community
Workers in western Europe	Workers in the United States
Crisis situations	Normal situations

Source: Seymour M. Lipset, Paul F. Lazarsfeld, Allen H. Barton, and Juan Linz, "The Psychology of Voting: An Analysis of Political Behavior," Gardner Lindzey (ed.), *Handbook of Social Psychology.* Cambridge, Addison Wesley Publishing Company, 1954, Vol. III, p. 1127.

Another factor to consider in analyzing the electorate is the extent to which the act of voting constitutes an act of discrimination on the part of the voter in preparation for which he sought information, weighed issues, and otherwise used his judgment. Estimates are not clear on the proportion of persons that can be called discriminatory, but it is uniformly held to be small. Perhaps as many as four voters out of five in national elections cast their ballot on the basis of traditional loyalty to one or the other of the major parties. About one-fifth of the voters consider themselves "independent" of either major political party; they constitute a much larger percentage of white-collar and business and professional workers than of manual workers and farmers.[22]

Certain conclusions can be made concerning the electorate. By failing to exercise its sovereignty, the electorate has surrendered basic political decision making (selection of candidates, delineation of issues, etc.) into the hands of professional organizations. It has been observed in earlier sections that the balance of organized pressure activity is

[22] Key, *op. cit.*, pp. 587–588.

weighted against social legislation. To this weight must be added the political machine, which, as Professor Key observes, is seldom counted among those interests supporting social change:

> One will search fruitlessly . . . for state or city organizations equipped to gather facts, make analyses, and arrive systematically at policy proposals. More often the more or less professionalized element of the organization achieves a massive inactivity in policy development. This state of affairs comes about in part because the party organization—Democratic or Republican—tends towards conservatism. It wants to upset no applecarts and conduct no crusades. Organization conservatism, in turn, flows from the fact that bureaucracies tend always to be attached to the *status quo* and from the fact that the funds for the maintenance of party organizations come from elements of the community attached to the *status quo*.[23]

An additional bias against social legislation must therefore be reckoned with, a bias for which those persons are responsible whose grievances are most often redressed through social legislation. Those "offsets" to bias against social legislation which were mentioned in a previous section assume greater importance as the full strength and influence of conservatism are realized.

The Political Process and Social Legislation: Concluding Remarks

The state, which we understand to be the association that legitimately exercises the use of force over citizens, has attained a central position among social institutions as social problems have become more complex. Its activities have come more and more to interfere with the unrestrained use of individual rights, particularly property rights, which the eighteenth and nineteenth centuries valued so highly. This deprivation of individual rights followed from a calculus which counseled the surrender of extreme forms of personal rights in order to provide for broadly conceived social rights. Social crises, which showed repeatedly how inadequate were the resources of individualism in industrial society, forced the issue, and social legislation is dependent fundamentally upon a belief in collective security at the expense of individual rights.

The American state carries on the functions of government through a formal and operative order of institutions at the state and national levels. Essentially the formal order was defined in the Constitution of 1787 and has been extended by the addition of important statutes

[23] *Ibid.*, pp. 372–373.

establishing government departments, court decisions, opinions of public attorneys, and customs. The operative order is not provided for in the basic law, but rather atones for the major shortcomings in the basic law; it provides apparatus through which to "get government business done." Political parties are the major institutions in the operative order.

Because the operative order is unrestrained by basic constitutional definitions of power, it is more prone to opportunism than the formal order, and the beneficiaries of this opportunism tend to be the major power groups in the society which are able to "influence" legislative organs. Yet the balance of pressure groups does not determine the enactment of legislation in a decisive way; a quantity of very considerable importance is the individual legislator who must, in the final analysis, personally decide how to cast his vote. Local influences on the individual legislator are of major importance in determining his position on legislation. But if local pressures (or other pressures) are opposed to their personal convictions, the legislator and his colleagues have available to them a number of "hedges" (delay, assurance of Presidential veto, etc.) which permit them to vote on the basis of conviction. In view of this dependence of the legislative output on the convictions of legislators, the research aids and assistance which have been made available at the national and, in some instances, the state level are very important. So much as research findings serve to define the "general welfare" more clearly, they increase the likelihood that the legislator will vote on the basis of conviction. For these and other reasons, the convictions of legislators constitute one of the most important determinants of social legislation.

This chapter has made it apparent that the American political system is not swift and positive in its provision for social needs through legislation. Rather it is slow and cumbersome, acting only when considerably more than a majority sentiment calls for redress of social grievances through legislation. This indictment of the process is offset to some extent, however, by the support normally given new social legislation programs once they are established. Programs instituted to carry out social legislation often obtain priority in such matters as funds and administrative personnel because they are recognized as being "long overdue." The lag between the initial demonstration of social need and the provision of relief by the political unit is a serious problem, nonetheless, and few advantages can be cited to compensate for the prolongation of such social evils as inadequate housing, inse-

curity of old age, and inadequate health services. The conditions fostering such lag are not inescapable shortcomings of the political machinery, but can be traced to the apathy and political passivity of the electorate. Political machines are not, on their own volition, responsive to social needs, as we have seen, but respond to organized sentiment in the process of mobilizing a majority for elections which ultimately determine their power. Only infrequently are citizens organized to bring pressure for social legislation in such strength as would attract political machines. More often a popular candidate for office, holding positive views about social legislation, is supported by the political machine and thus indirectly machine power is placed behind a social legislation program. To make the citizen aware that strong pressure groups with generally narrow interests attempt to effect legislation, the national government and thirty-eight of the states have passed laws which require lobbyists for vested interests to register and, in some states, to disclose the sources and uses of their funds. The national law requires lobbyists to report their expenditures, the names of their principals, and the legislation which they attempt to influence. An infinitesimally small number of citizens attempt to avail themselves of this information, which is reported quarterly in the *Congressional Record*. Their failure to do so largely nullifies the effect of the national law except as a few publicists, such as Stuart Chase and Karl Schriftgiesser, present an analysis of pressure tactics.[24] Thus, the faults of the American political process are to be traced to the electorate primarily, and only secondarily to the machinery. One cannot but wonder about the consequences for future social legislation of the growing strength represented by irresponsible political power, irresponsible in the sense that it is exercised without being reviewed at the polls because of mass passivity. MacIver properly holds the use of this kind of power up as the nemesis of democratic systems:

It is the eternal problem of democracy to keep them [power groups] in their place, subject to the democratic code. Every group that owns power without corresponding responsibility is a menace to it. Every monopoly, or approach to monopoly, is subversive of it. Any group whatever, if armed with the requisite power, destroys the reciprocity of interests that democ-

[24] Stuart Chase, *Democracy Under Pressure*, New York, The Twentieth Century Fund, 1945; and Karl Schriftgiesser, *The Lobbyists*, Boston, Little, Brown and Company, 1951. See also the excellent legislative histories prepared by James M. Burns, *Congress on Trial*, New York, Harper & Brothers, 1949, particularly chap. III, "The Story of Three Bills"; and Stephen K. Bailey, *Congress Makes a Law, The Story Behind the Employment Act of 1946*, New York, Columbia University Press, 1950.

racy postulates. Every group, if it is not restrained from so doing, puts its interest above the interest of the whole.[25]

It is a paradox that this irresponsibility emanates from the citizenry.

SELECTED REFERENCES

Brogan, Denis W., Politics in America, New York, Harper & Brothers, 1954.

Griffith, Ernest S., The American System of Government, New York, Frederick A. Praeger, 1954.

Key, V. O., Jr., Politics, Parties and Pressure Groups, New York, Thomas Y. Crowell Company, 1953.

Laswell, Harold D., Who Gets What, When, and How, New York, Whittlesey House, 1936.

MacIver, Robert M., The Web of Government, New York, The Macmillan Company, 1947.

Schattschneider, E. E., Party Government, New York, Farrar and Rinehart, 1942.

[25] R. M. MacIver, The Web of Government, New York, The Macmillan Company, 1947, p. 221.

PART III

FAMILY LEGISLATION

chapter 6

Family Legislation

In this chapter we shall inquire into the functioning of the most basic of human groups, the family. We shall attempt to explain its antiquity and describe society's actions to ensure its stability, a stability crucial to the orderly functioning of other social institutions. We shall go back into history to investigate the beginnings of family life, and we shall concern ourselves with both ancient and contemporary cultures to discover the rules by which society regulates the family. In succeeding chapters we shall look into the legislation which has resulted from our society's concern with American family life; but let us first consider the biological and psychosocial functions which characterize all families.

The Family as a Social Unit

Society is people and the basis of society and civilization is people living together. For it is in group life that human nature is born, nurtured, and regulated. As the incubator of human nature and teacher of the rules which regulate social relations, the family becomes the nucleus in the interaction of individual and society. Children are born, reared, socialized, and placed in society as members of families. And society guides the family in this service by providing a normative system of folkways, mores, and laws which has as one of its ends the assurance of stability in the familial institution.

In its role as formal regulator of relations among the members of society, the normative order operates concurrently through each of the several social institutions. Societies everywhere regulate their economic, political, and religious structures, but nowhere is this concern with social behavior more obvious than in societal control of the family. This solicitude is realistic, for it recognizes that, in addition to its

role in producing new members of the society, the family serves the key functions of defining the society's rules of conduct for the child and eventually placing him in the structure of the society. And the family does much more in addition to these crucial tasks. It acts as the centralizing agency for the behavioral influences of other institutional structures; it serves as the mentor of custom and tradition even while transferring to the child the results of social change. What we are in thought and behavior we owe largely to this social institution which molds our habits and attitudes, gives us our first tastes of the cultural heritage, and orients us in society.

Yet most of us have considerable difficulty in defining the family. This difficulty is in part a function of the common inability to construe familiar objects and partially the result of the variations one encounters in familial membership. For there are many forms of the family and, even within specific forms, many variations. We think of our family, which consists of father, mother, son, and daughter, and are prepared to define the family as two married people and their children; suddenly we recall the family down the street, wherein the grandchildren and perhaps even an uncle or two are coresident, and our two-generational concept of the family seems inadequate. If this is not perplexing enough, we remember the Wilsons around the corner, who have never had any children, and so have adopted some, or perhaps we even remember reading about some Near Eastern potentate who had many wives and many children, or the ruler of the West African Ashanti who is allowed 3333 wives. But a solution to our enigma is readily available if we agree that there are indeed many forms of the family, but that all families everywhere share certain functions in society. It is through these common functions that we shall be able to identify the family regardless of its manifest form.

There are many definitions of the family, but perhaps the most all-embracing and therefore definitive is the first paragraph of George Peter Murdock's already classic study of social structure:

The family is a social group characterized by common residence, economic cooperation, and reproduction. It includes adults of both sexes, at least two of whom maintain a socially approved sexual relationship, and one or more children, own or adopted, of the sexually cohabiting adults. The family is to be distinguished from marriage, which is a complex of customs centering upon the relationship between a sexually associating pair of adults within the family. Marriage defines the manner of establishing and terminating such a relationship, the normative behavior and re-

ciprocal obligations within it, and the locally accepted restrictions upon its personnel.[1]

Immediately several ideas emerge: the family is not a family unless it includes the parental relationship, it is not the same as a marriage (note that we call the mates "husband" and "wife" in the marital relationship, "father" and "mother" as parents), and there are several other key characteristics of the family. Most crucial is the characterization of the family as a social group, for it is within the enclave of the social group that the nonsocial neonate acquires his first taste and hence appetite for social contact and association. Here also he learns that he must curb his personalized drives and submit to rules, a lesson he transfers later to the larger society. Moreover, this protective and socializing function of the family is the primary reason for the emergence of this institution and is in large measure the explanation for its permanence. Mating, sex, parenthood, and kinship structure all revolve around this parent-child relationship.

Perhaps we can better focus these ideas about the family by a view of the family in two dimensions, temporally into the past for a glimpse at the probable bases for the formation of the family and spatially into our own and other societies for a view of the operation of the family within the framework of functioning society. These excursions from our own society should add some objectivity to our vistas and, since we shall be dealing primarily with simple, nonliterate societies, should give sharper perspective than our own complex culture. Let us first look at the bases of the family as a social group.

What was the first family like? Was it monogamous or characterized by promiscuity? Did the father wield the power, or was there even a functioning father? Was there a formally organized group with enough permanence to be called a family, or just a male with a harem of wives and their offspring? Questions of this nature hold a certain fascination, as do all searches for origins, but present the same problem as the riddle of the chicken and the egg: nontestability. We simply cannot know and must, therefore, hypothesize upon observation of simple "primitive" societies and modern anthropoid apes or sheer conjecture. Despite this difficulty, controversies have raged both within and outside social science over just these questions, with, however, just slightly more scientific success than the doctrinal dispute over Eve's possession of a navel. Therefore, we shall restrict our interests to

[1] George Peter Murdock, *Social Structure*, New York, The Macmillan Company, 1949, p. 1.

why the family was formed rather than how it originated or what was its earliest form.

Here we experience no such difficulty, for the family was formed to perform the same functions it performs today the world over: the reproduction, maintenance, and replacement of society's personnel. The basis of these universal functions of the family is the mother-child relationship born of the dependence of the human infant upon adults. In all mammalian societies, including our own, this dependent relationship is basically nutritional, for the mammalian offspring requires the continuous presence of the mother for the life-sustaining product of her breasts. Born in this dependent state, he has neither the stored food nor instinctive food-getting behavior we find in many other animal and insect forms. Human technology has provided substitutes for the mammary glands of the female (although exponents of breast feeding still abound), but even these nutritional alternatives must be discovered and administered by adults. Nor does this nutritional dependence diminish with rapidity as the infant matures, for he remains for a surprisingly long time in a semifetal state, an embryo outside his mother's body.

This continued dependence is the basis of all anthropoid and particularly human familialism. All mammalian offspring exhibit helplessness upon birth, but for most self-sufficiency comes in relatively short order. Not so our human infant. Born as a relatively small edition of the adult, a helpless animal with senses only partially functioning, he is dependent on his mother (or some food-supplying adult) for at least a year. The Rhesus monkey (Macaca rhesus), on the other hand, enters life as a relatively large animal with senses well developed and is dependent upon the mother monkey for only a few weeks. An even sharper contrast is given if we consider the flesh fly (Sarcophaga sarraciniae), which at birth is functionally quite similar to the adult. It will guide itself accurately in flight, escape would-be captors with dexterity, search out suitable food, and even recognize the opposite sex of its own species. How different from our helpless offspring. This birth as a functioning individual can also be viewed by any reader who invests in a pair of common guppies (Lebistes reticulatus) for visible evidence of almost complete self-sufficiency of the young upon birth.

Still another reason for the length of human infancy and the solicitous care of the young is the small number of offspring presented at each birth, which characterizes all primates. Now in other mammalian species a large number of puppies or piglets or kittens are born at one

time, so that a high infant mortality might be experienced with no danger of species extinction. But with single-order births, the rule in the human family, better and more extensive care is necessary for species survival. Finally, as we mentioned in an early chapter, the human animal is a generalized animal, lacking in specialization and requiring extensive training by adults to fill the gap left in adjustive behavior by our paucity of instinctive patterns of adjustment. Such an extended learning situation demands a stable, relatively permanent social group such as the family for even the minimum standards of humanization.

We seem to have neglected that long-suffering member of every family—the father. How do we explain his remaining a member of this group in human societies? In many mammals we find that the father is not permanently attached to the "family," which consists here of the mother and her offspring. Characteristically, he serves as the impregnator or progenitor and not as the "father." Consider, for example, the social life of the northern seal (Callorhinus alascanus), which is typical of the social relations of many mammals. During the greater part of the year the males and females live separately, so that cohabitation is seasonal. During the season of abundant food supply, the females gather on the beaches with their offspring and are joined by the males. Here "beachmasters" (dominant bulls) can acquire a coterie of females and establish harems. After this period of breeding, the sexes separate and the cubs are born when the mother is alone. Our seal cub never even knows who "father" is; for when he returns with the mother seal to the breeding grounds in the following season, she will quite probably breed with a new bull. This absence of social fatherhood was noted by Herodotus, 400 years before Christ, in his account of the domestic cat in ancient Egypt. Remarking on the large number of felines in Egypt, Herodotus noted that the number would be even greater if it were not for the attacking and killing of kittens by the older males, which view them as rivals. To Herodotus this killing of the young by the males is an artifice to obtain again the sexual companionship of the mother cat, who, upon the birth of kittens, no longer seeks the company of the males.[2] Nor should we assume that the male is always even given the opportunity to be the father of the child after conception. The male among black widow spiders (Latrodectus mactans), for example, never sees his offspring, for the female of the species devours the male immediately after mating, her self-

[2] George Rawlinson (tr.), *The History of Herodotus*, London, J. M. Dent and Sons, 1907, p. 147.

imposed widowhood accounting for her name. Why then do we find that the primate male remains with his newly formed family? Quite simply, he remains because of the female, not because of the child. For in anthropoid apes and men there is a permanent, nonseasonal sexual interest in the female by the dominant male. Thus there is no mating or rutting season, as we observed in the seal where sexual activity is cyclic, no absence of sexual motivation for cohabitation during the entire year. Therefore, while we find that other mammalian groups are formed during the seasonal oestrus or "heat," the anthropoid apes and man form permanent bisexual groups. No lofty ideals of pride or love motivate the male to protect the female and the child; these must await later rationalization as human society develops.

It appears, then, that man's sociability and group forming are not based upon some inherited "gregarious instinct," nor upon any unusual, human need for companionship, but rather, as we find in lower animal forms, upon quite simple biological drives and their satisfaction. The mother-child relationship exists as a result of the infant's nutritional and protective dependence upon the female, whose complex hormone structure has placed her in a milk-producing state of readiness to satisfy her offspring's hunger drive and, at the same time, gratify her own physiological needs through tension-releasing suckling. The male is sexually attracted to the female as an available source of sexual gratification, and hence he acquires a vested interest in protecting the female.

This analysis does not rule out the later importance of psychological and social factors in family cohesiveness. As Linton has pointed out, the psychological factors of security in personal relationship and the desire for congenial companionship, though less pressing in motivational power than the physiological satisfactions, are far more continuous in operation.[3] Later, as the group grows in permanence, a third set of factors, social in nature, adds further meaning and reason to group life. Primary among these is a system of dividing labor among family (group) members. In all societies labor is basically divided according to age and sex. When societies grow more complex and can support specialists, there is a greater diversity of tasks and chores assigned, but all societies recognize a difference in function among mothers, fathers, and their immature issue. Murdock, in his cross-cultural survey of 250 societies, observes that males are typically the providers

[3] Ralph Linton, "The Natural History of the Family," in Ruth Nanda Anshen (ed.), *The Family: Its Function and Destiny*, New York, Harper & Brothers, 1949, p. 22.

and women the preparers of raw materials for subsistence.[4] Characteristically, men, with their superior physical strength and greater mobility, perform the more strenuous tasks and those which require
absence from the household at some distance and for extended times.
Women, with decreased mobility as a result of pregnancy and motherhood, are bound to the household and must perform those tasks located in or near the dwelling. Similarly with age: the very young and
the very old lack the physical prowess to contribute materially to the
economy. The young, whose economic contributions are held in abey-
ance until maturation allows full productivity, receive training in what
they are later to do and gradually take over more productive tasks with
advancing maturity. But the very old cannot rejuvenate the physical
power needed for a full share of productivity. Characteristically, the
very old must, therefore, offer some new service, such as wise counsel
or experience or, in very rigorous subsistence economies, as among the
Eskimos, they may be disposed of as an economic burden. And so the
division of labor by sex becomes institutionalized and children are
trained for adulthood by learning those occupations which are assigned
to their sex. As new tasks arise, they are assigned in accordance with
the established pattern. The increased productivity and efficiency as a
result of specialization and the mutual benefits which can be shared
make the partnership of man and woman economically as well as phys-
iologically inevitable.

We may end our hurried journey back to seek the genesis of the
family with the realization that man, as a human animal, has biological
motives for the formation of the family, but that they are reinforced
and sustained by psychological and sociocultural factors which increase
in importance as man becomes more "human."

Society's Concern with Family Stability

As families are made up of associated individuals, so we also find
that societies are made up of associated families; and as the family develops an interest in the well-being of its personnel, society likewise
has an interest in the well-being of its member families. The proper
functioning of each depends upon the ability of its membership to
fulfill assigned roles. Every family is held together by the contribution
of father, mother, and child through a definitely established functional
role. Unless the role of the father as the provider and protector is performed by the male or his surrogate, the family cannot survive. With-

[4] Murdock, op. cit., p. 213.

out a female to bear and nourish new members, the family would disappear. And so it is with society; for without the family to provide, care for, and place new members, society would lose its continuity and existence. We may characterize society's primary concern with family stability, then, as a selfish one based upon the functions which are performed by the family for which no substitute has as yet appeared. Our first task will be to decide just what the universal functions of the family are and then to observe their operation in society. In this manner we may lay the groundwork for a later discussion of the manner in which every society seeks to ensure that the family performs these tasks.

The first of these functions grows directly out of the biological nature of the family. Families everywhere are charged with the reproductive function of replenishing society by creating new members. Now this function can and does occur outside the circle of the family, but illegitimacy is nowhere approved. Malinowski has drawn attention to this "principle of legitimacy" by pointing out that "The most important moral and legal rule concerning the physiological side of kinship is that no child should be brought into the world without a man—and one man at that—assuming the role of sociological father, that is, guardian and protector, the male link between the child and the rest of the community." [5] The import is clear: regardless of the action of the mores in allowing, accepting, or forbidding premarital and extramarital sexual experiences, conception must be limited to the family. We shall have more to say about this in a moment. But first let us look at the operation of the reproductive function among the mountain-dwelling Arapesh of New Guinea. Margaret Mead has described the role of the parent in procreation.

The procreative task of an Arapesh father is not finished with impregnation. The Arapesh have no idea that after the initial act which establishes physiological paternity, the father can go away and return nine months later to find his wife safely delivered of a child. Such a form of parenthood they would consider impossible, and furthermore, repellent. For the child is not the product of a moment's passion, but is made by both father and mother, carefully, over time. The Arapesh distinguish two kinds of sex-activity, play which is all sex-activity that is not known to have induced the growth of the child, and work, purposive sex-activity directed toward

[5] Bronislaw Malinowski, "Parenthood—The Basis of Social Structure," in V. F. Calverton and S. D. Schmalhausen (eds.), The New Generation, New York, Macaulay Company, 1930, p. 137.

making a particular child, towards feeding it and shaping it during the first weeks in the mother's womb.[6]

Among the Arapesh we see the emergence of rules governing procreation as separate from, though certainly the result of, sexual relations. Anthropological literature relates many instances of sexual license both before and after marriage, but almost universally parenthood is conditioned by a socially approved marital relationship. The purposive sexual activity of the Arapesh in making children recognizes the importance of creating new members, and the required presence of a father illustrates the concern that someone must act out the role of husband-father if we are to have a stable family. We shall have reason to recall this requirement later.

But just producing children is not, in itself, enough. If they are to survive and grow to maturity, they must be nurtured and protected by other human beings. For, as we have seen, the human infant is for a relatively long period unable to feed and protect himself. Again the family serves society, for in the absence of such a stable, permanent social group the rearing of the helpless neonate would be, at best, haphazardly effected. The family, therefore, provides for the care of this prolonged infancy. Moreover, it offers a source of protection to the mother during the periods of relative dependence occasioned by pregnancy, birth, and motherhood. In time the folkways and mores formally define the roles of the parents in caring for the child. Expectations of behavior, particularly on the part of the mother, become firmly entrenched. In all societies mothers provide certain basic care for their offspring. Among the Tanala of Madagascar, for example, Linton observes:

> The Tanala are extremely fond of children and take the best care of them possible with their limited knowledge of hygiene. Babies are kept clean, being bathed at least once a day with cold water. Very small children are carried in the arms almost constantly, husbands and older children doing their share. . . . Nursing seems to be continued as long as the mother's milk holds out, although the infant is given a little rice or soft food as soon as it will take it. There is no idea of regularity in feeding and the child is given the breast whenever it cries.[7]

Added to this responsibility for the physical care and development

---

[6] Margaret Mead, *Sex and Temperament in Three Primitive Societies*, London, George Routledge and Sons, 1935, p. 31.

[7] Ralph Linton, *The Tanala, A Hill Tribe of Madagascar*, Chicago, Field Museum of Natural History, Anthropological Series, Publication 317, Vol. XXII, 1933, p. 286.

of the child is the family's accountability for the transference of the customs and traditions, rules and values, of the group to the new member. It is the family's interpretation of the culture which prepares the child for his behavior in the larger society. In this role, the family comes also to control the developing personality of the growing child, for much that we do and must do is learned as a result of interaction within the group. Moreover, the family gets the child first, so that his attitudes toward other institutions and agencies originate within the family circle. We call this gradual implanting of skills, rules, and values in the child the socialization process. It transforms the nonsocial neonate into a social adult. Let us return to the mountain-dwelling Arapesh for a glimpse of the operation of the family in the socialization process:

How is the Arapesh baby moulded and shaped into the easy, gentle, receptive personality that is the Arapesh adult? What are the determinative factors in the early training of the child which assures that it will be placid and contented, unaggressive and non-initiatory, non-competitive and responsive, warm, docile, and trusting? It is true that in any simple and homogeneous society the children will show the same general personality-traits that their parents have shown before them. But it is not a matter of simple imitation. A more delicate and precise relationship obtains between the way in which the child is fed, put to sleep, disciplined, taught self-control, petted, punished, and encouraged, and the final adult adjustment. Furthermore, the way in which men and women treat their children is one of the most significant things about the adult personality of any people, and one of the points at which contrasts between the sexes come out most sharply. We can only understand the Arapesh, and the warm maternal temperament of both men and women, if we understand their childhood experience and the experience to which they in turn subject their children.[8]

The family adds continuity to society; for the learning of one generation will be transferred in similar, though modified, form and content to the next, which will in its turn give its knowledge and attitudes to the next generation. But, while the child will probably be molded into an adult with what his society considers an acceptable personality, no society can completely socialize the child. Parental differences in the interpretation of culture and individual differences and unique experience among children rule out such complete conformity. There-

[8] Mead, op. cit., p. 40.

fore, each of us is unique, and society must continue and extend the socializing and conformity producing role of family living.

One of the techniques of ensuring conformity behavior is the injunction to "know one's place." From childhood we are taught a system of superordination and subordination in society, within which we find our place. A large portion, actually a much larger portion than we are willing to admit, of this placement is a result of our being born into a particular family. This status-conferring function whereby the family places the child in the stratification system of his society is a third universal function of the family. The most immediate status is that of legitimacy as a result of birth within a sanctioned marital relationship. But this is only the beginning: while the individual's status in adult life is partially the result of his accomplishments or lack of them, the range of possible statuses he may eventually earn or hope to earn is limited by the position accorded him as a result of birth. Linton has called these statuses or positions given as a result of birth "ascribed" as contrasted to "achieved" status, which is earned or won by individual accomplishment.[9] Universal bases of status ascription are sex, age, family background, and, in heterogeneous societies, racial origin. It is from these family-determined characteristics that the child acquires his name, lineage, and general position in society. If the child eventually achieves a higher status, his children take their position from his new status. This is true in simple as well as complex societies. Observe the fixing of status among the Haidas, a highly competitive American Indian tribe of British Columbia:

The Haidas proper, excluding their slaves, fall into two great classes—those possessing status and those lacking it, often rather inaccurately called "nobles" and "commoners" respectively. A so-called "commoner" is simply a person whose parents have given no potlatches; a "noble" is one whose parents have acquired status for him by a distribution of wealth. (The potlatch is a ceremonial "give-away" wherein an individual attempts to gain status by extravagant distribution or conspicuous consumption of property.) There are, moreover, many intricate gradations of status, all arising directly from the number and quality of the parents' potlatches. . . . A person, of himself, can do little to affect his status. . . . He may show himself capable and industrious. He may accumulate great wealth and give lavish potlatches. By so doing he may confer status upon his children, making them the equals of any one in the village. He can even

[9] Ralph Linton, *The Study of Man*, New York, D. Appleton-Century Company, 1936, p. 115.

secure a measure of respect for himself and become technically a chief. But he can never escape the stigma of his low status. His situation is quite analogous to that of the *nouveau riche* in our society.[10]

It would seem that with the Haidas, as in all caste-type systems of stratification, the future position of the child is determined by birth. The child learns early in life what he can expect to become and what he cannot, what he may do and what he may not, just where he must set the upper limits of his aspirations. But what of a relatively "open" class system, such as our own, where the opportunity is presented to the individual to alter his status through achievement? Even here we find that the point of origin and perhaps even the zenith of his socioeconomic status are determined in large measure by the level of achievement, color, and other characteristics of his parents. We are placed in society as members of families.

A final major function of the family in society is its producer-consumer role as an economic unit. We have earlier discussed the coöperative division of labor which results from primary sex differences of males and females, and the operation of age as a differentiating factor in assigning the tasks of a society. To this we may add the economic behavior of the family as a consumer unit. In simple, nonindustrial societies where the immediate end of economic activity is survival, the operation of the family as the basic economic unit emerges with clarity. Embree, for example, has described the family as an economic unit in a Japanese village before the Second World War:

> Everyone in the family does some work. Old people help look after the small children and do simple handwork such as making straw rope, mending *geta*, and sweeping out the yard; children help their parents in whatever is being done and often carry young children on their backs. Young people of fifteen or over do regular work along with their parents. . . . Every member of the household works not for himself but for the house and, even if a member leaves home, he is expected, if successful elsewhere, to contribute money to his house. This co-operative unity of the household affects many relationships. In marriage, for instance, it is essential for the bride to be not only a good worker but also to forget her old home, to turn all her loyalty to the home of her husband. Similarly, in case of adoption of a son, it is desirable to choose a young boy and, whenever possible, a relative. Because the household is a unit, anyone from a house may represent it in *buraku* (hamlet) co-operative affairs—not only the head. . . .

[10] George Peter Murdock, "The Haidas of British Columbia," *Our Primitive Contemporaries*, New York, The Macmillan Company, 1934, pp. 245–246.

The household, as a working unit, is thus the basic co-operative group, and all other co-operation within the *buraku* depends on these constituent household groups.[11]

The early American rural family exhibited this same coöperative labor which is so characteristic of nonindustrial societies, moving William Graham Sumner to characterize marriage as primarily an economic matter, based upon the coöperative relationship of its members for self-maintenance.[12] Twenty years later, Murdock accorded the same importance to the economic function of the family in concluding that "marriage exists only when the economic and the sexual are combined into one relationship, and this combination exists only in marriage." [13] This economic bond also exists between parent and child in terms of reciprocal obligations for support during various periods of the life cycle and is manifested between siblings by mutual economic assistance and help patterns during periods of crisis, for, as we say, "Blood is thicker than water."

These, then, are the universal functions served by families throughout the world which are responsible for its origin and permanence. Despite this permanance, however, significant and far-reaching changes have taken place in the family under the impress of technological and social change. The family no longer serves as the locus of production. The education of the child has been moving from the family into the eager hands of the school, which now is getting the child sooner and keeping him longer than ever before. Family recreation is almost a thing of the past, the mass media of television and cinema, or in their absence a get-together with the "kids," replacing traditional family gatherings. Also weakened is family religious activity. For although most children follow the religion of their parents, and much emphasis has been given to the need for familial religious experience ("The family that prays together stays together"), religion (or the lack of it) has become a personal and individual activity. The family of today resembles the family of old only in terms of the functions it performs, for, like all institutions, it must adapt itself to the changing times.[14]

[11] John F. Embree, *Suye Mura, a Japanese Village*, Chicago, University of Chicago Press, 1939, p. 97.
[12] William G. Sumner and A. G. Keller, *The Science of Society*, New Haven, Yale University Press, 1929, Vol. III, pp. 1505, 1508.
[13] Murdock, *op. cit.*, p. 8.
[14] For a cogent description of the effect of change on social institutions, see F. Stuart Chapin, *Cultural Change*, New York, Century Company, 1928.

Social scientists have long been aware of this gradual weakening of family prerogatives. William F. Ogburn as early as 1933 called attention to the removal from the family of the economic, protective, religious, recreational, and educational functions.[15] He and other sociologists traced this gradual loss of institutional functions and consequent growth of personality and adaptive functions. This view has seen the family as moving "from an institution to a companionship." As stated by Burgess and Locke, the new form of the family is one based upon companionship, with a unity which "inheres less and less in community pressures and more and more in such interpersonal relations as mutual affection, the sympathetic understanding, and the comradeship of its members." [16] To us this seems an overstatement of the case. Certainly there have been changes in the family and resultant modifications of its functions. Indeed, some, such as religious and recreational functions, have been seriously impaired. But the family could not survive as either an institution or a companionship if its functions of child rearing and placement were completely usurped. Furthermore, there are certain functions which could not be performed by any existing institution. With the possible exception of the controlled-breeding experiments that took place in the Third Reich, reproduction is socially limited to the family. The family is still charged with the primary responsibility of maintenance of the young, although some aid of a supplementary and emergency nature is now obtained from governmental sources.

A better case might be made for the loss of the family's status-conferring, socializing, and economic functions. A closer examination, however, will reveal that even here the obvious indications of modification of service do not indicate the loss of the family's role in these areas.

We assume, for example, that as a result of increased social mobility one's status is now largely achieved and therefore not dependent upon family placement of the individual. This conception of our American social structure as a "rags to riches" system is not substantiated. Granted that mobility is relatively high in the class structure of the United States, the consequences of birth into a particular family still determine the level of entrance into the structure. In addition to the

---

[15] William F. Ogburn and Clark Tibbits, "The Family and Its Functions," *Recent Social Trends in the United States*, New York, McGraw-Hill Book Company, 1933, Vol. I, chap. XIII.

[16] Ernest W. Burgess and Harvey J. Locke, *The Family*, 2nd ed., New York, American Book Company, 1953, p. vii.

parents' socioeconomic standing, the color of their skin and their ethnic and religious background will greatly influence what has been termed the child's "life chances." Furthermore, the training given children for adult social and economic roles must begin long before the child shows any indications of ability or the lack of it. So the child born into a higher stratum starts early to receive training for roles which, while available to the more humbly born, are more likely to be assigned to the individual trained since childhood to fill them. As we saw in our earlier discussion of the American social structure, lifting oneself by one's bootstraps is dependent upon the quality of the boots with which one begins.

In the area of educating and training the child, the manifest evidence again seems to point to a continuing loss of function by the family. Again, however, we must proceed cautiously lest we too soon count the family out of this area of the child's life. For while it is obvious that the age of school attendance is being extended at both extremes and that the educator is more and more moving in the direction of educating the "whole" child, the chief function of the educational institution remains that of formal education. The family retains the major responsibility for his exposure to values and still serves as tutor in the formation of attitudes, even toward the school. The family's influence in socialization takes place during the formative early years of life, when molding of personality is most easily achieved and when the competition from other institutions is least. As one schoolteacher was heard to remark: "I have no patience with these mothers who expect us to make social butterflies out of their shy daughters or respectable young gentlemen out of their young hoodlums; don't they realize that by the time we get them their parents have done a pretty thorough job of making them what they are?"

The most frequently cited "lost function" of the family, and the one which is usually mentioned as the first to lose ground, is the economic function. The argument usually runs: the family at one time encompassed almost all of the economic functions of the individual, but such activities as baking, laundering, the shifting of occupations from the home to the factory, and the advent of the automatic stoker as the custodian of the family heating system have gradually weakened its economic function.[17] One receives the impression that the family as an economic unit passed out of existence when women stopped canning and men stopped directly producing the family food. Now

[17] Ogburn and Tibbits, loc. cit.

certainly the family was more of an economic institution during the agricultural period of the American economy; production was located within the family, wives and children contributed directly as extra hands on the farm, and children frequently kept close contact with parents after marriage. Today the canning, baking, clothesmaking, and laundering wife is an old-fashioned survival; few fathers have home-centered occupations and children frequently show financial value only as income-tax exemptions. But the present domestic division of labor still leaves the nonworking wife the important task of overseeing the accomplishment of her former duties as well as seeing to the preparation and consumption of the goods which the father-producer's earnings purchase. The male still "works for the family" and his relative success in his occupation is reflected in the economic standing of the entire family unit in the community. Children still perform light household chores and, as ego extensions, serve to stimulate the productivity of the father. Recent evidence indicates that the current sociological conception of generational independence, wherein the middle-class child strikes out on his own and forms a new independent family, may underestimate the economic ties between generations in American middle-class families.[18] Even if we allow that the family as a unit of production is a thing of the past, the household unit, and ultimately the family, still represent the basic consumer group in society. Perhaps we are no longer employed as families, but we still purchase as families the major home items: household appliances, automobiles, and food.

The family, then, has changed under the impress of a changing society, but the major functions of childbearing and rearing are still located with the family. It is because of this responsibility for the well-being of their newborn members that societies everywhere give great concern to establishing and maintaining a stable family system. The functions which the family serves are vital to societal continuity and must be protected at any cost if society itself is to remain a stable and going concern. Faced with this requisite, all societies seek to guarantee a stable family system through regulation of individual behavior within and toward families, and by defining implicitly the characteristics of a stable family. To do so, rules must be established and members must be taught certain values inherent in family life. Each society presents to its growing members a picture of the stable family and

---

[18] Marvin B. Sussman, "The Help Pattern in the Middle-Class Family," *American Sociological Review*, February, 1953, pp. 22–28.

then seeks to set him to striving for these same ends. The system of folkways, mores, and laws discourages or forbids him to behave in a way which might hinder family stability and devalues as taboo those ends which endanger the family. In time he comes to accept society's definition of the stable family as "good" and worthy of attainment.

But while this concept of the stable family is unconsciously assimilated by individuals, its presence in society is difficult to measure. A device often suggested for measuring family stability is the divorce rate in a society. The rationale here is quite simple: stable families are families which stay together; separation is, therefore, an indication of lack of family stability. A moment's reflection, however, indicates that divorce is not always the result of a family crisis, and merely serves as a legal sanction for separation where some form of disintegration has already taken place. Certainly a high divorce rate indicates that marriages and hence families lose permanence and therefore disturb the equilibrium of social life; but too frequently this concept of stability-instability leads to the further assumption that families which stay together are therefore stable, regardless of their ability to behave as families. The family wherein the father and mother do not speak to each other, keep separate rooms, and each seeks to alienate the children from the other, or the family where, through occupational requirements or preference, the parents live apart for the major portion of the year, are permanent families and remain together but do not produce a stable atmosphere for childbearing and growth.

The same difficulty is encountered with other external indices of stability, such as "successful" (economically) families. They represent cultural rather than universal concepts of stability. True family stability must be measured by the ability to carry out the functions assigned to it by the surrounding society. It is a family which "works," a family whose members are part of a unity of interacting personalities and the relationships among whom are strong enough to function even in times of crisis.[19]

To ensure this stability each society constructs a web of regulations to pattern the relationships among family members—between marital partners, between parents and their offspring, among siblings, and between the family and the larger community. This ordering is vested in the normative system of folkways, mores, and laws and is inherent

[19] For a more detailed discussion of the problems inherent in measuring family stability, see Ray H. Abrams, "The Concept of Family Stability," *The Annals*, November, 1950, pp. 1–8.

in the value system which prods members of society to follow these rules. For, in the words of St. Augustine, "it follows apparently, that the family's peace adheres unto the city's, that is, the orderly command, and obedience in the family, has real reference to the orderly rule and subjection in the city." [20]

Cultural Regulation of Family Behavior

In the preceding sections we have characterized the basic form of the family—father, mother, and dependent children—as a universal expression of society's need for trained members. Later, we saw that this "nuclear" family, to borrow Murdock's descriptive phrase, forms the basis of the kinship structure and lends continuity and stability to social organization. As befits so important an institution, society establishes norms of family behavior to ensure conformity. These norms, or rules, may not be rational or even functional; they may differ greatly from culture to culture and throughout history. But whatever their external form, they are basic to the stability of any society.

While our eventual interest will be the legislation which seeks to ensure this stability, a complete view of cultural regulation of the family must include the role of folkways and mores, customs and traditions. Laws cannot develop outside the impress of the social environment, and the legal order, even the enacted legislation of today, is rooted in the controls of the normative order. All social norms, however, are not necessarily written into codes. In simple, nonliterate societies, folkways and mores serve the same directive end as customary law in regulating behavior. They prescribe and prohibit behavior with as much success as our formal, written statutes, often more successfully, for they appear as natural behavior and are followed unconsciously. In time they form part of the heritage of custom and tradition that is handed down in the folkthought of the society. Eventually, as the society becomes more complex, conflicts of interests appear and elder members of the society may have to arbitrate the clash of interests; but characteristically they "find" the solutions in the cultural heritage of customary behavior.

Whether the norms be written or unwritten, "found" or enacted, there is always the need for regulation to avoid the chaos of completely free self-expression and gratification. Sex and hunger are no respecters of the rights of others, and every society provides a system

[20] St. Augustine, *The City of God* (John Healey, tr.) London, J. M. Dent and Sons, 1931, Bk. XV (Bk. XIX of the original text), chap. XVI, p. 152.

of control, and individuals sacrifice unrestricted expression of personal goals for the coöperative ends of group life. A network of regulations is woven by each society, and each new member must learn to operate within this web of rules or suffer the consequences prescribed by his society. These rules are first encountered when the child finds that his parents, as agents of society, have defined most situations for him and are prepared to manipulate a continuum of rewards and punishments to ensure his acceptance of these definitions. In time he may redefine these situations but by then he will have obtained a vested interest in the perpetuation of the same values which the society, operating through the family, taught him as a child, and which he will pass on in more or less modified form to his own children. Family customs and family law are slow to change, for they regulate a particularly sensitive region of human behavior.

We may now ask: what areas of family behavior are regulated by custom and law? Custom and law seek to regulate the relationships among family members by defining the rights and duties of each personal role within the family and by facilitating the interaction between family and community. Thus, society protects its interest in a functioning family by attempted control of patterns of interaction between husband and wife, parents and children, and brothers and sisters. Let us consider each of these relationships, which occur in every form of the family, as a means of discerning what behavior is controlled in the interactive process.

THE MARITAL RELATIONSHIP

Societies exhibit various degrees of control, but sexual relations are nowhere left unregulated. The potential havoc which unrestricted sexual behavior might cause necessitates the establishment of some kind of control over sex. There must be rules and, because of the compulsiveness of this appetite, powerful sanctions must be imposed to guard against their violation. Anthropological literature abounds with accounts of freedom in sexual relations, but too often freedom in prenuptial sexual behavior is confused with license after marriage. Few if any societies fail to impose restrictions on sexual activity after marriage. Murdock's data reveal that in only 5 of 148 societies studied was adultery freely allowed, and that even where it was not forbidden, various regulations on postmarital sexual behavior were imposed.[21]

---

[21] Murdock, *Social Structure*, p. 265.

But while the control of sexual behavior is a major aspect of regulation, it is by no means all that is controlled in the husband-wife relationship. Other regulations are concerned with (1) who may and who may not marry, (2) what constitutes a marriage, (3) the rights and duties of husbands and wives, and (4) the means whereby the marital relationship may be dissolved. Let us consider each separately and view the actual controls imposed by certain societies.

Who May and Who May Not Marry. All societies, including our own, impose limitations upon the free choice of the marital partner. Rules range from proscription to prescription, from forbidden marriages to required or at least preferred marriages. But everywhere rules govern the "choice." Some rules are universal, such as the incest taboo. There are many definitions of incest, but nowhere are sexual encounters between the parents and their children and between siblings permitted. Murdock's data are again conclusive: in none of the societies on which data concerning incest regulation were available were sexual relations between father and daughter, mother and son, or brother and sister allowed either before or after marriage. In each case, marriage was also forbidden.[22] Several outstanding exceptions have been recorded. Brother-sister marriage was preferred among ancient Egyptian and Inca royal families and among the old Hawaiian nobility; Balinese brother-and-sister twins are allowed to marry since they are assumed to have reached a degree of intimacy in the mother's womb, but these exceptions are indeed special cases. In no case was this permitted among the general population.

Many explanations have been advanced for the universality of the incest taboo. These range from the notion of instinctive aversion to the imputing of eugenic considerations to early man. Perhaps the most acceptable, in the light of cross-cultural knowledge, is Murdock's eclectic theory drawn from psychoanalysis, sociology, behavioristic psychology, and cultural anthropology.[23] Simply stated, this theory assumes a sexual attraction between parents and children of the opposite sex. These impulses, however, encounter resistances based upon sexual jealousy and the punitive attitude of the parents, who represent status figures to the siblings. Each parent blocks the impulses of the child of the same sex and each, as a result of inhibitions acquired in socialization, will experience anxiety over his own impulses. Both parents feel a threat to their own unconscious attachments to the

---

[22] *Ibid.*, p. 12.
[23] *Ibid.*, p. 292 f.

offspring of the opposite sex when the possibility of a sexual relation between son and daughter appears, and jealousy leads to parental punishment for sibling sexual encounters. These inhibitions become internalized and thus exclusive sex privileges and clear-cut statuses are preserved. Society accepts this arrangement since it tends to minimize sexual conflict within the family, ensuring a stable system of relationships within which the crucial family functions can be carried out. Moreover, the internalization of these restraints tends to add weight and support to parental authority. Through the psychological processes of association and stimulus generalization, these taboos are extended until they eventually include other relatives of the same sex and age grade as the sexually tabooed relative. Thus an uncle may represent a father image to his niece, an aunt a mother image to her nephew. This process of stimulus generalization is aided in those societies where the same kinship term may be applied to more than one relative, thus eliciting similar patterns toward each person within the relationship. As society develops, incest taboos come to serve the added social function of extending kinship outside the immediate family, allowing for trade alliances, friendly relations among groups, and other relationships of both personal and social utility.

In addition to incest taboos, societies establish restrictions against marrying within certain groups and requirements to marry within others. Preferred or required mating within a particular grouping is known as endogamy, the requirement that one marry outside a particular grouping as exogamy. Examples are numerous, but perhaps the most interesting system of endogamous-exogamous marriage regulation occurs among the Aranda, aborigines of Central Australia. Murdock's summary of Radcliffe-Brown's account of the workings of this system follows:

The social organization of the Aranda consists first of all in a primary division of the tribe into two halves or "moieties." These are not local divisions, for any group of moderate size will contain members of both. Each moiety is subdivided in turn into two "sections," likewise not local in character. Exogamy prevails with regard both to the moiety and to the section, i.e., a man cannot marry a woman of his own moiety, and consequently not of his own section either. He must obtain a wife from the other moiety—indeed from one particular section of that moiety.[24]

In our own society we are legally exogamous by sex, kinship, mental

[24] George Peter Murdock, "The Aranda of Central Australia," Our Primitive Contemporaries, New York, The Macmillan Company, 1934, p. 27.

defection, physical health, and certain character factors. We are endogamous legally by age and (in some states) race; and traditionally, if not legally, we are also endogamous to some extent by social class, religion, and ethnic background. In the next chapter we shall discuss some of the methods of regulating these preferences and proscriptions through licensing and recording marriages and through the prohibition of undesirable marriages.

What Constitutes a Marriage.   Every society seeks to prescribe for its members what constitutes a marriage. This task appears to present no problem until one considers that there are not only many forms of marriage, but sometimes several in one locality. In the African kingdom of Dahomey, for example, there are no fewer than thirteen types of legal marriage. The problem is not so complex, however, if we realize that all forms of marriage are merely variations of the two basic types: monogamy (the union of one man and one woman) and polygamy (plural mating). Polygamy may involve either one man and two or more women (polygyny) or, less frequently, one woman and two or more men (polyandry). Rarer still are the instances wherein societies allow the concurrent "marriage" of both plural husbands and plural wives (group marriage).

Of these four variations of marriage, monogamy is most prevalent, although few societies make it obligatory. The prevalence of monogamy is obviously related to the sex ratio, which nowhere is so unbalanced as to make bigamy, let alone more than two husbands or wives, feasible on a society-wide basis. As Dr. Johnson said to Boswell: "No man can have two wives, but by preventing somebody else from having one."

Polygyny is next most common, being much more frequently encountered than polyandry. This greater frequency of plural wives rather than husbands seems to be related to male dominance and mobility, taboos against coitus during and after pregnancy, higher male mortality, and masculine initiation of the marriage proposal. While we offer these explanations in an effort to account for the phenomenon in general, it must be remembered that the incidence of polygyny or any form of marriage in a particular society is related to its peculiar culture history. A word of caution must be added concerning our "natural" feeling that polygynous mating, for example, must inevitably result in sexual jealousy and degradation of women. The socialization process in childhood can justify whatever forms of behavior are found in the existing culture. Thus, the plural wives in a

polygynous marriage, having themselves come from polygynous families, usually accept this as "natural." They may even welcome the assistance and easing of labor afforded by additional wives. On the island of Madagascar, for example, the polygynous family seems quite stable.

Among the Ikongo, who hold land individually, each wife is assigned a share of the husband's land. He has to help her cultivate this on her day, while she feeds herself, her children, and the husband while with her, from its produce. . . . In spite of the separate housing for the wives and married sons, the Tanala family is well integrated. It is customary for the entire group to eat together in the house where the father is on that day and cooking is done in rotation. The wives aid each other in all their activities, look after each other's children, etc. There can be no doubt that polygyny does a great deal to lighten the labor of the women and they are quite as much in favor of it as the men.[25]

The incidence of polyandry is much less frequent, but where it does occur it seems to be related to female utility. Among the Eskimos, for example, while polygyny is common, polyandry is also found and seems to be associated with female services to the male. Rasmussen, in commenting on the marriage practices of the Netsilik Eskimos of Greenland, observes that:

Polyandry is also practiced, it being no rare occurrence for a woman to have two husbands. A grown man is a helpless being if he has no woman to make his clothes, and so it will happen that a man will call a good comrade who is alone to share his wife with him. It is seldom, however, that these marriages run smoothly, especially if the men are young, for it very often ends in one of them being killed. Naturally, a wife can never ask a good friend to come in as a partner in her marriage; this is a right that exclusively belongs to the husband.[26]

Concerning group marriage, the evidence seems to indicate that authentic instances are extremely rare, and that where it does occur it is usually an extension of sexual privileges among a group of males and females and does not represent a functioning family group as such.[27]

[25] Linton, The Tanala, pp. 132, 133.
[26] Knud Rasmussen, "The Social Eskimos," A Reader in General Anthropology, Carleton S. Coon, (ed.). New York, Henry Holt and Company, 1948, p. 135.
[27] Cf. Robert H. Lowie, Primitive Society, New York, Albert and Charles Boni, 1920, pp. 49–62, and Social Organization, New York, Rinehart and Company, 1948, pp. 122–124; Murdock, Social Structure, New York, The Macmillan Company, 1949, pp. 24–25.

Society also shows its concern for defining approved marriages in its requirement that some form of ceremony announce the changed status of the new mates. This marriage rite may be very simple, as among the Kutenai Indians of the Northern United States, where a feast or housewarming constituted the only public ceremonial; or very elaborate, as in the marriage of a member of the British royal family amid much regal pomp and ceremony. But whether simple or elaborate, the marriage rite serves the same purpose: the affirmation of social approval to the union.

Basically, the action of society in defining what constitutes a marriage seems to center around rules regulating the number and characteristics of the males and females involved, and the institutionalization of the marital relationship by a public proclamation that the union has social sanction. In our later discussion of the regulation of marriage, we shall see that our own society has attempted this regulation through laws governing multiple marriages; marriages contracted as a result of fraud, mistake, or duress in obtaining consent to marriage; common law marriages; and the form of solemnization ceremony.

The Rights and Duties of Husband and Wife. A third configuration of rules to regulate marital relationships concerns the rights and duties of husbands and wives. Here we may make good use of the concepts of status and role following the classical discussion by Linton.[28] By status we mean a particular position within a hierarchy of positions held by members of a group. To ensure common understanding, positions must be defined, and a status is defined by the rights and duties which are attached to the position. Within the family, for example, a male may have the status of husband, with certain rights and duties toward his wife, and also that of father, with a different set of rights and duties toward his children. To each status is attached a role, the dynamic behavioral component of the structural position (status). It represents the behavior which is necessary to put the rights and duties inherent in the status into effect. In the family, for example, the role played by the male as a father is not the same as the role he plays as a husband, and the two roles may even conflict.

Earlier we differentiated between status ascribed at birth and status earned as a measure of achievement. Both types of status play a part in the consideration of the husband-and-wife relationship. Certainly one "earns" the status of husband or wife just as both later "earn" the culturally valued status of parent. But whether one enters life as a

---

[28] Linton, *The Study of Man*, pp. 113–121.

male or female determines which of these roles one will eventually fill. As a result of this ascription of a later status, the child is able to begin very early the business of learning the role he will eventually play in the marital relationship. Here again the family is the primary teacher, for by observation of both parents the child learns not only the role he is to play, but, of equal importance, what he is to expect of his spouse. Small children at play illustrate this in their games of "house"; the discerning parent may observe many of his own behaviors if he observes his son in the play role of "daddy." These statuses have a continuity as they are passed from generation to generation, in some ways changed as society redefines the role of wife or husband, but in many ways unchanged, for universally there are certain things which must be done by the male and others which can only be done by the female.

Let us consider first the important elements in the role attached to the status of wife. But before we do this we must make the obvious, but nonetheless important, point that each wife has a dual status in the nuclear family; she is really a wife-mother. We recognize this difference by giving her the two titles; mother in her parent-child relationship, wife to her husband. The problem is to separate those elements of the wife-mother role which adhere to the marital relationship from her role as a mother. Universally she is responsible for the bearing of children, certainly an element of the parent-child relationship. But her refusal or inability to bear children is tantamount to abrogation of the marriage in most societies, and in Moslem cultures her "inability" to produce male heirs may lead to the setting aside of the marriage (rather enigmatic since it is male sperm not female ovum which sexes the child). But if we think of "clusters" of rights and duties centering about the adult female in the family rather than mutual distinctions, we need not complicate the wife-mother role. The clustered responsibilities of the wife status center around the bearing and rearing of her husband's children, the care and upkeep of the home, subordination to the husband in social and economic spheres, loyalty, and, more recently, affectional companionship for her husband. In return she receives the rights of financial and emotional security, status as a wife, and authority over certain domestic functions.

The specific components of the wifely role differ in various cultures and change over the course of time, but she is everywhere subordinate to her husband, although there are variations in the degree of subservience. Among the Mende, a West African people, the role of the

wife includes complete obedience: "The wife's duty is to obey and satisfy her husband in every way possible. She is expected to defer to him in everything except purely domestic matters, and traditional etiquette requires her to approach him on bended knee. If she comes into the household as a junior wife, however, she is under the immediate control of her husband's big wife and takes her orders directly from the latter." [29]

Among the Navajo Indians of the Southwest, however, where descent is traced through the mother and the maternal uncle functions as the sociological father, the role of the wife seems less dominated by masculine superordination: "Socially, the position of the Navajo woman is high. She has a voice in all family affairs and many times her decision on a matter is final since she may have control of the family purse strings according to the relative wealth of herself and her husband." [30]

But even in Navajo society the man enjoys privileges and prestige which mark him as the protector of the family, and even where the husband is "replaced" as social father by his brother-in-law, his children still have about the same attitude toward him as in our own society. Nowhere in human society do we find that women are assigned the role of protector; but everywhere they are assigned the tasks of childbearing and care of the household.

The superior physical strength and mobility of the male have caused him to be cast in the role of provider and protector of the family. Almost universally we find that authority within the family is vested in him; even where the mother serves as disciplinarian, she frequently has recourse to the father as the ultimate source of authority. This latter situation is illustrated by the threat frequently made by mothers to misbehaving youngsters in our own society to "Wait until your father comes home." Specifically, within the marital relationship the male is responsible for the protection and security of his wife and her offspring, the achievement of status for the entire family, and the provision of conjugal companionship to his wife. In return he may expect the rights of determining the domicile, the bearing of his (and only his) children, and the fidelity, emotional security, companionship, and coöperation of the wife. Again we shall find that the specific

[29] K. L. Little, The Mende of Sierra Leone, London, Routledge and Kegan Paul, 1951, p. 159.

[30] Gladys A. Reichard, "Social Life of the Navajo Indians with Some Attention to Minor Ceremonies," Columbia University Contributions to Anthropology, Vol. 7, 1928, p. 62.

elements which make up the role of husband differ in various cultures and with the passage of time; but he is universally the provider and protector in the human family. If we return to the polygynous Mende, among whom we recently observed the role of the wife, we find that he is a provider and protector to each of his wives: "The husband's obligations toward his wife are to maintain her so long as she remains with him and to provide her with clothing. He is expected to treat all of his wives in the same way, though an exception is made in the case of a senior wife." [31]

This duty of the husband to support and protect his wife and her offspring may even be prolonged to include care when the marriage has been dissolved. In modern American urban society, where women have come as near equality with men as anywhere, we characteristically have nonsupport laws for the protection of women and children; and where the male is no longer filling this role, the state will seek to carry out the obligation.

We have several times pointed to the effect of culture on human behavior and have seen that social action is relative to both time and place. Roles are also determined by culture and are shaped by our membership in groups and subgroups such as social class, ethnic background, and religion. Roles also reflect social and cultural change, for as society changes behavior changes to keep pace. In modern roles of husband and wife some elements have been lost and others added. For example, the emancipation of women, introduction of labor-saving devices into the home, and the generally changing character of marriage in America have changed the husband-wife relationship. We frequently view these changes in role behavior as a sign of the growing masculinity of women, her inroads into occupations once restricted to males, her new role as a companion in the family, and her indulgence in such "masculine" pursuits as smoking, drinking, and driving. Actually, there has been a concurrent, if less marked, movement in the opposite direction: the "feminization" of the male. The present generation of males seems willing to give much more aid in household tasks, such as drying dishes and caring for children, than were their fathers. It seems that what is actually occurring is that the roles of husband and wife are acquiring more elements which are shared in practice if not in societal assignment. Note that when husband and wife are both employed, the discredit for a poorly kept and untidy

[31] Little, *op. cit.*, p. 159.

house still falls upon the wife regardless of any degree of "sharing" of domestic responsibilities.

Roles, like most concepts in human behavior, have an ideal and an operational component. The ideal role of wife grows out of the customs and mores which are rooted in the past. They seek to fulfill the cultural values defining the mutual orientation of husband and wife in the ideal or traditional family. The operational role of wife is based upon current expectations of behavior—the ideal role redefined to fit existing social situations. The recent interest shown in the word "obey" as part of the marriage vows of the bride illustrates the subtle but realistic differences between these role definitions. Traditionally, the wife owes obedience to the husband as a result of the submissive character of the ideal role pattern of the female in marriage. But with the developing concept of individual freedom and the emancipation of women, the need to pledge obedience to the husband presented a rankling reminder of the subservient position of women, and some individuals sought to omit the word "obey" from the marital vows. Later, various religious groups allowed its omission, causing some dissension from groups dedicated to the ideal role of the wife as owing obedience to the man. See, for example, the encyclical letter of Pope Pius XI, entitled "On Christian Marriage," which proclaims: "The same false teachers who try to dim the luster of conjugal faith and purity do not scruple to do away with the honorable and trusting obedience which the woman owes the man. Many of them go even further and assert that such a subjection of one party to the other is unworthy of dignity, that the rights of the husband and wife are equal; wherefore, they boldly proclaim, the emancipation of women has been or ought to be effected." The conflict is, of course, between the traditional and "modern" conceptions of the rights and duties of the wife—between the ideal and operational roles.

It must be remembered that these changes in marital roles take place over a long period of time, for our concepts of behavior associated with the family show a high resistance to change. Thus at any given time there is general agreement as to the basic elements of the role, although alternative behaviors may be approved. A woman may or may not work as she sees fit, but regardless of which alternative she chooses, she is still held responsible by the community for the care of her children and for fidelity toward her husband. This agreement as to patterns of behavior leads to the establishment of what Max

Weber has called a "social relationship." [32] The action of each member of the marital relationship takes into account that of the other, so that there exists a probability of action which has meaning to both members. These expectations of marriage behavior come from many sources, but are largely derived from the partners' early environment, especially in their own childhood family. They are essential to the stability of marriage; for when the married couple do not share these expectations, one partner no longer experiences security in the knowledge of the other's probable behavior.

There have been many changes in the legal positions of husbands and wives as the legal position of women has changed. In the next chapter we shall discuss the changes which have taken place in the rights and duties of husbands and wives in terms of the changing position of women, and the liabilities of husband and wife.

Dissolving the Marriage Relationship. Every society regulates the dissolution of the marital relationship either through custom and tradition or laws (tempered by current attitudes). Thus, a state may have very rigorous controls on the granting of divorce by the device of limited grounds, but existing practice leads to falsifying of grounds or excessive use of annulment or desertion as substitutes for divorce. No other aspect of the marital relationship is so closely controlled by law, for this concern is but another expression of the interest of society in maintaining stable families. Once the marriage has been established and sanctioned, the legal system bows out of the picture in favor of the social controls, and folkways and mores direct the behavior of the members of the family. It is only when trouble strikes, when the stability of the family is threatened and the established social relationship is disrupted, that the legal order returns to concern itself with the marriage relationships. If the husband fails to carry out his responsibilities toward the wife or if she fails to act in accordance with the role of wife, then the legal order becomes involved.

Historically, western society has looked upon marriage as a sacrament, so that the disruption of this relationship for any reason other than death has been viewed as inadmissible. This concern with keeping marriages whole is honored in such tenets as "What God has joined together let no man put asunder" and "Until death us do part." In primitive societies, however, where marriage is usually a group covenant rather than a religious or civil function, divorce often

---

[32] Max Weber, *The Theory of Social and Economic Organization* (A. M. Henderson and Talcott Parsons trs.), New York, Oxford University Press, 1947, pp. 118–120.

may be obtained with little formality. This should not be taken to
mean that divorce is common among primitives, but where it does
occur it is not always obtained through litigation, as in American
society. Typical of attitudes toward divorce among a hunting and
gathering people are those found among the Flathead Indians of
Montana:

> There was no specific cause for divorce, nor did the act necessarily imply
> social culpability on the part of the divorced. A husband might leave his
> wife just because he was tired of her. In spite of the wife's theoretical right
> to divorce, such complete freedom was seldom exercised.
>
> Divorce was devoid of public regulation or ceremonial. The only act
> which might be construed as divorce ritual was the tying of a horse at the
> wife's door by the husband with divorce in mind. A woman who had her
> mobility thus increased considered it a gentle hint to move away.[33]

This ease of divorce is common among simple, nonliterate societies.
But if we turn to more complex and civilized societies, we find that
patterns of behavior relating to divorce are similar to our own. The
Aztecs treated the dissolution of marriage with some surprisingly
"modern" ideas. Vaillant has described the marital practices of this
great warrior nation.

> Desertion was frowned upon, but a court would grant a decree of di-
> vorce under certain circumstances. A man could obtain the right to cast
> out his wife if she were sterile, were subject to prolonged ill temper or neg-
> lected the household duty. The wife could be freed from a husband who
> failed to support her or educate the children or who ill-treated her in the
> physical sense, for the Aztecs had not invented mental cruelty.[34]

The differentiation between the action of the Flatheads in merely
broadly hinting to an unwanted wife that she might leave and the
court-decided divorce of the Aztecs or of modern society is not as
great as it first appears. Certainly there is a difference in procedure
and in the culturally determined refinements of the action, but in
both cases the action was aimed at the artificial interruption of the
marital relationship. As societies become more complex, it seems that
divorce becomes increasingly more institutionalized and religious and
legal restrictions are imposed upon the dissolving of the marriage
bond. Marriage comes to be looked upon as a sacrament and the bond

---

[33] Harry H. Turney-High, *The Flathead Indians of Montana*, Menasha, Wis.,
Memoir 48, American Anthropological Association, 1937, p. 96.

[34] George C. Vaillant, *The Aztecs of Mexico*, New York, Doubleday, Doran and
Company, 1944, p. 112.

which it creates as sacred and voidable only under extreme circumstances. Barriers are placed in the way of those individuals who seek to escape from the bond. In our own society, as in most modern societies, divorce cannot be obtained unless one party to the marriage can be proved guilty of some breach of the relationship. Actually, if a couple should decide that both want a divorce because, let us say, they feel that their marriage is a failure, they will soon discover that in this contract mutual consent is not sufficient reason for nullifying the obligations of each in the marriage. For in our society there can be no divorce without fault. It must be proven that, at some specific time prior to the suit for divorce, the marriage *de facto* has been destroyed by reason of any of the legal grounds for divorce designated by the state. As we have mentioned, divorce has become a contentious litigation whereby one party must theoretically be at fault.

The law is slow to change, however, and eventually public opinion concerning the "fault" involved may be relatively slight, and the grounds or faults cited by the couple seeking a divorce may be tailored to fit the law. Today we read of divorces granted as a result of the wife's charge of extreme cruelty with no great feeling of censure against the perpetrator of this deed, her husband. The reader does not react with fervor and loathing toward the husband and demand that he be punished as he might if he read of some member of the community severely beating his child or even mistreating a pet. In short, we accept the fact that this "extreme cruelty" is more a legally required definition of conduct than conduct in fact.

Society's concern with dissolving of the marriage bond does not stop with regulations concerning the divorce itself. The relationships among the members of the broken family are also regulated in terms of the adjudication of property rights, custody of children, and the payment of alimony. In the next chapter we shall look into the legislation which has been enacted to define these relationships, as well as those laws concerning the legal restrictions surrounding the obtaining of the divorce.

The Parent-Child Relationship. With the appearance of the first child the marriage becomes a family and a whole host of new relationships are born. New roles of parent and child bring with them new demands and different spheres of behavior from those which existed in the simple marital relationship. The care and protection of the child take precedence over the personal needs of the parents, and orderly patterns of experience gained in playing the roles of husband

and wife are disturbed by the necessity of adopting the new roles of father and mother. Not infrequently, jealousy may be aroused as one or both parents feel a loss of attention and affection from the other, and the demands of child care may conflict with the interests and desires of the new parents. In short, the new child creates the need for adjusting the dyad to a three-person group with new rights and duties.

The appearance of the child, however, represents the consummation of the marital relationship, the end for which the marriage was undertaken. We have previously discussed the genesis of the family in the mother-child relationship and commented on the importance attached by the community to the protection and training of the child. Modern society adds new reasons for concern. Freud and later social scientists have pointed to the importance of childhood and parent-child relationships in the formation of personality patterns. It has long been known that family relationships, while not the sole cause, play a critical role in the causation of juvenile delinquency. In 1934 the White House Conference Report indicated that one-half to two-thirds of all homes where delinquency was present were broken by the absence of one or both parents as a result of death, separation, desertion, or divorce. The report also stressed the importance of tensions and conflicts in the family as factors in delinquency, pointing out that a psychologically broken home is just as serious a drawback to adequate development of the child's personality as a legally broken one.[35] Subsequent studies have supported this view. Howard Bell, in a study of 13,500 young people between the ages of 16 and 24, found that 32.3 percent of the delinquents in his sample had experienced breaks in their families. The United States Children's Bureau reported in 1939 that, in the cases processed in sixty-four courts during the year 1936, broken homes were associated with 50 percent of the girls' cases and 36 percent of the boys' cases. In a separate study, Weeks found a positive relationship between broken homes and delinquency and again noted a much higher incidence of broken homes in the cases of delinquent girls than in the cases of boys.[36] In analyzing his data Weeks advances the interesting suggestion that the characteristic types of male and female delinquency explain this differential. While boys are most frequently committed

[35] White House Conference Report on Child Health and Protection, *The Adolescent in the Family*, New York, D. Appleton-Century Company, 1934.

[36] H. Ashley Weeks, "Male and Female Broken Home Rates by Types of Delinquency," *American Sociological Review*, August, 1940, pp. 601–609.

to institutions for crimes against property and traffic violations, females are committed primarily for sexual delinquency, ungovernability, and running away from home. The loss of parental influence which results from the disrupted relationship in a broken home would seem to be clearly related to the offenses characteristic of the girls. We may conclude that the presence of a stable family, characterized by secure relationships between parents and their children during the early formative years of the children's life, is an important element in maintaining order in society.

The important role of the family and its members in providing this stable platform for child development is dealt with by society. Folkways and mores urge and the laws order that, at least during the early period of the child's life, parents shall perform certain duties as a result of their responsibility to the child and, ultimately, to society. At the same time the parent is given certain rights and interests in connection with his offspring. While these rights and duties vary considerably from society to society, the universal nature of the parent-child relationship allows for certain cross-cultural similarities. Nonliterate, as well as civilized, peoples distinguish between the child born of a sanctioned marriage and the child of unmarried parents; adoption seems to be even more frequent among primitives than in modern industrial society. All societies regulate the parents' rights to custody and control of children while defining the new generation's behavior toward their parents. Our understanding of these controls will be increased if we consider characteristics of the parent-child relationship in several societies in terms of (1) the rights and duties of parents, (2) children born out of wedlock, and (3) adoption and the guardian-ward relationship.

The Rights and Duties of Parents and Children. Roscoe Pound, in his discussion of individual interests as distinguished from society's interest in domestic relations, discusses those interpersonal claims within the family relationship which must be secured as between the parties of the relation and against interference from the rest of the world.[37] He finds that the parents have an interest or claim in the society of which their children are a part, their custody and control, and the power to direct their training; a claim to the chastity of a female child; and an interest in the industrial services of the child. In

---

[37] Roscoe Pound, "Individual Interests in the Domestic Relations," in Association of American Law Schools, *Selected Essays on Family Law*, New York, The Foundation Press, 1950, pp. 1–19.

addition, as part of the parental role, he may claim respect and obedience from the child and, in the event of indigence, support from a child of age, capacity, and sufficient means.[38] Furthermore, the child may claim support during infancy, education and training dependent upon the ability of the parent to provide such services, and maintenance by the parent in the event of indigence during maturity.[39] However, the child's right to support in infancy and to education are not part of the legal tradition, but are actually expressions of the public or social interest. At common law, for example, there was no liability on the part of the parent to support the child, and the child had no legal recourse against the parent. Legislation has been enacted in recent years to compel support of the child, the state being empowered to remove a child from an inadequate home in the event of noncompliance. Thus, we have an expression of society's interest in the situation. We might characterize the legal tradition as concerning itself with the rights of parents and the duties of children while neglecting the duties of parents and the rights of children. The current direction of family legislation seems to be toward greater concern with the welfare of the dependent members of the family.

Morally, if not legally, the parents are responsible to the community for the welfare of their children in all societies. This embraces the biological necessities of nourishment and physical protection, and the more variable social requirement that the child be trained in the ways of his society. What and how children are taught about social behavior changes with history and culture, but the responsibility of the parent to provide at least the bare outline of socially approved values and norms is universally recognized. Even in modern society, with its highly developed system of formal education outside of the home, the importance of furnishing social orientation and transmitting social values is recognized as a responsibility of the parent toward the child. Every national conference on child welfare has stressed this fact.

Children are responsible to their parents in many ways. They are in all societies responsible, though in varying degrees, for obedience to the wishes of their parents, who, in addition to their greater physical size and strength, have the "law of the land" largely on their side. As members of the miniature society which is the family, they are expected to show loyalty to that group. This responsibility and loyalty may extend beyond marriage, so that in the traditional Chinese

---

[38] *Ibid*, pp. 5–6.
[39] *Ibid*, p. 9.

family, for example, a son's duty toward his parents must always take precedence over his obligations to his spouse. In many societies this loyalty includes the support of the parent in old age or indigence, the child often continuing his subordination to the parents nonetheless. Characteristically, the child's role toward the parent is one of dependency and subordination the world over. In Chapter 8 we shall see the extent to which the rights of parents in relation to their children have changed and legislation has moved to protect and enforce the rights of the child. In general, regulation of the parent-child role is in terms of the rights of the parents to the custody, punishment, and earnings and services of minor children and the duties of the parents to support, protect, and educate the child.

Children Born out of Wedlock. In our earlier discussion of legitimacy as a necessary feature of socially approved birth, we explained the institutional taboos against extramarital conception as a universal recognition of the need for a stable, permanent group to bear children and induct them into society. In an attempt to restrict the reproductive behavior to the family, society has used ridicule and scorn as well as a variety of legal punishments and penalties against the mother and the child. This is true of simple nonliterate as well as modern urban societies.

The problems brought on by the birth of a child out of wedlock are many and have consequences for society as well as for the child, the mother, and (to a lesser degree) the father. A child born outside of the family has no claim to paternity and therefore no established rights to name, support, inheritance, and all the intangible privileges which go with legitimate birth. At common law he was *nullius filius*, nobody's child. In ancient Rome he had but few of the rights assigned to legitimate children, and even in England he was, until the enactment of the Poor Law of 1576, a parish ward whose parents could not be made to support him. Our conceptions of legitimacy have changed somewhat since that time, primarily in terms of reducing the penalties imposed upon the child and to some extent the unwed mother while at the same time increasing the responsibility of the reputed father. But even with these changes, the attitude of society toward the unwed mother is still one of scorn and avoidance, and the stamp of illegitimacy a despised one.

Adoption of Children and the Guardian-Ward Relationship. Despite the primacy of the natural family relationship of parents and children in all societies, occasions arise where a decision must be made

as to the appointment of new protectors for the child. The inability of children to care for themselves and the necessity of the presence of adults to protect children have led to the practices of adoption (wherein new parents are appointed for the child) and the somewhat different guardian-ward relationship. For the present it is sufficient to say that adoption differs from the appointment of a guardian primarily in that, while the adopting parent acquires all of the rights and duties of the natural parent, the guardian is not required to supply the needs of his ward except from the ward's estate and is not entitled to the labor of the ward.

Adoption is by no means a phenomenon restricted to modern society, being widespread among primitive peoples. Radcliffe-Brown, commenting on the frequency of adoption among the Andaman Islanders of the Pacific, quotes an early visitor to the islands as follows: "It is said to be a rare occurrence to find any child above six or seven years of age residing with its parents, and this because it is considered a compliment and also a mark of friendship for a married man, after paying a visit, to ask his hosts to allow him to adopt one of their children." [40]

Even the guardian-ward relationship, which is usually associated with civilization and the protection of property rights of minor children, is approximated in nonliterate societies. The following description of Dobuan child claims sounds almost like the litigation of guardianship matters in a modern divorce case or custody fight.

> When a man marries a woman of a far away place he usually comes and settles permanently in his wife's place . . . if he dies away from his home, leaving a daughter by his wife this daughter may be required to leave her mother and her mother's place and go to her father's sister, far away. There she must stay until she bears a child in her father's place. She then has her choice of leaving her child to replace that place's loss of her father and coming home to her mother, or staying on in her father's place with her own child. [41]

While adoption seems to be most common in the earlier stages of cultural development, its legal control and institutionalization are peculiar to civilization. Here the child is artificially made a member of a new status in a kinship group other than that into which he was

---

[40] A. R. Radcliffe-Brown, *The Andaman Islanders*, Cambridge, The University Press, 1933, p. 77.

[41] Reo F. Fortune, *Sorcerers of Dobu*, New York, E. P. Dutton and Company, 1932, p. 20.

born. Society and the law accept this arrangement whereby the parentless child is afforded the protection of interested adults. In recent times we have added the interest in supplying the childless home with the privileges of parenthood.

The Sibling Relationship. The family relationship which in modern society receives least legal attention is that among brothers and sisters. It would appear that after the siblings have emerged as adults from the controlling and regulating family group into which they were born, they form new nuclear families of their own and society's concern, like that of the sibling, turns to the newly formed family. This lack of concern for adult patterns of sibling behavior is not, however, found in primitive societies. The relationships among brothers and sisters are frequently very formalized in adult life, and very definite patterns of rights and duties may be rigidly imposed. An example of such a relationship is the previously mentioned Navaho custom of the avunculate, wherein the maternal uncle functions as the sociological father, which could only exist where a strong sibling relationship persists into adulthood. A quite different type of control of adult sibling relationships is found among certain Plains Indian peoples where adults must characteristically avoid adult siblings of the opposite sex. It is sometimes improper, for example, for Menominee Indian males to utter their sisters' names. The sexual significance of these controls as extensions of incest taboos becomes apparent in the behavior of Menominee males in gathering behind barns and clandestinely whispering their sisters' names.

In our society, with the exception of laws concerning incestuous marriages, the chief control of sibling relationships would seem to be economic. Thus we shall discuss legislation affecting the sibling bond primarily in terms of laws governing the inheritance of property.

Contemporary Problems in Family Legislation

The history of any social institution is a history of adaptation and accommodation. The interplay of economic, political, and religious forces constantly remolds the basic social relationships of society. Major social institutions remain but must adapt to changing conditions, and as one institution changes the adaptations are radiated to other institutional structures. As we have seen, the family, basic though it is, important though it be, has not been immune to this process of change and has responded to the introduction of a new technology by modifying its characteristic functions. Factory-centered

production has moved the locus of economic activity outside the home, where a new division of labor has disturbed the ancient distribution of tasks by sex and age while creating an ever growing demand for technically trained personnel. The school, in response to this demand, has taken over the skill training once performed by the family and, at the same time, seems to be moving steadily in the direction of offering its own social attitudes to the child. The home has moved from the small, homogeneous community to the urban center and has responded to the new urban patterns of life by decreasing its size and modifying its kinship relations. In the small community the family was an integral part of a larger, extended kinship group; in the urban environment it has been freed from the control of extended kindred, and each generation forms nuclear families more independent than before. The social control once exercised by the extended kinship group loses meaning as the pattern of family separatism becomes established. Even the informal control by public opinion, sufficient to compel conformity in the small, homogeneous community, loses its effectiveness and must be bolstered by legal sanctions. Family behavior changes and established rules and conventions give way to new patterns oriented to the new values of the emergent industrial culture. Individualism replaces group orientation as more and more activities of individual family members move outside the home under the influence of competing secondary institutions. This individuation of family members upsets traditional roles within the family. Women, with lessened dependence upon men as their sole possible source of support, strive for equality and are freed from the restricted roles afforded by the home. They enter the labor market in increasing numbers, achieve political equality, and emerge with a status nearer full equality with men than at any previous time in history. But this freedom produces other effects as well: an increasing divorce rate related to feminine economic independence, loss of effectiveness of kin disapproval, and the acceptance of romantic love and individual happiness as the primary basis for marriage; and, because marriage becomes an end in itself rather than a vehicle for the formation of the family, the birth rate, already adversely affected by urbanization, decreases.

This growth of individualism has had equally important effects upon the parent-child relationship. Largely unprotected in the ancient law, the child now becomes an individual rather than a group member, and society develops an interest in his rights as an individual. The

growing attention which we have given to the rights of children has led to an age of child-centered family life. As in the past we were cautioned to "think of the family," so today we are more likely to be urged to "think of the children." As the birth rate declines, the number of brothers and sisters competing for family attention decreases and the child represents an even greater center of parental and social concern. Filial devotion, once the highest of childish virtues, gives way to an understanding between parents and children and (if we are to believe some modern reports) to a democratic situation where family behavior is decided by mutual agreement. The period of childhood, which was once preparatory to adulthood, when the individual became a completely productive member of society, has been extended and the youth culture becomes an end in itself largely devoid of any realistic orientation toward adult roles. There is a growing characterization of contemporary society as showing too much concern for the child while neglecting his preparation for responsibility to parents and society.[42] This emphasis upon the youth culture, the postponing of social and economic maturity, and the rapidity of social change has placed a gap between parents and their children, and the consequent difficulty in communication has resulted in parent-child conflict.

It seems clear that modern society has witnessed the emergence of a new kind of family lacking many of the stabilizing influences of the former agrarian family. This change has not come about from any internal revolution in the family itself, but represents an adaptive adjustment by the family to a changing social order. New family problems have resulted from this change and are added to the age-old problems of family life, which were retained and compounded as the family changed. As in the past, society's preoccupation with family stability has led to new attempts to enact legislation to bring about this family unity. In addition to the adjustment which family legislation has had to make to a new kind of family, the political institutions have themselves been subjected to the same pressures for change as the family. The specific responses which American family legislation has made to these pressures and to a changing family will be dealt with in the two following chapters. But we should first consider the

[42] Cf. Kingsley Davis, "The Child and the Social Structure," *Journal of Educational Sociology*, December, 1940, pp. 217–221; Roy Helton, "Are We Doing Too Much for Our Children?", *Annals of the American Academy of Political and Social Science*, November, 1940, pp. 231–243; and Edward A. Strecker, *Their Mothers' Sons*, Philadelphia, J. B. Lippincott Company, 1946.

general complexion of the changes which have been wrought and the current problems which will influence the direction of future legislation.

The Changing Character of American Family Legislation

The problem of discussing effects of social change on family legislation is very difficult. The various state legislatures have moved in many (and sometimes strange) ways to achieve the ultimate goal of all family legislation: family stability. Confronted with this confused and inchoate medley of laws, in describing how the body of family laws has changed we shall focus on the common goals of the legislation enacted by fifty-three jurisdictions.

Earlier we saw that the American colonists brought with them the common law of England. This great body of law, concerned with the legal rights and duties of individuals rather than social needs, soon became inadequate as the concept of individual dignity gained headway. New situations arose in the changing society, and the common law, rooted in the customs and mores of an earlier period, was modified by an increasingly large body of complementary enacted statutes. As progress accelerated in the later history of the country, technological change was rapid and social behavior moved to keep pace. To maintain order in the changing relationships which resulted from a new economic system and increased social mobility and urbanism, it became necessary to draft new laws which would redefine rights and obligations of family members. Each addition to the laws probably seemed adequate at the time of its enactment, but our individualism led us to label as suspect any centralization of power which might have given more uniformity to family legislation. Furthermore, colonial and later state jurisdictions differed markedly in their approaches to family legislation. Despite this variability there were many similarities in the family laws of the various jurisdictions as a result of the universality of family functions and the limited possibilities of safeguarding the performance of these functions.

In general, the tendency in the laws regulating marriage has been toward equalizing the rights and duties of husbands and wives as their social roles show greater similarity. Entrance into marriage has been made more difficult by more discriminating licensing procedures and by the addition of new restrictions, such as blood tests and the requirement that a longer period elapse between the announcement of intention to marry and the marriage. The law of divorce seems to

be moving in the direction of greater curbs on the addition of new grounds for divorce, while the procedure in obtaining a divorce is being eased in some states by reductions shortening residence requirements and expanding existing grounds for divorce.

The laws regulating the parent-child relationship show three tendencies, according to the late Chester G. Vernier: "(1) equalization of both the rights and the duties of the two parents; (2) amelioration of the condition of the illegitimate child; (3) increasing control by the state in adoption proceedings." [43] To this we might presently add the growing concern of legislation with child welfare through child-labor and school-attendance laws. A further expression of this interest in child welfare is the growing attention to preventive as well as correctional services in juvenile delinquency. The establishing of youth commissions, police training courses for prospective members of juvenile bureaus, special courts for young offenders, and legislative investigations attest the present realization that delinquency presents special problems which require specialized treatment.

Recent Trends in Family Legislation

Society is never static, and the recent problems which led to the legislative trends just described have already been superseded by contemporary problems. Again, there are special problems in each of the various jurisdictions, but all might be resolved into three common issues: (1) the advisability of uniform laws of marriage and the family to do away with the confusion resulting from multiple jurisdiction, (2) the right of the state to act in the interests of dependent members of the family, and, (3) legal realization of the need for a social-science approach to the problem of family unity.

Uniform Family Laws

There is a distinct body of laws for each of the fifty-three jurisdictions in the United States. The confusion which this can cause might be illustrated by the fact that a man may marry in one state, obtain a divorce in a second state, and remarry in a third only to find that he is single, married, or a bigamist depending upon which of the three states' laws he examines. Obviously a national marriage law would do away with such situations; but the fear of centralization is still strong, and many states and individuals view with alarm any movement to

---

[43] Chester G. Vernier and E. Perry Churchill, *American Family Laws,* Stanford University, Stanford University Press, 1936, Vol. 4, pp. 3–4.

obtain uniformity by the assumption of exclusive jurisdiction over marriage and family laws by the national government. Senator Capper repeatedly sought to introduce constitutional amendments granting Congress the right to make federal marriage and family laws which would be uniformly administered, but these bills met the usual opposition on the part of vested interests fearful of federal control.

Some progress in obtaining uniformity has been made by the institution of a National Conference of Commissioners on Uniform State Laws, an annual conclave of representatives of the various states to consider model laws drafted by committees. As an advisory group they have no power to enact changes of the law in any state, but they can urge, with the added support of the American Bar Association, that their uniform and model acts be adopted by each constituent jurisdiction.

State Intervention in the Interests of Dependent Family Members

At common law the position of women and children was one of almost complete subjection to the father, who stood forth as the representative of the family before the law. As the economic and social position of women changed, however, the legal rights and duties of the wife also changed. Her person has become her own; she has a right equal to her husband's in the control and custody of their children. But her legal responsibilities have also increased, and the same social forces which led to her independence have increased her legal liability for the support of an indigent husband and, in the event of divorce, even to pay alimony.

Laws concerning the employment and education of children, their treatment, and the growth of the state's role in problems concerning their adoption and custody are a further evidence of the action of the legislatures to intervene in behalf of the dependent members of the family. This movement has not been without some criticism of the right of any agency to interfere in the sensitive area of intrafamily relations. One court expressed this view in its opinion that "it would be intolerable if anyone who should choose to furnish a minor necessaries, under all circumstances could compel a father to answer to a court or jury concerning the propriety of the family discipline." [44] Despite the resistance, however, legislation seems to be moving increas-

[44] *Ramsey v. Ramsey*, 121 Ind. 215. 23 N.E. 69 (1889).

ingly in the direction of extending protection to dependent members of the family.

The Unitary Nature of Family Problems

There is a growing awareness within legal circles of an established principle in social science: all difficulties of the family are manifestations of the fundamental problem of the family's failure as a unit. Faced with this realization, and the implication that the treatment of any family discord or problem requires consultation with other specialists, the courts and the legislatures have sought the services of social scientists, social workers, psychiatrists, and the medical profession in the enactment and interpretation of family legislation. Publications in the field of family law devote whole sections to social-science interpretations; law schools sponsor conferences on the relationship between law and related social sciences and include social scientists on their faculties. This wedding of approaches to family study and social engineering may give greater perspective and depth to future legislation.

This new awareness of available help from social science has not, however, removed the influence of nonrational pressure groups representing vested interests that would keep modern family legislation geared to an outmoded and archaic approach to family problems. Every recent session of the New York State Legislature has witnessed attempts by realistic members to change the antiquated single-ground divorce law in that state. Despite the support of social scientists and professional legal guilds, the changes are always doomed as the result of pressures applied by religious groups which maintain that to change the law would weaken family stability.

Family Legislation: Concluding Remarks

In this chapter we have viewed the family from its beginnings in the simple nutritional bond between the primate mother and her helpless offspring to its modern complexity in an urban environment. There has emerged a picture of a social group which has been modifying many historical functions. Despite these modifications in function, the family persists as the only social institution which can perform the basic function of bearing and training new members of society. The importance of this role has led to a pronounced social interest in every society in maintaining a stable and continuous family group. But the strength of individual drives is such that strong pressures

must be brought to bear if members of the society are to be made to conform to social rather than individualistic values. To produce this conformity an elaborate system of rules and standards of behavior is developed to order the relationships among members of the family and between the family and other elements of the social structure. At first these rules operate through the force of public opinion and the informal social controls, but as society becomes more complex and heterogeneous, clashes of interest develop and it becomes necessary to apply the authority of legal sanctions to standards of family behavior. In time these rules form an established code of family law and become firmly entrenched in the normative order.

In the next two chapters we shall examine some of the specific changes and directions in family law under the impress of a changing society. The power of kinship control has been greatly weakened and competing institutions come to define many elements of family behavior. Group values give way to individual goals in a highly competitive society. The family legislation which has been enacted during this period shows the same concern for individual interests as the state becomes the champion of the dependent members of the family.

SELECTED REFERENCES

Flügel, J. C., *The Psychoanalytic Study of the Family*, London, Hogarth Press, 1931.

Harper, Fowler V., *Problems of the Family*, Indianapolis, Bobbs Merrill, 1952.

La Barre, Weston, *The Human Animal*, Chicago, University of Chicago Press, 1954.

Murdock, George Peter, *Social Structure*, New York, The Macmillan Company, 1949.

Pilpel, Harriet F., and Zavin, Theodora, *Your Marriage and the Law*, New York, Rinehart, 1952.

Richards, E. A. (ed.), *Proceedings of the Midcentury White House Conference on Children and Youth*, Raleigh, Health Publications Institute, 1951.

chapter **7**

Family Legislation:
The Marital Relationship

In the preceding chapter we observed in connection with the family that, biologically, marriage stems from the human animal's permanent, nonseasonal sexuality and from the existence of primary sex differences which require that a man and a woman form the basic unit in procreation. Regardless of its manifest form, marriage is everywhere reducible to a sexual relationship between a male and a female. It is upon this biological foundation that society builds the elaborate superstructure of cultural responses called marriage.

To assume, however, that sex is the exclusive factor in either the origin or maintenance of human marriage would be to misunderstand the relationship between marriage and the family. The union which results from sexual attraction produces offspring whose extended dependence requires a permanent and stable group for survival. So fluctuating and capricious a force as the sexual appetite could not have produced bisexual relationships with enough permanence to form the firm basis necessary for family-group building. It is human society that gives this necessary stability to marriage by institutionalizing the marital relationship into a pattern of attitudes, symbols, and material objects and surrounding the institution with written and oral specifications describing and ordering the marital relationship.[1] Thus, as Goodsell and others have pointed out, marriage grew out of rather than resulted in the formation of the family.[2]

---

[1] F. Stuart Chapin, *Cultural Change*, New York, Century Company, 1928, pp. 48–49.

[2] See Willystine Goodsell, *A History of Marriage and the Family*, New York, The Macmillan Company, 1934, p. 4; and E. A. Westermarck, *The History of Human Marriage*, New York, The Macmillan Company, 1926, p. 22.

The purpose of the present chapter is to examine the legislation which has resulted from regulation of the marital relationship in American society. Since fifty-three different jurisdictions enact our domestic laws, it will be impossible to state simple, comprehensive, nationally prevailing laws of marriage and divorce. There are, however, certain natural uniformities among the statutes of the various states as a result of a common legal tradition and recent pressures for uniformity. It is to these uniformities that we shall direct our attention, and we shall comment on variations among the states. This approach will permit us to deal with trends and the probable future directions of legislation affecting the marital relationship rather than merely to cite existing statutes which might very well change with each legislative year.

Marriage: A Social and Legal Definition

The individual and social consequences of marriage are great and the number and complexity of definitions of marriage are limited only by the frame of reference within which one seeks to define the marital relationship. Legally, marriage has been declared a contract, a relationship, and a status; in religion, it is a sacrament; to the social scientist, an institution or complex of customs and rules governing the marital relationship. Obviously, these differences in definition follow from a difference in emphasis, for all are describing the same relationship. The courts are interested in the legal rights and duties of the individuals involved and in the interests of society, the church in the spiritual relationship, and social science looks to the social functions of marriage. For our purposes it is only necessary that we consider a socio-legal definition of marriage.

Viewed in its social perspective, marriage is a socially approved method of establishing a family. Every society maintains a system of controls over the marriage of its members. These controls may be moral or legal, formal or informal. Religious precepts, for example, while not a part of the formal law, embody many of the moral norms and taboos which regulate marital behavior. Adultery, incest, bigamy, and fornication are condemned; conjugal fidelity, filial devotion, and parental solicitude are encouraged. It is within this social setting of formal and informal moral norms that the common law and, eventually, the legislatures and courts have sought to define and regulate marriage.

At law, marriage is a permanent, legalized relationship between a man and a woman. As such, it becomes a status or settled legal rela-

tionship between the parties entering into the marriage. Various courts have held that once placed in this relationship the principals take on a new status which can be changed only by the authority of the state.[3] In addition, marriage has been referred to as a "civil contract." It was Sir William Blackstone who first gave wide currency to this concept that in English law marriage is viewed solely and simply as a contract.[4] If marriage were indeed simply a contract, then a marriage would have to meet the same general requirements as any contract in the business world. This would seem to mean that, to be binding upon both parties, (1) an offer or proposal must be made and accepted, (2) there must be a "meeting of minds" or mutual assent from both parties, (3) there must be a legal consideration or promise to perform various duties or obligations, (4) both parties must have the legal capacity to make a contract, and (5) there must be an absence of fraud or duress and the subject matter must not be illegal.

Many courts, however, have held that marriage is not a contract "like any other." [5] Basically, the marriage contract differs from an ordinary contract in several ways:

1. While an ordinary business contract can be terminated at will, the marital contract cannot be changed or rescinded by the voluntary actions of the parties.

2. The marriage contract results in a status and merges the interests of the parties in the relationship for life. Most contracts do not result in relationships which become permanent upon the execution of the agreement, since they can be rescinded by the action of the parties without the consent of the state.[6]

3. The tests for capacity to enter into the marriage contract differ from those applied to ordinary contracts. Thus, "infants" (at common law, any person under 21 years of age) may not make legally binding contracts, but may make valid marriages if they are above certain age limits.

Fundamentally, these differences tend to cluster about two important characteristics of the marital relationship as a contract: (1) the inability of the parties to terminate the relationship by mutual con-

---

[3] State v. Bittick, 103 Mo. 183, 15 S.W. 325 (1891); Atkeson v. Sovereign Camp, 90 Okla. 154, 157, 216 Pac. 467, 469 (1923); Rocke v. Washington, 19 Ind. 53, 81 Am. Dec. 376 (1862).

[4] Cf. Sir William Blackstone, Commentaries on the Laws of England, Oxford, The Clarendon Press, 1765, Bk. I, p. 434.

[5] Maynard v. Hill, 125 U.S. 190, 8 S. Ct. 723 (1887); Adams v. Palmer, 51 Me. 480 (1863); Maguire v. Maguire, 7 Dana, 181, 183 (1838).

[6] Cf. Chester G. Vernier. American Family Laws, Stanford University, Stanford University Press, 1931, Vol. I, p. 51.

sent and (2) their inability to make the terms of the relationship. Many important consequences for marriage stem from these differences. Thus, while the parties to a private contract may specify the length of time during which their agreement remains in effect, or may state in advance the conditions under which the contract will terminate, such is not the case in marriage. If a man and a woman agree in advance that their marriage shall last for some stated period of time only, or that if either party is dissatisfied and desires a divorce, the other shall aid in obtaining grounds, such antenuptial agreements are legally worthless.

The basis for this special treatment of the marriage contract would appear to be the state's responsibility to make the terms of the marital relationship as manifest and standardized as possible. If every prospective pair of mates could draw up the terms and conditions of marriage without respect to the established norms, marriage would lose the stability which results from standardization. Therefore, society, in the person of the state which guards the interests of society, becomes a third party to the contract and insists upon conditions which it feels are in the best interests of private and public welfare. No individual or informal organization lacking the regulatory powers of the state could require these conditions so effectively. The state, wielding the powerful instrument of the law, can establish and enforce qualifications for entry into marriage and define the standards of acceptable marital behavior. As we shall see in succeeding sections of this chapter, legislatures have concentrated on the negative task of placing obstacles in the path of those desiring to enter into marriage.

The Legal Regulation of Marriage

An oft-quoted legal opinion holds that, for the purpose of promoting public and individual moral stability, every state is fully sovereign with respect to the regulation of marriages.[7] Our whole system of marriage laws is built upon the basic principle of the right of each state to decide who shall and who shall not marry within its borders. Although this multiple jurisdiction has produced a variety of statutes limited only by the number of states and territories involved, certain basic principles are true of every state's regulatory actions. In every state the business of deciding who shall marry is largely the result of the state's prior decision as to who shall not marry, since the role of matrimonial legislation seems to be one of placing obstacles in the

[7] *Tolar v. Oakwood Smokeless Coal Corp.*, 173 Va. 425; 127 ALR 430 (1930).

way of marriage. While the specific impediments cited by each state may differ somewhat, all seek to promote what is considered to be group welfare by controlling entrance into marriage. Practically, this can be done only if the state has some means of extending or withholding its approval prior to a marriage. In American jurisdictions, states have sought to accomplish this regulation by (1) controls imposed through the requirement of a license for marriage, (2) secular controls over the solemnization of the marriage, and (3) the prohibition of undesirable marriages.

THE MARRIAGE LICENSE

The imposition of legal controls over who enters into marriage and the conditions under which the marriage will take place necessitates some administrative means of signifying that sanction has been granted or withheld for each marriage. The most practical manner is for the state to require of all persons a license indicating that both parties meet all of the qualifications necessary for marriage in the particular jurisdiction. All fifty-three American jurisdictions have adopted this procedure.[8]

Historically, the marriage license had its origin in the early English practice of obtaining a bishop's license as a means of release from the requirement that banns, or announcements of the intent to marry, be published prior to marriage. On the Continent, similar dispensations had been authorized by the sixteenth-century Council of Trent in order to ensure that marriages were not "maliciously hindered." [9] With the gradual transfer of matrimonial control from the ecclesiastical courts to the civil courts, the requirement of a license became a state rather than a church regulation.

In this country, while we have an optional system of solemnization, wherein the officiant may be either an ecclesiastical or civil official, the issuance of a marriage license is a civil function. Each state has estab-

[8] The survey of the statutory provisions presented in this and the following chapter represents the latest and most complete information available to the authors concerning the family laws of the forty-eight states, the District of Columbia, Alaska, Hawaii, Puerto Rico, and the Virgin Islands. Sources from which information was obtained include (1) Vernier op. cit.; (2) the Martindale-Hubbel Law Directory, Summit, N.J., Martindale-Hubbel Inc., Vol. III, 1955; (3) pertinent government publications; (4) correspondence with legislative reference bureaus of several states; (5) the Women's Bureau of the Department of Labor; (6) appropriate professional journals and magazines; (7) the Council of State Governments' Book of the States, Chicago, the Council, 1954–55; and (8) newspaper and magazine coverage of specific changes in the laws of various states.

[9] Mary E. Richmond and Fred S. Hall, Marriage and the State, New York, Russell Sage Foundation, 1929, p. 17.

lished its own procedure for the issuance of the license, but basically all prescribe (1) the requirement of a license for marriage, (2) where and by whom licenses shall be issued, (3) the form and content of the application, and (4) the substantive regulations as to the qualifications of the parties and how these are to be determined.[10]

It is paradoxical that, while all American jurisdictions have laws which require a license in order to marry, a license is not essential to the validity of a marriage in every state. The laws of a state may be "mandatory" in that they require a license as a prerequisite to a valid marriage, or they may be "directory" in that they are merely suggestive of the steps necessary for marriage. Legislatures have specifically provided in some states that noncompliance with the license laws does not invalidate an otherwise valid marriage, while the courts in other states have produced the same results through decisions and judicial construction. An obvious example of valid marriage in the absence of licensing and solemnization is common-law marriage, which is still recognized in some states. Here, despite the obvious noncompliance with the requirement of the license and a ceremony, the individuals in the relationship are considered married. In three states, banns may be published as a substitute for a license and in other states specific groups, such as Quakers or American Indians, are exempted from both license and ceremony requirements. The intent of these provisions for marriage in the absence of complete compliance with the laws of marriage is clear; to allow the innocent omission of some requirement to invalidate an otherwise successful marriage would in most cases produce unnecessary anxiety and hardship. This does not mean, however, that the license requirement should not be strictly enforced and that obvious evasion should not be punished. The present direction of most legislation is toward improving the licensing process as a means of catching errors before they are committed.

No licensing process can be successful unless it is based upon valid and complete information collected by competent and efficient civil officials. The most efficient procedure would seem to require the presence of both prospective partners at the place of issuance with proof of their contentions as to the absence of any impediments to their marriage. Unfortunately, such is not always the case. While in a few states both parties must appear in person to apply for the license, most states require the presence of only one person, and in a few cases

[10] Vernier, *op. cit.*, Vol. I, p. 59.

it is even possible for a third person to make the application.[11] In some states the unsupported statement of the applicant is sufficient proof of the fitness of the parties to marry, and only a few states require the use of affidavits from a third party as to the validity of the information given. If the restrictions placed upon the right to marry have any realistic value and if the evasion of these restrictions is undesirable, then we must obviously require some means of establishing the validity of the statements made to the civil official issuing the license. The suggestions for the improvement of license issuance made in 1929 by Richmond and Hall, as a result of their exhaustive study of the operation of the license system in this country, would appear to be just as valid and necessary today: (1) Both candidates should be required to appear to apply for the license. (2) Verification of the statements of applicants in the case of certain easily verifiable information, such as age, residence, parental consent, and the legal dissolution of any prior marriages. (3) The verification of the statements of the applicants should be required under oath, with provision for penalties in the case of false oaths and for the challenging of incompetent or "professional" witnesses. (4) The refusal of one issuing district to license a marriage should be reported to neighboring licensing districts along with the reason for such refusal. (5) Licenses should be issued only during regular office hours except in grave, realistic emergencies. (6) Some central state agency should be charged with the responsibility for ensuring the familiarity of local issuing officials with the present marriage laws of that state. The issuer should, in turn, be responsible for the explanation of the provisions of the law to the applicants.[12]

Banns or Advance Notice of Marriage.   One of the important modern functions of licensing is to give advance public notice of the intention of community members to marry. In the past, this function was served by the publishing of the banns, or announced intention of marriage. This religious custom was a practice in many Christian countries even before the requirement of banns by the Lateran Council of A.D. 1215. As early as A.D. 802, for example, Charlemagne had instituted a system of inquiry into prospective marriages as a safeguard against clandestinity. The purpose of publishing the banns was to bring to light any knowledge of impediments to marriage on the part of either candidate. In a small, homogeneous community, lacking modern urban anonymity, such controls would be particularly effective. Today, while

---

[11] In Alabama, for example, neither party need appear to apply for the license.
[12] Richmond and Hall, *op. cit.*, chap. III, *passim.*

the practice of publishing the banns has remained as a custom in some religious groups, it has been replaced in civil practice by the licensing procedure. By requiring a waiting period either before the issuance of the license or between the issuance of the license and the marriage, the state is, in effect, allowing a period of time during which the community is placed on notice as to the intended marriage. In 1955, thirty-one states, the District of Columbia, Hawaii, and Alaska had laws which require some form of advance notice. Table 8 summarizes the general requirements of American jurisdictions.

TABLE 8. American Marriage Laws as of 1952.

State	Age of Consent to Marriage[a]		Age Below Which Parental Consent is Required		Common-Law Marriages Recognized	Prohibits Marriage of Those with Transmissible Disease in Infectious Stage	Physical Examination and Blood Test for Male and Female		Waiting Period	
	Male	Female	Male	Female			Date of Enactment	Scope of Laboratory Test[b]	Before Issuance of License	After Issuance of License
Alabama	17	14	21	18	★		e	30 da.	d		
Arizona	18	16	21	18							
Arkansas	18	16	21	18						3 da.	
California	•	•	21	18	f		1939	30 da.	g		
Colorado	•	•	21	18	★		1939	30 da.	i		
Connecticut	16	16	21	21			1935	40 da.	g	5 da.	h
Delaware	18	16	21	18		★				4 da.	
District of Columbia	18	16	21	18	★		1945	30 da.	g	3 da.	
Florida	18	16	21	21	★						
Georgia	17	14		18	★		1943	30 da.	i	5 da.	
Idaho	15	15	18	18	★		1943	30 da.	i		
Illinois	18	16	21	18	★		1939	15 da.	d		
Indiana	18	16	21	18	★		1939	30 da.	g		
Iowa	16	14	21	18	★		1941	20 da.	g		
Kansas	•	•	21	18	★		1947	30 da.	i	3 da.	
Kentucky	16	14	21	21			1940	15 da.	g	3 da.	
Louisiana	18	16	21	21			j				72hrs.
Maine	•	•	21	18	★	★	1941	30 da.	g	5 da.	
Maryland	18	16	21	18						2 da.	
Massachusetts	18	16	21	18			1943	30 da.	g	5 da.	
Michigan	18	16		18	★		1939	30 da.	d	5 da.	
Minnesota	18	16	21	18	k					5 da.	
Mississippi	•	•	21	18	★					5 da.	
Missouri	15	15	21	18	l		1943	15 da.	g	3 da.	
Montana	18	16	21	21	★		1947	20 da.	g		
Nebraska	18	16	21	21		★	1943	30 da.	g		
Nevada	18	16	21	18							
New Hampshire	20	18	20	18			1937	30 da.	g	5 da.	
New Jersey	•	•	21	18	m	★	1938	30 da.	g	3 da.	
New Mexico	18	16	21	18							
New York	16	14	21	18			1938n	30 da.	g	3 da.	24 hrs.
North Carolina	16	16	18	18			1941	30 da.	d,o	2 da.p	
North Dakota	18	15	21	18			1939	30 da.	o,q		
Ohio	18	16	21	21	★		1941	30 da.	g	5 da.	
Oklahoma	18	15	21	18	★	★r	1945	30 da.	g		
Oregon	18	15	21	18			1937	10 da.	s	3 da.	
Pennsylvania	16	16	21	21	★		1939	30 da.	g	3 da.	
Rhode Island	18	16	21	21	★		1938	40 da.	s,o	5 da.	
South Carolina	18	14	18	18	★					1 da.	
South Dakota	18	15	21	21			1939	20 da.	g		
Tennessee	16	16			★		1939	30 da.	d	3 da.	

TABLE 8. American Marriage Laws as of 1952. (Continued)

State	Age of Consent to Marriage[a]		Age Below Which Parental Consent is Required		Common-Law Marriages Recognized	Prohibits Marriage of Those with Trans-missible Disease In Infectious Stage	Physical Examination and Blood Test for Male and Female		Waiting Period	
	Male	Fe-male	Male	Fe-male			Date of Enact-ment	Scope of Labor-atory Test[b]	Before Issuance of License	After Issuance of License
Texas	16	14	21	18	★			15 da.	d	
Utah	16	14	21	18		★	1941	30 da.	i	
Vermont	16	14	21	18		★	1941	30 da.	g	5 da.
Virginia	18	16	21	21			1940	30 da.	g	
Washington	e	e	21	18		★	t			3 da.
West Virginia	18	16	21	21			1939	30 da.	g	3 da.
Wisconsin	18	15	21	18			1939	15 da.	g	5 da.
Wyoming	18	16	21	21	★		1943	30 da.	d	

★ Information furnished by the Women's Bureau, U. S. Department of Labor.
(*Source: Martindale-Hubbel Law Directory*, Vol. III, 1953 and individual State Codes).
a With parental consent.
b Time allowed between date of examination and issuance of license.
c In 1919 law adopted applying to male only; laboratory test authorized but not required. Amendments in 1947 and 1949 rewrote law and apply to both male and female applicants.
d Venereal diseases.
e Common-law age of consent to marriage in absence of statutory requirement 14 for males and 12 for females. California requires court approval where female is under 16 and male under 18.
f Valid if consummated prior to 1895.
g Syphilis.
h 24 hours, residents; 96 hours, nonresidents.
i Syphilis and other venereal diseases.
j In 1924 law adopted applying to male only; laboratory test authorized but not required.
k Valid if contracted on or before April 26, 1941.
l Valid if contracted prior to March 31, 1921.
m Valid if contracted prior to November 30, 1939.
n Amended in 1939.
o Tuberculosis in infectious stage.
p In one county if both applicants are nonresidents.
q Pulmonary tuberculosis in advanced stages or with any contagious venereal disease.
r Person infected with venereal disease who marries any other person guilty of a felony and upon conviction may be punished by penitentiary confinement from 1 to 5 years.
s Syphilis and gonorrhea.
t In 1929 law adopted applying to male only; no provision as to laboratory test.

Source: Council of State Governments, *The Book of the States, 1954-55*, Chicago, The Council, 1954, Vol. X, p. 323. Used by permission.

While the statutes of the various jurisdictions differ both in length and placement of the period, the most common form of advance-notice law requires a waiting period between the application for a license and its issuance. The period ranges from one to five days, with three and five days being most common. Three states presently place the waiting period between the issuance of the license and the marriage ceremony. In Virginia, the marriage must be delayed five days and in Louisiana three days. Delaware, the third state using this type of law, requires only a one-day waiting period for residents, but four days for nonresidents. New York uses a combination of both systems, dividing the waiting period into three days before and one day after the issuance of the license. In most states, these requirements may be waived under conditions which the court feels constitute an emergency, as in the case of pregnancy of the female.

The popularity of the first system, wherein the waiting period comes

before the actual issuance of the license, attests to its obvious advantages. Where the license has been issued, it is possible for the officiant, in effect, to "waive" the waiting period by marrying the couple at once, dating the certificate the proper number of days ahead, and not returning it for filing until the required period of time has expired. Also, placing the waiting period between the application and the issuance demands at least two appearances before the issuing office (unless the license is mailed) and allows for a somewhat more controlled and regulated waiting period.

The present direction of advance-notice laws would seem to be one of increased use both in terms of the number of states adopting such statutes and in the length of the waiting period. The benefits of such laws are twofold: (1) the period of advance notice offers a means of halting—or at least postponing—hasty, illegal, and freak marriages; and (2) they provide a "cooling off" period during which one or both parties may consider the advisability of the marriage. Still another benefit which should result from nation-wide use of advance-notice laws is the effect such legislation would have on marriage market towns or Gretna Greens. Elkton, Maryland, for example—once notorious as a "quickie" marriage mart—was dealt an effective blow by the enactment of Maryland's advance-notice law in 1938. The greater instability of marriages performed in these matrimonial automats makes their early demise a condition devoutly to be desired.[13]

Breach of Promise.   Since the common-law definition of marriage centers about its contractual nature, it is not surprising that a breach of the promise to marry is treated in our courts as a violation of a contract. This approach is peculiar to those countries whose legal tradition is rooted in the English common law. France and other civil-law countries have provisions for the recovery of expenses or pecuniary losses and for punitive damages in the event of seduction by reason of the promise to marry, but only the English-speaking countries have ever allowed unlimited damages for the mere breach of the promise to wed. The essential difference is that while the civil-law tradition focuses on the conditions surrounding the breaking of the contract, common-law emphasis is upon the breach itself, which is considered sufficient cause to bring court action. This emphasis in common-law jurisdictions came about as a result of the changing of jurisdiction in

[13] Cf. William G. Kephart and Ralph B. Strohm, "The Stability of Gretna Green Marriages," *Sociology and Social Research,* May-June, 1952, pp. 291–296.

such cases from the ecclesiastical to the common-law courts. The church courts had been interested in preserving the sacrament of marriage so that they would decree specific performance of the promise to marry. In the secular courts the emphasis fell upon the breach of the contract and the resulting right of the injured party to receive damages.

The right of the injured party to sue and collect damages, however, was not a part of the early common law. The right to sue was not established in the common-law courts until 1639 and a full discussion of the action did not come until 1672, when it was concluded that the action for breach of promise was maintainable at common law.[14] Although in modern practice the breach-of-promise suit has become almost entirely a feminine action, the right of both sexes to sue was established in 1698, when an action was brought against a woman who broke her contract to marry.[15] Later, it was held that definite proof of an express promise to marry by the plaintiff was unnecessary if consent could be inferred from circumstantial evidence.[16]

The breach-of-promise suit, a holdover from the days when dependent women required legal protection from predatory males, represents a distinct cultural lag in the present age of increasing economic independence of women; yet the specter of the wronged woman (who might have been the juror's daughter or sister) still produces resistance to the movement to do away with such suits. Certainly, much abuse of the intent of the law has taken place on the part of unscrupulous women who, coached by their even less scrupulous counsels, are willing to expose their intimate personal affairs in court for a profit. On the other hand, some type of protection would still seem necessary for women who sustain financial loss as a result of the man's capricious breaking of an engagement or in the case of seduction under promise of marriage. But, in either case, little real justice results from airing the situation in courts with the expectation of money compensation for romantic and sentimental injuries. The very nature of the promise to wed, which is almost always an oral statement exchanged between the parties to the action, makes verification difficult and, under the

[14] *Stretch v. Parker*, Rolle, Abridgement, 12 Car. Rot. 21 (1639), and *Holcraft v. Dickenson*, Carter 233, 124 Eng. Rep. 933 (1672).

[15] *Harrison v. Cage et uxor*, Carthew 467, 5 Mod. 411, 1 Salk, 24, 90 Eng. Rep. 870 (1698).

[16] *Hutton v. Mansell*, 6 Mod. 172 (1704). Vernier (*op. cit.*, Vol. I, p. 24) quotes a decision from the case of *Daniels v. Boles*, 2 C. and P. 533 (1826), which contains the astonishing statement that "it would be indelicate to expect that she [the plaintiff] should consent in words."

jury system, the persuasiveness of the counsel and the pulchritude of the plaintiff too frequently become the chief consideration. Also, the inclusion of such intangibles as wounded pride, damaged reputation, and reduction of marriageability has introduced factors which are very difficult if not impossible to compensate financially.

In the English Parliament, there have been frequent attempts to abolish or modify breach-of-promise laws since 1879 and continuing up to the present day. In the United States, the rash of "heart balm" cases in the twenties and thirties led to increased effort for abolition, and in 1935 seven states passed laws abolishing the breach-of-promise action.[17] Vernier, writing in 1931, contends that complete abolition of such suits would be in the best interests of society. Lacking complete repeal, the following regulations might make such suits more equitable and less distasteful: (1) require written proof of the promise to marry in all cases; (2) require separate suits for seduction; (3) restrict the type of evidence admissible and require corroboration; (4) limit damages to material loss incurred on the faith of the promise; (5) if sentimental or punitive damages are allowed, place a low and arbitrary limit, e.g., $1000.[18]

Not all legal authorities, however, agree that breach-of-promise suits should be repudiated. The suits are said to be needed to protect the more emotional sex from fraud and deceit by males, to enforce the performance of the contract to marry, and for numerous reasons centering about the desirability of maintaining what the courts have upheld. One of the strongest legal objections to abolition has been that such a step would be unconstitutional since it would violate the prohibition against the impairment of contract and the due-process clause of the Fourteenth Amendment. This objection was answered in a test case of New York's statute abrogating breach-of-promise suits. The Court of Appeals held that marriage is a unique contract, with the state as an interested party, and so does not come under the contract clause. Further, since the state has complete power to change or even destroy a common-law right of action, the repeal did not violate the due-process clause.[19] The trend of the states in abolishing breach-of-promise suits seems to be well established and can be expected to continue into the future until "heart balm" cases become a rarity.

[17] Alabama, Illinois, Indiana, Michigan, New Jersey, New York, and Pennsylvania.
[18] Vernier, op. cit., Vol. I, p. 29.
[19] Fearon v. Treanor, 272 N.Y. 268, 5 N.E. (2nd) 1815 (1936).

Solemnization and Recording of Marriages. In American jurisdictions, the statutes usually provide that either a civil or religious official may perform the marriage ceremony. This represents a merging of two traditions in our colonial history. Colonial New England, with the barren simplicity of its religious life, looked upon marriage as not so much a sacrament as a civil contract, so that the early laws of that region prescribed civil marriages before justices of the peace or magistrates. It was not until the close of the seventeenth century that the religious marriage ceremony began to receive equal footing in New England. In the southern colonies, where the Church of England was established, marriage was viewed primarily as a sacrament, so that the Anglican religious ceremony was prescribed by law. Gradually, civil ceremonies, which had been recognized under certain conditions since the days of the Revolution, gained equality with the religious rite. Today, only two states (West Virginia and Maryland) restrict the performance of the marriage ceremony to religious officiants only. Most states, however, provide that any one of a number of civil officials may officiate. Justices of the peace perform the largest number of civil marriages, although governors, mayors, judges, police magistrates, city clerks, and even notaries public may officiate. In many states, statutory provisions require that ministers and other religious officials, and in some cases civil officials, who are authorized to perform marriages must first receive official sanction from the state in the form of either registration or licensing.[20]

There is little regulation of the form of the marriage ceremony since more than half of the jurisdictions have no legislation at all. Where statutes do exist, they usually provide that the parties shall declare in the presence of the solemnizing officer that they take each other to be husband and wife, with a few requiring the declaration be made in each other's presence and most states requiring the presence of witnesses.[21] A large majority of states expressly permit the celebration of marriage according to the rites of particular religious groups or sects. Thus Quakers, whose ceremonies may not call for the intervention of a solemnizing officer, in many states are allowed to solemnize their

[20] The necessity for such laws is attested by the occasional disclosure of illegal marriages performed by unauthorized officiants. On February 3, 1954, for example, a bill was introduced into the New Jersey State Assembly to legalize the twenty-five marriages which had been performed by a 43-year-old unordained "student pastor" since 1947. New Jersey law requires that a religious officiant be an ordained minister.
[21] Vernier, *op. cit.*, Vol. I, p. 92.

marriages according to their own customs. In some states, this same privilege is extended to German Baptists, Mennonites, and Old Amish Mennonites. Some states, taking cognizance of the fact that some religious societies may not be generally recognized as denominations, specifically grant them and their officers the authority to solemnize marriages. The New York State statutes, for example, specifically authorize the leaders of the Society for Ethical Culture and the Brooklyn Society for Ethical Culture to perform marriage ceremonies.[22] Still another concession to local custom is found in statutes which authorize special procedure for American Indian marriages. Iowa, for example, allows for their marriage by superintendents of Indian agencies, New York allows Indian "peacemakers" to officiate, as does South Dakota, and Oklahoma specifically recognizes marriages performed according to Indian customs.

Recording Marriage Licenses and Certificates. It is exceedingly important that some record exist of both the issuance of the license and the celebration of the marriage. The absence of such records can have serious consequences for the parties and for the state, since they serve almost exclusively as evidence of marriage. In addition to their obvious value as social statistics, they are invaluable in later questions of the legitimacy of children, the existence of bigamy, and the property and pension rights of heirs and a surviving spouse. All American jurisdictions have recording statutes, which generally provide (1) that the issuing officer must record the license at the time of issuance, (2) that the officiant return the license or certificate or both following the marriage ceremony to the issuing officer, (3) that the returns be recorded, and (4) that the local recording officer transmit a copy of his records to the appropriate state bureau or officer.[23]

Common-Law Marriages. A common-law marriage is one which does not depend upon any ceremony or officiant for its validity and is based entirely upon the mutual assent of the parties. The history of these nonceremonial marriages is associated with the early conflict of jurisdiction between the English ecclesiastical and common-law courts. By the close of the twelfth century, the Church had gained undisputed jurisdiction over matrimonial cases except for those parts of the law concerned with the property rights of the parties, which remained under the administration of the common-law courts. As

[22] *Ibid.,* p. 191.
[23] *Ibid.,* pp. 145–146.

with most cases of divided jurisdiction, this arrangement eventually led to conflict since the church courts, jealously guarding their magistracy, attempted to retain as much of their jurisdiction as possible in the wake of the attempted expansion of dominion on the part of the common-law courts. This conflict emerged not only in the area of original jurisdiction but also over the principles of substantive law which should govern matrimonial cases. The ecclesiastical courts followed the Scholastic dogma that mere consent, secretly expressed in the present tense (*de praesenti*) was sufficient to validate a marriage. The common-law courts, charged with the determination of property rights, took a much stricter view, holding that some publicity, either through a public ceremony at the door of a church or the publication of banns, was necessary for an actual (*de facto*) marriage in determining property rights. If the marriage had been secretly and privately contracted, it was declared a *de jure* marriage and the common-law courts could and often did withhold dower rights from the widow and inheritance from any children.[24]

This dispute continued to grow in intensity until the eventual separation of the Church of England from papal jurisdiction between 1529 and 1536. When the Council of Trent (1545–1563) decreed that all Roman Catholic marriages should be contracted before a priest and several witnesses, England, no longer recognizing Roman Catholic decrees, continued to allow nonceremonial marriage. It was not until 1753, with the passage of the Hardwicke Act, that England abolished common-law marriage. This act provided that all marriages except those of Quakers, Jews, and members of the royal family were to be solemnized only after the securing of a license or the publication of banns and an Anglican ceremony. With some exceptions, no license was to be issued without four weeks' residence in the parish of one of the parties, and parental consent was required for all candidates under twenty-one years of age. The clergy were required to record each marriage, with death as the penalty for falsification or destruction of these records. In 1836, the intolerance of non-Anglican ceremonies was somewhat reduced by the passage of a bill permitting civil marriage for those unwilling to accept the Anglican ceremony.[25] At the same time, another bill was passed establishing a system of civil

---

[24] George Eliot Howard, *A History of Matrimonial Institutions*, Chicago, University of Chicago Press, 1904, Vol. I, pp. 355–356.

[25] 6 and 7 William IV, chap. 85.

registration of births, marriages, and deaths which has functioned to this day.[26]

The Hardwicke Act, however, applied only to England and not to Scotland, Ireland, or the English colonies, so that common-law marriage remained valid in these jurisdictions. In the United States they are still valid in twenty-three of the fifty-three jurisdictions. Table 8 (p. 194) summarizes this information. Vernier has grouped the various state laws concerning common-law marriage as follows: (1) those which recognize the validity of a marriage where certain of the imposed regulations are not complied with, (2) those which expressly declare common-law marriage to be valid, (3) those which specifically declare such marriages to be invalid, (4) those which declare void any marriage not licensed and solemnized by law, (5) those which impose marriage regulations of various kinds but do not specifically declare all marriages otherwise solemnized invalid. This latter type is the most common.[27] To these we should add two additional types of statutes presently found in some states: (6) those which do not permit common-law marriage within their own borders but recognize such marriages if permitted elsewhere, and (7) those states which have declared invalid common-law marriages contracted after some established date.

The great variation in the types of statutes dealing with these unions is indicative of the confusion and vulnerability to multiple interpretation of our statutes. As of 1955, for example, the status of common-law marriage in Alaska was still unsettled, and Maine legal experts could only report that such marriages were "probably not recognized" in their state.[28]

There is generally common agreement among legal authorities, social scientists, and social workers that common-law marriage should be abolished. These nonceremonial unions flaunt the established social and legal norms, destroy the validity of marriage statistics, and, in general, fail to impart any of the stability which society has attempted to legislate into the marital relationship. Arguments in favor of permitting such marriages to be valid usually point to the necessity of legitimizing the children of such liaisons or establishing the dower rights of a surviving member. The proponents of this view, however, fail to realize that such marriages are never validated unless some difficulty arises which calls the marriage to the attention of the courts.

[26] Ibid., chap. 86.
[27] Vernier, op. cit., Vol. I, p. 103.
[28] Cf. Martindale-Hubbel Law Directory, Vol. III, 1955. (This volume is alphabetized but not paginated.)

While this might still provide the opportunity to establish dower rights, it would seem to be too late to be of much help in enhancing the social standing of the children.

The number of states limiting common-law marriages is slowly increasing, yet few states have seen fit to declare these marriages unconditionally null and void. The same ends have been served, however, by judicial decisions declaring them invalid, by various laws stating that marriages contracted without proper licensing or solemnization are null and void, and by invalidating any common-law marriage performed after some established date. The future seems quite certain: all states will eventually abolish common-law marriage; such groups as the Committee on Uniform State Laws of the American Bar Association and other authoritative social-action groups continue to advocate this step.

THE PROHIBITION OF UNDESIRABLE MARRIAGES

Despite the popular belief that today one has free choice in selection of a mate, American jurisdictions, like societies the world over, prohibit the marriage of certain persons under certain conditions. The bases and origins of many of these proscriptions are to be found in outmoded religious, social, and economic thought, as we find in our irrational and scientifically untenable restrictions on miscegenation and the marriage of affinal relatives. Some, however, represent a paralleling of modern scientific concepts, as in the case of eugenic measures such as premarital examination for communicable venereal disease or the restrictions placed upon the marriage of the mentally deficient.

The evolution of these statutes is characterized by a long and tortuous path through centuries of uncoördinated attempts on the part of our legislatures, the courts, and various political and religious groups to regulate who may and who may not enter the marital relationship. That these agencies have not always been successful in producing a regulation consistent with social needs is a commentary on the static nature of the common law, which is the basis of most current matrimonial law. This individualistic body of laws, developed in an era of agrarian values and dedicated to the maintenance of the *status quo*, has not kept pace with social change and would seem to be a poor yardstick for the standards of marriage in today's rapidly changing industrialized society. The courts through their decisions furnish a ready means of adjusting the law to the current social milieu,

but the emphasis has too often been on upholding the precedents of the traditional law rather than promoting social welfare.

As a result of this common-law background, the regulations of our fifty-three jurisdictions are similar, but in no two are they the same. It would be too ambitious to state the laws of each jurisdiction in a volume of this sort, but a survey of the major points covered and the differences and similarities among the statutes of the various jurisdictions will reveal the basic ends which are sought through such prohibitions and the multitude of means which have been enacted to attempt these goals.

Age and Parental Consent. All jurisdictions have minimum-age requirements for those entering marriage, but not all of our states have established statutory minima. Where no such legislation exists, the common-law limits of 14 for males and 12 for females are still in effect. In 1954 there were still seven states which lacked definitive statutory requirements, and in at least three of these the 14 and 12 years' limits were still in effect. Table 8 (p. 194) presents the legal minimum-age requirements for marriage with parental consent in each of the states. The age standards generally adopted vary between 16 and 18 for males and 14 and 16 for females, with the 18–14 limit most frequent. New Hampshire has established the highest age requirement, 20 for males and 18 for females; Idaho and Missouri have the lowest statutory ages for males (15 years), and eight jurisdictions have legislation which places the minimum age for females at 14 years.

No information is available about the total number of marriages involving young people in their early teens. Some indication is given, however, by the information furnished by the National Office of Vital Statistics, which gives the ages of brides and grooms married during 1951 in twenty-three reporting states. These data indicate that, in that year, 4616 females and 52 males 15 years of age or younger and 16,360 females and 577 males 16 years of age were married.[29] The national figure would obviously be much higher since these data include only the twenty-three states reporting.

Despite the gradual decrease in the median age of marriage in the United States in this century, it is important that a distinction be made between the effects of youthful marriage and *child* marriage. Although it is biologically possible for females to bear children soon after the onset of puberty, the best interests of maternal health and

[29] National Office of Vital Statistics, *Vital Statistics of the United States,* 1952, Vol. I, Table 3, p. 62.

social development would not encourage marriage or childbirth at that time. The chances of maternal fatality in childbirth are five times as high in the age group 10–14 as at 20–24. Since the post-pubescent period is one of rapid physical growth, the shared nutrition necessary while nursing as well as during pregnancy produces a physical strain on the young mother. Socially, the effects of child marriage may be even more damaging and may be injurious to both sexes. In a society which lays such stress upon the youth culture and the heterosexual experiences of adolescence, child marriage deprives young people of experimental "dating" and social experience, an integral part of growing up in modern America. Even in these days of accelerated social maturity, a boy of 14 to 16 is barely emancipated from childhood games and associations and is rarely self-sufficient. A girl of 12 to 14 has so recently given up dolls as play objects that it is questionable if she can make the transition to caring for a human infant.

At common law, individuals beyond the minimum age for marriage could contract a valid marriage without the consent of their parents or guardian. American jurisdictions, however, have generally insisted on a delay of a few years between the attainment of minimum age and the age of permissive marriage without parental consent. The most common age below which parental consent to marriage is required is 21 for males and 18 for females, although there are some variations, as indicated in Table 8 (p. 194).

Consanguinity and Affinity. In the previous chapter, we observed that incest taboos generally forbid sexual relations or marriage between close relatives. The codification of these incest taboos into law has concerned both blood relationship (consanguinity) and relationship through marriage (affinity), but in American jurisdictions we find the greatest uniformity in the prohibition of marriage between close blood relatives. No state or territory permits marriage between parents and their children, grandparents and their grandchildren, brother and sister, an uncle and his niece, or an aunt and her nephew. Beyond this degree of relationship, however, uniformity gives way to the usual variability which we find among our marriage laws, as indicated in Table 9, which summarizes the restrictions based upon consanguinity and affinity among the several jurisdictions.

While there is some scientific support for the imputation of dysgenic effects to marriage of close blood relatives, no such rationalization can justify or explain the origin of our laws forbidding the marriage of affinal relatives. These restrictions, long a part of English

TABLE 9.   Number of Jurisdictions Prohibiting Marriage Within Specified Degrees
of Consanguineal and Affinal Relationship.

Consanguineal Relationship	Number of Jurisdictions Prohibiting	Affinal Relationship	Number of Jurisdictions Prohibiting
Parent, child, grandchild, grandparent, siblings, aunt, uncle, nephew, niece	53	Stepmother or stepfather, Stepchildren	24
		Son-in-law or daughter-in-law	21
Grandaunt or granduncle	7	Grandfather's wife, grand-	
Grandniece or grandnephew	10	mother's husband	10
First cousin	30	Grandson's wife, grand-	
First cousin once removed	6	daughter's husband	13
Half-siblings	31	Mother-in-law, father-in-law	13
Half-blood cousins	6	Wife's grandmother, hus-	
Half-blood aunts or uncles	6	band's grandfather	10
Half-blood nieces or		Wife's granddaughter,	
nephews	6	husband's grandson	20

Source: Adapted from Jessie Bernard, *American Family Behavior*, New York, Harper & Brothers, 1942, p. 120, and revised from the *Martindale-Hubbel Law Directory*, Summit, N.J., Martindale-Hubbel Inc., 1955, Vol. III.

law, resulted from the relentless logic of the medieval Church, which maintained that sexual relations made a man and woman one flesh. Therefore, reasoned the Church, a man's relatives became the kin of his wife and her kinsmen were in turn related to him. Such was the logic of the Church, and affinal relationship became an impediment to marriage along with blood relationship and was incorporated into the common law.

In the United States, while some jurisdictions have statutes prohibiting marriage between affinal relatives, the tendency has been away from such restrictions and, in the absence of any specific legislation, the courts have usually ruled against following the English law.[30] Twenty-four states, the District of Columbia, and Puerto Rico have statutes designed to prohibit marriage on grounds of affinity, but only nine of these are broad enough to include remote relationship.

While there is uniform social condemnation of incestuous marriage, there is no such unanimity in the legislation concerning the effect of these prohibitions upon incestuous marriages. The majority of jurisdictions, with varying degrees of clarity, take the view that such marriages are absolutely void without any legal process. Only three states make such marriages void only from the time when they are annulled by legal process, and seven jurisdictions are entirely silent on the ques-

[30] See *Blogget v. Brinsmaid*, 9 Vt. 27 (1837); *Back v. Back*, 148 Ia. 233, 125 N.W. 1009 (1910); and *Henderson v. State*, 26 Ala. App. 263, 157 Ao. 884 (1934).

tion.[31] Another question left unanswered in most jurisdictions is the effect on the grounds of affinity of the dissolution by death or divorce of the marriage which created the affinity. Only five states expressly state that the prohibitions remain in effect unless the divorce is granted because the marriage was originally unlawful or void.

Physical Diseases. Probably the most recent and certainly the most scientifically valid development in the field of prohibited marriage is the regulation of marriages by individuals with certain physical diseases. In recent years, this movement has led to the increasing adoption of statutes requiring premarital physical examinations to determine the presence of specified communicable diseases. The principal purpose of these examinations is to detect communicable venereal diseases, although three states prohibit marriage of persons with tuberculosis in an infectious stage, Hawaii allows for the annulment of marriages in which one party concealed the presence of leprosy, and several states have prohibitions concerning communicable diseases in general. The most important portion of the premarital physical examination is the blood test, which is intended to detect the presence of syphilis and thus prevent the subsequent infection of the intended spouse and prospective progeny.

Effective legislation in this area did not come until after 1935, when Connecticut passed its law. As early as 1913, several states had passed ineffective legislation in this area, but it was not until 1918 that a comprehensive, nation-wide program, aimed at the control of venereal disease, gave direction to state premarital-examination bills. In that year, a federal law established an Inter-Departmental Social Hygiene Board to aid the states in setting up a control program for the venereal diseases. By 1925, many states had adopted general legislation concerning enforcement; but after 1926, when federal aid was withdrawn, the attempted control of these diseases slowed down, although several states continued their programs with their own appropriations.[32]

When Connecticut passed the 1935 act, which has served as a model for subsequent legislation, several important new regulations were incorporated into the law. Prior statutes had merely required an affidavit of good health from persons desiring to marry, but this law required both parties to submit to a blood test for syphilis before marriage. The presence of syphilis in an infectious stage constituted an impediment to marriage.

[31] Vernier, *op. cit.*, Vol. I, p. 175.
[32] Thomas Parran, *Shadow on the Land: Syphilis*, New York, Reynal and Hitchcock, 1937, p. 69.

By 1955, premarital health examinations were required in forty
states and in the territories of Alaska and Hawaii.[33] The majority of
these jurisdictions require both the prospective bride and groom to take
a physical examination, including a blood test, prior to the issuance of
a license. The period of time during which the test must be made
varies from ten to forty days in different jurisdictions, with thirty days
being the most common. Table 10 indicates those jurisdictions which
had adopted premarital examination laws by 1955 and the date of
their adoption or revision.

As the number of states requiring premarital examinations has increased, steps have been taken to reduce the possibility of evasion.
Laboratory work must be done by the state health department or
an approved laboratory. Penalties are provided for physicians or
laboratory technicians who falsify health reports, and in some states
the parties to a marriage may be penalized for failure to comply with
the law. Several states have enacted statutes requiring residents marrying outside the state, in a jurisdiction where no health examination is
required, to undergo a blood test after returning to their home state.
Despite these precautions, many problems still exist in the administration of these laws. Applicants, cognizant or suspicious of their infection, may send a friend to take the test. A large source of evasion has
always been common-law marriage, where, since no license is required,
there is no effective method of compelling the parties to take the test.
Pennsylvania has attempted to resolve this difficulty by a 1939 amendment to its marriage laws requiring persons seeking to be married
under common law first to obtain a license and furnish a certificate
of freedom from syphilis. Since this law does not invalidate a common-
law marriage contracted without a license, it would seem to be ineffective. As the number of states barring common-law marriages increases,
however, many of these difficulties in the administration of premarital-
examination legislation will disappear.

The benefits derived from the requirement of a blood test should
prove conclusively to legislatures the wisdom of such legislation. In
addition to the controls placed upon the transmission of syphilis, the
blood test serves as a case-finding device. Of the 631,206 blood tests

---

[33] Correspondence with the Division of Special Health Services of the United States
Public Health Service reveals that Puerto Rico's requirement of a "medical certificate"
operates as a premarital health-examination law. Information received by that agency
reveals that "Applicants for a marriage license must submit to an examination by a
licensed Puerto Rican physician. There is space on each marriage license for the physician to state that applicants do not have mental disease, epilepsy, or syphilis. Such
statements must be issued within 10 days prior to the date of the marriage."

TABLE 10. Approval and Effective Dates of Premarital Laws.[a]

State	Date Approved	Date Effective
Alabama	July 11, 1947	Jan. 2, 1948
Arkansas	Feb. 23, 1953	July 1, 1953
California	June 5, 1939	Sept. 19, 1939
Colorado	Apr. 10, 1939	Oct. 10, 1939
Connecticut	May 23, 1935	Jan. 1, 1936
Delaware	Apr. 18, 1947	July 1, 1947
Florida	May 28, 1945	Oct. 1, 1945
Georgia	Feb. 25, 1949	Aug. 25, 1949
Idaho	Feb. 11, 1943	Apr. 29, 1943
Illinois	June 23, 1937	July 1, 1937
Indiana	Mar. 9, 1939	Mar. 1, 1940
Iowa	Apr. 5, 1941	Apr. 9, 1941
Kansas	Apr. 9, 1947	July 1, 1947
Kentucky	Feb. 28, 1940	Jan. 1, 1941
Louisiana	July 7, 1954	July 28, 1954
Maine	Apr. 10, 1941	July 25, 1941
Massachusetts	June 12, 1943	June 12, 1943
Michigan	July 20, 1937	Oct. 28, 1937
Missouri	Apr. 13, 1943	Jan. 1, 1944
Montana	Mar. 6, 1947	July 1, 1947
Nebraska	Mar. 27, 1943	Aug. 29, 1943
New Hampshire	Aug. 12, 1937	Oct. 1, 1938
New Jersey	May 3, 1938	July 1, 1938
New York	Apr. 12, 1938	July 1, 1938
North Carolina	Apr. 3, 1939	Apr. 3, 1939
North Dakota	Mar. 13, 1939	July 1, 1939
Ohio	May 16, 1941	Aug. 17, 1941
Oklahoma	Feb. 7, 1945	July 25, 1945
Oregon	Mar. 12, 1937	Dec. 1, 1938
Pennsylvania	May 17, 1939	May 17, 1940
Rhode Island	Mar. 29, 1938	Apr. 28, 1938
South Dakota	Mar. 10, 1939	July 1, 1939
Tennessee	Mar. 10, 1939	July 1, 1941
Texas	July 8, 1949	Oct. 4, 1949
Utah	Feb. 28, 1941	July 1, 1941
Vermont	Apr. 10, 1941	July 31, 1941
Virginia	Feb. 28, 1940	Aug. 1, 1940
West Virginia	Feb. 25, 1930	May 26, 1939
Wisconsin	June 29, 1937	July 31, 1937
Wyoming	Feb. 1, 1943	May 21, 1943
Alaska	Mar. 19, 1949	June 17, 1949
Hawaii	May 11, 1945	July 1, 1945

a Dates given are those when either new premarital examination laws were passed or existing laws were amended for better operation.
Source: *Premarital Health Examination Legislation,* U.S. Public Health Service Publication No. 383, 1954, p. v.

made from 1936 to 1941 in thirteen states, 8605 (1.4 percent) were positive for syphilis, and a majority of the positive cases interviewed reported no prior knowledge of the infection.[34] Those jurisdictions

[34] J. K. Shafer, "Premarital Health Examination Legislation: History and Analysis," *Public Health Reports,* May, 1954, pp. 487–493, reprinted in *Premarital Health Examination Legislation,* U.S. Public Health Service Publication No. 383, pp. 1–10.

which presently lack blood tests and premarital-health examinations will undoubtedly legislate in this direction in coming years.

Insanity, Feeble-mindedness, and Epilepsy. Restrictions are also placed upon the marriage of the mentally deficient and mentally ill in modern statutes. The legal basis of these prohibitions had its origin in the assumption that there can be no legal contract if either party is mentally incapable of understanding what he is doing and is therefore incompetent of giving consent. Contemporary scientific support is given to these prohibitions by the considerable evidence that heredity plays an important role in the development of psychotic disorders, as well as its established effect in determining the individual's level of intelligence.[35] Since the common-law requirements for marriage included consent as an essential element, lack of consent by reason of mental incapacity serves as an available ground in all jurisdictions for declaring such marriages invalid. Most jurisdictions have passed specific legislation in this area, and at the present time all jurisdictions except Alabama, Arizona, Colorado, Florida, Louisiana, Maryland, New Mexico, and Texas have statutes either forbidding the issuance of a license or providing for the annulment of such marriages.[36] The language of these statutes in identifying the mentally incompetent shows considerable variation, some statutes referring to "lunatics," "idiots," "imbeciles," and others using more inclusive terms, such as "insane," "feeble-minded," persons of "unsound mind," and those "incapable of consenting for want of sufficient understanding." [37] Although all of these categories are legally admissible in terms of the individual's ability to contract marriage, they are confusing and in some cases meaningless as scientifically valid diagnostic terms, and could better be replaced with more accurate psychiatric terminology. There is also some conflict among the various statutes as to the means by which such marriages should be discouraged. Many statutes do not specifically forbid such marriages or prohibit the issuance of a license to mental defectives, but are content to provide for the annulment of such marriages by court proceedings. A majority of those

[35] Cf. F. J. Kallman, *The Genetics of Schizophrenia*, New York, J. J. Augustin, 1938; G. L. Brown, "On the Constancy of the I.Q.," *Journal of Educational Research*, October 1950, pp. 151–153; Z. I. Hirt, "Another Study of Retests With the 1916 Stanford-Binet Scale," *Journal of Genetic Psychology*, March 1945, pp. 83–105; and A. M. Leahy, "Nature-Nurture and Intelligence," *Genetic Psychology Monographs*, August 1935, pp. 236–308.

[36] Vernier, *op. cit.*, Vol. I, p. 189, and the *Martindale-Hubbel Law Directory*, Vol. III, 1955, *passim.*

[37] *Ibid.*, p. 190.

states requiring court action are in effect making these marriages voidable only if one or the other of the parties sues for annulment. The Court of Appeals of New York State has even held that if the sane spouse is not included in the statutory list of persons authorized to sue for annulment in such cases, he or she does not have the right to seek annulment, although the afflicted party may do so upon being restored to sanity.[38]

If the protection of society is to become the chief concern of these eugenic prohibitions in our marriage laws, it would seem that preventing these marriages by the refusal of a license would provide the most adequate means. But even with this positive method there are possibilities of abuse. In some states which presently withhold licenses in such cases, officials will issue licenses if the applicants furnish affidavits that they are not insane, mentally deficient, or epileptic! Such a system is hardly foolproof and should be replaced by some more positive and valid form of scientific evidence.

Despite the fact that most modern authorities do not consider the hereditary tendencies to epilepsy strong enough to justify the laws against the marriage of epileptics, seventeen jurisdictions currently have such statutes, although they are seldom enforced.[39] Seven of these make exceptions in the case of women beyond the age of 45 and three permit "hereditary" epileptics to marry after sterilization. In nineteen states, there are statutes requiring the sterilization of epileptics upon their release from institutions. Many social-action groups, such as the American League Against Epilepsy and the Committee for Public Understanding of Epilepsy, have embarked upon a campaign to abolish these laws, which are no longer valid in the light of recent scientific research. In 1954, a report by Dean Roscoe E. Barrow, of the College of Law of the University of Cincinnati (on two years of research into the various statutes concerning epilepsy, conducted under a grant from the National Institute of Neurological Diseases and Blindness of the Public Health Service) scored these laws and presented legal proposals for their revision. In the same year, the United Epileptic Association set up a legislative committee to work toward the same ends. Concerted efforts by such organizations may result in a needed reconsideration of the legal treatment of epileptics.

[38] *Hoadley v. Hoadley*, 224 N.Y. 424, 155 N.E. 725 (1927).
[39] See, for example, William G. Lennox, *Science and Seizures*, New York, Harper & Brothers, 1953.

Miscegenation. Statutory prohibitions concerning racial inter-marriage are found in those sections of the country with large racial minorities. In the southern states, where the bulk of our Negro popula-tion is located, these laws are aimed at halting Negro-white marriages, while the western states show primary concern with Mongoloid-white intermarriage. Only two states prohibit the marriage of Mongoloids (American Indians in both cases) and Negroes. This distribution of anti-miscegenation legislation points to the social origins of such laws in local race prejudices and discrimination, and identifies such statutes with the doctrine of "white supremacy." Further, there is neither common-law precedent nor eugenic endorsement for these prohibi-tions. The common law places no barriers to the marriage of indi-viduals of diverse racial, religious, or social backgrounds, so that, in the absence of prohibitory legislation, interracial marriages are legal and valid. Neither is there any scientific evidence for the popular assump-tion that miscegenation results in race deterioration or any other biological blemish.[40]

There are twenty-eight states with laws prohibiting racial inter-marriage. In one state, California, the status of interracial marriages is uncertain, since the state supreme court found the prohibitory statute unconstitutional, but two subsequent sessions of the legislature failed to repeal the original law.[41] All of these states forbid the mar-riage of Negroes and whites. Fourteen states also mention Mongoloids of various descriptions and many states include "mulattoes." Four states specifically mention Indians and two include "mestizos" (the offspring of an Indian or Negro and a person of "European" stock).[42]

[40] Cf. Franz Boas, "Fallacies of Racial Inferiority," *Current History*, February, 1927, p. 676; Ernest A. Hooten, "When Races Intermarry," *Nation*, July 25, 1928, p. 84; W. E. Castle, "Biological and Social Consequences of Race Crossing," *American Journal of Physical Anthropology*, April–June, 1926, pp. 145–156, and M. F. Ashley-Montagu, *Statement on Race*, New York, Henry Schuman, 1951, p. 151.

[41] There were originally thirty states with laws against intermarriage, but the North Dakota Legislative Assembly repealed the statutes in that state prohibiting the marriage of Negro and white persons and removed the penalties for issuing a license or perform-ing the ceremony in such marriages. The repeal bill (H.B. 575) was approved February 10, 1955, and became effective on July 1, 1955 (personal correspondence with the Legislative Reference Committee of the North Dakota Legislative Assembly). As in-dicated above, the status of the California law is as yet unsettled. The Supreme Court of California held the statute barring interracial marriage unconstitutional in the case of *Perez v. Lippold*, 32 Cal. 2d 17 (1948). Bills were introduced and passed in the Assembly both in 1951 (A.B. 2182) and 1955 (A.B. 555), but both were defeated in the Senate (personal correspondence with the Office of the Legislative Counsel of California).

[42] Vernier, *op. cit.*, Vol. I, p. 205.

It is interesting that there is no uniformity or consistency in the terminology used in the various statutes to identify the members of the minority racial groups. Negroids are variously described as Negroes, mulattoes, Ethiopians, Africans, or members of the "black race"; Mongoloids are called Mongolians or separately specified as Malayans, Asiatic Indians, Koreans, persons of Kanaka blood, or members of the "yellow race." The categorical terms "colored person" and "persons of color" are also used in addition to the ambiguous "mestizos." Some states go into involved detail to compute the degree of admixture necessary to qualify an individual as a Caucasian and hence free him from marital restriction by reason of race. The ambiguity and ineptitude of their terminology serve to indicate the scientific invalidity of these laws.

In general, miscegenetic marriages are held to be null and void without the necessity of court action, with only West Virginia providing that they are void only from the time they are so declared by annulment or divorce.[43] Nearly all states which prohibit miscegenation also make it illegal, providing penalties for the parties and in some cases for anyone issuing a license or performing the ceremony in such marriages. Virginia also makes it a crime for a resident to intermarry out of the state in order to escape the Virginia statute.[44] Mississippi further provides that "any person, firm or corporation" guilty of "printing, publishing or circulating" written matter which urges or presents for public approval any arguments or suggestions in favor of social equality or racial intermarriage between whites and Negroes shall be guilty of a misdemeanor and subject to a fine not exceeding $500 or imprisonment not exceeding six months, or both.[45] The tendency of the courts in the past has been to uphold the constitutionality of such laws.[46]

Although there is almost universal condemnation of the antimiscegenation laws by social and biological scientists, their repeal in the immediate future would seem unlikely, particularly in the southern

[43] Ibid., Vol. I, p. 205.
[44] Code of Virginia, 1950, Title 20, chap. 4, secs. 20–59.
[45] Mississippi Code, 1930, Annotated, Vol. I, chap. 49, sec. 2361.
[46] As recently as November 22, 1954, the United States Supreme Court refused to rule on an Alabama law prohibiting the marriage of Negroes and Whites. In this case the attack on the constitutionality of the law was made in behalf of a Negro woman sentenced to two years in prison for miscegenation. For other leading cases, see Green v. State, 58 Ala. 190 (1877); Blake v. Sessions, 99 Okla. 59, 220 Pac. 876 (1923); and Dodson v. State, 61 Ark. 57, 31 S.W. 977 (1895).

states where the popular fear seems to be that the aim of all legislation to approximate racial equality is to encourage racial intermarriage.[47] In other parts of the country, efforts to repeal these laws have met with limited success. Although North Dakota repealed its statutes, bills of repeal failed in Colorado and Idaho, and California has yet to repeal its law now proclaimed unconstitutional by the state supreme court.

Polygamous Marriages. American social and legal policy allows an individual only one mate at a time, and in all fifty-three jurisdictions bigamous marriages are both criminally and civilly condemned. We find, however, that, notwithstanding uniform condemnation, our states use different legal paths to achieve the same end. Generally, the statutes barring bigamous marriages maintain (1) that whoever marries another while having a living husband or wife is guilty of bigamy, which is usually a felony, and (2) that such marriages are null and void from the beginning.[48] Not all states have prohibited bigamous marriages, however, eleven states being content to depend upon either common-law principles, judicial interpretation, or less positive legislation, such as making bigamy a ground for divorce or citing it as a crime.[49]

The courts have established that religious approval of polygyny in no way justifies or excuses the possession of two or more wives. This problem has occasionally arisen in the cases of Mormon plural marriages. Although polygyny was formerly practiced by the Mormons, at no time did any appreciable percentage of Mormon males have more than one wife. As early as 1882, federal legislation had been enacted against such marriages and eventually, with the passage of the Edmunds-Tucker Law, a strong campaign was waged against polygyny in those states settled by the Mormons. Parties to polygynous marriages were fined and imprisoned and the Mormon leaders driven into exile. It was not until the Supreme Court upheld the constitu-

---

[47] In 1954, following the historic decision by the United States Supreme Court holding segregation in the public schools unconstitutional, one of the frequently heard criticisms in the South was that this was merely a stepping stone to the approval of racial intermarriage. The Attorney General of Georgia, for example, in commenting on the decision, was quoted as stating that it "even opens the doors for a constitutional attack on our laws prohibiting the intermarriage of Negro and White people." *The New York Times*, May 24, 1954, p. 19.

[48] Vernier, *op. cit.*, Vol. I, p. 214.

[49] *Ibid.*, Vol. I, p. 216, and *Martindale-Hubbel Law Directory*, Vol. III, 1955.

tionality of the laws barring polygamous marriages [50] that the Mormon General Council withdrew its sanction from such marriages. In 1953, new trouble arose in Short Creek, Arizona, when an isolated community of fundamentalists, disowned by the Church of Jesus Christ of Latter-day Saints (Mormons) in 1939, was raided by a large force of peace officers, who discovered that 36 men, 86 women, and 263 children were living in a polygynous relationship. Some of the men were reputed to have as many as six wives. The authorities issued orders for arrest of the adults and resettlement of the children in new homes.

Fraud, Force, and Mistake. Most jurisdictions make some provision in their criminal or civil statutes for marriages involving some fraud or duress and for "freak" marriages contracted as the result of mistakes or in jest. A number of states provide that where fraud is present the marriage may be annulled, with the responsibility for bringing suit resting upon the innocent party, as was the case at common law. The decision as to what constitutes fraud has been left entirely to the courts since the statutes speak only in general terms and fail to define what constitutes fraud. Basically, the courts have held that the fraud must relate to some fact or act essential to the relationship, but there is no agreement among the various jurisdictions as to what these essentials are.

This same difficulty is present in defining the nature of duress that is necessary to make a marriage void or voidable. In general, any use of physical force or threats of violence which "overwhelm" the will and compel consent are sufficient to annul a marriage.[51] Marriages which have been contracted as the result of a mistake, such as in mistaken identity or a mistake as to the sex of the other party, have also been held to be voidable.

Moral Character. There is little legislation concerning the effect of the moral character of the parties upon the validity of the marriage, most jurisdictions leaving this to the discretion of the parties and their families. Common or habitual drunkards may not marry in North Dakota, Washington, and Delaware, and the latter state also bars the marriage of drug addicts. North Dakota, Washington, and Virginia forbid the marriage of habitual criminals, and in five states— Delaware, Indiana, Maine, Pennsylvania, and Vermont—paupers or indigent persons are not permitted to marry.[52]

[50] *Reynolds* v. *United States*, 98 U.S. 145, 25 L.Ed. 244 (1878).
[51] *Shoro* v. *Shoro*, 60 Vt. 268, 14 Atl. 177 (1888); and *Fowler* v. *Fowler*, 131 La. 1088, 60 So. 694 (1913).
[52] Vernier, *op. cit.*, Vol. I, pp. 224–228.

Marriage-Evasion Laws. The principle that every state has the right to regulate marriages within its borders and the resultant multiplicity of jurisdictions have created the related problems of conflicting laws and the possibility of out-of-state marriages by residents unable to qualify in their home state. Many possible motives might cause the residents of states with stringent marriage laws to seek the temporary haven of neighboring states with less strict requirements. They may not wish to wait the number of days required by their state's advance-notice laws; they may not have reached the minimum age for marriage in their state; or they may be unwilling or unable to qualify by complying with premarital health examinations. An example of this latter motivation is furnished by the recent experience of Connecticut with its premarital-examination law of 1935. When the implications of the new law became apparent, the marriage rate in that state dropped from the 7.1 per 1000 population rate of the two years preceding the enactment of the law to 6.8 in 1935, 5.9 in 1936, and 6.4 in 1937 despite an increase in the marriage rate of the nation as a whole during those same years. Much of this decrease has been attributed to evasion of the blood test through out-of-state marriages.[53] Such problems may call for some form of interstate coöperation in their enforcement. The Federal Constitution foresaw this difficulty and provided that "full faith and credit shall be given in each state to the public acts, records, and judicial proceedings of every other state," but the implementation of this provision has remained a problem.

Generally, the courts have held that the validity of a marriage is determined by the laws of the jurisdiction in which it was celebrated. From this it follows that if a marriage is valid where celebrated, it retains its validity even if it would have violated the statutes of the home state of either of the parties. There are, however, some important exceptions, depending upon the nature of the laws it would have violated in the home state. Out-of-state marriages in violation of the home state's directory laws, such as licensing or ceremonial procedure, retain their validity; those in violation of the *prohibitory* laws of that state, such as miscegenation and incest laws, do not.[54]

While some states and territories have statutory provisions concerning the validity of out-of-state marriages, many do not. Recent attempts to establish a Uniform Marriage Evasion Act by the Com-

[53] Shafer, *op. cit.*, p. 4.
[54] Helen I. Clarke, *Social Legislation*, New York, Appleton-Century-Crofts, 1940, p. 110.

missioners on Uniform State Laws have met with so little success that they are now considered obsolete by the parent body, the Council of State Governments. As more states establish advance-notice laws and require premarital health examinations, however, the problem of evasive extrastate marriages should resolve itself.

THE PROHIBITION OF UNDESIRABLE MARRIAGES: A SUMMARY

As must now be apparent to the reader, our marriage prohibitions present a confused and conflicting pattern of laws lacking in any logical or clearly defined overall policy. Not only is there a diversity of possible grounds for prohibiting marriage among our jurisdictions; there is not even a uniformity of means to enforce those prohibitions which are universally accepted. This confusion is a result of the diverse forces—religious, legal, social, and in recent years scientific—which have influenced our social legislation. The legal view of marriage as a contract requires the presence of full mutual consent, freely given, for a valid marriage. Prohibitions concerning age, mental capacity, fraud, and duress attempt to ascertain and ensure such mutual consent. To these are added other qualifications based upon social and religious values of the society. Some of these prohibitions, such as those concerning polygamous marriage, are common to all jurisdictions and so might be called "universals" since they affect all members of our society equally. Others are "specialties" and apply only in certain sections of the country to specific categories of individuals.[55] Examples of "specialties" would be laws concerning miscegenation or eugenic measures. Regardless of the scope or proportion of the population covered by such laws, however, all such prohibitions are the result of society's efforts to promote family stability by legislating standards for those who seek to establish families. Where this fails, means of dissolving undesirable marriages must be provided.

The Dissolution of Marriage

Once contracted, marriage may be terminated only by annulment, divorce, or death. Because the termination of a marriage relationship is of great individual and social importance, and involves the cessation of a contract and (in a religious sense) a sanctioned state, we should expect legislation to be grave and cautious.

[55] We are indebted to the late Ralph Linton for these terms, which he first used in his *The Study of Man*, New York, D. Appleton-Century, 1936, chap. XVI.

ANNULMENT

Annulment does not actually terminate a marriage, for an annulment is a legal decree that no marriage ever existed. It has the effect of declaring null and void any ceremony which established the marriage and returning the parties to their single state. All of our jurisdictions have some provision for annulment either by specific statute or, in a few cases, by their action in declaring certain marriages void or prohibited, or by making the parties to certain marriages subject to criminal action. The grounds generally coincide with the previously discussed causes for prohibiting marriage. Table 11 indicates those grounds which are expressly provided by the various jurisdictions.

TABLE 11. Statutory Grounds for Annulment in American Jurisdictions.

Jurisdiction	Fraud	Bigamy	Non-age	Mental Incapacity	Force or Duress	Impotence	Incest or Affinity	Miscegenation	Other Grounds
Alabama			Yes				Yes		
Alaska	Yes	Yes	Yes	Yes	Yes		Yes		
Arizona	Yes	Yes	Yes	Yes			Yes	Yes	a b c d
Arkansas	Yes	Yes	Yes	Yes	Yes	Yes			
California	Yes	Yes	Yes	Yes	Yes	Yes			
Colorado		Yes	Yes				Yes		
Connecticut							Yes		e
Delaware	Yes	Yes			Yes	Yes	Yes		
District of Columbia	Yes	Yes	Yes	Yes			Yes	Yes	
Florida^m	Yes				Yes			Yes	
Georgia	Yes	Yes				Yes	Yes		
Hawaii	Yes	Yes	Yes	Yes	Yes	Yes			
Idaho	Yes	Yes	Yes	Yes	Yes	Yes			
Illinois			Yes	Yes			Yes		
Indiana	Yes		Yes	Yes					
Iowa		Yes	Yes	Yes		Yes	Yes		
Kansas			Yes	Yes					
Kentucky	Yes	Yes	Yes	Yes	Yes		Yes	Yes	e
Louisiana		Yes			Yes		Yes		b
Maine		Yes	Yes	Yes			Yes		
Maryland		Yes					Yes	Yes	l
Massachusetts	Yes	Yes	Yes	Yes			Yes		k
Michigan	Yes	Yes	Yes	Yes	Yes		Yes		h
Minnesota	Yes		Yes	Yes	Yes				
Mississippi							Yes	Yes	
Missouri	Yes	Yes	Yes	Yes	Yes		Yes	Yes	
Montana	Yes	Yes	Yes	Yes	Yes	Yes			
Nebraska	Yes		Yes	Yes	Yes	Yes	Yes	Yes	
Nevada	Yes	Yes	Yes	Yes			Yes		
New Hampshire		Yes	Yes	Yes			Yes		
New Jersey	Yes	Yes	Yes	Yes		Yes	Yes		
New Mexico			Yes				Yes		
New York	Yes	Yes	Yes	Yes	Yes	Yes			a c d k
North Carolina		Yes	Yes	Yes		Yes	Yes	Yes	
North Dakota	Yes	Yes	Yes	Yes	Yes	Yes	Yes		
Ohio			Yes	Yes	Yes	Yes	Yes		
Oklahoma			Yes	Yes			Yes		
Oregon	Yes		Yes	Yes		Yes	Yes	Yes	
Pennsylvania				Yes			Yes		
Puerto Rico		Yes	Yes	Yes		Yes	Yes		

TABLE 11. Statutory Grounds for Annulment in American Jurisdictions. (Continued)

Jurisdiction	Fraud	Bigamy	Non-age	Mental Inca-pacity	Force or Duress	Impo-tence	Incest or Affinity	Misce-genation	Other Grounds
Rhode Island		Yes	Yes	Yes			Yes		
South Carolina			Yes	Yes			Yes	Yes	
South Dakota	Yes	Yes	Yes	Yes	Yes	Yes			
Tennessee	Yes	Yes	Yes	Yes	Yes				
Texas			Yes			Yes	Yes	Yes	
Utah	Yes		Yes	Yes	Yes		Yes		f
Vermont	Yes	Yes	Yes	Yes	Yes	Yes	Yes		
Virginia		Yes	Yes	Yes		Yes	Yes	Yes	
Virgin Islands			Yes	Yes	Yes				
Washington	Yes		Yes	Yes	Yes				
West Virginia		Yes	Yes	Yes		Yes	Yes	Yes	d, g
Wisconsin	Yes	Yes	Yes	Yes	Yes	Yes	Yes		
Wyoming	Yes	Yes	Yes	Yes	Yes		Yes	Yes	

a Concealment of previous marriage or divorce.
b Mistaken identity.
c Misrepresentation of position in life.
d Concealment of pregnancy.
e Not solemnized by the proper authority.
f Unchastity of the female.
g Concealment of a venereal disease.
h Imprisonment for life.
i Conviction of a felony.
j Concealment of leprosy or other loathsome disease.
k Refusal to consummate marriage.
l Wife's failure to disclose birth of illegitimate child by another man prior to marriage.
m No statutory provision for annulment.

Sources: Martindale-Hubbel Law Directory, Vol. III, 1955; 1953 addenda to the Women's Bureau Bulletins No. 157–48 and 157–49, The Legal Status of Women in the United States of America, January 1, 1948. The 1953 addenda include the pertinent statutory changes in the various states up to January 1, 1953.

The table reveals that lack of sufficient age, bigamy, fraud, force, incest and affinity, and mental inacapacity are the grounds most widely accepted in our jurisdictions. Of these, bigamy, fraud, and nonage are the grounds most frequently used in obtaining annulments, as can be seen in Table 11, which indicates the relative frequency of each of the major grounds in twenty-four states. These three grounds account for more than 90 percent of all annulments for which grounds were reported in 1951.

With the possible exception of New York and California, which use annulment as a handy divorce substitute, the number of annulments is extremely small when compared with divorce. The relative frequency can be seen in Table 12 (p. 220).

Since the causes of annulment are, theoretically at least, present at the time of marriage, the duration of marriages ending in annulment is also much shorter than that for marriages ending in divorce. Table 13 indicates that over two-fifths of all annulments occur within the first year of marriage and that three-fifths of all annulments occur within two years after marriage. Those marriages which end in divorce

TABLE 12.   Divorces and Annulments by Legal Grounds for Decree,
24 Reporting States, 1952.[a]

Legal Grounds for Decree	Annulment		Divorce	
	Number	Percent of Total Annulments [b]	Number	Percent of Total Divorces [b]
Cruelty	21	1.8	74,016	50.0
Desertion	6	—	28,585	19.3
Nonsupport	2	—	2,768	1.9
Drunkenness	16	1.0	3,493	2.4
Adultery	0	—	2,218	1.5
Conviction of crime	0	—	741	0.5
Bigamy	338	22.3	202	—
Fraud	223	14.7	116	—
Insanity	16	1.0	98	—
Nonage	82	5.4	1	—
Other grounds	153	10.0	34,392	23.3
Not stated	660	43.5	1,272	8.6
Total	1,517		147,902	

a These data are for the following states which reported this information in 1951:
Alabama, Georgia (estimated), Kansas, Ohio, Connecticut, Delaware, Florida, Idaho,
Iowa, Maine, Massachusetts, Michigan (incomplete), Mississippi, Missouri, Montana,
Nebraska, New Hampshire, North Dakota, Oregon, South Dakota, Tennessee, Vermont,
Virginia, and Wyoming (incomplete).
b Detail may not add to totals owing to rounding.

Source: Adapted from National Office of Vital Statistics, *Vital Statistics of the
United States, 1952*, 1955, Vol. I, Table 13, p. 82.

TABLE 13.   Divorces and Annulments by Duration of Marriage in Years,
19 Reporting States, 1951.[a]

Duration of Marriage	Annulment		Divorce	
	Number	Percent of Total Annulments [b]	Number	Percent of Total Divorces [b]
Under 1 year	365	42.2	5,206	6.4
1 year	171	19.8	7,683	9.5
2 years	70	8.1	7,280	9.0
3 years	39	4.5	7,288	9.0
4 years	33	3.8	6,987	8.6
5 years	17	2.0	6,408	7.9
Over 5 years or not stated	170	19.6	40,325	49.6
Total	865		81,177	

a These data are for the following states which reported this information in 1951:
Connecticut, Delaware, Florida, Idaho, Iowa, Maine, Michigan (incomplete), Mississippi, Missouri (incomplete), Montana, Nebraska, New Hampshire, North Dakota,
Oregon, South Dakota, Tennessee, Vermont, Virginia, and Wyoming (incomplete).
b Detail may not add to totals owing to rounding.

Source: National Office of Vital Statistics, *Vital Statistics of the United States, 1951*,
1954, Vol. I, Table 15, p. 97.

seem to have a greater comparative longevity despite their tendency to terminate in the early years also. Notice that 80 percent of all annulments occur in the first five years, while the incidence of divorce is only 50 percent in the same period of time.

Even though the law makes a distinction between annulment and divorce, the problems of property rights and the future of any children born are just as real in annulment. At common law it was held that since no valid marriage had occurred, neither party had acquired any marital rights. Once the decree was issued, both parties were again single and any children born were declared illegitimate. The harshness of these provisions was continued in American jurisdictions and, except for some statutes specifically to the contrary, still exist. At present, forty-three of the jurisdictions have legislation which to some extent modifies the common law concerning the issue of null-and-void marriages. The most common type of statute clearly provides that the children of such marriages are legitimate. The remaining states limit legitimacy to the children of certain annulled marriages, such as those resulting from bigamy or mental incapacity of one of the parents. Some states have passed legislation which specifically declares that the issue of certain prohibited marriages, such as miscegenetic unions, are illegitimate. The remaining states have passed no legislation in this area.

Regarding property rights, some states provide for the restoration of the property held by each of the parties at the time of the marriage, some provide for an equitable division of communal property, and others authorize the granting of temporary or permanent alimony. Again, however, many states are silent on these issues and leave decisions to the courts.

DIVORCE: ABSOLUTE AND LIMITED

The essential difference between divorce and annulment is that absolute divorce dissolves an existing marriage and leaves the parties as ex-spouses rather than single, as in an annulment. In American jurisdictions it is a litigious action—a judicial contest. This means that one party or the other must be at fault; must have theoretically caused the disruption of the marriage at some time in the past by the commission of some fault or wrongful act. These faults, or grounds, allow the supposedly injured party to sue for divorce since the marriage has been disrupted by the guilty party who, again theoretically, opposes

the divorce action. Thus, divorce does not destroy a marriage; it merely recognizes that at some time in the past the marriage has ceased to exist as the result of the operation of one of the legal grounds. The role of divorce is to regularize the proceedings in such cases, redetermine the status of the parties, and establish their future relationship. While this is the legal conception of divorce, such is obviously not a realistic picture of divorce in modern society. To begin with, in most cases both parties are to some degree guilty of the actual, if not the legal, causes of the disintegration of the relationship. Again, in most cases the manifest cause of cruelty, adultery, desertion, or nonsupport is but symptomatic of the latent cause, which may be quite different and result from mutual incompatibility rather than the fault of either of the parties. Finally, as we shall see later, both members of the unhappy marriage usually are in agreement that it should end, and hence there is no element of fault, no opposition, and certainly no spirit of contest.

As a result of this disparity between the ideal conception of divorce and its present social function, the laws which govern divorce actions are outmoded and ineffective. A brief summary of the important provisions among the various jurisdictions will reveal this cultural lag.

Establishing Residence. Since divorce is a legal action, the plaintiff must have established residence in the jurisdiction which will hear the suit. In the great majority of the jurisdictions this must be done by the injured party (or plaintiff), but in a few cases the residence may be established by the guilty party (or defendant), or by the place of occurrence of the marriage or the grounds. The length of time required for the plaintiff to establish residence varies from six weeks in Nevada, Idaho, and the Virgin Islands [56] to five years in Massachusetts (three years if both parties were residents at the time of the marriage). One year, however, is the most common residence requirement. Over three-fourths of the jurisdictions determine residence by the domicile of the plaintiff. Table 14 gives the time required to establish residence, based upon the plaintiff's residence in each of the fifty-three jurisdictions.

The primary importance of the length of required residence is not in its effect upon the bona fide residents of that jurisdiction, but consists in the fact that "migratory divorces" are attracted from states with longer requirements. The lure which such quickly met require-

[56] On April 11, 1955, the Supreme Court declared that the Virgin Islands' six-week-residence requirement without a declaration of intention to become a permanent resident was unconstitutional.

TABLE 14.   Residence Requirements for Divorce in American Jurisdiction.[a]

State	Period of Residence Required	State	Period of Residence Required
Alabama	1 year [b]	New Jersey	2 years
Arizona	1 year	New Mexico	1 year
Arkansas	2 months	New York	None [d]
California	1 year	North Carolina	6 months
Colorado	1 year	North Dakota	1 year
Connecticut	3 years	Ohio	1 year
Delaware	3 years	Oklahoma	1 year
Florida	90 days	Oregon	1 year
Georgia	6 months	Pennsylvania	1 year
Idaho	6 weeks	Rhode Island	2 years
Illinois	1 year	South Carolina	1 year
Indiana	1 year	South Dakota	1 year
Iowa	1 year	Tennessee	2 years
Kansas	1 year	Texas	1 year
Kentucky	1 year	Utah	6 months
Louisiana	None [c]	Vermont	6 months
Maine	1 year	Virginia	1 year
Maryland	1 year	Washington	1 year
Massachusetts	5 years	West Virginia	2 years
Michigan	1 year	Wisconsin	2 years
Minnesota	1 year	Wyoming	6 months
Mississippi	1 year	Alaska	2 years
Missouri	1 year	Hawaii	2 years
Montana	1 year	District of Columbia	1 year [e]
Nebraska	2 years	Puerto Rico	1 year
Nevada	6 weeks	Virgin Islands	6 weeks
New Hampshire	1 year		

a Periods stated refer to cases where the court's jurisdiction is based upon the plaintiff's "residence."

b In Alabama, plaintiff must have resided in the state for at least one year if defendant is a nonresident, except that (1) no particular or specific period of residence of plaintiff is required where court has jurisdiction over both parties, (2) plaintiff need not reside in state if defendant is a resident, and (3) a wife seeking divorce for nonsupport must have resided in the state for two years and the husband and wife must have been separated during that time.

c In Louisiana, there is no specified period of residence, but divorce for any grounds other than adultery or condemnation for an infamous crime may not be granted unless a separation from bed and board has been decreed and one year has elapsed without reconciliation.

d In New York, courts may not take jurisdiction of a divorce action unless (1) both parties reside in the state, (2) the cause of action arose in New York, or (3) the parties were married in the state.

e Two years if cause occurred outside of the District and prior to residence therein.

Sources: Based upon data from *Residence Required for Divorce in the United States,* 1954, a mimeographed publication of the Legislative Reference Service, State Capitol, Montgomery, Alabama, supplemented and corrected with additional data from the *Martindale-Hubbel Law Directory,* Summit, N.J., Martindale-Hubbel Inc., Vol. III, 1955.

ments can have for persons seeking a "quickie" divorce is illustrated in the divorce rates of two of the states with the lowest requirements. In one of these, Nevada with its famed divorce centers at Reno and Las Vegas, the 1950 divorce rate was 55.7 per thousand population, 22 *times* as *high* as the nation-wide rate of 2.5 per thousand. Another example is furnished by the experience of the Virgin Islands, which

TABLE 15. American Divorce Laws as of 1952.

State	Length of Residence Required Before Filing Suit	Adultery	Cruelty	Desertion	Alcoholism	Impotency	Felony Conviction	Neglect to Provide	Insanity	Pregnancy at Marriage	Bigamy	Separation	Imprisonment	Indignities	Drug Addict	Fraudulent Contract
Alabama	a	★	★	★	★	★	★	★	★[b]	★			★[c]			★
Arizona	1 year	★	★	★	★	★	★	★		★	★	★[b]		★		
Arkansas	90 days[f]	★	★	★	★	★	★	★	★		★	★[g]		★		
California	1 year	★	★	★	★		★	★	★[g]							
Colorado	1 year	★	★	★	★		★	★	★[b]	★					★	
Connecticut	3 years	★	★	★	★			★	★[b]				★			★
Delaware	2 years[i]	★	★	★	★			★	★[b]		★		★[l]			
Florida	90 days	★	★	★	★	★					★		★			
Georgia	6 months	★	★	★	★	★	★[n]		°,[g]	★		★[b]	[n]			★
Idaho	6 weeks	★	★	★	★		★	★	★[g]		★	★[b]				
Illinois	1 year[p]	★	★	★	★	★	★				★					
Indiana	1 year	★	★	★	★	★		★	★[b]							
Iowa	1 year	★	★	★	★		★			★						★
Kansas	1 year[s]	★	★	★	★	★	★	★	★[b]	★	★					★
Kentucky	1 year	★	★	★	★	★	★		★[b]			★[b]				
Louisiana	1 year[v]	★	★	★	★							★[j]				
Maine	1 year	★	★	★	★	★		★	★[g]			★[g]			★	
Maryland	1 year[z]	★		★	★	★	★[v]		★[g]		★			★[b]		★
Massachusetts	5 years[z]	★	★	★	★	★		★[aa]				★				
Michigan	1 year	★	★[aa]	★	★	★		★[aa]				★				
Minnesota	1 year	★	★	★	★	★			★[b]		★[j]	★				
Mississippi	1 year	★	★	★	★	★			★[g]	★	★			★		★
Missouri	1 year	★	★	★	★	★	★					★				
Montana	1 year	★	★	★	★	★	★	★	★[b]							
Nebraska	2 years[a][e]	★	★	★	★	★	★		★[b]			★[g]				
Nevada	6 weeks	★	★	★	★	★	★	★	★[j]			★[g]	★[ba]			
New Hampshire	1 year[aq]	★	★	★	★	★	★	★				★	★[ba]			
New Jersey	2 years	★	★	★												
New Mexico	1 year[ai]	★	★	★	★	★	★	★	★[b]	★			★			
New York	aj	★														
North Carolina	6 months	★			★				★[al]	★	★	★[j]				
North Dakota	1 year[s]	★	★	★	★		★	★	★[b]	[bb]	[bb]				★	[bb]
Ohio	1 year	★	★		★	★		★	★[an]	★	★		★			★
Oklahoma	1 year	★	★	★	★	★	★	★	★[an]	★	★					★
Oregon	1 year	★	★	★	★	★	★		★[b]					★		
Pennsylvania	1 year	★	★	★		★	★				★			★		★
Rhode Island	2 years	★	★	★	★	★	★	★				★[al]		★		
South Carolina	1 year	★	★	★	★											
South Dakota	1 year[ao]	★	★	★	★		★	★	★[b]		★	★		★		
Tennessee	2 years	★	★	★	★	★	★	★		★	★			★		
Texas	1 year	★	★	★		★	★[aq]		★[b]			★[al]				
Utah	90 days	★	★	★	★	★	★	★	★[b]			★[g]	★[l]			
Vermont	6 months[z]	★		★		★		★	★[b]		★		★[g]	★		
Virginia	1 year	★				★	★				★		★			
Washington	1 year	★	★	★	★	★		★	★[j]			★[b]	★	★	★	★
West Virginia	2 years[ae]	★	★	★	★		★					★[b]	★[l]			
Wisconsin	2 years	★	★	★	★[ah]	★	★[g]	★	★[j]	★	★	★[j]	★	★		
Wyoming	60 days	★	★	★	★	★	★	★	★[g]					★		
Alaska	2 years	★	★	★	★	★	★	★	★[g]					★		
Dis. of Columbia	2 years[au]	★	★[bc]	★			★					★[b]		★		
Hawaii	2 years	★	★	★	★			★	★[g]		★	★[g]		★		
Puerto Rico	1 year	★	★	★	★	★	★		★[h]			★[g]				★
Virgin Islands	6 weeks	★	★	★	★	★	★		★							

Note: explanatory notes for Table 15 are found on p. 226.

Felony Before Marriage	Violence	Absence	Infamous Crime	Loathsome Disease	Relationship Within Prohibited Degrees	Other Grounds	Plaintiff	Defendant	State
							— Grounds for Divorce —		
							— Period Before Parties May Remarry —		
	★★					d	60 days if no appeal	60 days if no appeal[e]	Alabama
★	★★						1 year	1 year	Arizona
		★					Immediately	Immediately	Arkansas
							1 year	1 year	California
							6 months	6 months	Colorado
			★[h]	★			Immediately	Immediately	Connecticut
						k	1 year	1 year	Delaware
					★	m	Immediately	Immediately	Florida
	★					★	Fixed by court	Fixed by court	Georgia
							6 months	6 months	Idaho
	★		★	★			Immediately	Immediately	Illinois
	★						2 years[q]	Immediately	Indiana
							1 year[r]	1 year[r]	Iowa
							6 months	6 months	Kansas
	★★			★		t,u	Immediately	Immediately	Kentucky
	★★		★			w	Wife, 10 mos.[ad]	Wife, 10 mos.[ad]	Louisiana
	★						Immediately	Immediately	Maine
							Immediately	Immediately	Maryland
							6 months	2 years	Massachusetts
	★[aa]					ab	6 months if children under 17[ac]	6 months if children under 17[ac]	Michigan
							6 months	6 months	Minnesota
					★	o	Immediately	Immediately[ad]	Mississippi
★			★			d	Immediately	Immediately	Missouri
	★						Immediately	Immediately	Montana
							6 months	6 months	Nebraska
							Immediately	Immediately	Nevada
			★[g]			t,af	Immediately	Immediately	New Hampshire
							3 months	3 months	New Jersey
							Immediately	Immediately	New Mexico
						ak	Immediately	3 years—consent of court	New York
						d	Immediately	Immediately	North Carolina
							Immediately[aa]	Immediately[aa]	North Dakota
			★[ba]			m	Immediately	Immediately	Ohio
							6 months	6 months	Oklahoma
							6 months	6 months	Oregon
					★		Immediately	Immediately[ad]	Pennsylvania
		★				d	6 months	6 months	Rhode Island
									South Carolina
							Immediately	Immediately[ad]	South Dakota
	★		★[j]	★		ap	Immediately	Immediately[ad]	Tennessee
							Immediately; Cruelty, 1 year	Immediately; Cruelty, 1 year	Texas
							6 months	6 months	Utah
			★[h]	★		d	6 months	2 years[r]	Vermont
				★		ar,as	4 months	4 months[ad]	Virginia
							Immediately	Immediately	Washington
	★						60 days	60 days[ad,at]	West Virginia
							1 year	1 year	Wisconsin
★	★			★		d	Immediately	Immediately	Wyoming
						d	Immediately	Immediately	Alaska
							6 months	6 months	Dist. of Columbia
					★		av,aw	av,aw	Hawaii
						ax	Immediately[ay]	Immediately[ay]	Puerto Rico
						d	az	az	Virgin Islands

Source: Council of State Governments, *The Book of the States, 1954–1955*, Chicago, The Council, 1954, Vol. X, pp. 324–325.

Explanatory notes for Table 15:

a   No specific period of residence required except when ground is abandonment or defendant is a nonresident, in which cases plaintiff must prove one year's residence; wife seeking divorce on non-support must prove 2 years' residence and spouses must have been separated during that time.

b   Five years.

c   Two years' imprisonment, sentence for 7 years or longer.

d   Alabama and North Carolina, crime against nature; Alaska, Virgin Islands, incompatibility; Mississippi, insanity at time of marriage; Missouri, Wyoming, husband a vagrant; Rhode Island, other gross misbehavior or wickedness; Vermont, intolerable severity.

e   Court may forbid remarriage.

f   Divorce suits may be filed after 60 days' residence, but an additional 30 days must elapse before decree granted.

g   Three years; also in New Hampshire wife's absence out of state 10 years.

h   Seven years.

i   Action for divorce based on adultery or bigamy may be commenced at time cause of action arose, when either party was bona fide resident of state and has continued to be so until commencement of action.

j   Two years.

k   Female under 16, male under 18, complaining party under age of consent at time of marriage not confirmed after reaching such age.

l   Habitual violent, and ungovernable temper.

m   Defendant obtained divorce from complainant in other state.

n   Felony conviction must comprehend sentence for 2 years to penitentiary.

o   Insanity at time of marriage.

p   Six months if offense committed in state.

q   Where obtained by default of notice on publication only.

r   Period can be shortened if approval of court is obtained.

s   Five years if on insanity grounds and insane spouse is inmate of out-of-state institution. Joining a religious sect disbelieving in marriage.

u   Unchaste behavior of wife after marriage.

v   In cases of separation of 2 or more years; no statutory requirement for other grounds.

w   Absence of reconciliation for 1 year after judgment of separation, or public defamation, or fugitive from justice.

x   Insanity 2 years.

y   Plus sentence of at least 3 years, 18 months of which has been served.

z   Three years if both parties were state residents at time of marriage.

aa   In the court's discretion.

ab   At court's discretion to resident of state whose spouse has obtained divorce in another state.

ac   At court's discretion time may be shortened in cases of unusual hardship or compelling necessity. For defendant court may prohibit remarriage within specified time not exceeding 2 years.

ad   One divorced for adultery may not marry the paramour. Special restrictions on remarriage exist in Mississippi, Virginia and West Virginia.

ae   One year where the cause of divorce arose within state.

af   When a wife of any alien or citizen of another state, living separate, has resided in the state, 3 years together, husband having left U. S. to become a foreign citizen and during that period has not come into state to claim marital rights or provide for wife.

ag   Three years on grounds of desertion.

ah   Husband habitual one year, wife given to intoxication.

ai   Time spent on military reservation shall count as residence.

aj   Parties residents when offense committed; married in state; plaintiff resident when offense committed and action commenced; offense committed in state and injured party resident when action commenced.

ak   The so-called Enoch Arden law provides for annulment of marriage upon showing that the other party has been absent for 5 successive years and that diligent search reveals no evidence that such other party is living.

al   Ten years.

an   Incurable insanity, the insane person having been an inmate of a state or private institution 5 years.

ao   Divorce suits may be commenced any time if married in state and residents then until action; action may be commenced after 6 months residence if cause of action arose in state.

ap   Refusal of wife to live with husband in the state and absenting herself 2 years.

aq   If imprisonment follows.

ar   Wife a prostitute; 2 years a fugitive from justice under indictment.

as   Sodomy and buggery.

at   Court may keep defendant from remarrying for a year.

au   Residence of 1 year is required where the cause of divorce occurred in the District.

av   Immediately, when marriage is dissolved for adultery.

aw   May be limited at court's discretion not to exceed 1 month.

ax   Attempt to corrupt sons or prostitute daughters; proposal of husband to prostitute wife; grave injury.

ay   Man immediately, woman after 301 days.

az   Neither plaintiff nor defendant may remarry with a third party until action has been heard and determined on appeal, and if no appeal be taken, until expiration of 30-day period allowed by law to take appeal.

ba   One year.

bb   May be grounds for annulment.

bc   Legal separation for cruelty which can be enlarged into an absolute divorce after 2 years.

also requires but six weeks, and, until recently, did not even require
a statement of intention to become a permanent resident, as is the
case in Nevada and Idaho (although no one gives them any serious
consideration). In the Virgin Islands, before it became known as a
sanctuary for those anxious to end their marital woes, the divorce
rate was very low. For example, in 1940 only thirty-four divorces were
granted in the islands. After the Second World War, however, when
travel restrictions were ended and knowledge of the short residence
period became known, it rose sharply, reaching a peak of 343 in 1952.
After a lower court first ruled that the six-week-residence law was in
error, the number dropped to 236 in 1953 and probably will approach
its original low figure now that the Supreme Court has affirmed its
unconstitutionality.

Grounds for Divorce. Each jurisdiction has a right to prescribe
which grounds may or may not lead to divorce within its borders. The
variability with which the several jurisdictions have reacted to this
privilege has created a multitude of dissimilar grounds which, even
where similar, are defined differently. The major legal grounds for
which absolute divorce may be granted in each of the fifty-three jurisdictions are presented in Table 15. Some of these grounds deserve
further comment.

Adultery. Adultery may be defined as extramarital sexual relations
or sexual intercourse by a married man with someone other than the
spouse. All jurisdictions allow adultery as a ground for divorce, and in
New York it is the only legal ground for absolute divorce. It is
popularly conceived that adultery is a major cause of divorce and
accounts for a large number of broken marriages. If such is the case,
it is not supported by evidence concerning the grounds given in court
as the cause of the marital disruption. As Table 12 indicates, less than
2 percent of the divorces granted in 1952 were based upon charges of
adultery. There is, of course, no way of knowing how many divorces,
actually a result of adultery, were sought under grounds carrying less
social stigma.

It is not necessary that the accused adulterer be discovered in the
actual performance of sexual relations, for the courts have held that
circumstantial evidence is sufficient.[57] To prove adultery in such cases,
however, it is usually necessary that the elements of opportunity and
inclination must be present, and the evidence must be such as to

---

[57] *Taft v. Taft,* 80 Vt. 256, 67 Atl. 703 (1907); *Snyder v. Snyder,* 159 Md.
391, 150 Atl. 837 (1930).

"carry conviction of the truth of the charge." Thus, if a married man should take some woman other than his wife to a hotel and register with her as man and wife, the assumption is that adultery could and did take place.

Cruelty. While it is the most frequent ground given in divorce actions, half of all grounds in 1952, not all states have established cruelty as a legal cause for absolute divorce. If we include Michigan, where it can serve at the court's discretion, and the District of Columbia, where a legal separation based upon cruelty can be enlarged into an absolute divorce after two years, forty-eight of the fifty-three jurisdictions accept cruelty as a ground. The determination of cruelty differs among the jurisdictions, with various definitions in terms of the degree of severity and the physical or mental nature of the cruelty. In respect to severity, it is variously required to be "extreme cruelty," "cruel and inhuman treatment," or simply "cruelty," with the assessment of severity necessary to qualify left to the courts. Seven states specifically add "mental cruelty" as a ground, but other jurisdictions can, with few exceptions, in effect allow it as a matter of judicial interpretation of what constitutes cruelty. In practice, judicial definition of cruelty has ranged from extreme, harsh physical punishment [58] to constant nagging by the husband or wife.[59] In general, however, the present tendency is to grant divorce in those cases where physical anguish or suffering as the result of repeated acts by one of the parties has taken place.[60]

Desertion. The period of absence required to constitute desertion as a cause of divorce ranges from six months in Hawaii to five years in Rhode Island, the most common period being one year. Every jurisdiction except New York, North Carolina, and Ohio recognizes it as a ground for absolute divorce. Once more we find a diversity of definitions of what constitutes desertion; "wilful desertion," "wilful and malicious desertion," and "utter and continued desertion" are specified in different states. In general, however, there usually must be a cessation of cohabitation by the deserter, with an unjustifiable intention to abandon without the consent of the injured party.[61] Even under these

---

[58] *French v. French*, 4 Mass. 587 (1808).

[59] *Barngrover v. Barngrover*, 57 Cal. App. 43, 206 Pac. 461 (1922).

[60] Max Rheinstein makes the interesting comment that the requirement of at least two acts of physical violence to constitute cruelty is similar to the law concerning dog bites wherein "the first bite is free." Quoted in the University of Chicago Law School, *Conference on Divorce*, February 29, 1952, p. 40.

[61] J. J. Madden, *Persons and Domestic Relations*, St. Paul, West Publishing Company, 1931, p. 276.

stringent requirements, it is a frequent cause of action and is second only to cruelty in the number of cases ending in divorce.

Nonsupport. Frequently confused with desertion, nonsupport (or neglect to provide, as it is also called) differs from desertion in that there is no requirement of cessation of cohabitation. Nonsupport assumes that a husband able to do so has not met his marital obligation to support his wife for a period of time ranging from sixty days in Hawaii to three years in New Hampshire. Thirty states recognize nonsupport, with the most frequent time requirement being one year.

Impotence. Although impotence existing at the time of marriage is usually a ground for annulment, thirty-seven jurisdictions make it a legal cause for divorce either as a substitute or concurrently with annulment.[62]

The legal conditions necessary to establish impotence are the same as in annulment, and usually it must have existed both at the time of the marriage and at the time when the action was brought. Another frequent requirement is that it be incurable.

Imprisonment or Conviction for a Crime. Statutes dealing with criminal behavior as grounds for divorce are found in forty-seven jurisdictions. The statutes mention several forms of crime: conviction of a felony, conviction of a felony before marriage, conviction of an infamous crime, imprisonment and conviction of an infamous crime. There is great diversity in the statutes concerning the length of the sentence (from one year to life), the place of confinement (state penitentiary, jail, jail in any state), and whether conviction need be followed by imprisonment. Few states discuss the effect of a pardon, but those which do state that the pardon in no way alters the grounds. Time off the sentence for good behavior has also been held to have no effect upon the qualification of the sentence in meeting the minimum number of years. Several states also maintain that the suit for divorce must be originated prior to the release of the defendant.

Alcoholism and Drug Addiction. Forty-four jurisdictions allow some degree of alcoholism to serve as grounds for absolute divorce, although there is in no case a definition of what degree of severity is required. Some states, for example, require "habitual drunkenness" for two years, which might be interpreted as being continually intoxicated for this length of time but in practice is usually construed in terms of an irresistible urge to use alcohol continuing for at least two years. It

[62] Vernier, *op. cit.*, Vol. II, p. 38, and *Martindale-Hubbel Law Directory*, Vol. III, 1955.

is interesting that Wisconsin requires one year of habitual drunkenness for males, but is satisfied to require of females only that they be "given to intoxication." Eleven jurisdictions currently add drug addiction as a legal cause for divorce, again with obscure definitions of what constitutes addiction.

Other Grounds. The grounds so far discussed are only the more frequent of the more than forty possible legal causes for divorce. Others found in one or more jurisdictions include living apart for a given number of years, attempt to corrupt sons or prostitute daughters, wife's (but not the husband's) unchastity before marriage, sodomy and buggery, defamation of spouse in public, joining a religious sect disbelieving in cohabitation, and incompatibility. It is interesting that the much publicized incompatibility of temperament, the butt of so many of our stories concerning the ease of obtaining a divorce, is found only in Alaska and New Mexico.

DEFENSES AGAINST ACTIONS FOR DIVORCE

We are so accustomed to thinking of divorce as the voluntary and coöperative action by both parties which it has become that we sometimes forget that it is actually a court contest and therefore must make allowances for defense against the grounds charged. The defense to actions for divorce may be either general, as would arise in any law suit, or one or more of the four special defenses allowed in divorce suits: collusion, connivance, condonation, and recrimination. Collusion is any agreement between the husband and wife to obtain a divorce by imposing upon the court.[63] Thus, a husband and wife who agree to arrange convenient grounds for a divorce, such as prearranged adultery, are guilty of collusion. Some fraud has been perpetrated upon the court, either by committing an offense for the express purpose of establishing grounds for a divorce, introducing false evidence into the suit concerning an offense that was actually never committed, or suppressing some valid defense.

Connivance is the corrupt consent of the husband or wife to the marital offenses of the other. If a husband, for example, consents to his wife's adultery, he cannot use this act of misconduct on her part as grounds for divorce since his consent constituted connivance. Condonation, on the other hand, refers to the later forgiveness by the injured spouse of some marital offense. Condonation might be exemplified by the husband or wife who welcomes back an adulterous spouse with full knowledge of his misconduct. An important element

[63] Vernier, op. cit., Vol. II, p. 75.

in establishing condonation is that of knowledge, for subsequent cohabitation by a spouse ignorant of the misconduct of the other party to the marriage would not constitute condonation. Recrimination may be defined as a countercharge that the plaintiff is also guilty of some offense which is sufficient grounds for divorce. If, for example, a husband is charged with adultery and he can establish that his wife also committed adultery, each suit cancels the other. In our peculiar legal fiction of divorce as a contentious action, two wrongs do not make for a more certain divorce but rather send the guilty parties back to the marriage both have violated.

Collusion is the most interesting of these defenses since, in practice, it would seem that the vast majority of divorce actions, particularly in states with limited grounds, are characterized by what amounts to collusion.[64] As we mentioned earlier, in most cases where divorce is sought both parties have agreed to the initiation of the suit and perhaps have (illegally) decided upon such matters as who shall have custody of the children, what grounds will provide the easiest, quietest, and quickest divorce, and what property settlements will be made. The frequency with which this happens is indicated by the large percentage of divorces which go uncontested, estimated to be as high as 80 to 90 percent by some legal authorities. In the absence of any realistic or possible means of enforcing this fictitious wrong, it would seem that the legislatures and the courts might do well to concede to reality and either renounce the litigious concept of the divorce action, abolish the unenforceable statutes concerning collusion, or do both.

THE RIGHT TO REMARRY

Absolute divorce grants to both parties the right to remarry, but in thirty-six jurisdictions certain restrictions are placed upon the plaintiff, the guilty party, or both. The defendant, or guilty party, may not remarry in some states for a period ranging from sixty days to three years depending upon the jurisdiction. In six states, the guilty party in a suit based upon adultery may not marry the paramour. The waiting period for the plaintiff varies from sixty days to one year. Louisiana takes exception by requiring twenty-two months if the plaintiff is a woman, but only one year if a man. In Puerto Rico, a man may remarry immediately after a divorce, but the woman must wait the 301 days

[64] Cf. Ray E. Baber, *Marriage and the Family*, New York, McGraw-Hill Book Company, 1953, pp. 478–479; John S. Bradway, "The Myth of the Innocent Spouse," Association of American Law Schools, *Selected Essays on Family Law*, Brooklyn, The Foundation Press, 1950, pp. 937–955, and, *ibid.*, "Collusive and Consensual Divorce," pp. 977–987.

which are also legally required after an annulment or the death of her husband.[65] Table 15 (p. 224) indicates the waiting period required in each of the fifty-three jurisdictions.

Alimony. As a result of divorce, and of annulment as well in some states, the court must make a decision as to the financial relationship between the parties in terms of property settlements and alimony. The theory of alimony grew out of the ecclesiastical-court doctrine that only death could dissolve a valid marriage and so free the husband of his marital obligation to support his wife. Today, even though absolute divorce is the rule, the concept of alimony continues, largely as an extension of the husband's matrimonial obligation, although it is possible for the husband to receive alimony in certain cases. Every jurisdiction makes some allowance for alimony in absolute divorce. Following the tradition of the ecclesiastical courts, alimony today represents a money judgment against the person of the husband, although some states have statutes authorizing alimony from the husband's property.

The amount of the award is usually within the discretion of the court, and most states also allow for revision of the award should there be some significant change in the needs of the wife or the ability of the husband to meet payments. Most jurisdictions allow for the payment of temporary alimony during the course of the court action and for the payment of the suit costs. Failure to pay alimony is punishable since it has been held to represent contempt of the court's order to pay.

Although most jurisdictions authorize alimony for husbands as well as wives, it is technically incorrect to call such payments alimony since the wife has no duty to support her husband. Since there is no common-law basis for such payments, they are usually found only in states which have statutory authorization for payments to the husband. Another radical departure from common law is the awarding of alimony to a wife who is the "guilty" party in the divorce action. At common law a wife could not obtain alimony when the legal cause of the divorce was her own misconduct, but in most jurisdictions this has been changed by specific statutes and in others through judicial interpretation. Some jurisdictions, however, do not allow alimony to a wife guilty of adultery.

CHILDREN IN DIVORCE ACTIONS

Where the parties to a divorce action are also parents, the courts must determine which of the parents is to have custody of the children

[65] *Martindale-Hubbel Law Directory*, Vol. III, 1955.

and make arrangements for their support. The present tendency of most courts seems to be a mixture of the philosophy that the welfare of the child is the primary concern and the widespread belief that a child belongs with his mother. The difficulties involved in deciding such issues are many and will be considered along with other aspects of the parent-child relationship in the next chapter.

LIMITED DIVORCE

Limited divorce, or divorce from bed and board, is what is popularly called a "separation." It differs from absolute divorce in that, while it has the effect of prohibiting cohabitation, it does not dissolve the marriage. It places the couple in a twilight zone between marriage and the single state, since they are unmarried as far as conjugal rights are concerned but married in terms of the ability to contract a new marriage.

As with so much of the law of divorce, the history and rationale of limited divorce go back to the English ecclesiastical courts. Under their jurisdiction, two types of "divorce" were possible: divorce a vinculo, or what we today know as annulment, and divorce a menso et thoro, or judicial separation. This meant, in effect, that unless a decree a vinculo was issued annulling the marriage, only death could dissolve the union, although the couple could obtain a limited divorce from bed and board (a menso et thoro). The Church allowed three exceptions to the rule that only death dissolved a valid marriage: a Christian abandoned by an infidel spouse, the acceptance by one of the parties of holy orders, and the dissolution of the marriage by papal dispensation. This approach to divorce remains the basic philosophy of the Roman Catholic Church and the Church of England today, and is the common-law basis for our present legal separation or limited divorce.

The methods of obtaining a limited divorce are basically the same as in absolute divorce. The grounds are usually the same except that there are more grounds available for limited divorce in many states, the most common being cruelty, desertion, adultery, intoxication, nonsupport, and imprisonment or conviction for a crime in that order. The number of limited divorces, even in New York, where there are many more grounds for limited divorce than the single ground of adultery for absolute divorce, is relatively low. The Bureau of the Census and the National Office of Vital Statistics combine limited and absolute divorces into one figure in their reports, so that there are no current figures available on the number of limited divorces granted, but

Marshall and May's study revealed that only one in seven of the applications for divorce at that time was for the limited type.[66]

Today, over half of American jurisdictions grant limited divorce or legal separation, and in Louisiana absolute divorce for any grounds other than adultery or condemnation for an infamous crime may not be granted unless a separation from bed and board has been previously granted and one year has elapsed without reconciliation. Florida is the only state in which the granting of limited divorces is expressly forbidden.

Modern American Divorce: A Summary

The confusion and contradiction of our divorce laws offer sufficient evidence of the need to revise our outmoded domestic-relations law. Yet we continue to deal with twentieth-century marital problems with nineteenth-century or even medieval sociolegal concepts. Why, then, has not the weight of public opinion operated to bring about the necessary revisions, as it has usually done where cultural lag is so obvious? The answer is a function both of the fragmentary nature of the public knowledge of matrimonial law and the public interest in divorce prevention which draws attention away from the need to make our domestic laws more equitable.

This concern with preventing divorce, a logical outgrowth of society's concern for a stable family, has been heightened in recent years by our anxiety over the "alarming" growth of divorces in this country. The daily press, specialty writers in popular magazines, social agencies, government spokesmen, and others seem to hold the opinion that immediate action is necessary to halt this growing tide of "broken families." We are told that the divorce rate is skyrocketing, that "one in three marriages ends in divorce," and that unless something is done our divorce rate will soon equal our marriage rate. In these warnings, some mention is usually made of the cruel effects of divorce upon the emotional life of family members, particularly the children. Law-enforcement officials, jurists, social workers, and the press remind us of the established relationship between the broken home and juvenile delinquency, and new urgency is added to our determination to "do something about the divorce situation." Once we enter into the discussion of what we can do, we are very likely to hear the popular suggestion that we should tighten our "lax" divorce laws. This solution is usually based upon the belief that our divorce rate has steadily in-

[66] Leon C. Marshall and Geoffrey May, The Divorce Court, Baltimore, Johns Hopkins Press, 1933, 2 vols.

creased as a result of the easing of our laws and the growth in the number of grounds available to individuals seeking divorce. Such has not, however, been the case, for, contrary to general belief, our divorce laws have changed surprisingly little in the last few decades. Those changes in the law which have taken place have been designed to make the existing laws more readily enforceable. The growth of legislation aimed at revision and better enforcement of residence requirements and the proper notification of a nonresident defendant typifies the general direction of these changes. Such measures are far more common than any addition of grounds or other steps to make divorce more readily obtained. What has changed in our jurisdictions is our procedure in divorce cases, which has become more lax as it responds to the changing mores. While we still think of divorce as a social evil, we have removed much of the stigma from the divorced person, and religious and social censure no longer exerts strong inhibitory pressures upon the individual contemplating divorce.

THE AMERICAN DIVORCE RATE AND SOCIAL FORCES

The widespread fear that the modern American family faces disintegration as it turns increasingly toward divorce as an escape from marriage is a result of the recent history of the divorce rate. Recent evidence suggests that a reappraisal of our fear is necessary. Prior to the First World War, our divorce rate seldom went as high as one divorce for every 1000 persons in our population, although from 1890 on there was a small but consistent increase every year. Just after the war, however, there was a sharp increase in the number of divorces—

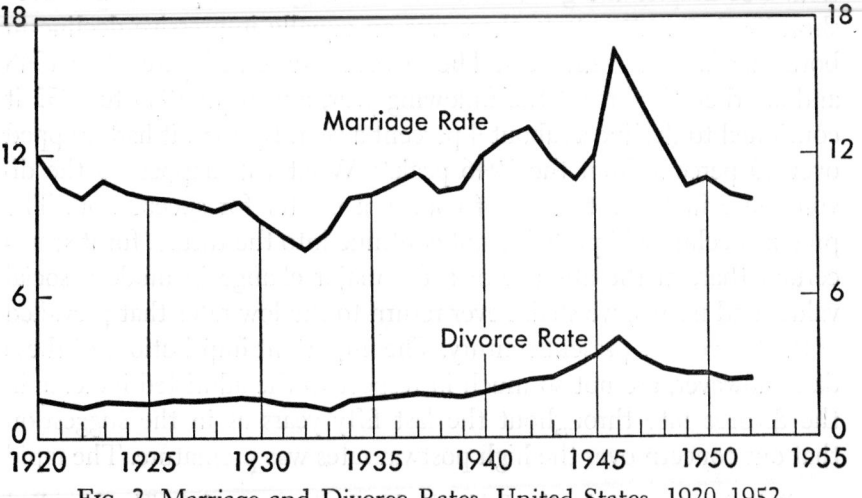

FIG. 2. Marriage and Divorce Rates, United States, 1920–1952.

the greatest increase in the divorce rate up until that time. Figure 2, which shows both the marriage and divorce rate in the United States from 1920 to 1952, illustrates what has happened to the rate since that first postwar increase. After a slight drop in 1922, the number of divorces again began to increase slowly but steadily for the remainder of the twenties. During the depression in the early thirties, there was a decided decrease in the number of divorces and at the same time the marriage rate showed an even sharper decrease, so that it reached an all-time low in 1932. Both decreases were the result of the economic pressures exerted by the depression, which caused the postponement of many marriages and divorces, a common occurrence when business is poor. With the gradual return of prosperity in the later thirties, the upward swing for both rates returned, presumably the result of the completion of postponed marriages and divorces and the usual effect of periods of prosperity to encourage both marriage and divorce. The divorce experience of the first war was repeated during and after World War II. Again we experienced a sharp increase in the divorce rate with the approach of war in 1940, and a significant increase in marriages both in 1940 during mobilization and in 1944 to 1945 as servicemen returned. It was immediately after the war, however, that the most spectacular jump took place in both marriage and divorce rates, reaching an all-time high in 1946. In that year, there were an estimated 610,000 divorces, or 4.3 per thousand population, twice the prewar rate. There was an even more impressive leap in the marriage rate with 2,291,045 marriages, or 16.4 per thousand population. But despite the great concern caused by these peaks, they were short-lived, for after 1946 there was an equally impressive decline in both marriages and divorces. The divorce rate fell 21 percent in 1948 and another 18 percent the following year, and from 1949 to 1952 it continued to decline at about 4 percent a year. By 1952 it had dropped over 40 percent from the 1946 peak.[67] What will happen to the divorce rate in the future is, of course, a matter for speculation. The present decline will probably not continue into the future, for it seems certain that, in the absence of some major change in modern social values and norms, we shall never return to the low rates that prevailed at the turn of the present century. The important implications of these data, however, are not so much in respect to the admitted increase in the divorce rate throughout the last fifty years as in the suggestion that our concern over the high postwar rates was premature. The rapid

[67] Preliminary reports by the Public Health Service reported in *The New York Times*, June 23, 1954, p. 20.

decline from these rates in the years following World War II suggests that our fears concerning the disintegration of the family may not be justified.

These trends also indicate that it is the social and economic milieu rather than the relaxing or strengthening of legal controls which has the greatest effect upon the divorce rate. There were no important prohibitive or restrictive divorce laws passed in the predepression days which could account for the decline in divorces during the depression. There were, however, economic factors of a very obvious nature which would operate to depress the divorce rate. Neither were there any important changes in our divorce laws during either war which would explain the increase in divorces which followed both conflicts. The explanation of postwar divorce booms would seem to center about the hasty and ill-advised marriages which frequently take place during such periods of rapid social change and the social and psychological problems of readjustment confronting returning servicemen. The correspondence between marriage and divorce rates in their response to the social milieu gives added weight to the position that the "divorce laws are the chief factor in divorce rates" approach is shallow and unrealistic in its negation of sociocultural factors.

Our understandable concern over the detrimental effects of divorce upon children is also guilty of a too frequent oversimplification in criticizing divorce. Granted that every child needs and deserves a full share of the emotional and physical security which is found only in an intact family of mother and father, it is still an oversimplification to assert that divorce breaks children's homes and disturbs intrafamilial relationships. At the risk of repetition and overemphasis, we must again point out that divorce merely recognizes the existence of an already broken or badly bent home. As any experienced social worker, psychiatrist, or correctional worker will testify, a psychologically broken home is as damaging to proper childhood development as a physically broken one and often represents a more intensive and prolonged period of anxiety for the child.[68] Divorce can and sometimes does offer a means of easing or relieving family tensions and domestic discord which can have lasting effects upon the developing personality of the child. Then again, not all marriages which end in divorce or annulment involve young children. The available evidence suggests that more childless marriages end in divorce and annulment than fruitful ones. Table 16 shows the number and percentage of all divorces and annulments which involved young children in 1952 in nineteen states.

[68] Cf. James H. S. Bossard, *The Sociology of Child Development*, New York, Harper & Brothers, 1954, p. 407.

TABLE 16. Divorces and Annulments by Number of Children Reported Under 18
Years of Age, 19 States Reported, 1952.[a]

| Number of Children | Annulments | | Divorces | |
Reported	Number	Percent of All Annulments	Number	Percent of All Divorces
None	856	67.6	73,819	54.2
One	70	5.4	29,635	21.8
Two	18	1.4	17,557	12.9
Three	3	—	6,291	4.6
Four	2	—	3,165	2.3
Five or more	—	—	1,487	1.1
Not stated	318	25.1	3,566	2.6
Total	1,267		136,150	100.0 [b]

a These data are for the following states, which reported this information separately
for annulment and divorce in 1952: Alabama, Florida, Georgia (estimated), Idaho,
Iowa, Kansas, Maine, Michigan (incomplete), Mississippi, Missouri, Nebraska, New
Hampshire, North Dakota, Ohio, Oregon, South Dakota, Tennessee, Virginia, and
Wyoming.
b Detail may not add to totals owing to rounding.
Source: Adapted from National Office of Vital Statistics, Vital Statistics of the
United States, 1952, 1955, Vol. I, Table 13, p. 82.

These data indicate that over half of all divorces and 90 percent of
annulments where data concerning the number of children are furnished were granted to couples without children under 18. If these
figures are representative of the nation as a whole, and there is no reason to suspect that they are not, it would appear that a good many
annulments and divorces do not result in broken homes for children.

THE REAL PROBLEMS OF DIVORCE LAW

The data presented above would seem to argue that the legislatures
of the various jurisdictions would contribute little to any solution of
the divorce problem by enacting more prohibitory or repressive legislation. They might well, however, turn their attention to the two most
basic problems in our divorce laws: antiquated laws out of tune with
modern society and confusion because of different procedures and laws
among the fifty-three jurisdictions. Attempts have been made to remedy both situations, but so far have met with little success.

The basic cultural lag in our divorce laws is our conception of the
divorce action as a litigation and the resultant necessity of a guilty
and an innocent party. Several solutions have been suggested which,
if implemented by public support, would seem to offer a means of
attuning the laws to the inescapable fact that most modern divorce is
mutually desired by both parties. Bradway, in his critique of the existing procedure in divorce cases, summarizes the suggested remedies as
follows:

1. Divorce should be rather a conciliatory than a contentious action.
2. The parties in interest should include the spouses and the members of the family.
3. The goal should be to work out whatever plan is best for the family as a whole.
4. The divorce court should be supplied with interprofessional personnel, tools and sanctions to enable it to cope with this most serious of domestic problems.[69]

The essence of this approach, variously called conciliatory or therapeutic, is that it removes the litigious procedure of accusation and guilt from the courtroom and substitutes a therapeutic procedure of family welfare. The court, in conjunction with experts in the field of family relations, considers not just questions of guilt and injury but the individual and collective welfare of all family members as well.

No such easy solution presents itself for the equally pressing problem of bringing some basic uniformity to the divorce laws of the several jurisdictions. The question is not one of a paucity of solutions but rather of choosing among several. Necessary revisions in the laws could come about as the result of individual efforts by each of the states and territories acting independently. A different approach suggests coöperative efforts of the various jurisdictions acting in concert through model legislation which would serve as a pattern for revision. A third solution is a federal law of divorce. Each of these solutions offers both advantages and pitfalls.

Ideally, in the perspective of our principle of state sovereignty over domestic-relations laws, we should hope for the enlightened self-interest of the several legislatures to produce the necessary modernization and conformity. Experience has shown, however, that such individual efforts rather have the effect of perpetuating the disparity among jurisdictions. Attempts at modernization become bogged down in the mire of conflicting views of various religious, political, and social factions. The recent experiences of New York State with its divorce law furnishes an example of the conflict of interests. Few people conversant with the operation of New York's single-ground divorce law would deny the existence of widespread fraud, perjury, and collusion in proving adultery. Another admitted evil which results from the single-ground law is the excessive use of annulment as a substitute for divorce. One woman, for example, was granted an annulment after thirteen years of marriage because her husband had concealed his be-

[69] John S. Bradway, "New Techniques in the Law," Association of American Law Schools, *Selected Essays on Family Law*, Brooklyn, The Foundation Press, 1950, p. 891.

lief in communism from her.[70] But while there is common agreement among many legal, social, and religious leaders that the laws need revision, any attempts to liberalize the law are met with immediate censure and condemnation by some religious and social factions which argue in favor of even stricter laws. These same forces have at times opposed even study of the laws by a commission for the purpose of discerning the needs, if any, of revision. In 1953, 1954, and 1955, bills were introduced into the New York legislature by Senator Dutton S. Peterson, a Methodist pastor, and Assemblywoman Janet Hill Gordon, asking that such a group be commissioned. The basic purpose was merely to analyze the divorce and matrimonial legislation of the state. Despite the active support of the New York State Council of Churches, the New York Board of Rabbis, the Bar of the City of New York, and many other organizations and individuals, the bill failed to win a majority in any of the three sessions. The principal opposition to the bill came from the New York State Catholic Welfare Commission, which argued that this was an attempt to liberalize the divorce laws.[71] The Catholic Welfare Commission did, however, support a set of five bills and a constitutional amendment introduced in 1954, for the purpose of tightening the divorce and annulment laws, as a response to those elements trying to liberalize the laws.[72] These bills resulted in a change in the law concerning annulments based on fraud which set a three-year limit on annulments dating from the *discovery* of the fraud by the injured party.[73] No legislation has as yet been enacted to prevent a person married thirty years from "discovering" an impediment after twenty-seven years of marriage.

New York's inability to satisfy all of the conflicting interests of religious, civic, and political factions is not an isolated incident. All jurisdictions are faced with this same problem and must necessarily seek some coöperative or centralized direction in revitalizing the laws of domestic relations.

UNIFORM MARRIAGE AND DIVORCE LAWS

Two possibilities exist for establishing nation-wide uniformity in our marriage and divorce laws: federal rather than state control of marital-relations legislation, and interstate coöperation in providing model laws to serve as examples of revision and future enactment of

---

[70] *The New York Times*, June 24, 1954, p. 39.
[71] *The New York Times*, January 21, 1955, p. 15.
[72] *Ibid.*, March 9, 1954, p. 19.
[73] *Ibid.*, April 15, 1954, p. 24.

statutes by the sovereign jurisdictions. Since the power to regulate marriage and divorce derives from the police power of the states, an amendment to the Constitution would probably be necessary to allow the Congress to legislate in this area. Attempts to produce such amendments have met with total failure to date. The most comprehensive movement in this direction came under the direction of Senator Arthur Capper of Kansas, who tried throughout his career in the Senate to initiate such an amendment. His first resolution on the subject was introduced in 1921 and almost annually after that time. In December of 1937, he proposed that "The Congress shall have power to make laws, which shall be uniform throughout the United States, on marriage and divorce, the legitimization of children, and the care and custody of children affected by annulment of marriage or divorce." The future of such attempts seems dark. At present a uniform, federal law of marriage and divorce would either have to offend some sections of the country by directly making changes in their social conception of marriage and divorce or it would have to be so watered down that it would be little better than the present diversity.

The model-law method of bringing uniformity through the coöperative efforts of the several jurisdictions presents the most promising approach at present. If the states could even agree upon uniform procedure in such matters as advance-notice laws, residence requirements for divorce, and premarital health examinations, many of the present reasons for migratory marriage and divorce and most of the resultant problems would disappear. The promotion of such uniformity has been one of the basic objectives of the previously mentioned National Conference of Commissioners on Uniform State Laws. First organized in 1892, the annual conference is composed of from one to five commissioners appointed by the governors of each state. At each conference, bills are drafted by committees and, if approved by the commissioners of at least twenty states and by the American Bar Association, the laws are released and are presented to the various legislatures as models. There is, of course, no obligation upon the legislatures to accept all or any of the provisions, but the hope of the Conference is that its research and coöperative insight will produce basic uniformity of statutes. In 1911, the Conference adopted a Uniform License Act defining the essentials of proper licensing and giving detailed provisions concerning their incorporation into the law. Again, in 1912 it adopted a Uniform Marriage Evasion Act aimed at reducing migratory marriages. While the Uniform Licensing Act made some headway and

was adopted by several states and served as a model for other states, the Uniform Marriage Evasion Act never was widely accepted and some of the states which adopted it have since dropped it.

Efforts for uniform divorce laws also have a respectable antiquity. As early as 1906, a conference of forty-two jurisdictions was called in an effort to halt the increase of migratory divorces. Backed by the American Bar Association, the conference drew up a proposed model divorce law, but only three states adopted this law and it has since passed into oblivion. Efforts since that time have met with little more success. Despite the failure of such model acts in the past, the concerted action of interstate study groups and the pressures for uniformity which are reaching a growing intensity from the American Bar Association, social work groups, social scientists, and jurists should result in at least basic uniformity in the future. It is virtually impossible to legislate rapid change in an area as sensitive as the marital relationship, but the success of such agencies as the Public Health Service in *educating* the legislatures and the citizenry concerning the need for premarital health-examination legislation suggests that progress, no matter how slow, is possible.

Family Legislation: Concluding Remarks

This chapter has purposed to describe the essential features of our polyglottous system of matrimonial and divorce legislation. Even the most dedicated states' rightist, confronted with this bewildering jumble of usages, must grant the need for revision in favor of greater conformity. But even the reduction of the confusion caused by multiple jurisdiction would not solve the greater problem of the lag of our marriage and divorce laws behind current social behavior.

The modern family is beset on all sides by constantly varying pressures of social and economic origin which operate to tear it asunder. Extrafamilial interests, lack of identification with kin, adjustment to a culture which glorifies individualism, are only a few of the elements in the modern American cultural pattern which operate to weaken marital and family ties. Yet our society still holds as inviolable the principles of stability and continuity in family living. It is the purpose of all matrimonial law to ensure this stability and continuity and of divorce law to allow for an orderly dissolution and readjustment when the marriage has been disrupted. The legislation we have just viewed represents an attempt to produce these ends through laws which were construed in an agrarian society lacking the complexity of modern

multigroup culture. Now, in any society, simple or complex, the law cannot be a thing apart, divorced from the social and economic milieu within which individuals must strive and behave. Laws do not function in a vacuum; neither can they be produced in one. A conservative, absolute legal system can produce stability by fiat, but it is an artificial stability based upon forced compliance to tradition and precedent. What is needed is a *science* of jurisprudence which, through adequate research by legislative bodies and the courts, in consultation with behavioral scientists, social workers, psychiatrists, and others expert in the study of human behavior, could produce a legal code in close articulation to the general welfare and needs of the people.

At best, however, the state can do little to *make* marriages secure. In the final analysis, it is the mores, not the legal norms, which set the acceptable standards of marital behavior. Those attitudes and values which produce stable marriages and secure families are the result of a long educational process beginning with each individual's early family-life experiences. It is in this early experience, modified and extended by extrafamilial influences such as religion, peer-group relations, and the mass media of communication, that one acquires the attitudes toward marriage and family living which serve as the basis for his future concepts of family living. Secure, happy families tend to produce stable families in the next generation by adequately preparing children for adult marital roles. Where these values and attitudes are missing or inadequate, the law can do little to order family life.

SELECTED REFERENCES

Association of American Law Schools, *Selected Essays on Family Law*, Brooklyn, The Foundation Press, 1950.

Baber, Ray E., *Marriage and the Family*, New York, McGraw-Hill Book Company, 1954.

Clarke, Helen I., *Social Legislation*, New York, Appleton-Century-Crofts, 1940.

Harper, Fowler G., *Problems of the American Family*, New Haven, Yale University Press, 1954.

Sahra, T. Knox, *The Family and the Law*, Chapel Hill, University of North Carolina Press, 1941.

Vernier, Chester G., *American Family Laws*, Stanford University, Stanford University Press, 4 vols., 1931–1936.

chapter 8

Family Legislation:
The Parent-Child Relationship

In Chapter 6 we examined the relationship among parents, children, and society, and the community's concern over the proper performance of parent-child roles. We observed that all societies charge the parents, or some kin substitute, with the care and social orientation of the children and require varying degrees of submission on the part of children to parental authority. In this chapter we shall look into the legislation which American jurisdictions have enacted to ensure the proper performance of these roles and to allow for some alternative where the parent-child relationship has not or cannot be appropriately fulfilled.

The fundamental and sensitive nature of the parent-child bond has made society reluctant to interfere, and it usually has done so only in extreme situations such as illegitimacy, parental neglect, or adoption. Even so, the amount of legislation in this area of family law is surprisingly large. As with marital-relations law, the large number of jurisdictions has resulted in a variety of statutes often quite dissimilar. Our approach must again be one of summarization and classification of laws whose goals are similar although the means of attainment differ. We shall describe the common characteristics of state and federal legislation affecting (1) rights and duties of parents and children, (2) illegitimacy and paternity proceedings, (3) adoption and guardianship, (4) fertility controls and parenthood, (5) child-welfare services, and (6) juvenile and family courts.[1]

---

[1] Principal sources for legislation were (1) the Women's Bureau publications: *The Legal Status of Women in the United States of America as of January 1, 1948,* for each state and the District of Columbia (Nos. 157–1 through 157–49), the summary volumes for the series, *The Legal Status of Women, United States Summary,* (No. 157–Revised), *Reports and Summary for the Territories and Possessions* (No. 157–50), and

Some important areas of legislation affecting children have been omitted from this chapter since they are more logically included in other chapters. Thus, child-welfare legislation concerning foster care, social casework, aid to dependent children, maternal and child health, and services to handicapped children will be discussed in Chapter 16.

The Rights and Duties of Parents and Children

While society defines the reciprocal rights and duties of parents and children, it is the responsibility of the state, operating through its laws, to give these standards the force of law. Recent American tendencies have been toward decreasing the once complete authority of the father while increasing the rights of the mother and of the child. At common law, the father was given almost complete authority over the custody, control, and services of his minor children while the mother was entitled only to their respect and reverence. What rights the child enjoyed were socially rather than legally protected, since the common-law courts did not feel qualified to interfere against the father in the child's behalf.[2] Furthermore, unless the father, through some fault of his own, contributed to the delinquency or injury of the child, his rights to custody could not be removed even in favor of the mother. Neither poverty, lack of industry, nor want of competence was sufficient ground for his disqualification.

This harsh common-law treatment of the dependent members of the family was never completely accepted in the United States. Our early laws and court decisions did grant the father the primary right to the custody and control of his children, but this bias is disappearing in the wake of growing emphasis upon the welfare of the child as the ultimate concern in parent-child laws. Basically, the parent has a right or interest in the custody, control, and earnings of his minor

the addenda to the individual state bulletins (No. 157–1 through 157–50), which include pertinent statutory changes and additions to the 1948 data up to January 1, 1953; (2) Chester G. Vernier, *American Family Laws*, Vol. IV, *Parent and Child*, Stanford University, Stanford University Press, 1936; (3) American Association of Social Workers, *Social Work Year Book*, New York, The Association, 10th, 11th, and 12th issues, 1952, 1953, and 1954; (4) Council of State Governments, *The Book of the States*, Chicago, the Council, 1954–55; (5) American Association of Law Schools, *Selected Essays on Family Law*, Brooklyn, The Foundation Press, 1950; (6) *Martindale-Hubbel Law Directory*, Martindale-Hubbell Inc., Summit, N.J., 1954, Vol. III; (7) pertinent legal and social-work professional journals; (8) various publications of the Children's Bureau, the Social Security Administration, and the Public Health Service; and (9) press and magazine coverage of recent judicial decisions in cases concerning the parent-child relationship.

[2] Roscoe Pound, "Individual Interests in Domestic Relations," Association of American Law Schools, *Selected Essays on Family Law*, Brooklyn, The Foundation Press, 1950, pp. 9–11.

child. His duties to the child, which are therefore the rights of the child, are for his support, protection, and education during minority.

PARENTAL RIGHTS TO CUSTODY, CONTROL, AND EARNINGS

The right to the custody of a minor child is vested in his biological parents, unless they are unfit, as natural guardians. All fifty-three jurisdictions have laws affecting this custody which provide for the removal of dependent, neglected, or delinquent children when it is deemed necessary for the welfare of the child and the community. By 1953, twenty-nine states had recognized, generally, both the father and mother as the joint natural guardians of their legitimate, unmarried children and so jointly entitled to their services and earnings as well.[3] In the eight community-property states,[4] where French, Spanish, or Mexican community-property traditions govern ownership rights within the marital relationship, the earnings of the child are part of the community and so owned mutually by the parents while living together.[5] The control of the property, however, and hence of the child's earnings as part of that property, is generally controlled by the father in these states, except in Nevada under certain circumstances.[6] California has recently declared by statute that the father is not superior to the mother in matters of custody, control, and education while the parents live separate and apart from each other.[7] Sixteen states and territories continue to give preference to the father in regard to the custody, earnings, and service of the children, although the mother succeeds to this right upon his death and, in some states, if he is found to be mentally incompetent or has deserted his family.[8]

The mother is the natural guardian of an illegitimate child and will usually be appointed guardian of his property unless there is evidence that this would be contrary to the welfare of the child or the community. If the father is known, he usually has superior rights to the custody of the child after the death of the mother and may be appointed as guardian at that time.

[3] Women's Bureau, The Legal Status of Women, United States Summary, (Bulletin No. 157–Revised as of January 1, 1951), p. 72, and addenda indicating changes up to January 1, 1953.

[4] Arizona, California, Idaho, Louisiana, Nevada, New Mexico, Texas, and Washington.

[5] Women's Bureau, op. cit. (1951), p. 272, and addenda.

[6] Ibid.

[7] Women's Bureau, "Addendum to Bull. 157–5—The Legal Status of Women in the United States of America, January 1, 1948, Report for California, as of January 1, 1953."

[8] Women's Bureau, The Legal Status of Women, United States Summary (1951), p. 272, and addenda.

Ordinarily, the legal question of custody does not arise unless (1) the marital relationship of the parents has been destroyed by death or legally dissolved; (2) there is some question as to the welfare of the child, as a result of dependency, neglect, or delinquency; or (3) he is mentally or physically handicapped. We have previously indicated that where the child's welfare or health is threatened, all jurisdictions allow for his removal from the parents. After separation or divorce, the custody of the child becomes a question as a result of the physical dissolution of his home. At common law, custody was usually awarded to the father, but today the courts have broad discretionary power in deciding which parent receives custody. The court may award custody to either parent or even to third parties if its appraisal of the situation reveals that this would best serve the interests of the child. If the child is old enough, his wishes may also be consulted.

If the parents remarry after the divorce, or if their respective financial conditions are materially altered, the custody decree may be reviewed to determine what effects the new conditions may have in making pertinent a reappraisal of the child's welfare. Similar action may be taken as the child grows older or if the parent awarded custody is subsequently found to be unfit.

With the parental right to the child's earnings at common law went the right to employ the child in the homestead or even in the community and to collect his wages. At present, however, the employment of minor children outside the home is subject to state and federal child-labor laws which affect this right. Another variation from the common law is the provision, found in several states, that the earnings of a minor child are not seizable for the debts of his parents.[9]

The right of the parent to punish and correct his child was established under the common law holding that the father was within his rights if he acted with moderation. About one-third of the jurisdictions currently have statutes dealing with parents' rights to punish and correct their children, but all fifty-three allow for the removal of the child when his welfare is threatened, which would normally include excessive or abusive punishment by the parent. Under early English common law the child could not bring suit against the father and, indeed, could not bring any suit except through his guardian. Several states have enacted legislation which permits the child to bring suit against the parent for excessive punishment or failure to fulfill his parental responsibilities, but most frequently it is through some third

[9] Vernier, op. cit., Vol. IV, p. 21.

party, such as a social agency or court, that such actions are initiated. The many states having criminal statutes concerning excessive punishment, injury, and neglect are again interjecting the state as a third party in the relationship between parent and child.

PARENTS' RIGHTS AGAINST THIRD PARTIES

Generally, the parents are not held responsible for the wrongdoing or negligence of their children. Should the child commit a tort without the express or implied knowledge and authority of his parents, they ordinarily could not be held accountable. Even the recent efforts to make parents legally responsible and accountable for repeated delinquency of their offspring have proceeded from the legal assumption of their negligence rather than their accountability.

Neither are parents generally responsible for a child's contracts made without their being parties to the contract. A minor child is responsible for necessaries, such as food, clothing, and medicines, furnished to him only if it can be demonstrated that he is obliged to obtain them for himself. In general, all other contracts by minors may be avoided, although Washington makes the minor wife of an adult husband legally bound by her contracts, and in Indiana a minor husband or wife may make a valid real estate contract in conjunction with the adult spouse with proper court approval.[10]

Where some third party wrongfully injures the child, the parents, in addition to the child, may bring suit under some circumstances. The child, for example, may sue for injuries received from some third party concurrently with a suit by the parent for the loss of services he has incurred as a result of the incapacitation of the child. The parent's legal right to the services of his child places the minor and even mature children who live at home in a master-servant relationship with him, and he therefore has a right to sue if he is deprived of these services.

An important outgrowth of this legal reasoning is the parental prerogative of bringing suit against a third party for the seduction or debauchment of his daughter or the abduction of any of his children. In the case of seduction, the common-law precedent seems more concerned with the loss of the daughter's services than her honor, for the basis of such suits is the father's right to just compensation for the loss of the daughter's services. In addition, the parent may also sue the wrongdoer for the shame and disgrace brought to his family and

---

[10] Women's Bureau, *op. cit.* (1951), p. 37, and addenda.

even for the corrupting example set for his other children. If aggravating circumstances are involved, punitive damages may also be levied as a social deterrent to other prospective seducers. Usually, if the girl is a minor her age is sufficient to establish her servitude, but if she is an adult the father must demonstrate that she was in his service. The seduction action is usually available to legal guardians and others acting in the place of the parents and so entitled to the child's services.

PARENTAL RIGHT TO SUPPORT FROM THE CHILD

While the common law places no burden upon the child to support even indigent parents, most American jurisdictions have done so by statute. Most make the child civilly liable for the support of indigent parents, a few criminally liable, and others make such failure to support both a civil and criminal liability. Other statutes may be found which make grandchildren and brothers and sisters responsible for paupers.[11] In all cases, however, the relative must be unable to support himself and it must be established that the liable individual is able to supply the necessary support. Some jurisdictions specifically exempt married women living with their husbands from liability.[12] The importance of these laws will be discussed in a later chapter in connection with the state's ability to require support of indigent parents applying for old-age assistance.

THE RIGHTS OF THE CHILD TO SUPPORT, PROTECTION, AND EDUCATION

As a result of the parent's right to the custody, control, and services of his minor children, they enjoy the reciprocal rights to support, protection, and education from the father. As we have previously observed, these rights of the child against the parent have been secured through social rather than legal sanctions, and where they exist in modern law they are likely to be in terms of the parent's liability to third persons rather than directly to the child. The common-law reluctance toward direct intervention in the child's behalf is well exemplified in Lord Eldon's famous dictum in the Wellesley case that "The courts of law can enforce the rights of the father but they are not equal to the office of enforcing the duties of the father." [13]

This extreme condition has been overcome in American jurisdictions through legislation and judicial interpretation. The courts have usually held that the father is legally liable for the support of his

[11] Vernier, op. cit., Vol. IV, p. 93.
[12] Ibid.
[13] Wellesley v. Duke of Beaufort, 2 Russ. 1, 23 (1827).

minor children even after the marriage has been dissolved. All jurisdictions have statutes which establish the criminal liability of the father for nonsupport of his children, and all save Kansas have civil statutes as well.[14] These provisions were usually made under the poor-relief laws and generally allow for the institution of court action by (1) civil officials of state, county, or municipal governments, (2) relatives, (3) the pauper himself, and in some cases any of the foregoing.[15] Many states also have laws which authorize juvenile or other courts having jurisdiction to order support of dependent, neglected, or delinquent children while they are in the care of a social agency or institution.

Today, the father's criminal liability for the nonsupport of his children is usually a part of the state's family-desertion law, which establishes parental nonsupport as a crime. The age of the child usually qualifies the desertion as a criminal action and is most frequently given as "under 16." In recent years, attempts to encourage reciprocal state legislation to enforce support of dependents where the father has deserted out of the state have had considerable success. After New York State's pioneering attempts in 1948, the National Conference of Commissioners on Uniform State Laws promulgated a Uniform Reciprocal Enforcement of Support Act at its 1950 sessions. Since that time the number of states and territories adopting this uniform act has grown rapidly, so that by 1955 every state but Nevada had adopted the law or some amended form.[16] Basically, these laws provide that the person to whom support duty is owed must petition the designated court in her home jurisdiction. Upon verification of the petition, the court certifies and forwards the petition to the corresponding court in the jurisdiction in which the deserter or person owing support has taken refuge. The responding state court takes jurisdiction of the case, ascertains whether and how much support duty is owed, and enters the appropriate support order. The court is also authorized to take depositions if the individual denies his liability.[17] The constitutional validity of these laws has been upheld in several state courts.[18]

[14] Women's Bureau, op. cit. (1951), p. 76, and addenda.
[15] Vernier, op. cit., Vol. IV, p. 57.
[16] Council of State Governments, op. cit., Vol. X, p. 147, and Martindale-Hubbel Law Directory, 1955, Vol. III.
[17] Brevard E. Crihfield, "Recent Developments in Reciprocal Support Legislation," Social Casework, March, 1955, p. 114.
[18] Duncan v. Smith, 262 Ky. S.W.2 d 373 (1953); Smith v. Smith, 270 Cal. P2d (1954); Commonwealth v. Shaffer, 103 Pa. A2d 430 (1954); and Warren v. Warren, 105 Md. A2d 488 (1954).

The extreme treatment and overconcern with property protection of the early English common law combined to deny the illegitimate child any rights to support from either father or mother. Under the present common law, the mother, as the child's natural guardian, is usually held responsible for his support, although there is still no legal obligation for support from the father unless paternity has been established through bastardy proceedings. In each of the fifty-three jurisdictions except Idaho, Missouri, and Texas, some statutory provision has been made to charge the father with support after paternity has been legally established.[19] The amount, terms, and duration of this support, however, vary widely among the several states and territories. Many states also provide that the adjudicated father may be required to contribute to the expenses occasioned by the birth of his child. A few states even provide for the imprisonment of the mother of an illegitimate child who refuses to divulge the name of the father or to furnish security for the child's support.[20]

There is little direct statutory legislation dealing with the support and maintenance of children in divorce actions. Unless they are denied custody as a result of unfitness, the duty of each parent to support the child continues as before the divorce and is generally the father's responsibility.

The common-law background of the child's right to protection by his parents was permissive rather than directory. That is to say, the father was *permitted* to use force and even homicide to protect the child, but the child had no legal right to expect that he would. Some states currently have laws which direct parental protection by making parents legally liable for their negligence in providing necessaries, including medical attention. Thus, if a parent refuses to obtain necessary medical attention for his children because of religious principles, he may be held liable and the child may be taken from his custody.

At common law the parent was responsible for the education and training of the child in so far as the familial status in life permitted, but there is some question as to whether this parental obligation was legally or morally sanctioned.[21] Modern American legislation dealing with compulsory school attendance, child labor, and the neglect clauses in juvenile-court laws has currently established this responsibility as a legal as well as a moral obligation.

[19] Women's Bureau, op. cit. (1951), p. 76, and addenda.
[20] Ibid.
[21] Pound, op. cit., p. 9.

The compulsory attendance of children at schools is provided for by state laws. This state prerogative is an outgrowth of the early principle that education is a state rather than a federal function, which led the framers of the Constitution to leave the chief responsibility for the establishment of school systems to the individual states. In a later chapter, we shall observe that many states still jealously guard their suzerainty against any suggestion of federal intervention in educational matters. This sensitivity is particularly potent in the areas of elementary and secondary education.

Every jurisdiction has laws which require school attendance by children between certain ages. Nearly all require this attendance for the entire school terms, but a few define the requirement in terms of a specified number of days per year. The laws usually refer to day school, but some jurisdictions also have laws requiring attendance of working children at night or continuation schools on a part-time basis. A few states have made the failure of the parents to provide the child with proper education a crime.

The age by which a normal child must have begun to attend day school varies between 6 and 8, but most frequently is placed at 7 years of age.[22] The child must usually attend school until he is 16 years old, although some states require attendance to the age of 17 or 18, making special exemptions for employed children beyond 16 years of age. This does not mean, however, that the laws declare that *all* children must attend school until they have attained the specified minimum age of termination. Many states allow for the exemption of children who have completed a certain grade in school and are above some specified age but below the statutory age of termination. Generally, these exemptions concern children who are needed at home for farm or domestic chores, have encountered emergencies in the home, or are required to leave school as a result of parental poverty. Recent legislation has attempted to do away with these exemptions, which were necessary under an agrarian economy in which children were needed seasonally for farmwork but have little justification in an age which demands an ever increasing amount of education for responsible adulthood.

Many states have also established enforcement facilities through the employment of attendance officers, visiting teachers, and other

[22] Data on compulsory-school-attendance laws from Ward W. Keesecker, *Compulsory School Attendance and Minimum Educational Requirements in the United States,* U.S. Office of Education, rev. March, 1955, by Alfred C. Allen.

personnel charged with the responsibility of aiding parents and children to utilize the available educational facilities to the maximum. Theoretically, at least, these enforcement officers are a far cry from the old truant officer, whose function was punitive and centered upon enforced attendance. The modern philosophy holds that a preventive program, aimed at discovering the causes of individual truancy, working with the child and the parent to correct the situation, and checking it before it develops into serious delinquency, is most effective. Such an approach obviously demands the employment of only fully qualified attendance officers and visiting teachers who have the necessary specialized training in educational guidance.

PARENTS AND CHILDREN: RESPECTIVE RIGHTS TO INHERITANCE

An important area of legislation which has meaning for marital, parent-child, and sibling relationships is our laws controlling inheritance. These laws have their origin in the common law of England or, in some cases, French and Spanish community-property tradition. While there is a considerable difference between the common law and community-property law of inheritance, all jurisdictions have enacted legislation dealing with the descent of property and, in general, it is these laws which govern inheritance.

At common law, a surviving husband or wife does not take an absolute inheritance in the real property of the deceased spouse. In the absence of a will, the claims of "dower" and "curtesy" were provided by law to regulate inheritance within the marital relationship. Dower refers to the widow's right to have for the remainder of her life the use of or income from one-third of the lands belonging to her husband during their marriage. A valid marriage is required to establish the wifely right to dower, but there is no requirement of issue to the marriage. Generally, the dower claim is superior to any liens or mortgages against the property in which the widow did not join. While this dower right cannot be disposed of by the husband's will, the wife may herself relinquish it by an antenuptial arrangement (jointure) or by conveying the property, in joint action with her husband, to some third party during the marriage. The husband's entitlement through a valid marriage to his wife's estate is called curtesy and, unlike dower rights, is conditioned by the live birth of a child who might inherit from the mother.

Today, where a married man dies without making a will, the disposition of his real and personal property is dependent upon the jurisdic-

tion in which he lives. There is considerable variety among these statutes, but they may be summarized as follows:

I. Where the deceased person leaves lineal descendants:
  A. Some states make no mention of the surviving spouse, who must, therefore, claim dower or curtesy rights or the statutory substitute for it in their jurisdiction.
  B. Some give the widow or widower equal shares in both real and personal property. The amount of the share varies according to the jurisdiction.
  C. Other states give equal rights to a widow or widower, but the share of the real property differs from that of the personal property of the deceased.
  D. In other states the widow, under certain circumstances, receives a larger share of the estate of a deceased husband than would a widower.
II. Where the deceased leaves no lineal descendants, but is survived by his relatives:
  A. In some states the surviving spouse takes the whole real- and personal-property estate of the deceased spouse.
  B. In other states the surviving spouse takes the entire estate up to a certain fixed value and one-half of all property, real and personal, in excess of this amount.
  C. Some states give the surviving spouse one-half of all real and personal property.
  D. There are miscellaneous provisions in other states.
III. Where neither lineal descendants nor relatives survive:
  A. Some states give the surviving spouse the entire estate, with certain exceptions in the case of parents.
  B. Others give the survivor the entire estate if there is no issue, parent, brother, sister, or descendant of a deceased brother or sister.
  C. Other states give the surviving spouse the entire estate if there are no blood relatives or heirs.
  D. There are other and varied provisions in the remaining states.
IV. Where the deceased is survived by neither spouse, lineal descendant, nor relatives:
  A. In all cases the estate is escheated to the state.[23]

A majority of the states have statutes which provide that husbands and wives may not be disinherited by the will. The surviving spouse

[23] Based upon John S. Bradway, "What Family Members Should Know About Law," Howard Becker and Reuben Hill (eds.), *Family, Marriage and Parenthood*, Boston, D. C. Heath and Company, 1955, pp. 482–483, and Women's Bureau, *op. cit.* (1951), p. 54.

may renounce the will in favor of the common-law right to dower or curtesy or any statutory share of the estate which replaces these common-law provisions. In the community-property states, there are no restrictions upon the will of either spouse in disposing of their separate property. The statutory portion of the community estate provided for husband or wife cannot be disturbed by the will of either, however, unless the other consents.[24]

Unlike the many societies which have age and sex restrictions upon the rights of inheritance of children, no such rules as primogeniture or ultimogeniture exist in American jurisdictions. Neither age, birth order, nor sex may disqualify a legitimate child from his equal share of the parents' estate. Nor is any legal distinction made concerning adoptive children, who inherit equally with the biological children of the deceased. A child unborn at the time of his father's death also shares equally in the estate even if no provision is made for him in the father's will.

Under the common law, parents and all other lineal ancestors were excluded from inheriting the estate of a child dying intestate. The early statutes in the United States, however, deviated from this rule to allow fathers to inherit from intestate children. The mother might inherit only such lands as came to the child through her ancestral line. This distinction has also disappeared, and there are no longer any distinctions made in the respective rights of parents to inherit from intestate legitimate offspring who die without descendants. A number of states give preference, however, to the surviving spouse over the claims of surviving parents.[25]

Illegitimate offspring had rights of inheritance from neither father nor mother under the early common law, but today it is well established that they may inherit from their mothers, and in a few states from her kin. A few states also provide for rights of inheritance from the father if he is known. The prohibition against inheritance from intestate children under the common law was equally true in the case of illegitimacy. Neither father, mother, nor lineal ancestors had any claim to an illegitimate's estate. At present, however, practically every jurisdiction allows the mother of an illegitimate child to inherit from his estate. In a few states the father may also share in the estate if he has acknowledged his paternity, but the mother and her heirs usually have prior rights to inheritance.

24 Women's Bureau, op. cit. (1951), p. 60.
25 Women's Bureau, op. cit. (1951), and addenda.

Adoption and the Guardian-Ward Relationship

The rights and duties acquired by natural parenthood may also be procured through legally assigned parenthood. This legal proceeding, called adoption, confers upon the child and the adoptive parents the legal relationship of parent and child. It has the social effects of providing a home and security for children whose natural parents cannot, for some reason, provide such an environment, and offering the satisfactions of the parental status to all couples desiring children.

While the practice of adoption has a background in antiquity—evidence of its use in ancient Babylonia, Egypt, Greece, and Rome being well established—there is no common-law basis for such legal paternity. In fact, it was not until the passage of the Adoption of Children Act in 1926 that statutory recognition was given adoption in England. There were, however, adoption statutes in the early history of the United States, but these provided for adoption by means of formally executed private instruments with none of the protective participation of the courts required by present adoptive practices. The intention of these early American laws seems to have been the neutral one of providing some legal, public record of the transfer of the child from his biological parents to the adopting parents. The role of the court as the guardian of the welfare of the child and both sets of parents did not emerge until later legislation was enacted.

There is some question as to the origin of court-centered adoption law in the United States. Texas and Alabama both passed legislation in 1850 dealing with adoption, but the concern of these laws seems to have been more with the heirship of the child than with any judicial protection of his welfare. Massachusetts in 1851 passed what is generally accepted as the first adoption law incorporating judicial ratification and following the current conception of child protection. Since that time each of the fifty-three jurisdictions has adopted some form of adoption legislation. These statutes, which have their roots in the Roman law, govern local adoptive procedure, which must be carried out in strict conformity to the laws of each particular jurisdiction. As in most areas of family law, the statutes vary widely among the states and territories, but certain principles are common.

CURRENT ADOPTION LAW AND PROCEDURE

All jurisdictions now have statutes requiring court proceedings in adoption, but there is some diversity in the court given jurisdiction. The current trend is toward giving jurisdiction to the juvenile courts

or specialized domestic-relations and family courts, particularly where the child is already in their legal care as a result of having been adjudicated a dependent, neglected, or delinquent child. A majority of the states, however, still give jurisdiction to probate, district, or county courts, which are not oriented to social-work principles and child-welfare concepts, and which often have little other contact with child and family welfare problems.[26]

There is also some variation in the procedure followed in adoption cases, but the steps followed are generally the same. The adopting parents must initiate a formal petition to the court, setting forth pertinent information concerning the child and both adoptive and biological parents. In essence, this petition requests the court to issue an adoption order transferring the parental role to the new legal parents. Notice must be given to the child's biological parents or their substitute in order to ensure their awareness of the proposed adoption, and it is also necessary to obtain the consent of certain interested parties. Generally, consent must be obtained from:

1. The child. If the child is considered old enough to give valid consent, it is required in almost every jurisdiction. The age necessary for such consent also varies among the jurisdictions, but is most frequently 14, less frequently 12.

2. The biological parents. Usually, the voluntary consent of both natural parents is required unless this is impossible or their parental rights have previously been legally removed. The courts have been very firm in their requirement that the parents must have forfeited their parental rights before adoption can take place in the absence of their consent.[27] Consent is usually not required from the father of an illegitimate child and adoption can usually take place with only the mother's consent. Other instances in which the parental consent is usually not required include abandonment of the child, transfer of the child to some public or social agency, parental lack of ability to give consent due to mental incapacity, habitual drunkenness of the parent, and where the parent has been divorced because of his or her adultery. As a general rule, however, court adjudication is necessary to remove the parental right to withhold consent.[28]

3. Guardians or others acting in place of the parents. Where the

[26] Cf. Children's Bureau, *Essentials of Adoption Law and Procedure*, Children's Bureau Publication No. 331, 1949, pp. 11–12.

[27] See, for example, Hershey v. Hershey, 271 Mass. 545 171 N.E. 815, 70 A.L.R. 518 (1930).

[28] See In re Mathew's Will, 198 Wis. 128, 233 N.W. 434 (1928).

child's natural parents cannot or need not give consent, the consent of the guardian or social agency having custody and control of the child is needed. If no guardian has been appointed subsequent to the death of the natural parents, the court will appoint a "friend" of the child or authorize the state welfare department to act as a parent substitute. Many states allow the parents to place the child in a licensed child-placement agency and to release all rights to the child. In such cases it is the consent of the child-placement agency which is required for adoption.

Another important step often required in the procedure is a social investigation into the situation surrounding the prospective adoption. Ideally, these investigations consider the physical and mental health of the child and the physical and psychological environments of both parental and adoptive homes. The results of this inquiry, along with the testimony of the various interested parties appearing at the adoption hearing, form the basis for the judicial decision.

The adoption order may be final or, as in roughly half of modern jurisdictions, interlocutory for a period ranging from six months to one year. The judge may, of course, deny a petition for adoption, in which case the custody and control of the child remain unchanged. The most frequently encountered reasons for denial are (1) religious or racial differences between the child and prospective adoptive parents, (2) lack of legal marriage by the prospective parents, (3) unsuitable home life or the presence of disease in the adoptive home, and (4) physical or mental disqualification of the child as adoptable.[29] In practice, however, these legal disqualifications are most frequently encountered before the petition is ever initiated, and the prospective parents' attorney or some social agency with which they have come in contact will dissuade them from seeking adoption in such circumstances.

Probably the most controversial of these prohibitions are the many statutes which forbid or discourage adoption across religious lines. Even where the statutes do not directly forbid such adoptions, child placement and judicial practice may achieve the same results. Despite the arbitrary and needless barrier which such laws place in the path of childless couples unable to find adoptable children of their own faith, the courts have upheld these prohibitions. As recently as 1955, the U.S. Supreme Court gave them added support by declining to hear

29 Vernier, op. cit., Vol. IV, pp. 280–286.

the appeal of a Jewish couple whose application to adopt two Catholic twins had earlier been denied by a probate court in Massachusetts.[30] The natural mother of the children, who were born out of wedlock, had agreed to the adoption and to the rearing of the children in the Jewish faith, but to no avail.[31] But even a promise on the part of the adoptive parents to rear the child in the faith of the natural parents does not seem to be sufficient to overcome these laws. A few months after the case described above, a similar one arose again in Massachusetts. In this instance, a Jewish couple attempted to adopt a 4-year-old girl whom they had reared as foster parents from the age of ten days. They were ordered by the court to return the child for placement in a Catholic home despite their offer to rear the child as a Catholic. When they failed to return the child within the allotted period of time, the court issued an order for their arrest.[32]

Once the adoption order has become final, the new parents acquire virtually the same rights as natural parents to the child's custody, control, and earnings. The child in turn receives similar rights to support, protection, and education. Nearly all jurisdictions expressly recognize the court's right to change the child's name if so desired, and most states even allow for a new certificate of birth.[33] All jurisdictions also deal with the rights of inheritance of the foster child. Generally, he may inherit from either of his adoptive parents, and a few states even allow him to inherit from the collateral kin or lineal descendants as well, although he usually may not do so in the absence of such statutes. Over half the jurisdictions also have statutes dealing with the rights of adoptive parents to inherit from their foster children.[34] While most of these laws establish the heirship of the new parents, a very few expressly deny such inheritance to foster parents.[35] A small number of states deny the child any right to a share in the estate of his natural parents, once he has been adopted. In general, however, it would appear that in the absence of any specific statute to the contrary, an adopted child may inherit from his natural and adoptive parents.[36] There are also laws in some states which affect the rights of the natural parents and their relatives to share in the in-

[30] Social Legislation Information Service, February 21, 1955, p. 43.
[31] Ibid.
[32] The New York Times, July 2, 1955, p. 17.
[33] Vernier, op. cit., Vol. IV, p. 453.
[34] Ibid., p. 413.
[35] Ibid.
[36] Ibid., p. 415.

heritance from the child once he has been adopted, but these are both positive and negative depending upon the jurisdiction.[37]

The adoption statutes of many of the states also provide for the annulment of and appeal from the decree even after it has become final. Generally, the provisions for annulment refer to the development of mental defects, epilepsy, insanity, or venereal infection within some stated period following the adoption. A few jurisdictions also make annulment possible where the terms or expectations of the adoption are not fulfilled by either the new parents or the foster child, or in cases where some fraud was involved in the petition or action.

Although adoption is popularly thought of only in connection with infants or young children, a number of states also make provision for the adoption of adults as well. These actions to establish legal parenthood of adults are often for the sole purpose of establishing legal rights of inheritance and do not involve the problems of child welfare and protection.

CURRENT PROBLEMS AND PRACTICES IN ADOPTION

As we have found in most other areas of family legislation, our adoption laws lag well behind scientific knowledge and social concepts. Despite many revisions in recent decades, the Children's Bureau has estimated that only about one-fourth of the states have adoption laws which are adequate with respect to the principles felt to be necessary.[38] These objectives, which succinctly summarize current thought concerning the social role of adoption laws, are:

1. To protect the child from unnecessary separation from parents who might give him a good home and loving care if sufficient help and guidance were available to them; from adoption by persons unfit to have responsibility for rearing a child; and from interference, after he has been happily established in his adoptive home, by his natural parents, who may have some legal claim because of defects in the adoption procedure.
2. To protect the natural parents from hurried decisions to give up a child, made under strain and anxiety.
3. To protect the adopting parents from taking responsibility for children about whose heredity or capacity for physical or mental development they know nothing; from later disturbance of their relationship to the

---

[37] *Ibid.*, pp. 414–415.
[38] Inter-Agency Committee on Background Materials for the National Conference on Family Life, Washington, The Conference, May, 1948, p. 354.

child by natural parents whose legal rights had not been given full consideration.[39]

The growing importance of these problems is testified to by the sharp increases in both the number of adoptions and the number of parents seeking to adopt children. It is estimated that the number of adoption petitions probably reached 90,000 in 1953—80 percent more than in 1944.[40]

It is possible, of course, to make private or voluntary adoptions unsupervised by any social agency. In such situations, the interests of the child and both sets of parents are jeopardized by their careless refusal to accept the skills and safeguards which a professionally staffed child-placement agency can offer. The superiority of the agency system of child placement has been established by research, as shown, for example, in the report of the Yale Child Development Clinic. Its findings indicate that while 75 of 100 Connecticut agency placements studied in 1945 were satisfactory, only 46 of 100 voluntary placements were satisfactory.[41] Since the number of couples wanting to adopt children is estimated at ten times the number of adoptable children, the problem of the private, independent placement becomes acute. Recent scandals involving multimillion-dollar "baby black markets" and clandestine adoptions suggest the abuses possible where social or public agency supervision is not required by law.

The pressure of couples seeking foster children has led to a reconsideration of the once "unadoptable" older or handicapped child. Recent evidence indicates that many children with minor mental or physical handicaps can benefit greatly from the care and affection of a foster home as contrasted with institutional care. Individual cases, of course, may involve such serious handicaps that institutionalization is the only feasible solution. Most prospective foster parents desire babies who are not only mentally and physically sound but are indeed "babies." This has created the problem of the older child, who was for many years considered a poor adoption risk. Today, child-placement agencies are turning increasingly to the opinion that these older children, if properly placed, benefit from the permanent home situation provided by adoption.[42]

[39] Children's Bureau, op. cit. (1949), p. 2.

[40] I. Richard Perlman and Jack Wiener, "Adoption of Children, 1953: A Statistical Analysis," Iowa Law Review, Winter, 1955, pp. 336–349.

[41] Yale Child Development Clinic, Report of Current Adoption Practices in Connecticut-Independent and Agency Placement, New Haven, the Clinic, 1949, passim.

[42] Cf. Ruth Taft, "Adoptive Families for 'Unadoptable' Children," Child Welfare, June, 1953.

Under the leadership of the Child Welfare League of America and the federal Children's Bureau, more uniform and effective practices are gradually spreading throughout the country. In 1948 and again in 1951, the Child Welfare League sponsored national workshops for a self-examination and reëvaluation of practices and procedures and for a consideration of the legal and administrative problems surrounding adoption.[43] Concurrently with these efforts for improvement, the Children's Bureau has prepared an outline of the principles of adoption, which serves as a guide for the necessary repeal and amendment of our conflicting laws of adoption. These principles offer an excellent summary of the necessary changes and the most socially advantageous future directions for our legislatures:

1. The termination of parental rights is as important as the establishment of new parental ties by adoption and should be as securely safeguarded.
2. Placement for adoption should be made only by an agency authorized to make such placements by the State Department of Public Welfare.
3. Adoption proceedings should be in a court of record having jurisdiction over children's cases, in the home state of the petitioners for adoption and preferably in the local community in which they live and are known and where the child is properly before the court.
4. In every proposed adoption of a child the court should have the benefit of a social study and a recommendation made by the State Department of Public Welfare, or by a local Department of Public Welfare or other public or private child-placing agency designated by the State Welfare Department.
5. Consent to adoption should be obtained from the natural parents, or, if their parental rights have been legally relinquished or terminated, from a person or agency having legal responsibility for the child and the right of consent to adoption.
6. Court hearings should be closed to the public and the records, because of their confidential nature, should be protected.
7. A period of residence in the adoptive home, preferably for one year, should be required before the hearing on the petition, so that the suitability of the proposed adoption may be determined.
8. In the event a final decree is not entered, provision should be made for the removal of a child from a home found to be unsuitable and for his care and guardianship after his removal.
9. Safeguards should be provided in related laws, such as those affecting relinquishment of parental rights, regulation of child-placing services, and determination of guardianship and custody of children, to assure

[43] See Child Welfare League of America, *Adoption Practices, Procedures and Problems*, New York, the League, 1952.

the welfare of the child in all such matters as well as in the adoption proceedings and to define the rights and the responsibilities of parents.[44]

GUARDIANSHIP AND WARDSHIP

The guardian-ward relationship is similar to adoption in that the child is legally established in a parent-child-like relationship by the action of a court. It differs significantly, however, in that guardianship affects only the care and custody of the child, with no change resulting in the child's name or rights to inheritance. There are several types of guardianship:

1. A *natural guardian* is a parent lawfully in control of the person of his child.
2. A *legal guardian* is anyone appointed by a proper court over the person, estate, or both of a child.
3. A *public guardian* is a public official empowered to accept court appointment to act as a legal guardian.
4. The terms *tutor* and *curator* are used in some states to describe, respectively, court-appointed guardians of person and guardians of estate.
5. A *testamentary guardian* is anyone designated guardian by the last will and testament of the child's parent.
6. A *guardian ad litem* is one appointed by a court to represent a child in a particular suit or legal proceeding who has no right of control over the child's person or estate.[45]

These various forms of guardianship can be separated into two major categories: (1) guardianship over the child's person and (2) guardianship over the child's estate. The guardian over the child's person becomes responsible for the care, custody, and control of the child and acquires the legal right to make important decisions concerning his ward's adoption, employment, marriage, and other matters respecting his well-being.[46] The guardian of the child's estate, however, has no right to interfere in the personal affairs of the minor, by law confining himself to the "prudent and economical" management of the estate entrusted him.[47] He is answerable to the court for his conduct of the guardianship and subject to its orders and to periodic accounting. In practice, the same person is frequently appointed to the guardianship of both the person and the estate of the minor child.

[44] Children's Bureau, *op. cit.* (1949), pp. 3–4.

[45] Irving Weissman, et al., *Guardianship, A Way of Fulfilling Public Responsibility for Children,* Children's Bureau Publication No. 330–1949 Washington, Government Printing Office, 1949, p. 184.

[46] *Ibid.*, p. 25.

[47] *Ibid.*, p. 26.

The necessity for the guardian-ward relationship results from the legal premise that an infant, or minor child, is incapable of prudent self-care and requires adult supervision. At common law, parents were natural guardians of their child's person but not of his property, yet the child was not generally considered capable of handling his own property. When some situation arose which required the appointment of a guardian over the minor child's property, as when he inherited from grandparents, his natural parents were given preference in appointment, but there was no legal right on their part, nor could the parent appoint a guardian for either the person or the property of his child under the early common law. It was not until the statutes of Charles II, in 1660, that the father was given the power to appoint a testamentary guardian, but no such power was invested in the mother.[48]

With the exception of Louisiana, early American jurisdictions followed the common-law position and the statutory changes made by Charles II concerning guardianship. The early statutes did, however, simplify the English law by reducing the types of guardians and minimizing the procedural regulations concerning their appointment and supervision.[49] They maintained the common-law emphasis of property protection rather than any concept of child welfare. These early statutes, among the first laws enacted affecting the child, have since received little legislative attention except to equalize the testamentary rights of the mother.[50] Today, the parental role still does not authorize either father or mother to take control over the property of their children without an express mandate from the court. Where such appointment is necessary, most jurisdictions allow either parent to qualify for appointment, although a few states still give preference to the father.[51] In Virginia and Florida, the mother is only eligible where the estate is a small one.[52] In the states lacking statutory mention of the respective rights of the father and mother, the paternal preference promulgated in the Charles II statutes continues.

The mother of an illegitimate child now has guardianship over his person and will usually be appointed as guardian of his property. Upon

---

[48] 12 Charles II, Ch. 24 (1660).
[49] Weissman et al., op. cit., p. 16.
[50] Hasseltine Byrd Taylor, Law of Guardian and Ward, Chicago, University of Chicago Press, 1935, p. 25.
[51] Children's Bureau, op. cit., 1951 p. 73, and addenda.
[52] Ibid.

her death, the father has superior rights to the child's custody and so may be appointed guardian.[53]

In all jurisdictions, the father may exercise his power to appoint a testamentary guardian for his children only after some consideration by the mother.[54] In some of these states, however, the right of the mother is conditional upon the death of the father or requires that the mother be a fit person.[55] The mother of an illegitimate child may appoint a guardian of her child's estate in seven states and of his person in three.[56]

When a child is under guardianship of the person, he is placed in a situation very similar to that of the parent and his child. The importance of this relationship is such that it demands more serious and prolonged attention from our legislators. Seeing this need, the Children's Bureau extended the pioneering studies of Sophonisba P. Breckenridge and her students into the problems and legal treatment of guardianship. The findings of the Children's Bureau study, which was restricted to an intensive study in six states,[57] indicate that:

1. The need for guardianship of the person is not being met.
2. Guardianship of estate is often provided unnecessarily.
3. Appointments are made in a perfunctory manner.
4. The courts are poorly equipped for the job.
5. Supervision of the guardian is lax.
6. Social agencies feel the impact of the lack of proper legislative consideration of guardianship and of the confusion in existing laws.
7. The increasing number of children who are becoming financial beneficiaries of veterans' and social security programs has enlarged the problem posed by our inadequate laws.
8. The basic need is for revision or replacement of our very old, inadequate and frequently inconsistent laws relating to guardianship.[58]

To meet these problems the Bureau has outlined an ambitious program for the revision of existing statutes by the various jurisdictions. The recommended changes include procedural separation of judicial consideration of the need for guardianship of the person and of the estate, giving jurisdiction of guardianship of the person to children's courts, making social services available to these courts, and allowing

[53] Ibid.
[54] Ibid., p. 74, and addenda.
[55] Ibid.
[56] Ibid., p. 75, and addenda.
[57] California, Connecticut, Florida, Louisiana, Michigan, and Missouri.
[58] Weissman et al., op. cit., pp. 168 ff.

guardians of the child's person to act for the child when his whole estate is $500 or less or where monthly payments to the child do not exceed $50.[59]

The Children of Unmarried Parents

In an earlier chapter we cited Malinowski's observation that all societies require some male to stand as father between the child and the greater community. The action of the law to limit social approval of children illegitimately conceived and born is well illustrated in the harsh treatment which the illegitimate child has received in the English and American legal tradition. At common law, children born to unmarried mothers were bastards, the illegitimate "children of no one." While there was a strong presumption of the legitimacy of children born to married women, the impotence or absence of the husband and birth subsequent to the annulment of a marriage were also sufficient to brand the innocent child with this shameful status.[60] Children conceived prior to marriage were legitimate if their birth followed the marriage, illegitimate if it preceded the ceremony. Likewise, children conceived in marriage were legitimate even if born after the death of the father or the dissolution of the marriage.[61]

This severe treatment of the illegitimate child was more the result of the property-conscious conservatism of the common law than an indictment of the parents. Certainly, any moral condemnation would not explain the action of the laws in withholding from the child (who after all had no control over his birth) many of the rights usually accorded children of legitimate birth.

In the early common law, no one was responsible for the illegitimate child's support—neither father, mother, nor state—consequently neither parent had any right to his custody. The child did not have rights of inheritance from either parent, nor could anyone but his own legitimate offspring inherit from him.

The harshness of the law was somewhat mitigated by the Elizabethan Bastardy Laws of 1576, which compelled either or both parents to support the illegitimate child. However, the motivation was economic rather than humanitarian, for the purpose of these laws was to relieve the parish from the burden of the child's support. The statute itself is the best evidence of this intention:

[59] *Ibid.*, pp. 180 ff.
[60] Frank H. Hankins, "Illegitimacy," *Encyclopedia of the Social Sciences*, New York, The Macmillan Company, 1932, Vol. VII, p. 579.
[61] Vernier, *op. cit.*, Vol. IV, p. 147.

Concerning bastards begotten and born out of lawful matrimony (an offence against God's law and man's law) the said bastards being now left to be kept at the charges of the parish where they be born, to the great burden of the same parish, and in defrauding of the relief of the impotent and aged true poor of the same parish, and to the evil example and encouragement of lewd life: it is ordained . . . that two justices of the peace . . . within such parish . . . shall and may by their direction take order, as will for the punishment of the mother and reputed father of such bastard child, as also for the better relief of every such parish in part or in all; and shall and may likewise by like discretion take order for the keeping of every such bastard child, by charging such mother or reputed father, with payment of money weekly or other such sustentation for the relief of such child, in such wise as they shall think meet and convenient and if . . . mother or reputed father . . . shall not for their part observe and perform the said order; that then every such party so making default in not performing the said order to be committed to ward to the common gaol. . . .[62]

From 1576 until the present century, the history of the statutory treatment of illegitimacy has seen relatively little change in the position of the illegitimate child or his relationship to his parents. Even these recent efforts to ease the lot of the child and the mother have not been completely successful. The term "bastard" and even the less strident "illegitimate child" have been removed in favor of less ignoble appellatives, such as "children born out of wedlock" or "children of unmarried parents," but the legitimate child is still legally and morally preferred.

RECENT LEGISLATIVE ATTITUDES TOWARD ILLEGITIMACY

What little legislative effort has been given to the relationships between the illegitimate child, his parents, and the community has primarily concerned the presumption of illegitimacy, the establishment of legal paternity, the legitimization of the child, and the respective rights of illegitimate children and their parents.

Current statutory provisions dealing with the presumption or proof of illegitimacy are found in a few states. In general, these follow the common-law presumption of legitimacy for a child born to a married woman. Today, however, the presumption is one of fact, and if it can be proved that the husband was impotent at the time of conception or that no sexual intercourse could have taken place, the child may be declared illegitimate. If, however, it can be proved that the husband

[62] 18 Elizabeth, Ch. 3 (1576).

had access to the wife, it is usually assumed that the sexual relations leading to impregnation took place.[63]

A few states limit the permissibility of disputing the legitimacy of a child to the husband or wife or to the descendants of one or both of them.[64] This represents a variation from the common-law ruling, which permitted any interested party to contest the legitimacy of a child, even when born to a married woman.[65] A further departure from the common law is the ruling of several states that one or both spouses may testify to the nonaccess. The competency of either spouse to testify to nonaccess has been affirmed in the common law since Lord Mansfield ruled that it was against the law of "decency" for either husband or wife to bastardize the child by their testimony.[66]

Any child born of a single woman is assumed to be illegitimate, unlike the case of a married woman, where it is necessary to disprove the legitimacy of the child. All fifty-three jurisdictions, however, allow the single mother access to the courts to establish the paternity of her offspring and to receive support from the putative father, a proceeding which was unknown at common law. These laws authorizing paternity proceedings, or affiliation statutes as they are commonly called, are the outgrowth of concern with public economy rather than with the child's protection. Their early appearance in the United States was a result of an attempt to spare the public the expense of supporting the unwed mother and her child.[67] Today, however, the more progressive and enlightened view is gaining favor—that these proceedings should attempt to secure the "health, welfare, and happiness" of the child.[68]

Modern legislation usually allows the complaint in affiliation cases to be made by the mother or her next of kin or by the child's guardian. Where the public-assistance laws require that the mother name the father of the child, the state department of public welfare is also authorized to institute the proceeding. In addition to the establishment of legal paternity, the duty of support may be levied by these same proceedings. The amount of this support varies considerably

[63] Vernier, op. cit., Vol. IV, p. 150; see also Cross v. Cross, 3 Paige (Ch. N.Y.) 139 (1832).

[64] Ibid., p. 151.

[65] Ibid.

[66] Goodright v. Moss, 2 Cowper 591 (1777); see also Vernier, op. cit., Vol. IV, p. 152.

[67] Sidney B. Schatkin, Disputed Paternity Proceedings, 3rd ed., Albany, Mathew Bender Company, 1953, pp. 47–48.

[68] Ibid., p. 43.

among the several jurisdictions from the $3-a-month-until-age-7 minimum of one southern state to the provision in one eastern state for $40 a month until the child is 16 years of age. Several states have no maxima, leaving the exact amount of the support to the discretion of the court.

To establish paternity in the courts the evidence, which may be either direct or circumstantial, must be "clear, convincing, and satisfactory," so that the burden of proof is in reality upon the mother or the state in American jurisdictions. Quite a different approach has been instituted in the Scandinavian countries, which presently place the full burden of proof upon the man named as the father of the child by an unwed mother. Upon being named by the woman as the father, he is summoned by the proper officials and unless he can establish conclusively the true paternity of the child, he is himself held liable for its support. The child receives the full rights of legitimate birth, including the use of the reputed father's name, inheritance, and support from both parents. It is a question of emphasis in deciding which system is most equitable. Where the mother is charged with the burden of proving the paternity of the child, there is always the difficulty of finding enough proof to convince the court and so protect the child from the stigma of "fatherless" birth. Where the man is held completely responsible for the charges made by the woman, there is the equally grave danger that the approach will be misused by compromising women. In both cases, however, it behooves the court to place its greatest concern in the protection and future welfare of the child.

Perhaps the most interesting development in recent years in paternity proceedings is the increased judicial reliance upon expert testimony from serologists and, to a lesser extent, from physical anthropologists. There is a growing, though slow, realization on the part of the nation's courts that blood-test information is an invaluable tool in at least *disproving* the possibility of physiological paternity. The present level of development in the science of serology allows for disproof of the charges made by women against falsely accused men in at least 50 percent of the cases.[69] The reluctance of the courts to accept blood-test information is an indictment of the conservative tendencies of jurisprudence; in one famous appeal, the court admitted the efficacy of blood-test information, but refused to reverse a decision against a man who had voluntarily sought a blood test to disprove

[69] *Ibid.*, p. vii.

incestuous paternity.[70] The man was eventually given a full pardon after serving six years of his sixteen-year sentence.

In 1952, the National Conference of Commissioners on Uniform State Laws adopted a Uniform Act on Blood Tests to Determine Paternity. The act, which has not as yet been widely adopted by the constituent states, recognizes "the infallibility of matching blood tests to determine, as conclusive fact, the impossibility of paternity." It does not recognize the tests "as conclusive proof of paternity but only as another fact for the courts to consider." [71]

Another example of the willingness of the courts to accept scientific evidence is the use, in a few cases, of expert anthropological testimony to establish the probability of paternity in miscegenous paternity proceedings. The anthropologist is called upon to testify, by means of the racial characteristics of the child whose paternity is in question, as to the possibility of the putative father's having sired the child.[72]

Every jurisdiction also makes provision for the legitimization of children born out of wedlock. The various jurisdictions provide for any or all of three methods: (1) the marriage of the parents subsequent to the child's birth, with the father accepting the child as his own; (2) a petition to the court by the father, asking for legitimization without marriage; and (3) the acknowledging of paternity by the father in taking the child into his own home.[73] Probably the most far-reaching of these provisions is found in the laws of Arizona and North Dakota, which have declared every child to be the legitimate issue of his natural parents even where the father is married to another woman. The Arizona statute provides that "Every child is hereby declared the legitimate child of its natural parents and as such is entitled to support and education to the same extent as if it had been born in lawful wedlock. It shall inherit from its natural parents and from their kindred heirs, lineal and collateral, in the same manner as children born in lawful wedlock." [74]

Both states, however, still require that the father acknowledge paternity and that the mother bring suit within one year after the birth of the child.[75] Since the accompanying provisions authorize only

[70] State v. Damm, 63 S.D. 252 N.W. 7, 104 A.L.R. 430 (1933).
[71] Council of State Governments, op. cit., p. 144.
[72] See, for example, Commissioner of Welfare v. Levy, Court of Special Sessions, New York County, Index 55, 56 (1945).
[73] Vernier, op. cit., Vol. IV, pp. 154–155.
[74] Arizona Laws of 1921, Ch. 144, Sec. 1.
[75] Vernier, op. cit., Vol. IV, p. 181.

the mother to bring such actions, her death prior to the fulfillment of her responsibility would create a difficult situation.[76]

Legitimization is the effect of rendering the illegitimate child eligible for all of the rights and responsibilities of legitimate birth. All states have some provision for establishing the newly legitimized child's rights of inheritance. Usually, he may inherit from the mother and, with less certainty, from the father, although Louisiana grants inheritance only in the absence of lawful issue.

ILLEGITIMACY IN MODERN AMERICA

The secrecy and social disapproval surrounding illegitimacy make accurate knowledge of its incidence and growth impossible. Recent evidence, however, indicates that both the number and ratio of such births are increasing. The Mid-Century White House Conference on Children and Youth reported that "nearly one-half again as many babies were known to be born out of wedlock in 1948 as in 1938 and the rate per thousand unmarried mothers was 80 percent higher in 1948 than in 1940." [77] This increase might be attributed to the rising total birth rate during the same period, but it would appear that the actual number of illegitimate births is on the rise. Freeman, commenting on this growth, states that the increase was "substantial in both white and non-white groups and was found among all age groups in the 15–44 year span." [78]

The effects of social factors in the incidence of illegitimacy are illustrated by the characteristics of unwed mothers. Table 17 presents the estimated number and ratio of illegitimate births by the age and race of the mother, and shows that in 1952 the ratio of illegitimate births to every 1000 births was over ten times as high among nonwhites as among whites. It also evidences the comparative youth of the unwed mother.

There is evidence that much illegitimacy stems from young unwed mothers who are bearing their first child. In the early thirties, one investigator found that one-third of 1600 unwed mothers studied were under 20 years af age and five out of every hundred were under 16; nearly seven-eighths of them were having their first child.[79] In 1946,

[76] Ibid.

[77] Helen L. Witmer and Ruth Kotinsky, (eds.), Personality in the Making, New York, Harper & Brothers, 1952, p. 177.

[78] Lucy Freeman, Children Who Never Had a Chance, Public Affairs Pamphlet No. 183, New York, The Public Affairs Committee, 1952.

[79] Ruth Reed, The Illegitimate Family in New York City, New York, Columbia University Press, 1934, passim.

TABLE 17.   Estimated Number and Ratio of Illegitimate Live Births, by Age of
Mother and Race, United States, 1952.[a]

Age of Mother	Number			Ratio		
	Total	White	Nonwhite	Total	White	Nonwhite
Total	150,300	54,100	96,200	39.1	16.3	183.4
Under 15 years	3,200	700	2,600	645.3	381.8	783.8
15–19 years	58,700	19,600	39,000	134.0	58.4	384.1
15–17 years	30,700	8,800	21,800	228.4	96.3	513.7
18–19 years	28,000	10,800	17,200	92.2	44.1	290.9
20–24 years	45,500	18,500	27,000	37.5	17.6	163.7
25–29 years	22,400	7,700	14,700	20.3	7.9	116.2
30–34 years	12,400	4,300	8,000	18.2	7.2	106.5
35–39 years	6,500	2,600	3,900	20.3	9.3	99.9
40 years and over	1,600	700	900	19.2	9.7	79.3

a In states for which legitimacy data were not available, estimates were derived by adding an estimate of the number of illegitimate births to the number of reported illegitimate live births based on a 50 percent sample for the reporting states. No estimates were included for misstatements in the birth record or for failures to register births. Estimates were rounded to the nearest hundred without being adjusted to group totals, which were independently rounded. Ratios are based on unrounded numbers per 1000 total births in each specified group.

Source: National Office of Vital Statistics, Vital Statistics of the United States, 1952, Vol. I, Table AA, p. xxxvii.

the Children's Bureau estimated that one-half of all unwed mothers were under 18 years of age.[80] The reasons for this preponderance of young unwed mothers are many; lack of parental consent or insufficient age to marry, improper parental supervision and sex education, poverty and neglect leading to a strong craving for affection, and heavy emphasis upon sexually stimulating advertising are just a few of the many causes. What is important here is that legislators and jurists realize that in many cases they are dealing not only with illegitimate children, but with child mothers, and in many cases probably with child fathers, and approach the problem from a child-welfare point of view rather than a punitive standpoint.

With the apparent increases in illegitimate births and our new concern for child protection, a reconsideration of our existing statutes dealing with children of unmarried parents would seem to be in order. Many of our laws are antiquated in their championship of the common-law predilection for ensuring that none but the legally born shall enjoy the rights of the parent-child relationship. We have come a long way from this view in many jurisdictions, but modern welfare

80 Maud Murdock and Hilary Campbell, Maternity Homes for Unmarried Mothers, Children's Bureau Publication No. 309 Washington, Government Printing Office, 1946, p. 13.

principles do not allow for its existence in any jurisdiction which would make childhood happy and secure.

Fertility Controls and Parenthood

Societies everywhere show concern with the quantity and quality of population. In primitive societies, population control is effected through informal, traditional rules which are passed through the family, folk lore, and the magico-religious realm. Modern society adds to these informal controls various laws which attempt, with different degrees of success, to regulate population.

Birth Control

The antiquity and ubiquity of population consciousness are attested to by the universality of population-control techniques. Even the Australian Bushman, reputedly ignorant of the facts of physiological paternity, makes use of abortion and infanticide as a means of checking population growth. These techniques are of many types and exhibit various degrees of effectiveness, but basically the three methods of birth control are:

1. Contraception, or the prevention of conception by the interception of the male sperm prior to its impregnation of the female ovum.

2. Abortion, or the expulsion of the fetus before it can sustain life. Abortions may be *spontaneous*, or those resulting from unintentional causes; *therapeutic*, or those which are intentionally produced with the health or safety of the mother as the primary end; and *induced*, or those where the abortion is purposely produced by the mother or some other person. This latter category includes the illegal, nontherapeutic abortion.

3. Infanticide, or the destruction of the neonate at birth or soon afterward.

While each of these methods is found in primitive society, effective, safe contraceptive devices and practices are relatively recent. Modern medical science has done much to remove the uncertainty and danger from this least drastic method of regulating childbirth. Yet controversy still rages over the moral and religious status of contraception.

The history of this antagonism is part of the larger controversy over birth control itself. This discord might properly be said to have begun in this country with the publication of Robert Dale Owen's *Moral Physiology* in 1830, although the arguments over the morality

of purposive birth control predate Owen's book. This volume, in which Owen espoused *coitus interruptus*, however, brought the question to the attention of the general public. Its original publication seems to have occasioned little notice in this country, but when it was published in England, along with Charles Knowlton's *Fruits of Philosophy*, which suggested vaginal douching as a technique, such was not the case. A series of arrests and prosecutions based upon charges of obscenity and corrupting the minds of the young soon brought the problem to the attention of the American as well as the British public.

Since that time a series of federal and state laws have been passed which still treat birth control as an obscene practice despite its widespread use throughout the civilized world. This incongruous situation is in part the result of the efforts by Anthony Comstock, the militant moral reformer, to ban obscenity and destroy indecency. He broadened his attack to include birth-control literature and devices. Under his zeal and direction, Congress was asked in 1873 to add what came to be known as the Comstock Law to its previous measures banning the importation of indecent pictures (1842) and their dissemination through the mail (1865). Still feeling the effects of the Crédit Mobilier scandal, Congress passed this bill with little discussion. The law prohibited the mailing of obscene matter in the United States, including literature or devices "for the prevention of conception."

Shortly after the passage of this law, Comstock himself was appointed to enforce it as a special agent of the Post Office Department. In his new capacity he diligently and extensively carried out the letter of the law.[81] It is difficult properly to assess Comstock's role in American social legislation. Certainly, he was responsible for the inexcusable labeling of contraceptive information as indecent before the federal law, and contributed to the rash of state legislation which followed the enactment of his law. Probably his energetic, even fanatic, hatred of obscenity did not allow him to see that his real target was *indecent* and *obscene* contraceptive literature and that his approach was overinclusive.

Since the passage of the Comstock Act, the interpretations of various federal courts have done much to soften its rigors. At present, it is generally held that *federal* laws do not prohibit the mailing, for

---

[81] Heywood Broun and Margaret Leech, *Anthony Comstock*, New York, Albert and Charles Boni, 1927, chap. X, "Comstock Shows His Badge," pp. 145–154.

medical use, of contraceptive devices to physicians or to laymen under a physician's direction.[82]

Following the lead of the Comstock Law, a majority of the states passed similar legislation. As late as 1955, twenty-nine states still had laws concerning the distribution of contraceptive information. Thirteen of these expressly exempted physicians in medical practice and fourteen others had laws which, in effect, produced the same exemptions, by implication or construction. Only two states, Massachusetts and Connecticut, had statutes which made it illegal for a physician to dispense birth-control information to his patients.[83] Connecticut goes further and also makes the use of contraceptive devices, even by husband and wife, punishable by a fine and imprisonment.

Repeated efforts to do away with these unrealistic and myopic laws have met with little success. In 1948, a referendum in Massachusetts, which sought to abolish the anti-birth-control laws of that state lost by a margin of 37 percent,[84] and a similar attempt in the Connecticut legislature was defeated in the State Senate in 1955.[85]

There are also state laws concerning abortion. Most states permit its therapeutic use, although illegally induced abortion is everywhere condemned. Unlike contraception, the use of abortion as a means of birth control poses a health problem as well as a religious and moral question. The universal condemnation of abortion to rid the mother of the child where there is no problem of health and safety has made such operations secretive and uncontrolled by health regulations. The possibility of infection is great, an estimated 3000 to 4000 maternal deaths resulting from this cause every year.[86] The growth of clandestine abortion mills, staffed by midwives and quacks, as well as unethical physicians, presents a sordid problem. The solution is difficult to find, for our knowledge of the problem is sketchy and second-hand. Certainly, better self-policing by medical groups would help, but this would not erase the even more dangerous problem of operations by quacks and midwives. One possible solution is to make the concept of therapeutic abortion more inclusive and more readily available, so

---

[82] *United States* v. *One Package*, 86 Fed. 2d737 (1936); *United States* v. *Dr. Jose Belaval*, U.S. District Court, Puerto Rico (1939).

[83] This summary of current state legislation affecting birth control is based on material furnished by the Planned Parenthood Federation of America.

[84] *The New York Times*, May 6, 1948, p. 32.

[85] *Ibid.*, May 24, 1955, p. 20.

[86] Ray E. Baber, *Marriage and the Family*, New York, McGraw-Hill Book Company, 1953, p. 616.

as to include many of the cases where childbirth would present a mental health if not a physiological danger.

THE BIRTH-CONTROL CONTROVERSY TODAY

Despite the concerted efforts of such groups as the National Birth Control League (Planned Parenthood Federation since 1942) to accomplish the repeal of restrictive legislation, the laws seem destined to be with us for a long time. Since about 1924, the approach of these organizations has been to work within the limitations of the laws and gain liberal interpretation in the courts. This approach, first utilized by Mrs. Margaret Sanger, the pioneering founder of the birth-control movement in this country, has met with some success.

The most powerful and vocal opposition to the practice and teaching of birth-control techniques is undoubtedly the Roman Catholic Church. The Church has long held that all mechanical means of birth control are unnatural and intrinsically evil.[87] There is also the feeling that widespread knowledge of these techniques would have a degenerating effect upon youth by removing the fear of pregnancy as a check upon premarital intercourse, and that if sexual relations are separated from procreation they become little more than acts of passion and lust. This approach is not characteristic of most other religious groups, which have accepted the practice of birth control while still teaching the virtues and blessings of parenthood.[88]

Despite the opposition of the Church, birth control and its social significance have profoundly affected modern society. The gradual dissemination of information about techniques has been widespread throughout western society and has wrought decreases in the birth rates over the last fifty years. It cannot be said to have caused the decreases, the motivation being a function of complex socioeconomic and cultural factors, but it has provided a safe and efficient means for man to check his population growth when he so wishes.

The future position of the Roman Catholic Church is difficult to predict. Many look upon her acceptance of the "rhythm method," where intercourse is avoided during the relatively short fertile period of the menstrual cycle, as a sign of the acceptance of the principles and ends of birth control if not the mechanical practices.

[87] Pope Pius XI, encyclical "On Christian Marriage," December 31, 1930.
[88] See, for example, Guy Emery Shipler, "Catholics and Birth Control," a series of articles in The Churchman, April 15, May 1, May 15, and June 1, 1941; J. H. J. Upham, "The Catholics and Planned Parenthood," The American Mercury, February, 1944.

STERILIZATION OF DEFECTIVES

The eugenic use of sterilization in American jurisdictions differs from other birth-control techniques in two important respects: (1) it is a permanent form of controlling childbirth since it renders impregnation impossible, and (2) it is most frequently used as a device for quality rather than quantity control. Although normal, healthy individuals may submit to surgical sterilization in order to prevent impregnation without the necessity of contraceptive devices, its primary use and importance are in reducing dysgenic characteristics such as feeble-mindedness, certain mental illnesses, and epilepsy thought to be inheritable.

The first sterilization bill was passed in Indiana in 1907, although previous unsuccessful attempts had taken place in Michigan (1897)

TABLE 18. States Having Sterilization Laws in 1954 with Year of Enactment, Types of State Laws, and Sterilizations Reported for All States to January 1, 1955.

State	Year of Enactment[a]	Voluntary[b]	Compulsory[c]	Voluntary and Compulsory[d]	Extra-mural[e]	Eugenics Board[f]	Total Sterilizations Reported[g]
Alabama[h]	1919		X				224
Arizona	1929		X				21
California	1909		X				19,937
Connecticut	1909		X				532
Delaware	1923		X		X		859
Georgia	1937		X			X	1,961
Idaho	1925		X		X	X	31
Indiana	1907		X				2,197
Iowa	1911		X		X	X	1,574
Kansas	1913		X				3,025
Maine	1925		X	X			278
Michigan	1913		X		X		3,462
Minnesota	1925	X					2,285
Mississippi	1928		X				596
Montana	1923		X			X	256
Nebraska	1915		X				829
New Hampshire	1917		X				658
New York[i]	1912						42
North Carolina	1919		X	X	X	X	3,967
North Dakota	1913		X				931
Oklahoma	1931		X				555
Oregon	1917		X		X	X	2,111
South Carolina	1935		X				128
South Dakota	1917		X	X	X		775
Utah	1925		X		X		708
Vermont	1931	X					252
Virginia	1924		X				6,485
Washington[j]	1909						685
West Virginia	1929		X				62
Wisconsin	1913		X				1,792
Total		2	26	3	8	6	57,218

[a] Date indicates year law passed.
[b] Consent of defective person, spouse, or guardian required.
[c] Consent of defective person not required.
[d] Law contains provision for either voluntary or compulsory sterilization.
[e] Law contains provision for individuals outside of institutions.
[f] Authorization agency for sterilization. (Other states designate state agencies.)
[g] Sterilizations performed from date of enactment to January 1, 1955.
[h] Law presently inoperative owing to 1935 State Supreme Court ruling adverse to broader legislation then pending.
[i] Declared unconstitutional in 1918.
[j] Declared unconstitutional in 1942.

Source: Based upon data in Human Betterment Association of America, *Sterilizations Reported in the United States to January 1, 1955*, a compilation of 1954 data from the states, published in February, 1955.

and Pennsylvania (1905). The fate of the Indiana law was short-lived, however, for it was declared unconstitutional in 1921 and subsequently replaced with a valid law. Since that time other states have passed similar legislation, and today twenty-eight states and Puerto Rico have laws permitting or directing sterilization under certain circumstances. These states are presented in Table 18, which also shows the year of enactment, type of law, and volume of sterilizations for the states with current legislation.

These laws may call for compulsory or, much less frequently, for voluntary sterilization, or both. The compulsory type of statute authorizes the sterilization of institutionalized or, in some cases, extramural defectives without the requirement of consent on their part. In most cases, however, an attempt is made to obtain the consent of the patient's nearest relative or guardian. In voluntary legislation, the consent of the patient, his legal guardian, or both is required. The administration of the law is variously delegated, often handled by the state departments covering institutions handling defectives. Six states [89] have shown the foresight to establish Eugenics Boards as the permanent authorization agency for passing upon cases where the operation has been recommended.

The operations involved are simple surgical techniques, much simpler and safer than the original technique of castration used to provide eunuchs and choir boys or as a punitive device. In the female, the Fallopian tubes are cut (salpingectomy) and in the male the vas deferens (vasectomy), neither requiring extensive, major surgery. Neither technique has any effect upon sexual appetite or performance.

There is still considerable opposition to the sterilization of defectives. Led by the Catholic Church, some religious leaders feel that sterilization, even where its sole purpose is to check the transmission of hereditary defects, is immoral and a presumption of divine powers by the state. The position of the Church was presented by Pope Pius XI, whose encyclical letter on Christian marriage condemned sterilization, since it denies that "the family is more sacred than the state and that men are begotten not for the earth and time but for heaven and eternity." [90] Opposition also comes from various social and civic organizations fearing the possibility of abuse. The argument is also presented that the decision to sterilize is an extremely difficult one since there are frequent borderline cases.

[89] See Table 18.
[90] Pope Pius XI, encyclical "On Christian Marriage," December 31, 1930.

A careful scrutiny of the extent to which sterilization is used should quiet most of the nonreligious objections. The volume has never been higher than five or six persons per 100,000 population in most states and it is usually well below that ratio. In the entire nation, only 57,218 legal sterilizations were reported up to January 1, 1955, a figure which does not even approach the number of defectives potentially eligible for sterilization under state laws. The arguments pointing to the severity of the action in rendering an individual permanently sterile are somewhat weakened by the fact that the operations are at least theoretically reversible and in the great majority of cases are only performed after obtaining the consent of the defective, his guardian, or both.

The benefits of the sterilization of defectives are several. Where it is carefully supervised, it offers a means of quality control in society which is individually as well as socially beneficent. It offers a safe and efficient safeguard against the perpetuation of inherited defects and protects the individual from parenthood, which is often beyond his or her ability to restrain in a socially acceptable manner. Finally, it offers the possibility of marriage to defectives who, in the absence of their sterilization, would not be permitted entry into the marital relationship because of society's desire to keep them from establishing unfortunate parent-child relationships.

ARTIFICIAL INSEMINATION

With the heavy backlog of prospective adoptive parents and the rapid progress of medical science, the need for artificial-insemination legislation assumes an ever increasing importance. As yet, however, no state or territory has proposed or enacted any adequate legislation concerning artificial insemination or its use. Consequently, the legal status of this means of enabling childless couples to become parents is an unsettled medico-legal question.

Artificial insemination is a method of introducing semen into the genital tract of the female without sexual contact with the male, instead of the "natural insemination" which follows normal coitus.[91] Technically, it is artificial impregnation, the result of artificial insemination, which produces the child, for, like normal coitus, artificial insemination is not always productive of pregnancy.

[91] Ernest Henry Breuer, "Artificial Insemination," unpublished bibliography, 1948, p. iii.

Long a practice with animals, the technique has been used with human beings in recent decades with high medical success but with much religious, moral, and legal controversy. If both husband and wife are fertile, but for some anatomical reason coitus or impregnation is impossible, the sperm may be taken from the husband and painlessly and safely introduced into the female. This is known as artificial insemination, with the husband as donor or A.I.H. This method presents little legal difficulty since the father of the child and the husband of the mother are one and the same person. Legal controversy enters, however, when the sperm must be obtained from some male other than the husband. When the wife is apparently fertile but the husband is incurably sterile, artificial impregnation with semen obtained from a donor other than the husband (A.I.D.) may be attempted.

The necessarily secret nature of both A.I.H. and A.I.D. makes any certain knowledge of the number of successful impregnations and births impossible, but estimates generally run to about 25,000 as a total in this country alone. Even more difficult to obtain are data concerning the relative frequency of A.I.D. and A.I.H., but one study in 1941 found 3649 children in the United States born as a result of A.I.D.[92] The same researchers report that A.I.H. was used in about two-thirds of the cases reported.[93]

The lack of legislation concerning artificial insemination leaves unanswered several important legal questions presented by A.I.D.:

1. Since his biological father is not his mother's husband, is the child of legitimate birth?
2. Has the mother been guilty of adultery in bearing a child sired by a male other than her husband?
3. Can the husband at some later date, even after having consented to the insemination, obtain a divorce on the grounds that his wife committed adultery?
4. Is the father responsible for the child's support and does the child have any rights of inheritance?

The answers to these problems cannot be found in the common law, developed before scientific knowledge permitted the artificial impregnation which has presented this legal quandary. The answer

---

[92] Frances I. Seymour and Alfred Koerner, "Artificial Insemination; Present Status in the United States as Shown by a Recent Survey," *Journal of the American Medical Association*, June 21, 1941, pp. 2747–2759.
[93] *Ibid.*

must await full judicial review or, more satisfactorily, enactment of cognizant legislation.

So far, there is still no clear-cut and definite judicial precedent established for handling these questions in A.I.D. cases where the husband has given his consent. New York's statute, which defines adultery as "the physical relationship between a woman or man with a partner other than the legal mate," would seem to rule out the problem of possible consideration of the wife as an adulteress, but it still leaves the other questions open. In 1948, for example, a New York judge denied a petition by a woman who sought to exclude custody of her child, born as a result of A.I.D. with her husband's consent, claiming the husband had no right of visitation since he was not the child's father. In refusing to grant her request, the court pointed out that, if it did so, this would harm her and brand her child and all others like it as illegitimate, and that the problem of the propriety of artificial procreation was one for sociology, morality, and religion.[94] No such reticence in a similar case, however, was shown by a Cook County, Illinois, Superior Court in 1954. In a custody case over a 5-year-old child, conceived through A.I.D. with the father's consent, the court ruled that the child was illegitimate and the mother guilty of adultery.[95] At the time of this writing the case is still in appeal, and the action of the judge, which could result in the branding of several thousand children as illegitimate and their mothers as adulteresses, is as yet inconclusive.

An even more difficult problem is presented in the rare case where the artificial insemination is obtained by the wife without her husband's knowledge or permission. In one such case, although the court found that the wife's "artificial impregnation" without her husband's knowledge was actually the result of natural adultery, the court proceeded to rule on the case as a model for such situations and found the wife's action to constitute adultery.[96]

In addition to these legal questions, there are many others of a psychological or moral nature. Will the husband be able to accept as his own a child fathered by another or will it represent a symbol of his own failure at paternity? Will the wife develop an overpowering curiosity to discover who is the actual father of her child and perhaps even feel some romantic attachment? What if the child discovers he

[94] Strnad v. Strnad, 190 Misc. 786, 78 N.Y. Supp. 2nd 390 (1948).
[95] Newsweek, December 27, 1954, p. 48.
[96] Orford v. Orford, 49 Ontario Law Reports 15 (1921).

is a "test-tube baby"—will he not feel impelled to find his actual father and will he not feel anxious over the situation surrounding his birth?

The precautions which ideally surround the insemination should do much to dispel these emotional fears and worries. Proper medical ethics calls for elaborate safeguards. Neither husband nor wife is to know the identity of the donor, who in turn does not know the identity of the female his semen will impregnate. The health, family heredity, and general character of the donor have been carefully checked. His race and religion are carefully matched with those of the prospective parents and, to guard against any possible incestuous taint or familial difficulty, he must not be a member of the husband's family. The wife and the donor never see each other, for the semen is obtained at some point other than the place of insemination. The inseminating physician should not double as the obstetrician, so that there may be no question or concern over how the birth certificate should be made out. As far as the physician attending the birth knows, the wife's husband is the father of the child.[97]

Strong opposition to A.I.D. may be found among religious, legal, and even medical groups. The Roman Catholic Church has spoken out against it on several occasions. Encyclical letters by Pope Leo XIII [98] and Pope Pius XI [99] have condemned the practice, and in 1949 Pope Pius XII told the Fourth International Convention of Catholic Doctors that A.I.D. was immoral and against nature. A similar position has been taken by the Anglican commission appointed by the Archbishop of Canterbury to study human artificial insemination.

There is no such unanimity of opinion among physicians and the legal profession, for opponents and proponents of the practice may be found in either group. The *Journal of the American Medical Association* has editorially concluded that children born of A.I.D. "would seem to be illegitimate" and suggests adoption by the husband soon after the birth of the child for the protection of the family.[100] Some opposition has also come from psychiatric medicine relating to the psychological effects of the artificial paternity. Dr. Ruth W. Berenda, a psychoanalyst and former staff member of the Psychiatric Clinic of

[97] Frances I. Seymour and Alfred Koerner, "Medicolegal Aspects of Artificial Insemination," *Journal of the American Medical Association*, November 7, 1936, pp. 1527–1534.

[98] Pope Leo XIII, "On Christian Marriage," March 17, 1897.

[99] Pope Pius XI, "On Christian Marriage," December 31, 1930.

[100] "Artificial Insemination and Illegitimacy," *Journal of the American Medical Association*, May 6, 1939, pp. 1832–1833.

the New York City Domestic Relations Court, has been quoted as maintaining that the resultant secrecy can be harmful to the couple's relationship and that most stable men would not consent to the artificial insemination of their wives by donors.[101]

The legal question must await further judicial reviews and the clear statement of the opinions of jurists concerning the complex and difficult problem of the legal status of this form of parent-child relationship. A more effective means of dealing with the problem would be through the enactment of legislation by the various states, a slow and tedious process. A bill was introduced into the New York State Senate in 1948 which sought to make a child born to a married woman by means of artificial insemination with the consent of the husband the legitimate and natural child of the couple.[102] The bill was referred to the Committee on Codes, amended, and referred again to the same committee, where it died.

Future legislation should be based upon adequate medical and psychiatric consultation by the legislatures and should embody the growing concept of the primacy of the child's welfare. The possibilities of artificial insemination as a device for parenthood for many otherwise childless couples requires more legislative consideration than a forthright rejection based upon emotionalized attitudes.

PRENATAL-HEALTH-EXAMINATION LAWS

One of the recent eugenic developments in social legislation is the addition of prenatal-health-examination laws to bolster the premarital-health-examination attack upon venereal diseases. These laws are aimed at the protection of the unborn child from congenital syphilis, which can be transferred from the infected mother to the fetus, causing stillbirth, crippling, or early death in the infant. Discovery of the disease in the mother during pregnancy allows ample opportunity for adequate treatment, which permits most of the babies to be born free of the disease.

The State of New York pioneered with the first prenatal-health-examination law in 1938 and was followed by other states, so that by 1955, forty-two states, Alaska, Hawaii, and the Virgin Islands had adopted similar laws. Table 19 presents the approval and effective dates of all prenatal-health-examination laws passed up to 1955.

[101] Daniel Lang, "Artificial Insemination—Legitimate or Illegitimate?" *McCall's*, May, 1955, p. 62.
[102] New York Senate Nos. 758, 2042. Int. 745 January 26, 1948.

TABLE 19. States and Territories Having Prenatal-Health-Examination Laws in 1955 with Approval and Effective Dates of the Laws.

State	Date Approved	Date Effective
Arizona	Mar. 5, 1945	June 9, 1945
Arkansas	Feb. 17, 1947	July 1, 1947
California	May 9, 1939	Sept. 19, 1939
Colorado	Apr. 10, 1939	Apr. 10, 1939
Connecticut	June 18, 1941	Oct. 1, 1941
Delaware	Mar. 8, 1939	Mar. 8, 1939
Florida	May 19, 1945	Oct. 1, 1945
Georgia	Mar. 18, 1943	July 1, 1943
Idaho	Feb. 5, 1943	Apr. 29, 1943
Illinois	July 21, 1939	July 21, 1939
Indiana	Feb. 18, 1939	Jan. 1, 1940
Iowa	May 17, 1939	July 4, 1939
Kansas	Mar. 22, 1943	June 28, 1943
Kentucky	Mar. 18, 1940	June 12, 1940
Louisiana	July 12, 1940	July 31, 1940
Maine	Apr. 20, 1939	July 20, 1939
Massachusetts	Aug. 3, 1939	Nov. 1, 1939
Michigan	May 16, 1939	May 16, 1939
Missouri	July 28, 1941	Oct. 10, 1941
Montana	Feb. 24, 1945	July 1, 1945
Nebraska	Mar. 27, 1943	Aug. 29, 1943
Nevada	Mar. 28, 1941	July 1, 1941
New Hampshire	July 1, 1947	July 1, 1947
New Jersey	Mar. 30, 1938	Jan. 1, 1939
New Mexico	Mar. 15, 1949	June 10, 1949
New York	Mar. 18, 1938	Mar. 18, 1938
North Carolina	Apr. 3, 1939	Jan. 1, 1940
North Dakota	Mar. 12, 1949	July 1, 1949
Ohio	May 23, 1945	Aug. 22, 1945
Oklahoma	Mar. 10, 1939	July 28, 1939
Oregon	Mar. 7, 1941	June 13, 1941
Pennsylvania	June 24, 1939	June 24, 1940
Rhode Island	Apr. 22, 1938	Apr. 22, 1938
South Carolina	Apr. 1, 1946	July 1, 1945 a
South Dakota	Mar. 8, 1939	July 1, 1939
Texas	July 8, 1949	Oct. 4, 1949
Utah	Feb. 28, 1941	May 13, 1941
Vermont	Apr. 10, 1941	July 31, 1941
Virginia	Mar. 4, 1950	July 1, 1950
Washington	Mar. 16, 1939	Jan. 2, 1940
West Virginia	Mar. 5, 1945	June 3, 1945
Wyoming	Feb. 20, 1941	Apr. 21, 1941
Alaska	Mar. 14, 1949	June 12, 1949
Hawaii	May 17, 1943	July 1, 1943
Virgin Islands	Dec 8, 1942	Dec. 4, 1943

a Original law contained this effective date.

Sources: U.S. Public Health Service, *Prenatal Health Examination Legislation*, Public Health Service Publication No. 369, 1954, p. 2. Personal correspondence with C. A. Smith, Medical Director, Chief, Venereal Disease Program, Division of Special Health Services of the Public Health Service, indicated that no prenatal-health-examination laws were enacted between the publication of this booklet and July 1, 1955.

There is some diversity among the various laws, but basically they all require a mandatory blood test for syphilis in a majority of the jurisdictions. Some laws, however, allow the woman to refuse and others make her consent essential to giving the test.[103] Most states require that the serological test be given on the first visit or examination for pregnancy or within fifteen days of this examination, while other states set some other time requirement. The test is often free if performed at a state laboratory, and all jurisdictions require that a state-approved laboratory perform the actual serological test, although the physician may obtain and submit the blood sample.

Provisions for filing the results of the tests also vary. In sixteen states, the results of all tests must be filed with the state department of health, four states require filing only if the results are positive, and four other states require the filing of only state-laboratory tests. The remaining states do not require filing.[104] A further check is made in all but seven of the states by the requirement that the birth certificate must show whether a blood test has been made prior to the child's birth. In twenty-four states, the certificate must indicate the reason for a failure to comply with the blood-test laws, and twenty-one states provide penalties for physicians who fail to comply.[105]

The efficacy of these laws is shown by California's experience with infant mortality from syphilis following the passage of a blood-test law in 1939. In 1938, one year prior to the passage of the law, the state recorded 51 deaths from syphilis among children under one year of age, a rate of 0.50 per thousand live births; by 1945, the number was 28, or 0.15 per thousand live births, and the number and rate of reported cases of congenital syphilis in the same age group showed a similar decline.[106] While this study could not definitely establish a cause-and-effect relationship between the law and the decreases, it does suggest that the laws contributed in some measure to the successful campaign against syphilis.

Further legislation is needed, not only in those states which have no law, but to strengthen existing legislation concerning the reporting and treatment requirements. With present-day case-finding and detection

[103] Laura M. Halse and Dominic V. Liberti, "Prenatal Health Examination Legislation," *Public Health Reports*, February, 1954, pp. 105–110, reprinted in *Prenatal Health Examination Legislation*, Public Health Service Publication No. 369, 1954.

[104] *Ibid.*, p. 108.

[105] *Ibid.*

[106] A. F. Brewer and F. E. Olson, "Evaluation of California's Prenatal Law Requiring a Serological Test for Syphilis," *American Journal of Syphilis, Gonorrhea and Venereal Diseases*, November, 1947, pp. 633–639.

techniques and the availability of penicillin as an effective therapeutic agent, there is no excuse for lax laws which continue to allow this deplorable disease to kill and maim infants.

CHILD WELFARE SERVICES

The omnibus term "child welfare" has come to encompass almost any activity which is directed toward the protection, care, and development of the child. As such, it presents a difficult subject for unified treatment and discussion. Added to this difficulty is the one posed by the fact that several types of agencies—federal, state, and private—administer and provide these services. We must, therefore, draw careful lines of distinction and rule out of the present discussion the activities of private agencies except as they result from and are affected by state and federal legislation. Since the enactment of the Social Security Act, the federal government has assumed a commanding role in this area through its program of grants to the states for establishing, strengthening, and extending welfare programs affecting children. Rather than produce an artificial division between the state and federal programs, which are usually coöperatively planned and financed, the primary treatment will come in our later discussion of the assistance features of the Social Security Act. In this section we shall briefly consider the major areas and recent developments in child-welfare services.

Public child-welfare services, which derive much of their financial support from state and local funds, are provided in all the states and territories. These services vary from state to state, but usually include most of the following:

1. Social casework services for children, youth and parents requiring help with reality problems in individual, family or community situations.
2. The development of services designed to promote and preserve wholesome and adequate family living. An example of this type of program is the homemaker or housekeeper service designed to reduce the necessity of parent-child separation when a parent is ill or incapacitated.
3. Foster care of children away from home in a family or institutional setting. These services may include: foster family care of children on a temporary or permanent basis; care in a small group setting when the child requires closer peer-group relationships and somewhat less individual attention from adults; institutional care for delinquent, emotionally disturbed or other children with specialized problems which would not respond to a foster family or small group setting; the assumption of partial responsibility for the child during certain periods of the day in day-care centers or other facilities outside the home.

4. Services to protect children who are being placed for adoption.
5. Services for the prevention and control of juvenile delinquency, including services to juvenile and children's courts, detention facilities and correctional institutions.
6. The care and training of mentally deficient children.
7. Services to private children's agencies through licensing, supervision and consultation of both agencies and institutions dealing with children.
8. Programs of cooperation with other public and private agencies in establishing a community-wide approach for the planning and organization of child welfare services.[107]

The responsibility for the implementation of these services is usually vested in a division of child welfare within the state department of public welfare. In some states, however, the responsibility and performance of these services are shared with other state agencies, such as departments of health, correction, and mental hygiene, and with specialized bureaus, such as state youth commissions or authorities. The state welfare department may function directly to provide services or do so indirectly through local public-welfare units. In most states, this local agency is the county welfare department, over which the state agency may exercise varying degrees of supervision and control. Some states charge the state department of public welfare with the establishment and supervision of county agencies, some give it the responsibility for training and selecting personnel, and others direct it to pay approved costs of the local unit. In some states, the state department has all of these powers and responsibilities. Where the specific program or service is not the direct responsibility of the state-level agency, it frequently supervises the performance of the service by the local agency and may even delegate some given service for which it is responsible to the local department.

The type of service, quality of performance, and training of personnel vary considerably among the various states. The assessment of causes for such variation, a difficult task, would seem to concern such factors as community resources and facilities, governmental organization, and intangibles, such as the prevailing philosophy of the state toward welfare problems. These differences also affect the type and amount of services which will be utilized by the particular jurisdiction in meeting its responsibility toward children. Some idea of the degree of variation among the jurisdictions may be obtained from Table 20,

[107] Council of State Governments, *op. cit.*, Vol. X, pp. 326–327; Spencer H. Crookes, "Child Welfare," American Association of Social Workers, *Social Work Year Book*, New York, The Association, 1954, p. 90.

which compares the states and territories in respect to the number and rate per 1000 children in the population receiving child-welfare case-work services from public agencies, and also indicates the number and percentage of these children in the various living arrangements described above.

TABLE 20. Children Receiving Child-Welfare Casework Service from Public-Welfare Agencies, by State and by Living Arrangements, March 31, 1954.

State and Reporting Coverage [a]	Total	Rate per 1000 Child Population [b]	In Homes of Parents or Relatives Number	%	In Foster-Family Homes Number	%	In Institutions and Elsewhere [c] Number	%
Total, 53 States	272,357[d]	e	104,947	e	119,651	e	47,486	e
Total, substantially complete reports	251,839[d]	4.9	101,080	40	105,530	42	44,956	18
Alabama	9,308	7.0	6,882	74	1,499	16	927	10
Alaska	702	16.1	236	34	218	31	248	35
Arizona	2,126	5.4	1,088	51	852	40	186	9
Arkansas	2,149	2.7	1,045	49	847	39	257	12
Colorado	2,520[d]	4.8	1,394	55	829	33	292	12
Connecticut	5,688[d]	8.1	807	14	3,652	65	1,182	21
Delaware	1,036	8.2	386	37	558	54	92	9
District of Columbia	2,857[d]	11.8	956	34	999	36	845	30
Florida	2,487	2.1	974	39	1,315	53	198	8
Georgia	3,273	2.2	1,134	35	1,714	52	425	13
Hawaii	1,745	8.0	735	42	780	45	230	13
Idaho	290	1.2	225	78	53	18	12	4
Illinois	4,383	1.5	820	19	3,248	74	315	7
Indiana	12,725	8.5	5,866	46	4,845	38	2,014	16
Iowa	2,858	3.0	2,180	76	412	15	266	9
Kansas	2,089[d]	2.9	670	32	751	36	655	32
Kentucky	5,403	4.5	2,872	53	1,391	26	1,140	21
Louisiana	3,703	3.1	927	25	2,456	66	320	9
Maine	2,921[d]	8.6	847	29	1,882	65	182	6
Maryland	4,966	5.5	1,148	23	3,137	63	681	14
Massachusetts	6,889	4.3	699	10	5,515	80	661	10
Michigan	2,116	0.8	677	32	1,356	64	83	4
Minnesota	10,650[d]	9.3	7,029	67	2,880	27	677	6
Mississippi	4,866	5.0	4,012	82	471	10	383	8
Missouri	3,515	2.5	1,614	46	1,606	46	295	8
Montana	910	3.8	446	49	360	40	104	11
Nebraska	1,792	3.7	884	49	443	25	465	26
New Hampshire	2,488	13.6	1,117	45	961	39	410	16

State and Reporting Coverage [a]	Total	Rate per 1000 Child Population [b]	In Homes of Parents or Relatives Number	%	In Foster-Family Homes Number	%	In Institutions and Elsewhere [c] Number	%
New Jersey	6,965	4.3	1,340	19	4,464	64	1,161	17
New Mexico	1,710	5.0	779	46	754	44	177	10
New York	38,814	8.1	3,985	10	21,178	55	13,651	35
North Carolina	13,151	7.4	7,264	55	3,265	25	2,622	20
North Dakota	3,662	14.2	3,376	92	145	4	141	4
Ohio	18,028[c]	6.1	5,294	29	8,357	47	4,314	24
Oklahoma	2,512	2.9	569	23	495	20	1,448	57
Oregon	2,525	4.4	967	38	1,427	57	131	5
Puerto Rico	10,213	8.4	7,363	72	555	5	2,295	23
Rhode Island	1,893	7.3	658	35	968	51	267	14
South Carolina	4,667	4.7	3,052	65	606	13	1,009	22
South Dakota	727	2.8	346	48	304	42	77	10
Tennessee	3,034	2.3	1,331	44	1,396	46	307	10
Texas	2,608	0.8	1,704	65	689	27	215	8
Utah	979	3.0	437	45	493	50	49	5
Vermont	1,776	12.5	721	41	819	46	236	13
Virgin Islands	238	18.2	131	55	48	20	59	25
Virginia	9,571	7.1	3,236	34	5,377	56	958	10
Washington	6,190	7.0	2,213	36	3,069	49	908	15
West Virginia	7,362	9.0	4,721	64	1,994	27	647	9
Wisconsin	8,306	6.4	3,656	44	3,941	47	709	9
Wyoming	453	3.8	267	59	156	34	30	7
Total Incomplete reports	20,518	[e]	3,867	[e]	14,121	[e]	2,530	[e]
California	15,904	[e]	1,890	[e]	12,311	[e]	1,703	[e]
Nevada	176	[e]	94	[e]	94	[e]	28	[e]
Pennsylvania	4,438	[e]	1,923	[e]	1,716	[e]	799	[e]

a States with substantially complete reports are those reporting 90 percent or more of the children served. States with incomplete reports are those reporting less than 90 percent of the children served.

b Estimated civilian population under 21 years of age, July 1, 1953. Bureau of the Census. 1950 population data used for Alaska, Puerto Rico, and Virgin Islands.

c Includes 37,180 children reported as living in institutions and 10,306 reported as living elsewhere. The children reported in institutions represent only those served by workers attached to state or local public-welfare agencies and not all children receiving institutional care.

d Includes a number of children for whom whereabouts are unknown. For the total, this is less than 1 percent.

e Not computed because of incomplete report.

Source: Children's Bureau, *Children Receiving Child Welfare Casework Service From Public Welfare Agencies—March 31, 1954*, December, 1944. Table 1, p. 2.

The federal level of the state-federal partnership in child welfare is generally administered by the United States Children's Bureau, an

operating unit of the Social Security Administration of the Department of Health, Education, and Welfare. The Bureau was originally established in 1912 under the then Department of Commerce and Labor, but has several times responded to changing governmental organization. When the Department of Labor was created as a separate entity in 1913, the Children's Bureau went with it and remained there until 1946, when it was transferred to the Federal Security Agency. When that agency became part of the newly formed Department of Health, Education, and Welfare in 1953, the Bureau entered and has since remained in that department. There have also been changes in the mandate of responsibilities given the Bureau. Originally a research agency, charged with the investigation and reporting of all matters relating to child health and welfare, it has since been granted important administrative and enforcement duties by the Sheppard-Towner Maternity and Infancy Act (1921), the Social Security Act (1935), and the Fair Labor Standards Act (1939).[108] Today, the Bureau is responsible for the investigation and reporting of information pertinent to child welfare, the administration of federal grants for maternal and child health, crippled-children and child-welfare services under the Social Security Act, and acts in an advisory capacity for voluntary and public agencies concerned with child welfare.

Another important aspect of child welfare in general is the occasional convening of White House Conferences to consider the needs of children and the efficacy of existing child-welfare practices in meeting these needs. The first such conference was called in 1909, when President Theodore Roosevelt invited leading representatives from every phase of child-welfare work to Washington for a Conference on the Care of Dependent Children. As its title implies, the primary purpose of the meeting was to consider the needs of dependent children and to discuss the means by which these needs might be met. Following two days of discussion, the Conference unanimously adopted a platform which included recommendations which had a substantial effect upon child-welfare practice and principles in the years following. It recommended that children should not be removed from their family homes for reasons of poverty; if special reasons necessitated the child's removal from the home, then wherever possible placement should be in a foster home rather than in an institutional setting; if institutionalization was inescapable, the institutional setting

---

[108] Walter A. Friedlander, *Introduction to Social Welfare*, New York, Prentice-Hall, 1955, p. 130.

should be one of small-group cottage residence rather than a dormitory arrangement. Licensing and inspection of children's agencies by state authorities were also suggested.

Two of the recommendations of the Conference brought almost immediate results. Probably the most important recommendation was for the establishment of the Children's Bureau, providing federal participation in child-welfare activities as a nation-wide clearing house. The idea had originally been suggested by Lillian D. Wald, famous as the founder of both the Henry Street Settlement in New York City and the Visiting Nurse Association, and an attempt had been made in 1905 to produce federal legislation calling for such an agency. It was the action of the Conference and the vigorous support of social agencies which eventually led to the creation of the Bureau.

Another recommendation of the Conference resulted in the establishment of the Child Welfare League of America in 1920, a nation-wide voluntary organization which formulates standards and attempts to improve methods in child care. The organization continues at present as a league of voluntary and public child-welfare agencies which meet the self-imposed standards of membership.

The second White House Conference was convened in 1919 by the Children's Bureau as The Children's Bureau Conference on Child Welfare Standards. This second gathering, sanctioned by President Woodrow Wilson, covered a wider range of interests than the 1909 meetings. It discussed problems of child labor, maternal and child health, the preschool and school-age child, child dependency, juvenile delinquency, and child-welfare legislation. The results of this Conference led to the enactment of the Sheppard-Towner Maternity and Infancy Act in 1921 and provided the impetus for the creation of child-welfare divisions in many state departments of public welfare.

This conference was followed by a third White House Conference on Child Health and Protection convened in 1930 by President Herbert Hoover. This Conference issued The Children's Charter, affirming every child's right to spiritual and moral training, a home with love and security, protection and understanding from birth through adolescence, and proper schooling, recreation, and preparation for adulthood.[109]

The White House Conference on Children in a Democracy was called by President Franklin D. Roosevelt in 1940 and covered a broad range of topics, emphasizing the interrelatedness of the family

[109] Ibid., p. 131.

with other institutions, such as religion, education, and the government, the specific problems of children of racial and religious minorities, and the social and economic needs of children. Its proposals for implementing the broad policies of tolerance, economic and social security for children, and the health and welfare of every child were entrusted to a voluntary National Citizens Committee which was to follow up the recommendations. Many state-wide meetings were held, but the intervention of the Second World War made extensive continuation of most of these proposals impractical.

The fifth Conference was convened as the Midcentury White House Conference on Children and Youth by President Harry S. Truman in 1950. The central concern of the series of meetings was the development of a healthy personality for every child. Several important procedural innovations marked this Conference. Previous conferences had drawn their invited attendance from professional groups and leading laymen throughout the country, but the Midcentury Conference included broad citizen and youth participation. A three-stage sequence was followed, with extensive preconference preparation of fact-finding reports and efforts to increase the effectiveness of the conferences. These preliminaries were followed by the actual conferences and these in turn by the third step, extensive follow-up activities by citizen and professional groups and through widespread publications of the results and recommendations of the Conference.

The platform adopted by the Conference cited the central inquiry of the proceedings as being concerned with how the necessary mental, emotional, and spiritual qualities may be developed in children; how we may assure the physical, economic, and social conditions favorable to such development.[110] A large number of recommendations were made with respect to the furthering of healthy personality development in children and youth; the role of the family, the church, the school, and other social institutions in this development; and the influence of certain social and economic forces. Further recommendations suggested citizen mobilization for the improvement of conditions affecting young people and a series of specific resolutions calling for follow-up programs and future action. In December of 1953, two groups, the Advisory Council on State and Local Action and the Advisory Council on Participation of National Organizations, were given

---

[110] Edward A. Richards (ed.), *Proceedings of the Midcentury White House Conference on Children and Youth*, Raleigh, N.C., Health Publications Institute, 1951, p. 29.

the primary responsibility for carrying on the follow-up program of the Midcentury Conference.

Other Legislation Affecting Child Welfare

There has been much legislation concerned with the welfare problems of specific groups of children. Most of these are discussed elsewhere in this chapter or in other sections of the book; legislation affecting illegitimate children, adoptive children and their parents, and compulsory-school-attendance legislation were discussed in earlier sections of the chapter; and the special problems of juvenile delinquency and dependent and neglected children will follow in the next section. Child-labor laws will be treated along with the protection of employment conditions in Chapter 9, and laws affecting other areas of child welfare in Chapters 15 and 16 on the Social Security Act.

Juvenile and Family Courts

We have previously observed the growing tendency in legislative and judicial circles to treat the family as a legal unit in the same manner as the social scientist has come to look upon it as a social unit. Nowhere is this more obvious or welcome than in the development of special courts to handle matters of law relating to individuals as family members. This has been a unified movement, growing as the national social conscience has matured. But since our primary interest here is with the parent-child relationship, we shall dwell more fully on the development of the juvenile court and then relate this development to the ever-growing interest and reliance on a court for the family.

THE JUVENILE COURT MOVEMENT IN AMERICA

What are today called juvenile or children's courts are of relatively recent origin, awaiting the reaction of American legislatures and courts against the classification and confinement of children as adult criminals. But even at common law, children were given special status under the law when they were involved in legal difficulty. A child under 7 years of age could not be found guilty of a crime because he was presumed to be incapable of the necessary guilty intent (*mens rea*), a necessary element of a crime. Children 7 to 14 were presumed to be incapable of the necessary intent also, but this presumption could be overcome by evidence indicating that the child was capable of distinguishing between right and wrong. Once beyond the age of 14, the

child was an adult in regard to his culpability for crimes and the penalty he might receive.[111]

The application of this rule led in many instances to the punishment and even execution of children deemed juvenile offenders under modern sociolegal definitions. In Plymouth Colony, for example, a law passed in 1671 provided the death penalty for stubbornness and rebelliousness by children toward their parents.[112] In 1828, a boy of 13 was hanged in New Jersey for a crime committed when he was 12 years old.[113] There is considerable evidence, however, that in many cases where such severe penalties were imposed upon children they were never actually carried out.[114]

It was during the early part of the nineteenth century that the states first began to enact legislation designed to eliminate the treatment of child lawbreakers as adults. The movement, which culminated in the development of specialized courts for children, consisted of three major phases of legislation. The first phase was the establishment of separate facilities for the confinement of juvenile offenders previously housed in the same institutions and even the same cells as adult criminals. New York established the first juvenile reformatory, the House of Refuge, in 1825, and was followed by Pennsylvania in 1828 and neighboring Massachusetts in 1847. Other states soon began to provide these separate facilities, either as separate institutions or in separate sections of existing facilities.

The second major development was legislative provision for separate hearings in cases involving minor children and for probation. Massachusetts pioneered in 1869 with a law providing that a visiting officer or agent of the State Board of Charities should attend cases involving children to protect the child's interests in court.[115] This was followed in the same state by an 1870 law which required that the Suffolk County (Boston) courts try children under 16 "separate from the general and ordinary criminal business," and established their jurisdiction in the probate courts elsewhere in the state.[116] In 1872, the provision

---

[111] Regina v. Smith, 1 Cox. C. C. 260 (1845).

[112] Grace Abbott, The Child and the State, Chicago, University of Chicago Press, 1938, Vol. II, p. 324.

[113] Herbert H. Lou, Juvenile Courts in the United States, Chapel Hill, University of North Carolina Press, 1927, p. 14, n. 3.

[114] Cf. Negley G. Teeters and John O. Reinemann, The Challenge of Delinquency, New York, Prentice-Hall, 1950, pp. 69 ff.

[115] Sheldon and Eleanor T. Glueck, One Thousand Juvenile Delinquents, Cambridge, Mass., Harvard University Press, 1934, p. 10. See also Abbott, op. cit., Vol. II, pp. 366–368; and Lou, op. cit., pp. 16–17.

[116] Glueck and Glueck, op. cit., p. 10.

for separate trials was extended to all pertinent courts in the state, and in 1877 a separate session for juvenile offenders was provided for with its own court records and docket.[117] To Massachusetts belongs similar credit for the first probation system, which placed juvenile offenders under supervision rather than in confinement.[118] This law, passed in 1880, was anticipated in some respects by Chicago's limited system of probation for boys, which began in 1861.

The final stage of the juvenile-court movement was the actual establishment of separate juvenile courts where children could be treated as wards of the state requiring special care and treatment usually unobtainable in a court with a criminal-law orientation. The world's first juvenile court was established in Illinois as the Juvenile Court of Cook County by an act of the legislature on July 1, 1899. This first law emerged as a remarkably "modern" concept of the court's responsibility to the child and society, as is illustrated by a section of the act itself:

This act shall be liberally construed, to the end that its purpose may be carried out, to wit: That the care, custody and discipline of a child shall approximate as nearly as may be that which should be given by its parents, and in all cases where it can properly be done the child be placed in an improved family home and become a member of the family by legal adoption or otherwise.[119]

The title of the act, An Act to Regulate the Treatment and Control of Dependent, Neglected and Delinquent Children, indicates the breadth of its coverage of children's problems. In actuality, however, the new law did not provide for separate courts, but for separate courtrooms where juvenile cases could be heard. The principal contribution of this law was its clear conception of the futility of attempting to treat children as criminals.

This first juvenile-court law was followed in rapid order by the passage of similar statutes in other states, so that by 1904, five years later, Colorado, Pennsylvania, Wisconsin, New York, Maryland, California, Missouri, New Jersey, Indiana, Iowa, and Ohio had passed legislation calling for juvenile courts. The next decade marked a period of great growth in the concept of separate courts for children, for by 1920 only three states lacked juvenile-court laws. Today, every American jurisdic-

[117] Ibid.
[118] Lou, op. cit., pp. 17–18.
[119] Laws of Illinois, 1899, Sec. 21, p. 137, reproduced in Glueck and Glueck, op. cit., p. 12.

tion has some form of juvenile-court legislation, although they differ widely and in some cases have not actually instituted functionally adequate courts for the treatment of juveniles.

The legal mandate for these courts may be found in the common-law and equity doctrines. The early equity or chancery courts had jurisdiction over cases in which the welfare or property of children was involved. This responsibility was delegated from the authority of the crown under the principle that "the care of all infants is lodged in the king, and by the king this care is delegated to his Courts of Chancery." [120] Thus, the designation of the king as the "father of his country" (parens patriae) and his duty to protect his wards established the jurisdiction of courts in the equity pattern over dependent and neglected children.

But since the equity courts lacked jurisdiction over children in criminal cases, the extension of this principle to include delinquent children represented a new departure from the common law by what Dean Roscoe Pound has characterized as an example of "judicial empiricism." [121] A new legal institution was created.

The laws providing for juvenile courts did not go without challenge as to their constitutionality. The bases for the several challenges were the contentions that they violated the right of the child to trial by jury, denied him the right of appeal, imposed unequal penalties, and in general deprived him of his liberty without due process of law. Almost unanimously, the courts have upheld the constitutionality of the laws against these attacks, explaining that, since the purpose of the juvenile court is therapeutic rather than punitive, it does not involve a criminal proceeding and need not accord such constitutional guarantees.[122]

CURRENT JUVENILE-COURT PROCEDURES

Juvenile delinquency has become a major social problem. This concern results from recent increases both in the number and severity of juvenile crimes. Since the beginning of the Second World War, the number of such crimes reported to the police and the number of court cases involving juveniles have shown a tendency to increase sharply. As Figure 3 indicates, the increase in juvenile-court cases was

[120] Eyre v. Shaftsbury, W. Peere Williams, 103 (1772); See also Wellesley v. Beaufort, 2 Russ. 1 (1827).
[121] Roscoe Pound, Interpretations of Legal History, Cambridge, Mass., Harvard University Press, 1923, p. 134.
[122] See Commonwealth v. Fisher, 213 Penn. 48 (1905), and also Ex parte Januszewski, 196 Fed. 123 (1911); Cinque v. Boyd, 99 Conn. 121 Atl. 678 (1923).

especially pronounced during the wartime period of social disorganization, but showed a decreasing trend in the three years following the
war. Beginning in 1949, however, the upward trend was renewed, until
in 1953 it was 45 percent higher than in 1948.

The explanations advanced for these increases are legion: family

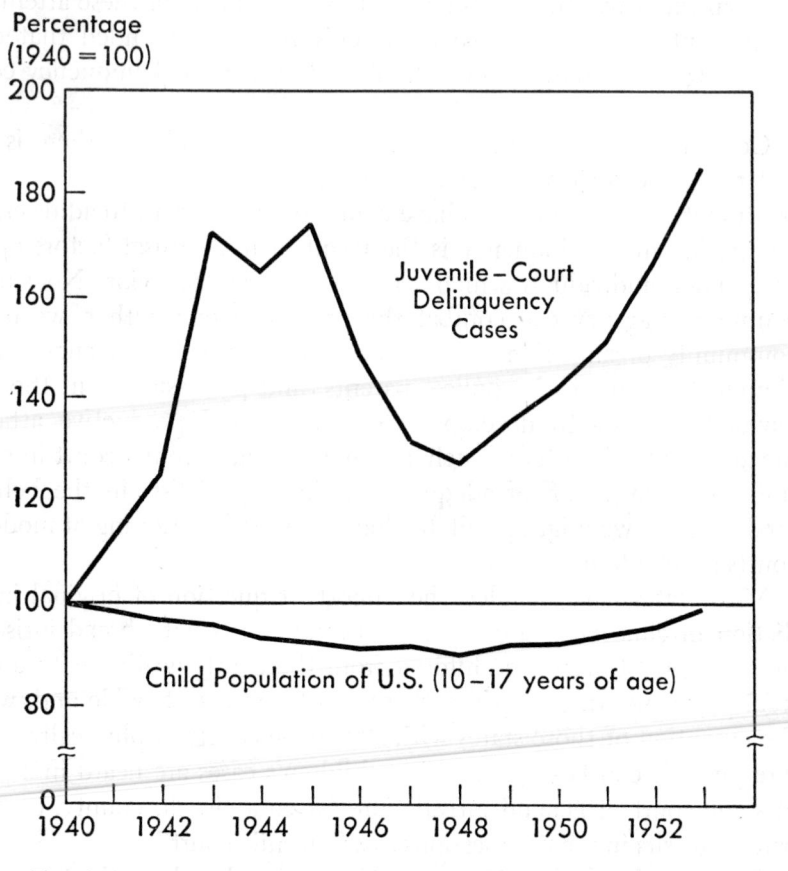

Fig. 3. Juvenile Court Cases and Child Population, 1940–1953.

disintegration, the loss of religious and moral values, rapid social
change, comic books and other mass media of communication, parental neglect, working mothers, and others too numerous to catalogue.
Some have found the explanation in better, or at least more frequent
diagnosis, pointing out that many of the delinquent acts of today were
mischief in our parents' generation, and hence the increases are paper
ones with no substance in fact. To combat these increases, an even
more impressive area of techniques and approaches has been suggested: environmental improvement through slum clearance, better

recreational and athletic facilities and boys' clubs, improvement of educational facilities, punishment of parents rather than the children, education of the parents for social responsibility, establishing curfews for children below certain ages, and numerous other techniques limited only by the number of proffered causes of delinquency. In 1954, after an extensive study of the effectiveness of many of these attempts to prevent delinquency, the Children's Bureau concluded that our knowledge at present is "uncertain" in the field of delinquency control.[123]

Certain points, however, do emerge with some clarity: there is no isolated cause of juvenile delinquency and hence no unitary cure or treatment. As criminologists have come to see in regard to adult criminality, juvenile delinquency is the result of multicausal factors operating upon individuals which lead to criminal behavior. No single community agency can combat the problem alone; rather, we need community organization of all interested and involved agencies—the church, the school, the police, parents, and professionals in the behavioral sciences—to develop an efficacious and productive attack. Since the logical center of such a program is the juvenile court in consultation with a staff of adequately trained specialists in the behavioral sciences, we might profitably look into the functioning of modern courts for children.

Most states have handled the important question of original jurisdiction in children's cases by establishing courts with broad jurisdiction designed to remove children from the courts dealing with adult legal problems. In most cases these courts are county-wide and, with the exception of those states with state-wide courts or physically separate juvenile courts in large cities, children's cases are heard in a part of some court of general jurisdiction. Often a circuit, county, or probate court sits in separate sessions as a "juvenile court."

Cases coming before these courts may involve dependent or neglected children; children charged with delinquent acts; those in which an adult commits some act or omission, such as a crime against a child or violation of the child-labor laws; and questions of guardianship or protection of children. A further limitation of jurisdiction is effected by imposing age limits which sometimes vary according to the child's sex or the nature of the case. The upper age limit varies between 16 and 21, but is most frequently set at 18 for both sexes, as suggested by

[123] Helen L. Witmer and Edith Tufts, *The Effectiveness of Delinquency Prevention Programs*, Children's Bureau Publication No. 350–1954, 1954, p. 47.

the Children's Bureau. All juvenile-court laws list the violation of the law or ordinances as sufficient cause for bringing a child before the court, but also list many other actions which constitute due cause. The most frequently listed are being habitually truant or incorrigible, knowingly associating with thieves or other immoral persons, growing up in idleness or crime, conduct injurious to self or others, immoral or indecent conduct, and absence from the home without just cause and consent. Some states except crimes punishable by death or life imprisonment from original jurisdiction in juvenile courts, and in some states "concurrent original jurisdiction" is established between the juvenile and criminal courts. Most of the states provide that the juvenile court may waive even exclusive jurisdiction and permit the minor to be tried in a criminal court. Many states also provide for the extension of jurisdiction up to 21 years of age once the case has been established in the juvenile court's jurisdiction.

Since the fundamental purpose of these courts differs considerably from that of the criminal courts, the procedure is also quite different. The proceedings are initiated by a petition rather than the complaint or indictment used in the criminal court. This petition should include at least the following information:

1. The facts alleged to bring the child before the court.
2. The name, age and residence of the child.
3. The names and residences of his parents or guardian of the person.
4. The names and residences of any other persons having legal custody or physical care of the child and of his nearest relative if he has neither parents nor guardian.
5. The child's spouse, in case of marriage.[124]

Following the filing of the petition by a police officer, social worker, probation officer, or the person making complaint, a summons is usually issued calling for the appearance of the child and his parent or guardian in the court at a specified time. Failure to comply may lead to a charge of contempt or to the issuance of a warrant to take the child into custody.

Most juvenile-court laws provide for a social history apart from the evidence necessary to establish the facts in the case. These histories usually cover the circumstances surrounding the cause of the child's difficulty, a family history, and other pertinent information regarding the child's environment and social-psychological background.

[124] Children's Bureau, *Standards for Specialized Courts Dealing with Children*, Children's Bureau Publication No. 346–1954, 1954, p. 48.

The actual hearings are kept as informal as possible in order to avoid the suggestion of criminal proceedings. In keeping with the conception of a therapeutic approach, the public is usually excluded and usual technicalities governing courtroom procedure are kept at a minimum. In many minor cases, the child never actually reaches the courtroom, the adjudication taking place in the judge's chambers or some action being taken by the probation staff prior to any contact between the child and the judge.

If the allegation against the child is accepted by the court, he is most often "adjudicated a juvenile delinquent" rather than convicted of a crime. Thus he is not liable for the civil disabilities which often go with criminal conviction and hinder his life in the community. Upon adjudicating the child as delinquent, the court may (1) find that no further action is necessary and dismiss or discharge the child; (2) place the child on probation; (3) remove legal custody of the child to an authorized agency, institution, or individual in a foster-home placement; or (4) commit the child to a juvenile-correction institution. The nature of the disposition is, of course, a function of the nature of the offense, the previous delinquency of the child, and other factors deemed pertinent by the court.

As a protective device in the child's interest, the court records are usually maintained as private and are not available for public inspection. Where the juvenile court is a part of some court of general jurisdiction, its records are usually separate from those of the larger court. Some states have even provided that the records of juvenile court cases must be destroyed after some specified period of time.

The juvenile court is a forward-looking development, but it can be no more effective than its personnel. These usually include the judge, various referees appointed by the judge to handle certain cases, the probation staff, and, frequently, a board or committee of lay-citizen advisers to the court. In recent years, juvenile courts have also added a clinical staff of physicians, psychiatrists, and clinical psychologists to aid the probation staff in garnering as much valuable information concerning the child as possible, and frequently to advise the court on matters relating to the physical and psychological well-being of the child.

The qualifications of the court personnel are an important factor in the effectiveness of the court. The judge, in addition to his legal training, should be vitally interested in children and their problems and

have some training in or awareness of the findings of modern psychology, psychiatry, and social work. The referee, who often functions as an "assistant judge," should possess the same qualifications as the judge wherever possible.

Probation officers should be selected on the basis of their fitness and training, although most states make little mention of qualifications other than that the individual should be a discreet and suitable person for the position. Minimum educational qualifications should be graduation from college, preferably with a major in one of the behavioral sciences and some experience in social casework, and the ultimate goal should be graduation from accredited schools of social work.[125]

The national government was slow to establish the principle of the juvenile court in the federal judiciary. A federal probation act which included juveniles who would come before the national courts on postal law, narcotics, or other federal charges was enacted in 1925, but needed additional legislation in later years to make it effective.[126] In conjunction with the 1930 White House Conference on Child Health and Protection, the Wickersham Commission on Law Observance and Enforcement made a study of federal juvenile offenders. The Commission's report resulted in the passage of a bill in 1932 authorizing federal district attorneys to surrender jurisdiction of offenders under 21 years of age to state jurisdiction if the offense could be brought under the laws of that state and if this was in the best interests of the federal government.[127] The law further required that the juvenile offender signify his willingness to be returned and that the state juvenile court concerned be willing to accept him.[128] If the executive authority of the state demanded the juvenile's return, his consent was unnecessary. Finally, in 1938, the Congress passed a bill which led to the establishment of juvenile-court proceedings for federal offenders under 18 not returned to state jurisdiction.[129]

Since that time, the federal government has operated national training schools and reform institutions for minors which are among the best in the country, and has taken the lead, through the Children's

---

[125] See the "Report on Juvenile Court Administration, National Conference on Prevention and Control of Juvenile Delinquency, Washington, Government Printing Office. 1946," 1947, pp. 8–9, in this respect. A summary of the recommendations concerning the necessary minimal qualifications for probation officers is included in Children's Bureau, op. cit., p. 86, n. 6.

[126] 43 U.S. Stats. Ch. 521 (1925).

[127] 37 U.S. Stats. 301 Ch. 243 (1932).

[128] Ibid.

[129] 52 U.S. Stats. 764 (1938).

Bureau, in establishing standards for juvenile-court procedure. In 1955, the Bureau established a Division of Juvenile Delinquency Service to provide technical advice and guidance to states and communities to aid them in dealing with the growing problems of juvenile delinquency.

THE FAMILY COURT

From the juvenile-court movement sprang the movement for the establishment of domestic-relations or family courts. The basic premise of this movement was that the proven procedures of the juvenile court could be applied with equal success to a wider range of family problems and domestic discords. The first tangible step in this direction was the establishment in 1910 of a domestic-relations division under the newly created city court in Buffalo. This court's domestic-relations division was given jurisdiction over all criminal matters relating to the family, such as illegitimacy and wayward minors over 16 but not yet 21 years of age.[130] In 1924, this jurisdiction was extended to include equity matters.

The first court combining domestic-relations and juvenile cases into one jurisdiction was opened in Cincinnati in 1914, and other Ohio cities soon followed suit. This marked the real beginning of the family-court tradition, for now most of the cases affecting individuals as family members were heard in one court. Other states have since followed this pattern in general, but with enough individualism so that today there are five different forms of family-type courts in the United States:

1. A family court with juvenile and broad adult jurisdiction hearing children's cases, and adult cases involving divorce, desertion, non-support, dependency and contributing to the child's delinquency.
2. A family court of juvenile and limited adult jurisdiction which is less inclusive than the range of cases in the first type.
3. A juvenile court with broad jurisdiction which includes adult cases but not divorce actions.
4. A domestic relations court which has jurisdiction over adult cases of desertion, non-support, certain offenses against children and sometimes bastardy cases as well although it has no juvenile division.
5. A municipal or district court which is granted juvenile and domestic

---

[130] Bernard Flexner, Reuben Oppenheimer, and Katherine F. Lenroot. *The Child, the Family and the Court*, Children's Bureau Publication No. 193, Washington, Government Printing Office 1929, p. 13.

relations jurisdiction and special organization for family court procedure.[131]

The procedure followed is also similar to the juvenile courts. The staff should include social workers with casework experience, trained probation officers whose qualifications approximate those described for the juvenile-court staff, physicians, psychiatrists, clinical psychologists, and, ideally, marriage counselors trained in the social sciences. The proceedings are informal and the court tries by every possible means to minimize the adversary nature of court cases.[132] Hearings are held only after careful study and analysis by the clinical staff and the summarization of the pertinent material for the judge's benefit. Since the court is essentially an "implemented caseworking agency," personal interviews, often in the client's home, are its most effective techniques.[133] The ideal situation calls for the absence of lawyers and juries at the actual hearing, which has a conciliatory orientation and becomes punitive only as a final resort. The skill, training, and dedication of the judge and his staff can develop a program of family-court techniques which can redesignate the courts, wherein so many families break up, into a therapeutic community where family problems are faced, discussed, and reconciled and families made whole again.

Family Legislation, The Parent-Child Relationship: Concluding Remarks

This survey of the history and current directions of legislation dealing with the relationship among parents, their children, and the community has pictured an extensive but confused attempt on the part of society to regulate equitably reciprocal rights and duties and so ensure a stable and functional family unit. In their attempts to bring about this universally sought end, the means of the lawmakers have often seemed capricious and wanting in any concept of concern for the dependent members of the family. Under the early common law, the father was supreme, with fully protected rights and legally impeccable duties toward his wife and children.

From the earliest history of this country, our legislation has been concerned with reducing the arbitrary powers of the father and bolstering the rights of his wife and children. Another characteristic of

[131] Ibid., pp. 15, 16. See also Paul W. Alexander, "What is a Family Court, Anyway?", Connecticut Bar Journal, September, 1952, pp. 243–278, and particularly the table on p. 278.

[132] Alexander, op. cit., p. 248.

[133] Ibid.

this legislation has been its emphasis upon the welfare of the child as an individual deserving the consideration of society. Where parental responsibilities have not or cannot be met, the state has stepped in and protected the health and well-being of the child; where he has become involved in acts which are socially condemned, society has learned to apply a mother's toleration to the child's misdeeds and hope that a therapeutic approach will develop adults properly adjusted to the societal values. Finally, we have come to treat the family unit as a unit in both legislation and before the courts by establishing laws and courts which attempt to ensure family unity by approaching the family as a functioning social unit.

SELECTED REFERENCES

Becker, Howard, and Hill, Reuben, *Family, Marriage and Parenthood*, Boston, D. C. Heath and Company, 1955.

Bossard, James H. S., *The Sociology of Child Development*, New York, Harper and Brothers, 1948.

Teeters, Negley G., and Reinemann, John O., *The Challenge of Delinquency*, New York, Prentice-Hall, 1950.

Vernier, Chester G., *American Family Laws*, Stanford University, Stanford University Press, 1931–1936.

Witmer, Helen L., and Kotinsky, Ruth (eds.), *Personality in the Making*, New York, Harper & Brothers, 1952.

PART IV

THE LABOR MOVEMENT AND LABOR LAW

The American Labor Movement and Labor Legislation

Labor problems, as we understand them, came into existence with the Industrial Revolution during the eighteenth century. Income insecurity, disabling accidents, protracted working hours, and old-age dependency all became social problems with the onset of the Industrial Revolution. It is likely, of course, that persons who depend for a livelihood on the use made of their labor by associations with which they have no familial relationship have always constituted a social problem. The burden of poverty and misery which has been associated with the basic producing, labor classes has always strained social relationships and threatened social stability. To the alleviation of the crushing burdens which life meted out to them, downtrodden workmen have at various times sought relief through combining their efforts, and the term "labor movement" carries the meaning of an organized effort with some continuity which seeks redress of labor problems through economic and political means.

Some historians have seen a continuity in the labor movement going back to Biblical times, and Wright hails the Exodus of the Jews from Egypt under Moses as "the greatest strike that has been recorded." [1] Similar observations are made concerning the uprising of the gladiators under Spartacus about 73 B.C. and the Peasants' War of the sixteenth century. Since these incidents were in most instances spontaneous and involved slaves and their masters, for the most part, their continuity with the modern labor movement is artificial. The modern labor movement is largely the story of how trade unions united to gain

[1] Carroll D. Wright, *The Battles of Labor*, Philadelphia, George W. Jacobs and Company, 1906, p. 29.

the title to legal existence and legal right to ply their weapons against employers. In this sense it is a phenomenon about 160 years old.

The American Labor Movement

Among organizations deliberately formed by laborers to contest the economic and legal power of employers, the American labor movement is unique in many respects. In the first place, the movement was long delayed. Because the availability of agricultural opportunities was general, at least until the mid-nineteenth century, laborers had an alternative to factory employment. There was less willingness to cast one's lot with the trade unions, then, when a simpler course could be followed. Furthermore, the American faith that any persevering young man could become a capitalist if he really applied himself gained many adherents, and, if the realities did not square with the ideal, at least mobility upward was sufficiently open to keep alive the faith. Men who do not expect to be laborers for an appreciable period of their lives are not enthusiasts about working for trade-union success. Leadership was also scarce within the labor movement during its early years because persons of real leadership capabilities found positions in industry, and virtually all of the leaders of the earlier American trade unions were drawn from within the labor ranks. The shortage of leaders who could or would devote their lifetimes to the labor movement added to the delay in the spread of the movement. In the second place, the American labor movement has been predominantly conservative, numbering itself among the advocates of free-enterprise capitalism, with only a few glaring exceptions. No labor party has ever gained the approval and support of the labor movement in the United States, except in a few cities, and the prospects of this form of political activity have not changed. Finally, it should be noted that the American labor movement gained its way in the most hostile kind of environment. Individualism and the Whig philosophy were deeply ingrained in the American myth complex, and the result has been an exceptionally violent history of labor-management relations.

Factors Motivating Employee Organization

Throughout the nineteenth century it was broadly true that diligence (and a little luck) could carry a man in his lifetime from laborer to entrepreneur or manager. Labor organizations gained importance before such opportunities seriously decreased, however, largely because of new developments which threatened the workingman. Primary

among these threats were increased mechanization, the arrival of the large corporation as an employer, the establishment of a nation-wide transportation and communication system, the decline of agriculture, and an increase in the immigration of unskilled Europeans. Organization on a significant scale, i.e., after 1867, stemmed from these factors.

MECHANIZATION

Beginning in the 1830's a veritable flood of techniques was developed for mechanizing previously hand-wrought operations. Drop forging, die stamping, power looming, and machine sewing are examples. First the cotton industry and then a whole series of industries, including iron, shoes, and glass, came within a factory system of operation. Craftsmen, particularly, felt the effects of this movement toward concentrated production within the factory. With the dilution of skill through division of labor, the uniqueness of skill attainment, the most valuable property possessed by the employee, became less and less important. Mobility among jobs increased and hence competition of laborers with one another. Furthermore, women and children who had, as employees, formerly lightened the burden on the individual craftsman in his home shop gradually became his competitors for factory employment. These developments prompted organizations of craftsmen, which had formerly sought merely to maintain standards, to adopt broad programs of operation.

THE LARGE CORPORATION AS AN EMPLOYER

Mechanization led to another development which spelled trouble for craftsmen. So large was the investment required for the installation and operation of the new machinery that master craftsmen could not afford to be self-employed capitalists. They entered into a relationship of dependency upon an organization which, for the profit of owners, purchased machinery and organized production. For less-skilled workmen the changes in scale were also significant. Whereas he may have been employed in a carpentry shop in a close relationship to his employer prior to the advent of the large corporation, the unskilled workman now worked for an organization with little chance of knowing the employer. Accordingly, the degree of understanding between employer and employee deteriorated. No machinery seemed to exist whereby employers and laborers could communicate their feelings. Competition among firms in similar lines of production forced an increasing pace of work or lower hourly wages, or both, in order to

decrease costs. To offset this change in bargaining position, some workmen sought to organize themselves.

ESTABLISHMENT OF A NATION-WIDE TRANSPORTATION AND COMMUNICATIONS SYSTEM

As the sectionalism of the country was broken down through the development of turnpikes, canals, and then railroads, the local advantages which had accrued to some workmen suffered. First of all, the competition among goods became more widespread, causing increased attention to cost reduction; and, where workmen had gained local advantages in wages and hours, they tended to decrease toward the wages-and-hours level of the least-advantageous competitive area. In a truly national market, therefore, the lowest wages paid tended to become the standard wages paid. Improved communications facilities also made information about local advantages more widespread, thus attracting other workmen and resulting in downward pressure on conditions of employment.

INCREASED IMMIGRATION

Large-scale immigration had characterized the American society throughout the nineteenth century. Beginning in the late 1840's, however, the pace of immigration accelerated rapidly as a result of revolutionary conditions in Prussia and famine in Ireland. For the two decades 1841–1880, immigration averaged 2,500,000 per decade. In each of the three decades 1881–1910, the average was 4,500,000 per decade. Until the 1880's, there was a tendency for immigrants to enter agriculture in large proportions, but thereafter the character of immigration changed and immigrants were largely unskilled common laborers. In an economy which had undergone wide-scale mechanization and division of labor, it was inevitable that employers would seek their labor supply from this influx because of their lower wage standards. More than any other factor, immigration provoked large-scale unionization, including unskilled and semiskilled workmen.

These factors constituted conditions of stress which, one might expect, would bring workmen into trade unions in large numbers. No mass enlistment took place, however, and it was not until the 1930's that workmen in any appreciable numbers entered unions. The reluctance of workmen to enter unions seems to be explained by such factors as (1) the general rise of real wages throughout the nineteenth century owing to mechanization and the shortage of labor; (2) the

hostile social environment, particularly in small towns; (3) such organizations as existed not being able to determine exactly what they wanted for labor, nor how they would obtain those objects upon which agreement was general; and (4) legal obstacles which held organizations of workmen to be conspiracies under the common law.

Early American Labor Organizations, 1791–1881

Craft organizations among carpenters, cordwainers, printers, and tailors arose in the large coastal cities before the end of the eighteenth century. Their programs stressed welfare functions for members in need, but enforcement of apprenticeship requirements and attempts to improve working conditions were also undertaken. The period of retrenchment embraces roughly the years 1800 to 1827 and was characterized by craft-union separateness, each craft carrying on its operations autonomously. During this period, two developments were noteworthy. First, the extension of the vote was accomplished as property qualifications disappeared. Second, the conspiracy doctrine which had seen a Philadelphia court find the Philadelphia Cordwainers guilty of two offenses—"one was a combination to raise wages, the other a combination to injure others"—was meliorated.[2] After 1827, the labor movement gained strength because of the suffering which had been occasioned by the panic of 1819 and the recognized need for coördination among city craft organizations. In 1827, building-trades workers in Philadelphia banded together in the first concerted movement among trade unions. They entered politics through the formation of the Working Men's party and held the balance of power in Philadelphia for several years. Strikes for the ten-hour-day became common. In these experiences, the cause of the labor movement was significantly strengthened. The real beginning of the American labor movement is usually dated from 1827.

During the period 1827–1850, the labor movement displayed many valences. On the one hand, there was the attempt to nationalize the city trade unions; and on the other, the flirtation with various movements outside of labor, including associationism, coöperation, and agrarianism. Two events are of utmost importance during the period, however: first, the Panic of 1837, which wiped out all but a few of the trade unions; and second, the *Commonwealth* v. *Hunt* decision issued by the Supreme Judicial Court of Massachusetts in 1842, which

---

[2] John R. Commons, et al., *History of Labour in the United States*, New York, The Macmillan Company, 1921, Vol. I, p. 140.

removed the legal impediments of the conspiracy doctrine from union operations. The period, all things considered, was not without importance to the labor movement. A labor press was created and pressures for free public education were rewarded. But the immediate ends of labor organizations—wages and hours—were largely unaffected. The National Trades Union, organized at the urging of the New York General Trades Union in 1834, in each of its three annual conventions called for a program of social, civic, and political reform. Because of the heterogeneity of its membership, it could not more precisely state its aims. Even the economic disturbances which were apparent in 1836, and would bring widespread misery in the following year, were dealt with only in general terms as committees to investigate "speculation" were set up. The depression of 1837 lasted until 1842, and it broke the strength of the labor movement. Following this defeat, workmen turned to promises of utopias: first, associations on the plans of Fourier, Brisbane, and Owen; and later, coöperatives under Horace Greeley's influence.

The decade of the 1850's saw the reëmergence of the labor movement in a very different form. Disillusioned over the failure of idealistic schemes to cushion them from economic shocks, workmen formed permanent and exclusive organizations concerned frankly with improving wages. The major labor weapon is clearly indicated by Commons in the following account of union activities:

In August 1849, the Boston tailors went on strike for a higher scale of prices. This was followed by a number of strikes in other places during 1850, 1851, 1852, many of them unsuccessful. In 1850 in New York there were strikes by boot makers, bricklayers, carpenters, painters, coopers, cordwainers, printers, and common labourers. In 1851 labourers, painters, and tailors went out on strike; in 1852 carpenters, cartmen, coopers, 'longshoremen, and sail makers. In 1850 the printers of Philadelphia took the initiative and were followed by eighteen other trades. In the absence of trade agreements, strikes and threats to strike were the only weapons available to the workers.[3]

Until the outbreak of the Civil War the strike remained the major operation of trade associations, the total number of strikes during the years 1853–1860 being estimated at 400.[4] When the depression of 1857 fell on the labor movement, the results were different from the 1837 experience. The attrition in strength was less, many unions

[3] *Ibid.*, Vol. I, p. 576.
[4] *Ibid.*, p. 607.

surviving and more determined than ever before to secure their wages. Rising prices and the competition of immigrants gave a sharper edge to their efforts.

The period following the Civil War was one of unparalleled action to better labor conditions. Between 1864 and 1873, some twenty-six national trade unions were established, and they attained a membership of nearly 300,000.[5] This was also the period of renewed attempts to form a national organization which would represent labor in general. The National Labor Union (1866) was such an attempt. It was the predecessor in direct line of the Knights of Labor and the American Federation of Labor. Among the changes sought by the National Labor Union was the eight-hour day, offered as "the most important change to us as workingmen." Within a year, the eight-hour day had been obtained on government contracts. Until 1870, annual congresses were held by the National Labor Union, but they barely served to hold the diverse membership together. The depression of 1873–1879 sealed its fate, and for the third time in the nineteenth century a severe blow was dealt to the labor movement by depression. The cycle of growing membership during prosperity and declining membership during depressions was repeated. One union with ambitions to organize all American labor survived the depression, and achieved notable success during the decade of the eighties—the Knights of Labor. Native American in leadership and largely in personnel, the Knights were skillfully led by Terence V. Powderly, who saw the necessity of abandoning the secret nature of the organization to obtain public confidence. The broad interests of the Knights are suggested by the exclusions which they made in their membership— "no person who either sells, or makes his living by the sale of, intoxicating drink, can be admitted, and no lawyer, doctor or banker can be admitted"—interests which narrowed to matters of wages when the decade of the eighties involved them in numerous strikes. In 1885, a strike against certain of Jay Gould's railroad interests was won by the Knights through the chance of their having caught the unscrupulous magnate when his resources were low. The effect on the labor movement was very fortunate, because many strikes had been lost in 1884. Commons describes the reaction of the laboring classes to the strike as follows:

Here a labour organization for the first time dealt on an equal footing

[5] Chester W. Wright, *Economic History of the United States*, New York, McGraw-Hill Book Company, 1949, p. 608.

with the most powerful capitalist in the country. It forced Jay Gould to recognise it as a power equal to himself, a fact which he amply conceded when he declared his readiness to arbitrate all labour difficulties that might arise. The oppressed labouring masses finally discovered a champion which could curb the power of a man stronger even than the government itself. All of the pentup feeling of bitterness and resentment which had accumulated during the two years of depression, in consequence of the repeated cuts in wages, and the intensified domination by employers, now found vent in a rush to organise under the banner of the powerful Knights of Labor.[6]

The rush was of sizable proportions. From a membership of about 100,000 in 1885, the Knights grew to 700,000 following the successful strike. On the horizon, however, was the Waterloo of the organization. It became identified in the public mind with the strike of 1886, in connection with its program for the eight-hour day, against the McCormick Harvester Works in Chicago. Following the dispersal of striking workmen who attacked strikebreakers as they left the McCormick plant, a call was issued for all strikers to assemble in Haymarket Square the following day. When the police again intervened to maintain order, a bomb was thrown which killed one person and fatally injured six more. The public reaction was intense, and the Knights, though on record against the demonstration, were held guilty by association with the anarchists, seven of whom were convicted of murder in the bomb incident. From this point on, the power of the Knights declined precipitously, falling to 100,000 by 1890. The union's place was to be taken by the American Federation of Labor.

The American Labor Movement, 1881–1936

In 1881, there had been formed a conspicuously unsuccessful federation called the Federation of Organized Trades and Labor Unions. Its agreement to merge with the newly formed American Federation of Labor in 1886 contributed little to the latter organization. The American Federation of Labor, however, was able to capitalize on the decline of the Knights of Labor in the years following 1887. In no small part this was owing to the Knights' policy of using skilled craftsmen as leverage to obtain greater benefits for the unskilled membership. The craftsmen were ready to support a new organization. After 1889, moreover, the Knights had come under the control of farmers.

The American Federation of Labor was a new venture in the labor

---

[6] Commons, *op. cit.*, Vol. II, p. 370.

movement. Formed as a loose federation of craft organizations for economic action, it had the advantage of homogeneous membership which the Knights of Labor had so obviously lacked. After weathering two serious setbacks during the decade of the nineties, the Homestead strike against Carnegie and the depression of 1893, the AF of L was prepared for almost anything. At its helm in the presidency was Samuel Gompers, who for thirty-eight years gave its operations the imprint of his personal convictions. Each constituent trade union was autonomous in order to retain strength at the local level, and partisan involvement in politics was not a general policy of the organization until after Gompers' death in 1924. With his death, the advance of the AF of L was imperiled and its vitality faltered between 1920 and 1935.

The growth of the AF of L is shown in Table 21. Between 1897 and 1904, the membership increased six times. On other occasions the membership doubled, as in the periods 1916–1920 and 1931–1942. Moreover, the membership increased nearly four times during the period 1933–1950.

TABLE 21. Membership of the American Federation of Labor, 1897–1950.

Period	Number of Affiliated Unions	Total Membership
1897–	58	265,000
1901	87	788,000
1904	120	1,676,000
1910	120	1,562,000
1916	111	2,073,000
1920	110	4,079,000
1924	107	2,866,000
1930	104	2,961,000
1935	109	3,045,000
1940	105	4,247,000
1945	102	6,931,000
1950	107	7,143,000
1952	109	8,043,000

Source: U.S. Department of Labor, Bureau of Labor Statistics, *Handbook of Labor Statistics,* 1950, p. 139.

The apparent ease with which membership in the AF of L increased should not obscure the contest which it waged for survival in a hostile environment. In 1903, the National Association of Manufacturers began its function as national spokesman for the open shop and against the labor movement, declaring against the recognition of unions at its

eighth annual convention. Under the aegis of the NAM, a Citizens' Industrial Alliance was constituted, which fought labor unions so successfully that it could by 1908 relax its influence and look upon a mission accomplished. The NAM also entered into political activity in an endeavor to defeat those congressmen who seemed friendly to labor, and in 1904 its efforts were crowned with success. In self-defense, the AF of L was forced to abandon its tradition of non-partisan political participation and seek to prevent the election of its enemies. The year 1906 saw the presentation by the AF of L of Labor's Bill of Grievances to the President of the United States and the chief officers of Congress, and the election of six union members to the House.[7] In 1908, the AF of L actually bested the NAM in a contest for the seat of Representative John J. Jenkins of Wisconsin. During the first decade of the present century, moreover, the "muck-rakers" were popularizing the abuses of business enterprise and the plight of the poor, all of which redounded to the benefit of those organizations which championed the laboring man's cause. President Theodore Roosevelt had written and spoken extensively in labor's behalf, and he arranged the settlement of the coal strike of 1902 to the benefit of the United Mine Workers. But one will search his two administrations in vain for positive evidence that he rendered material assistance to the labor movement. It is the verdict of historians that T.R. sponsored and dramatized those issues which were "popular"; and the labor movement was not such an issue. With the election of Woodrow Wilson in 1912, the stage was set for a reversal of the official indifference which had been labor's lot. In 1916, the AF of L was represented on the Council of National Defense by Samuel Gompers, and the philosophy of the War Labor Board was in sharp contrast to the position taken by the Citizens' Industrial Alliance a decade earlier. The legislation which issued from the eight-year tenure of the New Freedom will be reviewed in a later section (pp. 322–323) in order to point up the continuity of liberal administrations.

Following the cessation of World War I and the passing of labor's privileged position in the highest war councils, a sharp reversal of strength occurred in the labor movement. The contributing factors were many. Radicalism under the International Workers of the World, the success of the Russian Revolution in 1917, and skillful association of unfavorable symbols with the labor movement by labor's

[7] Selig Pearlman and Philip Taft, *History of Labor in the United States, 1896–1932*, New York, The Macmillan Company, 1935, p. 152.

foes all played a part. Two years after the war, the labor movement was suspect as an arm of international communism, and its program, particularly any alternative to the open shop, was labeled un-American. Capitalizing on this sentiment, the "American plan" was pressed by employers' associations, chambers of commerce, and other sympathetic organizations in a gigantic effort to erase the gains scored by the labor movement since 1912. Both the courts and the legislatures joined forces with business. Samuel Gompers, who had died in 1924, was sorely missed by the AF of L as this crusade wore on. As against the direct opposition to the labor movement evident in the propagandizing of the American plan, more subtle distractions from labor unions were employed, chiefly scientific wage determination (Taylorism), union-management coöperation, and welfare capitalism. Furthermore, owing to falling agricultural prices, buying power increased. However, as the decade of the twenties wore on, it began to appear that business interests had bitten off more than they could chew in proclaiming that the responsibility for maintaining prosperity rested in the policies of management, a view widely promulgated by Secretary of Commerce Hoover. The depression which began with the stock-market crash in October, 1929, led President Hoover to call together industrialists and labor leaders in an effort to prevent further deterioration of the economic situation. It was agreed that wage cuts would be disastrous, and it was decided that wages should be maintained. As the situation worsened and wage cuts became general in 1931, an era characterized by various forms of hostility to the labor movement came to a close. The responsibility for maintaining prosperity passed into the hands of the national government by default.

The American Labor Movement After 1936

The record of the AF of L during the early 1930's suggested little enthusiasm for the labor movement. Unable to agree on methods to alleviate the miseries of the depression, the organization was generally obstructionist. The Presidential campaign of 1932 found it apparently uninterested in the opportunity to gain relief through political means. With the New Deal program under way, the AF of L made only feeble efforts to capitalize on the new protection given unions and conducted no organizing campaigns of consequence until after 1935. The annual convention in 1931 rejected the principle of compulsory unemployment insurance, although a change in sentiment was regis-

tered in the 1932 convention and the endorsement of a carefully worded resolution was obtained.

One issue, which ultimately split the AF of L, concerned the vast number of workmen who were employed outside the crafts. Only small sections of steel and meat-packing industries were represented in the federation. The New Deal program, addressed to the relief of economic need and supporting labor as a general group to that end, seemed to be falling on barren ground as the craft-union leaders stubbornly refused to expand their operations to include labor as a whole. In the conventions of 1933 and 1934, a small group interested in industrial unionization sought to compromise the stand assumed by the powerful craft unions, but to no avail. After a third defeat in their attempt to obtain support for the organization of mass-production industries, John L. Lewis, Sidney Hillman, and David Dubinsky led the formation of a Committee for Industrial Organization to operate within the AF of L and carry on organization efforts. Eight national organizations with a membership of nearly 1,000,000 aligned their support with the Committee immediately, and four more organizations added their support shortly.[8] In 1936, the AF of L convention brought about the suspension of the Committee and its member union for promoting "dual unionism." Organization of the supposedly impregnable steel industry and the auto industry in 1937, with greater violence than at any previous stage in the American labor movement, assured the success of the Committee, which became a permanent separate organization calling itself the Congress of Industrial Organizations. As the membership rolls of the CIO increased and finally surpassed the AF of L at the end of 1937, a new era in the labor movement was instituted. The commencement of armament on a wide scale prior to World War II brought about a period of high wages and increased union membership. As during World War I, labor was represented at the highest war councils within the government. But some features of the post-World War I reversal of the labor movement reappeared following World War II, a matter of such importance in the labor movement that we shall deal with it in a separate chapter (Chapter 13).

[8] The organizations which formed the Committee were the United Mine Workers, the Amalgamated Clothing Workers, the International Ladies Garment Workers, the International Typographical Union, the United Textile Workers, the United Hatters, Cap and Millinery Workers, the International Union of Mine, Mill and Smelter Workers, the Oil Field, Gas, Well and Refinery Workers, the Federation of Flat Glass Workers, the Amalgamated Association of Iron, Steel and Tin Workers, the United Automobile Workers, and the United Rubber Workers.

For fifty years, from 1886 until 1936, the AF of L had led the labor movement. On the basis of the experiences of its predecessors, the AF of L sought first of all to achieve homogeneity and to avoid those excesses which had brought public disapproval. The organization was thus conservative and devoted to the interests of craftsmen, explaining that the whole labor movement would gain, though indirectly, from the gains achieved by craftsmen. By 1920, the achievements of the AF of L loomed impressively. A sympathetic President had arranged for organized labor to participate at the highest war councils, abetted organization of the railroads while they were operated by the government, and appointed a trade unionist as Commissioner of Labor. The following decade was one of serious reversals, however, and not until 1937 was the labor movement put back on the offensive. In a real sense, the AF of L had surrendered its right to exclusive direction of the American labor movement. Complacent acceptance of craft unionism, even in an environment which, after 1932, afforded opportunity for growth, brought about the organization of the CIO. Less respectful of tradition, dynamic and resourceful, the CIO gave the labor movement a new lease on life and ushered in the period of its greatest influence. The legislative side of the labor movement remains to be dealt with.

American Labor Legislation, 1896–1945

This analysis of labor legislation during the period after 1896 will be selective and will deal only with the more important phases of the subject. Its major purpose is to point up the paucity of legislation to relieve labor distress until very recent times and to show the role of the courts, which prevented effective relief for labor problems through the political unit until the 1930's. Health and safety legislation will be treated in Chapter 12, and the legislation in connection with social security will be dealt with in Chapters 14–17.

Two observations are to be made in connection with labor legislation. One is that, save for restriction of immigration, trade unions seldom pressed legislatures for preferential treatment until the first decade of the twentieth century. Second, the general framework of legal principles in the United States rejected labor organizations and their objects throughout most of the nineteenth century and, in some

cases, well into the twentieth century. As it turned out, the conversion of the legal framework was necessary before labor legislation could be assured unhampered application. This conversion was incomplete until 1937.

THE LEGAL BACKGROUND

English legal institutions from the mid-fourteenth century on had held concerted effort by workingmen to raise their wages to be unlawful. Accumulated piecemeal restrictions to this effect were given general application in 1799 and 1800, when Parliament passed the Combination Acts outlawing concerted action by employees and employers. In practice, the acts limited labor organizations. Complete relief from the earlier laws was obtained in 1824, when they were repealed. But in the following year, restrictions were reinstituted and the objects for which combination was permitted were reduced to matters of wages and hours and negotiations with employers in connection with those matters. Other combinations constituted a conspiracy. For forty years, the essentials of a master-servant relationship were upheld by the law, and complete relief in the form of permissive legislation for employees to combine was obtained only in 1871.

The American legal background of labor legislation must be understood as resting on the British common law. Throughout the nineteenth century, but particularly prior to 1842, trade associations fought an uphill battle against the doctrines of conspiracy and restraint of trade, the primary doctrines of the common law that found application to labor activities and labor legislation. There was, furthermore, the interpretation of the phrase, "nor deny to any person within its jurisdiction the equal protection of the laws," in Article XIV, Section 1 of the Constitution as a prohibition against labor "class" legislation.

In 1806, the first application of the conspiracy doctrine was made against some Philadelphia cordwainers. They were convicted of conspiracy to raise wages after the judge instructed the jury in these terms: "A combination of workmen to raise their wages may be considered in a twofold point of view: one is to benefit themselves . . . the other is to injure those who do not join the society. The rule of law condemns both." [9] Other cases were decided according to the same formula in New York and Pittsburgh. The conspiracy doctrine was of immense importance to labor in terms of at least two of its

[9] Commons, op. cit., Vol. I, pp. 140–141.

features, Professor Taylor points out: "First is the principle that when the purpose of a combination is illegal every act performed in pursuance of that act becomes illegal, though the act itself may be innocent. The second disturbing feature . . . is the fact that all conspirators are responsible for the acts of any of the conspirators done in pursuance of the common end." [10] Such innocent acts as using the press to draw workmen into labor organizations could, thus, be made illegal when used for the illegal purpose of forming labor organizations, though the act itself is innocent in its isolated exercise. And, according to the second feature, all persons engaged in the attempt to form a labor organization are guilty if any one of them should commit an act of violence. Gradually, distinctions came into use in employing the conspiracy doctrine by distinguishing between motive and intent, and malice in fact as against malice in law. In 1842, finally, the *Commonwealth v. Hunt* decision was rendered by the Supreme Judicial Court of Massachusetts, which specifically held labor organizations to be lawful associations and upheld an organization in its efforts to obtain a closed shop.[11]

The restraint-of-trade doctrine was often coupled with the conspiracy doctrine in early indictments of labor organizations as the unlawful purpose for which organization was sought. As part of the common-law protection accorded the lines of trade, however, the doctrine of restraint of trade seldom was employed by itself to prevent labor organization, the conspiracy doctrine being adequate to that need; and when it was applied, the existence of coercion, intimidation, or violence in achieving restraint was a factor. After the passage of the Sherman Antitrust Act in 1890, however, the prohibitions stated within the law making combinations in restraint of trade illegal found almost immediate application to labor organizations, a "misapplication" in view of the purposes for which the law was passed. Although applied in the Pullman strike of 1894 to obtain an injunction against the American Railway Union, the first important application of the Sherman Act to labor organizations was in the Danbury Hatters' case of 1908.[12] Because the National Hatters Union had sought to boycott the firm's product in the national market, it was sued for triple damages ($234,000) under the Sherman Act. Three years later, the

---

[10] Albion G. Taylor, *Labor Problems and Labor Law*, New York, 2nd ed., Prentice-Hall, 1950, p. 370.
[11] *Commonwealth v. Hunt*, 4 Metcalf 111, 45 Mass. 111 (1842).
[12] *Loewe v. Lawlor*, 208 U.S. 274 (1908).

law was applied in the Buck Stove case, in which the AF of L was forbidden by the Supreme Court to perform any act in furtherance of a boycott against the company.[13] So serious was the denial of the boycott weapon to labor organizations that the AF of L sought legislation that would specifically remove labor organizations from the odious provisions of the Sherman Act. In 1914, this effort produced the Clayton Act, which specifically removed labor organizations from the provisions of the antitrust laws and limited the purposes for which injunctive relief might be obtained in the federal courts. Also, jury trial was prescribed in contempt-of-court cases. The act was widely hailed as a kind of Magna Charta for labor, but the course of events in the 1920's was to prove otherwise.

The Duplex case saw the Machinists Union ordered to cease a boycott of printing presses in and around New York City.[14] By soliciting the coöperation of other unions, the Machinists had created a secondary boycott which the court held illegal. Other courts also were upheld against the union. Professor Taylor observes that four substantive issues were decided by the Supreme Court in its 6–3 decision: (1) ". . . the employer's business is a property right which, under Section 20 of the Clayton Act, may be protected by the injunction"; (2) ". . . the limitations placed upon the issuance of the injunction by Section 20 apply solely to disputes between the employer and his employees, thus providing no protection for union members not in his employ"; (3) ". . . Section 20 was not intended to legalize the secondary boycott"; (4) ". . . a labor organization becomes an illegal combination in restraint of trade when it departs from its lawful objects." [15] In this decision, the achievements of the Clayton Act were largely nullified. The most bitterly accepted decision of the Supreme Court occurred in 1927 in the famous Bedford case. In 1921, the Journeymen Stone Cutters Association sought to force the Bedford Cut Stone Company to renew trade agreements which, after many years of continuous renewal, had been summarily rejected. The Association ordered its members in other states not to work on Bedford stone. No violence accompanied the action and no additional action was taken by the Association. Following the filing of a suit by the Bedford Company and a decision rendered in the lower courts, the case went to the United States Supreme Court, which held that

---

[13] *Gompers v. Buck Stove and Range Company,* 221 U.S. 418 (1911).
[14] *Duplex Printing Company v. Deering,* 254 U.S. 443 (1921).
[15] Taylor, *op. cit.,* p. 470.

the Association was in violation of the Sherman Act.[16] In spite of the union's avoidance of illegal methods and the secondary boycott, it was, nonetheless, held guilty of conspiracy to restrain trade. The Clayton Act was by this action largely nullified. Justice Brandeis, in a dissenting opinion, noted that the decision made the Sherman and Clayton Acts "an instrument for imposing restraints upon labor which reminds me of involuntary servitude." Only the provision for jury trial in cases of contempt of court survived in the Clayton Act.

In concluding this discussion of the doctrines of conspiracy and restraint of trade, mention must be made of the injunction through which control of labor organizations was made effective with the advent of the Sherman Act. It was during the 1880's that the courts began to issue injunctions in the case of labor organizations, particularly in connection with railroad disputes. The court order requiring or enjoining action by labor organizations in pursuit of their objectives has been the major weapon used by employers since 1894, when the United States Department of Justice became an ally of the General Managers Association in breaking the Pullman strike. Wholesale issue of injunctions, many on application of the Department of Justice, characterized the strike, and ultimately the imprisonment of the president of the American Railway Union was secured through his conviction for contempt of court after failing to obey an injunction. The judge who issues an injunction assumes the responsibilities of prosecution, conviction, and sentencing when the injunction is not complied with, powers which we have seen fit to give to one man in no other instance. As applied to labor organizations, the whole theory of injunctive relief was radically altered. In the first place, injunctive relief is an extraordinary measure issued only when relief at law is inadequate, as when irreparable damage is threatened. The complainant in an injunction, furthermore, must come before the court guiltless in the matter for which injunctive relief is sought, and the relief granted must not bear more heavily on the defendant than the complainant. The most radical change in practice of injunctive relief was in the preference given the employer over the labor organization. Only rarely was the employer required to prove his own lack of guilt in obtaining an injunction. Neither was he required to restrain the specifications of his request to maintain the traditional "balance" of incidence mentioned above. Throughout the decade of the 1920's,

---

[16] *Bedford Cut Stone Company v. Journeymen Stone Cutters Association*, 274 U.S. 37 (1927).

labor organizations sought legislation to limit the injunction procedure both from the national government and from the states. Bills were introduced annually in Congress until, in 1932, the passage of the Norris-La Guardia Act was secured. United States courts were forbidden to issue injunctions against normal peaceful activities occasioning industrial disputes, and then only after open hearings on the request for injunction. Until 1937, when the Supreme Court revised its social philosophy, neither the national law nor any of the state anti-injunction laws secured union rights against the misuse of injunctions.

Union Security Legislation

The continuing legislative objective of the labor movement during the present century has been the safeguarding of individuals from reprisals at the hands of employers because of union membership. It is this kind of union security which will be discussed in this section.[17] The culmination of this effort has been legislation requiring employers to recognize unions as representatives of employees and to bargain with them collectively. During the 1890's, a number of states had passed laws which prohibited the practice of requiring an employee to sign a contract agreeing not to join a union as a condition of employment (yellow-dog contract). The first national legislation of a similar kind was the Erdman Act of 1898.

In this act, it was recognized for the first time that labor organizations might contribute to industrial peace. Thus, the Erdman Act, seeking to regulate disputes on the railroads, made it a misdemeanor for any employer to require any person seeking employment to enter into an agreement not to join a labor organization, or to discriminate against any employee because of his membership in a labor organization. Provision for voluntary arbitration of disputes was made in the act and proved highly successful. Commons notes that "from 1906 until the act was superseded (1913) there was no serious strike, actual or threatened, in which one of the parties did not seek settlement under its terms." [18] In 1908, however, Section 10 of the act outlawing yellow-dog contracts was declared unconstitutional; that is, the *dis-*

---

[17] In a later section (Chapter 13), the term "union security" will be used in connection with the attempt of a union to gain preference for its members, usually in the form of exclusive rights to employment, as in the closed shop. At this point, the term is employed simply because it is descriptive of the legislation sought to safeguard union members from discrimination.

[18] John R. Commons and John B. Andrews, *Principles of Labor Legislation*, New York, Harper & Brothers, 1927, p. 150.

charge of an employee because of union membership was upheld.[19] The requirement that an employee enter into a yellow-dog contract was not passed on. In declaring the law unconstitutional, the Supreme Court applied the due-process-of-law doctrine because the act limited the right of an employer to use his property according to his own determination. Three years later, the yellow-dog-contract section was also held unconstitutional in the case of *Hitchman Coal and Coke Company v. Mitchell*[20] because the act limited the individual's right to enter into a contract. The success of the mediation and arbitration features of the act led to the establishment of the Federal Board of Mediation and Arbitration in 1913. At the national level, until 1932, the yellow-dog contract enjoyed the protection of the courts. Many states had passed legislation against the practice, Indiana as early as 1893. The state laws were generally held unconstitutional after a Kansas case was brought before the United States Supreme Court in 1915.[21] Not until 1930 was the legality of laws prohibiting yellow-dog contracts established. In that year, a case arose under the Railway Labor Act of 1926. The law guaranteed parties to railway labor disputes the right to select representatives for negotiations in connection with disputes without interference, coercion, or influence. An obvious violation of the law was brought before the United States Supreme Court and the law was upheld.[22] The decision, in effect, removed the previous Adair interpretation. Two years later the Norris-La Guardia Act amended the Sherman Act and sought to relieve labor organizations of their two major obstacles at law, the yellow-dog contract and the injunction. Yellow-dog contracts were made unenforceable in the United States courts, and the issuance of injunctions was made contingent upon actual knowledge that "unlawful acts have been threatened and will be committed unless restrained" and "that substantial and irreparable damage to the complainant's property will follow"; in other words, the traditional rightful use of injunctions was reasserted.[23] No more than any other statute could this one protect labor organizations from hostile court action, and its constitutionality was not affirmed until 1937.[24]

[19] Adair v. United States, 208 U.S. 161 (1908).

[20] Hitchman Coal and Coke Company v. Mitchell, 245 U.S. 161 (1908).

[21] Coppage v. Kansas, 236 U.S. 1 (1915).

[22] Texas and New Orleans Railway Company et al. v. Brotherhood of Railway and Steamship Clerks et al., 281 U.S. 548 (1930).

[23] Henry Steele Commager, Documents of American History, New York, F. S. Crofts and Company, 1940, pp. 415, 416.

[24] Senn v. Tile Layers Protective Union, 301 U.S. 468 (1937).

When Franklin Delano Roosevelt was elected President in 1932, an era of official approval and sponsorship of the American labor movement was entered. For twenty years the government used its powers to fortify labor organizations against the forces which had rendered them largely ineffective during the first third of the twentieth century. In 1933, the national economic mechanism was halted at dead center and the first of many measures having the dual purpose of recovery and reform was enacted. The National Industrial Recovery Act in Section 7(a) provided:

> That employees shall have the right to organize and bargain collectively through representatives of their own choosing, and shall be free from the interference, restraint, or coercion of employers of labor, or their agents, in the designation of such representatives or in self-organization or in other concerted activities for the purpose of collective bargaining or other mutual aid or protection; that no employee and no one seeking employment shall be required as a condition of employment to join any company union or to refrain from joining, organizing, or assisting a labor organization of his own choosing . . .[25]

The "codes," which were to provide a kind of interindustry government, thus required employers to recognize unions and to refrain from interfering in the employee's exercise of his right of association. In 1935, the law was declared unconstitutional in the Schechter Poultry case,[26] and Congress set itself to the task of drafting a law which would embrace the specific provisions of Section 7(a) toward which the court had not expressed any antipathy. The National Labor Relations Act of 1935 resulted, and, after a half-century of struggle, the realities of industrial society and the supremacy of human rights over property rights were reflected in the law. In explaining the purpose of the law, it was asserted that employer practices in refusing to bargain collectively had led to strikes and other activities which impaired the flow of commerce. It further observed that employees in an unorganized status were deprived of equal bargaining power. To redress these wrongs, the act provided for a board of three persons (the National Labor Relations Board) to preserve the rights of employees as the rights were enumerated in the act, to investigate industrial conditions and prevent unfair labor practices (also enumerated in the act), and to determine the collective-bargaining agent by conducting elections in the appropriate labor unit. The rights of employees were stated in

[25] Commager, op. cit., p. 453.
[26] Schechter Poultry Corporation v. United States, 295 U.S. 495 (1935).

Section 7 as follows: "Employees shall have the right of self-organization, to form, join, or assist labor organizations, to bargain collectively through representatives of their own choosing, and to engage in concerted activities, for the purpose of collective bargaining or other mutual aid or protection." [27] The close relationship between this statement of rights and the statement cited above in the National Industrial Recovery Act will be obvious. In connection with employer unfair labor practices, the following statement was made:

It shall be an unfair labor practice for an employer—
1. To interfere with, restrain, or coerce employees in the exercise of the rights guaranteed in Section 7.
2. To dominate or interfere with the formation or administration of any labor organization or contribute financial or other support to it. . . .
3. By discrimination in regard to hire or tenure of employment or any term of condition of employment to encourage or discourage membership in any labor organization. . . .
4. To discharge or otherwise discriminate against an employee because he has filed charges or given testimony under this Act.
5. To refuse to bargain collectively with the representatives of his employees. . . . [28]

The constitutionality of the act was highly questionable, but the overwhelming endorsement given the Roosevelt administration in the election of 1936, together with the threat that reorganization of the Supreme Court, although recently defeated, might be accomplished in the future, caused the Court to uphold the law. The complaint was brought against the Jones and Laughlin Steel Company by the Amalgamated Association of Iron, Steel and Tin Workers of America, charging that the employer was coercing and intimidating his employees with respect to their self-organization.[29] In a 5-4 decision, the Supreme Court upheld the law against the employer. For twelve years after its passage, the National Labor Relations Act stood unamended as the basic American labor legislation.

With the commencement of World War II, legislation was passed restricting the right to strike, but only after the United Mine Workers had broken the "no strike–no lockout" pledge negotiated at the beginning of the war. The Smith-Connally Act of 1943 asserted the powers of the President to seize establishments where labor disputes

[27] Commager, op. cit., p. 495.
[28] Ibid., pp. 495–496.
[29] National Labor Relations Board v. Jones and Laughlin Steel Corporation, 301 U.S. 1 (1937).

threatened to disrupt the production of goods essential to the prosecution of the war. In addition, thirty days' notice was required in the case of strike action, and provision was made for the NLRB to conduct elections, a majority vote being required to make a strike "lawful."

This survey has dealt with measures enacted to secure labor organizations and their members from employer action. No better demonstration of the slow adjustment of institutions to new social demands could be cited. Time and again, as we have seen, the courts assumed a position which can only be called contemptuous with respect to the enactments of duly constituted representatives of the people, not to mention prevailing social thought. We shall see the recurrence of this hostility as we trace the development of legislation affecting wages and hours.

Minimum-Wage Legislation

The background of wage legislation shows the effect of social change upon social institutions. At the time of the founding of the American colonies, labor shortages in Britain had led Parliament to enact a series of measures to set maximum levels for wages in order to prevent the exploitation of employers. Later, in seventeenth-century America, similar legislation was enacted. With the development of the individualistic thought of the eighteenth century, and the onset of the Industrial Revolution, the removal of all restrictions to make way for the "invisible hand" was counseled. Wages fell, and Malthus and Ricardo added the force of moral rectitude to the prevailing conditions, which so well suited capital accumulation by British industrialists, proclaiming the subsistence theory of wages: higher wages would serve only to increase the population beyond the "fixed" supply of subsistence factors, thereby bringing more misery than attended the prevailing conditions. A century later, the automatic operation of nature's laws was challenged, and the resort to deliberate action in an effort to secure a minimum return for human labor seemed the rightful course of action. Thus, the transition in thinking from protection of the employer to protection of the employee was complete.

Throughout the nineteenth century in the United States, the objects sought in wage legislation were not concerned with minima for the most part, but with such matters as employer paternalism, attachments of wages by creditors, and the claims of employees against the employer's assets in the event of his default in paying wages. At the

close of the nineteenth century, many states had enacted legislation requiring wages to be paid in cash rather than in scrip, credits at the company store, or housing services, all of which had been used. The states also enacted legislation exempting large percentages of an employee's wage from attachment by creditors, and forbade imprisonment for debt. Finally, in most states frequent payment periods were required, and the rights of employees to the assets of an employer in default for wages constituted a prior claim except for the claim of governmental units.

At the close of the nineteenth century, however, sentiment for establishing minimum wages became stronger as New Zealand and Australia enacted such laws and Britain followed in 1909. Massachusetts passed a law in 1912, the first in the United States, providing for regulating minimum-wage levels of women. In the following year, eight other states passed similar laws, and it appeared that women would soon enjoy wage protection in all of the states. Five of the states provided that the level of wages should correspond to the cost of living, and set up boards to determine adequate levels; furthermore, punishment for noncompliance in the form of fine and imprisonment was provided.[30] While it had appeared that general enactment of minimum wages for women would soon come about, the prospect proved illusory. By 1919, only fifteen states had enacted such laws. The upholding of the Oregon law in 1917 seemed to remove doubts about the constitutionality of the laws, at least.[31] But in 1923, a severe blow was dealt to the movement when the United States Supreme Court reversed itself and found a District of Columbia law unconstitutional.[32] Among the objections was the primary one that the law deprived employers of the right to use their property as they saw fit, a violation of the Fifth Amendment; other objections included the view of Justice Sutherland that since the Nineteenth Amendment had given women the vote, they were on a basis of complete equality with men. Three justices dissented—offering somewhat more sophisticated views of human anatomy than those reflected by Justice Sutherland. A wave of suits brought about the invalidation of minimum-wage laws in six states, and, of the remaining eleven having such laws in 1923, most avoided any prosecution for offenses for fear of adverse decisions from the courts. With only the publication of information

[30] Elizabeth Brandeis, "Labor Legislation," in Commons, op. cit., p. 502.
[31] Stettler v. O-Hara, 243 U.S. 629 (1917).
[32] Adkins v. Children's Hospital, 261 U.S. 525 (1923).

identifying reluctant employers, the effectiveness of the state laws was severely limited and noncompliance became general.

An illuminating feature of the minimum-wage legislation of the period 1913–1923 was the lack of support from organized labor. Traditionally suspicious of "legislated economic justice," the AF of L refrained from endorsing the laws. Support came from outside the labor movement until the mid 1930's, chiefly from women's associations (the Women's Trade Union League being outstanding in the Massachusetts experience) and professional groups. The movement was, thus, a middle-class project motivated in large part by a desire to rid industrial society of one evil, substandard wages based on sex discrimination. Since 1900, various reports had been published by the United States Industrial Commission and the Department of Labor testifying to the facts about women's wages.

In 1937, the change in the United States Supreme Court's social philosophy which we noted previously found application in upholding the minimum-wage act of the State of Washington.[33] The decision in the case was split 5-4, and is interesting in that the Court had refused to uphold a similar New York law the previous year, also by a vote of 5 to 4.[34]

While the legislation we have been tracing dealt only with women, another series of acts concerned laborers working on government projects. The legislation is important in its own right, but particularly because it added to the precedents which finally produced the comprehensive national legislation of 1938. Since the Civil War period, laborers employed by the national government, especially those employed in military or naval installations, have been paid wages which shall not be less than those prevailing in the community for similar employment. In 1931, the Davis-Beacon Act provided for the payment of prevailing wages to private employees working on government projects in which the government contract exceeds $5000 (later $2000). In 1936, the Public Contracts Act (Walsh-Healey Act) was passed, requiring not only prevailing wages to be paid on projects in which the national government's contract exceeded $10,000 but also numerous other practices with respect to working conditions. The law was upheld by the Supreme Court in 1940.[35] This decision was of importance because the Court had invalidated a law passed in 1935 to

[34] Moorehead v. People ex rel. Tipaldo, 298 U.S. 597 (1936).
[33] West Coast Hotel Company v. Parrish, 300 U.S. 391 (1937).
[35] Frances Perkins v. Lukens Steel Company et al., 310 U.S. 113 (1940).

regulate wages of coal miners in accordance with the wages gained through collective bargaining, the collective-bargaining rate to be the minimum if collective bargaining for wages in the coal districts established was applicable to two-thirds of the coal mined and to one-half of the workers employed.[36]

Those features of the National Industrial Recovery Act which dealt with union security were reviewed above. The act also required that codes of fair competition within industries include the regulation of wages and hours. Accordingly, in most of the codes wage rates were established for unskilled labor which compared favorably with the rates established later in the Fair Labor Standards Act. When the National Industrial Recovery Act was declared unconstitutional in 1935, Congress immediately set about drafting laws which would deal exclusively with wages and hours. In 1938, the Fair Labor Standards Act was passed. As against the limited scope of previous wage legislation, this act applied to all industries (except agriculture and some minor exclusions) whose goods, or parts of whose goods, entered interstate commerce. A minimum wage was set at 25 cents per hour, and provision was made for automatic increases to 30 cents in 1939 and 40 cents in 1945. Procedures were established whereby wages could be raised during the six-year period 1939–1945 with the concurrence of industrial committees on which were represented labor and the public. By 1945, the minimum wage in all covered industries exceeded 40 cents, and in 1949 the act was amended to make the minimum wage 75 cents. Provision for an hourly minimum of $1 effective March 1, 1956, was made by the 85th Congress, 1st Session. In the same spirit as other cases after 1937, the Fair Labor Standards Act was upheld by the Supreme Court.[37]

After the favorable court decision in the West Coast Hotel case, many states enacted minimum-wage laws, and the states failing to make some provision for minimum wages at the present time are confined to the predominantly agricultural states in the South and West. However, laws covering minimum wages for men, women, and children are to be found in only seven states.

Regulation of wages during World War II became an exceedingly

[36] The Bituminous Coal Conservation Act, invalidated in *Carter v. Carter Coal Company*, 298 U.S. 238 (1936), because it regulated wages in violation of the due-process provisions of the Fifth Amendment and because it delegated wage-fixing power to private groups.

[37] *United States v. Darby Lumber Company*, 312 U.S. 100 (1941), and *Opp Cotton Mills v. Fleming*, 312 U.S. 657 (1941).

complex problem as the national government sought to maintain industrial peace, in part through wage incentives, and at the same time to prevent the scarcity of consumer goods from bringing serious inflation. The general features of these operations will be reviewed in Chapter 13, since they form the background for the labor movement and labor legislation in the postwar period.

Maximum-Hours Legislation

Hours of work, like combinations of workmen and the level of wages, have been a subject of importance to the political unit for centuries. In Britain and elsewhere, reduction in the length of working hours has come about primarily through legislation. The American experience has been different: until well into the present century, legislation regulating hours of employment for men, except in a few occupations, has been uncommon. Labor organizations have preferred to bargain directly for shorter hours with employers, and hence have limited their efforts in legislation to securing legal recognition of their efforts. Part of the explanation lies in the "do it yourself" attitude of the American Federation of Labor—despairing perhaps that the United States Supreme Court would ever awaken to the problems of human rights. But other factors, such as the traditional American fear of "feminizing" work relationships through the extension of protection, were also undoubtedly involved. At any rate, the reduction of the "sunrise to sunset" working conditions of the early nineteenth century, first to ten hours per day, then to eight, was chiefly accomplished through the use of economic power by labor organizations.

A strike for the ten-hour day occurred as early as 1791 among Philadelphia carpenters, and sporadic outbursts by craftsmen for shorter hours occurred throughout the nineteenth century. Public employees were the first to receive reductions in hours through the intervention of the political unit, many employees of the national government receiving the ten-hour day in 1840 and the eight-hour day in 1868. Following the Civil War, the agitation for the eight-hour day became general as the movement was carried on by the National Labor Union, the Knights of Labor, and the American Federation of Labor in succession. That the movement gained acceptance slowly is indicated by the fact that in 1909, after a half-century of striving, only 8 percent of the wage earners worked eight hours or fewer per day.[38] During World War I, hours were generally reduced, but the postwar

[38] Commons and Andrews, *op. cit.*, pp. 232–233.

years and the employer offensive against labor organizations saw a return to the prewar hours schedule, a majority of manufacturing employees working forty-eight hours per week or more. As the eight-hour day became general, agitation for a five-day week strengthened. During the decade of the twenties, virtually no authority, including the Bible itself, was overlooked in the campaign of businessmen against reductions in the work week. Amid great consternation, Henry Ford adopted the five-day week in his automobile company in 1926. It was only with the beginning of the depression in 1929 that the forty-hour week gained support, as a recovery measure.

There can be little doubt that the reluctance of organized labor to press for legislation to reduce hours substantially weakened that avenue to accomplishment. It was virtually impossible for organized labor to maintain national pressure for shorter hours, with the result that regional differences in their success worked hardship on industries that faced competitive markets. The need, therefore, was legislation to make regulation of hours uniform over the whole economy. Only in recent years has anything like general regulation been effected, and the first legislation enacted dealt with children. Women, public employees, and workmen in dangerous occupations were regulated before the enactment of legislation having wide coverage appeared in 1938.

CHILDREN

Legislation dealing with the employment of children was introduced in the United States in 1842, when the State of Massachusetts passed a law limiting the working day of children under age 12 to ten hours per day. Six other states then passed laws limiting the working day to from ten to thirteen hours. Because the laws were largely unenforced, except in Pennsylvania and New Jersey, they had little effectiveness and were, therefore, statements of sentiment on the question of child labor rather than regulatory. The motives for passing child-labor laws in most of the states rarely can be traced to humanitarian consideration of the health and morals of the child. Selfish desire to increase the scarcity of labor relative to jobs seems to have been the major factor responsible for support from labor organizations. At the turn of the century, interest in limiting the hours of children was rekindled and, beginning in 1903, the eight-hour standard day was established in about three-fourths of the states, but occupations covered varied greatly and enforcement was lax.[39] In large measure, the achievement

[39] *Ibid.*, pp. 244–245.

of expanded state protection was due to the support of the National
Child Labor Committee, formed in 1904 by private citizens. It became
apparent to this group that effective regulation would have to come
from the national government and legislation was pressed for and
obtained in 1916 and 1919. In the first law, Congress made it unlawful for any firm to ship goods in interstate commerce if any of the
farm products were produced by children under 14 years of age, or
where children between the ages of 14 and 16 had worked either more
than eight hours per day or forty-eight hours per week, or after 7 P.M.
and before 6 A.M. In the courts, the law fared badly, and on appeal
to the United States Supreme Court in 1918 it was declared unconstitutional.[40] The Court, while sympathetic to the aims of the act,
determined that it was an improper regulation of interstate commerce.
The 1919 act was passed to meet the objections of the earlier law and
it met a like fate at the hands of the Court, because it had sought to
regulate employment of children according to the same standards as
were stated in the 1916 act, by levying a 10 percent tax on annual net
profits of firms which produced goods in violation of those standards.[41]
This was held to be an abuse of the national taxing power. The advocates of limitations on the employment of children next turned to the
Constitutional amending process for their relief, and succeeded in
getting the Congress to propose an amendment to the Constitution
which would give it power to limit, regulate, and prohibit the labor
of children under 18 years of age. Proposed by Congress in 1924, the
amendment was ratified by only six states in 1933 and only twenty-
eight (of the necessary thirty-six) in 1937. Since the enactment of the
Fair Labor Standards Act in 1938, the proposal has been virtually
forgotten.

Within the National Industrial Recovery Act, provision had been
made for codes to regulate child labor; the standard age was 16 years,
below which employment in certain occupations was forbidden. When
the law was declared unconstitutional, an effort was made to secure a
law embracing the provisions which had dealt with wages and hours.
To effect limitations on the employment of children, goods are
excluded from interstate commerce if the firm produces goods manufactured under conditions where children under 16 years have been
employed in mining and manufacturing, on other jobs without certification, and on certain enumerated jobs if between 16 and 18. State

[40] *Hammer v. Dagenhart*, 247 U.S. 251 (1918).
[41] *Bailey v. Drexel Furniture Company*, 259 U.S. 20 (1922).

laws have reinforced the provisions of the Fair Labor Standards Act by enacting laws making the same standards effective within the states, and by providing for compulsory school attendance until age 16. Still, large numbers of children are employed in agriculture and in some of the street trades, which are largely exempt from regulation.

WOMEN

The need to regulate the hours of employment for women followed closely the adoption of limitations on the hours of children. In 1847, New Hampshire passed the first law providing for a ten-hour day, a law secured through the efforts of organized women in New Hampshire. Laws passed in other states were ineffective for various reasons, and the first enforceable law was not passed until 1879 by Massachusetts.[42] In 1908, an Oregon law limiting hours of employment for women to ten per day was upheld by the United States Supreme Court.[43] An eight-hour day for women was similarly upheld by the Court in 1915.[44] On the basis of these decisions, which upheld the protection of women as a means of improving the health of offspring, laws were passed in nearly half of the states regulating maximum daily and weekly hours. Night work, work without rest periods, and work preceding and following childbirth were also regulated. Since the enactment of the Fair Labor Standards Act, these regulations apply in the main to intrastate industries.

The Fair Labor Standards Act sought to accomplish reduction in the hours of work for women by requiring the payment of one and one-half times the basic rate when hours exceeded a maximum specified as forty-four in 1938, forty-two in 1939, and forty in 1940. Intrastate industries, agriculture, and some other industries are excluded from the provisions of the act.

MEN

Hampered by the indifference of labor organizations to legislation limiting hours of employment, and lacking such disabilities as achieved hours reduction for women (and cultural factors which stressed individualism and the "manly assuming of one's share"), men received little attention from legislators. Only in dangerous occupations, public

---

[42] Commons and Andrews, op. cit., p. 249.
[43] Muller v. Oregon, 208 U.S. 412 (1908).
[44] Miller v. Wilson, 236 U.S. 373 (1915).

employment, and occupations in which fatigue would endanger the public safety were hours regulated prior to 1938.

Even before the turn of the century, laws regulating the employment of miners for more than eight hours per day had been enacted. In 1898, a law passed by the State of Utah making such provisions was upheld by the United States Supreme Court.[45] In 1936, a national law (Bituminous Coal Conservation Act of 1935) was declared unconstitutional when it sought the same end.[46] Only a few states extended regulation of hours to factories and shops. Transportation employees have long enjoyed legal limitations on their hours of work because of the close connection between their hours and the public safety. In 1907, a limitation on the employment of railroad operating personnel to sixteen per day, with provisions for rest periods, was enacted by the national government.[47] The Adamson Act of 1916 sought to provide an eight-hour day by requiring the payment of overtime rates when hours exceeded eight per day. Provisions of the Walsh-Healey Act have been discussed above, and the general hours reductions provided in the Fair Labor Standards Act of 1938 were discussed above in connection with women.

The advent of World War II led to a relaxation of hours for children, women, and men in order to assure a labor force adequate to the needs of the nation. Moreover, the need to make up for a pent-up demand for consumers' goods caused this relaxation to be carried over into the postwar period. But in general, the trend at the present time is toward greater protection for children (a minimum age of 18 is often posted) and women. In the case of men, the power of organized labor in the postwar period has been such as to assure that hours will be modified by the terms of contracts struck between employers and employees. Rather than reducing hours, however, more attention has been given to such perquisites as vacations, rest periods, and other means of offsetting the fatigue which accompanies modern employment in highly mechanized industries. A review of these matters will be presented in Chapter 12.

An Appraisal of American Labor Legislation

This survey of labor legislation in terms of only three matters, union security, minimum wages, and maximum hours, reveals certain distin-

[45] *Holden v. Hardy*, 109 U.S. 366 (1898).
[46] *Carter v. Carter Coal Company*, 298 U.S. 238 (1936).
[47] Commons and Andrews, *op. cit.*, p. 270.

guishing features. The attitude of nonparticipation assumed by organized labor until recent years is difficult to understand. If the courts were hostile, then little was accomplished to lessen their hostility by giving the impression that legislation was unwanted, an interpretation of labor's passivity often offered by employer organizations. There is, too, the callous disregard for the effect of long hours on women and children in terms of health and morals. That the employment of children aged 14 and under for ten hours per day could have been thought of as other than the most barbarous kind of disregard for human personality until the beginning of the present century indicates how much we have grown in terms of our social conscience during the last two generations.

The American Labor Movement and Labor Legislation to 1945: Concluding Remarks

The period which we have surveyed in this chapter might be called the growth period of the labor movement and labor legislation. We were, by 1945, a very different people in terms of our thinking about these subjects from the people who had complacently assumed that the 1920's represented a level of social life never to be rivaled in terms of its bounty of material goods and underlying righteousness. The Great Depression and the Second World War, coupled with the leadership of a strong administration that was sensitive to the contradictions and inadequacies of twentieth-century industrial life and boldly pointed out ways in which social problems might be redressed, have made the difference. Because the scales had been too long weighted in favor of propertied interests, and accumulated discontent had reached proportions which, in other lands, might have produced revolution, the deliberate intervention of the national government on the side of employees led to problems of another character. Power long withheld is likely to be overindulged when first it is granted. Accordingly, the decade of the 1940's was accompanied by many excesses and examples of narrow selfishness on the part of labor organizations, and the heritage of the war period was the baffling problem of limiting irresponsibility in the labor movement without sapping its vitality. To approach this question properly, we must examine the major problems of employees generally in terms of their modern dimensions. Thus, the next three chapters will be devoted to a discussion of how American employees earn a living, their quest for income security, and their condi-

ns of employment. Chapter 13 then discusses the response of labor
ganizations and political units to these problems after 1945.

SELECTED REFERENCES

Commons, John R., et al., *History of Labour in the United States*, New
York, The Macmillan Company, 4 vols., 1918–1935.

Taylor, Albion G., *Labor Problems and Labor Law*, 2nd ed., New York,
Prentice-Hall, 1950.

Wright, Chester W., *Economic History of the United States*, New York,
McGraw-Hill Book Company, 1949.

chapter 10

How American Employees Earn a Living

In several instances, we have used the terms "labor," "workmen," and "labor force" in such a way that a homogeneity may have been implied which does not in fact exist. The American labor force is misunderstood if it is thought of as an aggregate that refers to manual workmen or unskilled and semiskilled factory employees, two interpretations which seem to have wide currency. A great variety of occupations are included in the labor force (the two-volume *Dictionary of Occupational Titles* issued by the Federal Security Agency in 1949 lists between 30,000 and 40,000 definitions of job titles), and it is appropriate to emphasize its heterogeneity rather than its sameness. Some important factors which show variability in the labor force include age and sex, industrial and geographical location, and skill attainment and occupational specialization. We should expect that these variations would show changes from one decade to another in response to those forces which cause all social change, particularly in response to depressions and wars. In this chapter, we will analyze the labor force and its composition, and then look into the social and economic characteristics of employment in some major industries. We should gain, as a result, an understanding of the groups to which social legislation is addressed, and thus appreciate somewhat more the present role of social legislation and the needs which it may attempt to meet in the future.

The Labor Force

The Bureau of the Census has used two classifications of the labor force, one until 1940 and another since the census of 1940. Prior to 1940, the concept used was "gainful workers" which included all persons 10 years of age or over who reported a gainful occupation, regard-

339

less of whether they were working or seeking work at the time of the census, and in general excluded new workers without previous experience in a gainful occupation. After 1940, the concept used was more carefully defined to include persons 14 years old and over who, during the census week, were either "at work" (those who did any work for pay or profit, or worked without pay for fifteen hours or more in a family farm or business) or "with a job, but not at work" (those who did not work and were not looking for work, but had a job or business

TABLE 22. Employment Status of the Population, 1820–1950.
(thousands)

Year	Population 10 or 14 Years and Older	In Labor Force	Percentage in Labor Force
All Persons 10 Years Old and Over			
1820	6,488	2,881	44.4
1830	8,639	3,932	45.5
1840	11,629	5,420	46.6
1850	16,453	7,697	46.8
1860	22,430	10,533	47.0
1870	29,124	12,925	44.4
1880	36,762	17,392	47.3
1890	47,414	23,318	49.2
1900	57,950	29,073	50.2
1910	71,580	37,371	52.2
1920	82,739	42,434	51.3
1930	98,723	48,830	49.5
All Persons 14 Years Old and Over [a]			
1940	101,102	51,742	50.1
1950	112,354	59,015	50.3

[a] Data for years after 1930 are not strictly comparable with data for other years because of the change made in the labor-force concept in 1940.
Sources: U.S. Bureau of the Census, *Historical Statistics of the United States,* 1945, 1949; *Statistical Abstract of the United States,* 1955, p. 185.

from which they were temporarily absent because of vacation, illness, industrial dispute, bad weather, or layoff with definite instructions to return to work within thirty days of layoff; also included were persons who had new jobs to which they were scheduled to report within thirty days).[1] The labor force has increased continuously since 1820, as Table 22 indicates. The data presented in Table 22 show that the number of persons employed and the proportion they represent of the population over 10 or 14 years of age have increased steadily since 1820. It should

[1] U.S. Bureau of the Census, *Statistical Abstract of the United States,* 1954, p. 89.

not be inferred that those persons not included in the labor force are idle or nonparticipants in the sense that they are unwilling to be employed. The proportion of the population not in the labor force is made up of retired persons, institutionalized persons, housewives, and persons in school. Of persons in the age group 14–64, all but a very small percentage are employed or otherwise occupied.

The growth of the labor force during the period 1820 to the present is related to two primary factors, the population net-reproduction rate and immigration. Data are not available concerning the net-reproduction rate (when the rate is 1000, then the population remains the same in the absence of net immigration) for the nineteenth century, but the data for the period 1905–1910 suggest that the rate during the nineteenth century may have been 1300 or more. At this rate, a generation would reproduce its numbers and add nearly one-third to the existing population. Immigration data are more complete, and they indicate that the contribution to the labor force from this source was substantial from 1840–1930. From 1840–1890, about 15,500,000 immigrants entered the United States, and from 1890–1930 about 21,000,-000 entered.[2] A very large source of labor, therefore, was immigration. Since the turn of the century, however, other factors have contributed to the growth of the labor force, chiefly the increasing participation of women in gainful employment. This increasing factor has to some extent been offset by the declining proportion of youthful participants in the labor force, as we shall see in the following discussion. Variations within the labor force which are not reflected in the totals are also important to us, and we shall now turn to age and sex characteristics.

Age and Sex Characteristics of the Labor Force

The total participation in the labor force (exclusive of the war years 1941–1946) seems to have been little affected by the changes in age and sex composition of the labor force. But the social importance of these changes has been considerable. Table 23 shows the relevant data for the period 1920–1950 and projections for future years.

Table 23 shows the remarkable changes that have taken place in the composition of the labor force during the past three decades. The following observations seem to be supported by the date: (1) participation of women in the labor force has increased markedly since 1920, except

[2] *Ibid.*, p. 101.

TABLE 23. Labor-Force Participation by Age and Sex, 1920–1975.[a]
(percentage of population 14 years old and over)

Age	1975	1965	1955	1950	1940	1930	1920
				Both Sexes			
14 years old and over	58.4	56.7	57.0	56.8	54.1	54.6	55.8
				Male			
14 years old and over	80.6	79.7	82.4	82.4	80.9	83.4	85.9
14 to 19 years	43.7	45.7	47.8	47.5	38.4	43.5	55.9
20 to 24 years	86.9	87.6	88.3	86.9	89.2	89.6	90.7
25 to 34 years	96.6	96.5	96.4	94.4	96.3	96.5	96.2
35 to 44 years	97.0	96.9	96.8	96.5	96.6	96.9	96.6
44 to 54 years	94.1	94.2	94.3	94.6	93.7	94.8	94.5
55 to 64 years	86.6	86.8	86.9	85.1	85.6	87.6	87.4
65 years and over	36.5	39.6	42.9	45.0	43.3	55.5	57.1
				Female			
14 years old and over	37.5	34.9	32.6	31.9	27.4	25.1	24.1
14 to 19 years	26.3	26.8	27.2	26.4	19.9	23.8	29.6
20 to 24 years	53.4	50.0	46.3	44.4	47.8	43.9	39.3
25 to 34 years	42.7	39.1	35.2	33.5	35.3	28.7	25.0
35 to 44 years	50.1	45.4	40.4	38.0	29.2	23.3	20.6
45 to 54 years	46.7	42.5	38.1	36.9	24.2	21.3	19.4
55 to 64 years	33.8	30.7	27.6	27.3	17.8	16.4	15.3
65 years and over	9.5	9.3	9.0	9.5	6.7	8.2	8.2

a The labor-force participation rate is the percentage of total population in the age group in the labor force. Projections assume a continuation of the high-level employment characteristic of the World War II period and are based on past trends.

Source: Conference Board, The Economic Almanac, 1953–54, New York, Thomas Y. Crowell Company, 1953, p. 426.

for the group over age 65; (2) participation of men in the labor force has decreased, and there has been a marked decrease in the participation of those in the age group 14–19 and in the age group over 65; (3) participation by women between the ages of 35 and 64 has greatly increased, and they undoubtedly constitute the major addition to the labor force since 1930; and (4) projections for the future indicate that the participation of men will remain essentially the same except for accelerated decreases in the participation of those over 65, the participation of men and women aged 14 to 19 will continue to decline, and the participation of women at all ages will increase, nearly doubling in some age groups. The implications of these observations will be dealt with in later chapters; but the general meanings to be attached to them may be suggested here. It was suggested in Chapter 4 (p. 94) that the increasing participation of women in the labor force had to be evaluated in terms of the increased economic security gained for the

family compared with the change in traditional family roles. On the whole, the advantages of greater income do not appear to balance the disadvantages of a changing role structure. (See Chapter 6, p. 159.) The data regarding participation in the labor force by persons aged 14 to 19 indicate clearly that school attendance has become more important for that group, and the social merits of the change in its status following the Civil War, from a condition where it represented perhaps one-third of the labor force, must be highly approved. Finally, the implications of the data regarding the participation in the labor force of persons over age 65 are not at all clear solely on the basis of the table, but the growing numbers of persons over 65 not participating in the labor force give the social-insurance programs of the United States increasing importance. We shall analyze this final consideration more fully in Chapter 15.

Industrial Classification of the Labor Force

The industrial classification of the labor force commonly utilizes three major classifications, within each of which subclassifications are made. Agricultural and nonagricultural industries are the major classifications, and the nonagricultural industries are further broken down into manufacturing industries and nonmanufacturing industries. Employment in manufacturing industries, moreover, is differentiated between durable goods (primary metal, transportation, machinery, etc.) and nondurable goods (food, textile, paper, etc.) industries, as well as by production workers and nonproduction workers. Table 24 shows the industrial composition of the labor force for the last half-century.

The table shows some very significant developments concerning the composition of the labor force. First, persons employed in agricultural pursuits not only have constituted a declining proportion of the labor force since 1900, but have decreased in absolute numbers as well. The rate of increase in nonagricultural employment, moreover, has been far more rapid than the rate of decline in agricultural employment. As late as 1880, persons employed in agricultural pursuits outnumbered those in nonagricultural pursuits, but after that date the proportion of the labor force in agriculture decreased steadily. Second, all nonagricultural industries except mining show increases in the number of persons employed, the increases in manufacturing, wholesale and retail trade, and government being very large. Finally, the decade of the 1940's accelerated trends which had begun to appear in the two pre-

TABLE 24. Industrial Classification of the Labor Force, 1900 and 1920–1954.

(thousands)

Industry	1900	1920	1930	1940a	1950	1954b
Agricultural	9,552	11,362	11,161	11,671	7,507	6,504
Nonagricultural	19,473	27,088	29,143	32,031	52,450	54,734
Manufacturing	6,090	10,534	9,401	10,780	14,967	15,989
Mining	819c	1,230	1,000	916	889	770
Contract Construction	1,639	848	1,372	1,294	2,333	2,527
Trans'ion and Pub. Util.	1,631	3,998	3,675	3,013	3,977	4,008
Wholesale and Ret. Trade	3,224	4,623	6,064	6,940	9,645	10,498
Service, incl. Finance	2,781	3,252	4,482	4,896	6,894	7,743
Government, incl. Milit.	1,161d	2,968	3,414	4,724	7,642	6,749

a Data after 1940 are not strictly comparable with data for previous years because the previous data are based on a "gainful workers" concept of the labor forces, and the data after 1940 are based on "the labor force" concept.
b Based on data for first quarter of 1954.
c Includes forestry and fishing.
d Estimate based on data from Solomon Fabricant, *The Rising Trend of Government Employment*, New York, National Bureau of Economic Research, 1949.

Sources: U. S. Bureau of the Census, *Historical Statistics of the United States, 1789–1945*, 1949; Conference Board, *The Economic Almanac, 1953–54*, New York, Thomas Y. Crowell Company, 1953; *Current Population Reports;* and U.S. Bureau of the Census, *Statistical Abstract*, 1955.

ceding decades, showing, again, the significance of the Second World War.

One can explain the decline in agricultural employment largely in terms of mechanization (in 1953, the value of farm machinery, including motor vehicles, was more than twelve times the 1910 value), which permitted a smaller number of agricultural employees to provide food and raw materials for the growing economy. The growth in nonagricultural employment reflects the very large increase in demand for consumer goods since 1900, the improvements in mass-production techniques, and the almost complete abandonment of home-centered production in favor of business organizations. In manufacturing industries, the increase in employment was accompanied by at least a fivefold increase in utilization of machine-generated horsepower, which suggests how extensive were the increases in demand for manufactured goods. In wholesale and retail trade, the increase in employment reflects the growing complexity of the distribution facilities for all kinds of goods during the present century. Government employment has increased since 1900 because the scope of government activities has constantly widened, and, after 1940, the number of persons in the armed forces causes the total employment to increase. A detailed pres-

TABLE 25. The Labor Force Classified by Occupation, 1910-1950.

Occupation a	Per cent					Change 1910-1950
	1950	1940	1930	1920	1910	
Major occupation group						
1. Professional and technical workers	8.7	6.5	6.1	5.0	4.4	+97.7
2. Proprietors, managers, and officials	(16.6)	(17.8)	(20.3)	(22.3)	(23.1)	—28.1
a. Agricultural	7.7	10.1	12.4	15.5	16.5	—53.3
b. Nonagricultural	8.9	7.7	7.6	6.8	6.6	+34.8
3. Clerical and kindred workers	(19.3)	(17.2)	(16.3)	(13.8)	(11.7)	+65.0
a. Sales	7.0	6.8	n. a.	n. a.	n. a.	2.9
4. Skilled workers and foremen	13.8	11.7	6.9	13.5	11.7	+17.9
5. Semiskilled workers	19.8	21.0	16.4	16.1	14.7	+34.7
6. Unskilled workers	(10.3)	(17.9)	(21.5)	(24.0)	(29.2)	—64.7
a. Agricultural	4.2	7.1	8.6	9.4	14.5	—71.0
b. Nonagricultural	6.1	10.7	12.9	14.6	14.7	—58.5
7. Service workers	(10.1)	(11.7)	(6.9)	(5.4)	(6.8)	+48.5
a. Household	2.5	4.6	n. a.	n. a.	n. a.	—45.7
b. Other	7.6	7.1	n. a.	n. a.	n. a.	+ 7.0
8. Total b	100.0	100.0	100.0	100.0	100.0	—
Class of worker c						
9. Self-employed and professional (1 + 2)	25.2	24.3	26.1	27.3	27.5	— 9.1
a. Non Agricultural (1 + 2b)	17.6	14.2	13.7	11.8	11.0	+60.0
b. Agricultural (2)	7.7	10.1	12.4	15.5	16.5	—53.3
10. Employees (3 + 4 + 5 + 6 + 7)	74.7	75.7	73.9	72.7	72.5	+ 3.0
11. White-collar workers (1 + 2b + 3)	36.9	31.4	30.6	25.6	21.2	+74.1
12. Manual workers (2a + 4 + 5 + 6 + 7)	63.1	68.6	69.4	74.4	78.8	—19.9

a Persons 14 years old and over, computed from "labor force" concept for years 1940 and after and from "gainful workers" concept for prior years. Occupational classifications are approximate equivalents and are not strictly comparable.

b Detail may not add to totals because of rounding and because unreported occupations are omitted (1.3 percent in 1950, and 0.9 percent in 1940).

c Considerable overlapping occurs within these classifications, especially the designation "Self-employed and professional employees."

Source: U. S. Bureau of the Census, *U. S. Census of Population, 1950,* Vol. II. *Characteristics of the Population,* Part I, "United States Summary," p. 102; and *Historical Statistics of the United States, 1789-1945,* 1949.

entation of the industrial composition of the labor force is included in the Appendix and it merits careful study.

The significance of these data for social legislation is varied. Obviously, the declining position of agriculture constitutes a special problem, and agricultural employees have only recently been brought within the coverage of social insurance and other social legislation, many forms of protection still not being provided. It is clear also that the social problems that derive from urbanization bear a relationship to the declining employment in agriculture which forced a steady stream of persons to emigrate to the cities. In many respects, the plight of low-income farm families surpasses the worst conditions in urban "slums." Among the employees of nonagricultural industries, those in mining and construction have special problems in connection with the sporadic employment characteristic of their industries. In a later section, we shall deal with problems of specific employment condition in the skill attainment of the labor force and the extent of service industries, wholesale and retail trade, and manufacturing has opened up employment opportunities for women which were previously limited, and the mixed social consequences of this development have been discussed previously.

Occupational Classification of the Labor Force

Cutting across all industries and age and sex is the classification of employees according to the type of function which they perform in earning their livelihood. We shall be primarily interested in this section in the skill attachment of the labor force and the extent of "employeeism." In Table 25 the data concerning the labor force occupational distribution are presented.

The data presented in the table reveal many changes which have taken place in the labor-force occupational structure since 1910. Some of the changes are striking: for example, the growth of professional and technical workers, who nearly doubled in importance; the growth of skilled and semiskilled workers, particularly the latter; the more than 60 percent decline in the proportion of unskilled workers; and the near doubling of the proportion of clerical and sales workers. Other changes are of particular importance to social legislation. The decline in the proportion of household-service workers and agricultural employees and in the proportion of proprietors, managers, and officials is of this nature.[3] Considering employees by their occupational class, it is im-

---

[3] The reader is referred to the Appendix for a breakdown of the exact occupations included in the classifications used in Table 25.

portant to note that the proportion of self-employed and professional persons seems to be decreasing; and the extent of the decrease is probably greater than the table suggests, since managers and officials are included in the "proprietor" classification and they have increased faster than the proprietor group. The employee group, at any rate, is increasing, and the proportion of persons dependent on wage or salary payments from an employer probably is four out of five persons in the labor force. White-collar workers, it will be noted, have nearly doubled in percentage terms since 1910, and the "blue collar" manual workers have decreased by nearly 20 percent. From the table, therefore, it seems probable that the following changes have occurred: (1) an increase in the proportion of technically trained workers; (2) an increase in the proportion of self-employed and professional persons outside agriculture, although the trend has abated since 1930; (3) an increase in the proportion of the labor force dependent upon an employer for wage and salary payments; (4) an increase in the proportion of skilled and semiskilled workmen, and a decrease in the proportion of workmen who possess no skill; (5) a large increase in the proportion of white-collar workers; and (6) an increase in the proportion of service workers outside households in the labor force.

These changes reflect technological advancement, which has created a need for specialized labor both in the production and distribution of economic goods. Technological advance in household appliances has, at the same time, freed women from the necessity of making housekeeping an all-day job. World War II, with its broadly based program for training skilled workmen, accelerated trends which had become apparent after 1910. Postwar programs of training for returning veterans likewise increased the number of technical and professional workers, and new industries, particularly electronics, have carried on training programs to provide technically trained personnel. These developments account in large measure for the growth of professional and technical workers. It would seem, on the surface, that the decline of the proportion of unskilled workers to less than one-third their proportion in 1910 has increased the security of workmen, since skill attainment has long been regarded as a valuable property right of workmen. But the kind of skill possessed by most workmen at the present time does not provide security in the measure to which the craftsmen at the turn of the century possessed skill. The skill which has increased since 1910 has been operative skill, that is, skill in operating machinery, and the skill can be learned in a very short time on

most jobs. The semiskilled workman can thus be replaced and his position taken up by a new worker without jeopardizing the operations of the firm. To this false security of skill attainment must be added the personal costs of machine-centered employment, which has eliminated the pride of craftsmanship from most semiskilled jobs and has left problems of boredom, fatigue, and dissatisfaction. Later in this chapter and again in Chapter 12 we shall discuss the consequences of skill dilution for the labor force. It should be noted that skilled workmen have increased also as a percentage of the labor force, but the trend since 1940 suggests that they will represent a declining proportion of the labor force in future years. White-collar workers, moreover, many of whom might be classified as skilled workmen in clerical positions, face a problem of skill dilution as expensive machinery is substituted for personal skill in office employment. Something akin to semiskilled machine tending has developed with the advent of complex billing and accounting machine operations.

The increase in employeeism and the dilution of skill attainment have unquestionably affected employees and the movement for social legislation. Labor organizations, for example, have taken the view that wages should be increased and hours decreased as machinery introduction reduces skill and increases monotony. Pensions have become more highly prized as a form of relief from boring work. Legislation to increase wages through a higher minimum wage, reduce hours, and raise pensions has resulted from organized efforts on the part of labor and other groups. Less closely, perhaps, legislation in education, housing, and other fields can be associated with these trends in the labor force.

THE LABOR FORCE: SUMMARY

From the preceding discussion, it should again be observed that American employees work in industries and occupations which differ widely in their conditions of work. It is important to realize how complex is the labor force and how varied its problems, because labor problems seldom are general to the entire labor force, but rather specific, relating to particular groups of industries and occupations. Still, some common denominators can be associated with all employment situations, and we shall discuss those basic factors now.

Social Aspects of Employment

When we say that one-quarter of the labor force is engaged in manufacturing employment or one-fifth in clerical and sales employment, we gain only the most general appreciation of the conditions of em-

ployment among these workers. Neither the types of tasks performed nor the special problems associated with employment in some industries are revealed. Data describing employment, even when presented in series, do not indicate the changes which have occurred in the character of work performed in specific industries. It is the purpose of this section to fill in some of the factors which relate so closely to conditions of work and job satisfaction, but are not revealed in the statistical data. In particular we shall evaluate the common observation that the work situation has become less demanding of the employee although wages have risen steadily, implying that many workers are "pampered."

CHARACTERISTICS OF A JOB

The component elements of a job include many elements beyond the actual tasks performed for an employer. When it is observed that John Doe has a "job" with the Acme Manufacturing Company as a semiskilled worker, relatively little is revealed about his work situation. If we were to understand his work situation more fully, we should have to know, in addition to wage conditions, the general features of these other factors: physical conditions of the plant or office, work loads, plant rules, length of work day, steadiness of employment, advancement possibilities, social status of the job, character of supervision, congeniality of fellow workers, and opportunity for self-expression.[4] Data which would permit an assessment of the changes which have taken place since 1900 in these matters are not readily available, but general changes may be suggested.

Physical conditions of the plant refer to all physical aspects of the job, functional and dysfunctional, including the layout of machinery, the presence of hoists and cranes, the method of handling material, temperature and humidity and their variations, illumination, space allowance, and similar factors. Office employees of a metropolitan insurance company may enjoy physical conditions of work that are carefully controlled in the interest of their comfort and safety. Bituminous-coal miners, on the other hand, may be employed a large share of the time at temperatures near 100 degrees and at nearly the same percentage of humidity, with dust and fumes creating serious hazards. Since the physical conditions of work are closely related to fatigue and frequency of injuries, they are of primary importance in many industries.

[4] Richard A. Lester, *Labor and Industrial Relations*, New York, The Macmillan Company, p. 39.

The work load must be considered in terms of both physical and emotional taxation. Unquestionably the physical exertion required of the average production worker has been greatly reduced in recent years owing to the introduction of automatic feeding, conveying, and lifting machinery. Those skills which formerly required a great deal of backwork have thus been moderated in terms of the physical taxation attached to them; and hours of work have also been reduced by perhaps 20 percent since the 1920's. But the fatigue and monotony which are produced by the machine-dictated pace of production may well have increased the total taxation, physical and emotional, of the modern semiskilled employee. It is generally felt that workers today work with greater intensity than they did fifty years ago.[5] The work load has primary importance for workers who for various reasons (age, recent illness, emotional problems, etc.) may not be at the required level of physical and emotional efficiency. Many semiskilled jobs permit little variation in the adaptation of an individual to operations whose sequence and timing are centrally determined. The very presence of machinery increases the hazards of employment, especially when the machinery involves crushing weights, rapidly revolving grinding wheels, and sharp boring apparatus. The work load may be influenced by many factors, including geographic location of the industry, the presence of a strong union, and the size of the plant.

Plant rules, which are an extension of the supervision role, figure prominently in the analyses of employment situations. In studies of job satisfaction, it has been found that restrictive supervision is among the foremost reasons for being dissatisfied with one's job.[6] Rules concerning factory discipline and operating procedure are most common. Some plant rules, however, concern the order of layoff and promotion, in union organized plants usually according to seniority of employment. When such rules are enforced, they bear heavily upon steadiness of employment and advancement possibilities.

In nearly all nonagricultural industries, the length of the working day has been decreased to eight hours and the work week to forty hours. However, employment in many industries has long called for an atypical work day, and in recent years other industries have introduced irregular employment hours. Continuous-process industries, such as the basic-steel industry, have always utilized shifts of workers on a round-the-clock basis. More recently, it has become common in

[5] Harry Ober, "The Worker and His Job," *Monthly Labor Review*, July, 1950, p. 22.
[6] Lloyd G. Reynolds and Joseph Shister, *Job Horizons: A Study of Job Satisfaction and Labor Mobility*, New York, Harper & Brothers, 1949, p. 88.

retail trade for employees to be employed at irregular hours in order to accommodate customers who are themselves employed during the regular work day. Many service trades likewise require irregular hours, as in the case of utilities employees, bus drivers, and others.

Steadiness of employment ideally means the continuation of full work weeks throughout the year. In many industries, however, this ideal is never realized. Certainly, a majority of production employees is employed less than the full potential of about 2000 hours annually. In the automobile, clothing, steel, and coal industries, slack periods have been assumed as a matter of course. Interruption of employment because of seasonal variations in consumer buying and the so-called normal business cycle introduces uncertainties into employment and differentiates the attractiveness of jobs. The order in which men are recalled to their jobs is also of importance. When an industry is organized by a union, various forms of preference may be employed, the most common being seniority.

For most production workers, advancement possibilities must be thought of in terms of advancement within the employee ranks, with advancement to the supervisory ranks limited to those few who become foremen. Seniority is likely to determine promotion in industries which are highly organized, and the implications of this procedure are profound when the individual renders meritorious service that does not count in his favor within the plant. In plants that are not organized by the union, the procedure may not be fairer, as the favoritism of minor supervisory officials and invalid rating forms play a part. In either case, the factor of advancement and its possibilities remain a significant factor in employment, though probably less so than formerly.

Social status of their jobs is sufficiently important to some workers that they forgo jobs at higher wages and shorter hours. White-collar workers have been an obvious example in the past. Minor supervisory jobs and jobs with "name" firms have been in the same group. Even within the same industry, the prestige attached to jobs may vary greatly, as in the case of the railroad engineer as compared with the baggage clerk, or the accounting-office stenographer as compared with the production-unit stenographer. Wherever skilled and semiskilled or unskilled workers are employed by the same industry, the higher status of the skilled workers is always prized.

The characteristics of supervision have been mentioned above, but other details may be added here. Supervision bears upon the em-

ployee most heavily when it is capricious and arbitrary. The want of a "personnel point of view," particularly among plants of such small size that the personnel function must be carried on as an extra duty by officials whose primary interest and duties are outside personnel, is a peculiarly unfortunate aspect of employment in such units. Among larger plants, and some small ones, the movement known as human relations in industry has proved that attention to the human-relations aspects of employment pays off in cost reduction. In the measure to which the principles underlying the human relations approach are implemented, some of the uncertainties of the work situation may be moderated.

Congeniality of fellow employees is highly important as a source of job satisfaction. The Reynolds-Shister study showed that employees who were satisfied with their jobs mentioned relations with fellow employees as the most important reason. Conversely, to be discriminated against because one's ethnic or racial background puts him in a minority classification can make a job dissatisfying when other factors are favorable.

Finally, opportunities for self-expression in terms of individualizing one's own role and work are widely held to be necessary goals in a work situation. Most of the developments in modern industry, particularly the technological aspects, have lessened the individual character of work, and opportunities for self-expression are limited. Few jobs in production work are likely to meet this need.

Thus, we have surveyed the components of the job situation and the kinds of on-the-job problems which may cause employer-employee disagreement. Among those aspects of the modern work situation which increase the probability of frustration, legislation can influence but a few—physical conditions, work loads, length of workday, and (in slight measure) steadiness of employment. The areas in which legislation may play an effective role are therefore likely to be pressed vigorously by employees when they are united. Other off-the-job factors may assume great importance similarly as compensatory objects to supplant the shortcomings of the work situation.

Characteristics of Employment in Major Industries

To describe the employment conditions of the major industries in the United States in terms of job components discussed above would be a very extensive undertaking. It is necessary, however, that we survey those general conditions of work in the more important indus-

tries in order better to understand the complexity of the labor force and the varied problems which are faced by employees in these industries. Only after such a survey can we understand the characteristics of the labor movement in such industries as coal mining and steel manufacture, and the type of legislation periodically pressed for relief of these and other groups of employees.

AGRICULTURAL EMPLOYMENT

We have already seen how employment in agriculture has been declining throughout the twentieth century owing to mechanization and the attractiveness of urban employment. In addition to declining opportunities, other features make agricultural employment unique. First of all, family workers constitute a large proportion (four-fifths) of agricultural employees, and the proportion has been increasing in recent years. About 8,000,000 family workers and more than 2,000,000 hired workers form the bulk of the agricultural labor force. Other groups of employees are also important in some regions of the United States, including a quarter of a million farm tenants and perhaps as large a number of migrant workers who follow the harvests.

Conditions of employment for agricultural workers are trying at best. For whole decades during the 1920's and 1930's, the parity conditions (ratio of level of prices paid by farmers to the level of prices received in a base period) of farmers have been disadvantageous, and a similar condition seems to be developing in the mid-1950's. When agriculture is beset for long periods by disadvantageous cost-price relationships, employees suffer economic hardship. Because farm employment is necessarily seasonal, employees are frequently dependent upon off-season "clutch" employment in order to obtain sufficient annual income. In those areas which are characterized by diversified industry balanced between agriculture and nonagricultural opportunities, this hardship may not be too serious, since logging, food packing, and other industries may permit the worker to enjoy year-round employment. Hours in agriculture are notoriously long, and the average wages paid to agricultural workers (without board) were only $124 monthly in 1952. Finally, the coverage of agricultural workers in public insurance and assistance programs has been very incomplete. In 1952, of more than 9,500,000 agricultural employees, about 6,000,000 were not covered by Old Age and Survivors Insurance. Recent legislation at the national level has afforded most of these workers the opportunity to become insured in OASI, but workmen's

compensation and unemployment insurance are generally not available to agricultural employees, a factor of great importance when the seasonal nature of the work and the high injury rates characteristic of agricultural employment are considered.

MINING

Within the mining industry in the United States, more than one-third of the total employees are employed in anthracite and bituminous coal mining, another third in the extraction of petroleum, and the remainder in iron, lead, copper, and nonmetallic mining. Our attention will center primarily on coal mining, since the problems of coal-mining employees have been a national problem for several decades. Nearly five times as many employees are engaged in mining bituminous coal, primarily for industrial use, as are engaged in the mining of anthracite for home use. Employment in the combined operations is only slightly more than half as large as it was three decades ago, and during that period an average of less than 200 days' employment per year has typified the industry. Injuries are a major consideration, the frequency rate being four times as high as in manufacturing, and the severity rate exceeding all other forms of employment. Falling roof material in the many-miles-long tunnels from which coal is obtained constitutes the chief hazard, although spectacular fires and explosions claim large numbers of lives annually. Simply in terms of the physical conditions of work, coal mining is a disagreeable form of employment. Dust, excessive heat and humidity, and the ever present dirt make this so. Power-driven machinery for cutting and loading coal has decreased the physical ordeal of mining somewhat in the more modern mines; but the machinery has also introduced factorylike methods and a more intensive pace of work. A rural industry often isolated from surrounding communities, coal mining offers little in the way of attractive living conditions for the miner's family. Finally, the inroads made into coal consumption by petroleum, water power, and natural gas—not to mention the possible effects of atomic energy as a fuel substitute—make the future of coal-mining employment uncertain. Thus, while hourly wage rates for coal miners have risen to be the highest of all employees, annual wages do not stand highest, and the conditions of work impose great burdens on the miner and his family.

Petroleum workers have enjoyed the fruits of a rapidly expanding industry. The hazards from explosions and various forms of dermatosis

caused by contact with petroleum products, as well as the essentially rural nature of the industry, are typical factors in employment.

CONSTRUCTION

One smaller group of employees in nonagricultural employment is in the construction industry, contract employees numbering more than 2,500,000. An industry employing a large proportion of highly skilled workmen, construction is typified by seasonal employment and a high injury frequency and severity rate (second only to logging and mining in 1952). During the year 1954, a variation of more than 500,000 employed distinguished the month of highest employment from that with lowest employment. Most of the more than twenty skilled trades involved in construction require training and apprentice periods, and the industry is highly unionized. In the nature of the work, sporadic employment is to be expected even beyond the seasonal fluctuations. Contractors bid for construction projects, and only the contractors who are fortunate enough to have their bids accepted frequently can employ a construction force continuously. When construction workers are employed continuously, their wages average well above the average for most other industries. The period since 1946 has been a period of unusually good times for construction workers, and the proportion of skilled workmen on construction work has steadily increased.[7] This latter factor, the continuously rising use of skilled labor, represents a departure from a tendency which set in during the 1940's and has threatened the traditional structure of employment in the industry, namely, the prefabrication of construction materials and whole units. It is probable, however, that the future will witness an expansion of assembly-line methods in prefabrication, with the effect of decreasing the amount of labor used at the site of construction.

MANUFACTURING

Manufacturing industries are divided into twenty groups, and the industries which make up each group often differ in fundamental ways. Working conditions, furthermore, tend to vary according to the geographic location and size of plant, and other similar factors; hence, few common denominators can be found which are in any meaningful sense descriptive of employment in manufacturing. The size of units has tended to increase in recent years, the growth in plants employing

[7] Cf. *Construction During Five Decades*, U.S. Department of Labor Bulletin No. 1146, p. 28.

over 2500 workmen having increased markedly, although accelerated growth in a few large-scale industries, such as automobiles and steel, may account for much of the trend. In textile, clothing, machinery, and other manufacturing industries, the small unit still predominates. One should be wary of the observation that smaller units usually favor the employee, as in closer relations with the employer, associations with employees, etc.; if these observations are true, it is also true that poorer physical conditions of work, lack of skilled staff services (e.g., personnel), and higher injury frequency and severity rates are associated with small units as compared with large ones. We shall now survey the distinctive conditions of work in some selected industries.

Textile-Mill Products. More than 1,000,000 persons are employed in the production of fabrics, knitted goods, carpets, and other similar goods. About four out of five of these employees are engaged in fabric mills. The units of the industry are small, more than three-fourths of the employees being in establishments with fewer than 250 employees. While variations in working conditions are to be found among the several industries in the group, it can be said that in general intense competition forces attention to costs and neither the physical conditions of work nor the level of wages and hours compare favorably with other manufacturing industries. The presence of lint and dust in the carding, combing, and spinning operations causes hazards, and looming is a noisy operation. Large numbers of women are employed in the industry, and they made up the bulk of the more than one-fourth of the textile employees who in 1954 were paid at a rate less than $1 per hour. Displacement of workers by machinery has been severe in some areas, and the industry's growth has lagged following the large increases in employment which characterized the war years. Competition from synthetic fibers has been the major cause of decline, and the probability is that it will become more serious.

Apparel and Related Products. An employee force slightly larger than that employed in the textile-mill industry is employed in the production of men's, women's, and children's clothing, including furs and millinery. As with the textile industry, the units of the apparel industry are small, more than four-fifths of the establishments having fewer than fifty employees, and nearly half having fewer than ten. Ten years ago, an appreciable amount of the work in the garment industry was processed in homes and small shops outside the main center of the firm, but the location of all operations within the plant now characterizes production. The industry is still centered in New York,

although to a lesser extent than formerly. Competition among the more than 28,000 establishments is intense, and the physical conditions of work reflect the effort to keep costs low. In the ladies' garment industry, however, the welfare and other services of a strong union make up for some of the inadequate shop conditions. Wage levels, in spite of the highly skilled character of the industry, stand well below the manufacturing average, and the industry is subject to extreme seasonal fluctuations which reduce annual wages. Skilled in a unique trade, unemployed persons in the industry are seldom able to locate comparable work in the off seasons.

Primary Metals. The industry within the primary-metals group to which we shall devote our attention is the basic steel industry. The blast furnace, rolling mills, foundries, and other operations employ more than 900,000 persons, an increase of about 60 percent over 1939. Because steel is a basic necessity in a large number of industries, its production is frequently used as a "barometer" or gauge of economic performance. The dependency of the steel industry upon the production of automobiles, machinery, and construction is very great; and when uncertainties appear in the production of these industries, the steel industry is immediately affected, with frequent wide-scale unemployment. The recession which began in the summer of 1953 and continued through 1954 reduced the manufacture of steel to an average of 70 percent of capacity. Conditions of work vary according to the location of the plant and the type of production method used. The introduction of the continuous-sheet rolling mill, power-driven lifting and conveying apparatus, and automatic stoking apparatus has removed much of the arduous labor attached to steel manufacture in the more modern plants. Extereme temperature variations are characteristic of some branches of the industry, and the huge masses of material as well as dust and fumes cause the accident frequency and severity rates to exceed all other manufacturing industries. Steel manufacture is a round-the-clock operation, and until the mid-1920's only two shifts were employed, with the work week being eighty-four hours in some instances. Three shifts are now employed at the customary eight-hour day and forty-hour week. Not infrequently, the steel mill is located in a semirural area apart from the urban center; and when unemployment hits, the towns that only have one industry must bear the effects. Only very recently have fringe benefits common in other industries been introduced. Threats to the future expansion of employment in the industry include the increasing use of plastics and alu-

minum, mechanization and consolidation, and the possible decrease in defense expenditures.

Machinery. More than 2,000,000 workers are employed in the manufacture of nonelectrical machinery in the United States, nearly three times as many as in 1939.[8] This is a very cycle-sensitive (variable according to the general level of business conditions) industry, and characterized by small units (nearly 17,000 in 1947), some 80 percent of which had fewer than fifty employees in 1947. Since the industry employs large numbers of skilled workmen, variations in employment are serious inasmuch as alternative employment of a comparable nature is difficult to find. Working conditions reflect the competitive situation which has been referred to above in connection with textiles and apparel, and the accident frequency and severity rates are among the highest in manufacturing. Conditions of business in the automobile, shoe, locomotive, and other industries determine the level of employment in a fundamental way.

Automotive. Within a half-century the automotive industry has moved from the small shop to the giant integrated corporation. The number of employees in the industry has doubled since 1939, but variations in employment even during the "good times" of the postwar period have been significant. In the four years beginning in 1950, the annual averages of employment were 825,000, 844,000, 790,000, 920,000, and 738,000. Not only is the year-to-year employment situation variable but sharp seasonal fluctuations also occur. For periods lasting from several weeks to several months, automobile workers are laid off while plant facilities are retooled and adapted for the next year's models. Furthermore, since the industry is concentrated in a relatively small number of cities in Michigan, Ohio, and Indiana, the impact of employment fluctuations falls with a heavy impact on a few communities. It should also be noted that large numbers of employees in the steel, glass, machine-tool, rubber, and textile industries are dependent for their jobs on the production of automobiles. Employment conditions in the automobile industry have for many years centered around the related problems of mechanization and work loads. Mechanization has allowed a rapidly rising number of automotive products to be produced by a slowly rising number of employees since 1947. Work loads have created a problem because of the tend-

---

[8] The nonelectrical-machinery industry is here used to include electrical transmission, distribution, and industrial apparatus in addition to the conventional "machinery, nonelectrical" classification used by the Bureau of Labor Statistics.

ency to speed up the assembly line by mechanically accelerating the conveyor system and by undermanning the line. The problem of monotony induced by too extensive subdivision of tasks has been continuous, and the industry is the classic example of semiskilled-personnel problems caused by division of labor. In some branches of the industry, machinery units are of enormous size and involve crushing weights, as in the cases of block boring and the pressing of body parts. Still, the injury severity and frequency rates have been well below the average for manufacturing as a whole. Working conditions are generally not substandard, owing, in all probability, to the activity of a strong union and the use of professional personnel in matters of personnel and safety.

TRANSPORTATION

Our discussion of the transportation industry will be confined to the problems which confront interstate railroad employees, who share some of the employment problems of coal miners in that the number of companies has decreased and the industry has had to make frequent resort to the national government in an effort to solve its problems. Some of the problems which confront transportation are shown in the following statistics: since 1920 the number of surface-railroad companies has decreased by about 50 percent, and since 1939 by about 25 percent; total freight revenue ton-miles have increased by about 60 per cent since 1920 and 90 percent since 1939. Passenger miles declined by nearly 25 percent since 1920, but have increased by nearly 50 percent since 1939; and employment has decreased by about 40 percent since 1920 and by about 14 percent since 1945. Thus, the volume of service rendered has increased while the volume of employment has decreased. In part this is owing to mechanization, but to a far greater extent it is due to the competition of buses, trucks, and airlines, which have taken a large share of the postwar increase in transportation service away from railroads. For skilled employees, loss of employment poses a real hardship. Working conditions vary between operating (train operation and maintenance) and nonoperating (track, maintenance, and other employees). Both seasonal and long-term variations in employment are characteristic, however, and seasonal unemployment has a close relationship to the volume of coal and other major revenue-producing items that are carried. The injury frequency and severity rates are very high in railroad transportation, although they have been much reduced from the 1916–1920 average

of nearly 3000 annual fatalities. The future of railroad employment may well come to a question of holding the present level of employment against competing transportation media, expansion of present levels being improbable.

WHOLESALE AND RETAIL TRADE

This final survey of employment conditions deals with an industry in which employment has nearly doubled since 1939, averaging nearly 10,000,000 in 1954. Twice as many persons are employed in retail trade as in wholesale trade. Few observations which might be made about employment in this group of industries would apply in general. Employment security is a problem, however, as it fluctuates with the level of expenditures by businesses and consumers. The mortality of enterprises in retail trade is unusually high. Concerning employment conditions, hours are apt to be irregular in order to adapt to the working hours of customers, and wage levels are considerably below those in manufacturing. In recent years, the shortage of persons available for sales positions (because in a period of full employment they apparently sought more desirable jobs) has led employers to offer extensive "fringe benefits" in the form of insurance protection, vacations, etc., which have somewhat increased the attractiveness of employment. Injuries are comparatively infrequent and the severity rate is low.

How American Employees Earn a Living: Concluding Remarks

The objective of this chapter, as stated in its introduction, has been to impress the reader with the varied composition of the labor force and the diversity of its problems. Some of the problems deal with hours of work, wage levels, and occupational safety—problems with which legislation can deal. Other problems concern the rising tide of employeeism and long-term fluctuations in employment, which are probably not readily dealt with through the instrument of government. Some problems, indeed, pose dilemmas, such as the problem of the workmen in steel mills and railroad transportation who are displaced as a result of mechanization and are not readily absorbed by other industries. The question in this instance involves how great a responsibility for moving away from attachments to home and family we are prepared to ask the workmen to bear. Should some form of activity be stimulated in the locality affected by unemployment through the government unit in order to prevent uprooting of persons who are unemployed owing to forces beyond their control? In the case of

agricultural labor, the problem is one of extending social-insurance coverage, improving wages, and meeting the still-existing problems of child labor.

Some industries confront American industrial society with problems which may require drastic changes in our traditional approaches if they are to be solved. Coal mining, rail transportation, textile mills, and apparel are examples. In each, the problem appears to be the lack of large operators or combinations of operators which might bring more stability into the industries through intraindustry government. Still, units with the strength to meet the problems of dispersion and over-production might pose problems of their own. Suffice it to say that the problems of American employees are sufficiently varied and complex to challenge the efforts of those who would approach them through legislation or other means.

SELECTED REFERENCES

Jaffe, Abram J., and Stewart, Charles D., *Manpower Resources and Utilization*, New York, Wiley, 1951.

Peterson, Florence, *Survey of Labor Economics*, New York, Harper & Brothers, 1947.

Reynolds, Lloyd G., and Shister, Joseph, *Job Horizons: A Study of Job Satisfaction and Labor Mobility*, New York, Harper & Brothers, 1949.

chapter 11

The Family's Quest for Income Security

The central fact of industrial society is the extent to which families have become dependent upon the income of one or more of their members who is employed outside the household. We have examined various aspects of employment conditions and dependency in the previous chapter, and in this chapter we shall pay special attention to the problem of income security. Our attention will be directed first to the structure of income payments, then to the nature of family needs, and finally to private and public approaches to promoting income security at levels which will permit families to live at levels of health and decency.

The Importance of Employee Income

Money income is at one and the same time the godsend and the curse of industrial society. On the one hand, individuals can specialize their productive roles and use money income to purchase those products and services which they would otherwise be obliged to supply for themselves. Specialization, of course, enables us to use our national resources more efficiently, and the amount of goods and services available to us is thereby increased. But the money payments made to employees for their contributions to production have showed a tendency to become very unequal in all industrialized societies, a tendency which has created the need for many forms of legislation to relieve the needs of those whose incomes are below the minimum level to maintain a decent and healthful living standard.

The reasons why modern production methods should produce this maldistribution of income have been a matter of importance for nearly two centuries, but the concern directed toward family income levels and their adequacy is comparatively recent. At the turn of the

nineteenth century, the attitude of society toward unequal distribution of income and its resulting poverty was one of resignation to the operation of inexorable natural laws. This attitude was sharply revised during the second half of the nineteenth century after John Stuart Mill insisted that social laws, not natural laws, determined the character of income distribution, and Karl Marx added his inflammatory doctrine of exploitation. At the close of the nineteenth century, the natural-law explanation of wage levels was being questioned on many sides, and it was generally thought that severe income inequality could be relieved through the political unit without harm to the economic mechanism. In the United States, particularly, this view gained popularity and expressed itself in the demand for an income tax. Still, the question was largely one of whether our social conscience would permit extremes of income which condemned millions of persons to lives of poverty. For three decades, our approach to the problem was restricted to the imposition of an income tax upon the very wealthy. But during the 1930's and the misery of the Great Depression, the views of those who saw serious problems for the economy because of underconsumption gained a wider audience and, where the humanitarian arguments had failed, the economic arguments succeeded. Legislation to deal with the problem of income security was enacted in many forms at the national level. The role of income security was thought sufficiently important to merit legislation to protect the family against loss of income caused by unemployment, industrial injury, loss of a wage earner, old age, and exploitation.

The Roles of Income Security

The role of income security has many facets. Personal security is enhanced and personal anxieties reduced when an individual's income adequacy is assured for long periods of time. Those fears which tax both the individual's productive capacity and his responsible citizenship are more frequently than not related to income uncertainty. If they can be lessened, the society will respond, as to relief from any other kind of stress, and achieve a new equilibrium. In the social system, the role of income could hardly be overestimated as a determinant of social behavior. It is not irresponsible to declare that family income level determines in some measure nutritional adequacy, neighborhood, marriage stability, life expectancy, birth rate, health and medical care, insurance protection, membership in associations, and

social status of family members, to mention the more important factors. Clearly, more is involved in the question of income distribution than simply providing the basic necessities of life, although we have not yet achieved that level of economic well-being which assures to all families even adequate food, clothing, and shelter. This observation follows from a comparison of family income data with standard budgets of family needs at various levels of living, data which give conservative answers to the problem of need, as we shall see in a later section.

The economic role of family income security is not less important than the personal and social roles mentioned above. As a matter of fact, it might be considered an element of the social role of income security. It has been pointed out that the importance of income distribution increased significantly when the conviction gained attention that mass-production techniques depended upon mass markets, and that national economic stability depended upon the stability of the mass-production industries. Some aspects of this relationship are highly complex, and a special appendix, Appendix A (pp. 410–421), has been added to this chapter to explain their basic character. The essential relationships can be simply stated, however. Mass-production industries depend upon mass markets, as we have said. All products, moreover, are sensitive in some measure to consumer resistance to their consumption when consumer income positions become uncertain, and some products (nonessentials) are keenly sensitive to consumer income positions. For a large proportion of the products upon which economic stability depends, therefore, the course of events seems to be as follows: (1) consumer incomes decrease; (2) consumption, particularly of durable goods, decreases; (3) retail and wholesale firms decrease their stocks and their orders from factories and processors; (4) factories and processors decrease their consumption of labor, equipment, and materials; (5) employment falls off in the primary industries which depend on consumer-goods production; (6) consumption is further reduced because of decreased incomes; and (7) other industries in the economic system also experience decreasing needs for employees and materials, ultimately adding to the loss of income. Although the above sequence is not meant to be a description of an actual downturn in economic activity, it suggests the role which family income plays in sustaining the level of economic activity. We should be sure to understand that consumer expenditures are a necessary but not a sufficient condition to maintain economic activity; other im-

portant factors include business expenditures on new plant and equipment, government purchases, and certain other factors. In recent years, legislation addressed to the problem of income security of employees has justified itself largely in terms of the economic advantages of sustained purchasing power, in addition to the traditional humanitarian grounds.

Factors upon Which Family Income Depends

Few programs of social legislation have proved more fruitless than those hastily conceived to "legislate" higher incomes for this or that needy group. The factors upon which income security depends are related to the efficiency of production, which is in turn related to such factors as the use of machinery, sufficiency of natural resources, cultural norms concerning work and material needs, health and age of the population, etc. Thus, legislation can operate only indirectly to influence income distribution in a capitalistic system. In the United States, however, machinery utilization is at very high levels; natural resources, cultural norms, and health are unusually favorable; and the functions which legislation can perform in the field of income security are therefore extensive. Let us approach a determination of those areas wherein legislation might be effective by analyzing the factors upon which family income depends.

A multiplicity of factors influences the size of a family annual income, but we shall deal only with the major factors. These include (1) the general level of business conditions; (2) the industry in which the major wage earner(s) is (are) employed; (3) age, sex, and race of the wage earner; (4) number of family wage earners; (5) family wealth and family income; and (6) the geographic location.

THE GENERAL LEVEL OF BUSINESS CONDITIONS

The level of business activity influences the income security of the family in a fundamental way through its consequences of underemployment (working less than a full work week) and unemployment. When the wage earner upon whom the family is dependent is employed fewer hours than normal or not employed at all for part of the work year, then the income available to the family decreases. If consumers decrease their purchases of goods and services (and compensating factors do not take effect), then the situation becomes worse. In most firms, a decrease in the level of sales (or simply a failure of the level of sales to increase) results in unemployment or underemploy-

ment for the employee force. Not only labor but also other factors of production feel the impact of falling sales revenue, and firms may decide not to replace equipment or not to build up normal inventories, with the consequence that employment in the machinery industries and in the factories which supply inventories and materials will fall off. Certain industries are highly sensitive to the level of business activity, as we shall see in the next section. Activities to halt this phenomenon of deteriorating business conditions constitute a controversial question; but it is clear that one of the activities will have to deal with the family income situation, because decreasing expenditures cause the lag in sales in the first place.

Falling income owing to the level of business activity severely affects the family income position, and the existence of unemployment insurance or other compensation payments only moderates the consequences of unemployment. The payments are nearly always much less than the average pay check to which the family has adjusted its consumption activity. In Table 26, the effect of the level of business conditions on family income can be seen. All of the income data are stated in terms of 1953 dollars, which makes each year comparable with the other years.

TABLE 26. Disposable Personal Income and Average Disposable Personal Income per Employee, Selected Years.

(billions of dollars)

Years	Civilian Labor Force	Disposable Personal Income [a]	Average Disposable Income Per Employee [c]
1929	49,180	$129.1	$2,627
1933	51,590	98.3	1,905
1939	55,230	139.8	2,531
1945	53,860	211.0	3,918
1948	61,442	211.4	3,441
1949	62,105	212.5	3,422
1953	63,418	248.0	3,911
1954	64,616	248.0 [b]	3,838

a Income actually available for consumption activity to the employee at 1953 prices.
b Estimated.
c Disposable personal income at 1953 prices divided by civilian labor force total.
Sources: Bureau of the Census, Statistical Abstract of the United States, 1954, p. 195, and Current Population Reports; U.S. Department of Labor, Monthly Labor Review, April, 1955; and U.S. Department of Commerce, Survey of Current Business, July, 1955.

The years 1933, 1949, and 1954 were years during which the level of economic activity was depressed and the variations which occurred in

average disposable income were considerable, as the table shows. In Appendix A to this chapter, we shall discuss approaches to the problem of economic activity, and the circumstances of family income being a causal factor in declining economic activity, and also the avenue through which the decline can be arrested.

THE INDUSTRY IN WHICH THE MAJOR WAGE EARNER IS EMPLOYED

Working conditions were seen to show considerable variation in the preceding chapter, and these variations also apply to wage conditions. Both the level of hourly wages and the total number of hours actually worked influence wages, and these factors are highly uncertain determinants of income in some industries. Seasonal fluctuations in business activity and the sensitivity of some industries to the business cycle also cause family income to be uncertain.

Low hourly wage rates may result from many factors, but chiefly from the low value of hourly output by the employee. The employee's hourly output (productivity) is, of course, dependent primarily on the machinery with which he performs his tasks. Other causes of low wage rates include exploitation of labor—chiefly based on race, sex, and age—and local labor-supply conditions where a larger number of workers offer their services in seasonal industries than the industries require. A Department of Labor survey conducted in 1954 disclosed that five major manufacturing-industry groups employed more than 10 percent of their workers at rates below 90 cents an hour.[1] In lumber and furniture, this percentage was 25, in leather and leather products 15.9, in textiles and apparel 13.9, in tobacco manufactures 12.9, and in food and kindred products 11.3.[2] Regional variations were far more revealing, as indicated by the fact that more than half of the lumber and furniture employees received wages averaging less than 90 cents per hour. We shall discuss regional variations in earnings in a later section. Outside manufacturing, earnings less than 90 cents an hour are received by large proportions of employees in agriculture and retail trade.

High hourly earnings do not necessarily ensure the income security of the employee and his family. The number of hours for which the employee actually receives wages is also an important factor. In 1954, an average work week of less than 40 hours was found in coal mining

---

[1] U.S. Department of Labor, "The Distribution of Factory Workers' Earnings," *Monthly Labor Review*, April, 1955, pp. 410–416.

[2] *Ibid.*, p. 415.

(30 hours in anthracite mining and 33 hours in bituminous mining), apparel (35 hours), contract construction (37 hours), leather and leather products (37 hours), textile-mill products (37 hours), rubber products (39 hours), and retail trade (39 hours).[3] It should be pointed out that the industries which are among the five highest in terms of average hourly earnings also are among the five highest in terms of annual earnings, although the ranks are different for the industries in each case. But wide disparities appear between hourly and annual earnings outside of the high-wage industries.

Seasonal variations in employment are particularly important in agriculture, some branches of the food-products industry, the apparel industry, the automotive industry, and other industries which have been mentioned previously. Mining, primary metals, machinery manufacture, transportation, and many service industries also are highly sensitive to business-cycle fluctuations. It is apparent, therefore, that the industry in which the major wage earner or wage earners on which the family is dependent for income is important in determining the adequacy and the security of its income. We shall see that the regional location of the industry is also significant in determining earnings.

AGE, SEX, AND RACE OF THE WAGE EARNER

Age, sex, and race are significant factors in determining the level of family income security. Considering the age factor in earnings first, in the case of both men and women the years 15–25 are ones of low earnings, the peak earnings being in the years 35–40, with a gradual decrease to age 50 and a rapid decrease thereafter.[4] Table 27 presents data showing the relationship between age of the family head and earnings.

From the table, it can be seen that in the age groups 18–24 and over 55, particularly age 65 and over, a far larger percentage of spending units fall below each income level indicated, and, in the age groups embraced by ages 25–55, more than half of the spending units fall above the $4000 level—three times as large a proportion as falls above $4000 in the 18–24 or over 65 group. It should also be noted that younger workers and older workers experience difficulty in becoming reëmployed if their employment is terminated.

Sex differences are likewise important as a determinant of family

    [3] Ibid., pp. 486–501.
    [4] W. S. Woytinski and Associates, *Employment and Wages in the United States*, New York, The Twentieth Century Fund, p. 448.

TABLE 27.   Family Income by Age of Family Unit Head, 1953.ᵃ

Age of Family Unit Head	1953 Income Before Taxes					
	Under $1000	Under $2000	Under $3000	Under $4000	Under $5000	Over $5000
	Percent of Family Units ᵇ					
18–24	9	39	68	81	93	7
25–34	3	9	21	42	62	38
35–44	5	13	25	41	59	41
45–54	6	16	28	45	60	40
55–64	9	22	37	50	66	34
65 and over	34	63	75	86	91	9

a "Family unit" is Federal Reserve Board "spending unit," defined as all persons living in the same dwelling and related by blood, marriage, or adoption who pool their income for their major expenses. Includes only spending units where husband and wife are present. Total number of families surveyed, 3000.
b Cumulated.

income. A *Fortune* survey of family incomes in 1953 indicated that of 22,000,000 supplementary earners in 17,000,000 families, 15,000,000 (more than three-fourths) were women.[5] More than one-tenth of the women who work are the only income earners in their families, and a large proportion of widowed and divorced women are the only earners in their families.[6]

Earnings of women workers are significantly lower than earnings of men in similar occupations. In 1952, the median annual income of men was $3105 and of women $1147, or about 40 percent as large as the median income of men.[7]

Table 28 shows the 1953 income pattern for men and women as reported by the Bureau of the Census.

Table 28 shows that 68.6 percent of women income earners fell below the $2000 level, while only 30.4 percent of men receivers fell below this level. In manufacturing, the proportion of women workers earning less than 90 cents an hour in 1954 was more than three times as large as the proportion of men having such earnings, 14.2 percent as compared with 4.0 percent.[8] At all occupational levels, from unskilled through managerial and professional, the median incomes of women are significantly less than the incomes of men.

[5] U.S. Department of Labor, *1954 Handbook on Women Workers*, Women's Bureau Bulletin No. 255, 1954, p. 34.
[6] *Ibid.*, p. 34.
[7] *Ibid.*, p. 21.
[8] U.S. Department of Labor, *Factory Workers' Earnings*, Bureau of Labor Statistics Bulletin No. 1179, p. 6.

TABLE 28.   Annual Income According to Sex of Earner, 1953.

Sex of Earner	1953 Income Before Taxes [a]					
	Under $1000	Under $2000	Under $3000	Under $4000	Under $5000	Over $5000
	Percent of Earners					
Male	16.5	30.4	47.2	70.1	83.6	16.4
Female	46.8	68.6	86.6	96.6	98.5	1.5

[a] Cumulated.

Source: U.S. Bureau of the Census, *Statistical Abstract of the United States, 1954,* 1955, p. 316. Board of Governors of the Federal Reserve System, "1954 Survey of Consumer Finances," reprinted from the *Federal Reserve Bulletin,* March, June, and July 1954, p. 9 (July 1954).

Finally, the racial factor must be seen as a determinant of family income, since nonwhite family heads receive incomes which place them farther down the income scale than white family heads. The Joint Committee on the Economic Report declared in 1949 that "families headed either by a woman or a non-white male comprised about 40 percent of all non-farm families with heads between the ages of 21 and 64 receiving incomes under $2,000; and only 10 percent of the families having incomes of $3,000 or more." [9] The disparity between the incomes received by whites and nonwhites has lessened since 1939, as Table 29 shows; but median wage and salary income of whites still exceeds the median of non-whites by 93.5 percent in the case of both sexes and 72.1 percent in the case of males.

TABLE 29.   Median Income of Nonfarm Families by Color, 1939 and 1952.[a]

Group	Both Sexes		Males	
	1939	1952	1939	1952
White	$959	$3309	$1112	$3507
Nonwhite	364	1570	460	2038

[a] Median wage and salary income of nonfarm families.

Sources: U.S. Bureau of the Census, *Statistical Abstract of the United States, 1954,* 1955, p. 318.

NUMBER OF FAMILY WAGE EARNERS

The total income available to the family has become more and more a function of the number of wage earners in the family. A

[9] Joint Committee on the Economic Report, *Low Income Families and Economic Stability*, Washington, Government Printing Office, 1949.

Census Bureau report of family income in 1950 reveals the role which "extra" wage earners play in bolstering the consumption power of families. Table 30 is based on those data.

TABLE 30. Median Family Income by Number of Wage Earners, 1950.

Number of Earners	Percent of Families	Median Family Income
0	6.6	$ 923
1	54.4	3,128
2	30.4	3,913
3 or more	8.6	5,268

Source: U.S. Bureau of the Census, Current Population Reports, Series P-60, No. 9, pp. 27–29.

The addition of one wage earner, the table shows, results in an increase of 25 percent, and the addition of another wage earner results in the increase of family income by nearly 60 percent. The breakdown of families according to income class and number of wage earners is given for 1953 in Table 31.

TABLE 31. Family-Income Levels According to Number of Wage Earners, 1953.[a]

Number of Earners	Income Size Class					
	Under $1000	Under $2000	Under $3000	Under $4000	Under $5000	Over $5000
	Percent of Families [b]					
1	12	27	42	59	75	25
2	3	11	22	37	54	46

a "Family unit" is Federal Reserve Board "spending unit," defined as all persons living in the same dwelling and related by blood, marriage, or adoption who pool their income for their major expenses. Includes only spending units where husband and wife are present. Total number of families in survey, 3000.
b Cumulated.

Sources: Board of Governors of the Federal Reserve System, "1954 Survey of Consumer Finances," reprinted from the Federal Reserve Bulletin, March, June, and July 1954, p. 9 (July 1954).

The table indicates that twice as large a proportion of families who have one wage earner fall below the $3000 level as those who have two or more wage earners. Similarly, twice as large a proportion of families having two or more earners receive incomes above $5000.

Supplemental wage earners are, as has been noted, women for the most part, and many enter the labor force when their incomes become necessary to safeguard the family income security and leave when

adequate economic security has been attained. The supplemental wage earner, therefore, is not typified by a career woman, but rather by a person whose primary interest is immediate income.

FAMILY WEALTH AND FAMILY INCOME

The proverbial warning that "it takes money to make money" appears to be borne out by family-income source data. At least, the higher the family income, the larger the proportion that is received from income-producing property. Income in the form of rents and royalties, dividends, interest, and profits is received only in very small amounts by families below the $10,000-annual-income level. Table 32 shows the sources of income for families at various income levels as between wages and salaries and property income.

TABLE 32.   Wage and Salary and Property Sources of Income at Various Levels of Annual Income, 1951.[a]

Income class	Wages and Salaries	Property Income [b]
Dollars	Percent of Adjusted Gross Income	
Under 1,000	82.2	17.8
1,000 to 2,000	83.9	16.1
2,000 to 3,000	86.3	13.7
3,000 to 4,000	89.9	10.1
4,000 to 5,000	91.0	9.0
5,000 to 10,000	85.2	14.8
10,000 to 15,000	56.7	43.3
15,000 to 25,000	44.2	55.8
25,000 to 50,000	36.6	43.4
50,000 to 100,000	31.6	68.4
100,000 to 500,000	20.8	79.2
500,000 to 1,000,000	6.9	93.1

a Adjusted Gross Income as reported to the Internal Revenue Service.
b Includes dividends, interest, annuities and pensions, rents and royalties, business and professional income, partnership net profit, net gain from the sale or exchange of capital and other assets, income from estates and trusts, and other income.

Source: U. S. Treasury Department, Statistics of Income for 1951, Internal Revenue Service Publication No. 79, Part I, 1955, pp. 30–32.

It is evident from the table that income receivers from the $10,000 level upward are progressively less dependent on wage and salary income, and earn a substantial portion of their annual income from the use of property. It is probable also that those income receivers below the $5000 level who receive an average of about 13 percent of their income from property fall above the median income in each of the income classes below that level. Rental income probably is the most

widely distributed form of property income below the $5000 level, particularly since homeowners who occupy their own homes can be viewed as receiving the rental value of their homes as income.[10]

Information about the holding of income-producing property is very inadequate. In early 1953, however, the *Survey of Consumer Finances* reported that 11 percent of the spending units surveyed had a net worth (the excess of assets over liabilities) of zero, 31 percent had a net worth less than $1000, and 54 percent had a net worth less than $5000.[11] The income return from property which might be held by families with a net worth less than $1000 would be minimal and relatively small for a net worth below $5000. Clearly, the structure of property holding revealed in these data does not permit significant amounts of property income to accrue to the vast majority of spending units.

REGIONAL VARIATIONS IN INCOME

Among the census regions into which the United States is divided, significant variations in family income are to be found. In 1949, the range of median family income was $1465 from the region of lowest per capita income to the region of highest per capita income. Table 33 summarizes this information.

The details of the large income differentiation among census regions of the United States are revealed in the table. Since the range is $341 above the national median and $684 below the national median, the table indicates that the areas having median family incomes below the national median are characterized by quite different income security problems from the more fortunate, predominantly industrial areas. Some of the implications of these data will be discussed in Chapter 14.

Factory-worker earnings also show wide variations among census regions, as shown in Table 34. These variations exist for comparable jobs and within the same industry. Straight-time hourly earnings vary by as much as 100 percent among census regions, as in the lumber and furniture industry, and in each industry the hourly rates are lowest in the South and highest in the Far West. The proportion of production workers who receive less than 90 cents an hour is from four to

[10] Interest income is undoubtedly the most widely received form of property income if one includes the interest received by life-insurance policyholders and the interest paid into the social-insurance funds by the national government.

[11] The Conference Board, *Economic Almanac, 1953–54*, New York, Thomas Y. Crowell Company, 1954, p. 478.

TABLE 33.   Median Income of Families and Unrelated Individuals by Census Region, 1949.[a]

Census Region	Median Income	Percent of U.S. Median
Continental United States	$2,619	100.0
Northeast	2,968	113.3
New England	2,801	106.9
Middle Atlantic	3,020	115.3
North Central	2,872	109.7
East North Central	3,063	117.0
West North Central	2,432	92.9
South	1,935	73.9
South Atlantic	2,081	79.5
East South Central	1,555	59.4
West South Central	2,021	77.2
West	2,907	110.0
Mountain	2,620	100.0
Pacific	3,004	114.7

a Based on 20 percent sample. Median income computed from $500 intervals.

Source: U.S. Bureau of Census, *U.S. Census of Population: 1950,* Vol. II, *Characteristics of the Population,* Part I, "United States Summary," 1953, p. 136.

six times as large in the South as the United States average for various branches of manufacturing.[12]

The factors which contribute to the inequality of family incomes among regions in the United States are complex. In some regions,

TABLE 34.   Average Hourly Earnings of Production Workers in Selected Manufacturing-Industry Groups by Census Regions, 1954.[a]

Industry Group	United States	Northeast	South	Middle West	Far West
Food and kindred products	$1.48	$1.55	$1.13	$1.58	$1.67
Textiles and apparel	1.33	1.47	1.15	1.27	n.a.
Lumber and furniture	1.41	n.a. [b]	.97	1.50	2.13
Paper and printing	1.84	1.82	1.67	1.87	2.16
Chemicals and petroleum	1.83	1.81	1.78	1.84	2.06
Leather and leather products	1.36	1.40	1.16	1.35	n.a.
Primary metals [c]	1.86	1.82	1.72	1.91	1.93
Transportation equipment	1.89	1.83	1.68	1.94	1.98

a Straight-time hourly earnings of production workers, April, 1954.
b Means data not available.
c Includes fabricated metal products.

Source: U.S. Department of Labor, "The Distribution of Factory Workers' Earnings," *Monthly Labor Review,* April, 1955, p. 414.

12 U.S. Department of Labor, "The Distribution of Factory Workers' Earnings," *Monthly Labor Review,* April, 1955, p. 415.

characteristically low-wage industries predominate, as the textile industry in the South. In others, the investment in machinery is relatively low per worker, and wage rates correlate highly with machinery investment. Education and skill attainment play a large part in explaining wage levels, as do health and climate factors. In some regions, unusually bountiful natural resources contribute to high earnings and high wage rates.

SUMMARY

Family income security has been discussed in connection with the major factors which seem to influence it in terms of size and steadiness. Many of the factors are of such a nature that legislation might aid in promoting greater income security, although the influence would be indirect. Legislation to aid in stabilizing business conditions through monetary and fiscal policies would appear to be of primary importance in this connection. Other assistance might be rendered through tax relief for low-income families during adverse business conditions, a factor which we shall discuss in the next section. Age, sex, and racial discrimination in wages has been approached through fair-employment-practices legislation and requires expansion on a broad front. National minimum-wage standards accompanied by regional development programs might significantly alter the income differentials which presently exist among census regions. Other areas of legislation might concern protection of labor organizations and their organizational drives. It is important that the problem of income-security legislation be not considered separately from labor productivity. Because the level of income and labor productivity are so closely related, aid to education and training in substantial amounts might well prove the most effective long-run program.

Income Distribution in the United States

Having discussed the general features of family income determination, we shall now turn to the income structure of the United States. This will lead us into a discussion of the problems involved in evaluating income adequacy and measures to promote income security. Our discussion will be largely in statistical terms.

One of the pitfalls for the unwary in analyzing income distribution is the type of statistical information presented. Particularly misleading is the use of "average" (arithmetic mean) data to show changes. If the average income per family increases between two selected years,

it may mean that the insecurity surrounding the typical family's income situation has abated. But it may also reflect merely a reduction in the proportion of very low incomes, an increase in the proportion of very high incomes, or a decrease in the proportion of very high incomes but an increase in the proportion of relatively high incomes, say, from $5000 to $10,000. The description of income data in terms of medians and percentage classes is therefore preferable. Other dangers surround the use of data for widely separated years without compensating for the factors of price inflation (decrease in the purchasing-power "value" of the dollar) and taxation. Other issues will arise concerning the character of data which we use, and where we feel it is necessary to do so, explanations will be made in the notes accompanying the tables.

The first comprehensive survey of family income was conducted by the National Resources Committee for the years 1935–1936.[13] Previous data are estimated to a large extent, but are valuable because they indicate trends in income distribution. Data for the period of World War II and the postwar period are not adequate to answer conclusively such questions as, "Has the income security of the first or second or third quartile of families increased since 1935–1936 or since 1945, and, if so, to what extent?" or "What are the characteristics of the families whose incomes fall in the lower two deciles of the distribution?" However, the data suggest answers to these questions, and we can assess the case for legislation to deal with the problem of income insecurity with a fair amount of confidence. From data reported by the United States Treasury, the Department of Commerce (the Bureau of the Census and the National Income Division), and the Board of Governors of the Federal Reserve System, we can develop a picture of the income structure since 1910.

Professor Kuznets reports that for the period 1919–1938, before taxes, the upper 1 percent of the nation's income receivers averaged 12.8 percent of total income payments, the upper 5 percent averaged 25.4 percent, and the lower 95 percent averaged 74.6 percent.[14] These data, according to Kuznets, probably understate the shares of total income payments going to the upper-income groups. Other data for these and earlier years are presented in Table 35. They are from National Industrial Conference Board estimates. These data, although

[13] National Resources Committee, Consumer Incomes in the United States, the Committee, Washington, 1938.
[14] Simon Kuznets, National Income, a Summary of Findings, New York, National Bureau of Economic Research, 1950.

TABLE 35.   Distribution of the National Income According to Proportion of
Recipients, 1910–1937.[a]

Percent of Income receivers	1910	1918	1921	1929	1934	1937
	Percent of National Income Received by Deciles					
Highest tenth	33.9	34.5	38.2	39.0	33.6	34.4
2nd tenth	12.3	12.9	12.8	12.3	13.1	14.1
3rd tenth	10.2	9.6	5.0	8.9	11.0	11.7
4th tenth	8.8	8.7	8.9	9.0	9.4	10.1
5th tenth	8.0	7.7	7.4	7.9	8.2	8.5
6th tenth	7.0	7.2	6.5	6.5	7.3	7.2
7th tenth	6.0	6.9	5.9	5.5	6.2	6.0
8th tenth	5.5	5.7	4.6	4.6	5.3	4.4
9th tenth	4.9	4.4	3.2	3.6	3.8	2.6
Lowest tenth	3.4	2.4	2.0	1.8	2.1	1.0
	Percent of National Income Received by Deciles, Cumulated [b]					
Lower nine-tenths	66.1	65.5	56.3	60.1	66.4	65.6
Lower eight-tenths	53.8	52.6	43.5	47.8	53.3	51.5
Lower seven-tenths	43.6	43.0	38.5	38.9	42.3	39.8
Lower six-tenths	34.8	34.3	29.6	29.9	32.9	29.7
Lower half	26.8	26.6	22.2	22.0	24.7	21.2
Lower four-tenths	19.8	19.4	15.7	15.5	17.4	14.0
Lower three-tenths	13.8	12.5	9.8	10.0	11.2	8.0
Lower two-tenths	8.3	6.8	5.2	5.4	5.9	3.6
Lowest tenth	3.4	2.4	2.0	1.8	2.1	1.0

[a] Total personal-income payments including capital gains, transfers, gifts, etc.
[b] Detail may not add to totals owing to rounding.

Source: National Industrial Conference Board; data reported in U. S. Bureau of
the Census, Historical Statistics of the United States, 1789–1945, 1949, p. 15.

they were derived through somewhat coarse statistical techniques,
have the merit of allowing data for various years to be compared
without considering the purchasing power of the dollar. The trends
revealed in the table are indicative of the concentration of income
in the hands of higher-income classes. During the period 1910–
1937, the highest tenth of the income receivers commanded a proportion of the national income, varying from ten to about fifteen
times the proportion received by the lowest tenth. Stated in another way, the highest tenth of the income receivers commanded
a larger proportion of the national income than the lower six-tenths
of the income receivers in each of the years indicated. Furthermore,
for the years indicated, the upper five deciles have increased their
shares of the national income at the expense of the lower five as a
general trend through the 1930's. Table 36 completes the series of
data for the period of World War II and the postwar period in terms
of shares of the national income. This table shows the distribution of

family personal income and is not strictly comparable with table 35, although the trends it reveals can be compared with the previous table.

TABLE 36. Distribution of Family Personal Income According to Proportion of Recipients.[a]

Income-Receiving Unit	1944	1947	1950	1953
	Percent of Family Personal Income Received by Quintiles			
Highest fifth	45.8	46.0	46.1	44.9
4th fifth	22.2	22.0	22.1	22.3
3rd fifth	16.2	16.0	16.1	16.5
2nd fifth	10.9	11.0	10.9	11.3
Lowest fifth	4.9	5.0	4.8	5.0
	Percent of Family Personal Income Received by Quintiles, Cumulated [b]			
Lower four-fifths	54.2	54.1	53.9	55.1
Lower three-fifths	32.0	32.1	31.8	32.8
Lower two-fifths	15.8	16.0	15.7	16.3
Lowest fifth	4.9	5.0	4.8	5.0
	Lower Income Limit of Each Quintile			
Highest fifth	$4,800	$5,130	$5,470	$5,960
4th fifth	3,410	3,650	3,830	4,200
3rd fifth	2,450	2,680	2,800	3,040
2nd fifth	1,510	1,660	1,730	1,840

[a] Includes social insurance and assistance payments and other transfers, but not capital gains.
[b] Detail may not add to totals owing to rounding.

Source: U. S. Department of Commerce, Income Distribution in the United States, 1953, p. 81, and Survey of Current Business, March, 1955, p. 20.

The data shown in Table 36 for the period since 1944 indicate that the fundamental structure of income distribution in the United States has changed but little during the disturbing conditions of reconversion from a completely mobilized economy. When the shares of income are analyzed, it appears that the highest fifth of income-receiving units receive an income share considerably larger than the three lower fifths and nearly as large a share as the four lower fifths. One measurement comparing the earlier data and the post-1940 period can be made: the ratios among the quintiles. When the ratios of the highest to the lowest quintile are computed, they vary only slightly for the period after 1921 except for the depression year 1937. Little change seems to have occurred in the relationship between the income shares of the highest and the lowest quintiles. The ratios of the highest to the fourth quintiles reveal a decreasing ratio from 1921 to the present, indicating that

the fourth quintile has gained at the expense of the highest quintile. Finally, when the ratios between the lowest and the fourth quintiles are computed, they show a generally increasing tendency, except for the year 1937, which bears out the probability that the fourth quintile has experienced the largest gain over the period since 1921.[15] The table also shows the lower limits of income-receiving units included in each of the quintiles.

The cautious conclusion that gains in the distribution of income shares may have been experienced largely by the two uppermost quintiles is supported by data gathered in the *Survey of Consumer Finances*. Table 37 presents these data for the period 1948–1955. It will be seen that the income classes which increased their percentages by the largest amount were the $5000 to $7500 and the $7500 and over

TABLE 37.   Spending Units Distributed According to Income Classes, 1948–1955.[a]

Income Class	1955[b]	1954	1953	1952	1951	1950	1949	1948
				Percent of Spending Units				
Under $1,000	10	10	11	13	13	14	12	14
$1,000 to $1,999	13	13	14	15	17	19	18	22
$2,000 to $2,999	14	14	16	18	19	21	23	23
$3,000 to $3,999	16	16	18	18	19	19	20	17
$4,000 to $4,999	15	16	15	15	12	11	12	10
$5,000 to $7,499	21	21	17	14	14	11	10	9
$7,500 to $10,000	6	5	5	4 }	6 }	5 }	5 }	5 }
$10,000 and over	5	5	4	3 }	}	}	}	}

a Based on an average survey of approximately 3000 spending units defined as all persons living in the same dwelling who are related by blood, marriage, or adoption and who pool their incomes for major expenses. Because the units surveyed in successive years are not identical, some lack of comparability is present. Income level is for previous year.
b Data for 1955 are preliminary.

Source: Board of Governors of the Federal Reserve System, "Preliminary Findings of the 1955 Survey of Consumer Finances," *Federal Reserve Bulletin*, March, 1955, p. 251.

classes, both of which more than doubled from 1948 to 1955. Considering the lower income limits shown in Table 36, it is probable that

[15] The relevant data upon which the above conclusions are based are presented in the following summary (computed from Tables 35 and 36):

Year	Ratio Highest to Lowest Quintile	Ratio Highest to Fourth Quintile	Ratio Fourth to Lowest Quintile
1910	5.6	2.4	2.3
1921	9.8	3.4	2.9
1929	9.5	2.9	3.3
1937	13.5	2.2	6.0
1944	9.3	2.1	4.5
1947	9.2	2.1	4.4
1950	9.6	2.1	4.6
1953	9.0	2.0	4.5

these income classes are in the fourth and highest quintiles. The data also show that the whole income structure has moved upward, a condition of improvement which is retained even after adjustments have been made to compensate for reductions in purchasing power actually available to the family. Still, the apparent gains made by "average" income receivers are substantially reduced when compensations for price inflation and taxation are made. In Table 38, we have presented data which permit some conclusions concerning the growth in actual (real) incomes for selected periods. These data will be of importance to us when, in the following section, we attempt to judge the extent to which incomes are "adequate" for the standards of consumption

TABLE 38. Income Distribution in the United States in 1948 Adjusted for Inflation and Taxes.[a]

Families Ranked by Income Size	In 1948 Dollars	Median Income of Each Group		
		In 1947–1949 Dollars [b]	After Federal Income Tax [c]	After Taxes, All Levels [d]
Highest fifth	$6000	$5837	$5259	$4226
Fourth fifth	3750	3648	3396	2696
Median fifth	2840	2763	2574	2047
Second fifth	2000	1946	1815	1473
Lowest fifth	860	837	811	601
All groups	2840	2763	2575	2047

a Family personal income, 1948.
b Adjusted for inflation by Consumers Price Index (1947–1949 = 100).
c Adjusted for "Effective tax rate according to adjusted gross income," as reported by the U.S. Treasury Department in *Statistics of Income, 1951*, 1955, p. 98.
d Adjusted for tax incidence, all levels of government, federal, state, and local according to schedule of rates given in Richard A. Musgrave and associates, "Distribution of Tax Payments by Income Groups: A Case Study for 1948," *National Tax Journal*, March, 1951, p. 26.

Source: Basic income data for 1948 from *Economic Report of the President to the Congress*, January, 1950, pp. 145–46.

that are called for in budgets drawn up for today's families. It can be appreciated from the table how important are changes in the price level (purchasing power of incomes) and the tax structure. Price inflation as a factor was not of serious consequence for 1948 because our 1947–1949 index was only 102.8. Taxes, however, were of considerable importance. After compensating for price inflation and taxes, the median income of the families included in the lowest fifth was reduced by more than 30 percent; the average reduction for all income groups was about 28 percent. One observation that should be made concerns the impact of other types of taxes in addition to the federal personal-income tax. As the table shows, far more income is taken by such taxes

as federal and state excises, corporation-income taxes,[16] and other taxes than by the federal personal-income tax. When the income-payments data for the years 1944–1953 are adjusted for the impact of inflation and taxation, they take on a very different appearance from the usually reported increasing trends. Table 39 reports the average family personal income (remember that average data overstate the level of income above and below which half of the families fall) for selected years 1944–1953 and adjusted for inflation and taxation.

TABLE 39. Family Personal Income, Adjusted for Inflation and Taxes, Selected Years, 1944–1953.[a]

Average Family Personal Income	1944	1947	1950	1953
Unadjusted [b]	$4027	$4574	$4969	$6002
In 1947–1949 dollars [c]	5355	4790	4834	5325
After federal personal-income taxes [d]	4654	4291	4352	4722
After taxes, all levels [e]	3961	3545	3577	3915

a Average family personal income.
b "Current dollars" unadjusted for price inflation or taxes.
c Average family personal income adjusted for changes in the purchasing power of the dollar through dividing by the Consumers Price Index (1947–1949 = 100).
d Average family personal income less the average federal personal-income tax for the income bracket (in $1000 intervals) and adjusted by the Consumers Price Index.
e Average family personal income less the average tax incidence, federal, state, and local governments according to the Musgrave study (see notes, Table 38), on the assumption (probably invalid for 1944 and 1953) that the rate structure for 1948 applied in 1944, 1947, 1950, and 1953, and adjusted by the Consumers Price Index.

Sources: Basic average family personal-income data from U.S. Department of Commerce, *Survey of Current Business,* March, 1955, p. 23; federal personal-income tax rate for 1953, *ibid.,* p. 24; and, other tax data as indicated in Table 38.

Table 39 suggests several observations in connection with our income structure since 1944. In the first place, what appears to be an increase of nearly one-third in family income, 1944–1953 ($4027 to $6002), is far less than that amount when the price inflation and taxation factors are considered. After federal personal-income taxes and the price-index adjustment, the increase is less than 1 percent and, when all levels of taxation are considered, an actual decrease is shown.[17] But

[16] Most authorities in the field of taxation agree that the corporation-income tax is shifted in some measure to the consumer through higher prices for products and other means. It is also roundly believed that the shifted taxes fall most heavily on the lowest-income receivers. Professor Richard A. Musgrave and associates believe that the distribution of corporation-income taxes shifted to the taxpayers describes a U-shaped curve, the lowest shifted-tax-to-income ratio being at the $7000 income level. That is, the ratio of shifted tax to taxpayers' income falls from the below $1000 to $7000 level and then rises. Cf. Richard A. Musgrave and associates, "Distribution of Tax Payments by Income Groups: A Case Study for 1948," *National Tax Journal,* March, 1951, pp. 1–5.

[17] Further corroboration of the contention that little gain in income actually available for spending has taken place in the postwar period is obtained from the Bureau of Labor

our analysis might better be confined to the years 1947–1953, which show the income gain after federal personal-income taxes, and after all taxes, to be about 10 percent. This annual rate of 1 percent is about half that rate on a per capita basis (average family personal income divided by the average number of persons per family), which compares somewhat unfavorably with the annual rate, 1929–1950, of about 2 percent annual increase.[18] One can also consider the tax inroads upon average family personal income as payments made for services rendered by government (including the provision by the government of protection for the American social system from its world foes). When this approach is used, we should consider only the effect on average family income of changes in the purchasing power of the dollar, and deal with the increased tax rate simply as a new expenditure in the family budget, an expenditure which, unfortunately, reduces the ability of the family having average personal income to increase its consumption standards beyond the 1944 level. In a succeeding section concerned with family budgets, we shall consider the family budget from this standpoint.

Income Adequacy in the United States

Only part of the income-security problem has been dealt with in our analysis of the income structure of American families. Income must be evaluated in relationship to expenditure needs at various levels of adequacy and comfort in order to determine whether or not government measures to reinforce family income security should be strengthened. In this section, we shall look into the characteristics of low-income groups and evaluate their income-expenditure problems with reference to standard budgets which set forth expenditure requirements for families at various levels of living.

Statistics data on "net spendable average earnings" (i.e., gross earnings adjusted for federal income and social-security taxes and price inflation) of factory workers. For the period 1944–1953, the "net spendable weekly earnings" of a factory worker with three dependents decreased from $58.59 to $58.20, although the period 1939–1953 shows an increase from $39.76 to $58.20. The factory worker with no dependents fared somewhat better, increasing his "net spendable earnings" from $39.70 in 1939 to $50.92 in 1944 and to $51.17 in 1953. U.S. Department of Labor, Bureau of Labor Statistics, "Spendable Earnings of Factory Workers, 1939–54," *Monthly Labor Review*, January, 1955, p. 55.

[18] The per capita personal income change from 1929–1950 was $700 to $1480; adjusted for changes in the purchasing power of the dollar, these data become $699 and $1053, respectively; and, adjusted for higher taxes, they become $677 and $957, or an increase of 41 percent for the twenty-one years. U.S. Department of Commerce, *National Income*, 1951, p. 9.

WHAT ARE THE CHARACTERISTICS OF LOW-INCOME GROUPS?

It has been the fashion in recent years for publicists to assert that the poverty problem has disappeared in the United States—a blessing of full employment—except for the rural poor, the newly arrived Puerto Ricans, and a few other "nontypical" groups.[19] Our discussion up to this point should suggest that the problem is more widespread than such assertions indicate. Substantial gains have been made in raising some groups out of the below-$2000 family level; but to deëmphasize the importance of those groups, to whom the income-security problem means inability to meet reasonable standards of consumption, implies that measures need not be undertaken (through the instrument of government or otherwise) to relieve the situation.

Income insecurity is a more serious problem in rural areas than in urban areas. This is not to say that the rural families with low income are more numerous than urban families, but their poverty is more desperate. In 1953, the median income of farm laborers and foremen was only $830, and the median income received by male heads of rural farm families was only $1790.[20] Urban-family heads received a median

[19] Other arguments with which the problem of low-income families is dismissed as unimportant include the allegation that most of the low-income units are recent graduates of schools and colleges who work only part of the year, but full time; and that, furthermore, they are only beginning their life income cycle and will improve their positions. The notion that the lower quintiles are composed of "transients" who will not remain in that income group also has a special appeal to some organizations. In 1953, nearly 10,000,000 families received incomes below $2000 ($2000 is used as a boundary for low-income groups because the Joint Committee on the Economic Report selected this level as the boundary in its study of low-income families and collected extensive data on their characteristics); and of the more than 2,000,000 graduates of schools and colleges, the number who are enumerated as family units following June graduation can scarcely account for a large proportion of the 10,000,000 total. More likely, a large number live with their families or with a working spouse, and their incomes then increase the incomes of established families or, with the income of working spouse, place them beyond the $2000 level. Those who are "unlucky" in any given income year—business proprietors, accident victims, etc.—may account for a larger proportion of the low-income group. However, their plight in many instances is of the kind that might be relieved by carefully drawn legislation, and the "unlucky" of another year might be spared the difficulties which accompany reduction in income. Some overstatement of income needs in the lower quintiles of income receivers does result from the fact that the number of persons per family in the lower quintiles is less than above the median quintile. Also, aged persons (who own their own homes) probably have more moderate needs than younger families, and the same may be true of "individuals not in families," who are more numerous within the lower quintiles (particularly the lowest quintile) than in quintiles above the median quintile. Also, if incomes were considered on a two-year basis rather than on an annual basis, income disparity between upper and lower quintiles would be less—those to whom a capricious fate metes out atypical losses and accidents, etc. being removed. However, 10,000,000 families are not to be hypothesized out of their low-income circumstances by these considerations.

[20] U.S. Bureau of the Census, Current Population Reports, Consumer Income, Series P–60, No. 16, May, 1955, p. 15.

income of $3987. In 1948, nearly two-fifths of American farms reported the value of farm products produced as less than $1000 (a proportion which approached one-half in the South), and nearly one-half of all farm families received less than $2000 annual income in that year.[21] Sex, age, and color factors influence farm income as well as urban income, and the plight of Negro farmers and aged farmers is particularly trying.

Underemployment is a serious problem in the American economy and results in extensive income insecurity. As a segment of the total group receiving annual incomes under $2000, underemployed workers are probably not numerous. But the task of adjusting family expenditures to an income level which cannot be accurately anticipated is very difficult for families which are unable to accumulate savings in liquid form. During the Bureau of the Census survey week in 1954, one-fifth of the persons at work were employed fewer than thirty-five hours per week; and for the year 1954, only in manufacturing, wholesale and retail trade, and public administration were the proportions of wage and salary workers employed full time (forty hours per week) the year round in excess of 50 percent.[22] Agricultural workers who worked fewer than twenty-five hours weekly on the average in 1954 accounted for 45 percent of all agricultural workers, and, outside agriculture, more than 25 percent of wage and salary workers in forestry, fishing and mining, construction, wholesale and retail trade, and services shared the same plight.[23] This latter group is apt to be unskilled, except in agriculture, where the problem is shared by laborers, foremen, and farm managers alike. The income consequences of underemployment, of course, are that the worker receives less than the full potential annual income for the type of service he is capable of rendering.

One of the largest elements within the low-income group consists of persons whose services simply are not sufficiently valuable to an employer or to the consuming public to command an annual income above $2000, even if they are fully employed. Agricultural workers included in the description above probably predominate in this group. Within the occupational classifications reported by the Bureau of the Census, women, Negroes, and the aged are in some measure victims of less valuable skills, although discrimination without any sound basis in actual value of services rendered plays a part, as we have previously

[21] Joint Committee on the Economic Report, *Low Income Families and Economic Stability*, Government Printing Office, Washington, 1949, pp. 36–37.

[22] U.S. Bureau of the Census, *Current Population Reports, Annual Report on the Labor Force*, Series P–50, No. 59, April, 1955, p. 7.

[23] *Ibid.*, p. 7.

noted. Still, a general increase in the educational or skill attainment of Negroes and, to some extent, women would almost certainly increase the payments made for their services. Capability to operate machines seems to be rewarded throughout the economy, although at differential rates which reflect traditional discrimination against certain groups. Educational attainment is not less closely related to earnings; the Joint Committee on the Economic Report found that 63 percent of the families with incomes below $2000 had received no schooling beyond elementary school.[24] Because we have previously discussed the income positions of the women, the aged, and nonwhites, we will not repeat the data here. Clearly, the typical family whose head is female, over 65, or nonwhite faces income-security problems more pressing than the family whose head is male, aged 44–64, and white.

Another group whose income problem might properly be dealt with in this discussion of skills which lack sufficient value is the disabled. Their income problem derives in part from the fact that their services are in many instances less valuable than persons who are not disabled. Nearly 5,000,000 persons aged 14–64 (outside institutions) must be considered in this group, more than half of whom were in the labor force prior to becoming disabled. Characteristics of the 53,000 disabled persons who were rehabilitated under the state-federal program in 1948 make clear that their income problems are serious. More than nine out of ten were earning less than $1500 per year prior to their rehabilitation, and following rehabilitation their incomes averaged only $1830.[25] Positions in industry and trade which disabled persons can fill satisfactorily are numerous. But the data available suggest that disabled workers, even following rehabilitation (most have not received rehabilitation training), receive incomes below the median for other workers.

Finally, a group of low-income families whose income insecurity is associated with the low-income status of women in the economy must be dealt with, the "broken families." Women who were family heads in 1953 received a median income of only $1497, and in the Bureau of the Census classifications of occupations, only female "professional, technical and kindred workers," "managers, officials and proprieters," and "clerical and kindred workers" received median annual incomes in excess of $2000.[26] Large numbers of working women are the sole earners in their families, and the problem of income security seems to be particularly serious in broken families. More than one-third of working

---

[24] Joint Committee on the Economic Report, op. cit., p. 15.
[25] Ibid., p. 20.
[26] U.S. Bureau of the Census, Current Population Reports, Consumer Income, Series P–60, No. 16, p. 17.

widows and nearly one-half of working divorced women are the sole earners in their families, according to a study made by the Women's Bureau.[27] The Joint Committee on the Economic Report added evidence to this report in noting that one-fourth of the more than 6,000,-000 nonfarm families having incomes below $2,000 were broken families headed by a widowed, divorced, or separated person.[28] The same report indicated that nearly three-fourths of the families receiving aid to dependent children from federal-state sources were broken by death or absence of a parent; and in terms of income, more than half of the families aided in 1948 had incomes less than $1000.[29]

The picture that we now have of low-income groups is not complete; but it is a composite of the groups whose income distress constitutes the major problem in the United States today. They are the rural poor, many of whom do not have sufficiently valuable services to command an adequate income; the underemployed, whose rates of pay may be adequate in hourly terms, but whose occupations or working situations are so unstable that they are deprived of the full value placed on their services over an annual period; those whose skills are not sufficiently valuable to employers, or whose services are not sufficiently valued by the consuming public to obtain for them an adequate income whether or not they are fully employed (including the aged and the disabled); and those whose incomes are low for reasons of tradition and prejudice—women, the aged, and nonwhites—the position of women being peculiarly unfortunate in view of their importance as sole earners in many broken families. That families whose incomes fall below the $2000 level cannot in most instances enjoy an adequate, socially satisfying standard of living would seem obvious. But we must look into the data concerning the expenditure requirements of families and individuals according to present-day standards to determine the nature of their unsatisfied needs.

Family Expenditure Requirements

The effort to determine how families spend the funds available to them has a long history. Frédéric Le Play's studies in France date from the early nineteenth century. In the United States, however, the national government followed the states in carrying out statistical studies of family expenditures. Congress instructed the Bureau of Labor to

[27] U.S. Department of Labor, *1954 Handbook on Women Workers*, Women's Bureau Bulletin No. 255, 1954, p. 34.

[28] Joint Committee on the Economic Report, *op. cit.*, p. 20.

[29] *Ibid.*, pp. 20–21.

ascertain family spending practices in 1888.[30] Of these early studies, the 1901 survey is most often cited for comparison with later dates. Until 1935, however, the budget data were derived simply by observing the spending practices of families and deriving an "average" budget of expenditure needs. The alternative approach calls for the development of a budget (based on surveys) which, followed by the average family with specific characteristics, would yield a given standard of living, and has developed only since 1935, when the Works Progress Administration used the technique. Since that time, the practice has been highly refined to produce the Bureau of Labor Statistics concept —City Workers Family Budget—expenditures for which have been published since 1946.

When the budgets for various years are compared, a number of conclusions about family needs come to light. (Because of price changes and the appearance of new items in the family budget, we are able to review only the percentages of the families' total budgets which are allocated for the necessities of life.) Table 40 presents budget data for the period since 1901, with notes giving detailed information about the standard measured in each budget study. One

TABLE 40. Family-Expenditure Patterns, 1901–1950.[a]

| Expenditures by Major Group | Proportion of Total Family Expenditures | | | | |
	1901[b]	1918–1919[c]	1935–1936[d]	1941[e]	1950[f]
Food and beverages	47	38.2	38.5	37.5	33.3
Housing, fuel, light, and refrigeration	21	23.9	31.4	26.8	25.1
Clothing	15	16.6	10.6	12.3	12.8
Other expenditures	17	21.3	19.5	23.3	28.8

a Data for 1901 and 1918–1919 are surveys of consumer expenditures; 1935–1936, 1941, and 1950 data are standards instituted to determine level of family living or to guide government programs dealing with family income.
b "Fair American standard" budget for a family of 4.76 persons in wage-earning and low-salaried clerical groups based on survey of 2567 urban families.
c Workingman's family budget for a family of 4.9 persons based on expenditures obtained from a survey of 92 cities in 42 states.
d "Minimum health and decency" standard for a family of 4.75 persons in wage-earning and low-salaried families as revealed in survey of 55 cities.
e "Maintenance level" budget for a family of four persons (maintenance level, but below the skilled-worker level) based on survey in 33 cities.
f "Modest but adequate" budget for a family of four persons, covering conventional and social as well as biological needs, based on data obtained from surveys in 34 cities.

Sources: Data for 1901 from Witt Bowden, "Changes in the Modes of Living," Monthly Labor Review, July, 1950, pp. 24, 129–132; 1918–1919 data from Bureau of Labor Statistics, Bulletin of the Bureau of Labor Statistics, 357, 1924, p. 5; 1935–1936 data from Margaret L. Stecker, Intercity Differences in Costs of Living, 1935–1936, Works Progress Administration, Research Monograph No. 12, 1937, p. xxvi; 1941 data from Bureau of Labor Statistics, Bulletin of the Bureau of Labor Statistics, No. 710, 1942, p. 36; 1950 data from U.S. Department of Labor, Handbook of Labor Statistics, Bureau of Labor Statistics Bulletin No. 1016, 1951, p. 122.

[30] Dorothy S. Brady, "Family Budgets: A Historical Survey," Monthly Labor Review, February, 1948, pp. 171–175.

obvious change that has taken place since 1901 has been the decreasing proportion of income which must be spent for the basic necessities food, clothing, and shelter. This is shown in the larger amount remaining after basic needs have been cared for (other expenditures), a percentage which increased from 17 to nearly 29 over the period 1901–1950. Since the budgets differ in terms of the fundamental standard they employ and in terms of the kinds of items included, conclusions must be drawn with caution. The observation that families in 1950 have a larger proportion of their income remaining after making expenditures for food, clothing, and shelter would seem tenable, however, even after allowing for the incomparability of budget concepts. Decreases in the proportions of income spent on food and clothing would appear to have contributed most to this larger percentage. A case could also be made that the quality of items purchased has increased.

Our analysis of the actual cost of family budgets will necessarily be limited to the post-World War II years. Not only have the budget data been more complete and varied since 1946, but the kinds of items purchased by the average family have changed to such an extent that even from 1941–1946 they are in many instances only roughly comparable. Among the new items which appeared in the 1950 City Workers Budget, but were not included in previous budgets, were frozen vegetables, fruits and juice concentrates, canned baby food, group hospital payments, home permanent-wave refills, television sets, "miracle fiber" clothing, chrome dinette sets, allowances for automobile purchase, etc.[31] There is also a prevalent opinion that the years since World War II have been sufficiently different from the prewar years to obviate comparisons of living levels except in the most general way. We shall be interested to ascertain how large a proportion of families are unable to maintain expenditures necessary to provide the "modest but adequate" level of living which is the present-day standard.

Standard Budgets and Income Adequacy

The comparison of income levels with standard budgets of expenditure requirements which are considered necessary to maintain a comfortable living level is not offered here as conclusive evidence of income inadequacy. Dorothy S. Brady, perhaps the outstanding

[31] Doris P. Rothwell, "Interim Adjustment of the Consumers Price Index," *Monthly Labor Review*, April, 1952, p. 422.

authority on living levels and their measurement, has commented as follows on the measurement of income adequacy: "The notion of a measurable boundary marking off the lower part of the income scale that can be designated substandard has crept into our thinking . . . practically unchallenged. Theorists of all persuasions utilize such a concept implicitly while proponents of various types of social policy exploit the 'poverty line' almost melodramatically. Yet, when faced directly with the problem of determining this measure for a given time and place, the theorist will deny the possibility of a unique answer and the propagandist will settle for any one of many solutions if the result suits his purposes." [32] In view of the nature of this abuse, Professor Brady's comment concerning the use to which income data and standard budgets have been put is a testament to her moderation. Studies of income requirements have been carelessly used for wholly partisan purposes. Budget data have been used to argue higher wages for workers whose income circumstances bear little relation to the limited group for which the studies have validity, and wages have been "adjusted" to the cost of living based on the costs of a Bureau of Labor Statistics standard budget, the protests and warnings of the Bureau notwithstanding. Furthermore, a kind of circularity in reasoning has been introduced by the fact that the same proportion of families is revealed by each budget study to be below the minimum level for "health and decency" (or some similar standard) from decade to decade. In other words, our concept of what constitutes an adequate or comfortable living standard matures with our income position, thus pointing at all times to a constant proportion of substandard incomes. Now, it is not objectionable that we should revise our ideas about income adequacy—indeed it would be objectionable if we were to consign some element of the population (whatever the level of national income) to an income standard determined in the past—but comparisons of budget studies for widely separated years or periods of very different economic circumstances are difficult to make in view of this tendency. One more warning must be given. Budgets of expenditure needs must be regarded as relevant and valid only within the circumstances of family size, location, and living standard.

Considering the substantive aspects of budgets now, we must realize what they represent. Uniformly, they postulate a schedule of expenditures which the prevailing income circumstances in the United

[32] Dorothy S. Brady, "Research on the Size Distribution of Income," *Studies on Research in Income and Wealth*, New York, National Bureau of Economic Research, 1951, Vol. 13, p. 30.

States would not permit even if total personal income were distributed on the basis of perfect equality to all families. Professor Brady has observed that postwar budgets "instead of describing the prevailing manner of living, have been a curious kind of forecast of the workers' pattern of living in the future." [33] Within the budgets, certain judgments must be made concerning what goods and services to include and what goods and services to exclude. Professor Reid has distinguished three classes of needs on which such judgments might be made: (1) things which families both use and need; (2) things which they use, but do not need; and (3) things which they need but do not have.[34] The determination whether to include items falling in the first class involved little difficulty. Items which the family uses and needs properly belong in the budget "basket of goods and services." The second and third classes are more controversial, the second even more than the first. A sizable bill is rung up by American families for alcoholic beverages and tobacco—items which surely do not contribute to family health and welfare. Should they, therefore, be excluded? In the framework of American culture and social philosophy, the answer must be no. On the assumption that the consumer should have free choice to experiment in allocating his income among various uses—taking the consequences of his folly and perhaps reappraising his decisions for the future—the portion of income which families in the basic survey allocate to these items must be included in the budget. Concerning the third classification, a large amount of room exists for expert opinion to assert itself. And the fact that budgets uniformly require expenditures beyond the reach of most families reflects the generosity with which this class of needs is usually treated.

Two budgets developed since World War II have been widely used, the Heller Committee budgets for executive, white-collar, and wage-earner families and the Bureau of Labor Statistics' City Workers Family Budget. The earlier Heller Committee budget permits some rough comparisons between prewar and postwar years, while the BLS budget, in addition to giving coverage for more cities, reflects the post-war sentiment concerning expenditure needs. Expenditures necessary to obtain a healthful and reasonably comfortable living in San Francisco for a family of four persons (a man, wife, boy aged 13, and girl

[33] Dorothy S. Brady, "Scales of Living and Wage Earners' Budgets," *Annals of the American Academy of Political and Social Science*, March, 1951, p. 37.

[34] Margaret G. Reid, "Distribution of Income and Consumption," *American Income and Its Use*, New York, Harper & Brothers, 1954, p. 179.

aged 8) for three income levels in 1949 as compared with 1939–1941 are given in Table 41.

TABLE 41.   Family Budgets for Three Income Levels, 1939–1941 and 1949.[a]

Budget Items	Executive		White Collar		Wage Earner	
	March 1939–1941	Sept. 1949[b]	March 1939–1941	Sept. 1949[c]	March 1939–1941	Sept. 1949[d]
Consumption	$6,582	$10,459	$2,913	$4,701	$2,272	$3,378
Food	1,012	2,116	708	1,546	632	1,321
Clothing	894	1,497	364	631	227	408
Housing [e]	2,087	2,840	866	980	195	267
Miscellaneous	2,589	4,006	975	1,545	807	1,325
Automobile	487	992	254	467	254	467
Medical and Dental care	369	537	168	291	168	291
Life insurance [f]	685	862	176	168	105	115
Other	1,048	1,684	377	619	280	451
Income and payroll taxes [g]	197	1,737	59	434	46	263
Total	$6,779	$12,196	$2,972	$5,135	$2,318	$4,051

a Average costs in San Francisco of budget to provide a healthful and reasonably comfortable standard of living for a family of four: a man, wife, and two children (boy aged 13 and girl aged 8).
b With home purchased in 1939–1941.
c With controlled rent.
d With controlled rent.
e Includes home operation and furnishings.
f Includes savings for emergencies.
g Includes federal income tax, state income tax, unemployment-insurance tax, and old-age-insurance tax.

Sources: Heller Committee for Research in Social Economics, Quantity and Cost Budgets for Three Income Levels, Prices for San Francisco, Berkeley, University of California Press, 1949 (mimeographed).

The Bureau of the Census reports that for the year 1949, 97,480 of the 202,440 families in San Francisco received less than $3999 income, or, in terms of the income necessary for a wage earner's family to maintain a healthful and reasonably comfortable living, about half of the families (including those with fewer than four persons) in the area under consideration lived below the required level. The Heller Committee differentiates between the standard and the plane of living, the former being admittedly beyond the present reach of most families. Still, the conclusion that a large number of the families in so economically favored an area as San Francisco have insufficient incomes to carry on a program of expenditures which would yield a level of living that the Committee considers "healthful and reasonably comfortable" is not without significance.

Turning now to the City Workers Family Budget, we may recognize variations in the cost of the budget among thirty-four large cities.

The budget has been prepared following the survey of expenditures in thirty-four cities to reveal the expenditures which would yield a "modest but adequate" standard of living for a family of four persons, including a husband, wife, and two children under age 15 where the husband is an urban worker. In 1951, the budget required expenditures as indicated in Table 42. In 1951, the lowest, second, and most of the third

TABLE 42.   City Workers Family Budget, 1951.[a]

Budget Items	Cost of Budget Items		
	Average for 34 Cities	Washington, D.C.	New Orleans, La.
Consumption	$3714	$3965	$3441
Food	1346	1352	1363
Housing [b]	802	1034	581
Other goods and services	1566	1579	1497
Life Insurance and other costs [c]	165	161	161
Personal taxes	287	328	210
Total	$4166	$4454	$3812

[a] City Workers Family Budget, as prepared by the Bureau of Labor Statistics to represent the estimated required expenditures to maintain the family at a level of adequate living, which includes conventional and social as well as biological needs. Costs are for October, 1951, in 34 large cities.
[b] Includes operation of home.
[c] Includes an allowance of $85 for life insurance, $22 for occupational expenses, $54 for old-age and survivors' insurance, and employee contributions for unemployment or disability insurance as required by state law in Alabama, California, and New York.

Source: U.S. Department of Labor, Handbook of Labor Statistics, 1951 Supplement, 1952, p. 43.

(median) quintile of family incomes fell below the average cost of the City Workers Family budget as priced in October, 1951. In Washington, D.C., 109,585 of the total 183,990 families with income (including those with fewer than four persons) received incomes substantially below the budget requirement in 1949 and half fell below $3800.[35] Similar figures apply to New Orleans, which had the lowest budget cost of the thirty-four cities. Clearly, the budget utilizes standards of consumption below which large proportions of the families in the areas where it is applied actually maintain themselves. Both the Heller Committee budget and the City Workers Family Budget utilize a four-person family for which necessary income data are not available. We can gain some idea of the proportion of families for which the budget is too large in terms of their income position by adjusting the budget

[35] U.S. Bureau of the Census, U.S. Census of Population: 1950, Vol. II, Characteristics of the Population, Part 9, "District of Columbia," Chapter B, 1952, p. 22.

for families of other sizes and determining the proportion of families which fall below the basic cost. In 1951, the average budget for three persons was $3499, for four persons $4166, for five persons $4749, and for six persons $5332. Data collected by the Joint Committee on the Economic Report for the year 1948 show that 41 percent of all nonfarm families received incomes below $3000; broken down to show the income positions of families having different sizes, the data show 53 percent of two-person families, 49 percent of three-person families, 44 percent of four-person families, and 32 percent of five-or-more-person families below the $3000 figure.[36] Allowing for some upward movement of incomes between 1948 and 1951, the indications are that for perhaps half of the families for which the City Workers Family Budget was designed, the expenditure requirements are in excess of their incomes. The conclusion must be made cautiously, however, and with the realization that conclusive evidence does not exist.

A budget of expenditure needs for elderly couples has also been developed by the Bureau of Labor Statistics to maintain the couple at a level of living comparable to that provided in the City Workers Family Budget. The data for aged persons (only 37 percent of whom were married couples in 1951) are especially valuable in view of the projections that show the rising trend in the proportion of persons in the over-age-65 group. We have already observed that the relationship between the median income of persons over age 65 and the income of other persons in the population has declined since 1947. Unless the expenditure needs of aged persons have declined in relationship to the expenditure needs of other persons, we should expect that their incomes would be inadequate to meet the level of living for which the Elderly Couple's Budget provides. In 1950, the budget average for thirty-four cities was $1765, with a range from $1602 in New Orleans to $1908 in Milwaukee, Wisconsin.[37] Dr. Henry W. Steinhaus estimated the cost of the budget in 1953 at $1788 when the couple owns its own home and at $2100 when it rents housing.[38] Income data, however, show that the percentage of couples aged 65 and over whose income is below the average budget requirement is very large; about three couples in five receive incomes less than $2000, and one couple

[36] Joint Committee on the Economic Report, op. cit., p. 21.
[37] The Conference Board, The Economic Almanac, 1953–54, New York, Thomas Y. Crowell Company, 1953, p. 440.
[38] Ibid., p. 440.

in three receives an income less than $1000.[39] Non-married men and women over 65 have lower incomes.

Another approach to income adequacy is to determine the extent to which families "overspend" their incomes. We can compare their expenditures with income receipts and determine whether surpluses or deficits exist. Table 43 presents expenditure and income data for wage-earner and clerical families in large cities obtained by the Bureau of Labor Statistics in 1950. The deficit, or overspending, ranged from $279 to $680 for cities with populations between 240,000 and

TABLE 43.　Income, Expenditures, and Savings of Wage Earners and Clerical Workers, 1950.[a]

Budget Items	Average for 18 Cities, 240,000 to 1,000,000 Population	Average for 11 Cities, 1,000,000 Population
Average expenditures for current consumption [b]	$3957	$4445
Insurance	175	192
Personal Taxes [c]	276	322
Total expenditures	$4408	$4959
Money income [d]	$3879	$4204
Total income	$3879	$4304
Deficit [e]	$ 529	$ 755
Deficit less insurance [f]	$ 354	$ 563

a Average money income per family of two or more persons for 52 weeks.
b Includes gifts and contributions.
c Includes federal and state income, poll, and personal-property taxes.
d Total money income from wages, salaries, self-employment, receipts from roomers and boarders, rents, interest. dividends, etc., after payment of personal taxes (federal and state income, poll, and personal property) and occupational expenses; includes other money receipts from inheritances, large gifts, and lump-sum settlements from accident and health insurance policies.
e The difference between total expenditures and total income.
f Deficit less insurance expenditures.

Source: U.S. Department of Labor, Bureau of Labor Statistics, *Family Income, Expenditures and Savings in 1950*, Bureau of Labor Statistics Bulletin No. 1097 (Revised), June, 1953, pp. 17–19, 21–23.

1,000,000, and from $562 to $928 for cities over 1,000,000. Saving is hardly the average practice for the families included in this survey. Corroboration of the fact that most families are not "savers" is given in the following data from the Economic Report of the President. The data in Table 44 are for the year 1948, a year for which we have analyzed income data at length in previous sections. As the table indicates, savings begin in the schedule of median income only when the median (third) quintile is reached, and the share of saving done

[39] Social Security Administration, "Size of Income and Personal Characteristics of the Aged," *Social Security Bulletin*, October, 1954, p. 8.

TABLE 44. Savings in the United States According to Family Income Level, 1948.[a]

Families Ranked by Size of Income	Percent of Total Money Income Before Taxes	Median Income of Each Class	Percent of Total Net Saving by Families [b]
Lowest fifth	4	$ 860	—24
Second fifth	11	2,000	— 3
Third fifth	16	2,840	7
Fourth fifth	22	3,750	21
Highest fifth	47	6,000	99
All groups	100	$2,840	100

a Average family personal income.
b The figure 99 percent is obtained by adding algebraically (— 24) + (— 3) + 7 + 21 + 1; 100 — 1 = 99.

Source: Economic Report of the President to the Congress, January, 1950, pp. 145–146.

by the highest quintile accounts for all but 1 percent of the total family net saving. This information and the information revealed in the Bureau of Labor Statistics survey will be useful when we consider the capacity of families to provide for their expenditure needs after the head of the family retires, or to bear the cost of adequate private retirement programs.

CONCLUDING REMARKS ON STANDARD BUDGETS AND INCOME ADEQUACY

Several conclusions are suggested by the data analyzed in the preceding section. All of the evidence examined points to a condition of inadequate power to consume at the level which standard budgets describe as "modest but adequate" or "healthful and reasonably comfortable" on the part of perhaps one-half of American families. The figure may be higher when it is considered that our data only have dealt with the nonfarm population in large cities. Furthermore, the budget which is recognized as standard today is almost certain to change in the near future, and a more pretentious budget will replace it. This is a natural consequence of the growth which takes place in our ideas about living standards. If budgets are anything other than an indication of the distance that needs be traveled to a condition of adequate consumption, then a question is posed for the economy: Will we be able to increase incomes in such proportions as to raise, say, four families out of five up to adequate levels of consumption? The answer turns on such varied factors as family size (which is increasing) and the stability of economic activity. In the next section, we shall analyze the methods which have been employed and might be employed to this end.

Measures to Promote Family Income Security

Income security can best be viewed as a community matter, a problem for employers, governments, business and professional groups, and families alike. Reductions in family income affect not only the consumption standards of individual families, but the stream of income payments to other sectors of the community as well. Furthermore, the potential danger that falling family incomes will have a compounding effect—ultimately causing tradesmen to reduce inventory stocks and factories to reduce their schedules of production, thus further reducing employment and income—means that complacency and inaction cannot be tolerated.

No approach to the income-security problem confined either to "private" or "public" programs can meet the needs of the situation. The factors which underlie the problem are too complex. Removing discrimination in wage payments based on age, sex, and color is not best accomplished through legslation, it seems from experience thus far. The guarantee of wages during periods of declining economic activity, or the indemnification of employees against the loss of income during periods of prolonged (nonjob-connected) disability resulting from illness or accident, may, on the other hand, be impossible without government assistance. Clearly, promoting income security must be viewed as a joint responsibility.

We should recall those factors relating to income insecurity which have figured in our discussion up to this point. They are the level of economic activity in the whole economy and within separate industries which causes unemployment and underemployment; traditionally "low-wage" industries; age, sex, and color discrimination; geographic location; value of the worker's services; and the levels of prices and taxes. It will be in connection with these factors that we shall discuss private and public action to reduce income insecurity.

Private Action

Analyses of employer attitudes toward programs to reduce income insecurity not infrequently suggest callous indifference to the whole problem. As a matter of fact, interest in the maintenance of employee income, both as a means of stimulating positive attitudes toward the firm and keeping purchasing power high, has (including the guarantee of annual wages) dated from the later years of the nineteenth century. The major efforts which have been made by employers and labor organizations to promote income stability can be sum-

marized under the headings of extraordinary-compensation plans, employment-stabilization plans, and fringe benefits.

Extraordinary-compensation plans include all forms of compensation that supplement regular hourly earnings or piece rates. Increased rates of pay for Sunday and holiday work, severance pay, reporting pay and call-in pay, profit sharing, annual-wage guarantees, and other similar kinds of compensation have been utilized to buttress the regular wage conditions of employees. Increased rates of compensation for work performed on holidays and Sundays are common features of labor-management agreements, double and even triple rates frequently applying. The latter, of course, is a reduction in the employment of labor on holidays except under urgent situations. Severance or dismissal pay is compensation immediately available to the employee whose employment has been terminated through no fault of his own. Length of service with the company and average level of wages are usually taken into consideration in computing the amount of payment, and an employee with long service may collect up to several thousand dollars when losing his job under such an agreement. The majority of plans, however, provide the equivalent of about two months' earnings. Although it is becoming a more common feature of labor-management agreements, only 8 percent of the 2137 agreements analyzed by the Bureau of Labor Statistics in 1949 provided for severance pay.[40] Reporting pay is paid when an employee scheduled to work reports for work and, lacking prior notice, finds his services are not required. The common provision in reporting-pay agreements is a "half-shift" compensation, although "full-shift" payments are often made. In 1953, 80 percent of labor-management agreements made provision for some form of reporting pay.[41] Call-back pay is paid when workers are called back to work without being put to work.

Profit sharing has a long history and was at one time regarded as a near cure-all for industrial-relations problems. The practice is very limited and has bred much discouragement. In 1946, the National Industrial Conference Board reported that 60 percent of the 161 plans it had analyzed in 1937 had been discontinued.[42] The idea of returning to the employee force some portion of the profits which it has helped

[40] Laura Chase and James C. Nix, "Dismissal Pay Provisions in Union Agreements, 1949," *Monthly Labor Review*, April, 1950, p. 386.

[41] Dena G. Weiss and Cordy Hammond, "Reporting and Call-Back Pay in Collective Bargaining Agreements," *Monthly Labor Review*, December, 1954, p. 1335.

[42] Dale Yoder, *Personnel Management and Industrial Relations*, New York, Prentice-Hall, 1948, p. 411.

make possible appeals to fairness and logic. However, the profits fund out of which payments are made is usually carefully defined, and the payments are not always made in cash or immediately convertible claims. Furthermore, the danger of such a plan substituting for regular wage increases, which are more permanent, is considered a drawback by organized labor. Perhaps 1 to 2 percent of all employees are employed under some form of profit-sharing arrangement.

Guaranteed wages have gained importance in labor-management relations since the advent of the Great Depression, and many of the better-known plans were introduced at that time or shortly afterward. In the postwar period, they have been an issue of prime importance in bargaining, one of the two or three goals upon which labor leaders were agreed as the Second World War came to a close. The well-known Hormel, Procter and Gamble, and Nunn-Bush plans have operated smoothly for two decades or more. Implied in the guarantee of wages is the establishment of a floor under wages which will give the worker income security regardless of economic conditions or the production schedule of his individual employer. Few plans are of such a character, however, and the most recently negotiated Ford and General Motors plans, which are likely to become the model for mass-production industries, make only limited guarantees. These plans call for some interrelationship between guaranteed wage payments and state unemployment insurance. Because they are regarded with such interest, it will be worth considering their general features. In 1946, the Bureau of Labor Statistics studied the characteristics of 196 guaranteed wage plans which it knew to be operating. They were largely found in small plants outside nonmanufacturing industries in the Middle Atlantic and Great Lakes regions.[43] Some 61,000 workers were covered under the plans. Basic questions about the operation of guaranteed-wage plans are the extent of worker eligibility and the duration and amount of payments. In 101 of the 196 plans, all or nearly all of the workers in the firm were covered, automatic coverage after thirty days' employment being a feature of 63 plans.[44] Limitations on coverage are very broad in many plans, however. The duration of the wage guarantee was a full year of 52 weeks at full-time pay in 140 of the 196 plans, and only 25 of the plans provided for less than 45 weeks of work.[45] Sixty-two of the 196 plans were studied in some detail

[43] Bureau of Labor Statistics, Guaranteed Wage Plans in the United States, Bulletin No. 925, 1947.
[44] Ibid., p. 10.
[45] Ibid., p. 13.

by the Bureau of Labor Statistics. The opinions of employers concerning the workability of the plans reveals optimism. In the words of the report: "Few employers reported disadvantages resulting from the plans. Costs were not regarded as disadvantages, but as necessary features of the guarantee, offset by compensating benefits. . . . In one-fourth of all the cases, the plans had been introduced at union behest, employers taking very little interest in them. In two-thirds of these cases, however, management reported that their experiences under the plans had been favorable, and that the plans had had a good effect on morale, turn-over, or efficiency." [46]

Advantages of the guaranteed-wage plans to the employee are obvious. Family expenditures from week to week can be undertaken in the confidence that extraordinary saving for periods of unemployment is unnecessary. Income will remain relatively constant even as essential expenditure needs remain constant. The psychological effects on the employee appear to contradict the expectations of those who would mourn any reduction in the "stimulus of fear" from the work situation. Employers operating under guarantee plans report continuing or increasing employee diligence.

Some anxiety has been aroused concerning the extremely high costs that would be incurred by a wage-guarantee program. The Bureau of Labor Statistics study indicated that employers operating under guaranteed-annual-wage plans found costs offset by savings (in more than half the cases) or so small that they were "reasonably certain" to be offset.[47] It should not be concluded from the above discussion that a single plan of wage guarantees can be applied in all industries, nor that all firms could operate such a program by simply agreeing to its introduction. All successful wage-guarantee plans were introduced after long study, and each is tailored to the circumstances of production and marketing peculiar to each firm.

It is probable that the modified plans negotiated in the automobile industry will become widely sought in other industries as new contracts are negotiated. The Ford and General Motors agreements,

---

[46] *Ibid.*, p. 49.

[47] *Ibid.*, pp. 42–43. Some of the sources of savings were given as reduction of unemployment taxes under merit-rating plans for employers with guaranteed wage plans, elimination of overtime payments required under the Fair Labor Standards Act for work in excess of forty hours, and lower wage rates than competitors. Indirect savings included reduction of costs of training new workers, reduction in turnover (dismissal and accession) costs, increased productivity, savings in overhead costs owing to constant use of equipment, recruitment of more efficient employees, and competitive advantage in serving customers out of accumulated stocks of goods.

even though they provide for a modified guarantee of wages, nonetheless increase tenfold the number of workers under some form of wage guarantee. An accurate designation of the guarantee negotiated in the automobile industry would be "supplemental unemployment benefits." Under the Ford agreement, eligible unemployed workers would receive up to $25 weekly benefits for a maximum of twenty-six weeks, subject to the principle that the total weekly payment not exceed 65 percent of the employee's weekly wages (after taxes) for the first four weeks, nor 60 percent of average community wages thereafter for the remaining twenty-two weeks. It has been estimated that this would raise the combined wage-guarantee and unemployment-insurance benefits for a man with a wife and one child from $42 to $52.21 (after the four-week special benefit of $56.56) in Detroit, Michigan, and from $36 to $47.95 in Buffalo, New York.[48] We shall discuss the legality of such combined payments in Chapter 13.

The very uncertain employment conditions in the automotive industry have not been eliminated by the newly adopted compensation plan, and the spectre of income insecurity has not disappeared. An important principle has been established, however: the liability for unemployment that grows out of variations in an employer's operations is mutual, falling on the employer as well as the employee. Until the General Motors and Ford pacts were signed, however, only about 7 percent of the labor-management contracts in force contained provisions for a wage guarantee.

Private employment-stabilization plans frequently accompany guaranteed-wage plans, but are more numerous. Where such plans exist, they are variations of two approaches: those related to production and marketing policies, and those relating to personnel policies. In the case of production and marketing policies, producing for "stock," timing the release of annual changes in models or fashions, routing work so as to prevent underutilization of specific kinds of employees, and similar kinds of policies can help to relieve the tendency to unemployment. Personnel policies range from transferring employees from their regular jobs to positions where shortages exist (which necessitates training for versatility if it is to be successful) to locating new jobs for dismissed workers. The degree in which production and personnel policies can cope with the problems of unemployment varies from industry to industry; but in such differing industries as meat packing and soap manufacture, a large degree of success has been experienced.

[48] *The New York Times*, June 7, 1955, p. 22.

Fringe benefits include employer payments for a wide range of job-related benefits, the most common being vacations with pay, paid holidays, insurance benefits, pensions, sick leave, and special stock distribution or sale at discount prices. During World War II, the control of inflation required curbs on wages as well as other prices, and the War Labor Board coined the concept of fringe benefits to refer to compensation which did not increase money wage payments, yet increased total remuneration. Perhaps the average money equivalent of such benefits is about 10 percent of total earnings, although much higher benefits are received in specific industries.[49] The value of fringe benefits is substantial, both in terms of money equivalents and in terms of the fact that insurance coverage which the employee might consider too expensive at his income level is provided for him and his family. Only 5 percent of plant and office workers are without some form of health insurance or pension benefits. Income is also freed for immediate-consumption expenditures. Vacation periods of two weeks per year have become standard for manufacturing employees, and those with fifteen years' service commonly receive three weeks or longer. Considering the tendencies toward automation in industry, vacations and holidays may well be the most valuable of the fringe benefits because they permit an employee to recharge his emotional apparatus.

Certain other efforts deserve brief mention, notably the nondiscrimination policies which have been initiated by employers, often in conjunction with labor-management agreements. Equal pay for equal work is more than a slogan; it can make a considerable difference in employee compensation where women, Negroes, and the aged are concerned. International Harvester's policies in this respect have had notable success in three southern cities.[50] Management policies aimed at increasing the skill attainment of employees through in-service training programs, extending in some cases to the payment of tuition expenses at adult-education institutions, are also noteworthy efforts.

Private Action: Summary. It would be unfortunate to underestimate the importance of private action in its relation to family income security. But the extent of guaranteed-wage plans and similar accomplishments indicates that employers' capabilities differ widely, even granting their willingness to promote income stabilization of employees. Public programs of social insurance and services must bear

---

[49] Woytinski and associates, *op. cit.*, p. 425.
[50] *The New York Times*, September 14, 1953, p. 22.

the brunt of income-security activity, particularly in the less wealthy regions of the country and in highly unstable industries.

PUBLIC ACTION

Concern with income security led many states and finally the national government to enact legislation providing for wage minima. This and related movements were traced in Chapter 9 from their inception in 1912 to the beginning of World War II. In recent years, the scope of public action has widened, and the potency of public policy has been generally recognized by social scientists. In this section, we shall briefly discuss new developments in full-employment legislation, minimum-wage legislation, taxation policy, and fair-employment-practices legislation. The American social-insurance and public-assistance programs, which are a basic framework of public action, will be discussed in Chapters 14–16. At the risk of repetition, it is important to observe again that higher or more regular income cannot, in the strictest sense, be "legislated"; machinery utilization, consumption and investment expenditure levels, industrial peace, and related factors determine the level of national income, which is a controlling factor. Public action can affect the distribution of income and may stimulate the factors which determine national income. Still, the influence is indirect. That scope of public action which might materially affect the level of the national income is impossible within the existing American cultural milieu. In Chapter 18, we shall discuss the proposals for "planning" economic activity, the most modest of which are greeted with hostility in the United States.

At the end of World War II, there was great uncertainty about the ability of the American economy to make the transition from war-goods production to consumer-goods production. Unless unusual precautions were taken, it was thought, unemployment would be severe, and the specter of the depression years loomed ominously. Widespread interest was developed in a national law which would fix responsibility with the national government for maintaining sufficient employment for everyone willing and able to work. In 1946, a bill addressed to the problem was passed by both Houses of Congress and signed by the President. It was called the Employment Act of 1946. The law scarcely satisfied the extremists, who would have required the government to provide jobs for those who could not find them in the private sector, but it did fix the government's responsibility in general terms.

Because the act is brief and its purpose so important, it has been appended to this chapter (Appendix B). Section 2 reads:

The Congress hereby declares that it is the continuing policy of the Federal Government to use all practical means consistent with its needs and obligations and other essential considerations of national policy with the assistance and cooperation of industry, agriculture, labor, and State and local governments, to coordinate and utilize all its plans, functions, and resources for the purpose of creating and maintaining, in a manner calculated to foster and promote free competitive enterprise and the general welfare, conditions under which there will be afforded useful employment, for those able, willing, and seeking to work, and to promote maximum employment, production, and purchasing power.

The law was hedged about with so many restrictions that it was of necessity ineffective.[51] To many persons, the phrase "all practicable means consistent with its needs and obligations" posed the danger that any program to carry out the purposes of the act would be subservient to a conservative debt-management policy such as making "balancing the budget" the primary object of government. Moreover, the phrase "in a manner calculated to foster and promote free competitive enterprise" could be interpreted to prohibit economic planning on any effective scale. The requirement in Section 3 that the President report to the Congress the "gap" which he and his advisers estimate would exist between a full-employment situation and the prospects in view was, in many ways, unrealistic. Experience in the United States indicates that the administration in power is held responsible for the nation's economic posture at any given time, and the reports issued thus far have tended to be overoptimistic. The Council of Economic Advisers created under the act has been burdened with administrative and personality problems, and never has taken a firm stand for specific actions to implement full employment, preferring instead the comparatively safer solicitation of coöperation from industry, agriculture, and labor. Neither in recession nor in inflation has the Council seen fit to press a program of action vigorously. Still, the information marshaled in the semiannual *Economic Report of the President* and the studies of the Joint Committee on the Economic Report have been very useful and have filled a void.

From one point of view, the effectiveness of the act remains unproved. Since its enactment, unusually favorable economic conditions

[51] For an excellent description of the legislative history of the law, see Stephen K. Bailey, *Congress Makes a Law*, New York, Columbia University Press, 1950.

have been enjoyed. But the control of inflation was accomplished slowly, and in the opinion of many persons the recessions of 1949 and 1953–1954 were prevented from being more serious by the sheer force of luck. At any rate, the weapons of fiscal and monetary policy have yet to be coördinated effectively in the service of full employment. How inadequate the full-employment bill was can be seen by comparing it with the British plan as proposed by Sir William Beveridge. In the latter plan, three essential conditions for full employment were recognized: (1) adequate total outlay, (2) controlled location of industry, and (3) organized mobility of labor. To the end of ensuring that these conditions would be met, new government machinery was urged with broad powers to regulate investment and consumption.

Minimum-wage legislation has been discussed earlier as one aspect of the growth which took place in American ideas about equity in labor-management relations. As a method of income protection for the family, minimum-wage legislation has serious disadvantages as compared with an effective full-employment policy. In a period of declining economic activity, an employer would reduce his costs by using less labor, either by laying off some members of the work force or reducing the hours of all. Family income would decline with economic activity, regardless of the minimum-wage level. Setting wage minima at the national level has motivated some states to pass lax laws for intrastate employees and benefit their particular region at the expense of states with higher minimum levels. Also, the effect of a minimum wage may be simply to drive workers out of low-wage interstate industries and into comparable jobs in intrastate industries. In normal times, the hope is that the setting of wage minima will operate to induce more efficient management, and shift competition to factors other than labor. As of 1949, the minimum-wage level was set at 75 cents an hour. The minimum to be in effect after March 1, 1956, is $1.[52] The 1949 amendments also strengthened a provision in the Fair Labor Standards Act which frees employers who guarantee from 1840 to 2080 hours of employment per year, for not less than forty-six work weeks of thirty hours per week, from the overtime-pay provisions of the act. The amendment act covers a majority of the labor force, but some exclusions are unfortunate. We shall discuss the exclusions and other features of the program in Chapter 12.

Taxation policy and inflation control are two areas of public policy

---

[52] By action of the 1st session, 85th Congress, the minimum was set at $1 after consideration of proposals ranging from 90 cents to $1.

TABLE 45. Distribution of Tax Payments by Income Groups, 1948.[a]

(millions of dollars)

Item	Spending-Unit Income Brackets (Thousands of Dollars)							
	Under 1	1–2	2–3	3–4	4–5	5–7.5	7.5 and over	Total
1. Percent of spending-unit income taken by tax								
A. Federal government	16.5	16.2	18.6	19.0	19.3	21.1	30.1	22.3
B. State and local	11.6	8.1	7.3	7.1	6.7	6.4	6.3	6.9
C. All levels	28.1	24.3	25.9	26.1	26.0	27.6	36.3	29.2
2. Percent of total tax receipts from each spending-unit income bracket								
A. Federal government	1.4	5.1	12.3	15.3	11.6	15.4	38.8	100.0
B. State and local	3.2	8.3	15.7	18.5	12.9	15.2	26.1	100.0
C. All levels	1.8	5.9	13.1	16.0	11.9	15.4	35.8	100.0
3. Percent of spending units in each income bracket	12.2	17.7	22.9	20.1	11.6	10.2	5.3	100.0

a Includes income imputed under standard corporation assumptions. Detail may not add to totals because of rounding.

Source: Richard A. Musgrave and Associates, "Distribution of Tax Payments by Income Group—1948: A Case Study," National Tax Journal, March, 1951, p. 26. Used with permission of author and National Tax Journal.

where substantial effects on income security can be realized. Furthermore, the instruments of control in each instance are relatively flexible
and (in the absence of millstone-like principles of action which frustrate flexibility) can be adjusted for changes in economic goals. We
have seen in previous sections of this chapter that taxes cut deeply
into the income positions of wage earners and have substantially modified the gains made in incomes since 1944. Unquestionably, there is
wisdom in the view that everyone should share in the payment of
direct taxes (as contrasted with "hidden" taxes), if only to point up
the costs of government and keep interest in government activities
keen. But having accepted the principle, we are not prevented from
working within its requisites to make tax policy contribute to income
security. Table 45 shows the effective rates of taxation of various
spending-unit income levels for each level of government.

For those who labor under the delusion that taxes are levied according to ability to pay (progressively) in the United States, the table will
hold some surprises. The total tax take from spending units when all
levels of government are taken into consideration (item 1C) is seen
to be larger in proportionate terms at the lower levels of income than
at the higher levels (until the $7500-and-over bracket is reached).
Especially when the percent of total spending units is considered, this
situation is inequitable. Almost 95 percent of American spending
units fall below the "7½ and over" bracket at which taxation becomes
"progressive." When we compare items 1A) and 1B), it becomes clear
that the inequity does not result from taxation policies at the national
level, but from the state and local levels. The latter jurisdictions levy
taxes which are generally considered regressive because they fall more
heavily on low-income spending units than on high-income spending
units. Correction of the basic inequities shown in the table will be
very difficult because the revenue sources available to state and local
governments are limited by the fact that the national government has
preëmpted income taxes, making it impossible for states to make
effective use of this tax form to the exclusion of other regressive taxes.
The problem at present is to hold the line against other regressive
state and local taxes, such as sales taxes.

Suggestions have been made for the removal of some inequities,
however, chiefly at the national level. The collection of income taxes
on dividends and interest at the source, as in the case of wages and
salaries, would yield an amount approximating $300 million according
to one observer, and rigorous enforcement of allowances for percentage

depletion and taxation of capital gains might yield an additional $500 million to $1 billion.[53] This amount of revenue, amounting to $1 billion or more, certainly would permit relaxation of the rates applied to the fourth of the spending units with incomes below $2000 without reducing total revenue. Low-income groups generally are taxed regressively by excise taxes and corporation taxes which have been shifted to consumers. And the federal income tax discriminates against wage earners in two separate ways, as Professor Heller observes: "1) it collects from wages and salaries a higher proportion of the liabilities legally due than it does from any other source of income, and (2) it allows, by law, more generous deductions and concessions to other forms of income than to wage and salary incomes." [54] The relief obtained by low-income receivers through equivalent treatment on these counts would not be great, but sufficient revenue might be obtained by the adoption of several reforms to permit the removal of some excise taxes and provide moderate relief to the lowest brackets.

At the opposite extreme of the income scale, beneficial results in the way of investment incentives might be obtained by scaling down the steeply progressive rates of taxation at the levels above $50,000. Leveling off the rates at, say, 50 percent would affect far less than 1 percent of those who file tax returns.

Some part of our discussion of taxation should point also to the increases in benefits which have occurred in recent years. In part, the family tax bill must be offset by the value of services received. The social-service benefits and benefits not related to national security are an extremely small portion of total government expenditures, however, and almost no information exists which would permit us to determine how spending units at any given income level are affected by them. Housing and education services provided through public authority are important areas of benefit to low-income groups, however, and we shall discuss the general features of legislation in this respect in Chapter 17.

Inflation control has been an important national issue since 1941. The basic condition which requires control consists simply in the expansion of people's ability to buy more rapidly than the production of goods can be expanded. Particularly during war periods, when part of the goods and services produced are not made available to the

[53] Walter H. Heller, "Taxation and Lower Income Groups," *Monthly Labor Review*, December, 1953, pp. 1285–1286.

[54] *Ibid.*, p. 1286.

private sector, inflation control becomes of primary importance. The question, actually, does not involve the adequacy of our knowledge or tools to conquer inflation, but rather our will and political ability to do so. When the ability of people to buy expands more rapidly than goods and services can be made available, the obvious remedy is to remove that portion of purchasing power which is overabundant.[55] But the target of anti-inflation measures must, in the main, be low- and middle-income groups, which do the preponderance of consuming. This makes inflation control inequitable; but if inflation were permitted to continue, it would produce even greater inequities by raising the prices of goods and services (including essentials, of course) and reducing living standards.

Since 1952, inflation control has been a less important issue because the Consumers Price Index has appeared to level off. Had not the prices of food items, particularly agricultural products, declined during that period, however, the index would almost certainly have increased moderately. Increases in the costs of housing (including rent, gas and electricity, furnishing, and household operation), transportation, medical care, and personal care have been registered in the index since 1952, some increases being substantial. The problem of controlling inflation while at the same time avoiding large-scale unemployment— conditions which have coexisted in our economy in the postwar years —may require far more extensive planning and control over the economy than we have seen fit to develop thus far. In Appendix A to this chapter and in Chapter 18, we will pursue the question at greater length.

Discriminatory wage policies based on sex and race have been the object of government policy, and the movement for legislation to regulate such practices has run a rocky course. Since the establishment of the Fair Employment Practices Committee by President Roosevelt in 1941, interest for some form of national legislation has run high. Bills have floundered after being introduced in Congress, however, and southern senators and representatives have not been averse to withholding their support for legislation unrelated to "fair-employment practices" in retaliation for progressive action in the field of antidiscrimination. In both the executive and the legislative branches of the national government, there has been an apparent unwillingness

---

[55] There are other options, of course, including increases in productivity by such amounts as will overcome the lag in the supply of goods and services, increased saving, and direct controls such as rationing.

to fight for the legislation.[56] The national government's experience has included the insertion of FEPC clauses in government contracts, provisions of which are administered by a committee of fifteen members. Bills to provide equal pay regardless of sex have been introduced repeatedly in the Congress, but have failed to gain the necessary support.

At the state level, legislation covering fair-employment practices is found in thirteen states. In nine of the states, provision is made for enforcement of the laws.[57] In the remainder, the laws are "educational." In operation, the laws have been something less than a huge success. Suits must be initiated to gain relief under most of the laws, and in spite of commissions and legal-aid groups the burden on the worker who has been treated illegally is great both financially and psychologically. An employer who has been forced to hire an employee can still make working conditions unpleasant for him if he wishes, and the atmosphere resulting from forcing an employer to hire a worker against his will could not fail to be unpleasant for the employee. Equal-pay legislation designed to protect women gained momentum during the war, and at present fourteen jurisdictions have laws forbidding discrimination in rates of pay based on sex. These states employ more than half of the women in the United States, and, except for two states (Illinois and Michigan), the laws apply generally to all private employment.

The areas of public action which may improve family income security are numerous, as we have seen. But the measures as they stand are far from adequate actually to safeguard family income. It is argued that with full or near-full employment, more comprehensive measures are unnecessary. But the contingencies which threaten income security are only partly dispelled by full employment, and the threats to income security from prolonged illness, nonwork-connected injuries, and other vicissitudes are unrelated to the level of economic activity. The social-security program, even in its expanded form, does not provide protection against these threats.

[56] See Louis Rouchames, Race, Jobs and Politics, New York, Columbia University Press, 1953, for the history of national efforts to enact fair-employment-practices legislation.

[57] Alaska, Connecticut, Massachusetts, New Jersey, New Mexico, New York, Oregon, Rhode Island, and Washington. In New Mexico, the law has been passed, but no budget for operation provided up to January, 1954. An additional state, Colorado, had a law which applied only to public employment. Beatrice McConnell, "State Labor Legislation in 1953," Monthly Labor Review, November, 1953, p. 1188.

The Family's Quest for Income Security: Concluding Remarks

We have discussed the role of income security in this chapter from the standpoint of maintaining the family against dependency, and have focused our attention largely upon material needs. Important as the provision for basic needs is, it should not be thought that guaranteeing the family against inability to provide essentials is a sufficient goal in modern industrial life. Independency is to be valued for its own sake in view of the conditions which we recognize as necessary in the development of personality. But the standard against which we measure income adequacy long ago passed the "minimum essentials" level and is maturing toward an ever larger margin for nonessentials. Because an uncomfortably large proportion of American families are presently in the position of failing to meet standard budget levels of expenditure, we must be concerned over the prospects for the future.

Both private and public programs of action have been developed to the end of sustaining family income security. And the protection afforded the family has increased beyond the dreams of the average wage earner a generation ago. But the permissible areas of action have not been developed to the fullest, and studies to determine income adequacy in future years have been neglected.[58] The question arises now, and will continue to arise, as to whether the course of economic activity, with its profound consequences for social life, can be permitted to set its own pace and goals without extensive participation by public authority.

Appendix A: National Income and Its Determination

This brief appendix is included to explain the basis whereby the performance of the national economy is measured. We shall try to understand what the national income is and what the factors are upon which its size depends. At the outset, we should understand that the performance of the economy is judged in economic terms on the basis of the total value of goods and services produced in a given year (less certain items which would result in overstating the total if left in). This total is the national income. To assess the economy's perform-

---

[58] The single comprehensive program of study has been carried on by The Twentieth Century Fund, and the most recent survey (J. Frederic Dewhurst and Associates, *America's Needs and Resources*, New York, The Twentieth Century Fund, 1955), although generally optimistic about the future, notes that inadequacies in our ability to consume will fall short of our needs in 1960 with respect to seven out of ten consumption areas, seriously falling short of our needs in the areas of medical care and religion (p. 107).

ance accurately, however, we must divide the national-income total by the national-population total to obtain a per capita national-income figure. Per capita national income tells us how large is the output of goods and services per person and, when compared with other years, reveals whether or not an improvement has taken place. Of course, if the value of the national income has changed owing simply to changes in prices, an adjustment must be made. Measured in comparable prices, however, per capita national income reveals whether the economy is satisfying the goal set for it: an ever larger production of goods and services. In Table 46, national income per capita in comparable prices is shown for the years 1939–1953.

TABLE 46. National Income per Capita in Constant Dollars.[a]

Year	National Income (Billions of Dollars)	Continental Population of the United States (Millions)	National Income Per Capita (Dollars)
1939	157.5	131,628	1,202
1940	171.6	132,122	1,299
1941	198.2	133,402	1,486
1942	223.6	134,860	1,658
1943	248.9	136,739	1,820
1944	268.2	138,397	1,938
1945	263.1	139,928	1,880
1946	233.8	141,389	1,654
1947	232.2	144,126	1,666
1948	243.9	146,631	1,663
1949	246.5	149,188	1,619
1950	264.7	151,677	1,745
1951	282.9	154,360	1,802
1952	294.2	156,981	1,874
1953	306.6	159,696	1,920

a This is not national income in the technical sense, but rather gross national product, measured in dollars of constant (1947) purchasing power.

Sources: U.S. Department of Commerce, National Income, 1954, p. 217; and U.S. Bureau of the Census, Statistical Abstract of the States, 1954, p. 13.

The table shows that, measured in per capita terms, we have not enjoyed anything like a continuous upward increase in economic growth. Over the fifteen-year period, an increase of 60 percent was registered, only one-third of which has been achieved in the postwar years.

DETERMINANTS OF NATIONAL-INCOME GROWTH

Factors which contribute to national-income growth are numerous, and they are embraced within the term *productivity*. By productivity

we mean the *rate* of production, or the value of output produced in a
given period of time, say, an hour. The key to productivity lies in using
our resources (land, labor, capital, and management) in their best use;
that is, so they will, in combination, yield the largest volume of goods
and services. Thus, workmen (labor) who can operate machinery and
thereby contribute to the total value of goods and services must not
be used in hand-loading trucks where their labor makes a relatively
smaller contribution to the total value of goods and services. Similarly,
land which will yield a more valuable crop of corn than cotton should
not be used for cotton production. And so on. Flexibility in the use
of resources, technological advance, utilization of machinery, labor-
management peace, and the levels of health and security all contribute
to national-income growth in the measure to which they promote
productivity. Still, using resources in their best use is not the whole
answer to rising national income; the extent to which resources can be
continuously employed in their best use is decisive. As a matter of
fact, failure to keep resources fully employed is the major threat to
income growth. It is this threat toward which the Employment Act
of 1946 was addressed. We will understand the nature of the threat,
and the kinds of public policy which can be utilized to keep resources
fully employed, if we look at the national-income framework more
closely.

National income is the total value of all the goods and services produced in the economy (less some deductions) in a given year, as we
have noted. It is also the total value of all *payments* made to the basic
resources (land, labor, capital, and management) for their part in producing these goods and services (actually payments to those who control the resources). That is, the sum of rent, wages and salaries, interest,
and profits on an annual basis equals the national income. This stream
of payments to landlords, wage and salary earners, lenders, and "managers" is of enormous importance in the operation of the economic
system. Ultimately, it becomes the income of households, business
firms (domestic and foreign), and governments, and what these groups
of units decide to do with the payments they receive determines the
size of the national income in the succeeding period. A diagram will
help us see what happens.

Figure 4 is a simplified representation of the economic system, showing how payments are passed along from sector to sector. At A we
begin the circuit of payments with *households*, of which there are
about 48,000,000; households receive income in the form of wages and
salaries, rents, interest, and profits, and spend a large portion, though

not all, of the total. Some portion of income received will be saved and flow into *savings* at E, rather than around the payments stream. Households are shown as beginning the spending process with purchases from the *business* sector (B), the *foreign* sector (C), and the *government* sector (D). Purchases from the business sector are for

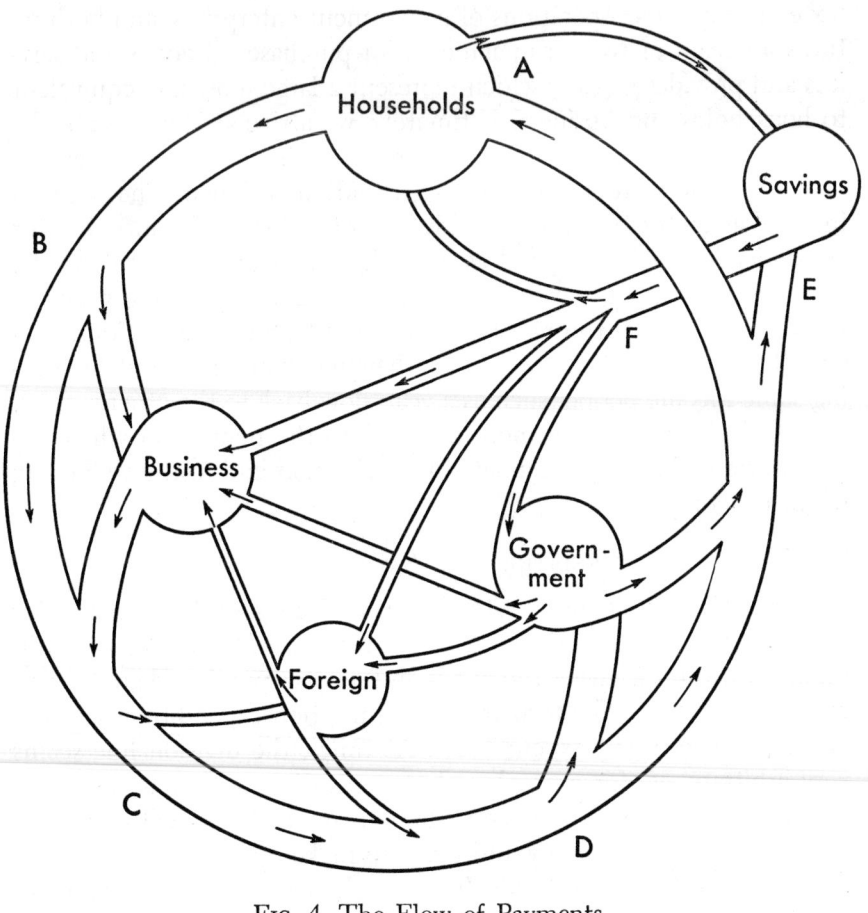

FIG. 4. The Flow of Payments.

obvious goods and services—food, clothing, shelter, haircuts, permanent waves, etc.—and the purchases from the foreign sector are for foreign goods and services (insurance and ocean-transportation services, for example). In the case of government, we may view the households as making compulsory purchases of services, such as military and police protection, social welfare, highway upkeep, etc. Of course, the purchases made by households result in a flow of funds to the remain-

ing sectors, which are also buying goods and services for their own accounts. The business sector employs workers (paying them wages and salaries) and purchases materials from other firms, as well as making compulsory purchases of government services. So also with the foreign sector, although the transactions here are more complicated. Finally, the government sector receives a flow of funds as a result of tax collections and operations of government enterprises, and both returns a stream of funds as payments for purchases of goods and services and provides services which represent a large monetary equivalent to households and business. Ultimately, we arrive at E in tracing the stream of payments, an "eddy" in the spending stream representing savings by the sectors that we have already mentioned. The position in the diagram of the savings "eddy" is not realistic, of course, but for convenience can be pictured as a residue of income unspent by the several sectors. At F we see the accumulated savings being returned to the other sectors through borrowing and lending transactions. It is a matter of the greatest importance that the savings accumulated during some income period, such as a year, flow back to the other sectors. It is time for us to look more deeply into the manner in which expenditures and savings are related to each other and to the well-being of the economy.

THE NATURE OF EXPENDITURES AND SAVING

Economists distinguish between expenditures that are made for *consumption* and expenditures that are made for *investment*. The difference turns on whether the goods and services purchased are for current or future use. The former are consumption expenditures and the latter are investment expenditures. At times, the division line seems very arbitrary, as, for example, when expenditures for business (net) inventories and residential construction are included with business expenditures on machinery and plant to make up *private investment*. A further distinction is made between domestic and foreign investment, but we shall neglect the precise nature of the latter to keep our discussion as simple as possible. Government expenditures must also be included in the total reckoning of consumption and investment, and, although a large part of the expenditures made by government are for future use, the total is nonetheless considered as consumption. Now, an important fact which we must realize is that national income is made up of investment expenditures plus consumption expenditures (after certain deductions for plant and equipment that are used up

and for indirect business taxes). For our purposes now, it will be helpful to separate these basic determinants of national income into three groups: consumption expenditures, investment expenditures, and government purchases of goods and services. As our discussion proceeds, it will be clear why the private and public expenditures ought to be considered separately.

A basic difference between consumption and investment expenditures is the relatively unstable character of investment expenditures. Those who make decisions to undertake expenditures for plant and equipment, inventories, and residential construction can delay and cancel their outlays. They would be led to do this if they considered the costs of borrowing funds to be too high or if the returns anticipated from their investments were not adequate to offset the risks assumed. In contrast to investment decisions, consumption decisions are relatively stable, chiefly because they involve expenditures for objects that are not postponable, such as food, clothing, and shelter. But let us see what effect this will have on national income, which is the sum of consumption and investment expenditures. If investment expenditures are reduced (and it is more likely that *they* rather than consumption expenditures will be reduced), national income will fall unless some compensating forces come into play. When we say that expenditures for investment are "reduced," we mean, of course, that the portion of the payments stream that would go into investment is channeled instead into savings. This is the case because the total amount of payments cannot be lost within the stream, but only transferred among the sectors. Hence the income received, but not spent, goes into savings. We can view the process in numerical terms as follows:

EXPENDITURES ON OUTPUT

	Consumption Expenditures	Investment Expenditures	Government Expenditures	National Income	Savings
(A)	200	50	25	275	0
(B)	200	25	25	falls	25
(C)	200	25	50	rises	0

Recalling again that the national income is equal to the sum of expenditures on consumption (C), investment (I), and government (G) purchases, we see in (A) a situation where C is 200, I is 50, and G is 25. National income becomes 275 and savings are 0. In situation (B), however, investment expenditures are reduced by 25 (falling from 50 to 25), savings increase by 25 (from 0 to 25), and the national-in-

come total falls ultimately by an amount larger than 25 because of what are called "multiplier effects." In situation (C), government expenditures are increased by 25 and savings decreased by 25, with the consequence that national income goes back to the 275 level and ultimately higher because of "multiplier effects." We should have observed the same effect if expenditures on investment or consumption had increased by 25, offsetting the savings item of the same amount. In terms of our diagram, the total amount of savings "eddying" out of the stream of payments at E must be returned to the various sectors (as shown at F) to maintain the level of national income. And, as one might anticipate, if the total investment expenditures are in excess of the total savings, national income will increase. But that area of the process is not essential for this discussion, and highly technical problems would crop up if we were to attempt to clarify it.

MANAGING THE CONSUMPTION AND INVESTMENT DETERMINANTS OF NATIONAL INCOME

The importance of ensuring that consumption and investment expenditures will remain at the levels required to maintain national income can readily be understood in view of the relationships we have noted between national income and employment. Only in recent years have citizens and their governments been willing to admit that adequate levels of consumption and investment do not result automatically from the flow of savings into investment. It was Sir William Beveridge who made the most succinct appraisal of the problem in a passage from his book, *Full Employment in a Free Society*, in which he sought to give the gist of the new approach to the problem of unemployment.

Employment depends on spending, which is of two kinds—for consumption and for investment; what people spend on consumption gives employment. What they save, i.e., do not spend on consumption gives employment only if it is invested, which means . . . expenditure in adding to capital equipment, such as factories, machinery, or ships, or in increasing stocks of raw material. There is not in the unplanned market economy anything that automatically keeps the total of spending of both kinds at the point of full employment, that is to say, high enough to employ all the available labour.[59]

Highly organized money markets in the United States perform their

[59] Sir William Beveridge, *Full Employment in a Free Society*, New York, W. W. Norton and Company, 1945, pp. 93–94.

task of getting people who have savings into contact with people who need savings for investment purposes. But in only a limited number of cases are the persons who decide to save (that is, decide "not to spend") also the persons who decide to invest. Aunt Jane may have accumulated a modest amount of savings within the year by going without certain goods and services which she could have consumed. Let us assume she has put her savings in a bank. The decision whether or not to employ the savings now rests with the bank officials. But they do not ordinarily make decisions to expand plant and equipment or otherwise invest the savings. Hence, they must await the application for funds of someone who *does* make such decisions, a businessman. Once the savings are in his hands, there still remains the final decision to employ the savings in investment, and any or all of the factors which we mentioned above as leading persons to postpone investment decisions may yet prevent the savings finding their way into actual expenditures on investment. Such failings in the private sectors of the economy can be counteracted in the public sector, of course, ignoring for the moment the question of increasing private *consumption* expenditures. And the power of public authority in this connection is impressive. Turning to Sir William Beveridge again, he calls attention to the fact that investment undertakings out of borrowed funds operate under the liability that they must produce profits in order to facilitate repayment. But, Beveridge observes, "the State is under no such restriction, since it possesses an unlimited command over the nation's credit, and therefore can use the savings of its citizens in any way that seems good to it. It can spend them on explosives or on milk for babies or on salaries for civil servants and still be able to repay with interest what it has borrowed." [60]

By reason of its great power and its freedom to make expenditures without necessarily being concerned with profitability, the state must assume responsibility for managing the major determinants of national income. In Chapter 11 we reviewed the activities of the state in this respect, and in Chapter 18 we shall extend our discussion when we discuss governmental planning for social and economic welfare.

Appendix B: Employment Act of 1946

An Act

To declare a national policy on employment, production, and purchasing power and for other purposes.

[60] *Ibid.*, p. 99.

Be it enacted by the Senate and House of Representatives of the United States of America in Congress assembled.

Sec. 1. This Act may be cited as the "Employment Act of 1946."

Declaration of Policy

Sec. 2. The Congress hereby declares that it is the continuing policy and responsibility of the Federal Government to use all practicable means consistent with its needs and obligations and other essential considerations of national policy with the assistance and cooperation of industry, agriculture, labor, and State and local governments, to coordinate and utilize all its plans, functions, and resources for the purpose of creating and maintaining, in a manner calculated to foster and promote free competitive enterprise and the general welfare, conditions under which there will be afforded useful employment, for those able, willing, and seeking to work, and to promote maximum employment, production, and purchasing power.

Economic Report of the President

Sec. 3(a) The President shall transmit to the Congress within sixty days after the beginning of each regular session (commencing with the year 1947) an economic report (hereinafter called the "Economic Report") setting forth (1) the levels of employment, production, and purchasing power obtaining in the United States and such levels needed to carry out the policy declared in Section 2; (2) current and foreseeable trends in the levels of employment, production, and purchasing power; (3) a review of the economic program of the Federal Government and a review of economic conditions affecting employment in the United States or any considerable portion thereof during the preceding year and of their effect upon employment, production, and purchasing power; and (4) a program for carrying out the policy declared in Section 2, together with such recommendations for legislation as he may deem necessary or desirable.

(b) The President may transmit from time to time to the Congress reports supplementary to the economic report, each of which shall include such supplementary or revised recommendations as he may deem necessary or desirable to achieve the policy declared in Section 2.

(c) The Economic Report, and all supplementary reports transmitted under subsection (B), shall, when transmitted to Congress, be referred to the Joint Committee created by Section 5.

Council of Economic Advisers to the President

Sec. 4(a) There is hereby created in the executive office of the President a Council of Economic Advisers (hereinafter called the "Council"). The Council shall be composed of three members who shall be appointed by the President, by and with the advice and consent of the Senate, and

each of whom shall be a person who, as a result of his training, experience, and attainments, is exceptionally qualified to analyze and interpret economic developments, to appraise programs and activities of the Government in the light of the policy declared in Section 2, and to formulate and recommend national economic policy to promote employment, production, and purchasing power under free competitive enterprise. Each member of the Council shall receive compensation at the rate of $15,000 per annum. The President shall designate one of the members of the Council as Chairman and one as Vice-Chairman, who shall act as Chairman in the absence of the Chairman.

(b) The Council is authorized to employ, and fix the compensation of, such specialists and other experts as may be necessary for the carrying out of its functions under this Act, without regard to the civil-service laws and the Classification Act of 1923, as amended, and is authorized, subject to the civil-service Laws, to employ such other officers and employees as may be necessary for carrying out its functions under this Act, and fix their compensation in accordance with the Classification Act of 1923, as amended.

(c) It shall be the duty and function of the Council:

   (1) To assist and advise the President in the preparation of the Economic Report:

   (2) To gather timely and authoritative information concerning economic developments and economic trends, both current and prospective, to analyze and interpret such information in the light of the policy declared in Section 2 for the purpose of determining whether such developments and trends are interfering, or are likely to interfere, with the achievement of such policy, and to compile and submit to the President studies relating to such developments and trends;

   (3) To appraise the various programs and activities of the Federal Government in the light of the policy declared in Section 2 for the purpose of determining the extent to which such programs and activities are contributing, and the extent to which they are not contributing, to the achievement of such policy, and to make recommendations to the President with respect thereto;

   (4) to develop and recommend to the President national economic policies to foster and promote free competitive enterprise, to avoid economic fluctuations or to diminish the effects thereof, and to maintain employment, production, and purchasing power;

   (5) to make and furnish such studies, reports thereon, and recommendations with respect to matters of Federal economic policy and legislation as the President may request.

(d) The Council shall make an annual report to the President in December of each year.

(e) In exercising its powers, functions, and duties under this Act:

    (1) the Council may constitute such advisory committees and may consult with such representatives of industry, agricultural, labor, consumers, State and local governments, and other groups, as it deems advisable;

    (2) The Council shall, to the fullest extent possible, utilize the services, facilities, and information (including statistical information) of other government agencies as well as of private research agencies, in order that duplication of effort and expense may be avoided.

(f) To enable the Council to exercise its powers, functions, and duties under this Act, there are authorized to be appropriated (except for the salaries of the members and the salaries of officers and employees of the Council) such sums as may be necessary. For the salaries of the members and the salaries of officers and employees of the Council, there is authorized to be appropriated not exceeding $345,000 in the aggregate for each fiscal year.

Joint Committee on the Economic Report

Sec. 5(a) There is hereby established a Joint Committee on the Economic Report, to be composed of seven members of the Senate, to be appointed by the President of the Senate, and seven members of the House of Representatives, to be appointed by the Speaker of the House of Representatives. The party representation on the joint committee shall as nearly as may be feasible reflect the relative membership of the majority and minority parties in the Senate and House of Representatives.

(b) It shall be the function of the joint committee—

    (1) to make a continuing study of matters related to the Economic Report;

    (2) to study means of coordinating programs in order to further the policy of this Act; and

    (3) as a guide to the several committees of the Congress dealing with legislation relating to the Economic Report, not later than May 1 of each year (beginning with the year 1947) to file a report with the Senate and the House of Representatives containing its findings and recommendations with respect to each of the main recommendations made by the President in the Economic Report, and from time to time to make such other reports and recommendations to the Senate and House of Representatives as it seems advisable.

(c) Vacancies in the membership of the joint committee shall not

affect the power of the remaining members to execute the functions of the joint committee, and shall be filled in the same manner as in the case of the original selection. The joint committee shall select a chairman and a vice chairman from among its members.

(d) The joint committee, or any duly authorized subcommittee thereof, is authorized to hold such hearings as it deems advisable, and, within the limitations of its appropriations, the joint committee is empowered to appoint and fix the compensation of such experts, consultants, technicians and clerical and stenographic assistants, to procure such printing and binding, and to make such expenditures, as it deems necessary and advisable. The cost of stenographic services to report hearings of the joint committee, or any subcommittee thereof, shall not exceed 25 cents per hundred words. The joint committee is authorized to utilize the departments and establishments of the Government, and also of private research agencies.

(e) There is hereby authorized to be appropriated for each fiscal year the sum of $50,000, or so much thereof as may be necessary, to carry out the provisions of this section, to be disbursed by the secretary of the Senate on vouchers signed by the Chairman and Vice Chairman.

SELECTED REFERENCES

Hoyt, E. E.; Reid, Margaret G.; McConnell, Joseph L.; and Hooks, Janet M., *American Income and Its Use*, New York, Harper & Brothers, 1954.

Rouchames, Louis, *Race, Jobs and Politics*, New York, Columbia University Press, 1953.

Ruggles, Richard, *An Introduction to National Income and Income Analysis*, New York, McGraw-Hill, 1949.

Yoder, Dale, *Personnel Management*, New York, Prentice-Hall, 1948.

Occupational Health and Safety and Workmen's-Compensation Legislation

This chapter initiates our study of American legislation to provide social security. In previous chapters, we have discussed laws to regulate wages and hours of workmen and to gain security for labor organizations. But in this chapter, we shall encounter for the first time legislation which purposes to protect the family from the consequences of injuries and sickness sustained by the breadwinner in connection with his job. We shall enter the substantive aspects of this legislation by discussing the kinds of threats which the employee faces in connection with his work, the costs (financial and social) of industrial injuries and disease, and the legislation which has been passed to promote occupational health and safety. Finally, we shall analyze the provisions of workmen's-compensation legislation in American jurisdictions, and determine how effective it is in safeguarding the worker's family against the loss of his income and his employability.

Threats to the Employee on the Job

In Chapter 10, we surveyed the characteristics of major occupations at which members of the labor force are employed. Many of the occupations that we discussed required employees to expose themselves to various kinds of hazards. Working in the presence of fumes and dust, beneath the ground, or in the presence of dangerous machinery and massive weights are examples of occupational conditions which greatly increase the dangers of injury and sickness. The Engineering Committee which reported to the President's Conference on Industrial Safety cited four categories of hazards related to

the problems of accidents and occupational diseases.[1] The categories and their subgroups were:

1. Uncontrolled movement of men, materials, and equipment, arising out of:
   a. Plant layout.
   b. Material-handling methods and transport.
   c. Congestion, arising out of inadequate permanent and temporary storage facilities.
   d. Waste-reject disposal.
2. Lack of foolproof installations, arising out of:
   a. Process equipment operation.
   b. Pressure and temperature controls.
   c. Flammable, explosive, and toxic dusts, gases, liquids, and solids.
   d. Electrical wiring and equipment.
3. Structural failure of:
   a. Cranes, hoists, and elevators.
   b. Permanent structures.
4. Practices of individual workers arising out of:
   a. Lack of knowledge of the controlled operation of machines and equipment.
   b. Lack of knowledge of the safe handling of hazardous materials.[2]

All students of industrial safety and hygiene recognize that only a small proportion of injuries are attributable to failures in mechanical processes and machines. An even smaller proportion of all disabilities can be traced to mechanical failures. The vast majority of accidents can be traced to human failings, such as failure to wear protective clothing or to abide by safe rules of procedure. But the Engineering Committee's viewpoint in this matter is different, as its conclusion shows; "An accident is almost always a symptom of something wrong in the production process—something wrong with the man, the machinery, the method, or the materials. Therefore practically all accidents are prima facie evidence of defects in the working environment, or inefficiency in supervision or of lack of adequate training of employees." [3] In other words, the Committee believes that nearly all accidents are preventable through perfecting the production process—men, machinery, methods, or materials.

---

[1] *President's Conference on Industrial Safety*, Washington, Government Printing Office, March 23, 24, and 25, 1949.
[2] *Ibid.*, p. 55.
[3] *Ibid.*, p. 37.

Dimensions of the Industrial Health and Injury Problem

The President's Commission on the Health Needs of the Nation reported in 1952 that "On an average working day in 1949–50 an estimated 1.2 to 1.6 million persons in the labor force were unable to work because of sickness or other disabling conditions. In addition, a large number of persons of working age are not in the labor force at all because of some disability. Each year we lose about a billion mandays from industry because of disability." [4] The gross problem is portrayed in the Commission's statement. However, there are several dimensions of the industrial injury and health problem that cause social concern.

Looking first at the human consequences, there is the anxiety felt by the family concerning the worker's recovery and the costs which may be entailed to enable him to resume his occupation. Furthermore, the loss of the worker's income if his convalescence is prolonged may work severe hardship on the family. In some of the highly specialized skilled occupations (which often have high injury frequency and severity rates), a disabling accident requires extensive and costly rehabilitation if the worker would maintain his level of living. We can enlarge on some of the statistical indications offered in the statement above concerning the magnitude of the injury and sickness problem. The Commissioner of the Bureau of Labor Statistics reported to the President's Conference on Industrial Safety that in 1948 about 16,500 workers were killed in on-the-job accidents, 1800 were permanently disabled to a degree which will prevent their ever resuming gainful employment, 83,700 experienced permanent impairments which will reduce their physical abilities for the rest of their lives, and 1,858,000 others experienced temporary injuries of sufficient severity to cause each of them to lose one or more full days from work.[5] The loss to the nation in production amounted in 1948 to 41,000,000 man-days actually lost, the equivalent of a full year's employment for 175,000 workers; but when the future losses in production ability arising from deaths and permanent impairments are taken into consideration, the loss rises to the astounding total of 219,000,000 man-days, or the equivalent of a full year's work for 730,000 workers.[6] The dollar cost to employers is estimated at more than $3 billion, of which one-fifth are direct costs for workmen's compensation, hospital,

[4] Building America's Health, A Report to the President by the President's Commission on the Health Needs of the Nation, Washington, Government Printing Office, Vol. I, p. 65.

[5] Ibid., p. 23.

[6] Ibid., p. 23.

and medical costs. Additional costs are borne by the injured worker, his family, and the community, causing the dollar-total cost to be far in excess of three billions. On the whole, since 1947 the experience in disability resulting from industrial injury has been highly encouraging. This is also true of industrial sickness, though to a lesser degree.

The Bureau of Labor Statistics conducts an annual survey of work injuries which reveals both the frequency-rate (number of disabling injuries per million hours of employee exposure) changes and the severity-rate (total days disability charged per thousand hours of employee exposure)[7] changes. The rates for the period since 1947 are

TABLE 47. Injury Frequency and Severity Rates, Selected Industries, 1947–1953.[a]

Industry	1947	1948	1949	1950	1951	1952	1953
			Frequency Rates [b]				
Manufacturing	18.8	17.2	14.5	14.7	15.1	14.3	13.4
Construction	40.9	36.7	39.9	41.0	39.3	34.6	32.9
Heat, light, and power	18.1	17.1	16.0	13.8	13.2	12.1	12.7
Waterworks	21.0	25.1	27.5	21.9	23.5	21.4	n.a.
Personal services	10.0	10.2	8.9	10.0	9.9	10.1	n.a.
Business services	4.5	4.4	3.9	3.9	4.4	4.3	n.a.
Educational services	8.0	8.3	7.6	7.9	8.2	8.5	8.3
Fire departments	24.8	30.9	32.1	35.5	30.4	34.7	31.8
Police departments	29.1	28.2	27.5	32.4	36.5	33.2	30.3
Trade	16.4	15.1	12.7	12.3	12.9	12.4	12.1
			Severity Rates [c]				
Manufacturing	140	150	140	120	130	130	120
Construction	360	500	390	380	420	370	320
Heat, light, and power	230	210	230	190	200	170	190
Waterworks	90	150	110	160	140	250	n.a.
Personal services	70	50	50	50	40	60	n.a.
Business services	30	30	30	30	20	30	n.a.
Educational services	50	40	40	30	60	40	56
Fire departments	240	160	250	190	210	180	320
Police departments	310	220	240	150	160	180	300
Trade	80	90	60	60	60	50	60

a Industries with very high injury rates, such as transportation, have not been included, and the classification of industries used tends to group industries with high frequency rates with those having low frequency rates; hence the data are useful primarily to indicate trends.
b Number of disabling injuries per million hours of exposure.
c The conventional base of 1000 hours of exposure has been increased one hundred times to minimize the tendency to discount the importance of severity data, which are frequently represented by numbers less than one. The data here, then, are the number of days disability charged per 100,000 hours of exposure.

Sources: Data for 1947–1952 taken from U.S. Bureau of the Census, *Statistical Abstract of the United States, 1954*, p. 234. Data for 1953 computed from U.S. Department of Labor, *Monthly Labor Review*, November, 1954, p. 1227.

[7] The severity-rate base was changed by the BLS to a million hours of employee exposure upon recommendation of the American Standards Association effective January 1, 1955. *Monthly Labor Review*, May, 1955, p. 565.

shown in Table 47. It will be seen from the table that both injury frequency rates and severity rates have been declining since 1947 in the large employee groups—manufacturing, construction, and trade. The rates have declined considerably from the high points which were reached in the period 1941–1943 and 1945–1947. Preliminary estimates for 1954 suggest further reductions from the 1953 figures, owing in part to a reduction in hours of work (total exposure). Another method of viewing the industrial-injury problem is according to the effect of injuries on the worker. Table 48 presents this information for the

TABLE 48. Estimated Number of Disabling Work Injuries and Nature of Disabilities Sustained, 1953 and 1954.[a]

(thousands)

Industry Division	All Disabling Injuries		Deaths		Permanent Impairments		Temporary-Total Disabilities	
	1954 [b]	1953	1954	1953	1954	1953	1954	1953
Agriculture [c]	310	320	3.8	3.8	[f]	[f]	[f]	[f]
Mining	52	61	.8	.9	[f]	[f]	[f]	[f]
Contract construction [d]	205	225	2.4	2.5	6.6	7.9	196.0	214.6
Manufacturing	390	480	2.0	2.4	20.0	23.6	368.0	454.0
Transportation	167	186	1.2	1.4	[f]	[f]	[f]	[f]
Public utilities	18	19	.2	.3	[f]	[f]	[f]	[f]
Trade [e]	340	363	1.3	1.4	7.7	8.2	331.0	353.4
Finance, service, government, and miscellaneous	378	380	2.3	2.3	[f]	[f]	[f]	[f]
Total	1860	2034	14.0	15.0	76.0	84.0	1770.0	1935.0

a Data apply to all workers, including proprietors, self-employed persons, and unpaid family workers as well as employees, but exclude domestic-service workers.
b Data for 1954 are preliminary.
c Based on cross-section surveys by the U.S. Department of Agriculture in 1947 and 1948, adjusted for changes in employment.
d Based on small sample survey.
e Based on small sample survey.
f Data not shown separately, but included in grand total.

Source: U.S. Department of Labor, *Monthly Labor Review*, April, 1955, p. 431.

years 1953 and 1954. The data reveal that the industrial injury problem is serious in spite of recent improvements. Fourteen thousand workers were killed, 76,000 permanently impaired, and 1,750,000 totally disabled temporarily in 1954. Again, composing the data according to industrial division masks large variations in experience among industries within each division.

Industrial illness is the other phase of the injury and health problem. Against the background of all illness in the nation, industrial illness may appear unimportant. However, a large proportion of indus-

trially caused illness can be prevented, and in many cases the illness traceable to occupational factors is unusually painful or in other respects unpleasant. Perhaps 2 percent of all disabilities arising from industrial causes are accounted for by occupational diseases.[8] It is impossible to know the exact proportions of the occupational-disease problem because reporting of such diseases is mandatory in only twenty-six states and nation-wide data are unobtainable. Information collected from eighteen states in which reporting did take place showed a total of 31,400 cases for the period July, 1947, to June, 1948.[9] The place of occupational disease in relationship to other aspects of the industrial health and injury problem is suggested in data reported by the American College of Surgeons: in 1947, the average days of work lost per employee owing to industrial injury were sixty times as great as those lost due to occupational disease, and the days lost due to non-industrial injuries and illnesses were more than 400 times as great.[10] Any program to relieve this toll must be broadly based and not confined to industrial injuries and illnesses alone. Arguing the case for a broad program of national health protection, the President's Commission commented on the relationship between industrial injuries and disease and the larger general problem as follows: "An industrial worker does not pick up his heart or his lungs or his body at the factory gate when he checks in. Nor does he leave them there when he checks out at the day's end. His health on the job is one-third of the picture of his health throughout the day. Industrial health is tied up with home health." [11]

Industrial-health hazards can be discussed within three general classifications—chemical hazards, biological hazards, and hazards related to environmental conditions.[12] Industrial poisons are the major hazard within the chemical classification. The total number to which industrial employees may be exposed is more than one hundred and includes aluminum, antimony, arsenic, barium, beryllium, bismuth, copper, iron, lead, tin and tungsten dusts. Poisonous gases to which

[8] Margaret C. Klem, Margaret F. McKiever, and Walter J. Lear, *Industrial Health and Medical Programs*, Public Health Service Publication No. 15, Washington, Government Printing Office, 1950, p. 97.

[9] *Ibid.*, p. 97.

[10] Gaylord R. Hess, "Analysis of Experience of Industry in the Medical Care of Employees—A Compilation," *Bulletin of the American College of Surgeons*, September, 1948, pp. 163–169. Based on a survey of 381 companies.

[11] President's Commission on the Health Needs of the Nation, *op. cit.*, p. 66.

[12] This discussion utilizes the classification developed by J. J. Bloomfield in "Industrial Health Hazards," Roland P. Blake (ed.), *Industrial Safety*, New York, Prentice-Hall, 1943.

workers are exposed in some industries include ammonia, carbon monoxide, carbon dioxide, chlorine, fluorine, hydrogen chloride, hydrogen sulfide and hydrogen phosphide. Other poisons include methy alcohol, benzene (and other coal-tar products), carbon disulfide, and chromic acid. In the case of the poisons which occur in the form of dust and gas, the danger is from inhalation. Liquid poisons are a hazard both from the standpoint of absorption through the skin and through inhalation of fumes. Biological hazards include infections of all kinds, including anthrax, tuberculosis, and many forms of respiratory disease. Anthrax results from the handling of contaminated hides and wool. In the cases of other forms of infection, it is uncertain whether the pathogen, or disease-causing agent, results directly from the performance of occupational tasks. Physically exhausting work, which may cause the individual to be more susceptible to infection, constitutes another hazard in this classification. Hazards related to the work environment account for a large majority of occupational diseases. The primary hazard is skin disease, which the Public Health Service found accounted for more than half of the cases of occupational disease in its study of reports in eighteen states.[13]

In addition to the poisonous dusts discussed above, there are many irritating dusts which produce diseases that fall under the general terms dermatosis and pneumonoconiosis. The main forms of the latter are silicosis and asbestosis. Other hazards include excessive heat and cold, humidity, illumination, noise, repeated motion, shock, exposure to radioactive materials, and abnormal atmospheric conditions.[14]

Many of these hazards have been reduced in recent years through special control programs, substitution of less harmful processes for dangerous ones, design of work situations to promote safety, and similar practices. Moreover, the consequences of industrial injury and sickness have been made less severe by the establishment of treatment facilities at the work site. The latter practice has been restricted to large organizations, unfortunately, and the great majority of workers are without adequate medical facilities at their place of employment. And it is the smaller plants which have the highest frequency and severity rates with respect to industrial injury.[15]

[13] Klem, McKiever, and Lear, op. cit., p. 97.

[14] Ibid., p. 112.

[15] The National Safety Council analysis of injury rates in 6454 reporting plants (exclusive of mining and quarrying) shows that the accident frequency rate for small business organizations (under 100 employees) averages approximately two and one-half times that of establishments employing more than 500 persons (26.39 as compared with

Meeting the Industrial Sickness and Injury Problem

The health hazards which are associated with certain occupations are not recent discoveries. Most of the poisonous dusts have been recognized as such for centuries, and lead poisoning was well recognized by the first century A.D. It was 1837, however, before a scientific paper was presented in the United States relating occupational factors to the cause of disease.[16] In the movement to reduce hours, the health effects of fatiguing work carried on for prolonged periods were recognized. But it was 1877 before a state passed a law requiring factory safeguards, and employers were protected from liability for accidents and diseases suffered by their employees until 1885. Not until 1902 was an official survey of industrial hygiene in the United States undertaken. In 1910, the first national conference on industrial diseases was convened.

State legislation requiring monthly physical examinations of workers in certain industries which had been shown to pose serious health hazards was first accomplished (by Illinois) in 1911. Congress enacted a law in 1908 granting the right of compensation for injuries to certain employees of the United States, a law which was broadened in 1916 to cover all federal civilian employees. Beginning in 1910, states began to enact workmen's-compensation legislation, but its constitutionality remained in doubt until 1917, when the United States Supreme Court held both elective and compulsory laws constitutional. Considering that all European industrial countries had enacted workmen's-compensation legislation by the turn of the present century, the American experience can hardly be called progressive. Interest in this legislation had become keen all of a sudden, and the motive force behind it has given rise to much speculation. The primary factor would appear to have been the growth which took place in our social conscience during the progressive era, as described in Chapter 3.

Already, private business firms had initiated preventive programs and developed medical-care facilities for employees. The earliest company-financed medical department with a full-time professional staff was established by the Homestake Mining Company (North Dakota) in 1887. Many industrial-health and medical-care programs had been established, especially in the railroad-transportation industry.

11.50). Severity is greater in a proportion of more than five to one (5.39 as compared with 1.05). *President's Conference on Industrial Safety*, p. 170.

[16] Benjamin W. McCready in 1837 wrote a prize essay entitled "On the Influence of Trades, Professions, and Occupations in the United States in the Production of Disease" for the Medical Society of the State of New York.

PRIVATE EFFORTS

The interest of employers in occupational safety and health goes beyond the humanitarian aspects involved. Accidents and illnesses are costly in terms both of money and morale. Far-sighted firms sought to reduce occupational hazards at an early date, and various organizations sought to assist them in their programs.[17]

Standards such as "maximum allowable concentrations," "permissible limits," and "safe limits" have been developed to aid in safety engineering. Air-purification systems have been adopted in many firms to remove atmospheric contaminants and meet safety standards. Special clothing and equipment are required for workers who are exposed in their work to such hazards as acids and alkalis, hot materials, moisture, flying particles, etc. Automatic feeding and ejecting equipment reduces mechanical hazards, and the danger of machinery and objects falling from overhead is reduced by counterweighting. Finally, in addition to providing medical care at the work site, personnel factors may play a part in reducing industrial hazards by the selection of employees for positions in terms of job specifications which include physical qualifications, and by detecting accident-prone employees and transferring them out of hazardous jobs.

In large industrial establishments, safety programs are often carried out with professional personnel and in the same spirit as production programs. But the great majority of workmen are employed in small establishments where safety programs tend to be neglected and treatment facilities are poor. The cost factor for small plants is a major drawback. One authority has observed that "usually, shops have around 2000 employees before much of an inplant [medical] program seems justified financially." [18] The same authority quotes a report of the Thirteenth Annual Congress on Industrial Health that "for the large industrial firm, health and safety programs cost $19 per worker per year, but that for the small or medium firm, the cost soars to $40 or $45 per year.[19] Mechanical equipment for feeding and ejecting materials, lifting heavy objects, and controlling atmospheric contamina-

[17] The National Safety Council assumed leadership of the safety movement at the time of its formation in 1912. The American Standards Association is now recognized as the coördinating agency in the formulation of safety codes. In addition, manufacturers' associations, such as the Manufacturing Chemists Association, and professional groups, such as the American Society of Mechanical Engineers, have promoted safe practices in industry through the development of safe procedures.

[18] William A. Sawyer, "Occupational Health: Opportunities for Labor Health Plans," Monthly Labor Review, April, 1954, p. 398.

[19] Ibid., p. 398.

tion is more extensively employed in large plants than small plants for reasons of cost. Hence, it has been necessary for public authority to intervene in the employer-employee relationship to protect workers from hazards.

Health plans promoted by labor organizations have become an important part of the protection afforded industrial workers. Some of the plans are administered by the labor organization unilaterally; others are under joint labor-management administration. The present health plans fall into four general classifications: (1) contracts purchased from commercial insurance companies providing cash indemnities to cover some part of medical and hospital costs; (2) Blue Cross and Blue Shield plans, for the most part to cover part of hospital and surgical expenses; (3) medical service for ambulatory cases, providing the diagnosis and treatment possible in a well-equipped medical center staffed by full-time and part-time physicians; and (4) complete, comprehensive medical service provided by a group-practice medical center, similar to the centers in the third group, but with the addition of home and hospital care.[20] Negotiated health plans primarily cover workers in large plants, and, as has been stated, the absence of protection for small-plant workers increases the problems of health and injury protection for that group.

Public Authority and Occupational Hazards

Public authority was very slow to assume responsibility in the safety movement, as we have already seen; Massachusetts passed the first law requiring factory safeguards in 1877. However, the safety movement caught on before state legislatures only after the first decade of the present century. Compulsory workmen's-compensation legislation induced employers to provide safeguards and, where occupational diseases were included among compensable risks, to avoid exposing employees to chemical and physical hazards. Many states enacted legislation beyond workmen's compensation in an attempt to control industrial-health hazards. But the President's Commission on the Health Needs of the Nation noted that eleven states still were without factory-inspection laws in 1952.[21]

Furthermore, the great majority of states are not able to enforce their laws adequately. Compensation for the worker who sustained injuries as a result of occupational duties was initiated by the United

[20] Ibid., p. 397.
[21] Ibid., p. 77.

States Government, as we have noted, first for selected groups of employees in 1908, and then for all civilian employees in 1916. The states began enacting similar laws in 1911 after an initial setback from the New York Court of Appeals.[22] At least thirty states had enacted compensation legislation in some form by the time the constitutionality of the laws was upheld by the United States Supreme Court in 1917. The American Association for Labor Legislation and in time the American Federation of Labor pressed the cause before state legislatures.

To appreciate the progressive character of the compensation laws, it is necessary to understand the plight of the injured worker prior to their enactment. The early English common-law rules of employer responsibility had been adopted in American jurisdictions, and these required the employer to exercise reasonable care in making the work site safe; but they also gave three defenses to the employer in case of injury to an employee—assumption of risk, contributory negligence, and fellow servant—which more than counterbalanced his duty. Under the assumption of risk defense, the employee (servant) was assumed to be capable of determining for himself the hazards involved in his work. If he continued to work under the hazardous conditions and sustained injury or sickness, the employer was not liable for any negligence of which he, himself, was guilty. Under the contributory-negligence defense, the injured employee could not recover damages if he had been negligent in any degree, the employer's negligence notwithstanding. A complex of degrees of negligence by the "master" and his "servant" came to be employed under this defense in time. The fellow-servant defense held that an injured employee could not recover damages if the injury could be shown to have resulted from the negligence of a fellow worker. The effect of the common-law doctrines was to make recovery of damages resulting from work-connected injury or sickness extremely difficult. Perhaps nine of every ten injuries went uncompensated. Compensation, when received, was inconsistent and lawyers took a lion's share in their contingent fees. Furthermore, the common law held that the right to damages for personal injuries died with the victim; consequently, the survivors of fatally injured workmen were unable to recover damages.

Public outrage over the absurd doctrines of the common law as applied in suits resulting from industrial injury and sickness led to legislation increasing employer liability in many jurisdictions after

[22] *Ives v. South Buffalo Railway Company*, 201 New York 27 (1911).

1885. But the relief obtained in court continued to be uncertain, and the expense accompanying litigation kept the number of awards low. A new approach already a generation old in Europe was required, and the decade 1910–1920 witnessed the enactment of workmen's-compensation laws in forty-one jurisdictions. Fifty-one such laws had been enacted in 1930 by forty-four states, the United States Congress, and three territories.

In the concluding sections of this chapter, we shall examine the existing occupational safety and health legislation and workmen's-compensation legislation in more detail.

Occupational Health and Safety Legislation

All of the industrial states have made some provision for controlling occupational hazards. Very few of the states are able to deal adequately with the occupational safety and hygiene problem; however, eleven states have not even enacted factory-inspection laws (although they have the legal authority to do so), and in others safety regulations do not have the force of law. Often jurisdictions of state agencies overlap and inefficient regulation results.

GENERAL FEATURES OF STATE LAWS

Occupational health and safety legislation is typically administered by at least two state agencies, departments of health, and departments of labor. In some states, provision is made for an industrial-accident board, a fire marshal, or other organization. State departments of health all have broad statutory authority to protect the health of citizens within the state; but twenty-one of fifty-one jurisdictions do not have statutory provisions directly related to occupational health.[23] Furthermore, twenty-three jurisdictions make no provision for the compulsory reporting of occupational disease to the state health department, and three others require only one disease to be reported. State labor departments ordinarily assume the major burden in matters of safety and hygiene. Only three jurisdictions (Idaho, North Dakota, and South Dakota) fail to make statutory provision for regulation of occupational health by the labor department, and they also fail to make such provisions in connection with the department of health. However, twenty-four jurisdictions have statutory provisions

[23] Based on analysis of fifty-one jurisdictions (forty-eight states, District of Columbia, Hawaii, and Alaska), as compiled in Victoria M. Trasko (ed.) *Occupational Health and Safety Legislation*, Public Health Service Publication No. 357, U.S. Department of Health, Education, and Welfare, 1954.

for the regulation of occupational health that apply both to health and to labor departments. Duplication of functions of dubious value exists. Occupational diseases are fully covered in the workmen's-compensation acts of only twenty-eight states. In twenty states, only schedule coverage of an average of twelve to fifteen diseases is provided, and three states (Mississippi, Montana, and Wyoming) make no provision for occupational-disease coverage.[24] Finally, vocational-rehabilitation service for workers disabled by disease or injury is provided in the laws of forty-eight jurisdictions; only Kentucky, Nebraska, and South Carolina are without such provisions.

This summary shows the lack of uniformity among state laws dealing with occupational health and safety. We must now deal with the adequacy of the laws. First, we shall look into the adequacy of safety laws and codes from the standpoint of coverage of hazards. Then we shall deal with the support given to their administration, which is the important factor in assessing their effectiveness.

The Engineering Committee that reported to the President's Conference on Industrial Safety analyzed the titles of state safety laws and codes to determine the extent to which they covered industrial-safety problems. Recognizing that needs differ among the states, they divided the forty-eight states into three groups: heavy industrial, medium industrial, and essentially nonindustrial. The determination of how to classify a given state was made on the basis of the number of industrial workers, the ratio of industrial to total population, and relative industrial activity.[25] With respect to each of the states, a classification of coverage as relatively high, average, or inadequate was made. The relative standing of the three groups of states was as follows: [26]

Group	Extent of Coverage		
	High	Average	Inadequate
Heavy industrial (12 states)	5	6	1
Medium industrial (18 states)	1	5	12
Nonindustrial (18 states)	0	3	15
Total	6	14	28

The problem of adequate protection, as the table shows, is most serious in the medium industrial and the nonindustrial groups. Two-

[24] Wyoming has special legislation with respect to victims of silicosis, under which monthly payments are available from public funds.
[25] *President's Conference on Industrial Safety*, p. 81.
[26] *Ibid.*, p. 81.

thirds of the safety laws and codes of the medium industrial states and a larger percentage of those of the nonindustrial states were judged inadequate.

Another committee which, like the Engineering Committee, reported to the President's Conference was the Committee on Laws and Regulations. It reviewed the results of a Bureau of Labor Standards survey concerning state safety programs as follows:

Forty-two of the 45 state labor departments . . . indicated that they have the necessary legal authority and responsibility to carry on a safety program. In general, this authority includes the right to inspect for compliance with existing safety laws, and to engage in safety promotion and educational activities. Many of these state safety agencies, however, have reported that they are not fully utilizing their authority, for various reasons . . . we cite the fact that in 29 states the labor departments reported that they have rule-making authority; 9 of these states reported, however, that very little or no action for promulgation or revision of safety codes has occurred within the last 10 years. Two states which possess rule-making authority have failed to issue any codes to date. Six workmen's compensation agencies have reported that they have rule-making authority. No codes have been issued, however, by one of the six, and very little code-making has been undertaken by one of the other five within the last 10 years.[26]

Expenditures on safety activities by state labor departments were gathered from thirty-seven states for which complete figures were available, and the Committee noted in describing the results of its findings that "one-fourth of these states spend on an industrial accident prevention program as much as 25 cents per year for each industrial worker; that less than two-thirds of the states spend as much as 10 cents per year per industrial worker; that only two states spend as much as 50 cents per industrial worker.[27] The effectiveness of industrial-safety programs is not wholly determined by money expenditures. But a range from $0.009 to $1.77 among the thirty-seven states suggests a wide diversity in the adequacy of programs. Personnel expenses bulk large within a safety program, and the disparity in expenditures is matched in data which show that the ratio of safety inspectors to the number of industrial wage earners ranges from one inspector per 5300 industrial workers to one per 236,600 industrial workers among the thirty-seven states analyzed.[28] The Committee

26 *Ibid.*, p. 99.
27 *Ibid.*, p. 112.
28 *Ibid.*, p. 113.

noted that "only four of the thirty-three state agencies reporting on the adequacy of staff considered that they could give satisfactory service." [29]

The structure of occupational-injury control is revealed in these data to be wholly inadequate in terms of the problem. Nor is the need lessening as the technique of production advances. New processes, whose hazards are not known from experience, are continuously being introduced. By-products of conventional production processes find economic use on an increasing scale, and a large proportion of them increases the chemical or physical hazards of employment.

Improving the legislation relating to occupational health and safety requires action on several fronts. Lack of uniformity is one problem that frustrates an adequate national program of control. To remedy the situation, suggested language for state legislation has been drawn up from time to time. The Committee on Laws and Regulations which reported to the President's Conference on Industrial Safety proposed language for a uniform statute, and the Council of State Governments included a model bill in its *Suggested State Legislation Program for 1953*.[30] The Council proposal would create a tripartite board with power to promulgate and enforce rules and regulations through the use of penalties and injunctions. To the extent that such legislation would fix responsibility and provide penalties for violations, it could be highly beneficial. But the problem of sufficient appropriations to make such laws effective is not solved by uniform statutes. Education and that kind of citizenship which is willing to be concerned are crucial.

ROLE OF THE FEDERAL GOVERNMENT

In matters of occupational health and safety, the role of the federal government is secondary to that of the states. It is in seeking to make state action effective that federal activity makes a contribution to the national problem. The President's conferences on industrial safety have already figured in our discussion. The Labor Standards Bureau of the Department of Labor provides many technical services to aid in the identification and solution of safety and hygiene problems. A Federal Safety Council also exists within the Department of Labor to coördinate safety programs among United States employees. The

---

[29] *Ibid.*, p. 113.

[30] Council of State Governments, *Suggested State Legislation Program for 1953*, Chicago, the Council, 1952, pp. 140–146. The bill was not given full approval of the Council's drafting committee and was included for information purposes only.

Public Health Service maintains a Division of Occupational Health, through which the resources of the Public Health Service are focused on occupational health and hygiene problems. Grants for research are made by the Public Health Service for several phases of research, including a program which seeks to identify the psychological factors in industrial injury. All of the federal programs are considered to be administered with a high degree of efficiency.

Workmen's-Compensation Legislation

We have discussed the development of workmen's-compensation legislation and will turn now to its current status and operational problems. Many of the problems which have been discussed in connection with state occupational health and safety legislation apply as well to workmen's-compensation legislation. There are great variations among state laws with respect to their type, insurance requirements, coverage, amounts and duration of benefits paid, and administrative procedures.[31]

TYPES OF LAWS

Laws establishing workmen's-compensation programs are classified as compulsory or elective. A compulsory law requires every employer within its scope to accept its provisions and pay compensation as specified. An elective law permits the employer to accept or reject the law; but if he fails to accept, he loses the right to employ the customary common-law defenses (assumption of risk, contributory negligence, and fellow servant).[32] In few states is the option left wholly to the employer whether to accept the law, even in states with elective-type laws. Nearly always, employers are required to insure employees in certain hazardous kinds of employment. Twenty-seven state compensation laws and the two federal laws are of the compulsory type, while twenty-five of the states have elective-type laws. However, a much greater proportion of workers fall under compulsory laws than under elective laws.

INSURANCE REQUIREMENTS

Another variation concerns the kind of insurance requirement provided in compensation laws. Some laws provide for state-fund

[31] These differences were analyzed recently by the Bureau of Labor Standards in its Bulletin No. 161, 1955. This survey draws heavily on the Bureau's analysis.

[32] In some states, an employer whose firm is exempted from coverage may "voluntarily" elect to come under the law; but he does not under those conditions lose his common-law defenses if he rejects coverage.

insurance on an exclusive or competitive basis. Other states permit insurance with a private company or self-insurance by the employer. Of the nineteen jurisdictions (eighteen states and Puerto Rico) having state-fund systems, eight make the system exclusive (thus, employers are required to insure with the state fund). The others are competitive funds and employers may choose between insuring with the state fund or with a private insurance company. In thirty-three jurisdictions,[33] the employer may insure with a private company or qualify as a self-insurer. Penalties for failure to comply with the laws range from small fines to $500 per day and imprisonment for each day of noncompliance in Pennsylvania. In some states, an employer may be enjoined from doing business after a period of noncompliance.

Coverage

Coverage under the workmen's-compensation laws is extensive, although major gaps are criticized by students of social insurance. Estimates analyzed by the Bureau of Labor Standards indicate that "at most not more than 75 percent of the workers in this country are covered, and the number may be less than 60 percent." [34] The major exemptions from coverage are establishments with fewer than a specified number of workers, those not in hazardous employment, those in public employment, and farm workers. In twenty-nine states and Puerto Rico, employers are exempted who have fewer than a stated number of employees, usually three or four. Twelve states make the law applicable mainly to hazardous or extrahazardous employments. Even allowing for liberal inclusions of employments, this deprives many workers of protection. Only in fourteen states and the territories of Hawaii and Puerto Rico are agricultural workers included, and more than half of these states discriminate on the basis of protection afforded agricultural workers as compared with other workers. Usually, agricultural workers must be employed in mechanical operations to obtain coverage.

Coverage under the workmen's-compensation laws is also restricted with respect to the injuries and diseases that are covered. Until recently, the major restriction on coverage was in connection with occupational diseases. At present, forty-five states and Alaska, the District of Columbia, Hawaii, and Puerto Rico cover disabilities resulting from occupational disease as well as other disabilities. In only

[33] Including Alaska, Hawaii, the District of Columbia, and the Federal Government.
[34] Bureau of Labor Standards, op. cit., p. 2.

thirty of the forty-nine jurisdictions is the coverage of occupational disease complete, however. Mississippi, Wyoming, and Montana have no provision in their workmen's-compensation laws for disability resulting from occupational disease, and twenty-one jurisdictions provide only limited (schedule) coverage.

BENEFITS

The amount of benefits and the term of payment received by an injured worker have been strongly criticized by students of social legislation because of the extreme variations among the states. This has been particularly true of the term or duration of benefits. The amount of compensation which an injured worker will receive is determined by the rate, usually a percentage of the weekly wage, the term or period of payment, the weekly maximum, and the aggregate amount.[35] Most laws base the compensation on a percentage of the worker's average wages, usually 66⅔ percent. In some states, the rate is dependent on the worker's family obligations. Four states and the territory of Alaska specify an amount of benefits rather than a percentage. In any case, the percentage formula and the specifications do not always determine the money payments. Other provisions, such as waiting periods and maximum limitations on weekly and aggregate dollar totals, reduce the compensation. Estimates are that payments have not kept pace with rising wages.[36] An Illinois report shows that the loss in compensation has been substantial: of the compensable cases closed for the first time in 1952, the wage loss compensated was estimated at 30 percent for temporary disability cases; but at only 13 percent for permanent total disabilities, 14 percent for permanent-partial disability, and less than 6 percent for fatal cases;[37] maximum periods which must elapse before compensation may be paid range from three to seven days, the seven-day period being most common.[38] Retroactive payments to the injured worker are made where the injury

[35] Ibid., p. 18.

[36] Dorothy McCamman and Alfred M. Skolnik, "Workmen's Compensation: Measures of Accomplishment," Social Security Bulletin, March, 1954, p. 6, show that the effectiveness of the compensation has declined in recent years: "To maintain the same relative effectiveness over a period of years, the growth in benefit payments would have to keep pace with the growth in insured payrolls, unless injuries were to decline in frequency and severity. Actually, the rise in benefit payments has lagged far behind that in insured payrolls during the period for which estimates are available (1940–53)."

[37] State of Illinois, Division of Statistics and Research, Annual Report on Compensable Injuries, 1952, Part II, Table 9, quoted in McCamman and Skolnik, op. cit., p. 9.

[38] Medical care and hospital charges are paid from the date of injury.

continues beyond a stated period of time, and the common period necessary is twenty-eight days. Maximum weekly payments are usually set by statutes in the range $30–$35. In some states, the figure exceeds $40 and in others it is below $30.

Benefits are related to the type of disability sustained by the worker, and there are variations within each type. Temporary total disabilities are by far the most common of all disabilities, accounting for nearly 95 percent of total disabilities in 1953. In these cases, the worker, although totally disabled temporarily, will return to work. The amount of benefits in all states except Washington and Wyoming is based on a percentage of average wages, usually 66⅔ percent. In more than half the states, the maximum weekly payment exceeds $35. In forty-two jurisdictions, the period during which benefits may be paid is limited, ranging from 104 to 700 weeks.[39] Permanent-partial disabilities are compensated according to specific (schedule) injuries and general (nonschedule) injuries. Schedule injuries are compensated on the basis of a percentage of average wages, and nonschedule injuries are compensated according to the difference between wages before injury and wages after injury. The maximum period of payments varies between 150 weeks and 500 weeks for schedule injuries, and between 260 weeks and 1000 weeks for nonschedule injuries.[40] In six states and the Federal Government the period is "during disability." Maximum weekly payments range from $15 to $126.92 and vary according to schedule or nonschedule injuries in four states and according to the number of dependents in six states. Furthermore, total aggregate payments have a maximum limit in the laws of twenty-one jurisdictions, the range being from $300 to $14,400. An average maximum for the twenty-one jurisdictions would be about $8500. In most states, compensation for permanent partial disability is made "in addition to" those payments, including medical payments, which are made during the disability and convalescence. Variations among the states concerning the compensation made for schedule injuries is one of the most unsatisfactory features of the workmen's-compensation system. One recent appraisal gave this view of the situation:

In Colorado, loss of a hand is worth 104 weeks of compensation—in New Jersey, 230 weeks. A New Jersey hand, in fact, is worth more than an entire arm in Alabama and 24 other States. The value of an arm varies between 500 weeks of compensation in Wisconsin to 150 weeks in Maine.

[39] Bureau of Labor Standards, *op. cit.*, pp. 23–24.
[40] *Ibid.*, pp. 26–27.

In only 6 states does it rate 300 weeks or more. A leg is worth 500 weeks in Wisconsin, 300 weeks in Rhode Island—but only 150 weeks in Maine, 160 in South Dakota, and 170 in Vermont. In Oregon, complete loss of hearing is worth 350 weeks; in Arizona, 260; and in Maine, as little as 65. And 15 states do not require additional compensation for the healing period when the injury calls for a "schedule" benefit, i.e., payment for a permanent impairment.[41]

Permanent total disability is paid for the duration of the disability or for life in twenty-four jurisdictions.[42] Limitations are made in the remaining jurisdictions with respect to duration, amount, or both. The time periods range from 260 to 800 weeks, and the money limitations range from $3500 to $15,000.[43] In some states, the amount of compensation depends on the number of dependents of the disabled worker. Death benefits are limited in the laws of two-thirds of the jurisdictions, the limitations applying to the period of benefits, the amount, or both. The periods range from 260 to 780 weeks, and the amounts are $10,000 or less.[44] In ten of the remaining jurisdictions, limitations apply to the maximum payment, but not to the number of weeks. Only in Arizona, the District of Columbia, Hawaii, Nevada, New York, North Dakota, Oregon, West Virginia and the Federal Government do compensation laws provide payments to widows until death or remarriage and to children until they reach a specified age. Most laws increase benefits to the survivors of the deceased if they have minor children. Variations in death benefits are a source of dissatisfaction with the compensation system, as in the case of other benefits. Kossoris describes the consequences for survivors as follows:

In about two-thirds of the states, a worker's life is worth $10,000 (about 2½ years' earnings) or less. The widow and four children of a worker who earned $75 a week before he was killed will receive $25 a week in Kansas up to a total of $6000. A widow in Indiana, under the same circumstances, would be paid $10,000, but minus the benefits paid before her husband's death. In Ohio, the death benefits would amount to $9000; in Tennessee, $7500; Kentucky, $9500; Virginia, $7500; Vermont, $6500; and in Maine, $6000. But, if the widow remarries, she forfeits all or most of the unpaid benefits.[45]

[41] Max D. Kossoris, "An Appraisal," in *Workmen's Compensation in the United States*, Bureau of Labor Statistics Bulletin No. 1149, 1954, pp. 4–5.

[42] Twenty-one states, the District of Columbia, Hawaii, and the Federal Government.

[43] Bureau of Labor Standards, *op. cit.*, pp. 32–33.

[44] *Ibid.*, pp. 35–36.

[45] Kossoris, *op. cit.*, p. 6.

The kinds of benefits discussed above, while they vary widely in terms of actual compensation, are uniform features of all compensation laws. Certain other benefits are found only in the laws of specific states. These include medical benefits, rehabilitation benefits, burial expenses, and provisions relating to compensation for second injuries. In the compensation laws of all states, medical aid must be furnished to injured employees. Only sixteen jurisdictions [46] have specific provisions in their laws for unlimited hospital and medical benefits, although eighteen additional jurisdictions have established administrative authority sufficiently broad to permit unlimited benefits in practice. In the remaining jurisdictions, the limitations regarding amounts and periods of payment are strict; the amounts range from $300 to $2500 and the periods range from four weeks to two years.[47] We have noted previously that all jurisdictions, with apparently four exceptions, make provision for some form of rehabilitation for disabled workmen. Thirty jurisdictions do not have special provisions in their workmen's-compensation laws dealing with this need, however. With few exceptions,[48] the state laws which recognize the need for rehabilitation services provide only for special maintenance during the rehabilitation period. The services of the federal-state rehabilitation program are available to all jurisdictions, thus filling some of the gaps in the state programs when the worker is eligible. Burial expenses are provided, subject to limitations on amounts, in the compensation acts of all jurisdictions except Oklahoma. The specified maximum ranges from $150 to $500, and in some instances is not payable in cases where there are no dependents. Finally, most states have made some provision against the contingency of a disabled worker's sustaining a second injury. The problems which arise in connection with such cases are numerous. Should the injured worker receive compensation concurrently for both injuries? For only the more serious one? Should the employer at the time of injury bear the full cost of disability if the impairment is increased? These questions have been answered in forty-seven jurisdictions [49] by the establishment of "second-injury" funds. The chief aim has been to prevent discrimination in employ-

[46] Twelve states, the District of Columbia, Hawaii, Puerto Rico, and the Federal Government.

[47] Bureau of Labor Standards, op. cit., p. 22.

[48] Rehabilitation centers are operated by Ohio, Oregon, Rhode Island, Washington, and Puerto Rico, with the goal of fully reëstablishing the employment capabilities of injured workers.

[49] Forty-two states, Alaska, the District of Columbia, Hawaii, Puerto Rico, and the Federal Government (with reference to the Longshoremen's Act only).

ment against handicapped workers by eliminating the threat of additional compensation costs to employers. Under the most progressive acts, compensation is made for the actual disability which results from the combined injuries. However, where a second-injury fund has been established, an employer has to pay only for the latest injury; the remainder of the award for disability from the combined injuries is paid from the fund. These special funds are financed in various ways, including the levying of assessments on employers, carriers, and self-insurers, and total-compensation awards, and, in some instances, by state appropriations.

ADMINISTRATIVE PROCEDURES

All workmen's-compensation jurisdictions face essentially the same problems of administration. In most jurisdictions, administration of the laws is the responsibility of an independent agency or an industrial commission. The proportions are about equal. Courts administer the laws in five states. Personnel problems are difficult in all jurisdictions regardless of the administrative authority. Paul E. Gurske accounts for this by noting that "Legislators are prone to regard workmen's compensation as just another governmental function requiring the usual run of clerical employees, whereas it is a highly specialized field of casualty insurance requiring experienced, well-trained personnel." [50]

Most workmen's-compensation cases are uncontested. Settlements under such circumstances take place according to one of four procedures—the agreement method, the direct-payment method, the hearing method, and the "triple-form" method.[51] A majority of states use the *agreement method*. Under this procedure, a settlement is proffered by the employer or his insurance carrier. If the injured worker signs an agreement to accept the settlement and the workmen's-compensation authority approves the settlement, payments begin immediately. The authority's supervision of the settlement ends if the case is not contested. It is a prevalent opinion among students of workmen's compensation that this method gives inadequate protection to the employee. *Direct-payment procedure* requires the employer or his insurance carrier to initiate settlements which are specified in the law. The right of the employee to compensation is presumed to be established by the injury. To make sure that the statu-

[50] Paul E. Gurske, "Problems of Administration," Bureau of Labor Statistics, *op. cit.,* p. 39.
[51] Herman Miles Somers and Anne Ramsay Somers, *Workmen's Compensation,* New York, John Wiley and Sons, 1954, p. 151.

tory provisions are being met, the compensation authority requires reports of the employer or his insurance carrier, and, in the event the reports indicate inadequate settlement or other irresponsibility, the authority may enter the case and direct proper settlement. Somers describes other functions of the authority as follows: "The commission, on its own initiative, writes to every injured employee advising him of his rights and investigates the case to determine whether settlement has been made in accordance with the law, although payment is not held up pending this investigation. If the case is uncontested it may be reopened within 6 years from the date of last payment. Either party may, within 1 year, challenge a settlement. The worker may, within a specified time period, challenge the amount received and a contested case will be created, but his interests will not be prejudiced by previous acceptance of the amounts tendered by the employer or carrier." [52] Under this system, the protection afforded the employee is far more extensive than under the agreement procedure. The *hearing procedure* was formerly employed in New York State, which now uses the direct-payment system. Its distinguishing feature was that a hearing was scheduled for every claim and payments were required to begin within eighteen days after injury, whether or not the extent of liability had been determined. In actual practice, formal hearings were frequently dispensed with through the use of "consent-type" judgments in which all parties agreed to the settlement. The *triple-form method* used in Ohio is described by Somers as follows: ". . . an injured worker, or his survivor, is required to fill out a long and detailed form and to get his employer and doctor each to fill out similar forms. . . . The worker must then send all three to the industrial commission, which administers the exclusive state fund." [53] The procedure proved very slow—three months elapsing in some instances before compensation actually was received by the injured worker.

The major objective in the adoption of workmen's-compensation systems was to expedite the claims of workmen and improve their protection in gaining settlement. However, the lags which characterize the system are notorious, and the methods discussed above for settling uncontested claims work out unsatisfactorily in most states.

Contested cases result when the parties involved cannot agree to an award. In most states, contested cases are first reviewed in hearings

[52] *Ibid.*, p. 152.
[53] *Ibid.*, p. 153.

with an administrative official, frequently one of the commissioners. Appeals may be made from the decision rendered by the official to the commission or appeals board and then to the courts if necessary. Few cases, proportionately, are appealed to the courts because of the time required and because settlements are reached in the initial hearings. On questions of law, however, the courts may review decisions by commissions and appeals boards, and the decisions which are rendered play an important role in the administration of all compensation claims. Questions of fact may be reviewed in twenty-two jurisdictions.

FEDERAL WORKMEN'S-COMPENSATION LEGISLATION

We have already discussed the role of the federal government in establishing workmen's-compensation systems for employees of the United States. In 1908, an act established limited benefits for certain federal employees in hazardous occupations. In 1916, this law was superseded by the Federal Employees Compensation Act, which applied to all civil employees of the United States. Certain workers fell outside the protection of state laws, however, because of the nature of their occupations, and the Longshoremen's and Harbor Workers' Compensation Act was passed in 1927 to provide them benefits. Coverage under the act has extended far beyond the limitations implied in the title. The act was extended in 1928 to include employees of private industry in the District of Columbia. Approximately 3,200,000 persons were estimated to be covered by these two laws in May, 1953.[54]

Coverage and benefits under the federal laws have been dealt with in the preceding discussion. Certain general features of the laws might

[54] John Petsko, "Federal Legislation," Bureau of Labor Statistics, *op. cit.*, p. 13. The groups to whom the federal laws provide compensation benefits include: (1) Under the Federal Employees Compensation Act—civil officers and employees of all three branches of the United States Government; employees of the government of the District of Columbia; and officers and enlisted personnel in the reserve corps of the armed services, including the Coast Guard, while on active duty or in training in time of peace. (2) Under the Longshoremen's and Harbor Workers' Act—longshoremen, ship repairmen, ship servicemen, harbor workers, and others performing maritime work on the navigable waters of the United States; all persons in private employment in the District of Columbia (except domestics and casuals); those employed at any military, air, or naval base acquired from any foreign government or occupied or used for military or naval purposes in the territories and possessions of the United States; those engaged by United States contractors in public work outside the continental United States; and those employed by government contractors during World War II who incurred injury, death, or detention as the direct result of a war-risk hazard, and the dependents of detained or captured employees (*Ibid.*, p. 14).

well be recalled, however, for comparison with the states and territories. Substantial differentials exist in the money-payments provisions of the two federal acts, the Federal Employees Compensation Act being more generous than the Longshoremen's Act.[55] In the first place, the federal laws are compulsory. Coverage of employees, moreover, although not complete, is less limited than state practices in most cases. Benefits exceed those paid in most states (even under the Longshoremen's Act, which is comparable to state acts) as a result of higher weekly maximum payments, shorter waiting periods, provision for medical benefits, and provision for compensation in cases of occupational disease. Rehabilitation provisions in the federal acts also mark them off from a majority of the state laws.

In addition to the two laws discussed above, Congress has passed legislation covering employees of railroads in interstate traffic and seamen of the merchant marine.[56] A distinguishing feature of these acts is that compensation is contingent on proof that disability resulted from negligence on the part of the employer.

Workmen's Compensation Acts: A General Evaluation

The brief survey just completed has included scarcely any evaluation of results. Nor can this section present an evaluation such as the workmen's-compensation experience justifies. But some comments are required concerning the very dubious success of the oldest of our programs to promote social security.

One can readily admit the improvements which have been wrought in compensation for industrial injury and sickness since 1910 without approving any single feature of the prevailing laws. Neither in terms of fulfilling its major objective—to compensate disabled workers fairly and expeditiously and refit them for employment service—nor in terms of adjusting to changes in the climate of social thought can the "movement" for workmen's compensation be called a success. Coverage still is limited to from six or eight of every ten workmen, and the compensable disabilities are so inconsistent from jurisdiction to jurisdiction that they appear absurd. Benefits are inadequate in most jurisdic-

[55] The Federal Employees Act cannot in fairness be compared with the various state laws, as Petsko points out, because an homogeneous group of workers under a single employer permits practices which would be impossible under the more varied conditions of private employment; and financing of the federal law is provided through Congressional appropriation. *Ibid.*, p. 18.

[56] The Federal Employer's Liability Act of 1908 and the Merchant Marine Act of 1920, which made the general provisions of the 1908 act applicable to seamen of the merchant marine.

tions and show extreme inconsistency. Medical and rehabilitation benefits—without which no act can claim to fulfill the goals of the original sponsors of workmen's compensation—are not provided for in sixteen and thirty jurisdictions respectively. Overhead costs in the program are high, reportedly running to half of the total costs of compensation, and the benefits paid to the worker are frequently reduced by 20 percent and more by attorneys' fees.

The question of radical departures from prevailing practices in workmen's-compensation legislation has been raised by the systems operating in the United Kingdom and in the Canadian Province of Ontario. Some of the features of these laws which have come under consideration include the denial of court review of decisions of the administrative agency, uniform compulsory insurance, employee contributions, and uniform benefits. In the discussion of these questions, interest has centered on the possibilities of employee contributions rather than the other features.

Occupational Health and Safety and Workmen's-Compensation Legislation: Concluding Remarks

Legislation which has as its purpose to reduce the incidence of industrial injury and sickness, and to compensate workmen who become disabled because of job-related injuries and diseases, has many shortcomings, which have been pointed out in this survey. The application of knowledge relating to the control of injury and disease has largely been left to the employer's discretion—usually by default. In the larger plants, accidents have in many instances been reduced to the minimum possible in the present stage of production technique. Labor unions have played their own role in matters of industrial safety and hygiene. But the great majority of workmen are employed under conditions where the application of existing knowledge would significantly reduce the injury and disease toll.

In the larger view, however, injury and disease control restricted to the employee's work life would be incomplete even if adequate. Some nine-tenths of employee absenteeism from work is attributable to non-work-connected sickness and injury. A comprehensive national health program promises to meet a large part of the industrial need in a broad approach to the whole health problem. In Chapter 15 we shall discuss proposals for insurance to meet this need.

SELECTED REFERENCES

Blake, Roland P. (ed.), *Industrial Safety*, New York, Prentice-Hall, 1953.

Hamilton, Alice, and Hardy, Harriet L., *Industrial Toxicology*, New York, Harper & Brothers, 1949.

Klem, Margaret C.; McKiever, Margaret F.; and Lear, Walter J., *Industrial Health and Medical Programs*, Washington, Government Printing Office, 1950.

Somers, Herman M. and Anne R., *Workmen's Compensation*, New York, John Wiley and Sons, 1955.

The American Labor Movement in World War II and the Postwar Reaction

After 1937, the outlook for the labor movement and labor legislation was indeed highly encouraging. As we have seen in Chapter 9, the legal basis of union security had been established and the first steps toward protection against economic insecurity enacted into law. All three branches of the national government were operating under a social philosophy which presumed a strong labor movement. Among the general public, it was thought that social justice had been served belatedly in legislative measures directed at equalizing the power of the underdog, labor, with that of the master, management. Middle-class leaders were, for the most part, thankful that a bulwark had been erected against national socialism (a credo which had found a frightening number of adherents in the United States) through a moderate and controlled movement to the left. In accordance with this sentiment, the principles of the New Deal were vindicated at the polls in 1940, 1944, and 1948, extending to twenty years the reform era which began in 1932.

The Character of the Labor Movement

Protective legislation was not the sole condition influencing the labor movement in the United States as the depression eased. An increase in organizational energy also was released with the formation of the CIO and its success in organizing mass-production industries. Younger leaders, unrestrained by traditions that had grown with the AF of L, organized industry after industry that had previously been considered unorganizable. By 1940, the ranks of the CIO had swollen to more than 3,500,000. Extreme violence accompanied the CIO

efforts to organize the steel and auto industries, which only solidified the ranks of the new federation in its fight for existence. Ultimately the AF of L, which had been without a rival since it succeeded the Knights of Labor, was jogged out of its lethargy and sought to consolidate its own ranks. Following the lead of the CIO, the AF of L also organized industrial workmen, and outdistanced its new rival steadily after 1941. As the war began, the labor movement was vibrant and its capabilities for service or obstruction very great.

Labor and the War

The demands made on a nation by total war are immense, and careful use of all resources is required to wage modern war effectively. More than ever before, the crucial battles are won on the production line. All peacetime objectives of necessity take a second place to the primary objective of winning the war, and World War II was especially noteworthy for the unanimity of response which it elicited from the American people. The nation had been wantonly attacked and this fact released all of the pent-up outrage which had been felt over excesses perpetrated by the European dictatorships, but suppressed under a neutrality policy. Because the logistical situation of the allied powers was so desperate, American production was even more important in 1942 than American military might. Accordingly, the task of organizing the war effort began immediately.

Regulation of labor and government supervision of labor-management relations had had a precedent during World War I under the National War Labor Board. The jurisdiction of the Board had extended to all disputes in the field of production necessary for the effective conduct of the war. In the course of its operations, the Board delivered judgment on a wide range of labor-management problems, including wages, hours, and discrimination against members of labor unions. A similar body was organized after the declaration of war in 1941 with extensive powers even beyond its World War I counterpart. It came into existence following a labor-management conference which concluded that, for the duration of the war, (1) there should be no strikes or lockouts, (2) all disputes should be settled by peaceful means, and (3) a proper War Labor Board should settle these disputes. By 1942, public feeling was growing doubtful about the responsible use of labor power. John L. Lewis, president of the United Mine Workers, had achieved the destruction of the National Defense Mediation Board (the forerunner of the National War Labor Board)

when he refused to honor its decision in a dispute even after three requests by the President of the United States.[1] This was neither the first nor the last instance in which John L. Lewis's activities harmed labor before the public.

Most of the dispute cases which the National War Labor Board decided concerned wages. The criteria used in granting wage increases survived the war and were influential both in private wage adjustments and decisions under postwar stabilization boards. Early in 1942, the foundation for settling wage disputes was established. In the "Little Steel" case, an increase in wages was permitted to compensate for changes which had taken place in the cost of living. Preservation of the employee's purchasing power in the face of rising costs of living thus became a major consideration. Coupled with the cost-of-living criterion was a "health and decency" wage criterion which implied that wages should be adjusted to a standard budget level. Wage differences within the same plant and substandard wages generally were given favorable consideration for adjustment. As the war progressed, the administration of wage policy sought to provide similar wage levels among large industries. Fringe benefits particularly gained importance in this kind of calculus.

During the war, public suspicion of labor organizations grew and suspicion turned to hostility. The number of strikes and the number of man-days lost through work stoppages provoked public resentment, particularly so in view of the unfavorable military situation, which was slow to improve. Editorials became bitter, noting that soldiers did not have the right to strike, being obliged to content themselves with $21 a month. Labor power exercised irresponsibly was called treasonous. Neither the editorials nor the pledge not to strike taken in 1942 restrained the United Mine Workers, and in 1943 Congress passed the War Labor Disputes Act (Smith-Connally Act) setting up machinery for disputes settlement. Prior notice of intent to strike was required, and, where strikes would interfere with war production, government possession of facilities was provided for. None of the provisions was extensively used, and neither the federal law nor the numerous state laws which were passed had much effect on the

[1] For a discussion of this case (Captive Coal Mines case) and other operations under government boards concerned with labor relations, see Abraham L. Gitlow, *Wage Determination under National Boards*, New York, Prentice-Hall, 1953. The failure of the National Defense Mediation Board's machinery in the Captive Coal Mines case was in no small part owing to the failure of President Roosevelt to uphold its decision. Following the adverse Board decision, the CIO members on the Board withdrew.

settlement of disputes. It was obvious that labor was rapidly losing the good will which the public had shown in the depression years. Production schedules were met and even surpassed, and the total working time lost during the 1942–1945 period was exceptionaly low; but the public reaction carried over into the postwar period.

Heritage of the War Period

The circumstances of the postwar adjustment appear very complicated in retrospect. In the first place, the economic circumstances which would attend the conversion from wartime to peacetime production were erroneously predicted. The predominating view was that a high level of unemployment would accompany reconversion unless extraordinary precautions were taken. Hence, labor pressure for protective measures was strong. Second, the war ended with unexpected suddenness following the employment of atomic weapons against Japan. The consequence was that national policy, especially labor policy, was developed hastily. Third, a concerted action was initiated by business interests to free the economy of all controls as soon as possible. This had many effects, but an important one was the sharpening of labor-organization hostility and suspicion. Finally, the shadow of communism and subversion lurked in the background, to become a national issue as the prospects for coexistence with the Soviet Union worsened. How reconversion could have proceeded without widespread dislocation and labor-management conflict under the circumstances is difficult to see.

Historians will argue the question in future years, but 1946 appears to have been a turning point in the history of the labor movement. In that year, the astounding total of 116,000,000 man-days were lost in work stoppages which numbered nearly 5000. For comparison, if the years 1935–1939 are given an index of 100, the index in 1946 for work stoppages is 174, for workers involved in stoppages 408, and for man-days idle 684.[2]

Nation-wide strikes brought essential industries to a standstill four times during the year, twice in the coal industry. The usually prolabor Congress considered bills to restrict union activities, and suggestions for compulsory arbitration of disputes in special labor courts received serious attention. Bills passed Congress and were signed to deal with irresponsible practices on the part of the Musicians and the Teamsters

[2] U.S. Bureau of the Census, *Statistical Abstract of the United States, 1954*, p. 236.

Unions.[3] Congressional elections in 1946 indicated the state of the public will as the Republican party won control of both Houses of Congress for the first time in twenty years. The new Eightieth Congress considered the election a mandate to change the nation's basic labor policy and surround unions with safeguards.

Labor's Postwar Objectives

Labor unions, for their part, came out of the war determined that the experiences of the post-World War I period would not be repeated. Following World War I, a concerted drive against unions had cost them the membership and wage gains achieved during the war. Labor's objectives were, in brief, to maintain wage levels regardless of reductions in the number of hours worked, to secure additional fringe benefits where wage demands met resistance, to secure some form of employment guarantees through public and private action, to organize hitherto unorganized workers, and to shift operations to a wider scope, such as market areas and regions.

It is noteworthy that the state of public feeling was largely neglected in framing these objectives. As if wearing blinders, union leaders led their membership in quest of the agreed-on objects and secured favorable action on most counts. Wage levels were maintained and no drop occurred in take-home pay as hours were reduced. Fringe benefits multiplied under the supervision of government boards. The Employment Act of 1946 was passed and stabilization of employment was sought through production planning in the private sector. Moderate success attended efforts to organize the South, white-collar workers, and government workers, and more frequently collective-bargaining contracts were negotiated for whole industries. But these objectives were reached at the cost of public support. A revision of the nation's basic labor law followed. It will be worth our while to review some of the policies and practices which provoked public disapproval and spurred restrictive legislation.

Union Policies and Practices

Outrage over union policies and practices was owing in some measure to misunderstanding, a large part of it cultivated by those whose interests led them to oppose labor unions. Particular instances of irresponsibility on the part of some unions were made in editorials and advertisements to appear typical of all unions. As a matter of

[3] These were the Hobbs Act and the Lea Act.

fact, no set of policies or practices could be drawn up in 1946, or now, which would apply to all labor unions. Some of them are more than a century old and are highly conservative in character. Others are new and seeking security through trial and error. From its beginning, the labor movement has suffered for want of professional-caliber leadership, and this lack has been a problem up to the present time, although it is gradually being relieved. In the public mind, however, certain broad aspects of policy and certain difficult-to-understand tactics were viewed with widespread suspicion.

Union Policies

Union policies reflect a concept of the union which seldom is understood or shared by the public at large. First of all, the union is thought of by its members as a defense against employers and their organizations without which employer-labor policies would be oppressive. Employers are viewed as conscious only of production costs and not of social costs, and they would, given the opportunity, attempt to destroy employee organizations in an effort to gain complete autonomy in matters relating to employment and production. On another plane, however, the union is an institution with profound psychological influences on the employee. It is "we" and gives "us" security against "them." Social services and benefits as well as fellowship are to be had within the union. It is a common role of professional union leaders to encourage a view of the union as an institution rather than as an instrument sheerly for obtaining wage advances. The fact that this view is held by a minority of the membership has created some of the problems that brought regulation.

The security of the union against the threats posed by its protagonists is therefore the abiding major policy of unions. Another major policy is directed at perfecting capitalism and countering its inherent tendency to subordinate social costs to production costs. To this end, all forms of protective legislation for employees are supported by labor organizations. Measures to aid in stabilizing economic activity have been especially important to labor, which sees its future position depending on an expanding national income of which the labor share also increases. Union policies are focused at the present time primarily on collective bargaining and the content of the collective agreement. Often long and detailed, the collective agreement sets forth the status of the union within the firm or industry, conditions of employment, methods for solving grievances, and related matters. A

typical contract contains sections dealing with the following matters: union security, management prerogatives, hours of work, wage policies, working conditions, grievance procedure, vacations and holidays, and other benefits. An important section also deals with the duration of the contract and renewal clauses. Some of these matters and the policies of unions with reference to them deserve special comment. Union security deals with matters implied in the phrase, and it sets forth the union's position in bargaining. Since the chief threat to the union's bargaining position lies in its failure to represent the major portion of the employee force, union security demands some control over hiring practices, restricting hiring to union members if possible.[4] Management prerogatives refer to provisions of the contract which differentiate the areas of policy determination belonging exclusively to the employer from those which are matters for collective bargaining. Usually, all matters not specifically delegated to the union are reserved to the employer. In recent years, union threats to infringe on traditional prerogatives of management have provoked stiff resistance on the part of management associations. Duration of the contract and renewal clauses would not require explanation except that the explicit language of the matter has changed in recent years. While the collective agreement has been regarded as binding both parties to its conditions for the period specified, a new concept known as the "living document" has provided that employers must bargain over issues which arise during the life of the agreement if they have not previously been the object of bargaining. Both union power and the National Labor Relations Board have forced such an interpretation. Other sections in the contract are self-explanatory. Union policies with reference to many items of the contract have been an important factor in turning public support away from unions. We should, therefore, discuss the union position in connection with some of the more controversial items.

Students of the labor movement will differ on the rationale advanced by labor leaders for their policies. But a broad area of agree-

---

[4] Common provisions for union security are the union shop (employees vote that within a stated period after joining a firm new employees must also join the union), maintenance of membership (while employees are not obligated to join the union as a condition of employment, if they are members at the time the agreement is signed, they must remain members in good standing for the duration of the agreement), and the preferential shop (union members are given preference in hiring and in retaining their jobs during periods of layoff). A related union security provision permits employers to deduct union dues at the source and is called the check-off.

ment can be found. Union security policies have as an ultimate goal the requirement that employees must join unions as a condition of employment. The advantage to the union of being able to bargain for a consolidated membership would be highly beneficial. In some industries, unions must bargain meekly in the knowledge that they represent only a small proportion of the total membership. Defending their position, union spokesmen point out that all employees benefit from the union's activities and should therefore share in the costs and responsibilities of membership. Union wage policies are complex and variable, but, in general, preference is given to nondiscriminatory wage policy (that is, equal compensation for identical jobs without regard to differentials in performance) and hourly rates as contrasted with incentive rates. Certainty is sought in the method of compensation, which leads unions to be suspicious of bonus plans, profit sharing, and other similar plans which allow a large margin of employer discretion. Of all of these wage policies, unions prefer equal pay without regard to performance initiative. Union spokesmen argue that certification of capability ought to be a prior determination before the employee enters the job and should result from union-management bargaining on job specifications. Any plan which includes rewards to individuals for differential performance is open to abuse by the employer and threatens to set the work standard beyond the capability of older workers, thus contributing to the superannuation problem. Union policies in connection with hours also vary, but in general greater amounts of leisure are sought both as a compensation for the intensified pace of work and to expand the leisure-time market for goods and services. Another aspect of union hours policy is defensive. The economies connected with replacement of men by machinery are dependent upon more or less continuous use of the machinery. Shortening hours of work decreases the advantage of machinery by increasing its cost of operation and thus reduces the incentive to substitute machinery for man power. When this policy is considered solely on economic grounds, it must be condemned because it discourages economic growth. Policies concerned with conditions of work bear upon illumination, atmospheric contamination, safety, and related matters. But the more controversial feature involves the pace of work. The term applied to efforts to "create" work is "featherbedding," and the practice has been so badly viewed by the public that special legislation was enacted to deal with it in 1946. A cloak of suspicion surrounds the practice from any viewpoint, but, as

pointed out in the preceeding chapter, in particular cases there may be a point to restrictions on the work load in order to accommodate workers who have passed their prime. Limitations on bricklaying may be based on a bona-fide consideration for older workers; forcing the employment of live orchestras to stand by while recorded music is played is far more dubious. In the matter of employment stabilization, unions have pressed for both private and public action. A preference for public measures seems to have continued in spite of the disappointing experience under the Employment Act of 1946. In matters of taxation and expenditure policies, unions have customarily favored compensatory spending, tax reductions for low-income groups, and planning for full employment.

These and other policies have not met with public favor, although they have become part of the operating background of business firms in general. Bitter debate centering around an "honest day's work," the "right to work," "labor monopoly power," and "inflationary wage increases" had become common at the war's end, and the labor movement was hard pressed to fight even a successful delaying action against restrictive legislation. It is not clear to date that the views of labor unions on the practices mentioned above are any nearer acceptance in the general framework of cultural values than a decade ago.

UNION PRACTICES

Criticism of union practices is a logical development from criticism of union policies. However, specific practices are most often criticized on the basis that they result from defects in union government. Policy determination and execution are held to be undemocratic and workers mere pawns in a power game. Great resources of power are supposed to reside in the executive offices of the AF of L-CIO, and this power is also supposed to be unhindered in its accumulation or exercise. In analyzing the basis for these contentions, we must thread our way carefully. Abuses of power do exist and union government scarcely measures up to the ideals of democracy in all cases. But such assertions fail to reveal the sources of irresponsibility and undemocratic practice which reside in the membership.

The seat of power in the American labor movement has never resided in the federations, nor the merger which has been accomplished between them. It is in the autonomous national and international unions (called international in some instances because they have chartered local unions outside of the continental United States) of

which the federation is composed. Sometimes the nationals represent workmen drawn from the same or related crafts (International Brotherhood of Carpenters and Joiners, formerly AF of L) or workmen in a common industry (United Automobile Workers, formerly CIO). Within the AF of L-CIO, the position of the nationals and inter-

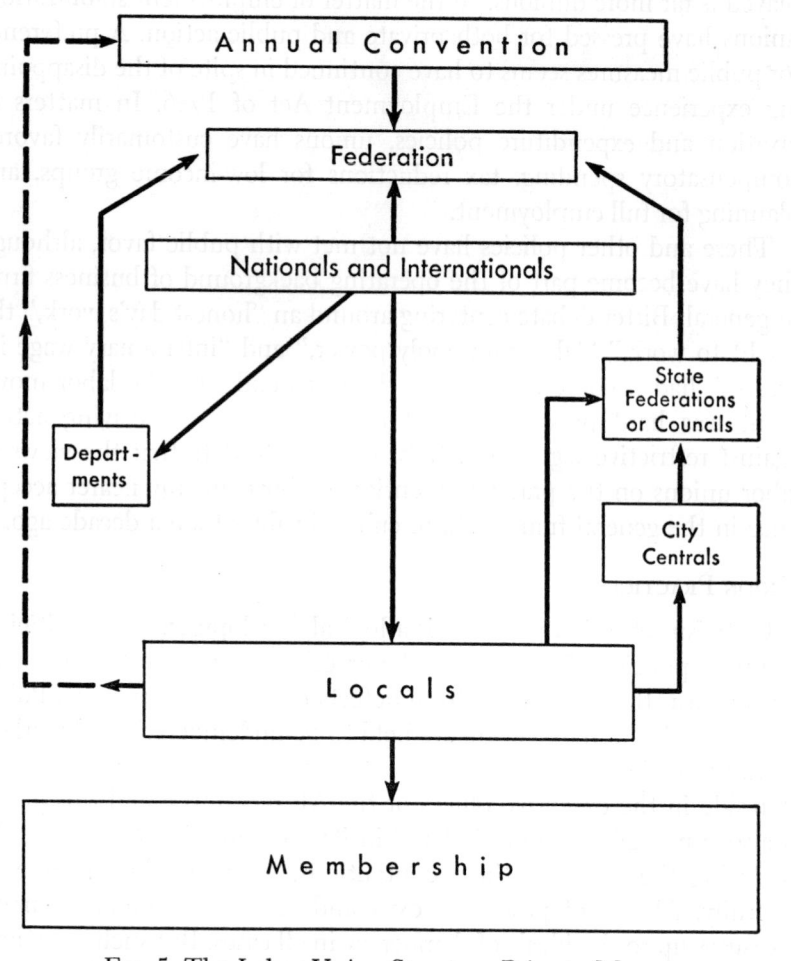

Fig. 5. The Labor Union Structure Prior to Merger.

nationals is analogous to the relationship of the states to the federal government under the Constitution. A chart will show how the several levels of the federation have been related to the membership and to each other. Figure 5 shows the organizational form which typified the AF of L and CIO prior to their merger.

It is hazardous to make any statements about the various levels of

the federation which would apply with equal validity to all of the units at any level below the federation level. The nationals may have comparatively few members or over a million,[5] and the policies of each union reflect the conditions peculiar to the industries from which the membership is drawn. Certain general functions can be assigned to each level of organization, however, keeping the limitations in mind. The federation is primarily concerned in political and public-relations activities. At the national level, the primary functions are organizing locals and assisting them in collective bargaining, deciding policy (ultimately through an annual convention), publishing news-papers, carrying on political activities, and related matters. Local unions are the first line of contact between the labor movement and the membership, and their activities are numerous. They collect dues, interpret national and federation policy for the membership (and communicate local preferences and feelings to the national and the federation), negotiate agreements, initiate grievance procedure, and generally are the "work horses" of the union structure. Intermediary stages of organization, such as departments and councils, carry on staff functions, and the state federations and councils attempt to represent the federation and the labor movement along lines paralleling the political organization of the nation. Conventions are the supreme policy-determining organs for both nationals and the federation. Delegates are apportioned to locals on the basis of paid-up member-ship, and an avenue for local participation in policy making is thus afforded. We shall see later that convention machinery and commit-tees not infrequently are controlled by the political organization assembled within the union by officials. A few union constitutions give broad policy-making powers to the chief official, but, in general, such powers are achieved through political organization not unlike that which achieves power for city bosses. Most constitutions thus provide a framework of operation in which democracy can operate—even as most municipal charters do—but bossism, racketeering, and dictatorship can make their way even in the most democratic struc-ture if the membership is apathetic. Disinterest and unwillingness to assume a responsible role on the part of the membership inevitably lead to someone's assuming interest and responsibility, for union busi-ness must get accomplished. In the wake of apathy, bosses will con-solidate their power, and few restraints exist on its irresponsible

---

[5] The five largest national unions have been the Teamsters, AF of L (1,300,000); the Automobile Workers, CIO (1,250,000); the Steel Workers, CIO (1,200,000); the Carpenters, AF of L (800,000); and the Machinists, AF of L (800,000).

exercise. American unions afford many examples of such practice. But they also afford shining examples of vigorous unions in which the membership is interested and holds the officialdom in check. The result has been a level of professional leadership responsible to the membership and required to win support for policies and practices by effective persuasion.

Within the union structure, there have developed, particularly since the war, tendencies which sap the vitality of the local organization. Collective bargaining has become an astonishingly complex operation as the scope of representation has moved to include whole industries. Economists, lawyers, statisticians, and professional-caliber negotiators must now be included in the bargaining situation, and they are reservoirs of talent too expensive for all but a few local organizations to support. Hence, the bargaining function has moved toward the national level and the consequence has been that the local's functions are reduced to less important matters. In the face of this situation, the membership loses interest, and the attendance at meetings, except when a matter of supreme importance is at stake, falls to a discouraging figure.[6] A small clique of interested persons is thus permitted to exercise authority over local matters. These criticisms of union government and policy determination require that the source of abuse—irresponsible citizenship—be recognized. However, the practices of unions have received the main scrutiny in the postwar period on the assumption that there is something inherent in the union organizational scheme which produces bossism and racketeering. Monopoly power, reckless and discriminatory financial practices, and susceptibility to subversive influences were the main charges made against the organizations. We shall examine each charge briefly in turn.

Before the end of World War II, the phrases "labor monopoly" and "laboristic economy" came into play as indictments of organized labor's power position. The factual basis for attributing a decisive or commanding position to labor unions in the economy is much exaggerated. In part, the fault lies with the term "labor monopoly," which has in no instance been defined according to traditional eco-

---

[6] Sayles and Strauss have reported that "attendance at regular meetings of large industrial unions averages from 2 percent to 8 percent of the total membership, whereas at extraordinary events, such as strike votes or contract negotiations, it averages from 40 percent to 80 percent. Leonard R. Sayles and George Strauss, "What the Worker Really Thinks of His Union," *Harvard Business Review*, May–June, 1953, p. 95.

nomic practice in evaluating the power of labor, and has been employed mainly by organizations hostile to labor which wished to capitalize on the opprobrium surrounding the term "monopoly" and, if possible, make labor organizations subject to the antitrust laws "like any other monopoly." Labor's chief weapon—the strike—is a double-edged weapon and it brings extreme suffering to union members if prolonged. Consequently, it is used only as a last resort and must be justified to the membership. Those who charge "labor monopoly" assume that strikes are glibly and frivolously entered into. The survival power of labor has been held by some critics to loom ominously over employers whose financial resources are "limited." Actually, the most superficial examination of the comparative financial power of corporations and unions reveals the wide disparity between unions and employers and the inferior position of unions. Probably, the total value (net worth) of all unions in the United States does not exceed $1 billion, of which a very small portion is in liquid funds. In 1950, only one union had assets as large as $50 million. However, the assets of sixty corporations each totaled in excess of $1 billion in 1950,[7] and 1284 corporations each had assets in excess of $50 million.[8] To the extent that "staying power" in a strike is measured by assets, the position of unions can only be called grossly inferior. It has also been charged that unemployment-insurance payments permit unions to prolong strikes, but, as we shall see in Chapter 15, no state permits its unemployment-insurance funds to be paid out to employees on strike. It is also contended that each corporation must individually stand off the massed power of unions. However, employers are in many cases better organized than unions, the typical bargaining session comes more and more to include trade-association representatives as well as employers, and some contracts are negotiated between employers' associations and labor unions. In another mistaken view, the power of labor organizations to deliver large blocs of votes in national elections is scored. However, the 1950 election of Senator Robert A. Taft in Ohio, in spite of labor-union opposition, and the election of President Eisenhower in 1952, also in spite of opposition, would seem to disprove the point. This result has been attributed to many factors (even the neutralizing of workmen's ballots by their wives' opposing ballots), but whatever the cause, labor's power in national politics is

[7] National City Bank of New York, *Monthly Letter*, June, 1952.
[8] U.S. Bureau of the Census, *Statistical Abstract of the United States*, 1954, p. 505.

far from decisive.[9] Labor-union officials are rarely elected to public office, and they share less in the distribution of patronage than other organized groups in the country. To these observations must be added the not inconsiderable handicap which labor has in access to the mass media. Newspapers and radio stations, primarily the latter, behave as business organizations and have their own share of labor problems. With rare exceptions, management's "press" is highly favorable and labor's "press" runs on a scale from suspicion to active hostility. Cultural factors, such as individualism, the Puritan ethic, and fear of centralized power, all operate in management's favor, making the public-relations job of labor extremely difficult. Finally, the "countervailing power" of employer's organizations, farm organizations, professional organizations, and, at times, veterans organizations all operate to limit the relative power of labor.

Intraunion power is another matter, and the concentration which has resulted from uncontested elections, the establishment of political machines, and domination by powerful personalities has caused anxiety even among labor's friends. But we have already located the source of the problem in the apathy of the membership.

Union finances have figured in a minor way in our discussion of relative power compared with corporations. Another phase of the financial-resources issue concerns the care with which funds are collected and accounted for. The size of dues and initiation fees has caused alarm, and the management of union funds has also been criticized. High dues, amounting to $10 or more monthly, and initiation fees, amounting to $500 and $1000, are known in some unions, but only in very small craft organizations and for extraordinary memberships which include death and pension benefits. Dues customarily average $1 to $3 per month, with the higher figure found mainly in the nationals formerly affiliated with the AF of L. Initiation fees are regularly $10 in the nationals formerly affiliated with the CIO and $25 or more in the former AF of L nationals. Defending the practice of charging initiation fees, unions cite the fact that a new member comes into the union and enjoys at once the benefits which older members secured at great sacrifices. The initiation fee is paid in recognition of this fact. Some initiation fees are set at a figure which limits the number of applicants. But, especially since the CIO was formed, the object of unions has been to expand their membership as much as

[9] For an excellent presentation of the labor-union side of the case, see Jack Kroll, "Labor's Political Role," *The Annals*, March, 1951.

possible and exclusion has been on the wane. The financial affairs of national unions are carried on with the same caution and according to the same accounting practices as in modern corporations. Certified public accountants audit the books regularly and every penny is accounted for to the membership in semiannual or quarterly reports. Bonding of officials who handle funds is a general practice. Locals carry on their financial affairs somewhat less carefully than the nationals, but the prevalent practice is for the nationals to audit the books of their locals and to encourage better accounting methods. Union treasuries have been mismanaged and welfare funds misappropriated in selected cases. But the source of the abuse again lies with the membership, who by their inattention and apathy permit questionable procedures to become established.

Subversive influences in unions have troubled students of the union movement since before World War I. The chief fear has been that agents of a pernicious social doctrine, whose interests only coincidentally matched those of American labor, would channel the idealism and energies of the labor movement to their own ends. It was inevitable that Communist agents would seek to influence the American labor movement, and the inconsistencies of public policy toward communism have nearly ensured that such efforts would in some instances succeed. Both the AF of L and the CIO have had Communist control problems, the latter especially, owing in part to John L. Lewis's "assimilation and control" policy with reference to communists in the CIO. The power position of the Soviet Union, and the gradual clarification that world revolution had survived the war alliance as a goal of international communism, led to counteraction by public and private groups in the United States. "Witch-hunters," operating in the post-World War I tradition, made sensational charges and were scorned. Then evidence of treachery was produced in the policy levels of the federal government itself, and the same charges became credible. Communists and their associates and sympathizers were publicly denounced without respect either for the circumstances or duration of the association. At its peak in 1953 and 1954, the most elementary considerations of constitutional rights and American fair play were roundly ignored in the opinion of many observers.

Soon after World War II, unions undertook to clean their own houses of Communists, a project which had been intensified in the AF of L from 1934 on. The activities of David Dubinsky, Philip

Murray, and Walter Reuther in winning control of their unions from Communist influence make one of the finest chapters in trade-union history. In the CIO, eleven unions under Communist influence or control were expelled in 1949 and 1950. Communist influence continued in some unions, and exists today, with the membership reluctant to change the situation. This is owing far less to Communist sympathies among the membership than to the fact that the membership is unwilling to heed the cry of "wolf" which has been so frequently made without basis in fact. Union members can recall that the labor movement, unemployment relief, social security, and related programs have uniformly drawn the cry of Communist influence from right-wing quarters. They have heard Philip Murray, Walter Reuther, and David Dubinsky called Reds and are inclined to discount the urgency of the present situation.

We might take notice, before we enter upon the substantive legislation passed in the postwar period to regulate labor, that dangerous tendencies are to be found in many union policies and practices, though scarcely in the measure which labor's opponents charge. Makework policies, bossism, irresponsibility in the possession of power, and other manifestations of immaturity are to be condemned where they are found. But it will be well to ponder the wisdom of enacting broadly based restrictive legislation and making basic alterations in the national labor policy to deal with scattered abuses and failings in union citizenship.

Amending Labor's Bill of Rights

Labor's protected position under the Wagner Act was little interfered with for twelve years in spite of a prevalent opinion even among labor's friends that the law should be amended when its object had been achieved, that is, when the unequal position of labor's bargaining power improved. Support for amendment was lacking, however, and when organized support was mustered in Congress it was thwarted by the Senate Labor Committee. In a previous chapter, we took notice that legislation seldom is enacted in response to social needs until the three branches of government have gained some sense of unanimity on the issue. When the need is recognized at last, the measures to cope with the situation are apt to be unnecessarily stringent if regulation is the course of action taken. The labor-management crises of 1946 were taken to mean that regulation of labor unions was long overdue. Union practices, as pictured in editorials,

speeches, and business-sponsored advertisements, were taken as immediate arguments for legislative action.

LEGISLATION

Bills introduced to meet the "labor question" increased markedly in number during 1946. Two of the bills were enacted into law, the Hobbs Act and the Lea Act. Only a veto by the President prevented the enactment of the Case Bill. This was fortunate in view of the fact that the provision for hearings on the bill had been inadequate and it was carelessly drafted. In 1946, the Republican party gained majorities in both Houses of Congress and the election result was considered a mandate from the public for restrictive labor legislation. Wage and salary controls were removed by executive order, and union pressure for wage increases was strong. A bill containing many features of the War Labor Disputes Act of 1943 [10] and the ill-fated Case Bill passed both Houses of Congress in the spring of 1947, was vetoed, and was passed again over the President's veto. The law, called the Labor-Management Relations Act, 1947, was an amendment to the National Labor Relations Act of 1935. However, the new amendment was a complicated piece of legislation as compared with the simple 1935 act, and it made basic changes in the nation's labor law.

The declaration of Congressional policy prefacing the new law stated: "Industrial strife which interferes with the normal flow of commerce and with the full production of articles and commodities for commerce, can be avoided or substantially minimized if employers, employees, and labor organizations each recognize under law one another's legitimate rights in their relation with each other, and above all recognize that neither party has any right in its relations with any other to engage in acts or practices which jeopardize the public health, safety, or interest."

This declaration was in accord with general feeling about the boundaries of labor-management conflict. In a following section, the law recognized the role of labor organizations in equalizing bargaining power and stabilizing wage rates as a beneficent factor in the economy. Title I amends the National Labor Relations Act, 1935, and the first section declared that "certain practices by some labor organizations have the intent or necessary effect of burdening or obstructing commerce." Other changes in the NLRA specified in the

---

[10] Basically, the bill drew on the Railway Labor Act of 1926 provisions for delay and fact finding in industrial disputes.

initial sections of the amendment enlarged the National Labor Relations Board to five members, and provided for the appointment of a General Counsel who would carry on investigations and prosecution activities that had formerly been vested in the Board. Section 7 stated a basic tenet of policy which pervades the whole law: "Employees shall have the right to self-organization, to form, join, or assist labor organizations, to bargain collectively . . . and shall also have the right to *refrain* from any and all such activities." We shall deal with the assumptions upon which this amendment of policy rests in a later section. The law did not prohibit employees from being required to join a union (after thirty days) as a condition of work, provided that such an agreement be negotiated by a labor organization certified by the Board as the exclusive bargaining agent and the Board decide (after a vote) that a majority of employees eligible to vote have authorized the labor organization to enter into such an agreement. Additional restraints were placed on union-security agreements by declaring that no such agreements were authorized if state laws prohibited them. In the same vein, the law declared in an intricately worded provision that "no employer shall justify any discrimination against an employee for *nonmembership* in a labor organization (A) if he has reasonable grounds for believing that such membership was not available to the employee on the same terms and conditions generally applicable to other members, or (B) if he has reasonable grounds for believing that membership was denied or terminated for reasons other than the failure of the employee to tender the periodic dues and the initiation fees uniformly required as a condition of acquiring or retaining membership." The unfair (employer) labor practices stated in the NLRA were modified slightly as indicated, but labor organizations were also restrained from certain unfair labor practices, including (1) restraining or coercing an employee in the exercise of the rights guaranteed to him in Section 7 (i.e., the right to refrain from labor-organization membership and activities); (2) causing or attempting to cause an employer to discriminate against an employee to whom membership has been denied for reasons other than failure to tender the periodic dues and the initiation fees uniformly required as a condition of acquiring or maintaining membership; (3) refusing to bargain collectively with the employer, provided he (or his agent) is the representative of his employees; (4) engaging in, or encouraging the employees of any employer to engage in, a strike or concerted refusal to handle materials, perform services, etc.,

where an object thereof is a boycott, furtherance of a jurisdictional dispute within the union, forcing recognition of the union other than a union certified by the Board, sympathy strike, reassignment of work tasks, or requiring an employer or self-employed person to join any labor or employer organization; (5) requiring of employees covered by a union-security agreement, authorized by the act, as a condition precedent to becoming a member, the payment of fees which the Board finds excessive or discriminating; and (6) forcing or requiring an employer to pay any money in the nature of an exaction for services which are not performed or not to be performed.[11] All of these restraints are in the spirit of that part of Section 7 which guarantees the right of employees to refrain from labor-organization membership and activities. A provision was added to Section 8 stating that expressions of any views, arguments, or opinions, or the dissemination thereof, whether in written, printed, graphic, or visual form, shall not constitute or be evidence of an unfair labor practice if they contain no threat of reprisal or force or promise of benefit. The purpose of the addition was to give employers an opportunity to persuade employees of their viewpoints in labor-management matters. Under the NLRA such practices would have constituted an unfair labor practice. Under Section 9, dealing with representation, other changes were made in the NLRA. An employee was permitted to adjust grievances with an employer directly without the intervention of the collective-bargaining representative, provided that the adjustment of the grievance was not inconsistent with the terms of the collective-bargaining agreement and provided the union representative was given an opportunity to be present at the adjustment. In an effort to regulate union internal government, the law required that no cases coming before the Board (including representation cases, union-shop elections, or charges of unfair labor practices initiated by a union) be processed unless specified financial and organizational reports had been filed with the Board and each officer of the union, and any national or international with which it is affiliated, files, or has filed within the past twelve months, an affidavit that he is not a member of the Communist party or affiliated with such party, and does not believe in, and is not a member of or supports any organization that believes in or teaches, the overthrow of the United States Government by force or by any illegal or unconstitutional methods. Under Section 9, employers as well as

[11] The unlawful practices listed here are based on a summary of the LMRA published in the *Monthly Labor Review*, July, 1947, pp. 58–59.

employees were permitted to file petitions for elections to certify (or decertify) a collective-bargaining representative. Employees on strike who were not eligible for reinstatement (by reason of having committed an unfair labor practice, or having struck within the sixty-day-notice period, etc.) were made ineligible to vote in NLRB elections. Other amendments to the NLRA dealt with administrative matters. The Board was empowered to authorize state labor-relations boards to take jurisdiction in some cases. At its discretion the Board might obtain an injunction against continuation of activities after an unfair-labor-practices complaint had been filed.

The remaining four titles of the LMRA deal with restrictions on dispute settlement, and only the major provisions of Titles II and III will be summarized. Title II transferred the United States Concilation Service out of the Department of Labor, creating in its stead an independent agency, the Federal Mediation and Conciliation Service. Procedures to be followed in the event of national-emergency disputes also were established. While declaring that "sound and stable industrial peace . . . can most satisfactorily be secured by the settlement of issues between employers and employees through the process of conference and collective bargaining between employers and the representatives of their employees," the LMRA provided elaborate machinery restricting reliance on private bargaining. Whenever in the opinion of the President of the United States a threatened or actual strike or lockout would, if permitted to occur or to continue, imperil the national health or safety, he was empowered to appoint a board to inquire into the issues. The report of the board had to be made public. Upon receiving a report from the board, the President was free to direct the Attorney General to obtain an injunction from any district court of the United States. At the end of the sixty-day period following the issuance of the restraining order (unless the dispute had been settled, of course), the board of inquiry was required to report to the President (1) the current position of the parties to the dispute and the efforts which had been made for settlement, (2) a statement by each party as to its position, and (3) a statement of the employer's last offer of settlement. The report then had to be made public, and the National Labor Relations Board was required within the succeeding fifteen days to take a secret ballot of the employees of each employer involved in the dispute on the question of whether they wished to accept the final offer of settlement as stated by the employer. Within five days, a report of the ballot had to be

filed with the Attorney General, whereupon the injunction would be removed. The President at this point had to file a complete report of all proceedings with the Congress together with his recommendations.

Title III permitted unions to be sued in the district courts for breach of contract. The union could be sued as an entity, although any money judgment could not be collected except from union assets. That is, individual members were not financially liable in such judgments. Broadly stated restrictions were placed on the transfer of any "money or other thing of value" between employers and employee representatives except for designated purposes, which include welfare and trust funds. Boycotts, sympathy strikes, and jurisdictional strikes were made unlawful and provision was made for damage suits.

Title III also prohibited contributions by corporations and labor organizations in connection with a federal election, amended existing legislation to prohibit "expenditures" as well as contributions, and applied the prohibition to primaries, caucuses, and conventions as well as elections.

Finally, employees of the United States or any agency thereof were prohibited from striking under penalties of discharge and forfeiture of Civil Service status.

ASSUMPTIONS OF THE LABOR-MANAGEMENT RELATIONS ACT

It will already be apparent that the provisions of the LMRA relate closely to those criticisms of union policies and practices which we discussed in the previous section. We shall be able to analyze the act only in the most general way here because it is so complex. Certainly, its most important single feature is the statement in Section 7 that employees shall have the right to *refrain* from union membership and activities. Many of the restraints and regulations which follow that section are based on the asumption that employees had been forced to join unions against their will; that the freely determined preferences of employees would be to remain outside labor organizations and bargain individually rather than collectively with their employers. There occur throughout the law provisions which assume that union officials had not properly reflected the wishes of the membership. This can be seen in the special elections required prior to the adoption of union security provisions and for the release of employees from such provisions, in the employer being prohibited from discriminating against an employee for *nonmembership*, in the addition of labor organizations within the unfair-labor-practices specifications under

Section 8, and in the permission granted in Section 9 for an employee to adjust his grievances directly with the employer without recourse to collective bargaining. The odious requirement that union officials certify their loyalty to the United States when employers were exempt from any such requirement unjustifiably lent credibility to reckless charges concerning loyalty of labor leaders which were being made in 1946 and have been made since.

The prohibition of political expenditures seemed to rest on the assumption that labor's political power was of great magnitude. Students of political science criticized the provision on the grounds that political activity should be encouraged rather than restricted.

An implicit assumption throughout the LMRA was that unions had become too strong and had put employers at a disadvantage. We have discussed the factual basis for this allegation previously. On the strength of the assumption, however, it was concluded in the act that union power should be scaled down through restraints on the right to strike, union security agreements, financial policies, etc. In view of the preference stated within the act for collective bargaining, the extreme care taken to promote individual bargaining through the provisions of the act is difficult to understand.

Finally, the intrusion of government into the most inner chambers of collective-bargaining procedure reveals scant attention to the lessons of labor-management-relations experience. Under the NLRA, the government took the side of labor, determined the bargaining agent, and required employers to bargain collectively. At the bargaining table, the intervention of government ceased. A healthy situation developed in that management and labor had to solve the problems by themselves. Under the LMRA, government power is committed on neither side. Equal government authority is available to certify or decertify a union. But the government's authority does not end at the bargaining table as before; prohibitions abound concerning what may or may not be included in the collective agreement. Dues and initiation fees, featherbedding provisions, union security clauses, inclusion of foremen and professional employees, and securing employer recognition of a union where another union already has been certified by the National Labor Relations Board within the year are some of the restraints imposed by the act on the contents of agreements.

Our discussion thus far has been critical of the assumptions upon which the LMRA was based. Consideration must be given to the refusal of labor officials to coöperate in framing the law, however, as

part of the explanation for its being so closely related to criticisms of union policies and practices as they were interpreted by employer organizations at the close of the war. It would also be shortsighted to overlook the substantial provisions to improve labor-management relations which were incorporated in the law. The requirement under Title I that unions bargain collectively in good faith with employers, even as employers were required to do, secured general approval from students of labor relations, as did the inclusion of union responsibility for unfair practices. The liability of unions for suit upon breach of contract also was generally approved. But the mistaken assumptions upon which the law rests led most students to urge early amendment or reënactment.

The Movement to Amend the Labor Management Relations Act

Few pieces of legislation have produced the bitterness which followed in the wake of the LMRA. Labor leaders denounced it as a "slave-labor law" and demanded its outright repeal, while employers' associations hailed it as a long-overdue first step. Several conclusions were justified by the first year under the act. In the first place, it did not prevent labor-management strife from interfering with the operations of the economy, nor did it reduce the number of work stoppages. Furthermore, it greatly increased the load of cases referred to the National Labor Relations Board, and some elections, for example, the union-shop elections, proved completely unnecessary since the results were a foregone conclusion. During the first year of the act, the ballots ran more than 95 percent in favor of the union shop. Emergency strikes were not stopped by the act. As a matter of fact, the emergency provisions over the five-year period 1948–1953 were used in but twelve cases, and in four of these strikes began after the law was involved.[12] The injunction period of sixty days and the additional period of twenty days required in the act were offered as a "cooling-off" period. But, far from "cooling off" the antagonisms relating to a dispute, they have aggravated the situation and permitted grievances to grow in importance while the disputants each build storm cellars for an all-out upheaval. The provision for employee ballots on the employer's last offer has resulted in uniform rejection, as students of labor relations had predicted. Moreover, the provision that striking workers not eligible for reinstatement could not vote in National Labor Relations

[12] See Sumner H. Slichter, "Revision of the Taft-Hartley Act," *Quarterly Journal of Economics*, May, 1953, p. 170, for a thorough discussion of the case for amendments.

Board elections left open the possibility that employers would employ strikebreakers, petition for an election to be held by the NLRB, and break the striking union by obtaining its decertification.

The LMRA did not result in any of the disasters for the labor movement which had been predicted by labor leaders. Wages rose, benefits were negotiated on an increasing scale, and employers with well-established union relationships spurned the provisions in most cases. Petitions for relief coming before the NLRB were initiated by the union in four out of five cases. Evidence also indicates that "consent" actions resulting from conferences by regional officials of the NLRB and parties to a dispute became much more common, particularly in representation elections.[13] But it does not follow that the law has been without serious effects, nor that its possible threat to the labor movement exists only in the imaginations of union leaders. During the period in which the law has been in operation, economic conditions have afforded generally full employment. It must also be remembered that the law has been neglected in large measure. Under prolonged recession and conditions of less-than-full employment, the law has features which, apart from being unnecessary to protect the public, might result in actual harm. There is uniform agreement among students of the question that the organization of southern industry and perhaps some other groups has been rendered much more difficult by the LMRA. That the general slowing down of the growth rate of the two major federations is in any significant way related to the act, however, has been disclaimed by most labor economists. The overriding consideration has been that the principal "hunting grounds" have already been organized.

It is the prevailing opinion that labor leaders badly managed their approach to securing legal changes in those threatening parts of the act. In the framing of the law, they had refused to coöperate, and when the issue of amendments came up in the year following its enactment, they refused again to coöperate. The general labor position was "complete repeal or nothing." The latter option came close to being an accurate description of the results obtained in the end. A wholly unrealistic view of its political power probably lay at the bottom of labor's ill-considered position. November, 1948, saw the election of Harry S. Truman to the Presidency, to the complete surprise of employers' organizations and their allies. Labor leaders rejoiced over the

[13] Sidney C. Sufrin and Robert C. Sedgwick, *Labor Law*, New York, Thomas Y. Crowell Company, 1954, p. 274.

exhibition of their power in the election. President Truman urged reënactment of the Wagner Act with minor changes, and the Secretary of Labor assured labor leaders that the law probably would be repealed in an early action of the Congress. Labor's position became more adamant and plans were laid to continue hunting the heads of those who were not labor's friends. Meanwhile, the principal sponsor of the LMRA, Senator Taft, prepared twenty-eight amendments which experience seemed to counsel should be made in the act.[14] The amendments were largely designed to meet labor's objections to the act and provided for modifications in the use of injunctions, the restrictions on election participation by certain strikers, the ban on secondary boycotts, election procedures to obtain the union shop, and restrictions on funds used in election campaigns. A bill providing these changes passed the Senate. Labor leaders held out for repeal, however, with the consequence that only one minor change (a 1951 amendment removing the union-shop-election requirement) was made during the entire tenure of the Democratic administration. In his bid for election, Mr. Eisenhower moderated considerably the approach that had been associated with the Republican Party in labor legislation by agreeing that the Taft-Hartley Act contained provisions that "could be used to break unions." Following his election, he appointed to his Cabinet a Democrat with known "anti-Taft-Hartley" convictions. The State of the Union Message in 1953 referred to the act only in declaring that it should be amended to produce a law "that merits the respect and support of both labor and management." Hearings in 1953 concerning the nature of provisions resulted in diametrically opposed suggestions being submitted by the employer and labor groups. The National Association of Manufacturers and the Chamber of Commerce of the U.S. declared that the LMRA should be strengthened with respect to secondary boycotts and jurisdictional strikes, and amendments added restricting industry-wide strikes for whatever cause and outlawing the union shop. Amendments urged by the AF of L and the CIO called for legalization of closed-shop agreements, elimination of all injunctions, abolition of non-Communist oaths, repeal of the "free speech" guarantees for employers, and reliance on persuasion and conciliation measures in national-emergency strikes. Nineteen

[14] See *Congressional Record*, June 28, 1949, Eighty-first Congress, First Session, pp. 8506–8508, 8513. Also see the proposals for amendment made by the New York State Bar Association, *Congressional Record*, March 18, 1949, Eighty-first Congress, First Session, pp. 2748–2751.

amendments were drawn up during the summer of 1953 by the President in consultation with his advisors, presumably for presentation in the State of the Union Message. Disclosure of the amendments [15] caused consternation among employers' associations, and when the message was delivered in January, 1954, its provisions were far less favorable to labor than had been the earlier draft. The President's message to Congress included some of the recommendations found in the earlier draft, for example, amendments permitting unions representing employees in the construction, amusement, and maritime industries to make prehiring agreements initially without certification elections; permitting a union-shop agreement to be negotiated calling for compulsory membership after seven days instead of thirty days; applying the common-law rules of "agency" to rule out a union's being held responsible for the acts of an employee solely on the basis of his union membership; making discretionary the requirement that the NLRB obtain an injunction in an emergency dispute; modifying the economic-strike provisions by prohibiting the consideration of an employer for a representation election for four months after the commencement of the strike; and restricting the definition of secondary boycott to permit strikes against employers who were assisting struck employers by taking their work on a "farming-out" basis. Other provisions had not been offered in the earlier draft, including recommendations that the states assume an increasing role in labor disputes, including emergency strikes; government-supervised elections be held in which employees would cast secret ballots to determine whether or not to strike; reiteration of the "free-speech" provision; and provisions for recommendations to be made by boards of inquiry under the emergency-disputes-settlement machinery. Congress responded by leaving the LMRA unamended for another year. A request by the President for enactment of the amendments in his January, 1955, message also had failed to produce any results by midyear, a not unexpected turn of events since the Democratic party had won control of Congress. Meanwhile labor leaders became alarmed over threats to

---

[15] The amendments had the approval of the Secretary of Labor, a former trade unionist, and among them were such provisions as removal of the certification elections in local and intermittent industries, with permission to negotiate agreements calling for a modified closed shop; removal of the requirement that state laws take preference over national laws when anti-union-shop considerations were concerned; modification of the emergency-strike-injunction provisions to make NLRB action discretionary; protection of strikers in economic strikes by prohibiting certification elections for four months following the commencement of the strike; reduction of the sixty-day-notice period to thirty days; and continuation of check-off agreements until revoked rather than for one year.

the labor movement from laws enacted by state legislatures to curb union activities and from the fact that three members of the National Labor Relations Board were appointees of President Eisenhower.

That the NLRB was willing to modify the harsh spirit of the Labor Management Relations Act was shown, however, in decisions requiring employers to make payroll data available to unions to assist them in bargaining and requiring employers to bargain on certain employer-inaugurated benefit plans.

State Labor Legislation

Following the passage of the National Labor Relations Act in 1935, many states, as we have seen, passed "little Wagner Acts" duplicating its major provisions. Similar experience followed the Labor Management Relations Act, 1947. Many states amended their labor legislation in the spirit of the LMRA. The objective of state legislation has been to regulate strike action and prohibit union security agreements. The latter laws have been the focus of controversy and are called (by their proponents) "right-to-work laws." The movement for regulation began in 1939, when Pennsylvania, Minnesota, and Michigan passed restrictive laws, but its pace was accelerated by the same forces which brought about revision of the National Labor Relations Act. Virtually all states at the present time have added some form of control to the generous provisions that had been found in the "little Wagner Acts." In fourteen states, legislation more stringent in some respects than Taft-Harley was enacted. In sixteen states, compulsory union membership in any form has been outlawed.[16]

The form of strike control legislated by the states varies widely. At the moderate end of the scale are provisions for advance filing of strike notices, usually with the state industrial commissioner. Michigan, Minnesota, and Missouri have favored this plan. At the other extreme of the scale, some states require compulsory arbitration and prohibit strike action. Indiana and Wisconsin first enacted such laws, followed by Florida, Pennsylvania, and Nebraska. The Wisconsin law was invalidated by the U.S. Supreme Court in 1951, and the other laws then ceased to operate. From 1948 to 1953, the tide was reversed and some of the states repealed their laws. In 1953, however, the movement for control was renewed, chiefly in the South. Experience under the laws, particularly those calling for elections in case of strike, has conformed

[16] W. R. Brown, "State Experience in Defending the Right to Work," *Proceedings of the Academy of Political Science*, May, 1954, p. 32.

to experience under the national law; decisions to strike have been uniformly upheld by the vast majority of the membership.

The state laws which contain the most restrictive provisions are found in agricultural states, largely in the South. Still, the group engaged in intrastate commerce, which potentially falls under the laws, may amount to 15,000,000 or more and is confined to industries which we have previously described as having relatively low standards with respect to wages, hours, and working conditions. In the South, the effect of the laws could be to perpetuate the feebleness of union power in some industries. The most important criticism is that the laws are based on erroneous assumptions. On balance, the state legislation must bear the same indictment as the LMRA; it approaches the problem of labor-management conflict with legal weapons and assumes that superior strength and ability to do harm lie with labor unions, and that unions do not represent the wishes of the membership.

Achievements of the Labor Movement Since 1945 in Wages, Hours, and Benefits

Frequently, criticism of the new national labor policy inaugurated with the Labor Management Relations Act, 1947, is countered by its advocates with evidence indicating an improvement since 1947 in wage-and-hour conditions as well as other benefits. That improvements have taken place is beyond argument, of course, but it does not at all follow that national and state legislation designed to curb unions is therefore less objectionable. A period of full employment offers opportunities for labor organizations to improve working conditions, and this is especially true of the conditions which have existed since 1945. Consumer demand for products of industry has been extremely active, and industries have chosen to settle wage and benefit matters rather than risk prolonged strikes. In 1950, the outbreak of hostilities in Korea produced a semiwar economy with government boards to settle wage and benefit matters. Whether a different set of demand conditions would have brought the same wage and hour conditions is debatable.

WAGES

In Chapter 9, we had an opportunity to analyze the income position of American families and concluded that their position had not improved in any substantial degree from 1944 to 1953 if increases in taxes

and prices were considered. Those who argue that wages have kept ahead of prices over the period since 1944 are generally basing their arguments on *wage rates,* not take-home pay.[17] It is the latter, obviously, which is important as an index of improvement. Table 49 presents data (some of which were presented in Chapter 9) showing the trend of net spendable weekly earnings from 1945 to 1954.

TABLE 49. Average Gross Weekly Earnings and Net Spendable Weekly Earnings, 1941–1954 [a]

| | Gross Weekly Earnings | | Net Spendable Weekly Earnings | | | |
| | | | Worker with No Dependents | | Worker with 3 Dependents | |
Year	Amount	Index (1947–1949 = 100)	Current Dollars	1947–1949 Dollars	Current Dollars	1947–1949 Dollars
1941	$29.58	55.9	$28.05	$44.59	$29.28	$46.55
1942	36.65	69.2	31.77	45.58	36.28	52.05
1943	43.14	81.5	36.01	48.66	41.39	55.93
1944	46.08	87.0	38.29	50.92	44.06	58.59
1945	44.39	83.8	36.97	48.08	42.74	55.58
1946	43.82	82.8	37.72	45.23	43.20	51.80
1947	49.97	94.4	42.76	44.77	48.24	50.51
1948	54.14	102.2	47.43	46.14	53.17	51.72
1949	54.92	103.7	48.09	47.24	53.83	52.88
1950	59.33	112.0	51.09	49.70	57.21	55.65
1951	64.71	122.2	54.04	48.68	61.28	55.21
1952	67.97	128.4	55.66	49.04	63.62	56.05
1953	71.69	135.4	58.54	51.17	66.58	58.20
1954 [b]	72.08	135.8	59.34	51.90	66.80	58.20

[a] Production workers in manufacturing. Net spendable earnings are obtained by deducting from gross weekly earnings, social security, and income taxes for which the specified worker is liable. The amount of the income-tax liability depends on the number of dependents supported by the worker as well as on the level of his gross income. Net spendable earnings have been computed, therefore, for two groups of workers: (1) those with no dependents, and (2) those with three dependents. Adjustment of disposable weekly earnings for price fluctuations was accomplished with the Consumers Price Index, 1947–1949 base.

[b] Data for 1954 are the means of monthly data as reported for the twelve months beginning with February, 1954, and ending with January, 1955.

Source: U.S. Department of Labor, *Monthly Labor Review,* May, 1955, p. 619.

The table shows clearly that weekly "spendable" earnings in constant (1947–1949) dollars have increased only very slowly in the postwar period. In 1946, the gross amount of weekly earnings actually decreased as compared with the previous year, owing to a reduction in hours of work. The upward movement of net spendable earnings has been interrupted several times. The data in the table are for production workers in manufacturing, whose wages tend to be higher than

[17] See, for example, Sumner H. Slichter, "Wage Policies Since World War II," *Commercial and Financial Chronicle,* December 4, 1952.

the national average. It will be recalled from Chapter 9 that sizable differences exist in the level of earnings among geographical locations. Also, weekly earnings vary considerably from industry to industry within a given geographical area.

Legislation affecting wages was largely ineffective over the period 1944–1954 because wage levels were considerably in excess of the minima required by national and state laws. We have noted previously that the minimum wage under the Fair Labor Standards Act was raised in 1949 to 75 cents. Further amendment was urged by the President in his January, 1955, address to the Congress. His recommendation was for a 90-cent hourly minimum and an increase in the coverage of the act. Action on the request was completed at midyear and an hourly minimum of $1 was provided, but with no increase in coverage.

State laws have been improved to give wider coverage and also higher minima since 1945. Up to 1949, only five states had made their minimum-wage provisions applicable to men. In 1955, however, at least twelve states introduced minimum-wage laws covering men as well as women and minors. Three of these proposals were enacted, bringing to eleven (eight states and three territories) the jurisdictions having minimum-wage laws that cover both men and women.[18] Thirty jurisdictions now have minimum-wage legislation on their statute books, and, although no state has enacted a law since 1941, wage orders have enabled many states to increase both the coverage and the minimum level. Of the more than fifty orders issued by sixteen jurisdictions between July 1, 1950, and January 1, 1953, two-thirds have been for the major trade and service occupations.[19] Thus, the effect of the state wage orders is likely to be felt in the industries where wage levels tend to be substandard. The minimum level established by wage orders in New York ranged from 65 to 80 cents an hour in July, 1955. With a higher national minimum, state minima probably will also be increased.

HOURS

Since we have already discussed legislative limitations on hours, we shall deal only with recent trends in hours here. During World War II, hours of work increased markedly, rising from 38.1 in 1940 (pro-

[18] Connecticut, Idaho, Massachusetts, New Hampshire, New Mexico, New York, Rhode Island, Wyoming, Alaska, Hawaii, and Puerto Rico.

[19] U.S. Department of Labor, *State Minimum Wage Laws and Orders*, Women's Bureau Bulletin No. 247, 1953, p. 12.

duction workers in manufacturing) to 45.2 in 1944. A decrease took place as the need for war production ended, and the average for the years 1946, 1947, and 1948 was 40.3 hours per week. In 1949, the average fell below 40 (39.2) for the first time in almost ten years, but an increase to 40.5 occurred in the following year. With the outbreak of the Korean hostilities, and renewed need for war production, the average weekly hours increased to 43.6 in 1951, 43.9 in 1952, and 43.3 in 1953. The end of hostilities and falling levels of economic activity brought a reduction in hours to 40.8 in 1954.

In many industries outside manufacturing, the weekly hours of work had been cut to 37.5 and even 35 hours by 1954. Furthermore, holidays and vacations have improved and the effect has been to reduce the actual hours of work by considerable amounts for the average employee. The Executive Council of the AF of L in September, 1954, proposed a reduction in weekly hours of work to 35, making the payment of overtime wage rates mandatory for hours in excess of 35 rather than the present 40. There is no doubt that pressures for reduction in the weekly hours of work have been great, and increasing attention has been directed toward the consequences of reductions below 40. The issues are too complex for us to treat them here. But students of industrial relations tend to be suspicious of claims that improvements in productivity would accompany further decreases in weekly hours of work. The earlier arguments put forth by proponents of the shorter work week stressed the value of leisure time in developing an informed and responsible citizenry. One indictment of the movement for shorter hours, however, has been the failure of any such improvement to take place. In few countries of the world has the use made of leisure time been more widely condemned than in the United States, the world's worst example of "creeping spectatoritis."

BENEFITS

Our discussion in Chapter 9 dealt with some aspects of the "fringe benefits," although not with the extent of the benefits or the scope which they have assumed in recent years. The Bureau of Labor Statistics survey of seventeen labor markets provides an indication of the characteristics and coverage of fringe benefits.[20] The Bureau studies establishment practices in seventeen labor markets in connection with retirement plans, life insurance, accidental death and dismember-

[20] U.S. Department of Labor, *Wage Differences and Establishment Practices*, Bureau of Labor Statistics Bulletin No. 1173, 1954.

ment, sickness and accident, hospitalization, surgical, medical, and catastrophe insurance, as well as sick-leave arrangements. Only about 5 percent of the approximately 6,000,000 plant and office workers in the establishments studied were not covered by any type of private health, insurance, or pension arrangements (financed at least in part by the employer).[21] About nine out of every ten plant and office workers were covered by life-insurance policies paid for in part or in whole by employer contributions.[22] Accidental-death-and-dismemberment insurance was provided by establishments employing slightly less than half of all plant and office employees; but only a few (2 percent) were covered by catastrophe insurance.[23] Retirement or pension plans (exclusive of those provided by law) were available to six of every ten employees included in the survey.[24] About half of the employees surveyed were eligible to receive sick-leave benefits, the vast majority receiving full pay.[25] Differences were reported between plant and office employees, but, except for pension plans, sickness-and-accident insurance, and sick leave, the coverage was essentially the same.

Other benefits studied included paid holidays and paid vacations. More than four-fifths of the plant and office workers, except for a few in small nonoffice jobs in the South, received these benefits. Both plant and office workers commonly became eligible for a vacation of one week with pay after one year of service, two weeks after five years, and three or more weeks after fifteen years of service. The proportions differed significantly among the seventeen markets.

There is every reason to expect that the kinds of benefits discussed above will become more widespread in the future. The benefits are costly to the employer, but the cost is deductible from business income taxes in most instances and the advantages to the employer in reducing turnover and maintaining efficiency are substantial.

Current Trends in the Labor Movement

At the present time, American labor leaders have departed almost completely from the position of antistatism which Samuel Gompers fastened on the labor movement. The realization has developed that permanent achievements for labor must be sought in the field of social

21 *Ibid.*, p. 23.
22 *Ibid.*, p. 23.
23 *Ibid.*, p. 23.
24 *Ibid.*, p. 23.
25 *Ibid.*, p. 25.

legislation. On December 5, 1955, the merger of the AF of L with the CIO was formally concluded, and one factor stimulating that achievement has been a feeling that labor was doing a second-rate job before legislative bodies.

The federation is devoting much more energy than formerly to the activities of state legislatures, which have enacted some of the most restrictive legislation in the postwar period. An added incentive has been produced by the supplemental unemployment-benefits plans negotiated by the United Automobile Workers. Whether or not such benefits may be received concurrently with state unemployment-insurance benefits turns on decisions of the states. Also, all forms of social legislation are being pressed more vigorously by the federation at the state and national levels. In general, labor organizations constitute the chief pressure system for social legislation at the present time.

The goals toward the achievement of which the merged federations will concentrate their future efforts include the control of automation (which provoked a CIO conference in April, 1955), extension of social insurance, adoption of private and public measures to gain employment security, and encouragement of collective bargaining on an increasingly wider geographic scale. In each instance, success will depend largely on the degree of acceptance which labor-organization policies and practices can gain with the public at large.

The American Labor Movement in World War II and the Postwar Reaction: Concluding Remarks

We have reviewed the major elements in the history of the American labor movement since World War II. Several observations can be made in connection with postwar experience. In the first place, public impatience with union policies and practices was largely ignored by the unions until it had expressed itself in law. Second, union leaders failed to coöperate in the revision of national labor policy which began with the close of hostilities, and have failed to coöperate in amending the national labor policy adopted at that time. Third, the coincidence of concern over subversion with the postwar reaction against labor-union practices made the task of defense virtually impossible for labor organizations, which were already condemned in the public mind. Finally, the political developments which began with the election of a Republican President and Congress in 1952 have lent support to the belief that labor's position in the social system will not be seriously damaged regardless of which political party is in power;

however, labor cannot expect substantial support for new programs from the President and the Congress under such conditions.

Labor legislation at the state and national levels since the war has rested on assumptions that are not supported in fact and are alien to the convictions held by students of labor-management relations. The bases of labor-management peace are assumed in postwar legislation to be legal and capable of being strengthened through the compulsive force of law. While the "human relations" approach has gained increasing respectability in industrial relations since the war, the legal context in which it is applied has constituted an antithesis of its point of view.

For solving the basic problem of labor-union responsibility, the outlook is not encouraging. We have traced most of the abuses of labor-union power to their source in membership apathy, and the conditions which promote such apathy are likely to increase rather than abate in the future. The real need, therefore, is for a strengthening of good citizenship at the local-union level, a need that cannot be legislated and requires for its realization a basic reorientation in public attitudes toward unions as a first step. Responsible citizenship is not the outcome of simple conviction, nor is it apt to be achieved through exhortation. Deliberate instruction and practice in the home and school planned to implant respect for its essentials remain the only long-run methods of building responsible democratic citizenship.

SELECTED REFERENCES

Bloom, Gordon F., and Northrup, Herbert R., Economics of Labor Relations, Revised Edition, Homewood, Ill., Richard D. Irwin, 1954.

Peterson, Florence, Survey of Labor Economics, New York, Harper & Brothers, 1947.

Reynolds, Lloyd G., and Shister, Joseph, Job Horizons: A Study of Job Satisfaction and Labor Mobility, New York, Harper & Brothers, 1949.

PART V

SOCIAL ASSISTANCE AND SOCIAL INSURANCE

chapter 14

Social Assistance and Social Insurance: Background and Philosophy

All over the world there has arisen the necessity for taking—even in "underdeveloped" countries—public action against the dependency which may engulf families in modern industrialized life. Poverty, the sheer inability of a family adequately to provide the essentials of life, is as old as man himself. But only in comparatively recent times has the threat of financial insecurity become acute, and "no money," as Bakke has put it, meant "no food, clothes, and rent." [1] Still, in the face of widespread dependency obvious from casual observation and documented by the reports of numerous commissions, public programs have been slow to develop. Some efforts to minimize the anguish which a family need bear as the result of old-age dependency, unemployment, sickness, and disability appeared before the present century, but the acceptance of social security as a primary aim of society to be ensured through the activities of government has not yet been achieved. The concept of "stopgap" aid for families in desperate need has lingered on in many countries.

We shall approach the adoption of legislative measures to gain social security by building on the material already analyzed in preceding chapters. Particularly pertinent will be Chapter 9, which evaluated the income-security situation for American families of which these chapters to follow are fundamentally a part. In keeping with earlier presentations, the actual provisions of legislation will be subordinated to the more enduring questions of growth and processes.

[1] E. Wight Bakke, *Insurance or Dole?*, New Haven, Yale University Press, 1935, p. 9.

World Backgrounds of the Movement for
Social-Security Legislation

Chapter 3 traced the stages whereby our social conscience has matured to the level where we must seek means of ameliorating human
suffering when it is brought to our attention. The growth of social
thought has a counterpart in public action. But the record, however
fascinating, would be long and only incidentally useful in the present
discussion. We are concerned simply with surveying the major developments in the movements for social security. The object is to
point out how belated were the American efforts in this respect and
to suggest the kinds of experiences upon which the United States
might draw when the necessity for legislation finally was recognized.

Recall that the state was formed and man began his political life so
that "social security" might be achieved for the group. We mean that
the marshaling of group efforts had been inadequate and had exposed
the group to insecurities connected with the needs for subsistence,
safety, etc. This close connection of the state with group welfare has
predominated in man's political life for more than ten centuries. But
many forces led to the castigation of the destitute in the group as the
territorial basis of political activity widened and class distinctions
sharpened. Accordingly care of the dependent fell upon those who
would provide aid out of various motives and impulses.

In the teachings of the Hebrew prophets and Jesus, brotherhood
and mutual service were made the highest objects of personal duty,
and the requirements laid down for the wealthy were no less than
that they dedicate all of their resources to the relief of the downtrodden. The Greeks and the Romans employed various forms of
public relief, including the distribution of grain, the granting of pensions, and even slavery and euthanasia. But the chief means of relief,
when the family system failed to care adequately for some of its members, seems to have been through private almsgiving.

As Christianity increased its influence, the practice of private almsgiving received inducements beyond the fulfillment of compassion:
failing in deeds of mercy and compassion, one could not hope to enter
Heaven. With the organization of the Church on the Roman imperial
model, the resources to care for the dependent were vastly increased,
although the practices of the Church in many ways aggravated the
very miseries which it sought through its hospitals, orphanages, and
poor relief to alleviate. Forces which brought ultimate limitation on

the Church's role in society—the rise of commerce and national states—also affected poor relief and related services. Secularization was under way in the sixteenth century, and in the eighteenth individualism added its force to the movement. Local civil authorities took on the obligations of poor relief with somewhat less tender mercies than the Church had exercised, since the blessings won by the benefactors of the poor came to count for less than the worthiness of the recipient. Upon the recipient fell an increasingly stern requirement that he use his personal resources to the limit. Recent centuries have seen the near sanctification of individualism and limitations on "government interference" regardless of the cause. But the laissez-faire policy in caring for indigence was waning by the end of the nineteenth century as country after country began to substitute public pensions and benefits for the security of agricultural life, which had passed so quickly before industrialization. Significantly, the states where laissez faire made the least impression pioneered the movement for such legislation.

In Britain, the fortress of laissez faire, relief of the dependent elements in the society took a form which greatly influenced American practice until very recent times. At first, the object of public action was simply to immobilize paupers whose itineracy was a threat to the citizenry. Later, the scope of relief broadened to include some allowances to indigent persons. The development of the system was by fits and starts, and into the twentieth century Britain, like ourselves, retained the fundamental attitudes established in the poor laws. It was the 1388 law that sought to restrain the wanderings of the paupers, an indignity and probably a hasty action since the wandering paupers were often in search of employment. Still, the "settlement and removal" tactics (paupers were either forbidden to move from their place of residence at the time of the act or were returned to the town in which they had been born) were a great improvement over the "branding" technique which had found use under the law of 1360. Another condition of the 1388 act has bearing on recent and existing practice in poor relief. The distinction was made between "sturdy" beggars and those whose dependency resulted from casualty or impotence, and the community's wrath fell on the former, who could look to confinement. The local resources of many of the parishes were inadequate, however, and administration crude. Neither licensing and branding of beggars nor compulsory apprenticing, two methods which were adopted in 1562, reduced their numbers in the long run.

After centuries of experience under this kind of approach, the principle that the community should be assessed for the care of the poor and the indigent was established in the Poor Law of 1601 (43 Eliz. Ch. 3). Civil officials took over functions previously undertaken by ecclesiastics. Those who would not work were sent to houses of correction if adults, or were apprenticed if minors. Before the middle of the seventeenth century, however, local autonomy had been reëstablished, and aside from local variations in practice, which in some instances included allowances to supplement wages, no major changes were made. Steadily mounting costs and deteriorating standards of performance forced a Royal Commission to study the problem of poor-law administration in 1832. The law of 1834 was the consequence of its handiwork. On the principle that pauperism was only to be discouraged by making the lot of the pauper measurably worse than even the lowliest "independent" laborers, the law established uniform administration for the whole land. The level of care was scaled down (where necessary!); provision for the separation of women, children, the aged, and other groups was made; and workhouses for the able-bodied became a national institution. Apprenticeship was largely confined to dependent children. In practice, many provisions of the law were ignored, and the year 1905 saw the appointment of another Royal Commission to reëvaluate the harsh justice of the 1834 law. When the report was issued, all members agreed that the changes should be made in the law. But a minority under Beatrice Webb saw no possibility of renovating the poor-law system. For them a system of social insurance—already a generation old on the Continent—was the only answer to the hazards of industrial life that brought those conditions which the poor laws sought to meet. In 1911, modest social-insurance measures came at last to replace Corporations of Guardians of the Poor, workhouses, loss of civil rights through indigency, and other ill-famed approaches to the problems of poverty and dependency.

The development of social insurance on the Continent, which played a part in Britain's adoption of social-insurance measures, began with Germany. This fact might occasion some surprise in view of the pattern of German history in the latter half of the nineteenth century. The explanation is that social insurance was an extraordinary development in Germany spurred by no compassion for the plight of German workmen and their families. In 1862, a crisis in Prussia led William I to recognize Otto von Bismarck as his chief minister. Thus began

three decades of intrigue and war to accomplish the tough-minded
Bismarck's single goal, consolidation of central power among the heterogeneous German states. Hindered in the fulfillment of this end on
the one hand by the Catholic Church and on the other by the Socialists, Bismarck sought to "steal the thunder" of the latter group by
giving German workmen all that the Socialists had promised and
more, through a comprehensive system of compulsory social insurance.
Accident insurance was legislated in 1881 under a system which
required employers to shoulder two-thirds of the cost. Sickness insurance followed in 1883, with one-third of the cost falling on employers,
the remainder on the employees. In 1889, an old-age-and-invalidity
insurance measure was passed calling for equal contributions by employers and employees. A generation later, in 1927, the program was
rounded out by the provision of unemployment insurance.

So influential was the program adopted in Germany that other
states quickly followed with similar measures, most of them compulsory. By 1930, when the Great Depression was multiplying the
miseries of normal hazards, eighteen countries had established programs of unemployment insurance, thirty-nine old-age insurance or
pensions, and twenty-eight country-wide sickness or health insurance.[2]
Many of the programs provided only modest benefits, but a floor was
provided against the worst effects of these contingencies which was
largely absent in the United States, as we shall see in the following
section.

Social Security in the United States

We have come to anticipate a pattern of action in the achievement
of social legislation in the United States. Initiative nearly always rests
with the states that take up a movement fostered by trade unions or
other groups. At some stage, the revelations of commissions and general
dissatisfaction with state activity result in pressure for legislation to

[2] Unemployment- and old-age-insurance data based on U.S. Department of Labor,
*Unemployment-Benefit Plans in the United States and Unemployment Insurance in
Foreign Countries*, Bureau of Labor Statistics Bulletin No. 544, July, 1931; and *Public
Old-Age Pensions in the United States and in Foreign Countries*, Bureau of Labor Sta-
tistics Bulletin No. 561, February, 1932; Sickness and health insurance data based on
Barbara Nachtrieb Armstrong, *Insuring the Essentials*, New York, The Macmillan Company, 1932, pp. 565–567. Adoption of social insurance measures by major countries was
as follows: *sickness insurance:* Germany (1883), Denmark (1892), France (1898 [sub-
sidies] and 1920), and Great Britain (1911); *old-age insurance:* France (1886),
Germany (1889), Denmark (1891), Italy (1898), and Great Britain (1925); *Unemployment insurance:* France (1905 [subsidies] and 1930), Great Britain (1911), Italy
(1919), Germany (1927), and Denmark (1927).

meet on a national basis the need for which the state legislation was devised. At length, the national government may, but often does not, attempt to systematize the state efforts. Seldom are the measures enacted as an initial response to such pressures based on the programs of action in the most progressive states. The movement for national social-security legislation could be put in such a mold with a comfortable fit.

THE POOR-LAW BACKGROUND

We have discussed in earlier chapters that rich heritage which the English colonists brought from their homeland. Law, religion, and marriage each conformed to the English institutional model. Dependency in the colonies was also dealt with after British custom.

Local regulations were made necessary because of the peculiar problems encountered in settling a new territory. Efforts were made, for example, to select immigrants carefully on the basis of resources and character, so as to prevent the emergence of a dependency problem. Still, the fundamental English customs were most influential.[3] Kelso's study of public poor relief in Massachusetts [4] reveals how public policy moved from discriminatory admission of immigrants through such nefarious practices as auctions, at which the care of the poor was bid for, to locally administered almshouses supported in part by the commonwealth. By 1720, the principle of commonwealth aid to dependent persons had gained acceptance. More than a century passed, however, before the protests of citizens and the reports of investigating commissions led to support and operation of relief facilities by the commonwealth. And once established, these facilities became dumping grounds for all of the human refuse that the rapidly industrializing New England society produced: the sick, the aged, the insane, and the criminal. In 1877, local administration of relief with commonwealth funds was readopted.[5] Meanwhile, the establishment in 1863

---

[3] Helen I. Clarke, *Social Legislation, American Laws Dealing with Family, Child and Dependent*, New York, Appleton-Century-Crofts, 1940, p. 417. The historical principles of English poor-relief legislation which have found application in this country include, according to Clarke, (1) the repression of vagrancy; (2) provision of funds through taxes; (3) local parish responsibility; (4) obligations of close relatives; (5) apprenticeship of young persons; (6) the provision of workhouses, almshouses, bridewells; (7) the union of parishes; (8) public subsidy of low wages; (9) less eligibility (the theory that the pauper's condition of life must be less desirable than that of even the lowliest dependent workman); and (10) national uniformity.

[4] Robert W. Kelso, *The History of Public Poor Relief in Massachusetts, 1620–1720*, Boston, Houghton Mifflin Company, 1922.

[5] *Ibid.*, p. 149.

of the Massachusetts Board of State Charities broke the ground, ultimately ushering in such reforms as segregation of the mentally ill from the general indigent, family care for dependent children, and public-health agencies with investigative powers.

Other states developed their systems of poor relief along lines similar to those in Massachusetts. On the basis of European experience with social insurance, however, the issue of public pensions for the aged as an alternative to almshouse care was forced before public officials. A Massachusetts commission appointed in 1907 investigated the subject of old-age pensions and reported cautiously that such pensions "would take away in part the filial obligation for support of aged parents, which is a main bond of family solidarity." [6] We shall not look into the bases for such a judgment at this point, but will turn to the generation of discussion and state action that preceded national legislation.

Public Relief of Dependency to 1935

At various times in the present century, public action was initiated at the state level to deal with dependency of the aged, survivors, the unemployed, and those injured while at work. The amount of relief provided differed widely from state to state, and frequently the states paying smaller benefits actually sacrificed more of their available resources than the progressive states with their larger benefits and wider coverage. At all times, a limiting factor was the hostility of organized opponents to systematic relief activity, who pressed into service every argument, from attributing agitation for social insurance to treasonable foreign influences to pious concern for filial devotion. With the onset of the Great Depression, the misery which unorganized relief resources permitted stiffened the resistance of the general public and its officials to the dire predictions of what would follow if the national resources were used in local relief activities.

We have already traced the development of workmen's-compensation legislation in Chapter 12. Now we shall fill in the general character of state provision against dependency resulting from other hazards.

Dependent survivors were among the first groups whose protection against dependency was given primary consideration by the states. It will be recalled that most states by 1930 awarded pensions to survivors of workmen who were killed under job-connected circumstances,

---

[6] Quoted in I. M. Rubinow, *The Quest for Security*, New York, Henry Holt and Company, 1934, p. 267.

generally without proof of need. Survivors generally, including those whose dependency was attributable to nonjob-connected fatality of the breadwinner, were first afforded "mother's aid" in 1911 by the State of Illinois, and by 1930 all of the states except Alabama, Georgia, and South Carolina had passed similar legislation.[7] Enactment of the laws was in part a response to the national child-welfare movement, which produced White House Conferences in 1909 and 1919. Much of the good intent of the legislation was lost, however, in the failure of most states to provide funds to put it into operation.

Investigations to determine the extent of dependency among aged persons were begun in 1907 by the State of Massachusetts and other states followed, beginning with Wisconsin in 1915. Private organizations devoted their energies to the problem, and the turning point in the movement for old-age pensions was 1926, when a group of fraternal organizations sponsored publication of Harry Carroll Evans' study, *The American Poor Farm and Its Inmates*. Where public investigations pointing to excessive costs and inhumanity had failed to awaken an indifferent public, this study succeeded. Considered with the evidence produced by state commissions, it made public action necessary. Arizona had passed a badly worded statute to provide old-age pensions in 1914, which was declared unconstitutional because of its ambiguity. Alaska then passed a law in 1915, the first actually to operate, and twenty-nine states followed by 1935.[8] At the beginning of 1932, however, a Bureau of Labor Statistics study showed that only nine states had actually put their statutes into operation, aiding 10,307 aged persons with an average payment of $14.32 per month.[9] The recipients, moreover, were carefully limited, a state-residence requirement of fifteen years or more typified most of the laws, and the number of aged public-pension receivers was only 236,000 as late as 1935—six years after the depresison began—with maximum benefits ranging from $15 to $30.[10] The depression caused many counties to curtail sharply the statutory provisions of the statutes existing in their states merely to aid more-needy persons, and in some states payments were halted altogether.

[7] Barbara Nachtrieb Armstrong, *Insuring the Essentials*, New York, The Macmillan Company, 1932, pp. 442–443.

[8] Committee on Economic Security, *Social Security in America, the Factual Background of the Social Security Act as Summarized from Staff Reports to the Committee on Economic Security*, Washington, Social Security Board, 1937, pp. 156–157.

[9] U.S. Department of Labor, *Public Old Age Pensions and Insurance in the United States and in Foreign Countries*, p. 5.

[10] Committee on Economic Security, op. cit., pp. 156–157.

Unemployment had been a major source of insecurity to the workingman for nearly a century before public action sought to relieve the major threat of income loss through unemployment insurance. The Great Depression had been pyramiding unemployment for five years before the first state law began operation. Significantly, the Bureau of Labor Statistics entitled a study made in 1931 *Unemployment-Benefit Plans in the United States and Unemployment Insurance in Foreign Countries*. Total provision for the unemployed was summed up in fifteen plans established by employers, sixteen established by agreement between trade unions and management, and forty-eight maintained solely by trade unions—a total potential coverage of 226,000 employees.[11] Wisconsin enacted the first law in 1932 (to begin operation in 1934) and precipitated a bitter debate over administrative alternatives in the provision of unemployment insurance. Wisconsin's objective was to promote steady employment by requiring the adoption of employer stabilization funds. Barring the establishment of such reserve funds on their own initiative, employers in Wisconsin would be required to contribute an amount equal to 2 percent of the employees' earnings, subject after two years to a reduction if the fund exceeded $55 per employee. Contributions by the employer would be the sole means of financing the system and the state would only indirectly control the fund. John R. Commons of the University of Wisconsin was the moving power behind the plan. Differing in fundamental respects from the Wisconsin plan was the Ohio plan. This method of meeting the unemployment contingency was based on joint contributions by the employer and the employee, and more nearly approximated the insurance concept in which payments are made to offset a future contingency the incidence of which is known with some precision. I. M. Rubinow had gathered data on the incidence of unemployment in Ohio and pioneered the adoption of the Ohio plan. Organized labor was more favorably disposed toward the Ohio plan because the fund would be administered by the state and would appear to give more protection against the actual income loss attending unemployment. Both measures were modest in the protection they extended, however. A waiting period of three weeks was required under the Wisconsin plan and two weeks under the Ohio plan before benefits could be collected following loss of employment. The size of the benefits ranged from $5 to $10 under the Wisconsin plan and up

[11] U.S. Department of Labor, *Unemployment-Benefit Plans in the United States and Unemployment Insurance in Foreign Countries*, p. 6.

to $15 under the Ohio plan, the duration of benefits being ten weeks and sixteen weeks respectively. Title III of the Social Security Act stimulated state action, and by 1935 eight more states had followed Wisconsin in passing unemployment insurance legislation, seven of them adopting the general features of the Ohio plan.[12]

This summary has intended only to indicate the general nature of state response to the social hazards which the Social Security Act attempted to meet. It is clear that action at the national level was a necessity in view of the scant protection afforded their citizens by the states. A more detailed account of the needs which state action failed to satisfy will be presented in the following section.

THE SCOPE OF AMERICAN NEEDS

It is a popular but erroneous belief that the Great Depression disrupted an otherwise economically secure American society in a kind of spontaneous combustion. Adequate provision had been made, this belief holds, against all *normal* contingencies; but the extraordinary catastrophe that began in 1929 proved too great a burden for even our best efforts. The previous section has established the inadequacy of the existing poor-relief and insurance systems to cope with social hazards. Furthermore, the experiences of 1921–1922 and 1927 suggest that *normal* "less-than-catastrophic" depressions severely tested the flimsy safeguards hopefully provided against their effects.[13] One more point needs to be dealt with: the "spontaneous" nature of the vast drain on poor-relief facilities which began in 1929. Many students of social legislation and interested organizations had long warned how inadequate were the provisions that had been made against dependency.[14] President Hoover's own Committee on Recent Social Trends in the United States, appointed a few months before the stock-market crash, signaled a warning that among indispensable public policies to cope with the built-in hazards of industrial life, the first must be "willingness and determination to undertake important integral

[12] Paul H. Douglas, *Social Security in the United States,* New York, McGraw-Hill Book Company, 1936, 1939, p. 309.

[13] Leah Hannah Feder, *Unemployment Relief in Periods of Depression,* New York, Russell Sage Foundation, 1936, pp. 325–353, *passim.*

[14] Isaac M. Rubinow, Abraham Epstein, Paul H. Douglas, E. Wight Bakke, and others pressed the case for more adequate measures—including social insurance—for two decades prior to the Great Depression. The American Association for Labor Legislation, the American Association for Old Age Security, and the American Association for Social Security were among the active organizations which focused attention on unpreparedness to meet social hazards.

changes in the reorganization of social life, including the economic and political orders, rather than the pursuance of a policy of drift." [15] The consequences of inaction were deftly suggested in the Committee's findings: "Unless there can be a more impressive integration of social skills and fusing of social purposes than is revealed in current trends, there can be no assurance that . . . alternatives with their accompaniments of violent revolution, dark periods of serious repression of libertarian and democratic forms, the proscription and loss of many useful elements in the present productive system, can be averted." [16] For public-policy purposes, however, the more illusory report prepared by the Committee on Recent Economic Changes, which scarcely mentioned any dark spots in the social-economic system, was used.[17] Meanwhile, the dimensions of the nation's needs mounted steadily, to portray a grim picture of suffering when the data were brought to light by the Committee on Economic Security in 1934.

Dependent mothers and children were in need of greatly increased assistance as local resources were exhausted. The Committee estimated that perhaps 300,000 families should be given regular long-term aid to reduce their dependency status.[18] Twice that number of orphans and children from fatherless homes were on the relief rolls in 1934, but the total scope of need remains in doubt.

Old-age dependency must be estimated from state surveys since no comprehensive data were assembled. From a limited survey conducted in 1930, New York State found that 74.5 percent of New York City aged and 43.4 percent in a limited state survey had incomes below $300 annually and less than $5000 worth of property.[19] The Connecticut average of 45.7 percent having the same characteristics in 1932 suggests that perhaps half of the aged in eastern industrial states were in a position of need. Massachusetts in 1925 and New York in

[15] President's Research Committee on Social Trends, *Recent Social Trends in the United States*, New York, McGraw-Hill Book Company, 1933, p. lxxi.

[16] *Ibid.*, p. lxxiv.

[17] Committee on Recent Economic Changes of the President's Conference on Unemployment, *Recent Economic Changes in the United States*, New York, McGraw-Hill Book Company, 1929, 2 vols.

[18] Committee on Economic Security, *op. cit.*, p. 248. Total expenditures for dependent mothers and children totaled approximately $90 million in 1934—including a grant from the federal government of $45 million—although assistance at standards below the level of adequacy required expenditures of "something over $120 million." Prior to the institution of federal aid, the dimensions of the need probably exceeded $75 million.

[19] *Ibid.*, p. 151.

1929 had established that aged persons were primarily dependent on relatives and friends, half of all of New York's population over age 65 and three-quarters of all dependent persons over 65 receiving such aid.[20] A small percentage of all aged persons was eligible for old-age assistance under state laws; New York estimated 12.7, New Jersey 9.9, and Connecticut 11.2.[21] The extent of need among aged persons who were colored or disabled was substantially greater than for other aged persons.

Unemployment was the key to a substantial portion of the dependency which existed from mid-1928 on. In part, the seriousness of the problem lay in the differing incidence of unemployment among the states and among industries. The 1930–1933 average of unemployment for the United States was 25.8 percent, but it was 34.3 percent in Michigan.[22] In 1933, Michigan and Pennsylvania had unemployment rates exceeding 40 percent and no Middle Atlantic state fell below 35 percent.[23] On an industry basis, unemployment was most severe in manufacturing and mining and relatively less severe in the service industries. Robert R. Nathan estimated the 1933 level of unemployment at 13,176,000.[24] In the face of this enormous figure, no public authority had adopted a social-insurance scheme that had been in operation for more than two decades on the European Continent, and no grant of federal funds had been made available to alleviate the suffering.

Private philanthropy, which never had accounted for as much as one-third of relief expenditures, had proved signally unequal to the demands made upon it. The efforts which were put forth by private organizations are well known, and the ability of the city of Chicago to raise $100,000,000 for relief indicates the dimensions of the effort. Private insurance had also been considered by many as the answer to all forms of hazard. But the expense even of moderate life insurance was beyond the reach of the mass of people, and the overhead expenses of industrial insurance made this form of protection an uneconomical form of protection. Furthermore, no company was prepared to insure workingmen against the income loss occasioned by unemployment. Hence, never having been equal to meeting a large propor-

[20] *Ibid.*, pp. 152–53.
[21] *Ibid.*, p. 154.
[22] *Ibid.*, p. 58.
[23] *Ibid.*, p. 58.
[24] Robert R. Nathan, "Estimates of Unemployment in the United States, 1929–35," *International Labour Review*, January, 1936, p. 49.

tion of the nation's relief needs, private efforts were overwhelmed by the needs that arose with the Great Depression.

THE RESPONSE OF THE NATIONAL GOVERNMENT

A quarter-century of investigation and reinterpretation by social scientists has not altered the conclusion drawn by critics of the Hoover administration that it permitted needless suffering occasioned by the Great Depression. The administration at first concealed statistical data relating to the seriousness of unemployment and, when the seriousness was so great as to preclude concealment, then launched into dissertations on the moral rectitude of local responsibilities. Rugged individualism, a philosophy championed by the President personally, became an end in itself and stood in the way of all efforts to meet a national disaster with national resources. On the assumption that the United States Government must be run according to the same principles of finance as a business enterprise, the virtue of maintaining a tidy balance between income and outgo assumed primary importance, human suffering notwithstanding. Other business organizations, it was reasoned, would be stimulated to order their own financial houses by the example of the national government.

Assistance to localities took the form of slogans and national campaigns—"Give a Job" campaigns, "Block-Aid" programs, and "Back to the Land" movements. But bills to provide federal grants for unemployment relief were rejected by Congress or vetoed by the President. In the fourth winter of the depression, Senator Robert La Follette sent questionnaires to the mayors of American cities. The replies showed how desperate was the need for federal aid to the localities, which were on the verge of bankruptcy. The 810 replies were read into the February 2, 1932, Congressional Record, a 193-page-long documentation. A clear majority of the municipalities favored federal aid.[25] It was revealed in the record that the chairman of the President's Committee on Unemployment Relief had not collected a single written report on the scale of unemployment, although he had indicated in a statement that the situation was well in hand. Additional information supplied in testimony before the Senate Committee on Manufacturers by the American Association of Social Workers left no doubt that local conditions were desperate.[26] In July, 1932, a bill finally

[25] *Congressional Record*, February 2, 1932, 72nd Congress, 1st Session, p. 3099.
[26] Josephine Chapin Brown, *Public Relief, 1929–39*, New York, Henry Holt and Company, p. 122.

cleared both houses of Congress and was vetoed by the President on grounds that it would cause the budget to be unbalanced (the deficit for the previous year had amounted to nearly $1 billion, so a really Spartan attempt was in order), aid too few persons, etc. Alongside the very large grants made available to the business and commercial sectors of the nation through the Reconstruction Finance Corporation, this attitude was difficult to understand; but persons who criticized the policy were chided by administration spokesmen for not understanding how depressions must be solved. Broadus Mitchell has appraised the administration program and public reaction as follows:

. . . Hoover's persistent objection to direct federal money relief to the millions of unemployed did not prevent him from creating with alacrity the Reconstruction Finance Corporation, which gave enormous immediate aid to the largest business enterprises. Earlier, the Farm Board had taken as its aim the artificial raising of price of prime essentials of life. . . . So the sincerity as well as the wisdom of Hoover's professed preference for individual, voluntary, and local aid to the needy was sharply in question. Hoover himself, and his apologists, with all their reasoning, were not able to make his tenderness for railroads, banks, and staple agriculture consistent with his obduracy toward the unemployed. The springs of private enterprise, for the purity of which he held such solicitude, would not be polluted by direct national grants.[27]

At length the President's hand was forced, and on July 21, less than a fortnight after his rejection of a similar measure, he grudgingly signed the Wagner-Rainey Bill, which authorized the Reconstruction Finance Corporation to grant loans to the states. Forty-two states and two territories ultimately received funds. In November, the American people went to the polls to elect a President; outside of New England, the electoral representatives of only two states cast votes for a continuation of the hard-bitten philosophy of rugged individualism. The end of an era was signaled as the new President solemnly warned a Congress filled with members of his own party:

I am prepared under my constitutional duty to recommend the measures that a stricken Nation in the midst of a stricken world may require. These measures, or such other measures as the Congress may build out of its experience and wisdom, I shall seek, within my constitutional authority, to bring to speedy adoption. But in the event the Congress shall fail to take one of these two courses, I shall not evade the clear course of duty

[27] Broadus Mitchell, *Depression Decade, from New Era Through New Deal, 1929–41,* New York, Rinehart and Company, 1947, p. 87.

that will confront me. I shall ask the Congress for the one remaining instrument to meet the crisis—broad Executive power to wage a war against the emergency, as great as the power that would be given me if we were in fact invaded by a foreign foe.[28]

In May, 1933, four years after the depression began, federal responsibility was assumed under the Federal Emergency Relief Act. Through the FERA, Federal funds totaling more than $3 billion were granted to the states and more than 20,000,000 persons received aid under the various programs when the peak was reached in January, 1935.[29] With the conclusion of this program, other public works and conservation programs continued the work of relief throughout the decade of the 1930's. In the offing, however, was a program of economic-security measures which might assure against future contingencies requiring extraordinary relief measures.

THE SOCIAL SECURITY ACT

After making funds available to the states for the relief of unemployment, the new administration turned to the preparation of permanent programs of security that would be preventive rather than palliative. In June, 1934, studies were initiated to prepare for a program of national social and economic security. The Committee on Economic Security and numerous technical advisory committees were created. Their reports and recommendations became the basis for the Social Security Act of 1935. Citing the widely differing capacities of the states to care for the economic security of their citizens, the Committee on Economic Security warned that there was not the remotest possibility of securing the nation's citizens against the vicissitudes of modern life without financial aid from the national government.[30]

Not all of the recommendations contained in the research reports were adopted in the bill which was signed by the President on August 14, 1935. Those who had labored for comprehensive social-security legislation were disappointed. But a bold start had been made and, in general, the Social Security Act was probably as ambitious as the prevailing cultural milieu would permit. Legislative opinion was favorable to social-security legislation in 1935. The persistent efforts of organizations hostile to the plan, however (particularly the Chamber of Com-

[28] Samuel I. Rosenman (ed.), *The Public Papers and Addresses of Franklin D. Roosevelt*, New York, Random House, 1938, Vol. II, p. 15.
[29] Works Progress Administration, *Final Statistical Report of the Federal Emergency Relief Administration*, Washington, 1942, p. iii.
[30] Committee on Economic Security, op. cit., pp. 369–372.

merce of the United States), to misrepresent both the issues in the legislation and the experience of other countries kept public opinion indecisive.

Under the Social Security Act, the role of the federal government in social insurance and public assistance was defined in three programs —grants of funds to the states, tax levies with offset provisions, and the establishment of a compulsory old-age and benefit system. The scope of the program and the services undertaken are shown in the following summary:

Grants to the States
1. Old-age assistance
2. Aid to dependent children
3. Maternal and child welfare
   A. Maternal and child health services
   B. Services for crippled children
   C. Child welfare services
   D. Vocational rehabilitation
   E. Administration
4. Public-health work
5. Aid to the blind
Insurance Benefit Systems
1. Federal old-age benefits
2. Unemployment Compensation Administration

Old-age assistance was to be provided out of federal funds for the support of state programs. If the program met the conditions stated in the act, the Social Security Board would approve a plan if (1) it should be in effect in all political subdivisions of the state, and, if administered by them, be mandatory upon them; (2) it provided for financial participation by the state; (3) it either provided for the establishment or designation of a single agency to administer the plan or for the establishment or designation of a single state agency to supervise the administration of the plan; (4) it provided for granting to any individual, whose claim for old-age assistance was denied, an opportunity for a fair hearing before such state agency; (5) it provided such methods of administration (other than those relating to selection, tenure of office, and compensation of personnel) as were found by the Board to be necessary for the efficient operation of the plan; (6) it provided that the state agency make such reports, in such form and containing such information, as the Board might from time to time require, and complied with such provisions as the Board might

find necessary to assure the correctness and verification of such reports; and (7) it provided that, if the state or any of its political subdivisions collected from the estate of any recipient of old-age assistance any amount with respect to old-age assistance furnished him under the plan, one-half of the net amount so collected should be promptly paid to the United States. The Board, furthermore, refused to approve any plan which set an age requirement of more than 65 years (with exceptions up to January 1, 1940), or a residence requirement of more than five years of the preceding nine years when the person had been resident one continuous year prior to application. All citizens of the United States had to be eligible.

Aid to dependent children was made available on the same terms, except that the plan would not be approved if it imposed as a condition of eligibility for aid a residence requirement which denied aid with respect to any child residing in the state (1) who had resided in the state for one year immediately preceding application for aid, or (2) who was born within the state within one year immediately preceding the application, if its mother had resided in the state for one year immediately preceding the birth.

Maternal and child welfare grants were made available on essentially the same basis as old-age assistance insofar as plans were required to meet the conditions (1) through (4). However, the regulating authority was the Department of Labor and additional requirements were imposed. Plans were required to provide for the extension and improvement of local maternal and child health services administered by local health units; coöperation with medical, nursing, and welfare groups and organizations; and for the development of demonstration services in needy areas and among groups in special need. The three forms of services provided by the grants for maternal and child welfare were each required to meet the general terms of plans described above except as the peculiar characteristics of each service called for special provisions.

Public-health work grants were to be made available to the states on the basis of population, special health problems, and financial needs and for the purpose of assisting the states and their subdivisions in establishing and maintaining adequate public-health services, including the training of personnel. Responsibility rested with the Surgeon General of the Public Health Service and the Secretary of the Treasury.

Grants for aid to the blind followed the procedure established for

old-age assistance of requiring a plan to be submitted by the states and approved by the Social Security Board. A blind person was prohibited from receiving old-age assistance and aid to the blind concurrently.

Common features of the assistance services were that they depended on the applicant's need and required the states to take the initiative in developing programs. The federal government then entered most of the programs with matching funds. We shall reserve extended discussion of the assistance services for the next chapter, which will trace the development of the assistance functions and evaluate the effectiveness of assistance as a method of meeting the problems of dependency.

Insurance benefits for the aged were made available under the Federal Old-Age Benefits title of the Social Security Act. Every qualified individual, Title II provided, *shall be entitled* upon reaching age 65, or on January 1, 1942 (whichever was later), to an old-age benefit to continue until the day of his death. About 26,000,000 persons were eligible to contribute under the qualifications that were laid down. Excluded from coverage were the following types of employment: agricultural labor; domestic service performed in a private home; casual labor; service performed as an officer or member of a crew of a vessel documented under the laws of the United States or any foreign country; service performed in the employ of the United States Government or any of its instrumentalities; service performed in the employ of a state, a political subdivision thereof, or an instrumentality of any one or more states or political subdivisions; and service performed in the employ of most charitable organizations. Aged persons who met the qualifications, however, could look to a monthly benefit of from $10 to $85, the amounts to be based on the level of their wages and the period during which contributions were made to the fund. The arithmetic of the benefit formula will be discussed in Chapter 16.

Unemployment compensation was to be paid through the states, with federal grants being given directly only for administration expenses incurred by the states in the operation of their programs. To be eligible for grants to assist states in meeting the expenses of their unemployment-insurance programs, the program was required to meet certain requirements set down in Title XII of the act. In general, these requirements were the same as those which pertained to the tax offset feature of Title IX, which was the important provision of the employment-insurance system. In Title IX, a tax on employer payrolls was

imposed, to be 1 percent of the payroll in 1936, 2 percent in 1937, and 3 percent after 1937. However, if the employer should make contributions to an approved state unemployment-insurance program, he might credit 90 percent of such contributions against the federal tax. Under certain conditions, additional credit also could be sought. To be approved, a state program was required to provide that (1) all compensation be paid through public employment agencies in the state, or such other agencies as the Board might approve; (2) no compensation should be payable with respect to any day of unemployment occurring within two years after the first day of the first period with respect to which contributions were required; (3) all money received in the unemployment fund should upon receipt immediately be paid over to the Secretary of the Treasury to the credit of the Unemployment Trust Fund; (4) all money withdrawn from the Unemployment Trust Fund by the state agency should be used solely in the payment of compensation, exclusive of exenses of administration; (5) Compensation should not be denied in such state to any otherwise eligible individual for refusing to accept new work under any of the following conditions: (A) if the position vacant was owing directly to a strike, lockout, or other labor disputes; (B) if the wages, hours, or other conditions of the work offered were substantially less favorable to the individual than those prevailing for similar work in the locality; (C) if as a condition of being employed the individual would be required to join a company union or to resign from or refrain from joining any bona-fide labor organization; (6) all the rights, privileges, or immunities conferred by such law or by acts done pursuant thereto should exist subject to the power of the legislature to amend or repeal such law at any time. The law applied only to employers of eight or more employees, and set no standards with respect to amount or duration of benefits.

The Social Security Act was criticized by its friends and foes alike. In general, advocates of a comprehensive program disapproved of the limited federal participation in programs other than federal old-age benefits. The absence of any continuing provision for the survivors of an insured worker was difficult to accept in view of the widespread incidence of dependency resulting from loss of the breadwinner. Failure to provide for dependency resulting from disability and sickness was equally disappointing. In terms of technical features, the offset provisions with respect to the federal tax on payrolls seemed an unwise choice in view of the express advice of professional experts and

their warning that the whole program depended on the dubious constitutionality of such a use of the tax power. Hopeful states read into their unemployment-compensation bills a provision that its continuation was contingent upon the constitutionality of the federal law. The decision to adhere to actuarial principles of private insurance in administering the federal insurance benefit programs *in the long run* seemed to be an unnecessary concession to private business methods. It was because adequate relief was not available elsewhere that the federal program was being instituted; hence, merely adding the factor of compulsion and joint contributions would fail to give adequate relief if the insurance principle were maintained in the strictest sense. Other criticisms were in the form of basic issues which existed prior to and following the enactment of the Social Security Act. We shall reserve discussion of them to the following section.

The dissatisfaction with the act led to its early amendment in 1939. Before any benefits were paid under the Federal Old-Age Benefits title, major changes had been made. Important changes were likewise made in the titles dealing with assistance and unemployment compensation. The character of the amendments was related to some basic criticisms which had been affirmed by the Advisory Council on Social Security. We shall simply mention them here because the legislative history of the Social Security Act will be dealt with in Chapter 15. After the 1939 amendments, the strict actuarial connections between contributions and benefits under the federal old-age benefits program were materially altered, although the proportionality principle was maintained. Benefits for those in low-wage groups and those who were already approaching retirement age were increased by revising the benefit formula, and allowances were instituted for aged wives and young dependent children of the beneficiaries. Monthly benefits for survivors also were provided under the amended act. The coverage of the program received modest increases, although the fundamental exclusions were maintained. Finally, the financial management of the reserve fund was liberalized.

Assistance programs also were amended, although the changes instituted were not far-reaching. All of the states had by 1940 made the granting of assistance by the counties mandatory. Confidential record keeping was instituted in 1939 and appeals systems were provided for those who were denied aid. Furthermore, payments were to be made in cash, as compared with the practice which prevailed in many states of giving assistance in kind. In contrast to these liberaliza-

tions in the assistance programs, there were indications of retrenchment in some states. These actions took the form of unreasonable restrictions on those who sold property in order to become eligible for assistance and exaggerating the emphasis of relatives' responsibility for those in need. On the eve of World War II, an extensive list of improvements remained to be made if social security were to be something other than an empty term.

World War II, after the manner of all wars, seemed to solve all forms of economic insecurity in the single task of producing war material financed from a bottomless Treasury war chest. The problem of finding jobs for men was suddenly reversed. As attention was detracted from the fundamental built-in insecurities of American life, social security became a dead issue in the United States in contrast to the vigorous activities along these lines in Great Britain and other countries. The end of the war, at any rate, again directed attention at the problems of unemployment that would attend the process of "reconversion," and at length amendments were enacted which substantially extended coverage and liberalized benefits.

Issues in Social-Security Legislation

The big issues in social-security legislation have persisted in spite of gradual liberalization of the original programs. Informed opinion can in most instances be distinguished when the basic questions are debated. Still, there remains a range of questions which men who know what they are talking about will debate from opposite points of view with the conviction that righteousness demands the acceptance of their position. Senator Eugene Millikan read into the Congressional Record on June 13, 1950, a list of 100 questions which the Advisory Council on Social Security had considered before going out of existence in 1948.[31] The questions fall into broad groups of issues, which might be summarized as follows:

1. Can we afford to indemnify a population whose future characteristics are in doubt against an ever wider range of hazards?
2. In what measure should we prefer insurance as against assistance methods?
3. Ought a pay-as-you-go program to be maintained, or should financing from general tax revenues be permitted?

[31] *Congressional Record*, June 13, 1950, 81st Congress, 2nd Session, pp. 497–498, 498.

4. What objectives ought to guide the determination of adequate benefit levels?
5. What are the incentive effects of a comprehensive social-security program?

Not all of these questions can be answered here. But some attention must be given to the kinds of problems which arise in connection with various answers to them. Detailed discussion will be reserved for the two chapters that follow.

Bearing the Costs

Appraising our ability to afford a comprehensive program of social security to relieve dependency turns on two primary considerations: (1) social-security costs are not "added costs," but costs which we must inescapably bear in some manner, and (2) long-term rates of growth in the American economy permit us to expand the program of social-security benefits. In part, the program of social-security benefits can be defended on the grounds that the inadequate resources of less-wealthy states and subdivisions to relieve dependency are enhanced by national action, thereby permitting more equitable relief. The apparent lower costs of failing adequately to relieve dependency in poorer states are deceiving in any case because the costs not borne directly in money terms will in all likelihood be borne in terms of irresponsible citizenship, deliquency, and family disruption.

Another side of the question concerns our ability to administer an expanded program of social-security benefits on strictly actuarial terms, "pay as you go." The answer to the suggestion that we should do so is simple: we cannot. But the program need not be restricted to a rigid scale of benefits and services for that reason. Supplementing contributions with funds from general government revenues is an alternative. The impressive growth prospects for the American economy, perhaps even exceeding the 3 percent annual figure often quoted, weighs heavily in support of our ability to continue an expanding program. Income stabilization measures, which we have previously discussed, would, of course, permit us to enter into expanded social-security protection with more assurance about the future.

Administrative Alternatives

The question of relying on insurance as against assistance methods is a primary question in the United States. We shall have to try to distinguish between the two methods before we evaluate their relative

merits. The fundamental distinction—and the only one that can be maintained—has been stated by Eveline Burns: "The essential and objective difference . . . lies in two characteristics of social insurance that are not found in public assistance. First, the law specifies with precision the conditions governing eligibility, and the nature and the amount of the benefit. Second, the specific conditions do not include a requirement to undergo a means test." [32] Thus, the essential difference comes down to whether administrative discretion can be exercised in granting benefits. Under assistance programs, a large measure of discretion is allowed in spite of state laws which require benefits to be given as a right.[33] The contributory versus noncontributory aspect is a less valid distinction simply because few social-insurance systems have ever collected contributions sufficient to defray the costs based on strict actuarial considerations. Nor have persons who at the time of establishing social-insurance programs were already victims of an insured contingency ordinarily been denied access to benefits.

The preference for social insurance over public assistance rests on numerous considerations. It seems that the preference first was established for budgetary reasons, since the scale of benefits could better be predicted and the costs borne by the Treasury thus controlled. In the United States, the preference for social insurance has rested on cultural factors. First, there is the contributory element, which removes some of the fear of being "kept" by the government. Second, the absence of a "means test" removes the stigma of dependency, with its innuendoes of failure.

Under the Social Security Act of 1935, it was acknowledged that income received through the federal old-age benefit program would be inadequate to support aged beneficiaries. Assistance was therefore expected to make up the gap between necessary income required by the beneficiary and that received through FOAB. As a matter of fact the number of assistance beneficiaries exceeded the number of insurance (FOAB) beneficiaries until 1953.

Nearly all students of social-security legislation in the United States agree on maintaining the distinctions between the insurance and assistance programs, although there is not complete satisfaction with the present scope and operations of either program. Discussion in recent years on the question has been concerned with the proposal of

[32] Eveline M. Burns, *The American Social Security System*, Boston, Houghton Mifflin Company, 1949, p. 31.
[33] See Ch. 16.

the Chamber of Commerce of the United States to discontinue the grants made to the states for old-age assistance. This proposal is unsound from any point of view, but the fundamental question at stake concerns financing the social-security program; hence, we shall reserve discussion until the financial aspects of the program are discussed in Chapter 15. We shall follow the same procedure as far as consideration of question 3 is concerned.

ADEQUACY OF BENEFITS

In an earlier section, we came across the concept of "less eligibility" which governed the administration of the English Poor Law and has found application in the United States. According to this concept, the lot of beneficiaries under programs of public aid should be perceptibly less adequate than the lot of independent persons. Whether based on this concept or not, the level of benefits in the United States has tended to stay below the adequacy level in both assistance and insurance programs. Increases in benefits have been made through amendments of the aid formulas, but the increase in living costs has caused the effective level of benefits to remain largely unchanged until recently.

Back of the concept of paying less than adequate benefits is the fear that the programs will be abused. Unemployment-insurance benefits, it is held, must be much less than the prevailing wage level to discourage people from accepting benefits instead of income. Assistance payments must not be so high as to discourage "initiative." There is relatively little evidence in the accumulated research connected with incentives to give substance to such fears. In percentage terms, as we shall see, abuse is relatively small in all of the programs. The level of adequacy tends to be thought of now in terms of needs—needs established by budget surveys—and legislation has sought to adjust the level of old-age and survivors' benefits to such a level. As the concepts of adequacy mature, we might expect benefits to increase if administered according to this procedure.

PROTECTING INCENTIVES

It is a curious fact that the Puritan ethic should be applied within the framework of social-security programs. The fundamental objective of relieving dependency is humanitarian; yet the effort to make the circumstances of benefits unpleasant and thereby discourage persons—the worthy and the unworthy—from making recourse to them

is entirely out of harmony with humanitarian practice. It might be supposed that the nonfulfillment of all the dire prophecies made at the time the Social Security Act was under consideration [34] would be taken at face value. But every proposal to broaden coverage or increase benefits is met by the same predictions of abuse offered by the same traditional opponents of social legislation. Studies of the effects of the social-security program on incentives have not been numerous and none has sought to determine the effects on a nation-wide basis. Various phases of research in social psychology and industrial relations, however, have associated levels of work performance with conditions of individual security. The proposition that people operate better under conditions of threat than under conditions secure from threat would find scant support among social scientists. Moreover, productivity has continued to rise, indicating that the insurance and assistance programs thus far established have failed to "sap the moral fiber" of the nation.

Guidelines to Social-Security Legislation

A half-century after most industrial nations put programs of social insurance and assistance into operation there has accumulated a body of thought concerning the dimensions of social-security programs. Debate now centers on administrative alternatives and coverage rather than on needs. A broad segment of world legislative opinion has indicated acceptance of the need for such legislation, and in many countries it has come to take precedence over all other domestic functions of the state.

The classic statement on social-security programs was prepared by Sir William Beveridge in 1942 and still stands as the authoritative statement. Few comparable "white papers" have been produced in other nations, but the contributions of the academic community, program administrators, and world organizations have rounded out the Beveridge proposals. From a notion of stopgap public aid in times of crisis, there have emerged carefully prepared concepts of minimum social-security standards which cover all of the major contingencies in modern life. In this section we shall review representative reports of public authorities and private groups, so as to gain an appreciation of advanced concepts of social security at the conclusion of World War II.

[34] For example, see "Social Insurance," *The Annals*, November, 1933.

NATIONAL RESOURCES PLANNING BOARD

The very week in which the United States entered World War II the Technical Committee on Long-Range Work and Relief Policies submitted its report to the President. Entitled *Security, Work and Relief Policies,*[35] it defined the problem of public aid and set forth the objectives of programs. The report read:

I. The Public-Aid Problem

The American people should base public-aid policy upon the acceptance of the following facts:

1. The need for public aid will be both large and persistent for some time to come.
2. The need for public aid is in large measure caused by serious maladjustments in the operation of our economy and by personal, physical or psychological defects, many of which can be remedied.
3. The social problem created by economic insecurity is many-sided and requires for its solution a series of diversified programs.

II. Broad Objective of Public Aid

The over-all objective of public aid should be the assurance of access to minimum security for all our people, wherever they may reside, and the maintenance of the social stability and values threatened when people lack jobs or income.

III. Specific Objectives

The specific objectives of public-aid policy should be:

1. Increasing emphasis upon policies aiming at the prevention of economic insecurity through a fuller utilization of our productive resources, including labor, and by more comprehensive measures to improve the health of our people.
2. Government provision of work for all adults who are willing and able to work, if private industry is unable to provide employment.
3. Appropriate measures to equip young persons beyond the compulsory school-attendance age for assuming the full responsibilities of citizenship.
4. Assurance of basic minimum security through social insurance, so far as possible.
5. Establishment of a comprehensive underpinning general public assistance system providing aid on the basis of need, to complete the framework of protection against economic insecurity.
6. Expansion of social services which are essential for the health,

[35] *Security, Work and Relief Policies, Report of the Committee on Long-Range Work and Relief Policies to the National Resources Planning Board,* House Document No. 128, Part 3, Seventy-eighth Congress, First Session.

welfare, and efficiency of the whole population; this expansion
should be as wide and as rapid as possible.[36]

Several aspects of this summary of recommendations by the Committee deserve attention. Throughout the report, the continuing need for public assistance was emphasized. The guarantee of employment was a progressive recommendation which culminated in the Employment Act of 1946. Health measures in the existing legislation were held to be inadequate. Finally, the broad objective was stated to emphasize social stability as a function of economic security. Thus, although stated in general terms, the report was a step beyond previous thought on social-security legislation.

The Beveridge Report

Sir William Beveridge was chairman of the British Interdepartmental Committee on Social Insurance and Allied Services, formed in 1941. The Committee's obligations were to survey existing programs and to recommend changes. A few simply stated guiding principles included in the first pages of the Committee report have been appraised with special appreciation. They read:

In proceeding from the first comprehensive survey of social insurance to the next task—of making recommendations—three guiding principles may be laid down at the outset.

The first principle is that any proposals for the future, while they should use to the full the experience gathered in the past, should not be restricted by consideration of sectional interests established in the obtaining of that experience. Now, when the war is abolishing landmarks of every kind, is the opportunity for using experience in a clear field. A revolutionary moment in the world's history is a time for revolutions, not for patching.

The second principle is that organizations of social insurance should be treated as one part only of a comprehensive policy of social progress. Social insurance fully developed may provide income security; it is an attack upon Want. But Want is one only of five giants on the road of reconstruction and in some ways the easiest to attack. The others are Disease, Ignorance, Squalor and Idleness.

The third principle is that social security must be achieved between the State and the individual. The State should offer security for service and contribution. The State in organizing security should not stifle incentive, opportunity, responsibility; in establishing a national minimum, it should

---

[36] *Ibid.*, p. 545.

leave room and encouragement for voluntary action by each individual to provide more than that minimum for himself and his family.[37]

This report, which responded cogently to the major criticisms of social-security programs in the content of three principles, was not advanced as something to aim for, a future set of conditions. It was advanced as "a limited contribution to a wider social policy, though as something that could be achieved now without waiting for the whole of that policy." [38] Dependency, furthermore, was seen as merely one phase of a larger comprehensive policy that would concern itself with health and disease, education, living and working conditions, and personal efficiency. Within the broad scale of this comprehensive policy, however, the need for security was not to be saturated by the efforts of the state; a margin was to be left that would permit individual action. In a later section we shall have occasion to compare the operation of the plan as adopted with the program of social security operating in the United States at present.

The Universal Declaration of Human Rights

In 1948, the General Assembly of the United Nations passed and proclaimed the Universal Declaration of Human Rights. Many aspects of the Declaration mark an advance in international human relations. But the provisions which are pertinent to this discussion were contained in Article 22 of the 1948 declaration. "Everyone," the Declaration declared, "as a member of society, has the right to social security and is entitled to realization, through national effort and international cooperation and in accordance with the organization and resources of each state, of the economic, social and cultural rights indispensable for his dignity and the free development of his personality." [39] In this declaration, a truly advanced concept of social security was framed; beyond the satisfaction of economic needs, it would include conditions of security which might permit an individual to realize the full potentialities of his personality.

International Labor Conference

At its 34th Session in 1951, the International Labor Conference took up a resolution to adopt one or more conventions or recommenda-

---

[37] Sir William Beveridge, *Social Insurance and Allied Services*, New York, The Macmillan Company, 1942, pp. 6–7.

[38] *Ibid.*, p. 7.

[39] United States Department of Public Information, *Universal Declaration of Human Rights*, Washington, 1949.

tions, relating to minimum standards of social security. The convention adopted in the 35th Session was to serve as a framework for revision of existing conventions. The recommendations of the Conference Committee, considering a proposed convention for the 35th Session, were that the following contingencies be included in a scheme of protection: medical benefits; sickness allowances; unemployment allowances; old-age pensions or allowances; medical benefits, sickness allowances, invalidity pensions, or allowances, and survivors' pensions or allowances, in case of employment injury; family allowances; medical benefits in case of maternity, and maternity allowances; invalidity pensions or allowances; and survivors' pensions or allowances.[40]

In drawing up the convention, it was recognized that the resources of nations would be the deciding factor in the scope of protection against each contingency. It was pointed out, however, that the classical system of social security had already been superseded by package programs of insurance and assistance in most countries and, in New Zealand and Great Britain, by the provision of many services through public-service media. When we come to analyze the American social security program, we shall be primarily interested in its unfavorable comparison with the medical-benefits and family-allowances sections of the International Labor Conference standards.

AMERICAN STUDENTS OF SOCIAL SECURITY

In 1942, the American Council on Public Affairs arranged for the presentation of views by American students of social security on the outlines of an expanded program. The editor, Wilbur Cohen, summarized the concept of security which should guide postwar changes in the program:

Our goal should be the establishment of a well-rounded system of social insurance to provide at least a minimum security to individuals and their families who suffer loss of income due to unemployment, sickness, disability, old age and death. In addition, we must provide a series of constructive social services to supplement social insurance. A basic system of public assistance, a national network of public unemployment services and similar community services are essential to the proper functioning of social insurance and to the protection of the individual. Under such a program every individual could be assured that these unforeseen con-

[40] International Labor Conference, *Minimum Standards of Social Security*, Geneva International Labor Office, 1951, p. 10. As finally ratified, the convention required only three of the nine types of programs.

tingencies would not leave him or his family dependent upon others but rather that should he meet with any of these unfortunate circumstances there would be a minimum regular cash income supplemented by other necessary services and assistance.[41]

This concept accepts the framework of insurance and assistance set up by the Social Security Act of 1935. An expansion of coverage is called for, however, and the scope of basic services beyond insurance and assistance must be extended. The goal is a minimum regular cash income available to those whose independence is threatened by the contingencies of unemployment, sickness, disability, old age, and death.

SOCIAL SECURITY ADMINISTRATION

The Annual Report of the Social Security Administration in 1947 contained positively stated recommendations for a comprehensive program of social security. Three major recommendations were made:

1. A comprehensive basic national system of contributory social insurance.
2. A comprehensive program of public welfare, including public assistance and family and child welfare services.
3. A comprehensive program of health and welfare services for children and research in child life.[42]

To round out the existing program in keeping with these objectives, the report recommended extending coverage to all gainful workers under old-age and survivors' insurance, extension of unemployment insurance to all employers with one or more employees, and improved standards of benefits, provisions for disability insurance, provision for medical-care insurance, special grants to increase the standards of public-assistance benefits in low-income states, and legislation providing for a progressive state-administered program of child services and research in child life.

THE AMERICAN SOCIAL-SECURITY PROGRAM AND ADVANCED CONCEPTS OF SOCIAL SECURITY

Analyzed in the light of the concepts which have been presented in the above survey, the American program of protection against the major contingencies of modern life seems inadequate in many re-

[41] Wilbur J. Cohen (ed.), "Next Steps and Future Goals," *War and Post-War Social Security*, Washington, American Council on Public Affairs, 1942, p. 31.

[42] Federal Security Agency, *Annual Report of the Social Security Administration*, Washington, 1947, *passim*.

spects. The most obvious gap is the absence of medical-care protection, a service included even in the classical concept of social security which is now outdated. Disability protection and general family allowances are also wanting. On a higher plane of consideration, the unwillingness of legislators and other persons whose action affects the program to provide a consolidated program of benefits which are comparable in terms of adequacy among the states weakens the scope of security the nation enjoys. In the next two chapters, we shall measure the adequacy of present programs against advanced concepts in respect to social insurance and social assistance.

Social-Security Legislation, Background and Philosophy: Concluding Remarks

This survey of the background and philosophy of social-security legislation has brought us to the point where we can profitably go on in the following chapters to consider the details of the American social-security system. Several factors brought out in the foregoing discussion are of special interest. In the first place, the American social-security program has progressed slowly toward its implied goals, and its growth has been related to the cultural beliefs about individual responsibility, fear of centralization, and human wickedness. But its progress has been steady in recent years and we should be far less secure as a people without the modest protection which the American system affords against dependent old age, survivorship, and unemployment. Second, the immature programs of public assistance and social insurance in the United States are still unconsolidated at a time when advanced concepts of social security call for consolidation and far less wealthy countries have proceeded with universal public coverage against all of the major vicissitudes of social life. Third, there is no widespread belief among students of social-security legislation that the American program should be altered in its fundamental characteristics.

SELECTED REFERENCES

Armstrong, Barbara N., *Insuring the Essentials*, New York, The Macmillan Company, 1932.

Bloom, Gordon F., and Northrup, Herbert R., *Economics of Labor Relations*, Chicago, Richard D. Irwin, 1954.

Burns, Eveline M., *The American Social Security System*, Boston, Houghton-Mifflin Company, 1949.

Douglas, Paul H., *Social Security in the United States*, 2nd ed., New York, Whittlesey House, 1939.

Lester, Richard A., *Labor and Industrial Relations*, New York, The Macmillan Company, 1951.

Rubinow, I. M., *Social Insurance*, New York, Henry Holt and Company, 1913.

chapter 15

The Social Security Act:
Insurance Features

This chapter and the chapter to follow will discuss the insurance and assistance programs established by the Social Security Act of 1935. Since we have already dealt with the rationale for social-security legislation and advanced concepts by which legislative changes should be guided, we shall concern ourselves only with changes in coverage and benefits and major gaps which exist in present legislation. In this chapter, our concern shall be with the insurance benefit systems—federal old-age and survivors' insurance benefits and grants for unemployment-compensation administration.

Federal Old-Age and Survivors' Insurance Benefits

The Social Security Act of 1935 was already legislative history when payments first were made under Title II in 1940. Established as a personal retirement system in 1935, it had been transformed into a personal retirement and survivors' benefit system by the 1939 amendments. In addition to the primary benefit payable to fully insured workmen who attained the age of 65 and filed application, there were also benefits payable to wives and widowers, surviving children, widows and husbands, parents, and other designated survivors of retired workers. The major provisions of the 1935 act as amended in 1939 have been maintained to the present time. Changes have been concerned in the main with coverage, insured status, benefits, and administrative matters, chiefly financial.

COVERAGE

The original Social Security Act excluded eight groups of employees from coverage, the largest being self-employed agricultural labor,

domestic-service workers, casual labor, and service in the United States Government, states, and their subdivisions. Amendment in 1939 added nearly an equal number of excluded groups, raising the total to fifteen. However, the groups excluded did not include large numbers of employees and the exclusions were in many instances connected with employment in educational institutions. Two increases in coverage were enacted, bringing into the system persons over 65 in covered employment and employees of national banks. In 1943, an extension of coverage was made to include seamen employed by the War Shipping Administration. Temporary changes instituted in 1946 included suvivors of World War II veterans who should die within a specified period following separation from active military or naval service. Coverage was withdrawn from individuals under 18 years of age whose employment consisted of delivery of newspapers and from newspaper and magazine vendors in 1948. In addition, the status of "employee" was defined more closely in accordance with common-law rules. By the end of 1948, more than 90,000,000 old-age and survivors' insurance accounts were kept by the Social Security Administration, which was more than double the 1940 number.

Sentiment was favorable to changes in the Social Security Act following World War II, and the amendments legislated in 1950 and 1954 made important contributions to the program coverage. The Advisory Council on Social Security of 1948 had pointed out the weaknesses in the program. Most obvious was the restricted coverage; the other shortcomings included unduly restrictive eligibility requirements and inadequate benefits. Accordingly, in 1950, coverage was extended to nearly 8,000,000 persons, the largest numbers of whom had been excluded as agricultural and domestic service workers, employees of nonprofit institutions, or the federal, state, and local governments. Wage credits of $160 per month also were provided for service in the armed forces. Still excluded were farm owners and operators, many farm workers, members of state and local government retirement systems, some domestic-service workers, ministers and members of religious orders, self-employed professional persons, and certain other groups, most of which were employees of international organizations, foreign laborers, and employees of certain tax-exempt instrumentalities of the United States Government. Most of these groups were admitted to coverage in comprehensive amendments enacted in 1954. Ten million persons were added to coverage, 6,000,000 persons on a compulsory basis and 4,000,000 on an elective basis. At the beginning of 1955,

coverage was thus expanded to 90 percent of employed persons. Still excluded were members of the armed forces of the United States, most federal civilian employees, self-employed physicians and dentists, and policemen and firemen in state retirement systems.

INSURED STATUS

The fact that a person is in "covered employment" does not automatically entitle him or his survivors to benefits under OASI. Under the original act a person in covered employment whose contributions met the statutory requirement and who filed an application could receive benefits beginning January 1, 1952, if (1) total wages received after December 31, 1936, and before age 65 were not less than $2000, and (2) wages were paid to the individual on some day in each of five years after December 31, 1936, and before age 65. Beginning in 1939, the concept of insured status was defined more clearly as "fully insured" and "currently insured." The act defined a fully insured individual as one "with respect to whom it appears to the [Social Security] Board that (1) he had not less than one quarter of coverage for each two of the (calendar) quarters elapsing after 1936, or after the quarter in which he attained the age of twenty-one, which ever quarter is later, and up to but excluding the quarter in which he attained the age of sixty-five, or died, whichever first occurred, and in no case less than six quarters of coverage; or (2) He had at least forty quarters of coverage." A quarter of coverage was defined as a calendar quarter of covered employment in which not less than $50 in wages was received, or each quarter of an annual period in which $3000 or more had been received in wages following the first quarter of coverage. Thus, fully insured status depended upon a minimum number of quarters' employment in covered occupations and on minimum earnings. The second concept, "currently insured" status, was defined in the 1939 amendments to include "any individual with respect to whom it appears to the satisfaction of the Board that he has been paid wages of not less than $50 for each of not less than six of the twelve calendar quarters, immediately preceding the quarter in which he died." Benefits were payable to qualified survivors without discrimination based on status, except for parents', widows', and widowers' sured individuals. The definitions remained unchanged under the 1946 amendments with minor exceptions, but were changed in the 1950 and 1954 amendments.[1] As amended in 1954, a "fully insured"

[1] Also, the maximum earnings figure, previously $3000, became $3600 in 1951 and $4200 in 1955.

status is affected by the time of death and the occurrence of a period of disability. Thus, in the case of an individual who died prior to September 1, 1950, and had the minimum six quarters' coverage, fully insured status could be obtained by having had one quarter of coverage, regardless of where acquired, for each two of the quarters elapsing after 1936, subject, as before, to the date at which age 21 was attained or death occurred. Some 200,000 persons received benefits as a result of these provisions relating to individuals whose death occurred prior to September, 1950. The fully insured status was also liberalized. Individuals who did not die prior to September 1, 1950, became fully insured if they had the minimum six quarters of coverage and not less than one quarter of coverage (regardless of when acquired) for each two of the quarters elapsing after 1950, or after the quarter in which they attained age 21, but excluding the quarter in which retirement age was attained or death occurred, as previously stated. All covered persons dying or retiring prior to September 1, 1958,[2] therefore, are able to achieve fully insured status without fulfilling the "one quarter of coverage for each two elapsing quarters" provision. The regular requirements will govern insured status after the third quarter of 1958. Under the 1954 amendments, quarters elapsing during which the individual is disabled are not included in determining whether the one-in-two" requirement has been met. This is called the "disability freeze."

In summary, fully insured status may be achieved (excepting the special provisions for newly covered persons under the 1954 amendments) by (1) obtaining forty quarters of coverage over any period which permanently fully insures the individual, or (2) acquiring one quarter of coverage for each two quarters elasping after 1950, subject to an absolute minimum of six quarters.

Changes wrought in the currently insured status resulted in its being defined more carefully. At present, an individual who is currently insured must have not less than six quarters of coverage during the thirteen-quarter period ending with (1) the quarter in which he dies, (2) the quarter in which he becomes entitled to old-age-insurance

---

[2] By that date, any person continuously employed from January 1, 1955, through September 1, 1958, would meet the insured-status requirements of the 1950 amendment, namely, that he have one quarter of coverage for each two elapsing quarters after 1950—the total is thirty-one elapsing quarters, half of which is fifteen and one-half, and this reduces to fifteen because the total numbers of quarters, if odd, is reduced by one. Fifteen quarters' coverage would be obtained by continuous employment from January 1, 1954, through September 1, 1958, because the quarter in which retirement age is attained or death occurs is excluded.

benefits, or (3) the quarter in which he becomes entitled to primary insurance benefits as defined prior to the 1950 revision subject to the "disability freeze" provisions mentioned above. This permits an individual who does not meet the one-in-two requirement to achieve a status which qualifies his survivors for benefits.

BENEFITS

The primary-benefit formula contained in the original Social Security Act was changed substantially by amendments enacted in 1939, 1950, 1952, and 1954. All other benefits depend on this formula. Table 50 shows the benefit formulas under the Social Security Act of 1935 and its subsequent amendments. It will be seen that average

TABLE 50. Benefit Formulas Under the Social Security Act and Its Amendments.

Legislation	Monthly Benefit of Retired Worker	Period Over Which Monthly Wage Is Computed
1935	½% of first $3000 of cumulative wage credits + ½₂% of next $42,000 + ½₄% of next $84,000	Not applicable
1939	40% of first $50 of average monthly wage + 10% of next $200, all increased by 1% for each year of coverage	Entire period of potential coverage under system
1950	50% of first $100 of average monthly wage + 15% of next $200	Entire period of potential coverage under system after 1950
1952	55% of first $100 of average monthly wage + 15% of next $200	Entire period of potential coverage under system after 1950
1955	55% of first $110 of average monthly wage + 20% of next $240	Entire period of potential coverage under system after 1950, excluding the periods of extended disability and 4 or 5 years of lowest earnings

Source: Robert J. Myers, "Old Age and Survivors Insurance: History of the Benefit Formula," Social Security Bulletin, May, 1955, p. 13.

monthly wages (and maximum annual amounts creditable) and the period over which wages shall be computed determine the size of the benefit. Once these factors are known, computation of benefits becomes a simple clerical problem. The 1935 and 1939 laws permitted a maximum annual-wage credit of $3000; the 1950 and 1952 laws, $3600; and the 1954 law, $4200. Workers who retired at the earliest

time date of eligibility would receive the monthly benefits, as shown in the following illustration: [3]

Act	Maximum annual creditable wage	Average monthly wage	Monthly old-age benefit	Benefit as percent of average wage
1935	$3000	$250	$25.00	10%
1939	3000	250	41.20	16.5
1950	3600	300	80.00	26.7
1952	3600	300	85.00	28.3
1954	4200	350	108.50	31.0

The increases brought about in workers' retirement benefits are shown in the table and indicate an increase of more than 300 percent in the monthly benefits. The minimum and maximum benefits are not shown, however, and the considerable benefits established for dependents and survivors are not shown. In Table 51, data are presented relating to old-age benefits, family benefits, and death benefits.

TABLE 51. Minimum and Maximum Benefit Provisions Under the Social Security Act and Its Amendments

Benefit	1935	1939	1950	1952	1954
	Monthly Amounts Except Lump-Sum Death Payments				
Old-age benefit					
minimum	$10.00	$10.00	$20.00	$25.00	$30.00
maximum	85.00	60.00 [a]	80.00	85.00	108.50
Family benefit [b]					
minimum	n.a.[c]	$10.00	$15.00	$18.80	$30.00
maximum	n.a.	85.00	150.00	168.80	200.00
Lump-sum death payments [d]					
minimum	n.a.[e]	$60.00	$60.00	$75.00	$90.00
maximum	n.a.	360.00	240.00	255.00	255.00

[a] Assume fifty years as maximum coverage possible.
[b] Payable to retired worker and dependents or to survivor beneficiaries. Maximum provision of 80 percent of average monthly wage also applicable, but application may not reduce benefits to less than $25 for 1939 law, $40 for 1950 law, $45 for 1952 law, and $50 or one and one-half times the primary insurance benefit for 1954 law.
[c] Not applicable under 1935 act, which did not provide for family or survivor benefits.
[d] Under the 1939 and later laws, the lump-sum payment is made to the surviving widow or widower who lives with the deceased person at time of death. When there is no such survivor, the lump-sum payment cannot exceed burial expenses.
[e] No minimum or maximum provided—potential maximum was $5000.

Source: Robert J. Myers, "Old Age and Survivors Insurance: History of the Benefit Formula," Social Security Bulletin, May, 1955, p. 14.

One conclusion that is obvious from the table is that the proportionate increases in minimum old-age and family benefits have exceeded the increases in maximum benefits. For example, a 200 percent increase took place in the minimum old-age benefit from 1939 to 1954, as compared with a 81 percent change in the maximum benefit,

[3] Ibid., p. 15.

minimum family benefits also increased by 200 percent from 1939 to 1954, but the increase in maximum benefits, though large, was only 136 percent. The increases established by the amendments of 1950 and 1952 were motivated primarily by the desire to maintain the purchasing power of benefits in the face of rising costs. The 1954 changes recognized higher standards of adequacy and increased earnings.

Changes made in the other benefits derived from the insured worker's primary benefit have been increased by the several amendments, as shown in the table, but since 1939 the conditions which establish the right of dependents and survivors to receive benefits have undergone only minor change. In the case of each benefit type, the basis for computing benefits or payments is the insured worker's primary benefit, as discussed above.

Benefits payable to dependent family members if the worker is *fully insured* include monthly payments to a wife if 65 years of age or over (one-half primary benefit), to a child under 18 (one-half primary benefit), and to a wife, regardless of age, if caring for a child entitled to benefits (one-half primary benefit). Dependent husbands over 65 years of age may receive payments (one-half primary benefit) if the wife retires in both a fully insured and currently insured status. General requirements are that applications be filed for benefits; that in the case of wives and dependent husbands, the wife and husband be living together at the time application for benefits is made, the marriage having been in effect at least three years (except where the couple are parents of a child); that parent beneficiaries must be dependent and benefits can be paid only if no widow, widower, or child can qualify for benefits. Certain limitations on benefits will be discussed in a succeeding section. Survivors' benefits are made to a widow age 65 or over (three-fourths primary benefit); to a widow or dependent divorced wife, regardless of age, if caring for a child (three-fourths primary benefit); to a child under 18 years of age (three-fourths primary benefit); [4] to a dependent widower age 65 or over (three-fourths primary benefit). In the case of benefits to a widow age 65 or over and to dependent parents age 65 or over, *fully insured* status of the worker at death is required. The other survivor benefits, excepting the minor category of widowers' benefits, are payable on the basis of fully insured or currently insured status. The qualifications which apply to family

---

[4] In case of more than one surviving child, each gets half the primary benefit plus one-fourth the primary benefit divided by the number of children.

benefits for a retired worker also apply in general to survivors' benefits. However, unless the couple were parents of a child, an aged widow or widower must have been married to the insured worker for at least a year prior to death. The widow or widower must have been living with the insured at the time of his death, and must not have remarried. As in the case of family benefits, there are provisions for limitations on benefits, which will be discussed later. Lump-sum death payments in the amount of three times the primary benefit, or $255, whichever is smaller, are paid in behalf of fully or currently insured individuals to the widow or widower of the deceased (if determined to have been living with the deceased at the time of death); or, if no such person exists, then to persons "equitably entitled" to receive such payments although the amount thereof cannot exceed the burial expenses they may have paid.

LIMITATIONS ON BENEFITS

Each of the benefits described above may be reduced or withheld under certain conditions. In general, these conditions relate to the receipt of two or more monthly benefits, earnings from employment beyond the allowable limits stated in the statute, or failure to comply with certain administrative requirements.

Insurance benefits may be paid to the wife of an insured retired worker or a dependent husband only if the beneficiary is not entitled to a primary benefit or is entitled to old-age benefits each of which is less than one-half of the spouse's primary benefit. Widows' and widowers' insurance benefits may be paid only if the beneficiary is entitled to old age insurance benefits each of which is less than three-fourths of the primary insurance amount of the deceased husband or wife. Insurance benefits of widows with dependent minor children may only be paid if the beneficiary's old-age-insurance benefits remain less than three-fourths the primary insurance amount of the deceased. Parents' benefits are subject to the same rule and continue only while the parents receive old-age-insurance benefits less than three-fourths of the primary insurance amount of the deceased. A child is entitled to only one insurance benefit, based on the greatest primary insurance amount applicable.

Reduction of benefits is specifically provided where (1) individuals receive monthly benefits based on the wages and self-employment income of an insured individual which total more than $50 and exceed either 80 percent of his average monthly wage or one and one-

half times his primary insurance amount, whichever is greater to a maximum of $200; or (2) one of the individual beneficiaries receiving monthly benefits based on the wages and self-employment income of an insured individual is a surviving child whose father and mother died fully or currently insured, in which case the total monthly benefit will not be reduced below 80 percent of the sum of the average monthly wages of both parents, except that the total may not exceed $200. Gagliardo has given the following example of the reductions in operation.

Assume, for example, that an insured man with an average monthly wage of $250 and a primary insurance amount of $88.50 dies, leaving a wife and three children entitled to benefits. Her unreduced benefit will be $66.38 and each child's unreduced benefit will be $51.63. The unreduced total for all will be $221.27. This exceeds both 80 percent of the average monthly wage and one and one-half times the primary insurance amount, and it exceeds the absolute maximum of $200. It will have to be reduced to $200. Ten parts are involved: three-fourths for the mother and seven-fourths for the children combined, and each part of the $21.27 is $2.126. Reducing the mother's benefit by three parts leaves it at $60, and reducing the children's benefits by seven parts leaves their total at $140. In most cases a single check for the maximum total amount allowed is issued. When the oldest child reaches eighteen, the benefits are recomputed. The mother will receives $66.38 and each child $55.31; this is less than any prescribed maximum and therefore they receive the full amount of their benefits for that combination of beneficiaries. When the second child is eighteen, the mother and the remaining child will each get $66.38. When the third child reaches eighteen, all benefits cease. If the deceased husband was fully insured and if the mother meets the required conditions, she will become entitled to a widow's benefit at age sixty-five.[5]

The reductions in benefits are made proportionately, as Gagliardo shows. The justification for such reductions will be dealt with in the general evaluation of old-age and survivors' benefits.

Deductions in benefit payments are required on account of work after retirement and failure to have a child "in care" for whom benefits are received.

Deductions from monthly benefits are required when an individual entitled to benefits, but less than 72 years of age, earns more than $1200 in wages or self-employment income. Benefits will continue to be paid, though with increasing deductions, until earnings amount to

[5] Domenico Gagliardo, *American Social Insurance*, rev. ed., New York, Harper & Brothers, 1955, pp. 92–93.

more than $2080 through employment in all months of the year. Regardless of annual earnings, however, benefits are payable for any month in which earnings are $80 or less and the beneficiary does not render "substantial services" in self-employment. Rendering "substantial services" means actively engaging in the operation of a trade or business. Restrictions apply also to a beneficiary under age 72 who works outside the United States in uncovered employment for seven or more days in any month. The whole monthly benefit is lost. After attaining the age 72, the beneficiary may earn unlimited amounts of income without affecting benefits. A wife under retirement age entitled to a wife's insurance benefit, who does not have under her care a child of her husband (individually or jointly with her husband), or a widow or divorced wife entitled to a mother's insurance benefit, not having under her care a child of her deceased husband, suffers deductions from benefits.

Other deductions result from failure to report earnings properly to the Secretary. The amount of deduction may amount to a total from wife's, husband's, or child's insurance benefits equal to the amount of the last monthly benefit of the year for the first failure, twice that amount for the second failure, and so on.

An important phase of old-age and survivors' insurance relates to the adequacy of benefits. We shall deal with this problem in the final section.

ADMINISTRATIVE CHANGES

Amendments to the Social Security Act and other changes in the structure of federal welfare operations have affected the social insurances several times. Most recently (April, 1953), the Social Security Administration was lodged in the Department of Health, Education, and Welfare. In this move, the insurance and assistance programs were recognized with cabinet rank, signifying the vital role of social insurance, social assistance, and other programs in national life. The system of appeals and the decisions rendered are interesting aspects of administration.

The controversial administrative problems have been concerned with financing the insurance programs, however, and we shall limit ourselves in this discussion to cost and revenue considerations in the main.

In previous discussion we have made the point that the expenses of old-age dependency must inescapably be borne in some manner, even

though inadequately from the standpoint of relieving misery. Prior to the Social Security Act, which initiated old age benefits as a right, the costs were assumed without proper planning and with the burden of support falling unequally on individual families and private and public agencies. The transfer of costs in part to the states through public-assistance grants and in part to individual beneficiaries and their employers through compulsory premium payments resulted in a far more adequate system of security for the aged and survivors, at an increase in costs considerably less than proportionate to the increase in benefits. Centralized administration, with its consequent reductions in overhead expense, and the assumption of administrative expenses by the federal government in the early years of the program resulted in economies.

The expenses entailed in the OASI program are indicated in Table 52, which shows the magnitude of operations at the end of March,

TABLE 52. Old-Age and Survivors' Insurance, Monthly Benefits in Current Payment Status.

Beneficiaries	Number	Amounts	Average Monthly Benefits
Old age	3,984,511	$240,345,900	$60.32
Wife or husband	1,075,282	34,828,100	32.39
Child	1,182,866	42,067,800	35.56
Widow or widower	662,406	30,746,100	46.42
Mother	270,486	12,046,300	44.54
Parents	25,254	1,202,700	47.62
Total	7,200,805	$361,237,000	$50.17

Source: Social Security Bulletin, June, 1955, p. 27.

1955. The cumulative amount of tax receipts from January, 1937, through the end of March, 1955, amounted to nearly $34 billion, from which benefit expenditures of nearly $16 billion had been made. The annual amount of OASI benefits for 1955 (based on first quarter, 1955) will be close to $5 billion.

Financing the program of OASI benefits has always been accomplished through the imposition of taxes on the employer's payroll and the employee's wages. Initially, these taxes were to be 1 percent for the years 1937–1939, 1.5 percent for 1940–1942, 2 percent for 1943–1945, 2.5 percent for 1946–1948, and 3 percent in 1949 and years thereafter. Under the 1939 amendments, the 1937–1939 rate was to be retained through 1942, going to 2 percent at the end of 1942, 2.5 percent at the end of 1945, and 3 percent at the end of 1948. Actually

the 1 percent rate was retained through 1950. Since 1939, the OASI benefits taxes have been collected under a subchapter of the Internal Revenue Code and both collections and disbursements have been made by the U.S. Treasury Department. In 1946, amendments retained the 1 percent rate through 1947 and provided for an increase to 2.5 percent in 1948 and 3 percent thereafter. In 1947, a new tax rate was established freezing the rates at 1 percent until 1950, when it would increase to 1.5 percent; in 1952, it would increase to 2 percent and remain at that rate until changed by Congress. The 1950 amendments changed the applicable tax rate to 1.5 percent for 1950–1952, 2 percent for 1954–1959, 2.5 percent for 1960–1964, 3 percent for 1965–1969, and 3.25 percent for the years thereafter. At present, the tax rates under the 1954 amendments are 2 percent for the years 1955–1959, 2.5 percent for 1960–1964, 3 percent for 1965–1969, 3.5 percent for 1970–1974, and 4 percent for the years after 1974. The rate applicable to self-employed persons is one and one-half times the rates which apply to employees and is levied on their net earnings. These changes are summarized in Table 53.

TABLE 53. Changes in Applicable Tax Rates, Old-Age and Survivors' Insurance, 1935–1954.[a]
(percentages)

Years to Which Tax Applies	Original Act [b]	1939 Amendments [c]	1946 Amendments [d]	1947 Amendments [e]	1950 Amendments [f]	1954 Amendments [g]
1937–1939	1	1	—	—	—	—
1940–1942	1½	1	—	—	—	—
1943–1945	2	2	—	—	—	—
1946–1947	2½	2½	1	—	—	—
1948	2½	2½	2½	1	—	—
1949	3	3	3	1	—	—
1950–1951				1½	1½	—
1952				2	1½	—
1953					1½	—
1954					2	—
1955–1959					2	2
1960–1964					2½	2½
1965–1969					3	3
1970–1974					3¼	3½
1974–					3¼	4

a Workers in covered employment.
b Applicable to $3000 earnings base.
c Applicable to $3000 earnings base.
d Applicable to $3000 earnings base.
e Applicable to $3000 earnings base.
f Applicable to $3600 earnings base.
g Applicable to $4200 earnings base.

Source: Various compilations of social-security laws, Washington, Government Printing Office.

The frequent delay in increasing taxes to support the OASI program requires some explanation. In 1939, the fundamental reorientation of the program to serve families in retirement and survivors of insured workmen brought a change in tax rates. After 1939, concern was felt for the enormous reserve fund that would be accumulated at the given rates, and Congress took steps to ensure that the fund would be at least adequate to meet three times the highest annual expenditures anticipated during the ensuing five fiscal years. During the 1940's, the idea of a contingency reserve fund gained favor and freezing of tax rates reflected the view that a self-sustaining program was not necessary for the foreseeable future. If outgo should exceed income, then liquidation of trust-fund securities would make up the balance. Actually, the high levels of employment enabled the fund to increase by large amounts, as we shall see. By 1950, the proposals for expansion of coverage and increases in benefits had created doubts about a "contingency reserve," and efforts were made in some quarters to get the program on an annual "pay-as-you-go" basis. The rate increases provided in the 1950 and 1954 amendments reflect a more conservative view of financing. The hope is that the excess of collections over payments at present will permit the growth of a reserve fund, the interest return on which will be sufficiently large to offset years in which payments exceed collections. Before the end of the present century, it is expected by some critics of OASI financing that collctions plus interest earnings will be insufficient to finance the program.

The future cost of the OASI program is dependent on "natural factors" (birth and death rates, marriage rates, disability rates, and age distribution of the population) and "economic and political factors" (levels of earnings, distribution of income, levels of price, and propensity to retire on benefits when eligible).[6] Since each of these factors is variable, studies which seek to determine future costs cannot possibly be carried out with accuracy. Such studies have frequently yielded results which differ by more than 50 percent simply as a consequence of using high-cost or low-cost estimates.[7]

---

[6] Lewis Meriam and Karl Schlotterbeck, *The Cost and Financing of Social Security*, Washington, Brookings Institution, 1950, pp. 25–26.

[7] See, for example, Robert J. Myers and E. A. Rasor, *Long Range Cost Estimates for Expanded Coverage and Liberalized Benefits Proposed to the Old-Age and Survivors Insurance System by H.R. 2893*, Security Administration, Actuarial Study No. 28, February, 1949, pp. 11–17; and *Old-Age and Survivors Insurance, a Report to the Senate Committee on Finance from the Advisory Council on Social Security*, Senate Document No. 149, Eightieth Congress, 2nd Session, 1948, pp. 55–56.

Schemes for financing the OASI program are highly complex, and we can merely note the more important factors involved and relate them to material already discussed. A potentially dangerous financial scheme proposed by the Chamber of Commerce of the United States has been widely discussed in recent years, and we should evaluate it. The role of taxes and the nature of the reserve fund are the two financial factors that we shall discuss.

Taxes which take income disproportionately from lower-income spending units are regressive and violate the "ability-to-pay" principle of fair and equitable taxation. Since the income on which the OASI tax is levied is uniformly $4200 for all persons in covered employment, regardless of income levels, it is a regressive tax. Furthermore, the tax paid by the employer, which is levied at the same rate as that paid by the employee, is probably shifted in large part to consumers in the form of higher prices for goods and services. It is not known to what extent the shifting of taxes results in greater regressivity. Referring back to our discussion in Chapter 11 regarding the flow of income payments, we can recognize another problem associated with OASI taxes; the government sector removes a larger amount from the payments stream in collections than it returns in benefit payments. Thus the household units (as a whole) must carry on their consumption of goods and services with reduced income. Except for the first three years of operation under the system, this effect has not been felt because the federal government has more than replaced the tax collections with total payments other than OASI benefits. In a period when inflationary pressures are strong, i.e., when the tendency for money payments to outstrip the availability of goods does not appear to be controllable through credit policy, this reduction in money payments is desirable of course. And the whole question of regressive taxes is thus related to whether the fundamental characteristic of economy is inflation or deflation. No agreement on this question would satisfy all economists, and we have already observed that the economy is "mixed," often experiencing inflation and deflation concurrently. If the reader is dissatisfied with the lack of finality and decisiveness in this kind of conclusion, he shares his plight with most economists!

The reserve fund has been accumulated as a natural consequence of the OASI system being in its youth. Because most persons contributing to the system will not become entitled to benefits for many years, tax collections exceed benefit payments. Thus, in the 1953–1954 fiscal

year, contributions and transfers to the fund totaled nearly $4.6 billion, and the fund earned in interest nearly $439 million. Benefit payments totaled $3.3 billion and expenses about $89 million, permitting the fund to increase by more than $1.6 billion (from $18.4 billion in 1952–1953 to more than $20 billion in 1953–1954). The question arises whether the fund is useful or even necessary. Obviously, in the future money for payments will have to be found from some source outside the fund since total benefit payments are going to increase steadily as larger numbers of persons gain entitlements and tax rates and interest earnings will be insufficient to provide necessary revenues. But we are not left with the single choice of building a reserve fund large enough to cover anticipated benefits, though levying tax rates sufficiently high to produce such a fund is one possible solution. Such a "level-premium" plan to enable the program to sustain itself would call for much higher tax rates at present than are warranted by benefit payments. The other options are to impose moderate increases in taxes in the future and bear part of the deficits from general revenues, or bear the deficits which will appear out of general revenues, i.e., by appropriations from the public treasury.

Advocates of the level-premium reserve plan claim these advantages for it: (1) it would safeguard the rights of contributors by setting aside funds to be used exclusively for benefit payments, and (2) interest payments on the reserve would lighten the burden of future generations, which otherwise would be called on to defray deficits that would arise under any other method of finance. Concerning the first argument, the federal government borrows the contributions which are in excess of the amounts required to pay current benefits anyway, and those who become entitled to benefits have a claim against only the general fiscal capacity of the nation, not against a private fund. The second argument is ill founded in assuming that an economic burden can be shifted in real terms, and that an increasing fund of forced savings would in fact be matched by investment levels necessary to maintain national income at full-employment levels. Disadvantages cited by critics, in addition to those already noted, are that a huge fund is apt to lead legislators either to liberalize benefits beyond the extent necessary or to use the fund more irresponsibly. At the opposite extreme, the pay-as-you-go plan, if it allows for no accumulation of reserves, has even more disadvantages, the most important of which is that it would probably restrict increases in coverage and benefit levels. Furthermore, the interest earnings on the trust fund would be

foregone, so that ultimately taxes for this specific purpose would have to be higher.

The expedient system which the United States has employed since 1951 is a modification of the pay-as-you-go and reserve plans. It allows for moderate tax increases to enable the program to sustain itself with interest earnings, yet permits the accumulation of a reserve fund. This method, it is hoped, will permit dividing costs equitably over the years and absorbing short-term fluctuations in benefits and tax collections.

One other proposal for financing OASI has been given extensive advertisement by the Chamber of Commerce of the United States.[8] It is more than a proposal dealing with costs, but its financing recommendations have drawn the most fire. Basically, the plan would discontinue federal support of the various public-assistance programs and pay benefits out of the present OASI fund until it was exhausted. In the meanwhile, taxes would be frozen at the 1951 rates. When the fund finally was exhausted, taxes on payrolls would be imposed at sufficiently high rates to meet the costs of benefits and administration on a year-to-year basis. Many students of American social legislation have criticized the plan. The most serious objections have concerned the tax rates that would be necessary to cover the expenses of the program upon exhaustion of the trust fund. Rates as high as 10 percent have been anticipated. It is extremely doubtful that a future Congress would be prepared to impose such rates, probably the key to the whole plan. Professor Burns pointed out a major shortcoming in the tax proposals, noting that ". . . it would shift the burden of supporting the mass of the present aged (those receiving assistance payments) from taxation levied on all income receivers (including income from property and persons subject to high rates of taxation) and place it on the first $3600 of income earned by workers (or paid by their employers) who would all pay at a nongraduated rate and with no exceptions. This seems a real step backward." [9] Another criticism concerned the assumption that assistance benefits might somehow be financed out of existence by the expedient of a strict contributory plan. It is generally agreed that assistance payments will continue to be an important part of the Social Security system and that assistance needs are both real and difficult to insure. Insurance on a contributory basis could provide against only average risks. The Chamber of Com-

[8] Proposed Policy Declaration: Federal Social Security Program for the Aged, Referendum No. 93, Washington, Chamber of Commerce of the United States, 1952.

[9] Eveline M. Burns, Comments on the Chamber of Commerce Social Security Proposals (mimeographed), Chicago, American Public Welfare Association, 1953.

merce proposal would of course forego interest earnings, but some of its defenders have countered any objections by assuming that the OASI trust fund is irregular anyway because its assets are in the form of United States Government securities. The apparent reasoning is that the securities would not exist if the trust fund did not purchase them. In this connection, the Advisory Council on Social Security explained in defense of the investment of the fund in government securities that ". . . such investment is as reasonable and proper as is the investment by life insurance companies of their own reserve funds in Government securities. The fact that the Government uses the proceeds received from the sales of securities to pay the costs of the War and its other expenses is entirely legitimate. It no more implies mishandling of moneys received from the sale of securities to the trust fund than it does of the moneys received from the sale of United States securities to life insurance companies, banks, or individuals." [10] In spite of their many shortcomings, pay-as-you-go methods of financing and some variation of the Chamber's proposals will be pressed from time to time. A more sophisticated plan having some of the features of the Chamber of Commerce plan was prepared by the National Planning Association.[11] It would accomplish the transfer of assistance beneficiaries to the OASI system by having the costs of their past service credits paid to the trust fund out of general tax revenues. It meets only some of the objections mentioned in connection with the Chamber's proposals.

Participation by the federal government in financing of OASI has been proposed by many students of social security. The position taken by the Advisory Council on Social Security is illustrative: "The Council believes that the Federal Government should participate in financing the old-age and survivors' insurance system. A government contribution would be a recognition of the interest of the nation as a whole in the welfare of the aged and of widows and children." [12] The extent of the Government contribution, as seen by the Council, is revealed in the suggestion that "Old-Age and Survivors Insurance benefits should be planned on the assumption that general taxation will eventually share more or less equally with employer and employee contributions in financing future benefit outlays and administrative

---

[10] *Old-Age and Survivors Insurance*, p. 47.

[11] Joint Committee on the Economic Report, *Pensions in the United States* (prepared by the National Planning Association), Eighty-second Congress, 2nd Session, 1952.

[12] *Old-Age and Survivors Insurance*, pp. 45–46.

costs." [13] It would appear that the Council urges eventual participation by the federal government to the extent of one-third or more. Justification for such participation is founded on two main propositions. First, the OASI system when initiated took on accrued liabilities, with the result that many persons in the present generation will retire and draw benefits without having worked a full lifetime. It is inequitable, therefore, to require those who enter the system later to pay for this extraordinary benefit load in addition to their own protection. The second proposition is that OASI taxes are regressive and the full cost of insuring against the hazards of dependent old age and survivorship ought to be borne in part by property income (rent, interest, profits, etc.) rather than exclusively by labor income (wages, salaries, and self-employment income). Professor Burns has commented on the fact that the choice is not between participation or nonparticipation through general tax revenues, but a choice among the programs to which such a subsidy shall be given: "A large proportion of low-paid workers if excluded from coverage or granted grossly inadequate OASI benefits, will apply for Old-Age Assistance which is financed entirely by the general taxpayer." [14]

Current Operations and Issues

In our discussion thus far, we have discussed the mechanics of OASI. Only incidentally have we mentioned the adequacy of benefits, proposals for reform, and similar issues. More than 105,000,000 people had built up wage credits by the beginning of 1955, of whom nearly 95,200,000 were living. Fully insured status had been achieved by 69,800,000, 25,100,000 of them being permanently fully insured. Insurance protection for the aged had been extended to nearly all eligible persons outside government employment and the armed forces. Benefits payable under OASI have increased markedly in recent years, and the proportion of persons age 65 and over receiving OASI benefits more than quadrupled between 1946 and 1955, increasing from 9 percent to 41 percent of all such persons.[15] Moreover, the value of benefits has increased sufficiently to maintain the income position of aged persons in the face of strong inflationary pressures, as the following comparison shows: [16]

---

[13] Ibid.
[14] Burns, The American Social Security System, p. 121.
[15] Lenore A. Epstein, "Money Income Sources for Persons Aged 65 and Over, June 1955," Social Security Bulletin, December, 1955, p. 22.
[16] Ibid., p. 9.

TABLE 54. Median Income of Aged Persons and the Consumers Price Index (1945 = 100), 1945–1952.

Year	Median income (1945 = 100)	CPI (1945 = 100)
1945	100	100
1946	n.a.	108
1947	132	124
1948	140	134
1949	134	132
1950	145	134
1951	162	144
1952	170	148

By 1955 the OASI program was established as a major factor in the workaday life of aged persons. The debates which remained concerned administrative alternatives in such matters as finance and benefit restrictions.

ISSUES

Not all of the shortcomings of the OASI system were corrected in the liberalizations enacted in 1950 and 1954. Coverage of public employees, members of the armed forces, and certain other groups on a compulsory basis is still sought by some legislators. In the waning days of the Eighty-fourth Congress, 1st Session, a bill passed the House of Representatives (H.R. 7225) which called for these changes in the Social Security Act: (1) benefits to begin for women at age 62 instead of age 65; (2) payments equivalent to full retirement benefits for totally disabled workers at age 50; (3) continuation of benefits to mentally and physically disabled dependent children past the present limit of age 18; (4) coverage of all self-employed professional persons, excluding physicians, on a compulsory basis; and (5) increases in taxes beginning January 1, 1956, to 2.5 percent each for employers and employees and 3¾ percent for self-employed persons, and increases of 0.5 percent and 0.75 percent for employers-employees and self-employed persons respectively in 1960, 1965, 1970, and 1975. Another bill (H.R. 7089) passed by the House would have included personnel of the armed forces on the same basis as civilian employees.

Some of the proposed changes are undoubtedly justified by the principle of increasing social-insurance coverage. The reduction in age at which women gain entitlement to benefits, for example, would permit many people to retire who presently must delay retirement

until the wife attains age 65—because the retirement benefits obtainable on the basis of one person's earnings are inadequate to support the couple. However, there is considerable sentiment at the present time for delaying the retirement of workers in their own interest as well as the interest of the OASI system. The relative merits of permitting or postponing retirement and other similar questions might have been aired in hearings connected with the bill, but none were held. One of the major objections to the proposed amendments is that they constitute a one-party measure that was proposed and passed within thirty days. Bipartisan agreement on amendments of the social-insurance programs, even at the cost of compromises which reduce the effect of changes, seems necessary if the future growth of the programs is to be assured.

Unemployment Compensation

Participation by the federal government in the provision of insurance against loss of earnings owing to unemployment is indirect. As we noted in Chapter 12, tax credits are given by the federal government against a payroll tax which it levies on employers, provided the employer makes contributions to an approved state unemployment-insurance system. The requirements for approval of state plans have changed very little from the provisions laid down in the original Social Security Act. Provisions regulating the use of withdrawn funds and recovery of moneys erroneously paid into the funds are typical of the changes made. A 1939 provision required that the states select administrative personnel according to the merit system. The conditions surrounding the imposition of the tax have also been changed, notably with respect to excluded employment. At the state level, the changes have been numerous and have concerned essentially the same matters which we considered in connection with old-age and survivors' insurance, namely, coverage, eligibility, benefits, and administrative matters. In contrast to the simple provisions of a single jurisdiction which characterized OASI, unemployment compensation is characterized by wide diversity among the fifty-one jurisdictions.

COVERAGE

Workers build up rights to compensation under unemployment-insurance compensation, but limitations on the proportion of workers who have actually accrued such rights are numerous. Only employers who meet certain criteria are liable to the provisions of the Federal

Unemployment Tax Act, and the criteria include (1) size of firm, (2) employee status, (3) location of employment, and (4) type of employment.[17]

The size-of-firm provision which requires employers to pay taxes usually is determined by the number of employees in the establishment.[18] Under the original act, the tax was applied to employers of *eight* or more workers, but this was amended in 1954 to apply to employers of *four* or more workers after 1955. However, by August, 1954, only twenty-four states had failed to make their laws applicable to employers of four or more workers.[19] In seventeen states, employers of one worker are taxed.[20] A time period is introduced in nine states, as in the Minnesota law, which covers employers of "eight or more employees in twenty weeks." [21] Care has been taken in the laws of most states to prevent the splitting of employment units to avoid coverage. Also, each state permits employers to enter the unemployment-insurance system voluntarily if they wish.

The tests applied in nearly all states to ascertain whether a person is an employee under the terms of the compensation acts involve each of the following tests (twenty-five states) or one or more of them (seventeen states): unless service for remuneration is considered employment, (1) the worker is free from control or direction of the performance of his work under his contract of service, and in fact (2) the service is outside the usual course of business for which it is performed; and (3) the individual is customarily engaged in an independent trade, occupation, profession, or business. The remaining states define employment status in terms of a master-servant relationship under common law or accept a contract for hire as sufficient evidence of employee status.

One condition of coverage, location of work, is uniform throughout all jurisdictions. The provisions relating to location of work attempt to meet the problem which arises when individuals work in more than one state. Under the uniform provisions, coverage of a multistate worker is restricted to a single state. Two approaches are used to this

[17] U.S. Department of Labor, Bureau of Employment Security, *Comparison of State Unemployment Insurance Laws*, 1954, pp. 1–13. This discussion draws extensively on the Bureau's compilation, which includes state legislation as of August, 1954.

[18] In thirteen states the amount of wages paid is a factor, the *only* factor in California, Idaho, Nevada, Utah, and Wyoming. (We shall employ the term "states" throughout to include Alaska, Hawaii, and the District of Columbia.)

[19] Bureau of Employment Security, *op. cit.*, p. 2.

[20] *Ibid.*

[21] *Ibid.*, p. 3.

end. The first permits employers to elect coverage of employees who perform their services entirely outside the state if they are not covered by any other state or federal unemployment-insurance law, while the second enables states to enter into reciprocal agreements with reference to coverage.[22]

All state laws exclude certain employments from coverage, and the exclusions are relatively uniform because they follow those exclusions listed in the Federal Unemployment Tax Act. Exclusions under the state laws apply to agricultural labor (every jurisdiction except the District of Columbia), domestic service in private homes (every jurisdiction except New York), service performed for relatives (every jurisdiction except Wisconsin), nonprofit organizations (every jurisdiction except Hawaii), service for state and federal governments (thirty-eight states exclude state and local employees, but only one state limits coverage of federal workers to the extent permitted by Congress), and maritime workers (seven jurisdictions).[23]

As a result of these coverage provisions, many workers (about one of every three) are excluded from the protection of the laws. Gagliardo points out that, in 1951, nearly one-half of covered employment was in six highly industrialized states, while the six states having the smallest percentage had a combined total of less than 1 per cent.[24] Variations in coverage among industries are also extensive, being highest in manufacturing and lowest in agriculture and mining.

ELIGIBILITY

As in the case of old-age and survivors' insurance, the simple fact of being in covered employment does not by itself establish entitlement to unemployment benefits. Every state has eligibility requirements and enumerates certain disqualifications which produce ineligibility. All state laws require that the person filing a claim for benefits be able to work and available for work. "Able to work" requires physical (and in some cases mental) fitness in a few states, but most often is established by the registration of the claimant at a public employment office on a weekly basis. The conditions which surround "availability for work" show much more variation. In seven states, a claimant is required to be available for suitable work, and six states specify suitability for the individual claimant in terms of

[22] *Ibid.*, p. 8.
[23] *Ibid.*, pp. 9–13.
[24] Gagliardo, *op. cit.*, p. 280.

work in his usual occupation or for which he is reasonably fitted by training and experience.[25] Other provisions require availability for full-time work and active seeking of work. Evidence for availability consists in the claimant's regularly presenting himself for work at a local public-employment office. Several types of disqualification below constitute evidence of nonavailability.

Disqualification from benefits may result from voluntary separation of the claimant from work, refusal of suitable work as defined in the various statutes, discharge for misconduct, and unemployment owing to a labor dispute. It is important to distinguish between the status of unavailability for work or inability to work and disqualification from benefits. The latter ineligibility is imposed for a specified period, such as the week in which the disqualifying act occurs. For voluntarily leaving work, the nature of disqualification is postponement of benefits for a specified number of weeks in thirteen states, a variable number in twenty-three states, and for the duration of unemployment in sixteen states.[26] Furthermore, in seventeen states reduction of benefits or their cancellation is imposed. In every state except Montana, a distinction is made between leaving work voluntarily "for good cause" and other conditions of voluntary separation. Definitions of "good cause" are complex; illustrative conditions relate to fault on the part of the employer, returning to a regular apprenticeable trade, leaving to join the armed forces, etc. Refusal to accept suitable work is a condition which results in disqualification in all states. The extent of disqualification varies considerably from state to state. Refusal to accept new work may not result in disqualification (1) where the position offered is vacant owing to a strike, lockout, or other labor dispute; (2) if the wages, hours, or other conditions of work are substantially less favorable than those prevailing for similar work in the locality; or (3) if as a condition of being employed the individual would be required to join a company union or to resign from or refrain from joining any bona-fide labor organization. These prohibitions on the states are contained in Section 3304(a) of the Federal Unemployment Tax Act. When disqualifications are imposed, it is generally because the claimants refused to apply for suitable work when directed by the employment office or when such work was offered. The disqualification imposed is reduction or cancellation of benefits. In twenty-five states, the disqualification lasts for a variable

---

[25] Ibid., p. 76.
[26] Ibid., p. 76.

number of weeks; but it is for the duration of employment in fifteen states, and ten of these specify an amount that the claimant must earn or a period of time he must work to remove the disqualification.[27] Some states reduce or cancel benefit rights for any such disqualification. Discharge for misconduct results in postponement of benefits or their reduction or cancellation. Disqualification varies with the nature of the misconduct. Aggravated and gross misconduct result in heavier disqualifications. In thirty-two states, the period of disqualification is variable, being from one to twenty-four weeks; disqualification is for the entire period of unemployment in nine states; and reduction or cancellation of benefits is a consequence of such separation in seventeen states.[28]

Disqualification for unemployment caused by labor disputes differs from the conditions thus far discussed. When a worker is unemployed owing to an employer's lockout, reduction or postponement of benefits is hardly justified. Such action would work to the employer's advantage and be inconsistent with the labor-standards provisions of the Federal Unemployment Tax Act. Again, there is the likelihood that an employee not directly connected with a labor dispute might nonetheless become unemployed owing to strike action of workers upon whose work performance his own job depends. These and other difficulties faced in the general application of the labor-disputes disqualification have been recognized in the provisions of state laws. Nine states exclude lockouts, and other states exclude disputes where the employer is involved in a breach of the labor-management agreement or is being struck as a protest against substandard working conditions.[29] Unless a worker actively participates in, finances, or directly interests himself in a dispute, he is protected from disqualification if he becomes unemployed as a consequence of the dispute.[30] In nearly all jurisdictions, disqualifications last for the duration of the labor dispute. Variations in the actual period of disqualification result from the use of such phrases as "period during which the dispute is in active progress."

The disqualification of certain other groups is provided in most unemployment-compensation laws. Most common are students who are not available for unemployment while attending school, women who are unable to work because of pregnancy, and women who separate

---

[27] Bureau of Employment Security, op. cit., p. 89.
[28] Ibid., p. 86.
[29] Ibid., p. 91.
[30] Ibid., p. 95.

themselves from employment owing to marital obligations. In each instance, the disqualifying factor relates to unavailability. Those who make fraudulent statements in connection with the filing of claims for benefits are automatically disqualified by the attempt to defraud. Finally, all states disqualify claimants who receive benefits under any other unemployment-insurance law, and most states include dismissal wages and severance pay. A few states include workmen's-compensation benefits and old-age and survivors' insurance benefits as disqualifying income. The disqualifications normally take the form of reductions in benefits.

Qualifications relating to the worker's earnings and employment have the purpose of establishing his connection with the labor force, of which he must be a member.

The base period refers, as we have noted, to the employee's record of covered work over a period of time. When the individual worker's base period is known, a "benefit year," during which his rights to compensation remain in force, can be computed. All the states with one exception use the same base period for establishing wage and employment qualification, weekly benefit amounts, and duration of benefits. This period is fifty-two weeks in most states and usually the last four quarters preceding the benefit year or four of the last five quarters. In thirty-six states, an individual "benefit year" begins with the week in which a worker first files a claim that is valid in terms of the wage qualification.[31] The base period (which does not coincide exactly with the benefit year in twenty-eight states) in forty-two states begins and terminates according to the date when the worker applies for benefits or begins drawing benefits. The importance of the base period and benefit year can be appreciated by the fact that, to draw benefits, a worker who uses up his entitlement to compensation before the expiration of a benefit year must wait until a new benefit year begins. The benefits will be based on a new base period.

BENEFITS

Benefits under the state unemployment-insurance laws have changed markedly since the first laws were introduced. Initially, benefits were based on a percentage of full-time average wages. At present, benefits depend on the employee's experience in covered employment during a specified period of time called the "base period." Important determinants of the benefits paid are amount of employment and

[31] Ibid., p. 46.

wages required to establish entitlement to benefits, the period for which wages are counted, the method of computing the weekly benefit amount, and the method of determining the duration of benefits paid.[32] These factors show great diversity among the states. Three variations are to be distinguished in the qualifying conditions that have been established—wages equal to a multiple of the weekly benefit (twenty-one states), a flat qualifying amount (twelve states), or a specified number of weeks of employment (six states).[33] The multiplier in states having such a requirement ranges from twenty to thirty-five, and is applied to the weekly benefit amount. Where a flat amount of wages is required, the amount varies between $200 and $600. Each of the six states with employment requirements has unique provisions. In Michigan, New Jersey, New York, and Wisconsin, only those weeks are covered in which the average wage is above a minimum figure. Some states impose an additional requirement with respect to total earnings in the highest quarter of the base period.

A waiting period, during which an employee's loss of earnings cannot be compensated, is provided for in all but three states. Nearly all of the states impose a period of one week of total unemployment. In a few states periods of partial unemployment are combined, such as two weeks partial unemployment being equivalent to a week of total unemployment.

The weekly benefit amount is payable, therefore, when the following conditions have been met: (1) the unemployed individual has filed a claim for benefits, (2) the claimant registers his ability and availability for work, (3) the claimant has not left his previous job under any of the disqualifying conditions discussed above, (4) the claimant must have met the earnings and employment qualification, and (5) the claimant must have served a waiting period. We can now analyze the arithmetic of benefit calculation.

Unemployment time is measured in some states according to the amount of remuneration received, if any. New York uses a unit called an "effective day," explained as follows: "The first three days of unemployment in any week are Qualifying Days and are not compensated. Any additional days of unemployment are 'Effective Days' which are compensable." [34] Benefits are paid for each accumulation

---

[32] Ibid., p. 42.
[33] Ibid., p. 50.
[34] Handbook for Employers, New York State Department of Labor, Division of Employment, Albany, 1954, p. 24.

of effective days within a week. Actual computation of benefits, however, is based on the employee's past record of earnings, subject to certain provisions relating to minima and maxima. In thirty-eight states, the benefit formula is applied to that quarter in the base period in which the employee's wages were highest. The formula is 1/26 of the earnings in the highest quarter in six states, 1/25 in eleven states, 1/24 in one state, 1/23 in one state and 1/20 in eight states.[35] In eleven states, a weighted formula designed to compensate workers in the lower pay brackets is used, and in nine states the benefit is a percentage of annual wages.[36] Average weekly wages are the basis for computing the weekly benefit in Michigan, New Jersey, New York, and Wisconsin and the percentage of the wage compensated averages about 65 percent.[37] Minimum and maximum provisions show very wide variation. In Missouri, the weekly minimum is 50 cents and in Oregon it is $15. The eleven states which increase benefits when the claimants have dependents provide a higher minimum. Maximum benefits depend closely upon the dependents supported by the claimant. Claimants without dependents face a maximum weekly benefit ranging from $20 to $35, while claimants with dependents face limits of $26 to $70 (except in Massachusetts, where no maximum is imposed).[38] Benefits for partial unemployment are, of course, less than for total unemployment, the differential most frequently being the benefit amount less wages earned. Limits are imposed on the amount of wages which can be disregarded in computing the weekly benefit.

Unemployment compensation is more accurately referred to as temporary unemployment compensation because the duration of benefits is limited in all States. A uniform period of entitlement for claimants meeting the wage requirements is provided in fourteen states. In no case does the maximum potential period exceed twenty-six and one-half weeks, nor the maximum amount exceed $910 for claimants without dependents or $1,820 for claimants with dependents. The common maximum period of entitlement tends toward the twenty-six weeks noted, but the average maximum amount of benefits (without dependents' allowances) is less than $800 in forty-nine jurisdictions.[39]

[35] Bureau of Employment Security, *op. cit.*, pp. 56–57.
[36] *Ibid.*, p. 58.
[37] *Ibid.*, p. 58.
[38] *Ibid.*, p. 60.
[39] *Ibid.*, p. 72.

ADMINISTRATIVE MATTERS

Decentralized administration has produced a system of unemployment compensation characterized by gross inequities in benefit payments. We shall see shortly that employers also are inequitably—even arbitrarily—treated under the existing system. Following a brief survey of the general characteristics of unemployment administration, we shall discuss the more controversial financial factors.

Three administrative arrangements are employed by the states to carry out their programs of unemployment compensation. In nineteen states, independent boards or commissions administer the laws. In each state, bipartisan or tripartite representation is required. Independent departments of the state government are the administering agencies in fourteen states, and the remaining eighteen states operate programs through the department of labor or the workmen's-compensation agency.[40] Most states make provision for an advisory council to aid in formulating policies and smoothing operating difficulties. Numbers are drawn on a state-wide basis, and labor, management, and the public are represented in most states.

Appeals machinery was required in state programs by the Social Security Act and, hence, all states have an appeals procedure. Two stages of appeal are ordinarily specified before an appeal can be made to the courts. The procedure is similar to that described in connection with workmen's compensation in that an initial hearing is held before a referee or examiner, and a second appeal is held before a larger body, usually an appeals board or the commission charged with administration of the compensation law.

FINANCING UNEMPLOYMENT INSURANCE

Funds to support benefits in state unemployment-insurance programs are obtained from employer contributions based on the wages of covered employees, although in two states (Alabama and New Jersey) contributions are also collected from employees.[41] Administrative costs are borne by the federal government, and these grants are in such amounts as will meet the total cost of "proper and efficient administration." Other sources of revenue are the excess of collections over administrative costs in connection with the 0.3 percent of the 3

[40] *Ibid.*, pp. 108–110.

[41] Seven other states have previously collected employee contributions at some time, including California, Indiana, Kentucky, Louisiana, Massachusetts, New Hampshire, and Rhode Island.

percent unemployment tax collected by the federal government, which is credited to the federal unemployment account, and moneys received through fines, penalties, etc., by the states. The funds from which payments are made are of two types: "pooled funds" (in fifty jurisdictions) and, in a combination of reserve-account and pooled-fund situation, benefits are paid out of generally collected funds rather than from the specific account of an employer. Under Kentucky's system, the pooled fund is a contingency fund out of which benefits are paid after an employer's reserve account has been exhausted.

EXPERIENCE RATING

Since 1938, a movement to vary the contributions of employers according to their experience with unemployment risk has gained general acceptance. The Federal Unemployment Tax Act as amended in 1939 permitted pooled-fund systems to give employers an additional credit for reduced rates of contribution justified by their experience with unemployment. Barring this provision, a reduced rate of contribution at the state level would not benefit the employer because he would be liable to the federal government for the difference between 90 percent of the federal tax and his state contribution anyway. But at present an employer meeting the necessary requirements may deduct from the federal tax the full amount of the maximum contribution within the state regardless of the amounts actually contributed. Amendments to the basic law in 1954 liberalized the three-year experience qualification previously imposed.

The formulas for determination of experience rating are intricate and vary greatly among the states. Each has as a common denominator a measurement of the relative incidence of unemployment among employers. On this basis, the insurance contribution is reduced. Five distinct systems of experience rating are in use at the present time. Because they permit reductions in the effective tax rate, these provisions have been of immense benefit to employers. It is estimated that the average tax rate instead of being 2.7 percent is actually about 1.6 percent as a consequence of these deductions.[42]

Economists have frequently pointed out the fallacy in the assumptions upon which experience rating rests. The unemployment experience of a particular employer's labor force is seldom within his control to any appreciable extent. Yet the employer whose labor force

[42] William J. Shultz and C. Lowell Harriss, *American Public Finance*, 6th ed., New York, Prentice-Hall, 1954, p. 323.

maintains a stable employment record is rewarded on the assumption that the result is his handiwork. Employers in industries which are sensitive in an abnormal degree to business conditions are thus penalized. Probably, the legislators who provided for such an unsound policy in 1939 were victims of a mistaken analogy involving workmen's compensation. In that case, incentive tax reductions did accomplish a reduction in industrial injury. But the degree of control possible in the area of unemployment is much less than in the case of occupational injury.

One last financial factor must be included in our discussion—the Federal Unemployment Account established in 1944. The excess collections of the Federal Unemployment Tax Act beyond the actual costs of administration, and certain other sums, were made available to states which would exhaust their reserve in the state account. Abolished in 1952, the Federal Loan Account was reëstablished in 1954, and the excess collections were made payable to the Unemployment Trust Fund. When the level of the fund exceeds $200 million, the excess is credited to state accounts. Loans to the states are made out of the fund, and the security of the state systems has, thereby, become an interest of the federal government.

ISSUES IN UNEMPLOYMENT COMPENSATION

Coverage, eligibility requirements, and the adequacy of benefits have been continued sources of discontent in unemployment compensation. But the major issues involve larger considerations than simply benefit liberalization. Predominating the whole concept of insuring persons against the loss of wages for temporary periods is the fear of abuse. If benefits are made more freely available, it is argued, there will be a continuous stream of claimants who choose to draw unemployment checks rather than wage checks. This is an application of the theory of less eligibility within an insurance system. So we are in a dilemma; we must either compensate loss of wages carefully and at inadequate benefit levels or aid and abet sloth and dishonesty. Studies of abuse in the benefit system have been neither numerous nor comprehensive, but they do not yield evidence which will support the charge of rampant deceit and misrepresentation frequently alleged.[43]

[43] A sampling of claims in forty-one states by the Department of Labor's Bureau of Employment Security placed fraudulent claims which were willful on the part of the claimant at 3 percent of the total, some of which claims were in the appeal process. A New York State survey yielded a figure of 2.5 percent. *The New York Times*, January

Certainly, studies in connection with the "human relations in in-dustry" approach to industrial relations do not support the suspicion that workers are prepared to draw unemployment-compensation checks as a substitute for payroll checks. The several primary groups with which the employee has strong identifications function in accordance with belief systems, and violation of the norms produces role conflicts and stress situations that are important elements of be-havior control. Only if the reinforcements of "rightness" in such belief systems should become inoperative would the dangers of wide-spread abuse constitute a serious problem. If the controls exercised by small primary groups should deteriorate in the measure which would justify the dire predictions of those who fear abuse, then we would indeed have cause for alarm. We would not have to search for evidence that such a change had occurred; society would cease to function effectively and the evidence would be all about us. Our only recourse would be to try to "legislate" rightness into the social system, an impossible task.

There would appear to be ample room for extension and liberaliza-tion of the unemployment-insurance system if no other indictment than susceptibility to uncontrollable abuse can be lodged against it. Improving on the present system may call for as radical a departure as the establishment of a national insurance system. In that way, a measure of uniformity might be achieved, which is doubtful if sought through the normal process of state initiative. Proposals for re-insurance of state programs by the federal government might similarly achieve desirable features of uniformity and would have the advantage of retaining state initiative. However, this proposal would have its main benefit in stabilizing state funds, some of which were drawn down to low levels in the recession of 1953–1954. Liberalization of benefits is being gradually achieved by the states. In 1954, benefits were increased in five states; and in 1955, twenty-three states were reported to have increased their benefits by midyear, 1955.[44]

A technical issue which appeared on the scene in 1955 relates to the supplemental benefits provided in the pacts negotiated by the United Automobile Workers with the Ford and General Motors Corporations. It will be recalled from Chapter 9 that these pacts pro-vided for the payment of benefits to unemployed workers covered by

30, 1955, p. 57. See also Joseph M. Becker, *The Problem of Abuse in Unemployment Benefits*, New York, Columbia University Press, 1953.

[44] *The New York Times*, June 12, 1955, p. 8.

the agreement, in addition to the unemployment-insurance benefits they would receive under the state programs. Five states (Connecticut, Indiana, Minnesota, Oregon, and Pennsylvania) have provisions in their unemployment-compensation laws which would exclude simultaneous receipt of unemployment compensation and the proposed benefits. This is not a large proportion of the fifty-one jurisdictions which administer unemployment-compensation systems, but resistance to such plans could produce restrictive legislation in other states. According to the Ford agreement, unless states whose unemployment-benefit systems cover two-thirds of the company's workers by 1957 approve the concurrent receipt of unemployment compensation and supplemental benefits, the agreement will not go into effect.

Areas of Future Social-Insurance Coverage

The insurance method of spreading risks over a large number of persons has found ready acceptance in the United States for economic and cultural reasons which we have already discussed. In the fields of job-connected injuries, old age and survivorship, and loss of earnings through involuntary unemployment, the method has proved its worth. Proposals for covering new risks have been advanced frequently by those who appreciate the role of social insurance in relieving the stress caused by a capricious fate which selects the victims of yet-uninsured risks. One area of coverage which has been a feature of European systems of social insurance for decades is health insurance. By January, 1954, forty-four countries had instituted "compulsory health and maternity insurance programs or voluntary subsidized programs with broad coverage, providing cash benefits to partly replace wage loss and medical care services for insured persons or a public medical service for all or most of the population." [45] The United States was not among the countries which had instituted such a program.

We shall not discuss the issue of national health insurance at length in this survey of social legislation. The issues which we shall survey briefly are the obvious ones—the need, the extent to which medical service is available to American families on terms which their economic circumstances will permit, and the fate of plans which have sought to make medical care a right to which a person is entitled irrespective of his social and economic circumstances. For the reader

[45] Carl H. Farman, *Old-Age, Survivors, and Invalidity Programs Throughout the World*, Social Security Administration, Division of Research and Statistics Report No. 19, 1954, p. x.

who would understand the history of American efforts in this area, and the fate which all plans to date have met, there exists a plethora of material.[46]

THE NEED

The need for some alternative method of distributing medical services besides the "ability to pay" doctrine rests on a demonstration that the existing system is inequitable; that it fails to bring about the widest availability of medical care possible on the basis purely of need. There is the related issue of whether or not the resources of the medical community are efficiently employed. Oscar R. Ewing's report to the President on the nation's health stated concisely the relationship between a family's income level and the availability of medical care:

Perhaps the basic lack of our entire health effort is the absence of any method that would permit the individual, regardless of the level of his personal income, to obtain the kind of services he needs to achieve better health. A scant 20 percent of our people are able to afford all of the medical care they need. About half our families—those with incomes of $3000 or less—find it hard, if not impossible, to pay for even routine medical care. Another 30 percent of American families with incomes between $3000 and $5000 would have to make great sacrifices or go into debt to meet the costs of a severe or chronic illness.[47]

The fact of the matter is that individuals do go into debt for medical expenses, as all surveys of the problem show. It is not the size of the average expenditure for medical care that drives families into debt, for the average is usually estimated at about $200 per family and the median close to $100. Rather, the problem is the unanticipated character of medical-care costs and the extraordinary costs borne by a small proportion of all families in any given year. An unlucky one-

[46] An indispensable volume is Oliver Garceau, *The Political Life of the American Medical Association*, Cambridge, Mass., Harvard University Press, 1941. It enables one to understand the operations of the group whose militant hostility has prevented the enactment of legislation concerning national health insurance. The dimensions of the need in the United States for more freely available medical care are set forth in the five-volume report of the President's Commission on the Health Needs of the Nation, *Building America's Health*, Washington, Government Printing Office, 1952; and a program to meet the nation's health needs is set forth in a report to the President by Oscar R. Ewing, *The Nation's Health, A Ten Year Program*, Washington, Government Printing Office, 1948. Domenico Gagliardo has evaluated several proposals for meeting the health needs of the country in his *American Social Insurance*.

[47] Ewing, *op. cit.*, p. 11.

sixth of our families bear nearly one-half of our total costs of medical care in any given year according to some surveys.[48]

Indebtedness occasioned by the cost of personal health services was reported by the Health Information Foundation to have the following dimensions as of July 1953:

1. Among all families, 15 percent are in debt to hospitals, physicians, dentists and other providers of medical goods and services, and their total debt is $900 million.
2. In absolute terms this means that approximately 7.5 million families have a medical debt and about one million of these families owe $195 or more.
3. The average debt among all families for bills owed to hospitals, physicians, dentists and other providers of medical goods and services is $121.
4. When debts to financial institutions and individuals are included, the national total is $1.1 billion.
5. A greater proportion, 21 percent, of the families with children have a medical debt than those without children.
6. Four percent of the families reported borrowing from financial institutions and individuals to pay charges for personal health services.
7. The greater the proportion of family income paid out for personal health services, the greater is the likelihood that the family seeks a loan.[49]

The 1955 Survey of Consumer Finances, using a larger number of cases, bears out the general pattern shown by the Health Information Foundation report. In addition, the characteristics of those in debt are shown in the 1955 survey according to income class and age of family head; these data are presented in Table 55. Not so large a proportion of persons are shown to be free of debt in these data. Several other observations of importance are to be made on the basis of the table. In the first place, medical indebtedness hits low- and middle-income groups harder than income groups above those levels. Second, medical indebtedness is a greater problem for families in which the family head is relatively young. Finally, the largest amounts of indebtedness are found in low-income spending units and those spending units in which the head is young. The picture of total medical indebtedness is not complete in these data, of course, because debts incurred with

[48] Emily H. Huntington, *Cost of Medical Care: The Expenditures for Medical Care of 455 Families in the San Francisco Bay Area*, Berkeley, University of California Press, 1951, p. 93.
[49] Odin W. Anderson, *National Family Survey of Medical Costs and Voluntary Health Insurance*, New York, Health Information Foundation, 1954, p. 65. The survey included 2809 families.

TABLE 55. Debts to Doctors, Dentists, and Hospitals for Medical Services.[a]

Group Characteristics	Number of Cases	Some Debt	Amount of Debt		
			$1–$99	$100–$199	$200 and over
			Percent of Spending Units Within Groups		
All spending units	3119	20	13	4	3
Money income before taxes, preceding year					
Under $1000	240	20	12	3	5
$1000–$1999	363	23	14	4	4
$2000–$2999	385	19	13	3	3
$3000–$3999	484	24	15	5	4
$4000–$4999	439	24	16	4	4
$5000–$7499	730	21	14	4	3
$7500 and over	478	10	5	3	2
Age of head of spending unit					
18–24	228	14	10	3	1
25–34	709	27	16	5	6
35–44	718	23	16	4	3
45–54	556	24	14	6	4
55–64	447	14	9	3	2
65 and over	394	12	9	1	2

[a] Includes debt at the beginning of each year. Excludes debts to other individuals and financial institutions which were incurred to pay for medical services.

Source: Board of Governors, Federal Reserve System, "1955 Survey of Consumer Finances—the Financial Position of Consumers," Federal Reserve Bulletin, June, 1955, p. 620.

financial institutions are not included. Furthermore, the data give no indication of how many families forgo needed medical services simply because their income status forces them to do so.

AVAILABILITY OF MEDICAL SERVICES

There are many facets to this element of the medical-care problem in the United States. Regional and urban-rural differentials in the availability of care would be anticipated, and we shall review that aspect of the problem briefly. The other factor that we shall discuss is the extent of medical-care insurance coverage, the expansion of which has, in the opinion of those who oppose national health insurance, rendered any comprehensive program of planning unnecessary.

In the South and Southwest there is a serious shortage of general hospital facilities, which becomes more serious as specialized facilities

such as tuberculosis hospitals and mental hospitals are considered. The problem is national, however, and the poorer regions of the country simply have a greater relative problem. Rural areas have less access to medical services in general and the standards of care and treatment are apt to be less modern. Specialized medical personnel are drawn to large cities and lucrative practices.

Private insurance against medical-care bills is extensive in the United States, as we have seen in Chapter 13. Data obtained by the Health Information Foundation in its 1953 survey indicate plainly, however, that voluntary insurance has not solved the cost problem for American families. The following summarization shows the costs on an aggregate basis and the nature of the burden of medical expenses for the American people:

1. The total annual charges for personal health services incurred by families in the United States is $10.2 billion.
2. Of these $10.2 billion, physicians charge $3.8 billion (37 percent), hospitals $2.0 billion (20 percent), prescriptions and medicines $1.5 billion (15 percent), other medical goods and services $1.3 billion (13 percent), and dentists $1.6 billion (16 percent).
3. Of all charges incurred by families 15 percent is covered by insurance benefits. Broken down by type of service: hospital services, 50 percent; all physicians' services, 13 per cent; surgery, 38 percent; obstetrics, 25 percent. The proportion paid by insurance for other benefits was non-existent or negligible because they are not usually covered.
4. The average charges for all personal health services is approximately $207 per family; one-half of the families have more than $110.
5. The families with insurance incurred a total median cost over twice as great as those without insurance, $145 compared with $63.
6. Seven percent of the families, or approximately 3,500,000 families, incurred charges in excess of $495.
7. Approximately one million families paid out amounts equalling or exceeding one-half of their annual incomes, of which approximately 500,000 families paid out amounts equalling or exceeding 100 percent of their incomes.[50]

The picture of medical-care costs and insurance coverage to meet that cost is made quite clear by the data quoted. In the first place, insurance which meets only the expenses of medical personnel or only the expenses of the hospital leaves nearly half of the medical bill uncovered. Existing insurance programs, moreover, pay only fractions of

[50] Ibid., p. 25.

total bills, seldom the total costs of an illness or injury. For reasons that are speculative, the families with insurance coverage have a larger total outlay for medical services than uninsured individuals. Perhaps families who become insured do so in recognition of their above-average risk or perhaps they are led to make outlays on non-covered items, thus increasing their expenses beyond the expenses incurred by noninsured individuals. The premium expense is an item of considerable cost even under group plans, and Blue Cross–Blue Shield (the former covering hospital expenses and the latter the expenses of physicians) coverage can run in excess of $100 annually.[51]

The Fate of Proposed Remedies Through Social Insurance

While the data presented above are recent, they are not revelations, and the general character of the medical-care problem has been known for decades. But at the state and the federal levels, every proposal for social medical insurance has been beaten down without regard for its merits, largely by the American Medical Association and its affiliates. A comprehensive national health survey conducted in the waning years of the Great Depression made the needs of the nation painfully obvious, and in 1939 a National Health Bill (S. 1620) was introduced in the Senate. It was a bill providing for grants in aid to the states, but the American Medical Association assailed it so vigorously that it never was reported out of committee. In 1940, Senator Capper, on whose shoulders many lost causes were borne, introduced a bill (S. 3660) patterned after the unemployment-insurance program in that it would make grants to states with approved compulsory-health-insurance laws. The bill was technically inferior to that which had been introduced in 1939, and it lost for this and other reasons. More recently, the bill introduced in the Senate in 1945 (S. 1606), called the Wagner-Murray-Dingell Bill, has sought to insure medical care. The objective was a compulsory national health-insurance system, and the bill pleased the American Medical Association no more than its predecessors. Bills introduced in 1947 (S. 1320 and S. 545) likewise failed to pass, and a measure calling for a much-watered-down "re-insurance service" introduced in 1955 failed to survive committee action.

The Ewing report mentioned earlier in our discussion asserted that

[51] Gagliardo, op. cit., p. 564, reports the premium-charge ranges in 1953 as follows: for contracts providing surgical and in-hospital medical benefits, the range in fifty-one plans was from $1.75 to $6.45 monthly; most commonly it was between $2.50 and $3.00. This would give an annual total cost of from $30 to $36.

we might prevent nearly one of every four of the 3800 deaths that occur in the United States each day by planning for that objective.[52] There is a real question raised by the continued frustration of attempts to fulfill that challenge by an organization of professional men in whose hands the nation's medical care resides. In 1949, the American Medical Association spent $1,522,683 to influence legislation, all of which was collected from members of the Association in the form of $25 assessments.[53] That total made the American Medical Association the largest single spender reported in 1949 under the Lobbying Regulation Act. The 43,000,000 pieces of literature which were distributed by the American Medical Association in 1950 pleaded the case against "government medicine" in terms which made much of solicitude for the nation's health; but in the opinion of many students of social insurance, the object being sought is the preservation of an economic position which puts physicians in an average income bracket more than one-third higher than their closest professional rivals.

The Social Security Act, Insurance Features: Concluding Remarks

We have carried the insurance features of the Social Security Act forward from their operation at the close of the Great Depression to their present status. Because the "rights" features and the contributory principle appeal to the American cultural complex, the insurance programs have been given preferment over assistance, and this measure of preference has been maintained—even pressed for extension.

By 1955, the coverage and benefits levels of the old-age and survivors' insurance program had made the program rather satisfactory to students of social legislation. Only a few fringe groups, each with protection of its own, remained outside the program. On these counts, the OASI program was in sharp contrast to the workmen's-compensation program and the unemployment-insurance system, both of which face problems of diversity in benefits and coverage.

On the horizon is the problem of adequate health care, frustrated in its solution for the second decade, and with little hope of immediate relief. To the natural American fears of government authority there have now been added the fears that national health insurance

---

[52] Ewing, op. cit., p. 3.

[53] Data from the *Congressional Quarterly*, February 24, 1950, and read into the *Congressional Record*, February 27, 1950, A 1415.

will bring socialism and worse down upon our heads. Symbols of treason, aggression, and despotism are now associated with the proposal to make medical care a right. In 1945, Franz Goldman, M.D. wrote these words in the Preface to his book. "Adequate medical care is a fundamental human right. It is as much a necessity of life as food, shelter, clothing, or education. It is no less indispensable to the well-being of society than to the welfare of the individual. It is an essential component of any program for individual and social security." [54] This seems to reflect the appropriate social conscience for a profession devoted to the health of the people.

SELECTED REFERENCES

Burns, Eveline M., *The American Social Security System*, Boston, Houghton Mifflin Company, 1949.

Gagliardo, Domenico, *American Social Insurance*, New York, Harper & Brothers, 1954.

[54] Franz Goldman, *Public Medical Care*, New York, Columbia University Press, 1945.

chapter 16

The Social Security Act:
Assistance Features

One of the distinguishing characteristics of social-assistance programs has been their resistance to comprehensive change. As social and economic conditions change, policies and procedures in programs of assistance should respond with corresponding changes in an effort to rearticulate the programs with the existing socioeconomic milieu. But, although the Social Security Act of 1935 has been amended several times by Congress, the changes in the assistance programs have been, for the most part, minor ones. The social-insurance features have been more often changed in terms of basic policy. The 1950 revisions represented the most basic changes in policy and practices thus far.

In this chapter, we shall examine the results of these changes and their effects on the present operation of the assistance programs established by the 1935 act. Our emphasis will be on operations, processes, and trends rather than on the citation of legislative provisions. First, we shall review the general administrative policies which have developed since 1935, and then inquire into the present status of the several programs of public assistance, and determine their adequacy in meeting the needs of those whose protection was sought by their enactment into law.

General Administrative Policies and Procedures

Today, public assistance embraces five major programs: old-age assistance (OAA), aid to dependent children (ADC), aid to the blind (AB), aid to the permanently and totally disabled (AD), and general assistance (GA). The first four of these programs are ad-

ministered by the individual states with the help of grants of financial aid from the national government under the Social Security Act and subsequent amendments. General assistance, however, is a state and local responsibility and receives no support from the national government. Actually a survival of the "poor relief" of pre-Social Security Act days, it provides aid for needy persons ineligible for any of the four federally aided programs. Supplementing these public assistance programs is a system of federally aided health and welfare services which provides social and professional services to meet needs in the areas of vocational rehabilitation, child welfare, and psychiatric and medical care for mothers, children, and certain handicapped groups in the population.

While the principal legal foundation of these programs is in the Social Security Act, subsequent amendments and policy changes have altered their operations to some extent. These changes, which have come in almost every legislative year, result from both national and state legislation. Recall that the original act maintained the control of the individual states over the administration of aid to the needy. The federal government has no power to impose a legal obligation upon any jurisdiction to accept its suggested programs, but acts rather in the capacity of defining standards, setting forth minimal requirements which must be met by state programs if they are to become eligible for federal grants. The states retain control over decisions as to how the programs are to be administered, the eligibility requirements, and the size of the grants, all within the limits of the federal standards, of course. This means that much of the legislative history of public assistance resides in state legislatures and makes any full summarization of legislative changes impossible within the space and subject limitations of this volume. What we may profitably accomplish, however, is a summary of the important legislative and policy changes in the federal assistance programs and the state legislative activity in response to these changes.

As we have seen in Chapter 14, the individual state must provide a plan for the operation of each of the programs for which it would receive federal funds. In order to secure the approval of the Secretary of the Department of Health, Education, and Welfare, the programs must now provide for:

1. State-wide operation of the plan in all political subdivisions. If the

plan is to be locally rather than state-administered, it must be mandatory upon the local subdivision.

2. State financial participation in the program. Essentially, this requirement makes the awarding of federal grants in aid to the county or
   town conditional upon some state contribution to the program,
   thereby utilizing the vastly greater taxing power of the state as contrasted to smaller political units.

3. The establishment or designation of a single state agency to administer the plan or, if it is to be locally administered, provide for a single
   state agency to supervise the administration of the plan.

4. Granting an opportunity to any individual for a fair hearing and
   appeal before the state agency when his application has been denied.
   The amendments of 1950 added that, effective July 1, 1951, this
   opportunity must also be provided to individuals whose applications
   are not acted upon with reasonable promptness.

5. Such methods of administration (including, after January 1, 1940,
   methods relating to the establishment and maintenance of personnel
   standards on a merit basis, but not with respect to the selection, tenure
   of office, or compensation of an individual employed in accordance
   with such methods) as are found necessary by the Social Security
   Administration for the proper and efficient operation of the plan.

6. The submittal to the Social Security Administration of reports in the
   form and bearing the information required by the Administration.

7. Effective July 1, 1941, the consideration of any income and resources
   of a claimant for assistance in determining his need. A partial exception was made in the case of earned income in aid-to-the-blind programs by the amendments of 1950. To encourage the needy blind to
   become as self-maintaining as possible, earned income up to $50 a
   month must be disregarded in assessing the need of blind persons.

8. Safeguards for the restriction of information concerning applicants
   or recipients to purposes directly connected with the administration
   of public assistance. This provision, adopted by Congress in 1939, to
   become effective July 1, 1941, was emasculated by the so-called Jenner
   Amendment to the Revenue Act of 1951, which allows the states to
   adopt legislation permitting exceptions to the restriction of assistance
   information without loss of federal funds. The Jenner Amendment
   does require that the state legislation contain safeguards against the
   commercial or political use of the information obtained. Since this
   amendment was permissive rather than mandatory, the provisions for
   the restriction of assistance information adopted in 1939 remain in
   force in the absence of specific state legislation opening the assistance
   rolls to public inspection.

9. An opportunity for all individuals wishing to make application for any

of the forms of categorical assistance to do so and for the furnishing of assistance to all eligible applicants with reasonable promptness. This provision was made by the amendments of 1950 to become effective July 1, 1951. The same 1950 amendments added aid to the permanently and totally disabled to the assistance programs for the first time, and the provision for an opportunity to make application was also included as one of the requirements for the approval of state plans for this form of assistance.

10. Designation of a state authority or authorities responsible for establishing and maintaining standards for private or public institutions in which the state plan permits needy persons to receive public assistance. This provision, added in 1950 to become effective July 1, 1953, is applicable to each of the programs except aid to dependent children.

11. Prompt notification of law-enforcement officials when children who have been deserted or abandoned by a parent are furnished with aid to dependent children. The intended purpose of this provision is to reduce assistance costs by enlisting the aid of law-enforcement officers in obtaining support from the missing parent. This provision was one of the amendments added in 1950 and became effective July 1, 1952.

12. Examination by a physician skilled in diseases of the eye or by an optometrist, whichever the individual may select, in determining blindness for the aid-to-the-blind program. This provision was added by the amendments of 1950 and became effective July 1, 1952.

13. Preventing the receipt of more than one type of federally aided public assistance at one time by the same individual. This provision, included in each of the programs by the 1950 amendments, was intended to strengthen existing limitations rather than to institute any new policy.[1]

There has been virtually no change in the list of conditions which, if imposed by the state, preclude any approval of the state plan. Currently, the plan may not include:

1. Any residence requirement more restrictive than five years of residence within the state in the last nine years and one year continuously preceding application for aid to the aged, the blind, and the permanently and totally disabled. In the case of aid to dependent children, the state may not require more than one year of residence.

2. Any citizenship requirement which excludes any citizen of the United States otherwise eligible. This provision does not require that the state render categorical assistance only to citizens of the United States, however, and noncitizens may be included under the state provisions.

[1] These required provisions originally appeared as parts of Sections 2(a), 402(a), 503(a), 513(a) and 1002(a) of the Social Security Act of 1935 and in various sections of the Amendments of 1939 and 1950.

3. In the case of old-age assistance, an age requirement of more than 65, although up until January 1, 1940, an age requirement of as much as 70 years was permissible.

The effects of some of these amendments are obvious. The provision making if possible for states to permit public inspection of the names of persons receiving assistance has resulted in an increasing number of state laws making assistance lists public documents. The history of this rather dramatic reversal of policy on the part of the national government presents an interesting example of the previously mentioned interplay between state and federal legislation in the area of public assistance.

The original provisions establishing the confidentiality of public-assistance information were added to the act after evidence appeared that there was widespread misuse of the assistance rolls to circularize old-age-assistance recipients during the 1938 elections. What appears to have happened was that worried incumbents in gubernatorial elections in some states obtained the names of recipients and sent them form letters suggesting that the size and very existence of assistance grants were contingent upon the reëlection of the party in power.

At the same time, there was a growing feeling among social-work leaders and public-welfare officials that an individual enjoyed a *right* to public assistance and he should be spared the discomfort of publicity concerning his needy situation. This feeling had led some agencies to insist on confidentiality, which they felt was necessary as a policy in the absence of legal safeguards. With the passage of the 1939 amendments, these policies had the force of law.

The onset of the Second World War drew legislative attention away from the effects of the new confidentiality, but, following the war, legislative interest in several states was directed toward what were felt to be serious wrongs resulting from the "secrecy" surrounding assistance records. The bases of these objections were several: concern over what seemed to be an increasing growth in the case load and cost of assistance programs; the problem of "alimony skippers" leaving families to be supported by ADC; the eruption of a series of scandals in several states, with obviously ineligible recipients being taken to court; and charges of inefficiency and paternalism leveled at local welfare agencies. Added to these were the older claims that aid to dependent children was giving license to mothers of illegitimate children, since the state not only supported them but protected their identity, and similar complaints concerning financially

able children unwilling to support or even contribute to their indigent parents. To correct these wrongs, many public officials openly called for public inspection of the assistance lists as a device to identify chiselers and chronic "professional" recipients.

To these assertions the public-welfare experts and numerous social-work groups answered that many of the charges were twisted versions of actual conditions or had been misconstrued. They pointed out that the mounting costs of public assistance resulted from population growth and the decrease in the purchasing power of original benefits rather than any great increase in the proportion of the population receiving assistance, and that irresponsible journalism and zealous judges were overemphasizing the number of recipients who were misusing public assistance.

The ferment came to a head in 1951, when Indiana passed a law, over a gubernatorial veto, opening its assistance lists to public inspection. When the bill had first been proposed, Oscar Ewing, then Federal Security Administrator, had threatened to suspend all payments of grants in aid for assistance programs to that state since its program would be in violation of the 1939 provision of confidentiality. With the passage of the bill, he promptly did so. Indiana took its case to the courts, but before any judicial decision was reached, Mr. Ewing's forthright position was vitiated by the passage of the Revenue Act of 1951 with the Jenner Amendment appended. This amendment, which represented a surrender of the principle of confidentiality in the face of strong pressure from certain states, made Indiana's law acceptable and paved the way for other states to enact similar legislation. Since that time, twenty-eight states have enacted legislation permitting at least limited public access to assistance information.[2]

Yet despite this seeming solution, the controversy over the value of making such information public continues. Some interested persons and groups maintain that the laws have done much to reduce the size of case loads and the costs of public assistance, but just as many are prepared to argue that they have had little effect, if any, and have added to the anxiety of the vast proportion of recipients

[2] Alabama, Arkansas, Florida, Georgia, Illinois, Indiana, Kansas, Louisiana, Michigan, Mississippi, Missouri, Montana, Nebraska, North Carolina, North Dakota, Ohio, Oregon, Pennsylvania, South Carolina, South Dakota, Tennessee, Utah, Vermont, Virginia, and Wisconsin have passed laws opening the welfare lists to public inspection. Two other states, New York and Washington, allow limited public access to assistance rolls. We are indebted to the Division of Program Statistics and Analysis of the United States Bureau of Public Assistance for these data.

who are deserving beneficiaries. The Indiana State Department of Welfare reports that "Most of our counties have chosen not to publish the names of recipients since they feel that such publication does not have any deterrent effect on applications for assistance. If it has any effect at all it probably deters the most deserving from making application. It certainly doesn't deter the applicant who is usually the subject of public criticism." [3]

But one of the original sponsors of the "Indiana Revolt" feels that the opening of the rolls has materially reduced the number of unworthy recipients in that state and that the overall costs may also be reduced.[4] What the total effectiveness of these laws will be we may never know, since it is difficult to discern any direct results. Many interested individuals and agencies, however, are making follow-up studies, and some future analysis of the experiences of the various states may prove of value.

Another important change in the provisions for state plans has been the amendment calling for standards to protect the health and safety of needy persons in institutions. Many states have established safeguards for hospitals and institutions caring for children, but little similar protection has ever been given to aged or infirm adults in many institutions.[5] The substandard conditions in many such institutions, whose resident populations include public-assistance recipients, is evidenced by the too frequent disastrous fires which take a shocking toll as they sweep through the antiquated and dangerous buildings.

In many states, the effect of the provision has been to extend the authority of existing standard-setting agencies rather than to demand the establishment of new agencies, since most states already have such bodies. The Federal Hospital Survey and Construction Act, for example, had previously required all states receiving federal grants for hospital construction to establish standards for such hospitals.[6] With the help of an advisory group of interested governmental and volun-

[3] Indiana State Department of Public Welfare, "Concerning Senate Bill 86 Introduced by Bontrager and Malone and Passed by the Senate on February 13, 1951" (mimeographed statement), quoted in Hilary M. Leyendecker, *Problems and Policy in Public Assistance*, New York, Harper & Brothers, 1955, p. 106.

[4] See Craig Thompson, "Indiana's Revolt: What's Happened Since," *Nation's Business*, March, 1954, pp. 23–28.

[5] Department of Health, Education, and Welfare, *Annual Report of the U.S. Department of Health, Education, and Welfare*, 1954, p. 36.

[6] Drafting Committee of State Officials of the Council of State Governments, *Suggested State Legislation Program for 1953*, Chicago, Council of State Governments, November, 1952, p. 147.

tary organizations, the Federal Bureau of Public Assistance aided the states in drawing up legislation to fit the requirements of the amendment, and since that time has furnished consultative advice on problems as they arose. It is still too early in the history of this amendment to assess its overall effect in raising the standards of institutions, but concerted effort on the part of both government and voluntary agencies to implement the spirit of the provision would seem to assure its success.

The 1950 Amendment calling for notice to law-enforcement officials when deserted or abandoned children are receiving ADC benefits became effective July 1, 1952. Again, it is too soon to pass any final judgment upon its ultimate effect in reducing the case load and costs of aid to dependent children. What evidence does exist suggests that it will do little to reduce substantially either the number of cases or the overall costs. In June of 1952, one month before it became effective, about one-fourth of the cases receiving aid to dependent children—about 375,000 children in 160,000 families—were affected by this amendment.[7] As an immediate result of the operation of the amendment, about 5000 families, including about 9000 children, had their cases closed or assistance payments reduced because the deserted parent did not wish to have the notice to the appropriate law-enforcement official sent.[8] Representing a little more than 3 percent of the cases affected by the amendment, but less than 1 percent of the total ADC case load in June of 1952, the total reduction in payments was $165,000 a month or about 0.5 percent of the total cost.[9]

FINANCING AND ADMINISTERING THE PROGRAMS

Assistance under the categorical programs is rendered in money payments and, since 1950, in payments for medical treatment to doctors, hospitals, clinics, and pharmacists. It is the state agency which determines the size of the payment which will be made to the individual recipient and enacts its own laws to this end. The federal government establishes ceilings for each of the programs of assistance and will share in assistance payments only up to that level. Thus, for adult recipients it will pay four-fifths of the first $25 assistance payment and one-half of the balance between $25 and $55 monthly. This system means, of course, that the national government pays a large

[7] Department of Health, Education, and Welfare, op. cit., p. 39.
[8] Ibid., p. 39.
[9] Ibid., p. 39.

proportion of the assistance costs in states whose assistance standards are low, and only a modest proportion of the actual assistance payments in the wealthier states with higher standards.

The formula used in computing the federal government's share in each of the programs has historically provided for matching grants, the size of the federal grant to the state depending upon the state's expenditure for assistance and administration. While this matching principle has not changed, there have been changes in the reimbursement formula since the passage of the original act. The original act had called for federal reimbursement to cover one-half of the individual OAA and AB grants up to a maximum of $30 per month, and one-third of the individual ADC grant up to a maximum of $18 a month for the first child and one-third of the individual grant up to $12 per month for each additional child. The 1939 amendments raised the level of federal participation from one-third to one-half of these amounts in the ADC program and to one-half of the individual grant up to a monthly maximum of $40 in the OAA and AB programs. Prior to 1946, the federal government also paid 5 percent of the individual grant in OAA and AB programs and one-third of the actual administrative costs of the ADC program to help defray the expenses of administering the programs. Since 1946, the federal reimbursement for administrative costs has been equal to one-half of such costs in all programs. The formulas for reimbursement for assistance costs were also changed in that year to two-thirds of the first $15 of average monthly payment and one-half of the remainder up to an average monthly grant of $45 in OAA and AB programs, and two-thirds of the first $9 of average monthly payment for the first child and one-half of the remainder up to a maximum of $24 per month for aid to dependent children. The new formula for ADC also allowed the same percentage up to a monthly maximum of $15 for each additional child. The formulas were changed again in 1948 to allow the federal government to pay three-fourths of the first $20 of average monthly payment and one-half of the remainder to a maximum of $50 for the OAA and AB programs, and three-fourths of the first $12 of average monthly payment for the first child and one-half of the balance to a maximum of $27 per month in ADC. The percentage was the same for each additional child to a maximum of $18.

In 1950, aid to the permanently and totally disabled joined the other categorical-assistance programs and was included in the new formulas established in that year along with the other programs con-

cerning adults—old-age assistance and aid to the blind. In the same year a bill was introduced in the House of Representatives to increase federal participation in each of the categorical programs. The proposed formula raised the national government's participation to four-fifths of the first $25 of average monthly payment, one-half of the next $10, and one-third of the remainder to a maximum of $50 in the OAA, AB, and AD programs. The reimbursement formula for ADC was changed to four-fifths of the first $15 average monthly payment per recipient, one-third of the next $6 to a maximum of $27 for the first child, and a maximum of $18 for each additional child. The new formulas were eliminated from the bill by the Senate, and federal participation remained at the levels set by the 1948 amendments. A change in the ADC program, however, permitted reimbursement for aid furnished to the needy relative caring for the dependent children in addition to the children themselves. This reimbursement was to be at the same rate as the children and to a maximum of $27 per month.

Since 1952, the federal rate of reimbursement has been at four-fifths of the first $25 and one-half of the balance between $25 and $55 for monthly OAA, AB, and AD payments. Reimbursement for ADC has been at four-fifths of the first $15 of a state's average monthly payment per recipient, plus half the balance, within individual maximums of $30 for the adult and for the first child and $21 for each additional child in the family. The 1952 amendments had made these rates effective through September 30, 1954, but they were extended until September 30, 1956, by the 1954 amendments to the act. At the time of this extension, Congress reported that it had taken this action pending possible consideration of basic amendments in the present system of matching formulas, and to allow the states time to plan for operations under any revised law.[10]

Several significant characteristics of the financing of state assistance programs emerge from the history of these formulas. First, they have consistently allowed for a higher proportionate sharing of the costs of old-age assistance, aid to the blind, and aid to the permanently and totally disabled than to recipients of aid to dependent children. The reasons for this apparent neglect of the needs of dependent children are many, but center around a greater acceptance of aid to aged and infirm individuals as a governmental function. Leyendecker makes the

[10] Wilbur J. Cohen, Robert M. Ball, and Robert J. Myers, "Social Security Act Amendments of 1954: A Summary and Legislative History," *Social Security Bulletin*, September, 1954, pp. 3–18.

TABLE 56. Special Types of Public Assistance Under Plans Approved by the Social Security Administration, 1954.

(includes vendor payments for medical care; amounts in thousands; data corrected to October 25, 1954)

State	Federal Grants to States[a]				
	Total	Old-age Assistance	Aid to Dependent Children	Aid to the Blind	Aid to the Permanently and Totally Disabled
Fiscal year:					
1952	$1,177,688	$799,845	$303,280	$29,397	$45,165
1953	1,338,989	903,241	343,321	33,017	59,410
1954	1,386,931	931,711	347,236	35,561	72,423
Alabama	27,308	17,803	6,831	383	2,291
Alaska	1,311	667	620	25	
Arizona	8,985	5,563	3,116	307	
Arkansas	20,707	15,507	3,916	629	656
California	156,126	113,426	37,636	5,064	
Colorado	26,590	20,502	4,092	147	1,848
Connecticut	9,866	6,497	3,021	124	223
Delaware	1,284	575	569	105	34
District of Columbia	3,651	1,095	1,774	101	680
Florida	35,709	24,392	10,121	1,195	
Georgia	42,767	31,004	8,248	1,121	2,394
Hawaii	3,282	656	2,125	40	463
Idaho	5,275	3,446	1,392	82	354
Illinois	59,720	40,011	15,777	1,574	2,359
Indiana	18,755	12,774	5,317	665	
Iowa	21,807	16,947	4,288	573	
Kansas	18,522	14,257	2,771	243	1,251
Kentucky	28,854	17,021	11,009	824	
Louisiana	65,314	48,742	11,372	741	4,459
Maine	8,031	4,928	2,883	220	
Maryland	9,446	3,744	3,962	175	1,565
Massachusetts	54,328	39,931	9,196	717	4,483
Michigan	43,399	29,719	12,222	717	741
Minnesota	25,110	19,461	5,018	528	103
Mississippi	22,355	17,069	3,771	963	552
Missouri	71,975	53,044	11,928	1,238	5,764
Montana	6,204	3,891	1,548	208	557
Nebraska	9,079	7,036	1,741	302	
Nevada	1,160	1,119	d	40	
New Hampshire	3,679	2,650	848	117	64
New Jersey	12,962	7,715	3,641	357	1,249
New Mexico	9,309	4,338	4,124	165	681
New York	98,077	44,231	36,114	1,981	15,752
North Carolina	28,581	14,256	10,009	1,696	2,620
North Dakota	4,498	3,149	1,016	45	288
Ohio	53,378	39,445	9,552	1,541	2,839
Oklahoma	50,638	38,099	9,715	905	1,919
Oregon	11,919	8,328	2,394	147	1,050
Pennsylvania	48,435	22,094	18,470	3,686	4,185
Puerto Rico	4,250	1,779	1,800	53	617
Rhode Island	6,074	3,322	2,199	80	472
South Carolina	18,302	12,466	3,270	547	2,019
South Dakota	6,117	3,992	1,858	75	193
Tennessee	34,900	20,853	12,667	1,075	305
Texas	86,564	72,732	11,577	2,254	
Utah	6,738	3,772	2,213	92	662
Vermont	3,319	2,445	688	67	119
Virgin Islands	108	69	28	3	8
Virginia	11,447	4,728	4,872	425	1,423
Washington	34,047	24,838	6,390	328	2,491
West Virginia	21,368	7,168	11,802	360	2,039
Wisconsin	23,036	16,746	5,343	479	468
Wyoming	2,267	1,671	380	32	183

TABLE 56 (*Cont.*). Special Types of Public Assistance Under Plans Approved by the Social Security Administration, 1954.

			Expenditures for Assistance and Administration				
Old-Age Assistance		Aid to Dependent Children		Aid to the Blind		Aid to the Permanently and Totally Disabled	
Amount	Percent from Federal Funds	Amount	Percent from Federal Funds	Amount	Percent from Federal Funds	Amount	Percent from Federal Funds
$1,572,790	52.5	$598,629	52.0	$62,942	47.0	$85,922	49.2
1,671,805	55.0	618,294	55.8	69,498	48.8	116,971	51.0
1,684,075	56.0	619,064	57.2	72,102	49.6	141,284	51.2
23,161	75.0	8,871	77.2	509	76.0	2,964	75.7
1,277	52.8	973	65.9	45	53.5		
9,598	58.2	4,545	68.1	549	54.9		
21,100	72.4	4,919	78.2	904	68.7	952	71.0
237,873	47.9	83,561	45.7	13,140	39.1		
51,385	39.6	7,398	56.3	297	48.6	3,284	54.9
16,741	41.4	7,007	43.1	352	37.5	768[b]	17.7
862	67.2	857	66.5	187	55.8	71	54.7
1,938	57.9	2,966	60.3	176	57.5	1,259	55.4
37,990	64.6	13,227	76.7	1,825	64.8	8[c]	[c]
44,911	69.2	12,051	70.4	1,684	66.8	3,476	66.4
1,020	64.0	3,579	59.7	71	58.6	859	51.9
6,132	56.5	2,845	48.2	149	53.2	649	53.7
76,274	53.8	32,545	50.0	3,119	51.4	5,304	44.3
23,270	58.2	8,515	63.4	1,211	54.4		
31,818	55.3	8,974	48.5	1,262	46.0		
28,185	50.7	7,576	51.9	537	47.5	2,601	47.7
24,201	70.6	14,592	74.0	1,195	69.6		
77,412	63.2	15,666	73.5	1,257	58.8	7,173	63.1
7,647	65.2	4,327	67.8	345	64.2		
6,104	62.2	6,586	62.8	301	59.4	2,719	57.5
88,873	44.2	19,522	45.4	1,897	38.5	11,307	38.0
53,926	56.7	24,204	53.0	1,342	53.4	1,561	47.7
41,470	48.8	10,487	49.2	1,170	43.8	281	57.7
22,730	75.1	4,920	76.0	1,362	70.7	745	75.1
82,060	64.5	16,859	72.3	2,610	47.3	9,151	63.7
7,235	54.8	2,870	55.4	406	51.0	1,070	51.8
12,916	56.3	2,968	59.7	582	51.2		
1,941	57.8	[d]	[d]	77	48.0		
5,080	53.2	1,793	47.4	228	50.9	134	45.2
17,242	49.8	7,312	49.7	734	49.8	2,436	44.7
6,924	62.8	5,866	70.4	259	65.0	1,059	64.4
105,414	43.8	84,618	45.6	4,930	41.4	39,224	41.9
19,432	73.4	13,172	76.5	2,530	66.4	3,864	69.2
6,331	51.4	2,075	52.0	84	54.3	659	47.0
74,115	56.3	15,364	62.4	2,664	57.5	4,501	63.1
68,675	55.3	14,383	68.0	1,833	49.7	3,382	55.4
16,941	49.3	5,244	48.4	329	45.6	2,439	44.5
38,318	59.6	35,035	55.9	10,459	35.3	8,400	50.3
4,632	38.4	4,990	36.2	151	33.5	1,820	33.7
6,312	53.0	4,419	50.5	173	45.9	925	46.7
17,478	71.6	4,338	77.2	802	68.5	2,802	71.2
6,462	65.6	2,871	64.6	116	65.7	303	64.4
29,640	69.8	17,756	72.6	1,595	67.5	474	63.2
105,815	68.9	15,277	77.3	3,401	67.6		
7,124	54.5	4,280	50.8	175	52.1	1,294	51.8
3,783	66.4	1,012	69.2	100	65.0	186	64.5
135	49.9	58	49.7	7	49.8	15	49.9
6,564	72.4	6,874	71.7	625	68.0	2,134	66.0
49,360	50.4	11,797	53.2	779	42.8	5,119	46.8
9,689	73.9	16,030	71.4	505	70.2	2,604	70.5
35,470	49.6	12,367	44.1	1,001	48.7	1,170	40.1
3,089	54.4	724	53.7	60	52.7	335	55.2

[a] Based on checks issued; differ slightly from fiscal-year expenditures from federal funds reported by states.
[b] Program approved for federal participation beginning January 1, 1954.
[c] Program not yet approved for federal participation.
[d] No approved plan in operation in 1954.
Source: Prerelease data furnished by the Department of Health, Education, and Welfare.

interesting suggestion that one of the reasons for the discrimination in favor of the aged is their growing proportion in the population and consequent voting power combined with the active lobbying in their behalf.[11]

A second characteristic follows from the fact that the lower the state's monthly grant for assistance, the higher becomes the proportionate share of the federal contribution. The method whereby the federal government's contribution is determined as a proportion of the average monthly payment, first introduced in 1946 and continued since that time, provides the means to this end. The rationale of this system is that in the poorer states, particularly in the South, the assistance needs are usually greater; but, since their available resources are lower, assistance grants are consequently smaller. By bolstering these lower grants with a greater share of federal aid, the poorer states are enabled to maintain better assistance standards. The consequence of this greater aid to poorer states is, of course, that the wealthier states must bear a larger burden of their own assistance costs.

The problem of equalizing assistance levels in the various states has attracted widespread interest in governmental and private welfare agencies. Table 56 shows the total expenditure for each type of assistance, the amount of federal grants, and the percentage of total expenditures for each type of assistance which came from federal funds in 1954. The table shows that there are wide differences in the relative contribution of federal grants in aid. The federal government pays 75 percent of the total expenditure for old-age assistance in Alabama, but only a little over 41 percent in Connecticut. It pays 78 percent of Arkansas's aid to dependent children expenditures, but only 42 percent of Connecticut's. These disparities are evident in each of the forms of assistance. The argument that this tends to raise the level of assistance in the poorer states is countered by the wealthier states' contention that the money for this uplift comes largely from their federal tax dollars. In the meantime, the standards of assistance in the poorer southern states remain low, as is evidenced by the large amount of "migratory application," in which southern families come to the northern states for the benefits of the higher levels of assistance payments.

One of the suggested means for equalizing the financial burden of aid to the needy among the states is an amendment to the Social Security Act calling for a system of variable grants in aid based upon

---

[11] Leyendecker, *op. cit.*, p. 113.

the state's ability to meet its obligations. The proposal has had the expressed approval of the Social Security Administration, the National Resources Planning Board, the American Public Welfare Association, the social-security technical staff of the House Committee on Ways and Means (1946), and, less forcefully, of the Advisory Council on Social Security to the Senate Committee on Finance (1948).[12] The original draft of the Social Security Act amendments submitted to the Eighty-first Congress (H.R. 2892) included proposals designed to effect these changes, but they were not in the bill as passed in 1950. Despite continued pressure, they were also absent from the 1952 amendments, and the 1954 decision to extend the 1952 formula again postponed the introduction of this new concept in federal-state coöperation in public assistance.

The primary opposition comes, of course, from the wealthier states. If such a plan were to be adopted, they would be in the position of supplying an even larger share of the assistance funds of poorer states, while their own grants in aid would be proportionately cut. In the face of this attitude, it is difficult to foresee the time when an identification by wealthier states with the nation as a whole will permit the welfare of the needy to be placed above their own self-interest.

In addition to the deterring effects of this opposition from the wealthier states, there is the practical problem of just how the federal government could go about setting up criteria to determine the relative needs of each state. While the concept of need is a condition of each assistance program, it is nowhere defined by the federal government. Each state is entitled to determine what constitutes need within its own borders—a privilege which has produced wide variations in its application. The considerable differences in judgment as to what constitutes a minimum decent standard of living found among the several jurisdictions would require compromise and still would meet criticism from states feeling neglected or mistreated. Also, the superior performance of some states would be scaled down. Despite both concerted opposition and administrative pitfalls, however, the obvious benefits of the plan and its widespread support among public-welfare leaders make its eventual acceptance almost a certainty.

Finally, these data reveal that federal participation has been relatively slow to increase as the costs of assistance have increased with the cost of living. As the costs of basic commodities increase, the costs of meeting the minimum needs of recipients show corresponding

[12] *Ibid.*, p. 118.

increase and public-assistance costs mount. Since the care of the needy in the several programs is supposed to be a shared state-federal responsibility, the payments by the federal government should help to meet this burden. The very slow increase in the maxima which the amendments have allowed as the basis for reimbursement indicates that such has not been the case.

For the individual recipient, the amount of the assistance payment is a function of the budget established by his jurisdiction. This budget, which is based upon the particular agency's policy, includes the cost figures of the minimum essentials of food, shelter, fuel, utilities, and clothing. In most states, standardized budgets are supplied by the state for the use of the county or local agency. In addition, most states also make provisions for meeting such special requirements of recipients as medical care and confinement in nursing homes. The costs of these basic essentials are previewed from time to time and new budgets prepared to meet changed economic conditions. These budgets represent the agency's appraisal of the minimum level of "decent and healthful" living for the individual. The difference between this level and that at which the individual is able to maintain himself through his own income and resources commonly represents his "need."

Specific Eligibility Requirements for Individual Applicants

In addition to the general administrative requirements we have just described, the Social Security Act and its subsequent amendments also discuss need and certain other characteristics of individuals applying for assistance under the aid programs. Certain of these characteristics, such as the degree of blindness for aid to the blind and the nature of the disability in aid to the permanently and totally disabled, are related to specific programs. Others, such as need and residence, concern all four programs. In this section, we shall discuss those requirements which affect the total program and consider in later sections the categorical-eligibility requirements dealing with the status of the specific programs.

THE DETERMINATION OF NEED

We have previously commented upon the fact that, while the basic function of the assistance features of the Social Security Act is to provide aid for the needy, the determination of need is left to the individual states. The amended act does, however, require that the

state take into consideration the income or resources of an individual in establishing his need (excepting, of course, the previously mentioned first $50 of earned monthly income in AB) if the state plan is to win approval. Even this control was not forcefully stated until the 1939 amendments sought to end the practices of California and a few other states, which had ignored income in their early programs.

When the claimant applies for public assistance, he usually must furnish information concerning his resources. These resources normally include any income or property which is readily available to the claimant. Thus, it may mean real-estate holdings, home ownership, personal savings, and contributions from relatives and insurance policies as well as actual income. The agency must then verify and evaluate these resources to determine the extent of the claimant's need—a process which is known as the means test. The states have established varied policies concerning the weight of home ownership, savings, cash reserves, and insurance in this means test. Many state and local agencies impose liens on real-estate holdings of recipients to permit recovery from the estate after the death of the recipient or his surviving spouse. Some states even provide for recovery prior to the recipient's death should his financial condition improve during his lifetime. In effect, these regulations require that an applicant must first utilize all but a limited amount of his cash or property assets before he may be considered needy and granted assistance.

Most states also have laws establishing the responsibility of a claimant's close relatives for his support when he becomes needy. All jurisdictions take into consideration any contributions actually made by relatives, but they differ considerably in their policies concerning the requirement that such contributions must be made by relatives. As we observed in Chapter 7, support duty is usually limited to the marital and parent-child relationships, but there is still considerable diversity in the states' recognition of this responsibility. Some states encourage but do not legally require contributions from relatives, and they do not consider the potential contribution as a resource to be included in the means test. Another group of states makes relatives legally responsible and will take legal action to force such payment, but they do not consider the contribution as a resource affecting the claimant's need until it is actually received. A final group of states considers the potential contribution as a resource to be considered in computing the claimant's eligibility and the size of his grant, regardless of whether it is actually received.

What effect this "relatives' responsibility" doctrine has upon the social function of public assistance is a matter of some controversy. One group of opponents holds that the relative-responsibility laws are archaic survivals of the agrarian family. They argue that when the extended family cared for its own indigent members, the responsibility was voluntarily assumed as part of the value structure of family living. To force such responsibility in the modern age of independent-nuclear family life is held to be an attempt to create an artificial family solidarity. They point out that most individuals financially able to support indigent close relatives would probably do so without legal pressure, and that the only use of the laws is to harry the few recalcitrants and to enforce payment on legally responsible but financially helpless relatives.

There is also a group of proponents who maintain that the laws are not only valid but should be made more extensive and enforceable. To them the laws are a necessary result of the all-too-willing reliance of children to accept the state's responsibility for the support of their parents while shirking their own moral responsibility in this direction. Crucial to this point of view is the belief that family solidarity and stability are based upon mutual responsibility, and that the state has neither the right nor reason to relieve children of the responsibility for the care of indigent parents, nor parents for their children. Any relaxation of relative-responsibility laws would further demoralize family life.

The important question is, of course, do contributions from relatives reduce the cost of public assistance materially enough to warrant the costs and unpleasantness of bringing legal action against relatives? Until recently, no reliable information was available on the proportion or magnitude of recipient cases involving help from relatives. In mid-1955, however, the Division of Program Statistics and Analysis of the Bureau of Public Assistance released a report of the findings from a Study of Requirements, Incomes, Resources, and Social Characteristics of Recipients of Old-Age Assistance.[13] This study, the largest undertaking of its kind in the history of the program, was a joint project of the Bureau and each of the fifty-three jurisdictions. Among its findings was certain detailed information concerning the extent of aid given by children of the recipients. In the early months of 1953, nearly three-fourths (73.4 percent) of all OAA recipients either had

[13] United States Bureau of Public Assistance, *Recipients of Old-Age Assistance in Early 1953; Part I—State Data*, Public Assistance Report No. 26, June, 1955.

no children or lived in household units separately from their children. There were wide regional differences in the proportion of recipients sharing households with their children—from 11.6 percent in New York to 48.3 percent in North Carolina.

Slightly more than half of the recipients sharing households with their children received contributions from the children, the item most frequently contributed being shelter. Relatively few of the children sharing households with parents contributed cash in addition to the shelter. For all states combined, the percentage receiving cash contributions from children was a mere 6.7 percent, and even in the highest state, Massachusetts, it was only 20.3 percent.

Children living apart from parents contributed even less frequently to recipient parents than the children living in the same home. Five out of every six recipients with children living elsewhere received no contributions of any kind from them. These children contributed cash to their parents in about the same proportion as the children sharing households with their parents.

Summary statistics give some idea of the magnitude of cases involving contributions of various sorts by children to recipients. Among all the states, the proportion of recipients receiving cash contributions varied from less than 1 to 22.9 percent, the proportion receiving shelter from less than 1 to 14.5 percent, and the proportion receiving "other items" from less than 1 percent to 19.4 percent.

While these data refer only to the contributions by children to recipient parents in the aid-to-the-aged program, they give the most complete picture yet available of the role of relatives' contributions to needy persons in public assistance. We still do not know, of course, what proportion of this aid is voluntary and in how many cases the contribution is obtained by the agency involved. The small proportion of contributing children does, however, suggest that relatives' contributions do not greatly reduce public-assistance costs. When added to the possible danger to family relationships between the recipient and the relative and to the possibility of an added financial burden being imposed upon the relative, these data suggest that relatives' responsibility is not entirely successful. Perhaps the best approach is the middle-of-the road position that relatives should remain legally responsible but the agency should adopt a broad and liberal philosophy of seeking voluntary rather than enforced contributions.

Generally, any cash resources, such as money kept in a bank or at home and all negotiable instruments, are considered to be resources

which must be utilized by the claimant before he can be considered as needy. Where an old-age-assistance applicant has no life-insurance policy to meet burial expenses, he may generally keep a small amount of cash resources aside for this inevitable expense.

All insurance policies held by the claimant are subject to inspection by the agency to determine the potential resources represented. Lewis Meriam has given an excellent summary of the present trend concerning the consideration of insurance policies as resources:

Two different points of view may be taken with respect to insurance. The first is that the family is not in need if it can even for a short period get along on the cash which can be obtained by surrendering the policy. The other is that it is in the best interest of both the family and the public treasury to appraise the situation and take action with consideration of the probable future. What are the chances that the insured will again earn and be able to continue the policy in force? What are the facts with respect to his expectation of life? To take a possible case, let it be assumed that the need arises from the disability of insured and that the prognosis of the physician is unfavorable. Under such circumstances, it is clearly in the interest of the public treasury that the policy be maintained in full force if there are dependents for whom provision will have to be made. The insurance, in other words, is, from the standpoint of the public treasury, worth far more than is its cash surrender value.[14]

Other sources of potential income are differentially treated by the various jurisdictions. Many states require claimants to dispose of personal property such as jewelry, objects of art, expensive fur coats, and automobiles. Usually the agency establishes a limit on the value of personal property which an applicant may retain and still be considered as needy. Often it seems excessively harsh to require that a needy family dispose of antique furniture and other luxury items, but the position of the agency is that unless these items are essential to the livelihood of the applicant, he should be willing to convert them into means for his own support.

The modern trend in need determination is toward a greater standardization of levels of "health and decency." The investment of responsibility in the several jurisdictions makes such a national level a difficult task, however. The differing economic conditions and philosophies of adequate and proper standards tend to perpetuate the disparities which presently exist. For the past several years, however,

---

[14] Lewis Meriam, *Relief and Social Security*, Washington, Brookings Institution, 1946, p. 258.

the Social Security Administration, through its program of technical consultation to the states, has attempted to develop uniformity by giving advice and data on proper standards of budgeting and payment levels.[15]

There is a growing pressure from the states to get Congress to enact legislation which will permit, without loss of Federal funds, them to disregard the income of recipients in programs other than aid to the blind. In 1953, Colorado decided to submit a constitutional amendment to the voters at the next general election to permit income to be disregarded in old-age assistance.[16] The same year the Missouri legislature adopted a bill to permit the state welfare department to disregard earned income wherever possible under existing federal legislation, and Nebraska passed a similar provision for old-age assistance.[17] The legislatures of California, New Mexico, Oregon, Washington, and Wisconsin adopted resolutions recommending to Congress that the states be permitted to disregard income of assistance recipients without loss of federal funds.[18]

The 1955 legislative year witnessed a renewal of the campaign. As yet, however, no Congressional action has responded to these demands for legislation to encourage recipients to engage in some productive activity without fear of loss of eligibility or reduction of grants.

RESIDENCE REQUIREMENTS

As in the case of need, the Social Security Act does not define the precise residence requirements which determine ligibility for assistance. Although the act does establish maxima for each program, it is the state which decides what length of residence entitles an individual to legal "settlement," or the responsibility of a community for his care should he become indigent. Thus, local public-assistance agencies are not required to aid indigent nonresidents and may return them to their home jurisdictions if they do not meet the state's settlement requirements.

The history of these settlement laws goes back to the Elizabethan poor laws, which made the local county or township responsible for its own needy. Since this responsibility was extended only to members

15 For a description of this movement, see Eveline M. Burns, *The American Social Security System*, Boston, Houghton Mifflin Company, 1949, chap. 12.

16 Jules H. Berman and George J. Blaetus, "State Public Assistance Legislation, 1953," *Social Security Bulletin*, January, 1954, p. 4.

17 *Ibid.*, p. 4.

18 *Ibid.*, p. 4.

of the local community, the counties and townships developed a caution toward admitting to full residence "outsiders" who might become public charges. In the Colonies, these precautions developed into an elaborate system of settlement laws for the financial protection of the community.[19] Even today, the intricacies of these laws in the several states is such that it is still possible for an individual to reside in one state and have settlement in another, or to be completely without legal settlement. Migratory workers, for example, may lack legal settlement in any state unless special provisions covering them have been enacted.

In establishing the residence requirements for assistance programs, the states have frequently followed the federal maxima, although some have shown a tendency to establish requirements below these maxima in certain programs. Less than half the states now require as long a period of residence for OAA as the "five in nine years' " maximum provided under the Social Security Act. By January 1, 1955, twenty of the fifty-three jurisdictions had reduced their requirements to one year immediately preceding application.[20]

The same federal maximum applies for aid to the blind and aid to the permanently and totally disabled as for old-age assistance, and the states have exhibited an even greater tendency to lower the residence requirements for these programs. Only sixteen states require periods up to the federal maximum for AB applicants, and many of these reduce or remove the requirements if the applicant became blind while a resident of the state. Of the forty-four jurisdictions which had federally approved AD programs on January 1, 1955, only five had residence requirements as high as the federal maximum and most required only one year. Four states had removed all residence requirements for applicants for aid under this program.

For aid to dependent children, the most common requirement (thirty-nine jurisdictions) is the federal maximum of one year's residence by the child, or by the child's mother or other responsible relative if the child is not yet 1 year old. The popularity of this federal

[19] For an excellent description of the early American settlement laws, see Robert Kelso, *History of Public Poor Relief in Massachusetts*, Boston, Houghton Mifflin, 1922; or David Schneider and Albert Deutsch, *History of Public Welfare in New York*, Chicago, University of Chicago Press, 1938.

[20] The data concerning residence requirements of the various jurisdictions presented in this section were computed from the American Public Welfare Association's *The Public Welfare Directory, 1955*, Chicago, the Association, Tables I and II, pp. 368–378. This directory, which is published annually, will provide the reader with the most recent compilation of the residence requirements of the various states.

maximum among the states is that it is low enough so that there would be little reason for the state further to reduce the requirement. Several states allow for reciprocal agreements concerning ADC with other states, and six states have abolished all residence requirements for this form of assistance.

General assistance, which as a local program receives no federal support and hence has no federally imposed maximum residence requirement, shows somewhat more variation than the federally supported programs. The residence required by the several states varies from six months to five years, but is most frequently placed at one year. Several states make no legal provisions for residence in general assistance either meeting need regardless of the indigent's residence or leaving the determination of eligibility to the county welfare officials or to judicial officers.

The residence requirements we have just described refer only to the physical presence of the individual within the borders of the jurisdiction granting settlement rights. Many states as well impose specific conditions upon how the residence is to be acquired. Some demand that the applicant must have lived within the particular locality in which he makes application, and others that he must intend to remain in the state. Some states will not give settlement if the individual receives private or public assistance during the period he is establishing residence, or if it is spent in a public institution.

While the states seem reluctant to remove the arbitrary inconsistencies and inequities of these settlement laws, the Social Security Administration and many other public-welfare groups have for years suggested that they be abolished or at least made consistent with modern social-welfare practice. Suggestions have been made that the states adopt uniform settlement laws or provide for reciprocal settlement rights as a means of easing the discrimination against migratory workers and others who must change residence. Perhaps the most plausible proposal, in terms of the states' willingness to accept change in this area, is for a new federally supported general assistance program which would provide aid to needy nonresidents without regard for residence.

Some states have already abolished residence requirements for assistance or reduced them to the point where the needy person is only required to be present in the state at the time of application and plan to remain there to qualify under the state plan. Rhode Island was the first state to pass such legislation (1943) and has since been followed

by New York and Tennessee. The territories of Hawaii, Puerto Rico, and the Virgin Islands also grant assistance without regard to residence.

OTHER ELIGIBILITY REQUIREMENTS

Certain other specific eligibility requirements are found in some states, but are not common. Several states still require United States citizenship as a condition to the receipt of assistance, most frequently in old-age-assistance programs. Less frequently, states have retained certain of the tests of character and fitness which are vestigial remains of the concept of aid only to the "deserving" poor. Although these tests are not prohibited by the Social Security Act, the current opinion in public-welfare circles is that the assessment of character is not one of the functions of a public-assistance program.

A final group of eligibility requirements refers to the individual's entitlement under the specific programs. These include the age minimum for old-age assistance, degree of blindness for aid to the blind, extent of disablement for aid to the permanently and totally disabled, and the definition of dependent children and persons caring for them. These eligibility requirements will be discussed within the framework of the specific programs which follow.

The Present Status of Assistance Programs

In Chapter 14, we commented upon the strong feeling evident in the United States that social insurance is more in keeping with the American system of values than is public assistance. When the Social Security Act was still in its infancy, the assistance features of this revolutionary new legislation were considered by many to represent "stopgap" programs designed to see us through the depression until the new era of prosperity. When the social-insurance programs reached maturity and began paying benefits, it was reasoned, American social security would largely be borne by the contributory system. The federal grants in aid to the states, having filled a temporary need, would disappear or at least be substantially reduced; certainly they would not continue indefinitely.

The development of the public-assistance programs of the act since 1936 indicates that this view, still harbored by some leaders of government and business, is unrealistic and short-sighted. Not only has public assistance survived recovery of the economy and the maturing of the social-insurance programs; it has shown a steady increase in both

the number of recipients and in the size of their grants as well. Table 57, which shows the number of recipients in each of the programs from 1936 to 1954, traces this growth. Prior to the establishment of

TABLE 57. Public-Assistance Recipients by Program, 1936–1954.[a]
(recipients in thousands)[b]

| Year | Old-Age Assistance | Aid to Dependent Children | | | Aid to the Blind | Aid to the Permanently and Totally Disabled [d] | General Assistance (Cases) [e] |
		Families	Total Recipients [c]	Children			
1936	1106	162	—	404	45	—	1510
1937	1577	228	—	565	56	—	1626
1938	1776	280	—	648	67	—	1631
1939	1909	315	—	760	70	—	1558
1940	2066	370	—	891	73	—	1239
1941	2234	390	—	941	77	—	798
1942	2227	348	—	849	79	—	460
1943	2149	272	—	676	76	—	292
1944	2066	254	—	639	72	—	258
1945	2056	274	—	701	71	—	257
1946	2196	346	—	885	77	—	315
1947	2332	416	—	1060	81	—	356
1948	2498	475	—	1214	86	—	398
1949	2736	599	—	1521	93	—	562
1950	2789	652	2234	1662	98	69	413
1951	2708	593	2044	1524	97	127	323
1952	2646	570	1992	1495	99	164	280
1953	2591	548	1942	1464	100	195	270
1954	2564	603	2137	1639	102	224	351

a Data through 1942 cover only continental United States; thereafter include Alaska and Hawaii. Programs for the special types of public assistance in Puerto Rico and the Virgin Islands initiated October, 1950, under Social Security Act amendments of 1950. See also notes c and d.
b Data shown are for December of each year.
c Includes as recipients the children and one parent or other adult relative in families in which the requirement of at least one such adult were considered in determining the amount of assistance. Beginning October, 1950, federal funds available for payments to these adults under the Social Security Act amendments of 1950.
d Program initiated October, 1950, under the Social Security Act amendments of 1950.
e Beginning September, 1952, excludes Nebraska; data not available.

Source: Adapted from Social Security Bulletin, September, 1954, Table 50, p. 65; and March, 1955, Table 9, p. 31.

the categorical-aid programs, general assistance, or poor relief, represented the most common means of providing aid to the needy. As the table indicates, this program still served the largest numbers during the early years of the act, and it was not until 1938 that the new old-age assistance began to surpass general assistance. Since that time OAA has continued to develop as a program serving far greater numbers than any of the other categorical programs, despite its promise of

an early death in the face of growing old-age and survivors' insurance benefits. As the categorical programs have grown, there has been a consequent decrease in the number of general-assistance cases, which, after a slight post-World War II upsurge, have continued to decline.

A growing program in both importance and number of recipients has been the aid-to-dependent-children program. If we should add the services and supplementary-aid programs to financial assistance, the growth would be even more apparent. This growth has paralleled the trends in old-age assistance, indicating once again that public-assistance programs, with the exception of the stable aid to handicapped groups in the population, respond to changing economic and social conditions. Notice that during the war years both OAA and ADC showed marked decreases as many older workers, mothers, and adolescents found employment in war industries. During the postwar period, as readjustment took place and servicemen returned to reclaim their positions in the labor market, both programs began the increases which have since been characteristic of all public-assistance programs.

The programs designed to assist the needy handicapped—aid to the blind and, since 1950, aid to the permanently and totally disabled—have always served much smaller numbers than ADC and OAA programs. This is, of course, a function of the proportionately smaller representation of this group in the population. The importance of these programs, however, is much greater than the numbers of recipients would indicate, for they usually provide aid over a much longer period of an individual's life.

Despite the obvious growth of the aid programs, there are still vocal segments of the population which annually call for the end of these "socialistic" policies. It seems incredible to these organizations and individuals that a nation as richly endowed as the United States should contain individuals who have legitimate need for assistance—blind people, handicapped individuals, perhaps even a few neglected and abandoned children, but certainly no significant numbers of adult, healthy, and industrious needy. The myopia of this view, as exemplified by the proposal of the Chamber of Commerce of the United States that old-age assistance be discontinued, and insurance methods be used exclusively, precludes the acceptance of the obvious fact that we are always going to have a proportion of the population in need of assistance. This proportion may decline, but it will not conveniently disappear.

While we are attempting to disband our assistance programs in

favor of contributory programs, the European countries, nearly always far ahead of us in social-security planning, are moving more and more toward social welfare programs based on right to aid as the central concept in social security. The growth of family-allowance programs is one manifestation of this development. Denmark, for example, pays rent subsidies to its aged and also subsidizes low-rent apartments for its pensioners, as does Sweden. Sweden's new national health program provides hospital and medical care and free medicine for everyone. Germany, though struggling to rebuild a war-ravaged nation, provides free medical care and hospitalization to pensioners under its compulsory-insurance system.

OLD-AGE ASSISTANCE

State-federal old-age-assistance plans are now in effect in each of the forty-eight states, the District of Columbia, Alaska, and Hawaii. Puerto Rico and the Virgin Islands received federal grants in aid for assistance to their needy aged for the first time under the 1950 amendments to the Social Security Act, which made this form of assistance available in all fifty-three American jurisdictions. Under the federal-state partnership plan, all needy individuals 65 years of age and older become eligible. In Colorado, which also aids needy persons from 60 to 64 under certain conditions, the federal grants do not match the cost of the aid program for those individuals under 65, and this portion of the state's aid to needy older persons must be financed entirely from state funds.

Although the proportion of persons 65 and over receiving help under this program varies among the several jurisdictions, ranging in 1953 from over 60 percent in Louisiana to only 6 percent in Delaware, the national average was about one-fifth in 1953. The average monthly grant which these individuals receive also exhibits a wide variation among the jurisdictions, from $7.81 in Puerto Rico and $27.70 in West Virginia to $82.49 in Connecticut in March, 1955. The national average for the same month was $51.85. At that time, there were 2,552,881 recipients of old-age assistance in the United States.

Recently, information concerning the characteristics of these recipients has become available as a result of the previously described Federal-State Study of Requirements, Incomes, Resources, and Social Characteristics of Recipients of Old-Age Assistance in the United States in early 1953. The findings of this study were that in early 1953:

1. A majority of aged recipients lived in rural areas and small towns. The proportion of aged persons receiving assistance in such areas was two-thirds higher than in metropolitan areas.

2. One-half of the persons receiving old-age assistance were aged 75 or over. The proportion of aged persons receiving assistance increased with age. Among all persons 65–69, one in ten received aid; among those 80 and over, one in three received aid.

3. Half of the recipients of OAA had been on the rolls less than five years.

4. Women outnumbered men by at least three to two among recipients. One-half million more women than men received aid.

5. Five of every six recipients were able to care for themselves insofar as activities of daily living are concerned. About one in thirty was bedfast. The remainder required considerable care from other persons because of their physical or mental condition.

6. Approximately two-thirds of the aged recipients maintained their own households, including slightly more than one-fourth who lived alone and somewhat less than one-fourth who lived with spouse only. About one recipient in twenty lived in an institution—most of them in private nursing homes.

7. The median number of rooms used by households in which recipients lived was four. Ninety-five percent of recipients (excluding those in institutions) had cooking facilities; seven-eighths had electricity; 36 percent had telephones either in their homes or available in the same building; three-fourths had some type of refrigeration, including 55 percent who had mechanical refrigeration; slightly more than two-thirds had running water available.

8. Nearly half of the married recipients owned their homes, while fewer than one out of five nonmarried recipients owned homes.

9. Forty-four percent of the married couples with two OAA payments and one-third of the other recipients had cash income from sources in addition to OAA. For the couples with such additional income, the median amount was $37.25; for the other recipients, $28.73.

10. Thirty-eight percent of OAA recipients received goods or services in some form other than cash, thereby further reducing their need for assistance. Such income in kind was common in rural areas, relatively infrequent in urban ones.

11. Median requirements for married couples both receiving OAA were $108.66 ($54.33 each); for other recipients, $66.86.

In addition to money payments for assistance, payments may be made for medical, surgical, and dental care under the existing program. Since the 1950 amendments, most states provide for recipients in public

institutions as well as in nonprofit homes for older people if the standards of such homes are not luxurious. Individuals may, and often do, receive old-age and survivors' insurance and old-age assistance concurrently if they are needy. At the end of 1950, some 300,000 persons aged 65 and over were receiving income from both programs, and the number has been gradually increasing, so that by February, 1955, some 500,000 persons were receiving both OASI benefits and OAA grants.[21] In February, 1954, 18.0 percent of old-age-assistance recipients and 9.7 percent of old-age and survivors' insurance beneficiaries were in both programs at the same time.[22]

Recent years have witnessed a gradual decline in the number of recipients in the continental United States—about 250,000 between December, 1950, and December, 1954—but this decline does not indicate any loss of importance of this program.[23] As we have previously indicated, over half of the recipients in the early months of 1953 were 75 years of age and over, and women outnumbered men three to two. This group, which includes many who are not covered by OASI, may be expected to decline even more as the coverage of the social-insurance program is extended, but there is some question whether OASI payments alone will suffice to furnish even the basic needs of older persons. In the absence of private or occupational retirement provisions or some other source of income, assistance would seem to serve as the one remaining avenue of income security.

AID TO DEPENDENT CHILDREN

In March, 1955, Nevada passed an enabling act to provide a program for aid to dependent children, thus extending the protection of ADC to the children of all fifty-three jurisdictions for the first time. Under the Federal-state program, grants are made to the states for any child who is ". . . a needy child under the age of sixteen, or under the age of eighteen if found by the State agency to be regularly attending school, who has been deprived of parental support or care by reason of the death, continued absence from the home, or physical or mental incapacity of a parent, and who is living with his father, mother, grandfather, grandmother, brother, sister, stepfather, stepmother, stepbrother, stepsister, uncle or aunt, in a place of residence

[21] Lenore A. Epstein, "Economic Resources of Persons Aged 65 and Over," *Social Security Bulletin*, June, 1955, p. 9.
[22] *Social Security Bulletin*, August, 1954, p. 15.
[23] *Ibid.*

maintained by one or more of such relatives as his or their own home." [24] As presently interpreted by the Bureau of Public Assistance, this definition means that any child meeting the stated age requirements who has been deprived of parental support as the result of the death, desertion, or continued absence from the home, or physical or mental incapacitation, of a parent is eligible for state aid supported by federal government funds. Since 1950, the federal government has also shared in aid given to the child's mother or any of the other relatives specified in the act who is caring for the child in the absence of the mother. This latter provision has done much to raise the level of ADC programs and grants. Prior to 1950, the federal government shared only in state aid extended to children, which placed the responsibility for the needy mother or relative entirely upon the state.

The present interpretation given to the concept of the dependent child also marks a step in the direction of liberal construction. Under the early state "mothers' aid" programs, relatively few children whose need resulted from the absence or incapacity of their parents received assistance since "dependent child" was construed to mean "fatherless child." Today the realization is growing that desertion or ineffectiveness of one or both parents presents just as serious a problem to the psychological and financial security of the child. The extension of social-insurance benefits to surviving children, which first became available in 1940, has further strengthened our provisions for dependent children and their families.

As with OAA, there is considerable disparity among the various jurisdictions in the number of recipients and the size of grants in ADC programs. In March, 1955, there were 1,699,626 children in 624,235 families receiving an average grant of $86.63 per family or $24 per child from federal-state aid-to-dependent-children programs.[25] The range in number of recipients ran from 1554 children in 572 families in Wyoming to 144,662 children in 56,594 families in California. Much of this disparity is, of course, owing to population size, but the operation of socioeconomic factors becomes apparent when we realize that Puerto Rico, which was not eligible for federal grants until 1950, had 110,152 recipient children in 42,262 families by March, 1955, the third largest number of recipients of ADC in the nation at that time. The size of the grants also varies: from $3.01 per recipient or $10.26 per family in Puerto Rico to $41.93 per recipient or $136.40 per

---

[24] Section 406(a) of the Social Security Act of 1935 as amended.
[25] *Social Security Bulletin*, June, 1955, p. 35.

family in Connecticut. The lowest grants in the continental United States in a state having a fully operating program were found in Mississippi, which paid $6.63 per recipient or $25.12 per family in March, 1955.

Assistance under this program is in the form of money payments, but provision is also made for payment for medical or remedial care for either the dependent child or the relative caring for him. Recent studies have shown, however, that, in terms of the existing needs of dependent children and their families, the grants in most states are barely at the level of minimum standards.[26] A less serious problem is posed by the fact that orphans without close relatives, who must consequently be placed in institutions or foster homes, are ineligible for aid to dependent children. Although they represent a very small proportion of all needy children, occasional situations do arise where foster-home care would be improved if orphans were included in the federal provisions.

AID TO THE BLIND

Nevada was also the last of the fifty-three jurisdictions to enact legislation providing for a federal-state program of aid to the blind. Each state is permitted to develop its own definition of blindness under the act, but they have generally established "economic blindness"—impairment of vision sufficient to disable an individual from employability—as the criterion. To this end, age limits are also imposed, usually excluding children below a minimum age, which ranges from 16 to 21, and, in one case, individuals over 65 who become eligible for old-age assistance. Since 1952, the determination of blindness must be made by a physician skilled in the diseases of the eye or, if the applicant prefers, by an optometrist.

The number of recipients in this program has never been large, owing to the specialized nature of the category. In March, 1955, there were 103,045 recipients of AB in the United States, whose average monthly grant was $56.74. Variations in the number of blind persons served, again a function of population size, ranged from 35 in the Virgin Islands to 16,312 in Pennsylvania. Grants varied from $7.74 in Puerto Rico and $32.23 in West Virginia to $93.46 in Massachusetts.

The new federal provision which encourages productive employment by exempting the first $50 a month earned by recipients of AB

[26] See Gordon M. Blackwell and Raymond F. Gould, *Future Citizens All*, Chicago, American Public Welfare Association, 1952.

is also being independently established by some of the states themselves. California's Aid to Partially Self-Supporting Blind Residents, for example, permits blind recipients to earn up to $1000 a year without any reduction in their standard monthly grant. Many states provide prevention and rehabilitation services as well, in the form of free examination and treatment of the eyes and vocational counseling and training for individuals disabled as a result of blindness.

AID TO THE PERMANENTLY AND TOTALLY DISABLED

The most recently established of the categorical programs, aid to the permanently and totally disabled, has been rapidly established by the various jurisdictions; and by 1955, forty-two states and territories had operating federal-state programs. When this category was first included under the 1950 amendments, it represented an almost entirely new type of assistance. Unlike the other forms of aid, which represented an attempt by the federal government to strengthen existing programs in the states, only Wisconsin and a few counties and cities in other parts of the nation had similar programs in operation.[27] Before the federal program was inaugurated, most of the disabled persons receiving aid were on general assistance or were incapacitated fathers of children in ADC programs.[28]

In the states having programs in March, 1955, 229,893 disabled persons received an average monthly grant of $55.03. Puerto Rico again paid the lowest average monthly payment, $8.54 to 18,863 persons, while Connecticut paid its 1,750 recipients an average of $103.52 a month. The largest number of recipients, 40,405, was found in New York; the smallest in Delaware, where 187 persons received such aid.[29] A mid-1951 study of the medical and social characteristics of the then almost 100,000 AD recipients indicated that four groups of diseases constituted the disabling impairment of about 65 percent of the recipients.[30] More than three of every ten recipients suffered from diseases of the heart and circulatory system; at least one of every ten was disabled by arthritis, paralyzing conditions, or congenital conditions.[31] The recipients, whose median age was 56, were equally

---

[27] Anne E. Geddes and Charles E. Hawkins, "Public Assistance," American Association of Social Workers, New York, the Association, 1954, p. 402.

[28] *Ibid.*, p. 402.

[29] *Social Security Bulletin*, June, 1955, Table 19, p. 36.

[30] United States Bureau of Public Assistance, *Characteristics of Recipients of Aid to the Permanently and Totally Disabled, Mid-1951*, Bulletin No. 22, 1953. Cited in Geddes and Hawkins, *op. cit.*, pp. 402–403.

[31] *Ibid.*, p. 402.

divided among men and women, and 70 percent of the total had a history of paid employment at some time.[32]

The definition of "permanently and totally disabled" is left to the individual state within the limits established by the act. The Bureau of Public Assistance has interpreted the category as follows: "Permanently and totally disabled" means that the individual has some physical or mental impairment, disease, or loss that substantially precludes him from engaging in useful occupations within his competence, such as holding a job or homemaking. It has been suggested that the disability factor be considered as consisting of two parts—one dependent upon medical findings and one on a social study of the individual and his ability to carry out his responsibilities, as for example, wage earner or homemaker." [33]

Within these limits, the states have accepted various degrees of disability as establishing eligibility; some states require almost complete physical disability, while others take a more liberal construction and emphasize the unemployability of the disabled person as the primary concern. Complementing this form of assistance is the vocational-rehabilitation program we shall discuss in a later section.

GENERAL ASSISTANCE

General assistance, financed and supported entirely from state and local funds, presents an example of the inequities of assistance programs lacking the standard-setting influence of the federal government. Administered by nearly 10,000 local units, the standards, number of recipients, and size of grants vary markedly throughout the United States. In March, 1955, 381,000 cases of this type of aid throughout the nation received an average monthly grant of $57.46. If we consider the average monthly payments to these cases in the various jurisdictions, we receive some idea of the disparity in treatment given to these individuals. In March, 1955, the average grants varied as follows: Puerto Rico paid $10.67 per case, Mississippi $13.73 per case, Tennessee $16.56 per case, Georgia $22.74 per case, Wisconsin $77.16 per case, New Jersey $80.37 per case, and New York $84.73 per case.[34] These differences are not entirely explained by population size and relative wealth of the states alone, but indicate a difference of

[32] *Ibid.*, p. 402.
[33] Phyllis Hill, "Aid to the Permanently and Totally Disabled," *Social Security Bulletin*, December, 1950, pp. 12–13.
[34] *Social Security Bulletin*, June, 1955, Table 20, p. 36.

philosophy and standards in the various states. The more liberal philosophy of the northern states, admittedly coupled with greater resources, has generally produced higher standards of general assistance than in the southern states.

Even the administrative level of authority varies widely among the states. In 1952, ten states assumed full burden for general assistance, fifteen states allowed the local unit to pay the entire costs of GA, and of the remainder fifteen states paid half or more of the costs of this program in their political subdivisions.[35] While the administration of this program by the different states acting individually presents unlimited possibilities for arbitrary standards and practices, the administration of the program by large numbers of local units greatly compounds the diversity. Some local units will give assistance only to individuals in the most extreme need and then only if they meet rigid settlement requirements. If a migratory worker should become indigent in some one of these localities, there is no assurance that his needs would be met unless some private agency should assume his care. Adding to the discrimination in this category is the fact that many people still find it difficult to believe that healthy, able-bodied adults should ever be in need of assistance in the United States. There is a strong feeling that the needs of these individuals are engendered by laziness and immorality and that they are not the "deserving poor."

Two primary methods of dealing with the problems presented by the varied nature of the general-assistance programs throughout the nation have been advanced: (1) integrating all types of public assistance into one unified program without the categorical requirements, and (2) establishing general assistance as one of the categorical programs, broadly defined, under the present federal-state grant system. Both suggestions have merit. The arguments for abolishing the categorical system in favor of a "generalized assistance" program include the abolition of present inequities among the various programs with old-age assistance, for example, receiving a disproportionately larger share of the assistance dollar as compared with the other assistance categories. Criticism has also been leveled at the administrative difficulties presented in financing and managing several different yet related programs.[36]

[35] Geddes and Hawkins, op. cit., p. 403.

[36] See, for example, the reports of the Committee on Federal-State Relations of the Hoover Commission and Robert T. Lansdale, "A Major Problem of Public Welfare: The Growing Complexity of Administering Public Assistance," Public Welfare, April, 1953, pp. 7–12.

The harsh reality is, however, that the extension of the categorical system to include the new general assistance under federal-state coöperation would probably meet less resistance from the critics of public assistance than the consolidation of the several programs into one comprehensive federal-state program. As we have mentioned on several occasions, any program which proposed to aid *all* needy persons, regardless of their possession of social or physical characteristics which qualify them as "unfortunates," would almost certainly be labeled as socialistic today and stand little chance of success. Regardless of the social and economic advantages of a unitary program, this opposition precludes any radical change in the present categorical system.

MATERNAL AND CHILD WELFARE SERVICES

Under the provisions of Title V of the Social Security Act, the federal government also allocates grants in aid to the states for four services for maternal and child welfare: maternal and child health services, services to crippled children, child welfare services, and vocational rehabilitation. Each of these health and welfare services is designed to protect and care for specific groups within the population.

Grants for maternal and child health services totaling $1 million a year for five years were first authorized by the Sheppard-Towner Act in 1921, but owing to strong opposition they were allowed to expire during the Hoover administration in 1929. Reinstituted in the Social Security Act of 1935, the program has operated without interruption since that time. The purpose of the program, which is now available in all fifty-three jurisdictions of the United States, is to "extend and improve . . . services for promoting the health of mothers and children, especially in rural areas and in areas suffering from severe economic distress." The federal allotment to the states is drawn from two separate funds of the appropriation—"MCH Fund A" and "MCH Fund B." From Fund A each state receives an amount based upon a flat grant ($43,373 in 1954) and the ratio of live births in the state to the total in the United States. Twenty-five percent of Fund B is set aside as a reserve for special and emergency programs, and the remaining 75 percent is apportioned among the states on the basis of the individual need of each state for financial assistance to carry out its approved program. Grants from Fund A must be matched by the state on a dollar-for-dollar basis, and grants from Fund B do not require state matching.

An analysis of MCH programs reveals the federal-state funds are used by the State health departments to:

1. Develop, support, extend, and improve services for mothers and children such as: maternity clinics for prenatal care; well-child clinics for the health supervision of infants and preschool children; health services for school children including health supervision by physicians, dentists, public health nurses, and nutritionists; dental hygiene and prophylaxis dental care; nutrition education; advice to hospitals on maternity and new-born services; licensing and inspection of maternity homes; and provision of incubators and hospital care for premature infants. The programs of the several states vary considerably in relative emphasis among the foregoing, and

2. Provide for postgraduate training for physicians, nurses and nutritionists through in-service training and institute, and through payment of stipends and tuition at universities.[37]

As in the case of the assistance programs, the state must submit a plan for its program to the Secretary of Health, Education, and Welfare for approval. In addition to the usual requirement concerning financial participation by the state, the administration or supervision of the program by the state agency (in this case the state health department), the submission by that agency of such reports as are required by the Secretary of Health, Education, and Welfare, and the selection of personnel on a merit basis, the plan must also provide for (1) the extension and improvement of local maternal and child-health services administered by local child-health units; (2) coöperation with medical, health, nursing, and welfare groups and organizations; (3) the development of demonstration services in needy areas and among groups in special need.

In recent years, this program has placed an increasing emphasis upon the emotional growth and physical well-being of children. Originaly conceived as a preventive program, it has also developed in the direction of providing medical care and demonstration services in an effort to reduce infant and fetal mortality throughout the country. Some estimate of the size of maternal and child health services is provided by the number of mothers and children served in 1952: 180,000 expectant mothers attended prenatal clinics, about 434,000 infants and 576,000 preschool children attended well-children clinics, approximately 2,500,000 children received dental inspections, and

---

[37] Commission on Intergovernmental Relations, *A Description of Twenty-Five Federal Grant-in-Aid Programs*, Washington, Government Printing Office, June, 1955.

about 3,600,000 smallpox and diphtheria immunizations were given under the program.[38]

Like the maternal and child health program, services for crippled children are administered on the federal level by the Division of Health Services of the Children's Bureau in the Department of Health, Education, and Welfare. The grants further resemble the maternal and child health provisions in that they are designed to give preference to rural and economically distressed areas. Under the Social Security Act, the grants are to be used for locating crippled children; providing medical, surgical, corrective, and other services and care; and for facilities for diagnosis, hospitalization, and aftercare of crippled children and children with conditions which lead to crippling.

At the state level, the program is administered by different agencies in the various states. The state health department administers the program in thirty-three jurisdictions, the state welfare department in eight states, the State health and welfare departments in two states, a crippled-children's commission in four states, the state education department in three states, and the state medical school in three states.[39] The Children's Bureau specifies that the state plan must include requirements for (1) contributions to be made by profesisonal personnel, such as physicians, medical social workers, nurses, physical therapists, etc.; (2) appropriate cross-referencing of crippled-children's projects with other phases of the state health program (e.g., dental care of crippled children); (3) significant health needs and administrative problems as related to crippled children; (4) program activities envisaged over the next two years for each principal diagnostic group, such as orthopedic, plastic, rheumatic fever, and speech and hearing; (5) measures being employed to measure progress and evaluate services; (7) various required descriptive materials; and (8) special projects to be financed from the reserve fund.[40]

The federal financing of crippled-children's grants is also split into two funds, termed "CC Fund A" and "CC Fund B." From Fund A, each state receives a flat grant (again $43,373 in the fiscal year 1954) and its proportionate share of the remaining funds based upon the number of children under 21 in the state. From Fund B, 25 percent is reserved for special projects and each state receives a prorated share based upon the number of children under 21 in both rural and urban

[38] *Ibid., passim.*
[39] *Ibid.,* p. 99.
[40] *Ibid.,* p. 101.

areas, with the number of rural children being doubly weighted. The size of the grant from Fund B is also affected by the ratio of the state's per capita income to United States per capita income, the size of the state's grant varying inversely with its per capita income. Grants received from Fund A must be fully matched by the state, but Fund B requires no matching.

To win the approval of the Secretary of Health, Education, and Welfare, the state plan must make the same general administrative provisions as those for maternal and child health services and, in addition, provide for (1) carrying out the purpose of the crippled-children's program as envisaged in the act, and (2) coöperation with medical, health, nursing, and welfare groups and organizations and with any state agency charged with the vocational rehabilitation of handicapped children. About 238,000 children received care under the state-federal crippled-children's programs in 1952.[41]

We have previously discussed some of the child-welfare services provided by local and voluntary agencies in communities for various groups of children. Under the provisions of Title V of the Social Security Act, the Division of Social Services of the Children's Bureau administers a program of child-welfare services which is preventive and protective in nature in "areas predominantly rural and other areas of special need." These funds, which are not granted on a matching basis, are to be used for establishing, extending, and strengthening public-welfare services for the protection and care of homeless, dependent, and neglected children and children in danger of becoming delinquent. In practice, these services include a wide range of activities: counseling services on the problems of children; case finding and treatment of children with physical, mental, or emotional handicaps; arranging substitute foster-home or institutional care of children on a permanent or temporary basis; safeguarding children who are born out of wedlock; assisting the courts when children's cases are involved; working with mental-hygiene clinics and other specialized health and welfare services in developing programs for special children; and promoting community-wide planning for child welfare.[42]

The plan for the program is developed jointly by the state and federal governments, with the federal government paying only about one-fourth of the actual child-welfare costs ($5,113,476 of the $23,-

[41] *Ibid.*, p. 100.

[42] Spencer H. Crookes, "Child Welfare," American Association of Social Workers," *Social Work Year Book, 1954*, New York, the Association, 1954, pp. 90–91.

270,956 expended in the fiscal year ending June 30, 1952).[43] The actual federal allotment to the states is made in the amount of $40,000 to each state, with the remainder of the sum appropriated by Congress apportioned to each state on the basis of the ratio of its rural population under 18 to the rural population of the United States of the same age. The exactness of the requirements practically precludes the use of the funds in the urban areas. There is some justification for this seeming discrimination, however, since the welfare and health services furnished by local governmental and voluntary agencies in most rural areas are below the standards found in most urban areas.

In an earlier chapter, we described the history of federal legislation concerning vocational rehabilitation and its use as a means of employee protection. In 1954, the vocational-rehabilitation features of the Social Security Act were extensively altered by Congress (P.L. 565, Eighty-third Congress) both in respect to financing and administering the program.

Currently, three types of grants in aid are provided to the state for vocational-rehabilitation services. Grants are now authorized for the support of basic vocational-rehabilitation services, extension and improvement of new and existing services, and special projects, including research and personnel training programs. Designed to aid those individuals who have substantial physical or mental handicaps, which make them unemployable but who can be reasonably expected to regain employability, the program is presently available in each of the forty-eight states. Each individual receives such services as are considered necessary to render him fit to engage in productive, remunerative employment.

The state must submit a plan for the approval of the Secretary of Health, Education, and Welfare, which is judged on the basis of its feasibility within the conditions established by the act.[44]

The rehabilitation services covered by federal grants include diagnostic and related services, such as transportation, and training, guidance, and placement services, including financial aid if required to make the handicapped individual employable. If a needy handicapped individual requires hospitalization, prosthetic devices, subsistence, or tools and equipment for training purposes, these may also be furnished.

[43] Commission on Intergovernmental Relations, op. cit., p. 122.

[44] For a review of the several specific requirements for approval, the reader is referred to the report of the Commission on Intergovernmental Relations, A Description of Twenty-Five Federal Grant-in-Aid Programs, op. cit., pp. 124–125.

The allotments for each of the three grants are determined by criteria established under the 1954 amendments to the Social Security Act. For basic services each state receives a grant based on its population and an allotment percentage determined by its per capita income. The allotment for basic services is protected by the act, which establishes the 1954 state grant as a "base allotment" for future grants in order to provide for uninterrupted service. The federal share of basic-service expenses ranges from 50 to 75 percent depending upon the state. Grants for the extension and improvement of these services are allocated on the basis of the state's population and require that the federal government provide 75 percent of the program costs. Federal participation in any project is limited to three years. The determination of the grants and required state matching of federal funds for special projects are left to the discretion of the Secretary of Health, Education, and Welfare. Congress in 1955, however, enacted legislation which requires that the state shall contribute not less than $1 for every $2 provided by the Federal Government for special projects.

PUBLIC-HEALTH SERVICES

The Social Security Act also provides for public-health services under Title VI, in addition to the public-health services administered by the Children's Bureau under Title V as just described. Under Title VI, the United States Public Health Service of the Department of Health, Education, and Welfare is authorized to assist "states, counties, health districts and other political subdivisions of the States in establishing and maintaining adequate public-health services, including the training of personnel for state and local health work." In addition, the Public Health Service Act of 1954 authorizes grants for general public health, tuberculosis control, venereal-disease control, mental-health, and heart-disease programs, and the Annual Appropriation Act (P.L. 170, 1954) added a cancer-control grant program and amplified the project-grant authority of the venereal-disease-control program.

Each state must submit to the Public Health Service for its approval a complete health program or plan which includes the following information: (1) major health and administrative problems, (2) what the state proposes to do, (3) where the state proposes to do it, (4) the method the state proposes to use, and (5) what specific plans the state has made for measuring progress and evaluating each pro-

gram and component thereof.[45] Funds for the specific grant programs in the several areas of public-health activities are made available to the states on the basis of their population, the general health needs of the state, the extent of the specific health problem presented in the disease covered by the grant, and the state's relative financial need. Each of the specific program grants is made by weighting each of these factors in various proportions for each program except venereal-disease control, which is handled on a project basis at the discretion of the Surgeon General of the United States.

While these federal grants have proved very helpful in the states' public-health needs, personnel-training programs, and, more recently, demonstration and research activities, they by no means cover a large portion of the states' public-health expenditure. In the fiscal year 1953, for example, federal grants accounted for less than 10 percent of the total expenditures for all programs of public health.[46]

Closely related to these programs is the long-awaited National Mental Health Act, which was passed in 1946 after many years of neglect of the great and growing problem of the nation's mental health. The act provides for programs of research, training of clinical personnel for mental-health teams, and the development of community-wide services for mental-health programs which are both preventive and therapeutically oriented. The federal grants in aid under this program are allocated to the states on a matching basis and cannot be used for the construction of hospitals and clinics. Rather, the programs are directed toward providing more efficient diagnostic and therapeutic services to a larger group of people by raising the level of training of mental-health personnel, providing for larger numbers of trained workers in this field, and providing funds for needed research in mental health.

The Social Security Act, Assistance Features: Concluding Remarks

When the extended family was the basic unit of social and economic activity, the problems of dependent individuals were family problems, solved by family-help patterns. In the family unit of production, there was always some functional role for even the aged and infirm and consequently always a source of lifelong security. As our economy has expanded and manufacturing and commerce have dis-

---

[45] Commission on Intergovernmental Relations, *op. cit.*, p. 82.
[46] *Ibid.*, p. 86.

placed agriculture as the center of economic activity, the family has sent its members into the greater community in search of income and individual success. When they can no longer care for themselves, some of the responsibility for the care of these members has been transferred to the community. At first this transfer was to private "charities," and later to local communities and their systems of poor relief. More recently, however, it has been the federal government which has undertaken to promote the welfare of individuals whose income security and welfare are threatened.

The federal government has not, however, accepted this responsibility without some misgivings. Until recent decades, the relief of human misery was primarily the responsibility of the local community, with little state aid and less federal aid. So strong was this division of responsibility that when the first effects of the Great Depression began to emphasize the need for some comprehensive system of assistance, the Hoover administration refused to render aid which would encroach upon the responsibility that had been assigned to the local community. It took the Great Depression and a progressive new administration to provide the limited federal intervention into public welfare which we enjoy today.

The passage of the Social Security Act of 1935 marked the turning point in American public welfare. For the first time in our history, the federal government was committed to a broad and multifaceted program which put it squarely in the center of assistance activities as a partner of the states. Even this step, however, was envisaged by many as a temporary expedient, which would disappear as the economy was bolstered and the more "Puritan" social-insurance features of the act began to provide for the income security of the nation. Yet the need for assistance has remained and, in an economic sense, increased, for the programs have grown rather than diminished.

What the future of these assistance features will be is still in question. Strong opposition, particularly from the United States Chamber of Commerce, to their continuation, and the belief that social insurance offers the soundest means of providing income security, operate in the direction of reduction and even abandonment of the programs. The more liberal approach of providing a comprehensive coverage of all needy individuals in one federally supported program rather than the present categorical system finds favor with social-work and welfare organizations, but apparently is not in our immediate future. Meanwhile, European countries have extended rather than reduced their

welfare programs, particularly in terms of making childhood secure through a system of family allowances as well as providing services for older citizens. We should do well to consider the costs of abandoning our programs or allowing them to become inoperative through a gradual process of neglect before we allow our consideration of money costs to control our actions.

SELECTED REFERENCES

Burns, Eveline M., *The American Social Security System*, Boston, Houghton Mifflin Company, 1949.

Friedlander, Walter A., *Introduction to Social Welfare*, New York, Prentice-Hall, 1955.

Leyendecker, Hilary M., *Problems and Policy in Public Assistance*, New York, Harper & Brothers, 1955.

Russell, James E. (ed.), *National Policies for Education, Health and Social Services*, Garden City, N. Y., Doubleday and Company, 1955.

chapter 17

Other Social-Legislation Programs

Our discussion of family legislation, labor legislation, and social-security legislation has limited its coverage to programs which definitely fall within each classification. In some instances, this has meant the omission of important programs in each area. This chapter is intended to pick up some major programs that were by-passed. We shall discuss briefly (1) federal housing legislation, (2) federal education legislation, and (3) legislation in behalf of special groups, of which war veterans and railroad-transportation employees will serve as examples.

Federal Housing Legislation

Assistance in the form of land or shelter has been provided in American legislation since before the Constitution. The liberalization of the government's land policies during the 1820's was based on an attempt to assist those who could not lay out the cash for large sections of the public domain. That kind of public relief which would attempt to lessen the pressure of people on scarce dwellings and would plan for the removal of slums on grounds of social policy is quite recent, however. The background of public housing sometimes is traced from the First National Conference on Housing, which convened for three days in 1911; but by the time the Conference convened, New York State already had in operation a tenement-house law applicable to cities of the first class—a product of the New York State Tenement House Commission appointed by Governor Theodore Roosevelt in 1900. A note sounded during the Conference by the speaker on housing legislation has a familiar ring: "With the broadening scope of legislative control, which is gradually assuming greater and greater proportions, we are beginning to regulate almost every

field of human activity, the State thus gradually assuming responsibility. The danger of relieving the individual of his moral responsibility to some extent and transferring the burden to the State, lies in the tendency to weaken the individual conscience, making the written law instead of the moral law the defined limit of transgression." [1] Hearings by a Congressional committee considering public aid to housing would, in all probability, bring forth similar statements from opponents of the proposals.

During World War I, the federal government gave modest aid to housing insofar as it was necessary to promote war production. The Great Depression brought the housing problem to the fore, primarily because the construction industry was in a state of economic prostration. The Home Loan Act of 1932 and the Home Owner's Refinancing Act of 1933 sought merely to enable mortgaged householders to hold their property. In 1934, however, the passage of the National Housing Act set in operation a program to stimulate construction of new housing through reinsurance of mortgages. Private construction could not, however, by itself and without aid relieve the housing needs of low-income groups. A start in relieving this area of housing need was made under the Public Works Administration purely as an employment-producing activity. In 1937, the legislation to provide federal aid for the construction of low-rent housing was passed (the United States Housing Act), and the essential features of the plan have remained largely the same to the present day. The administrative organ is the Public Housing Administration and its operations include approving plans drawn up by local communities in accordance with federal standards, providing for loans to carry out the programs of approved plans, and subsidizing local owners in order to permit rental of new construction at a price that will permit low-income groups to take advantage of facilities. The war period brought about federal participation in public housing on a scale that has not been exceeded since. More than one-half million units were constructed by the government. At the war's end, a powerful interest group, the veterans, emerged as a force favorable to public housing, and in 1946 the Veterans Emergency Housing Program came into existence. Long-term financing, guarantee of parts of loans, and relatively low interest rates enabled the nation to catch up somewhat on the demand carried over from depression days. The following year, all housing agencies of

---

[1] *Housing Problems in America*, Proceedings of the First National Conference on Housing, 1911, Cambridge, University Press, 1911, p. 15.

the federal government, which had been centralized within the National Housing Agency in 1942, were transferred to the Housing and Home Finance Agency by executive order. There was considerable marking of time by proponents of public housing aid in deference to well-organized opponents, notably the National Association of Real Estate Boards, the National Association of Home Builders, and the Mortgage Bankers Association. Moreover, the public housing-aid program became a convenient vehicle on which to pile all manner of arguments against the welfare state. Ample time was allowed for study and restudy of this state of affairs, and bills introduced after the most careful preparation and documentation passed the Senate (where Senator Robert A. Taft guided their progress) and floundered in the House of Representatives. Finally, in 1949, enabling legislation for a comprehensive beginning in federal aid was passed.

The Housing Act of 1949 retained the best features of previous legislation and added some new programs. Assistance became available for slum clearance, public housing, housing research, and farm housing. The purpose of the act was explained by the administering agency: "From any angle—citizenship, health, appearance, taxes, or property protection—it is better to pay now for the cost of clearing slums and thereby get rid of them than to continue paying the mounting costs of slums and suffer their destructive effects upon human lives and property indefinitely." [2] Title I dealt with slum clearance and advancement of funds; loans and capital grants were provided for redevelopment of two kinds of "blighted" areas and two kinds of "open" areas that posed problems of diverse ownership (thus preventing assemblage of the necessary plot for redevelopment) or neglected opportunity for construction. Many states had to enact special legislation to vest local communities with the powers required to participate in the federal program. Title II provided for extension of certain powers of the Federal Housing Administration. Title III amended the United States Housing Act of 1937 by authorizing federal contributions and loans for local programs not to exceed 810,000 units of low-rent public housing over a six-year period. The President was, however, authorized to accelerate the annual rate of the program to 200,000 units per year or to retard it to 50,000 units per year subject to the 810,000 maximum for the six-year period. A fund of $1.5 billion was made available for loans primarily for construction advances. Selection

---

[2] Housing and Home Finance Agency, A *Handbook of Information on Provisions of The Housing Act of 1949*, Washington, Government Printing Office, 1949.

of families for the projects aided by federal funds was made on the basis that their annual income not exceed five times the rent, with appropriate deductions from income provided for each minor dependent. Preference was given to veterans who were displaced from their existing housing by the program. Local authorities were required to set the monthly rental levels at least 20 percent below rental levels at which private enterprise unaided by subsidies "is providing an adequate supply of decent housing" in the respective localities. Units were to be kept simple in design and limitations on costs were provided in the act, although the figures of $1750 per room with increases of $750 in some instances seemed liberal enough. Title IV recognized a condition of sclerosis in the construction of public housing. Custom-made houses erected piece by piece with skilled labor were strangely out of keeping with mass-production efficiency in other industries. Hence, the act authorized the Housing and Home Finance Administrators to undertake and conduct technical research and studies which would promote reduction in housing construction and maintenance costs and stimulate the increased production of housing. Building codes, design, materials, credit, housing needs, and use and improvement were some of the areas into which research was authorized. Under Title V, the Secretary of Agriculture was authorized to extend financial assistance to farmers to enable them to construct, improve, or repair farm housing or other farm buildings within specified limitations.

Hardly had the housing program provided in the 1949 act got under way than the outbreak of hostilities in Korea brought supplies under restriction and the housing problem grew more desperate. The actual accomplishment was disheartening to the proponents of public housing. Of 135,000 units authorized in 1949, only 43,800 were actually started the following year. The scope of the program over the last two decades is reviewed in Table 58.

When it is considered that the estimated need in 1937 was judged by the National Resources Planning Board to be 800,000 new non-farm dwellings per year and was estimated in 1944 by the National Housing Agency at 1,260,000 per year, the response indicated in the table can be seen for the pittance which it is in terms of the housing problem. Since 1953, the housing program has been drastically reduced.[3] A compromise measure was before the President for his signature at the end of the 1st Session of the Eighty-fourth Congress. It

[3] Except that the Housing Act of 1954 broadened slum clearance and redevelopment provisions of the 1949 Act.

TABLE 58. Number of Federal Public Housing Units Completed
for Occupancy, 1935–1953.

Year	All Public Housing [a]	U.S. Housing Act (low rent)	War and Defense	Veterans
1935	3,932			
1936	1,213			
1937	7,849			
1938	17,319			
1939	3,858	3,858		
1940	31,940	31,940		
1941	119,634	59,848	59,786	
1942	158,266	37,537	120,729	
1943	374,729	27,325	347,404	
1944	153,158	2,831	150,327	
1945	45,026	2,949	40,171	1,906
1946	134,726	1,084	4,051	128,871
1947	107,097	466		106,631
1948	30,054	1,336	1,550	27,168
1949	1,242	547		695
1950	1,582	1,201		381
1951	10,246	10,246		
1952	63,533	57,956	5,577	
1953	64,773	58,214	6,559	
Total	1,330,227 [b]	298,058	736,154	265,652

a Programs administered by the Housing and Home Finance Agency or Public Housing Administration.
b Includes 30,313 Low Rent units completed under emergency legislation, 1935–1938.

Source: U.S. Bureau of the Census, *Statistical Abstract of the United States, 1954,* p. 788.

provided for 45,000 new housing units in the immediate twelve-month period, 10,000 more than the President had seen fit to request in his message to the Congress. The House of Representatives had passed a bill allowing for no units at all.

The census of 1950 had thrown new light on our housing needs. It clearly indicated that we were living on the housing we inherited from our parents and grandparents. Nearly half (45 percent) of the dwellings had been built before 1920, 20 percent from 1920 to 1929, and only 35 percent since 1930.[4] Seventy percent met acceptable standards and 30 percent were deficient in plumbing or dilapidated.[5] Forty percent had more than one person per room.[6]

In this matter the needs are obvious enough, nor are the issues

[4] U.S. Bureau of the Census, *U.S. Census of Housing, 1950,* Vol. I, *General Characteristics,* Part I, "U.S. Summary," p. xxxi.

[5] *Ibid.,* p. xxx.

[6] *Ibid.*

necessarily complicated, although assembling property, carrying out condemnation proceedings, and related factors make for difficulties. Expenses for public units run higher than for comparable private units, but the extra costs entailed in government-subsidized housing arise from the predatory tactics of contractors and unions who have come to consider the federal government legitimate prey. The year 1955 has revealed treachery and collusion in the administration of the housing programs, but that is scarcely an argument for failing to fill housing needs. Neither states and local units nor private contractors can meet the need for low-rent housing. Hence, the charge of unfair competition with private industry is strangely inappropriate. On balance, there is no problem so loaded with danger as a consequence of procrastination as housing, for the population growth in the next two decades is already determined and will be unusually large.

Legislation Relating to Education

The minor role which the federal government has played in the administration of American education is in sharp contrast to the nationally controlled school systems of Europe. This peculiarity of our public-school system is the result of its birth in an era of small communities, relatively isolated owing to rudimentary communication and transportation facilities, and of the American tradition of decentralization of authority. Educational control has continued to reside at the state and local level despite the fact that the economy, communication, and other features of the society have become significantly national in character. The modern exponents of localized control posit many reasons for the retention of the decentralized system. Regional differences in educational and social philosophy, the fostering of the democratic process, and adaptability to community needs are some of the usual arguments given whenever national coördination of federal control of education is suggested. Yet the system of local control has not been sufficient to provide adequately for the educational needs of the nation's children. The United States Office of Education estimated in 1955 that by the school year 1959–1960 there would be a deficit of 176,000 classrooms throughout the country.[7]

[7] This estimate was made by the Secretary of Health, Education, and Welfare to the House Committee on Education and Welfare and reported in the *Social Legislation Information Service*, April 11, 1955, p. 86. The estimate was based upon state reports projected on a national basis, and replaced a previous estimate of a deficit of 407,000 classrooms by the school year 1959–1960 made in 1951.

Even this figure assumes a continuation of the present construction rate of about 60,000 classrooms a year.

A further difficulty of localized administration is that not forty-eight states but over 80,000 local school districts within the states guide educational policy. The premise that such autonomy is in keeping with the principles of democracy is questionable if one considers that individual school districts are often controlled by school boards whose regionalism and traditionalism often conflict with the professional supervision within the schools.

Still further problems are presented by the unequal financial base which the various states (not to mention local subdivisions) provide for educational services. Table 59, which presents the value of school property by totals and per pupil, and the total and per-pupil school expenditures for the year 1950 by the various regions of the United States, indicates the disparity that exists in the financing of public education throughout the nation. With pupil enrollment predicted to reach new highs in coming decades, state-local financing will come under additional stresses. Rising costs of construction merely add to the coming dilemma.

TABLE 59. Public Elementary and Secondary Schools, Value of Property and Expenditures, by Geographical Regions, 1950.[a]

Region	Value of School Property		Current Expenditures for Full-Time Day Schools Chargeable to Pupils	
	Total Amount	Per Pupil [b]	Total Amount	Per Pupil [b]
Continental U.S.	$ 11,396,804	$ 511	$ 4,653,464	$ 208.83
New England	710,597	615	262,535	227.10
Middle Atlantic	2,842,606	770	968,675	262.38
East North Central	2,580,437	619	949,687	227.93
West North Central	1,127,028	531	456,214	214.76
South Atlantic	1,215,914	337	548,288	152.09
East South Central	399,869	187	242,810	113.78
West South Central	921,295	396	452,919	194.68
Mountain	439,781	505	191,909	220.48
Pacific	1,159,277	525	580,426	262.73

a In thousands of dollars, except averages per pupil.
b Average per pupil in average daily attendance.

Source: Adapted from U.S. Bureau of the Census, *Statistical Abstract of the United States, 1954*, Table 145, p. 130.

In the context of this traditional localization of control, the efforts of the federal government in recent years to establish aid to the school

programs become the central issue of social legislation in this area. There are many and varied areas of state legislation affecting education, and over half the states provide financial assistance to local schools; but since our interests are in the overall effects of legislation, we shall dwell most fully on federal programs.

Despite the rebuffs which efforts to institute widespread federal aid to education have received, there are many existing federal-state programs affecting education. While federal aid to school construction has received the most popular attention in recent years, there are other federal programs which relate to education, including (1) federal aid for maintaining and operating schools in certain areas, (2) federal contributions to vocational education, (3) national school lunch and school milk programs, and (4) provisions which make federal surplus property available for use by local educational institutions.

The history of these federal programs begins with the original land grants for education, which predate the Constitution, but it has been in the period since 1930 that the present direction of federal influence in educational programs has taken shape. The effects of the Great Depression on the schools, and on the ability of localities to finance education, led to such programs as the Civilian Conservation Corps, National Youth Administration, and the Works Progress Administration program of school construction, all designed as relief measures. These projects were abandoned, however, when the economic conditions which led to their introduction were improved.

As these programs were gradually disbanded, there was little new federal legislation of import to education until another crisis, the Second World War, again provided an emergency which called for federal action. Programs were developed for the education and training of armed-forces personnel, defense workers, and for specialists needed in the emergency; but, almost unnoticed, a plan of federal participation in education was instituted, under the provisions of the Lanham Act (1941), which was to have a more lasting effect upon federal-state relations in education. The act provided for the distribution of federal funds for school maintenance and operation in communities where war-incurred federal activity had created undue financial burdens. Of similar importance was the Surplus Property Act of 1944, which, in setting up the procedure for the disposal of the stockpiles of property which the federal government had acquired during the war, provided for the transfer of surplus property to tax-

supported and tax-exempt nonprofit educational institutions. These two war-born programs have both been since extended and broadened.

As the war drew to a close, federal participation in education was again extended through the Servicemen's Readjustment Act of 1944 (Public Law 346), popularly known as the G.I. Bill of Rights. Through its provisions, hundreds of millions of dollars were paid to institutions of higher learning and to various training schools for the education of eligible veterans. The effects of this development upon the colleges and universities of the nation are still debated. No one denies the tremendous financial advantages of the program to American higher education; but there are some who feel that we have glutted the market with college graduates, and that the quality of education which the colleges have given under this influx of students has suffered. In 1952, following the conflict in Korea, a modified version of the original G.I. Bill (P.L. 550) was passed by the Eighty-second Congress.

The postwar period saw an increasing volume of legislation designed to extend further federal aid to the schools. The George-Barden Act of 1946 authorized further development of the vocational education established under the Smith-Hughes Act in 1917. Under the new program, funds are made available to the states and territories for establishing apprentice training and vocational instruction and guidance programs, for the costs of training and supervising the necessary teachers, and for administrative and physical-plant costs.

As has happened previously in the history of federal school legislation, a new crisis led to renewed efforts to help the states. The postwar "baby boom" of 1946–1948, once it became apparent, brought speculation as to the adequacy of the school system to answer the demands which the increased birth rate would produce. Hurried projections of the growing number of children quickly added up to a gloomy forecast. State and local revenues were already overtaxed, and the gradual transfer of wealth from "tangible" to "intangible" property had further reduced the real-property tax source for paying of school bonds. Again the need for federal action was certain, but equally certain was the resistance to federal aid to education, which again negated any direct aid. Indirectly, however, such aid did come about. The Federal Property and Administrative Services Act of 1949 made the donation of surplus federal property to educational institutions a permanent program. The scope of the program was broadened by P.L. 754, approved in 1950, which provided for the donation of

surplus personal property to tax-supported and tax-exempt educational and health organizations. Between 1950 and 1954, $171 million in personal property and $58 million in real property have been transferred or donated to the educational or health institutions.[8]

The Eighty-first Congress passed two bills which continued the principle of the Lanham Act of granting assistance to schools in federally affected areas. P.L. 874, which was passed in September, 1950, authorized the Commissioner of Education to provide financial assistance for current maintenance and operational expenses of local educational agencies which have had financial burdens placed upon them as a result of [9] (1) acquisition by the federal government of a considerable portion of all the real property in a school district; (2) ownership by the federal government of tax-exempt property on which children reside or on which their parents reside; or (3) establishment or reactivation of federal activity in an area, thereby creating a sudden and substantial increase in school attendance.

A separate act, P.L. 815, also passed in September of 1950, provided for federal funds to aid in schoolhouse construction in federally affected areas. The law proposed to help construct school facilities in areas with substantially increased numbers of school children which met the same requirements listed above for the aid for maintenance and operation costs. Together, the bills sought to help ease the burden on schools whose sources of revenue had been reduced as a result of loss of taxable wealth to federal ownership. Nothing, however, was done to aid other areas where the need for assistance was great and where promised increases in enrollment threatened to compound school problems.

Both laws were amended by the first session of the Eighty-third Congress following a request for such amendment in the President's State of the Union Message in 1953. P.L. 248 extended aid for current operating expenses and maintenance for two additional years until June 30, 1956. The original law was also modified, and the net result was that while payments to some school districts were increased in 1954, almost all school districts would suffer reductions in federal funds in the school years 1954–1955 and 1955–1956.[10]

The school-construction program established under P.L. 815 was

[8] Clayton D. Hutchins, Albert Munse, and Edna D. Booher, *Federal Funds for Education*, U.S. Office of Education Bulletin No. 514, 1954, p. 48.

[9] U.S. Office of Education, *Administration of Public Laws 874 and 815; Fourth Annual Report of the Commissioner of Education, June 30, 1954*, 1955.

[10] Hutchins, Munse, and Booher, *op. cit.*, p. 31.

also amended in the same session of Congress by the New P.L. 246, which extended the construction program to June 30, 1954. The bases for eligibility were made more difficult, and increases in school enrollment owing to federal activity between June, 1952, and 1954 became the new grant criterion. In the fiscal year 1952–1953, federal aid to the states and territories for the maintenance and operation of affected areas totaled $65,994,668.51 and for schoolhouse construction another $134,089,151.07 was expended.[11] Still, however, nothing was done to provide direct aid to the states for schools.

Late in 1954, one of the federal aid-to-education programs which has suffered least criticism, the school lunch program established in 1935, received additional support from a new special school milk program. Under the original act, aid to the schools for children's lunches was in commodities as one method of providing additional outlets for agricultural products. Cash assistance did not come until the establishment in 1940 of the school milk program, which reimbursed schools for a portion of the cost of the milk they served to children. Here again the motivation was more to remove surplus milk than to aid education. The National School Lunch Act of 1946 further extended the principle of cash payments, but also included commodity distribution to schools to aid nonprofit school lunch programs. The 1954 special milk program is a two-year project authorizing the Commodity Credit Corporation to use $50,000,000 annually to increase milk consumption by schoolchildren.

The apparent reluctance of states and of the federal government to develop some comprehensive school-construction program was nowhere more apparent than in the debate which centered over the plan for aid to school construction proposed by President Dwight D. Eisenhower in February, 1955. Growing agitation for federal aid had come from numerous parent-teacher, educational, and civic organizations, and the National Education Association had called for a yearly $1 billion federal program. When the Administration bill was finally presented to Congress, it called for a $7 billion federal-state program to cover a three-year construction program, but only a small portion of the money was to come from the federal government. The major portion of the money was to come from the states themselves, which would thus be primarily responsible for helping the local communities. The role of the federal government was fourfold:

[11] *Ibid.*, Table 3, p. 22.

1. If the communities themselves could not sell their school bonds at a 3.5 percent rate of interest, then the federal government would purchase them. An appropriation of $750,000,000 for the three-year period was asked to cover these purchases.
2. The states would be encouraged to create new agencies to build $6 billion worth of schools during the three-year periods. These new state agencies would build schools and rent them to local school districts which had exceeded their legal borrowing powers. The proceeds from these rents would repay the initial federal and state grants.
3. Those communities which could not possibly finance their own school-building programs would receive federal-state grants. Two hundred million dollars was asked for the federal grant program during the three years. The states were to contribute an amount equal to the federal contribution.
4. The states were to receive grants from a $20 million fund to pay half of the administrative costs of special studies to be conducted by the states for the establishment of long-run financing programs.

The reaction to the President's proposals was immediate and, for the most part, critical. Charges of "too little and too late" and of slavish adherence to the state-responsibility principle were most common. Many leaders in the field of public education denounced the program as hopelessly inadequate.[12]

Even this inadequate program did not survive the Congress, and as yet no program of aid to school construction for the entire nation has come forth. The continuation of the resistance to federal intervention in education provides the chief barrier to such comprehensive legislation. Other programs of the federal government have aided education with no evidence of dictatorial control of the beneficiaries. In the fiscal year 1952–1953, for example, almost $1.4 billion in federal aid was allotted to the states and territories for educational programs under the direction of various federal agencies.[13] The benefits to edu-

[12] See, for example, Benjamin Fine, "Education in Review," *The New York Times*, February 13, 1955, p. 11, which quotes several educational leaders concerning the then new proposal.

[13] Clayton, Munse, and Booher, *op. cit.*, Table 6, pp. 21–25. This figure represents the total of federal funds allotted for education by the Department of Health, Education, and Welfare. The Department of Agriculture, the Veterans Administration, and all other departments and agencies allotting funds for this purpose are reported in this bulletin. Major programs concerned include vocational rehabilitation, Public Health Service grants for education and training, support of land-grant colleges, aid to federally affected areas, surplus property transferred to the states, school lunch programs, and others.

cation of these expenditures have been many and it seems questionable if any undemocratic controls have resulted.

Legislation in Behalf of Specific Groups

We come now to legislative programs which differ from those enacted for the general welfare. In the following two sections we shall consider the legislation enacted to aid veterans of American wars and railroad-transportation workers. These serve only as examples and do not by any means exhaust the list of beneficiaries of this kind of legislation.

VETERANS' LEGISLATION

American legislatures have shown considerable interest in veterans' problems, particularly in postwar periods. As early as 1776, the Continental Congress provided pensions for wounded veterans and widows of soldiers killed in the Revolutionary War. Land grants and pensions were given to veterans of the Civil War also. It was during and after the First World War, however, that comprehensive veterans' legislation first began. The War Risk Insurance Act of 1917 established the pattern of government insurance compensation for death or disability resulting from war injuries, and vocational rehabilitation and hospitalization provisions were added to existing veterans' benefits. In the period immediately following the war, it became apparent that the several agencies serving veterans required consolidation, so that in 1921 the Veterans Bureau was established, becoming the present Veterans Administration in 1930.

World War II marked the beginning of a new era in veterans' benefits as the concept of compensatory help through pensions, hospitalization for the war disabled, and the care of survivors of the war dead was joined by a new philosophy that the government (and the public) should aid the veteran to readjust to civilian life. Since his normal educational, occupational, and social development had been interrupted by the requirement of military service, the government which he had served should help him return to his place in society with as few conflicts and strains as possible. Added to this rationale was the strong feeling that we should "do something for the boys" to show the nation's gratitude for their services; and, as in much of our legislation, pressure applied by veterans' groups and the potential voting power of 11,000,000 men and women and their families helped the legislators to see their indebtedness.

Although the largest and best-known veterans' programs are federally operated, there has also been much state legislation for veterans. Immediately after the war, many states established veterans' bureaus, authorized the payment of bonuses, set up veterans' assistance and public-welfare programs, and in many ways supplemented the programs of the federal government. While some of these state services had previously been given to veterans of World War I, nothing of the magnitude of the new programs had ever been attempted. In many cases, the new state services, particularly the bonuses, called for new systems of taxation or increases in existing levies to offset the cost of our gratitude.

The many services and benefits provided veterans and their families may be conveniently grouped under five major categories: (1) medical and dental care and hospitalization; (2) economic compensation to veterans and their families through pensions to disabled veterans and to the survivors of deceased veterans, and life and social-insurance benefits; (3) educational and occupational training programs and vocational rehabilitation; (4) employment benefits through civil-service preferences, job reinstatement, and employment services; and (5) economic privileges through provisions for mustering-out pay, readjustment allowance, and guarantees for loans made to veterans for the purchase of a home, farm, or business.[14] Each of these programs will be discussed in terms of its present operation.

The Veterans Administration provides medical care for veterans in its nearly 160 hospitals; in civil, state, or federal hospitals on a contract basis; and through out-patient treatment in VA hospitals or with private physicians and dentists. Honorably discharged veterans may receive hospital treatment for service-connected ailments in a VA or other authorized hospital. He (or she) may also be admitted to a hospital for treatment of nonservice-connected disabilities when beds are available and the veteran is unable to pay the necessary costs of hospitalization. Emergency treatment of veterans in VA hospitals, however, is permitted without restriction as to means.

Honorably discharged veterans may also receive out-patient treatment for service-connected disabilities when the VA has previously authorized such treatment. The Eighty-first Congress removed the requirement of service connection for veterans of the Spanish-American War, the Philippine Insurrection, and the Boxer Rebellion.

[14] Walter A. Friedlander, *Introduction to Social Welfare*, New York, Prentice-Hall, 1955, pp. 483–484.

Necessary medical treatment may be obtained in a VA hospital or field station or by an approved private physician under the home-town medical-care program. Out-patient dental service, with eligibility requirements similar to those for medical treatment, may also be provided. Recent criticism of the out-patient dental program has brought a tightening of the requirements, and, unless it can be shown that the dental condition is compensable, treatment is on a one-time, satisfactory-completion basis.[15]

The VA also provides domiciliary care in its special homes to veterans with chronic conditions which incapacitate them for employment and which do not require major medical care. To be eligible, the veteran must have served in wartime or after the fighting broke out in Korea, although peacetime veterans with service-connected disabilities for which they are receiving VA compensation are also eligible.[16] Blind veterans may also receive "seeing-eye dogs," or electronic and mechanical equipment, if they are entitled to compensation for service-connected disabilities, although the blindness itself need not have resulted from service-incurred injuries or illness. If a veteran has lost the use of one or both hands or feet or has permanently impaired vision as the result of service in World War II or after June 27, 1950, the VA will pay up to $1600 for the purchase of a specially equipped automobile or other conveyance. Honorably discharged veterans may also be buried in national cemeteries or have a suitable headstone provided for their graves if buried elsewhere.

Veterans with disabilities resulting from disease or injury incurred in or aggravated by military service in wartime or peacetime may also qualify for monthly compensation benefits. If the disability results from wartime service, the monthly compensation may range from $17 for 10 percent disability to $181 for total disability. Peacetime service entitles the veteran to compensation at 80 percent of the wartime rate for the same condition. Permanently and totally disabled veterans with nonservice-connected disabilities receive pensions at the rate of $66.15 per month, increased to $78.75 per month at age 65 and beyond, or after continuous receipt for ten years. For regular pension and attendance aid, the disabled veteran receives $135.45 per month. Receipt of these pensions is based upon need, and annual income limits of $1400 for single veterans and $2700 for veterans with a wife

[15] Social Information Legislation Service, November 15, 1954, p. 511.

[16] Roger Cumming, "Veterans' Benefits and Services," American Association of Social Workers, Social Work Year Book, 1954, New York, the Association, 1954, p. 526.

or minor child are observed. Special eligibility requirements give preference to Spanish-American War veterans. Following the death of the veteran, as a result of the service-connected disability, his wife, children, and dependent parents are also entitled to compensation payments. In the case of nonservice-connected-disability pensions, the widow and minor children may also receive payment if need can be established.

There are currently three systems of insurance administered by the VA: U.S. Government Life Insurance for veterans of the First World War, National Service Life Insurance for veterans of the Second World War, and, for those veterans who served after the fighting broke out in Korea, the new insurance under the Indemnity and Insurance Act of 1951. The insurance programs for World War I and World War II veterans were similar in that they permitted the veteran to purchase insurance from the government in any amount from $1000 to $10,000 in multiples of $500. Insurance was available under term plans. The Indemnity and Insurance Act of 1951 provided for the automatic coverage without payment of premiums of any individual with service in Korea (and certain other groups) for $10,000 up to a period of 120 days following his separation from the service.

We have previously noted that wage credits of $160 per month are granted for military service until March 1956. Survivors of veterans who served between September 16, 1940 and July 24, 1947, and were not dishonorably discharged, are also entitled to social-security insurance benefits under OASI if the veteran dies within three years after discharge. This special death benefit is not available to survivors of veterans separated after July 26, 1951. Relatives of deceased veterans may also receive up to $150 as reimbursement for burial expenses.

We have previously described the history of the legislation providing educational and training benefits for veterans. Veterans of World War II with ninety days service, part of which was served between September 16, 1940, and July 25, 1947, are entitled to one year of education or training plus the time spent in military service up to a maximum of four years. All expenses for tuition, books, fees, and so on are paid by the VA directly to the school or training institution within limits of $500 for the full school year. The veteran receives monthly subsistence payments of $75 if he is without dependents, $105 for one dependent, and $120 for more than one dependent while he is attending a full-time educational institution. Veterans receiving on-the-job training receive monthly subsistence allowances of $65 if

they are without dependents and $90 with dependents. The influence of this program on American colleges and other training institutions is apparent in the fact that over one-half of all veterans of World War II—7,800,000 in all—had taken some form of education or training under the G.I. Bill by the end of 1952.[17]

For those veterans with service on or after June 27, 1950, and prior to a date as yet undetermined by Congress, educational and training benefits are available under P.L. 550, already known as the Korean G.I. Bill of Rights. Educational entitlement under this act is computed at a rate of one and one-half times the duration of the active service period, not to exceed thirty-six months. Payment for tuition, fees, books, and so forth is made directly to the veteran rather than to the institution, as under the World War II plan. Current rates are at $110 a month for a veteran with no dependents, $135 a month if one dependent, and $160 a month if more than one dependent. From this allowance the veteran must meet all of his educational or training costs and his subsistence needs.

Vocational rehabilitation for disabled veterans is provided under P.L. 16 (1943) to restore them to employability. Basically, the program provides for education and training at government expense, with additional payment of such expenses as special equipment, travel allowance, and other necessary training expenses. To be eligible, the veteran must have seen service during the Second World War or the as-yet-undetermined period of the conflict in Korea, be honorably discharged, and have a minimum of 10 percent service-connected disability. The minimum monthly allowances under this program are the same as in the G.I. Bill educational program and are added to the compensation which the veteran receives under the disabled veterans' compensation program already described. When these two payments are combined, they must total at least $105 a month for veterans with no dependents and $115 a month with a dependent where the disability is less than 30 percent, and at least $115 a month for veterans without dependents and $135 per month for those with dependents where the disability is greater than 30 percent. Counseling is mandatory in this program and the veteran must work toward a definite job objective.

To insure that returning servicemen would regain their former jobs with as little difficulty as possible, the Veterans Readjustment Act

17 *Ibid.*, p. 524.

also provided that each veteran had a right to reëmployment in the job he left to enter the service unless special circumstances intervened. Other steps were taken to ensure that he would have as much assistance as possible in finding new employment. The federal government and most of the states now give a special priority of 5 percent for veterans and 10 percent for disabled veterans in civil-service examinations. Such preference is also extended in some cases to wives of disabled veterans and to certain mothers of deceased veterans. Additional preferences are provided in the establishment of homestead rights to public lands and in job counseling from the United States Employment Service.

Upon his discharge from the service under honorable conditions, the veteran also received mustering-out pay of $100 for less than sixty days' service, $200 for more than sixty days' service, and $300 if he had sixty days' or more service, part of which was overseas. The purpose of this separation bonus was to aid the veteran in the first period of readjustment to civilian life. Further aid was supplied through a federally financed unemployment program, known as a "readjustment allowance" but popularly called "52–20." This nickname came from the fact that the veteran was to receive $20 a week for a maximum of fifty-two weeks if he had seen sufficient service. At present, veterans may receive unemployment benefits from two different programs. If they have established their benefit rights under the state requirement since their discharge, or if their state has made special provision for the entitlement of veterans, they may receive benefits from the general state unemployment program. Those veterans with service on or after June 27, 1950, and prior to a date yet to be established, may receive benefits of $26 per week of unemployment for a total of twenty-six weeks under the Veterans Readjustment Assistance Act of 1952. The veteran must first exhaust his mustering-out pay and claim any benefits for which he is entitled under the state unemployment program or the Railroad Unemployment Insurance Act. Benefits received under other unemployment programs may be supplemented to a maximum of $26 a week. Administration of the new program is by the United States Department of Labor through the unemployment-compensation agencies of the various states. There are also provisions which protect self-employed veterans by entitling them to readjustment allowances to bring their monthly earnings up to a minimum of $100 a month.

To assist veterans and veterans' widows in the purchase or construc-

tion of a home, farm, or business property, the VA is authorized to guarantee up to 60 percent of a real-estate loan and 50 percent of nonreal-estate loans. The maximum guaranty limits are $7500 and $2500 respectively. Direct loans for homes or farmhouses are authorized up to $10,000 in areas where private capital is unavailable.

There are many other special provisions for veterans, such as preferences in naturalization, priority in purchasing war-surplus supplies and in obtaining low-cost federal housing, and grants up to $10,000 for suitable "wheel chair" housing for veterans who have lost both legs or the use of them. The programs which have been described above, however, are the major ones now in operation. Other legislation for veterans' benefits and services will certainly come in the future. Already, efforts are being made to obtain a federal bonus for veterans of the Second World War similar to those received by World War I veterans. The success of veterans' legislation is an example of the benefits which special groups in the population may obtain by combined effort and through powerful lobbies.

RAILROAD-TRANSPORTATION WORKERS

The railroad industry has been a chronic "sick" industry and legislation both with respect to its operations and the protection of its employees has been atypical in comparison with other industries. Sometimes it is said that railroad employees have achieved "super social security" for themselves owing to the strategic position which they hold in the economy. Enough has been said about the industry in previous chapters to indicate the tenuousness of such a statement.

Some features of the Labor Management Relations Act of 1947 were anticipated in the Railway Labor Act of 1926. The obligation of employers and employees was stated more positively than in any other legislation until 1947 in that a "duty" was placed on both to make "every reasonable effort" to make agreements (and keep them) and settle disputes. Procedures leading to the convening of fact-finding boards were instituted, and while the boards investigated disputes a compulsory waiting period was provided during which time no changes should take place in the terms of employment. Amendments in 1934 added substantially to the security enjoyed by railroad unions, and control of bargaining units by employees was affirmed. In contrast to the restrictive provisions of the Labor Management Relations Act, 1947, the Railway Labor Act was amended to permit union shops and checkoffs in 1951. Beyond these provisions for union

security and settlement of disputes, there is legislation relating to retirement benefits and unemployment-insurance benefits which should receive our attention.

Railroad Retirement Act. Prior to the Great Depression there had already developed a considerable movement for retirement benefits in the railroad industry. Nearly 100 plans were in operation, covering a large majority of railroad employees. In 1934, a compulsory retirement system was established, the first covering private employees. The law provided for a retirement system of annuities based on average monthly compensation and would be financed by joint contributions of employees and employers. But the law ran afoul of the courts and was declared unconstitutional. The tax provision was held to be a violation of the due-process clause of the Fifth Amendment. A law providing similar benefits to the 1934 law—but separating the tax feature—was passed the following year, only to be assailed again in the courts. Finally, after a Presidential conference, an agreement for a retirement system amicable to the railroads and employees was reached. Amendments to the 1935 act enacted in 1937 made the retirement system operational.

Very extensive coverage was provided for all employees of the railroads with virtually any connection to the industry. Benefits are of three types—old age, survivorship, and disability. A retirement age of 60 is established for women with full retirement benefits (upon attaining thirty years of service) and for men at the same age with reduction of benefits. Average monthly compensation and number of years' creditable service determine the amount of benefits.[18] We will summarize the average benefit levels currently paid at the end of this section. Since 1946, a system of survivors benefits has been included in the program. Requirements are somewhat similar to the old-age and survivors' insurance system for widows' and widowers' annuities. A minimum of six quarters' coverage and one quarter's coverage for every two elapsing quarters since a base date are features of the system. Furthermore, a distinction is made between "completely insured" status and "partially insured" status. Widows of completely insured employees receive the full "basic amount" to which the insured worker is entitled. The same amount would be paid to a widow of a completely insured or partially insured employee who had in her care

---

[18] The formula for determining benefits is 2.76 percent of the first $50 of average monthly compensation, 2.07 percent of the next $100, and 1.38 percent of the next $200; the sum is multiplied by the number of years' creditable service to obtain the benefit.

a child entitled to its own annuity. The benefit for a child of an individual who died either completely or partially insured is two-thirds of the basic amount. A similar benefit may be made to surviving parents in the absence of a widow or child beneficiary. In all instances, the qualifying age is 60. Disability benefits are provided both for employees who suffer a mental or physical impairment which probihits their employment in the railroad industry and for impairment which disables them for any kind of regular employment.

A relationship between Railroad Retirement benefits and OASI benefits has been developed. Survivors are assured a benefit at least as large as the wage record of the insured would have provided under OASI.

The tax moneys from assessments on employees and employers (6.25 percent each) go into a general fund administered by the Railroad Retirement Board and held by the United States Treasury. Benefits paid under the system are relatively high in keeping with the taxes imposed. Table 60 shows the benefits payable to a retired worker and to his survivors, assuming thirty years of service.

TABLE 60. Monthly Retirement Annuities Under the Railroad Retirement Act.

Average Monthly Compensation	Retired Worker		Survivors	
	Married	Unmarried	Widow, Age 60	Widow, 2 Children
$100	$108.68	$72.45	$45.00 [a]	$98.58
150	143.50	103.50	51.40	120.00
200	164.20	124.20	58.90	157.10
250	184.90	144.90	66.40	177.20
300	205.60	165.60	73.90	197.10
350	226.30	186.30	81.40	200.00

[a] Individual is assumed to enter railroad service at age 21 in 1955 or later and to remain in steady employment therein at a level wage. Figures indicate survivor benefits should death occur at ages 31, 41, 51, and 61 respectively.

Source: Robert J. Myers and John A. MacDougall, "The Railroad Retirement Act in 1954," *Social Security Bulletin,* February, 1955, pp. 10–11.

The Railroad Unemployment Insurance Act. The interstate character of much railroad employment and certain peculiar characteristics of the industry created early sentiment for a system of unemployment insurance for railroad employees. The Social Security Act permitted the inclusion of railroad employees under the state plans; but, in anticipation of federal legislation specifically directed at relieving this problem, the states did not all bring railroad employees within their systems. When an act finally was passed in 1946, it established a

nation-wide system of payments for unemployment and sickness for qualified workers.

The coverage of the act corresponds to the coverage provided in the Railroad Retirement Act, and the two programs are administered by the same body. In order to qualify for benefits under the Unemployment Insurance Act, a worker must have earned at least $400 from covered employers in the preceding calendar (base) year. General ability to work and availability for work provisions apply as in the Social Security Act system. The cost of the insurance is borne wholly by the carriers, and the contribution rate varies from 0.5 to 3 percent depending upon the balance in the railroad unemployment-insurance account. Benefit amounts which apply at various earnings levels are given in the following schedule:

Base Year Earnings	Daily Benefit Rate
$400–499.00	$3.50
500–749.99	4.00
750–999.99	4.50
1000–1299.99	5.00
1300–1599.99	5.50
1600–1999.99	6.00
2000–2499.99	6.50
2500–299.99	7.00
3000–3499.99	7.50
3500–399.99	8.00
4000 and over	8.50

A maximum number of days that may be compensated is established in the act, 130 days, which applies to unemployment and sickness benefits. In the first fourteen-day registration period in a benefit year in which an employee is unemployed for seven or more days, he is paid for all days over seven. In all later fourteen-day periods in that year, he is paid for all days over four. Two appeals levels below the courts are provided in the act for disputed claims.

Other Social-Legislation Programs: Concluding Remarks

We have seen in this chapter how income security can be enhanced by the provision of services in the form of assistance in housing costs and free education facilities. In neither area of need has our effort at the national level approached the demands of the current situation. School construction and housing have been casualties of regional bickering and organized selfishness. The danger is, of course, that the present needs will cumulate a definite development in school construction.

Beyond the more general housing and education legislation which has been enacted in recent years, there is the unique legislation which is oriented to the benefit of special groups. An important observation in connection with these programs is that they go considerably beyond measures enacted in behalf of unselected groups. This has the effect of placing in operation a program of benefits which is more liberal than existing general programs, which results in maturation of the more general programs toward the levels of the special programs. Also, the special programs, once the benefit structure differential which they enjoy has been removed, press for reëstablishment of the differential and, hence, higher benefit levels. Particularly during periods of inflation, this has the effect of benefit escalation, which is not the soundest method of achieving mature programs.

SELECTED REFERENCES

Abram, Charles, *The Future of Housing*, New York, Harper & Brothers, 1946.

Armstrong, Barbara N., *Insuring the Essentials*, New York, The Macmillan Company, 1937.

Burns, Eveline M., *The American Social Security System*, Boston, Houghton Mifflin Company, 1949.

Epstein, Abraham, *Insecurity, A Challenge to America*, New York, Random House, 1936.

Rubinow, I. M., *The Quest for Security*, New York, Henry Holt and Company, 1934.

PART VI
ANALYSIS OF AMERICAN SOCIAL LEGISLATION

chapter 18

Planning for Social Goals

It is fitting to begin the concluding part of this survey with the most comprehensive proposal that has been made to remedy the uncertain and uncoördinated relief of social needs afforded by American social legislation. Planning is a highly controversial subject, and the intent of the authors is simply to offer for the reader's cogitation the pros and cons as they have appeared in the extensive literature pertinent to the subject.

Origins of the Planning Concept

This will not be a historical discourse on planning because the dates involved in the growth of the planning concept are irrelevant. The "origins" referred to in the title to this section might have been called "bases," because it is the realization of their necessity on the part of those who were moved to advocate planning that we wish to examine.

No better account of the origins of planning has been set forth than that prepared by Lewis Mumford in the Foreword to a symposium on planning that appeared nearly two decades ago:

In the nineteenth century, capitalistic industry sought to work on the assumption that economic life was self-equilibrating. Human needs would be satisfied, and human progress served, if each economic agent acted with no thought for anything but his immediate aim: the largest possible profit in the shortest time. Behind this theory was a sublime and now incredible theology: the conception that order is so far preordained in human affairs that a multitude of blind actions and reactions will bring it to pass.

This theology was a superstition and its practical results were disastrous. The waste of natural resources, the unbalance of regional life, the misbuilding of cities, the pauperization of labor, the duplication of effort, the

recurrent jars and wrenches in the economic organizations—themselves all these characteristics of industrial society during the last century showed that order was something less than providential.[1]

The realization that waste and unsystematic provision for human need had produced severe stresses and strains in the social order is the origin of those proposals for "planning" order in social life rather than leaving order to happenstance. We did not at once embrace the idea of planning the results of social interaction. From the first concerted challenge to laissez faire in the latter half of the nineteenth century until the Great Depression, we made compromises among three ameliorates—limited government interference in economic affairs, internal stabilization of economic life by large business units, and government planning on a comprehensive scale in limited areas. The classic arguments concerning planning have not originated in the United States, but on the European Continent. England and the United States, having been peculiarly influenced by the doctrine of laissez faire, maintained a state economic policy that only in exceptional instances violated the laissez-faire principle.

Of course, no economic system is "planless" in the sense that the consequences of its operation are completely arbitrary. A system based on the profit motive in which institutional apparatus has been developed to make production and distribution possible has an inherent element of control based on the coincidence of wants of buyers and sellers. But even the ingenious structure described by the high priest of laissez faire, Adam Smith, provided for an economic game which had to be kept going and had to prevent a "winner" from emerging. The choice, therefore, is between conscious, deliberate, external planning and more or less complete reliance on an inherent order-producing system, as the argument customarily has been put.

The Issues in Planning

Since the 1930's, planning has been discussed primarily in economic terms. This seems to be a natural consequence of the Great Depression, which was fundamentally an economic crisis. Hence, the imperfections which produced the catastrophe must be economic, it was reasoned. However, the assumption that attention to economic factors is sufficient in planning to reduce the imperfections is very dubious. The whole system of cultural responses, of which the eco-

[1] Findlay Mackenzie (ed.), *Planned Society, Yesterday, Today and Tomorrow,* New York, Prentice-Hall, 1937, p. v.

nomic responses are only a part, is involved in planning changes to prevent crisis. Only because economic responses are so basic to a social system based on materialism do they merit any primary consideration. The goals toward which planning is directed are social—implying that the consequences for the whole cultural complex are of significance—and economic responses are simply a means to the end.

As we seek to understand the choices upon which the acceptance of planning depends, the reader may profitably turn back to Chapter 1 and the guideposts to social legislation there presented. One fact is obvious: very basic questions must be weighed in deciding to consign to a central government power to plan the consequences of economic activity. The questions begin with what is to be sought through planning and end with administrative alternatives for carrying out the planning function.

THE FUNDAMENTAL GOALS

A group of wise men at their leisure might set down and draw up a schedule of goals for American society that would find a wide measure of acceptance save for the order in which they were presented. The goals would reflect basic needs, perhaps corresponding to the needs set forth by Malinowski (see Chapter 2). But if they reflected merely needs corresponding to metabolism, reproduction, safety, health, etc., the goals would be hopelessly inadequate. Satisfaction of basic life processes is a minimum requisite of the social order, but scarcely appropriate as a goal of social planning, say, in the United States of the 1950's. There are myth structures and dysfunctional elements of the American social system that are on a par with satisfaction of basic needs so far as the prevailing value system is concerned. Planning, therefore, if it is to find favor with those whose welfare it proposes to enhance, must take on a larger task than merely satisfying basic needs.

SECURITY AS A GOOD

We have discussed measures which have as their aim the accomplishment of some kind of security—social-security legislation, for example. In our discussion we have proceeded on the assumption that reducing insecurity is a desirable goal and security might be reduced to a theoretical minimum of zero without any question of desirability. There are many reasons to doubt the validity of such an assumption. Bertrand Russell has put the argument as follows:

Security, though undoubtedly a good thing, may be sought excessively and become a fetish. A secure life is not necessarily a happy life; it may be rendered dismal by boredom and monotony. Many people, especially while they are young, welcome a spice of dangerous adventure, and may even find relief in war as an escape from humdrum safety. Security by itself is a negative aim inspired by fear; a satisfactory life must have a positive aim inspired by hope. This sort of adventurous hope involves risk and therefore fear. But fear deliberately chosen is not such an evil thing as fear forced upon a man by outward circumstances. We cannot therefore be content with security alone, or imagine that it can bring the millennium.[2]

Security, then, might be carried to a point where it would sap the vitality of men. In the foreseeable future, such a likelihood is remote, and if the danger zone ever should be reached, the stage would be set for wise counselors to point out the dangers involved and persuade the citizenry to their viewpoint. Nor would this be necessary, perhaps, if education were oriented toward the objective of encouraging citizens to develop the full potentialities of their personalities.

There is the further requisite that if we are to jettison a system which has, despite temporary breakdowns and the cruel dilemmas which it has occasionally fostered, provided a higher material living standard than any presently operating alternative, the superiority of the successor system must be established. This would fail to be the case only if the continuation of the present system's performance were gravely in doubt. American capitalism has grown in strength, however, since 1940, and the case for a radical modification is far less convincing now than in 1933 or 1937. This observation does not render further discussion useless, however, because there is the question whether we are making the best use of the energies and resources available to us. Are we, for example, sufficiently proof against such a catastrophe as befell us in 1929? Would we not better improve on the structural strength of our social system if we planned so to do than if we passively awaited such improvements?

FREEDOM AND SECURITY

The primary issue which has divided American students of social policy on the question of planning is freedom versus security. Opponents of planning note that it would require, to fulfill its objectives, vastly increased power in the hands of the federal government and

---

[2] Bertrand Russell, *Authority and the Individual*, New York, Simon and Schuster, 1949, pp. 18–19.

that such power would inevitably be abused. This view has been countered by proponents of planning, who argue that the additional power that need be lodged with the federal government depends on the scope of planning, and that the primary protection of citizens against governmental power is their right to vote, change the Constitution, or otherwise impose restrictions on government activity.

Between these two positions there is the important question of whether we have the ability to plan social consequences from a technical standpoint. Presumably, economic factors are to be the basic *modus operandi* in any planned social system, and a precise determination of what factors produce a desirable state of economic affairs is beyond the capabilities of economics at the present time. Nor is economics able to tell us with precision whether the economic outlook (level of employment, for example) is favorable for the foreseeable future. A real question, therefore, concerns the state of our knowledge about the operation of those elements of the social system that would be liable to control. Proponents of planning meet this issue by noting that the state of social-science theory is continuously improving and warning that change will take place whether we plan for it or not, and that we would better employ the tools we have in controlling its direction, learning as we proceed.

Another observation is sometimes made in connection with freedom. Perhaps freedom is not a condition of life that is in opposition to security. It may, in fact, be effective only under conditions of security. R. B. Perry noted in 1929 that:

> The whole recent movement of democracy may be said to be directed toward providing the conditions for *effective* freedom, by raising the standard of living through cooperative government effort, by public education, by facilities for research, by social insurance. Man is not, as Rousseau had said, born free and everywhere in chains; man is as free as the public roads to freedom provided by all for all. In primitive society men are chained by custom; in our society by technical complexity and economic inequality.[3]

Security—reducing the conditions of stress on the family unit—is thus seen as a fulfillment of freedom rather than a competitor. As a matter of fact, the major threat to freedom may lie in conditions of insecurity. Charles E. Merriam has made this point in the following observation:

[3] Ralph Barton Perry, *Puritanism and Democracy*, New York, The Vanguard Press, 1944, p. 520.

One of the surest roads to totalitarianism is unwillingness to trust our-selves enough to build up an adequate planning structure. Those who oppose planning are unintentionally making planning necessary, but not democratic planning. The alternative is not between planning and no planning, between planning in a free society and planning under a dictator-ship, whether Fascist or Communist Doubtless many well-meaning persons who are critical of all planning believe that they are contributing to freedom. On the contrary they are helping to make it impossible. It cannot be too strongly stated that the real foes of freedom are those who refuse to co-operate in setting up machinery for democratic dealing with the difficulties of our time. Planning is coming. Of this there can be no doubt. The only question is whether it will be the democratic planning of a free society, or totalitarian in character.[4]

The Requisites of Social Planning

We have already taken notice that planning social consequences requires a highly developed state of technical knowledge concerning causes and results in the social system. Given this technical knowledge, however, there are additional requisites of planning that must be met if planning activities are to be successful in practice. These requisites include consumer sovereignty, the capacity to make compromises for the general welfare, and reliable administrators and civil servants.

Consumer Sovereignty

This is a necessary concomitant of all discussions of planning in Britain and the United States. The phrase implies that final approval in planning the consequences of social action must lie with those whose actions are the target of planning. Barbara Wootton approaches her discussion of consumer sovereignty by asserting that what people want to do must be treated as something to be discovered, not changed.[5] This position rests upon two premises: first, that freedom must be guarded cautiously simply because in the course of human history it has proved so illusive; and second, that any other system for guiding uses of resources than consumer preferences as expressed through a price system is unworkable. Landauer defines his concept of consumer sovereignty in terms of this second premise: "Consumer sovereignty . . . means that consumers decide how each available

---

[4] Charles E. Merriam, "The Place of Planning," Seymour E. Harris (ed.), *Saving American Capitalism*, New York, Alfred A. Knopf, 1948, p. 161.

[5] Barbara Wootton, *Freedom Under Planning*, Chapel Hill, University of North Caro-lina Press, 1945, p. 43.

unit of resources should be used. The consumer through the "pull" of his demand steers production." [6]

On the question of consumer sovereignty, there is a difference of opinion among students of social planning as to whether effective planning could be carried on if a full measure of consumer sovereignty were retained. Barbara Wootton, for example, concluded that full consumer sovereignty was incompatible with economic planning if the sovereignty in question "implies a claim that the choices which consumers do actually make should continuously determine the pattern of production." [7] In the opinion of some American students, however, she underestimates the degree of freedom which could be permitted consumers while still carrying out a planned program.[8] It should be understood, of course, that in no operating economic system could it be demonstrated that the unique wishes and desires of each individual consumer determine in their separate state the course of production. The productive apparatus which is massed in the United States responds to needs when it is probable that such a response can be made profitably.[9] Thus, the alternatives available for consideration must be weighed in relationship to the existing situation, not the theoretical maximum of consumer sovereignty.

THE CAPACITY TO MAKE COMPROMISES

Planning for social goals is defended primarily in terms of the greater orderliness and efficiency it promises. It would fulfill this brief held for it if it fostered full use of resources and facilitated the achievement of consensus as to priorities that should be given to competing demands for resources. It is obvious that the establishment of priorities means for some demands a low priority that may preclude their satisfaction. Barbara Wootton has made the point with characteristic clarity: ". . . it is not, to begin with, axiomatic that in every community some common good exists in the sense of ends which would

[6] Carl Landauer, *Theory of National Economic Planning*, Berkeley, University of California Press, 1947, p. 17.

[7] Wootton, *op. cit.*, p. 43.

[8] For example, see Landauer, *op. cit.*, pp. 28 ff.; Joseph Rosenfarb, *Freedom and the Administrative State*, New York, Harper & Brothers, 1948, pp. 84 ff.; Sidney Hook, "The Philosophical Implications of Economic Planning," in Mackenzie, *op. cit.*, pp. 669 ff.

[9] There is a phase of this observation which cannot be discussed here, the role of monopoly power. Substantial control over the productive facilities in a given market region by a giant corporation as effectively limits the sovereignty of consumers—and possibly in the end their range of choices—as would any scheme of planning that has been proposed in the United States. Hence, the restriction of consumer sovereignty is a matter of comparative degree.

be freely chosen by all members of that community. Thus, if three people wish to spend a holiday together, and one wants to go to Margate, one to Bath and one to Edinburgh, no planner can decide, on behalf of all, and according to the wishes of all, where the holiday is to be spent." [10] We could dismiss this problem of resolving competing demands by simply pointing to the political machinery of democracies, which processes competing demands in other areas of workaday life. But the issue is not that simple. There is, in the matter of allocating economic resources, an almost unanimous belief on the part of economists that the price system is the only workable way to decide among competing uses for scarce resources. Whether retention of the basic price system while restricting the choices with reference to which it operates would deprive it of its efficiency is a matter of the greatest consequence. Nor is there a unanimity or near unanimity of judgment on the part of students concerning this basic problem.

Proponents of planning point to the fact that adjustment of demand and supply as brought about by the price system is wasteful because of the magnitude of fluctuations and adjustments required. It would be better to plan for a simpler and more precise process. Thus, Landauer states that ". . . the most important advantage of planning lies in the possibility of performing these [adjustment] operations on paper before they have to be performed in reality, thereby cutting out the costly fluctuations through which the market has to seek its equilibrium." [11] Opponents of planning emphasize the complete incompatibility of planning and the "competitive" price system. One of the most bitter opponents of planning, Friedrich A. Hayek, argues to the point that we must either plan everything or nothing: "Nothing, indeed, seems at first more plausible, or is more likely to appeal to more reasonable people, than the idea that our goal must be neither the extreme decentralization of free competition nor the complete centralization of a single plan but some judicious mixture of the two methods. Yet mere common sense proves a treacherous guide in this field. Although competition can bear some admixture of regulation, it cannot be combined with planning to any extent we like without ceasing to operate as an effective guide to production." [12] This is not the sole argument with which Hayek has assailed planning, but it is a crucial one and his opposition would be commonplace but for the

[10] Wootton, op. cit., p. 20.
[11] Landauer, op. cit., pp. 74–75.
[12] Friedrich A. Hayek, The Road to Serfdom, Chicago, University of Chicago Press, 1944, p. 36.

vehemence with which he presses this single argument. The fact that "competition" is a conceptual tool of economics, not an actual condition of economic activity, therefore, deprives his argument of its value on this count. Edwin G. Nourse analyzed Hayek's case against planning in these terms: ". . . Hayek's case rests on his assumption of the practicability and beneficence of the system of economic individualism in a free market, or on the ideal quality of atomistic competition. Admitting the beauty of this as a textbook model for exposition in the early weeks of an undergraduate class, it seems amazing to hear Hayek put it forward as a real situation that once obtained and to which we should seek to return." [13] In a later section, we shall consider the possibilities of "mixing" planning and essentially free-enterprise economic activities.

RELIABLE ADMINISTRATION

When it became apparent that nations whose systems of government were democratic had decided to plan more or less methodically for social goals, the reaction in the United States was (especially in the case of Great Britain) to regard the character and reliability of the civil service as the major factor in their success. If the splendid British civil service could not make planning work, then once and for all we should abandon its concepts. Our discussion thus far has made it apparent that other factors, particularly technical knowledge, are the keys to success in planning. Administrative factors certainly are not unimportant, however, and a substantial literature has developed in connection with the requisites for planning in this area.

Administration is not a process in the political sector which embraces easily defined antecedents and neatly enumerated functions. Certainly, the conventional definition of public administration as mere execution of policies determined by the people's representatives poorly defines its operations. We saw in Chapter 5 that administrative agencies often urge expansion of those programs for which they are responsible. That is to say, administration is an active political process having policy-determining functions as well as policy-executing functions. In no sense is this a novel observation; most treatises in political theory, which have been concerned primarily with power and its control, have warned of the problem to be faced in the custody of the custodians. When the custodians may have at their disposal vast

[13] Edwin G. Nourse, "Serfdom, Utopia, or Democratic Opportunity?", *Public Administration Review*, Spring, 1946, p. 179.

power of economic life and death, even though judgment is rendered periodically at the ballot box, the issue cannot be avoided.

Barbara Wootton has set the administrative problem as an essential condition of planning; if "our frustrations are [to be] diminished and our freedom enlarged," then we must be assured "that the men and women on whom lies the duty of making decisions 'for the benefit of all and on behalf of all' will in fact continuously pursue these objectives." [14] In one sense, of course, this problem is a phase of consumer sovereignty. But it is obviously of such importance as to merit consideration in its own right. In a statement somewhat similar to that of Wootton, Barbara Ward has offered the following administrative requisites of democratic planning: ". . . the civil service must be reasonably efficient and honest, citizens must be reasonably ready to pay their taxes and in general, the conception of obeying the regulations laid down by the government must be reasonably widespread." [15] Both Wootton and Ward assume that the area of permissible choice for those in whose behalf planning is carried on must be very much more restricted under planning than otherwise would be the case. Under those circumstances, the whole idea of planning for social goals takes on a danger that otherwise would be secondary.

Apart from the problem of its "all-interestedness," administration by government entities frequently is challenged from the standpoint of its efficiency and adaptability. Great difficulties are encountered in any effort to judge the efficiency of public administration on an "input-output" basis. That which is being "put out" is service, which rarely bears a price tag that would enable comparison with costs at various stages in its "production." But the common allegation holds that, in comparison with private industry, government administration must necessarily be less efficient simply because the factor of competition with other producers is absent as a spur to greater efficiency. Paul Appleby questions the lack of competition in government administration as a spur to efficiency, noting that "Each of thousands of budget estimates competes strenuously with all others for appropriations. Each bureau, each program, each project, has to fight for life and funds. A section head is under tremendous pressure in preparing estimates to justify his askings; he has to play down, skimp, or reduce estimates for projects that he cannot hope to justify effectively in con-

[14] Wootton, op. cit., p. 20.
[15] Barbara Ward, "Limits of Economic Planning," Foreign Affairs, January, 1949, p. 247.

trast with other items from other sections." [16] The budget process, therefore, is apt to be as rigorous in producing efficiency as would be adjustment of costs vis-à-vis competing firms in private industry. Furthermore, where competition is restricted in its effect (for example, under monopolistic competition and administered or subsidized prices), the incentive of private industry to reduce costs may be less than in the public sphere. Few economists doubt that the reduction or elimination of competition is a prime object of most business firms, the protests of trade associations notwithstanding.

Concerning the adaptability of public agencies, the argument has been broached that sheer size makes them unwieldy and hinders their adjustment to changing conditions. As a counterargument, however, it can be said that only in the public sphere can the money costs of change be subordinated to the desirability of change irrespective of cost. American economic history is not without examples of inventions and processes suppressed in an attempt to shelter investments already "sunk." On the matter of size, proponents of planning have pointed out that the magnitude of many American corporations— some of which conduct operations which dwarf those carried on by American states and even groups of states—makes them as susceptible to inadaptability as public agencies. The task of management and planning is scarcely different in the two cases.

Appraisal of Planning in the American Cultural Context

Our discussion thus far has been in general terms with only occasional references to the American scene. When planning is seriously argued in terms of its applicability to the United States, it is a form of the classical argument that is criticized or defended—a form that takes into consideration the "ultimate values" of American culture and accepts many factors as given. Thus, planning for social goals as debated in the United States is very different from its counterpart on the European Continent. The amount of change in the existing social order necessary to meet the proposals of those who advocate planning is far less than in Europe.

THE AMERICAN LIMITS

Certain changes in the existing order and certain requisites of planning are rarely suggested by American students of planning, regardless of their attachment to the idea. No one suggests nationaliza-

[16] Paul H. Appleby, *Big Democracy*, New York, Alfred A. Knopf, 1945, p. 54.

tion of basic industries or government determination of what should be produced, how much, and by whom. Furthermore, an economic system of large enterprises is taken as the point of departure, if for no other reason than that reducing the units to conform with the doctrines of perfect competition would be too upsetting. More important, however, has been the recognition that large units better serve American wants in terms of "standard brands" and "standard prices."

AMERICAN CONCEPTS

Proposals for planning compatible with American cultural values have tended to emphasize full employment, particularly since 1944. Accepting in large measure the theory that full employment is a function of savings and investment dynamics, American students have tended to argue for government responsibility to ensure levels of investment which would produce full employment of American resources, particularly labor. There is the assumption that for most social problems full-employment levels of national income are a solution or an ameliorant. To the end of maintaining full employment, the government is urged to take action with respect to consumption, public and private investment, and foreign trade. In Chapter 11, we discussed some of these techniques. The important point, of course, is that all measures would be adapted to the existing institutional structure.

Regardless of their moderate scope in comparison with European planning concepts, American concepts have been bitterly opposed. The opposition which can be mustered by conservative forces in the United States would be something to contend with under any circumstances. But in the postwar period, the tactics of Soviet imperialism have focused opposition on all phases of Communist activity, and it is a fact that planning (with a big stick) is a mainstay of the Soviet economy. Hence, the most moderate of proposals relating to planning have become cloaked with suspicion and sinister motives have been ascribed to them. Furthermore, the American economy has performed adequately in the postwar period and the recessions of 1949 and 1953–1954 were negotiated with only minor damage, which removes planning from the list of compelling needs.

We have seen how proposals for the extension of social-insurance programs have been scorned on account of the costs they would entail and the "big government" which they would inevitably usher in. So

TABLE 61. Per Capita Expenditures of the Federal Government, 1940–1954.
(constant 1939 dollars)

Function	1940	1941	1942	1943	1944	1945	1946	1947	1948	1949	1950	1951	1952	1953	1954
Military services	$11.25	$39.07	$157.63	$373.75	$450.35	$467.23	$196.23	$53.81	$39.00	$40.80	$39.68	$63.34	$114.81	$126.80	$129.03
Veterans' services, benefits	4.14	3.46	3.03	3.23	4.00	11.56	19.19	22.70	23.36	22.83	21.37	16.53	14.05	12.99	11.80
International security and foreign relations	.37	.85	3.45	.88	1.31	3.74	6.35	24.59	17.01	22.11	15.49	14.63	15.22	17.24	21.80
Housing and Community development	.21	1.57	1.13	1.61	1.65	1.06	.86	1.30	.29	.96	.84	1.86	2.12	2.16	2.23
Social security, welfare, and health	23.66	16.09	10.44	6.36	5.44	5.77	4.55	4.93	6.65	6.55	7.13	7.10	7.19	7.41	5.52
Education and general research	.48	.40	.31	.24	.47	.82	.34	.24	.22	.23	.36	.35	.49	.78	.52
Agriculture and agricultural resources	11.63	8.06	8.08	.317	6.46	8.89	3.25	4.67	2.04	8.60	8.98	2.01	3.02	5.55	7.09
Natural resources	2.95	2.19	2.40	2.18	1.75	1.34	1.07	2.33	3.91	5.17	5.01	6.34	8.52	9.63	3.36
Transportation and communication	4.18	3.01	6.20	19.12	23.17	18.60	3.43	2.06	4.25	5.55	5.65	5.21	5.55	5.87	4.47
Finance, commerce, industry	—	—	.18	.41	.91	.58	.13	.38	.31	.41	.73	.54	.69	1.31	.37
Labor	.08	.47	1.14	1.28	1.20	1.12	.75	.72	.65	.66	.84	.70	.70	.72	.76
General government	2.57	2.41	1.84	1.79	3.50	5.06	3.82	4.91	5.12	3.70	3.57	3.99	4.08	3.96	3.35
Interest	7.82	6.88	6.88	9.75	14.10	20.22	20.93	18.84	18.67	18.64	18.73	17.96	17.15	18.63	17.94
Adjustment to daily Treasury statement	- .06	-.56	-5.04	-1.05	-1.93	1.39	4.68	1.14	-1.38	.93	1.06	-2.18	-2.47	—	—
Total	$69.24	$84.46	$202.71	$426.78	$547.44	$547.34	$265.61	$147.42	$121.48	$137.14	$129.44	$138.38	$193.53	$213.12	$207.54
Implicit price deflators	100.9	122.7	135.9	139.5	136.2	137.1	163.6	185.2	192.4	196.7	204.4	217.0	220.8	221.0	222.0
Continental population, U.S. (thousands)	131,936	133,058	133,752	133,971	132,622	132,137	139,893	143,375	146,045	148,558	151,240	153,377	156,700	158,375	162,414

Sources: Budget of the United States, 1946–1955; National Income, 1954; Survey of Current Business, July, 1953.

too with planning. As conventionally pressed, the argument runs that we have already allowed the "welfare state" to expand beyond all reasonable proportions and the cost is reflected in each citizen's tax bill. Because the government cannot balance its budget, moreover, it has had to borrow money and contribute to inflation. What greater indictment could be made of proposals to plan for social goals that would increase welfare expenditures beyond even their existing levels? The argument that welfare expenditures in the United States have reached levels which have "broken" the government would seem shallow enough if only in view of the fact that most other countries, all of whom are much poorer than the United States, have in operation comprehensive programs of social insurance, social welfare, and assistance beyond anything known here, and excepting those in which war damage was extensive, fiscal problems have not limited their accomplishments. The fact is that the American tax burden has been necessitated by a turn which was taken in world affairs at the time it became apparent the Soviet Union would be a threat to the peace of the free world. As a matter of fact, the cost burden of "welfare programs" has been a relatively small portion of total costs. Table 61 shows the expenditures by the federal government on all of its functions since 1940. The figures in the table are on a per capita basis and have been adjusted for depreciation of the dollar by implicit price deflators for gross national product; hence they are comparable for the years shown.

The data make it very clear that the cost of government is not related to "welfare programs" in any significant way. The pattern of expenditures that existed in 1940 and 1941 is barely being maintained, or has been reduced, in housing and community development, social security, welfare and health, education and general research, natural resources,[17] an dlabor. On the other hand, military services, veterans' benefits, international security and foreign relations, and other costs of past or future wars have increased as much as fifty times over the 1940 level. The implications of these data could constitute a chapter by themselves, but we shall be content with only a few observations. In the first place, the nation's fiscal capacity is not being sorely tested by welfare expenditures. Moreover, by failing to meet current needs we are probably making larger outlays necessary in future years.

---

[17] The precipitous drop for 1954 which appears in the table is the result of removing the atomic-energy programs from the "natural resources" classification. For the same reason, the "swollen" expenditures in this area that appear for the years 1949–1953 reflect the inclusion of the atomic-energy programs.

Finally, the states are not, by their increased efforts, making up for the defaults of the federal government in these areas.[18]

Planning for Social and Economic Goals: Concluding Remarks

The logical culmination of our previous discussion of American social legislation with its diversity and shortcomings was consideration of comprehensive action to plan the consequences of social life. Especially when it is known that the resources of the United States are so vast and its productive capacity so great, we should consider planning to meet needs that presently are not met or are met inadequately. Considered in this sense, planning is simply a means of promoting efficiency and fulfilling humanitarian ideals.

But the decision to extend the planning concept to production of goods and services—in whatever degree—poses dangers which we should do well to consider. Almost certainly, effective planning would interfere with people doing as they please in workaday life as it presently exists. And the willingness of those whose activities would in some degree be restricted to consign that restricting authority to government—even when its exercise is reviewed periodically at the ballot box—must rest on the importance of the security that might be won. Probably the chief danger in the United States is not that government authority will needlessly extend its power, but the opposite. The danger lies in atrophy permitted by apathy and irresponsible citizenship.

Whatever be the arguments concerning the extension of planning in the American social system, they have not been reviewed widely by the people. In some measure this is a consequence of the full-employment period that began with the close of World War II. But it is also owing in part to the misrepresentation of the planning function and the burden of existing welfare programs. Measured in terms of fiscal effort devoted to their execution, welfare programs hardly appear to have run wild. Changes in the composition of the American population, knowledge of our needs, and like factors might have been expected to increase real welfare expenditures beyond their present proportions. Regardless of what other arguments may be lodged

[18] This is particularly true of housing and community development, but data presently in a preliminary state have been prepared by the author and they show that the wealthiest states are falling behind in the pattern of expenditures that they experienced in 1940. New York State, for example, seems to be spending less (exclusive of capital outlays) on such functions as conservation, correction, education, and labor on a constant-dollar per capita basis in the 1950's than was the case in 1940.

against the extension of planning for social goals, the argument that we cannot afford it seems to have little validity. It may be argued legitimately that the assumption of welfare operations and the expenses accompanying their expansion have been less easily borne owing to our having to maintain a large military establishment in the face of the Russian threat. But it is very dubious that we shall improve our position vis-à-vis the Russians if we permit stresses to exist in our society that could as well be countered by a slightly greater effort.

SELECTED REFERENCES

Hayek, Friedrich A., *The Road to Serfdom*, Chicago, University of Chicago Press, 1944.

Landauer, Carl, *Theory of National Economic Planning*, Berkeley, University of California Press, 1947.

Mackenzie, Findlay (ed.), *Planned Society, Yesterday, Today and Tomorrow*, New York, Prentice-Hall, 1937.

Wootton, Barbara, *Freedom under Planning*, Chapel Hill, University of North Carolina Press, 1945.

chapter 19

Social Legislation and the Social Structure

When Plato described his ideal society, he pictured a division of labor which at once provided the greatest community good and the optimum of individual happiness and well-being. Sir Thomas More's *Utopia* also managed to make community service and individual happiness synonymous. Unfortunately, such a happy equation is found only in the Utopian society, for in the world of reality societies must constantly balance these variables one against the other. By its very nature society operates to restrict the unhampered satisfaction of individual needs while seeking to impose a system of social values which substitutes group-oriented goals for individualistic ends. Yet it is only through group life that individuals can satisfy their needs.

In Chapter 4, we recounted the role of American culture in shaping these values and in providing the social goals for which men strive. The present chapter is designed to extend that analysis by relating the role of the American social legislation we have since described in modifying and changing the structure of American society. We shall first review the requisite elements of our social structure and how they are affected by social change. From this vantage point, we may then proceed to consider how social legislation is affected by and in turn affects that structure. In the next chapter, we shall look into the consequences of these changes for individual behavior within the social system.

Requisites of the American Social Structure

In earlier chapters, we have described certain requisite elements common to all social systems. We have portrayed societies as sharing certain structural and functional characteristics: a system of statuses and roles, a set of values, a normative order, personnel, and a system

of social relations among these individuals. The behavior of individuals within this structure results from the compromise between imperious individual drives and the social forces which control the expression of these drives.

Every society also establishes devices to regulate an orderly functioning of social life within that unit. Thus, a means of meeting subsistence needs must be devised and some plan established for the division of labor necessary to this end. This is accomplished by a series of statuses and roles which place and direct the activity of each member of the society. If we return to Plato's ideal society for a moment, we see that he did just this. He provided for three broad status groups: the commoners, the soldiers and administrators, and the guardians or rulers. Each of these status groups was to perform a different functional role: the commoners were to supply the necessary labor, the soldiers and administrators to conduct warfare and maintain domestic order, and the guardians to rule. Modern American society is much more highly stratified, but basically we do the same thing. We supply each person with a series of statuses which define for him what he is to do in society. His status determines his position in the hierarchy of inferior-superior relationships and establishes limits and conditions to his behavior. In large measure, what we do is conditioned by what we are.

Talcott Parsons has described the behavior which takes place within this system as "social action" and has defined the elements of the typical act.[1] Any act, from the point of view of the actor, contains certain indispensable and irreducible elements. First, there is the "actor" himself, a biosocial being who thinks, feels, and perceives and who is capable of decision making. Each time this actor is impelled to action, he is oriented to some "end" or future state of affairs toward which he believes his activity is aimed. All of this behavior takes place within a total situation which includes two important sets of elements called "conditions" and "means." Conditions are aspects of the situation over which the actor has no control, obstacles in the path of the achievement of his desired goal. One's desire to become a concert pianist, for example, might require overcoming such conditions as the lack of talent or of the financial resources for the necessary training. Each situation also presents means by which the actor may achieve his desired goal. The actor does have control over these aspects of the

[1] Talcott Parsons, *The Structure of Social Action*, New York, McGraw-Hill Book Company, 1937, pp. 43 ff.

situation and usually a choice among several possible means of reaching the same end. Thus, wealth may be obtained by vigorous and diligent industry, by gambling, by marrying the boss's daughter, or by holding up a bank. Yet each of these means is not equally acceptable, for the final element of social action, a "normative orientation," affects the choice of means insofar as any choice is possible. Bank robbery may present the fastest and least tedious means of obtaining the desired wealth, but it is not the "right" course of action.

Each of these elements of social action is affected by the culture within which the action takes place. Ends are derived in part from individual drives, but are also related to the social goals found in the ideology of that culture. Inculcated in the socialization process, they are for the most part uncritically accepted by the members of the society, who come to desire those objects and states of being which are valued. The means of achieving these valued ends are weighed and judged according to the standards of the society, and conditions may present sociocultural obstacles as well as natural barriers. Modern American society, for example, has established education, training, and experience as conditions to be met on the path of success.

As culture and society change, ends, means, and conditions also undergo modification and change in response to the new ideology and normative order. In the individualistic American society of the nineteenth century, one accepted the conditions imposed upon him by his "lot" and sought, through diligence and thrift, to fulfill his niche in the *status quo*. Modern Americans are more prone to seek the "unlimited" possibilities of success which the mobility of our industrial society promises to anyone with the necessary "ambition." We might explain these behavioral changes as resulting from industrialization, but this would identify only the impetus to the change and neglect the middle range of forces which operate directly to modify behavior. As the economy changes, the roles of the society must also change. The father, a patriarchal and dominating figure in agrarian society, becomes a wage earner. Away from the home for a large part of the day, he must surrender much of his dominance as his children and even his wife become potential wage earners as well. The expanding base of extrafamilial relationships from the kinship area to the larger community tends to weaken family ties, and family solidarity gives way to greater identification with social units larger than the family. The value systems of the agricultural or semi-industrial society no longer answer the problems posed by urban-industrial life. New, vital-

ized values of some flexibility replace the passive and rigid agrarian value system. Robert Lynd has pointed to the dualism which results from the retention of some of these values as ideals while social action is based upon the current operational values.[2] Thus, "hard work and thrift are signs of character and the way to get ahead," but "no shrewd person tries to get ahead today by just working hard, and nobody gets rich nowadays by pinching nickels."

These seemingly contradictory assumptions are merely the result of the tenacity of the values which frequently remain as ideals long after they have been discarded as guides for current behavior. The normative order of folkways, mores, and laws also responds to sociocultural change. The rules which were sufficient to produce conformity in the small, homogeneous agrarian community, where social pressure alone could often regulate behavior, lack authority in the larger, more dynamic, and culturally heterogeneous society.

As social change becomes more rapid, the folkways and mores, no longer sufficient in themselves to regulate behavior, surrender control over more and more areas of social behavior in the face of the growing importance of enacted laws. More deliberate and consciously wrought than folkways and mores, enacted law represents a more adaptable device of conscious planning for adjustment to change. Thus, with the advent of new technological devices, such as the automobile, new regulatory laws are almost immediately enacted, while the customary controls over behavior associated with the new device respond more slowly.

Since they are the result of deliberate and conscious construction, laws are, of course, influenced by the value system of the society. Laws openly contrary to the established mores have little chance of successful enforcement. The Eighteenth Amendment, for example, was successful in producing prohibition, but, since it was the result of lobbying by a vocal but small prohibitionist lobby whose position was actually in opposition to the general acceptance of drinking in American society, enforcement was impossible and the amendment was eventually repealed.

A further problem in the relationship between custom and the enacted law occurs when laws do not respond to change and consequently lag behind existing behavior patterns. Our divorce laws fur-

2 Robert S. Lynd, *Knowledge for What?*, Princeton, Princeton University Press, 1948, pp. 60–62. These "assumptions" also appear in Robert S. and Helen M. Lynd, *Middletown in Transition*, New York, Harcourt, Brace and Company, 1937, chap. XII.

nish a timely example of just such a situation. Based upon the static common law, they still define the divorce action as a contentious litigation involving a "guilty" and an "innocent" party. Divorce today is frequently mutually sought, and the fiction of the injured party has led to widespread collusion between couples who seek the most practical grounds furnished the "injured" party by the state. Our values concerning the sanctity of marriage, the controls exerted by religious pressure groups, and the reluctance of legislators to intervene in the sensitive area of family relationships have all contributed to the lag of divorce law behind divorce behavior.

Often, however, the enacted law serves as an instrument to produce social change long before the slower, less deliberate customary controls of behavior are ready to produce or even accept such change. The Social Security Act, for example, proposed innovations in social relationships which were probably in advance of the then accepted concepts of government-sponsored security and certainly ahead of the social thought of the more conservative elements in the population. The frequency and bitterness of the condemnation which the act received verify its progressiveness. Enacted law, then, may serve as a means of maintaining stability by adjusting social relations to changes in the technological and social orders. It may also become an instrument of social change by legislating adjustments in the framework within which social action takes place.

Finally, every social system organizes its folkways, mores, and laws into institutions which pattern the goal-seeking activity of its members and at the same time serve the functional needs of the society. The major insitutions fulfill societal needs for (1) a means of obtaining and distributing subsistence needs (the economy); (2) a system of authority which regulates behavior and enforces the legal norms (government); (3) the procreation, care, and placement of new members of the society (the family); (4) the training and indoctrination of these members in the skills and values of the culture (education); and (5) the reaffirmation of the ultimate and sacred values of the society (religion). There are other institutions in society, just as there are other functional needs, but these five combine to provide for the basic social needs of any society.

The social institutions are no more immutable to sociocultural change than any of the other elements of the social structure we have previously discussed. Social and technological changes produce im-

portant changes in each of these fields of social activity. The introduction of the automobile, for example, has mobilized the economy
and fostered new industries, provided new sources of revenue and new
areas of regulation for the government, helped produce the suburban-
ization of the American family, and, in recent years, affected the folkways of church attendance and introduced the drive-in church. All of
the basic institutions tend to resist rapid change since the elaborate
structures which they have developed to satisfy particular social functions are often too cumbersome to allow for quick adjustments. One
final point concerning social institutions and social change: alterations
in one of the basic institutions usually effect changes in other institutions. We shall have reason to consider this interrelatedness in connection with the later section on the relationship between social
legislation and institutions (pp. 650–657).

Social Legislation and the Requisites of the Social Structure

Now that we have identified the requisite elements of the social
structure and their response to sociocultural change, we may turn to
the more specific problems of the operation of that structure to meet
the individual and social needs of its members and the role of social
legislation in providing for their welfare. We should like to know this:
What does a member of society have a right to expect from the social
system and how does social legislation protect these rights?

Answers to these questions may be found in political slogans such
as "Life, liberty, and the pursuit of happiness" or "Freedom from
want," but these are abstractions from the problems which daily face
mankind. They represent abstract states of mind rather than the
answers to the immediate problems of earning a living, raising a
family, and protecting one's health. They present the further problem
of being very difficult to legislate in any direct fashion. More specifically, we may say that society owes to its members the maintenance of
order and justice in its social relations and the protection of the individual from unnecessary stresses. Essentially, it must provide for his
"welfare." Bentham, who used the word "happiness" in the same sense
as we have used the word "welfare," has described its components in
his discussion of the objectives of civil legislation:

In prescribing and distributing rights and obligations, the legislator
should, as we have pointed out, seek as his end and aim the happiness of
the body politic. Inquiring more particularly wherein this happiness

consists, we find four subordinate objects: "Subsistence," "Abundance," "Equality," "Security." The more perfect the enjoyment in all these respects, the greater the sum of social happiness, and especially that happiness which is dependent upon the laws. Hence we conclude that all of the functions of law may be referred to one or other of these four heads: to provide subsistence, to aim at abundance, to encourage equality, and to maintain security.[3]

Bentham's four goals for civil legislation furnish us with a convenient classification of the major objectives for modern American social legislation. If our legislative action is to promote the public welfare, it must (1) provide subsistence protection and promote an equitable distribution of the means of subsistence, (2) provide for the amelioration of the conditions which result from poverty or the unequal distribution of the means of subsistence, (3) provide a social regulation consistent with equality of opportunity and equal protection under the law, (4) provide for the social and economic security of all members of society. These objectives represent the ultimate ends of social legislation, and, as we learned in our discussion of the elements of social action, the path to the achievement of ends is always blocked by conditions or obstacles which must be circumvented or overcome. Vested interests, cultural lags, public apathy, and legislative inefficiency are but a few of the barriers in the way of effective social legislation. Further difficulty is encountered when it becomes necessary to choose among the several means which are proposed by factional interests for reaching these goals. John G. Winant, the first chairman of the Social Security Board, has documented the differences of opinion which occasioned the Social Security Act:

No one assumes that this act is the final word in social insurance. For, since society is a growing organism, there can never be any finality in the treatment of its problems. What the present law does represent is a sincere effort to reconcile the divergent views of a large number of thoughtful and public-spirited men and women who cared enough to do something about present insecurity. Though all agreed on the basic principle of social insurance, there were natural differences of opinion as to the means and techniques to be used in attaining the ends on which there was common agreement.

The framers of the law were also compelled to take account of certain fundamental cleavages in American political and social philosophies. This

---

[3] Quoted in L. L. Bernard, *Social Control and Its Sociological Aspects*, New York, The Macmillan Company, 1939, pp. 587–588.

involved an attempt to strike a working balance between the proper claims of the federal government and the states.[4]

In our survey of existing social legislation, we have often pointed to these clashes of interests and to the sociocultural barriers which stand in the way of an adequate and effective social legislation in America. In our family legislation and in our attempts to legislate income security, they have produced confused and inefficient laws inconsistent with the goals we have just described. Social well-being and individual security have suffered as a result.

Social Change and the Concept of the Public Welfare

We have discussed the concept of the public welfare proposed in the previous section as if it represented a constant and common assessment of the responsibility of society, and of its legal agent the state, toward individuals. Insofar as government has been for the benefit of the governed, the public welfare has always been one of its major concerns; but, as we saw in Chapters 3 and 4, the social philosophy which has approved public-welfare activities as a legitimate function of the state is of relatively recent origin. The individualistic values and behavior standards of the agrarian society did not allow for the extension of any protective concern on the part of the government. Had any been proffered, it would probably have been viewed as paternalistic and an accusation of inadequacy by the recipient. Security, insofar as it existed, resulted from self-sufficiency, and only the family and kindred served to protect needy and dependent individuals.

Even the Elizabethan Poor Laws, which placed the responsibility for the poor and indigent upon the local community, established a principle of local responsibility which to this day results in the charge of "government intervention" and "creeping socialism" whenever the federal government attempts to extend its welfare functions. Our own exaggerated fears of a strong centralized authority have compounded our antagonism to national welfare programs.

With the emergence of the Industrial Revolution and the maturity of democracy in England, the traditional controls over behavior soon became antiquated, but they were not soon replaced by values and standards fitted to the new dependency produced by wage labor. Rather, there emerged the self-regulating, self-restoring economy which was part and parcel of the "simple system of natural liberty,"

---

[4] John G. Winant, "Social Security Begins," *Survey Graphic*, January, 1937, pp. 7–15.

the laissez-faire state.[5] This doctrine of no government intervention, free competition, and the labor market produced widespread misery and squalor, but eschewed any attempt on the part of the government to alleviate the consequent suffering. William Graham Sumner, the great American exponent of laissez faire, has typified this attitude with an eloquence that almost masks its indifference to human suffering:

Now you know that "the poor and the weak" are continually put forward as objects of public interest and public obligation. In the appeals which are made, the terms "the poor" and "the weak" are used as if they were terms of exact definition. Except the pauper, that is to say, the man who cannot earn his living or pay his way, there is no possible definition of a poor man. Except a man who is incapacitated by vice or by physical infirmity, there is no definition of a weak man. The paupers and the physically incapacitated are an inevitable charge on society. About them no more need be said. But the weak who constantly arouse the pity of humanitarians and philanthropists are the shiftless, the impractical, and the inefficient, or they are the idle, the intemperate, the extravagant, and the vicious. . . . Whatever capital you divert to the support of a shiftless and good-for-nothing person is so much diverted from some other employment, and that means from somebody else. . . . If you give a loaf of bread to a pauper you cannot give the same loaf to a laborer.[6]

It was the reaction against these conditions of misery which went unattended in the laissez-faire society, coupled with the growing number and authority of new urban-industrial values and norms, which eventually led to the legitimization of government activity for the social welfare. As the new industrial age developed, the increased social mobility, the weakening of family and kinship ties, the new hazards of unemployment, and the heterogeneity of urban life weakened the control of the agrarian values and behavior standards. Self-sufficiency and family-help patterns were no longer sufficient to protect the individual from the vicissitudes of life in the industrial order. Our value system was modified to allow for governmental services to

[5] Robert M. MacIver, The Web of Government, New York, The Macmillan Company, 1947, p. 333.

[6] Sumner originally delivered the lecture "The Forgotten Man," from which this is an excerpt, in the Brooklyn Historical Museum on January 30, 1883. Since then it has been reproduced in several places. This quotation came from Maurice R. Davie (ed.), Sumner Today, New Haven, Yale University Press, 1940, pp. 10–11. It is interesting that the New Deal used some of Sumner's concepts and that President Franklin D. Roosevelt used the phrase "the forgotten man" to mean the needy and dependent individuals against whom this essay is directed. To Sumner, however, the forgotten man was the industrious and hard-working taxpayer whose tax dollars were used to support Roosevelt's "forgotten man."

protect wage earners and dependent individuals, and the government was established in the area of welfare services.

In our earlier discussion of the American culture pattern, we have traced the development of this social-welfare concept and assessed the relative importance of such factors as the Great Depression, the American character, and the various belief systems which have influenced American culture. We need not recount this story again in explaining that social legislation is limited and oriented by the social structure within which it operates. The brief history of our attitudes toward government activity in the field of public welfare should suffice to illustrate that such milestones in American social legislation as the Social Security Act would have been impossible if previous changes had not taken place in the sociocultural system of behavior standards, values, and attitudes.

Like all enacted law, social legislation is itself an agent of change in the social structure. Family legislation, income-protection laws, and other areas of social legislation produce changes in the social relations which they regulate and consequently change institutional activities. Before we can consider this effect of social legislation, however, we must first explain how group reactions to new situations result in legislation.

THE SOCIETAL REACTION PATTERN [7]

When we examined the operation of the social system and its response to sociocultural change, we noted that new situations, or significant alterations of existing ones, require new rules and standards of behavior. Once the existing rules have become established, they represent adjustment to the situation and become comfortable for individual actors since they provoke no stress. When the situation is altered, there is an initial resistance to any change of the rules, since actors have become habituated to them and they represent the "right" way of doing things, but soon the inappropriateness of the existing rules creates a stress and the old mores lose their comfortable feeling. Faced with the necessity of finding rules to fit new situations with which they have as yet had little experience, the first efforts of actors to change the rules are experimental as different expedients are at-

[7] This section is based upon F. Stuart Chapin's theory of the societal reaction pattern first written in 1926 and published under the title "A Theory of the Societal Reaction Pattern" as a chapter in the *Franklin H. Giddings' Memorial Volume*, 1928. This treatment is adapted from the theory as presented in Professor Chapin's *Cultural Change*, New York, Century Company, 1928, chap. VIII, especially pp. 226–233.

tempted and found wanting. In this trial-and-error phase, there is generally little coördination of effort, and rules are tried, judged, and either discarded or retained depending upon their efficacy in adapting means to specific ends. Finally, after much experimentation, an integrated and effective system of rules is established by the combination of those experimental norms which proved successful. The newly adopted pattern of rules becomes the "right" thing to do and represents adjustment until a new change in the situation again requires readjustment.

Chapin has applied this theory of the societal reaction pattern to the process of legislation, and suggests a threefold sequence of action when social change disturbs existing adaptations:

Phase   I.   Enforcement of the mores. This process is formal, inelastic, undifferentiated and indiscriminate. The lag of mores behind the requirements of a changing order creates strain toward a better adaptation of means to ends, and toward greater consistency among the mores, consequently there is a shift to the next phase of the pattern.

Phase II.   Special legislation of a trial-and-error or experimental type. Laws are enacted to deal separately with each case. The process is particularistic, largely uncoordinated, and shows the beginnings of rational differentiation.

Phase III.   General legislation that integrates successful group practices. Based upon study of the problem and centralizes policy and method of administration. Efficient adjustment and necessary elasticity in group response attained by new administrative machinery and of a secondary group type. Use of specialized administrative personnel. Considerable range of administrative discretion rather than minute mechanical regulation. High element of personal responsibility. Result: Integrated, coordinated, highly differentiated, discriminating, and elastic group response made possible.[8]

This pattern sequence will also serve to explain the development of social legislation as a means of readjusting social relationships to changing situations. Perhaps a concrete example will best illustrate societal reaction through social legislation.

In the previous section, we traced the development of the concept

[8] Chapin, op. cit., pp. 236–237.

of governmental activity in the area of the public welfare. Recall that when industrialization first began to alter the social structure of agrarian society and disturb existing behavior patterns, the first attempts at adjustment represented an obstinate reenforcement of the existing social norms. The Elizabethan Poor Laws, while extending responsibility for indigents to the community, retained the censure of those who lacked the valued self-sufficiency. Even the doctrine of laissez faire represented a retrenchment of established beliefs and standards concerning the dignity and responsibility of individuals. Gradually, as the ineffectiveness of these standards became increasingly apparent, new and highly experimental plans for the care of the indigent began to appear. In Colonial America, this second phase of societal reaction was characterized by the appearance of legislation designed to help special groups of individuals and uncoördinated efforts by local units of administration.

The eventual consolidation of welfare activities on a state-wide level and the still later intervention of the federal government in this area mark the beginnings of the third phase of integration of successful legislative practices. Even today, however, the social legislation in the nation is still not completely integrated and coördination is as yet tentative. The involvement of the several states and the federal government in welfare programs which might better be singly administered on a national level, the existence of many and often uncoördinated programs of welfare, such as the categorical-assistance approach, and our diverse state laws of marriage and divorce are evidences of the incompleteness of the integration of social legislation.

In time, the changing structure of American society may call for further and even more dramatic adjustments in the normative order and in enacted legislation. New technologies, population changes, changing ideologies, and fluctuations in the economy might well reorder social relations in such a way that existing legislation will soon become dysfunctional and no longer serve its adjustive role. When social change reaches this point, the three-phase cycle must begin again the process of readjustment.

Social Legislation and the Institutional Structure
of American Society

Once an institution has become established, it tends to grow and to expand its influence. Eventually, conflicts of interest develop among the various institutions as several attempt to meet the same needs at

once. In American society, we have witnessed such clashes between the family and the school, the government and the economic system, and generally among all of the institutions as they have sought to adjust to an ever more complex social system. As social change has become more rapid, these conflicts have increased and the fundamental integration of institutions which served our agrarian period has been replaced by a new division of responsibility oriented to the urban-industrial order. In this process of adjusting institutional controls, there has been no loss of function, but rather a reassertion of control over need satisfaction. These changes have been necessitated by the introduction of new or better means of meeting existing needs or by innovations in the social system which produced new needs. Thus the family has lost much of its educational function to the school as the training requirements of industrial society have produced educational goals impossible for the limited family facilities.

The equilibrium which exists in the structure of a society rests upon the capacity of the basic institutions to work out a division of responsibilities. Thus, there must be a constant readjustment in institutions to the changing functions and practices of all other institutions. By way of illustration, the laissez-faire economic system of the early part of the last century produced basic insecurity among those individuals whose labor had become a commodity, the price of which was set by impersonal forces. Economic threats of this nature had previously been the concern of the family and, to a lesser degree, the church, but their facilities were hopelessly inadequate to the magnitude of the task. Also, they had themselves undergone change as the result of the new industrial order and were in the process of readjustment. Clearly, some other social institution had to step in to develop some means of compensating for these new threats to need satisfaction. In response to this demand, the state developed legislation which culminated in fundamental changes in the roles of employer and employee, as we have described.

The role of social legislation in relation to the institutional structure and its social functions is clear: it is primarily to regulate and modify that structure in such a way that social institutions continue to meet the basic problems of human life in the best interests of the general welfare. The degree to which it is able to meet this responsibility in the face of a changing social milieu is the index of its adequacy. Let us now examine each of the major social institutions in their Ameri-

can setting to determine how social legislation has affected their functions.

GOVERNMENT

Probably the greatest changes that have taken place in the American government in the last century have consisted in the gradual transfer of authority from small, independent political units to state-wide and eventually nation-wide control and the extension of political action into areas once served by the other social institutions. Social legislation produced these changes.

When the patterns of American government were first established, limited transportation and communication facilities, population concentration in rural areas, an agricultural economy, and a fear of centralization of authority combined to limit authority to local government. The localized nature of the problems facing an agrarian society allowed for such a development. As the nation grew, however, and as these problems became more complex, the ability of local units to meet adequately the needs of citizens diminished and the original pattern of government has been slowly reorganized. Throughout this volume, we have described the various programs of federal social legislation which have been enacted to meet these needs and have consequently transferred responsibility for their satisfaction to the larger political unit. The process is as yet incomplete. Our continuing fear of centralization has operated to restrict the transfer of many of these legislative areas to nation-wide control; family laws, state welfare programs, and education are but a few examples. It is probably in the area of income protection that we have provided for the greatest amount of federal control. Conversely, the more sensitive areas of family law, education, and public welfare have shown the greatest resistance to change.

As government has grown in size and authority, it has also reached out to meet needs once served by the family, the economic system, the school, and the church. One of the symbols of modern American society is "big government." Government programs relating to family life, for example, have done much to alter the family's functions. Programs for old-age security, maternal and child welfare, and family-support laws have provided a security to family living that promises to meet the threats occasioned by urban-industrial life. In place of kinship security, the family has been provided with the new security in government concern for the public welfare.

THE ECONOMIC SYSTEM

In the economic system, social legislation has framed one of our greatest controversies concerning the proper relationship between the government and the economy. Briefly, the debate centers on whether, by providing income security and protecting wage earners and their families from the insecurities attending production based solely on the profit motive, we have not reduced the efficiency of production. The question of the effect of fear and insecurity as motives for individual activity will be dealt with in Chapter 20, but this controversy also has important implications concerning the relationship between social legislation and the economic order.

Recall that we portrayed the doctrine of laissez faire as espousing a self-regulating economy, free of governmental interference, in which the profit motive and "free and equal" competition contrived to motivate man's economic behavior. Any attempt by government to regulate the exchange of goods and services or to enact legislation relating to working conditions, wages, or unemployment was condemned as an intrusion into a natural order of life. The hope and belief of this doctrine was that if the economic system was left to its own course, free competition would serve to develop a "natural" and "fair" system which would penalize the inefficient.

This harsh doctrine which came to the Colonies with our English heritage evolved into the present conservative political position, helped on its way by a generation of conservative stalwarts, including William Graham Sumner, Andrew Carnegie, Stephen Field, and others.

Opposed to this traditional view was the growing belief that industrialization and the laissez-faire principles produced unnecessary suffering. The new economic and social structure which had developed was seen as creating gross inequalities and producing insecurities based upon fear of depression, technological unemployment, class conflicts, and the gradual sublimation of the family, religion, and government. Only the government seemed strong and persuasive enough to intervene between the wage earner and the economic process. The process of readjustment and amelioration was slow and often inconsistent, as we have seen, but gradually the principle of legislative intervention in the economic relationships of society came to be accepted.

The principle is still grudgingly accepted by some conservative

elements which retain the values of the earlier social and economic structure of the nation. The perpetuation of these principles continues the opposition which has met every effort to ensure that free competition and free enterprise are indeed free of gross inequalities. The fundamental error of the champions of unbridled free enterprise is that they urge us to approach the modern complex structure of the American economy with the values of a small individual-oriented society. They overlook the fact that when any structure in society becomes large and complex it develops a pattern of bureaucratic organization in which the individual is submerged, and for which the principles of individual motivation and activity are no longer sufficient.

The present conflict between American free enterprise and totalitarian communism adds especial urgency to social legislation to meet individual economic needs. Any social system will survive only so long as it continues to meet the needs of its members. If we are to wage any sort of a successful ideological and economic struggle with Communism, we must control want, inequality, and insecurity in the American economy before we exhibit our model system for foreign and domestic inspection.

THE FAMILY

There have also been frequent criticisms of the effects of social legislation on the structure and functions of the family. These attacks usually take one of two directions: (1) that the liberalization of divorce laws has increased family instability by furnishing an "easy out" for dissatisfied mates who would otherwise remain married, and (2) that such legislation as old-age and aid-to-dependent-children programs have weakened the interdependence which once characterized family relationships by interfering in the balance of rights and obligations among family members. We have dealt with each of these charges in describing the legislation concerned, but we would reiterate once again the basic fallacy of these views: social legislation has more often followed than led changes in family values and usually merely recognizes the structural and functional changes which have already taken place in family life. As we have said before, liberal divorce legislation does not cause a high divorce rate but simply recognizes that the mores concerning divorce have changed, and so removes needless administrative barriers in the way of those whose marriage

has suffered some casualty. That there are fewer divorces in countries with stringent and rigid divorce laws does not mean that family relationships are any more stable in these countries, but merely that divorce is more difficult to obtain. Similarly, public-assistance legislation has not weakened filial piety or the sense of responsibility which children feel toward their aged parents. Such discontinuities in the family-help pattern result from the breakdown of the extended family, urbanization and the decreased size of family dwelling units, the position of aged parents as economic burdens in adult children's attempts at status betterment, and other changes in the social relationships within the family. Old-age assistance serves to ensure that some alternative method of support is provided for such aged parents. Neither has aid to dependent children "weakened our moral fiber" by granting license to unwed mothers to continue having illegitimate children nor encouraged paternal desertions. Again, these assistance provisions seek to substitute governmental concern for children in the absence of adequate family protection. Had the family not been previously weakened by its new locus in an urban-industrial society, such measures would probably never have come about.

American social legislation has, however, done much to strengthen the structure of the family. By extending social protection to the once completely dependent mother and child, who were virtually without rights against the father, it has adjusted the once patriarchal family structure to the new demands of modern society. It has provided security to all members of the family by removing the threats of income deprivation and by establishing a pattern of rights and duties more consistent with current principles of individual dignity and responsibility. These measures have bolstered family life at all ages from childhood through adulthood and extending into old age. Even special family problems such as illegitimate birth, orphanhood, parental neglect, and family health problems have received legislative consideration. Considered in their total impact, social laws which are related to family living have done more to strengthen family life and security than any other single agency.

Yet this is not to say that these laws have been completely successful or are entirely adequate to the modern social needs of the family. In our concern for the aged, we have neglected the crucial younger years of the individual's life. By our dependence on the common-law precedents and in our submission to conservative pressure groups, we

have at times allowed antiquated values to dissociate family related legislation from the reality of our modern scientific knowledge concerning family tensions and problems and their solutions. Social legislation cannot operate outside of the framework provided by social-science research and knowledge, and the need for a science of social legislation is nowhere greater than in family legislation.

EDUCATION

The effects of social legislation on the educational institution have been conditioned by our reluctance to accept planning and financing for educational needs on a national level. What legislation has taken place has either been confined to the state and local level or has had to deal with education in an indirect fashion. There have, however, been some important alterations in educational policy and practices as the result of the total program of social legislation.

At the state level, there has been direct legislation which has served to increase the educational level of the population through compulsory-school-attendance laws and child-labor laws. Bolstered by federal legislation in the same area, these laws have enabled the educational institution to offer its services to an increased number of children over a longer period of their lives. Standards of education have also been affected by state legislation which has provided funds for educational activities in political subdivisions, by state licensing and certification of teachers, and by the establishing of state-wide scholarship programs and student examination.

While there has been little direct federal legislation, the indirect effect of welfare legislation has been of importance in education. The security provided by social-insurance and social-assistance programs has enabled children to remain in school for a longer period of time by reducing the necessity of childhood employment to assist in family income. More directly, veterans' educational benefits and government scholarship programs for the training of health specialists and technicians of various types have also served to enlarge the services of the schools and universities of the country.

The resistances to federal aid to education, resulting from provincial interests and regional antagonisms, offer one of the most serious problems to adequate social legislation. The measure to which widespread differences in the standards of education exist throughout the nation is in part a result of these resistances.

RELIGION

Of the five basic institutions, religion has been least affected directly by social legislation. The American doctrine of the separation of Church and State, and the conservative nature of religious values and institutions, are primarily responsible for this situation. In addition, the very personal relationship which exists between the individual and his religious beliefs serves to prohibit any legislative intrusion into this area. There have, however, been some important indirect results of social legislation on the religious institution. The extension of the government into the area of public assistance has lessened the role of religious charities, which once played an important role in aid to the needy. Insofar as legislation has provided for secular public education, it has likewise removed another of the services once dominated by the church, which once shared this function with the family. In the field of family law, social legislation has often been in conflict with religions which seek to perpetuate the family system described in the religious values. The most vocal challenges to liberalization of divorce laws have come from religious bodies. The provisions for the care of illegitimate children and of unwed mothers is another example of the secularization of services once located in the parish or carried out by religious orders dedicated to social service. The growth of secular control over marriage further illustrates this movement.

Religion has also had important effects upon social legislation. In Chapter 7, we saw the extent to which our matrimonial laws developed from religious precepts and continue to follow religious values. Many of our concepts of individual and social well-being also have their origin in religious teachings. The principles of social justice inherent in the Judaeo-Christian tradition have often served to influence our social conscience and shaped our legislative attempts to produce a society consistent with the dictates of that conscience.

The Problem of Conflicting Values

The essence of the problem presented in any attempt to appraise the functional or dysfunctional role of what we have called "welfare legislation" is the relative merit of the planned versus the individualistic society. Opinion in this area is represented by two polar views. One holds that society, and particularly its socioeconomic system, is better left to its own devices since meddling attempts at conscious change can only destroy the natural balances which have evolved over

time. Opposed is the belief that there is no inevitability in social systems, and that when dysfunctional elements become apparent something should and can be done about them. The basic problem is one of conflicting values.

This conflict is really at two levels of social action. There is first a conflict as to whether the condition (e.g., child labor, poverty, or unemployment) actually presents any hazard to the society. Thus an individualistic interpretation of unemployment would hold that it is part of "the nature of things" and that it has the functional value of providing increased competition and thus increasing individual motivation. Opposing values would insist that unemployment is dysfunctional to society since it produces want and insecurity, and rather than increasing motivation has a tendency to reduce human dignity and efficiency.

Further conflict develops when means for solving conditions accepted as dysfunctional are discussed. Once again, the exponent of the *status quo* is prone to insist that if nothing at all is done about the condition, it will probably right itself. Not infrequently, he adds that it is probably present in society as the result of the inefficiency or ineptness of the people involved anyway. The concept of the "deserving poor," which holds that some people are in poverty because of laziness or vice, is an example of this position. Even the proponent of the planned economy is sometimes confronted with conflict as to the means which society should employ to right the objectionable feature. He differs significantly from the exponents of "natural order," however, in that he believes that something can be done and that adequate planning represents the medium of solution. From the fluidity of this approach comes an important advantage over the intransigence of the negativistic "do nothing" approach to social problems. Passivity toward the social structure connotes acceptance of the nature and functioning of that structure. Its values become permanent values, and means for obtaining the ends enjoined by the value system become static and are measured by tradition rather than utility, but conditions are constantly changing and require reappraisal and modification of existing means. If we adopt the laissez-faire orientation to the social system, we are faced with the burden of unchanging means in a world of constantly changing conditions. Social planning provides an experimental attitude toward means and allows for the abandonment of dysfunctional and ineffective means and their re-

placement by new or modified means which may be tested in the light of changing social conditions.

Social Legislation and the Social Structure: Concluding Remarks

Like all social action, legislation is influenced by the social system within which it is cast. The social legislation which we have reviewed in this volume had its origin within the structure of American society and so represents the type of social activity our society is prepared to require of its members. The values which American society reveres become the ends of social legislation, and the success of any legislative program must ultimately be measured by the degree to which it provides means for the attainment of these goals.

The primary functions of all social legislation are two: (1) to provide for the orderly regulation of social relationships, and (2) to provide for the welfare and security of all individuals in the social unit. Difficulty arises in the definition of what constitutes an orderly (and just) regulation and the magnitude and type of individual needs encompassed within the "general welfare" concept. Different periods of history have provided different answers. In the individualistic society of agricultural enterprise, the valued conception of individual self-sufficiency greatly restricted the social needs served in the general welfare; the laissez-faire doctrine of the early years of industrialization retained this same restricted view. It was not until the dependency-producing effects of industrialization became extreme that the general welfare embraced the concepts of physical and psychological security which we include today.

The effects of social legislation in altering and modifying the social structure have been many. Changes in the relationship among social classes, between employer and employee and between governed and governors, have resulted. The value system of American society has embraced some of the legislated changes in social behavior as experimental programs of social legislation have provided new values or demonstrated the dysfunctional effects of old values. No less responsive to legislated change have been the major social institutions. Government, economy, family, school, and church have struck a new equilibrium as their functions have been modified by social change and by the more deliberate changes wrought by social legislation. The role of the government has been greatly expanded as church and family have transferred functional prerogatives to secular control. Social legislation has also resulted in increased governmental activity

in the economy as the laissez-faire principle of a self-regulating economy toward which the government was to adopt a "hands-off" policy has proved inadequate for social and individual need satisfaction. These changes have not gone without critical comment from modern-day exponents of the *status quo*.

SELECTED REFERENCES

Bernard, L. L., *Social Control and Its Sociological Aspects*, New York, The Macmillan Company, 1939.

Chapin, F. Stuart, *Cultural Change*, New York, Century Company, 1928.

Lynd, Robert S., *Knowledge for What?*, Princeton, Princeton University Press, 1948.

MacIver, Robert M., *The Web of Government*, New York, The Macmillan Company, 1947.

Murdock, George Peter, *Social Organization*, New York, The Macmillan Company, 1949.

Parsons, Talcott, *The Structure of Social Action*, New York, McGraw-Hill Book Company, 1937.

Parsons, Talcott, *The Social System*, Glencoe, Ill., The Free Press, 1951.

chapter 20

Social Legislation and the Individual

We have previously described equilibrium in social life as a relationship which allows for the maximum exercise of human talents and creativeness consistent with maximum conditions of physical and mental health. This concept was introduced in connection with the relationship between the social framework and its human fabric. We raised the question as to whether man was equal to the demands which society makes of him. We suggested that deliberate legislation might enhance the personal and social equipment with which he meets demands. There is a certain urgency to this question because adjustment, the criterion of mental health, is dependent upon a comfortable relationship between individual needs and social conditions. Since setting forth the problem of man's resources as compared with his needs, we have examined a major portion of the social legislation American society has wrought in the belief that society and man are both perfectible. More recently, we have made additional inquiries into (1) the nature and the efficacy of the social planning that has been involved in these attempts at conscious social change, and (2) the impact of these changes on the social structure. Now we turn again to the fundamental issue of human resources and social demands to consider the consequences of social legislation for individual well-being. There are many dimensions of this question which we might consider: the effects of legislation on the utilization of human resources, changes in standards of health and nutrition, family stability, and many other areas. Our primary interest is the consequences of social legislation for mental health and individual well-being. We shall restrict our analysis to the two major areas—goal fulfillment and role behavior. Within the context of these processes, we shall deal with the relationship between individual goal fulfillment

and the sense of personal well-being, the effect of social legislation on goal fulfillment, and finally the role of legislation in redefining and regulating social roles.

Individual Goal Fulfillment and the Sense of Personal Well-Being

Each of us is interested in being well. The popularity of books and magazine articles, mail-order courses, and lectures on the attainment of physical and mental well-being testifies to the intensity of this interest in modern American society; but, even after reading the books or listening to the lectures, most of us would be hard-pressed to describe the state of being "well." When we become more specific, however, some of this difficulty disappears. When we speak of being physically well, we mean that we are not ill or that we are not suffering from physically injurious conditions such as disease, hunger, exposure, or fatigue. If we refer to mental well-being, we are a little less definite since we do not have such well-established criteria for the measurement of adequacy and satisfaction in subjective mental states. Still, we can say that if we are happy and are able to cope with the usual worries and problems, we are well off.

Two important elements enter into this measurement of well-being. First, there is a standard of adequacy against which we may compare our present condition. When we say that we are physically well, we have some criterion to furnish us with a point of origin. In the area of health, the criterion becomes simple. One is ill or injured or otherwise incapacitated in terms we use to denote physical ailments, or one is well. There are also degrees of being in between these polar conditions. A whole series of graduations exist to express degrees of being well or unwell. Such standards also exist in the area of mental health, but with somewhat less definiteness than in physical health.

A second important element in the determination of personal wellbeing is that of value orientation. Every social system establishes rather definite consensus concerning the relative desirability of certain conditions or states of being as compared with opposing ones. Thus, there is fairly common agreement in American society that it is desirable and pleasant to be happy, healthy, successful, or popular; while it is unpleasant and undesirable to be unhappy, ill, a failure, or unpopular. There are, of course, many areas of behavior where there is no such common agreement, but even here the perception of the condition or state of being is based upon values.

We might now define a sense of personal well-being as the result of the possession or acquisition of certain valued conditions or states of being in a quantity or of a quality deemed adequate. To put it another way, a sense of personal well-being results from the successful attainment of a goal or goals. As such, it is a result of goal fulfillment and has an important bearing on mental health.

GOAL FULFILLMENT

We can describe goal fulfillment as a process which begins when an actor is selectively oriented toward some object or future state of affairs and ends when he has successfully attained the desired goal. This description is, of course, solely in terms of the polar ends of the process, for there is much else that occurs between selective orientation and goal fulfillment. The orientation toward the goal is the result of a drive or mobilization of bodily energy which has its origin in biological and social stimuli. When the actor is under this stimulation, he may be said to be motivated or to have mobilized energy to be used in goal-oriented behavior.

Now motivation also connotes activity, for once a drive is activated it produces a restlessness or tension state in the individual which requires relief or removal. This is not to say that all drives are uncomfortable, but rather that, once established, the drive creates an energy potential which must be expended in some activity. Table tapping, floor thumping, hair twisting, and pencil chewing are all examples of dissipation of energy built up under tension. The pacing and too-frequent clock glancing of the commuter waiting for a late train are other examples of the displacement of energy potential blocked from goal-oriented expenditure. Such interferences caused by barriers or conditions which stand in the way of the goal fulfillment of motivated individuals are called frustrations.

FRUSTRATION AND MENTAL HEALTH

Frustrations have serious consequences on mental health and, as we shall see later, on individual efficiency as well. Since the blocking of any goal-oriented activity means that some need has been left unanswered, any situation which produces frustration causes an unpleasant emotional strain called stress. Because man has so many needs, he is constantly faced with frustrations and a certain amount of stress, but these are usually merely annoying. When frustration affects any of man's basic needs and threatens his "survival," his whole

conception of well-being is shattered and he becomes oriented to the blocking situation (or what he believes to be the blocking situation) in terms of threat. Other emotionally harmful conditions, such as a feeling of inadequacy, a loss of self-esteem, and feelings of insecurity, may result from the threat to the individual's ego. He becomes anxious and casts about for some relief from the new tensions caused by his anxiety. The many possible reactions—aggression, defense, withdrawal, and compromises such as sublimation—which may be induced in order to do away with the discomfort of security-shattering anxiety are the subject for mental-health treatises and are not of great importance here.[1] Suffice it to say that anxiety is personally harmful and socially dysfunctional and to be avoided.

One further point requires clarification before we may consider some of the important consequences of failure to provide opportunities for goal fulfillment. This has to do with the determination of what constitutes adequate need satisfaction, and thus defines adequate goal fulfillment.

CULTURE AND ADEQUACY OF SATISFACTION

In describing human behavior, we have depicted man as a bundle of capabilities and energy with a resource-using schedule to allocate the expenditure of these resources into action. Priorities are established in terms of the pressure of drives which impel man to action and of goals which provide ends for the action. The stimuli which prod man to act may be physiological, such as hunger pangs, or they may be culturally determined, as in the case of the success motive or "popularity." It is erroneous, however, to assume that the physiological drives of man are divorced from his culture and derive their satisfaction from sheer material implementation. For it is abundantly evident that even man's most basic needs are modified by the culture in which he seeks their satisfaction. The cultural variability which attends man's food-seeking behavior offers a convenient if overworked example. All men must eat, but they will eat different foods at different times of the day depending upon what their culture prescribes as diet and etiquette. Moreover, even the degree of satisfaction required

---

[1] The interested reader is referred to Sigmund Freud's "Morning and Melancholia," *The Collected Papers of Sigmund Freud*, London, Hogarth Press, 1934; and *A General Introduction to Psychoanalysis*, New York, Boni and Liveright, 1920, also available in Permabook form, New York, Doubleday and Company. A further source is John Dollard, Leonard Doob, and Neal Miller, *Frustration and Aggression*, New Haven, Yale University Press, 1939.

is to some extent culturally determined once the sheer needs of survival have been met.

If we accept the principle that culture determines levels of adequate need satisfaction, we may proceed to an important generalization concerning goal fulfillment and the individual's appraisal of his personal well-being. Threats to man's security may come from the inability or refusal of the socioeconomic system to satisfy his needs at the "survival plus" level which he has come to expect. Thus, insecurity, fear, feelings of inadequacy, and emotional stress may result which adversely affect his sense of personal gratification from energy expenditure.

Social Stress

We may further generalize that social conditions have an impact on the individual's sense of well-being to the extent that he views them as threats. Thus, unemployment may be interpreted quite differently by two employees both of whom have lost their jobs, but who differ significantly in their orientation to "unemployment." To one with adequate resources or some source of income security, loss of employment is interpreted in terms of deprivation and, while he may react hostilely and even with discomfort, the conditions does not involve threat or anxiety since he is assured that his needs and those of his family will be met. The reaction of a worker without resources and without any means of income security may be quite different. He perceives the loss of his job as jeopardizing the satisfaction of his needs and those of his family, and so the loss is more than deprivation to him and his orientation is one of threat. Fear, anxiety, stress, and feelings of inadequacy and insecurity are the wages of his threat orientation.

The importance of this generalization for any analysis of social legislation is clear. The provision of alternative means of need satisfaction by legislative action may also provide the means of replacing dysfunctional and harmful threat orientation with uncomfortable but less ego-involving deprivation. We shall pursue this point further in the next section, but first we must make a further generalization prior to applying these postulates to the analysis of legislation.

We have described stress as if it were entirely a product of failure to satisfy needs. This might give the impression that unless some basic biological drive is involved, stress will not occur. This is not the case. Individuals may be placed under stress by many situations, some

of which have little relation to biological needs. Leighton has supplied a convenient classification of specific types of stress which are disturbing to the emotions and thoughts of the individual:

1. Threats to life and health
2. Discomfort from pain, heat, cold, dampness, fatigue and poor food
3. Loss of means of subsistence, whether in the form of money, job, business or property
4. Deprivation of sexual satisfaction
5. Enforced idleness
6. Restriction of movement
7. Isolation
8. Threats to children, family members and friends
9. Rejection, dislike and ridicule from other people
10. Capricious and unpredictable behavior on the part of those in authority upon whom one's welfare depends

Furthermore:

The following general types of stress are derived from the more specific types, but are in themselves particularly disturbing to the emotions and thoughts of the individual:
1. Persistent frustration of goals, desires, needs, intentions and plans
2. Circumstances that promote the dilemma of conflicting and mutually incompatible desires and intentions
3. Circumstances creating confusion and uncertainty as to what is happening in the present and what can be expected in the future [2]

Scrutiny of this list of stress-provoking situations reveals the psychological or social origin of several. We are primarily interested in the last listed of the basic stress-provoking situations and in all three of the derived conditions.

These might be combined to state that "Stress will result when there is no regulation and hence no predictability in social relationships." Now, we have previously alluded to the chaos which would result from unbridled expression of individual drives. Rules, moral norms, laws, and institutions do more than regulate behavior; they provide a predictability which reduces the possibility of "capricious behavior," "conflicting intentions," and "confusion and uncertainty" in society. This final generalization produces another standard for the analysis of social legislation. In the previous chapter, we proposed the "orderly regulation of social relationships" as one of the functions of

[2] Alexander H. Leighton, *The Governing of Men*, Princeton, Princeton University Press, 1945, pp. 252, 260.

social legislation in the social system. This role of social legislation has an equally important contribution to individual behavior. If lack of predictability in social relations is a source of individual stress, then the degree to which social legislation has given predictability to social relations becomes a criterion of its social utility.

Goal Fulfillment in American Society

Poets, philosophers, and psychoanalysts have depicted modern industrial society as "an age of anxiety." [3] They are in agreement that urban-industrial culture has produced many of modern man's anxious attitudes toward himself and society. He is less secure, less self-reliant, and faced with infinitely more stress-provoking situations than were his agrarian predecessors. He has lost consciousness of his unity with his fellow man and has in many instances lost the sense of belonging which he once felt with his community, family, and work. As a result, he has become an isolate in a competitive society where he must constantly strive with others for scarce goals with the constant threat of failure and feelings of inadequacy. Many of the goals are synthetic contrivances of ad men and other guardians of the present order.

All of this has fairly obvious application to the questions we have raised in connection with goal fulfillment. Under conditions such as those described above, the individual is hard-pressed to maintain his sense of well-being. Isolated from his family and community, he is forced to strive for goals as an individual rather than as a member of a group. Intense competition makes goal-fulfilling experiences infrequent and individual self-esteem would be threatened. Such conditions are both individually harmful and socially dysfunctional. Social action to alleviate such conditions is one of the charges that has been placed on social legislation. We must ask: What has social legislation done to better man's lot in this age of anxiety? An examination of all of the laws aimed at reducing man's anxiety would be impossible. We can, however, consider the effects of the legislation which has been most directly involved in ameliorating anxiety, that which seeks to reduce income security. First, let us review what has already been said about stress and then turn to the questions of how modern man's security was destroyed and what social legislation did to restore it.

[3] See, for example, W. H. Auden, *The Age of Anxiety: A Baroque Eclogue*, New York, Random House, 1941; R. H. Tawney, *The Acquisitive Society*, New York, Harcourt, Brace and Company, 1921; Erich Fromm, *Escape From Freedom*, New York, Farrar and Rinehart, 1941; Karen Horney, *The Neurotic Personality of Our Time*, New York, W. W. Norton and Company, 1937; and Abram Kardiner, *The Psychological Frontiers of Society*, New York, Columbia University Press, 1945.

So far, we have seen that a sense of personal well-being, a necessary feature of adjustment and mental health, results from the attainment of goals to which one is oriented in the environment. When some obstacle stands in the way of the achievement of these goals, frustration results, a sense of well-being is lost, and mental health may be adversely affected. We have suggested that social legislation offers a means of reducing frustrations and accompanying stress by (1) providing for individual and collective welfare and so reducing the insecurity caused by inadequate need satisfaction, and (2) regulating social relations in such a way that there is a minimum of the stress that results from inability to anticipate the responses of other individuals and of the society to one's actions.

We may extend this analysis by adding another postulate to our growing list. How a person feels will determine what he thinks, how he acts, and how he utilizes the limited resources of energy he commands. Now, a large part of what we have already said was meant to demonstrate that one of the most important determinants of the feeling of well-being is a sense of security. We have previously said that survival is undoubtedly man's most elementary motive and that it is interpreted by individuals in terms of the satisfaction of their basic needs. We might even propose to define "basic" security as a feeling of relative certainty that one will continue to be able to satisfy his needs. It is the phrase "continue to be able" that furnishes us with the real meaning of "a sense of security." Perhaps an example will best illustrate the importance of continuity in need satisfaction. If an impoverished and hungry migrant worker receives a bowl of soup at a mission kitchen, we may say that his *immediate* need for food has been satisfied, and even add that there has been a reduction of tension because of removal of the immediate hunger drives; but unless he has been provided with some certainty (or at least a belief that such certainty exists) that his needs will be met tomorrow and the next day, we may not say that he has a sense of security. It is the certainty or belief that one's needs will continue to be met that produces the sense of security.

If we analyze the changes which have produced modern American society in terms of the corresponding change in certainty of need satisfaction, we shall gain further insight into the importance of social legislation for individual goal fulfillment. We mentioned in an earlier chapter that the chronic fear of unemployment is of relatively recent origin. There was, of course, intense fear, anxiety, and uncertainty in

agrarian society, but they were not characteristically related to un-employment. The threats which plagued the agrarian were natural phenomena over which neither he nor society had any control—drought, pestilence, fire, flood, and so on. He probably viewed these threats in much the same way we do today: as acts of God over which we have no control and from which society can do little to protect us.

He was also a member of a family which was both a social and an economic unit and which provided each of its members with security. Since he shared his home with his adult children, old age posed no survival problems or threats, for it merely meant that he would pass into a new status category and that his functional role in the family would be somewhat altered. Agrarian security, then, was family-oriented or group security.

Compared to his agricultural forebears, the modern industrial worker has considerably less reason to feel secure. Although industrial-ization has provided greater efficiency in producing goods and services, it has also produced a new form of threat to challenge his security and sense of well-being. As a wage earner, his security is dependent on the sale of his labor. The market-place character of such a relationship is well illustrated in Auden's poem, *The Age of Anxiety*, when a young man seeking a useful vocation is told by another character:

> . . . Well, you will soon
> Not bother but acknowledge yourself
> As market made, a commodity
> Whose value varies, a vendor who has
> To obey his buyer . . .[4]

Even after the modern worker obtains employment, there is always the fear that he will lose it as the result of depression, sickness, or other conditions over which he has no control. His need satisfaction is to a surprising extent a day-to-day affair, for his job represents the one source of the income he needs for survival. The loss of his job comes to represent a threat to his survival (and to his family's), and he feels secure only to the extent that his employment is secure.

Neither has he the security of the agrarian's strong and all-embracing family system. When he marries, he leaves home to establish his new family as a relatively independent unit. As the breadwinner, he is solely responsible for the need satisfaction of his dependent wife and children, and the loss of his job becomes even more damaging to his

[4] Auden, *op. cit.*, p. 42.

self-conception as he adds his loss of status as a breadwinner in the eyes of his family and the community to his own feelings of inadequacy. When his children marry, they will also strike out on their own and form new families. When he reaches old age, he has (in the absence of social legislation) none of the assurance of his agrarian ancestors that there will be a place for him in the family life of his children.

Threats to the modern wage earner may be described as immediate, personal, and man-made. Under stress by these threats, he has none of the group security of the agrarian simply because there is no longer any institution which can provide him with the feeling of "group belongingness" necessary. He faces life alone. His relationship with the socioeconomic milieu has been aptly described by Erich Fromm, who states that "certain factors in the modern industrial system in general and in its monopolistic phase in particular make for the development of a personality which feels powerless and alone, anxious and insecure." [5] Karen Horney has further characterized this feeling of aloneness and isolation in a competitive culture as the source of the basic anxiety of our time.[6] The serious consequences of such conditions to mental health and social well-being made some new source of security imperative.

Since we have spent a considerable portion of this volume in describing the growth and procedures of income-protection and public-assistance legislation, we need not recount the history of the gradual movement on the part of government to replace the wage earner's lost security with a new government-sponsored security. We would only add by way of summary that these government programs came about as a response of government to the inability of the family (and apparent refusal of the economy) to provide security for wage earners.

Concerning the success of these government programs, we must begin with a word of caution. Two serious problems are encountered by anyone who would attempt an objective analysis. First, there is the problem of values. As we shall see in a few moments, not everyone is in agreement that income security is a valuable thing. Obviously, one's view concerning the social and individual value of income security will greatly affect his appraisal, unless some objective standard of measurement is found.

The second problem has to do with the frame of reference within

[5] Fromm, *op. cit.*, p. 240.
[6] Horney, *op. cit.*, p. 286.

which the measurement is made. There are two dimensions of success involved. First, there is the question of the success of the program when viewed in terms of its objective. The question here is: Has the program provided the *means for promoting* a feeling of security in the wage earner? Measurement here is relatively precise. Adopting the standard we proposed earlier, we may say that the income-protection and public-assistance programs have provided at least the essentials for individual security. The social-insurance programs supply alternative sources of income for the jobless or superannuated worker; social-assistance programs have provided protection for parents whose children cannot (or will not) support them and for those disabled through blindness and certain other diseases. The value of these programs is also in that they present to the worker a potential alternative source of income should he be unable to work. Thus, knowledge that if one loses his job he may receive unemployment compensation can have a depressive effect on the individual's threat orientation to unemployment.

There is a second area of measurement, however, where any evaluation of the effectiveness of social legislation on individuals becomes almost entirely speculative. In terms of our present problem, an important question is: Have income-protection and public-assistance laws actually succeeded in producing a *feeling of security* in the worker? The subjective nature of such a measurement makes any objective evaluation difficult. The difficulties do not stop there, for there are certain other problems involved.

RESENTMENT

Money means different things to different people. To one person, it may be a symbol of status; to another, it may represent only purchasing power. Equally variable is the reaction which individuals show to being given public-assistance or social-insurance benefits. Combined, these present the problem of the attitude which the recipient or beneficiary will take toward assistance or benefits. For convenience, we shall restrict our discussion to assistance recipients, since the unsettled nature of our value orientation toward assistance allows for a wider range of behavior.

If security were simply a matter of meeting basic needs, it would matter little where the objects used to satisfy the need came from, but earlier we saw that basic drives are affected by culture and that there is a cultural dimension to survival. If, therefore, the need satisfaction

is not culturally satisfying, security is not obtained. An example might serve to illustrate this point. If a wage earner loses his job because of technological unemployment and remains idle for a considerable period of time, he may require public assistance. We shall assume that he is eligible for and begins to receive a grant. If his attitude toward public assistance has been structured in such a way that he considers this assistance as "a dole" or as a sign of feministic dependency, his receipt of assistance may actually injure rather than improve his feelings of security. He may feel inadequate and helpless. Requiring assistance and yet threatened by its receipt, he may become inwardly resentful and this resentment may in itself cause further anxiety. Harry Stack Sullivan described the stress-provoking effects of resentment:

> I said years ago that if one swallows much resentment it will ruin one's belly; there are few better established hypotheses than that which sees in unrecognized recurring resentment the prime factor in troubles from the stomach onward in the alimentary canal. Resentment itself often if not always includes anxiety in its composition.[7]

ATTITUDES

There is the further problem of the public attitude toward the receipt of assistance and insurance benefits. We have said elsewhere that there is a greater acceptance of the principle of social insurance, with its concept of individual initiative in providing for one's own needs in advance, than of social assistance, which is considered by many to be, at best, a necessary evil. Our point here is that two factors—the individual's conception of the morality and "manliness" of receiving assistance and his perception of what the community at large thinks about it—govern his attitude toward assistance. If he conceives or perceives that what he is doing is somehow wrong, there can be important consequences for mental health.

MOTIVATION

A final problem related to the measurement of subjective security provided by legislation concerns motivation. Briefly, the issues are these. There seem to be two persistent beliefs concerning income-security programs and motivation. One holds that most people who require assistance are somehow "evilly" motivated by laziness, avarice,

---

[7] Harry Stack Sullivan, "The Meaning of Anxiety in Psychiatry and Life," *Proceedings on the Occasion of the First William Alanson White Memorial Fund*, New York, William Alanson White Institute, 1948, p. 12.

and so forth, and that they are on the "dole" because they would rather sit idly at home and let others work. The second proposition concerning income security is that if we make life too secure, we shall remove the valuable motive force of fear from the socioeconomic system. Let us examine each of these propositions in terms of their accuracy in motivation theory.

We need only return to our discussion of the basis of motivation to see the error of the first proposition. We characterized motivation as activity and said that the individual is impelled to action when he is motivated because there is a tension produced by energy mobilization. This energy requires expenditure, and if it is not used in goal-oriented behavior it will be dissipated in other directions. Thus activity, not passivity, is the condition of being motivated. Furthermore, there is abundant scientific evidence that work represents more than a means of obtaining need-satisfying objects to most individuals.[8] Long-enforced periods of idleness are frustrating since energy potential from biological and social stimulation maintains a level of tension which requires some activity for dissipation. Finally, there is a strong emphasis upon "achievement" and "success" in American society, which places a premium on "doing," and an individual's value is largely measured by whether and *how* he has achieved symbols which mark the path of success. We do not suggest that there is no such things as "lack of industry" or that all individuals are equally motivated toward work. Our point is rather that under normal conditions, most individuals would rather work (expend energy) than be subjected to the frustration of prolonged idleness.

Nor will the second proposition, which pictures fear as the primary motive force in industriousness and efficiency, stand the test of scientific scrutiny. It errs in two important directions: (1) it confuses "fear" with "anxiety," and (2) there is a misunderstanding concerning the normal reactions to fear and anxiety.

Fear and anxiety are very much alike; both involve apprehension and both are disturbing to the individual. They differ in a significant way. Fear is directional, one is afraid of *something* and his fear is attached to the object which aroused the apprehension. Thus we are afraid of the dark, the ocean, the lightning, or high places. Anxiety, however, is nondirectional, or perhaps we should say that it is multi-

---

[8] See, for example, Abram Kardiner, *The Individual and His Society*, New York, Columbia University Press, 1939; E. Wight Bakke, *Citizens Without Work*, New Haven, Yale University Press, 1940; and Edith Abbott, "People Prefer to Work," *Social Service Review*, March, 1944.

directional, for it is a general "free-floating" fear. The individual is afraid, but he does not know what frightens him. Thus, while he is afraid of "nothing," he is afraid of everything and has a "feeling of impending doom."

Returning to the proposition, we quickly observe that what is called "fear" in this proposition is actually "anxiety." The worker whose security has been destroyed by social change and for whom the laissez-faire economy would do nothing is not afraid of any one object or state. Rather, he is suspended in a state of objectless fear, generally apprehensive, frequently depressed and dejected. The scientific literature concerning his "efficiency" and "industry" while in an anxious state is vast but conclusive. Individuals under anxiety have neither efficiency nor industry when these are defined in terms of realistic goals, for one of the most common characteristics of the anxious person is the expenditure of energy into some mechanism or defense against the uncomfortable anxiety.

The proposition also suggests that the worker, when he is kept insecure, becomes "aggressive" since he must then compete more actively for the scarce goals. Aggression, as popularly and psychologically construed, is quite different. When we describe a salesman as "aggressive," we are really saying that he has initiative and enterprise. It is goal-oriented behavior. This is, of course, the aggression which the exponents of laissez faire wanted in the socioeconomic system; but as Freud and later behavioral scientists have described the aggression which results from frustration, it is the result of blocked goal-oriented behavior and can have serious consequences for individual and social well-being. Once aggression is aroused through frustration, it must, like all mobilized energy, be used. Logically, it should be used against the blocking situation, but under stress the individual seldom reacts with logic. The energy of the aggression may be expended in the form of *regression*, or a symbolic return to an earlier level of satisfaction; *fixation*, or failure to outgrow a satisfying level of behavior; *redirection*, or displacing the aggression from the blocking situation to some third person or object; and finally, *self-direction*, or the displacement of the aggression back toward oneself.

Each of these forms of aggression displacement is found in society in relation to need satisfaction. Racial and religious prejudices and intergroup conflict are increased as insecurity leads to a search for a scapegoat; most social workers have at one time or another observed

the emergence of "childish" behavior in a client whose needs are seriously threatened; and we have previously exemplified the self-castigating, threatened individual who feels a personal inadequacy and inferiority.

The meaning for social legislation is clear: the optimum conditions of personal and social well-being demand a culturally adequate level of need satisfaction. There is abundant evidence that if these conditions are not met, mental and physical health are endangered and inefficiency results.

CHANGING ROLES VIA SOCIAL LEGISLATION

One important function of social legislation remains: the redefinition of roles which guide the behavior of the members of the social system. It is this system of roles which gives predictability and hence security to social life. Just one brief example will describe the role of social legislation in ensuring social regulation and predictability.

As social relationships are altered and relative placement of individuals changes, the content of the roles they must play undergoes constant revision. When social change is rapid, the consequent readjustment of roles may be confusing to the actor and may produce frustration, anxiety, and inefficiency. If, on the other hand, roles are held static and no longer fit the existing socioeconomic milieu, the dangers to individual personality development and to society are equally grave. This first situation is well portrayed in Arnold Green's analysis of the factors making for neurosis in the modern middle-class American family.[9] Each member of the family is required to play contradictory roles. The father's affectional obligations toward the child and the necessary expenditure of time, money, and effort in caring for the child conflict with his role as a businessman seeking success and status. The mother's role as a housewife requires behavior which is no longer valued in the new conception of the wife as a companion. Finally, the child is faced with the conflicting role demands of meek and humble acquiescence to his parents while he is constantly enjoined to become an aggressive and independent personality in a competitive society. In each of these role conflicts there is an element of conflicting values and norms as the traditional roles in family relationships have slowly given way to the new ideals of the urban-industrial family.

[9] Arnold W. Green, "The Middle-Class Child and Neurosis," *American Sociological Review*, February, 1946, pp. 31–41.

Examples of roles held constant in the face of social change are also common. The traditional conception of the role of the adolescent in American society furnishes a timely and well-known example. Despite the many and significant changes which have taken place in our youth culture over the past few generations, we still expect the attributes of filial devotion, submission, and dependence which we attach to the role of the adolescent to be fulfilled. Exposed to the maturity-provoking effects of multigroup contacts and the mass media of communication and to societal pressures toward self-expression and independence, the confused and bewildered adolescent can only seek escape in adverse and often openly hostile behavior. This produces further conflict and widens the gap between parental expectations and adolescent behavior.

Social legislation provides the means for adjusting social roles to the existing socioeconomic order. We have previously discussed the changes which have been effected in the role of the father through the intervention of the state in the marital and parent-child relationship. The role of the father as the dominant member of the family vested with almost complete authority over his wife and children has been altered as their economic dependence has declined. Many sociocultural factors have led to this decline, but the chief instrument has been legislation protecting and increasing the rights of his wife and children. In Chapters 7 and 8, we traced the development of some of this legislation; the equalization of the rights of the mother to the custody and control of her children, the enactment of child-welfare laws, provisions for the institution of divorce actions by the wife as well as the husband, and support laws are only a few of the many examples. Legislative programs for the protection of wage earners and their families and for the amelioration of the economically distressed, the dependent, and the aged have also had profound effects in changing social roles.

Social Legislation and the Individual: Concluding Remarks

We have described the state of equilibrium between man and his society as a relationship which allows the maximum exercise of his talents and capabilities consistent with maximum conditions of physical and mental well-being. The achievement of this relationship is a basic function of social legislation.

When the biosocial individual first comes into contact with his society, it is as a bundle of energy which is often randomly expended.

As he grows and learns in the socialization process, he comes to control these energies and establishes a resource-using schedule. No longer randomly expended, the energies are now directed to certain definite ends which result from both biological and cultural definition as valuable.

Once this resource-using schedule has been established, the individual reacts to any interruption in the schedule with discomfort and displeasure. If he has been motivated to seek out some object in the environment, he builds up his energies in that direction, and any object, person, or situation which blocks his path to the goal causes further discomfort. In short, he becomes frustrated.

If the object he is seeking represents the satisfaction of some basic need, then any block becomes even more disturbing since his survival is now threatened. He views the blocking situation as a threat and, under the stress of the frustration he feels, may develop anxiety or objectless fear toward that object.

If our imaginary and anxious example is continually faced with frustrations of his basic drives, he develops a characteristic orientation toward his social and personal world, which is best described as "a sense of insecurity." He has no certainty that his needs are going to be met. A rational and intelligent animal, he can see the discomfort ahead of him as a result of the interruption of need satisfaction. His insecurity is then even greater.

If this uncertainty becomes chronic, he may feel a deepening sense of social rejection and disapproval; for he has come to believe that since society provides for its own, he must be an outcast. Added to this feeling of societal rejection is the feeling that his family and neighbors no longer look up to him, and he feels a loss of social status.

All of this is damaging to his sense of personal well-being, and the adjustment which he has worked out between his own needs and society's demands becomes inadequate. He is no longer adjusted to his social world and his mental health is adversely affected.

This brief excursion into the personal and social disorganization which results from inadequate need satisfaction is intended to develop two principles: (1) social legislation is a means of providing the "sense of security" which comes from the knowledge of subsistence (income) security; (2) it further serves the individual by providing a predictability to behavior. From there it follows that social legislation serves as the means whereby social planning can create a society-individual equilibrium that serves the welfare and happiness of both.

SELECTED REFERENCES

Dollard, John; Doob, Leonard; and Miller, Neal, *Frustration and Aggression*, New Haven, Yale University Press, 1939.

Horney, Karen, *The Neurotic Personality of Our Time*, New York, W. W. Norton and Company, 1937.

Freud, Sigmund, *A General Introduction to Psychoanalysis*, New York, Boni and Liveright, 1920.

Fromm, Erich, *Escape from Freedom*, New York, Farrar and Rinehart, 1941.

Symonds, P. M., *The Dynamics of Human Adjustment*, New York, D. Appleton-Century Company, 1946.

chapter **21**

Future Directions of Social Legislation

The brief analysis to be included in this chapter is not concerned with predicting future trends of social legislation. It is rather an attempt to point up those forces and eventualities which will have an effect on the course of legislative action. In the past, the role of crises in sparking accomplishments in social legislation has been paramount. There is no good reason to believe that we would have the limited legislation presently in operation but for the advent of the Great Depression and an administration which was willing to experiment in social planning. And the present limits are widely interpreted as excessive or as maxima beyond which further legislation need not or ought not to go. In the postwar period, sentiment to scale down welfare functions within the federal government has had powerful and influential support. Beyond the legitimate issues which might be debated in the area of social legislation, there has come into operation another obstacle extraneous to the legitimate issues. This is the manipulation of fear and the deliberate pairing of advocacy of change with treasonous purposes as an agency of world communism. In what measure social legislation is a casualty of that cultivated disrespect and suspicion of heterodoxy it is difficult to say. One thing is clear: the safe position for those who would make their way in the present context of American culture is enthusiastic acceptance of the *status quo.* Such a value system cannot fail to register its effect on those who otherwise would champion the liberal strain in American social thought that runs back to Jefferson.

In specific areas of social legislation, some observations are to be made. Family legislation is bound to be affected by the cross-fertilization which is gradually occurring between law and the social sciences. The blame aspect of divorce may be affected by this tend-

ency, not through changes in the law, but through changes in judicial interpretation. In the future, an enlightened attitude may produce a therapeutic role in the courts which will be a logical culmination of the sociology of jurisprudence that Roscoe Pound spelled out so well. Labor legislation has run a rough course in the postwar period, and the fundamental trend is not at all clear. Restrictive legislation on unions has been imposed and removed, only to leave the situation largely unchanged on a net basis. Certainly, the level of economic activity and the achievement of continued full employment will be of basic importance in determining the character of future legislation. The terrible cost of strikes requires that some workable solution to industrial conflict be found, and there is reason to believe that we shall seek solutions in legal prohibitions and proscriptions—ignoring the fundamental bases of peaceful coexistence in labor-management relations. A danger which lurks on the horizon is thought to present the greatest threat because it is not recognized as dangerous. That is labor-management coöperation. It is frequently held that if labor and management could just see eye to eye, we should be able to establish a greater harmony. Unquestionably this is true; but the "new harmony" could be distasteful if it were achieved at the expense of unorganized groups such as consumers. Experience in some areas—Seattle, Washington, with coöperation engineered by the Teamsters Union and its employer confederates, for example—has cast suspicion on the merit of coöperation between labor and management without qualifications as to the objectives which such coöperation seeks to fulfill.

Social-insurance and social-assistance legislation faces forces not very different from labor legislation in the future. The trend of the economy in economic performance will obviously be a factor. It is unlikely that we shall decide to abandon the preference which we have for contributory programs of insurance, and the principle may be extended to workmen's compensation and unemployment insurance with good effects. Health insurance on a compulsory basis is difficult to evaluate. The 74th Congress found that even a mild reinsurance program for existing group-insurance programs was unpalatable. Given that kind of sentiment, we shall be a long time making up for the seveny-five-year lag which we presently have in comparison with programs of insurance on the European Continent.

Planning for social consequences is so sensitive a point at the present time that the mildest suggestions are decried on all counts exclusive of their merits. Cultural values antagonistic to central authority,

combined with the present enthusiasm for removing "government" from business, augur a dismal future for even the present ventures in this area. The Tennessee Valley Authority, for example, which is acclaimed the world over as an example of what intelligent planning can accomplish, is presently accepted with shame by the administration and the Authority must fight for its life. The extension of its methods to other valleys—the Missouri, for example—is vigorously opposed by traditional opponents of social legislation because it would "bring socialism in by the back door." Meanwhile, the unbridled rivers carry people and topsoil to the sea in an annual rampage and the vast energy potential remains unexploited.

Throughout this volume, the reader will have realized that education for specific achievements is an answer to many questionable aspects of social legislation. If people presently abuse unemployment-insurance benefits, it is high time that the school systems orient their programs to the inculcation of values which would prevent such behaviors. The same is no less true of the homes of the nation. If people would be distraught over the failure of a more fully planned economy than we now have to respond to their separate idiosyncrasies, then we should spread somewhat more widely the principles of consumer buymanship and point out the costs of present adjustment in an economy left to its own devices. The point is clear: there is no insuperable barrier to the employment of knowledge to make certain that goals upon which we can all agree are achieved.

combined with the present enthusiasm for removing "government" from business, augur a dismal future for even the present ventures in this area. The Tennessee Valley Authority, for example, which is ac- claimed the world over as an example of what intelligent planning can accomplish, is presently accepted with shame by the administration and the Authority must fight for its life. The extension of its methods to other valleys—the Missouri, for example—is vigorously opposed by traditional opponents of social legislation because it would "bring socialism in by the back door." Meanwhile, the unbridled rivers carry people and topsoil to the sea in an annual rampage and the vast energy potential remains unexploited.

Throughout this volume, the reader will have realized that educa- tion for specific achievements is an answer to many questionable aspects of social legislation. If people presently abuse unemployment- insurance benefits, it is high time that the school systems orient their programs to the inculcation of values which would prevent such be- haviors. The same is no less true of the homes of the nation. If people would be distraught over the failure of a more fully planned economy than we now have to respond to their separate idiosyncrasies, then we should spread somewhat more widely the principles of consumer buymanship and point out the perils of present adjustment in an economy left to its own devices. The point is clear: there is no in- superable barrier to the employment of knowledge to make certain that goals upon which we can all agree are achieved.

APPENDIX

APPENDIX. Detailed Occupation of the Experienced Civilian Labor Force, 1950 Census

Detailed Occupation	Total
Total, 14 years old and over	58,998,943
Professional, Technical, and Kindred Workers	4,988,012
Accountants and auditors	383,676
Actors and actresses	18,453
Airplane pilots and navigators	14,191
Architects	25,000
Artists and art teachers	80,535
Athletes	12,389
Authors	16,184
Chemists	75,747
Chiropractors	13,084
Clergymen	168,419
College presidents, professors, and instructors (n.e.c.) [a]	125,583
Dancers and dancing teachers	17,239
Dentists	75,025
Designers	40,108
Dietitians and nutritionists	22,826
Draftsmen	124,749
Editors and reporters	91,472
Engineers, technical	534,424
Entertainers (n.e.c.)	16,311
Farm and home management advisers	12,316
Foresters and conservationists	27,052
Funeral directors and embalmers	39,914
Lawyers and judges	181,226
Librarians	55,750
Musicians and music teachers	161,307
Natural scientists (n.e.c.)	40,698
Nurses, professional	403,793
Nurses, student professional	76,671
Optometrists	14,711
Osteopaths	5,167
Personnel and labor relations workers	52,858
Pharmacists	88,998
Photographers	54,734
Physicians and surgeons	192,317
Radio operators	16,421

[a] Not elsewhere classified.

Recreation and group workers	16,799
Religious workers	41,698
Social and welfare workers, except group	76,467
Social scientists	35,893
Sports instructors and officials	45,823
Surveyors	26,229
Teachers (n.e.c.)	1,127,845
Technicians, medical and dental	78,033
Technicians, testing	76,962
Technicians (n.e.c.)	27,471
Therapists and healers (n.e.c.)	24,864
Veterinarians	13,489
Professional, technical, and kindred workers (n.e.c.)	117,091
Farmers and Farm Managers	4,320,576
Farmers (owners and tenants)	4,285,462
Farm managers	35,114
Managers, Officials, and Proprietors, Except Farm	5,076,436
Buyers and department heads, store	144,566
Buyers and shippers, farm products	28,809
Conductors, railroad	56,036
Credit men	33,326
Floormen and floor managers, store	11,051
Inspectors, public administration	56,807
Managers and superintendents, building	66,620
Officers, pilots, pursers, and engineers, ship	41,387
Officials and administrators (n.e.c.), public administration	155,303
Officials, lodge, society, union, etc.	27,060
Postmasters	38,831
Purchasing agents and buyers (n.e.c.)	64,147
Managers, officials, and proprietors (n.e.c.), salaried	1,811,448
Construction	88,164
Manufacturing	416,443
Transportation	96,683
Telecommunications, and utilities and sanitary services	61,564
Wholesale trade	158,749
Retail trade	521,373
Food and dairy products stores, and milk retailing	103,039
General merchandise and five-and-ten-cent stores	60,165
Apparel and accessories stores	42,530
Furniture, home furnishings, and equipment stores	27,820
Motor vehicles and accessories retailing	57,015
Gasoline service stations	36,058
Eating and drinking places	70,991

Hardware, farm implement, and building material, retail	43,901
Other retail trade	79,854
Banking and other finance	119,264
Insurance and real estate	70,429
Business services	28,162
Automobile repair services and garages	24,045
Miscellaneous repair services	4,374
Personal services	66,688
All other industries (incl. not reported)	155,510
Managers, officials, and proprietors (n.e.c.), self-employed	2,541,045
Construction	203,087
Manufacturing	239,138
Transportation	51,926
Telecommunications, and utilities and sanitary services	5,782
Wholesale trade	179,404
Retail trade	1,426,316
Food and dairy products stores, and milk retailing	401,110
General merchandise and five-and-ten-cent stores	65,531
Apparel and accessories stores	85,209
Furniture, home furnishings, and equipment stores	68,538
Motor vehicles and accessories retailing	60,118
Gasoline service stations	147,763
Eating and drinking places	292,640
Hardware, farm implement, and building material, retail	85,201
Other retail trade	220,206
Banking and other finance	21,995
Insurance and real estate	45,019
Business services	34,101
Automobile repair services and garages	60,458
Miscellaneous repair services	29,806
Personal services	145,380
All other industries (incl. not reported)	98,633
Clerical and Kindred Workers	7,070,023
Agents (n.e.c.)	126,085
Attendants and assistants, library	12,674
Attendants, physician's and dentist's office	41,880
Baggagemen, transportation	8,101
Bank tellers	64,497
Bookkeepers	736,097
Cashiers	234,335
Collectors, bill and account	23,953
Dispatchers and starters, vehicle	31,508
Express messengers and railway mail clerks	18,881

Mail carriers	167,880
Messengers and office boys	58,813
Office machine operators	145,943
Shipping and receiving clerks	297,125
Stenographers, typists, and secretaries	1,621,863
Telegraph messengers	8,038
Telephone operators	365,708
Ticket, station, and express agents	59,895
Clerical and kindred workers (n.e.c.)	3,011,832
Sales Workers	4,044,143
Advertising agents and salesmen	33,734
Auctioneers	5,453
Demonstrators	14,003
Hucksters and peddlers	23,197
Insurance agents and brokers	307,442
Newsboys	99,222
Real-estate agents and brokers	142,564
Stock and bond salesmen	11,257
Salesmen and sales clerks (n.e.c.)	3,407,271
Manufacturing	326,846
Wholesale trade	414,588
Retail trade	2,530,545
Other industries (incl. not reported)	135,292
Craftsmen, Foremen, and Kindred Workers	8,152,743
Bakers	124,833
Blacksmiths	45,132
Boilermakers	38,896
Bookbinders	32,393
Brickmasons, stonemasons, and tile setters	175,828
Cabinetmakers	76,421
Carpenters	985,443
Cement and concrete finishers	32,653
Compositors and typesetters	178,696
Cranemen, derrickmen, and hoistmen	106,864
Decorators and window dressers	45,029
Electricians	324,046
Electrotypers and stereotypers	11,941
Engravers, except photoengravers	10,039
Excavating, grading, and road machinery operators	111,026
Foremen (n.e.c.)	853,448
Construction	60,439
Manufacturing	516,662
Metal industries	83,985

Machinery, including electrical	80,808
Transportation equipment	50,531
Other durable goods	76,510
Textiles, textile products, and apparel	70,274
Other nondurable goods (incl. not specified by mfgr.)	154,554
Railroads and railway express service	54,169
Transportation, except railroad	20,020
Telecommunications, and utilities and sanitary services	40,378
Other industries (incl. not reported)	161,780
Foremen and hammermen	13,631
Furriers	12,888
Glaziers	10,665
Heat treaters, annealers, and temperers	18,296
Inspectors, scalers, and graders, log and lumber	17,851
Inspectors (n.e.c.)	97,300
Construction	8,272
Railroads and railway express service	37,000
Transport, except railroad communication and other public utilities	12,598
Other industries (incl. not reported)	39,430
Jewelers, watchmakers, goldsmiths, and silversmiths	47,804
Job setters, metal	25,015
Linemen and servicemen, telegraph, telephone and power	215,948
Locomotive engineers	73,306
Locomotive firemen	56,032
Loom fixers	30,969
Machinists	533,726
Mechanics and repairmen	1,767,618
Airplane	73,720
Automobile	677,569
Office machine	16,289
Radio and television	78,259
Railroad and car shop	48,339
Not elsewhere classified	873,442
Millers, grain, flour, feed, etc.	9,777
Millwrights	60,193
Molders, metal	63,567
Motion picture projectionists	26,567
Opticians, and lens grinders and polishers	19,814
Painters, construction and maintenance	431,109
Paperhangers	22,536
Pattern and model makers, except paper	37,338
Photoengravers and lithographers	28,991

Piano and organ tuners and repairmen	7,989
Plasterers	64,351
Plumbers and pipe fitters	295,990
Pressmen and plate printers, printing	50,238
Rollers and roll hands, metal	31,016
Roofers and slaters	48,528
Shoemakers and repairers, except factory	58,909
Stationary engineers	218,146
Stone cutters and stone carvers	9,073
Structural metal workers	55,133
Tailors and tailoresses	85,945
Tinsmiths, coppersmiths, and sheet-metal workers	129,639
Toolmakers, and die makers and setters	156,992
Upholsterers	63,787
Craftsmen and kindred workers (n.e.c.)	74,052
Members of the armed forces	29,326
Operatives and Kindred Workers	11,715,606
Apprentices	119,848
Auto mechanics	3,879
Bricklayers and masons	6,471
Carpenters	10,753
Electricians	9,194
Machinists and toolmakers	15,704
Mechanics, except auto	6,539
Plumbers and pipe fitters	12,373
Building trades (n.e.c.)	4,254
Metalworking trades (n.e.c.)	6,848
Printing trades	15,569
Other specified trades	13,124
Trade not specified	15,140
Asbestos and insulation workers	16,425
Attendants, auto service and parking	247,420
Blasters and powdermen	11,485
Boatmen, canalmen, and lock keepers	8,450
Brakemen, railroad	80,522
Bus drivers	157,222
Chainmen, rodmen, and axmen, surveying	7,397
Conductors, bus and street railway	11,439
Deliverymen and routemen	247,403
Dressmakers and seamstresses, except factory	142,680
Dyers	25,389
Filers, grinders, and polishers, metal	155,701
Fruit, nut, and vegetable graders and packers, except factory	34,369

Furnacemen, smeltermen, and pourers	57,547
Heaters, metal	9,679
Laundry and dry-cleaning operatives	448,636
Meat cutters, except slaughter and packing house	176,315
Milliners	12,858
Mine operatives and laborers (n.e.c.)	604,583
Coal mining	381,209
Crude petroleum and natural-gas extraction	108,317
Mining and quarrying, except fuel	115,057
Motormen, street, subway, and elevated railway	26,795
Motormen, mine, factory, logging camp, etc.	24,322
Oilers and greasers, except auto	61,461
Painters, except construction and maintenance	122,833
Photographic process workers	29,289
Power station operators	21,613
Sailors and deck hands	51,109
Sawyers	97,614
Spinners, textile	84,946
Stationary firemen	126,806
Switchmen, railroad	62,146
Taxicab drivers and chauffeurs	212,422
Truck and tractor drivers	1,396,594
Weavers, textile	102,624
Welders and flame-cutters	275,545
Operatives and kindred workers (n.e.c.)	6,444,119
Manufacturing	5,686,303
Durable goods	2,525,737
Furniture and fixtures	129,125
Stone, clay, and glass products	188,309
Metal industries	545,742
Primary metal industries	267,914
Fabricated-metal industries (incl. unspecified metal)	277,828
Machinery, except electrical	356,694
Electrical machinery, equipment, and supplies	347,188
Transportation equipment	458,185
Motor vehicles and motor vehicle equipment	359,699
Aircraft and parts	65,607
Ship and boat building and repairing	14,772
Railroad and misc. transportation equipment	18,107
Professional and photographic equipment and watches	78,431
Miscellaneous manufacturing industries	229,155
Nondurable goods	3,119,098
Food and kindred products	530,883

Tobacco manufacturers	67,603
Textile-mill products	694,998
Knitting mills	150,391
Dyeing and finishing textiles, except knit goods	25,208
Carpets, rugs, and other floor coverings	25,157
Yarn, thread, and fabric mills	463,390
Miscellaneous textile-mill products	30,852
Apparel and other textile products	855,210
Apparel and accessories	798,580
Miscellaneous fabricated textile products	56,630
Paper and allied products	225,490
Printing, publishing, and allied industries	78,276
Chemicals and allied products	189,913
Synthetic fibers	26,427
Drugs and medicines	14,752
Paints, varnishes, and related products	18,046
Miscellaneous chemicals and allied products	130,688
Petroleum and coal products	53,739
Petroleum refining	47,086
Miscellaneous petroleum and coal products	6,653
Rubber products	123,586
Leather and leather products	299,400
Leather, tanned, curried, and finished	30,820
Footwear, except rubber	219,962
Leather products, except footwear	48,618
Not specified manufacturing industries	41,468
Nonmanufacturing industries (incl. not reported)	757,816
Construction	69,233
Railroads and railway express service	93,979
Transportation, except railroad	36,211
Telecommunications, and utilities and sanitary services	51,212
Wholesale and retail trade	301,860
Business and repair services	52,411
Personal services	21,051
Public administration	52,492
All other industries (incl. not reported)	79,367
Private Household Workers	1,487,574
Housekeepers, private household	145,453
Living in	52,755
Living out	92,698
Laundresses, private household	73,485
Living in	643
Living out	72,842

Private household workers (n.e.c.)	1,268,636
Living in	162,142
Living out	1,106,494
Service Workers, Except Private Household	4,511,996
Attendants, hospital and other institution	210,756
Attendants, professional and personal service (n.e.c.)	50,081
Attendants, recreation and amusement	64,206
Barbers, beauticians, and manicurists	388,806
Bartenders	207,836
Boarding and lodging house keepers	29,190
Bootblacks	14,794
Charwomen and cleaners	124,336
Cooks, except private household	463,234
Counter and fountain workers	92,939
Elevator operators	94,167
Firemen, fire protection	110,773
Guards, watchmen, and doorkeepers	248,979
Housekeepers and stewards, except private household	108,971
Janitors and sextons	471,750
Marshals and constables	6,581
Midwives	1,794
Policemen and detectives	194,313
Government	173,672
Private	20,641
Porters	173,784
Practical nurses	144,240
Sheriffs and bailiffs	18,710
Ushers, recreation and amusement	25,185
Waiters and waitresses	713,112
Watchmen (crossing) and bridge tenders	11,717
Service workers, except private household (n.e.c.)	541,743
Farm Laborers and Foremen	2,514,780
Farm foremen	17,143
Farm laborers, wage workers	1,569,106
Farm laborers, unpaid family workers	918,904
Farm service laborers, self-employed	9,627
Laborers, Except Farm and Mine	3,750,990
Fishermen and oystermen	72,428
Garage laborers and car washers and greasers	70,154
Gardeners, except farm and groundskeepers	155,003
Longshoremen and stevedores	69,822
Lumbermen, raftsmen, and wood choppers	188,972
Teamsters	22,254

Laborers (n.e.c.)	3,172,357
Manufacturing	1,172,981
Durable goods	734,353
Sawmills, planing mills, and misc. wood products	165,503
Sawmills, planing mills, and mill work	147,947
Miscellaneous wood products	17,556
Furniture and fixtures	20,918
Stone, clay, and glass products	82,052
Metal industries	281,635
Primary metal industries	221,068
Fabricated-metal industries (incl. unspecified metal)	60,567
Machinery, except electrical	56,392
Electrical machinery, equipment, and supplies	31,655
Transportation equipment	74,702
Motor vehicles and motor vehicle equipment	49,775
Aircraft and parts	3,842
Ship and boat building and repairing	15,205
Railroad and misc. transportation equipment	5,880
Professional and photographic equipment and watches	4,594
Nondurable goods	427,918
Food and kindred products	155,733
Tobacco manufactures	9,191
Textile-mill products	63,919
Knitting mills	2,967
Dyeing and finishing textiles, except knit goods	3,144
Carpets, rugs, and other floor coverings	5,938
Yarn, thread, and fabric mills	48,145
Miscellaneous textile-mill products	3,725
Apparel and other fabricated textile products	11,255
Apparel and accessories	8,541
Miscellaneous fabricated textile products	2,714
Paper and allied products	46,273
Printing, publishing, and allied industries	11,738
Chemicals and allied products	67,213
Synthetic fibers	3,239
Drugs and medicines	1,954
Paints, varnishes, and related products	4,777
Miscellaneous chemicals and allied products	57,243
Petroleum and coal products	30,682
Petroleum refining	24,728
Miscellaneous petroleum and coal products	5,954
Rubber products	16,962
Leather and leather products	14,952

Leather, tanned, curried, and finished	7,236
Footwear, except rubber	5,706
Leather products, except footwear	2,010
Not specified manufacturing industries	10,710
Nonmanufacturing industries (incl. not reported)	1,999,376
Construction	752,847
Railroads and railway express service	283,817
Transportation, except railroad	114,477
Telecommunications, and utilities and sanitary services	131,994
Wholesale and retail trade	334,652
Business and repair services	14,532
Personal services	79,599
Public administration	104,554
All other industries (incl. not reported)	182,904
Occupations Not Reported	1,366,064

INDEXES

Index of Names and Cases

Index of Subjects

Abortion, current legal problems, 275–276; defined, 273; in primitive society, 273

Adoption, current legal procedures, 256–260; current problems, 260–263; in human society, 177–179; legal regulation of, 256–263

Adoption of Children Act (1926), 256

Advisory Council on Participation and National Organizations, 292

Advisory Council on Social Security, 504, 518, 533, 534

Advisory Council on State and Local Action, 292

Adultery, and artificial insemination, 281; and collusion, 231, 239; as grounds for divorce, 227; in primitive society, 151

Affiliation statutes, see Illegitimacy

Affinity, see Consanguinity and affinity

Age, minimum requirements in marriage, 204–205

Aged, role of in American society, 98–100

Aggression, as a response in public assistance, 674

Aid to the Blind, 501–502, 564–565, 585–586

Aid to Dependent Children, 500–501, 564–565, 583–585

Aid to Partially Self-Supporting Blind Residents (California), 586

Aid to the Totally and Permanently Disabled, 565, 586–587

Alimony, 232

Amalgamated Association of Iron, Steel and Tin Workers of America, 327

American Association for Labor Legislation, 432

American Association for Old Age Security, 494 n.

American Association for Social Security, 494 n.

American Association of Social Workers, 245 n., 497

American Association of Law Schools, 243, 245 n.

American Association of University Women, 128

American Bankers Association, 125

American Bar Association, 127, 184, 203, 241, 242

American College of Surgeons, 427

American Council on Public Affairs, 513

American culture, American character, 72–77; centralization, fears of, 79–80; nineteenth century, 77–78; pragmatism, 86–87; Puritanism, 84–86; social mobility, 80–84; socialization, 75–78, 89, 95–98; twentieth century, 75, 78

American Economic Association, 63

American Farm Bureau Federation, 123, 126

American Federation of Labor, 125, 313, 314, 318, 319, 332, 432, 449, 450, 458, 459 n., 462, 463, 481

American labor movement, Employment Act of 1946, 402, 412, 417–420, 453; Hobbs Act, 453, 465; Lea Act, 453, 465; National Defense Mediation Board, 450–451; National War Labor Board, 450–451; Norris LaGuardia Act, 324, 325; Sherman Anti-Trust Act, 321, 322; state legislation, 475–476; Taft-Hartley Act, 465–475, 467, 468, 469, 473, 475, 616; Walsh-Hartley Act, 326, 330; War Labor Disputes Act, 405, 451

American League Against Epilepsy, 211

American Legion, 127

American Medical Association, 123, 127, 553, 554

American Petroleum Institute, 125

American Public Welfare Association, 569, 576 n.

American Railway Union, 321, 323

American social system, 624–625; goal fulfillment and, 667–671; requisites of, 639–644; social legislation and, 644–646

American Society of Mechanical Engineers, 430 n.

American Standards Association, 430 n.

American Veterans Committee, 127

Annual Appropriations Act (1954), 594

Annulment, children in, 218–219; grounds for, 218–219; property rights in, 221; rate in United States, 219–221

Anxiety, as a reaction to stress, 664; in American society, 668–671

Archbishop of Canterbury, 282

Artificial insemination, current legal status of, 281; defined, 279–280; legal history of, 280–281, 283; medicolegal proce-

705

concerning, 213; laws concerning, 212–213

Monogamy, 164

Moral idealism, 30

Mormons, 214–215

Mortgage Bankers Association, 600

Mother-child relationship, basis of human family, 146–147

Motivation, as activity, 7–8, 663; as goal-oriented behavior, 662; of individuals receiving public assistance, 672–674

National Association of Home Builders, 600

National Association of Manufacturers, 123, 124, 177, 315, 316, 473

National Association of Real Estate Boards, 600

National Birth Control League, 276

National Child Labor Committee, 334

National Conference of Commissioners on Uniform State Laws, 184, 241

National Conference on Prevention and Control of Juvenile Delinquency, 301 n.

National Defense Mediation Board, 450

National Education Association, 608

National Federation of Business and Professional Women's Clubs, 128

National Hatters Union, 321

National Health Bill, proposed, 553

National Housing Act (1934), 599

National Housing Agency, 600, 601

National income determination, 410–417

National Industrial Conference Board, 376, 377 n., 397

National Institute of Neurological Diseases and Blindness, 211

National Labor Relations Act (1935), 326, 327, 465, 466, 467, 468, 469, 473, 475

National Labor Relations Board, 326, 328, 455, 466, 467, 468, 469, 470, 471, 474, 475

National Labor Union, 313, 332

National Mental Health Act (1946), 595

National Planning Association, 533

National Resources Committee, 376

National Retail Dry Goods Association, 125

National Safety Council, 428 n., 430 n.

National School Lunch Act (1946), 608

National Securities Resources Planning Board, 119

National Service Life Insurance, 613

National Trades Union, 312

National unions, expanded role of, 449–453, 480–481; powers of, 453–464, 457–458; structure of, 457–463

National War Labor Board, 450, 451

National Youth Administration, 605

Natural Resources Planning Board, 510–511, 569, 601

Need, as requirement in public assistance, 570–575; human, 20

Need-satisfaction, and mental health, 662, 663; in American society, 668–671

New Deal, 62, 70, 75, 317, 318, 449

New Freedom, 62, 64, 69, 70, 316

New Harmony, 14

    See also Communistic experiments

New York Board of Rabbis, 240

New York General Trades Union, 312

New York State Council of Churches, 240

New York State Tenement House Commission (1900), 598

Non-seasonal sexuality, as basis for human family, 147–148

Old-Age Assistance, 501, 572–573, 581–583

Occupational health and safety, general problem of occupational health and safety, 422–423; injury frequency and severity, 424–426; job hazards, 423; legislation, 433–437; President's Conference on, 422, 423, 434, 435, 436

Occupations of civilian labor force in Census of 1950, 685–694

Parent-child relationship, adoption, 256–259; artificial insemination, 279–283; birth control, 273–279; child-welfare services, 286–293, 500, 501, 589–594; guardian-ward relationship, 263–266; illegitimacy, 266–273; inheritance in, 253–255; prenatal health examinations, 283–286; rights and duties in, 175–177, 245–256

Parents, responsibility for support, protection and education, 249–253; rights against third parties, 248–249; rights of inheritance, 253–255; rights to custody, 246–247; rights to support, 249

    See also Parent-child relationship

Paternity proceedings, 267–271

Personality, 17–19

Planned Parenthood Federation of America, 275 n., 276

Planning for social goals, issues in, 624–628; requisites of, 628–633

Political process, 105–107; formal and operative, 117; legislative, 129–133; political machines, 133–137; political parties, 119–122; pressure groups, 122–129; voting behavior, 134–137

Polyandry, see Polygamy